INTRODUCTION TO
MANAGERIAL ACCOUNTING

Fifth Canadian Edition

Peter C. Brewer
Miami University, Oxford, Ohio

Ray H. Garrison
Professor Emeritus, Brigham Young University

Eric W. Noreen
University of Washington and INSEAD

Suresh S. Kalagnanam
University of Saskatchewan

Ganesh Vaidyanathan
University of Saskatchewan

McGraw Hill Education

Introduction to Managerial Accounting

Fifth Canadian Edition

ISBN-13: 978-1-25-910570-8
ISBN-10: 1-25-910570-9

1 2 3 4 5 6 7 8 9 0 WEB 1 9 8 7

Printed and bound in Canada.

Care has been taken to trace ownership of copyright material contained in this text; however, the publisher will welcome any information that enables it to rectify any reference or credit for subsequent editions.

Portfolio and Program Manager: *Karen Fozard*
Product Manager: *Keara Emmett*
Executive Marketing Manager: *Joy Armitage Taylor*
Product Developer: *Amy Rydzanicz*
Photo/Permissions Research: *Maria DeCambra*
Senior Product Team Associate: *Stephanie Giles*
Supervising Editor: *Joanne Limebeer*
Copy Editor: *Laurel Sparrow*
Plant Production Coordinator: *Sarah Strynatka*
Manufacturing Production Coordinator: *Emily Hickey*
Cover Design: *Dave Murphy*
Cover Image: *George Clerk / Getty Images*
Interior Design: *Michelle Losier*
Page Layout: *Aptara, Inc.*
Printer: *Webcom*

About the Authors

Peter C. Brewer is a professor in the Department of Accountancy at Miami University, Oxford, Ohio. He holds a BS degree in accounting from Penn State University, an MS degree in accounting from the University of Virginia, and a PhD from the University of Tennessee. He has published more than 35 articles in a variety of journals, including *Management Accounting Research, The Journal of Information Systems, Cost Management, Strategic Finance, The Journal of Accountancy, Issues in Accounting Education,* and *The Journal of Business Logistics.*

Ray H. Garrison is emeritus professor of accounting at Brigham Young University, Provo, Utah. He received his BS and MS degrees from Brigham Young University and his DBA degree from Indiana University.

As a certified public accountant, Professor Garrison has been involved in management consulting work with both national and regional accounting firms. He has published articles in *The Accounting Review, Management Accounting,* and other professional journals. Innovation in the classroom has earned Professor Garrison the Karl G. Maeser Distinguished Teaching Award from Brigham Young University.

Eric W. Noreen has held appointments at institutions in the United States, Europe, and Asia. He is emeritus professor of accounting at the University of Washington.

Professor Noreen has served as associate editor of *The Accounting Review* and the *Journal of Accounting and Economics.* He has numerous articles in academic journals, including the *Journal of Accounting Research, The Accounting Review, The Journal of Accounting and Economics, Accounting Horizons, Accounting, Organizations and Society, Contemporary Accounting Research, The Journal of Management Accounting Research,* and *The Review of Accounting Studies.*

Suresh Kalagnanam is an associate professor of accounting at the Edwards School of Business, University of Saskatchewan, where he currently teaches and researches managerial accounting. He is a graduate of the University of Madras in India, where he obtained his bachelor of engineering degree. He subsequently obtained an MBA from Gujarat University in India, an MBA and a master of science in accounting from the University of Saskatchewan, and a PhD from the University of Wisconsin–Madison in the United States. He is also a Canadian Chartered Professional Accountant (CPA). His scholarly work has been published in *Accounting Organizations and Society, Accounting Perspectives, IMA Educational Case Journal, Qualitative Research in Accounting and Management,* and other academic publications. Dr. Kalagnanam is a member of the American Accounting Association, Canadian Academic Accounting Association, CPA Canada, and the Institute of Management Accountants. In his spare time, he is involved in cultural activities and community service.

Ganesh Vaidyanathan is an associate professor and scholar at the Centre for Accounting Education, and head of the Department of Accounting in the Edwards School of Business at the University of Saskatchewan. He has a BA from the University of Toronto, an MA in economics from the University of Waterloo, and an MASc and PhD in management sciences from the University of Waterloo. He holds the FCPA (Fellow of the Chartered Professional Accountants) and CPA, FCGA, CMA designations.

Dr. Vaidyanathan has more than 20 years of university teaching experience. He has taught a wide range of courses in management accounting and control, accounting information systems, microeconomics, finance, strategy, statistics, and management science. Prior to his current appointment at the University of Saskatchewan, he was an associate professor and chair of the Department of Business Administration at Brandon University, Brandon, Manitoba, from 1991 to 2001. He has also taught at Wilfrid Laurier University, the Conestoga College of Applied Arts and Technology, and the University of Waterloo, in Waterloo, Ontario. Dr. Vaidyanathan has co-written a text in business statistics with his father, Raja Vaidyanathan. His research has been published in *The Wall Street Journal, Journal of Applied Corporate Finance, Issues in Accounting Education, Accounting Perspectives,* and other scholarly publications. He is a member of CPA-Saskatchewan, the Canadian Academic Accounting Association, and the American Accounting Association. Outside of his professional interests, Dr. Vaidyanathan is an avid fan of blues music and Bollywood movies. For the past 13 years he has been cycling for recreation and fitness. He commutes to work daily on his bike year-round.

College of Applied Arts and Technology, and the University of Waterloo, in Waterloo, Ontario. Dr. Vaidyanathan has co-written a text in business statistics with his father, Raja Vaidyanathan. His research has been published in *The Wall Street Journal, Journal of Applied Corporate Finance, Issues in Accounting Education, Accounting Perspectives,* and other scholarly publications. He is a member of CPA-Saskatchewan, the Canadian Academic Accounting Association, and the American Accounting Association. Outside of his professional interests, Dr. Vaidyanathan is an avid fan of blues music and Bollywood movies. For the past 13 years he has been cycling for recreation and fitness. He commutes to work daily on his bike year-round.

Brief Contents

Contents

Preface

PART I: PRODUCT AND SERVICE COSTING

Chapter 2

Chapter 3

Chapter 4

Chapter 5

PART II: PLANNING AND DECISION MAKING

Chapter 6

Cost Behaviour: Analysis and Use   285

Chapter 7

Budgeting   339

Chapter 8

Cost–Volume–Profit Relationships

THE BASICS OF CVP ANALYSIS

ASSUMPTIONS OF CVP ANALYSIS

SOME APPLICATIONS OF CVP CONCEPTS

Chapter 9

Relevant Costs: The Key to Decision Making 496

Chapter 10

Capital Budgeting Decisions   573

PART III: PERFORMANCE MANAGEMENT

Chapter 11

Chapter 12

RESIDUAL INCOME—ANOTHER MEASURE OF INVESTMENT CENTRE PERFORMANCE

MULTI-DIMENSIONAL PERFORMANCE MEASUREMENT: THE BALANCED SCORECARD

Chapter 13

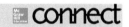

"How Well Am I Doing?"—Financial Statement Analysis — Online

LIMITATIONS OF FINANCIAL STATEMENT ANALYSIS IN BUSINESS TODAY

Comparison of Financial Data
The Need to Look Beyond Ratios

STATEMENTS IN COMPARATIVE AND COMMON-SIZE FORMS

Dollar and Percentage Changes on Statements
Common-Size Statements

RATIO ANALYSIS—THE COMMON SHAREHOLDER

Earnings per Share
Price–Earnings Ratio
Dividend Payout and Yield Ratios
Return on Total Assets
Return on Common Shareholders' Equity
Financial Leverage
Book Value per Share

RATIO ANALYSIS—THE SHORT-TERM CREDITOR

Working Capital
Current Ratio
Acid-Test (Quick) Ratio
Accounts Receivable Turnover
Inventory Turnover

Chapter 14

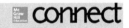

Index

Empowering Students to Rise to New Levels

Concise Coverage

Students want a text that is concise, clear, and readable. *Introduction to Managerial Accounting* presents everything students need to know, keeping the material accessible and avoiding advanced topics related to cost management. Students' biggest concern is making sure they can solve the end-of-chapter problem material after reading the chapter. Market research indicates that *Introduction to Managerial Accounting* achieves—and helps students achieve—this better than any other concise managerial accounting text on the market.

"When will I ever use managerial accounting?"

Many students ask this and similar questions about the relevance of their managerial accounting course. *Introduction to Managerial Accounting,* Fifth Canadian Edition, by Brewer et al., teaches students not only managerial accounting skills but also how to apply them in the real world.

More importantly, students will learn the critical thinking skills crucial to success in business. This combination of conceptual understanding and the ability to apply this knowledge in the real world empowers students to make business decisions and ascend to new heights.

Decision Making Focus

All students need to know how accounting information is used to make business decisions, especially if they plan to be future managers. That's why Brewer et al. have made decision making a pivotal component of *Introduction to Managerial Accounting.* In every chapter, you'll find important features designed to teach students how to use accounting information like a manager. **Decision Point** boxes challenge students to develop analytical and critical thinking skills in solving managerial accounting problems in both corporate and entrepreneurial settings. **Building Your Skills** cases give students' decision making skills an added boost by presenting them with more in-depth scenarios to work through.

Spotlight on Service

To reflect Canada's growing service based economy, this text is filled with examples from service based businesses. These examples are much more relevant and meaningful to non-majors than are the manufacturing examples typically used in managerial accounting texts. In keeping with the text's decision making focus, every service example is presented to help students relate the concepts in this book to the decisions made by real-world working managers. A student reading *Introduction to Managerial Accounting* should never have to ask, "Why am I learning this?"

Powerful Pedagogy

Introduction to Managerial Accounting has a variety of pedagogy designed to make studying productive. On the following pages, you'll see the kind of engaging, helpful pedagogical features that have made *Introduction to Managerial Accounting* one of the best-selling managerial accounting texts on the market.

On the Job

Each chapter opens with a feature titled **On the Job** that provides a real-world example for students, allowing them to see how the chapter's information and insights apply to the world outside the classroom. A critical thinking question is asked at the end of the feature to enhance students' critical thinking abilities.

> **ON THE JOB**
>
> **UNDERSTANDING COSTS KEEPS AIR CANADA FLYING HIGH**
>
> Air Canada is Canada's largest provider of passenger services, with an asset base of over $13.1 billion at the end of 2015. At just over 57% of its 2015 revenue of $13.9 billion, aircraft fuel, regional airline expenses, and wages, salaries, and benefits are the highest operating expenses. Like many other airlines and businesses, Air Canada has faced significant challenges due to rising oil prices and the global financial crisis.

Managerial Accounting in Action

These highly praised vignettes depict cross-functional teams working together in real-life settings on products and services that students recognize from their own lives. Students are shown step by step how managerial accounting concepts are implemented in organizations and how these concepts are applied to everyday business problems. First, "The Issue" is introduced through a dialogue. The student then works through the implementation process. Finally, "The Wrap-Up" summarizes the big picture.

MANAGERIAL ACCOUNTING IN ACTION
THE ISSUE

Samantha Trivers, is the president of Double Diamond Skis. After a rocky start, the company had come out with a completely redesigned ski called X-Factor, made of exotic materials and featuring flashy graphics. The steps in the manufacturing process are shown below. The ski was a runaway bestseller—particularly among younger skiers— and had provided the company with much-needed cash for two years. However, last year, a dismal snowfall in the Canadian Rockies had depressed sales, and Double Diamond was once again short of cash. Trivers was worried that another bad ski season would force Double Diamond into bankruptcy. The company typically made and sold all of

In Business

These helpful boxed features offer a glimpse into how real companies use the managerial accounting concepts discussed within the chapter. Each chapter contains these current examples.

IN BUSINESS

COST MANAGEMENT IS CRUCIAL IN THE NEW ECONOMIC ENVIRONMENT

Nearly a decade has passed since the 2008 global financial crisis, yet many businesses and other organizations are still facing challenges as the world's economy remains sluggish. In times of uncertainty and challenging economic environment, cost-cutting has continued to be a priority for businesses. For example, the oil and gas sector has cut thousands of jobs and reduced spending by billions of dollars to competitively reposition itself in the market. The ripple effect of this is that other sectors also undertaking cost-cutting measures in hopes of maintaining (or at least not significantly reducing) profit levels.

Decision Point

This boxed feature fosters critical thinking and decision-making skills by providing real-world business scenarios that require the resolution of a business issue. The suggested solution is located on Connect.

DECISION POINT

FINANCIAL ANALYST

You are a financial analyst for several clients who are interested in making investments in stable companies. You become aware of a privately owned airline that has been in business for 20 years and is in need of $75 million in new capital. When you call one of your clients, she replies that she avoids investing in airlines because of the high proportion of fixed costs in this industry. How would you respond to this statement?

*Note to student: See **Guidance Answers** online.*

Concept Check

These questions reinforce the student's understanding of basic concepts presented in each chapter. The answers are located on Connect.

CONCEPT CHECK

1. Which of the following cost behaviour assumptions are true? (You may select more than one answer.)
   a. Variable costs are constant when expressed on a per-unit basis.
   b. Total variable costs increase as the level of activity increases.
   c. The average fixed cost per unit increases as the level of activity increases.
   d. Total fixed costs decrease as the level of activity decreases.
2. Which of the following statements are true? (You may select more than one answer.)

Helpful Hints

Helpful Hint boxes are found several times throughout each chapter and highlight a variety of common mistakes, key points, and "pulling it all together" insights for students.

HELPFUL HINT

Students often assume that fixed costs expressed on a per-unit basis behave like variable costs. This is not true! If the average fixed cost per cellphone is $5 at a production level of 100,000 phones, it means the total amount of the fixed cost is $500,000. If the activity level/volume increases to 100,001 units, it does not mean that fixed costs will increase by $5. The total fixed cost remains constant at $500,000 within a relevant range of production.

Working It Out

These boxes illustrate the application of concepts and techniques through a worked example.

WORKING IT OUT

CanLube Corporation manufactures lubricants for industrial applications. The company uses the weighted average cost method of process costing to compute costs; its cost accountant recorded the following information for the most recent quarter.

Beginning WIP inventory	26,000 litres (80% complete as to materials; 70% complete as to conversion costs)
Units started into production this period	307,000 litres
Units completed and transferred out	313,000 litres

Application Competency Summary

Each chapter opener identifies Know and Apply competencies covered in that chapter, organizing them by Learning Objective. A summary at the end of the chapter provides a snapshot of each action-oriented application competency by highlighting its key information, documents, steps, and concepts. These summaries enhance student learning by reinforcing the essential tools of managerial accounting.

LEARNING OBJECTIVES AND CHAPTER COMPETENCIES

After studying Chapter 2, you should be able to demonstrate the following competencies:

COMPETENCY		Know	Apply
LO1	**UNDERSTAND COST CLASSIFICATION BY BEHAVIOUR.**		
CC1	Define variable and fixed costs, and give examples.	•	•
LO2	**UNDERSTAND COST CLASSIFICATION BY TRACEABILITY.**		
CC2	Define direct and indirect costs, and give examples.	•	•
LO3	**UNDERSTAND COST CLASSIFICATION BY RELEVANCE.**		
CC3	Define differential costs, opportunity costs, and sunk costs, and give examples.	•	•
LO4	**UNDERSTAND COST CLASSIFICATION BY FUNCTION.**		
CC4	Distinguish between manufacturing and nonmanufacturing costs.	•	
CC5	Identify and give examples of direct materials, direct labour, and manufacturing overhead costs.	•	•
CC6	Identify and give examples of marketing or selling and administrative costs.	•	•
CC7	Distinguish between product and period costs, and give examples.	•	•
CC8	Explain how costs are classified in financial statements of merchandising and manufacturing companies.	•	
LO5	**PREPARE FINANCIAL REPORTS.**		
CC9	Prepare an income statement.		•
CC10	Prepare a schedule of cost of goods sold.		•
LO6	**UNDERSTAND AND PREPARE MANUFACTURING REPORTS.**		

APPLICATION COMPETENCY	DELIVERABLE	SOURCE DOCUMENTS AND KEY INFORMATION	STEPS	KNOWLEDGE COMPETENCY
Compute the net income for the period. • **LO5–CC9**	*Key Information* Gross margin and net income *Report/Document* Income statement	*Sales Ledger* Actual sales revenue *Schedule of Cost of Goods Sold* Actual cost of goods sold (COGS) *Selling, General, and Administrative Expenses Ledgers* Actual selling, general, and administrative expenses	1. Obtain the sales revenues from the sales ledger. 2. Obtain the COGS from the schedule of COGS. 3. Obtain the selling, general, and administrative expenses from the ledgers. 4. Compute net income as sales revenue *less* COGS *less* selling, general, and administrative expenses.	Manufacturing versus nonmanufacturing costs • **LO4–CC4** Product vs. period costs • **LO4–CC7**

End-of-Chapter Material

Introduction to Managerial Accounting has earned a reputation for having a wealth and variety of end-of-chapter review and discussion material to support student learning, including Brief Exercises, Exercises, Problems, and Building Your Skills material. The Building Your Skills section contains comprehensive problems, analytical problems, communication projects, teamwork projects, and ethics challenges. The problem and case material makes a great starting point for class discussions and group projects. Other helpful features are as follows:

- To assist students in understanding how budgets look in a spreadsheet, Microsoft® Excel® spreadsheet templates have been made available for use with select problems and cases.

- Ethics assignments serve as a reminder that good conduct is vital in business.
- Group projects can be assigned either as homework or as in-class discussion projects.

- The writing icon denotes problems that require students to use critical thinking, as well as writing skills, to explain their decisions.

New to the Fifth Canadian Edition

In Response to Faculty Suggestions:

- Many of the *On the Job* boxes are revised.
- Many of the *In Business* boxes are new and/or revised. Drawing from recent events, these boxes provide interesting examples of how managerial accounting concepts are used by real businesses.
- The end-of-chapter material has been expanded. In addition, the authors have also refreshed and updated the end-of-chapter Brief Exercises, Exercises, and Problems.

Other Changes Include the Following:

- In response to user feedback, the chapter on cost behaviour has been positioned just ahead of the chapters on budgeting, cost–volume–profit analysis, and relevant costing.
- To aid student comprehension, the material throughout has been revised, simplified, or rewritten; many exhibits have been modified, and the flow of the narrative has been greatly improved.
- With regard to the material on standard costing and variance analysis, the end-of-chapter material has been revised extensively, however the challenge of the problems has not been diluted.
- An exciting new visual text design has been implemented to aid in student learning.
- NEW "Foundational 15"—Each chapter now contains one Foundational 15 exercise that includes 15 "building-block" questions related to one concise set of data.
- NEW Connect Insight provides instructors with a visual analytics dashboard regarding student performance in the course.

Market Leading Technology

Learn Without Limits

McGraw-Hill Education Connect® is an award-winning digital teaching and learning platform that gives students the means to better connect with their coursework, with their instructors, and with the important concepts that they will need to know for success now and in the future. With Connect, instructors can take advantage of McGraw-Hill's trusted content to seamlessly deliver assignments, quizzes, and tests online. McGraw-Hill Connect is a learning platform that continually adapts to each student, delivering precisely what they need, when they need it, so class time is more engaging and effective. Connect makes teaching and learning personal, easy, and proven.

Connect Key Features:

SmartBook®

As the first and only adaptive reading experience, SmartBook is changing the way students read and learn. SmartBook creates a personalized reading experience by highlighting the most important concepts a student needs to learn at that moment in time. As a student engages with SmartBook, the reading experience continuously adapts by highlighting content based on what each student knows and doesn't know. This ensures that he or she is focused on the content needed to close specific knowledge gaps, while it simultaneously promotes long-term learning.

Connect Insight®

Connect Insight is Connect's new visual analytics dashboard—now available for instructors—that provides at-a-glance information regarding student performance, which is immediately actionable. By presenting assignment, assessment, and topical performance results together with a time metric that is easily visible for aggregate or individual results, Connect Insight gives instructors the ability to take a just-in-time approach to teaching and learning, which was never before available. Connect Insight presents data that helps instructors improve class performance in a way that is efficient and effective.

Simple Assignment Management

With Connect, creating assignments is easier than ever, so instructors can spend more time teaching and less time managing.

- Assign SmartBook learning modules.
- Edit existing questions and create your own questions.
- Draw from a variety of text specific exercises and problems (static and algorithmic format), resources, and test bank material to assign online.
- Streamline lesson planning, student progress reporting, and assignment grading to make classroom management more efficient than ever.

Smart Grading

When it comes to studying, time is precious. Connect helps students learn more efficiently by providing feedback and practice material when they need it, where they need it.

- Automatically score assignments, giving students immediate feedback on their work and comparisons with correct answers.
- Access and review each response; manually change grades or leave comments for students to review.
- Track individual student performance—by question, by assignment, or in relation to the class overall—with detailed grade reports.
- Reinforce classroom concepts with practice tests and instant quizzes.
- Integrate grade reports easily with learning management systems including Blackboard, D2L, and Moodle.

Instructor Library

The Connect Instructor Library is a repository for additional resources to improve student engagement in and out of the class. It provides all the critical resources instructors need to build their course.

- Access instructor resources.
- View assignments and resources created for past sections.
- Post your own resources for students to use.

Instructor Resources

The following instructor resources are available on Connect:

- **Instructor's Manual:** Includes chapter overviews, lecture notes and tips, Application Competency Summary charts, and more.
- **Solutions Manual:** This resource contains completely worked-out solutions to all exercises, problems, and Building Your Skills assignments.
- **Computerized Test Bank:** Approximately 2,000 questions are organized by chapter and include true/false, multiple choice, and essay questions plus computational problems. Each test bank question is identified by level of difficulty and its related learning objective.
- **Microsoft® PowerPoint® Slides:** These slides offer a great visual complement for your lectures. A complete set of slides covers each chapter.
- **Microsoft® Excel® templates:** These are the solutions to the Excel templates offered online.
- **Image Bank:** This is a collection of helpful photos, exhibits, and other visuals for classroom use.

Superior Learning Solutions and Support

The McGraw-Hill Education team is ready to help instructors assess and integrate any of our products, technology, and services into your course for optimal teaching and learning performance. Whether it's helping your students improve their grades, or putting your entire course online, the McGraw-Hill Education team is here to help you do it. Contact your Learning Solutions Consultant today to learn how to maximize all of McGraw-Hill Education's resources.

For more information, please visit us online: http://www.mheducation.ca/highereducation/

Reviewers

The efforts of many people are needed to develop and improve a text. Among these people are the reviewers and consultants who point out areas of concern, cite areas of strength, and make recommendations for change. In this regard, the following professors provided feedback that was enormously helpful in preparing the Fifth Canadian Edition of *Introduction to Managerial Accounting:*

Orlando Brown, *Sheridan College*

Terry Cole, *Red Deer College*

Brenda Collings, *University of New Brunswick*

Rob Delcourt, *Algonquin College*

Tamara Ebl, *University of British Columbia, Okanagan*

Pamela Quan, *Athabasca University*

Michael Shih, *University of Windsor*

Thank you to the professors who contributed their expertise in reviewing the previous editions of *Introduction to Managerial Accounting.*

Thank you also to the technical checker, Brent Li, CPA, CMA.

Dedication

Suresh Kalagnanam wishes to dedicate this book to his wife, Viji, and his children, Pallavi and Siddharth.

Ganesh Vaidyanathan wishes to dedicate this text to his children, Saumya and Akul, to his mother, Sulochana, and to the memory of his late father, Sri Rajagopala Vaidyanathan.

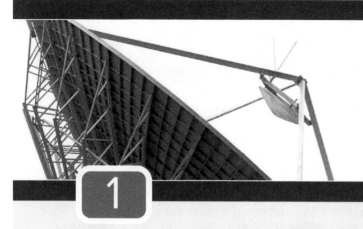

1

An Introduction to Managerial Accounting

LEARNING OBJECTIVES AND CHAPTER COMPETENCIES			
After studying Chapter 1, you should be able to demonstrate the following competencies:			
COMPETENCY		Know	Apply
LO1	**UNDERSTAND THE BASICS OF MANAGERIAL ACCOUNTING.**		
CC1	Describe the management cycle and the need for managerial accounting information.	●	
CC2	Differentiate between financial and managerial accounting.	●	
LO2	**UNDERSTAND THE ROLE OF GLOBALIZATION AND THE LEAN BUSINESS MODEL IN INFLUENCING MANAGERIAL ACCOUNTING.**		
CC3	Describe the impact of globalization on business.	●	
CC4	Explain the lean business model and its corresponding management practices.	●	
LO3	**UNDERSTAND THE IMPORTANCE OF PROFESSIONAL RESPONSIBILITY.**		
CC5	Explain the importance of ethical responsibility, corporate governance, and codes of conduct.	●	
CC6^A	Understand the code of ethics for professional accountants.	●	

ON THE JOB

OK TIRE STORES INC.: MAKING FACT-BASED DECISIONS IN REAL TIME

Getting relevant information in a timely manner is critical to the success and growth of an organization. One company that understands this is Vancouver-based OK Tire Stores Inc., which has grown significantly since it came into existence in 1953.

With the intention of offering a wider selection of tires to the consumer, as well as better service, a group of independently owned and operated tire retailers joined hands to form the company, which in 2016 had grown to over 300 locations across Canada. OK Tire offers all the benefits of a large franchise operation, while retaining customer satisfaction through the personal service of a local owner/manager. This is possible because each store is independently owned and its owner decides what tire brands and automotive services will be offered, including brakes, shocks, alignments, tuneups, oil changes, exhaust, cooling systems, and road service.

Each store has the freedom to determine how it tracks costs, margins, performance, employee performance, etc. For example, three local stores prepare weekly reports and charts comparing budgeted and actual sales and gross margins. As noted by Rod Janzen, one of the store managers, "timeliness of the reports is of the essence" because he must know about weekly sales decreases/increases to be able to make timely adjustments in order to meet his targets.

A key operating principle of the organization is that the individual stores should be involved in their local communities. The store owners wholeheartedly invest in the communities in which they live. From mud bogs and rodeos to hockey games and car racing, the owners are proud to be involved as both sponsors and participants. Just as important as their commitment to community is their dedication to making the country a better place to live. Owners are actively involved in local charities and work with groups fighting breast cancer, stamping out hunger, and promoting community wellness.

OK Tire owners keep their community top of mind in all areas of their life, including their stores. They provide honest advice and fair prices, while treating their customers as they would want to be treated—like a neighbour. And

Imagestate Media (John Foxx)

like any good neighbour, customers can count on them for the right advice and a helping hand whenever it is required.

Sources: Personal conversation with Devin Jaspar, CGA, and Rod Janzen; OK Tire Stores Inc. website, http://www.oktire.com.

Critical thinking question *"OK Tire's weekly reports are not simply a control tool; they help in planning and implementation, too."* Do you agree?

*Note to student: See **Guidance Answers** online.*

▶ A Look at This Chapter	▶▶ A Look Ahead
After describing the three major activities of managers and the need for managerial accounting information, this chapter compares and contrasts financial and managerial accounting information. It then exposes you to the changes taking place in the business environment. The design of an appropriate managerial accounting system is critical for managers to be able to make solid decisions.	Chapter 2 focuses on the basics of a managerial accounting system by defining and explaining many terms used to classify costs in business. Because these terms will be used throughout the text, you should be familiar with each of them.

Running a company like the Bank of Montreal, Magna, PotashCorp, or OK Tire is by no means an easy task. Senior managers must constantly study the company's business environment, the economy, competition, technological developments, and government regulations. Public companies must also report their activities to investors (shareholders). Reporting to investors requires that companies record accounting transactions and prepare a balance sheet, an income statement, and a statement of cash flows. Most of you are already familiar with these financial statements from your study of **financial accounting**.

A manager's duties do not end with reporting to investors. Managers must also ensure that the business is properly guided so that its objectives are achieved (this may include earning at a certain level of profitability or maintaining a certain level of market share). In order to do this, managers must *plan* for the future, *implement* or *execute* the plans, and *control* the operations—tasks that must be carried out *within* the organization. For this purpose, managers need information that focuses on internal activities. **Managerial accounting** provides managers with the essential information they can use to run organizations.

This chapter introduces the main functions of management and then explains the need for managerial accounting information. Finally, it examines the changes taking place in the business environment and their impact on the design of managerial accounting systems.

The Management Cycle and the Need for Managerial Accounting Information

LO1 • Know

CC1: Describe the management cycle and the need for managerial accounting information.

Broadly speaking, there are three types of business organizations: service, merchandising, and manufacturing. Service firms include such organizations as a doctor's clinic, an advertising agency, and a financial institution. Merchandising firms largely refer to retail and wholesale outlets that buy goods from suppliers and resell them to customers (e.g., Canadian Tire or Costco). Manufacturing firms engage in the production and sale of different types of products, ranging from small consumer goods (such as chewing gum) to large products (such as ships and aircraft).

Most organizations, ranging from a large hospital to a local Mac's Convenience Store, have a mission (purpose), a vision (long-term goal), and strategies for achieving the mission and vision. They typically follow the management cycle shown in Exhibit 1–1 (or some variation of it). Managerial accounting systems are designed to provide relevant information to assist managers in managing processes and activities aimed at achieving the mission and vision.

EXHIBIT 1–1 The Management Cycle

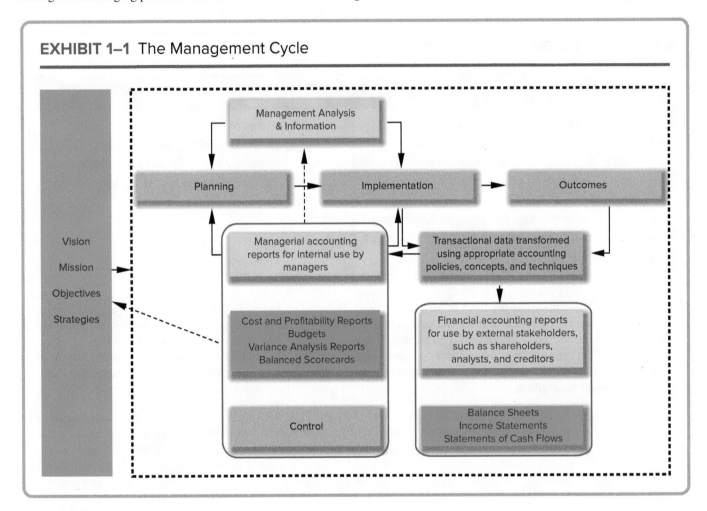

Strategy

In today's globally competitive environment, companies must develop a viable strategy to achieve their goals and objectives and succeed in the marketplace. Most businesses develop objectives along multiple dimensions, such as finances, customers, employees, the environment, and society. The company's goals and objectives are generally derived from the organization's stated mission (its purpose) and vision (how it wants to be perceived by the outside world).

Although a single accepted definition of *strategy* does not exist, most people agree that **strategy** pertains to the general direction in which an organization plans to move to achieve its goals and objectives.[1] Guided by the company's vision, mission, and strategy, managers carry out the three main activities of planning, implementation, and control. We illustrate the management cycle using the example of Pick Your Music, Inc., below.

Planning

Planning involves selecting a course of action and specifying how the action will be implemented. The first step in planning is to identify alternatives and then to select the one that does the best job of furthering the organization's objectives.

When making this and other choices, management must balance the opportunities against the demands made on the company's resources. Managers often rely upon critical information and analysis to aid planning; one example is **budgets**, which express a company's plans in quantitative (often financial) terms and are prepared annually, quarterly, or even monthly (see the Management Analysis & Information section in Exhibit 1–1).

Implementation

Once the plans are made, managers must implement them. **Implementation** involves carrying out day-to-day activities, making short-term and long-term decisions, organizing and allocating resources, and managing people by directing and motivating them. Managers assign tasks to employees, arbitrate disputes, answer questions, solve on-the-spot problems, and make many decisions that affect customers and employees (which, in turn, will likely influence future financial and nonfinancial performance, such as profitability and customer satisfaction, respectively). Examples of decisions are whether to automate the existing manual payroll system and whether to increase advertising expense or decrease sales price (or both) in order to increase sales. In effect, implementation is action oriented, and decisions must be made after carefully analyzing the situation and the available alternative courses of action. Managerial accounting concepts/tools, such as relevant cost analysis and cost–volume–profit analysis, can be used to make such decisions. Proper implementation of plans is expected to lead to the desired outcomes.

Control

Control involves instituting procedures and then obtaining feedback to ensure that all parts of the organization are functioning effectively and moving toward overall company goals. Control is largely achieved through internal management reports produced on a frequent basis; these reports provide **feedback**, which signals whether operations (and performance) are on track. Informal reporting, largely through verbal communication, may work in small organizations; however, larger organizations require more formal reporting. One example of a formal report, simply known as a **performance report**, compares budgeted results with actual results.

Pick Your Music, Inc.—Illustration of the Management Cycle

Pick Your Music, Inc.—a retailer of music CDs, DVDs, games, and other entertainment items—runs a chain of retail stores that are concentrated in Pacific Rim cities such as Sydney, Singapore, Hong Kong, Beijing, Tokyo, and Vancouver. An important financial objective of Pick Your Music is to earn profits; this helps the company achieve some of its other equally important objectives pertaining to customers and the local communities in which individual stores are located.

A key strategy that the company adopts to achieve its profitability objective is expansion to attract customers in as many markets as possible. To further this objective, every year, top management carefully considers a number of alternatives for expanding into new geographic markets. This year, management is considering opening new stores in Shanghai, Los Angeles, and Auckland. Managers at Pick Your Music, like managers everywhere, carry out three major activities: planning, implementation, and control.

PLANNING

Management of Pick Your Music knows from bitter experience that opening a store in a major new market is a big step that cannot be taken lightly. When the company attempted to open stores in both Beijing and Vancouver in the same year, resources were overextended, which resulted in delays. Therefore, entry to new markets is planned very, very carefully, using any lessons learned from previous experience.

Among other data, top management looks at the sales volumes, profit margins, and costs of the company's established stores in similar markets. These data, supplied by the managerial accountant, are combined with projected sales volume data at the proposed new locations to estimate the profits that would be generated by the new stores. In general, virtually all alternatives considered by management in the planning process have some effect on revenues or costs, and managerial accounting data are essential in estimating those effects.

After considering the alternatives, top management of Pick Your Music decided to open a store in only the burgeoning Shanghai market in the third quarter. Soon after, detailed plans were drawn up for all parts of the company, especially the human resources (HR) and marketing departments, which will play a big role in getting the Shanghai store up and running.

IMPLEMENTATION

Soon after the plans were finalized, key marketing and HR personnel became busy putting the plans into action. A critical decision for the marketing department was to start advertising the store. After doing the relevant analysis, management decided to advertise heavily on social media as well as on television. The HR department concentrated on hiring staff to run the store. Management analyzed the industry data as well as data on the local labour supply and demand patterns to decide the salary and benefits to be offered to new employees.

CONTROL

Before the opening of the new Shanghai store in the third quarter of the year, the store's manager was given sales volume, profit, and expense targets for the fourth quarter of the year. As the fourth quarter progresses, periodic reports will be prepared in which the actual sales volume, profit, and expenses are compared with the targets. If the actual results don't hit the targets, top management is alerted that the Shanghai store requires more attention. Experienced personnel can be flown in to help the new manager with the implementation of the plans (including the analysis part), or top management may conclude that plans will have to be revised.

Financial and Managerial Accounting

The final result of managers' activities is the achievement of the organization's objectives. The implementation of plans results in transactions (e.g., purchasing capital equipment, materials, and supplies; implementing marketing programs; and hiring people) and outcomes (e.g., customer order, sales contract) that have financial consequences. Management uses the *same set of data* pertaining to the transactions and outcomes to develop a variety of reports (see Exhibit 1–1). Financial accounting systems use these data to produce periodic financial statements (e.g., the balance sheet, the income statement, and the statement of cash flows). In contrast, a managerial accounting system uses the data to develop internal reports to provide key information to managers to aid them in the management cycle. However, there are some key differences between financial and managerial accounting, as illustrated in Exhibit 1–2.

EXHIBIT 1–2 Financial and Managerial Accounting

	Financial Accounting	Managerial Accounting
Users	Primarily external to the organization—investors, creditors, regulatory bodies	Primarily internal to the organization—managers and other decision makers
Time horizon	Historical perspective	Historical and future perspective
Verifiability vs. relevance	Emphasis on verifiability	Emphasis on relevance
Precision vs. timeliness	Emphasis on precision	Emphasis on timeliness
Unit of analysis	Entire organization	Individual organizational units or the entire organization as necessary
Regulation	Must follow prescribed accounting standards (e.g., international financial reporting standards—IFRS)	No prescribed standards or prescribed format; extent of detail decided by management
Requirement	Mandatory	Not mandatory

For the Managers

LO1 • **Know**

CC2: Differentiate between financial and managerial accounting.

Financial accounting reports are prepared primarily for the use of external parties such as shareholders and creditors, whereas managerial accounting information is used primarily by managers within the organization. This contrast in basic orientation results in a number of important differences between financial and managerial accounting, even though both financial and managerial accounting rely on the same underlying set of data.

Emphasis on the Future

Since planning is such an important part of the manager's job, managerial accounting has a strong orientation toward the future. In contrast, financial accounting adopts a more historical perspective in that it captures the financial implications of the transactions carried out and the results obtained during the most recent accounting period. These summaries may be of only limited use in planning because the future is not a simple reflection of the past. Constant changes in economic conditions, customer needs and desires, competitive conditions, and so on demand that the manager's planning be based, in large part, on estimates of what will happen rather than on summaries of what has happened.

Relevance and Flexibility of Data

Financial accounting data are expected to be objective and verifiable. However, for internal uses, the manager wants information that is relevant even if not completely objective or verifiable. By *relevant,* we mean *appropriate for the decision at hand.* For example, it is difficult to verify estimated sales volumes for a proposed new Pick Your Music store, but this is exactly the type of information that would be most useful to managers in their decision making. In addition to monetary information, managers often need nonmonetary information to aid the decision-making process (e.g., impact on customer satisfaction). The managerial accounting information system should be flexible enough to provide whatever data are relevant for a particular decision. We further discuss relevant costs and benefits in Chapter 9.

Emphasis on Timeliness

Precise information obtained in a timely manner is always desirable for the purposes of planning, implementation, and control. However, collecting precise information often requires more time and more resources. Consider the situation in which a manager has to wait an additional week for precise cost information regarding a customer's urgent order. In a situation like this, the manager may have to make a decision using immediately available cost information that is less precise but is a reasonably good estimate, rather than waiting longer for more accurate information. Timeliness is important because a potential consequence of waiting longer is that the manager may lose this customer's business. Financial accounting reports, on the other hand, present information pertaining to past transactions for which more precise information is readily available.

Focus on Segments of an Organization

Financial accounting is primarily concerned with reporting for the organization as a whole. In contrast, managerial accounting focuses much more on the parts, or **segments**, of an organization. These segments may be product lines, sales territories, divisions, departments, branch offices, or any other categorization of the company's activities that management finds useful—that is, localized units of analysis. This is because planning and decision making often occur at the segment level. Financial accounting does require some breakdowns of revenues and costs by major segments in external reports, but this is a secondary matter.

Regulation

Canadian organizations must prepare their financial statements in accordance with **International Financial Reporting Standards (IFRS)** if they are publicly traded, or the Accounting Standards for Private Enterprises (ASPE) if they are private enterprises. External users must have some assurance that the reports have been prepared in accordance with a common set of ground rules. Such ground rules enhance comparability and help reduce fraud and misrepresentation, but they do not necessarily lead to the types of reports that would be most useful for internal decision making.

Managerial accounting reports are not bound by such standards. Instead, organizations may establish their own guidelines concerning the content and form of internal reports. The only constraint is that the expected benefits from using the information should outweigh the costs of collecting, analyzing, and summarizing the data.

Managerial Accounting—Not Mandatory

Financial accounting is mandatory; that is, it has to be done. Various (external) regulatory bodies such as the Ontario Securities Commission (OSC) and the tax authorities require periodic financial statements. Managerial accounting, on the other hand, is not mandatory. An organization is completely free to do as much or as little as it wishes. There are no regulatory bodies or other outside agencies that specify what is to be done or, for that matter, whether anything is to be done at all. Since managerial accounting is completely optional, the important question is always "Is the information useful?" rather than "Is the information required?"

As previously explained, the management cycle focuses on (1) planning, which includes setting objectives and outlining how to attain these objectives, (2) implementation, which involves putting the plans into effect, and (3) control, which provides required periodic feedback to monitor the organization's progress toward achieving its stated objectives. To carry out these responsibilities, managers need *information* about the organization. From an accounting point of view, this information often relates to the *costs* of the organization. In managerial accounting, the term *cost* is used in many different ways, as explained in Chapter 2.

Are Financial and Managerial Accounting Independent?

Our discussion of the differences between financial and managerial accounting might suggest that they are independent of each other, but this is not true. Usually, organizations have a common database to capture the financial data that will be used for both financial and managerial accounting purposes (refer back to Exhibit 1–1). For example, accounting ledgers are an important primary source of data. Moreover, information from managerial accounting reports often feeds into financial accounting reports. Therefore, although there are important differences between financial and managerial accounting, they are not independent of each other.

Increased Relevance of Managerial Accounting

Although managerial accounting information has always been useful to managers, its relevance and importance have greatly increased in the past four decades during a period of tremendous change in the business environment. First, competitive boundaries have expanded due to globalization, which has been good for consumers because the increased competition has led to lower prices, higher quality, and more choices. However, this means that organizations must find new ways of doing business, which is the second aspect of change. The third issue is one of ethical responsibility and corporate governance among businesses and other organizations. More and more allegations are being made of management misconduct in many businesses, governments, and not-for-profit and charitable organizations. And, to add even more dynamism, the Internet has changed the face of business in several industries.

These changes are having a profound effect on managerial accounting practices, as we will see throughout this text. Managers require timely information not only on costs and profits but also on key drivers of these outcomes. We will now elaborate upon the changes in the business environment.

Globalization

LO2 • **Know**

CC3: Describe the impact of globalization on business.

Over the past three decades, several factors have led to an increase in worldwide competition in many industries. These include reductions in tariffs, quotas, and other barriers to free trade; improvements in global transportation systems; and increasing sophistication in international trade markets. These factors work together to reduce the costs of conducting international trade and make it possible for foreign companies to compete on a more equal footing with domestic firms. These changes have been most dramatic within the European Union (EU) and the North American Free Trade Agreement (NAFTA) free trade zones.

Very few organizations can now afford to be complacent. An organization that is successful in its local market can suddenly face competition from halfway around the globe. Consequently, businesses face increasing levels of risk and must always be vigilant about events taking place around the world; the recent financial crisis is a good example. Global organizations must also be careful about natural disasters, such as tsunamis and earthquakes, as well as disasters caused by humans, businesses, or organized groups, such as environmental disasters, cyber attacks, and terrorist attacks. All such events have severe consequences for businesses and other organizations, including different levels of government. It is likely that risks will become even more potent as business migrates more and more to the Internet. On the bright side, however, globalization offers the potential for greater opportunities (e.g., networking possibilities with new business partners and access to new markets). Similarly, more choices are available to customers: a greater variety of goods and services, higher quality, and lower price.

What are the implications of globalization? One major implication is that organizations must find new ways of conducting business: new strategies, new management practices, and more sophisticated managerial accounting systems. Another implication is that organizations must conduct their affairs in a responsible manner. We will now discuss each of these implications in greater detail.

The Lean Business Model

LO2 • **Know**

CC4: Explain the lean business model and its corresponding management practices.

Global competition has forced companies to find new ways of doing business in order to offer better products/services and to deliver them faster and at a cheaper price. Since the early 1980s, companies have adopted different kinds of improvement programs; these fall under the umbrella of what experts call the **lean business model**. The main idea underlying this model is the elimination of waste.

Consider a grocery store that sells fresh produce (fruits and vegetables) and bakery products, among other things. The fresh produce that gets damaged in transit and the excess quantity ordered that sits on the shelves too long (and rots) are examples of waste. They cost the grocery store money; this cost cannot be recovered because the damaged and rotten produce cannot be sold to customers. Similarly, manufacturing companies may produce too much just to keep people and machines busy; such excess production is also a form of waste if the products become obsolete in a short period of time. Even if the excess products do not become obsolete, they tie up financial and other resources that a business can utilize elsewhere. Moreover, businesses cannot *always* pass these increased costs on to the consumer in the form of higher prices because doing that may lead to lower demand.

IN BUSINESS

IS A LEAN BUSINESS MODEL THE ONLY ANSWER?

In times of economic uncertainty, consumption behaviours of consumers can change rapidly. As businesses are looking for sustainable means of growth, many experts point out that the focus of supply chain management to achieve a lean business model is no longer as effective as it once was. Others are exploring the option of a hybrid supply chain—one which combines lean processes with agile concepts. While lean processes are still effective for businesses whose key focus is to eliminate waste and non-value-added activities, there are benefits to incorporating agile concepts in their supply chain strategies. Agile concepts allow for a flexible and fast system when dealing with unexpected change in demand for a certain product, and they are particularly useful when faced with constraints and external environmental factors. Research shows that when businesses adopt these concepts, they are more adaptable to constraints and volatility from the external environment, and are more productive in general.

Sources: Paul A. Myerson, "A Lean and Agile Supply Chain: Not an Option, But a Necessity," October 2014; Dan Woods, "Why Lean and Agile Go Together", December 1, 2010; Vivek Sehgal, "Supply Chain Strategy: Lean and Agile at The Same Time?", October 28, 2010; Michael Fournier, "How the Demand Chain Will Change the Future of Agile and Lean Procurement," August 12, 2014.

In order to eliminate waste, companies must adopt and implement one or more management practices that focus on different aspects of the lean business model. Examples of these management practices include *just-in-time, total quality management, process reengineering,* and *theory of constraints.* These management practices, or programs of continuous improvement, if properly implemented, can enhance quality, increase efficiencies, eliminate delays, and reduce costs, thereby adding to the profits. Unfortunately, they have not always been properly implemented; as a result, considerable controversy exists about their ultimate economic value. Although each of the previously mentioned programs is worthy of extended study, we will discuss them only briefly, leaving the details to operations management courses.

In addition to adopting these management practices, companies have also refined their managerial accounting systems. For example, many companies now use the concepts of *activity-based costing* (ABC) and *multi-dimensional performance measurement systems* (e.g., the balanced scorecard)—these concepts are discussed in later chapters.

Just-in-Time

Traditionally, companies generally maintained large amounts of inventory to shield themselves from any unanticipated disruptions such as late shipments from suppliers, machine breakdowns, and unexpectedly large orders from customers. This means they maintained large amounts of raw materials inventory, work-in-process inventory, and finished goods inventory.

While these inventories provide some insurance against unforeseen events, they come at a cost. According to experts, in addition to tying up money, maintaining inventories encourages inefficient and sloppy work, results in too many defects, and dramatically increases the amount of time required to complete a product. Large inventories of partially completed goods create many other operating problems, which are best discussed in more advanced courses. These problems are not obvious—if they were, companies would have long ago reduced their inventories. Managers at Toyota are credited with the insight that large inventories often create many more problems than they solve, a realization that led Toyota to pioneer the *just-in-time (JIT) approach.*

The JIT Approach

Companies such as Dell, Inc. that use the **just-in-time (JIT) approach** purchase materials and components and build products only as needed to meet actual customer demand. In contrast to the traditional approach, the theory is that simply producing goods does the company no good unless someone buys them.

Few companies have been able to reach the ideal of "zero inventory," but many have been able to reduce inventories to a small fraction of previous levels. The results have been (1) a substantial reduction in ordering and warehousing costs and in waste due to obsolescence, pilferage, and other reasons, and (2) much more effective operations.

The change from a traditional to a JIT approach is more profound than it might seem. Among other things, producing only in response to a customer order means that workers will be idle whenever demand falls below the company's production capacity. This cultural change can be extremely difficult for an organization to make. It challenges the core beliefs of many managers and raises anxiety among workers who have become accustomed to being kept busy all the time.

Zero Defects and JIT

Given that JIT requires smooth operations, the existence of quality problems can create havoc. At a minimum, this creates a delay in shipping the order and may generate a ripple effect that delays other orders. For this and other reasons, defects cannot be tolerated in a JIT system. Companies deeply involved in JIT tend to become zealously committed to a goal of **zero defects**. Even though it may be next to impossible to achieve this goal, companies have found they can come very close. For example, Motorola, Allied Signal, and many other companies now measure the number of defects per *million* units of product.

Total Quality Management

Many companies working toward achieving the goal of zero defects have chosen to adopt a management practice known as **total quality management (TQM)**. There are two major characteristics of TQM: (1) a focus on serving customers, and (2) systematic problem solving using teams made up of front-line workers. A variety of specific tools are available to aid teams in their problem solving. One of these tools, **benchmarking**, involves studying organizations that are among the best in the world at performing a particular task. For example, when Xerox wanted to improve its procedures for filling customer orders, it studied how L. L. Bean, the mail-order company, processed its customer orders.

The Plan–Do–Check–Act Cycle

Perhaps the most important and pervasive TQM problem-solving tool is the **plan–do–check–act (PDCA) cycle**, also referred to as the **Deming Wheel**.[2] The PDCA cycle is a systematic, fact-based approach to continuous improvement. Its basic elements are illustrated in Exhibit 1–3. The cycle applies a scientific method to problem solving.

EXHIBIT 1–3 The Plan–Do–Check–Act Cycle

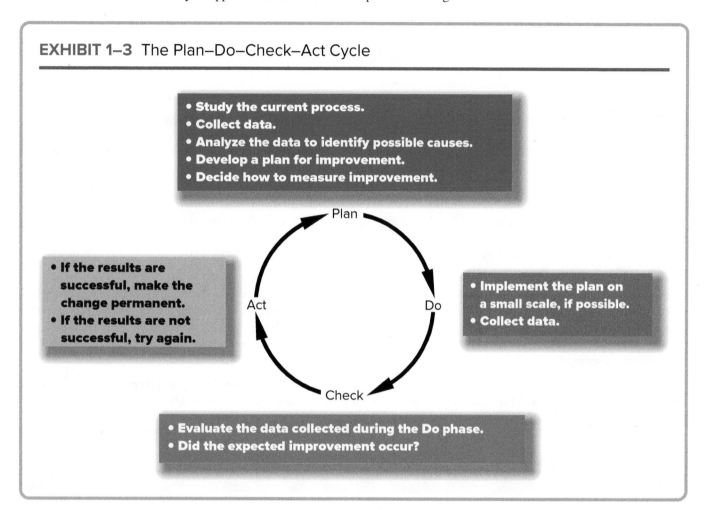

- Study the current process.
- Collect data.
- Analyze the data to identify possible causes.
- Develop a plan for improvement.
- Decide how to measure improvement.

- If the results are successful, make the change permanent.
- If the results are not successful, try again.

- Implement the plan on a small scale, if possible.
- Collect data.

- Evaluate the data collected during the Do phase.
- Did the expected improvement occur?

Plan

Act

Do

Check

In the Plan phase, the problem-solving team analyzes data to identify possible causes of the problem and then proposes a solution. In the Do phase, the team conducts an experiment. In the Check phase, it analyzes the results, and in the Act phase, if the results of the experiment are favourable, it implements the plan. If the results of the experiment are not favourable, the team goes back to the original data and starts all over again.

IN BUSINESS

QUALITY MANAGEMENT IS IMPORTANT WORLDWIDE

Quality management became popular over five decades ago and continues to remain important the world over. The importance attached to quality can be understood by the fact that many countries around the world award prizes to organizations and individuals practising the highest level of quality management principles in their journey toward excellence. While some countries (such as Mauritius, Morocco, Singapore, China, and Egypt) have developed their quality award based on the American Baldrige Award or the European Framework for Quality

Management (EFQM) Excellence Award, others (such as Canada, India, Korea, Malaysia, and Luxembourg) have developed their own unique frameworks. In Canada, the Canada Awards for Excellence are administered by Excellence Canada; awards recipients include private businesses, schools, hospitals, and local, provincial, and federal government agencies/departments.

Sources: http://www.excellence.ca/en/awards/; http://www.nist.gov/baldrige/; http://www.efqm.org/what-we-do/recognition/efqm-excellence-award; http://qcin.org/nbqp/DLShah-Award/index.php.

Process Reengineering

A **business process** is any series of steps followed to carry out a task in a business. For example, the steps followed to make a large pineapple and Canadian bacon pizza at Godfather's Pizza or those followed by your bank when you deposit a cheque represent a business process. **Process reengineering** is a radical approach to improvement that managers can use to remove waste from business processes. Process reengineering diagrams a business process in detail, questions it, and then completely redesigns it to eliminate unnecessary steps, reduce opportunities for errors, and reduce costs. This is in direct contrast to approaches in which an existing process is continuously tweaked to generate incremental improvements.

Process reengineering focuses on *simplification* and *elimination of wasted effort*. Activities that do not add value to a product or service that customers are willing to pay for are known as **non-value-added activities**. A central idea of process reengineering is that all non-value-added activities should be eliminated. For example, moving large batches of partially completed goods from one workstation to another is a non-value-added activity that can be eliminated by redesigning the factory layout to bring the workstations closer together.[3]

One potential consequence of process reengineering is layoffs. Organizations that focus on process reengineering (or improvement) may not always be able to prevent job losses; in such situations they must manage the communication and the process to minimize the negative impacts resulting from job losses.

The Theory of Constraints

A **constraint** is a hurdle (or an obstacle) that prevents people from getting more of what they want. For example, that each day has only 24 hours is a constraint for many of us. We have to juggle our activities so as to be able to complete them (or at least some of them) within the available time. Every individual and every organization faces at least one constraint. For example, gas companies such as Petro-Canada have a limited number of pumps at each of their gas stations, which means customers have to wait their turn to fill gas or go to a competitor.

The **theory of constraints (TOC)** framework focuses on effectively managing constraints as the key to success. For example, Petro-Canada could consider one of several options: (1) install additional pumps (but this may be prohibitively expensive), (2) increase pumping speed, or (3) introduce fast checkout. All of these can help in reducing customer waiting time and potentially increase revenues.

An Example of TOC

ProSport Equipment, Inc. manufactures aluminum tennis racquets using the production process illustrated in Exhibit 1–4. The capacity of each workstation is stated in terms of the maximum number of racquets that can be processed in a week. A careful examination shows that frame assembly is the *bottleneck* operation with the lowest capacity of 1,800 racquets per week. How can management increase the output of the production process?

EXHIBIT 1–4 A Flowchart of an Aluminum Tennis Racquet Production Line

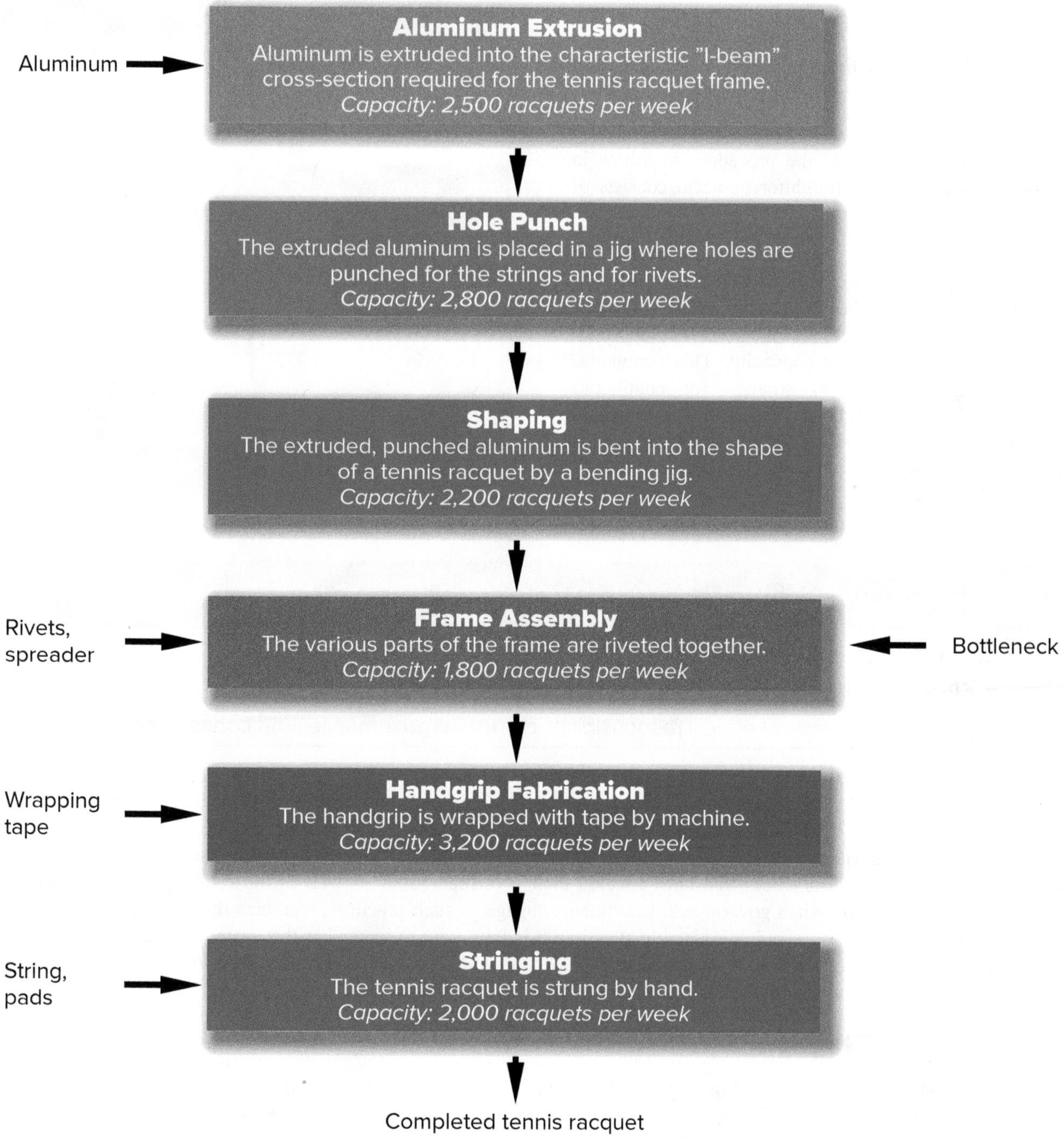

Aluminum →

Aluminum Extrusion
Aluminum is extruded into the characteristic "I-beam" cross-section required for the tennis racquet frame.
Capacity: 2,500 racquets per week

↓

Hole Punch
The extruded aluminum is placed in a jig where holes are punched for the strings and for rivets.
Capacity: 2,800 racquets per week

↓

Shaping
The extruded, punched aluminum is bent into the shape of a tennis racquet by a bending jig.
Capacity: 2,200 racquets per week

↓

Rivets, spreader →

Frame Assembly
The various parts of the frame are riveted together.
Capacity: 1,800 racquets per week

← Bottleneck

↓

Wrapping tape →

Handgrip Fabrication
The handgrip is wrapped with tape by machine.
Capacity: 3,200 racquets per week

↓

String, pads →

Stringing
The tennis racquet is strung by hand.
Capacity: 2,000 racquets per week

↓

Completed tennis racquet

TOC and Continuous Improvement

In TOC, an analogy is often drawn between a business process—such as the tennis racquet production line—and a chain. What is the most effective way to increase the strength of a chain? Should you concentrate your efforts on strengthening the strongest link, the largest link, all the links, or the weakest link? Clearly, focusing effort on the weakest link will bring the biggest benefit.

Continuing with this analogy, the procedure to follow in strengthening the chain is straightforward and consists of three steps.

If the improvement efforts are successful, eventually the weakest link will improve to the point where it is no longer the weakest. At this point, the new weakest link (i.e., the new constraint) must be identified, and the three-step approach must be adopted for the new constraint. This continuous process provides a powerful strategy for continuous improvement. The TOC approach is a perfect complement to TQM and process reengineering—it focuses improvement efforts where they are likely to be most effective.

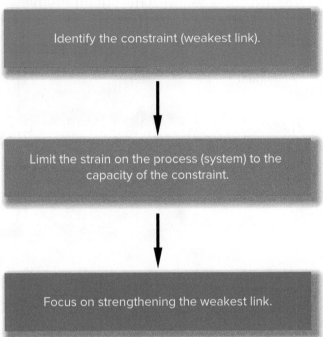

Identify the constraint (weakest link).

Limit the strain on the process (system) to the capacity of the constraint.

Focus on strengthening the weakest link.

Ethical Responsibility and Corporate Governance

LO3 ● **Know**

CC5: Explain the importance of ethical responsibility, corporate governance, and codes of conduct.

As previously mentioned, the conduct of organizations is an extremely important global issue. As businesses interact more and more with organizations in different parts of the world, they must be cautious that the companies they deal with are worth their time and effort. Unfortunately, we find that many businesses, governments, and not-for-profit and charitable organizations have engaged in questionable practices that have affected their own reputations as well as those of other stakeholders (such as employees and investors). When government departments engage in such practices, it affects the taxpayer. Although these allegations and scandals have received considerable attention, it is important to remember that many other businesses and other organizations conduct their affairs in a responsible manner. Nonetheless, no organization can claim to be 100% immune to the possibility of such events taking place in the future.

Professional Ethics

Often, unethical behaviour is the result of managers and other top executives focusing exclusively on achieving short-term results *at any cost*. This can be very dangerous, as it may drive employees to act unethically in order to meet the expectations of their superiors. Managers may also ignore unethical behaviour when the results are good or if there is something to lose by recognizing it. In fact, it is sometimes hard to notice when behaviour deteriorates gradually.[4]

To prevent unethical behaviour, many organizations have implemented formal ethical codes of conduct. For example, Manitoba Hydro's purchasing department expects all of its buyers to abide by the Purchasing Management Association of Canada's Professional Code of Ethics. These codes are generally broad-based statements of an organization's responsibilities to its employees, its customers, its suppliers, and the communities in which it operates. Codes rarely spell out specific dos and don'ts or suggest proper behaviour in specific situations. Instead, they provide broad guidelines.

DECISION POINT

TO DO OR NOT TO DO

You are the treasurer of a charitable organization. An organization member tells you about his noble intention to help three hospitals in his country of origin. He has written a sizeable cheque to the charity and requests two things from you: (1) a tax deduction receipt, and (2) a cheque in his name that he can use to help the hospitals "back home." Is there an ethical dilemma? What would you do?

*Note to student: See **Guidance Answers** online.*

Accountants are generally considered the *guardians* of an organization's money. But what if accountants themselves behave irresponsibly? To prevent this, professional accounting bodies in most parts of the world have developed codes of conduct to guide appropriate behaviour of accounting professionals. The Code of Ethics for Professional Accountants, first issued in June 2005 by the International Federation of Accountants (IFAC), governs the activities of *all* professional accountants throughout the world, regardless of whether they are in public practice or employed in government service or private industry.[5] The recently formed Canadian Chartered Professional Accountant (CPA) designation, unifying the previously existing accounting designations (CA, CGA, CMA), is governed by a common code of conduct.

Canadian companies dealing with foreign governments are bound by the *Corruption of Foreign Public Officials Act,* which prohibits company executives from offering gifts, payments, or other benefits to foreign government officials in order to receive favourable business treatment.

These ethical standards provide sound, practical advice for professional accountants and managers. Most of the rules in the ethical standards are motivated by a very practical consideration: if these rules are not generally followed in business, the economy will come to a screeching halt.

Corporate Governance

Corporate governance is the system by which an organization is directed and controlled. Properly implemented, it should encourage the board of directors and top management to pursue objectives that are in the interests of the company's owners, and it should provide for effective monitoring of performance.[6] Effective corporate governance enhances stakeholders' confidence that an organization is being managed in their best interests rather than solely in the interests of top management and certain key individuals.

Unfortunately, history has repeatedly shown that unscrupulous top managers, unchecked, can exploit their power to defraud stakeholders. This unpleasant reality became all too clear in 2001 when the fall of Enron started an unprecedented wave of corporate scandals—scandals characterized by financial reporting fraud and misuse of corporate funds at the very highest levels, including among CEOs and CFOs. While this was disturbing in itself, it also indicated that the institutions intended to prevent such abuses were not working, raising fundamental questions about the adequacy of the existing corporate governance system. In an attempt to respond to these concerns, the U.S. Congress passed the most important reform of corporate governance in many decades—the **Sarbanes-Oxley Act** of 2002, which is intended to protect the interests of those who invest in publicly traded companies by improving the reliability and accuracy of corporate financial reports and disclosures.

IN BUSINESS

TOYOTA ENCOUNTERS MAJOR PROBLEMS

When Toyota Motor Corporation failed to meet its profit targets, the company set an aggressive goal of reducing the cost of its auto parts by 30%. The quality and safety of the company's automobiles eventually suffered mightily, resulting in recalls, litigation, incentive campaigns, and marketing efforts that analysts estimate will cost the company more than $5 billion. The car maker's president, Akio Toyoda, blamed his company's massive quality lapses on an excessive focus on profits and market share. Similarly, Jim Press, Toyota's former top U.S. executive, said the problems were caused by "financially oriented pirates who didn't have the character to maintain a customer-first focus."

Sources: Yoshio Takahashi, "Toyota Accelerates Its Cost-Cutting Efforts," *The Wall Street Journal*, December 23, 2009, p. B4; Norihiko Shirouzu, "Toyoda Rues Excessive Profit Focus," *The Wall Street Journal*, March 2, 2010, p. B3; and Mariko Sanchanta and Yoshio Takahashi, "Toyota's Recall May Top $5 Billion," *The Wall Street Journal*, March 10, 2010, p. B2.

Implications of the Changing Business Environment on Managerial Accounting

What are the implications of the business environment changes previously described? Modern organizations cannot use systems designed in the early 1900s to implement their strategies and achieve their objectives. To compete in a global economy, organizations must have well-designed managerial accounting systems to guide managers. Organizations must question the usefulness of their existing managerial accounting tool kit and replace obsolete tools and techniques with more relevant ones. The past three decades have seen the introduction of several new concepts and methodologies, including activity-based costing/management (ABC/ABM), activity-based budgeting (ABB), the balanced scorecard (BSC), and strategic cost management (SCM). Moreover, successful modern companies are effectively using computerized systems to track and analyze data and to generate reports. Large companies routinely use enterprise resource planning (ERP) systems. Many also effectively use the Internet to disseminate information. In brief, managers must employ methods that take into consideration the factors that drive costs, revenues, and profits. An excellent managerial accounting system will not guarantee success by itself, but a poorly designed system will certainly lead to failure.

Organization of the Text

This text is designed to give you a basic overview of the types of managerial (or *internal*) accounting information useful to managers to ensure that the main purpose of their organization is achieved. In doing so, the text begins by introducing cost terminology that will be used throughout. It proceeds to describe different systems used to determine the cost per unit of providing a service or manufacturing a product. The text then focuses on the information required for planning, decision making, and control. In explaining each topic (conceptually and procedurally), the text briefly examines the impact of the lean business model. Although each chapter may focus on one or more specific topics, you are encouraged to integrate topics in an attempt to understand the interrelationships among them.

Learning Objectives Summary

LO1 **UNDERSTAND THE BASICS OF MANAGERIAL ACCOUNTING.**

Managerial accounting provides managers with the essential information they need to run organizations in a way that fulfills the mission and achieves the vision established by senior management. A managerial accounting system provides information that helps managers in the planning, implementation, and control cycle. In contrast, a financial accounting system provides information primarily for the use of external stakeholders (e.g., shareholders, analysts, and creditors).

LO2 **UNDERSTAND THE ROLE OF GLOBALIZATION AND THE LEAN BUSINESS MODEL IN INFLUENCING MANAGERIAL ACCOUNTING.**

Over the years, businesses have increasingly become globalized. Many have responded to the increasing competition by adopting a variety of lean business practices, such as total quality management and just-in-time systems. Managerial accounting systems have evolved to meet the needs of the changing management practices.

LO3 **UNDERSTAND THE IMPORTANCE OF PROFESSIONAL RESPONSIBILITY.**

The conduct of organizations (and individuals within the organization) is an extremely important global issue. Often, unethical behaviour is the result of managers and other top executives focusing exclusively on achieving short-term results *at any cost*. To prevent unethical behaviour, many organizations have implemented formal ethical codes of conduct. Also, professionals are required to follow the code of conduct established by their professional organization.

Questions

1–1 What is the basic difference in orientation between financial and managerial accounting?
1–2 What are the three major activities of a manager?
1–3 Describe the steps in the planning, implementation and control cycle.
1–4 What are the major differences between financial and managerial accounting?
1–5 Describe the lean business model and its corresponding management practices.
1–6 What are the pros and cons of a JIT system?
1–7 "It is vital that management accountants abide by a code of ethics." Do you agree or disagree? Explain.

Exercises

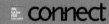

EXERCISE 1–1
Differentiating Between Managerial and Financial Accounting [LO1 – CC2]

Classify the following activities as *primarily* managerial accounting or financial accounting:

a. Preparing a cash budget for the next quarter.
b. Analyzing the profitability of a request from a potential customer.
c. Accumulating the transactions for the previous six months to prepare an income statement.

d.   Preparing a weekly performance report for the branch manager.

e.   Preparing an announcement to be released to the financial analysts.

EXERCISE 1–2
Differentiating Between Planning, Implementation, and Control [LO1 – CC1]

Classify the following activities as *primarily* planning, implementation, or control:

a.   Doing a cost–benefit analysis of adding a new branch versus installing three new automated teller machines (ATMs).

b.   Estimating the cost of raw materials to be purchased during the next quarter.

c.   Analyzing market demand to assist in the preparation of the sales budget.

d.   Compiling the labour report for the past week.

e.   Outlining the changes to a process based on a process reengineering team report.

f.   Documenting the savings from reductions in raw materials inventory resulting from the adoption of a JIT inventory system.

Problems

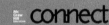

PROBLEM 1–1
Applying Professional Responsibility [LO3 – CC5]

As a professional accountant, you adhere to the code of ethics set forth by the International Federation of Accountants (see Appendix 1A). Keeping the IFAC Code in mind, determine if there are any clear ethical considerations in the following scenarios:

a.   Cleo Patra is the managerial accountant for a multinational company. An industry stock analyst has invited her to spend two weeks in Aruba at no cost to her. In return for this favour, Cleo would send him any financial press release before it became public.

b.   Your company is a large multinational highly esteemed by investors. The shares are overpriced in your opinion. As the managerial accountant, you know that the company's earnings cannot sustain investor expectations, and you believe that the share price will fall dramatically within the next year. Your parents are thinking of investing a large part of their retirement income in the company. Do you tell them not to, on the basis of what you know?

PROBLEM 1–2
Applying Ethical Responsibility [LO3 – CC5]

A month after the mid-semester examination, a student approaches his instructor with a doctor's note and requests the instructor to ignore his poor exam performance by not including it in the computation of his final course mark. This student is aiming to become a manager. Do you see an ethical dilemma (or dilemmas)? Explain. What should be the conduct of a student who intends to become a manager? What would you do if you were the instructor for the course?

Appendix 1A: Code of Ethics for Professional Accountants—International Federation of Accountants

LO3   • **Know**

CC6^A: Understand the code of ethics for professional accountants.

A professional accountant shall comply with the following fundamental principles:

1. *Integrity*—to be straightforward and honest in all professional and business relationships.
2. *Objectivity*—to not allow bias, conflict of interest, or undue influence of others to override professional or business judgments.
3. *Professional Competence and Due Care*—to maintain professional knowledge and skill at the level required to ensure that a client or employer receives competent professional service based on current developments in practice, legislation, and techniques and act diligently and in accordance with applicable technical and professional standards.
4. *Confidentiality*—to respect the confidentiality of information acquired as a result of professional and business relationships and, therefore, not disclose any such information to third parties without proper and specific authority, unless there is a legal or professional right or duty to disclose, nor use the information for the personal advantage of the professional accountant or third parties.
5. *Professional Behavior*—to comply with relevant laws and regulations and avoid any action that discredits the profession.

Source: This text is an extract from the 2015 edition of the *Handbook of the Code of Ethics for Professional Accountants* (Section 100.5) of the International Ethics Standards Board for Accountants, published by the International Federation of Accountants (IFAC), and is used with permission of IFAC.

Endnotes

1. R. S. Kaplan and D. P. Norton, *The Execution Premium: Linking Strategy to Operations for Competitive Advantage* (Boston: Harvard Business Press, 2008), p. 38; M. E. Porter, "What Is Strategy?" *Harvard Business Review,* November/December 1996, pp. 61–78; R. N. Anthony and V. Govindarajan, *Management Control Systems,* 12th ed. (Toronto: McGraw-Hill Ryerson, 2007), p. 57.
2. Dr. W. Edwards Deming, a pioneer in TQM, introduced many of the elements of TQM to Japanese industry after World War II. TQM was further refined and developed at Japanese companies such as Toyota.
3. Activity-based costing and activity-based management, both of which are discussed in Chapter 5, can be helpful in identifying areas in the company that might benefit from process reengineering.
4. Max A. Bazerman and Ann E. Tenbrunsel, "Ethical Breakdowns: Good People Often Let Bad Things Happen. Why?" *Harvard Business Review,* April 2011, pp. 58–65.
5. For the fundamental principles of IFAC's code of ethics, see Appendix 1A to Chapter 1.
6. This definition of corporate governance was adapted from the 2004 report *OECD Principles of Corporate Governance,* published by the Organization for Economic Cooperation and Development.

2

Cost Concepts

ON THE JOB

UNDERSTANDING COSTS KEEPS AIR CANADA FLYING HIGH

Air Canada is Canada's largest provider of passenger services, with an asset base of over $13.1 billion at the end of 2015. At just over 57% of its 2015 revenue of $13.9 billion, aircraft fuel, regional airline expenses, and wages, salaries, and benefits are the highest operating expenses. Like many other airlines and businesses, Air Canada has faced significant challenges due to rising oil prices and the global financial crisis.

The airline pays close attention to costs. At least 90% of its costs are fixed with respect to the number of passengers; fuel costs vary with the number of routes and flights rather than just the number of passengers. Significant cost savings can potentially be achieved through eliminating or reorganizing its routes, according to an analyst. The airline introduced Rouge, a low-cost leisure airline, to address the cost issues; this move is in line with what Australia's Qantas has already done, as well as rival WestJet's proposal to launch a short-haul carrier.

Large airlines usually have a high proportion of fixed costs due to the infrastructure required to provide services to customers. Automating processes performed by humans usually means a reduction in recurring salary expenses but a corresponding increase in depreciation expenses and maintenance costs. Understanding the nature of costs and the implications of alternative cost reduction programs is very important in order to decide which program to implement.

Royalty-free/CORBIS

Sources: Air Canada Annual Report, December 31, 2015; R. Marowits, "Air Canada Needs to Take Axe to Service to Survive, Says Analyst," *The Canadian Press*, April 2, 2009; S. Deveau, "Air Canada Weighs Costs; Airline Looking at Several New Carriers: Sources," *National Post*, February 10, 2012, p. FP.1; S. Deveau, "WestJet to Move Ahead With Its Regional Carrier; Employee Support," *National Post*, February 9, 2012, p. FP.4; S. Deveau, "Rouge, a More Casual Way to Take Flight; Air Canada's Profitability Hope," *National Post*, December 19, 2012, p. FP.1.

Critical thinking question *How should a company decide when, and how much, to invest in additional infrastructure and other fixed costs?*

*Note to student: See **Guidance Answers** online.*

◀◀ A Look Back	▶ A Look at This Chapter	▶▶ A Look Ahead
In Chapter 1, we introduced the three main activities of a manager and the need for managerial accounting information. We then compared financial and managerial accounting information. We also addressed some of the challenges faced by management and described the lean business model.	We define many of the terms that managers use to classify costs. Because these terms are used throughout the text, be sure you are familiar with them.	Chapters 3, 4, and 5 build on the introduction to cost concepts in Chapter 2 and describe costing systems that are used to compute product/service costs. Specifically, Chapters 3 and 4 describe two contrasting cost accounting systems, whereas Chapter 5 describes a different approach to cost allocation and cost management.

C osts are incurred by all kinds of organizations: governments (e.g., City of Windsor); hospitals (e.g., Concordia Hospital, Winnipeg); educational institutions (e.g., Simon Fraser University); and merchandising, service, and manufacturing companies (e.g., Canadian Tire, Myers Norris Penny, and Toyota Canada). The costs incurred may be one-time or recurring and may differ depending on the need. Managers find it useful to classify costs in different ways in order to facilitate their analysis. In general, costs can be classified using four broad categories: behaviour, traceability, relevance, and function. In this chapter, we will discuss each of the cost classification categories.

Why Cost Classification Is Important to Managers

Costs are costs; why should we care about classifying costs in different ways? In Chapter 1, we listed the three main activities of a manager. All three of the activities involve dealing with cost information by way of estimation (for planning), analysis (for implementation), and reporting (for control). Managers cannot estimate, analyze, and report if they do not have a good understanding of costs. Cost classification enables a manager to better understand costs. The rest of Chapter 2 discusses the different ways in which costs can be classified; later chapters discuss cost estimation, cost analysis, and cost and profitability reporting.

Cost Classification by Behaviour

LO1   ● **Know**   ● **Apply**

CC1: Define variable and fixed costs, and give examples.

Managers often need to understand how costs will behave in response to changes in activity level; this knowledge is useful for cost estimation, planning, and cost–profitability analysis. For instance, a manager at Air Canada may want to estimate the impact of a 10% increase in the number of passengers on its catering costs. It seems reasonable to assume that an increase in the number of passengers will result in a proportionate increase in catering costs. The airline will have to acquire 10% more food and beverages. Therefore, we will say that catering costs *vary* with respect to the number of passengers. On the other hand, a 10% increase in the number of passengers will not require additional fuel or even additional flight crew; this means that fuel and flight crew costs do not vary, or are *fixed,* with respect to the number of passengers.

Cost behaviour is the way a cost will respond to changes in the level of an organization's business activity (such as the number of passengers flying Air Canada). As the level of activity rises or falls, a particular cost may rise or fall, respectively, or may remain constant. For planning purposes, a manager must be able to estimate how different costs will behave with respect to changes in business activity. Classifying costs as variable or fixed helps a manager make such predictions.

Variable Cost

A **variable cost** is one that changes in direct proportion to fluctuations in the level of activity. The activity can be expressed in many ways, such as the number of customers served (restaurant), units produced or sold (manufacturing company), beds occupied (hospital), or students registered (educational institution). As an example, consider the Optima Hybrid manufactured by KIA. Each car requires one lithium polymer battery pack. Therefore, if car production goes up 10%, then the number of battery packs used and the corresponding costs will also go up 10%, assuming that the cost of each battery pack purchased from the supplier does not change.

It is important to note that when we speak of a cost as being variable, we mean the amount in *total* rises and falls as the activity level rises and falls. However, the cost *per unit* of activity remains constant. This idea is presented below, assuming that each battery pack costs $100. The concept of a variable cost is shown in graphical form in Exhibit 2–1.

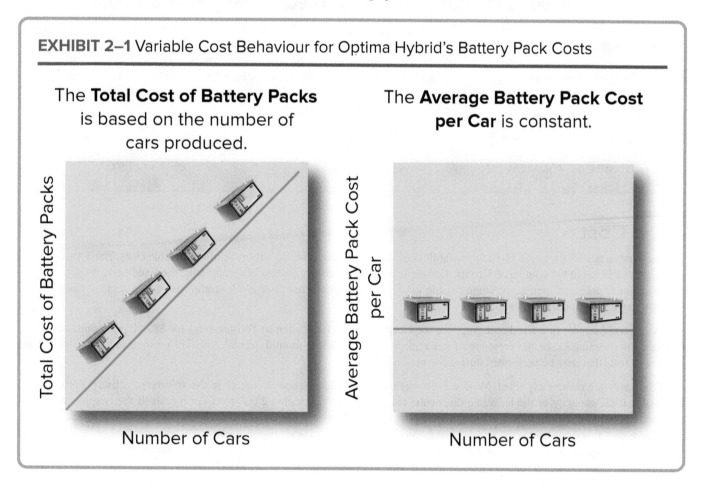

EXHIBIT 2–1 Variable Cost Behaviour for Optima Hybrid's Battery Pack Costs

The **Total Cost of Battery Packs** is based on the number of cars produced.

The **Average Battery Pack Cost per Car** is constant.

Number of Cars Produced	Cost per Battery Pack	Total Variable Cost—Battery Packs
100	$100	$ 10,000
1,000	100	100,000
2,000	100	200,000

There are many examples of costs that are variable with respect to the volume of products/services provided by a company. In a merchandising company, variable costs include such items as cost of goods sold, commissions to salespeople, and billing costs. In a hospital, the variable costs of providing healthcare services to patients include the costs of the supplies, drugs, and meals. In a manufacturing company, variable costs include such items as materials used in the product, wages of operators, lubricants, supplies, shipping costs, and sales commissions.

The activity causing changes in a variable cost need not be how much output is produced or sold. For example, the wages paid to employees at an Extreme Pita outlet will depend on the number of hours worked per day (or week) and not strictly on the number of customers served. In this case, we would say that wage costs are variable with respect to the hours worked. Nevertheless when we say that a cost is variable, we *ordinarily* mean it is variable with respect to the volume of revenue-generating output—in other words, the number of customers served, patients treated, cars sold, and so on.

IN BUSINESS

COST MANAGEMENT IS CRUCIAL IN THE NEW ECONOMIC ENVIRONMENT

Nearly a decade has passed since the 2008 global financial crisis, yet many businesses and other organizations are still facing challenges as the world's economy remains sluggish. In times of uncertainty and challenging economic environment, cost-cutting has continued to be a priority for businesses. For example, the oil and gas sector has cut thousands of jobs and reduced spending by billions of dollars to competitively reposition itself in the market. The ripple effect of this is that other sectors also undertaking cost-cutting measures in hopes of maintaining (or at least not significantly reducing) profit levels.

Sources: K. Bakx, "Energy Industry Layoffs in Calgary a Boon for HR Companies," *CBC News*, March 18, 2015; Y. Hussain, "Cost-Cutting Fever Grips Big Oil," *Calgary Herald,* August 22, 2014; S. Deveau, "Bombardier Blames Economy for Shortfall," *National Post,* January 21, 2014; D. Berman & B. Milner, "Falling Markets—and Canada's Suddenly Vulnerable Energy Sector," *The Globe and Mail*, October 15, 2014.

Fixed Cost

A **fixed cost** is one that remains constant, regardless of changes in the level of activity. Unlike variable costs, fixed costs are not affected by changes in the volume of activity. Consequently, as the activity volume rises and falls, the fixed costs remain constant in total amount unless influenced by some outside force, such as a price change or a substantial increase in demand leading to an increase in the resource requirement.

Rent is a good example of a fixed cost. Suppose the Hospital for Sick Children in Toronto rents for $8,000 per month a machine that tests blood samples for the presence of leukemia cells. The $8,000 monthly rental cost will be incurred regardless of the number of tests that may be performed during the month.

Very few costs are completely fixed. Most will change if there is a large enough change in the volume of activity. For example, suppose that the capacity of the leukemia diagnostic machine at the hospital is 2,000 tests per month. If the hospital wished to perform more than 2,000 tests in a month, it would be necessary to rent an additional machine, which would cause a jump in the fixed costs. When we say a cost is *fixed,* we mean it is fixed within some *relevant range*. The **relevant range** is the range of activity within which the assumptions about variable and fixed costs are valid. For example, the assumption that the rent for a diagnostic machine is $8,000 per month is valid within the relevant range of 0 to 2,000 tests per month.

Fixed costs can create confusion if they are expressed on a per-unit basis. This is because the average fixed cost per unit increases and decreases *inversely* with changes in activity volume. In the Hospital for Sick Children example, the average cost per test will fall as the number of tests performed increases because the $8,000 rental cost will be spread over more tests. Conversely, as the number of tests performed in the hospital declines, the average cost per test will rise, as the $8,000 rental cost is spread over fewer tests. This concept is illustrated in the table below:

Monthly Rental Cost	Number of Tests Performed	Average Cost per Test
$8,000	100	$80
8,000	1,000	8
8,000	2,000	4

Note that if the hospital performs only 100 tests each month, the rental cost of the equipment will average $80 per test. But if 2,000 tests are performed each month, the average cost will drop to only $4 per test. More will be said later about the problems created for both the accountant and the manager by this variation in *average* unit costs.

Examples of fixed costs include straight-line depreciation/amortization, insurance, property taxes, rent, supervisory salaries, administrative salaries, and advertising.[1]

A summary of the fixed cost behaviour is presented in Exhibit 2–2.

EXHIBIT 2–2 Fixed Cost Behaviour for Machine Rental Costs

Hospital for Sick Children's **Monthly Machine Rental Cost** does not change regardless of how many tests are performed within a relevant range.

Hospital for Sick Children's **Average Machine Rental Cost per Test** decreases as more tests are done.

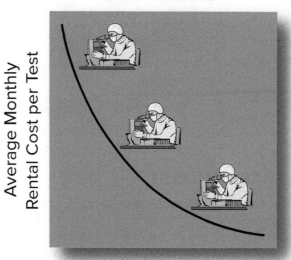

Monthly Rental Cost

Number of Tests Performed

Average Monthly Rental Cost per Test

Number of Tests Performed

HELPFUL HINT

Students often assume that fixed costs expressed on a per-unit basis behave like variable costs. This is not true! If the average fixed cost per cellphone is $5 at a production level of 100,000 phones, it means the total amount of the fixed cost is $500,000. If the activity level/volume increases to 100,001 units, it does not mean that fixed costs will increase by $5. The total fixed cost remains constant at $500,000 within a relevant range of production.

IN BUSINESS

THE COST OF A NEW HOME

With real estate sales and prices on the rise across Canada, it is beneficial for homebuyers to understand the costs associated with acquiring a new home so that they have a better understanding of what they are paying for. According to a new study, over a quarter of the costs for a new home in Manitoba comprise government fees, taxes, and infrastructure requirements. During the 17th annual Housing Forum and Building Trade Show, the Manitoba Home Builders' Association (MHBA), along with a large home builder, provided a breakdown of all the government-imposed costs related to the construction of a standard new home in Winnipeg.

Using the average price of a two-storey, single-detached home as an example, they found out that over 27.6% was for government-imposed costs such as provincial land-transfer taxes, Canada Mortgage and Housing Corporation's mortgage insurance fees, city building permits and related fees, infrastructure costs, and federal, provincial, and municipal taxes. Over a quarter of these government-imposed costs were paid by the homebuyer, 13.5% by the builder, and the remaining amount (about 60%) was borne by the developer. However, a portion of the costs borne by the builder and the developer will likely be passed on to the buyer so that the developer can generate a profit.

Being aware of other important unassociated costs (such as appraisals, legal services, insurance, moving costs, etc.) will help homebuyers prepare a more comprehensive budget that properly informs them of the commitments they will be making.

Sources: G. Marr, "Canada Home Prices Keep Rising Despite Slowdown in Prairies," *Financial Post*, March 13, 2015; M. McNeill, "Nailing Down Cost of Homebuilding," *Winnipeg Free Press*, November 5, 2014; Canadian Home Builders' Association website (www.chba.ca), accessed on April 3, 2015.

DECISION POINT

FINANCIAL ANALYST

You are a financial analyst for several clients who are interested in making investments in stable companies. You become aware of a privately owned airline that has been in business for 20 years and is in need of $75 million in new capital. When you call one of your clients, she replies that she avoids investing in airlines because of the high proportion of fixed costs in this industry. How would you respond to this statement?

*Note to student: See **Guidance Answers** online.*

Cost Classification by Traceability

LO2   ● **Know**   ● **Apply**

CC2: Define direct and indirect costs, and give examples.

In addition to understanding costs by behaviour, managers also need to know whether costs can be traced to specific cost objects; this helps managers in accurately assigning costs. A **cost object** is anything for which cost data are desired—department, division, product, product line, customer, or geographical territory. Costs can be classified as either *direct* or *indirect* based on traceability. Let's go back to our Air Canada example and assume that management is interested in tracking costs relating to specific flights; each such flight is considered a cost object.

Direct Cost

A **direct cost** is one that pertains to a certain cost object and can be easily and economically traced to that cost object. In the case of Air Canada, fuel costs can be traced to individual flights and therefore are considered direct costs.

Indirect Cost

An **indirect cost** is one that cannot be easily and conveniently traced to a particular cost object under consideration. For instance, costs such as the salaries of the baggage handling staff, ticketing staff, and other office staff, or the expenses incurred in running the airline's marketing and accounting departments, cannot be traced to specific flights and therefore are classified as indirect costs. This is because these costs are not driven by any one specific flight; they are incurred as a result of running the airline. Exhibit 2–3 illustrates the concept of direct and indirect costs.

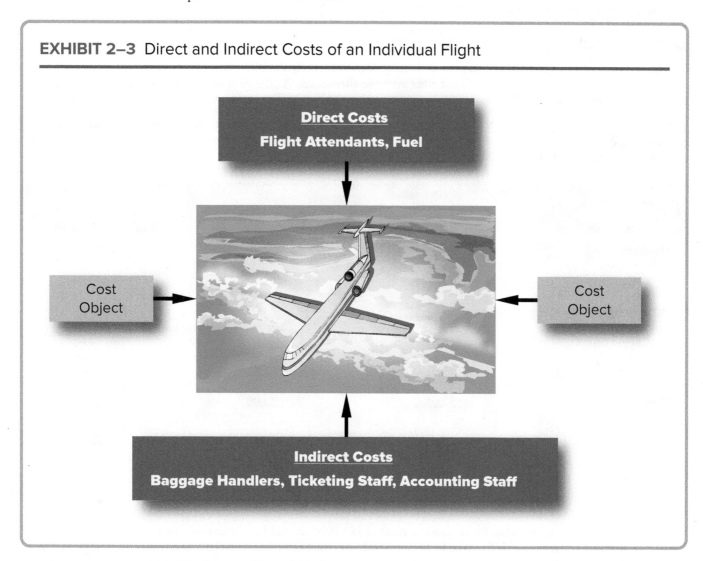

EXHIBIT 2–3 Direct and Indirect Costs of an Individual Flight

To be traced to a cost object, such as a specific flight, the cost must be caused by the cost object. The airline's baggage handling, ticketing, and marketing costs are common to multiple flights. An indirect cost or a **common cost** is one that is incurred to support a number of cost objects (e.g., different flights) but cannot be traced to individual cost objects.

Whether a cost is classified as direct or indirect depends upon the cost object. For example, although salaries of the baggage handling staff are indirect to individual flights offered by Air Canada, they are direct to the baggage handling department. In the second case, the cost object is the baggage handling department.

Cost Classification by Relevance

CC3: Define differential costs, opportunity costs, and sunk costs, and give examples.

Given the importance of cost information for decision making, managers must be able to identify costs that are relevant for individual decisions. Cost classification by relevance helps in decision making. Only costs that are relevant to individual decisions must be used in the analysis preceding decision making. In general, *differential* and *opportunity* costs are relevant for most decisions, whereas *sunk* costs are irrelevant for any decision.

Differential Cost and Revenue

Decisions involve choosing among alternatives. In business decisions, each alternative will have certain costs and benefits that must be compared with the costs and benefits of other available alternatives. A difference in costs between any two alternatives is known as a **differential cost.** A difference in revenues between any two alternatives is known as a **differential revenue.**

Differential costs can be either fixed or variable. To illustrate, assume that Nature Made Cosmetics, Inc. is considering changing its marketing method from distribution through retailers to online sale. Present costs and revenues are compared with projected costs and revenues in the following table:

	Retailer Distribution (current)	Online Selling (proposed)	Differential Costs and Revenues
Revenues (V)*	$700,000	$800,000	$100,000
Cost of goods sold (V)	350,000	400,000	50,000
Advertising (F)	80,000	115,000	35,000
Warehouse depreciation (F)	50,000	80,000	30,000
Other expenses (F)	60,000	60,000	–0–
Total	540,000	655,000	115,000
Net income	$160,000	$145,000	$(15,000)

*V = Variable; F = Fixed.

According to the preceding analysis, the differential revenue is $100,000, and the differential costs total $115,000, leaving a negative differential net income of $15,000 under the proposed marketing plan. The financial analysis suggests that Nature Made Cosmetics should not implement the proposed plan. However, before making any changes, management must also consider nonfinancial factors, such as the effect of the proposed online selling policy on brand image, competitors' actions, and the current trend of online shopping (which may result in future sales).

In general, only the differences between alternatives are relevant in decisions. Those items that are the same under all alternatives are not affected by the decision and can be ignored. For example, in the Nature Made Cosmetics example, the "other expenses" category, which is $60,000 under both alternatives, can be ignored because it is not affected by the decision. If it were removed from the calculations, the retailer distribution method would still be preferred by $15,000. This is an extremely important principle in managerial accounting that we will return to in later chapters.

Opportunity Cost

Opportunity cost is the potential benefit that is given up when one alternative is selected over another. To illustrate this important concept, suppose Walmart Canada is considering investing a large sum of money in land that may be a site for a future store. Rather than invest the funds in land, the company could invest the funds in high-grade securities. If the land is acquired, the opportunity cost will be the investment income that could have been realized if the securities had been purchased instead.

Opportunity cost is not incurred by the organization and therefore is not recorded in the accounts, but it is a cost that must be explicitly considered in every decision a manager makes. Virtually every alternative has some opportunity cost attached to it.

DECISION POINT

YOUR DECISION TO ATTEND CLASS

When you make the decision to attend class, what opportunity costs are inherent in that decision?

*Note to student: See **Guidance Answers** online.*

Sunk Cost

A **sunk cost** is one that has already been incurred and cannot be changed by any decision made now or in the future. Since sunk costs cannot be changed by any decision, they are not differential costs. Therefore, they can and should be ignored when making a decision; in other words, sunk costs are irrelevant.

To illustrate a sunk cost, assume that a company paid $50,000 several years ago for a special-purpose machine. The machine was used to make a product that is now obsolete and is no longer being sold. Even though in hindsight the purchase of the machine may have been unwise, no amount of regret can undo that decision. And it would be foolish to continue making the obsolete product in a misguided attempt to recover the original cost of the machine. In short, the $50,000 originally paid for the machine has already been incurred and cannot be a differential cost in any future decision. For this reason, such costs are said to be *sunk* and should be ignored in decisions. However, any revenue recognized from the future sale of the machine may be treated as a relevant cost depending on the situation.

CONCEPT CHECK

1. Which of the following cost behaviour assumptions are true? (You may select more than one answer.)
   a. Variable costs are constant when expressed on a per-unit basis.
   b. Total variable costs increase as the level of activity increases.
   c. The average fixed cost per unit increases as the level of activity increases.
   d. Total fixed costs decrease as the level of activity decreases.
2. Which of the following statements are true? (You may select more than one answer.)
   a. A common cost is one type of direct cost.
   b. A sunk cost is usually a differential cost.
   c. Opportunity costs are not usually recorded in the accounts of an organization.
   d. A particular cost may be direct or indirect depending on the cost object.

*Note to student: See **Guidance Answers** online.*

Cost Classification by Function

Another cost classification is based on function. Before we discuss this further, it might be useful to understand that every organization carries out a sequence of steps (tasks) to fulfill its mission. Such a sequence of steps (tasks) is known as the **value chain** of that organization.

Acadian Seaplants, located in Dartmouth, Nova Scotia, is a diversified, technology-based manufacturer of natural specialty fertilizers, crop biostimulants, feed, food, food ingredients, and brewery supplies derived from select species of marine plants. Acadian is a fully integrated company involved in activities ranging from marine plant cultivation and the hand harvesting of pure seaweeds to product and application development, manufacturing, and technical customer support. Acadian's value chain is considerably broad (see Exhibit 2–4). In contrast, some competitors of Acadian may be less integrated—involved only in product and application development or in manufacturing. Such competitors must depend on other organizations for the cultivation and harvesting of seaweeds (front end of the value chain) and customer support (back end of the value chain).

EXHIBIT 2–4 Acadian Seaplants' Value Chain

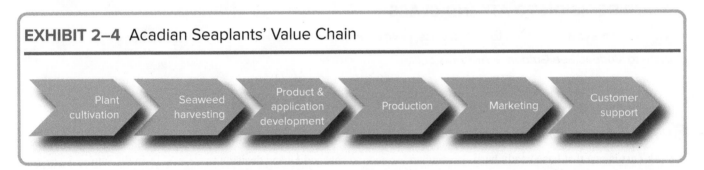

Cost classification by function consists of associating costs with the type of activity for which that cost is incurred (e.g., manufacturing, marketing, or administration). For a retailer, such as Best Buy, the cost of products purchased from suppliers (e.g., laptop computers, cellphones and iPads) including delivery would be classified as merchandise costs (or cost of merchandise sold). Advertising costs and the costs of the accountants and legal personnel may be classified under selling and administrative costs. Such a distinction is more pronounced for manufacturing companies; we can distinguish between manufacturing and nonmanufacturing costs.

Manufacturing Costs

LO4 • **Know**

CC4: Distinguish between manufacturing and nonmanufacturing costs.

Similar to merchandising companies that must procure the goods they sell, manufacturing companies must produce the goods they sell. We use the term **manufacturing costs** to identify the costs associated with production activity. Typically, there are three types of manufacturing costs; we discuss each of these below as they might pertain to AmbuTech, a division of Winnipeg-based Melet Plastics, Inc., which produces a variety of canes for visually impaired and physically challenged customers.

DIRECT MATERIALS

The materials that go into the final product are called **raw materials.** At the least, the raw materials required for one line of AmbuTech's canes would include aluminum for the body of the cane and plastic or wood for the handle.

LO4 • **Know** • **Apply**

CC5: Identify and give examples of direct materials, direct labour, and manufacturing overhead costs.

The term *raw materials* is somewhat misleading because it seems to imply unprocessed natural resources. Actually, raw materials refer to any materials that are used in the final (finished) product of a company. Note, however, that the finished product of one company can be the raw material for another company. For example, AmbuTech might be purchasing ready-to-assemble plastic cane handles from a supplier, rather than producing them in-house. Whether to make the cane handles or buy them from outside can be an important decision that would influence AmbuTech's costs; we will examine such decisions in Chapter 9.

The aluminum sheets and plastic cane handles can also be called **direct materials,** since they become an integral part of the cane. As you can see, the quantity of direct materials required varies proportionately with the number of units produced. Therefore, the cost of direct materials is a variable cost with respect to production activity.

In addition to the direct materials, AmbuTech would also be using other **indirect materials** in the manufacturing process (e.g., screws, glue, solder, and other supplies) that are not integral parts of the cane. Indirect materials are relatively insignificant in value, and their costs are either not traceable to, or not worth tracing directly to, the finished product. The cost of indirect materials is included as part of manufacturing overhead, which is discussed later in this section.

DIRECT LABOUR

Direct labour refers to those labour costs that can be easily (i.e., physically and conveniently) traced to individual units of product. In the case of AmbuTech, this would include the wages and benefits of the individuals directly involved in rolling the aluminum sheets to form the body of the canes and those involved in assembling the canes. Whether direct labour costs should be classified as variable (with respect to output) or fixed is debatable. It is reasonable to classify direct labour cost as a variable cost because the amount of direct labour hours required varies in proportion to the level of production. However, in many organizations, direct labour may be paid a fixed monthly salary regardless of how much is produced. *For our purposes, we will generally classify direct labour as a variable cost.*

Labour costs that cannot be physically traced to the creation of products, or that can be traced only at great cost and inconvenience, are termed **indirect labour** and treated as part of manufacturing overhead, along with indirect materials. Indirect labour includes the labour costs of janitors, supervisors, materials handlers, and night security guards. Although the efforts of these workers are essential to production, it would be either impractical or impossible to accurately trace their costs to specific units of product.

In some industries, major shifts are taking place in the structure of labour costs. Sophisticated automated equipment, operated and maintained by skilled indirect workers, is increasingly replacing direct labour. In a few companies, direct labour has become such a minor element of cost that it has disappeared altogether as a separate cost category. More is said in later chapters about this trend and about the impact it is having on cost systems. However, the vast majority of manufacturing and service companies throughout the world continue to recognize direct labour as a separate cost category. In service companies, labour can often be a significant portion of the total cost of providing a service.

MANUFACTURING OVERHEAD

In addition to direct materials and direct labour, AmbuTech would also be incurring other costs related to manufacturing. These might include indirect materials and indirect labour (discussed previously), factory maintenance, utilities, property taxes, and depreciation on equipment and factory buildings. Such costs are included in a separate category called **manufacturing overhead.** It is important to remember that AmbuTech will incur utility, maintenance, and depreciation expenses associated with its selling and administrative functions; however, these costs are *not* recorded as part of manufacturing overhead. Only costs that are associated with the manufacturing function (i.e., operating the factory) are included in the manufacturing overhead category.

Various names are used for manufacturing overhead, such as *indirect manufacturing cost, factory overhead,* and *factory burden.* All of these terms are synonymous with *manufacturing overhead.*

Manufacturing overhead combined with direct labour is called **conversion cost.** This term stems from the fact that direct labour costs and overhead costs are incurred to convert raw materials into finished products. Direct labour combined with direct materials is called **prime cost.**

Nonmanufacturing Costs

LO4   • Know   • Apply

CC6: Identify and give examples of marketing or selling and administrative costs.

Generally, nonmanufacturing costs are subclassified into two categories: marketing or selling costs, and administrative costs.

Marketing or selling costs include all costs necessary to secure customer orders and get the finished product or service into the hands of the customer. These costs are often called *order-getting* and *order-filling costs.* Examples of marketing (selling) costs include market research, advertising, shipping, sales travel, sales commissions, sales salaries, and costs of finished goods warehouses.

Administrative costs include all executive, organizational, and clerical costs associated with the general management of an organization, rather than with manufacturing, marketing, or selling. Examples of administrative costs include executive compensation, general accounting, secretarial, public relations, and similar costs involved in the general administration of the organization *as a whole*.

IN BUSINESS

THE CHALLENGE OF MANAGING CHARITABLE ORGANIZATIONS

Charitable organizations—such as the United Way of Canada, KidSport Canada, the Canadian Red Cross, and the Canadian Cancer Society—experience challenges of their own. How they spend their money is definitely a matter of concern. United Way's 2013 annual report states that on average it spends 15% of total revenue on fundraising and administration costs, while the Canadian Red Cross averaged close to 20% over the last five years. These figures compare very favourably with the Canadian Cancer Society, which, in 2013–14, spent close to 35%. A recent report noted that the Canadian Cancer Society's cost of fundraising and administration has increased significantly compared to a decade ago. The CEO claimed that this cost increase was necessary due to the expansion and diversification of fundraising activity across the country.

Many charitable organizations are starting to seek gifts explicitly to fund administrative expenses. Their argument is simple—they cannot do good deeds for other people without incurring such costs.

Sources: United Way of Canada Annual Report, 2013, p. 14; Canadian Red Cross Annual Report, 2013–14; Canadian Cancer Society Annual Report, 2013–14; S. Ubelacker, "Cancer Society Defends Spending After Research Dollars Questioned: Cancer Society Defends Research Spending," *The Canadian Press*, July 6, 2011; R. E. Silverman and S. Beatty, "Save the Children (But Pay the Bills Too)," *The Wall Street Journal*, December 26, 2006, pp. D1–D2.

Product Costs versus Period Costs

LO4   ● **Know**   ● **Apply**

CC7: Distinguish between product and period costs, and give examples.

Another classification by function, often used synonymously with manufacturing versus nonmanufacturing costs, is that of *product* versus *period* costs. To understand the distinction between the two, we must first refresh our understanding of the matching principle from financial accounting.

The *matching principle* is based on the accrual concept and states that *costs incurred to generate a particular revenue should be recognized as expenses in the same period that the revenue is recognized*. This means that if a cost is incurred to acquire or make something that will eventually be sold, then the cost should be recognized as an expense only when the sale takes place—that is, when the benefit occurs. Such costs are called *product costs*.

Product Costs

For financial accounting purposes, **product costs** include all of the costs that are involved in acquiring or making a product. In the case of a merchandising firm, such as Hudson's Bay Company (HBC), product costs would include the costs associated with procuring (or acquiring) the merchandise HBC sells. For a manufacturing company, product costs include direct materials and labour and manufacturing overhead. Product costs are *attached* to goods when they are acquired or produced and are carried forward to an inventory account that appears on the balance sheet. Consequently, product costs are also known as **inventoriable costs.** Canadian Tire's 2015 annual report showed a merchandise inventory balance of $1,764.5 million (14.4% of sales revenue). Loblaw's annual report for the same period showed a merchandise inventory balance of $4,322 million (9.5% of sales revenue).

When the inventory is sold, the product costs attached to the quantities sold are *expensed* (i.e., matched against sales revenue) and carried forward to the cost of goods sold account, which appears on the income statement. It is important to note that product costs may not be expensed in the period in which they are incurred; instead, the period when the goods are sold is critical for determining when to expense the product costs.

EXHIBIT 2–5 Summary of Cost Classifications by Function

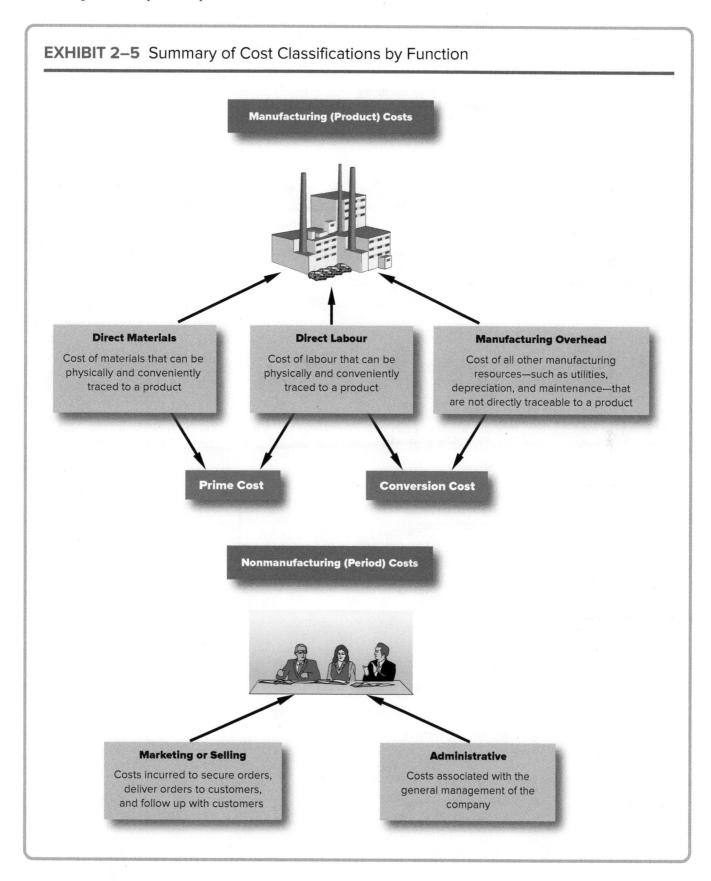

Period Costs

Period costs are all the costs not included in product costs. These are expensed on the income statement in the period in which they are incurred, using the usual rules of accrual accounting that you have already learned in financial accounting.

Period costs are not included as part of the cost of either purchased or manufactured goods. Sales commissions and office rent are good examples of period costs. Neither commission nor office rent is included as part of the cost of purchased or manufactured goods. Rather, both items are treated as expenses on the income statement in the period in which they are incurred.

As suggested previously, *all nonmanufacturing costs are considered to be period costs*. Therefore, advertising, executive salaries, sales commissions, public relations, and other nonmanufacturing costs discussed previously would all be period costs. They will appear on the income statement as expenses in the period in which they are incurred.

Exhibit 2–5 summarizes cost classifications by function.

HELPFUL HINT

For a manufacturing company, the terms *manufacturing costs, product costs,* and *inventoriable costs* have the same meaning. These costs are first carried to an inventory account until the goods are sold, at which time they are expensed. This practice follows the matching principle.

WORKING IT OUT

For a bicycle manufacturer, indicate whether each item listed below is a prime cost, a conversion cost, both, or neither. Also, indicate whether each item is fixed or variable with respect to the number of bicycles sold.

- **a.** Salary of the marketing manager.
- **b.** Cost of bicycle tires.
- **c.** Wages of employees who assemble the bicycles.
- **d.** Salary of the assembly shop supervisor.
- **e.** Commission paid to the salesperson as a percentage of sales revenue.
- **f.** Monthly rent on the manufacturing facility.
- **g.** Wages of employees who paint the bicycles.

SOLUTION TO WORKING IT OUT

- **a.** Salary of the marketing manager.

    | NEITHER | This is *not* product cost. |
    | FIXED | This cost does not vary with the number of bicycles sold. |

- **b.** Cost of bicycle tires.

    | PRIME | This is a direct materials cost. |
    | VARIABLE | This cost varies with the number of bicycles sold. |

- **c.** Wages of employees who assemble the bicycles.

    | BOTH | This is a direct labour cost. |
    | VARIABLE | For our purposes we classify direct labour cost as variable. |

d. Salary of the assembly shop supervisor.

CONVERSION   This is a manufacturing overhead cost.

FIXED   This cost does not vary with the number of bicycles sold.

e. Commission paid to the salesperson as a percentage of sales revenue.

NEITHER   This is *not* a product cost.

VARIABLE   This cost varies with the number of bicycles sold.

f. Monthly rent on the manufacturing facility.

CONVERSION   This is a manufacturing overhead cost.

FIXED   This cost does not vary with the number of bicycles sold.

g. Wages of employees who paint the bicycles.

BOTH   This is a direct labour cost.

VARIABLE   For our purposes we classify direct labour cost as variable.

Cost Classifications on Financial Statements

LO4 • **Know**

CC8: Explain how costs are classified in financial statements of merchandising and manufacturing companies.

In your prior accounting training, you learned that firms prepare periodic financial reports for creditors, shareholders, and others to show the financial condition of the firm and the firm's earnings performance over some specified interval.

The financial statements prepared by a *manufacturing* company are more complex than the statements prepared by a *merchandising* company. Manufacturing companies are more complex organizations than merchandising companies because the manufacturing company must produce its goods as well as market them. The production process gives rise to many costs that do not exist in a merchandising company, and these costs must be accounted for on the manufacturing company's financial statements. In this section, we focus our attention on how this accounting is carried out on the balance sheet and in the income statement.

The Balance Sheet

LO5 • **Apply**

CC9: Prepare an income statement.

CC10: Prepare a schedule of cost of goods sold.

The balance sheet of a manufacturing company is similar to that of a merchandising company. However, the inventory accounts differ between the two types of companies. A merchandising company has only one type of inventory—goods purchased from suppliers that are awaiting resale to customers. In contrast, manufacturing companies have three types of inventories—*raw materials, work in process,* and *finished goods*. Raw materials, as we have noted, are the materials that are used to make a product. **Work in process** (also known as *goods in process*) consists of units of product that are partially complete and will require further work before they are ready for sale to a customer. **Finished goods** consist of units of product that have been completed and are available for sale to customers.

We will use two companies—Halifax Manufacturing Corporation and Brandon Bookstore—to illustrate the concepts discussed in this section. Halifax Manufacturing Corporation makes precision brass fittings for yachts, and Brandon Bookstore specializes in books about Canadian history.

The balance sheets of both companies will likely include a single line item pertaining to inventory. However, notes to Halifax Manufacturing Corporation's annual report will reveal the following information concerning its inventories:

HALIFAX MANUFACTURING CORPORATION Inventory Accounts		
	Beginning Balance	Ending Balance
Raw materials	$ 60,000	$ 50,000
Work in process	90,000	60,000
Finished goods	125,000	175,000
Total inventory accounts	$275,000	$285,000

Halifax Manufacturing Corporation's raw materials inventory would consist largely of brass rods and brass blocks. The work-in-process inventory would consist of partially completed brass fittings, and the finished goods inventory would consist of brass fittings that are available for sale to customers.

In contrast, the inventory account at Brandon Bookstore would consist entirely of the costs of books the company has purchased from publishers for resale to the public. In merchandising companies such as Brandon, these inventories may be called *merchandise inventory*.

The beginning and ending balances in this account appear as follows:

BRANDON BOOKSTORE Inventory Accounts		
	Beginning Balance	Ending Balance
Merchandise inventory	$100,000	$150,000

The Income Statement

Exhibit 2–6 compares the income statements of Brandon Bookstore and Halifax Manufacturing Corporation. For the purposes of illustration, these statements contain more detail about cost of goods sold than you will generally find in published financial statements.

 **LO6** • **Know**

CC11: Explain the basic inventory flow equation.

At first glance, the income statements of merchandising and manufacturing firms such as Brandon Bookstore and Halifax Manufacturing Corporation are very similar. The only apparent difference is in the labels of some of the entries in the computation of the cost of goods sold. In Exhibit 2–6, the computation of cost of goods sold relies on the following basic equation for inventory accounts:

BASIC EQUATION FOR INVENTORY ACCOUNTS

Beginning		Additions		Withdrawals		Ending
	+		−		=	
balance		to inventory		from inventory		balance

The preceding equation provides the mathematics for calculating the cost of goods sold in both merchandising and manufacturing organizations. The logic underlying this equation, which applies to any inventory account, is illustrated in Exhibit 2–7A. During a period, additions to the inventory account come through purchases (in the case of merchandising companies) or production (in the case of manufacturing companies). The sum of the additions to the account and the beginning balance represents the total amount of inventory available for use during the period. During the period, a portion of the inventory is withdrawn, leaving a certain balance at the end of the period.

EXHIBIT 2–6 Comparative Income Statements: Merchandising and Manufacturing Companies

MERCHANDISING COMPANY
Brandon Bookstore

Sales		$1,000,000
Cost of goods sold:		
Beginning merchandise inventory	$100,000	
Add: Purchases	650,000	
Goods available for sale	750,000	
Deduct: Ending merchandise inventory	150,000	600,000
Gross margin		400,000
Deduct: Operating expenses:		
Selling expense	100,000	
Administrative expense	200,000	300,000
Net income		$ 100,000

The cost of merchandise inventory purchased from outside suppliers during the period.

MANUFACTURING COMPANY
Halifax Manufacturing Corporation

Sales		$1,500,000
Cost of goods sold:		
Beginning finished goods inventory	$125,000	
Add: Cost of goods manufactured	850,000	
Goods available for sale	975,000	
Deduct: Ending finished goods inventory	175,000	800,000
Gross margin		700,000
Deduct: Operating expenses:		
Selling expense	250,000	
Administrative expense	300,000	550,000
Net income		$ 150,000

The manufacturing costs associated with the goods that were finished during the period. (See Exhibit 2–8 for details.)

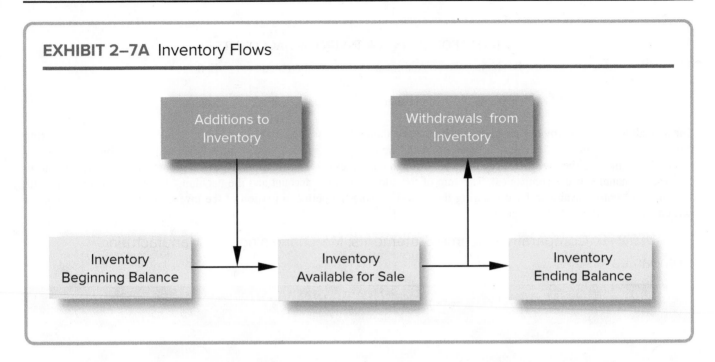

EXHIBIT 2–7A Inventory Flows

There are two methods to keep track of inventory and compute the cost of goods sold. A **perpetual inventory system** maintains a continuous record of the inventory. Additions to inventory are debited to the account, and withdrawals from inventory are transferred to the cost of goods sold (COGS) account as and when individual transactions take place. These transactions can be captured in the inventory and COGS T-accounts as illustrated in Exhibit 2–7B. This means that the inventory and the cost of goods sold balances are readily available assuming that there are no delays in recording the transactions. Retail companies like Best Buy and Walmart use computerized systems to track inventory transactions on a daily basis.

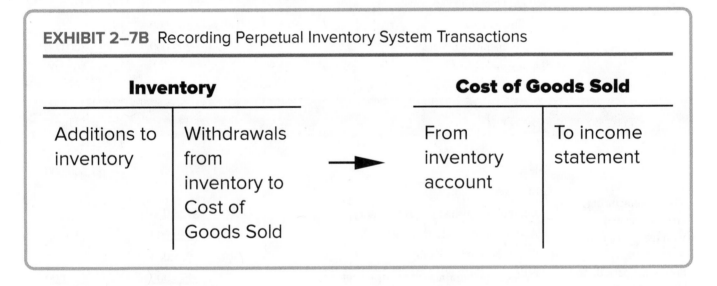

EXHIBIT 2–7B Recording Perpetual Inventory System Transactions

On the other hand, in a **periodic inventory system,** the inventory account is updated at the end of a period. To determine the cost of goods sold in a merchandising company such as Brandon Bookstore, we only need to know the beginning and ending balances in the merchandise inventory account, and the purchases (see Exhibit 2–7C). Total purchases can easily be determined in a merchandising company by simply adding up all purchases from suppliers.

EXHIBIT 2–7C Inventory Flows and Cost of Goods Sold

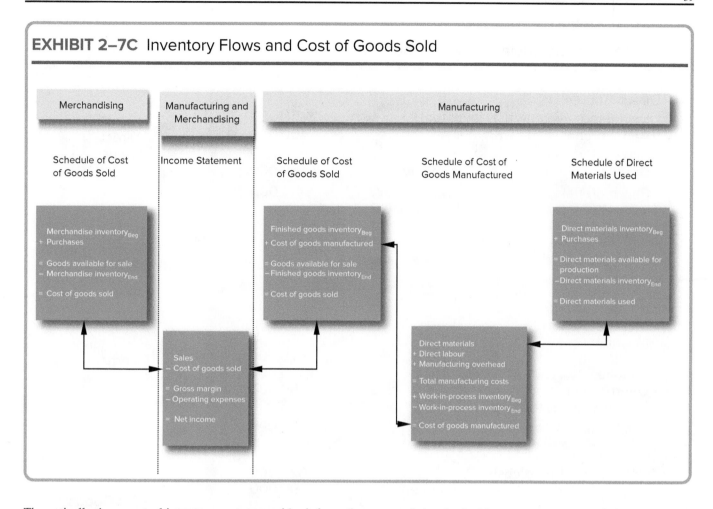

Theoretically the perpetual inventory system provides information on a real-time basis. Most managers want real-time (or at least daily) information about production or sales quantity. However, they will likely not want cost and profitability information on a real-time basis. Cost and profitability reports are prepared on a periodic basis (e.g., quarterly); therefore, a periodic system may be adequate for such reporting.

To determine the cost of goods sold in a manufacturing company such as Halifax Manufacturing Corporation, we must know the cost of goods manufactured and the beginning and ending balances in the finished goods inventory account (see Exhibit 2–7C). The **cost of goods manufactured** consists of the manufacturing costs associated with goods that were *finished* during the period. The cost of goods manufactured figure for Halifax Manufacturing Corporation is computed in Exhibit 2–8, which contains a *schedule of cost of goods manufactured.*

Schedule of Cost of Goods Manufactured

LO6 • **Apply**

CC12: Prepare a schedule of cost of goods manufactured, including the computation of the cost of direct materials used.

At first glance, the **schedule of cost of goods manufactured** in Exhibit 2–8 looks complex and perhaps even intimidating. However, it is all quite logical. Note that the schedule of cost of goods manufactured contains the three elements of product costs that we discussed earlier—direct materials, direct labour, and manufacturing overhead.

The cost of direct materials used is computed by taking into consideration the cost of direct materials in inventory at the start and the end of a period, and the cost of purchases during the period (see the schedule of direct materials used in Exhibit 2–7C). Once the cost of direct materials used is computed, direct labour and manufacturing overhead costs are added, which results in the total manufacturing costs incurred during the period ($820,000 in Exhibit 2–8). This amount, however, is *not* the cost of goods manufactured for the period.

EXHIBIT 2–8 Schedule of Cost of Goods Manufactured

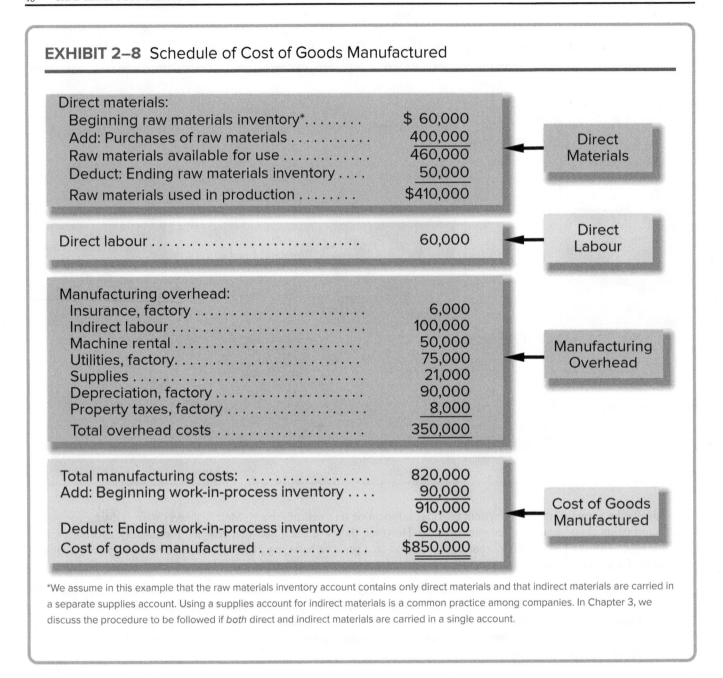

Direct materials:
Beginning raw materials inventory*.......	$ 60,000	
Add: Purchases of raw materials..........	400,000	Direct Materials
Raw materials available for use...........	460,000	
Deduct: Ending raw materials inventory....	50,000	
Raw materials used in production........	$410,000	

Direct labour.............................	60,000	Direct Labour

Manufacturing overhead:
Insurance, factory........................	6,000	
Indirect labour..........................	100,000	
Machine rental..........................	50,000	Manufacturing Overhead
Utilities, factory........................	75,000	
Supplies................................	21,000	
Depreciation, factory....................	90,000	
Property taxes, factory..................	8,000	
Total overhead costs....................	350,000	

Total manufacturing costs:	820,000	
Add: Beginning work-in-process inventory....	90,000	
	910,000	Cost of Goods Manufactured
Deduct: Ending work-in-process inventory....	60,000	
Cost of goods manufactured..............	$850,000	

*We assume in this example that the raw materials inventory account contains only direct materials and that indirect materials are carried in a separate supplies account. Using a supplies account for indirect materials is a common practice among companies. In Chapter 3, we discuss the procedure to be followed if *both* direct and indirect materials are carried in a single account.

The total units manufactured in any period often include partially completed units carried forward from the previous period (called *beginning work-in-process inventory*). Similarly, manufacturing activity in the current period often includes partially completed units that will be carried forward to the next period (called *ending work-in-process inventory*). To compute the cost of goods manufactured, prior period costs associated with the beginning work-in-process inventory must be added to the manufacturing costs, whereas costs associated with the ending work-in-process inventory must be deducted from the manufacturing costs (see the schedule of cost of goods manufactured in Exhibit 2–7C). This adjustment of the costs associated with the beginning and ending work-in-process inventories is also shown at the bottom of Exhibit 2–8 and results in the cost of goods manufactured for the current period amounting to $850,000.

HELPFUL HINT

The cost of goods manufactured (COGM) includes the costs of direct materials, direct labour, and manufacturing overhead that relate to the units *produced* during a certain period. The cost of goods sold (COGS), on the other hand, includes the costs of direct materials, direct labour, and manufacturing overhead that relate to the units *sold* in that same period. The COGM and COGS amounts will rarely be the same during a given period.

Product Costs—A Closer Look

Previously in the chapter, we defined product costs as those costs that are involved in either the purchase or manufacture of goods. For manufactured goods, we stated that these costs consist of direct materials, direct labour, and manufacturing overhead. To understand product costs more fully, it will be helpful at this point to look briefly at the flow of costs in a manufacturing company. By doing so, we will be able to see how product costs move through the various accounts and affect the balance sheet and the income statement in the course of producing and selling products.

Exhibit 2–9 illustrates the flow of costs in a manufacturing company. Raw materials purchases are recorded in the raw materials inventory account. When raw materials are used in production, their costs are transferred to the work-in-process inventory account as direct materials. Note that direct labour cost and manufacturing overhead cost are added directly to work in process. Work in process can be viewed most simply as an assembly line where workers are stationed and where products slowly take shape as they move from one end of the line to the other. The direct materials, direct labour, and manufacturing overhead costs added to work in process in Exhibit 2–8 are the costs needed to complete these products as they move along this assembly line.

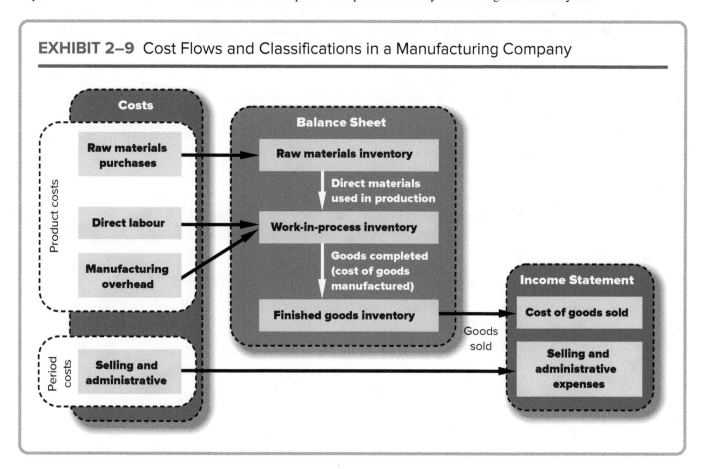

EXHIBIT 2–9 Cost Flows and Classifications in a Manufacturing Company

Note from Exhibit 2–9 that as goods are completed, their cost is transferred from work in process to finished goods. Here the goods await sale to a customer. As goods are sold, their cost is transferred from finished goods to cost of goods sold. At this point, the various materials, labour, and overhead costs that are required to make the product are finally treated as expenses.

As stated previously, product costs are often called *inventoriable costs* because these costs go directly into inventory accounts as they are incurred (first into work in process and then into finished goods), rather than going into expense accounts. *This is a key concept, since such costs can end up on the balance sheet as assets if goods are only partially completed or are unsold at the end of a period.*

Selling and administrative expenses are not involved in the manufacture of a product. For this reason, they are not treated as product costs but, rather, as period costs that go directly into expense accounts as they are incurred (and onto the income statement), as shown in Exhibit 2–9.

DECISION POINT

COST MANAGER

Your company has recently implemented a just-in-time inventory program, and the company's operations manager questions your method of recording all purchases and production to the inventory account. According to her, the company's goal is zero inventories; therefore, the inventory account should be eliminated from the books. How would you respond?

*Note to student: See **Guidance Answers** online.*

An Example of Cost Flows

To provide a numerical example of cost flows in a manufacturing company, assume that a company's annual insurance cost is $2,000. Three-fourths of this amount ($1,500) applies to factory operations, and one-fourth ($500) applies to selling and administrative activities. Therefore, $1,500 of the $2,000 insurance cost would be a product (*inventoriable*) cost and would be added to the cost of the goods produced during the year. This portion of the year's insurance cost will not become an expense until the goods that are produced during the year are sold—which may not happen until the following year or even later. Until the goods are sold, the $1,500 will remain as part of inventory (either as part of work in process or as part of finished goods), along with the other costs of producing the goods.

In contrast, the $500 of insurance cost that applies to the company's selling and administrative activities will go into an expense account immediately as a charge against the period's revenue.

CONCEPT CHECK

3. Which of the following statements are true? (You may select more than one answer.)

   a. Conversion costs include direct materials and direct labour.
   b. Indirect materials are included in manufacturing overhead.
   c. Prime costs are included in manufacturing overhead.
   d. Selling costs are considered period costs.

4. If the cost of goods sold is $100,000 and the ending finished goods inventory is $30,000 higher than the beginning finished goods inventory, what must be the amount of the cost of goods manufactured?

    a. $30,000   c. $130,000

    b. $100,000   d. $70,000

Note to student: See **Guidance Answers** *online.*

Cost Classification Summary

As explained previously in the chapter, costs can be classified in various ways to meet the information needs of managers; Exhibit 2–10 provides a summary of these different classifications. Indeed, the same cost item may be classified in more than one way. For example, the salary of Holiday Inn's catering department manager is a fixed cost with respect to the number of guests staying at the hotel. It is directly traceable to the catering department, but not to the sales department. It is a period cost, because the individual's services cannot be *banked*. Finally, it is a relevant cost when deciding whether to eliminate the department and outsource catering. When to use which classification depends on the purpose of the classification. The purposes and corresponding cost classifications are summarized in Exhibit 2–11. You will find it useful to understand the notion of "different costs for different purposes" as you progress through the text.

EXHIBIT 2–10 Cost Classification Summary

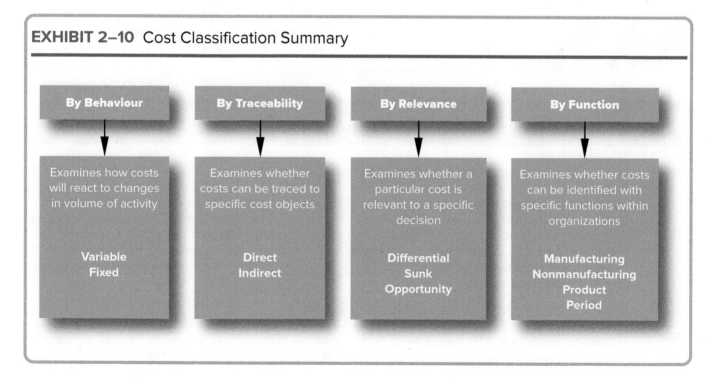

EXHIBIT 2–11 Cost Classifications for Different Purposes

Purpose of Cost Classification	Cost Classifications
Preparing external financial statements	Product costs (inventoriable) • Direct materials • Direct labour • Manufacturing overhead Period costs (expensed) • Nonmanufacturing costs • Marketing or selling costs • Administrative costs
Predicting cost behaviour in response to changes in activity	Variable cost (proportional to activity) Fixed cost (constant in total)
Assigning costs to cost objects, such as departments or products	Direct cost (can be easily traced) Indirect cost (cannot be easily traced; must be allocated)
Making decisions	Differential cost (differs between alternatives) Sunk cost (past cost not affecting a decision) Opportunity cost (forgone benefit)

Learning Objectives Summary

LO1   UNDERSTAND COST CLASSIFICATION BY BEHAVIOUR.

Managers often need to understand how costs will behave in response to changes in activity level; such an understanding is useful for cost estimation, planning, and cost–profitability analysis. Costs are commonly classified as variable or fixed with respect to changes in activity level. A variable cost remains constant when expressed per unit of activity, but increases or decreases in total proportionate to changes in activity level. In contrast, a fixed cost remains constant in total for a certain relevant range of activity; however, it fluctuates per unit of activity.

LO2   UNDERSTAND COST CLASSIFICATION BY TRACEABILITY.

Classification by traceability means being able to associate costs with individual cost objects. A direct cost is one that can be easily and conveniently traced to a cost object; for example, the cost of a hard drive can be directly traced to a computer. An indirect cost is one that is common to multiple cost objects; for example, the salary of a hospital administrator is common to multiple cost objects, such as patients, wards, and departments.

LO3   UNDERSTAND COST CLASSIFICATION BY RELEVANCE.

For the purpose of decision making, managers like to classify costs as being relevant or not relevant to specific decisions. Relevant costs (and revenues) differ between alternatives and are also called differential costs. An example of a relevant cost item is opportunity cost, which pertains to the benefit forgone when one alternative is chosen over another. Any cost that does not differ between alternatives is not relevant. An example of an irrelevant cost is the sunk cost, which is a cost that occurred in the past and cannot be changed.

LO4   UNDERSTAND COST CLASSIFICATION BY FUNCTION.

In manufacturing companies, costs are classified as manufacturing and nonmanufacturing costs. Manufacturing costs include the costs of direct materials, direct labour, and overhead; they are also called product costs. Nonmanufacturing costs include selling and administration costs; they are also called period costs. Product costs are first recorded in inventory accounts and then expensed through the cost of goods sold account when inventory is sold. In contrast period costs are expensed on the income statement in the same period when they are incurred.

LO5   PREPARE FINANCIAL REPORTS.

The income statements of both merchandising and manufacturing companies look similar. However, the calculation of the cost of goods sold (COGS) amount differs. In merchandising companies, COGS is calculated by adding the cost of merchandise purchases in a given period to beginning inventory and subtracting the ending merchandise inventory. In manufacturing companies, COGS is calculated by adding the cost of goods manufactured in a given period to beginning finished goods inventory and subtracting the ending finished goods inventory.

LO6   UNDERSTAND AND PREPARE MANUFACTURING REPORTS.

The cost of goods manufactured (COGM) includes the costs of direct materials, direct labour, and manufacturing overhead. The total of these three cost items for a period is added to the beginning work-in-process inventory; from this total the ending work-in-process inventory is subtracted.

Application Competency Summary

Starting with this chapter, you will find at the end of each chapter an Application Competency Summary, which is designed to serve as a reference manual. The length and the detail of these summaries vary across chapters largely due to the nature of the chapter content and the level of intricacy associated with the concepts and procedures covered. We also wanted to ensure that each technique and procedure is addressed in enough detail so as to be able to serve as a practical summary and checklist when solving problems and preparing for exams.

APPLICATION COMPETENCY	DELIVERABLE	SOURCE DOCUMENTS AND KEY INFORMATION	STEPS	KNOWLEDGE COMPETENCY
Compute the net income for the period. • LO5–CC9	*Key Information* Gross margin and net income *Report/ Document*	*Sales Ledger* Actual sales revenue *Schedule of Cost of Goods Sold*	1. Obtain the sales revenues from the sales ledger. 2. Obtain the COGS from the schedule of COGS. 3. Obtain the selling, general, and administrative expenses from the ledgers.	Manufacturing versus nonmanufacturing costs • LO4–CC4 Product vs. period costs • LO4–CC7

APPLICATION COMPETENCY	DELIVERABLE	SOURCE DOCUMENTS AND KEY INFORMATION	STEPS	KNOWLEDGE COMPETENCY
	Income statement	Actual cost of goods sold (COGS) *Selling, General, and Administrative Expenses Ledgers* Actual selling, general, and administrative expenses	4. Compute net income as sales revenue *less* COGS *less* selling, general, and administrative expenses.	
Compute the COGS for the period. ● **LO5–CC10**	*Key Information* Cost of goods available for sale and COGS *Report/ Document* Schedule of COGS	*Schedule of Cost of Goods Manufactured* Cost of goods manufactured (COGM) *Finished Goods Inventory Ledger* Cost of beginning and ending finished goods inventory	1. Obtain the beginning and ending finished goods inventory amounts from the finished goods inventory ledger. 2. Obtain the COGM from the schedule of the COGM. 3. Compute the COGS as beginning finished goods inventory *plus* COGM *less* ending finished goods inventory.	Manufacturing versus nonmanufacturing costs ● **LO4–CC4** Product vs. period costs ● **LO4–CC7** Inventory flow equation ● **LO6–CC11**
Compute the COGM for the period. ● **LO6–CC12**	*Key Information* Manufacturing costs and the COGM *Report/ Document* Schedule of COGM	*Schedule of Cost of Materials Used* Cost of materials used *Direct Labour Ledger* Cost of direct labour *Various Manufacturing Overhead Ledgers* Cost of manufacturing overhead *Work-in-Process Inventory Ledger* Cost of beginning and	1. Obtain the cost of direct materials used from the schedule of cost of materials used. 2. Obtain the cost of direct labour from the labour cost ledger. 3. Obtain the cost of manufacturing overhead from the overhead cost ledger. 4. Obtain the beginning and ending work-in-process inventory amounts from the work-in-process inventory ledger. 5. Compute COGM as costs of direct materials used *plus* direct labour *plus* manufacturing overhead *plus* beginning work-in-process inventory *less* ending work-in-process inventory.	Direct vs. indirect costs ● **LO2–CC2** Materials, labour, and overhead costs ● **LO4–CC4, 5** Inventory flow equation ● **LO6–CC11**

APPLICATION COMPETENCY	DELIVERABLE	SOURCE DOCUMENTS AND KEY INFORMATION	STEPS	KNOWLEDGE COMPETENCY
		ending work-in-process inventory		
Compute the cost of direct materials used during the period. ● **LO6–CC12**	*Key Information* Cost of direct materials used *Report/ Document* Schedule of cost of materials used	*Raw Materials Inventory Ledger* Cost of beginning and ending materials inventory *Materials Purchases Ledgers* Cost of materials purchased	1. Obtain the beginning and ending materials inventory amounts from the materials inventory ledger. 2. Obtain the cost of materials purchased from the cost of materials purchased ledger. 3. Compute the cost of direct materials used as the cost of beginning materials inventory *plus* the cost of purchases *less* the cost of ending materials inventory.	Inventory flow equation ● **LO6–CC11**

Review Problem 1: Cost Terms

You have been introduced to many new cost terms in this chapter. It will take you some time to learn what each means and how to properly classify costs in an organization. Consider the following example.

Porter Company manufactures furniture, including tables. Selected costs are given below:

1. The tables are made of wood, which costs $100 per table.
2. The tables are assembled by workers, at a wage cost of $40 per table.
3. Workers assembling the tables are supervised by a factory supervisor, who is paid $25,000 per year.
4. Electrical costs are $2 per machine-hour. Four machine-hours are required to produce a table.
5. The straight-line depreciation cost of the machines used to make the tables totals $10,000 per year.
6. The salary of the president of Porter Company is $100,000 per year.
7. Porter Company spends $250,000 per year to advertise its products.
8. Salespeople are paid a commission of $30 for each table sold.
9. Instead of producing the tables, Porter Company could rent its factory space out at a rental income of $50,000 per year.

Required:

Classify these costs according to various cost terms used in the chapter. *Carefully study the classification of each cost* . If you do not understand why a particular cost is classified the way it is, reread the section of the chapter discussing the particular cost term. The terms *variable cost* and *fixed cost* refer to how costs behave with respect to the number of tables produced in a year.

SOLUTION TO REVIEW PROBLEM 1

	To Units of Product Sold		Period (Selling and Administrative) Cost	Product Cost			To Units of Product Sold		Sunk Cost	Opportunity Cost
	Variable Cost	Fixed Cost		Direct Materials	Direct Labour	Manufacturing Overhead	Direct	Indirect		
1. Wood used in a table ($100 per table)	X			X			X			
2. Labour cost to assemble a table ($40 per table)	X				X		X			
3. Salary of the factory supervisor ($25,000 per year)		X				X		X		
4. Cost of electricity to produce tables ($2 per machine-hour)	X					X		X		
5. Depreciation of machines used to produce tables ($10,000 per year)		X				X		X	X*	
6. Salary of the company president ($100,000 per year)		X	X					X		
7. Advertising expense ($250,000 per year)		X	X					X		
8. Commissions paid to salespeople ($30 per table sold)	X		X				X			
9. Rental income forgone on factory space ($50,000 per year)										X†

*This is a sunk cost, since the equipment has already been purchased.

†This is an opportunity cost, since it represents the potential benefit that is lost or sacrificed as a result of using the factory space to produce tables.

Opportunity cost is a special category of cost not ordinarily recorded in an organization's accounting books. To avoid confusion with other costs, we will not attempt to classify this cost in any other way except as an opportunity cost.

Review Problem 2: Schedule of Cost of Goods Manufactured and Income Statement

The following information was taken from the accounting records of Klear-Seal Company for last year. Management wants these data organized in a better format so that financial statements can be prepared for the year.

Selling expenses	$ 165,000
Raw materials inventory, January 1	120,000
Raw materials inventory, December 31	82,000
Utilities, factory	38,500
Direct labour cost	157,300
Depreciation, factory	155,000
Purchases of raw materials	723,000
Sales	2,500,000
Insurance, factory	42,000
Supplies, factory	14,000
Administrative expenses	283,000
Indirect labour	306,000
Maintenance, factory	89,000
Work-in-process inventory, January 1	180,000
Work-in-process inventory, December 31	100,000
Finished goods inventory, January 1	260,000
Finished goods inventory, December 31	210,000

Required:

1. Prepare a schedule of cost of goods manufactured, similar to Exhibit 2–8.
2. Compute the cost of goods sold.
3. Using data as needed from parts (1) and (2), prepare an income statement.

SOLUTION TO REVIEW PROBLEM 2

1.

KLEAR-SEAL COMPANY
Schedule of Cost of Goods Manufactured
For the Year Ended December 31

Direct materials:		
Raw materials inventory, January 1	$120,000	
Add: Purchases of raw materials	723,000	
Raw materials available for use	843,000	
Deduct: Raw materials inventory, December 31	82,000	
Raw materials used in production		$ 761,000
Direct labour		157,300
Manufacturing overhead:		
Utilities, factory	38,500	
Depreciation, factory	155,000	
Insurance, factory	42,000	
Supplies, factory	14,000	
Indirect labour	306,000	
Maintenance, factory	89,000	
Total overhead costs		644,500
Total manufacturing costs		1,562,800
Add: Work-in-process inventory, January 1		180,000
		1,742,800
Deduct: Work-in-process inventory, December 31		100,000
Cost of goods manufactured		$1,642,800

2.

The cost of goods sold would be computed as follows:

Finished goods inventory, January 1	$ 260,000
Add: Cost of goods manufactured	1,642,800
Goods available for sale	1,902,800
Deduct: Finished goods inventory, December 31	210,000
Cost of goods sold	$1,692,800

3.

KLEAR-SEAL COMPANY
Income Statement
For the Year Ended December 31

Sales		$2,500,000
Less: Cost of goods sold (see above)		1,692,800
Gross margin		807,200
Less: Selling and administrative expenses:		
Selling expenses	$165,000	
Administrative expenses	283,000	
Total expenses		448,000
Net income		$ 359,200

Questions

2–1   What is meant by the term *cost behaviour*?

2–2   "A variable cost varies per unit of activity, whereas a fixed cost is constant per unit of activity." Do you agree with this statement? Explain why, or why not.

2–3   How do fixed costs create difficulties in costing units of product?

2–4   Give two examples each of variable and fixed costs.

2–5   "Fixed costs are inversely proportional to volume. As volume decreases, fixed costs increase, and as volume increases, fixed costs decrease." Do you agree with this statement? Explain why, or why not.

2–6   Why is manufacturing overhead considered an indirect cost of a unit of product?

2–7   Define the following terms: *differential cost, opportunity cost,* and *sunk cost.*

2–8   "Only variable costs can be differential costs." Do you agree with this statement? Explain your reasoning.

2–9   What are the three major elements of product costs in a manufacturing company?

2–10   Distinguish among the following: (a) direct materials, (b) indirect materials, (c) direct labour, (d) indirect labour, and (e) manufacturing overhead.

2–11   Use the following abbreviations:

- Prime costs = PC

- Conversion costs = CC

- Direct materials costs = DM

- Direct labour costs = DL

- Manufacturing overhead costs = MOH

Develop an equation that connects PC and CC.

2–12   Explain the difference between a product cost and a period cost.

2–13   Describe how the income statement of a manufacturing company differs from the income statement of a merchandising company.

2–14   Of what value is the schedule of cost of goods manufactured? How does it tie into the income statement?

2–15   Describe how the inventory accounts of a manufacturing company differ from the inventory accounts of a merchandising company.

2–16   Why are product costs sometimes called inventoriable costs? Describe the flow of such costs in a manufacturing company from the point of incurrence until they finally become expenses on the income statement.

2–17   Is it possible for such costs as salaries and depreciation to end up as assets on the balance sheet? Explain your answer.

The Foundational 15

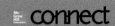

[LO1 – CC1; LO2 – CC2; LO3 – CC3; LO4 – CC4, 5, 6, 7]

Martinez Company's relevant range of production is 7,500 units to 12,500 units. When it produces and sells 10,000 units, its unit costs are as follows:

	Amount per Unit
Direct materials	$6.00
Direct labour	$3.50
Variable manufacturing overhead	$1.50
Fixed manufacturing overhead	$4.00
Fixed selling expense	$3.00
Fixed administrative expense	$2.00
Sales commissions	$1.00
Variable administrative expense	$0.50

Required:

2–1   For financial accounting purposes, what is the total amount of product costs incurred to make 10,000 units?

2–2   For financial accounting purposes, what is the total amount of period costs incurred to sell 10,000 units?

2–3   If 8,000 units are sold, what is the variable cost per unit sold?

2–4   If 12,500 units are sold, what is the variable cost per unit sold?

2–5   If 8,000 units are sold, what is the total amount of variable costs related to the units sold?

2–6   If 12,500 units are sold, what is the total amount of variable costs related to the units sold?

2–7   If 8,000 units are produced, what is the average fixed manufacturing cost per unit produced?

2–8   If 12,500 units are produced, what is the average fixed manufacturing cost per unit produced?

2–9   If 8,000 units are produced, what is the total amount of fixed manufacturing cost incurred to support this level of production?

2–10   If 12,500 units are produced, what is the total amount of fixed manufacturing cost incurred to support this level of production?

2–11   If 8,000 units are produced, what is the total amount of manufacturing overhead cost incurred to support this level of production? What is this total amount expressed on a per unit basis?

2–12   If 12,500 units are produced, what is the total amount of manufacturing overhead cost incurred to support this level of production? What is this total amount expressed on a per unit basis?

2–13   If the selling price is $22 per unit, what is the gross margin when 10,000 units are sold?

2–14   If 11,000 units are produced, what are the total amounts of direct and indirect manufacturing costs incurred to support this level of production?

2–15   What total incremental cost will Martinez incur if it increases production from 10,000 to 10,001 units?

Brief Exercises

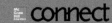

BRIEF EXERCISE 2–1
Identifying Opportunity Costs [LO3 – CC3]

Bill is the manager of the product development division at Fiao Company. He has been invited to a company lunch with several colleagues. He is also expected to prepare a quarterly financial performance report on his division. The report is due in two days, and Bill estimates that there are approximately 16 to 20 hours of work remaining. A colleague remarks to Bill, while they discuss if Bill should attend the lunch, "You are not one to refuse a free lunch! You should go." Bill responds by saying, "In this case, I am not sure there is such a thing as a free lunch."

Required:

Explain the cost concept that best applies to Bill's response.

BRIEF EXERCISE 2–2
Identifying Variable and Fixed Costs [LO1 – CC1]

Following are a number of costs that are incurred in a variety of organizations.

Required:

Classify each cost as variable or fixed with respect to the number of units sold or services provided by the organization by placing an X in the appropriate column.

Cost Item	Cost Behaviour	
	Variable	Fixed
The costs of advertising a U2 rock concert in Vancouver.		
Depreciation on the Hard Rock Café building in Ottawa.		
The electrical costs of running a roller coaster at West Edmonton Mall.		
Property taxes on your local cinema.		
The costs of synthetic materials used to make Reebok running shoes.		
The costs of shipping Apple iPods to retail stores.		
The cost of leasing a CT-scan diagnostic machine at the American Hospital in Paris.		

BRIEF EXERCISE 2–3
Identifying Differential, Opportunity, and Sunk Costs [LO3 – CC3]

The University of Keen Learning's printing department is considering replacing an old, inefficient production printing machine with a state-of-the-art digital DocuTech 180 HighLight Colour machine. The new machine will provide higher-quality prints in less time and at a lower cost per page. Instead of investing in the new machine, the university's administrative department is lobbying the university management to buy a new, state-of-the-art scanner.

Required:

For each of the following items, indicate by placing an X in the appropriate column whether it should be considered a differential cost, an opportunity cost, or a sunk cost in the decision to replace the old printing machine with a new one. If for any particular item none of the categories applies, leave all columns blank.

Item	Differential Cost	Opportunity Cost	Sunk Cost
Example: Costs of toner used in the old machine.	X		
Cost of the old printing machine.			
Salary of the head of the printing department.			
Salary of the head of the finance department.			
Rent on the space occupied by the printing department.			
Cost of maintaining the old printer.			
Benefits from a new, state-of-the art scanner.			
Cost of electricity to run the printing machine.			

BRIEF EXERCISE 2–4
Classifying Manufacturing Costs [LO4 – CC4, 5, 6]

Your Computer, Inc. assembles custom computers from components supplied by various manufacturers. The company is very small, and its assembly shop and retail sales store are housed in a single facility in North Vancouver. Following are some of the costs that are incurred at the company.

Required:

For each cost, indicate whether it would most likely be classified as direct labour, direct materials, manufacturing overhead, marketing and selling, or administrative cost. List all classifications that apply to a specific cost item.

1. Monthly salary of the company's accountant.
2. Cost of a fan installed in a computer.
3. Rental on equipment used to assemble computers.
4. Cost of advertising in the local community newspaper.
5. Monthly charge paid to an outside company for quality testing (20% of the computers assembled are sent for testing).
6. Wages of employees who assemble computers from components.
7. Salary of the assembly shop's supervisor.
8. Sales commissions paid to the company's salespeople.
9. Rent on the facility.

BRIEF EXERCISE 2–5
Identifying Product and Period Costs [LO4 – CC7]

A product cost is also known as an *inventoriable cost*.

Required:

Classify the following costs as either product (inventoriable) costs or period (non-inventoriable) costs in a manufacturing company:

1. Depreciation on salespeople's cars.
2. Rent on equipment used in the factory.
3. Lubricants used for maintenance of factory equipment.
4. Salaries of finished goods warehouse personnel.
5. Soap and paper towels used by factory workers.
6. Sales supervisors' salaries.
7. Property taxes on the factory building.
8. Materials used in boxing units of finished product for shipment overseas. (Units are not normally boxed.)
9. Advertising outlays.
10. Workers' compensation insurance on factory employees.
11. Depreciation on chairs and tables in the administrative boardroom.
12. Salary of the production quality supervisor for the company.
13. Depreciation on a Learjet used by the company's executives.
14. Rent on rooms at a Florida resort for a manufacturing conference.
15. Attractively designed box for packaging breakfast cereal.

BRIEF EXERCISE 2–6
Constructing an Income Statement [LO5 – CC9, 10; LO6 – CC11]

Last month Bims, a wedding dress retailer, had total sales of $3,000,000, selling expenses of $315,000, and administrative expenses of $385,000. The company had beginning merchandise inventory of $250,000, purchased additional merchandise inventory for $950,000, and had ending merchandise inventory of $100,000.

Required:

Prepare an income statement for the company for the month in good form.

BRIEF EXERCISE 2–7
Preparing a Schedule of Cost of Goods Manufactured [LO6 – CC11, 12]

Lompac Products manufactures a variety of products in its factory. Data for the most recent month's operations follow:

Beginning raw materials inventory	$170,000
Purchases of raw materials	870,000
Ending raw materials inventory	150,000
Direct labour	245,000
Manufacturing overhead	560,000
Beginning work-in-process inventory	210,000
Ending work-in-process inventory	340,000

Required:

Prepare in good form a schedule of cost of goods manufactured for the company for the month.

Exercises

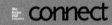

EXERCISE 2–1
Identifying Costs [LO1 – CC1; LO3 – CC3; LO4 – CC4, 5, 6, 7]

Royal Group Ltd. of Medicine Hat, Alberta, acquired its factory building about 20 years ago. For several years, the company has rented out a small annex attached to the rear of the building. The company has received a rental income of $50,000 per year on this space. The renter's lease will expire soon, and rather than renew the lease, the company has decided to use the space itself to manufacture a new product.

Direct materials cost for the new product will total $60 per unit. To have a place to store finished units of product, the company will rent a small warehouse nearby. The rental cost will be $1,000 per month. In addition, the company must rent equipment for use in producing the new product; the rental cost will be $15,000 per month. Workers will be hired to manufacture the new product, with direct labour costs amounting to $80 per unit. The space in the annex will continue to be depreciated on a straight-line basis, as in prior years. This depreciation is $5,000 per year.

Advertising costs for the new product will total $150,000 per year. A supervisor will be hired to oversee production, with a salary of $3,500 per month. Electricity for operating machines will be $1.80 per unit. Costs of shipping the new product to customers will be $12 per unit.

To provide funds to purchase materials, meet payrolls, and so forth, the company will have to liquidate some temporary investments. These investments are currently yielding an average return of about $5,000 per year.

Required:

Prepare an answer sheet with the following column headings:

Name of the Cost	Product Cost					Period (Selling and Administrative) Cost	Opportunity Cost	Sunk Cost
	Variable Cost	Fixed Cost	Direct Materials	Direct Labour	Manufacturing Overhead			

List the different costs associated with the new product decision down the extreme left column (under "Name of the Cost"). Then place an X under each heading that helps describe the type of cost involved. There may be Xs under several column headings for a single cost. (For example, a cost may be a fixed cost, a period cost, and a sunk cost; you would put an X under each of these headings opposite the cost.)

EXERCISE 2–2
Defining Cost Terms [LO1 – CC1; LO3 – CC3; LO4 – CC7]

Following are a number of cost terms introduced in the chapter:

Variable cost	Product cost
Fixed cost	Sunk cost
Prime cost	Conversion cost
Opportunity cost	Period cost

Required:

Choose the term or terms that most appropriately describe the cost identified in each of the following situations. A term can be used more than once.

1. Lake Company produces a tote bag that is very popular with students. The cloth used in the manufacture of the bag would be called direct materials and classified as a(n) _____cost. In terms of cost behaviour, the cloth could also be described as a(n) _____cost.

2. The direct labour cost required to produce the tote bags, combined with the manufacturing overhead cost involved, would be known as a(n) _____cost.

3. The company could have taken the funds that it has invested in production equipment and invested them in interest-bearing securities instead. The interest forgone on the securities would be called a(n) _____cost.

4. Taken together, the direct materials cost and the direct labour cost required to produce tote bags would be called a(n) _____cost.

5. The company used to produce a smaller tote bag that was not very popular. Some 300 of these smaller bags are stored in one of the company's warehouses. The amount invested in these bags would be called a(n) _____cost.

6. The tote bags are sold through agents who are paid a commission on each bag sold. These commissions would be classified by Lake Company as a(n) _____cost. In terms of cost behaviour, commissions would be classified as a(n) _____cost.

7. Depreciation on the equipment used to produce tote bags would be classified by Lake Company as a(n) _____cost. However, depreciation on any equipment used by the company in selling and administrative activities would be classified as a(n) _____cost. In terms of cost behaviour, depreciation would probably be classified as a(n) _____cost.

8. A(n) _____cost is also known as an inventoriable cost, since such costs go into the work-in-process inventory account and then into the finished goods inventory account before appearing on the income statement as part of cost of goods sold.

9. The salary of Lake Company's president would be classified as a(n) _____cost, since the salary will appear on the income statement as an expense in the time period in which it is incurred.

10. Costs can often be classified in several ways. For example, Lake Company pays $5,000 rent each month on its factory building. The rent would be part of manufacturing overhead. In terms of cost behaviour, it would be classified as a(n) _____ cost. The rent can also be classified as a(n) _____ cost and as part of _____ cost.

EXERCISE 2–3
Classifying Variable, Fixed, Direct, and Indirect Costs [LO1 – CC1; LO2 – CC2]

Various costs, as given below, are associated with running a commercial bakery that supplies baked goods to local coffee shops:

1. Account manager's salary.
2. Rent on building.
3. Flour used in the making of croissants.
4. Bakery manager's salary.
5. Wages of bakers who are paid on a piecework basis.
6. Depreciation of commercial ovens used in baking.
7. Insurance on the building.

Required:

Classify each cost as being either variable or fixed with respect to the quantity of baked goods supplied. Also, indicate whether each cost would typically be treated as a direct cost or an indirect cost with respect to the quantity of baked goods supplied. Prepare your answer sheet as shown below:

	Cost Behaviour		To Quantity of Baked Goods Supplied	
Cost Item	Variable	Fixed	Direct	Indirect

EXERCISE 2–4
Classifying Variable, Fixed, Period, and Product Costs [LO1 – CC1; LO4 – CC7]

Following are various costs that are found in organizations:

1. Advertising by a dental office.
2. Shipping canned apples from a Del Monte plant to customers.
3. Apples processed and canned by Del Monte Corporation.
4. Insurance on IBM's corporate headquarters.
5. Commissions paid to Future Shop salespeople.
6. Hamburger buns in a McDonald's outlet.
7. Depreciation of factory lunchroom facilities at a General Electric plant.
8. Insurance on a Bausch & Lomb factory producing contact lenses.
9. Salary of a supervisor overseeing production of circuit boards at Hewlett-Packard.
10. Steering wheels installed in BMWs.

Required:

Classify each cost as being either variable or fixed with respect to the number of units sold. Also, classify each cost as either a selling and administrative cost or a product cost. Prepare your answer sheet as shown below:

| | Cost Behaviour | | Selling and Administrative | |
Cost Item	Variable	Fixed	Cost	Product Cost

Place an X in the appropriate columns to show the proper classification of each cost.

EXERCISE 2–5
Determining Cost of Goods Sold [LO5 – CC10; LO6 – CC11, 12]

The following cost and inventory data are taken from the accounting records of Mason Company for the year just completed:

Costs incurred:	
Direct labour cost	$ 70,000
Purchases of raw materials	120,000
Indirect labour	45,000
Maintenance, factory equipment	6,000
Advertising expense	90,000
Insurance, factory equipment	1,900
Sales salaries	50,000
Rent, factory facilities	24,000
Supplies	3,600
Depreciation, office equipment	4,500
Depreciation, factory equipment	17,000

	Beginning of the Year	End of the Year
Inventories:		
Raw materials	$18,000	$12,500
Work in process	10,300	15,150
Finished goods	23,000	18,100

Required:

1. Prepare a schedule of cost of goods manufactured in good form.
2. Prepare the cost of goods sold section of Mason Company's income statement for the year.

EXERCISE 2–6
Identifying Cost Flows [LO4 – CC8]

The Ningbo Fortune Company produces custom-made linens for the hospitality industry. During the month of June, the company purchased 10,000 bolts of spun polyester fabric at the cost of $80 per bolt. Ningbo withdrew 9,200 bolts from the storeroom during the month. Of these, 200 were used as customer samples and swatches for promotional purposes. The remaining 9,000 bolts of polyester withdrawn from the storeroom were used in the production of custom-made table and bed linens. Of the linens produced in June, 90% were completed and transferred from work in process to finished goods. Of the linens completed during the month, 30% were unsold at June 30. There were no inventories of any type on June 1.

Required:

1. Determine the cost of bolts of polyester that would appear in each of the following accounts at June 30:
   a. Raw materials.
   b. Work in process.
   c. Finished goods.
   d. Cost of goods sold.
   e. Selling expense.
2. Specify whether each of the previous accounts would appear on the balance sheet or on the income statement at June 30.

EXERCISE 2–7
Calculating Cost of Goods Manufactured [LO6 – CC12]

The following cost information is presented for Phoenix Ltd. for the most recent period.

Cost of direct material used in manufacturing	$62,000
Direct labour costs	15,000
Manufacturing overhead	6,500
Sales commissions at 8% of sales	22,000
Opening finished goods inventory	5,000
Opening work-in-process inventory	3,000
Ending finished goods inventory	12,000
Ending work-in-process inventory	12,000

Required:

What was the cost of goods manufactured for Phoenix?

EXERCISE 2–8
Calculating Cost of Goods Manufactured [LO5 – CC10; LO6 – CC11, 12]

Sage Ltd. had the following results for the month of March.

Sales	$1,700,000
Opening finished goods inventory	$130,000
Gross margin	40% of sales
Ending finished goods inventory	$85,000

Required:

What was the cost of goods manufactured in March?

Problems

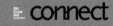

PROBLEM 2–1
Identifying Costs [LO1 – CC1; LO4 – CC4, 5, 6, 7]

Staci Valek began making pottery several years ago as a hobby. Her work is quite creative, and it has become so popular that she has decided to quit her job with an aerospace firm and manufacture pottery full-time. The salary from Staci's aerospace job is $70,000 per year.

Staci will rent for $2,500 per month a small building in which to make the pottery. She estimates that the cost of clay and glaze will be $3.50 for each finished piece of pottery. She will hire workers to produce the pottery at a labour rate of $12 per pot. To sell her pots, Staci must advertise heavily in the local area. An advertising agency will handle all advertising for a fee of $2,600 per month. Staci's brother will sell the pots for a commission of $4 per pot sold. Equipment needed to manufacture the pots will be rented at a cost of $1,300 per month.

Staci has already paid the $5,000 legal and filing fees associated with incorporating her business. Staci's sales office will be a small room rented for $1,250 per month in a tourist area. A phone for taking orders will cost $40 per month. In addition, the phone will be equipped with voice mail for taking after-hours messages.

Staci has some money in savings that is earning interest of $1,200 per year. These savings will be withdrawn and used to get the business going. For the time being, Staci does not intend to draw any salary from the new company.

Required:

1. Prepare an answer sheet with the following column headings:

			Product Cost			Period		
Name of the Cost	Vari- able Cost	Fixed Cost	Direct Materi- als	Direct Labour	Manufactur- ing Overhead	(Selling and Administra- tive) Cost	Opportunity Cost	Sunk Cost

List the different costs associated with the new company down the extreme left column (under "Name of the Cost"). Then place an X under each heading that describes the type of cost involved. There may be Xs under several column headings for a single cost. (That is, a cost may be a fixed cost, a period cost, and a sunk cost; you would put an X under each of these column headings opposite the cost.)

Under the "Variable Cost" column, list only those costs that would be variable with respect to the number of units of pottery that are produced and sold.

2. All of the costs you have listed above, except one, would be differential costs between the alternatives of Staci producing pottery or staying with the aerospace firm. Which cost is *not* differential? Explain.

PROBLEM 2–2
Classifying Costs [LO1 – CC1; LO2 – CC2; LO4 – CC4, 5, 6]

Following are a number of costs typically found in organizations:

1. Property taxes, factory.
2. Boxes used for packaging detergent.
3. Salespeople's commissions.
4. Supervisor's salary, factory.
5. Depreciation, executive automobiles.
6. Wages of workers assembling computers.
7. Packing supplies for out-of-province shipments.
8. Insurance, finished goods warehouses.
9. Lubricants for machines.
10. Advertising costs.
11. Chips used in producing calculators.
12. Shipping costs on merchandise sold.
13. Magazine subscriptions, factory lunchroom.
14. Thread in a garment factory.
15. Billing costs.
16. Executive life insurance.
17. Ink used in textbook production.
18. Fringe benefits, assembly-line workers.
19. Yarn used in sweater production.
20. Wages of receptionist, executive offices.

CHECK FIGURE

Boxes for packaging: variable, direct

Required:

Prepare an answer sheet with column headings as shown below. For each cost item, indicate whether it would be variable or fixed with respect to the number of units produced and sold and then whether it would be a selling cost, an administrative cost, or a manufacturing cost. If it is a manufacturing cost, indicate whether it would typically be treated as a direct cost or an indirect cost with respect to units of product. Three sample answers are provided for illustration.

Cost Item	Variable or Fixed	Selling Cost	Administrative Cost	Manufacturing (Product) Cost	
				Direct	Indirect
Direct labour	V			X	
Executive salaries	F		X		
Factory rent	F				X

PROBLEM 2–3
Identifying Costs, Cost Concepts [LO1 – CC1; LO2 – CC2; LO4 – CC4, 6]

The Mahela Company specializes in producing sets of wooden patio furniture consisting of a table and four chairs. The company has ample orders to keep production going at its full capacity of 2,000 sets per quarter. Quarterly cost data at full capacity follow:

> **CHECK FIGURE**
> (1) Total variable cost: $402,000

Factory labour, direct	$168,000
Advertising	50,000
Factory supervision	50,000
Property taxes, factory building	4,500
Sales commissions	80,000
Insurance, factory	3,500
Depreciation, office equipment	14,000
Lease cost, factory equipment	6,000
Indirect materials, factory	6,000
Depreciation, factory building	8,000
General office supplies (billing)	4,000
General office salaries	50,000
Direct materials used (wood, bolts, etc.)	114,000
Utilities, factory	30,000

Required:

1. Prepare an answer sheet with the column headings shown below. Enter each cost item on your answer sheet, placing the dollar amount under the appropriate headings. As examples, this has been done already for the first two items in the preceding list. Note that each cost item is classified in two ways: first, as variable or fixed, with respect to the number of units produced and sold, and, second, as a selling and administrative cost or a product cost. (If the item is a product cost, it should also be classified as being either direct or indirect, as shown.)

| Cost Item | Cost Behaviour | | Selling and Administrative Cost | Product Cost | |
	Variable*	Fixed		Direct	Indirect*
Factory labour, direct		$168,000			$168,000
Advertising			$50,000	$50,000	

*To units of product.

2. Total the dollar amounts in each of the columns in part (1). Compute the average product cost per patio set.

3. Assume that production drops to only 1,000 sets quarterly. Would you expect the average product cost per patio set to increase, decrease, or remain unchanged? Explain. No computations are necessary.

4. Refer to the original data. The president's brother-in-law has considered making a patio set and has priced the necessary materials at a building supply store. He has asked the president if he could purchase a patio set from the Mahela Company "at cost," and the president has agreed to let him do so.

   a. Would you expect any disagreement over the price the brother-in-law should pay? Explain. What price does the president probably have in mind? The brother-in-law?

   b. Since the company is operating at full capacity, what cost term used in the chapter might be justification for the president to charge the full, regular price to the brother-in-law and still be selling "at cost"?

PROBLEM 2–4
Classifying Salary Cost [LO4 – CC7]

You have just been hired by Ogden Company to fill a new position that was created in response to rapid growth in sales. It is your responsibility to coordinate shipments of finished goods from the factory to distribution warehouses located in various parts of Canada so that goods will be available as orders are received from customers.

The company is unsure how to classify your annual salary in its cost records. The company's cost analyst says your salary should be classified as a manufacturing (product) cost, the controller says it should be classified as a selling expense, and the president says it does not matter how your salary cost is classified.

Required:

1. Which viewpoint is correct? Why?

2. From the point of view of the reported net income for the year, is the president correct? Explain.

PROBLEM 2–5
Supplying Missing Data [LO5 – CC10; LO6 – CC11, 12]

Required:

Supply the missing data in the following cases. Each case is independent of the others.

CHECK FIGURE

Case 1: Goods available for sale = $69,000

	Case			
	1	2	3	4
Direct materials	$14,500	$ 60,000	$ 5,000	$23,000
Direct labour	?	23,000	7,000	14,000
Manufacturing overhead	25,000	44,000	?	19,000
Total manufacturing costs	58,500	?	20,000	?
Beginning work-in-process inventory	3,500	?	3,000	?
Ending work-in-process inventory	?	4,000	4,000	8,500
Cost of goods manufactured	58,000	131,000	?	?
Sales	80,000	201,000	36,000	90,000
Beginning finished goods inventory	10,000	12,500	?	12,000
Cost of goods manufactured	?	?	?	47,500
Goods available for sale	?	?	?	?
Ending finished goods inventory	?	11,500	4,000	3,500
Cost of goods sold	67,000	?	18,500	?
Gross margin	13,000	?	17,500	?
Operating expenses	?	33,500	?	?
Net income	4,000	?	5,000	9,000

PROBLEM 2–6
Preparing Financial Statements for a Manufacturer [LO5 – CC9, 10; LO6 – CC11, 12]

Swift Company was organized on March 1 of the current year. After five months of startup losses, management had expected to earn a profit during August, the most recent month. Management was disappointed, however, when the income statement for August also showed a loss. August's income statement follows:

CHECK FIGURE

(1) COGM: $375,900

SWIFT COMPANY Income Statement For the Month Ended August 31		
Sales		$530,000
Less: Operating expenses:		
Indirect labour cost	$ 9,000	
Utilities	25,000	
Direct labour cost	80,000	
Depreciation, factory equipment	21,000	
Raw materials purchased	226,000	
Depreciation, sales equipment	8,000	
Insurance	8,000	
Rent on facilities	80,000	
Selling and administrative salaries	22,000	
Advertising	65,000	544,000
Net loss		$(14,000)

The company's controller resigned a month ago. Sam, a new assistant in the controller's office, prepared the income statement above. Sam has had little experience in manufacturing operations. After seeing the $14,000 loss for August, Swift's president stated, "I was sure we'd be profitable within six months, but our six months are up and this loss for August is even worse than July's. I think it's time to start looking for someone to buy out the company's assets—if we don't, within a few months there won't be any assets to sell. By the way, I don't see any reason to look for a new controller. We'll just limp along with Sam for the time being."

Additional information about the company follows:

a. Some 50% of the utilities cost and 80% of the insurance apply to factory operations. The remaining amounts apply to selling and administrative activities.

b. Inventory balances at the beginning and end of August were as follows: ·

	August 1	August 31
Raw materials	$31,000	$78,000
Work in process	18,000	10,000
Finished goods	55,000	50,000

c. Only 75% of the rent on facilities applies to factory operations; the remainder applies to selling and administrative activities.

The president has asked you to check over the income statement and make a recommendation about whether the company should look for a buyer for its assets.

Required:

1. As one step in gathering data for a recommendation to the president, prepare a schedule of cost of goods manufactured in good form for August.
2. As a second step, prepare a new income statement for August.
3. On the basis of your statements prepared in parts (1) and (2), would you recommend that the company look for a buyer?

PROBLEM 2–7
Preparing Financial Statements; Cost Behaviour [LO1 – CC1; LO5 – CC9, 10; LO6 – CC11, 12]

Various cost and sales data for Meriwell Company for the just-completed year follow:

CHECK FIGURE
(1) COGM: $290,000

	A	B
1	Finished goods inventory, beginning	$ 20,000
2	Finished goods inventory, ending	40,000
3	Depreciation, factory	27,000
4	Administrative expenses	110,000
5	Utilities, factory	8,000
6	Maintenance, factory	40,000
7	Supplies, factory	11,000
8	Insurance, factory	4,000
9	Purchases of raw materials	125,000
10	Raw materials inventory, beginning	9,000

	A	B
11	Raw materials inventory, ending	6,000
12	Direct labour	70,000
13	Indirect labour	15,000
14	Work-in-process inventory, beginning	17,000
15	Work-in-process inventory, ending	30,000
16	Sales	500,000
17	Selling expenses	80,000

Required:

1. Prepare a schedule of cost of goods manufactured.
2. Prepare an income statement.
3. Assume that the company produced the equivalent of 10,000 units of product during the year just completed. What was the average cost per unit for direct materials? What was the average cost per unit for factory depreciation?
4. Assume that the company expects to produce 15,000 units of product during the coming year. What average cost per unit and what total cost would you expect the company to incur for direct materials at this level of activity? For factory depreciation? (In preparing your answer, assume that direct materials are a variable cost and that depreciation is a fixed cost; also, assume that depreciation is computed on a straight-line basis.)
5. As the manager responsible for production costs, explain to the president any difference in the average cost per unit between parts (3) and (4).

PROBLEM 2–8
Preparing Financial Statements; Cost Behaviour [LO1 – CC1; LO5 – CC9, 10; LO6 – CC11, 12]

Selected account balances for the year ended December 31 are provided below for Superior Company:

CHECK FIGURE
(1) COGM: $770,000

Selling and administrative salaries	$110,000
Insurance, factory	8,000
Utilities, factory	65,000
Purchases of raw materials	390,000
Indirect labour	60,000

Direct labour	?
Advertising expense	70,000
Cleaning supplies, factory	7,000
Sales commissions	50,000
Rent, factory building	90,000
Maintenance, factory	40,000

Inventory balances at the beginning and end of the year were as follows:

	Beginning of the Year	End of the Year
Raw materials	$30,000	$10,000
Work in process	?	20,000
Finished goods	20,000	?

The total manufacturing costs for the year were $753,000, the goods available for sale totalled $790,000, and the cost of goods sold totalled $740,000.

Required:

1. Prepare a schedule of cost of goods manufactured in good form and the cost of goods sold section of the company's income statement for the year.

2. Assume that the dollar amounts given above are for the equivalent of 40,000 units produced during the year. Compute the average cost per unit for direct materials used and the average cost per unit for rent on the factory building.

3. Assume that in the following year the company expects to produce 50,000 units. What average cost per unit and total cost would you expect to be incurred for direct materials? For rent on the factory building? (In preparing your answer, you may assume that direct materials are a variable cost and that rent is a fixed cost.)

4. As the manager in charge of production costs, explain to the president the reason for any difference in average cost per unit between parts (2) and (3).

PROBLEM 2–9
Classifying Costs, Preparing an Income Statement [LO1 – CC1; LO2 – CC2; LO4 – CC5, 6, 7; LO5 – CC9]

The following data is available for Crater Corporation's North American division for the years 2014 and 2015. During these years there were no inventories in the system.

CHECK FIGURE
(2) Period cost $5,944,699

	2015	2014
Production quantity	40,000	44,000
Number of customers	12,600	11,000
Revenues	$23,200,000	$24,640,000
Expenses		
Direct materials & components	$3,200,000	$3,533,200
Direct production wages (1)	$1,448,000	$1,590,600
Production supervisory salaries	$261,400	$238,100
Salaries paid to sales representatives (2)	$548,000	$569,600
Advertising	$675,300	$568,400
Insurance (3)	$115,670	$110,600
Building rent (4)	$258,640	$256,800
Other salaries (5)	$1,160,000	$1,232,000
Honorarium to the members of the board	$430,200	$430,200
Production quality control (6)	$130,650	$135,870
Market research	$346,200	$303,160
Depreciation (7)	$1,326,700	$1,168,900
Facilities management (8)	$884,230	$746,200
Legal	$685,600	$618,200
Personnel department	$196,500	$194,200
Utilities—production (9)	$852,600	$762,700
Utilities—other (10)	$360,340	$301,500
Customer service (11)	$917,400	$924,600
	$13,797,430	$13,684,830

Note:

1. Paid on the basis of production quantity
2. Ten representatives @ $20,000 per person + 1.5% of sales revenue
3. Manufacturing - 65%; remaining - general liability
4. Manufacturing - 60%; Marketing - 15%; remaining for Administration
5. Manufacturing - 50%; Marketing - 20%; remaining for Administration
6. Variable - 40%
7. Manufacturing - 60%; Sales & Marketing - 20%; remaining for Adminsitration (all straight line)
8. Factory maintenance - 40%; General maintenance - 60%
9. Fixed - 35%
10. Equally divided between Sales & Marketing and Administration; variable - 40%
11. Variable - 15%

Required:

1. Classify the expense items by behaviour (based on the number of units produced/sold) and by function (manufacturing, sales/marketing, and administration). Write the amount for each item using 2015 data.

2. What were the total amounts for product costs and period costs during 2015? Classify the product costs as direct or indirect.

3. Prepare an income statement in good form for the year 2015. Compute the gross margin *per unit* for the year.

PROBLEM 2–10
Computing Income and Cost of Goods Manufactured [LO5 – CC9; LO6 – CC12]

Margaret Rosenthal, accountant for Russell Manufacturing Company, prepared the following income statement for the quarter ending December 31, 2016.

CHECK FIGURE

(2) $853,611

Sales	$1,367,600
Purchases of materials (1)	245,640
Payroll (2)	266,786
Advertising	37,000
Administrative travel	27,600
Manufacturing utilities	49,400
Facility rental (3)	90,000
Depreciation (4)	63,500
Sales commissions	41,000
Annual insurance (manufacturing)	40,000
Office utilities	22,400
Management salaries (5)	388,000
Net income	$ 96,274

Notes:

(1) 80% of the materials were direct

(2) 70% direct labour; 30% indirect labour

(3) 90% related to manufacturing

(4) 75% related to manufacturing

(5) 40% related to manufacturing

Furthermore Rosenthal compiled the following information with respect to inventories for the quarter (note that the company does not maintain inventories of indirect materials).

	Beginning	Ending
Direct materials	$ 6,870	$7,860
Work-in-progress	8,070	9,120
Finished goods	11,280	7,420

Required:

1. Identify the conceptual errors, if any, in the quarterly income statement presented above.
2. Prepare a cost of goods manufactured statement for the quarter.
3. Prepare a revised income statement for the quarter.

PROBLEM 2–11
Computing Manufacturing Costs; Calculating Inventory [LO4 – CC5; LO5 – CC9, 10; LO6 – CC11, 12]

Discon Corporation manufactures a popular doll called Teardrops. Last year the company started with 10,000 dolls, produced 240,000 dolls, and ended the year with 8,000 dolls. Each doll was sold for $20. The actual unit cost for Teardrops is given below:

CHECK FIGURE

(1) $532,000

Direct material	$ 2.00
Direct labour	0.50
Variable overhead	2.50
Fixed overhead	7.00
Total unit cost	$12.00

The only selling expenses were a commission of $2 per unit sold and advertising amounting to $350,000. Administrative expenses, all fixed, equaled $270,000. There were no beginning and ending work-in-process inventories.

Required:

1. Prepare an income statement.
2. Calculate the following per unit costs:
   a. Prime cost
   b. Conversion cost
   c. Variable cost

Building Your Skills

COMPREHENSIVE PROBLEM [LO1 – CC1; LO3 – CC3; LO4 – CC4, 5, 6, 7]

Ahmedabad Manufacturing Corporation (AMC) is based in western India and uses India's currency, the rupee (symbol: ₹). AMC has been operating in its own manufacturing facility for over 15 years. Given the size of the facility, AMC has been able to rent the back portion of the building to a local retailer to use as a warehouse. It has now decided not to renew the lease and instead to use the area to manufacture a new product. AMC will lose a rental income of ₹1,800,000 per year.

CHECK FIGURE

(2) ₹6,588.44 per unit

The direct materials and direct labour per unit for the new product will amount to ₹4,000 and ₹2,200, respectively. AMC does not have sufficient equipment to produce the product; hence, it will rent the required equipment at a cost of ₹250,000 per month. The company will require additional space to store the raw material and work-in-process inventories associated with the new product; space can be rented in a nearby facility for ₹26,500 per month. AMC has always amortized its building on a straight-line basis and will continue to do so. The depreciation amount for the back portion of the building is ₹300,000 per year.

Other costs include the following:

Production supervisor salary	₹52,000 per month
Electricity for operating the machines	₹54 per unit
Delivery costs	₹390 per unit
Advertising	₹3,100,000 per year

Rather than borrow money to buy raw materials, pay workers' salaries, and meet other expenses, AMC's management has decided to liquidate some temporary investments that provided a return of ₹92,000 per year.

Required:

1. Classify the above costs using the following categories: behaviour, function, and relevance.
2. Assume that AMC will produce 1,800 units per month (90% of its capacity of 2,000 units per month). Compute the product cost per unit. Round your answer to two decimal places.
3. Assume AMC receives an order for 300 new units (i.e., total production will be 2,100 units). Compute the *additional* or *incremental* costs that AMC will incur in the manufacture and delivery of these 300 units.

THINKING ANALYTICALLY [LO4 – CC4, 5, 6, 7; LO5 – CC9, 10; LO6 – CC11, 12]

On December 31, 2016, the accounting records of a medium-sized company in Winnipeg were severely damaged by an accidental fire. The company did have access to certain incomplete accounting records, which revealed the following:

CHECK FIGURE

Direct materials purchased: $16,403,000

a. Beginning inventories, January 1, 2016:

Direct materials	= $24,000
Work-in-process	= $48,000
Finished goods	= $40,000

b. Key ratios for 2016:

Net income	= 10% of sales revenue
Manufacturing overhead	= two-thirds of conversion costs

c. Operational data for 2016:

Sales	= $76,500,000
Cost of goods manufactured	= $53,540,000
Direct labour	= $12,375,000

d. Ending inventories, December 31, 2016:

Direct materials	= $20,000
Work-in-process	= $40,000
Finished goods	= $30,000

Required:

From the above data, prepare *in good form* (1) the statement of cost of goods manufactured and (2) the income statement. Your statements must clearly show (1) the cost of direct materials purchased and used, (2) direct labour, (3) manufacturing overhead, (4) total manufacturing costs, (5) cost of goods sold, and (6) the SG&A expenses.

COMMUNICATING IN PRACTICE [LO4 – CC7, 8; LO5 – CC9, 10; LO6 – CC11, 12]

"I was sure that when our cellphone hit the market it would be an instant success," said Brittany Patel, founder and president of Sun Power Communications, Inc. "But just look at the gusher of red ink for the first quarter. It's obvious that we're better scientists than we are businesspeople." The data to which Patel was referring follow:

CHECK FIGURE

(2) COGM: $1,014,000

SUN POWER COMMUNICATIONS, INC. Income Statement For the Quarter Ended March 31		
Sales (32,000 cellphones)		$1,280,000
Less: Operating expenses:		
Selling and administrative salaries	$150,000	
Advertising	90,000	
Maintenance, production	73,000	
Indirect labour cost	120,000	
Cleaning supplies, production	7,000	
Purchases of raw materials	460,000	
Rental cost, facilities	95,000	
Insurance, production	18,000	

SUN POWER COMMUNICATIONS, INC. Income Statement For the Quarter Ended March 31		
Depreciation, office equipment	47,000	
Utilities	100,000	
Depreciation, production equipment	140,000	
Direct labour cost	90,000	
Travel, salespeople	40,000	
Total operating expenses		1,430,000
Net loss		$(150,000)

"At this rate we'll be out of business within a year," said Peter Merchant, the company's accountant. "But I've double-checked these figures, so I know they're right."

Sun Power Communications was organized at the beginning of the current year to produce and market a revolutionary new solar-powered cellphone. The company's accounting system was set up by Margie Wallace, an experienced accountant who recently left the company to do independent consulting work. The statement above was prepared by Merchant, her assistant.

"We may not last a year if the insurance company doesn't pay the $286,000 it owes us for the 8,000 cellphones lost in the warehouse fire last week," said Patel. "The insurance adjuster says our claim is inflated, but he's just trying to pressure us into a lower figure. We have the data to back up our claim, and it will stand up in any court."

On April 3, just after the end of the first quarter, the company's finished goods storage area was swept by fire and all 8,000 unsold cellphones were destroyed. (These phones were part of the 40,000 units completed during the first quarter.) The company's insurance policy states that the company will be reimbursed for the "cost" of any finished phones destroyed or stolen. Merchant has determined this cost as follows:

$$\frac{\text{Total costs for the quarter, } \$1,430,000}{\text{Batteries produced during the quarter, } 40,000} = \$35.75 \text{ per cellphone}$$

$$8,000 \text{ cellphones} \times \$35.75 \text{ per cellphone} = \$286,000$$

The following additional information is available on the company's activities during the quarter ended March 31:

a. Inventories at the beginning and end of the quarter were as follows:

	Beginning of the Quarter	End of the Quarter
Raw materials	–0–	$10,000
Work in process	–0–	50,000
Finished goods	–0–	?

b. 80% of the rental cost for facilities and 90% of the utilities cost relates to manufacturing operations. The remaining amounts relate to selling and administrative activities.

Required:

1. Write a brief memorandum to the president identifying what conceptual errors, if any, were made in preparing the income statement above.

2. Prepare a schedule of cost of goods manufactured for the first quarter.

3. Prepare a corrected income statement for the first quarter. Your statement should show in detail how the cost of goods sold is computed.

4. Do you agree that the insurance company owes Sun Power Communications, Inc. $286,000? Explain your answer in another brief memorandum to the president.

ETHICS CHALLENGE [LO4 – CC7]

M. K. Gallant is president of Kranbrack Corporation, a company whose shares are traded on a national exchange. In a meeting with investment analysts at the beginning of the year, Gallant had predicted that the company's earnings would grow by 20% this year. Unfortunately, sales have been less than expected for the year, and Gallant concluded within two weeks of the end of the fiscal year that it would ultimately be impossible to report an increase in earnings as large as predicted unless some drastic action were taken. Accordingly, Gallant has ordered that wherever possible, expenditures should be postponed to the new year—including cancelling or postponing orders with suppliers, delaying planned maintenance and training, and cutting back on end-of-year advertising and travel. Additionally, Gallant ordered the company's controller to carefully scrutinize all costs that are currently classified as period costs and reclassify as many as possible as product costs. The company is expected to have substantial inventories of work in process and finished goods at the end of the year.

Required:

1. Why would reclassifying period costs as product costs increase this period's reported earnings?
2. Do you believe Gallant's actions to be ethical? Why, or why not?

TEAMWORK IN ACTION [LO1 – CC1]

Steel production involves a large amount of fixed costs. Since competition is defined primarily in terms of price, steel manufacturers (and many of their manufacturing and service industry counterparts) try to gain a competitive advantage by using economies of scale and investment in technology to increase productivity and drive unit costs lower. Their substantial fixed costs are the result of their size.

Required:

1. The team should discuss and then write descriptions of the definitions of fixed costs and variable costs.
2. Each member of the team should select one of the following types of businesses and do the following: (i) give examples of fixed costs and variable costs that would be incurred by that type of business, (ii) choose a relevant measure of production or service activity for that type of business, and (iii) explain the relationship between the production (or service) output and each of the following: total fixed costs, fixed cost per unit, total variable costs, and variable cost per unit.
   a. Steel company.
   b. Hospital.
   c. University.
   d. Auto manufacturer.

   Each team member should present his or her notes to the other teammates, who should confirm or correct the presentation. Then work together as a team to complete parts (3) through (6) below.

3. Using the examples of fixed and variable costs for steel companies from part (2a) above, explain the relationship between production output at a steel company and each of the following: total fixed costs, fixed cost per unit, total variable costs, variable cost per unit, total costs, and average unit cost.

4. With an X-axis (horizontal axis) of tonnes produced and a Y-axis (vertical axis) of total costs, graph total fixed costs, total variable costs, and total costs against tonnes produced.

5. With an X-axis of tonnes produced and a Y-axis of unit costs, graph fixed cost per unit, variable cost per unit, and total (or average) cost per unit against tonnes produced.

6. Explain how costs (total and per unit) behave with changes in demand once capacity has been set.

Endnotes

1. As per the International Financial Reporting Standards (IFRS), we use *depreciation* for plant, property, and equipment, and *amortization* for intangible assets.

3

Systems Design: Job-Order Costing

LEARNING OBJECTIVES AND CHAPTER COMPETENCIES			
After studying Chapter 3, you should be able to demonstrate the following competencies:			
COMPETENCY		**Know**	**Apply**
LO1	**UNDERSTAND THE CONTEXT FOR COSTING SYSTEMS.**		
CC1	Distinguish between process costing and job-order costing by identifying companies that would use each costing method.	●	
CC2	Describe the key decisions management must make when applying a system to determine costs.	●	
CC3	Distinguish between absorption and variable costing and between normal and actual costing.	●	
LO2	**COMPUTE THE COSTS OF A SPECIFIC JOB.**		
CC4	Determine the cost of a specific job in a job-order costing system.		●
LO3	**UNDERSTAND THE IMPORTANCE OF THE CONCEPT OF OVERHEAD COST AND ITS COMPUTATION.**		
CC5	Compute predetermined overhead rates, and use these rates to apply overhead to individual jobs.		●
CC6	Explain why applied overhead costs, not actual overhead costs, are preferred in the costing process.	●	
CC7	Explain the importance of an overhead allocation base when allocating overhead costs to products and services.	●	
LO4	**DETERMINE COSTS INCURRED IN A JOB-ORDER PRODUCTION SYSTEM OVER A SPECIFIED PERIOD AND DESCRIBE THE FLOW OF COSTS THROUGH THE COST ACCOUNTING SYSTEM.**		

COMPETENCY		Know	Apply
CC8	Prepare journal entries to record costs incurred over a specific period of operations in a job-order costing system.		●
CC9	Differentiate between the process for determining the cost of a specific product and the accounting for the costs incurred in a job-order costing system during a specific period of operations.	●	
LO5	**UNDERSTAND THE INCURRENCE AND APPLICATION OF OVERHEAD COSTS.**		
CC10	Describe how incurred overhead costs are recorded in the accounting system, and apply overhead to work in process using a predetermined overhead rate.	●	●
CC11	Explain the concept of a clearing account.	●	
LO6	**PREPARE ACCOUNTING SCHEDULES DOCUMENTING THE COSTS INCURRED.**		
CC12	Prepare T-accounts to show the flow of costs in a job-order costing system.		●
CC13	Prepare schedules of cost of goods manufactured (COGM) and cost of goods sold (COGS).		●
LO7	**RECONCILE THE DIFFERENCE BETWEEN ACTUAL AND APPLIED OVERHEAD COSTS.**		
CC14	Compute under- or overapplied overhead cost, and prepare the journal entry to close the balance in manufacturing overhead to the appropriate accounts.		●
CC15	Describe the causes of under- and overapplied overhead.	●	
CC16	Explain why the under- or overapplied overhead balance must be disposed of at period-end.	●	
CC17	Distinguish between a plantwide overhead rate and a multiple overhead rate.	●	
LO8	**PREPARE PROFITABILITY REPORTS FOR MANAGEMENT USING INFORMATION FROM THE COST ACCOUNTING SYSTEM.**		
CC18	Prepare an income statement from the information accumulated in a job-order costing system.		●

ON THE JOB

COST OF UNINTERRUPTED SATELLITE COMMUNICATION

What do spacecraft orbiting Mars, Jupiter, and Venus—controlled by deep-space antennas—have in common with the XM Radio in your car? They rely on uninterrupted satellite communication links to keep them going 24 hours a day, seven days a week. Customers in Canada, Europe, India, Mexico, New Zealand, and the United States turn to the SED Systems division of Ottawa-based Calian Technologies to provide them with reliable and high-quality satellite products and services.

Ray Basler, president and CEO of Calian Technologies, loves to talk about the great projects that SED Systems is doing around the world. "Each project is unique," says Basler. "They draw upon the common skill set of engineers, but no two projects are alike." A lot of thought and action goes into each project, from the conceptualization stage to the design, build, ship, site installation, and commissioning stages. Individual projects may take as long as four years to complete; however, the average is about one and a half years.

Calian Technologies Ltd.

Every individual project has a unique identifier. Once the job specifications are understood, SED Systems prepares a bid with detailed estimates of materials, subcontracts, components, labour, and overhead costs. A firm fixed-price contract means that SED Systems has very few opportunities to change the price—this means that managing costs is essential to earning the estimated financial return from that project. All costs incurred for a project are captured separately, which helps a great deal, and management relies heavily on the expertise of its accountants to produce accurate budgets and prepare reliable project control reports that capture performance against planned timelines and against budgeted costs for the portion of the work completed.

What else does SED Systems do with its technical expertise? It serves customers over a broad spectrum: from the European Space Agency to the Canadian Armed Forces. It has also developed a suite of communication products that are used on internal projects as well as being sold to third parties.

Does the business face any risks? Absolutely! Satellite communication failure poses a huge risk; SED Systems overcomes this risk by emphasizing the importance of quality and reliability. Fluctuations in foreign currency rates are another risk, which the company manages through an active hedging program. Finally, not meeting established timelines poses both a liquidity risk and a reputational risk, both of which the company simply cannot afford to take.

Sources: Personal conversation with Ray Basler, president and CEO, and recent annual reports, available at https://www.calian.com/en/annual-reports.

Critical thinking question   *Think about the different types of jobs that SED Systems will bid on during a typical year. What are some of the challenges the company faces when preparing bids?*

*Note to student: See **Guidance Answers** online.*

◀◀ A Look Back	▶ A Look at This Chapter	▶▶ A Look Ahead
Chapter 1 described the three major activities of managers and compared and contrasted financial and managerial accounting. In Chapter 2, we defined many of the terms that are used to classify costs in business.	Chapter 3 distinguishes between two costing systems—job-order and process costing—and then provides an in-depth look at a job-order costing system. We describe how direct materials and direct labour costs are	Chapter 4 continues the discussion of cost determination in the process costing system. We show that many of the issues relating to cost accumulation in a job-order costing system also carry over to the process costing

◀◀ A Look Back	▶ A Look at This Chapter	▶▶ A Look Ahead
	accumulated on jobs. Then we address manufacturing overhead, an indirect cost that must be allocated (or applied) to jobs. Finally, we take a more detailed look at the flow of costs through a company's accounting system using journal entries.	system. Nonetheless, important differences are highlighted in that chapter.

P roduct costing is the process of assigning costs to a company's products and services. An understanding of this process is vital to managers because the cost data provided by the costing systems will help them plan, control, direct, and make decisions.

MANAGERIAL ACCOUNTING IN ACTION

THE ISSUE

It was a cold, gusty, and wet Friday in October as Joel Stebbins and Tamara Wilson sat down to dinner at a Winnipeg restaurant. Stebbins and Wilson had met several years before at university, where they had both majored in accounting. The dinner was a Thanksgiving tradition, and this year was their first meeting after their graduation. Stebbins had teamed up with his brother at Your Home Looked After, a small but growing business providing landscaping and home renovation services in Thunder Bay, Ontario. Wilson worked as a junior accountant for the Rand Company in Winnipeg, which specializes in producing gold and silver commemorative medallions. Both had been looking forward to this dinner to share their on-the-job experiences.

Sentre Square

Stebbins: So ... how is the new job?

Wilson: I was going to ask you the same question!

Stebbins: I love every minute of it. I started a business with my older brother Bill, whom you may have met.

Wilson: Yes, I remember meeting Bill. Tell me all about your business.

Stebbins: Bill had completed college and was already in it by the time I finished. Here's the conversation we had on the day I joined him.

Bill: It's good to have someone who knows a thing or two about accounting. This is a good time for you to join me because competition is picking up and I need your expertise more than ever before.

Stebbins: Glad to help out, Bill. Where do you want me to start?

Bill: I have been giving a lot of thought to how to get you involved with what we do and the best way for you to become immersed in the business. We are going after a pretty substantial contract with Sentre Square, a commercial building. The owner wants to convert this into a fancy place, including an area for fitness and recreation.

Stebbins: That sounds great, Bill; it looks like you are expanding to commercial buildings.

Bill: Yes, we are. But the owner first wants us to do some sample work on the west side of the building; this involves replacing the carpet on two floors of one portion of the building, replacing two windows, and painting two small rooms. They will then assess our work and decide whether to offer a portion of that large renovation contract to us. For this sample work, I want to charge them just at our cost.

Stebbins: This means we have to closely track costs.

Bill: Absolutely. I want you to follow this job as it progresses. I want you to pay attention to the activities performed and capture the costs. You know your accounting stuff; this is a good opportunity to apply your knowledge. After the job is completed, I want you to provide me with a report of the documentation created, the costs incurred, and, finally, the price we should be charging Sentre Square.

Stebbins: So this sample work will give us a good idea of our costs and therefore our future price for a similar contract.

Bill: You've got that right. There's one other thing. The accounting system that we currently use is too simplistic; I just accumulate all the costs and figure out how much we spent at the end of the year. I hope you can do better than that.

Stebbins: I will certainly try to do better than that. We have to be more proactive in terms of estimating our costs so that we can compete with other contractors out there.

Bill: Sure. That's why I need a reliable and knowledgeable accounting guy like you.

Stebbins: Bill, I am really excited by this assignment.

Bill: Right, then. Off you go. I reckon you are going to be busy over the next week. So, let's plan to meet in one week to discuss your experience.

Stebbins: You bet!

... So off I went and had the most interesting and instructive first week on the job.

The Purpose of Costing Systems

The purpose of costing systems is to accumulate and record the incurrence of costs and to assign the costs to the cost objects. Examples of cost objects include products, customers, divisions, and market territories. Every costing system must accomplish two things:

1. It should tell you which costs are *traceable* to the cost object, including how much has been incurred. These are the cost object's *direct costs*.
2. For those costs that cannot be traced directly to a product or activity—such as the costs of using physical facilities, utility and power costs, shop supplies costs, and so on—the costing system or approach must tell you how to *allocate* those costs to the product or activity whose cost you are trying to compute. These are the *indirect costs*.

Types of Costing Systems

LO1 ● **Know**

CC1: Distinguish between process costing and job-order costing by identifying companies that would use each costing method.

Costs are typically incurred when the company makes goods for or provides services to customers. Therefore, the nature of the costing system is intimately tied to the type of production system used by the company. For simplicity, we use *production* to refer to the production of tangible goods as well as the provision of services. Two types of production systems are common: job shops and flow shops. The two types of costing systems that correspond to the job shop and the flow shop are the **job-order costing system** and the **process costing system**, respectively.

Job Shops and Job-Order Costing

Job shops typically make a large variety of products in small quantities called *batches*. Each order, or batch, is also referred to as a *job. Flow shops* produce a much smaller variety of products in large volumes, using a standardized and fixed sequence of operations.

Job shops usually *produce to order*. These production facilities are capable of making special, one-of-a-kind, custom orders. Small metal fabrication companies, for example, can make custom components for use in machinery. Golf equipment maker MacGregor Golf, for example, can custom-forge its irons by grinding the top-line and the sole of the club in addition to setting the lie angle according to the specifications of the customer. Some companies that use this type of production system are Bombardier, de Havilland, Hallmark (the greeting card maker), and LSG Sky Chefs (which prepares airline meals). Many service companies are also job shops. For example, each client of a law firm is a job. The example we have used (Your Home Looked After) is also a service company. Similarly, in a movie studio such as Columbia Pictures, each film produced by the studio is a job.

Flow Shops and Process Costing

Flow shops typically *produce to stock,* and the products made by these systems are sold from inventory. Examples include J. G. Schneider Foods in Kitchener, Ontario, which makes processed meats; any soft-drink bottler; the Potash Corporation of Saskatchewan; and Reynolds Aluminum. Television and appliance makers also fall into this category, as do flour mills, cement manufacturers, and oil refiners. The difference between an appliance maker and an oil refiner is that oil refining is a *continuous* process, meaning the output is one continuous stream; you cannot distinguish between the first litre and the last litre of oil. Appliance production, however, is a *discrete* process, which means it is possible to distinguish the first unit from the last unit. The mail-processing centres of Canada Post, and many other postal organizations across the world, use an automated continuous process, thereby resembling a flow shop.

Because production occurs continuously in large volumes in a flow shop, the concept of a batch is not meaningful over a period. Therefore, in process costing, costs of production over a period are first accumulated within a process and then divided by the volume of production to compute unit costs. This technique results in a broad average unit cost figure that applies to homogeneous units flowing in a continuous stream out of the production process. Process costing is covered in the next chapter.

Approaches to Costing—Key Management Decisions

Absorption Versus Variable Costing Approaches

LO1 ● **Know**

CC2: Describe the key decisions management must make when applying a system to determine costs.

Before a costing system is used to determine product costs, management must make certain important decisions. A firm will incur both fixed and variable costs when engaged in providing goods and services. One important decision for managers to make is whether to include *both* fixed and variable costs when computing the cost of a product. When management wishes to determine the profitability of a certain product, it must include both variable and fixed costs when computing product costs. This approach to product costing is called **absorption costing** (or **full costing**): All costs are completely assigned to products. In contrast, when management wishes to determine the additional cost of supplying 10 extra units of a product, it may consider only the variable costs of these 10 additional units. In this situation, management determines that fixed costs are *not relevant* to the purpose for which product cost information is desired, and a different approach called **variable costing** is used. In the variable costing approach, only variable costs of the product are considered in the analysis of the product's contribution to the firm's profits.

LO1   ● **Know**

CC3: Distinguish between absorption and variable costing and between normal and actual costing.

The absorption costing approach is common to many businesses, since (1) external financial reporting and tax reporting requirements dictate the use of this approach and (2) many companies have found this approach useful for managerial accounting purposes. For this reason, in this chapter and in the two that follow, we will use the absorption costing approach to determine product costs. Variable costing will be considered in later chapters.

Normal Versus Actual Costing Approaches

It is reasonable to assume that the actual cost of a product (service) is not known until the product is made (service is provided). However, managers often require cost information in order to make important decisions before a service is provided (e.g., in a situation where the company might be bidding for a contract). Managers might be able to estimate and predict the incurrence of direct costs before these costs are incurred. But what about the incurrence of indirect costs—overhead costs? Should managers wait until after the overhead costs have been incurred and then allocate these *actual* overhead costs to the product? Or should managers first *budget* the manufacturing overhead costs, then *apply* these *budgeted* manufacturing overhead costs to the products? If managers allocate *actual* overhead costs to jobs, they are said to be using the **actual costing system**. If managers use the *budgeted* overhead costs and apply them to the product, they are said to be using a **normal costing system**.

Managers must decide whether to use a normal costing system or the actual costing system. For our purposes, we will follow a normal costing approach in this chapter and the next two. In a normal costing system, actual overhead costs are never assigned to products, and these costs do not flow through the inventory accounts. Instead of actual costs, budgeted overhead costs are applied to products, and it is these budgeted overhead costs that flow through to the inventory accounts.

Certainly, managers are aware that the amount of the actual costs can vary (more or less) from the amount budgeted. Such differences will have to be reconciled at period-end to bring normal costs in line with actual costs, especially when preparing and reporting financial results. Choosing a method of reconciliation is another decision for managers to make, and several approaches can be used for adjusting normal costs. Regardless of the method of adjustment chosen, product costs are never adjusted in a normal costing system in the reconciliation process. In this text, we will adjust the cost of goods sold at the end of the operating cycle for the difference between actual and applied overhead costs.

Overhead Cost Allocation Approaches

One of the main challenges for management accountants is the problem of overhead allocation. Indirect costs—budgeted or actual—by their very nature are not traceable to the product and therefore have to be allocated to products using an allocation method. Choosing the allocation method is another important decision for managers because different methods can lead to different allocations of manufacturing overhead.

We are now ready to proceed to a detailed look at the job-order costing system. Our illustration of the job-order costing system will deal with a home renovation and landscaping firm, but the same concepts and procedures may be used by manufacturing companies as well as other service organizations such as hospitals, auto repair shops, movie studios, and professional service firms (e.g., law offices and accounting firms). We will assume that management has decided to follow the absorption costing approach and the normal costing system.

IN BUSINESS

PROCESS-FLOW OR JOB-FLOW?

CONTINUOUS-FLOW OR BATCH-FLOW?

Should companies use a continuous-flow or a batch-flow approach to production? Or can they utilize both? One industry that is gearing toward continuous-flow processing is the pharmaceutical industry. While batch-flow production has been the industry norm for many years, many pharmaceutical companies these days are realizing the advantages of adopting continuous-flow processing for high-demand drugs. Even regulatory bodies are acknowledging the benefits of adopting continuous-flow for the industry. It is widely believed that adopting continuous-flow will increase production efficiency and result in a significant reduction in drug manufacturing costs. Continuous-flow will also bring two main technical advantages: waste minimization and reduced raw materials consumption. Although implementing this change requires a substantial amount of time and careful planning, as well as more research and development to address potential issues in the new adoption, many stakeholders still hold a strong belief that the change will inevitably take place in the years to come. A change in the production process is necessary when existing practices can no longer meet the ever changing demands of the business.

Sources: Tibi Puiu, "Switch From Batch to Continuous Mass Production May Drastically Cut Cost and Speed of Medicine Manufacturing", *ZME Science*, September 9, 2013; R. Bowen, "Does Pharma Really Need Continuous Processing?", *Parenteral Drug Association*, January 30, 2015; C. Challener, "The Mainstreaming of Continuous Flow API Synthesis", *PharmTech*, July 2, 2014.

An Overview of Job-Order Costing—Determining the Cost of a Specific Job

LO2   • **Apply**

CC4: Determine the cost of a specific job in a job-order costing system.

To introduce job-order costing, let us return to Your Home Looked After (YHLA) and describe what Joel Stebbins learned that first week on his job as he followed the activities and the costs of work on the west side of Sentre Square.

Recall that, to secure Sentre Square's business, YHLA has agreed to provide the sample service at its cost of goods sold. This means that YHLA must carefully document its costs while completing the job. This is the responsibility of YHLA's job-order costing system. The cost of the work will be determined by recording and accumulating the costs of direct materials, direct labour, and overhead incurred to complete the job.

Measuring Direct Materials Cost

The costing system kicks into gear when a work order is issued authorizing the job. The department concerned then prepares a *materials requisition form* for the job. The **materials requisition form** is a detailed source document that (1) specifies the type and quantity of materials to be drawn from the storeroom and (2) identifies the job to which the costs of materials are to be charged. The form is used for controlling the flow of materials into production and also for making entries in the accounting records. The information on the materials requisition form about the quantity and type of materials required is typically taken from the job's *bill of materials*. The **bill of materials** is a document that lists the type and quantity of each item required to complete the job (a single unit of product in the case of a manufacturing firm). The bill of materials itself is determined initially from blueprints and engineering specifications and may undergo many revisions depending on the complexity of the job.

Exhibit 3–1 illustrates a materials requisition slip, which lists direct materials to be drawn from the storeroom. This completed form is presented to the storeroom clerk, who then issues the necessary materials. The storeroom clerk is not allowed to release materials without such a form bearing an authorized signature. (*With advances in technology, companies may prepare the materials requisition slip [and other documents illustrated in this chapter] electronically rather than manually.*) Note that multiple materials requisition slips may be prepared for a single job—this is so because it is not prudent to request and issue all materials at one time.

EXHIBIT 3–1 Materials Requisition Form

Materials Requisition

| Number | 2017-36 | | Date | 2-Mar-17 |

Job to be Charged   2017-4

Department   Commercial

Description	Quantity	Unit Cost	Total Cost	Remarks
Carpet	200	$ 4.50	$ 900	square yards
Paint	2	$ 80.00	$ 160	5-gallon containers
Windows	2	$120.00	$ 240	includes frame & glass
			$ 1,300	
			To Job Cost Sheet (#2017-4)	

Authorized Signature

Job Cost Sheet

After being notified that the work order has been issued, the accounting department prepares a *job cost sheet* similar to the one presented in Exhibit 3–2. A **job cost sheet** is a form prepared for each separate job that records the materials, labour, and overhead costs charged to the job.

EXHIBIT 3–2 Job Cost Sheet

JOB COST SHEET

Number	2017-4		Date Initiated	2-Mar-17
			Date Completed	
Department	Commercial		Units Completed	
Description	Renovation			

Direct Materials		Direct Labour			Overhead		
Req. No.	Amount	Time Sheet	Hours	Amount	Hours	Rate	Amount
From materials requisition forms		From time sheets			Applied overhead		

Cost Summary			Job Completion Status	
Direct Materials			Date	Progress to Date
Direct Labour				
Overhead				
Total Cost				
Unit Cost				

In addition to serving as a means for charging costs to jobs, the job cost sheet serves as a key part of a firm's accounting records. The job cost sheets form a subsidiary ledger to the work-in-process account. They are detailed records for the jobs in process that add up to the balance in work in process.

Measuring Direct Labour Cost

Direct labour cost is handled in much the same way as direct materials cost. Labour charges that cannot be easily traced directly to any job are treated as part of overhead. As discussed in Chapter 2, this latter category of labour costs is called *indirect labour* and includes the costs of such tasks as maintenance, supervision, and cleanup.

Workers use *time sheets* to record the time they spend on each job and task. A completed **time sheet** is a summary of the employee's activities throughout the day, along with the time taken to perform those activities. An example of an employee time sheet is shown in Exhibit 3–3. In many service organizations, such as accounting firms and law firms, having an accurate record of the time taken to perform different activities is crucial because billing is often based on the time taken (or required) to complete a job.

EXHIBIT 3–3 Employee Time Sheet

EMPLOYEE TIME SHEET					
Time Sheet No.		2017-47		Date	2-Mar-17
Employee		Mary Holden			
Time					
Started	Ended	Spent	Rate	Amount	Job Number
7:00	12:00	5.0	20	$ 100	2017-4
12:30	3:30	3.0	20	$ 60	2017-4
Totals		8.0		$ 160	
Supervisor					

An individual employee may prepare a time sheet either by writing the details manually on a printed form or by entering the data into a computer. Some companies with sophisticated systems may capture the time by requiring employees to swipe electronic cards each time they start and stop an activity; the data are then automatically recorded into a computer. What is important is that relevant data about the time taken are captured as accurately as possible, regardless of the method used.

When working on a specific job, the employee enters the job number on the time sheet and notes the amount of time spent on that job. When not assigned to a particular job, the employee records the nature of the indirect labour task (such as cleanup and maintenance) and the amount of time spent on the task.

At the end of the day, the time sheets are gathered, and the accounting department enters the direct labour-hours and costs on individual job cost sheets. (See Exhibit 3–2 for an example of how direct labour costs are entered on the job cost sheet.) The daily time sheets are source documents that are used as the basis for labour cost entries into the accounting records.

IN BUSINESS

THE POTENTIAL FOR INACCURATE PRODUCT COSTS

Labour costs were a large portion of total manufacturing costs as recently as 25 years ago. However, a shortage of skilled labour, increasing price competition, and a strong focus on quality and reliability have forced many manufacturers to automate many of their processes. A 2014 management issues survey conducted by Canadian Manufacturers & Exporters in conjunction with BDO LLP suggests that many Canadian manufacturers are facing labour shortages, especially a shortage of skilled production labour. This is seen as critical because 47% of survey respondents already felt that their businesses' growth is impeded by labour shortages, and 56% of the respondents felt that labour costs are being driven up by labour shortages. Businesses are trying to overcome labour shortages in many different ways, one of which is to automate many of their processes. The survey shows that 40% of respondents are investing in automation to overcome labour shortages, and 64% of respondents plan to increase investment on new machinery and equipment. A direct result of automation is that direct labour is becoming less important and also represents a smaller portion of total manufacturing costs. This raises two issues: (1) Should companies maintain elaborate systems to track direct labour-hours and costs? and (2) Is direct labour still an appropriate base to allocate manufacturing overhead costs?

Sources: Canadian Manufacturers & Exporters, BDO LLP, http://www.cme-mec.ca/_uploads/_media/51wjbzblm.pdf

Application of Overhead

LO3   ● **Apply**

CC5: Compute predetermined overhead rates, and use these rates to apply overhead to individual jobs.

Overhead must be included with direct materials and direct labour on the job cost sheet, since overhead is also a part of the job cost. However, determining the amount of overhead a specific job may consume can be a difficult task. There are three reasons for this:

1. Overhead is an *indirect cost*. This means that it is either impossible or difficult to trace these costs to a particular product or job.
2. Overhead consists of many different items, such as supplies (nails, screws, glue), maintenance, utilities, and the annual salary of the department manager.
3. Even though output may fluctuate due to seasonal or other factors, overhead costs tend to remain relatively constant due to the presence of fixed costs.

Given these problems, the only way to assign overhead costs to products is to use an application (allocation) process. This application of overhead costs is accomplished by selecting an **allocation base** that is common to all of the company's products and services. Examples include direct labour-hours and machine-hours.

The allocation base is used to compute the **predetermined overhead rate** in the following formula:

$$\text{Predetermined overhead rate} = \frac{\text{Estimated total manufacturing overhead cost}}{\text{Estimated total activity volume of the allocation base}}$$

Note that the predetermined overhead rate is based on *estimates* rather than on actual amounts. This is because the *predetermined* overhead rate is computed *before* the period begins and is used to *apply* overhead cost to jobs throughout the period. The process of assigning overhead cost to jobs is called **overhead application**. The formula for determining the amount of overhead cost to apply to a particular job is as follows:

Overhead applied to a particular job = Predetermined overhead rate × Quantity of the allocation base consumed by the job

When the allocation base is the direct labour-hour (DLH), the formula becomes

Overhead applied to a particular job = Predetermined overhead rate per DLH × Actual DLHs charged to the job

For example, if the predetermined overhead rate is $8 per direct labour-hour, then $8 of overhead cost is *applied* to a job for each direct labour-hour incurred by the job.

USING THE PREDETERMINED OVERHEAD RATE

To illustrate the steps involved in computing and using a predetermined overhead rate, let us return to Your Home Looked After. The company has estimated its total overhead costs to be $630,000 for the year and its total direct labour-hours (DLHs) to be 28,000. Its predetermined overhead rate for the year would be $22.50 per direct labour-hour, as shown below:

$$\text{Predetermined overhead rate} = \frac{\text{Estimated total overhead cost}}{\text{Estimated total activity volume of the allocation base}}$$

$$= \frac{\$630,000}{28,000 \text{ DLHs}}$$

$$= \$22.50 \text{ per DLH}$$

The job cost sheet in Exhibit 3–4 indicates that 48 direct labour-hours were charged to job 2017-4. Therefore, a total of $1,080 of overhead cost would be applied to the job:

$$\text{Overhead applied to job 2017-4} = \text{Predetermined overhead rate} \times \text{Actual DLHs charged to job 2017-4}$$

$$= \$22.50 \text{ per DLH} \times 48 \text{ DLHs}$$

$$= \$1,080 \text{ of overhead applied to job 2017-4}$$

This amount of overhead has been entered on the job cost sheet in Exhibit 3–4. Note that this is *not* the actual amount of overhead caused by the job. There is no attempt to trace actual overhead costs to jobs—if that could be done, the costs would be direct costs, not overhead. The overhead assigned to the job is simply a share of the total overhead that was estimated at the beginning of the year. When a company applies overhead cost to jobs as we have done—that is, by multiplying actual activity by the predetermined overhead rate—it is called a *normal costing system*.

The overhead may be applied when direct labour-hours are charged to jobs, or all of the overhead can be applied at once when the job is completed. The choice is up to the company. If a job is still incomplete at the end of the accounting period, all applicable overhead must be applied to the job so that work-in-process inventory can be assigned a value in accordance with the standards for inventory valuation.

HELPFUL HINT

This chapter is based on the concept of normal costing. A normal cost system assigns actual direct materials and direct labour costs to jobs; however, it does *not* assign actual overhead costs to jobs. Instead, a predetermined overhead rate is used to apply overhead cost to jobs. The predetermined overhead rate is multiplied by the actual quantity of the allocation base consumed by a job to apply overhead cost to that job. Many companies use normal cost systems; however, companies can also use other types of cost systems, such as actual costing and standard costing, which will be discussed in later chapters.

EXHIBIT 3–4 A Completed Job Cost Sheet

JOB COST SHEET							
Number	2017-4			Date Initiated		2-Mar-17	
				Date Completed		18-Mar-17	
Department	Commercial			Units Completed		N/A	
Description	Renovation						

Direct Materials		Direct Labour			Overhead		
Req. No.	Amount	Time Sheet	Hours	Amount	Hours	Rate	Amount
2017-36	$ 1,300	2017-47	8	$ 160	48	$ 22.50	<u>$ 1,080</u>
2017-39	$ 2,650	2017-52	8	$ 160			
2017-46	<u>$ 680</u>	2017-56	8	$ 160			
	<u>$ 4,630</u>	2017-57	8	$ 160			
		2017-62	8	$ 160			
		2017-66	8	<u>$ 160</u>			
				<u>$ 960</u>			

Cost Summary			Job Completion Status		
Direct Materials	$ 4,630		Date	Progress to-date	
Direct Labour	$ 960		18-Mar-17	Completed	
Overhead	<u>$ 1,080</u>				
Total Cost	<u>$ 6,670</u>				
Unit Cost					

THE NEED FOR A PREDETERMINED RATE

LO3 • **Know**

CC6: Explain why applied overhead costs, not actual overhead costs, are preferred in the costing process.

Instead of using a predetermined rate, a company could wait until the end of the accounting period to compute an actual overhead rate based on the *actual* total manufacturing costs and the *actual* total units in the allocation base for the period. However, managers cite several reasons for using predetermined overhead rates instead of actual overhead rates:

- Companies like YHLA are often required to quote a price prior to receiving a customer order. In such situations it is important to assign overhead costs to potential jobs so that a realistic quote can be prepared.

- Managers would like to know the accounting system's valuation of completed jobs *before* the end of the accounting period. Suppose, for example, that YHLA waited until the end of the year to compute its overhead rate. Then there would be no way for managers to know the cost of job 2017-4 until the close of the year, even though the job was completed in March. The seriousness of this problem can be reduced to some extent by computing the actual overhead more frequently, but that immediately leads to another problem, as described in the next point.

- If actual overhead rates are computed frequently, seasonal factors in overhead costs or in the allocation base can produce fluctuations in the overhead rates. Managers generally feel that such fluctuations in overhead rates serve no useful purpose and are misleading.

- The use of a predetermined overhead rate simplifies recordkeeping. To determine the overhead cost to apply to a job, the accounting staff at YHLA simply multiply the direct labour-hours recorded for the job by the predetermined overhead rate of $22.50 per direct labour-hour.

Properly estimating overhead costs and the volume of the allocation base is extremely important to ensure that the resultant predetermined overhead rate is not significantly distorted.

Choice of an Allocation Base for Overhead Cost

LO3 • **Know**

CC7: Explain the importance of an overhead allocation base when allocating overhead costs to products and services.

Ideally, the allocation base should be a *cost driver* of the overhead cost. A **cost driver** is a factor that causes overhead costs. Examples of cost drivers include machine-hours, direct labour-hours, maintenance-hours, inspection-hours (manufacturing company), beds occupied (hospital), rooms occupied (hotel), or flight-hours (airline). If the base used to compute overhead rates does not "drive" overhead costs, then the result will be inaccurate overhead rates and distorted product costs. For example, if direct labour and overhead costs have been moving in opposite directions in a company because of a shift toward automation and the increased use of highly skilled indirect labour such as engineers, direct labour should not be used as the allocation base. If direct labour is used in this situation, then products with high direct labour-hour requirements will be overcosted and products with low direct labour-hour requirements will be undercosted. The debate about which allocation base is appropriate has spurred the redesign of costing systems according to the principles of *activity-based costing* (ABC), which is discussed in Chapter 5.

IN BUSINESS

COST DRIVERS IN HEALTHCARE

The healthcare industry is one of the largest and most complicated industries in Canada. In recent years, the cost of healthcare has climbed significantly in Canada, leaving many stakeholders wondering how to address the issue. The rising costs are attributed to significant inefficiencies in the system. One of the reasons for these inefficiencies, says Jacques Bédard, senior vice-president of the healthcare sector for Siemens Canada, is the way budgets are created. He notes that hospitals in Canada operate on a fixed-budget system that is not related to the number of patients treated or the number of days a patient spends in the hospital. According to Bédard, one way to address the inefficiencies in the healthcare system is to carefully identify the cost drivers and make funding allocations on the basis of these activities. Specifically, the cost drivers include patient-days and patient treatments.

Sources: "Healthcare in Canada: Can We Fix It—And How?" *Canadian Business*, July 20, 2009. Courtesy Siemens Canada.

Computation of Job Costs

With the application of YHLA's $1,080 overhead to the job cost sheet in Exhibit 3–4, the job cost sheet is almost complete. The totals for direct materials, direct labour, and overhead are transferred to the cost summary section of the sheet and added to obtain the total cost for the job ($6,670). In the case of a manufacturing company, a single job may consist of producing multiple units of a custom product (say, 50 units of a designer pen ordered by a gift shop). The cost of one designer pen can be computed by dividing the total job cost by the 50 pens produced.

The completed job cost sheet is now ready to be transferred to the finished goods inventory account, where it will serve as the basis for valuing unsold units in ending inventory and determining cost of goods sold.

The sequence of events discussed previously is summarized in Exhibit 3–5. A careful study of the flow of documents in this exhibit will provide a good overview of the overall operation of a job-order costing system.

EXHIBIT 3–5 The Flow of Documents in a Job-Order Costing System

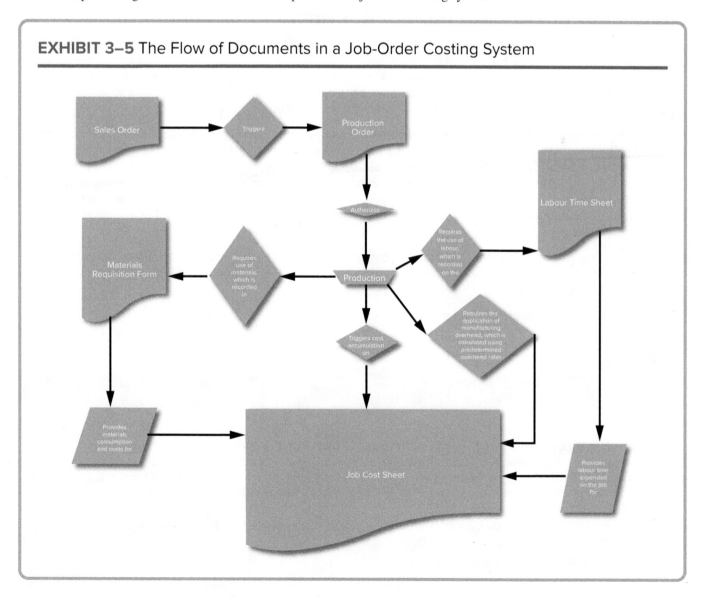

MANAGERIAL ACOUNTING IN ACTION

THE ISSUE

Stebbins: The next week I went to see Bill, and I walked him through the cost accumulation process using a flow chart [Exhibit 3–5] to describe the accumulation of the job costs. I showed him the various documents and accounting records that were created, and concluded with my job cost sheet for the sample work completed [Exhibits 3–1 to 3–4]. Finally, I ended with a suggestion that the company should abandon the actual costing system in favour of a normal costing system. This system is better when job costs must be estimated in advance.

DECISION POINT

TREASURER OF THE CLASS REUNION COMMITTEE

It is hard to believe that 10 years have passed since your high school graduation. After high school, you attended the local community college, transferred to a university, and graduated on time. You are now juggling a successful career, classes in an evening MBA program, and a new family. What's more, after reminiscing with one of your high school classmates, you have somehow agreed to handle the financial arrangements for your 10-year reunion. What were you thinking? Well, at least you can fall back on those accounting skills.

You call the restaurant where the reunion will be held and jot down the most important information. The meal cost (including beverages) will be $30 per person plus a 15% gratuity. An additional $200 will be charged for a banquet room with a dance floor. A band has been hired for $500. One of the members of the reunion committee informs you that there is just enough money left in the class bank account to cover the printing and mailing costs. He mentions that at least one-half of the class of 400 will attend the reunion and wonders if he should add the 15% gratuity to the $30 per person meal cost when he drafts the invitation, which will indicate that a cheque must be returned with the reply card.

How should you respond? How much should you charge to cover the various costs? After making your decision, label your answer with the managerial accounting terms covered in this chapter. Finally, identify any issues that should be investigated further.

*Note to student: See **Guidance Answers** online.*

CONCEPT CHECK

1. Which of the following statements are false? (You may select more than one answer.)
   a. Absorption costing assigns fixed and variable manufacturing overhead costs to products.
   b. Job-order costing systems are used when companies produce many different types of products.
   c. A normal costing system assigns costs to products by multiplying the actual overhead rate by the actual amount of the allocation base.
   d. A company such as Coca-Cola is more likely to use a process costing system than a job-order costing system.

*Note to student: See **Guidance Answers** online.*

MANAGERIAL ACCOUNTING IN ACTION

THE ISSUE

Joel Stebbins and Tamara Wilson continued their dinner conversation sharing their job experiences.

Sentre Square

Stebbins: Well, it's your turn. Tell me about your job at Rand Company.

Wilson: All right. I have a similar experience to share with you. Like yours, my first assignment was designed to let me learn about our accounting system and our operations. Your task was to follow one job from start to finish. I, on the other hand, had to consider all of the activities occurring during a single month—April—and trace the flow of costs through the accounting system. There was one job, job A, to supply 1,000 gold medallions commemorating the invention of motion pictures, which was started in March. It had a total of $30,000 in manufacturing costs recorded by the end of March. On April 1, we started a second job, job B, for 10,000 silver coins commemorating the fall of the Berlin Wall. So my assignment boiled down to tracking the activities performed during April through the accounting system records and determining the costs incurred to complete jobs A and B. I was to summarize the entries in the accounting system that traced the activities and the costs in April, and then prepare a schedule of the cost of goods manufactured, the schedule of cost of goods sold, and finally an income statement for April.

Stebbins: So where did you begin?

Cost Flows in a Job-Order System

We are now ready to look at the *flow of costs* through the company's formal accounting system. To illustrate, we shall trace Tamara Wilson's journey in her first week on the job at Rand Company (a manufacturing company) as she focused on tracing the activities for the month of April. The starting point is with the acquisition of materials.

The Purchase and Issue of Materials

LO4 ● **Apply**

CC8: Prepare journal entries to record costs incurred over a specific period of operations in a job-order costing system.

On April 1, Rand Company had $7,000 in raw materials on hand. During the month, the company purchased an additional $60,000 in raw materials. The purchase is recorded in journal entry (1) below:

(1)

Raw Materials	60,000	
Accounts Payable		60,000

As explained in Chapter 2, the raw materials account is an asset account. Thus, when raw materials are purchased, they are initially recorded as an asset—not as an expense.

ISSUE OF DIRECT AND INDIRECT MATERIALS

LO4 • Know

CC9: Differentiate between the process for determining the cost of a specific product and the accounting for the costs incurred in a job-order costing system during a specific period of operations.

During April, $52,000 in raw materials were requisitioned from the storeroom for use in production. Entry (2) records the issue of the materials to the production departments.

	(2)	
Work in Process	50,000	
Manufacturing Overhead	2,000	
Raw Materials		52,000

The materials charged to work in process represent direct materials for specific jobs. As these materials are entered into the work-in-process account, they are also recorded on the appropriate job cost sheets. This point is illustrated in Exhibit 3–6, where $28,000 of the $50,000 in direct materials is charged to job A's cost sheet, and the remaining $22,000 is charged to job B's cost sheet. (In this example, all data are presented in summary form, and the job cost sheet is abbreviated.)

The $2,000 charged to manufacturing overhead in entry (2) represents indirect materials used in production during April. Observe that the manufacturing overhead account is separate from the work-in-process account. The purpose of the manufacturing overhead account is to accumulate all manufacturing overhead costs as they are incurred during a period.

Before leaving Exhibit 3–6, note that the job cost sheet for job A contains a beginning balance of $30,000. We stated previously that this balance represents the cost of work done during March that has been carried forward to April. Also note that the work-in-process account contains the same $30,000 balance. *The $30,000 appears in both places because the work-in-process account is a control account and the job cost sheets form a subsidiary ledger. Thus, the work-in-process account contains a summarized total of all costs appearing on the individual job cost sheets for all jobs in process at any given point in time.* Since Rand Company had only job A in process at the beginning of April, job A's $30,000 balance on that date is equal to the balance in the work-in-process account.

EXHIBIT 3–6 Raw Materials Cost Flows

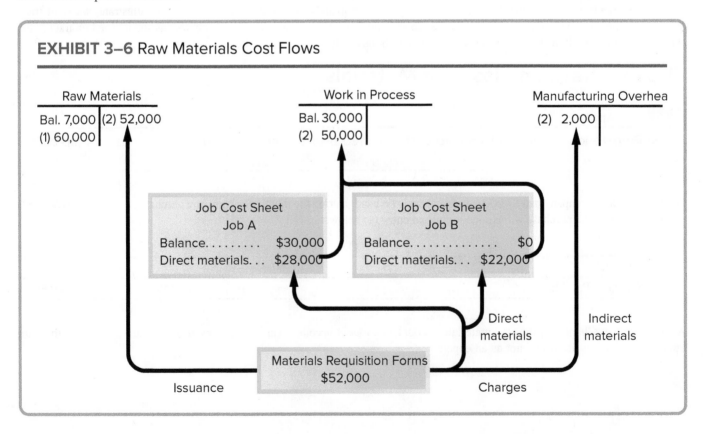

MANAGERIAL ACCOUNTING IN ACTION

THE ISSUE

Joel Stebbins and Tamara Wilson continued their dinner conversation sharing their job experiences.

Stebbins: Well, it's your turn. Tell me about your job at Rand Company.

Wilson: All right. I have a similar experience to share with you. Like yours, my first assignment was designed to let me learn about our accounting system and our operations. Your task was to follow one job from start to finish. I, on the other hand, had to consider all of the activities occurring during a single month—April—and trace the flow of costs through the accounting system. There was one job, job A, to supply 1,000 gold medallions commemorating the invention of motion pictures, which was started in March. It had a total of $30,000 in manufacturing costs recorded by the end of March. On April 1, we started a second job, job B, for 10,000 silver coins commemorating the fall of the Berlin Wall. So my assignment boiled down to tracking the activities performed during April through the accounting system records and determining the costs incurred to complete jobs A and B. I was to summarize the entries in the accounting system that traced the activities and the costs in April, and then prepare a schedule of the cost of goods manufactured, the schedule of cost of goods sold, and finally an income statement for April.

Stebbins: So where did you begin?

Cost Flows in a Job-Order System

We are now ready to look at the *flow of costs* through the company's formal accounting system. To illustrate, we shall trace Tamara Wilson's journey in her first week on the job at Rand Company (a manufacturing company) as she focused on tracing the activities for the month of April. The starting point is with the acquisition of materials.

The Purchase and Issue of Materials

LO4 • **Apply**

CC8: Prepare journal entries to record costs incurred over a specific period of operations in a job-order costing system.

On April 1, Rand Company had $7,000 in raw materials on hand. During the month, the company purchased an additional $60,000 in raw materials. The purchase is recorded in journal entry (1) below:

(1)

Raw Materials	60,000	
Accounts Payable		60,000

As explained in Chapter 2, the raw materials account is an asset account. Thus, when raw materials are purchased, they are initially recorded as an asset—not as an expense.

ISSUE OF DIRECT AND INDIRECT MATERIALS

LO4   • Know

CC9: Differentiate between the process for determining the cost of a specific product and the accounting for the costs incurred in a job-order costing system during a specific period of operations.

During April, $52,000 in raw materials were requisitioned from the storeroom for use in production. Entry (2) records the issue of the materials to the production departments.

	(2)	
Work in Process	50,000	
Manufacturing Overhead	2,000	
Raw Materials		52,000

The materials charged to work in process represent direct materials for specific jobs. As these materials are entered into the work-in-process account, they are also recorded on the appropriate job cost sheets. This point is illustrated in Exhibit 3–6, where $28,000 of the $50,000 in direct materials is charged to job A's cost sheet, and the remaining $22,000 is charged to job B's cost sheet. (In this example, all data are presented in summary form, and the job cost sheet is abbreviated.)

The $2,000 charged to manufacturing overhead in entry (2) represents indirect materials used in production during April. Observe that the manufacturing overhead account is separate from the work-in-process account. The purpose of the manufacturing overhead account is to accumulate all manufacturing overhead costs as they are incurred during a period.

Before leaving Exhibit 3–6, note that the job cost sheet for job A contains a beginning balance of $30,000. We stated previously that this balance represents the cost of work done during March that has been carried forward to April. Also note that the work-in-process account contains the same $30,000 balance. *The $30,000 appears in both places because the work-in-process account is a control account and the job cost sheets form a subsidiary ledger. Thus, the work-in-process account contains a summarized total of all costs appearing on the individual job cost sheets for all jobs in process at any given point in time.* Since Rand Company had only job A in process at the beginning of April, job A's $30,000 balance on that date is equal to the balance in the work-in-process account.

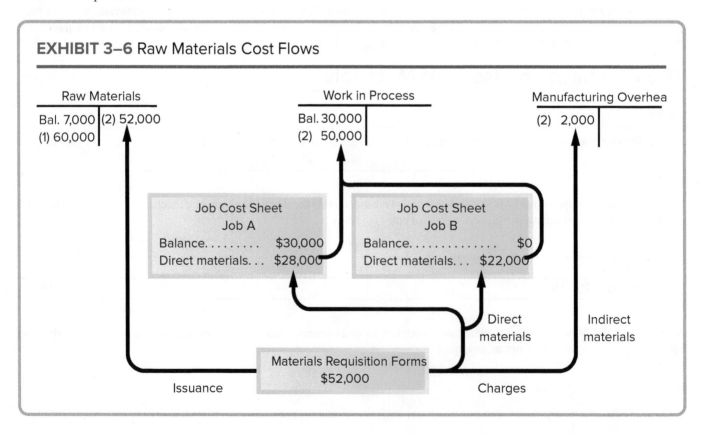

EXHIBIT 3–6 Raw Materials Cost Flows

Raw Materials	Work in Process	Manufacturing Overhea
Bal. 7,000 | (2) 52,000	Bal. 30,000	(2) 2,000
(1) 60,000 |	(2) 50,000	

Job Cost Sheet
Job A
Balance......... $30,000
Direct materials... $28,000

Job Cost Sheet
Job B
Balance............. $0
Direct materials... $22,000

Direct materials

Indirect materials

Materials Requisition Forms
$52,000

Issuance

Charges

ISSUE OF DIRECT MATERIALS ONLY

Sometimes, the materials drawn from the raw materials inventory account are all direct materials. In this case, the entry to record the issue of the materials into production would be as follows:

Work in Process	XXX	
Raw Materials		XXX

Labour Cost

As work is performed each day in various departments of Rand Company, employees fill out time sheets, which are then forwarded to the accounting department. In the accounting department, information from the time sheets, along with employee wage rates, is used to compute labour cost. Costs pertaining to direct labour are transferred to the work-in-process account, whereas the indirect labour costs are treated as overhead costs. This costing and classification for April resulted in the following summary entry:

(3)		
Work in Process	60,000	
Manufacturing Overhead	15,000	
Salaries and Wages Payable		75,000

At the same time that direct labour costs are added to work in process, they are also added to the individual job cost sheets, as shown in Exhibit 3–7. During April, $40,000 of direct labour cost was charged to job A and the remaining $20,000 was charged to job B.

The labour costs charged to manufacturing overhead represent the indirect labour costs of the period, such as supervision, janitorial work, and maintenance.

EXHIBIT 3–7 Labour Cost Flows

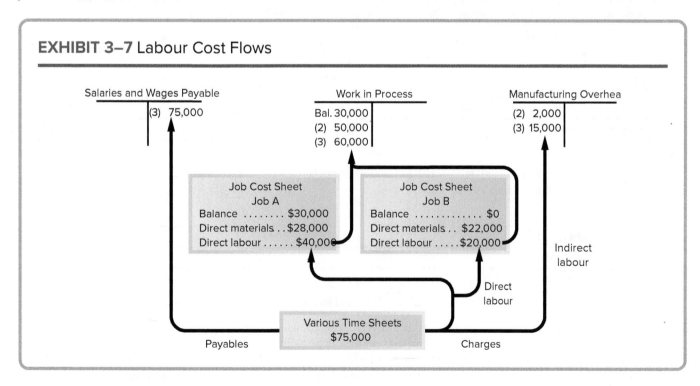

Manufacturing Overhead Costs

LO5   • Know   • Apply

CC10: Describe how incurred overhead costs are recorded in the accounting system, and apply overhead to work in process using a predetermined overhead rate.

Recall that all costs of operating the factory, other than direct materials and direct labour, are classified as manufacturing overhead costs. We will follow a simplified approach to recording the incurrence of these costs by entering them directly into the manufacturing overhead account as they are incurred. To illustrate, assume that Rand Company *incurred* the following general factory costs during April:

Utilities (heat, water, and power)	$21,000
Rent on factory equipment	16,000
Miscellaneous factory costs	3,000
Total	$40,000

The following entry records the incurrence of these costs:

(4)

Manufacturing Overhead	40,000	
Accounts Payable		40,000

In addition, let us assume that during April, Rand Company recognized $13,000 in accrued property taxes and that $7,000 in prepaid insurance expired on factory buildings and equipment. The following entry records these items:

(5)

Manufacturing Overhead	20,000	
Property Taxes Payable		13,000
Prepaid Insurance		7,000

Finally, let us assume that the company recognized $18,000 in depreciation on factory equipment during April. The following entry records the accrual of this depreciation:

(6)

Manufacturing Overhead	18,000	
Accumulated Depreciation		18,000

Recall that we have already recorded indirect materials ($2,000) and indirect labour ($15,000) as manufacturing overhead costs.

In short, *all* manufacturing overhead costs are recorded directly into the manufacturing overhead account as they are incurred, day by day, throughout a period. It is important to understand that, in actuality, manufacturing overhead is a control account for many—perhaps thousands of—subsidiary accounts, such as indirect materials, indirect labour, factory utilities, and so on. In the preceding example and also in the end-of-chapter material for this chapter, we omit the entries to the subsidiary accounts for the sake of brevity.

THE APPLICATION OF MANUFACTURING OVERHEAD

Since actual manufacturing costs are charged to the manufacturing overhead control account, rather than to work in process, how are manufacturing overhead costs assigned to work in process? They are assigned by using a predetermined overhead rate. Recall from our previous discussion that a predetermined overhead rate is established at the beginning of each year. The rate is calculated by dividing the estimated total manufacturing overhead cost for the year by the estimated total units in the allocation base (measured in machine-hours, direct labour-hours, or some other base). The predetermined overhead rate is then used to apply overhead costs to jobs. For example, if direct labour-hours are the allocation base, overhead cost is applied to each job by multiplying the number of direct labour-hours charged to the job by the predetermined overhead rate.

To illustrate, assume that Rand Company uses a predetermined overhead rate of $6 per machine-hour. Also, assume that during April 15,000 machine-hours were consumed (10,000 by job A and 5,000 by job B). Thus, $90,000 in overhead cost (15,000 machine-hours × $6 per machine-hour = $90,000) would be applied to work in process. The following entry records the application of manufacturing overhead to work in process:

(7)

Work in Process	90,000	
Manufacturing Overhead		90,000

The flow of costs through the manufacturing overhead account is shown in Exhibit 3–8.

EXHIBIT 3–8 The Flow of Costs in Overhead Application

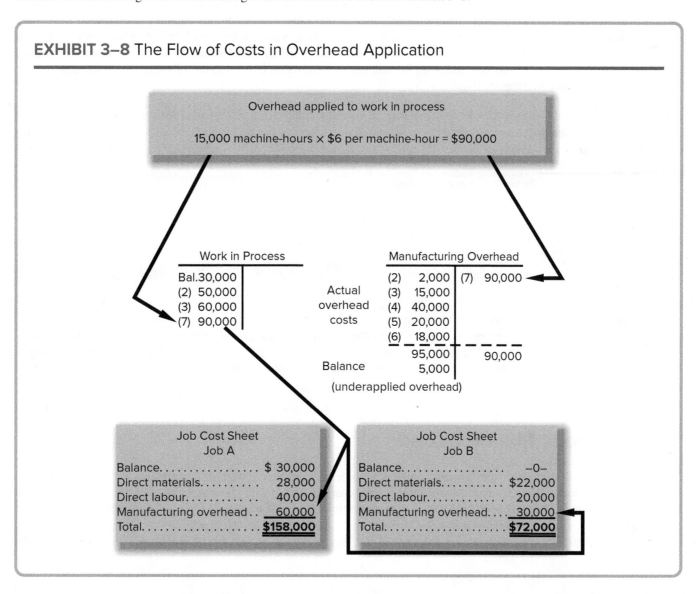

The "actual overhead costs" in the manufacturing overhead account in Exhibit 3–8 are the costs that were added to the account in entries (2)–(6). Observe that the incurrence of these actual overhead costs (entries (2)–(6)) and the application of overhead to work in process (entry (7)) represent two separate and entirely distinct processes.

THE CONCEPT OF A CLEARING ACCOUNT

LO5   ● **Know**

CC11: Explain the concept of a clearing account.

The manufacturing overhead account operates as a clearing account. As we have noted, actual factory overhead costs are debited to the accounts as they are incurred day by day throughout the year. At certain intervals during the year, usually when a job is completed, overhead cost is applied to the work-in-process account by means of the predetermined overhead rate. This sequence of events is illustrated as follows:

Manufacturing Overhead (a clearing account)

Actual overhead costs are charged to the account as these costs are incurred day by day throughout the period.	Overhead is applied to work in process using the predetermined overhead rate.

As we emphasized previously, the predetermined overhead rate is based entirely on estimates of what overhead costs are *expected* to be, and it is established before the year begins. As a result, the overhead cost applied during a year will almost certainly turn out to be different from the overhead cost that is actually incurred. For example, note from Exhibit 3–8 that Rand Company's actual overhead costs for the period are $5,000 greater than the overhead cost that has been applied to work in process. The resulting $5,000 debit balance in the manufacturing overhead account is called *underapplied overhead* because the applied amount ($90,000) is less than the actual amount ($95,000). We will reserve discussion of what to do with this $5,000 balance until the next section, "Under- and Overapplied Overheads."

For the moment, we can conclude from Exhibit 3–8 that the cost of a completed job consists of the actual materials cost of the job, the actual labour cost of the job, and the overhead cost *applied* to the job. Pay particular attention to the following subtle but important point: *Actual overhead costs are not charged to jobs; actual overhead costs do not appear on the job cost sheet, nor do they appear in the work-in-process account. Only the applied overhead cost, based on the predetermined overhead rate, appears on the job cost sheet and in the work-in-process account.*

HELPFUL HINT

Actual manufacturing overhead costs are recorded as debits to the manufacturing overhead account. The amount of manufacturing overhead applied to all jobs using the predetermined overhead rate is recorded on the credit side of the manufacturing overhead account. The manufacturing overhead cost added to all job cost sheets during a period will equal the amount of the credits recorded in the manufacturing overhead account during that period.

Cost of Goods Manufactured

When a job has been completed, the finished output is transferred from the production departments to the finished goods warehouse. By this time, the accounting department will have charged the job with direct materials and direct labour cost, and manufacturing overhead will have been applied using the predetermined rate. A transfer of these costs must be made within the costing system that *parallels* the physical transfer of the goods to the finished goods warehouse. The costs of the completed job are transferred out of the work-in-process account and into the finished goods account. The sum of all amounts transferred between these two accounts represents the cost of goods manufactured (COGM) for the period. (This point was illustrated earlier in Exhibit 2–8 in Chapter 2.)

In the case of Rand Company, let us assume that job A was completed during April. The following entry transfers the cost of job A from work in process to finished goods:

(8)		
Finished Goods	158,000	
Work in Process		158,000

The $158,000 represents the completed cost of job A, as shown on the job cost sheet in Exhibit 3–8. Since job A was the only job completed during April, the $158,000 also represents the cost of goods manufactured for the month.

Job B was not completed by month-end, and so its cost will remain in the work-in-process account, carrying over to the next month. If a balance sheet is prepared at the end of April, the cost accumulated thus far on job B will appear as *work-in-process inventory* in the assets section.

Cost of Goods Sold

As units in finished goods are shipped to fill customers' orders, the unit cost appearing on the job cost sheets is used as a basis for transferring the cost of the items sold from the finished goods account into the cost of goods sold (COGS) account. If a complete job is shipped, as in the case where a job has been done to a customer's specifications, then it is a simple matter to transfer the entire cost appearing on the job cost sheet into the cost of goods sold account. In most cases, however, only a portion of the units involved in a particular job will be immediately sold. In these situations, the unit cost must be used to determine how much product cost should be removed from finished goods and charged to cost of goods sold.

For Rand Company, we will assume that 750 of the 1,000 gold medallions in job A were shipped to customers by the end of the month for total sales revenue of $225,000. Since 1,000 units were produced and the total cost of the job from the job cost sheet was $158,000, the unit product cost was $158. The following journal entries would record the sale (all sales are on account):

(9)		
Accounts Receivable	225,000	
Sales		225,000
(10)		
Cost of Goods Sold	118,500	
Finished Goods		118,500
($158 per unit × 750 units = $118,500)		

With entry (10), the flow of costs through our job-order costing system is completed.

Summary of Manufacturing Cost Flows

LO6 • **Apply**

CC12: Prepare T-accounts to show the flow of costs in a job-order costing system.

CC13: Prepare schedules of cost of goods manufactured (COGM) and cost of goods sold (COGS).

To pull the entire example together, journal entries (1)–(10) are summarized in Exhibit 3–9. The flow of costs through the accounts is presented in T-account form in Exhibit 3–10. The corresponding model summarizing the cost flows in a job-order system appears in Exhibit 3–11. Study Exhibits 3–10 and 3–11 together. (Note that for the sake of completeness, Exhibit 3–10 shows some of the entries to the accounts that will have been made prior to starting the manufacturing process. The end-of-chapter material will not require that such entries be presented and explained.) A good grasp of the logic of the cost flows will be very helpful in understanding how an income statement for a manufacturing concern is constructed. We have illustrated this process in Exhibit 3–12. This exhibit presents the supporting cost schedules as a series of "waterfalls" that cascade down into the income statement. It is easy to see how the various schedules articulate with each other and where the data in the schedules come from. To illustrate, compare the T-accounts in Exhibit 3–10 with the schedules in Exhibit 3–12. Note that the quantity of direct materials used is calculated from the raw materials T-account. Direct materials used then flow into the work-in-process account. The entries in the work-in-process account provide the basis for determining cost of goods manufactured. Then the cost of goods manufactured flows into the finished goods account. The inventory balances in finished goods along with cost of goods manufactured determine cost of goods sold, which finally flows into the income statement.

EXHIBIT 3–9 Summary of Rand Company Journal Entries

(1)		
Raw Materials	60,000	
Accounts Payable		60,000
(2)		
Work in Process	50,000	
Manufacturing Overhead	2,000	
Raw Materials		52,000
(3)		
Work in Process	60,000	
Manufacturing Overhead	15,000	
Salaries and Wages Payable		75,000
(4)		
Manufacturing Overhead	40,000	
Accounts Payable		40,000
(5)		
Manufacturing Overhead	20,000	
Property Taxes Payable		13,000
Prepaid Insurance		7,000
(6)		
Manufacturing Overhead	18,000	
Accumulated Depreciation		18,000
(7)		
Work in Process	90,000	
Manufacturing Overhead		90,000
(8)		
Finished Goods	158,000	
Work in Process		158,000
(9)		
Accounts Receivable	225,000	
Sales		225,000
(10)		
Cost of Goods Sold	118,500	
Finished Goods		118,500

EXHIBIT 3–10 Flow of Costs Through T-Accounts: Rand Company

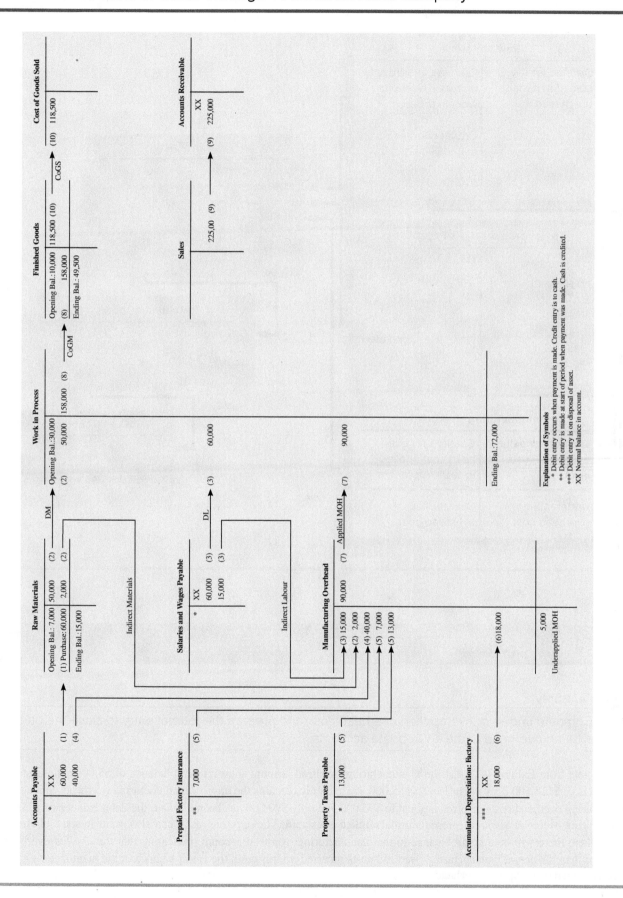

EXHIBIT 3–11 A General Model of Cost Flows

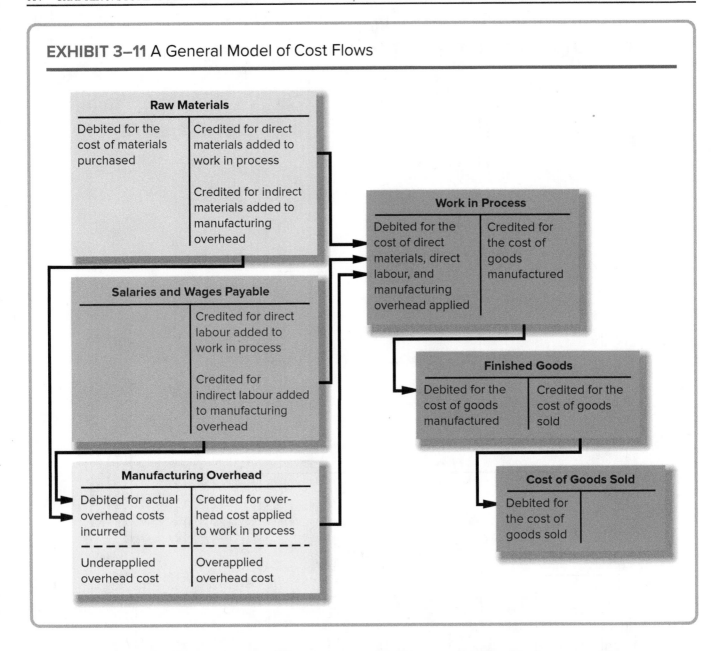

Under- and Overapplied Overheads

CC14: Compute under- or overapplied overhead cost, and prepare the journal entry to close the balance in manufacturing overhead to the appropriate accounts.

You will note from Exhibit 3–10 that the manufacturing overhead account shows a debit balance of $5,000. The cost of goods sold amount of $118,500 does not reflect this $5,000, since it only contains the *applied* manufacturing overhead. Since the *actual* manufacturing overhead costs incurred amount to $95,000 and only $90,000 has been *applied,* the debit balance of $5,000 in the manufacturing overhead account represents **underapplied overhead**. The opposite result can also occur in some circumstances. This is where there will be a credit balance in the manufacturing overhead account, indicating that the *applied* overhead costs are greater than the *actual* manufacturing overhead costs incurred. In this case, the credit balance in the manufacturing overhead account is called **overapplied overhead**.

EXHIBIT 3–12 Flow of Supporting Cost Schedules to the Income Statement

Direct Materials

Opening balance:	$ 7,000
Add: Purchases	60,000
RM available for use	$67,000
Deduct: Ending balance:	15,000
RM used	$52,000
Deduct: Indirect RM	2,000
DM used	$50,000 >>>>>>

COGM

DM	$ 50,000
DL	60,000
Applied MOH	90,000
Total mfg. costs	$200,000
Add: Beginning	
WIP	30,000
Mfg. cost to account	$230,000
Deduct: Ending WIP	72,000
COGM	$158,000 >>>>>>

COGS

Opening bal. FG	$ 10,000
COGM	158,000
Goods avail. for sale	$168,000
Deduct: End. bal.	
FG	49,500
COGS	$118,500 >>>>>

Income Statement

Sales	$225,000
COGS	118,500
GM	$106,500
Deduct: Nonmfg costs	
Net Income	

Note: The schedules shown in this exhibit are not in good form. They are presented in the format shown only to illustrate how the various schedules relate to each other. RM = raw materials; DM = direct materials; DL = direct labour; MOH = manufacturing overhead; WIP = work in process; FG = finished goods; COGM = cost of goods manufactured; COGS = (unadjusted) cost of goods sold; GM = gross margin.

Causes of Under- and Overapplied Overheads

LO7 • Know

CC15: Describe the causes of under- and overapplied overhead.

What causes underapplied or overapplied overhead? Applied overhead is calculated using a predetermined overhead rate and the actual volume consumed of the allocation base. Actual overhead, on the other hand, reflects the actual amounts paid to acquire the individual overhead resources. Moreover, for the purposes of allocation, different overhead items are often combined and a representative allocation base is used to calculate a predetermined overhead rate and to apply overhead costs to individual jobs. Therefore, applied overhead is at best an approximation of the actual overhead incurred.

The difference between the applied and actual amounts can have several causes:

- The estimated and actual prices of the individual overhead items are different
- The estimated and actual amounts of the allocation base are different
- The allocation base used to apply overhead may not be representative of the various factors that potentially drive the different overhead cost items
- The rate computed and used effectively treats overhead as a variable cost, whereas many individual overhead items may be fixed in nature

Disposition of Under- or Overapplied Overhead Balances

Now that we understand why over- or underapplied overhead balances exist, we can ask the question, "What disposition of any under- or overapplied balance remaining in the manufacturing overhead account should managers make at the end of the period?" Two common methods exist for dealing with the over- or underapplied overhead balance. One approach is to prorate the under- or overapplied overhead to cost of goods sold and the two inventory accounts (finished goods and work in process) based on the amounts in these accounts at the end of the year. This would be the preferred approach if the amount of under- or overapplied overhead is considered material. Recall that Rand Company had underapplied overhead of $5,000; this amount is over 5% of the actual manufacturing overhead amount of $95,000 and may be considered as material. The entry to close the underapplied overhead using this method would be as follows:

(11)

Cost of Goods Sold	2,469	
Finished Goods Inventory	1,031	
Work-in-Process Inventory	1,500	
Manufacturing Overhead		5,000

The simpler method is to close out the balance to cost of goods sold. The entry to close this underapplied overhead to cost of goods sold would be as follows:

(12)

Cost of Goods Sold	5,000	
Manufacturing Overhead		5,000

It is important to note that the first method affects both the balance sheet and the income statement, whereas the second (simpler) method affects only the income statement. However, companies that adopt a just-in-time inventory system will have low inventory levels; therefore, the second method can be adopted even if the under- or overapplied overhead amount is significant.

LO7 • Know

CC16: Explain why the under- or overapplied overhead balance must be disposed of at period-end.

Observe that since the manufacturing overhead account has a debit balance, manufacturing overhead must be credited to close out the account. This has the effect of increasing cost of goods sold for April to $123,500:

Unadjusted cost of goods sold (from entry (10))	$ 118,500
Add: Underapplied overhead (entry (11) above)	5,000
Adjusted cost of goods sold	$ 123,500

After this adjustment has been made, Rand Company's schedules of cost of goods manufactured and cost of goods sold for April will appear as shown in Exhibit 3–13 (no adjustment is made to the cost of goods manufactured schedule).

EXHIBIT 3–13 Schedules of Cost of Goods Manufactured and Cost of Goods Sold

Cost of Goods Manufactured

Direct materials:		
Raw materials inventory, beginning	$ 7,000	
Add: Purchases of raw materials	60,000	
Total raw materials available	67,000	
Deduct: Raw materials inventory, ending	15,000	
Raw materials used in production	52,000	
Deduct: Indirect materials included in manufacturing overhead	2,000	$ 50,000
Direct labour		60,000
Manufacturing overhead applied to work in process		90,000
Total manufacturing costs		200,000
Add: Beginning work-in-process inventory		30,000
		230,000
Deduct: Ending work-in-process inventory		72,000
Cost of goods manufactured		$158,000

Cost of Goods Sold

Finished goods inventory, beginning	$ 10,000
Add: Cost of goods manufactured	158,000
Goods available for sale	168,000
Deduct: Finished goods inventory, ending	49,500
Unadjusted cost of goods sold	118,500
Add: Underapplied overhead	5,000
Adjusted cost of goods sold	$123,500

*Note that the underapplied overhead is added to cost of goods sold. If overhead were overapplied, it would be deducted from cost of goods sold.

WORKING IT OUT

Gilbert Company is a job-order manufacturer specializing in manufacturing gear boxes to meet customers' individual requirements. For 2018, it estimated the overhead costs to be $12,560,000—to be allocated using a predetermined rate based on machine-hours. Tanner Gilbert, the production manager, estimated that his company will use 160,000 machine-hours in 2018. During the month of January, Gilbert worked on two jobs, which consumed the following resources:

	Job 2018-A1	Job 2018-A2
Direct materials cost	$ 6,500	$ 22,000
Direct labour cost	$42,000	$165,000
Machine-hours	1,800	7,000
Number of units	20	100

At the end of the year, Gilbert recorded the consumption of 158,700 machine-hours and incurred actual manufacturing overhead amounting to $12,538,250.

Required:

1. Compute the predetermined overhead allocation rate for 2018.
2. Compute the total cost *per unit* for each job.
3. Determine the total manufacturing overhead applied to jobs during the year.
4. Calculate the under- or overapplied overhead for the year and show how you will dispose this amount at the end of the year.

SOLUTION TO WORKING IT OUT

1. Predetermined overhead rate $= \dfrac{\text{Estimated total overhead cost}}{\text{Estimated total activity volume of the allocation base}}$

   $= \dfrac{\$12,560,000}{160,000 \text{ MHs}}$

   $= \$78.50 \text{ per MH}$

2. The total cost of each job includes the cost of direct materials, direct labour, and applied overhead.

   For Job **A1,** total job cost is as follows:

Direct materials:	$ 6,500
Direct labour:	42,000
Applied overhead (1,800 MH × $78.50):	141,300
Total job cost:	$189,800

   Cost per unit $= \dfrac{\$189,800}{20 \text{ units}} = \$9,490$

   For Job **A2,** total job cost is as follows:

Direct materials:	$ 22,000
Direct labour:	165,000
Applied overhead (7,000 MH × $78.50):	549,500
Total job cost:	$ 736,500

   Cost per unit $= \dfrac{\$736,500}{100 \text{ units}} = \$7,365$

3. Manufacturing overhead applied during the year:

158,700 machine-hours × $78.50 = $12,457,950

4.

Actual overhead	$12,538,250
Applied overhead	12,457,950
Underapplied overhead	$ 80,300

Underapplied overhead means that less overhead has been applied compared to actual; therefore, COGS must be debited by this amount. The appropriate journal entry to record the disposition of the underapplied overhead amount is as follows:

Cost of goods sold	80,300	
Manufacturing overhead		80,300

HELPFUL HINT

Students struggle to understand two key points with respect to underapplied or overapplied overhead. First, underapplied or overapplied overhead is *not* computed for each job. It is computed for the company as a whole (if a single [plantwide] overhead rate is used) or for each department (if departmental overhead rates are used). Second, students often fail to grasp the chronology of events in a normal costing system. Predetermined overhead rates are computed at the *beginning* of the period. Overhead is applied to jobs *throughout* the period. Underapplied or overapplied overhead is computed at the *end* of the period.

DECISION POINT

REMAINING BALANCE IN THE OVERHEAD ACCOUNT

The simplest method for disposing of any balance remaining in the overhead account is to close it out to cost of goods sold. If there is a debit balance (i.e., overhead has been underapplied), the entry to dispose of the balance will include a debit to cost of goods sold. This debit will increase the balance in the cost of goods sold account. If there is a credit balance, on the other hand, the entry to dispose of the balance will include a credit to cost of goods sold. That credit will decrease the balance in the cost of goods sold account.

If you were the company's controller, would you want a debit balance, a credit balance, or no balance in the overhead account at the end of the period?

*Note to student: See **Guidance Answers** online.*

Multiple Predetermined Overhead Rates

LO7 • **Know**

CC17: Distinguish between a plantwide overhead rate and a multiple overhead rate.

Our discussion in this chapter has assumed that there is a single predetermined overhead rate for the entire company, usually called a **plantwide overhead rate**. This is, in fact, a common practice—particularly in smaller companies. But in larger companies, *multiple predetermined overhead rates* are often used. In a **multiple predetermined overhead rate** system, each department will usually have a different overhead rate. Such a system, while more complex, is considered to be more accurate, since it can reflect differences in how overhead costs are incurred across departments. For example, overhead might be allocated on the basis of direct labour-hours in departments that are relatively labour intensive and machine-hours in departments that are relatively machine intensive. When multiple predetermined overhead rates are used, overhead is applied in each department according to its own overhead rate as a job proceeds through the department.

CONCEPT CHECK

2. Which of the following statements are true? (You may select more than one answer.)
   a. The manufacturing overhead account is debited when manufacturing overhead is applied to work in process.
   b. Job cost sheets accumulate the actual overhead costs incurred to complete a job.
   c. When products are transferred from work in process to finished goods, it results in a debit to finished goods and a credit to work in process.
   d. Selling expenses are applied to production using a predetermined overhead rate that is computed at the beginning of the period.

3. The predetermined overhead rate is $50 per machine-hour, underapplied overhead is $5,000, and the actual number of machine-hours is 2,000. What is the actual amount of total manufacturing overhead incurred during the period?
   a. $105,000
   b. $95,000
   c. $150,000
   d. $110,000

*Note to student: See **Guidance Answers** online.*

Nonmanufacturing Costs

In addition to manufacturing costs, companies also incur marketing and selling costs. These costs should be treated as period expenses and charged directly to the income statement. *Nonmanufacturing costs should not go into the manufacturing overhead account.* To illustrate the correct treatment of nonmanufacturing costs, assume that Rand Company incurred the following selling and administrative costs during April:

Top-management salaries	$21,000
Other office salaries	9,000
Total salaries	$30,000

The following entry records these salaries:

(13)		
Salaries Expense	30,000	
Salaries and Wages Payable		30,000

Assume that depreciation on office equipment during April was $7,000. The entry would be as follows:

(14)		
Depreciation Expense	7,000	
Accumulated Depreciation		7,000

Pay particular attention to the difference between this entry and entry (6), where we recorded depreciation on factory equipment. In journal entry (6), depreciation on factory equipment was debited to manufacturing overhead and is therefore a product cost. In journal entry (9), depreciation on office equipment was debited to depreciation expense. Depreciation on office equipment is considered a period expense rather than a product cost.

Finally, assume that advertising was $42,000 and that other selling and administrative expenses in April totalled $8,000. The following entry records these items:

(15)		
Advertising Expense	42,000	
Other Selling and Administrative Expense	8,000	
Accounts Payable		50,000

LO8 • **Apply**

CC18: Prepare an income statement from the information accumulated in a job-order costing system.

Since the amounts in entries (13) through (15) all go directly into expense accounts, they will have no effect on the costing of Rand Company's production for April. The same will be true of any other selling and administrative expenses incurred during April, including sales commissions, depreciation on sales equipment, rent on office facilities, insurance on office facilities, and related costs. The income statement showing these costs appears in Exhibit 3–14.

EXHIBIT 3–14 Income Statement Including Nonmanufacturing Costs

RAND COMPANY Income Statement For the Month Ending April 30		
Sales		$225,000
Less: Cost of goods sold ($118,500 + $5,000)		123,500
Gross margin		101,500
Less: Selling and administrative expenses:		
Salaries expense	$ 30,000	

RAND COMPANY
Income Statement
For the Month Ending April 30

Depreciation expense	7,000	
Advertising expense	42,000	
Other expense	8,000	87,000
Net Income		$ 4,500

MANAGERIAL ACCOUNTING IN ACTION

WRAP-UP

Joel Stebbins and Tamara Wilson, friends from university, are catching up at dinner at a Winnipeg restaurant.

Wilson: And so that was what my first assignment was like. Our company has been using a normal costing system for some time, so I knew I would be looking at the allocation of budgeted overhead costs to the jobs. This was going to create a complication when I prepared the income statement because I would have to reconcile the discrepancy between the actual overhead costs and the budgeted overhead costs. Our company practice was to close out the balance remaining in the overhead account to cost of goods sold, and that is what I followed. It was very instructive to tie the accounting entries to the schedules of costs and to the income statement. I sure learned a lot that first week!

Stebbins: You know, I think our experiences show how closely the accounting system, especially the costing system, is related to the operations and the activities of the business. When I finished my first assignment I was really pumped up because I felt I had made significant progress in understanding my company's business.

Wilson: Likewise! Let's toast to that!

Learning Objectives Summary

LO1   UNDERSTAND THE CONTEXT FOR COSTING SYSTEMS.

Companies may use a job-order costing system or a process costing system, depending on whether they are a job shop or a continuous flow operation. Managers may choose to use an absorption costing method in which all costs are recorded, or a variable costing method in which only variable costs are recorded (fixed costs are deemed to be irrelevant). Finally, the company must also decide whether to apply overhead using a normal costing approach or the actual costing approach. Under normal costing, overhead is applied using a predetermined overhead rate; however, under actual costing, actual overhead costs are used.

LO2   COMPUTE THE COSTS OF A SPECIFIC JOB.

Job costs typically include direct materi als, direct labour, and overhead. Direct materials consumed are tracked using a materials requisition form; similarly, labour is tracked using a time sheet. Total job costs are recorded on a job cost sheet; a separate job cost sheet is maintained for each job.

LO3   UNDERSTAND THE IMPORTANCE OF THE CONCEPT OF OVERHEAD COST AND ITS COMPUTATION.

Overhead is an important component of job costs even though these costs cannot be directly traced to individual jobs. Therefore, overhead is applied to individual jobs using a predetermined overhead rate. The use of a predetermined overhead rate computed at the start of the year helps companies to calculate costs on a timely basis.

LO4   DETERMINE COSTS INCURRED IN A JOB-ORDER PRODUCTION SYSTEM OVER A SPECIFIED PERIOD AND DESCRIBE THE FLOW OF COSTS THROUGH THE COST ACCOUNTING SYSTEM.

Costs incurred in a job-order costing system flow through the appropriate accounts (raw materials, labour, overhead, work in process). While the individual T-accounts capture total costs incurred during a certain period, the job cost sheets record the costs pertaining to individual jobs.

LO5   UNDERSTAND THE INCURRENCE AND APPLICATION OF OVERHEAD COSTS.

Overhead costs are incurred throughout the year and debited to the manufacturing overhead account as they are incurred. They are then applied to specific jobs using the predetermined overhead rate; the total applied overhead amount is credited to the manufacturing overhead account.

LO6   PREPARE ACCOUNTING SCHEDULES DOCUMENTING THE COSTS INCURRED.

The cost of goods manufactured schedule captures the costs of all jobs worked on during the specified accounting period (usually a year). It includes the cost of direct materials, direct labour, and applied overhead. The cost of goods sold schedule accounts for the cost of jobs that are completed and for which a sale is recorded. This amount is computed by adjusting the cost of goods manufactured by the amounts of beginning and ending finished goods inventory.

LO7   RECONCILE THE DIFFERENCE BETWEEN ACTUAL AND APPLIED OVERHEAD COSTS.

Finding a difference between actual and applied overhead is quite common due to a variety of reasons. When the amount of applied overhead is lower than the amount of actual overhead, the difference is called underapplied overhead. When the amount of applied overhead is higher than the amount of actual overhead, the difference is called overapplied overhead. In order to ensure that financial statements contain accurate information, the under- or overapplied overhead must be reconciled. This may be done by closing the differential amount to the cost of goods sold account, or by apportioning the amount to three accounts: cost of goods sold, finished goods inventory, and work-in-process inventory.

LO8   PREPARE PROFITABILITY REPORTS FOR MANAGEMENT USING INFORMATION FROM THE COST ACCOUNTING SYSTEM.

Information contained in the cost of goods sold account (after reconciling the under- or overapplied overhead) can be used to prepare an income statement for a given period. Similarly, information contained in the job cost sheets can be used to prepare profitability reports for individual jobs.

Application Competency Summary

APPLICATION COMPETENCY	DELIVERABLE	SOURCE DOCUMENTS AND KEY INFORMATION	STEPS	KNOWLEDGE COMPETENCY
Determine the cost of a job (including computing and applying a predetermined overhead allocation rate). • **LO2–CC4** • **LO3–CC5**	*Key Information* Cost of the job and the cost of each unit produced in the job *Report/ Document* Job cost sheet	*Materials Requisition Forms* Direct materials costs incurred by individual jobs *Employee Time Sheets* Direct labour hours supplied by each employee to individual jobs Employee wage rate *Annual Budget Documents* Budgeted amount of annual manufacturing overhead Budgeted quantity of overhead allocation base *Inventory and Production Records* Number of units produced of each job, and number of units in work-in-process (WIP) inventory Actual consumption of machine-hours and other resources that are used as bases to allocate overhead	1. Record the costs of direct materials from the various materials requisition forms on the job cost sheet and calculate the total material cost. 2. Record the wage costs of each employee from the employee time sheet on the job cost sheet and calculate the total direct labour cost. 3. Calculate the predetermined overhead allocation rate per unit of allocation base (by dividing the budgeted overhead amount by the budgeted quantity of the overhead allocation base). 4. Apply the predetermined rate to the quantity of the overhead allocation base consumed by the job (multiply the actual quantity of the allocation base consumed by the predetermined overhead allocation rate). 5. Add the costs of actual direct materials and labour and the applied overhead to compute the total costs of a job.	Actual costing and normal costing • **LO1–CC1, 3**

APPLICATION COMPETENCY	DELIVERABLE	SOURCE DOCUMENTS AND KEY INFORMATION	STEPS	KNOWLEDGE COMPETENCY
Account for the cost of jobs worked on and completed during an operating cycle (e.g., a year). ● **LO4–CC8** ● **LO5–CC10** ● **LO6–CC12**	*Key Information* Description of manufacturing cost flows occurring during the period and the calculation of the cost of goods manufactured (COGM) *Report/Document* T-account analysis of cost flows Schedule of COGM	*Materials Requisition Forms* Direct materials (DM) requisitioned and used during the period for the jobs Indirect materials used during the period *Employee Time Sheets* Cost of direct labour consumed during the period Indirect labour cost incurred during the period *Various Accounts in the General Ledger* Other manufacturing overhead (MOH) costs incurred during the period *Individual Job Cost Sheets* Quantity of overhead allocation base consumed in the period	1. Post transactions to T-accounts: • Use of DM in jobs • Use of indirect materials • Use of direct labour • Use of indirect labour • Incurrence of actual overhead costs • Application of MOH to WIP • Cost of jobs completed and transferred from WIP to finished goods inventory	Costing of a specific job versus accounting for all manufacturing cost flows occurring during a selected operating period ● **LO4–CC9** ● **LO5–CC10**
Determine the overapplied or underapplied overhead for the period. ● **LO7–CC14**	*Key Information* Amount of over- or underapplied overhead *Report/Document* None	*Manufacturing Overhead Account in the General Ledger* Actual MOH costs incurred—sum of all debit entries *Individual Job Cost Sheets* Total of MOH applied to various jobs—sum of all the credit entries in the MOH account. Applied MOH is the predetermined MOH rate times the quantity of overhead allocation base consumed by jobs in the period.	1. Calculate the balance in the MOH account at the end of the period: a debit balance is the amount of underapplied MOH, and a credit balance is the amount of overapplied MOH.	Actual and normal costing ● **LO1–CC3** Predetermined overhead rate ● **LO3–CC5** Disposition of balance in MOH account ● **LO6–CC12** ● **LO7–CC15, 16**

APPLICATION COMPETENCY	DELIVERABLE	SOURCE DOCUMENTS AND KEY INFORMATION	STEPS	KNOWLEDGE COMPETENCY
Prepare schedules of COGM and COGS. • **LO6–CC13**	*Key Information* The cost of jobs sold *Report/ Document* Schedule of cost of goods sold (COGS)	*Individual Job Cost Sheets* Cost of each unit sold (or job, if entire job is sold)	1. Total the cost of all the jobs sold and the cost of the units sold from jobs (normal costs).	Actual and normal costing • **LO1–CC3** Application of overhead • **LO3–CC5**
Determine the profitability of operations for the period given the nonmanufacturing costs • **LO8–CC18**	*Key Information* Net income for the period *Report/ Document* Income statement	*Sales/Revenue Account in the General Ledger* Revenue from sales in the period *Schedule of COGS* COGS before disposition of over- or underapplied overhead *MOH Account in the General Ledger* Actual and applied overhead amounts, and the amount of over- or underapplied manufacturing overhead for the period *Nonmanufacturing Accounts in the General Ledger* All nonmanufacturing costs incurred in the period	1. Dispose of the over- or underapplied MOH by closing it out to COGS. 2. Make the appropriate entry (debit or credit) to MOH to reduce the MOH balance to zero. 3. Make the opposite entry to COGS and determine the revised balance in the COGS account. 4. Enter this amount for COGS on the income statement. 5. Complete the income statement.	Actual and normal costing • **LO1–CC3** Disposition of under- or overapplied overhead • **LO6–CC12** • **LO7–CC15, 16**

Review Problem: Job-Order Costing

Hogle Company is a manufacturing firm that uses job-order costing. On January 1, the beginning of its fiscal year, the company's inventory balances were as follows:

Raw materials	$20,000
Work in process	15,000
Finished goods	30,000

The company applies overhead cost to jobs on the basis of machine-hours worked. For the current year, the company estimated that it would work 75,000 machine-hours and incur $450,000 in manufacturing overhead cost. The following transactions were recorded for the year:

a. Raw materials were purchased on account, $410,000.

b. Raw materials were requisitioned for use in production, $380,000 ($360,000 direct materials and $20,000 indirect materials).

c. The following costs were incurred for employee services: direct labour, $75,000; indirect labour, $110,000; sales commissions, $90,000; administrative salaries, $200,000.

d. Sales travel costs were incurred, $17,000.

e. Utility costs were incurred in the factory, $43,000.

f. Advertising costs were incurred, $180,000.

g. Depreciation was recorded for the year, $350,000 (80% relates to factory operations, and 20% relates to selling and administrative activities).

h. Insurance expired during the year, $10,000 (70% relates to factory operations, and the remaining 30% relates to selling and administrative activities).

i. Manufacturing overhead was applied to production. Due to greater than expected demand for its products, the company worked 80,000 machine-hours during the year.

j. Goods costing $900,000 to manufacture according to their job cost sheets were completed during the year.

k. Goods were sold on account to customers during the year at a total selling price of $1,500,000. The goods cost $870,000 to manufacture according to their job cost sheets.

Required:

1. Prepare journal entries to record the preceding transactions.

2. Post the entries in part (1) to T-accounts (do not forget to enter the opening balances in the inventory accounts).

3. Is manufacturing overhead underapplied or overapplied for the year? Prepare a journal entry to close any balance in the manufacturing overhead account to cost of goods sold.

4. Prepare an income statement for the year.

SOLUTION TO REVIEW PROBLEM

1.

a.	Raw Materials	410,000	
	Accounts Payable		410,000
b.	Work in Process	360,000	
	Manufacturing Overhead	20,000	
	Raw Materials		380,000

c.	Work in Process	75,000	
	Manufacturing Overhead	110,000	
	Sales Commissions Expense	90,000	
	Administrative Salaries Expense	200,000	
	Salaries and Wages Payable		475,000
d.	Sales Travel Expense	17,000	
	Accounts Payable		17,000
e.	Manufacturing Overhead	43,000	
	Accounts Payable		43,000
f.	Advertising Expense	180,000	
	Accounts Payable		180,000
g.	Manufacturing Overhead	280,000	
	Depreciation Expense	70,000	
	Accumulated Depreciation		350,000
h.	Manufacturing Overhead	7,000	
	Insurance Expense	3,000	
	Prepaid Insurance		10,000
i.	The predetermined overhead rate for the year is computed as follows:		

$$\frac{\text{Estimated manufacturing overhead, \$450,000}}{\text{Estimated machine-hours, 75,000}} = \$6 \text{ per machine-hour}$$

	Work in Process	480,000	
	Manufacturing Overhead		480,000
j.	Finished Goods	900,000	
	Work in Process		900,000
k.	Accounts Receivable	1,500,000	
	Sales		1,500,000
	Cost of Goods Sold	870,000	
	Finished Goods		870,000

2.

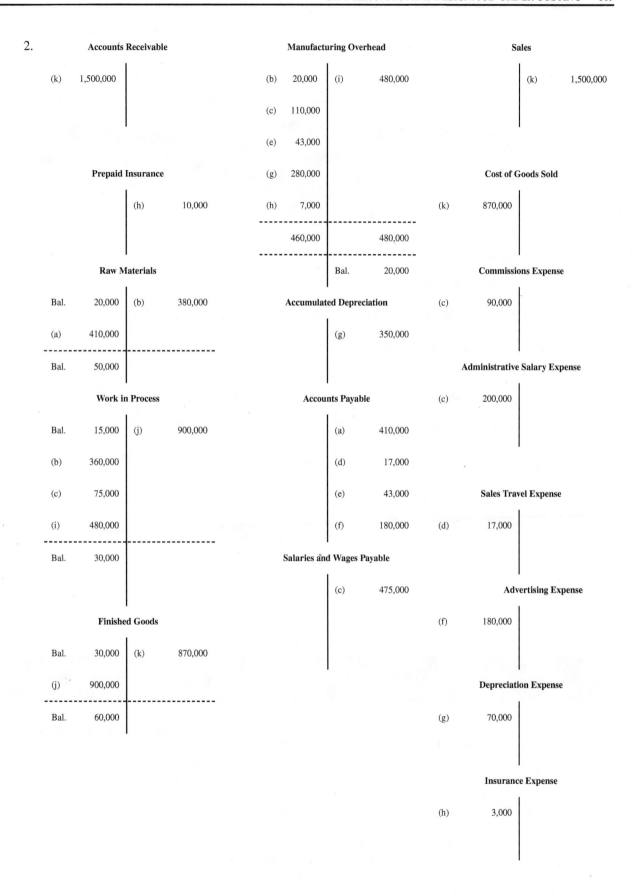

Accounts Receivable

(k)   1,500,000

Prepaid Insurance

(h)   10,000

Raw Materials

Bal.	20,000	(b)	380,000
(a)	410,000		
Bal.	50,000		

Work in Process

Bal.	15,000	(j)	900,000
(b)	360,000		
(c)	75,000		
(i)	480,000		
Bal.	30,000		

Finished Goods

Bal.	30,000	(k)	870,000
(j)	900,000		
Bal.	60,000		

Manufacturing Overhead

(b)	20,000	(i)	480,000
(c)	110,000		
(e)	43,000		
(g)	280,000		
(h)	7,000		
	460,000		480,000
		Bal.	20,000

Accumulated Depreciation

(g)   350,000

Accounts Payable

(a)	410,000
(d)	17,000
(e)	43,000
(f)	180,000

Salaries and Wages Payable

(c)   475,000

Sales

(k)   1,500,000

Cost of Goods Sold

(k)   870,000

Commissions Expense

(c)   90,000

Administrative Salary Expense

(c)   200,000

Sales Travel Expense

(d)   17,000

Advertising Expense

(f)   180,000

Depreciation Expense

(g)   70,000

Insurance Expense

(h)   3,000

3. Manufacturing overhead is overapplied for the year. The entry to close it out to cost of goods sold is as follows:

Manufacturing Overhead	20,000	
Cost of Goods Sold		20,000

4.

HOGLE COMPANY
Income Statement
For the Year Ended December 31

Sales		$1,500,000
Less: Cost of goods sold ($870,000 − $20,000)		850,000
Gross margin		650,000
Less: Selling and administrative expenses:		
Commissions expense	$ 90,000	
Administrative salaries expense	200,000	
Sales travel expense	17,000	
Advertising expense	180,000	
Depreciation expense	70,000	
Insurance expense	3,000	560,000
Net income		$ 90,000

Questions

3–1 Why are actual overhead costs not traced to jobs just as direct materials and direct labour costs are traced to jobs?

3–2 When would job-order costing be used in preference to process costing?

3–3 What is the purpose of the job cost sheet in a job-order costing system?

3–4 What is a predetermined overhead rate, and how is it computed?

3–5 Explain how a sales order, a production order, a materials requisition form, and a labour time sheet are involved in producing and costing products.

3–6 Explain why some production costs must be assigned to products through an allocation process. Name several such costs. Would such costs be classified as *direct* or as *indirect* costs?

3–7 Why do firms use predetermined overhead rates, rather than actual manufacturing overhead costs, in applying overhead to jobs?

3–8 What factors should be considered in selecting a base to be used in computing the predetermined overhead rate?

3–9   If a company fully allocates all of its overhead costs to jobs, does this guarantee that a profit will be earned for the period?

3–10   What account is credited when overhead cost is applied to work in process? Would you expect the amount applied for a period to equal the actual overhead costs of the period? Why, or why not?

3–11   What is underapplied overhead? Overapplied overhead? What disposition is made of these amounts at the end of the period?

3–12   Give two reasons why overhead might be underapplied in a given year.

3–13   What adjustment is made for underapplied overhead on the schedule of cost of goods sold? What adjustment is made for overapplied overhead?

3–14   Sigma Company applies overhead cost to jobs on the basis of direct labour cost. Job A, which was started and completed during the current period, shows charges of $5,000 for direct materials, $8,000 for direct labour, and $6,000 for overhead on its job cost sheet. Job B, which is still in process at year-end, shows charges of $2,500 for direct materials and $4,000 for direct labour. Should any overhead cost be added to job B at year-end? Explain.

3–15   A company assigns overhead cost to completed jobs on the basis of 125% of direct labour cost. The job cost sheet for job 313 shows that $10,000 in direct materials have been used on the job and that $12,000 in direct labour cost has been incurred. If 1,000 units were produced in job 313, what is the cost per unit?

3–16   What is a plantwide overhead rate? Why are multiple overhead rates, rather than a plantwide rate, used in some companies?

3–17   What happens to overhead rates based on direct labour when automated equipment replaces direct labour?

The Foundational 15   connect

[LO2 – CC4; LO3 – CC5; LO4 – CC8; LO5 – CC10; LO6 – CC13; LO7 – CC14; LO8 – CC18]

Sweeten Company had no jobs in progress at the beginning of March and no beginning inventories. It started only two jobs during March—job P and job Q. Job P was completed and sold by the end of the March and job Q was incomplete at the end of the March. The company uses a plantwide predetermined overhead rate based on direct labour-hours. The following additional information is available for the company as a whole and for jobs P and Q (all data and questions relate to the month of March):

Estimated total fixed manufacturing overhead	$10,000
Estimated variable manufacturing overhead per direct labour-hour	$1.00
Estimated total direct labour-hours to be worked	2,000
Total actual manufacturing overhead costs incurred	$12,500

	Job P	Job Q
Direct materials	$13,000	$8,000
Direct labour cost	$21,000	$7,500
Actual direct labour-hours worked	1,400	500

Required:

3–1   What is the company's predetermined overhead rate?

3–2   How much manufacturing overhead was applied to job P and job Q?

3–3   What is the direct labour hourly wage rate?

3–4   If job P included 20 units, what is its unit product cost? What is the total amount of manufacturing cost assigned to job Q as of the end of March (including applied overhead)?

3–5   Assume the ending raw materials inventory is $1,000 and the company does not use any indirect materials. Prepare the journal entries to record raw materials purchases and the issuance of direct materials for use in production.

3–6   Assume that the company does not use any indirect labour. Prepare the journal entry to record the direct labour costs added to production.

3–7   Prepare the journal entry to apply manufacturing overhead to production.

3–8   Assume the ending raw materials inventory is $1,000 and the company does not use any indirect materials. Prepare a schedule of cost of goods manufactured.

3–9   Prepare the journal entry to transfer costs from work in process to finished goods.

3–10   Prepare a completed work in process T-account including the beginning and ending balances and all debits and credits posted to the account.

3–11   Prepare a schedule of cost of goods sold. (Stop after computing the unadjusted cost of goods sold.)

3–12   Prepare the journal entry to transfer costs from finished goods to cost of goods sold.

3–13   What is the amount of underapplied or overapplied overhead?

3–14   Prepare the journal entry to close the amount of underapplied or overapplied overhead to cost of goods sold.

3–15   Assume that job P includes 20 units that each sell for $3,000 and that the company's selling and administrative expenses in March were $14,000. Prepare an absorption costing income statement for March.

Brief Exercises

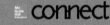

BRIEF EXERCISE 3–1
Assigning Process versus Job-Order Costing [LO1 – CC1]

Which method of determining product costs—job-order costing or process costing—would be more appropriate in each of the following situations?

1. A Husky oil refinery.
2. A shop that customizes vans.
3. An Elmer's glue factory.
4. A facility that makes Minute Maid frozen orange juice.
5. A Scott paper mill.
6. A custom home builder.
7. A textbook publisher, such as McGraw-Hill.
8. A manufacturer of specialty chemicals.
9. A law office.
10. A Firestone tire manufacturing plant.
11. An advertising agency.
12. An auto repair shop.

Required:

Identify the appropriate method of determining product costs for each situation.

BRIEF EXERCISE 3–2
Using Job-Order Costing Documents [LO2 – CC4]

Cycle Gear Corporation has incurred the following costs on job W456, an order for 20 special sprockets to be delivered at the end of next month:

Direct materials:

- On April 10, requisition number 15673 was issued for 40 titanium blanks to be used in the special order. The blanks cost $15 each.
- On April 11, requisition number 15678 was issued for 420 hardened nibs also to be used in the special order. The nibs cost $1.25 each.

Direct labour:

- On April 12, Jamie Unser worked from 11:00 a.m. until 2:45 p.m. on job W456. He is paid $12.60 per hour.
- On April 18, Melissa Chan worked from 8:15 a.m. until 11:30 a.m. on job W456. She is paid $13.20 per hour.

Required:

1. On what documents would these costs be recorded?
2. How much cost should have been recorded on each of the documents for job W456?

BRIEF EXERCISE 3–3
Computing the Predetermined Overhead Rate [LO3 – CC5]

Harris Fabrics computes its predetermined overhead rate annually on the basis of direct labour-hours. At the beginning of the year, it estimated that its total manufacturing overhead would be $540,000 and the total direct labour would be 30,000 hours. Its actual total manufacturing overhead for the year was $547,900, and its actual total direct labour was 31,000 hours.

Required:

Compute the company's predetermined overhead rate for the year.

BRIEF EXERCISE 3–4
Preparing Journal Entries [LO4 – CC8]

Larned Corporation recorded the following transactions for the past month:

a. $180,000 in raw materials were purchased on account.
b. $171,000 in raw materials were requisitioned for use in production. Of this amount, $152,000 was for direct materials, and the remainder was for indirect materials.
c. Total labour costs of $221,000 were incurred. Of this amount, $201,000 was for direct labour, and the remainder was for indirect labour.
d. Manufacturing overhead costs of $375,000 were incurred.

Required:

Record the preceding transactions in journal entries.

BRIEF EXERCISE 3–5
Applying Overhead [LO5 – CC10]

Luthan Company uses a predetermined overhead rate of $13.40 per direct labour-hour. This predetermined rate was based on 19,000 estimated direct labour-hours and $254,600 of estimated total manufacturing overhead.

The company used 19,800 labour-hours during the period and incurred actual total manufacturing overhead costs of $249,000.

Required:

Determine the amount of manufacturing overhead that would have been applied to units of product during the period.

BRIEF EXERCISE 3–6
Preparing T-Accounts [LO6 – CC12; LO7 – CC14]

Jurvin Enterprises recorded the following transactions for the past month. The company had no beginning inventories.

  a. $114,000 in raw materials were purchased for cash.
  b. $99,000 in raw materials were requisitioned for use in production. Of this amount, $88,000 was for direct materials, and the remainder was for indirect materials.
  c. Total labour wages of $146,000 were incurred and paid. Of this amount, $132,000 was for direct labour, and the remainder was for indirect labour.
  d. Manufacturing overhead costs of $103,000 were incurred and paid.
  e. Manufacturing overhead costs of $112,000 were applied to jobs using the company's predetermined overhead rate.
  f. All of the jobs in progress at the end of the month were completed and shipped to customers.
  g. The underapplied or overapplied overhead for the period was closed out to cost of goods sold.

Required:

  1. Post the preceding transactions to T-accounts.
  2. Determine the cost of goods sold for the period.

BRIEF EXERCISE 3–7
Determining Under- and Overapplied Overhead [LO7 – CC14]

Osborn Manufacturing uses a predetermined overhead rate of $28.20 per direct labour-hour. This predetermined rate was based on 12,000 estimated direct labour-hours and $338,400 of estimated total manufacturing overhead.

The company incurred actual total manufacturing overhead costs of $315,000 and 11,500 total direct labour-hours during the period.

Required:

  1. Determine the amount of underapplied or overapplied manufacturing overhead for the period.
  2. Assuming that the entire amount of the underapplied or overapplied overhead is closed out to cost of goods sold, what would be the effect of the underapplied or overapplied overhead on the company's gross margin for the period?

Exercises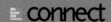

EXERCISE 3–1
Preparing a Job Cost Sheet [LO2 – CC4]

Biotechnologies Unlimited, Inc. (BUI), located in Sydney, Nova Scotia, is a small but growing biotech quality analysis organization that tests pesticides before they are used by farmers. The testing procedures are specific to the individual pesticides used because reagents used for testing react differently based on their composition and the quantity used. How they are introduced into the pesticides for testing is also important.

During the month of December 2016, it completed one job (reference number: KS 2016-337); records pertaining to this job are as follows:

Date	Document	Amount
2/12/16	M-3316	$ 890
4/12/16	L-4423	230
11/12/16	L-4437	530
13/12/16	M-3399	1,750
20/12/16	M-3407	200
22/12/16	L-4509	700

The documents with the references M and L pertain to direct materials and direct labour, respectively. BUI currently allocates overhead using direct labour cost as the allocation base. For the year 2016, it estimated $590,000 as the overhead amount and $472,000 for direct labour costs.

Required:

1. Compute the overhead allocation rate for 2016.
2. Compute the total costs of the job (show direct materials, direct labour, and overhead as separate line items).
3. Prepare a job cost sheet for job KS 2016-337 (use Exhibit 3–4 as a guide).

EXERCISE 3–2
Applying Overhead in a Service Firm [LO3 – CC5]

Leeds Architectural Consultants began operations on January 2. The following activity was recorded in the company's work-in-process account for the first month of operations:

Work in Process

Costs of subcontracted work	520,000	To completed projects	890,000
Direct staff costs	165,000		
Studio overhead	234,300		

Leeds Architectural Consultants is a service firm; thus, the names of its accounts differ from those used in manufacturing firms. Costs of subcontracted work are basically the same as direct materials; direct staff costs are the same as direct labour, studio overhead is the same as manufacturing overhead, and completed projects are the same as finished goods. Apart from the difference in terms, the accounting methods used by the company are identical to the methods used by manufacturing companies.

Leeds uses a job-order costing system, applying studio overhead to work in process on the basis of direct staff costs. At the end of January, only one job was still in process. This job (Lexington Gardens Project) had been charged with $4,000 in direct staff costs.

Required:

1. Compute the predetermined overhead rate that was in use during January.
2. Complete the following job cost sheet for the partially completed Lexington Gardens Project:

LEXINGTON GARDENS PROJECT Job Cost Sheet As of January 31	
Costs of subcontracted work	$?
Direct staff costs	?
Studio overhead	?
Total cost to January 31	$?

EXERCISE 3–3
Using Varying Predetermined Overhead Rates [LO3 – CC5]

Kingsport Containers, Ltd. of the Bahamas experiences wide variation in demand for the 200-litre steel drums it fabricates. The leakproof, rustproof steel drums have a variety of uses, from storing liquids and bulk materials to serving as makeshift musical instruments. The drums are made to order and are painted according to the customer's specifications—often in bright patterns and designs. The company is well known for the artwork that appears on its drums. Unit costs are computed on a quarterly basis by dividing each quarter's manufacturing costs (materials, labour, and overhead) by the quarter's production in units. The company's estimated costs, by quarter, for the coming year are as follows:

	Quarter			
	First	Second	Third	Fourth
Direct materials	$260,000	$130,000	$ 65,000	$195,000
Direct labour	200,000	100,000	50,000	150,000
Manufacturing overhead	320,000	240,000	190,000	290,000
Total manufacturing costs	$780,000	470,000	$305,000	$635,000
Number of units to be produced	80,000	40,000	20,000	60,000
Estimated cost per unit	$ 9.75	$ 11.75	$ 15.25	$ 10.58

Management finds the variation in unit costs to be confusing and difficult to work with. It has been suggested that the problem lies with manufacturing overhead, since it is the largest element of cost. Accordingly, you have been asked to find a more appropriate way of assigning manufacturing overhead cost to units of product. After some analysis, you have determined that the company's overhead costs are mostly fixed and therefore show little sensitivity to changes in the level of production.

Required:

1. The company uses a job-order costing system. How would you recommend that the manufacturing overhead cost be assigned to production? Be specific, and show computations.
2. Recompute the company's unit costs in accordance with your recommendations in part (1).

EXERCISE 3–4
Preparing Journal Entries and T-Accounts [LO3 – CC5; LO4 – CC8; LO5 – CC10; LO6 – CC12]

The Polaris Company uses a job-order costing system. The following data relate to October, the first month of the company's fiscal year:

a. Raw materials were purchased on account, $300,000.
b. Raw materials were issued to production, $290,000 ($228,000 direct materials and $62,000 indirect materials).
c. Direct labour cost was incurred, $110,000; indirect labour cost was incurred, $90,000.
d. Depreciation was recorded on factory equipment, $70,000.
e. Other manufacturing overhead costs were incurred during October, $140,000 (credit accounts payable).
f. The company applies manufacturing overhead cost to production on the basis of $12.60 per machine-hour. There were 30,000 machine-hours recorded for October.
g. Production orders costing $720,000 according to their job cost sheets were completed during October and transferred to finished goods.
h. Production orders that had cost $680,000 to complete according to their job cost sheets were shipped to customers during the month. These goods were sold at 25% above cost. The goods were sold on account.

Required:

1. Prepare journal entries to record the preceding information.
2. Prepare T-accounts for manufacturing overhead and work in process. Post the relevant information above to each account. Compute the ending balance in each account, assuming that work in process has a beginning balance of $42,000.

EXERCISE 3–5
Preparing Journal Entries; Applying Overhead [LO4 – CC8; LO7 – CC14]

The following information is taken from the accounts of Latta Company. The entries in the T-accounts are summaries of the transactions that affected those accounts during the year.

Manufacturing Overhead

(a)	460,000	(b)	390,000
Bal.	70,000		

Work in Process

Bal.	5,000	(c)	710,000
	270,000		
	85,000		
(b)	390,000		
Bal.	40,000		

Finished Goods

Bal	50,000	(d)	640,000
(c)	710,000		
Bal.	120,000		

Cost of Goods Sold

(d)	640,000	

The overhead that was applied to work in process during the year is distributed among the ending balances in the accounts as follows:

Work in process, ending	$ 19,500
Finished goods, ending	58,500
Cost of goods sold	312,000
Overhead applied	$390,000

For example, of the $40,000 ending balance in work in process, $19,500 was overhead that had been applied during the year.

Required:

1. Identify reasons for entries (a) through (d).
2. Assume that the company closes any balance in the manufacturing overhead account directly to cost of goods sold. Prepare the necessary journal entry.

EXERCISE 3–6
Applying Overhead; Cost of Goods Manufactured [LO6 – CC13; LO7 – CC14]

The following cost data relate to the manufacturing activities of Chang Company during the past year:

Manufacturing overhead costs incurred:	
Indirect materials	$ 34,000
Indirect labour	19,000
Property taxes, factory	19,500
Utilities, factory	102,000
Depreciation, factory	290,000
Insurance, factory	15,000
Total actual costs incurred	$650,500
Other costs incurred:	
Purchases of raw materials (both direct and indirect)	$500,000
Direct labour cost	85,000
Inventories:	
Raw materials, beginning	$ 30,000
Raw materials, ending	40,000
Work in process, beginning	50,000
Work in process, ending	80,000

The company uses a predetermined overhead rate to apply overhead cost to production. The rate for the year was $33 per machine-hour. A total of 20,000 machine-hours were recorded for the year.

Required:

1. Compute the amount of under- or overapplied overhead cost for the year.
2. Prepare a schedule of cost of goods manufactured for the year.

EXERCISE 3–7
Applying Overhead With Differing Bases [LO3 – CC5; LO7 – CC14]

Estimated cost and operating data for three companies for the upcoming year follow:

	Company		
	X	Y	Z
Direct labour-hours	80,000	45,000	60,000
Machine-hours	30,000	125,000	21,000
Direct materials cost	$400,000	$290,000	$300,000
Manufacturing overhead cost	$536,000	$520,000	$480,000

Predetermined overhead rates are computed using the following bases in the three companies:

Company	Overhead Rate Based On
X	Direct labour-hours
Y	Machine-hours
Z	Direct materials cost

Required:

1. Compute the predetermined overhead rate to be used in each company during the upcoming year.
2. Assume that Company X works on three jobs during the upcoming year. Direct labour-hours recorded by job are as follows: job 418, 18,000 hours; job 419, 26,000 hours; job 420, 38,000 hours. How much overhead cost will the company apply to work in process for the year? If actual overhead costs total $530,000 for the year, will overhead be under- or overapplied? By how much?

EXERCISE 3–8
Using Predetermined Overhead Rate; Overhead; Job Cost; Over- or Underapplied Overhead; Journal Entries [LO2 – CC4, LO3 – CC5; LO7 – CC14]

Answer each question independently.

Required:

1. Mirage Mirror's predetermined overhead rate for manufacturing overhead is $18 per direct labour-hour. The direct labour rate is $24 per hour. If the budgeted direct labour cost was $300,000, what was the budgeted manufacturing overhead?
2. Zion wants to compute the total cost for preparing a corporate tax return for his client. His labour is the only direct cost at $65 per hour. He estimates monthly overhead costs at $7,500 for 150 direct labour-hours. If the tax return requires 13 hours to prepare, what will be the total direct cost, indirect cost, and job cost, respectively?
3. Kyle Corporation had the following account balances at the end of this year:

Direct materials inventory	$1,000	
Work in process	680	
Finished goods	450	
Manufacturing overhead control	122	credit
Cost of goods sold	800	

Assuming that over- or underapplied overhead is written off to cost of goods sold, prepare the appropriate journal entry, and compute the adjusted balance in the cost of goods sold account.

EXERCISE 3–9

Actual, Applied and Overapplied or Underapplied Manufacturing Overhead [LO3 – CC5; LO5 – CC10; LO7 – CC14]

Cool Company applies manufacturing overhead on the basis of machine-hours. On December 31, the company's manufacturing overhead control T-account included the following amounts for the whole year.

Manufacturing Overhead Control	
3,832,546	4,192,000

At the beginning of the year, management estimated overhead to be $4 million and the allocation base to be 250,000 machine-hours.

Required:

1. Compute the predetermined overhead rate for the year. How many machine-hours were actually consumed during the year?
2. What is the amount of actual overhead cost incurred for the year?
3. At the end of the year, did the company overapply or underapply overhead, and by how much?

EXERCISE 3–10

Applying Overhead; Journal Entries; T-Accounts [LO2 – CC4; LO3 – CC5; LO4 – CC8; LO6 – CC12]

Dillon Products manufactures various machined parts to customer specifications. The company uses a job-order costing system and applies overhead cost to jobs on the basis of machine-hours. At the beginning of the year, it was estimated that the company would work 200,000 machine-hours and incur $4,800,000 in manufacturing overhead costs.

The company spent the entire month of January working on a large order for 12,000 custom-made machined parts. The company had no work in process at the beginning of January. Cost data relating to January follow:

a. Raw materials purchased on account, $452,000.
b. Raw materials requisitioned for production, $390,000 (80% direct materials and 20% indirect materials).
c. Labour cost incurred in the factory, $180,000 (one-third direct labour and two-thirds indirect labour).
d. Depreciation recorded on factory equipment, $175,000.
e. Other manufacturing overhead costs incurred, $92,000 (credit accounts payable).
f. Manufacturing overhead cost applied to production on the basis of 15,000 machine-hours actually worked during the month.
g. Completed job moved into finished goods warehouse on January 31 to await delivery to customer. (In computing the dollar amount for this entry, remember that the cost of a completed job consists of direct materials, direct labour, and *applied* overhead.)

Required:

1. Prepare journal entries to record items (a) through (f) above (ignore item (g) for the moment).
2. Prepare T-accounts for manufacturing overhead and work in process. Post the relevant items from your journal entries to these T-accounts.
3. Prepare a journal entry for item (g).
4. Compute the unit cost that will appear on the job cost sheet.

EXERCISE 3–11
Calculating Over- or Underapplied Manufacturing Overhead [LO7 – CC14]

Maurice Company allocates overhead using direct labour-hours. For 2016, the estimated and actual labour-hours were 180,000 and 167,000 respectively, and the predetermined overhead rate used to apply overhead for the year was $24.80 per direct labour-hour. The manufacturing overhead control T-account showed a debit balance of $183,550 at the end of the year, and this balance was disposed of at the end of the year by closing it to cost of goods sold.

Required:

1. Was manufacturing overhead under- or overapplied?
2. Compute the actual overhead amount incurred over the year.
3. How will end-of-period disposal of this amount impact net income?

Problems   connect

PROBLEM 3–1
Applying Overhead; Job Costs [LO2 – CC4; LO3 – CC5]

Case Construction Company, a three-year-old business, provides contracting and construction services to a variety of clients. Given that each construction job is different from the others, Susan Byrd, the company's accountant, decided to use a job-order costing system to allocate costs to the different jobs. She decided to use construction labour-hours as the basis for overhead allocation. In December 2016, she estimated the following amounts for the year 2017:

> **CHECK FIGURE**
> (1) Predetermined overhead allocation rate = $15.02 per DLH

Direct materials	$14,560,000
Construction labour	$9,800,000
Overhead	$7,510,000
Construction labour-hours	500,000

Byrd recorded the following for the second quarter of 2017 for the three jobs that the company started and completed during the quarter.

	School	Residential	Cinema
Direct materials	$824,000	$1,034,600	$1,425,000
Construction labour-hours	66,400	37,200	18,500

Required:

1. Compute the predetermined overhead allocation rate for 2017 and apply overhead to the three jobs.
2. Compute the cost of each job.

PROBLEM 3–2
Computing Departmental Overhead Rates [LO3 – CC5, 7; LO7 – CC17]

White Company has two departments: cutting and finishing. The company uses a job-order costing system and computes a predetermined overhead rate in each department. The cutting department bases its rate on machine-hours, and the finishing department bases its rate on direct labour cost. At the beginning of the year, the company made the following estimates:

CHECK FIGURE

(2) Overhead applied to job 203: $1,227.50

	Department	
	Cutting	Finishing
Direct labour-hours	5,000	21,000
Machine-hours	45,000	3,000
Manufacturing overhead cost	$382,500	$499,500
Direct labour cost	$ 75,000	$270,000

Required:

1. Compute the predetermined overhead rate to be used in each department.
2. Assume that the overhead rates that you computed in part (1) are in effect. The job cost sheet for job 203, which was started and completed during the year, showed the following:

	Department	
	Cutting	Finishing
Direct labour-hours	6	20
Machine-hours	90	4
Materials requisitioned	$500	$380
Direct labour cost	$ 85	$250

Compute the total overhead cost applied to job 203.

3. Would you expect substantially different amounts of overhead cost to be assigned to some jobs if the company used a plantwide overhead rate based on direct labour cost, rather than using departmental rates? Explain your answer. No computations are necessary.

PROBLEM 3–3
Applying Overhead; T-Accounts; Journal Entries [LO3 – CC5; LO4 – CC8; LO5 – CC10; LO6 – CC12; LO7 – CC14, 15]

Harwood Company is a manufacturing firm that operates a job-order costing system. Overhead costs are applied to jobs on the basis of machine-hours. At the beginning of the year, management estimated that the company would incur $192,000 in manufacturing overhead costs and work 80,000 machine-hours.

Required:

1. Compute the company's predetermined overhead rate.
2. Assume that during the year the company works only 75,000 machine-hours and incurs the following costs in the manufacturing overhead and work-in-process accounts:

Manufacturing Overhead

(Maintenance)	19,000	?
(Indirect materials)	6,000	
(Indirect labour)	60,000	
(Utilities)	30,000	
(Insurance)	7,000	
(Depreciation)	54,000	
(Property taxes)	8,000	

Work in Process

(Direct materials)	710,000	
(Direct labour)	90,000	
(Overhead)	?	

Copy the data in the previous T-accounts onto your answer sheet. Compute the amount of overhead cost that would be applied to work in process for the year, and make the entry in your T-accounts.

3. Compute the amount of under- or overapplied overhead for the year, and show the balance in your manufacturing overhead T-account. Prepare a general journal entry to close out the balance in this account to cost of goods sold.
4. Explain why the manufacturing overhead was under- or overapplied for the year.

PROBLEM 3–4

Preparing T-Accounts; Over- and Underallocated Overhead; Income [LO2 – CC4; LO3 – CC5; LO5 – CC10; LO6 – CC12; LO7 – CC14; LO8 – CC18]

Weyakwin Enterprises specializes in offering architectural consulting and design services to large clients. Given the nature of the services it provides, the company does not work on more than six jobs at a time. At the beginning of 2018, it estimated the following amounts:

CHECK FIGURE
(4) Operating income = $858,404

Direct materials (blueprints and other supplies)	$ 486,000
Direct professional labour (consulting)	2,500,000
Direct professional labour (design)	1,800,000
Consulting support	2,875,000
Design support	3,060,000

Support costs are allocated using predetermined overhead rates computed at the beginning of the year and are based on direct professional labour costs. Senior management recently changed its policy of allocating overhead costs. Separate rates are computed for the two types of support costs based on the *corresponding* direct professional labour costs. The company uses a *normal* costing system to track costs.

At the beginning of the third quarter in 2018, job 2018Q2-5 was unfinished. The following amounts were traced to it: direct materials, $22,460; professional labour (consulting), $180,520. During the third quarter, three new jobs were started: 2018Q3-1, 2018Q3-2, and 2018Q3-3. The following amounts were incurred during the quarter:

Direct materials (blueprints and other supplies)	$ 149,580
Direct professional labour (consulting)	930,060
Direct professional labour (design)	776,230
Consulting support	982,110
Design support	1,317,564

At the end of the quarter, job 2018Q3-2 was still unfinished, and the following amounts were traced to it: direct materials, $36,764; professional labour (design), $198,060.

Required:

1. Summarize the quarter's transactions by preparing T-accounts for jobs-in-process control; cost of jobs billed; direct professional labour control; support overhead control; and cash control. (Assume that all payments are made in cash.)
2. Compute the beginning and ending amounts in the jobs-in-process account.
3. Compute the over- or underallocated overhead amount(s) for the quarter. Close this amount to the cost of jobs billed account using the appropriate journal entry.
4. Assume that the revenue earned during the quarter was $4,853,000. Compute the company's operating income for the third quarter.

PROBLEM 3–5
Analyzing Cost Flows Using T-Accounts [LO6 – CC12; LO7 – CC14]

Selected ledger accounts of Moore Company are given below for the past year:

Raw Materials

Bal. 1/1	15,000	Credits	?
Debits	140,000		
Bal. 12/31	35,000		

Work in Process

Bal. 1/1	20,000	Credits	470,000
Direct materials	90,000		
Direct labour	160,000		
Overhead	240,000		
Bal. 12/31	?		

Finished Goods

Bal. 1/1	40,000	Credits	?
Debits	?		
Bal. 12/31	60,000		

Manufacturing Overhead

Debits	250,000	Credits	?

Factory Wages Payable

Debits	185,000	Bal. 1/1	9,000
		Credits	180,000
		Bal. 12/31	4,000

Cost of Goods Sold

Debits	?		

Required:

1. What was the cost of raw materials put into production during the year?
2. How much of the materials in part (1) consisted of indirect materials?
3. How much of the factory labour cost for the year consisted of indirect labour?
4. What was the cost of goods manufactured for the year?
5. What was the cost of goods sold for the year (before considering under- or overapplied overhead)?
6. If overhead is applied to production on the basis of direct labour cost, what rate was in effect during the year?
7. Was manufacturing overhead under- or overapplied? By how much?
8. Compute the ending balance in the work-in-process inventory account. Assume that this balance consists entirely of goods started during the year. If $8,000 of this balance is direct labour cost, how much of it is direct materials cost? Manufacturing overhead cost?

PROBLEM 3–6

Analyzing Overhead; Schedule of Cost of Goods Manufactured [LO3 – CC5; LO6 – CC13; LO7 – CC14]

Gitano Products operates a job-order costing system and applies overhead cost to jobs on the basis of direct materials *used in production* (*not* on the basis of raw materials purchased). In computing a predetermined overhead rate at the beginning of the year, the company's estimates were as follows: manufacturing overhead cost, $800,000; direct materials to be used in production, $500,000. The company's inventory accounts at the beginning and end of the year were as follows:

CHECK FIGURE
(2) COGM: $1,340,000

	A	B	C
1		*Beginning*	*Ending*
2	Raw materials	$ 20,000	$ 80,000
3	Work in process	150,000	70,000
4	Finished goods	260,000	400,000
5			
6	*The following actual costs were incurred during the year:*		
7	Purchase of raw materials (all direct)		$510,000
8	Direct labour cost		90,000
9	Manufacturing overhead costs:		
10	Indirect labour		170,000
11	Property taxes		48,000
12	Depreciation of equipment		260,000
13	Maintenance		95,000
14	Insurance		7,000
15	Rent, building		180,000
16			

Required:

1.   a.   Compute the predetermined overhead rate for the year.
     b.   Compute the amount of under- or overapplied overhead for the year.
2.   Prepare a schedule of cost of goods manufactured for the year.
3.   Compute the cost of goods sold for the year. (Do not include any under- or overapplied overhead in your cost of goods sold figure.)

4. Job 215 was started and completed during the year. What price would have been charged to the customer if the job required $8,500 in direct materials and $2,700 in direct labour cost and the company priced its jobs at 25% above cost to manufacture?

5. Direct materials made up $24,000 of the $70,000 ending work-in-process inventory balance. Supply the information missing below:

Direct materials	$24,000
Direct labour	?
Manufacturing overhead	?
Work-in-process inventory	$70,000

PROBLEM 3–7
Determining Overhead Allocation Rate; Computing Amounts [LO3 – CC5; LO5 – CC10, 11; LO8 – CC18]

MNC provides customized engineering services to large manufacturing companies and uses a job-order costing system. The system provided the following information:

CHECK FIGURE

(2b) Gross profit = $1,190,800

	June 30, 2016	July 31, 2016
Inventories:		
Jobs in process	$22,800	$ 34,600
Information about July:		
Materials purchases		50,000
Payroll		970,000
Actual overhead *incurred:*		
Supplies		6,000
Indirect labour		170,000
Other overhead costs		120,000
Selling & administration		640,000
Sales		2,325,000

MNC purchases materials as needed and consumes them during the accounting period. Therefore, it does not need to maintain a materials inventory account. The payroll amount includes salaries/wages paid to professional (direct) labour as well as indirect labour. Overhead is allocated to jobs using a predetermined overhead allocation rate based on professional labour costs computed at the beginning of the year. For 2016, MNC estimated its professional labour and overhead amounts to be $3 million and $960,000 respectively.

Required:

1. Compute the predetermined overhead allocation rate for the year.
2. Compute the following amounts for the month of July:
    a. Cost of jobs completed.
    b. Gross profit.
    c. Net income.

 PROBLEM 3–8

Using Multiple Departments; Applying Overhead [LO2 – CC4; LO3 – CC5; LO7 – CC14]

High Desert Potteryworks makes a variety of pottery products that it sells to retailers, such as Home Depot. The company uses a job-order costing system in which predetermined overhead rates are used to apply manufacturing overhead cost to jobs. The predetermined overhead rate in the moulding department is based on machine-hours, and the rate in the painting department is based on direct labour cost. At the beginning of the year, the company's management made the following estimates:

> CHECK FIGURE
> (3) $73.78 per unit

	Department	
	Moulding	**Painting**
Direct labour-hours	12,000	60,000
Machine-hours	70,000	8,000
Direct materials cost	$510,000	$650,000
Direct labour cost	$130,000	$420,000
Manufacturing overhead cost	$602,000	$735,000

Job 205 was started on August 1 and completed on August 10. The company's cost records show the following information concerning the job:

	Department	
	Moulding	**Painting**
Direct labour-hours	40	75
Machine-hours	90	25
Materials placed into production	$480	$340
Direct labour cost	$280	$660

Required:

1. Compute the predetermined overhead rate used during the year in the moulding department. Compute the rate used in the painting department.
2. Compute the total overhead cost applied to job 205.
3. What would be the total cost recorded for job 205? If the job contained 50 units, what would be the cost per unit?
4. At the end of the year, the records of High Desert Potteryworks revealed the following actual cost and operating data for all jobs worked on during the year:

	Department	
	Moulding	Painting
Direct labour-hours	11,000	61,000
Machine-hours	68,000	8,800
Direct materials cost	$430,000	$680,000
Direct labour cost	$108,000	$436,000
Manufacturing overhead cost	$620,000	$705,000

What was the amount of under- or overapplied overhead in each department at the end of the year?

PROBLEM 3–9
Preparing Journal Entries; T-Accounts; Cost Flows [LO4 – CC8; LO6 – CC12; LO7 – CC14; LO8 – CC18]

Almeda Products, Inc. uses a job-order costing system. The company's inventory balances on April 1, the start of its fiscal year, were as follows:

CHECK FIGURES
(3) Underapplied by $11,000
(4) NI: $23,000

Raw materials	$52,000
Work in process	40,000
Finished goods	38,000

During the year, the following transactions were completed:

a. Raw materials were purchased on account, $170,000.
b. Raw materials were issued from the storeroom for use in production, $200,000 (80% direct and 20% indirect).
c. Employee salaries and wages were accrued as follows: direct labour, $200,000; indirect labour, $82,000; selling and administrative salaries, $120,000.
d. Utility costs were incurred in the factory, $75,000.
e. Advertising costs were incurred, $90,000.
f. Prepaid insurance expired during the year, $20,000 (70% related to factory operations, and 30% related to selling and administrative activities).
g. Depreciation was recorded, $150,000 (80% related to factory assets, and 20% related to selling and administrative assets).
h. Manufacturing overhead was applied to jobs at the rate of 160% of direct labour cost.

i. Goods that cost $700,000 to manufacture according to their job cost sheets were transferred to the finished goods warehouse.

j. Sales for the year totalled $1,000,000 and were all on account. The total cost to manufacture these goods according to their job cost sheets was $720,000.

Required:

1. Prepare journal entries to record the transactions for the year.

2. Prepare T-accounts for raw materials, work in process, finished goods, manufacturing overhead, and cost of goods sold. Post the appropriate parts of your journal entries to these T-accounts. Compute the ending balance in each account. (Do not forget to enter the beginning balances in the inventory accounts.)

3. Is manufacturing overhead underapplied or overapplied for the year? Prepare a journal entry to close this balance to cost of goods sold.

4. Prepare an income statement for the year. (Do not prepare a schedule of cost of goods manufactured; all of the information needed for the income statement is available in the journal entries and T-accounts you have prepared.)

PROBLEM 3–10
Computing Costs and Overhead [LO2 – CC4, LO3 – CC5; LO5 – CC10; LO7 – CC14]

Kay Kee Limited (KKL) is a company that manufactures customized toy racing cars complete with all kinds of gadgetry. KKL purchases all the components (direct materials) but assembles and finishes the cars in two departments: assembly and finishing. Assembly is a *labour*-intensive process, whereas finishing is *machine* intensive. For 2018, KKL has developed the following estimates:

> CHECK FIGURE
> (2) Finishing department overhead applied: $59,850

	Assembly	Finishing
Overhead amount	$409,600	$637,650
Direct labour-hours	128,400	46,600
Direct labour rate per hour	$18.00	$12.00
Machine-hours	5,780	18,220

During January 2015, it received and started processing orders from three customers, whose details are as follows:

	Job 2018-K001	Job 2018-S001	Job 2018-M001
Number of cars	600	200	300
Direct materials/unit	$86	$112	$38
Direct labour-hours/unit (assembly)	12.0	9.0	7.0
Direct labour-hours/unit (finishing)	3.0	2.0	1.5
Machine-hours/unit (assembly)	0.5	0.5	0.5
Machine-hours/unit (finishing)	1.8	1.5	2.0

Assume the direct labour rate during January was the same as estimated at the beginning of the year. During the month, KKL completed jobs 2018-S001 and 2018-M001 but was able to complete only 75% of the units required to complete job 2018-K001. The assembly department incurred overhead amounting to $38,260 during the month, whereas the finishing department incurred $66,560.

Required:

1. Compute the prime costs incurred by each job during the month.

2. Compute the amount of overhead that would have been applied to the jobs during the month in the assembly and finishing departments.

3. Compute the total cost of the jobs completed during the month. What is the amount of work (jobs) in process at the end of the month?

4. Compute the under- or overapplied overhead for the month in each department and in total, labelling as appropriate. How should KKL adjust the over- or underapplied overhead amount in its financial statements for the month?

PROBLEM 3–11
Computing Job Cost [LO2 – CC4; LO3 – CC5; LO7 – CC17]

Nutratask, Inc., is a manufacturer of amino-acid-chelated minerals and vitamin supplements. The company was founded in 2004 and is capable of performing all manufacturing functions, including packaging and laboratory functions. Currently, the company markets its products in the United States, Canada, Australia, Japan, and Belgium.

> CHECK FIGURE
>
> (2) Approximately $763

The production of all mineral chelates follows a similar pattern. Upon receiving an order, the company's chemist prepares a bill of materials (BoM) that specifies the product, the theoretical yield, and the quantities of raw materials that should be used. Once the BoM is received by production, the materials are requisitioned and sent to the blending room. The chemicals and minerals are added in the order specified and blended for two to eight hours, depending on the product. After blending, the mix is put on long trays and sent to the drying room, where it is allowed to dry until the moisture content is 7–9%. Drying time for most products is from one to three days.

After the product is dry, several small samples are taken and sent to laboratory to be checked for bacteria levels and to see whether the product meets customer specifications. If the product is not fit for human consumption or if it fails to meet customer specifications, additional materials are added under the chemist's direction to bring the product up to standard. Once the product passes inspection, it is ground into a powder of different meshes (particle sizes) according to customer specifications. The powder is then placed in heavy cardboard drums and shipped to the customer (or, if requested, put in tablet or capsule form and then shipped).

Since each order is customized to meet the special needs of its customers, Nutratask uses a job-order costing system. Recently, Nutratask received a request for a 300-kilogram order of potassium aspartate. The customer offered to pay $12.40 per kilogram. Upon receiving the request and the customer's specifications, marketing manager Lanny Smith requested a BoM from the company's chemist. The BoM indicated the following material requirements:

Material	Required Quantity (Kilograms)	Price ($) per Kilogram
Aspartic Acid	195.00	5.75
Citric Acid	15.00	2.02
K_2CO_3	121.50	4.64
Rice	30.00	0.43

Lanny also reviewed past jobs that were similar to the requested order and discovered that the expected direct labour time was 16 hours. The production workers at Nutratask earn an average of $16.50 per hour; Nutratask incurs an additional $2 per hour for taxes, insurance, and additional benefits. Overhead is applied using two departmental rates: one based on the cost of direct materials, and the other based on direct labour costs. At the start of the year,

Nutratask estimated as follows: (1) Materials-related overhead: $586,000, (2) Direct materials costs: $1,831,250, (3) Labour-related overhead: $1,960,000, (4) Direct labour cost: $1,225,000.

Whenever a customer requests a bid, Nutratask usually estimates the manufacturing costs of the job and then adds a markup of 30%. This markup varies depending on the competition and general economic conditions. Currently, the industry is doing well, and Nutratask is operating at capacity.

Required:

1. Prepare a job cost sheet for the proposed job. What is the expected cost per kilogram? Should Nutratask accept the price offered by the prospective customer? Why or why not?
2. Suppose Nutratask and the prospective customer agree on a price of cost plus 25%. What is the gross margin that Nutratask expects to earn on the job?
3. Assume that the actual production level was only 280 kilograms despite using the expected quantity of materials and labour. What are the possible effects of this loss in production?

Building Your Skills

COMPREHENSIVE PROBLEM [LO3 – CC5; LO4 – CC8; LO5 – CC10; LO7 – CC14]

Grass Roots Consulting Company (GRCC) provides a variety of services to clients. For the year 2016, it had established the following budget (i.e., estimated amounts):

> CHECK FIGURE
>
> (2) Amount transferred to the cost of jobs completed account: $1,165,250

Materials and supplies		$ 586,400
Consulting hours	128,000	
Processing hours	91,900	
Consulting overhead		$ 622,080
Processing overhead		$1,654,200

Consultants are paid at the rate of $45 per hour (there was no difference between the budgeted and the actual rates). GRCC has two types of overhead as shown above and uses two different bases to allocate overhead to client jobs (consulting hours and processing hours). During December 2016, the company started three major client jobs and incurred the following actual costs. Jobs 2016-12-1 and 2016-12-3 were completed during the month but the other job was still incomplete at month-end (there were no incomplete jobs at the start of the month).

	Job 2016-12-1	Job 2016-12-2	Job 2016-12-3
Materials and supplies	$10,460	$7,664	$13,880
Consulting hours	9,580	7,140	7,490
Processing hours	6,950	7,140	9,150

Required:

1. Compute the total overhead costs applied during the month. Show all the steps in your computation (e.g., calculation of the predetermined overhead rate and the allocation).

2. What is the amount of total costs that GRCC would have transferred to the cost of jobs completed account during the month? (*Note:* This account is equivalent to the cost of goods sold account.) What is your estimate of the balance in this account at the beginning of December?

3. What is the amount of total costs that GRCC would have transferred to the jobs-in-process account during the month? (*Note:* This account is equivalent to a work-in-process account.) What is your estimate of the balance in this account at the end of the month assuming zero beginning balance?

4. During the month of December, GRCC debited the consulting overhead account in the amount of $123,450 and debited the processing overhead account in the amount of $413,920. Compute the balance in the overhead accounts at the end of the month after crediting the overhead accounts with the applied overhead amounts. What will you call these balances? What will be the impact on income when you close the balances in the two overhead accounts to the cost of jobs completed account?

THINKING ANALYTICALLY [LO2 – CC4; LO3 – CC5, 6, 7; LO8 – CC18]

Kelvin Aerospace, Inc. manufactures parts, such as rudder hinges, for the aerospace industry. The company uses a job-order costing system with a plantwide predetermined overhead rate based on direct labour-hours. On December 16, 2016, the company's controller made a preliminary estimate of the predetermined overhead rate for 2017. The new rate was based on the estimated total manufacturing overhead cost of $3,402,000 and the estimated 63,000 total direct labour-hours for 2017:

$$\text{Predetermined overhead rate} = \frac{\$3,402,000}{63,000 \text{ direct labour-hours}}$$

$$= \$54 \text{ per direct labour-hour}$$

This new predetermined overhead rate was communicated to top managers in a meeting on December 19. The rate did not cause any comment because it was within a few pennies of the overhead rate that had been used during 2016. One of the subjects discussed at the meeting was a proposal by the production manager to purchase an automated milling machine built by Sunghi Industries. The president of Kelvin Aerospace, Harry Arcany, agreed to meet with the sales representative from Sunghi Industries to discuss the proposal.

On the day after the meeting, Harry Arcany met with Jasmine Chang, Sunghi Industries' sales representative. The following discussion took place:

Arcany: Wally, our production manager, asked me to meet with you, since he is interested in installing an automated milling machine. Frankly, I'm skeptical. You're going to have to show me that this isn't just another expensive toy for Wally's people to play with.

Chang: This is a great machine with direct bottom-line benefits. The automated milling machine has three major advantages. First, it is much faster than the manual methods you are using. It can process about twice as many parts per hour as your present milling machines. Second, it is much more flexible. There are some upfront programming costs, but once those have been incurred, almost no setup is required to run a standard operation. You just punch in the code for the standard operation, load the machine's hopper with raw material, and the machine does the rest.

Arcany: What about cost? Having twice the capacity in the milling machine area won't do us much good. That centre is idle much of the time anyway.

Chang: I was getting there. The third advantage of the automated milling machine is lower cost. Wally and I looked over your present operations, and we estimated that the automated equipment would eliminate the need for about 6,000 direct labour-hours a year. What is your direct labour cost per hour?

Arcany: The wage rate in the milling area averages about $32 per hour. Fringe benefits raise that figure to about $41 per hour.

Chang: Don't forget your overhead.

Arcany: Next year, the overhead rate will be $54 per hour.

Chang: So, including fringe benefits and overhead, the cost per direct labour-hour is about $95.

Arcany: That's right.

Chang: Since you can save 6,000 direct labour-hours per year, the cost savings would amount to about $570,000 a year. And our 60-month lease plan would require payments of only $348,000 per year.

Arcany: That sounds like a no-brainer. When can you install the equipment?

Shortly after this meeting, Harry Arcany informed the company's controller of the decision to lease the new equipment, which would be installed over the Christmas vacation period. The controller realized that this decision would require a recomputation of the predetermined overhead rate for 2017, since the decision would affect both the manufacturing overhead and the direct labour-hours for the year. After talking with both the production manager and the sales representative from Sunghi Industries, the controller discovered that in addition to the annual lease cost of $348,000, the new machine would also require a skilled technician/programmer who would have to be hired at a cost of $50,000 per year to maintain and program the equipment. Both of these costs would be included in factory overhead. There would be no other changes in total manufacturing overhead cost, which is almost entirely fixed. The controller assumed that the new machine would result in a reduction of 6,000 direct labour-hours for the year from the levels that had initially been planned.

When the revised predetermined overhead rate for 2017 was circulated among the company's top managers, there was considerable dismay.

Required:

1. Recompute the predetermined rate assuming that the new machine will be installed. Explain why the new predetermined overhead rate is higher (or lower) than the rate that was originally estimated for 2017.
2. What effect (if any) would this new rate have on the cost of jobs that do not use the new automated milling machine?
3. Why would managers be concerned about the new overhead rate?
4. After seeing the new predetermined overhead rate, the production manager admitted that he probably would not be able to eliminate all of the 6,000 direct labour-hours. He had been hoping to accomplish the reduction by not replacing workers who retired or quit, but that had not been possible. As a result, the real labour savings would be only about 2,000 hours—one worker. In the light of this additional information, evaluate the original decision to acquire the automated milling machine from Sunghi Industries.

COMMUNICATING IN PRACTICE [LO1 – CC1; LO3 – CC5, 7; LO7 – CC17]

Look in the Yellow Pages or contact your local chamber of commerce or local chapter of CMA-Canada to find the names of manufacturing companies in your area. Call or make an appointment to meet with the controller or chief financial officer of one of these companies.

Required:

Ask the following questions and write a brief memorandum to your instructor that addresses what you found out.

1. What are the company's main products?
2. Does the company use job-order costing, process costing, or some other method of determining product costs?
3. How is overhead assigned to products? What is the overhead rate? What is the basis of allocation? Is more than one overhead rate used?
4. Has the company recently changed its costing system, or is it considering changing its costing system? If so, why? What changes were made, or what changes are being considered?

ETHICS CHALLENGE [LO3 – CC5, 7; LO8 – CC18]

Terri Ronsin was recently transferred to the home security systems division of National Home Products. Shortly after taking over her new position as divisional controller, she was asked to develop the division's predetermined overhead rate for the upcoming year. The accuracy of the rate is of some importance, since it is used throughout the year, and any overapplied or underapplied overhead is closed out to cost of goods sold only at the end of the year. National Home Products uses direct labour-hours in all of its divisions as the allocation base for manufacturing overhead.

To compute the predetermined overhead rate, Terri divided her estimate of the total manufacturing overhead for the coming year by the production manager's estimate of the total direct labour-hours for the coming year. She took her computations to the division's general manager for approval but was quite surprised when he suggested a modification in the base. Her conversation with the general manager of the home security systems division, Harry Irving, went like this:

Ronsin: Here are my calculations for next year's predetermined overhead rate. If you approve, we can enter the rate into the computer on January 1 and be up and running in the job-order costing system right away this year.

Irving: Thanks for coming up with the calculations so quickly, and they look just fine. There is, however, one slight modification I would like to see. Your estimate of the total direct labour-hours for the year is 440,000 hours. How about cutting that to about 420,000 hours?

Ronsin: I don't know if I can do that. The production manager says she will need about 440,000 direct labour-hours to meet the sales projections for the year. Besides, there are going to be over 430,000 direct labour-hours during the current year, and sales are projected to be higher next year.

Irving: Terri, I know all that. I would still like to reduce the direct labour-hours in the base to something like 420,000 hours. You probably don't know that I had an agreement with your predecessor as divisional controller to shave 5% or so off the estimated direct labour-hours every year. That way, we kept a reserve that usually resulted in a big boost to net income at the end of the fiscal year in December. We called it our holiday bonus. Corporate headquarters always seemed very pleased that we could pull off such a miracle at the end of the year. This system has worked well for many years, and I don't want to change it now.

Required:

1. Explain how shaving 5% off the estimated direct labour-hours in the base for the predetermined overhead rate usually results in a big boost in net income at the end of the fiscal year.

2. Should Terri Ronsin go along with the general manager's request to reduce the direct labour-hours in the predetermined overhead rate computation to 420,000 direct labour-hours?

TEAMWORK IN ACTION [LO3 – CC5; LO4 – CC8; LO5 – CC10; LO7 – CC14]

In an attempt to conceal a theft of funds, Snake N. Grass, controller of Bucolic Products, Inc., placed a bomb in the company's record vault. The ensuing explosion left only fragments of the company's factory ledger, as shown below:

> **CHECK FIGURE**
> (3) WIP inventory: $14,300

Raw Materials	
Bal. 6/1 8,000	

Work in Process	
Bal. 6/1 7,200	

Finished Goods

Bal. 6/30	21,000		

Manufacturing Overhead

Actual costs for June	79,000		
		Overapplied overhead	6,100

Accounts Payable

		Bal. 6/30	16,000

Cost of Goods Sold

To bring Mr. Grass to justice, the company must reconstruct its activities for June. Your team has been assigned to perform the task of reconstruction. After interviewing selected employees and sifting through charred fragments, you have determined the following additional information:

a. According to the company's treasurer, the accounts payable are for purchases of raw materials only. The company's balance sheet, dated May 31, shows that accounts payable had a $20,000 balance at the beginning of June. The company's bank has provided photocopies of all cheques that cleared the bank during June. These photocopies show that payments to suppliers during June totalled $119,000. (All materials used during the month were direct materials.)

b. The production superintendent states that manufacturing overhead cost is applied to jobs on the basis of direct labour-hours. However, he does not remember the rate currently being used by the company.

c. Cost sheets kept in the production superintendent's office show that only one job was in process on June 30, at the time of the explosion. The job had been charged with $6,600 in materials, and 500 direct labour-hours at $11 per hour had been worked on the job.

d. A log is kept in the finished goods warehouse showing all goods transferred in from the factory. This log shows that the cost of goods transferred into the finished goods warehouse from the factory during June totalled $313,000.

e. The company's May 31 balance sheet indicates that the finished goods inventory totalled $36,000 at the beginning of June.

f. A charred piece of the payroll ledger, found after sifting through piles of smoking debris, indicates that 11,500 direct labour-hours were recorded for June. The company's human resources department has verified that, as a result of a union contract, all factory employees earn the same $11 per hour rate.

g. The production superintendent states that there was no under- or overapplied overhead in the manufacturing overhead account at May 31.

Required:

1. Each member of the team should determine what types of transactions would be posted to one of the following sets of accounts:
   a. Raw materials and accounts payable.
   b. Work in process and manufacturing overhead.
   c. Finished goods and cost of goods sold.

   Each team member should present a summary of the types of transactions that would be posted to the accounts to the other team members, who should confirm or correct the summary. Then, the team should work together to complete steps 2 through 8.

2. Determine the transaction that should be reflected in the manufacturing overhead account, and then determine the company's predetermined overhead rate.

3. Determine the June 30 balance in the company's work-in-process account.

4. Determine the transactions that should be reflected in the work-in-process account.

5. Determine the transactions that should be reflected in the finished goods account.

6. Determine the transactions that should be reflected in the cost of goods sold account.

7. Determine the transactions that should be reflected in the accounts payable account.

8. Determine the transactions that should be reflected in the raw materials account.

(*Hint:* A good method for determining the transactions that were recorded in a given account is to update the related, fragmented T-account by posting whatever entries can be developed from the information provided above.)

4

Process Costing

After studying Chapter 4, you should be able to demonstrate the following competencies:

COMPETENCY		Know	Apply
LO1	**UNDERSTAND THE DISTINCTION BETWEEN JOB-ORDER AND PROCESS COSTING SYSTEMS.**		
CC1	Compare and contrast job-order and process costing systems.	●	
CC2	Explain a production report.	●	
CC3	Describe a processing department.	●	
CC4	Describe the flow of costs through a process costing system.	●	
LO2	**DESCRIBE THE COST CONCEPTS RELEVANT TO PROCESS COSTING AND THE FLOW OF COSTS THROUGH THE COSTING SYSTEM.**		
CC5	Define transferred-in costs.	●	
CC6	Prepare journal entries to record the incurrence and flow of costs through a process costing system.		●
CC7	Describe the cost categories commonly used in a process costing system.	●	
CC8	Explain the use of the conversion cost category in process costing.	●	
LO3	**UNDERSTAND THE CONCEPT OF EQUIVALENT UNITS OF PRODUCTION AND ITS COMPUTATION.**		
CC9	Explain the concept of degree of completion.	●	
CC10	Explain the concept of equivalent units of production and the role of work-in-process (WIP) inventories.	●	
CC11	Compute the equivalent units of production for each cost category.		●

COMPETENCY		Know	Apply
LO4	**APPLY THE WEIGHTED AVERAGE COST METHOD TO ACCOUNT FOR THE FLOW OF PRODUCTION AND COST AND PREPARE A PRODUCTION REPORT.**		
CC12	Account for the flow of production and the computation of equivalent units by preparing a quantity schedule using the weighted average cost method.		●
CC13	Compute the cost per equivalent unit of production using the weighted average cost method.		●
CC14	Account for the costs of production in a given period by preparing a cost reconciliation using the weighted average cost method.		●
LO5	**APPLY THE FIRST-IN-FIRST-OUT (FIFO) METHOD TO DETERMINE THE EQUIVALENT UNITS OF PRODUCTION.**		
CC15	Explain the concept of equivalent units of production, including the roles of the number of units started and completed in a given period and WIP inventories in the FIFO method.	●	
CC16	Compute the equivalent units of production for each cost category using the first-in-first-out (FIFO) method.		●
LO6	**PREPARE A PRODUCTION COST REPORT USING THE FIFO METHOD TO ACCOUNT FOR THE FLOW OF PRODUCTION AND THE PRODUCTION COST.**		
CC17	Prepare a production report using the FIFO method.		●
LO7	**COMPARE THE WACM AND FIFO APPROACHES.**		
CC18	Distinguish between the FIFO and weighted average cost methods of costing and know when the two methods will provide the same result.	●	

ON THE JOB

QUALITY AND COSTS ARE IMPORTANT IN BEER MAKING, TOO!

Whether you are drinking Grasshopper Wheat Ale, Traditional Ale, or Black Amber Ale, you care about deriving value for the money you spend. For Big Rock Brewery of Calgary, value means offering distinctive premium-quality beers at competitive prices.

Big Rock Brewery ©2012

Like many other industries, the beer industry is fiercely competitive. However, companies such as Big Rock Brewery have thrived in the marketplace by developing specialty beers that offer superior quality, taste, and value by controlling costs. And management's efforts have certainly paid off! From 1999 to 2009, net sales grew by over 277%, and the profit margin (percentage of net sales) increased from −3.3% in 1999 to over 16% in 2009 (it was 5.6% in 2011).

Big Rock understands that it cannot afford to be complacent, however. In an effort to further control costs, the company has invested in a computer system that allows managers to implement more effective cost controls in many areas. The system generates detailed cost information on weekly and monthly bases. This is important, given the number of different processes that add to the costs of brewing a good beer. Knowing the cost added at each stage of the entire process is essential to identifying potential avenues for cost management. Managers at Big Rock may also decide to adopt the lean business model to improve quality and efficiency (cost), two important factors in enhancing the value that the company's beers offer their drinkers.

Source: Big Rock Brewery Annual Reports, 2003, 2009, and 2011, http://www.bigrockbeer.com/corporate/investors. Big Rock Brewery © 2012.

 Critical thinking question *In what ways do you think determining the product cost of beer is different from, say, determining the cost of the coins that Rand Company in Chapter 3 specialized in making?*

*Note to student: See **Guidance Answers** online.*

◀◀ A Look Back	▶ A Look at This Chapter	▶▶ A Look Ahead
We described a basic job-order costing system in Chapter 3. In this system, a predetermined single plant-wide overhead rate is used to *apply* overhead costs to jobs by multiplying the overhead rate and the actual amount of the allocation base used to complete the jobs. This is a normal costing approach: Only *applied* (as opposed to *actual*) overhead costs flow through work in process to finished goods and then to cost of goods sold. At period-end, the difference between the actual and applied overhead (underapplied or overapplied overhead) is used to convert the cost of goods sold to actual cost of goods sold when preparing the financial statements.	In Chapter 4, we continue the discussion of the accumulation of product cost by describing a basic process costing system. This is applicable to production environments in which essentially homogeneous units of product are produced in large volumes. We stick to the normal costing approach for the allocation of manufacturing overhead costs.	In Chapter 5, we will look at activity-based costing, a more sophisticated technique that uses a variety of allocation bases to assign overhead costs to products.

Process costing is an approach to costing products used in industries that produce essentially homogeneous (i.e., uniform) products on a continuous basis, such as bricks, corn flakes, or paper. Process costing is used in such companies as Reynolds Aluminum (aluminum ingots), Scott Paper (toilet paper), General Mills (flour), Petro-Canada (gasoline and lubricating oils), Coppertone (sunscreens), and Kellogg (breakfast cereals). In addition, process costing is often used in companies with assembly operations, such as Panasonic (televisions), Dell (personal computers), General Electric (refrigerators), Toyota (automobiles), Amana (washing machines), and Sony (MP3 players). As suggested by the length of this list, process costing is widely used.

In this chapter, we will explain how product costing occurs in a process costing system.

MANAGERIAL ACCOUNTING IN ACTION

THE ISSUE

Samantha Trivers, is the president of Double Diamond Skis. After a rocky start, the company had come out with a completely redesigned ski called X-Factor, made of exotic materials and featuring flashy graphics. The steps in the manufacturing process are shown below. The ski was a runaway bestseller—particularly among younger skiers—and had provided the company with much-needed cash for two years. However, last year, a dismal snowfall in the Canadian Rockies had depressed sales, and Double Diamond was once again short of cash. Trivers was worried that another bad ski season would force Double Diamond into bankruptcy. The company typically made and sold all of its skis in a single year and had a policy of not carrying work-in-process inventories to provide maximum flexibility for making model changes. Also, until now Trivers had relied on annual reports for financial information, and she felt that this was too infrequent.

The Production Process at Double Diamond Skis

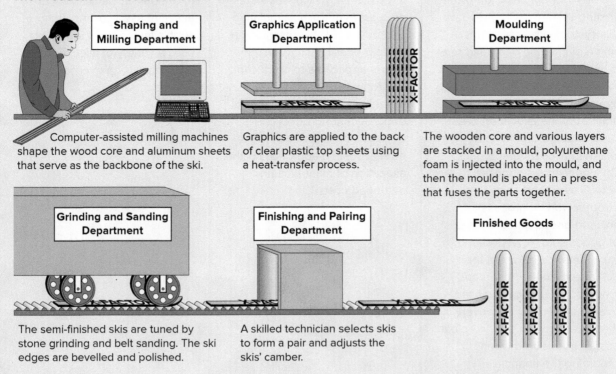

Shaping and Milling Department

Computer-assisted milling machines shape the wood core and aluminum sheets that serve as the backbone of the ski.

Graphics Application Department

Graphics are applied to the back of clear plastic top sheets using a heat-transfer process.

Moulding Department

The wooden core and various layers are stacked in a mould, polyurethane foam is injected into the mould, and then the mould is placed in a press that fuses the parts together.

Grinding and Sanding Department

The semi-finished skis are tuned by stone grinding and belt sanding. The ski edges are bevelled and polished.

Finishing and Pairing Department

A skilled technician selects skis to form a pair and adjusts the skis' camber.

Finished Goods

Source: Adapted from Bill Gout, Jesse James Doquilo, and Studio-MD, "Capped Crusaders," *Skiing*, October 1993, pp. 138–144.

On May 4, with the production of next year's model of X-Factor having been underway since the start of the year, Trivers called Jerry Madison, the company controller, into her office to discuss the reports she would need henceforth.

Trivers: Jerry, I am going to need more frequent cost information starting right away. I really have to stay on top of things.

Madison: What do you have in mind?

Trivers: I'd like reports once a month that detail our production costs for each department and for each pair of skis. I would like this practice to begin with a report for May.

Madison: That shouldn't be much of a problem. We already compile almost all of the necessary data for the annual report. The only complication is our work-in-process inventories. This has not been a problem in our annual reports, since our fiscal year ends at a time when we have finished producing skis for the last model year and haven't yet started producing for the new model year. Consequently, there aren't any work-in-process inventories to value for the annual report. But that won't be true for monthly reports.

Trivers: I'm not sure why that is a problem, Jerry. But I'm confident you can figure out how to solve it.

Madison: Let me prepare the report for the Shaping and Milling Department for May. You can then review it and decide if it meets your needs; after that, starting in June, I can prepare reports for all of the processing departments. Is that all right?

Trivers: I like this idea. Before you spend a lot of time preparing reports for all the departments, it is a good idea for me to see what you come up with for one department.

It is now June 1. Jerry has been provided with the information in Exhibit 4–1 on the production activity and the manufacturing costs in the Shaping and Milling Department for May. With this information in hand, Jerry sets about preparing the report for Trivers.

EXHIBIT 4–1 Production and Cost Information for May, Shaping and Milling Department, Double Diamond Skis

Shaping and Milling Department			
Production Activity for the Month of May			
		Degree of Completion of Production	
	Units	Direct Material	Labour Plus Overhead*
Beginning work in process	200	50%	30%
Ending work in process	400	40%	25%
Started into production	5,000	n.a.	n.a.
Completed in the month	4,800	100%	100%

Shaping and Milling Department			
Manufacturing Cost Information for the Month of May			
	Direct Materials	Labour Plus Overhead*	Total
Beginning work in process	$ 3,000	$ 1,000	$ 4,000
Cost incurred during May	$74,000	$70,000	$144,000
Total cost to account for	$77,000	$71,000	$148,000

n.a. Not Applicable

* Because the degree of completion is identical for direct labour and manufacturing overhead and because labour costs are a small fraction of total manufacturing costs these two inputs are combined into a single category at Double Diamond Skis.

We begin with an explanation of the meaning of the "costing" task in "process costing." We will use the data for May in the Shaping and Milling Department in Exhibit 4–1 to explain. During May, this department was charged a total of $148,000 for direct materials (DM), direct labour (DL), and manufacturing overhead (MOH). Notice that the company has combined direct labour and manufacturing overhead costs; this combination is called "conversion costs (CC)" in management accounting. We will explain the practice a bit later; for now, consider the $148,000 that has been charged to the department. The "process costing" activity is the task of "accounting" for this total by calculating the amount to be charged to the 4,800 units completed in May and the amount to the 400 units of ending work in process inventory. This is illustrated in Exhibit 4–2.

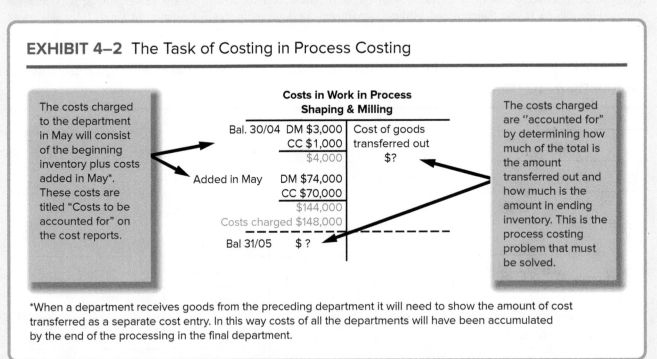

EXHIBIT 4–2 The Task of Costing in Process Costing

The costs charged to the department in May will consist of the beginning inventory plus costs added in May*. These costs are titled "Costs to be accounted for" on the cost reports.

Costs in Work in Process
Shaping & Milling

Bal. 30/04	DM $3,000	Cost of goods
	CC $1,000	transferred out
	$4,000	$?
Added in May	DM $74,000	
	CC $70,000	
	$144,000	
Costs charged	$148,000	
Bal 31/05	$?	

The costs charged are "accounted for" by determining how much of the total is the amount transferred out and how much is the amount in ending inventory. This is the process costing problem that must be solved.

*When a department receives goods from the preceding department it will need to show the amount of cost transferred as a separate cost entry. In this way costs of all the departments will have been accumulated by the end of the processing in the final department.

So what is difficult about this task? Notice that the costs are charged by type of input (direct materials and conversion cost—labour plus overhead) when the costs are incurred; this separation is important for costing inventory and also the cost of goods transferred out. "Process costing" is the procedure that management accountants have developed to allocate each input type's charged cost to completed units and to in-process units, and this is what you are going to learn in this chapter. Each cost category has to be treated separately because, even though we know the physical quantity of the in-process inventories, these units are at different stages of completion with respect to direct materials and conversion. The degree of completion indicates how far production has advanced with regard to the application of an input in the manufacturing process. We will explain how to overcome this complication, which is the key challenge in process costing.

Comparison of Job-Order and Process Costing

Similarities Between Job-Order and Process Costing

LO1 • **Know**

CC1: Compare and contrast job-order and process costing systems.

The similarities between job-order and process costing can be summarized as follows:

- The two systems have a common purpose, which is to assign materials, labour, and overhead costs to products and to provide a mechanism for computing unit costs.
- The two systems maintain and use the same basic accounts, including manufacturing overhead, raw materials, work in process, and finished goods, and the flow of costs through the accounts is basically the same in both systems.

As can be seen from this comparison, much of the knowledge that we have already acquired about job-order costing is applicable to process costing. Our task now is simply to refine and extend this knowledge to process costing.

Differences Between Job-Order and Process Costing

LO1 • **Know**

CC2: Explain a production report.

The differences between job-order and process costing are caused by the following factors: (1) the flow of units in a process costing system is more or less continuous, (2) these units are indistinguishable from one another, and (3) each order is just one of many that are filled from a continuous flow of virtually identical units from the production line, unlike in a job-order setting, where each order is unique.

In a process costing situation, note that although each unit of product will absorb an input in the same way as another unit; the inputs themselves need not be applied during production at the same time (stage of production) or at the same rate (gradually or in lumps or all together). For example, during production, at a given stage of the process, the in-process units may have 80% materials added, while only 60% of labour plus overhead has been applied to those units. Therefore the cost per unit has to be determined separately for each type of input (direct materials cost per unit, conversion cost per unit) first. And only then is the cost of the product calculated as the sum of the different input costs per unit. Thus the product cost in a flow shop is an "assemblage" of the individual input cost per unit.

In a job-order shop, the cost object is the job; at any given stage in the production process of a job, exactly the same percentage of completion will have occurred for every type of input. This allows you to combine the input costs first—the total is the cost of the job—and then calculate a cost per unit; in other words in the job shop, the costs of the inputs are assembled first into a total and then unitized.

The job cost sheet is not used in process costing because the focus of this method is on departments. Instead of using job cost sheets, a **production report** is prepared for each department in which work is done on products. The production report serves several functions. It provides a summary of the number of units moving through a department during a period and also provides a computation of unit costs, showing the details of the costing by input type. In addition, it shows the costs that were charged to the department and the disposition made of these costs, again by input type and by total. The department production report is the key document in a process costing system.

The major differences between job-order and process costing are summarized in Exhibit 4–3.

EXHIBIT 4–3   Differences Between Job-Order and Process Costing

Job-Order Costing	Process Costing
1. Many different jobs are worked on during each period, with each job having different production requirements.	1. A single product is produced either on a continuous basis or for long periods. All units of product are identical.
2. Costs are accumulated by individual job.	2. Costs are accumulated by department or process. Cost of each input is allocated separately, to account for the fact that, in a continuous process, inputs may not be added at the same rate or at the same time in the production process.
3. The *job cost sheet* is the key document controlling the accumulation of costs by a job.	3. The *department production report* is the key document showing the accumulation and disposition of costs by department.
4. Unit costs are computed *by job* on the job cost sheet.	4. Unit costs are computed *by department* on the department production report.

IN BUSINESS

MIXED FLOW SYSTEMS

Job shops and process flow systems are like two ends of a production process continuum. Can a business combine the two systems to exploit business opportunities? CEL Packaging Pvt. Ltd., a manufacturer of a variety of corrugated packaging products based in western India, has done just that. CEL manufactures a variety of boxes to pack eggs, electronic products, and even bicycles. It also uses the corrugated medium to produce a variety of other products, including display cases, library boxes, storage pallets, point of purchase displays, and much more. Moreover, its order size ranges from 10,000 boxes to fewer than 200. The proportion of low- to medium-volume orders increased from 10% in 1995 to 40% in 2009 (a fourfold increase). There was also a significant difference in terms of the quality requirements from the diverse set of customers.

CEL has responded to these changes by skillfully combining the characteristics of job production and process production to cater to the diverse needs of its customers. CEL uses a process flow to manufacture the corrugated sheets that form the main raw material for all its products. The job shop component is critical in handling the custom orders that require careful design, planning, and additional steps in the manufacturing process. This mixed production system poses significant costing challenges to the company.

Source: Personal conversations with executives of CEL Packaging Private Ltd; http://www.coreemb.com.

Process Cost Flows

CC3: Describe a processing department.

Cost accumulation is simpler in a process costing system than in a job-order costing system. In a process costing system, instead of having to trace costs to hundreds of different jobs, costs are traced to only a few processing departments. A **processing department** is any location in an organization where work is performed on a product and where materials, labour, or overhead costs are added to the product.

With regard to each input, the activity which causes the cost must be performed uniformly on all of the units passing through the department. This means that each unit must be treated in an identical fashion when an input is applied to production. But, as explained before, the activity of adding materials can be performed differently than the activity relating to another input like direct labour. Therefore it is possible for degree of completion of production for an input like materials to be different from the degree of completion of production for another input like conversion.

Some products and services may go through several processing departments. For example, making frozen pizza involves several steps that may be carried out in three processing departments: (1) dough making, (2) cooking, and (3) freezing and packaging. Processing departments are normally organized in a sequential pattern. By sequential processing, we mean that units flow in sequence from one department to another, as shown previously for Double Diamond Skis.

The Flow of Materials, Labour, and Overhead Costs

CC4: Describe the flow of costs through a process costing system.

A T-account model of materials, labour, and overhead cost flows in a process costing system is given in Exhibit 4–4. We have used the data for May that Jerry Madison at Double Diamond Skis is looking at. Several key points should be taken from this exhibit. First, note that a separate work-in-process account is maintained for *each processing department*. In contrast, in a job-order costing system, there may be only a single work-in-process account for the entire company.

Second, note that the cost of completed production of the first processing department (department A in the exhibit), $144,067, is transferred into the work-in-process account of the second processing department (department B). In department B, completed production received from department A undergoes additional work, leading to costs being incurred in department B. After this additional work, the completed units are then transferred into the next department in the sequence. In the exhibit, we show only two processing departments, although you know there are five departments at Double Diamond Skis.

CC5: Define transferred-in costs.

Third, note that materials, labour, and overhead costs can be added in *any* processing department—not just the first. Costs charged to department B's work-in-process account would consist of the materials, labour, and overhead costs incurred in department B ($XXX, $YYY, $ZZZ) plus the costs attached to partially completed units transferred in from department A called **transferred-in costs**—the $144,067. As the product moves from one department to the next, the transferred-in costs will be the accumulation of the costs added in all of the previous departments—think of a snowball rolling down a hill gathering more and more snow!

EXHIBIT 4–4 T-Account Model of Process Costing Flows

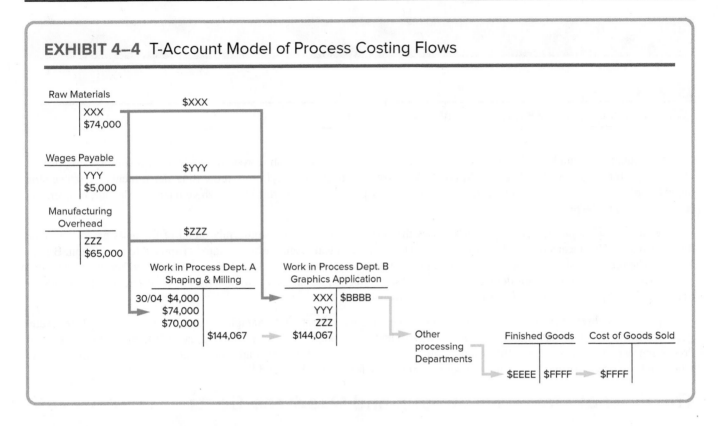

Materials, Labour, and Overhead Cost Entries

Mirroring the physical flow of units and the flow of costs through the various processing departments will be the accounting system's activities of entering and tracking the cost information in the accounting journals. To complete our discussion of cost flows in a process costing system, in the following paragraphs we show journal entries relating to materials, labour, and overhead costs.

MATERIALS COSTS

LO2 • **Apply**

CC6: Prepare journal entries to record the incurrence and flow of costs through a process costing system.

As in job-order costing, materials are drawn from the storeroom using a materials requisition form. As stated previously, materials (or any input) can be added in any processing department if required by the production technology.

Looking at the first processing department, department A, the journal entry for placing materials into production is as follows:

Work in Process—Department A	74,000	
Raw Materials		74,000

If other materials are subsequently added in department B, the entry is the following:

Work in Process—Department B	XXX	
Raw Materials		XXX

LABOUR COSTS

In process costing, it is necessary to keep track of only the amount of labour cost incurred in each department because labour costs do not have to be traced to specific jobs. The following journal entry will record the labour costs for a period in department A:

Work in Process—Department A	5,000	
Salaries and Wages Payable		5,000

OVERHEAD COSTS

In process costing, predetermined overhead rates are usually used to apply overhead costs to departments (or processes); each department receives a portion of the total overhead based on this rate. Overhead cost is then charged to units of product as the units move through the department using a journal entry, such as the following for department A:

Work in Process—Department A	65,000	
Manufacturing Overhead Applied		65,000

COMPLETING THE COST FLOWS

After processing has been completed in a department, the units are transferred to the next department for further processing. Of course, figuring out the cost of these units is the main objective of the method of process costing and we have not yet shown this. Therefore, assume for the moment that the cost of the completed units in department A is $144,067. The following journal entry is used to transfer the costs of the processed units from department A to department B (i.e., from Shaping and Milling to Graphics Application):

Work in Process—Department B (Graphics)	144,067	
Work in Process—Department A		144,067

We will show later how the $144,067 is calculated.

After processing has been completed in department E, the last processing department, the costs of the completed units are then transferred to the finished goods inventory account:

Finished Goods	EEEE	
Work in Process—Department E		EEEE

Finally, when a customer's order is filled and units are sold, the cost of the units is transferred to cost of goods sold:

Cost of Goods Sold	FFFF	
Finished Goods		FFFF

To summarize, cost flows between accounts are basically the same in a process costing system as they are in a job-order costing system. The only noticeable difference at this point is that in a process costing system, there is a separate work-in-process account for each department.

IN BUSINESS

COSTING HOMOGENOUS PRODUCTS

If you have a remote control to change the channel on your TV, chances are that batteries are used to power the remote. Alkaline batteries are the most frequently used variety. Because battery technology is not new or exotic, quality control has taken precedence in competitions between battery brands.

Battery manufacturing has two distinct stages: the cathode stage and the anode stage. Beginning with the cathode stage, massive quantities of ingredients such as manganese dioxide, graphite, and an electrolyte solution are brought in to be mixed in batches. The mixture is then processed into hollow cylinders called "preforms." In another section of the facility, rolls of steel sheets are cut and formed into standard battery cans. Depending on the size of the battery being made, the amount of preforms placed within the cans will also change.

A special paper is also brought in, cut, and soaked in electrolyte before it is inserted inside the preform cylinder space. This acts as a separator to prevent the cathode material from making contact with the anode material.

As the process moves into the anode stage, a suspension consisting mostly of zinc-based gel and potassium hydroxide electrolyte is injected into the cylinder space where the paper separator was previously inserted. The battery is then sealed and labelled before shipping out of the facility.

With this type of manufacturing process, costs for a single battery cannot be easily attributed. However given that the product is homogenous in nature, the total costs incurred in the cathode mixing stage can be spread uniformly across the number of batteries produced in that batch. Likewise the costs incurred during the anode stage can be transferred in and spread uniformly across the amount of batteries produced in the same batch.

Source: Craig Carmichael, "How to Make Economical, Green, High-Energy Batteries," March 11, 2012, http://members.shaw.ca/Craig-C/hybridize/BatteryMaking/BatteryMaking.html.

Product Cost Categories in a Process Costing System

LO2 • Know

CC7: Describe the cost categories commonly used in a process costing system.

Production environments that use a process costing system for determining product costs are typically highly capital intensive; labour is usually a small proportion of total manufacturing cost. In such environments, it may not be meaningful to separate product costs into three separate product cost categories for internal decision making purposes. Consequently, labour costs and manufacturing overhead are commonly combined into a single cost category called **conversion cost**. It is important to realize that this is usually relevant for cost reporting on a production report and illustrates the managerial accounting philosophy of "different costs for different purposes." The company's cost accounts will record labour and manufacturing overhead cost incurrence separately, and managers will be able to obtain this information, if needed. The manufacturing overhead cost component of conversion cost will still come from assigning it using an overhead allocation rate.

LO2 • Know

CC8: Explain the use of the conversion cost category in process costing.

CUTTING CONVERSION COSTS

CEMEX S.A.B., the world's third-largest cement maker, owns 54 plants that each consume 726 tonnes of fuel a day heating kilns to 1,482 degrees Celsius. Not surprisingly, energy costs account for 40% of the company's overall operating costs. Historically, CEMEX relied exclusively on coal to heat its kilns; however, faced with soaring coal prices and shrinking profits, the company desperately needed a lower-cost heat source. In 2004, CEMEX turned its attention to finding other sources of energy to cut costs, achieving a 17% reduction. In 2014, the company's use of alternative fuel comprised 28% of the total, up from 5% in 2005. This, along with interest savings from refinancing $1.9 billion of debt, enabled it to improve its profit from $76 million in 2014 to $116 million in 2015. Now facing slumping sales in Mexico and Europe, the company plans to improve its bond rating through sales of assets and further cost cutting. One key to improving its operating model has been an internal collaboration platform called Shift. According to the company, "Through Shift-based business networks, we achieved several important advantages, including shorter production cycles, faster speed to market, and real-time process improvements." These are elements of conversion costs and highlight the importance of properly managing these costs for achieving profit targets.

Sources: John Lyons, "Expensive Energy? Burn Other Stuff, One Firm Decides," *The Wall Street Journal*, September 1, 2004, pp. A1 and A8; CEMEX Annual Report 2011, http://www.cemex.com/MediaCenter/AnnualReports.aspx; Christine Murray and Gabriela Lopez, "UPDATE 1-Mexico's Cemex Profit Jumps but Sales Slump on Mexico, Europe," July 22, 2015, http://www.reuters.com/article/2015/07/22/cemex-results-idUSL1N1020L720150722; http://www.cemex.com/CEMEX_AR2014/operating_model.html.

Measuring Production Volume in a Process Costing Environment: The Quantity Schedule

The time has now come for us to address the task that Samantha Trivers has given Jerry Madison at Double Diamond Skis. The situation at the company introduced at the beginning of the chapter in Exhibit 4–1 is depicted in a "T-account" format in Exhibit 4–5. The key to the task of process costing is to realize that measuring the volume of production activity undertaken by the processing department during the production period by the number of physical units processed and completed will not work. For example, suppose two units are processed by a department, and one unit is completed but the other is still in process. Because one completed physical unit and one partially completed physical unit are not the same, the volume of production of the department cannot be measured as two physical units. Another method of measurement must be found.

EXHIBIT 4–5 T-Account View of the Production Activity and Production Costs for May, Shaping and Milling Department

Work in process, units				Costs in Work in Process	
	Units		Units	Bal 30/04 DM $3,000	Cost of goods
Bal 01/05 (50% DM, 30% CC)	200	Completed (50% DM, 70% CC), from Bal 01/05	200	CC $1,000	transferred out
Added in May	5,000	Completed (100%) from units added in May	4,600	$4,000	$?
		Total	4,800	Added in May DM $74,000	
				CC $70,000	
Bal 31/05 (40% DM, 25% CC)	400			$144,000	
				Costs charged $148,000	
				Bal 31/05 $?	

The Flow of Physical Units

Examine Exhibit 4–5. The flow of the *physical* units for May is shown in the T-account on the left. The debit side of the T-account shows that there are 200 units in beginning work-in-process inventory (50% complete with respect to direct materials and 30% complete with respect to conversion); 5,000 units were added during the period, thus a total of 5,200 units were processed. The credit side of the T-account shows that 4,800 units were fully completed (100% complete); the debit balance tells us that there are 400 physical units in ending work-in-process inventory (40% complete, direct materials and 25% complete, conversion). Note that these data obey the inventory balance relationship for physical units:

Number of units in beginning work in process (BWIP)	+	Number of units started	=	Number of units finished	+	Number of units in ending work in process (EWIP)
200	+	5,000	=	4,800	+	400

The T-account also shows that the 4,800 completed units include the 200 units from beginning work in process. These 200 physical units were the first units on which production activity in May was performed. Following their completion, management started 5,000 units and completed 4,600 of these. Thus the 400 units in ending inventory are the units that were started in May; they do not include any of the 200 units brought forward from April. The amount 4,600 is the quantity *started and finished* in May.[1]

The T-account on the right in the diagram depicts the flow of the costs through work in process. The question marks remind us that the cost accounting task is to compute the cost of goods transferred out—the cost of 4,800 units transferred, and the cost of the 400 units still in process at the end of May. This must be calculated by determining the cost of direct materials separately from the conversion cost and then putting the costs together, because the degree of completion of production is different for materials and conversion.

Challenge of Measuring Production Activity: Whole Units versus Partially Completed Units

As mentioned, the volume of production activity should not be measured in *physical* units. To understand why, ask, "What volume of production in May is responsible for the costs of $144,000 incurred in the month?" Consider a couple of possible choices for production volume measured in physical units. Suppose you take 5,200 to be the production volume. During May, 5,200 physical units were indeed *processed* (i.e., worked on in May), and the activity of working on these 5,200 units during the month led to the costs being incurred. But 5,200 units is not a true measure of May's production activity responsible for the costs. The department had 200 units partially complete and there are 400 units remaining unfinished. Therefore, if 5,200 is taken to be the production volume responsible for the costs, this will assign the same cost to each completed unit and also to each partially completed unit in ending inventory. This would be incorrect since a fully completed unit and a partially completed unit cannot be responsible for the same amount of cost. A whole unit should bear more burden than a partially completed unit. Therefore, taking the volume of production for May to be 5,200 units would be a mistake.

Suppose instead you take 4,800 as the production volume. Now you are saying that 4,800 units are responsible for the entire costs of May and that the 400 units in ending inventory are not responsible for any of the cost. This is clearly not true since we know that units in ending inventory are partially complete: 40% with respect to DM and 25% with respect to CC. What about the 200 units in beginning work-in-process inventory? Asserting that the production volume for May is 4,800 units also says that the 200 units from beginning inventory are like the 4,600 full units begun and completed in May and should bear the same burden. This would be incorrect because the 200 units are already partially complete to the degree of 50% for direct materials and 30% for conversion costs. Consequently, taking the volume of production for May to be 4,800 would be a mistake.

The lesson to take away is that when we measure production activity using physical units, the fundamental error being made is either treating a partially completed unit as if it were a fully completed unit or ignoring a partially completed unit entirely. Clearly, we need a way to express a partially completed unit and a fully completed unit that enables us to add them up to determine the volume of production. A different measurement scale than physical units is required to measure production volume.

The Concept of Degree of Completion

LO3 ● **Know**

CC9: Explain the concept of degree of completion.

The **degree of completion (percentage complete)** of a physical unit describes how much work has been done on the product. The figure of 100% means that the physical unit is fully completed; 30% indicates that the physical unit is 30% complete; and so on. At Double Diamond, the 200 units in beginning work in process are 50% complete with respect to direct materials and 70% complete with respect to conversion cost. The 400 units in ending work in process are incomplete because only 40% of direct materials have been applied and 25% of conversion cost has been applied.

Notice that the production activity has advanced to *different degrees of completion* with regard to direct materials as compared to conversion costs. Therefore the production activity must be separately measured for direct materials and conversion costs.

Until Jerry resolves the issue of how to measure the production activity for May and derives a measure for each input separately—direct materials and conversion costs—he will not be able to complete the task for Samantha Trivers.

HELPFUL HINT

The degree of completion with respect to direct materials can be different from that for conversion costs. Consider the example of baking bread. When baking bread, normally all of the ingredients are assembled before mixing and baking. In this case, you can see that all of the required direct materials are added right at the beginning of the bread-making process. Thus, the degree of completion of partially made bread with respect to the direct materials can be said to be 100%, whereas the degree of completion with respect to conversion costs will not be 100%; it will be some percentage less than 100%. When preparing a cake, on the other hand, even though most of the ingredients are introduced at the beginning, the icing is not put on until after the cake has been baked. Thus, some direct materials are added only toward the end, and therefore, in the case of a partially completed cake, the degree of completion with respect to direct materials (as well as conversion costs) will not be 100%. From this, it should be clear that each cost category must be separately considered when allocating cost because the degree of completion need not be the same for each cost category.

Equivalent Units of Production

LO3 ● **Know** ● **Apply**

CC10: Explain the concept of equivalent units of production and the role of work-in-process (WIP) inventories.

● **Apply**

CC11: Compute the equivalent units of production for each cost category.

The solution to Jerry's problem of measuring production activity in a way that properly accounts for partially completed units is the concept of **equivalent units of production (EU).** Using the degree of completion, the volume of physical units can be expressed in terms of a new scale of measurement, called equivalent units, as follows (each cost category must be treated separately):

Number of equivalent units = Number of physical units × Degree of completion of the units

The concept of equivalent units of production provides us the means to measure the production activity in a process costing environment. When there is work-in-process inventory, production quantity should be expressed in equivalent units of production using the percentage completion information and *not as the number of physical units processed*. For example, there are 200 physical units in beginning work in process. These are 30% complete with respect to conversion. This means the volume of production in beginning inventory with respect to direct materials is: $200 \times 30\% = 60$ EU. The key to process costing is to express all the physical quantities in terms of equivalent units before undertaking the cost accounting. This is accomplished in a schedule called the quantity schedule.

HELPFUL HINT

Make a clear distinction between a physical unit, a fully completed unit, and an equivalent unit. One physical unit 100% complete will be one equivalent unit. One fully completed unit is one equivalent unit and also one physical unit. A physical unit will be half an equivalent unit if it is 50% complete. Eighty physical units that are 40% completed will be $80 \times 40\% = 32$ equivalent units. The scale of measurement for production volume is no longer a physical unit. It is instead an equivalent unit. The beauty of the concept is that we can express any physical quantity of product using this common measurement scale regardless of whether the quantity represents fully or partially completed product. Given the formula to convert physical units to equivalent units, you can go from one scale to the other and back. For example, if there are 72 equivalent units in inventory which are 80% along the production process, the number of physical units in process must be $72/0.8 = 90$.

The Quantity Schedule

The quantity schedule expressing the production activity of May in the Shaping and Milling Department is shown in Exhibit 4–6. The number of equivalent units is obtained by multiplying the degree of completion and the number of physical units.

EXHIBIT 4–6 The Quantity Schedule: Physical and Equivalent Units of Production Processed in May in the Shaping and Milling Department

	Physical Units		Equivalent Units Processed	
	(1)	(2)	Direct Materials	Conversion Cost
Beginning work in process, May 1	200		$200 \times 50\% = \quad 100$	$200 \times 30\% = \quad 60$
May's production activity:				
Beginning work in process		200	$200 \times 50\% = \quad 100$	$200 \times 70\% = \quad 140$
Units introduced in May	5,000			
Started and completed in May*		4,600	$4,600 \times 100\% = 4,600$	$4,600 \times 100\% = 4,600$
Completed units, May 31		4,800	4,800	4,800
Ending work in process, May 31		400	$400 \times 40\% = \quad 160$	$400 \times 25\% = \quad 100$
Total physical and equivalent units processed	5,200	5,200	4,960	4,900
Less EUs from May 1			100	60
EUs of May production			4,860	4,840

* Started and completed = Completed units − BWIP or Units introduced − EWIP

Study this exhibit carefully. Columns (1) and (2) account for the flow of physical units. These two columns are the left and right sides of the flow of units equation presented earlier. Column (1) is a depiction of the physical units *to account for*. Column (2) *accounts for* the physical units. When accounting for the units in column (2), notice that the 5,000 units introduced in May are accounted for in terms of units completed (4,600) and units in ending inventory (400). These two columns in the quantity schedule may also be seen as the left side and the right side of the T-account of the physical units in the work in process account in Exhibit 4–5.

The computation of the equivalent units is depicted in the last two columns of the schedule, with each input separately considered when determining the equivalent units because the degree of completion *is not the same* for direct materials and conversion cost. Each cell shows the application of the formula to calculate the equivalent units:

$$\text{EU} = \text{Physical units} \times \text{Degree of completion.}$$

The schedule clarifies that even though 5,200 physical units were processed during May, when production activity is expressed in terms of equivalent units of production, 4,960 EU were processed during May for direct materials and 4,900 EU were processed for conversion cost during May.

It is important to understand how the total EU processed in May is derived. We will use direct materials as an example. At the start of May, there are already 100 EU in beginning work in process representing the materials added to the 200 physical units during April: $200 \times 50\% = 100$. When production activity started in May, the department first focused on completing the 200 units from April. Given these units were 50% already complete, the remaining $100\% - 50\% = 50\%$ of direct materials were added by the production system in May. Thus in May 100 EU of work was done to complete the beginning work in process. Notice that at this point 200 units are fully completed. Next, the department began production on 5,000 units in May and completed 4,600 of these. Thus the number of EU of units started and completed is $100\% \times 4,600 = 4,600$ EU. Adding the 100 EU from April, the 100 EU to complete the beginning work in process, and the 4,600 EU of units started and completed gives us the total number of units completed in May: 4,800. Finally, there are 400 physical units in ending inventory that are 40% complete. Thus the number of EU in ending inventory is $400 \times 40\% = 160$. Altogether, the department has processed 4,800 EU plus 160 EU for a total of 4,960 EU with respect to direct materials. A similar analysis tells us that a total of 4,900 EU were processed in May for conversion cost.

This discussion tells us that, to compute the total EU processed in a given production period for a given input, the formula is:

$$\text{Total EU processed} = \text{Total units completed} + \text{EU in ending inventory}$$

Thus—say, for conversion cost—this formula gives:

$$\text{Total EU processed} = 4{,}800 \text{ EU} + 400 \times 25\% = 4{,}900 \text{ EU.}$$

Exhibit 4–6 also shows one additional important point. Although the department *processed* 4,960 EU with respect to direct materials and 4,900 EU with respect to conversion cost, these EU *do not* represent the volume of *production* (i.e., production activity) which occurred *in* May and was responsible for the costs incurred *during* May. This is because the total EU processed in May also include the 100 EU from April for direct material and 60 EU from April for conversion cost. These EU represent work performed in April. They do not represent work done in May, therefore we must remove the EU of April's activity in beginning work-in-process inventory from the total EU processed in May to derive the EU for May. For direct materials the volume of production in May responsible for May's production costs of $74,000 is 4,960 EU – 100 EU = 4,860 EU. For conversion cost 4,900 EU – 60 EU = 4,840 EU measures the production volume responsible for the cost of conversion of $70,000 incurred in May.

The above paragraph tells us that if you want to calculate the volume *produced* in a period as opposed to the volume *processed* (i.e., *handled*) during the period, measured in EU, the formula to do so is:

$$\text{Volume of production, in EU} = \text{Total EU processed} - \text{EU in beginning inventory}$$

HELPFUL HINT

The equivalent units *processed* and the equivalent units of *production* are different concepts. The volume processed will include the EU from the previous period; it can be thought of as the units that must be handled in the current period in order to finish them. It can also be thought as the total EU to account for. But the act of finishing these units should be distinct from the activity performed in the previous period. Therefore, when measuring the production activity for the current period, we must remove the EU that represent the previous period's production activity from the total volume of units handled in the period.

Product Costing in a Process Costing Environment: The Weighted Average Cost Method

The previous section showed that the production activity in May must be measured in EU and not physical units. We computed two measures of volume for the production activity for May: the volume of EU *processed* and the volume of EU *produced*. We now turn to the task of the cost allocation. There are two approaches corresponding to the two measures of volume of production activity. The first approach to cost allocation that we will consider focuses on the total volume of EU processed. This approach is called the **weighted average cost method** (WACM). Since the volume measure chosen is the total EU processed, which includes the EU in beginning work in process, the costs to allocate must, logically, also include the costs from beginning inventory which are attached to those EUs. Therefore, the cost to allocate in the WACM is the sum of the cost in beginning inventory and the cost incurred in the period. This total is called the *costs to account for*.

The process costing steps are:

1. Measure the production activity.
2. Calculate the costs to allocate.
3. Calculate the cost per equivalent unit.
4. Apply the calculated cost per unit to completed units and to units in ending inventory, measured in EU.
5. Confirm that the costs after allocation equal the costs that were to be allocated.

Measuring Production Activity—WACM

LO4 • **Apply**

CC12: Account for the flow of production and the computation of equivalent units by preparing a quantity schedule using the weighted average cost method.

In the WACM approach, the volume of production activity is the volume of EU *processed*. The first step in the costing process is therefore to calculate the total EU processed in May for each type of input. The total EU processed for May is:

WACM EU, direct materials = EU of completed units + EU in EWIP = $4,800 + 400 \times 40\% = 4,960$ EU.
WACM EU, conversion cost = EU of completed units + EU in EWIP = $4,800 + 400 \times 25\% = 4,900$ EU.

This indicates that the total EU processed during May is in fact the WACM EU. The calculation shown earlier in Exhibit 4–6 is also illustrated in a T-account format in Exhibit 4–7.

EXHIBIT 4–7 Flow of Physical Units and Equivalent Units of Production: The Weighted Average Cost Method

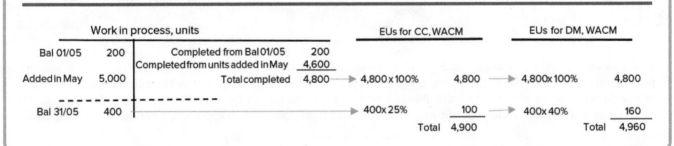

The calculation of the EU is usually presented by preparing a quantity schedule like the one in Exhibit 4–6. Using a schedule is convenient both for carrying out the computation and for presenting the information to management.

Cost per Equivalent Unit—WACM

LO4 • **Apply**

CC13: Compute the cost per equivalent unit of production using the weighted average cost method.

The next task is to determine the costs to allocate and calculate the cost per EU. The costs to allocate to the production activity of May, as measured by the total EU processed, are *the total costs to account for*. This is logically all the costs charged to the department; for direct materials, the total costs to account for are $3,000 + $74,000 = $77,000, and for the conversion cost, the total costs to account for are $1,000 + $70,000 = $71,000. The cost per equivalent unit can be now calculated.

WACM cost per EU, direct materials = Total cost charged to dept. / WACM EU = $77,000 / 4,960 = $15.52
WACM cost per EU, conversion = Total cost charged to dept. / WACM EU = $71,000 /4,900 = $14.49

The total (i.e., combined) cost per EU is $15.52 + $14.49 = $30.01. See the schedule below showing the calculation of cost per EU.

	Costs per Equivalent Unit			
	Total Cost	**Materials**	**Conversion**	**Whole Unit**
Cost to be accounted for:				
Work in process, May 1	$ 4,000	$ 3,000	$ 1,000	
Cost added in the Shaping and Milling Department	144,000	74,000	70,000	
Total cost (a)	$148,000	$77,000	$71,000	
Equivalent units processed (Exhibit 4–6) (b)		4,960	4,900	
Cost per EU, (a) ÷ (b)		$15.524 +	$14.490 =	$30.014

Remember that the costs allocated in WACM are the *total* costs (costs in BWIP plus the costs of the period) and the volume of production is measured by the EU *processed* by the department.

Cost Accounting—WACM Approach

LO4 • **Apply**

CC14: Account for the costs of production in a given period by preparing a cost reconciliation using the weighted average cost method.

With the cost per EU calculated, the cost allocation between the completed units and the EU in ending inventory can be made. This is the final step of the costing process. The cost allocation is shown below. The 4,800 completed units are transferred at a total cost of $15.52 + $14.49 = $30.01 per EU, for a value of $144,067.20. The breakdown of the total between the direct materials portion and the conversion cost portion is also shown. The cost of ending work in process is the sum of the costs of direct materials and conversion cost absorbed by the corresponding 160 and 100 EUs. The total value is $3,993.00.

| | Cost Allocation | | |
| | | Equivalent Units | |
	Total Cost	Materials	Conversion
Cost accounted for as follows:			
Transferred to next department:			
4,800 units × $30.01 per unit	$144,067	4,800	4,800
Work in process, May 31:			
Materials, at $15.524 per EU	2,484	160	
Conversion, at $14.490 per EU	1,449		100
Total work in process, May 31	3,933		
Total cost	$148,000		

The preceding presentation of the cost allocation confirms that all of the $148,000 charged to the department has been accounted for as the sum of the cost of production transferred out ($144,067) and the cost in ending inventory ($3,993). This confirmation that the costs to account for are fully accounted for is called **cost reconciliation**. This completes the costing process. If you go back and look at Exhibit 4–5, you will see that, having completed the costing process, we now know that the amount of cost transferred is $144,067 and the cost of the ending inventory is $3,933.

 HELPFUL HINT

To help you understand the logic of cost reconciliation, imagine that you have a non–interest-bearing chequing account with a balance on March 1 of $200. Also, assume that during March you earned pay cheques totalling $1,000. On March 31, you would have $1,200 to be accounted for. Each dollar of this $1,200 must be accounted for at the end of the month in one of two ways: Either it remains in your chequing account as of March 31, or it has been transferred out during the month (perhaps to your landlord, to the supermarket, or to your savings account). The ending balance in your chequing account plus the total amount of cash transferred out during the month must equal $1,200.

The same concepts apply to the cost accounting in the process costing environment. The cost of beginning work-in-process inventory plus the costs added to production during the period equals the total cost to be accounted for. The cost of ending work-in-process inventory plus the cost of units transferred out equals the total cost accounted for. The total cost to be accounted for must always equal the total cost accounted for.

The Production Report: WACM

The production report is simply a presentation of the costing procedure just described. The report combines all the previously developed schedules into a single integrated document. The production report takes the place of a job cost sheet in a process costing system. The production report will comprise:

- A quantity schedule, which shows the flow of units through the department and a computation of equivalent units.
- A schedule of computation of the costs per equivalent unit.
- A schedule showing the reconciliation of all cost flows into and out of the department during the period (this is the cost accounting previously shown in the T-account for flow of costs).

Exhibit 4–8 presents the production report for the WACM.

EXHIBIT 4–8 Production Report—Weighted Average Cost Method

DOUBLE DIAMOND SKIS

Shaping and Milling Department Production Report (weighted average cost method)

Quantity Schedule and Equivalent Units

	Physical Units		Equivalent Units Processed	
	(1)	(2)	Direct Materials	Conversion Cost
Beginning work in process, May 1	200		$200 \times 50\% =$ 100	$200 \times 30\% =$ 60
May's production activity:				
Beginning work in process		200	$200 \times 50\% =$ 100	$200 \times 70\% =$ 140
Units introduced in May	5,000			
Started and completed in May*		4,600	$4,600 \times 100\% =$ 4,600	$4,600 \times 100\% =$ 4,600
Completed units, May 31		4,800	4,800	4,800
Ending work in process, May 31		400	$400 \times 40\% =$ 160	$400 \times 25\% =$ 100
Total physical and equivalent units processed	5,200	5,200	4,960	4,900
Less EUs from May 1			100	60
EUs of May production			4,860	4,840

* Started and completed = Completed units − BWIP or Units introduced − EWIP

Costs per Equivalent Unit

	Total Cost	Materials	Conversion	Whole Unit
Cost to be accounted for:				
Work in process, May 1	$ 4,000	$ 3,000	$ 1,000	
Cost added in the Shaping and Milling Department	144,000	74,000	70,000	
Total cost (a)	$148,000	$77,000	$71,000	

	Costs per Equivalent Unit			
	Total Cost	Materials	Conversion	Whole Unit
Equivalent units of production (b)		4,960	4,900	
Cost per EU, (a) ÷ (b)		$15.524	+$14.490 =	$30.014

	Cost Reconciliation		
		Equivalent Units	
	Total Cost	Materials	Conversion
Cost accounted for as follows:			
Transferred to next department:			
4,800 units × $30.014 per unit	$144.067	4,800	4,800
Work in process, May 31:			
Materials, at $15.524 per EU	2,484	160	
Conversion, at $14.490 per EU	1,449		100
Total work in process, May 31	3,933		
Total cost	$148,000		

DECISION POINT

WRITER OF TERM PAPERS

Assume that all of your professors have assigned short papers this term. In fact, you have to submit four separate five-page papers early next month. During the month, you purchased all of the paper that you will need, began and finished two papers, and wrote the first two-and-a-half pages of the other two papers. You turned in the papers that you had finished to your instructors on the last day of the month.

If instead you had focused all your efforts into starting *and* completing papers this month, how many papers would you have written this month? After answering that question, reconfigure your answer as a computation of equivalent units of production by (1) preparing a quantity schedule and (2) computing the number of equivalent units for labour.

*Note to student: See **Guidance Answers** online.*

DECISION POINT

COST ANALYST

Assume you are a cost analyst in the Rawlings plant in Costa Rica that supplies baseballs to Major League Baseball. Your assignment is to identify the production departments in that facility. How many production reports will be needed to summarize the activity in each department?

*Note to student: See **Guidance Answers** online.*

WORKING IT OUT

CanLube Corporation manufactures lubricants for industrial applications. The company uses the weighted average cost method of process costing to compute costs; its cost accountant recorded the following information for the most recent quarter.

Beginning WIP inventory	26,000 litres (80% complete as to materials; 70% complete as to conversion costs)
Units started into production this period	307,000 litres
Units completed and transferred out	313,000 litres
Ending WIP inventory	? litres (50% complete as to materials; 60% complete as to conversion costs)
Costs in beginning inventory	$232,128 materials; $368,550 conversion
Current period costs	$3,388,702 materials; $6,193,200 conversion

Required:

Prepare a complete production report for the period using the weighted average cost method. What is the volume of EU processed in the quarter for direct materials and conversion cost and what is the production volume of EU for the quarter for direct materials and conversion cost?

SOLUTION TO WORKING IT OUT

The production report consists of the following schedules: (1) quantity schedule and equivalent units, (2) cost per equivalent unit, and (3) cost reconciliation.

Quantity Schedule and Equivalent Units

	Quantity Schedule					
	Physical Units		**Equivalent Units Processed**			
			Direct Materials		**Conversion Cost**	
	To account for	Accounted for	(EU = DOC × Physical units)		(EU = DOC × Physical units)	
			DOC*	EU	DOC*	EU
Beginning work in process	26,000		80%	20,800	70%	18,200
Production activity in the quarter:						
Beginning work in process		26,000	100 − 80% = 20%	5,200	100 − 70% = 30%	7,800
Units introduced	307,000					
Started and completed in the quarter		287,000	100%	287,000	100%	287,000
Completed units, quarter-end		313,000		313,000		313,000
Ending work in process, quarter-end		20,000	50%	10,000	60%	12,000
Total volume processed	333,000	333,000	WACM EU	323,000	WACM EU	325,000
Less EU from beginning of quarter				20,800		18,200
Quarterly production volume in EU				302,200		306,800

*DOC is degree of completion

Cost per Equivalent Unit

	Total Cost	Materials	Conversion	Whole Unit
Cost to be accounted for:				
Prior-period cost in work in process, beginning	$ 600,678	$ 232,128	$ 368,550	
Costs incurred during the month (a)	9,581,902	3,388,702	6,193,200	
Total cost	$10,182,580	$3,602,830	$6,561,750	
Equivalent units of production processed, WACM (b)		323,000	325,000	
Cost per EU (a) ÷ (b)		$11.21 +	$20.19 =	$31.40

Cost Reconciliation

		Equivalent Units (EU)	
	Total Cost	Materials	Conversion
Cost accounted for as follows:			
Transferred to next department: 313,000 units at $31.40 per unit (a)	$ 9,828,200	313,000	313,000
To partially complete units in work in process, ending			
Materials, at $11.21 per EU	112,100	10,000	
Conversion, at $20.19 per EU	242,280		12,000
Total (b)	354,380		
Total cost (a) + (b)	$10,182,580		

The quantity schedule shows that during the quarter the company *processed* 323,000 EU with respect to direct materials and 325,000 EU with respect to conversion cost. The quarterly production volume measured in EU is 302,200 for direct materials and 306,800 for conversion cost. Production volume is less than the volume processed because EU in beginning inventory from the previous quarter are also included when measuring the volume processed, whereas the production volume measures the activity performed in the quarter only. Note the slight reformatting of the quantity schedule. This was done to enable us to implement the schedule on a spreadsheet as a template.

Product Costing in a Process Costing Environment—FIFO Approach

The analysis of the production activity that was made in Exhibit 4–6 resulted in two alternative measures of production activity for May. One measure of the activity is the volume of EU processed, and the other measure is the volume of EU produced in the period. The WACM uses the volume of EU processed; we now consider an alternative costing approach which uses the volume of EU *produced* as the measure of production activity for May. This approach is called the **first-in-first-out (FIFO) method**.

Costs to Allocate: FIFO

LO5   • **Know**

CC15: Explain the concept of equivalent units of production, including the roles of the number of units started and completed in a given period and WIP inventories in the FIFO method.

In the FIFO approach, the cost accounting is about accounting for the costs of May using the production volume for May. Only the production activity of May and the costs of May are relevant. April costs and the EU from April are not relevant. These costs are attached to beginning work in process and will flow out when these units are completed. The costs to allocate will be the costs from May *only* and not the total costs to account for. In the FIFO approach, therefore, the sole concern is with accounting for the $144,000 costs incurred in May, comprising $74,000 in DM costs and $70,000 in CC costs.

Measuring the Volume of Production—FIFO

LO5   • **Apply**

CC16: Compute the equivalent units of production for each cost category using the first-in-first-out (FIFO) method.

Consider the production activity for May. Jerry wants to focus only on the activities of May since it is these activities that, logically, are responsible for the costs incurred during the month. This means that Jerry would need to measure the volume of production activity for May in terms of EU resulting from the work done in May. The WACM EU, which is the total number of EU processed, is not the correct volume measure if the intent of the accounting is to account for the costs of May only.

The volume of production for May, measured in EU was computed in the quantity schedule shown in Exhibit 4–6 according to the formula,

$$\text{FIFO EU, for an input} = \text{Total EU processed} - \text{EU in beginning inventory}$$

or

$$\text{FIFO EU, for an input} = \text{WACM EU} - \text{EU in beginning inventory.}$$

Thus,

FIFO EU, direct materials = 4,960 EU − 100 EU = 4,860 EU

FIFO EU, conversion = 4,900 EU − 60 EU = 4,840 EU

There is an alternative way to do this calculation. Think of the activities that occurred in the department during May resulting in costs being incurred. The production activity would have occurred in May and therefore costs were incurred for three reasons:

(1)   to complete the 200 physical units from April,
(2)   to make the 4,600 units that were started and fully finished in the month, and
(3)   to partially complete the 400 physical units in the ending inventory.

This is the *first-in-first-out* (FIFO) production logic. To measure the production activity correctly, we apply the concept of equivalent units of production to each of these above three types of activity.

1. The equivalent units of production to complete the 200 physical units in beginning work in process:

   Direct materials: (1 − percentage completion) × Physical units = (100% − 50%) × 200 = 100 EU.
   Conversion cost: (1 − percentage completion) × Physical units = (100% − 30%) × 200 = 140 EU.

   Note that since the 200 units are already partially complete, during May the production system will have worked to complete the work *remaining*. For direct materials, the work remaining is 100% − percentage completed = 100% − 50% = 50%. For conversion cost, the work remaining is 100% − percentage completed = 100% − 30% = 70%.

2. The equivalent units of production to start and complete 4,600 units in May:

   Direct materials: Percentage completion × Physical units = 100% × 4,600 = 4,600 EU.
   Conversion cost: Percentage completion × Physical units = 100% × 4,600 = 4,600 EU.

3. The equivalent units of production from work performed on the 400 physical units in ending work in process:

   Direct materials: Percentage completion × Physical units = 40% × 400 = 160 EU.
   Conversion cost: Percentage completion × Physical units = 25% × 400 = 100 EU.

The total production for May, measured in EU, is therefore:

FIFO Direct materials = 50% × 200 + 4,600 + 40% × 400 = 100 + 4,600 + 160 = 4,860 EU
FIFO Conversion cost = 70% × 200 + 4,600 + 25% × 400 = 140 + 4,600 + 100 = 4,840 EU

This calculation is shown in Exhibit 4–9, which reproduces Exhibit 4–6 except that the relevant amounts are found under the figures for May's activity and are set in bold face type. Only the activities of May are counted.

EXHIBIT 4–9 Flow of Physical Units and the Calculation of Equivalent Units Produced: FIFO

	Physical Units		**Equivalent Units Processed**			
	To account for (1)	Accounted for (2)	**Direct Materials** (EU = DOC × Physical units)		**Conversion Cost** (EU = DOC × Physical units)	
			DOC*	EU	DOC*	EU
Beginning work in process, May 1	200		50%	100	30%	60
May's production activity:						
Beginning work in process		200	100−50% = 50%	**100**	100 − 30% = 70%	**140**
Units introduced	5,000					
Started and completed in May		4,600	100%	**4,600**	100%	**4,600**
Completed units, May 31		4,800		4,800		4,800
Ending work in process, May 31		400	40%	**160**	25%	**100**
Total volume processed	5,200	5,200	WACM EU	4,960	WACM EU	4,900
Less EU from May 1				100		60
Production volume of EU, May			FIFO EU	**4,860**	FIFO EU	**4,840**

*DOC is *degree of completion*

To summarize, the volume of production in the month of May responsible for the incurrence of $74,000 of direct materials cost is 4,860 EU, and not the 5,200 physical units or the 4,960 EU processed during the month. And for conversion cost, the production volume responsible for the cost of $70,000 is 4,840 EU, not 5,200 physical units or the 4,900 EU that were processed.

Cost per Equivalent Unit: FIFO

Given that we know the costs to allocate and the number of FIFO EU over which to allocate the costs, the cost per EU under the FIFO approach is:

Direct materials = Current period cost / FIFO EU = $74,000 / 4,860 = $15.226 per EU
Conversion Costs = Current period cost / FIFO EU = $70,000 / 4,840 = $14.463 per EU

This is shown in the schedule below.

Cost per Equivalent Unit				
	Total Costs	Materials	Conversion	Whole Unit
Cost to be accounted for:				
Prior-period cost in work in process, May 1	$ 4,000	$ 3,000	$ 1,000	
Costs incurred during May (a)	144,000	74,000	70,000	
Total cost	$148,000	$77,000	$71,000	
Equivalent units of production (b)		4,860 EU	4,840 EU	
Cost per EU (a) ÷ (b)		$15.226	$14.463	$29.689

Cost Accounting—FIFO Approach

The final step is the presentation of the cost allocation. Using the cost per EU calculated, Jerry can determine the cost of goods transferred out and the cost of units in ending inventory. The cost accounting is shown below:

Cost Reconciliation—FIFO Approach			
		Equivalent Units	
	Total Costs	Materials	Conversion
Cost accounted for:			
Prior-period cost in work in process, May 1 (1)	$ 4,000		
Cost incurred during May:			
To complete units in work in process, May 1			
Direct material at $15.226 per EU	1,522.60	100	
Conversion at $14.463 per EU	2,024.82		140
Total (2)	3,547.42		
To bring into production and fully complete 4,600			
units during May at $29.689 per unit (3)	136,569.40		
To partially complete units in work in process, May 31:			
Direct material at $15.226 per EU	2,436.16	160	

Cost Reconciliation—FIFO Approach		Equivalent Units	
	Total Costs	Materials	Conversion
Conversion at $14.463 per EU	<u>1,446.30</u>		100
Total (4)	<u>3,882.46</u>		
Total cost	$147,999.28*		
Cost transferred out to Graphics Application Department, May 31 (1) + (2) + (3)	$ 144,116.82		

*Rounding error

In the FIFO method, costs are accounted for as follows:

1. Costs in the beginning work-in-process inventory from the previous period
2. Materials and conversion costs added to complete the units in beginning work-in-process inventory
3. Materials and conversion costs incurred to start and fully complete units in the current period
4. Materials and conversion costs added to partially complete the units in ending work-in-process inventory

Let us consider each of the above. The costs from the prior period are $4,000 (direct materials plus conversion).

During May, costs were incurred to complete beginning work-in-process inventory. For direct materials, of the $74,000 incurred in May, an amount of 100 EU @ $15.22 = $1,522.60 is allocated as the cost to complete beginning work-in-process inventory. For conversion cost, of the $70,000 incurred in May, an amount of 140 EU × $14.463 = $2,204.82 is allocated as the cost to complete beginning work-in-process inventory. Altogether the department spent $3,547.42 to complete the beginning work in process.

The department introduced 5,000 units to production in May. Of this 5,000 units, 4,600 were completed in the month. The cost of these whole units is 4,600 EU × $29.889 = $136,569.40. This is shown in the schedule. Note that this total comprises direct materials cost of 4,600 EU × $15.22 = $70,039.60, plus conversion cost of 4,600 EU × $14.463 = $66,529.80. This breakdown is not shown in the schedule.

There are 400 physical units in ending inventory. This inventory measured in EU is 160 EU for direct materials. These EU absorb 160 EU × $15.22 = $2,436.21 of the costs of May incurred for direct materials use. With respect to conversion cost, the ending inventory measured in EU is 100 EU. These EU absorb 100 EU × $14.46 = $1,446.30 of the costs incurred in May for conversion.

The sum of the costs of $4,000 and the costs of May allocated as above is $148,000, which equals the total costs charged to the department in May.

COST OF GOODS TRANSFERRED OUT—FIFO

The cost of goods transferred is calculated in one of two ways.

Cost of goods transferred (FIFO) = Total costs to account for − Cost in ending inventory

= $148,000 − $3,882.46 = $144,117   (rounded)

Alternatively,

Cost of goods transferred (FIFO) = Costs from beginning work in process

+ Cost in May to complete beginning work in process

+ Cost to start and finish units introduced in the period

This is the sum of items (1), (2) and (3) on the schedule: $4,000 + $3,547.42 + $136,569.40 = $144,117. The sum of the costs transferred and the cost in ending work in process is $148,000. Thus all the costs charged to the department are accounted for.

Jerry Madison can now report the following regarding May's production activity and the costs in the Shaping and Milling Department of Double Diamond Skis: the department was charged a total of $148,000 in May and he had to account for this total. He determines the cost of the 4,800 physical units transferred out is $144,116.82 and the cost of the 400 physical units in ending work in process inventory is $3,882.46.

Production Report—The FIFO Method

LO6 ● **Apply**

CC17: Prepare a production report using the FIFO method.

The production report is a formal document that provides management with the accounting of the costs in a processing department. It gathers the relevant schedules developed as part of the costing process into a single integrated document. A production report is prepared for each processing department. Remember that Jerry is planning to show the production report to Trivers; once she has approved the report, the plan is to prepare and present the production reports for all the departments in the production process each month.

Refer to Exhibit 4–10, which shows the production report from the FIFO method for the month of May in the Shaping and Milling Department. The report is made up of three schedules. As you read through the production report, make sure you see the parallel to the steps described in the previous section. Exhibit 4–10 presents the quantity schedule in a format that is slightly different from Exhibit 4–9. This format is an alternative way to present a quantity schedule. The total EU processed in the month is not shown in this format.

EXHIBIT 4–10 Production Report—FIFO Method

DOUBLE DIAMOND SKIS
Shaping and Milling Department—Production Report
(FIFO Method)

Quantity Schedule

(I) Units to Be Accounted For

Units to be accounted for:	
Work in process, May 1 (50% materials; 30% conversion added last month)	200
Started into production	5,000
Total units	5,200

(II) Units Accounted For and Equivalent Units (EU)

		Equivalent Units	
	Physical Units	**Materials**	**Conversion**
Units accounted for:			
Work in process, May 1 (50% materials, 70% conversion added this month)*	200	100†	140‡
Units brought into production and fully completed during May	4,600§	4,600	4,600

DOUBLE DIAMOND SKIS
Shaping and Milling Department—Production Report
(FIFO Method)

Work in process, May 31 (40% materials, 25% conversion added this month)	<u>400</u>	<u>160‖</u>	<u>100#</u>
Total units and equivalent units of production	<u><u>5,200</u></u>	<u><u>4,860</u></u>	<u><u>4,840</u></u>

*From the quantity schedule, work in process, May 1 was 50% complete with respect to materials; therefore, during May, 100% − 50% = 50% materials was added. Similarly 100% − 30% = 70% of conversion was added during May.

†50% × 200 units = 100 equivalent units

‡70% × 200 units = 140 equivalent units

§Units started − units in work in process May 31 = 5,000 − 400 = 4,600 units, or, alternatively, Units completed in May − units in work in process May 1 = 4,800 − 200 = 4,600 units

‖40% × 400 units = 160 equivalent units

#25% × 400 units = 100 equivalent units

Cost per Equivalent Unit

	Total Costs	Materials	Conversion	Whole Unit
Cost to be accounted for:				
Prior-period cost in work in process, May 1	$ 4,000	$ 3,000	$ 1,000	
Costs incurred during May (a)	<u>144,000</u>	<u>74,000</u>	<u>70,000</u>	
Total cost	<u><u>$148,000</u></u>	<u><u>$77,000</u></u>	<u><u>$71,000</u></u>	
Equivalent units of production (b)		4,860 units	4,840 units	
Cost per EU* (a) ÷ (b)		$15.226	$14.463	$29.689

*EU = Equivalent unit

Cost Reconciliation

	Total Costs	Equivalent Units	
		Materials	Conversion
Cost accounted for:			
Prior-period cost in work in process, May 1 (1)	$ 4,000		
Cost incurred during May:			
To complete units in work in process, May 1			
Direct material at $15.226 per EU	1,522.60	100	

DOUBLE DIAMOND SKIS
Shaping and Milling Department—Production Report
(FIFO Method)

Conversion at $14.463 per EU	<u>2,024.82</u>	140
Total (2)	3,547.42	
To bring into production and fully complete 4,600 units during May at $29.689 per unit (3)	136,569.40	
To partially complete units in work in process, May 31:		
Direct material at $15.226 per EU	2,436.16	160
Conversion at $14.463 per EU	1,446.30	100
Total (4)	<u>3,882.46</u>	
Total cost	$147,999.28*	
Cost transferred out to graphics application department, May 31 (1) + (2) + (3)	$ 144,116.82	

*Total does not add up to $148,000 due to rounding.

MANAGERIAL ACCOUNTING IN ACTION

WRAP-UP

Madison: Here are two examples of the kind of report I can put together for you each month. These particular reports are for the Shaping and Milling Department. Each report follows a fairly standard format for industries like ours and is called a *production report*. I hope that the information they provide is what you had in mind.

Trivers: The quantity schedule makes sense to me. I can see we had a total of 5,200 units to account for in the department for May. We completed 4,800 units and had 400 units remaining to be finished in June. I can also see from the FIFO-based report that we completed the 200 units that were in process at the beginning of May and then began processing 5,000 units from scratch in May. So, we must have started and completed 4,600 units during May. What are these "equivalent units"?

Madison: That is the problem I mentioned earlier. The 400 units still in process at the end of May, for example, are far from complete. When we compute unit costs, it wouldn't make sense to count each of these as a whole unit.

Trivers: I suppose not. Since the 400 units in process at the end of May are only 25% complete with respect to our conversion costs, we should count these as 100 units when we compute the conversion cost per unit.

Madison: That's right. I hope the rest of each of the reports is clear.

Trivers: Yes, they seem pretty clear, although I need to study each of them to decide which method I prefer. It appears that the weighted average cost method calculates the costs per unit by including the prior-period costs with the current-period costs, whereas the FIFO method only considers the current-period costs when determining the cost per unit.

Madison: You are right again! The FIFO method gives you a better idea of how the work done and the costs incurred as a result, in a period, are allocated between units in process at the beginning, units brought into production and completed, and units in process at the end of the period. But the weighted average cost method is less complicated, and depending on your specific needs it may be sufficient. The less inventory we have in our system at the end of each month, the less it will matter which method we use.

Trivers: In any event, I think I have enough information to help me understand our cost side better. I can focus my efforts on cost control knowing more about how our costs are determined. This information will also help me for planning purposes. Thanks, Jerry.

A Comparison of Costing Methods

LO7 • Know

CC18: Distinguish between the FIFO and weighted average cost methods of costing and know when the two methods will provide the same result.

This chapter has presented two methods of determining the cost of output in a processing department: the weighted average cost method and the FIFO method. Which is better? The answer, not surprisingly, is, "It depends." The table below captures the key differences between the two methods.

Weighted Average Cost Method	FIFO Method
Combines beginning work-in-process inventory (units and cost) with the current period's units and costs.	Separates beginning work-in-process inventory (units and cost) from the current period's units and costs.
Simple and less detailed.	Detail oriented and therefore more involved.
Uses a cost per equivalent unit that is an average number and is therefore not reflective of the current period's performance.	Uses a cost per equivalent unit that is specific to the current period and is therefore reflective of the current period's performance.
Not very useful to assess cost control when beginning inventory levels are substantial.	Can be used to assess cost control even when inventory levels are substantial.

Clearly, with FIFO there is more detail and more choice and discretion about how to group costs and present the information. The table below illustrates the flexibility of reporting provided by the FIFO approach. The cost is broken down by work done and then by input category. Management can ask for one or even both styles of cost breakdown and reconciliation. Such flexibility is not available in the WACM approach, which provides a more aggregated breakdown of the costs allocated.

Type of Work		DM	CC	Total
		Type of Input		
		Cost per EU = $15.23	Cost per EU = $14.46	Cost per EU = $29.73
To complete BWIP		(100 EU) $1,522.60	(140 EU) $2,024.00	$3,547.00 (a)
To start and finish		(4,600 EU) $70,039.60	(4,600 EU) $68,529.80	$136,569.40 (b)
To start EWIP		$2,436.16	$1,446.30	$3,882.46 (A)
Total for the period		$74,000	$70,000	$144,000
Cost in BWIP		$3,000	$1,000	$4,000 (c)
Total charged		$77,000	$71,000	$148,000 (B)
Transferred out (B − A) or (a + b + c)		$74,563.84	69,553.70	$144,116.82

The Logic of the WACM Calculation of Cost per EU

Before we close the chapter, we will explain what costs are being weighted in the WACM and where the name originates. Refer to the schedule below in Exhibit 4–11. You can see that the costs being averaged are the cost per EU in beginning inventory and the cost EU produced in May. This latter cost per EU is FIFO EU since FIFO is only focused on the production activity in May. Using the direct materials to illustrate the computation, you can see that there are 100 EU in opening inventory with a cost of $3,000. Thus the cost per EU from April is $30. The department produced 4,860 EU at a cost of $74,000 in May. Thus the cost per EU, considering only May's production and May's cost, is $15.23. This is of course the FIFO cost per EU for direct materials. Therefore the costs being averaged are cost per EU from April of $30 and the cost per EU from May of $15.23. The weights are April's EU of 100 as a percentage of the total EU processed in May of 4,960 and the percentage of the May EU of 4,860 calculated as a percentage of total EU processed of 4,960. The weighted average cost per EU is $15.52.

EXHIBIT 4–11 Illustrating the Calculation of the Weighted Average Cost per Equivalent Unit: Direct Materials

	Equivalent Units	Weight	Cost per EU, Direct Materials	Weighted Cost
Beginning work in process, May 1	200 × 50% = 100 EU (from April)	100EU/4,960EU = 2.02%	$3,000/100 EU = $30 per EU	$30 × 2.02% = $0.61
May production volume (FIFO EU)	4,860 EU (FIFO EU)	4,860 EU/4,960 EU = 97.98%	$74,000/4,860 EU = $15.23 per EU (FIFO)	$15.23 × 97.98% = $14.92
Total	4,960 (total volume of EU processed)	100%	($3,000 + $74,000)/(100 EU + 4,860 EU) = $15.52	$15.52 per EU, WACM

You can now see how the WACM formula works: The method calculates the total EU processed in May: 4,960 EU. In the weighted average cost method, the total cost that is allocated is the sum of the cost in BWIP of $3,000 and the cost from May of $74,000, for a total of $77,000. The WACM cost per EU is $77,000/4,960 EU = $15.52. The table shows that this WACM cost per EU is in fact a weighted average in the last column.

WACM and FIFO Method: A Summary

To summarize:

1. The WACM and FIFO method are alternative methods to allocate the costs of production to cost of goods transferred (manufactured) and ending work in process.

2. To allocate costs, a cost allocation rate—a cost per unit—is calculated. The numerator is the costs to allocate—which will differ between FIFO and WACM. The FIFO method allocates *only* the current costs. The WACM allocates the *total costs charged to the department*. The denominator will be the number of *equivalent units of production*.

3. When there are work-in-process inventories, these equivalent units will not correspond one-to-one to the physical units of the product processed in work-in-process inventory. The total EU will not equal the total physical units processed. The total EU will also differ between FIFO and WACM. With FIFO, the number of EU must relate ONLY to the current period production activity. With WACM, the EU must also include the EU already in BWIP.

4. FIFO EU and WACM EU are related as follows:

$$\text{WACM EU} = \text{FIFO EU} + \text{EU in BWIP}.$$

5. The formula for WACM EU is: Number of completed units + EU in EWIP.

6. The FIFO EU may be calculated using the formula: FIFO EU = WACM EU − EU in BWIP.

7. The FIFO method and the WACM also result in slightly different detail with regard to how the allocation is reported. Note that with the FIFO method, a considerable amount of detail is available for reporting and accounting for the costs; if management desires this information, it is available. With the WACM, the detail is hidden.

8. The choice between the methods will come down to how large the beginning inventories are, how much work remains to be completed in the current period, and the magnitude of the costs already incurred. When beginning inventories are zero or not material either in quantity (EU) or in the cost already expended, the WACM will provide results similar to FIFO and therefore can be used due to its simplicity.

IN BUSINESS

MONKS MAKE A LIVING SELLING BEER

The Trappist monks of St. Sixtus monastery in Belgium have been brewing beer since 1839. Customers must make an appointment with the monastery to buy a maximum of two 24-bottle cases per month. The scarce and highly prized beer sells for more than $15 per 11-ounce bottle.

The monks' brewing ingredients include water, malt, hops, sugar, and yeast. The sequential steps of the beer-making process include grinding and crushing the malt grain, brewing by adding water to the crushed malt; filtering to separate a liquid called wort from undissolved grain particles; boiling to sterilize the wort (including adding sugar to increase the density of the wort); fermenting by adding yeast to convert sugar into alcohol and carbon dioxide; storing and aging the beer for at least three weeks; and bottling, where more sugar and yeast are added to enable two weeks of additional fermentation in the bottle.

Unlike growth-oriented for-profit companies, the monastery has not expanded its production capacity since 1946, seeking instead to sell just enough beer to sustain the monks' modest lifestyle. However, in a rare move, the monastery in December 2012 sold its beer through gift packs in select cities in the United States and Canada. The revenue generated from this sale was used toward the cost of restoring and renovating the abbey.

Sources: John W. Miller, "Trappist Command: Thou Shalt Not Buy Too Much of Our Beer," *The Wall Street Journal*, November 29, 2007, pp. A1 and A14; Bruce Kennedy, "$85 for a 6-Pack? Beer Fans Shell Out for Rare Brew," *MSN Money*, December 14, 2012, http://money.msn.com/now/post.aspx?post=02715333-e404-477d-bc90-8786cc5a3a5d; T. Alamenciak, "Rare Belgian Beer Sells Out at LCBO in Four Minutes," *The Star.com*, December 12, 2012, http://www.thestar.com/news/gta/2012/12/12/rare_belgian_beer_sells_out_in_four_minutes.html.

CONCEPT CHECK

1. Beginning work in process includes 400 units that are 20% complete with respect to conversion and 30% complete with respect to materials. Ending work in process includes 200 units that are 40% complete with respect to conversion and 50% complete with respect to materials. If 2,000 units were started during the period, what are the equivalent units of production for the period according to the weighted average cost method?

   a. Conversion equivalent units = 2,280 units; material equivalent units = 2,100 units

   b. Conversion equivalent units = 1,980 units; material equivalent units = 2,080 units

   c. Conversion equivalent units = 2,480 units; material equivalent units = 1,980 units

   d. Conversion equivalent units = 2,280 units; material equivalent units = 2,300 units

2. Assume the same facts as above in Concept Check 1. Also, assume that $9,900 of material costs and $14,880 of conversion costs were in the beginning inventory and $180,080 of materials and $409,200 of conversion costs were added to production during the period. What is the total cost per equivalent unit using the weighted average cost method?

   a. $268.60

   b. $267.85

   c. $280.00

   d. $265.00

*Note to student: See **Guidance Answers** online.*

Learning Objectives Summary

LO1   UNDERSTAND THE DISTINCTION BETWEEN JOB-ORDER AND PROCESS COSTING SYSTEMS.

Job-order and process costing systems have both similarities and differences. Both systems have a common purpose, which is to assign materials, labour, and overhead costs in order to compute product costs. However, the flow of costs is different between the two systems. Job-order costing tracks costs by job, whereas process costing tracks costs by department. In job-order costing, the main report is a job cost sheet for each job, whereas in process costing, it is a production report for each processing department.

LO2   DESCRIBE THE COST CONCEPTS RELEVANT TO PROCESS COSTING AND THE FLOW OF COSTS THROUGH THE COSTING SYSTEM.

In process costing, direct materials and direct labour are traced to each processing department; similarly, overhead is assigned to each department using an appropriate allocation method. It is common to combine labour and overhead into a single cost category known as conversion cost. The direct materials and conversion costs are accumulated in (debited to) a work-in-process account for the department. Once the process is complete, the costs are transferred to finished goods inventory or to the next department if further processing is required. In the latter case, costs of the completed units are credited to the work-in-process account for the first department and debited to the work-in-process account for the second department.

LO3   UNDERSTAND THE CONCEPT OF EQUIVALENT UNITS OF PRODUCTION AND ITS COMPUTATION.

Partially completed units are expressed in terms of the number of equivalent units fully completed. Equivalent units are computed by multiplying the number of units by the percentage of completion at the end of the period for which the computation is required. The units completed and transferred out are always 100% complete with respect to materials and conversion. The partially completed units in work-in-process inventory are always less than 100% complete with respect to conversion; they may also be less than 100% complete with respect to direct materials. Equivalent units are computed separately for direct materials and conversion.

LO4   APPLY THE WEIGHTED AVERAGE COST METHOD TO ACCOUNT FOR THE FLOW OF PRODUCTION AND COST AND PREPARE A PRODUCTION REPORT.

The activity in a processing department is summarized in a production report consisting of three sections: (1) quantity schedule, which includes the computation of equivalent units and shows the flow of units through the department during the period; (2) cost per equivalent unit, which gives the cost per equivalent unit for direct materials and conversion; and (3) cost reconciliation, in which the costs of beginning work-in-process inventory and costs added during the period are reconciled with the costs assigned to units transferred out of the department and to the equivalent units of ending work-in-process inventory.

LO5   APPLY THE FIRST-IN-FIRST-OUT (FIFO) METHOD TO DETERMINE THE EQUIVALENT UNITS OF PRODUCTION..

Partially completed units are expressed in terms of the number of equivalent units fully completed. Equivalent units are computed by multiplying the number of units by the percentage of completion at the end of the period for which the computation is required. Under the FIFO method, we first look for units in beginning work-in-process inventory; the physical quantity is multiplied by the percentage to be completed during the current period. To this, the units started and completed during the current period are added (these are 100% completed during the current period). Finally, the physical units in ending work-in-process inventory are multiplied by the percentage of completion during the current period. Adding all three components provides the total equivalent units for the period. Note that the computation is done separately for materials and conversion.

LO6   PREPARE A PRODUCTION COST REPORT USING THE FIFO METHOD TO ACCOUNT FOR THE FLOW OF PRODUCTION AND THE PRODUCTION COST.

The activity in a processing department is summarized in a production report consisting of three sections: (1) quantity schedule, which includes the computation of equivalent units and shows the flow of units through the department during the period; (2) cost per equivalent unit, which gives the cost per equivalent unit for direct materials and conversion; and (3) cost reconciliation, in which the costs of beginning work-in-process inventory and costs added during the period are reconciled with the costs assigned to units transferred out of the department and to the equivalent units of ending work-in-process inventory. When using the FIFO method, the units transferred out are separated into (1) units from beginning work-in-process inventory completed during the current period and (2) units started and completed during the current period.

LO7   COMPARE THE WACM AND FIFO APPROACHES.

There are advantages to both the WACM and FIFO method. WACM is simpler since the beginning work in process inventories are treated as whole units since they are completed and transferred out. With FIFO, the focus is on accounting for the activities of the period, which will include the activity and cost to complete the units in beginning inventory. The FIFO method allows for more detail to be reported. Management must decide if this detail is helpful; when beginning inventory is inconsequential or does not exist, the WACM can be used with low risk of introducing errors in costing.

Application Competency Summary

APPLICATION COMPETENCY	DELIVERABLE	SOURCE DOCUMENTS AND KEY INFORMATION	STEPS	KNOWLEDGE COMPETENCY
Prepare journal entries to record the incurrence and flow of costs through a process costing system. ● **LO2–CC6**	*Key Information* Transactional information describing the incurrence of costs in a processing department *Report/Document* T-accounts analysis with appropriately journalized entries	*Materials Requisition Forms* Direct materials (DM) costs for individual departments *Labour Time Sheets* Labour hours and wage rates for individual departments *Annual Budget Documents* Quantity of overhead (OH) driver consumed and the OH allocation rate	1. Record the issuance of DM (dr. work in process [WIP] and cr. DM), the application of labour to production (dr. WIP and cr. wages payable), and the application of manufacturing OH (MOH) to production (dr. WIP and cr. MOH control).	Actual and normal costing ● **LO1–CC3 (Ch. 3)** Overhead cost driver and allocation base; overhead application rate ● **LO3–CC6 (Ch. 3)** Applied versus actual overhead ● **LO4–CC9 (Ch. 3)**
Compute the equivalent units (EU) of production for each cost category using the weighted average cost method. ● **LO3–CC11**	*Key Information* EU for each cost category as per the weighted average cost method *Report/Document* No specific document	*Inventory and Production Records* Percentage of completion information with respect to each cost category of the units in ending WIP inventory Quantity completed and transferred out of the department; number of units in ending WIP	1. EU for a cost category is the sum of the percentage completion for the cost category for the units in ending WIP multiplied by the number of units in ending WIP plus the number of units completed and transferred out from the department.	Cost categories ● **LO2–CC7** Degree of completion ● **LO3–CC9** EUs of production and the role of WIP inventories in the weighted-average method ● **LO3–CC10**
Account for the flow of production by preparing a quantity schedule using the weighted	*Key Information* The number of units in beginning WIP and the number of units brought into	*Inventory and Production Records* Number of units in beginning WIP	1. Determine the number of physical units to account for; this will be the units in beginning WIP and the units	Cost categories ● **LO2–CC7** Degree of completion ● **LO3–CC9**

APPLICATION COMPETENCY	DELIVERABLE	SOURCE DOCUMENTS AND KEY INFORMATION	STEPS	KNOWLEDGE COMPETENCY
average cost method. ● **LO4–CC12**	production during the period The number of units completed and transferred out during the period and the number of units in ending WIP The number of EUs for each cost category *Report/Document* Quantity schedule	Number of units brought into production Number of units completed and transferred out Number of units in ending WIP Percentage completion of production for each cost category	brought into production. 2. Account for the above total of physical units by determining that it equals the number of physical units completed and transferred out plus the number of physical units in ending WIP. 3. Compute the number of EUs for each category (multiply the physical units by the corresponding degree of completion for each cost category).	EUs ● **LO3–CC10, 11**
Compute the cost per EU of production using the weighted average cost method. ● **LO4–CC13**	*Key Information* Per-EU cost for each type of cost *Report/Document* Schedule of the cost per EU	*Quantity Schedule* Flow of production during the period *Cost Records* Cost of DM, labour, and MOH accumulated to perform the period's production activity Cost of DM, labour, and MOH accumulated in the previous period and assigned to units in beginning WIP	1. Compute the total DM cost (sum of DM cost in beginning WIP and DM cost added in the department during the period). 2. Combine direct labour and MOH costs to obtain the conversion cost. 3. Compute the total conversion cost. (Use the approach used for DM.) 4. Compute the cost per EU for DM and for conversion by dividing the total cost in each category by the corresponding EUs. 5. Add the cost per EU for each cost category to compute the total cost per EU.	Cost categories ● **LO2–CC7** Conversion costs ● **LO2–CC8** EUs of production ● **LO3–CC10, 11**
Account for the costs of production in a given period by preparing a cost reconciliation	*Key Information* The costs charged to the department and an accounting of these costs broken down into the portion	*Quantity Schedule* Flow of production during the period Number of units completed and transferred out	1. Determine the costs to account for. These are (a) costs in beginning WIP and (b) costs added in the department during the period.	Cost categories ● **LO2–CC7** EUs of production ● **LO3–CC10, 11**

APPLICATION COMPETENCY	DELIVERABLE	SOURCE DOCUMENTS AND KEY INFORMATION	STEPS	KNOWLEDGE COMPETENCY
using the weighted average cost method. • **LO4–CC14**	transferred out and the portion remaining in ending WIP and carried forward to the next period *Report/Document* Cost reconciliation schedule (part of a production report)	during the period and number of units in ending WIP Number of EUs for each cost category *Schedule of the Cost per EU* Cost per EU for each cost category	2. Determine the cost of the units completed and transferred out (total cost per EU multiplied by the number of units completed and transferred out). 3. Determine the cost of DM in ending WIP (DM cost per EU multiplied by the number of EUs for DM in ending WIP). 4. Determine conversion costs in ending WIP (conversion cost per EU multiplied by the number of EUs for DM in ending WIP). 5. Reconcile the costs to account for with the sum of the costs assigned to the units transferred out and the EUs in ending WIP.	Flow of production • **LO4–CC12** Cost per EU • **LO4–CC13**
Compute the EUs of production for each cost category using the first-in-first-out (FIFO) method. • **LO5–CC16**	*Key Information* EU for each cost category per the FIFO method *Report/Document* No specific document	*Inventory and Production Records* Percentage of completion information with respect to each cost category of (1) the units in beginning WIP inventory and (2) the units in ending WIP inventory Quantity completed and transferred out of the department; number of units in beginning WIP and number in ending WIP	1. Compute the units that were started and finished during the period. 2. Compute the percentage remaining to be completed of the units in beginning WIP for each cost category. 3. EU for a cost category is the sum of the percentage remaining multiplied by units in beginning WIP, the percentage completion for the cost category of the units in ending WIP multiplied by the number of units in ending WIP, and the number of units begun and finished during the period.	Cost categories • **LO2–CC7** Degree of completion • **LO3–CC9** EUs of production and the role of WIP inventories in the FIFO method • **LO5–CC15**

APPLICATION COMPETENCY	DELIVERABLE	SOURCE DOCUMENTS AND KEY INFORMATION	STEPS	KNOWLEDGE COMPETENCY
Account for the flow of production by preparing a quantity schedule using the FIFO method. ● **LO6–CC17**	*Key Information* The number of units in beginning WIP and the number of units brought into production during the period The number of units completed and transferred out during the period and the number of units in ending WIP The number of EUs for each cost category *Report/Document* Quantity schedule	*Inventory and Production Records* Number of units in beginning WIP Number of units brought into production Number of units completed and transferred out Number of units in ending WIP Percentage completion of production for each cost category	1. Determine the number of physical units to account for. This will be the physical units in beginning WIP and the physical units brought into production. 2. Account for the above total by determining that it equals the sum of (a) the number of physical units in beginning WIP, (b) the number of units started and completed during the period, and (c) the number of units in ending WIP. 3. Compute the number of EUs for each cost category (for beginning WIP, multiply the physical units by the portion remaining to be completed; for units started and completed and the ending WIP, multiply the physical units by the percentage of completion).	Cost categories ● **LO2–CC7** Degree of completion ● **LO3–CC9** EUs ● **LO5–CC15, 16**
Compute the cost per EU of production using the FIFO method. ● **LO6–CC17**	*Key Information* Per-EU cost for each type of cost *Report/Document* Schedule showing the calculation of cost per EU	*Quantity Schedule* Flow of production during the period *Cost Records* Cost of DM, labour, and MOH accumulated to perform the period's production activity Cost of DM, labour, and MOH accumulated in the previous period and assigned to units in beginning WIP	1. Determine the DM costs incurred during the period. 2. Combine direct labour and MOH costs to obtain the conversion cost. 3. Compute the total conversion cost. (Use the approach used for DM.) 4. Compute the cost per EU for DM and for conversion by dividing the cost incurred during the period in each category by the corresponding EUs.	Cost categories ● **LO2–CC7** Conversion costs ● **LO2–CC8** EUs of production ● **LO5–CC15, 16**

APPLICATION COMPETENCY	DELIVERABLE	SOURCE DOCUMENTS AND KEY INFORMATION	STEPS	KNOWLEDGE COMPETENCY
			5. Add the cost per EU for each cost category to compute the total cost per EU.	
Account for the costs of production in a given period by preparing a cost reconciliation using the FIFO method. • **LO6–CC17**	*Key Information* The costs charged to the department and an accounting of these costs broken down into the portion transferred out and the portion remaining in ending WIP and carried forward to the next period *Report/Document* Cost reconciliation schedule	*Quantity Schedule* Flow of production during the period Number of units completed and transferred out during the period and number of units in ending WIP Number of EUs for each cost category *Schedule of the Cost per EU* Cost per EU for each cost category	1. Determine the costs to account for. These are (a) costs in beginning WIP and (b) costs added in the department during the period. 2. Determine the cost of the units completed and transferred out (total cost per EU multiplied by the number of units completed and transferred out). 3. Determine the cost of DM in ending WIP (DM cost per EU multiplied by the number of EUs for DM in ending WIP). 4. Determine the conversion costs in ending WIP (conversion cost per EU multiplied by the number of EUs for DM in ending WIP). 5. Reconcile the costs to account for with the sum of the costs assigned to the units transferred out and the EUs in ending WIP.	Cost categories • **LO2–CC7** EUs of production • **LO5–CC15, 16** Flow of production • **LO6–CC17** Cost per EU • **LO6–CC17**

Review Problem: Process Cost Flows and Reports

Luxguard Home Paint Company produces exterior latex paint, which it sells in four-litre containers. The company has two processing departments—(1) Base Fab and (2) Finishing. White paint, which is used as a base for all the company's paints, is mixed from raw ingredients in the Base Fab Department. Pigments are added to the basic white paint, the pigmented paint is squirted under pressure into four-litre containers, and the containers are labelled and packed for shipping in the Finishing Department. Information relating to the company's operations for April follows:

a. Raw materials were issued for use in production: Base Fab Department, $851,000; Finishing Department, $629,000.

b. Direct labour costs were incurred: Base Fab Department, $330,000; Finishing Department, $270,000.

c. Manufacturing overhead cost was applied: Base Fab Department, $665,000; Finishing Department, $405,000.

d. The cost of basic white paint transferred from the Base Fab Department to the Finishing Department was $1,850,000.

e. Paint that had been prepared for shipping was transferred from the Finishing Department to finished goods. Its cost according to the company's cost system was $3,200,000.

Additional information:

Production data:

Units* in process, April 1: 100% complete as to materials, 60% complete as to labour and overhead	30,000
Units started into production during April	420,000
Units completed and transferred to the Finishing Department	370,000
Units in process, April 30: 50% complete as to materials, 25% complete as to labour and overhead	80,000

Cost data:

Work-in-process inventory, April 1:

Materials	$ 92,000
Labour	21,000
Overhead	37,000
Total cost	$150,000

One unit represents a four-litre container.

Required:

1. Prepare journal entries to record items (a) through (e).

2. Post the journal entries from part (1) to T-accounts. The balance in the Base Fab Department's work-in-process account on April 1 was $150,000; the balance in the Finishing Department's work-in-process account was $70,000. After posting entries to the T-accounts, find the ending balance in each department's work-in-process account.

3. Prepare a production report for the Base Fab Department for April using the weighted average cost method. Combine labour cost and manufacturing overhead cost into the conversion cost category before preparing the report. Use the format of Exhibit 4–6 to present the quantity schedule.

4. What information in the problem allows you to combine the cost of labour with that for manufacturing overhead into a single cost category?

5. Prepare a production report for the Base Fab Department for April using the FIFO method. Use two cost categories: materials and conversion costs.

6. Why is the cost per EU for WACM different from the cost per EU for FIFO?

7. Examine the quantity schedule in the FIFO production report and explain when the cost allocation using FIFO will be identical to that of WACM (or vice-versa).

SOLUTION TO REVIEW PROBLEM

1.

a.	Work in Process—Base Fab Department	851,000	
	Work in Process—Finishing Department	629,000	
	Raw Materials		1,480,000
b.	Work in Process—Base Fab Department	330,000	
	Work in Process—Finishing Department	270,000	
	Salaries and Wages Payable		600,000
c.	Work in Process—Base Fab Department	665,000	
	Work in Process—Finishing Department	405,000	
	Manufacturing Overhead		1,070,000
d.	Work in Process—Finishing Department	1,850,000	
	Work in Process—Base Fab Department		1,850,000
e.	Finished Goods	3,200,000	
	Work in Process—Finishing Department		3,200,000

2.

Raw Materials

Bal.	XXX	(a)	1,480,000

Salaries and Wages Payable

	(b)	600,000

Work in Process—Base Fab Department

Bal.	150,000	(d)	1,850,000
(a)	851,000		
(b)	330,000		
(c)	665,000		
Bal.	146,000		

Manufacturing Overhead

(Various actual costs)		(c)	1,070,000

Work in Process—Finishing Department				Finished Goods		
Bal.	70,000	(e)	3,200,000	Bal.	XXX	
(a)	629,000			(e)	3,200,000	
(b)	270,000					
(c)	405,000					
(d)	1,850,000					
Bal.	24,000					

3.

LUXGUARD HOME PAINT COMPANY
Production Report—Base Fab Department for the Month Ended April 30
(weighted average cost method)

Quantity Schedule and Equivalent Units

	Physical Units		Equivalent Units Processed			
			Direct Materials		**Conversion Cost**	
	To account for	Accounted for	(EU = DOC × Physical units)		(EU = DOC × Physical units)	
			DOC	EU	DOC	EU
Beginning work in process, April 1	30,000		100%	30,000	60%	18,000
Production activity in April:						
Beginning work in process		30,000	100 − 100% = 0%	0	100 − 60% = 40%	12,000
Units introduced	420,000					
Started and completed in April		340,000	100%	340,000	100%	340,000
Completed units, April end		370,000		370,000		370,000
Ending work in process, April end		80,000	50%	40,000	25%	20,000
Total volume processed	450,000	450,000		410,000		390,000
Less EU from beginning of April				30,000		18,000
April production volume in EU				380,000		372,000

Costs per EU	Total Cost	Materials	Labour	Overhead	Conversion	Whole Unit
Cost to be accounted for:						
Work in process, April 1	$ 150,000	$ 92,000	$ 21,000	$ 37,000	$ 58,000	
Cost added by the BaseFab						
Department	1,846,000	851,000	330,000	665,000	995,000	
Total cost (a)	$1,996,000	$943,000	$351,000	$702,000	$1,053,000	
EUs processed (b)		410,000	390,000	390,000	390,000	
Cost per EU, (a) ÷ (b)		$2.30	$0.90	$1.80	$2.70	$5.00

Cost Reconciliation	Total Cost	Equivalent Units	
		Materials	Conversion
Cost accounted for as follows:			
Transferred to Finishing Department:			
370,000 units × $5.00 each	$1,850,000	370,000	370,000
Work in process, April 30:			
Materials, at $2.30 per EU	92,000	40,000	
Conversion, at $2.70 per EU	54,000		20,000
Total work in process	146,000		
Total cost	$1,996,000		

4. The degree of completion for labour is the same as that for overhead and thus we can combine the costs of these categories into a single category called conversion cost.

5.

LUXGUARD HOME PAINT COMPANY
Base Fab Department Production Report
(FIFO method)

Quantity Schedule and Equivalent Units

	Physical Units		Equivalent Units Processed			
			Direct Materials		Conversion Cost	
	To account for	Accounted for	(EU = DOC × Physical units)		(EU = DOC × Physical units)	
			DOC	EU	DOC	EU
Beginning work in process	30,000		100%	30,000	60%	18,000
Production activity in April:						
Beginning work in process		30,000	100 − 100% = 0%	0	100 − 60% = 40%	12,000
Units introduced	420,000					
Started and completed in April*		340,000	100%	340,000	100%	340,000
Completed units, April end		370,000		370,000		370,000
Ending work in process, April end		80,000	50%	40,000	25%	20,000
Total volume processed	450,000	450,000		410,000		390,000
Less EU from beginning of April				30,000		18,000
April production volume in EU				380,000		372,000

*Units started − units in work in process April 30 = 420,000 − 80,000 = 340,000 units, or units completed in April − units in work in process April 1 = 370,000 − 30,000 = 340,000 units

Cost per EU				
	Total Cost	Materials	Conversion	Whole Unit
Cost to be accounted for:				
Prior-period cost in work in process, April 1	$ 150,000	$ 92,000	$ 58,000	
Costs incurred during April (a)	1,846,000	851,000	995,000	
Total cost	$ 1,996,000	$ 943,000	$ 1,053,000	
EUs of production, April (b)		380,000 units	372,000 units	
Cost per EU (a) ÷ (b)		$2.24	$2.675	$4.915

Cost Reconciliation		Equivalent Units	
	Total Cost	Materials	Conversion
Cost accounted for:			
Prior-period cost in work in process, April 1 (1)	$ 150,000		
Cost incurred during April to complete units in work in process, April 1			
Direct material at $2.24 per EU	0	0	
Conversion at $2.675 per EU	32,100		12,000
Total (2)		$ 32,100	
To bring into production and fully complete 340,000 units during April at $4.915 per unit (3)	$1,671,100		
To partially complete units in work in process,			
April 30:			
Direct material at $2.24 per EU	89,600	40,000	
Conversion at $2.675 per EU	53,500		20,000
Total (4)		$ 143,100	
Total cost		$1,996,300*	
Cost transferred out to Finishing Department, April 30 (1) + (2) + (3)		$1,853,200	

*Total exceeds $1,996,000 due to rounding errors.

6. The cost per EU WACM is different from cost per EU FIFO because both the amount of costs allocated and the volume of production activity over which the costs are allocated are different between the two approaches. With WACM, the focus is on total costs to account for, which includes the cost in BWIP from March, and the volume of production activity is the volume of EU processed in the month, which includes the EU from activity

in April. With FIFO, the focus is on the current period's (i.e., April's) cost and the volume of production activity performed in April.

7. The quantity schedule shows that when BWIP is zero, there is no cost from the prior period to account for and also there are no EU from the prior period. The total EU processed and the EU of production for April will be identical. The total cost to account for will be identical to the cost of the period. Then the FIFO and WACM will provide the same cost per EU.

Questions

4–1   Under what conditions would it be appropriate to use a process costing system?

4–2   In what ways are job-order costing and process costing similar?

4–3   Costs are accumulated by job in a job-order costing system. How are costs accumulated in a process costing system?

4–4   Why is cost accumulation easier under a process costing system than it is under a job-order costing system?

4–5   How many work-in-process accounts are maintained in a company using process costing?

4–6   Assume that a company has two processing departments: Mixing and Firing. Prepare a journal entry to show a transfer of partially completed units from the Mixing Department to the Firing Department.

4–7   Assume again that a company has two processing departments: Mixing and Firing. Explain what costs might be added to the Firing Department's work-in-process account during a period.

4–8   What is meant by the term *equivalent units of production* when the weighted average cost method is used?

4–9   What is a quantity schedule, and what purpose does it serve?

4–10   Under process costing, it is often suggested that a product is like a rolling snowball as it moves from department to department. Why is this an apt comparison?

4–11   Watkins Trophies Inc. produces thousands of medallions made of bronze, silver, and gold. The medallions are identical except for the materials used in their manufacture. What costing system would you advise the company to use?

The Foundational 15

connect

[LO2 – CC6; LO3 – CC11; LO4 – CC13, 14]

Clopack Company manufactures one product that goes through one processing department called Mixing. All raw materials are introduced at the start of work in the Mixing Department. The company uses the weighted average cost method to account for units and costs. Its work-in-process T-account for the Mixing Department for June follows (all forthcoming questions pertain to June):

Work in Process—Mixing Department

June 1 balance	28,000	Completed and transferred to Finished Goods	?
Materials	120,000		
Direct labour	79,500		
Overhead	97,000		
June 30 balance	?		

The June 1 work-in-process inventory consisted of 5,000 pounds with $16,000 in materials cost and $12,000 in conversion cost. The June 1 work-in-process inventory was 100% complete with respect to materials and 50% complete with respect to conversion. During June, 37,500 pounds were started into production. The June 30 work-in-process inventory consisted of 8,000 pounds that were 100% complete with respect to materials and 40% complete with respect to conversion.

Required:

4–1   Prepare the journal entries to record the raw materials used in production and the direct labour cost incurred.
4–2   Prepare the journal entry to record the overhead cost applied to production.
4–3   How many units were completed and transferred to finished goods during the period?
4–4   Compute the equivalent units of production for materials.
4–5   Compute the equivalent units of production for conversion.
4–6   What is the amount of the cost of beginning work-in-process inventory plus the cost added during the period for materials?
4–7   What is the amount of the cost of beginning work-in-process inventory plus the cost added during the period for conversion?
4–8   What is the cost per equivalent unit for materials?
4–9   What is the cost per equivalent unit for conversion?
4–10   What is the cost of ending work-in-process for materials?
4–11   What is the cost of ending work-in-process for conversion?
4–12   What is the cost of materials transferred to finished goods?
4–13   What is the amount of conversion cost transferred to finished goods?
4–14   Prepare the journal entry to record the transfer of costs from work in process to finished goods.
4–15   What is the total cost to be accounted for? What is the total cost accounted for?

Brief Exercises

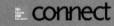

BRIEF EXERCISE 4–1
Preparing Process Costing Journal Entries [LO2 – CC8]

Quality Brick Company produces bricks in two processing departments—Moulding and Firing. Information relating to the company's operations in March follows:

a. Raw materials were issued for use in production: Moulding Department, $25,000; Firing Department, $10,000.
b. Direct labour costs were incurred: Moulding Department, $15,000; Firing Department, $10,000.
c. Manufacturing overhead was applied: Moulding Department, $29,000; Firing Department, $40,000.
d. Unfired, moulded bricks were transferred from the Moulding Department to the Firing Department. According to the company's process costing system, the cost of the unfired moulded bricks was $61,000.
e. Finished bricks were transferred from the Firing Department to the finished goods warehouse. According to the company's process costing system, the cost of the finished bricks was $110,000.
f. Finished bricks were sold to customers. According to the company's process costing system, the cost of the finished bricks sold was $107,000.

Required:

Prepare journal entries to record items (a) through (f).

BRIEF EXERCISE 4–2
Computing Equivalent Units—Weighted Average Cost Method [LO3 – CC11]

Clonex Labs, Inc. uses a process costing system. The following data are available for one department for October:

		Percentage Completed	
	Units	Materials	Conversion
Work in process, October 1	45,000	60%	70%
Work in process, October 31	20,000	50%	20%

The department started 175,000 units into production during the month and transferred 200,000 completed units to the next department.

Required:

Compute the equivalent units of production for October, assuming that the company uses the weighted average cost method of accounting for units and costs.

BRIEF EXERCISE 4–3
Preparing a Quantity Schedule—Weighted Average Cost Method [LO4 – CC12]

Hielta Oy, a Finnish company, processes wood pulp for various manufacturers of paper products. Data relating to tonnes of pulp processed during June are provided below:

		Percentage Completed	
	Tonnes of Pulp	Materials	Labour and Overhead
Work in process, June 1	20,000	90%	80%
Work in process, June 30	30,000	60%	40%
Started into processing during June	190,000	—	—

Required:

1. Compute the number of tonnes of pulp completed and transferred out during June.
2. Prepare a quantity schedule for June assuming that the company uses the weighted average cost method.

BRIEF EXERCISE 4–4
Preparing a Quantity Schedule—FIFO Method [LO6 – CC17]

Refer to the data in Brief Exercise 4–3.

Required:

Prepare a quantity schedule for June assuming that Hielta Oy uses the FIFO method.

BRIEF EXERCISE 4–5
Calculating Cost per Equivalent Unit—Weighted Average Cost Method [LO4 – CC13]

Superior Micro Products uses the weighted average cost method in its process costing system. Data for the assembly department for May are given below:

	Materials	Labour	Overhead
Work in process, May 1	$55,000	$11,000	$36,000
Cost added during May	$338,900	$80,300	$285,000
Equivalent units of production	54,450	44,380	44,380

Required:

1. Compute the cost per equivalent unit for materials, labour, and overhead.
2. Compute the total cost per equivalent whole unit.

BRIEF EXERCISE 4–6
Reconciling Costs—Weighted Average Cost Method [LO4 – CC14]

Superior Micro Products uses the weighted average cost method in its process costing system. During January, the Delta Assembly Department completed its processing of 25,000 units and transferred them to the next department. The cost of beginning inventory and the costs added during January amounted to $599,780 in total. The ending inventory in January consisted of 3,000 units, which were 80% complete with respect to materials and 60% complete with respect to labour and overhead. The costs per equivalent unit for the month were as follows:

	Materials	Labour	Overhead
Cost per equivalent unit	$12.50	$3.20	$6.40

Required:

1. Compute the total cost per equivalent unit for the month.
2. Compute the equivalent units of materials, labour, and overhead in the ending inventory for the month.
3. Prepare the cost reconciliation portion of the department's production report for January.

BRIEF EXERCISE 4–7
Calculating Cost of Units [LO7 – CC18]

In June, 4,750 units were completed and transferred out of the mixing process at Mudslide Industries Ltd. The ending work-in-process inventory was 500 units, 40% complete as to conversion costs and 50% complete as to materials costs. The month's charges were $19,800 for conversion costs and $25,000 for materials costs. There was no beginning inventory in June.

Required:

Does it matter whether the company uses FIFO or WACM to allocate costs? What is the value of the inventory at the end of June?

(Adapted © CPA Canada)

BRIEF EXERCISE 4–8
Valuing Inventory: FIFO Method [LO3 – CC10; LO5 – CC16; LO6 – CC17]

Lambda Company made an error in computing the percentage of completion of the current year's beginning work-in-process inventory. The error resulted in the assignment of a higher percentage of completion to each unit of the inventory than actually was the case. There was no ending work-in-process inventory this year-end. The company uses the FIFO cost flow method.

Required:

State and explain the effect in the current year of the error on the computation of equivalent units produced (overstated or understated) and the computation of costs per equivalent unit (overstated or understated)?

(Adapted © CPA Canada)

BRIEF EXERCISE 4–9
Calculating Cost of Units: Weighted Average Cost Method [LO4 – CC13]

Sauron Company incurred $140,000 in direct materials costs during May. Additionally, the 12,000 units in the work-in-process inventory on May 1 had a direct materials balance of $40,000 but were only 5% complete as to direct materials. No additional units were transferred into work-in-process inventory during May, and there was no work-in-process inventory at the end of May.

Required:

What is the cost per equivalent unit for materials for May, assuming Sauron uses the weighted average cost method of costing?

Exercises

connect

EXERCISE 4–1
Preparing Process Costing Journal Entries [LO2 – CC8]

Chocolaterie de Geneve, SA is located in a French-speaking canton of Switzerland. The company makes chocolate truffles that are sold in popular embossed tins. The company has two processing departments: Cooking and Moulding. In the Cooking Department, the raw ingredients for the truffles are mixed and then cooked in special candy-making vats. In the Moulding Department, the melted chocolate and other ingredients from the Cooking Department are carefully poured into moulds and decorative flourishes are applied by hand. After cooling, the truffles are packed for sale. The company uses a process costing system. The following T-accounts show the flow of costs through the two departments in April (all amounts are in Swiss francs):

Work in Process—Cooking

Bal. April 1	8,000	Transferred out	160,000
Direct materials	42,000		
Direct labour	50,000		
Overhead	75,000		

Work in Process—Moulding

Bal. April 1	4,000	Transferred out	240,000
Transferred in	160,000		
Direct labour	36,000		
Overhead	45,000		

Required:

Prepare journal entries showing the flow of costs through the two processing departments during April.

EXERCISE 4–2
Preparing Quantity Schedules and Equivalent Units—Weighted Average Cost Method
[LO3 – CC11; LO4 – CC12]

Alaskan Fisheries, Inc. processes salmon for various distributors. Two departments are involved—Department 1 and Department 2. Data relating to pounds of salmon processed in Department 1 during July are presented below:

	Pounds of Salmon	Percentage Completed*
Work in process, July 1	20,000	30%
Started into processing during July	380,000	—
Work in process, July 31	25,000	60%

*Labour and overhead only.

All materials are added at the beginning of processing in Department 1. Labour and overhead (conversion) costs are incurred uniformly throughout processing.

Required:

Prepare quantity schedules and a computation of equivalent units for July for Department 1 according to the weighted average cost method of accounting for units. Use the format of Exhibit 4–8/4–9.

EXERCISE 4–3

Preparing Quantity Schedules and Equivalent Units—FIFO Method [LO5 – CC16; LO6 – CC17)

Refer to the data in Exercise 4–2.

Required:

Prepare quantity schedules and a computation of equivalent units for July for Department 1 using the FIFO method. Use the format of Exhibit 4–8/4-9.

EXERCISE 4–4

Calculating Equivalent Units and Cost per Equivalent Unit—Weighted Average Cost Method [LO3 – CC11; LO4 – CC13)

Helox, Inc. manufactures a product that passes through two production processes. A quantity schedule for a recent month for the first process follows:

Quantity Schedule	
Units to be accounted for:	
Work in process, April 1 (60% materials, 75% conversion cost added last month)	20,000
Started into production	180,000
Total units	200,000

		EUs	
		Materials	Conversion
Units accounted for as follows:			
Transferred to the next process	190,000	?	?
Work in process, May 31 (all materials, 60% conversion cost added this month)	10,000	?	?
Total units	200,000	?	?

Costs in the beginning work-in-process inventory of the first processing department were materials, $4,000, and conversion cost, $14,200. Costs added during the month were materials, $56,000, and conversion cost, $360,360.

Required:

1. Assume that the company uses the weighted average cost method of accounting for units and costs. Determine the equivalent units for the month for the first process.
2. Compute the costs per equivalent unit for the month for the first process.

EXERCISE 4–5
Reconciling Costs—Weighted Average Cost Method [LO4 – CC14]

(*This exercise should be assigned only if Exercise 4–4 is also assigned.*) Refer to the data for Helox, Inc. in Exercise 4–4 and to the equivalent units and costs per equivalent unit you have computed there.

Required:

Complete the following cost reconciliation for the first process:

Cost Reconciliation			
	Total Cost	EUs Materials	Conversion
Cost accounted for as follows:			
Transferred to the next process: (? units × $?)	$?		
Work in process, May 31:			
Materials, at _____ per EU	?	?	
Conversion, at _____ per EU	?		?
Total work in process	?		
Total cost	$?		

EXERCISE 4–6
Preparing a Quantity Schedule, Equivalent Units, and Cost per Equivalent Unit—Weighted Average Cost Method and FIFO Method [LO3 – CC11; LO4 – CC12, 13; LO5 – CC16; LO6 – CC17]

Pureform, Inc. manufactures a product that passes through two departments. Data for a recent month for the first department follow:

	Units	Materials	Labour	Overhead
Work in process, beginning	5,000	$ 4,500	$ 1,250	$ 1,875
Units started in process	45,000			
Units transferred out	42,000			
Work in process, ending	8,000			
Cost added during the month	—	52,800	21,500	32,250

The beginning work-in-process inventory was 80% complete as to materials and 60% complete as to processing labour and overhead. The ending work-in-process inventory was 75% complete as to materials and 50% complete as to processing labour and overhead. The company combines labour and overhead to form the conversion cost category.

Required:

1. Assume that the company uses the weighted average cost method of accounting for units and costs. Prepare a quantity schedule and a computation of equivalent units for the month. Use the format of Exhibit 4–9.
2. Determine the costs per equivalent unit for the month.
3. Repeat Requirements (1) and (2) using the FIFO method. Do not prepare a new quantity schedule.

EXERCISE 4–7

Calculating Equivalent Units: Weighted Average Cost Method [LO3 – CC11; LO4 – CC13]

Iron Inc. manufactures paint in a highly automated process. Its costing system uses two cost categories: direct materials and conversion costs. Each batch of product must pass through the Mixing Department and the Testing Department. Direct materials are all added at the beginning of the production process, and conversion costs are incurred evenly throughout production. Forge uses the weighted-average method for costing.

Data for the Mixing Department for September
Work in process, beginning inventory: 500 units

Conversion costs: 30% complete

Units started during September: 1,600 units

Work in process, ending inventory: 300 units

Conversion costs: 75% complete

Costs for September
Cost of work in process, beginning, direct materials: $360,000

Conversion costs: $540,000

Costs added in September
Direct materials: $2,000,000

Conversion costs: $2,000,000

Required:

1. What is the direct materials cost per equivalent unit for September?
2. What are the equivalent units of production for conversion during September?

(Adapted © CPA Canada)

EXERCISE 4–8

Calculating Equivalent Units: FIFO Method [LO5 – CC15; LO7 – CC18]

Victor Company had 30,000 units in process on December 31, 2014, 80% complete as to materials and 40% complete as to conversion costs. The company's records show that 60,000 units were transferred to the finished goods inventory during 2015. Furthermore, 22,500 units were on hand at the end of 2015, 60% complete as to materials and 30% complete as to conversion costs.

Required:

Calculate the equivalent units of production for direct materials and conversion costs for the FIFO method from the WACM equivalent units.

(Adapted © CPA Canada)

EXERCISE 4–9
Calculating Equivalent Units and Cost per Equivalent Unit [LO5 – CC16; LO6 – CC17; LO7 – CC18]

The Mixing Department of Saiorise Ltd., a producer of fabric for Broadway shows, has the following information regarding costs and output for March:

Units:	Costs:
Opening work-in-process inventory: 0 units	Direct materials: $840,000
Started and completed: 150,000 units	Direct labour: $40,000
Started and still in process at March 31: 50,000 units	Factory overhead: $310,000
Direct materials: 100% complete	
Conversion costs: 50% complete	

Required:

1. Prepare a quantity schedule showing the computation of the equivalent units of production for March. The company is interested in learning if there will be a difference between the WACM and FIFO approaches for data for March. Comment.
2. Calculate the cost of 150,000 units transferred out in March.
3. Calculate the cost of ending inventory in March.

(Adapted © CPA Canada)

EXERCISE 4–10
Calculating Cost Flows: Weighted Average Cost Method [LO4 – CC14]

Omartian Inc. uses the weighted average cost method in its process costing system. Information for department A for July is as follows:

	Materials	Conversion
Work in process, beginning	$8,000	$6,000
Current costs added	$40,000	$32,000
Equivalent units	100,000 units	95,000 units
Costs per equivalent unit	$0.48	$0.40
Goods completed: 90,000 units		
Work in process, ending: 10,000 units		

Required:

1. Calculate the degree of completion for direct materials and conversion cost in ending inventory.

2. How would the "total costs accounted for" be distributed between units completed and transferred out, and units in ending work-in-process inventory?

(Adapted © CPA Canada)

EXERCISE 4–11

Calculating Equivalent Units: Weighted Average Cost Method [LO3 – CC11; LO4 – CC12, 13]

MacroMin Co. uses a weighted average process costing system. The following data are for the production department for December.

The December ending work-in-process inventory was 75% complete with respect to both materials and conversion costs. The department completed and transferred 60,000 units.

	Units	Materials Percentage Complete	Conversion Percentage Complete
Work in process, beginning	4,000	$ 9,000 (60%)	$ 11,000 (60%)
Units started into production	68,000		
Costs added in December		$159,000	$161,000

Required:

1. Calculate the cost of ending inventory for December.

2. Assume that the equivalent number of units processed for materials for December was 71,100. Calculate the number of units introduced and the DM cost of product in ending inventory for December (rounded to the nearest cent).

3. Calculate the number of units in ending inventory, assuming that 71,100 EUs were completed in December by the department.

(Adapted © CPA Canada)

EXERCISE 4–12

Calculating Equivalent Units: Weighted Average Cost Method and FIFO Method [LO3 – CC11; LO5 – CC16]

Last month, the Finishing Department of Rohirrim Inc. started 12,000 units into production. The department had 3,600 units in process at the beginning of the month, and these units were 50% complete with respect to conversion costs. There were 4,800 units in process at the end of the month, and these units were 40% complete with respect to conversion costs. A total of 10,800 units were completed and transferred to the next department during the month.

Required:

1. For the last month, compute the equivalent units for conversion using the weighted average cost method.

2. Using the answer to Requirement (1), calculate the equivalent units for conversion using the FIFO method.

(Adapted © CPA Canada)

EXERCISE 4–13
Calculating Cost per Equivalent Unit [LO3 – CC11; LO4 – CC12, 13; LO7 – CC18]

Saskatchewan Pulses Company makes flour from high-protein lentils. It uses a process costing system. In the month of January, the company started 12,000 units and completed and transferred out 8,000 units. There were no beginning inventories in January. January's ending inventories were 75% complete with respect to labour and overhead and 100% complete with respect to materials. The company incurred $21,200 in conversion costs and $24,000 in direct materials costs during January.

Required:

What will be the total cost per equivalent unit?

(Adapted © CPA Canada)

EXERCISE 4–14
Calculating Cost per Equivalent Unit [LO3 – CC11; LO4 – CC12; LO7 – CC18]

At the end of April, Department Z at the Tucumcare Glue Factory transferred all production to finished goods inventory. During May, the department started and fully completed 800 units. The month-end work in process (WIP) was 100% complete with respect to direct materials and 0% complete with respect to conversion costs. Manufacturing costs for May were as follows:

Direct materials	$12,000,000
Conversion	8,000,000

The cost per equivalent unit (EU) for direct materials was $10,000.

Required:

1. Using the weighted average cost method, compute the following:
   a. Units in ending work-in-process inventory at the end of May.
   b. Cost per equivalent unit for conversion costs.
2. Will the FIFO method produce a different result? Explain.

(Adapted © CPA Canada)

Problems

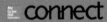

PROBLEM 4–1
Calculating Equivalent Units; Cost Reconciliation—Weighted Average Cost Method
[LO3 – CC11; LO4 – CC14]

Martin Company manufactures a single product. The company uses the weighted average cost method in its process costing system. Activity for June has just been completed. An incomplete production report for the first processing department follows:

> CHECK FIGURE
> (2) June 30 WIP: $9,020

Quantity Schedule and Equivalent Units	Quantity Schedule			
Units to be accounted for:				
Work in process, June 1 (all materials, 75% labour and overhead added last month)	16,000			
Started into production	90,000			
Total units	106,000			

		EUs		
		Materials	**Labour**	**Overhead**
Units accounted for as follows:				
Transferred to the next department	96,000	?	?	?
Work in process, June 30 (all materials, 40% labour and overhead added this month)	10,000	?	?	?
Total units	106,000	? =	? =	? =

Costs per EU

	Total Cost	Materials	Labour	Overhead	Whole Unit
Cost to be accounted for:					
Work in process, June 1	$ 14,260	$10,300	$ 1,320	$ 2,640	
Cost added by the department	117,640	58,600	19,680	39,360	
Total cost (a)	$131,900	$68,900	$21,000	$42,000	
Equivalent units (b)		?	?	?	
Cost per EU, (a) ÷ (b)		$? +	$? +	$? =	$1.28

Cost Reconciliation

	Total Cost	
Cost accounted for as follows:		
?	?	

Required:

1. Prepare a schedule showing how the equivalent units were computed for the first processing department.
2. Complete the cost reconciliation part of the production report for the first processing department.

PROBLEM 4–2
Interpreting a Production Report—Weighted Average Cost Method [LO3 – CC11; LO4 – CC12, 13, 14]

Cooperative San José of southern Sonora state in Mexico makes a unique syrup using cane sugar and local herbs. The syrup is sold in small bottles and is prized as a flavouring for drinks and desserts. The bottles are sold for $12 each. (The Mexican currency is the peso, denoted by $.) The first stage in the production process is carried out in the Mixing Department, which removes foreign matter from the raw materials and mixes the raw materials in the proper proportions in large vats. The company uses the weighted average cost method in its process costing system.

CHECK FIGURES
(1) Materials: 194,000 equivalent units
(2) Conversion: $1.412 per unit
(3) 150,000 units

A hastily prepared report for the Mixing Department for April follows:

Quantity Schedule

Units to be accounted for:	
Work in process, April 1 (60% materials, 75% conversion cost added last month)	20,000
Started into production	180,000
Total units	200,000
Units accounted for as follows:	
Transferred to the next department	170,000
Work in process, April 30 (80% materials, 90% conversion cost added this month)	30,000
Total units	200,000

Total Cost

Cost to be accounted for:	
Work in process, April 1	$ 98,000
Cost added during the month	827,000
Total cost	$925,000

Cost Reconciliation

Cost accounted for as follows:	
Transferred to the next department	$806,855
Work in process, April 30	118,145
Total cost	$925,000

Cooperative San José has just been acquired by another company, and the management of the acquiring company wants some additional information about Cooperative San José's operations.

Required:

1. What were the equivalent units for the month?

2. What were the costs per equivalent unit for the month? The beginning inventory consisted of the following costs: materials, $67,800; conversion cost, $30,200. The costs added during the month consisted of materials, $579,000; conversion cost, $248,000.

3. How many of the units transferred to the next department were started and completed during the month?

4. The manager of the Mixing Department, anxious to make a good impression on the new owners, stated, "Materials prices jumped from about $3.00 per unit in March to more than $3.50 per unit in April, but due to good cost control, I was able to hold our materials cost to less than $3.40 per unit for the month." Should this manager be rewarded for good cost control? Explain.

PROBLEM 4–3
Preparing a Production Report—Weighted Average Cost Method [LO3 – CC11; LO4 – CC12, 13, 14]

Sunspot Beverages, Ltd. of Fiji makes blended tropical fruit drinks in two stages. Fruit juices are extracted from fresh fruits and then blended in the Blending Department. The blended juices are then bottled and packed for shipping in the Bottling Department. The following information pertains to the operations of the Blending Department for June. (The currency in Fiji is the Fijian dollar [FJ$].)

CHECK FIGURE
June 30 WIP: $87,500

	A	B	C	D
1			Percentage Completed	
2		Units	Materials	Conversion
3	Work in process, beginning	20,000	100%	75%
4	Started into production	180,000		
5	Completed and transferred out	160,000		
6	Work in process, ending	40,000	100%	25%
7				
8			Materials	Conversion
9	Work in process, beginning		FJ$ 25,200	FJ$ 24,800
10	Cost added during June		334,800	238,700
11				

Required:

Prepare a production report for the Blending Department for June assuming that the company uses the weighted average cost method.

PROBLEM 4–4

Preparing a Step-by-Step Production Report—Weighted Average Cost Method and FIFO Method [LO3 – CC11; LO4 – CC12, 13, 14; LO5 – CC16; LO6 – CC17]

Builder Products, Inc. manufactures a caulking compound that goes through three processing stages prior to completion. Information on work in the first department, Cooking, is given below for May:

CHECK FIGURES
(2) Materials: $1.409 per unit
(3) May 31 WIP: $26,010

Production data:	
Units in process, May 1: 100% complete as to materials and 80% complete as to labour and overhead	15,000
Units started into production during May	110,000
Units completed and transferred out	100,000
Units in process, May 31: 60% complete as to materials and 20% complete as to labour and overhead	?
Cost data:	
Work-in-process inventory, May 1:	
Materials cost	$ 2,000
Labour cost	2,400
Overhead cost	6,000
Cost added during May:	
Materials cost	160,000
Labour cost	24,000
Overhead cost	70,000

Materials are added at several stages during the cooking process, whereas labour and overhead costs are incurred uniformly. The company uses the weighted average cost method. The company combines labour and overhead into a single cost category—conversion cost.

Required:

Prepare a production report for the Cooking Department for May. Use the following steps in preparing your report:

1. Prepare a quantity schedule and a computation of equivalent units. You may wish to follow the format of Exhibit 4–9 for the quantity schedule.
2. Compute the costs per equivalent unit for the month.
3. Using the data from Requirements (1) and (2), prepare a cost reconciliation.
4. Repeat Requirements (1) to (3) using the FIFO method. Do not redo the quantity schedule if following the format of Exhibit 4–9.

PROBLEM 4–5

Preparing a Production Report from Analysis of Work in Process— Weighted Average Cost Method [LO3 – CC11; LO4 – CC12, 13, 14]

Weston Products manufactures an industrial cleaning compound that goes through three processing departments—Grinding, Mixing, and Cooking. All raw materials are introduced at the start of work in the Grinding Department, with conversion costs being incurred evenly throughout the grinding process. The work-in-process T-account for the Grinding Department for May follows:

Work in Process—Grinding Department

Inventory, May 1 (20,000 kg, 1/3 processed)	$25,000	Completed and transferred to mixing (_?_ kg)	$?
May costs added:			
Raw materials (160,000 kg)	154,400		
Labour and overhead	285,600		
Inventory, May 31 (15,000 kg, 2/3 processed)	$?		

The May 1 work-in-process inventory consists of $16,600 in materials cost and $8,400 in labour and overhead cost. The company uses the weighted average cost method to account for units and costs.

Required:

1. Prepare a production report for the Grinding Department for the month.
2. What criticism can be made of the unit costs that you have computed on your production report?

PROBLEM 4–6

Costing Inventories; Journal Entries; Cost of Goods Sold—Weighted Average Cost Method [LO2 – CC8; LO3 – CC11; LO4 – CC12, 13, 14)

Earth Company is a manufacturer of circuit boards. The company's chief financial officer is trying to verify the accuracy of the ending work-in-process and finished goods inventories prior to closing the books for the year. You have been asked to assist in this verification. The year-end balances shown on Earth Company's books are as follows:

	Units	Costs
Work in process, December 31 (50% complete as to labour and overhead)	250,000	$ 700,000
Finished goods, December 31	150,000	1,000,000

Materials are added to production at the beginning of the manufacturing process, and overhead is applied to each product at the rate of 70% of direct labour cost. There was no finished goods inventory at the beginning of the year. A review of Earth Company's inventory and cost records has disclosed the following data, all of which are accurate:

		Costs	
	Units	Materials	Labour
Work in process, January 1 (80% complete as to labour and overhead)	100,000	$ 200,000	$ 315,000
Units started into production	900,000		
Cost added during the year:			
Materials cost		1,300,000	
Labour cost			1,985,000
Units completed during the year	750,000		

The company uses the weighted average cost method.

Required:

1. Determine the equivalent units and costs per equivalent unit for materials, labour, and overhead for the year.
2. Determine the amount of cost that should be assigned to the ending work-in-process and finished goods inventories.
3. Prepare the necessary correcting journal entry to adjust the work-in-process and finished goods inventories to the correct balances as of December 31.
4. Determine the cost of goods sold for the year assuming there is no under- or overapplied overhead.

(Adapted © CPA Canada)

 PROBLEM 4–7

Preparing Journal Entries, Production Reports—Weighted Average Cost Method and FIFO Method [LO2 – CC8; LO3 – CC11; LO4 – CC12, 13, 14; LO5 – CC15, 16; LO6 – CC17]

Lubricants, Inc. produces a special kind of grease that is widely used by race car drivers. The grease is produced in two processes: refining and blending. Raw oil products are introduced at various points in the Refining Department; labour and overhead costs are incurred evenly throughout the refining operation. The refined output is then transferred to the Blending Department.

> **CHECK FIGURE**
>
> (2) March 31 Refining Dept. WIP: $46,000

The following incomplete work-in-process account is available for the refining department for March:

Work in Process—Refining Department

March 1 inventory (20,000 litres; 100% complete as to materials; 90% complete as to labour and overhead)	$ 38,000	Completed and transferred to Blending Department (? litres)	?
March costs added:			
Raw oil materials (390,000 litres)	495,000		
Direct labour	72,000		
Overhead	181,000		
March 31 inventory (40,000 litres; 75% complete as to materials; 25% complete as to labour and overhead)	$?		

The March 1 work-in-process inventory in the Refining Department consists of the following cost elements: raw materials, $25,000; direct labour, $4,000; overhead, $9,000.

Costs incurred during March in the Blending Department were as follows: materials used, $115,000; direct labour, $18,000; overhead cost applied to production, $42,000. The company accounts for units and costs by the weighted average cost method.

Required:

1. Prepare journal entries to record the costs incurred in both the Refining Department and the Blending Department during March. Key your entries to items (a) through (g):
   a. Raw materials were issued for use in production.
   b. Direct labour costs were incurred.
   c. Manufacturing overhead costs for the entire factory were incurred, $225,000. (Credit accounts payable.)
   d. Manufacturing overhead cost was applied to production using a predetermined overhead rate.
   e. Units that were complete as to processing in the Refining Department were transferred to the Blending Department, $740,000.
   f. Units that were complete as to processing in the Blending Department were transferred to finished goods, $950,000.
   g. Completed units were sold on account, $1,500,000. The cost of goods sold was $900,000.

2. Post the journal entries from Requirement (1) to T-accounts. The following account balances existed at the beginning of March. (The beginning balance in the Refining Department's work-in-process account is given above.)

Raw Materials	$618,000
Work in Process—Blending Department	65,000
Finished Goods	20,000

After posting the entries to the T-accounts, find the ending balance in the inventory accounts and the manufacturing overhead account.

3. Prepare a production report for the Refining Department for March using the weighted average cost method. You may follow the format of Exhibit 4–9 for the quantity schedule.

4. Prepare a production report for the refining department for March, assuming that the company uses the FIFO method. Do not prepare a new quantity schedule if you have followed the format of Exhibit 4–9 for the quantity schedule.

PROBLEM 4–8
Calculating Cost per Equivalent Unit: Weighted Average Cost Method [LO4 – CC13, 14]

The following information pertains to production activities in the Refining Department of Storm Corporation. All units in work in process were costed using the weighted average cost flow assumption.

> **CHECK FIGURE**
> (2) $28,575

Refining Department	Units	Percentage of Complete Completion	Costs
WIP, November 1	18,750	80%	$ 16,500
Units started and cost incurred during November	101,250		$107,250
Units completed and transferred to the Mixing Department	75,000		
WIP, November 28	?	50%	$?

Required:

1. What were the conversion costs per equivalent unit of production last period and this period?
2. What was the conversion cost in the work-in-process inventory account at November 28?

PROBLEM 4–9
Preparing a Production Report: Weighted Average Cost Method [LO4 – CC12, 13, 14]

Callisto Company manufactures chemical additives for industrial applications. As the new cost accountant for Callisto, you have been assigned the task of completing the production cost report for the most recent period. Callisto uses the weighted average cost method of process costing. The following information pertains to the most recent period:

> **CHECK FIGURE**
> Cost per EU, Materials;
> $9.846

Beginning WIP inventory	16,000 units (75% complete as to materials; 70% complete as to conversion costs)
Units started into production this period	27,000 units
Units completed and transferred out	33,000 units
Ending WIP inventory	10,000 units (60% complete as to materials; 50% complete as to conversion costs)

| Costs in beginning inventory | $132,000 materials; $164,000 conversion costs |
| Current-period costs | $252,000 materials; $440,000 conversion costs |

Required:

Prepare a complete production report for the period using the weighted average cost method. (Round the cost per equivalent unit to three decimal places; round the costs in the cost report to the nearest dollar.)

PROBLEM 4–10
Calculating Equivalent Units and Costs: FIFO Method [LO5 – CC16; LO6 – CC17]

Below is information about Gandalf Corp., a chemical producer, for October:

CHECK FIGURE
(1)   40,000

Work in process, beginning inventory	50,000 units
Transferred in	100% complete
Direct materials	0% complete
Conversion costs	80% complete
Transferred in during October	200,000 units
Completed and transferred out during October	210,000 units
Work in process, ending inventory	? units
Transferred in	100% complete
Direct materials	0% complete
Conversion costs	40% complete

Required:

Compute the following using the FIFO method.

1. Number of units in work-in-process inventory at the end of the month.
2. Equivalent units of production for the month with respect to materials.
3. Equivalent units of production for the month with respect to conversion costs.

PROBLEM 4–11
Reconciling Costs: FIFO Cost Method [LO6 – CC17]

The BerryPhoenix BrickWorks, in Saskatoon, Saskatchewan, manufactures high-quality bricks used in residential and commercial construction. The firm is small but highly automated and typically produces about 300,000 bricks per month. A brick is created in a continuous production operation. In the initial step, the raw material, a mixture of soils and water, is forced into a mould moving along a conveyor belt. No other materials are actually required. Each brick takes about three days to complete. Approximately the last 36 hours on the conveyor belt are spent in an oven that removes moisture from the product. The belt speed is monitored and controlled by computer. The firm uses a process costing system based on actual costs in three cost pools—direct materials, direct labour, and factory overhead—to assign production costs to output. Here are cost and production data for May:

Beginning work-in-process inventory	25,000 bricks
100% complete as to direct materials	
60% complete as to direct labour	
36% complete as to factory overhead	
Started this period	305,000 bricks
Ending work-in-process inventory	30,000 bricks
100% complete as to direct materials	
50% complete as to direct labour	
40% complete as to factory overhead	

	Costs		
	Materials	Direct Labour	Overhead
Beginning inventory	$ 1,330	$ 835	$ 552
Costs added in May	16,200	15,000	18,180

Required:

Determine the cost of bricks transferred to finished goods inventory and the cost of bricks in ending work-in-process inventory for May. Assume the company uses the FIFO method of process costing.

Building Your Skills

COMPREHENSIVE PROBLEM [LO2 – CC8; LO3 – CC11; LO4 – CC12, 13, 14; LO5 – CC16; LO6 – CC17]

Hilox, Inc. produces an antacid product that goes through two departments—Cooking and Bottling. The company has recently hired a new assistant accountant, who has prepared the following summary of production and costs for the Cooking Department for March using the weighted average cost method:

Cooking Department costs:	
Work-in-process inventory, March 1: 70,000 litres,	
60% complete as to materials and 30% complete as to labour and overhead	$ 61,000*
Materials added during March	570,000
Labour added during March	100,000
Overhead applied during March	235,000
Total departmental costs	$966,000
Cooking Department costs assigned to:	
Litres completed and transferred to the bottling department: 400,000 litres at ? per litre	$?
Work-in-process inventory, May 31: 50,000 litres, 70% complete as to materials and 40% complete as to labour and overhead	?
Total departmental costs assigned	$?

*Consists of materials, $39,000; labour, $5,000; and overhead, $17,000.

The new assistant accountant has determined the cost per litre transferred to be $2.415, as follows:

$$\frac{\text{Total departmental costs, } \$966,000}{\text{Litres completed and transferred, } 400,000} = \$2.415 \text{ per litre}$$

However, the assistant accountant is unsure how to use this unit-cost figure in assigning cost to the ending work-in-process inventory. In addition, the company's general ledger shows only $900,000 in cost transferred from the Cooking Department to the Bottling Department, which does not agree with the $966,000 figure above.

The general ledger also shows the following costs incurred in the Bottling Department during March: materials used, $130,000; direct labour cost incurred, $80,000; and overhead cost applied to products, $158,000.

Required:

1. Prepare journal entries as follows to record activity in the company during March. Key your entries to the letters (a) through (g):
   a. Raw materials were issued to the two departments for use in production.
   b. Direct labour costs were incurred in the two departments.

c. Manufacturing overhead costs were incurred, $400,000. (Credit accounts payable.) The company maintains a single manufacturing overhead account for the entire plant.

d. Manufacturing overhead cost was applied to production in each department using predetermined overhead rates.

e. Units completed as to processing in the Cooking Department were transferred to the bottling department, $900,000.

f. Units completed as to processing in the Bottling Department were transferred to finished goods, $1,300,000.

g. Units were sold on account, $2,000,000. The cost of goods sold was $1,250,000.

2. Post the journal entries from Requirement (1) to T-accounts. Balances in selected accounts on March 1 are as follows:

Raw Materials	$710,000
Work in Process—Bottling Department	85,000
Finished Goods	45,000

After posting the entries to the T-accounts, find the ending balance in the inventory accounts and the manufacturing overhead account.

3. Prepare a production report for the Cooking Department for March using the weighted average cost method.

4. Prepare a production report for the Cooking Department for March using the FIFO method.

THINKING ANALYTICALLY [LO3 – CC11; LO4 – CC12, 13, 14]

"I think we goofed when we hired that new assistant controller," said Ruth Scarpino, president of Provost Industries. "Just look at this production report that he prepared for last month for the Finishing Department. I can't make any sense of it."

Finishing Department costs:	
Work-in-process inventory, March 1, 450 units; 100% complete as to materials; 60% complete as to conversion costs	$ 8,208*
Costs transferred in during the month from the preceding department, 1,950 units	17,940
Materials cost added during the month (materials are added when processing is 50% complete in the Finishing Department)	6,210
Conversion costs incurred during the month	13,920
Total departmental costs	$46,278
Finishing Department costs assigned to:	
Units completed and transferred to finished goods, 1,800 units at $25.71 per unit	$46,278

Work-in-process inventory, March 31, 600 units; 0% complete as to materials; 35% complete as to processing	$ –0–
Total departmental costs assigned	$46,278

*Consists of cost transferred in, $4,068; materials cost, $1,980; and conversion cost, $2,160.

"He's struggling to learn our system," replied Frank Harrop, the operations manager. "The problem is that he's been away from process costing for a long time, and it's coming back slowly."

"It's not just the format of his report I'm concerned about. Look at that $25.71 unit cost he's come up with for April. Doesn't that seem high to you?" said Scarpino.

"Yes, it does; but on the other hand, I know we had an increase in materials prices during April, and that may be the explanation," replied Harrop. "I'll get someone to redo this report and then we may be able to see what's going on."

Provost Industries manufactures a ceramic product that goes through two processing departments—Moulding and Finishing. The company uses the weighted average cost method to account for units and costs.

Required:

1. Prepare a revised production report for the Finishing Department.
   (*Hint:* Include transferred-in costs as a separate cost category and let the percentage of completion for this category be 100%. Why?)
2. Explain to the president why the unit cost on the new assistant controller's report is so high.

COMMUNICATING IN PRACTICE [LO2 – CC8; LO4 – CC14]

Assume you are the cost analyst who prepared the production report that appears in Exhibit 4–8. You receive a call from Minesh Patel, a new hire in the company's Accounting Department, who is not sure about what needs to be done with the cost reconciliation portion of the report. He wants to know what journal entries should be prepared and what balances need to be checked in the company's accounts.

Required:

Write a memorandum to Patel that explains the steps that should be taken. Refer to specific amounts on the cost reconciliation portion of the production report to ensure that he properly completes the steps.

ETHICS CHALLENGE [LO3 – CC9; LO4 – CC14]

Gary Stevens and Mary James are production managers in the Consumer Electronics Division of General Electronics Company, which has several dozen plants scattered in locations throughout the world. James manages the plant located in Hamilton, Ontario, while Stevens manages the plant in El Segundo, California. Production managers are paid a salary and get an additional bonus equal to 5% of their base salary if the entire division meets or exceeds its target profits for the year. The bonus is determined in March after the company's annual report has been prepared and issued to shareholders.

Shortly after the beginning of the new year, James received a phone call from Stevens that went like this:

Stevens: How's it going, Mary?

James: Fine, Gary. How's it going with you?

Stevens: Great! I just got the preliminary profit figures for the division for last year and we are within $200,000 of making the year's target profits. All we have to do is to pull a few strings, and we'll be over the top!

James: What do you mean?

Stevens: Well, one thing that would be easy to change is your estimate of the percentage completion of your ending work-in-process inventories.

James: I don't know if I can do that, Gary. Those percentage completion figures are supplied by Tom Winthrop, my lead supervisor, whom I have always trusted to provide us with good estimates. Besides, I have already sent the percentage completion figures to corporate headquarters.

Stevens: You can always tell them there was a mistake. Think about it, Mary. All of us managers are doing as much as we can to pull this bonus out of the hat. You may not want the bonus cheque, but the rest of us sure could use it.

The final processing department in James's production facility began the year with no work-in-process inventories. During the year, 210,000 units were transferred in from the prior processing department and 200,000 units were completed and sold. Costs transferred in from the prior department totalled $39,375,000. No materials are added in the final processing department. A total of $20,807,500 of conversion cost was incurred in the final processing department during the year.

Required:

1. Tom Winthrop estimated that the units in ending inventory in the final processing department were 30% complete with respect to the conversion costs of the final processing department. If this estimate of the percentage completion were used, what would be the cost of goods sold for the year?
2. Does Gary Stevens want the estimated percentage completion to be increased or decreased? Explain why.
3. What percentage completion would result in increasing reported net income by $200,000 over the net income that would be reported if the 30% figure were used?
4. Do you think Mary James should go along with the request to alter estimates of the percentage completion?

TEAMWORK IN ACTION [LO3 – CC11; LO4 – CC12, 13, 14]

The production report includes a quantity schedule, the computation of equivalent costs and costs per equivalent units, and a cost reconciliation.

Required:

1. *Learning teams* of three (or more) members should be formed. Each team member must select one of the following sections of the production report (as illustrated in Exhibit 4–7) as an area of expertise (each team must have at least one expert in each section).
   a. Quantity schedule and equivalent units.
   b. Costs per equivalent unit.
   c. Cost reconciliation.
2. *Expert teams* should be formed from the individuals who have selected the same area of expertise. Expert teams should discuss and write a brief summary that each expert will present to his or her learning team that addresses the following:
   a. The purpose of the section of the production report.
   b. The manner in which the amounts appearing in this section of the report are determined.
3. Each expert should return to his or her learning team. In rotation, each member should present his or her expert team's report to the learning team.

Endnotes

1. The quantity started and finished can be easily calculated using the T-account of the product flows. From the debit side: Quantity started and finished = the number of units started minus the units in ending inventory. Thus, 4,600 = 5,000 − 400. Alternatively, from the credit side of the T-account: Quantity started and finished = number of units completed minus the units in beginning inventory. Thus, 4,600 = 4,800 − 200.

5

Activity-Based Costing

LEARNING OBJECTIVES AND CHAPTER COMPETENCIES

After studying Chapter 5, you should be able to demonstrate the following competencies:

COMPETENCY		Know	Apply
LO1	**EXPLAIN THE BASICS OF ACTIVITY-BASED COSTING.**		
CC1	Outline the limitations of plantwide and departmental overhead allocation.	●	
CC2	Describe the basic approach underlying activity-based costing.	●	
LO2	**APPLY ACTIVITY-BASED COSTING.**		
CC3	Design an activity-based costing system.		●
CC4	Describe the hierarchical classification of activities.	●	
CC5	Distinguish between unit-, batch-, product-, and facility-level activities.	●	
CC6	Compute activity rates used to allocate costs to cost objects.		●
CC7	Assign activity costs to cost objects, and compute unit costs.		●
CC8	Describe the use of activity-based costing in nonmanufacturing organizations.	●	
LO3	**UNDERSTAND THE BENEFITS AND LIMITATIONS OF ACTIVITY-BASED COSTING.**		
CC9	Explain the benefits and limitations of activity-based costing.	●	
LO4	**EXPLAIN COST FLOWS IN AN ACTIVITY-BASED COSTING SYSTEM.**		
CC10[A]	Describe the flow of costs in an activity-based costing system.	●	
CC11[A]	Record the flow of costs in an activity-based costing system.		●
LO5	**UNDERSTAND QUALITY COSTS.**		
CC12[B]	Identify the four types of quality costs.	●	
CC13[B]	Explain how the different quality costs interact.	●	
CC14[B]	Prepare a cost of quality report.		●

Note: The superscripts "A" and "B" refer to Appendix 5A and Appendix 5B, respectively; both appendices are available on Connect.

ON THE JOB

UNDERSTANDING COSTS USING CUTTING-EDGE TOOLS

Understanding costs is fundamental to better planning and decision making, as realized by Quebec-based RONA Inc. Founded in 1939, RONA is the largest Canadian distributor and retailer of hardware, home renovation, and gardening products. In 2012, it operated a network of over 800 stores and distribution centres, and generated $4.9 billion in consolidated sales and just under $126 million in operating profit (excluding unusual and nonrecurring items).

In recent years, the company has placed significant emphasis on profitability, efficiency, and productivity. But the focus on efficiency is not totally new. A secret of RONA's success is its efficient and effective handling of supply chain management—distribution and purchasing activities. However, to operate efficiently, managers needed a better understanding of costs. Using an average costing system to allocate costs and determine the cost per supplier provided little information. Managers knew that something was wrong; costs could not be uniform across products and suppliers. Therefore, the company turned to activity-based management (ABM) for help. ABM includes activity-based costing (ABC), which is the topic of this chapter. ABM (and ABC) are founded on the philosophy that "Doing something—an activity—is the reason for costs to

Royalty-free/CORBIS

exist." An activity focus helps organizations better manage activities and thereby understand why costs occur and the factors that affect the costs. Implementing the ABM system allowed managers to obtain details on the costs that were previously not available.

Sources: R. Colman and J. Demers, "Route-to-Market Knowledge Builders," *CMA Management,* February 2004, pp. 14–15; RONA, Inc. Annual Reports 2003, 2009, and 2012, http://www.rona.ca/corporate/document-center.

Critical thinking question *What features of an activity-based costing system allow managers to "obtain details on the costs that were previously not available"?*

Note to student: See **Guidance Answers** *online.*

◀◀ A Look Back	▶ A Look at This Chapter	▶▶ A Look Ahead
The previous two chapters introduced two contrasting systems: job-order costing and process costing. The approach to	Chapter 5 continues the discussion of overhead cost allocation by introducing the concept of activity-based costing,	The next chapter deals with the behaviour of costs. This topic is the foundation for understanding

◀◀ A Look Back	▶ A Look at This Chapter	▶▶ A Look Ahead
overhead allocation in both systems was to use a single plantwide overhead rate.	a technique that uses a number of allocation bases to assign overhead costs to cost objects.	how costs figure into making decisions that improve profitability.

C onsider the costs of making a product. The cost of direct materials and direct labour costs can easily be traced to the desired cost object (e.g., product, job, or process). Overhead costs, in contrast, cannot be traced to cost objects and must be allocated to the cost object. Chapter 3 introduced the concept of overhead allocation using direct labour as an allocation base. The accuracy of the allocation depends on how well consumption of labour by the production activity tracks the incurrence of the overhead costs. If the incurrence of overhead is unrelated to the consumption of direct labour, the allocation of overhead to the cost object using labour as the allocation base will contain significant errors. You should realize the choice of *any* allocation base will introduce some errors since the correlation between the overhead cost incurrence and the use of the allocation base will be less than perfect (otherwise there is no need for allocation; all costs are directly traceable!). Overhead cost allocation is a fundamental challenge in product costing. This chapter further elaborates on the concept and process of cost allocation. It introduces activity-based costing (ABC) as an alternative approach to cost allocation that aims to improve the accuracy of the cost allocation and provide reliable estimates of product costs.

MANAGERIAL ACCOUNTING IN ACTION

THE ISSUE

Comtek Sound, Inc. makes two products: a Blu-ray disc player and a radio with a built-in DVD player. Both of these products are sold to automobile manufacturers for installation in new vehicles. The president of the company, Sarah Kastler, recently returned from a management conference at which activity-based costing was discussed. Following the conference, she called a meeting of the top managers in the company to share what she had learned. Attending the meeting were production manager Frank Hines, marketing manager Nicole Sermone, and accounting manager Tom Frazier.

comtek
SOUND, INC.

Kastler: I learned some things at the conference I just attended that may help resolve some long-standing puzzles here at Comtek Sound.

Sermone: Did they tell you why we've been losing all those bids lately on our bread-and-butter DVD player and winning every bid on our specialty Blu-ray disc player?

Kastler: Nicole, you probably weren't expecting this answer, but yes, there may be a simple explanation. We may have been shooting ourselves in the foot.

Sermone: How so? I don't know about anyone else, but we have been hustling like crazy to get more business for the company.

Kastler: Nicole, when you talk with our customers, what reasons do they give for taking their DVD player business to our competitors? Is it a problem with quality or on-time delivery?

Sermone: No, our customers readily admit that we're among the best in the business.

Kastler: Then what's the problem?

Sermone: Price. The competition is undercutting our price on the DVD player and then bidding high on the Blu-ray disc player. As a result, they're stealing our high-volume DVD business and leaving us with just the low-volume Blu-ray business.

Kastler: Why is our price so high for the DVD players that the competition is able to undercut us?

Sermone: Our price isn't too high. Theirs is too low. Our competitors must be pricing below their costs on the DVD player.

Kastler: Why do you think that?

Sermone: Well, if we charged the prices for our DVD player that our competitors are quoting, we'd be pricing below *our* cost, and I know we're just as efficient as any competitor.

Hines: Nicole, why would our competitors price below their cost?

Sermone: They're out to grab market share.

Hines: Does that make any sense? What good does more market share do them if they're pricing below their cost?

Kastler: I think Frank has a point. Tom, you're the expert with the numbers. Can you suggest another explanation?

Frazier: I was hoping you'd ask that. Those product cost figures my department reports to you are primarily intended to be used to value inventories and determine cost of goods sold for our external financial statements. I am awfully uncomfortable about using them for bidding. In fact, I have mentioned this several times, but no one was interested.

Kastler: Now I'm interested. Tom, are you telling us that the product cost figures we have been using for bidding may be wrong? Are you suggesting that we really don't know what the manufacturing cost is for either the DVD player or the Blu-ray disc player?

Frazier: Yes, that could be the problem. Our cost system isn't designed to generate accurate costs for decision-making purposes. It fails to recognize that our two products make different demands on our resources, especially overhead. The DVD player is simple to manufacture, and the Blu-ray disc player is more complex. We need a cost system that recognizes this difference in demand on resources.

Kastler: That's exactly the point made at the conference. The conference speakers suggested we recost our products using something called activity-based costing. Tom, can we do this?

Frazier: You bet! But we need to do it as a team. Can each person in the room appoint one of their top people to work with me?

Kastler: Let's do it! I'd like the special activity-based costing team to report back to this group as soon as possible. If there's a problem with our costs, we need to know it before the competition plows us under.

Assigning Overhead Costs to Cost Objects

We introduced the concept of overhead in Chapter 2 and overhead allocation in Chapter 3. We mentioned that overhead includes all those costs that cannot be traced directly to individual cost objects, such as the DVD player and the Blu-ray disc player in the case of Comtek, whose costs we are interested in computing (we will do the cost calculations later in this chapter). What we did not elaborate much is that overhead can consist of many different cost items. Should we accumulate all the cost items in one large cost bucket (or cost pool), or should we capture the cost of each item separately? Exhibit 5–1 illustrates this idea of accumulating costs in one or more cost pools.

Once we accumulate the overhead costs in cost pools, we can begin to think about allocating them to desired cost objects. This section describes three different methods of overhead cost allocation (the focus of this chapter is on the third method). The discussion of overhead allocation is largely couched within a manufacturing context, although the principles can be applied to nonmanufacturing settings, as we will see later in this chapter.

EXHIBIT 5–1 Accumulation of Overhead Costs

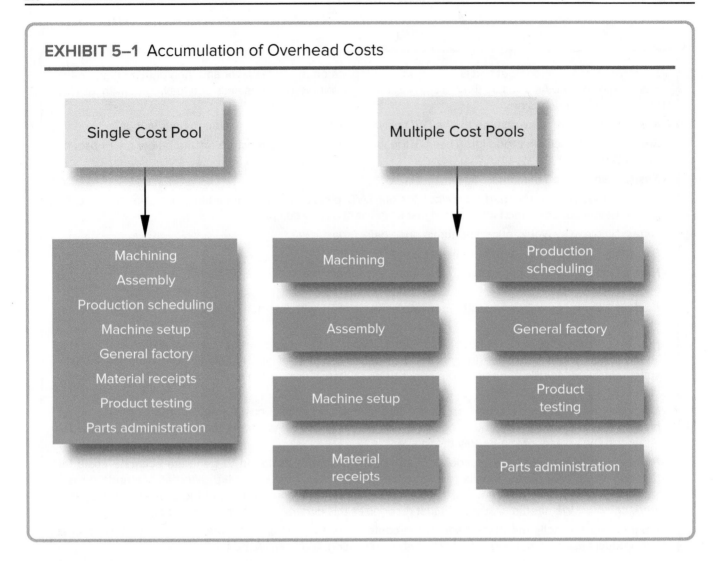

Plantwide Overhead Rate

LO1   • **Know**

CC1: Outline the limitations of plantwide and departmental overhead allocation.

The simplest method of assigning overhead involves using a single allocation base and rate, known as a *plantwide overhead rate*. This method is based on the convenience it offers in that the cost accounting system must capture only two pieces of information: total overhead costs (accumulated in a single cost pool), and the volume of the allocation base (such as total direct labour-hours). As suggested in Chapter 3, direct labour-hours were widely used largely because direct labour was a significant component of the total conversion costs (i.e., labour and overhead) and the designers of cost accounting systems believed that direct labour influenced overhead costs. Moreover, direct labour-hours were always meticulously recorded, which means that the information was readily available.

Conceptually, the use of a plantwide rate assumes the following: (1) all overhead costs in the organization are *driven* (or caused) by the single allocation base used, and (2) cost objects (e.g., products) consume overhead resources in the same proportion in which they consume the allocation base. Both assumptions are weak; therefore, using a single plantwide overhead rate has serious limitations, which can lead to cost distortions. A manager using distorted cost information can make flawed decisions that may have serious implications for the future of the organization.

Departmental Overhead Rate

As a first step to improving the allocation method, many companies use multiple cost pools (as shown in Exhibit 5–1) and multiple overhead rates along *departmental* lines. Each cost pool captures the overhead costs incurred by a specific department. As an example, consider a manufacturing company with three departments: machining, assembly, and maintenance. Overhead costs *within* each department are accumulated in a single *overhead cost pool;* thus, there will be three overhead cost pools in our example. An appropriate allocation base for each pool must then be identified and a predetermined overhead rate computed for each of the three pools. The allocation bases typically depend upon the nature of the work performed in each department. For example, machine-hours may be used to assign overhead incurred by the machining department, assembly labour-hours to allocate the assembly department's overhead costs, and maintenance-hours to allocate the maintenance department's overhead costs.

Unfortunately, even departmental overhead allocation makes the same assumptions made in the case of plantwide overhead allocation (but at a departmental rather than a plantwide level). These assumptions may not hold true in situations in which a company offers a diverse range of products and has a complex set of overhead costs. As a result, this method of overhead allocation can also lead to product cost distortions.

Activity-Based Costing

A serious limitation in the case of both plantwide and departmental overhead allocation is the failure by both methods to recognize two facts: (1) the total overhead cost pool in an organization is an accumulation of the costs of numerous resources that are consumed by the organization to serve its customers, and (2) the individual overhead costs may be *driven* by different factors. While some overhead costs may be caused by the level of production or service volume, others may be caused by the number of transactions processed, and still others may be caused by other drivers. Moreover, the two previous methods also fail to recognize that different cost objects (i.e., products, services, and customers) may consume the different overhead resources in varying proportions.

For example, consider two customers of a large organization—both customers may consume the same amount of resources with respect to order processing, but there may be significant differences between the two customers in terms of the consumption of resources relating to after-sales service. A simple (usually referred to as *conventional* or *traditional*) cost allocation system using a single allocation base (and rate) will not be able to capture these differences in the resource consumption patterns of the two customers. A good cost allocation system must recognize these differences and must consider them when assigning costs.

Also, as explained in Chapter 1, the business environment has changed considerably over the past 30 years. In adopting the lean business model, many organizations have automated their operations to a significant extent. As a result, overhead has increased and direct labour has decreased. Therefore, direct labour is no longer a good predictor of overhead. Moreover, increased competition has resulted in organizations offering a diverse range of products and services to their customers. Diverse products and services generally consume overhead resources in different proportions; this diversity cannot be fully captured by traditional costing systems.

HELPFUL HINT

Conventional cost systems that use plantwide or departmental overhead rates suffer from an important limitation: they tend to assign too much overhead to high-volume products and too little overhead to low-volume products. This distortion occurs because conventional cost systems rely exclusively on allocation bases, such as direct labour-hours and machine-hours, that are highly correlated with (or move in tandem with) the volume of production. You will notice a recurring theme throughout this chapter—activity-based costing systems usually reveal that low-volume products cost more and high-volume products cost less than reported by conventional cost systems.

LO1   • **Know**

CC2: Describe the basic approach underlying activity-based costing.

Activity-based costing (ABC) is a method of cost allocation that attempts to assign overhead costs to cost objects more accurately than the methods discussed so far. The basic idea underlying ABC is as follows: a customer order for a product or a service triggers a number of activities, a number of different types of resources are required to carry out these activities, and resources cost money. If the Hudson's Bay Company orders a line of women's dresses from Calvin Klein, a production order is generated, materials are ordered, patterns are created, textiles are cut to pattern and then sewn, and the finished dresses are packed for shipping. Each of these activities consumes resources. For example, designing patterns consumes the designer's time, a resource the company has to pay for. In activity-based costing, an attempt is made to trace these costs directly to the activities that cause them. The activities are believed to drive the costs; therefore, they are called **cost drivers**. This series of relationships is illustrated in Exhibit 5–2.

EXHIBIT 5–2 The Activity-Based Costing Model

Cost Objects

Customer Orders Require:

Activities

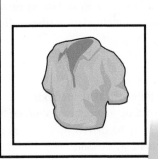   

Scheduling   Sewing   Inspection   Shipping

Activities Consume:

Resources

 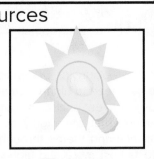  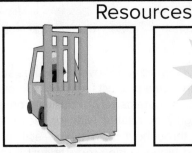

Labour   Equipment   Energy   Supplies

Resources Cost Money.

Switching to an ABC system will require a company to use a number of allocation bases to assign costs to cost objects. Each allocation base in an ABC system represents a major *activity* that causes overhead costs. An **activity** is a task (or a series of tasks) carried out to fulfill the organization's purpose. Exhibit 5–3 gives examples of activities.

EXHIBIT 5–3 Examples of Activities

CUSTOMER SERVICE COST POOL

Receiving customer orders

Handling customer complaints

Billing customers

MANUFACTURING COST

Machining

Assembly

Production scheduling

Product testing

ACCOUNTING COST POOL

Processing payroll

Processing a credit application

Preparing performance reports

Processing accounts payable or accounts receivable

Activity-based costing is centred on these activities. Each major activity has its own overhead cost pool (also known as an *activity cost pool*), its own *activity measure,* and its own predetermined overhead rate (also known as an *activity rate*). An **activity cost pool** is a *cost bucket* in which costs related to a particular activity are accumulated. The **activity measure** expresses how much of the activity is carried out (i.e., activity volume) and is used as the allocation base for applying overhead costs to products and services. For example, *the number of customer complaints* is a natural choice of an activity measure for the activity *handling customer complaints.* An **activity rate** is a predetermined overhead rate in an ABC system, as is illustrated in Exhibit 5–4. Each activity has its own activity rate that is used to apply overhead costs.

For example, the activity *maintenance* would have its own activity cost pool. If the total cost in this activity cost pool is $150,000 and the total expected activity is 1,000 maintenance-hours, the predetermined overhead rate (i.e., activity rate) for this activity will be $150 per maintenance-hour ($150,000 ÷ 1,000 maintenance-hours = $150 per maintenance-hour). Note that this amount does not depend on how many jobs are completed or how many units are produced during a month. A small job requiring maintenance would be charged $150 per maintenance-hour—just the same as a large job.

Taking each activity in isolation, this system works exactly like it does in the job-order costing system described in Chapter 3. A predetermined overhead rate is computed for each activity and then applied to cost objects based on the volume of activity consumed by that cost object. The ABC system can be used by organizations with a job-order costing system or a process costing system. In job-order costing, the desired cost object is a specific job, whereas in a process-costing system, it is a process (or a department).

EXHIBIT 5–4 Activity Rate

$$\text{Predetermined activity rate} = \frac{\text{Estimated activity costs}}{\text{Estimated activity volume}}$$

Designing an Activity-Based Costing System

LO2   • **Apply**

CC3: Design an activity-based costing system.

We illustrate the design of an activity-based costing system using the example of Comtek Sound, Inc. (see the Managerial Accounting in Action box at the beginning of this chapter). Designing an ABC system includes at least the following seven steps:

1. Identify activities and create an activity dictionary.
2. Create activity cost pools.
3. Identify the resources consumed by individual activity cost pools.
4. Identify the activity measure for each activity cost pool.
5. Estimate the total activity volume for each measure.
6. Compute a predetermined activity rate for each activity cost pool.
7. Allocate activity costs to desired cost objects.

Step 1: Identify Activities and Create an Activity Dictionary

In most companies, hundreds or even thousands of different activities cause overhead costs. Examples are taking a telephone order, filling out an invoice, training new employees, applying lubricant to machines, etc. Designing and maintaining a complex costing system that includes every activity would be prohibitively expensive.

The challenge in designing an activity-based costing system is to identify a manageable number of activities that explain the bulk of the variation in overhead costs. This is usually done by interviewing a broad range of managers in the organization to identify the activities they think are important and consume most of the resources they manage. This often results in a long list of potential activities that might be included in the ABC system. This list is refined and pruned in consultation with top managers; related activities are combined to reduce the amount of detail and recordkeeping costs. For example, several tasks might be involved in handling and moving raw materials, but these might be combined into a single activity called *materials handling*. The end result of this stage of the design process is an *activity dictionary* that defines each of the activities to be included in the system and specifies how each will be measured.

Step 2: Create Activity Cost Pools

In a manufacturing firm, should we expect all activities to be *directly* related to production volume? In other words, must the organization perform every activity listed in the activity dictionary *each* time an additional unit is manufactured? The answer is no. Some activities will be performed each time, but others may not be.

HIERARCHY OF ACTIVITIES

LO2 ● **Know**

CC4: Describe the hierarchical classification of activities.

Generally, a manufacturing organization can classify its activities into four types: (1) unit level, (2) batch level, (3) product level, and (4) facility level. Exhibit 5–5 lists the activities in Comtek Sound, Inc. using this four-level hierarchical classification scheme. Using such a classification scheme allows designers of an ABC system to examine whether activities can be meaningfully combined to simplify the system and to identify appropriate activity measures that can be used to allocate activity costs to cost objects.

EXHIBIT 5–5 Examples of Activities and Activity Measures in Comtek Sound, Inc.

Activity Type	Activity	Activity Measure
Unit level	Machining	Machine-hours
	Assembly	Direct labour-hours
Batch level	Machine setup	Number of setups
	Production scheduling	Number of production orders
	Product testing	Number of tests
	Materials receipts	Number of receipts
Product level	Parts administration	Number of part numbers
Facility level*	General factory administration	Direct labour-hours

*Facility-level costs cannot be traced on a cause-and-effect basis to individual products.

LO2 ● **Know**

CC5: Distinguish between unit-, batch-, product-, and facility-level activities.

Unit-level activities are performed every time a unit is produced. The costs of unit-level activities should be proportional to the number of units produced. For example, the assembly of a Blu-ray disc player (in Comtek) would be a unit-level activity, since every unit has to be assembled.

Batch-level activities consist of tasks performed every time a batch (or lot) is processed to accomplish an objective. Examples of processing objectives include scheduling production orders, setting up equipment (i.e., getting equipment ready for producing the next batch of products), and receiving materials that are purchased from several suppliers. Costs are incurred each time a production order is scheduled, each time equipment is set up, and whenever materials are received from suppliers. These are the batch-level costs; they depend on *the number of batches processed (the number of schedules, number of setups, number of materials receipts),* rather than on the number of units produced when the process is performed. For example, the cost of processing a purchase order is the same, regardless of whether one unit or 5,000 units of an item are ordered. Thus, the total cost of a batch-level activity, such as purchasing, is a function of the *number* of orders placed.

Product-level activities (sometimes called *product-sustaining activities*) relate to specific products and typically must be carried out regardless of how many batches or units of the product are manufactured. Product-level activities include maintaining information regarding the parts for a product (also known as *parts administration*), issuing engineering change notices to modify a product to meet a customer's specifications, and developing special test routines when a product is first placed into production. These activities generally depend on the number of different products a company produces.

Facility-level activities (also called *organization-sustaining activities*) are carried out regardless of which products are produced, how many batches are run, or how many units are made. Facility-level costs include such items as factory management salaries, insurance, property taxes, and building depreciation. The costs of facility-level activities are often combined into a single cost pool and allocated to products using an *arbitrary* basis such as direct labour-hours. Allocating such costs to products can result in misleading data and bad decisions (especially if facility-level costs are a significant portion of total overhead costs). However, facility-level costs must be allocated to meet external reporting requirements as well as to hold managers accountable for the costs of resources which, unless allocated, would be considered by them to be free. This would mean that the consumption of the resource and its cost would be uncontrolled.

HELPFUL HINT

Students often struggle to grasp the meaning of unit-level, batch-level, and product-level activities. Imagine a professor who teaches one section of managerial accounting that includes 35 students, and one section of financial accounting that includes 25 students. In this example, the two courses represent two separate products. The activity *preparing a syllabus* would be a product-level activity because it needs to be performed once for each course regardless of the number of class meetings during the semester or the number of enrolled students per class. The activity *preparing a lesson plan* would be a batch-level activity because it needs to be performed once for each class session regardless of the number of enrolled students in each class—the class (i.e., batch) size. The activity *marking exams* would be a unit-level activity because it needs to be performed once for each student enrolled in each class.

IN BUSINESS

HOW MUCH DOES IT COST TO HANDLE A PIECE OF LUGGAGE?

Back in 2008, it cost an airline about $15 to carry a piece of checked luggage from one destination to another. The activity *transporting luggage* consists of numerous sub-activities, such as tagging bags, sorting them, placing them on carts, transporting them planeside, loading them into the airplane, and delivering them to carousels and connecting flights.

A variety of employees—including ground personnel, check-in agents, service clerks, baggage service managers, and maintenance workers—spend a portion of their labour-hours handling and transporting luggage. In total, in 2008, labour costs were $9 per bag. Airlines also spend millions of dollars on baggage equipment, sorting systems, carts, tractors, and conveyors, as well as rental costs related to bag rooms, carousels, and offices. They also pay to deliver misplaced bags to customers' homes and to compensate customers for lost bags that are never found. These expenses add up to about $4 per bag. The final expense related to transporting luggage is fuel costs, which average about $2 per bag.

Now it is commonplace for many major airlines to charge fees for checked luggage. In fact, U.S. airlines raked in a record-breaking $1.6 billion in checked bag and change fees during the first quarter of 2015. In Canada, WestJet and Air Canada have started charging between $25 and $30 for the first checked bag instead of offering it free.

Sources: Scott McCartney, "What It Costs an Airline to Fly Your Luggage," *The Wall Street Journal*, November 25, 2008, pp. D1 and D8; Jelisa Castrodale, "U.S. Airlines Collected Record $1.6Bn in Baggage and Change Fees During Q1 of 2015. Here's How to Avoid Paying," *Road Warrior Voices*, June 23, 2015, http://roadwarriorvoices.com/2015/06/23/u-s-airlines-collected-record-1-6bn-in-baggage-and-change-fees-during-q1-of-2015-heres-how-to-avoid-paying/ ; Ross Marowits, "Air Canada Now Charging $25 for First Checked Bag on Domestic Flights," CTV News, September 18, 2014, http://www.ctvnews.ca/business/air-canada-now-charging-25-for-first-checked-bag-on-domestic-flights-1.2012701

Step 3: Identify the Resources Consumed by Individual Activity Cost Pools

An important step after creating the activity cost pools is to identify the resources consumed by the activity cost pools. As an example, let us identify the resources consumed by the activity cost pool *product testing*. It will include time supplied by testers, depreciation of testing equipment, and the testing supplies that can be directly traced to the cost pool. The cost of these resources is calculated. Other resources will include utilities, maintenance, and building space (or depreciation) that may be common across all activity cost pools. Such resources must be assigned to the individual cost pools and the cost determined. As an example, the building rental cost may be assigned on the basis of the space consumed by product testing activity. For instance, suppose the activities included in the product testing activity cost pool are carried out using 20% of the total space in the facility. This would mean that 20% of the building-related costs must be allocated to the product testing activity cost pool. Exhibit 5–6 illustrates Steps 3 to 7.

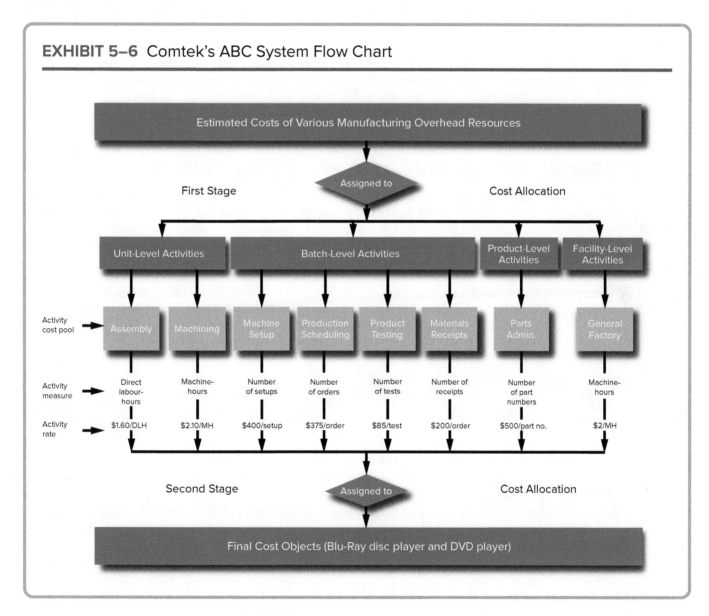

EXHIBIT 5–6 Comtek's ABC System Flow Chart

Step 4: Identify the Activity Measure for Each Activity Cost Pool

Once the amount of cost assigned to each activity pool has been determined, the next step is to assign the cost of the pool to the cost objects using an activity measure to allocate the cost. For example, when the amount of the cost assigned to the product testing activity cost pool is known, the next step is to identify an activity measure that will be used to assign the cost of this activity cost pool to final cost objects; in Exhibit 5–6, the activity measure chosen is number of tests. An alternative measure could be testing time. Ideally, the activity measure should be the cost driver for this activity cost pool (i.e., the variable that causes costs to increase or decrease). However, it may not always be possible to identify the best or even any cost driver for each activity cost pool. This is particularly the case for facility-level activities. In these cases, a selection of the cost driver is made arbitrarily and the possibility of error occurring in the cost allocation is noted.

Step 5: Estimate the Total Activity Volume for Each Measure

The remaining steps are about the mechanics of allocating the pool cost to the cost objects. Continuing with the product testing activity cost pool, the activity volume will be the estimated number of tests conducted during a certain period. Since product testing is a batch-level activity, the volume of the activity measure will depend on the estimated number of batches to be produced as well as the testing policy (e.g., five tests per batch).

Step 6: Compute a Predetermined Activity Rate for Each Activity Cost Pool

Next, we compute an activity rate using the formula presented in Exhibit 5–4. Assume that, after completing Step 1 of the ABC process, an amount of $1.7 million was allocated to the product testing cost pool at the beginning of the period, and that after completing Step 5, the total activity volume was estimated at 20,000 tests (4,000 tests for the DVD player and 16,000 for the Blu-ray player). The predetermined activity rate is then computed as $85 per test ($1,700,000 ÷ 20,000).

Steps 3 to 6 explained above are included in the *first stage* of cost allocation, as illustrated in Exhibit 5–6.

Step 7: Allocate Activity Costs to Desired Cost Objects

Step 7 represents the *second stage* of the cost allocation process. In the second stage, costs from the different pools are allocated to the desired cost objects using the activity rate and the volume of activity measure consumed by that cost object. The $85 rate computed above for the product testing cost pool is used to assign costs to the desired cost objects (say, products). If the DVD player required, as planned, 4,000 tests to be conducted, $340,000 (= $85 × 4,000) would be assigned to this product. Note that this procedure is similar to what was explained in Chapter 3; the only difference is that the ABC system has multiple overhead cost pools that are based on activities. This means that activity consumption information must be collected for individual cost objects. Thus the accounting system should track and record the information that 4,000 tests were performed on the DVD players. If this information was not previously gathered, the implementation of the ABC system now makes it a requirement that the information be gathered. This information facilitates both cost management and cost control, which may have been absent in a legacy non-ABC system and is often mentioned as a key advantage of the ABC system by its proponents.

CONCEPT CHECK

1. Which of the following statements are false? (You may select more than one answer.)
   a. In recent years, most companies have experienced increasing manufacturing overhead costs in relation to direct labour costs.
   b. Activity-based costing systems may use direct labour-hours and/or machine-hours to assign unit-level costs to products.
   c. Facility-level costs are not caused by particular products.
   d. Product-level costs are larger for high-volume products than for low-volume products.

*Note to student: See **Guidance Answers** online.*

Using Activity-Based Costing

Different products make different demands on overhead resources. This difference in demand on resources is not recognized by traditional costing systems, which assume that overhead resources are consumed in direct proportion to a single allocation base, such as direct labour-hours. Let us go back to Comtek Sound, Inc. and examine how ABC costs are different from the costs calculated using a traditional costing system.

The Traditional Costing System

COMTEK SOUND, INC.'S BASIC DATA

Tom Frazier and the ABC team immediately began gathering basic information relating to the company's two products. As a basis for its study, the team decided to use the cost and other data planned for the current year. A summary of some of this information follows. For the current year, the company has budgeted to sell 50,000 Blu-ray disc players and 200,000 DVD players. Both products require two direct labour-hours to complete. Therefore, the company plans to work 500,000 direct labour-hours (DLHs) during the current year, computed as follows:

	Hours
Blu-ray disc player: 50,000 units × 2 DLHs per unit	100,000
DVD player: 200,000 units × 2 DLHs per unit	400,000
Total direct labour-hours	500,000

Costs for materials and labour for one unit of each product are given below:

	Blu-Ray Disc Player	DVD Player
Direct materials	$90	$50
Direct labour (at $10 per DLH)	20	20

The company's estimated manufacturing overhead costs for the current year amount to $10 million. The company has always used DLHs as the base for assigning overhead costs to its products. The ABC team discovered that both products use the same number of DLHs per unit, but the Blu-ray disc player uses more machine-hours per unit and requires greater testing. Moreover, the Blu-ray disc player is produced in much smaller lot (batch) sizes than the DVD player. As a result, machines are required to be set up more frequently, thereby requiring more setups.

With these data in hand, the ABC team was prepared to begin the design of the new activity-based costing system. But first, they wanted to compute the cost of each product using the company's existing cost system.

HELPFUL HINT

As you continue to read through the Comtek Sound, Inc. example, keep the following "big picture" insight in mind. The company's existing cost system and the ABC system will both assign a total of $10 million in manufacturing overhead costs to the two products. In other words, the total amount of the "pie" being assigned to DVD players and Blu-ray disc players will be the same in both cost systems. However, the two cost systems will assign different portions of the pie to each product—as you will see.

DIRECT LABOUR-HOURS AS A BASE

Under the company's existing costing system, the company's predetermined overhead rate would be $20 per direct labour-hour. The rate is computed as follows:

$$\text{Predetermined overhead rate} = \frac{\text{Estimated total manufacturing overhead}}{\text{Estimated total direct labour-hours (DLHs)}}$$

$$= \frac{\$10,000,000}{500,000 \text{ DLHs}}$$

$$= \$20 \text{ per DLH}$$

Using this rate, the ABC team then computed the unit product costs as given below:

	Blu-Ray Disc Player	DVD Player
Direct materials (above)	$ 90	$ 50
Direct labour (above)	20	20
Manufacturing overhead (2 DLHs × $20 per DLH)	40	40
Unit product cost	$150	$110

Tom Frazier explained to the ABC team that the problem with this costing approach is that it relies only on labour time in assigning overhead cost to products and does not consider the impact of other factors—such as setups and testing—in determining the costs of the two products. Since these other factors are being ignored and the two products require equal amounts of labour time, they are assigned equal amounts of overhead cost.

The ABC System

Frazier said that while this method of computing costs is fast and simple, it is accurate only in those situations where other factors affecting overhead costs are not significant. Frazier stated that he believed these other factors to be significant in the case of Comtek Sound, Inc., and he was anxious for the team to analyze the various activities of the company to see their impact on costs.

COMPUTING ACTIVITY RATES

 LO2 • Apply

CC6: Compute activity rates used to allocate costs to cost objects.

The ABC team then analyzed Comtek Sound, Inc.'s operations and identified eight major activities to be included in the new activity-based costing system. (These eight activities are identical to those illustrated previously in Exhibit 5–6.) Cost and other data relating to the activities are presented in Exhibit 5–7.

EXHIBIT 5–7 Comtek Sound's Activity-Based Costing System

Panel A Basic Data

Activities and Activity Measures	Estimated Overhead Cost	Expected Activity Volume		
		DVD Player	Blu-Ray Disc Player	Total
Assembly (direct labour-hours)	$ 800,000	400,000	100,000	500,000
Machining (machine-hours)	2,100,000	700,000	300,000	1,000,000
Machine setups (setups)	1,600,000	1,000	3,000	4,000
Production scheduling (orders)	450,000	800	400	1,200
Product testing (tests)	1,700,000	4,000	16,000	20,000
Materials receipts (receipts)	1,000,000	3,200	1,800	5,000
Parts administration (part types)	350,000	300	400	700
General factory (machine-hours)	2,000,000	700,000	300,000	1,000,000
	$10,000,000			

Panel B Computation of Activity Rates

Activities	Overhead Estimated Cost (a)	Total Expected Activity Volume (b)		Activity Rate (a) ÷ (b)	
Assembly	$ 800,000	500,000	DLHs	$ 1.60	per DLH
Machining	2,100,000	1,000,000	MHs	2.10	per MH
Machine setups	1,600,000	4,000	setups	400.00	per setup
Production scheduling	450,000	1,200	orders	375.00	per order
Product testing	1,700,000	20,000	tests	85.00	per test
Materials receipts	1,000,000	5,000	receipts	200.00	per receipt
Parts administration	350,000	700	part numbers	500.00	per part number
General factory	2,000,000	1,000,000	MHs	2.00	per MH

Panel C Computation of the Overhead Cost per Unit of Product

| | Blu-Ray Disc Player | | | DVD Player | | |
| | Expected Activity | | | Expected Activity | | |
Activities and Activity Rates	Volume		Amount	Volume		Amount
Assembly, at $1.60 per DLH	100,000	DLH	$ 160,000	400,000	DLH	$ 640,000
Machining, at $2.10 per MH	300,000	MH	630,000	700,000	MH	1,470,000
Machine setups, at $400 per setup	3,000	setups	1,200,000	1,000	setups	400,000
Production scheduling, at $375 per order	400	orders	150,000	800	orders	300,000
Product testing, at $85 per test	16,000	tests	1,360,000	4,000	tests	340,000
Materials receipts, at $200 per receipt	1,800	receipts	360,000	3,200	receipts	640,000
Parts administration, at $500 per part number	400	part numbers	200,000	300	part numbers	150,000
General factory, at $2 per MH	300,000	MH	600,000	700,000	MH	1,400,000
Total overhead costs assigned (a)			$4,660,000			$5,340,000
Number of units produced (b)			50,000			200,000
Overhead cost per unit (a) ÷ (b)			$ 93.20			$ 26.70

As shown in the Basic Data panel (Panel A at the top of Exhibit 5–7), the ABC team estimated the amount of overhead cost for each activity cost pool, along with the expected activity volume for the current year. The machine setups activity cost pool, for example, has been assigned $1,600,000 in overhead cost. The company expects to complete 4,000 setups during the year, of which 3,000 will be for the Blu-ray disc player and 1,000 will be for the DVD player. Data for other activities are also shown in the exhibit.

The ABC team then determined an activity rate for each activity (see Panel B in Exhibit 5–7). The rate for machine setups, for example, was calculated by dividing the total estimated overhead cost in the activity cost pool, $1,600,000, by the expected amount of activity, 4,000 setups. The result was the activity rate of $400 per setup. This process was repeated for each of the other activities in the ABC system.

HELPFUL HINT

Students often make the mistake of trying to determine an activity rate for each product. This is incorrect; you should compute only one activity rate for each activity cost pool. The activity rate is then multiplied by the amount of the activity measure used by each product to assign overhead costs to that product. The key assumption is that the activity is exactly the same for each product, for example the DVD player and the Blu-ray player are assumed to be tested in exactly the same way. If there is reason to doubt this, then you should re-examine the assumption that a single activity pool for testing is sufficient.

Computing Product Costs

LO2 • **Apply**

CC7: Assign activity costs to cost objects, and compute unit costs.

Once the activity rates were determined, it was then possible to compute the overhead cost that would be allocated to each product (see Panel C of Exhibit 5–7). For example, the amount of machine setup cost allocated to the Blu-ray disc player was determined by multiplying the activity rate of $400 per setup by the 3,000 expected setups for Blu-ray disc players during the year. This yielded a total of $1,200,000 in machine setup costs to be assigned to the Blu-ray disc players.

Observe from the exhibit that the use of an activity approach has resulted in $93.20 in overhead cost being assigned to each Blu-ray disc player and $26.70 to each DVD player. The ABC team then used these amounts to determine unit product costs under activity-based costing, as presented in the table below. For comparison, the table also shows the unit costs derived earlier when direct labour was used as the only base for assigning overhead costs to the products:

	Activity-Based Costing		Direct Labour–Based Costing	
	Blu-Ray Disc Player	**DVD Player**	**Blu-Ray Disc Player**	**DVD Player**
Direct materials	$ 90.00	$50.00	$ 90.00	$ 50.00
Direct labour	20.00	20.00	20.00	20.00
Manufacturing overhead	93.20	26.70	40.00	40.00
Unit product cost	$203.20	$96.70	$150.00	$110.00

The ABC team members were shocked by their findings, which Tom Frazier summarized as follows in the team's report: "In the past, the company has been charging $40 in overhead cost per unit to both the products, whereas it should have been charging $93.20 in overhead cost to each Blu-ray disc player and only $26.70 to each DVD player. Thus, as a result of using direct labour as the base for overhead costing, unit product costs have been badly distorted. The company may even have been suffering a loss on the Blu-ray disc player without knowing it because the cost of these units has been so vastly understated. Through activity-based costing, we have been able to better identify the overhead costs of each product and thus derive more accurate cost data."

Comparison of the Two Approaches

Why is there such a large difference between the overhead costs under the two systems? To answer this, first note the ratio in which the *total* direct labour-hours are consumed by the DVD player and the Blu-ray player respectively. This is 4:1, which results from the relative production volume of each product. Now go back to Panel A of Exhibit 5–7, which shows the consumption of the activities to produce 200,000 DVD players and 50,000 Blu-ray disc players. While the consumption of direct labour-hours is in the ratio of 4:1, the consumption of other activities does not follow the same pattern. For example, the consumption of the machine setups activity is in the ratio of 1:3, and that of production scheduling is in the ratio of 2:1. Each product is charged for a resource according to the proportion of that resource which it consumes. Costing accuracy is improved when this occurs. The use of a single plantwide overhead allocation rate does not allow Comtek's managers to capture the above differences in activity consumption. On the other hand, the use of multiple activities and multiple activity measures provides for a better understanding and assignment of the overhead costs.

The pattern of cost distortion induced by the traditional system relative to the ABC system shown by the ABC team's findings is quite common. The difference between the cost of making a more complex and specialized product and making one that is relatively simple is much greater in the ABC system than the traditional system since ABC accumulates the cost across a variety of resources consumed by each product, whereas the traditional system relied only on direct labour consumption. Such a distortion can happen in any company that relies on a single allocation base in assigning overhead cost to products, ignoring other significant factors affecting overhead cost incurrence. In these situations, the allocation is driven by the relative volume of production—the high-volume product consumes more of the allocation base and is burdened with more of the overhead cost. When a company implements activity-based costing, overhead cost often shifts from high-volume products to low-volume products, with a higher unit product cost resulting for the low-volume products. This results from the existence of batch-level and product-level costs, which do not vary with the number of units produced.

CONCEPT CHECK

2. Carlson Company uses activity-based costing to compute product costs for external reports. The company has three activity cost pools and applies overhead using predetermined overhead rates for each activity cost pool. The current year's estimated costs and activities as well as the actual activities are presented below:

	Estimated Overhead Cost	Expected Activity	Actual Activity
Activity 1	$34,300	1,400	1,415
Activity 2	20,520	1,800	1,805
Activity 3	36,112	1,600	1,585

The amount of overhead applied for Activity 3 during the year was closest to
  a. $38,832
  b. $36,107
  c. $36,112
  d. $35,773

*Note to student: See **Guidance Answers** online.*

MANAGERIAL ACCOUNTING IN ACTION

THE WRAP-UP

The ABC team presented the results of their work in a meeting attended by all the top managers of Comtek Sound, including president Sarah Kastler, production manager Frank Hines, marketing manager Nicole Sermone, and accounting manager Tom Frazier. After the formal presentation by the ABC team, the following discussion took place:

comtek
S O U N D , I N C .

Kastler: I would like to thank the ABC team for all the work they have done. I am now beginning to wonder about some of the decisions we made in the past using our old cost accounting system.

Sermone: It's obvious from this ABC information that we had everything backward. We thought the competition was pricing below cost on the DVD player, but in fact *we* were overcharging because our costs were overstated. And we thought the competition was overpricing the Blu-ray disc player, but, in fact, *our* prices were way too low because our costs for these units were understated. I'll bet the competition has really been laughing behind our backs!

Kastler: You can bet they won't be laughing when they see our next bids.

Sermone: Tom, I am beginning to think that the ABC method could be used to better understand our other costs as well.

Frazier: You bet! The principles of ABC will not change—only the activities and the activity bases will change. Should I think of this as my next project?

Activity-Based Costing in Nonmanufacturing Functions and Organizations

LO2 ● **Know**

CC8: Describe the use of activity-based costing in nonmanufacturing organizations.

Although initially developed as a tool for computing product costs in manufacturing companies, activity-based costing is now also being used to assign their marketing and administrative costs to desired cost objects. For example, many companies assign marketing costs to different customer groups to analyze customer profitability. Activity-based costing has also been implemented by various service organizations, such as banks, hospitals, cities, and data service companies. Successful implementation of an activity-based costing system depends on identifying the key activities that generate costs and tracking how many of those activities are performed for each service the organization provides. As a result, companies can move beyond product profitability analysis to customer profitability analysis and even channel profitability analysis (see the examples given below).

Examples of Using Activity-Based Costing in Allocating Nonmanufacturing Costs

Activity-based costing can be used to assign selling and administrative expenses. Often, manufacturing companies have a diverse customer base, and companies might use different combinations of marketing strategies and distribution channels to serve their diverse customer groups. For example, Ireland-based Dublin Shirt Company,[1] a wholly owned subsidiary of an American parent, has three different types of customer groups and uses three different marketing approaches to obtain business from its customer groups (including independent commission-based salespeople and advertising). Moreover, there are significant differences in the number of individual customers within each group (fewer than 10 in one group versus more than 800 in another). The use of activity-based costing, as opposed to allocating marketing and sales costs using sales revenues as an allocation base, provided a better understanding of the marketing resources consumed by each customer group. Similarly, Shell Gabon, a wholly owned subsidiary of Royal Dutch Shell in the business of oil exploration and production,[2] decided to apply activity-based costing to assign its business management department's costs. The business management department housed a number of diverse processes, including procurement, information technology, financial services, and internal audit; each of these processes consisted of several activities. Management found that the implementation of an ABC system helped them better understand the diverse range of activities being carried out, and thus helped them manage activities and therefore costs.

The use of activity-based costing allowed managers in both these organizations to enhance their understanding of costs as well as assess the performance of the cost objects (e.g., customer groups in the case of Dublin Shirt Company).

Example of Using Activity-Based Costing in Service Companies[3]

Organizations such as banks deal with significant variety in terms of the needs of their clients. Moreover, individual clients can obtain financial services through different channels, such as a local branch, a centralized call centre, the bank's online services, or brokers. Airlines face a similar situation, in the sense that a traveller has a choice of channels for buying a ticket (online at the airline's or a third party's website, through a travel agent, or by calling the airline). While there might be differences on the revenue side for the organization (e.g., fare differences, depending upon how a ticket is purchased), there might also be significant differences on the cost side. For example, maintaining the online reservation system calls on resources quite different from those required for maintaining the ticketing activity using travel agents. Traditional cost systems that allocate costs using a single allocation base (e.g., sales revenue) are not designed to capture the differences in costs pertaining to the different channels. On the other hand, a properly designed activity-based costing system can allow for these differences, which would then enable the organization to prepare a channel profitability report. Such a report can be helpful to the organization in making decisions regarding the different channels.

WORKING IT OUT

(Note: This is a continuation of the Working It Out question in Chapter 3.)

Gilbert Company is a job-order manufacturer specializing in manufacturing gear boxes to meet customers' individual requirements. For 2018, it estimated overhead costs of $12,560,000 to be allocated using an activity-based costing system (see the table below). Gilbert also estimated that direct labour will be paid at the rate of $15 per hour.

Activity Cost Pool	Estimated Cost	Cost Driver (allocation base)	Total Quantity of Allocation Base
Indirect materials	$ 1,450,000	Direct materials	$6,590,910
Indirect labour and supervision	2,000,000	Direct labour	100,000 hours
Utilities	3,598,000	Power consumption	20,000 kilowatt-hours (kWh)
Inspection	4,200,000	Inspection	15,000 inspections
Depreciation	1,312,000	Machine usage	160,000 machine-hours
	$12,560,000		

During January 2018, Gilbert worked on two jobs, which consumed the following resources:

	Job 2018-A1	Job 2018-A2
Direct materials cost	$ 6,500	$ 22,000
Direct labour cost	$42,000	$165,000
Machine-hours	1,800	7,000
Number of inspections	200	200
Power consumed (kWh)	800	800
Number of units	20	100

At the end of the year, Gilbert recorded the consumption of resources as follows: direct materials, $6,660,800; direct labour, 101,540 hours; machine-hours, 158,700; power consumption, 20,370 kilowatt-hours; number of inspections, 14,780. The company also recorded actual overhead amounting to $12,538,250.

Required:

1. Compute the activity rate for each activity cost pool.
2. Compute the cost *per unit* using activity-based costing.
3. Determine the total manufacturing overhead applied to jobs during the year.
4. Calculate the under- or overapplied overhead for the year, and show how you will dispose of this amount at the end of the year.

SOLUTION TO WORKING IT OUT

1. The activity rates are as follows:

Activity Cost Pool	Estimated Cost	Total Quantity of Allocation Base	Activity Rate
Indirect materials	$ 1,450,000	$6,590,910	22% of direct labour cost
Indirect labour and supervision	2,000,000	100,000	$20 per direct labour-hour
Utilities	3,598,000	20,000	$179.90 per kilowatt-hour
Inspection	4,200,000	15,000	$280 per inspection
Depreciation	1,312,000	160,000	$8.20 per machine-hour
	$12,560,000		

As an example, the computation of the activity rate for inspection is shown below:

$$\text{Activity rate} = \frac{\text{Estimated activity cost}}{\text{Estimated activity volume}}$$

$$= \frac{\$4,200,000}{15,000 \text{ inspections}}$$

$$= \$280 \text{ per inspection}$$

1. The per-unit costs for each of the two jobs are as follows:

	Job 2018-A1	Job 2018-A2
Direct materials cost	$ 6,500	$ 22,000
Direct labour	42,000	165,000
Indirect materials	1,430[a]	4,840[b]
Indirect labour and supervision	56,000[c]	220,000[d]
Utilities	143,920[e]	143,920[f]
Inspection	56,000[g]	56,000[h]
Depreciation	14,760[i]	57,400[j]
Total job cost	$ 380,670	$ 669,160
Number of units	20	100
Cost per unit	$16,030.50	$6,691.60

Calculations:
[a] $1,430 = 22% of $6,500
[b] $4,840 = 22% of $22,000
[c] $56,000 = $20 × ($42,000 ÷ $15 per hour)
[d] $220,000 = $20 × ($165,000 ÷ $15 per hour)
[e] $143,920 = $179.90 × 800
[f] $143,920 = $179.90 × 800
[g] $56,000 = $280 × 200
[h] $56,000 = $280 × 200
[i] $14,760 = $8.20 × 1,800
[j] $57,400 = $8.20 × 7,000

We now contrast the costs calculated here with those calculated in Chapter 3, where we applied overhead using a single plantwide overhead allocation rate using machine-hours as the allocation base (see table below):

		Plantwide Overhead Allocation Rate	Activity-Based Costing
Job A1	Total cost	$189,800	$380,670.00
	Cost per unit	9,490	16,030.50
Job A2	Total cost	736,500	669,160.00
	Cost per unit	7,365	6,691.60

The use of multiple overhead rates in ABC results in very different overhead amounts being assigned to each of the two jobs; the total cost of job A1 increased by 69%, whereas the total cost of job A2 decreased by over 9%. Moreover, it helps in understanding activities as well as investigating them to identify areas of improvement (this process is known as activity-based management, which we discuss a little later in the chapter).

2. Total manufacturing overhead applied to all jobs during the year amounted to $12,600,479 (see computations below).

Indirect materials	22% of $6,660,800 of direct materials	$ 1,465,376
Indirect labour and supervision	$20 × 101,540 DLH	2,030,800
Utilities	$179.90 × 20,370 kWh	3,664,563
Inspection	$280 × 14,780 inspections	4,138,400
Depreciation	$8.20 × 158,700 machine-hours	1,301,340
Total overhead applied		$12,600,479

3.

Applied overhead	=	$12,600,479
Actual overhead	=	2,538,250
Overapplied overhead	=	$ 62,229

Note: Compare the applied overhead amount in this question to the amount in the same question in Chapter 3; when machine-hours are used as the allocation base, the amount of overhead applied is $12,457,950. This will result in underapplied overhead of $80,300. In contrast, when overhead is applied using activity-based costing, the applied overhead is $12,600,479, which results in overapplied overhead of $62,229. The difference in applied overhead under the two methods is $142,529. Although the applied overhead can rarely be equal to the actual overhead, it is expected that a more elaborate overhead allocation method (like ABC) can help in reducing the difference between the two amounts. This is because a better understanding of activities can help managers to more accurately estimate costs.

DECISION POINT

LEGAL FIRM BUSINESS MANAGER

You have been hired to manage the business dealings of a local legal firm with a staff of six attorneys, 10 paralegals, and five support staff. Clients of the firm are billed a fixed amount per hour of attorney time. The fixed hourly charge is determined each year by dividing the total cost of the legal office for the preceding year by the total billed hours of attorney time for that year. A markup of 25% is then added to this average cost per hour of billed attorney time to provide for a profit and for inflation.

The firm's partners are concerned because the business has been unprofitable for several years. The firm has been losing its smaller clients to other local firms—largely because its fees have become uncompetitive. In addition, the firm has been attracting larger clients with more complex legal problems from its competitors. To serve these demanding larger clients, the firm must subscribe to expensive online legal reference services, hire additional paralegals and staff, and lease additional office space.

What do you think might be the reason for the unprofitable operations in recent years? What might be done to improve the situation for the coming year?

*Note to student: See **Guidance Answers** online.*

Evaluating Activity-Based Costing

LO3   • **Know**

CC9: Explain the benefits and limitations of activity-based costing.

Although the discussion of activity-based costing suggests that it might be a useful tool for managers, it is important to examine ABC in greater detail, including its potential limitations.

Benefits of Activity-Based Costing

There are at least three different benefits of implementing an activity-based costing system, as discussed below.

ACCURATE COSTING

The initial purpose of implementing an activity-based costing system was to improve the accuracy of costs assigned to cost objects (e.g., product costs). ABC improves the accuracy of product costs in three ways. First, it usually accumulates overhead costs in multiple activity cost pools that represent the major activities, instead of in just one or two pools. As a result, the allocation is based on a better matching of the consumption of resources by cost objects.

Second, the activity cost pools are more homogeneous than departmental cost pools. In principle, all the costs in a single activity cost pool pertain to a single activity or a set of related activities. In contrast, departmental cost pools contain costs of many different activities carried out in a department.

Third, ABC does not rely just on *volume-based* allocation bases (such as direct labour-hours or machine-hours) to assign overhead. Instead, managers use a combination of *volume-based* and *non-volume-based* activity measures to assign overhead costs to cost objects. The non-volume-based activity measures include the batch-level and product-level activity measures illustrated previously in the chapter. The focus of ABC is to identify the activities or factors that cause or drive costs and use them as allocation bases. In doing so, the system attempts to establish a *cause–effect* relationship between the overhead costs and the allocation bases.

COST ESTIMATION

Increased accuracy in overhead allocation means that companies can do a better job of estimating costs. In today's competitive world, many companies are finding that they have less flexibility in setting their prices; they are largely market driven. Consequently, managers in these companies must identify a target cost that they can work toward to generate a desired profit margin. Activity-based costing can be a valuable tool in providing relevant cost information to managers in identifying the target costs and also in monitoring a company's progress toward achieving the target costs. It can also help in estimating costs related to quality. (See Appendix 6A on Connect.)

ACTIVITY-BASED MANAGEMENT

An important benefit of using ABC is that it allows managers to identify activities that could be improved, resulting in greater efficiency and lower costs. Indeed, this is the benefit of activity-based costing most widely cited by managers.[4] When used in this manner, it is often called *activity-based management*. Essentially, **activity-based management (ABM)** involves focusing on activities to eliminate waste. In other words, ABM is a tool that can supplement management practices such as total quality management and process reengineering, which were described in Chapter 1. As mentioned at the beginning of the chapter, RONA Inc. used ABM to identify waste in order to reduce costs.

The first step in any improvement program is to decide what to improve. The theory of constraints (TOC) approach discussed in Chapter 1 is a powerful tool for targeting the area in an organization whose improvement will yield the greatest benefit. An ABC system can provide valuable information. For example, Comtek's managers may wonder why it costs $375, on average, to process a purchase order (see Exhibit 5–7). Such a question arises when organizations decide on **benchmarking** their costs against the costs of similar organizations known for their outstanding performance. Once the activity is targeted for improvement, managers can use the ABM approach to study the activity in greater detail and identify ways to eliminate the wasteful consumption of resources. Some activities deemed not to add any value (i.e., non-value-added activities) are targeted for elimination. However, managers must ensure that eliminating a certain activity does not negatively impact other activities. There is scope for improvement in how value-added activities are carried out. Managers can look for ways to eliminate redundancies and improve efficiencies.

IN BUSINESS

ABC HELPING CANADIAN BLOOD SERVICES

Activity-based costing (ABC) has given Canadian Blood Services (CBS) a better understanding of its business processes. The Ottawa-based nonprofit group is responsible for Canada's blood supply and fulfills this mission by collecting blood products from donors and supplying them to hospitals across the country (except in Quebec). Since the implementation of ABC, CBS has gradually reduced its cost per unit, which represents an integrated measure of performance.

One benefit of implementing ABC is that it encourages organizations to better understand their activities and processes, which is the aim of the broader concept of activity-based management (ABM). The costing aspect enhances this benefit by identifying the cost of the resources required by an organization to carry out its activities or processes. User-friendly and versatile ABC software further enhances the usefulness of ABC, because it serves as a good tool not only for costing but also for planning and budgeting, as observed by Alex Reyes, CBS's manager for cost accounting.

A recent survey by Kaufman Hall showed that 65% of respondents in the health care sector agreed on the high importance of creating and maintaining a patient-level activity-based costing. Approximately 80% of the respondents plan to shift toward activity-based costing as well as time-driven activity-based costing.

Sources: John DeGaspari, June 26, 2014, "Healthcare Costing Survey Results Released at HFMA ANI Conference," Healthcare Informatics, http://www.healthcare-informatics.com/news-item/healthcare-costing-survey-results-released-hfma-ani-conference; Jeff Jedras, "Canadian Blood Services Learns Its ABCs," *Computer World Canada* 21(23). © Laurentian Technomedia Inc., 2005, http://www.itworldcanada.com/a/Daily-News/71728d69-cb9d-482d-89d3-3796eea28e09.html; Canadian Blood Services Annual Reports, 2007 and 2012, http://www.bloodservices.ca/centreapps/internet/uw_v502_mainengine.nsf/page/E_Annual-Reports?OpenDocument

Limitations of Activity-Based Costing

Any discussion of activity-based costing is incomplete without some cautions. First, the cost of implementing and maintaining an ABC system may outweigh the benefits. Second, it would be naive to assume that all the costs comprising the product cost—even when provided by an activity-based costing system—are all relevant when making decisions. These limitations are discussed below.

THE COST OF IMPLEMENTING ACTIVITY-BASED COSTING

Implementing ABC is a major project that involves a great deal of effort. First, to be most useful, the cost system must be designed by a cross-functional team, which necessitates taking valued employees away from other tasks for a major project. In addition, the data used in the ABC system must be collected and verified. In some cases, this requires collecting data that have never been collected before. In short, implementing and maintaining an ABC system can present a formidable challenge, and management may decide that the costs are too great to justify the expected benefits. Nevertheless, keep in mind that the costs of collecting and processing data have dropped dramatically in the last two decades due to barcoding and other technologies, and this trend is expected to continue.

When are the benefits of activity-based costing most likely to be worth the cost? Companies that have some of the following characteristics are most likely to benefit from ABC:

1. Products differ substantially in volume, in lot size, and in the activities they require.
2. Conditions have changed substantially since the existing cost system was established.
3. Overhead costs are high and increasing, and no one seems to understand why.
4. Management does not trust the existing cost system and ignores cost data from the system when making decisions.

LIMITATIONS OF THE ABC MODEL

The ABC model relies on a number of critical assumptions, the most important of which is that the cost in each activity cost pool is strictly proportional to its activity measure. The issue of whether overhead costs are proportional to the driver is of universal concern. What little evidence we have on this suggests that overhead costs are less than proportional to activity.[5] As a practical matter, this means that product costs will be overstated for the purpose of making decisions. The product costs generated by activity-based costing are almost certainly more accurate than those generated by a traditional costing system, but the product costs should nevertheless be viewed with caution. Managers should be particularly alert to product costs that contain allocations of facility-level costs, which are always arbitrary. Such product costs can mislead managers.

MODIFYING THE ABC MODEL

The discussion in this chapter has focused on allocating manufacturing overhead costs to products. The ABC model can also be used to apply selling and administrative expenses to products, customers, or other cost objects as desired by management. Service organizations, in particular, may find that different types of customers require different resources (e.g., number of sales calls, handling customer complaints) to satisfy their needs. Such organizations may find the ABC approach helpful in allocating customer-related costs. For more complete coverage of the use of ABC in decisions, see more advanced texts.

IN BUSINESS

AND THE SURVEYS SAY . . .

What methods do companies use to compute product costs? To allocate overhead? Surveys reveal mixed results. A survey of approximately 272 members of the Chartered Institute of Management Accountants working in the British manufacturing sector revealed that 80.9% of respondents used full costing methods to allocate overhead costs, while ABC only has a usage rate of 7%. The survey also revealed that small and medium enterprises (SMEs) are less likely to adopt ABC compared to large companies due to the size factor and the nature of the processes involved. However other surveys provide different results. With sponsorship, Business Research and Analysis Group (BRAG) conducted a survey of 348 companies across various industries located in different regions to study the use of ABC. The survey showed that ABC has a usage rate of just below 50%. More importantly, over 87% of respondents' ideal costing system would include certain attributes of ABC, suggesting the use of ABC or some elements of it is likely to continue to be examined for feasibility of implementation by many organizations in the future.

Sources: J. A. Brierley, (2011), "A Comparison of the Product Costing Practices of Large and Small-to-Medium-Sized Enterprises: A Survey of British Manufacturing Firms," *International Journal of Management, 28(4)*, 184–193, 195, http://search.proquest.com/docview/902631524?accountid=14739; W. O. Stratton, D. Desroches, R. A. Lawson, & T. Hatch, (2009). "Activity-Based Costing: Is It Still Relevant?" *Management Accounting Quarterly, 10(3)*, 31–40; http://search.proquest.com/docview/222805126?accountid=14739

DECISION POINT

CITY CONTROLLER

You are the controller of your city office. The managers responsible for utilities and property taxes have complained to you regarding the charges from support services departments, such as information systems and maintenance. The city recently decided to "charge" the internal users of support services an "appropriate" amount to reflect the cost of these services. After meeting with the cost analyst for the city, you discover that the city uses a single citywide rate to allocate overhead costs. You are puzzled, because you know that the support services departments are quite different from one another and that it does not make sense to combine the overhead costs into one single pool. How do you proceed to resolve the issue?

*Note to student: See **Guidance Answers** online.*

CONCEPT CHECK

3. Which of the following statements are false? (You may select more than one answer.)
    a. Activity-based costing systems usually shift costs from low-volume products to high-volume products.
    b. Benchmarking can be used to identify activities with the greatest potential for improvement.
    c. Activity-based costing is most valuable to companies that manufacture products that are similar in terms of their volume of production, batch size, and complexity.
    d. Activity-based costing systems are based on the assumption that the costs included in each activity cost pool are strictly proportional to the cost pool's activity measure.

*Note to student: See **Guidance Answers** online.*

Learning Objectives Summary

LO1 **EXPLAIN THE BASICS OF ACTIVITY-BASED COSTING.**

Activity-based costing (ABC) is a method of applying overhead costs on the basis of activities that are carried out by organizations to provide goods and services. ABC differs from traditional costing in two ways. First, unlike in traditional costing, where a single allocation base is used to assign overhead costs, ABC uses multiple allocation bases that each represent an activity cost pool. Second, the activity cost pools are diverse, and both volume-based and non-volume-based activity measures are used to assign the overhead costs.

LO2 **APPLY ACTIVITY-BASED COSTING.**

The allocation of overhead costs using ABC consists of two stages: (1) estimating the costs to be included in each activity cost pool, identifying and estimating the volume of each activity measure, and computing the predetermined rate for each activity cost pool, and (2) assigning costs from the activity cost pools to desired cost objects by applying the predetermined activity rate to the actual volume of individual activity measures. Activities are generally classified as unit level, batch level, product level, and facility level.

LO3 **UNDERSTAND THE BENEFITS AND LIMITATIONS OF ACTIVITY-BASED COSTING.**

Activity-based costing offers at least three benefits: (1) more accurate costs, (2) better cost estimation, and (3) cost management (called activity-based management). However, ABC is not without its limitations. Three major limitations are (1) implementation (including the cost), (2) limitations of the ABC model in that it will still not result in 100% true costs, and (3) the requirement that the model be adapted for decision-making purposes.

Application Competency Summary

APPLICATION COMPETENCY	DELIVERABLE	SOURCE DOCUMENTS AND KEY INFORMATION	STEPS	KNOWLEDGE COMPETENCY
Design an ABC system. ● **LO2–CC3**	*Key Information* Activities Costs assigned to individual activities Activity rates *Report/Document* No specific document	*Work Flow Chart* Work flow *Interview Transcripts* Notes from interviews regarding work done and activities	1. Identify activities, and prepare an activity dictionary. 2. Identify activities as unit-, batch-, product-, and facility-level activities. 3. Identify the appropriate activity measure (allocation base) for each activity.	
Compute activity rates used to allocate costs	*Key Information* Activity rates *Report/Document*	*Annual Budget Documents* Budgeted activity costs	1. Assign costs to individual activities. 2. Estimate the volume for the corresponding activity measure.	Basic approach underlying ABC ● **LO1–CC2**

APPLICATION COMPETENCY	DELIVERABLE	SOURCE DOCUMENTS AND KEY INFORMATION	STEPS	KNOWLEDGE COMPETENCY
to cost objects. • **LO2–CC6**	No specific document Can be used in preparing other reports for planning and decision making (e.g., standard cost card)	Budgeted activity volume for each activity measure	3. Divide activity costs by the volume of the activity measure (activity volume) to determine the activity rate.	Unit-, batch-, product-, and facility-level classification of activities • **LO2–CC3, 4**
Assign activity costs to cost objects, and compute unit costs. • **LO2–CC7**	*Key Information* Total activity costs assigned to individual cost objects Cost per unit of individual cost objects *Report/Document* Product cost report	*Activity Consumption Report* Activity rates Activity volume consumed by individual cost objects Volume of the cost object (e.g., production volume)	1. Identify the activity volume consumed by an individual cost object (e.g., individual product). 2. Multiply the activity volume for each cost object by the corresponding activity cost rate to determine the total activity costs assigned to each cost object. 3. Divide total activity costs by the volume of the cost object (e.g., production volume) to determine the cost per unit of the cost object.	

Review Problem: Activity-Based Costing

Fine Deck, Inc. manufactures and sells two types of wooden deck chairs: deluxe and tourist. Annual sales in units, direct labour-hours (DLHs) per unit, and total direct labour-hours per year are provided below:

	Total Hours
Deluxe deck chair: 2,000 units × 5 DLHs per unit	10,000
Tourist deck chair: 10,000 units × 4 DLHs per unit	40,000
Total DLHs	50,000

Costs for materials and labour for one unit of each product are given below:

	Deluxe	Tourist
Direct materials	$25	$17
Direct labour (at $12 per DLH)	60	48

Manufacturing overhead costs total $800,000 each year. The breakdown of these costs among the company's six activity cost pools is given below. The activity measures are shown in parentheses.

Activities and Activity Measures	Estimated Overhead Cost	Expected Activity		
		Deluxe	Tourist	Total
Labour related (DLHs)	$ 80,000	10,000	40,000	50,000
Machine setups (number of setups)	150,000	3,000	2,000	5,000
Parts administration (number of parts)	160,000	50	30	80
Production orders (number of orders)	70,000	100	300	400
Materials receipts (number of receipts)	90,000	150	600	750
General factory (machine-hours)	250,000	12,000	28,000	40,000
	$800,000			

Required:

1. Classify each of Fine Deck's activities as unit level, batch level, product level, or facility level.
2. Assume that the company applies overhead cost to products on the basis of direct labour-hours.
   a. Compute the predetermined overhead rate that would be used.
   b. Determine the unit product cost of each product, using the predetermined overhead rate computed in part (2a).
3. Assume that the company uses ABC to calculate overhead rates.
   a. Identify the activity rate (i.e., predetermined overhead rate) for each of the six activity cost pools listed above.
   b. Using the rates developed in part (3a), determine the amount of overhead cost that would be assigned to a unit of each product.
   c. Determine the unit product cost of each product, and compare this cost with the cost computed in part (2b).

SOLUTION TO REVIEW PROBLEM

1.

Activity Cost Pool	Type of Activity
Labour related	Unit level
Machine setups	Batch level
Parts administration	Product level
Production orders	Batch level
Materials receipts	Batch level
General factory	Facility level

2.

a.

$$\text{Predetermined overhead rate} = \frac{\text{Estimated total manufacturing overhead}}{\text{Estimated total direct labour-hours (DLHs)}}$$

$$= \frac{\$800,000}{50,000 \text{ DLHs}} = \$16 \text{ per DLH}$$

b.

	Deluxe	Tourist
Direct materials	$ 25	$ 17
Direct labour	60	48
Manufacturing overhead applied:		
Deluxe: 5 DLHs × $16 per DLH	80	
Tourist: 4 DLHs × $16 per DLH	___	64
Unit product cost	$165	$129

3.

a.

Activities	Estimated Overhead Cost (a)	Total Expected Activity (b)		Activity Rate (a) ÷ (b)	
Labour related	$ 80,000	50,000	DLHs	$ 1.60	per DLH
Machine setups	150,000	5,000	setups	$ 30.00	per setup
Parts administration	160,000	80	parts	$2,000.00	per part
Production orders	70,000	400	orders	$ 175.00	per order
Materials receipts	90,000	750	receipts	$ 120.00	per receipt
General factory	250,000	40,000	MHs	$ 6.25	per MH

b.

Activities and Activity Rates	Deluxe		Tourist	
	Expected Activity	Amount	Expected Activity	Amount
Labour related, at $1.60 per DLH	10,000	$ 16,000	40,000	$ 64,000
Machine setups, at $30 per setup	3,000	90,000	2,000	60,000
Parts administration, at $2,000 per part	50	100,000	30	60,000
Production orders, at $175 per order	100	17,500	300	52,500
Materials receipts, at $120 per receipt	150	18,000	600	72,000
General factory, at $6.25 per MH	12,000	75,000	28,000	175,000
Total overhead cost assigned (a)		$316,500		$483,500
Number of units produced (b)		2,000		10,000
Overhead cost per unit, (a) ÷ (b)		$ 158.25		$ 48.35

c.

	Deluxe	Tourist
Direct materials	$ 25.00	$ 17.00
Direct labour	60.00	48.00
Manufacturing overhead (see above)	158.25	48.35
Unit product cost	$243.25	$113.35

Under ABC, the unit product cost of the deluxe deck chair is much greater than the cost computed in part (2b), and the unit product cost of the tourist deck chair is much less. Using volume (direct labour-hours) in part (2b) as a basis for applying overhead cost to products has resulted in too little overhead cost being applied to the deluxe deck chair (the low-volume product) and too much overhead cost being applied to the tourist deck chair (the high-volume product).

Questions

5–1 What are the three common approaches for assigning overhead costs to products?
5–2 Why is ABC growing in popularity?
5–3 Why do departmental overhead rates sometimes result in inaccurate product costs?
5–4 What are the four hierarchical levels of activity discussed in the chapter?
5–5 Why is ABC described as a "two-stage" costing method?
5–6 Why do overhead costs often shift from high-volume products to low-volume products when a company switches from a traditional costing method to ABC?
5–7 What are the three major ways in which ABC improves the accuracy of product costs?
5–8 What are the major limitations of ABC?

The Foundational 15

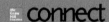

[LO2 – CC6, 7, 8]

Hickory Company manufactures two products—14,000 units of Product Y and 6,000 units of Product Z. The company uses a plantwide overhead rate based on direct labour-hours. It is considering implementing an activity-based costing (ABC) system that allocates all of its manufacturing overhead to four cost pools. The following additional information is available for the company as a whole and for Products Y and Z:

Activity Cost Pool	Activity Measure	Estimated Overhead Cost	Expected Activity	
Machining	Machine-hours	$200,000	10,000	MHs
Machine setups	Number of setups	$100,000	200	setups
Production design	Number of products	$ 84,000	2	products
General factory	Direct labour-hours	$300,000	12,000	DLHs

Activity Measure	Product Y	Product Z
Machining	7,000	3,000
Number of setups	50	150
Number of products	1	1
Direct labour-hours	8,000	4,000

Required:

5–1 What is the company's plantwide overhead rate?
5–2 Using the plantwide overhead rate, how much manufacturing overhead cost is allocated to Product Y? How much is allocated to Product Z?
5–3 What is the activity rate for the Machining activity cost pool?

5–4   What is the activity rate for the Machine Setups activity cost pool?

5–5   What is the activity rate for the Product Design activity cost pool?

5–6   What is the activity rate for the General Factory activity cost pool?

5–7   Which of the four activities is a batch-level activity? Why?

5–8   Which of the four activities is a product-level activity? Why?

5–9   Using the ABC system, how much total manufacturing overhead cost would be assigned to Product Y?

5–10   Using the ABC system, how much total manufacturing overhead cost would be assigned to Product Z?

5–11   Using the plantwide overhead rate, what percentage of the total overhead cost is allocated to Product Y? What percentage is allocated to Product Z?

5–12   Using the ABC system, what percentage of the Machining costs is assigned to Product Y? What percentage is assigned to Product Z? Are these percentages similar to those obtained in Question 11? Why?

5–13   Using the ABC system, what percentage of Machine Setups cost is assigned to Product Y? What percentage is assigned to Product Z? Are these percentages similar to those obtained in Question 11? Why?

5–14   Using the ABC system, what percentage of the Product Design cost is assigned to Product Y? What percentage is assigned to Product Z? Are these percentages similar to those obtained in Question 11? Why?

5–15   Using the ABC system, what percentage of the General Factory cost is assigned to Product Y? What percentage is assigned to Product Z? Are these percentages similar to those obtained in Question 11? Why?

Brief Exercises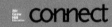

BRIEF EXERCISE 5–1
Applying ABC Cost Hierarchy [LO2 – CC4, 5]

The following activities occur at Greenwich Corporation, a company that manufactures a variety of products:

a.   Receive raw materials from suppliers.

b.   Manage parts inventories.

c.   Do rough milling work on products.

d.   Interview and process new employees in the human resources department.

e.   Design new products.

f.   Perform periodic preventative maintenance on general-use equipment.

g.   Use the general factory building.

h.   Issue purchase orders for a job.

Required:

Classify each of the activities as a unit-level, batch-level, product-level, or facility-level cost activity.

BRIEF EXERCISE 5–2
Computing Activity Rates [LO1 – CC1; LO2 – CC6]

Kramer Corporation is a diversified manufacturer of consumer goods. The company's activity-based costing system has the following seven activity cost pools:

Activity Cost Pool	Estimated Overhead Cost	Expected Activity	
Labour related	$ 48,000	10,000	direct labour-hours
Machine related	67,500	30,000	machine-hours
Machine setups	84,000	600	setups
Production orders	112,000	4,000	orders
Product testing	58,500	1,800	tests
Packaging	90,000	4,500	packages
General factory	672,000	10,000	direct labour-hours

Required:

1. Compute the activity rate for each activity cost pool.
2. Compute the company's predetermined overhead rate, assuming that the company uses a single plantwide, predetermined overhead rate based on direct labour-hours.

BRIEF EXERCISE 5–3
Computing ABC Product Costs [LO1 – CC2; LO2 – CC3, 6, 7]

Klumper Corporation is a diversified manufacturer of industrial goods. The company's ABC system has the following six activity cost pools and activity rates:

Activity Cost Pool	Activity Rates	
Labour related	$ 18.00	per direct labour-hour
Machine related	18.00	per machine-hour
Machine setups	50.00	per setup
Production orders	120.00	per order
Shipments	18.00	per shipment
General factory	38.00	per direct labour-hour

Cost and activity data have been supplied for the following products:

	K425	M67
Direct materials cost per unit	$126.00	$212.00
Direct labour cost per unit	$7.20	$4.50
Number of units produced per year	400	4,000

	Total Expected Activity	
	K425	M67
Direct labour-hours	160	1,000
Machine-hours	200	3,000
Machine setups	2	8
Production orders	2	8
Shipments	2	20

Required:

Compute the unit product cost of each of the products listed above.

BRIEF EXERCISE 5–4
Contrasting ABC and Traditional Product Costs [LO1 – CC2; LO2 – CC3, 6, 7]

Midwest Industrial Products Corporation makes two products: product H and product L. Product H is expected to sell 30,000 units and product L 50,000 units next year. A unit of either product requires 0.2 direct labour-hours.

The company's total manufacturing overhead for the year is expected to be $2,920,000.

Required:

1. The company currently applies manufacturing overhead to products using direct labour-hours as the allocation base. If this method is followed, how much overhead cost will be applied to each product? Compute both the overhead cost per unit and the total amount of overhead cost that will be applied to each product. (In other words, how much overhead cost will be applied to a unit of product H? Product L? How much overhead cost will be applied in total to all the units of product H? Product L?)

2. Management is considering an activity-based costing system and would like to know what impact this change might have on product costs. For the purpose of discussion, it has been suggested that all of the manufacturing overhead be treated as a product-level cost. The total manufacturing overhead would be divided in half between the two products, with $1,460,000 assigned to product H and $1,460,000 assigned to product L.

    If this suggestion is followed, how much overhead cost per unit will be applied to each product?

3. Explain the impact on unit product costs of the switch in costing systems.

Exercises

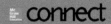

EXERCISE 5–1
Applying ABC Cost Hierarchy [LO1 – CC2; LO2 – CC3, 4, 5]

The following activities are carried out in Greenberry Company, a manufacturer of consumer goods:

a. Direct labour workers assemble a product.

b. Engineers design a new product.

c. A machine is set up to process a batch.

d. Automated machines cut and shape materials.

e. The HR department trains new employees concerning company policies.

f. Raw materials are moved from the receiving dock to the production line.

g. A random sample of 10 units is inspected for defects in each batch.

Required:

1. Classify each activity as a unit-level, batch-level, product-level, or facility-level cost.

2. Provide at least one example of an allocation base (i.e., activity measure) that could be used to allocate the cost of each activity listed above.

EXERCISE 5–2
Contrasting ABC and Traditional Product Costs [LO1 – CC1, 2; LO2 – CC6, 7]

Harrison Company makes two products and uses a conventional costing system in which a single plantwide, predetermined overhead rate is computed based on direct labour-hours. These products are customized to some degree for specific customers. Data for the two products for the upcoming year follow:

	Rascon	Parcel
Direct materials cost per unit	$29.50	$23.00
Direct labour cost per unit	$18.00	$4.50
Direct labour-hours per unit	0.80	0.30
Number of units produced	30,000	120,000

Required:

1. The company's manufacturing overhead costs for the year are expected to be $864,000. Using the company's traditional costing system, compute the unit product costs for the two products.

2. Management is considering an ABC system in which half of the overhead would continue to be allocated on the basis of direct labour-hours and half would be allocated on the basis of engineering design time. This time is expected to be distributed as follows during the upcoming year:

	Rascon	Parcel	Total
Engineering design time (in hours)	6,000	3,000	9,000

Compute the unit product costs for the two products using the proposed ABC system.

3. Explain why the product costs differ between the two systems.

EXERCISE 5–3
Computing Activity Rates and Assigning Activity Costs [LO2 – CC6, 7; Chapter 4 LO7 – CC18]

Sylvan Company uses activity-based costing to determine product costs for external financial reports. Some of the entries have been completed to the manufacturing overhead account for the current year, as shown by entry (a) below:

Manufacturing Overhead		
(a)	2,402,000	

Required:

1. What does entry (a) represent?
2. At the beginning of the year, the company made the following estimates of cost and activity for its five activity cost pools:

Activity Cost Pool	Activity Measure	Estimated Overhead Cost	Expected Activity
Labour related	Direct labour-hours	$560,000	40,000 DLHs
Purchase orders	Number of orders	45,000	1,500 orders
Parts management	Number of part types	360,000	400 part types
Board etching	Number of boards	450,000	2,000 boards
General factory	Machine-hours	600,000	80,000 MHs

Compute the activity rate (i.e., predetermined overhead rate) for each of the activity cost pools.

3. During the year, actual activity was recorded as follows:

Activity Cost Pool	Actual Activity
Labour related	41,000 DLHs
Purchase orders	1,300 orders
Parts management	420 part types
Board etching	2,150 boards
General factory	82,000 MHs

Determine the amount of manufacturing overhead cost applied to production for the year.

4. Determine the amount of underapplied or overapplied overhead cost for the year.

EXERCISE 5–4
Assigning Overhead to Products in ABC [LO2 – CC7]

Refer to the data in Exercise 5–3 for Sylvan Company. The activities during the year were distributed across the company's four products as follows:

Activity Cost Pool	Actual Activity	Product A	Product B	Product C	Product D
Labour related	41,000 DLHs	13,500	7,500	10,500	9,500
Purchase orders	1,300 orders	90	350	310	550
Parts management	420 part types	70	115	110	125
Board etching	2,150 boards	450	1,000	500	200
General factory	82,000 MHs	24,000	20,000	20,000	18,000

Required:

Compute the amount of overhead cost applied to each product during the year.

EXERCISE 5–5
Identifying Activity-Based Costing in Marketing and Sales [LO1 – CC1, 2; LO2 – CC6, 7, 8]

Kramer Corporation is an office supplier dealing in a number of different products. It currently allocates its ordering and delivery costs to its residential and business customer groups on the basis of order value. However, the company has recently decided to implement activity-based costing starting in 20X4 to assign these costs to customers. Key data for 20X3 are as follows:

Activity	Activity Cost	Activity Base	Activity Volume Residential	Activity Volume Business	Total Activity Volume
Sales (order value)			$3,600,000	$3,000,000	$6,600,000
Order processing	$ 960,000	No. of orders	6,000	2,000	8,000
Generating sales	750,000	No. of sales calls	2,000	4,000	6,000
Sales follow-up	810,000	No. of follow-ups	100	400	500
Processing change orders	60,000	No. of change orders	200	200	400
Delivery	1,250,000	No. of deliveries	6,000	4,000	10,000
Total	$3,830,000				

Kramer has 3,000 residential customers and 750 business customers.

Required:

1. Compute the cost per customer for residential and business customers for 20X3, using the current system of cost allocation.

2. Assume that the 20X3 data will hold for 20X4. Compute the cost per customer for residential and business customers for 20X4 using the proposed system of cost allocation. In doing so, calculate the overhead allocation rate for each activity, and use these rates to assign costs to the two customer groups.

3. Explain the difference between the two cost allocation systems.

EXERCISE 5–6
Assigning Overhead Cost to Products in ABC [LO2 – CC3, 6, 7]

PoseiDon Inc. (PDI) recently started operations to obtain a share of the growing golfing market. PDI manufactures two models of specialty drivers: the Thunderbolt model and the Earthquake model. The company was formed as a partnership by two professional engineers and a professional golfer, none of whom had any accounting experience. The business has been very successful, and to cope with the increased level of activity, the partners have hired a professional accountant as their controller. One of the first improvements the controller wants is an update of the costing system, changing from a single overhead application rate using direct labour-hours to activity-based costing. The controller has identified the following three activities as cost drivers, along with the related cost pools:

Model	Number of Materials Requisitions	Number of Product Inspections	Number of Orders Shipped
Thunderbolt	460	170	167
Earthquake	620	240	129
Total costs in the cost pool	$594,000	$82,000	$185,000

Required:

Using ABC, prepare a schedule that shows the allocation of the costs of each cost pool for each model. Show your calculations.

EXERCISE 5–7
Reviewing ABC [LO1 – CC1, 2; LO2 – CC3, 6, 7; LO3 – CC9]

Review what you have learned about activity-based costing.

Required:

1. Identify the four steps involved in an ABC system.
2. Identify *one* benefit of ABC compared with a traditional costing system.
3. Identify *one* limitation of ABC.

Problems

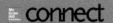

PROBLEM 5–1
Applying an ABC Cost Hierarchy [LO2 – CC3, 4, 5]

Juneau Company manufactures a variety of products in a single facility. Consultants hired by the company to do an ABC analysis have identified the following activities carried out in the company on a routine basis:

   a. Machines are set up between batches of different products.

   b. The company's grounds crew maintains planted areas surrounding the factory.

   c. A percentage of all completed goods are inspected on a random basis.

   d. Milling machines are used to make components for products.

   e. Employees are trained in general procedures.

   f. Purchase orders are issued for materials required in production.

   g. The maintenance crew does routine periodic maintenance on general-purpose equipment.

   h. The plant controller prepares periodic accounting reports.

   i. Materials are received on the receiving dock and moved to the production area.

   j. The engineering department makes modifications in the designs of products.

   k. The human resources department screens and hires new employees.

   l. Production orders are issued for jobs.

Required:

1. Classify each of the previous activities as a unit-level, batch-level, product-level, or facility-level activity.

2. For each of the above activities, suggest an activity measure that could be used to allocate its costs to products.

PROBLEM 5–2
Contrasting ABC and Traditional Product Costs [LO1 – CC1; LO2 – CC3, 6, 7]

Siegel Corporation manufactures a product available in both a deluxe and a regular model. The company has made the regular model for years; the deluxe model was introduced several years ago to capture a new segment of the market. Since the introduction of the deluxe model, the company's profits have steadily declined, and management has become concerned about the accuracy of its costing system. Sales of the deluxe model have been increasing rapidly.

> **CHECK FIGURE**
> (3b) Regular: $202.94 per unit

Overhead is applied to products on the basis of direct labour-hours. At the beginning of the current year, management estimated that $5,184,000 in overhead costs would be incurred and the company would produce and sell 5,000 units of the deluxe model and 40,000 units of the regular model. The deluxe model requires 3.2 hours of direct labour time per unit, and the regular model requires 0.8 hours. Materials and labour costs per unit follow:

	Deluxe	Regular
Direct materials cost per unit	$150	$112
Direct labour cost per hour	14	16

Required:

1. Compute the predetermined overhead rate using direct labour-hours as the basis for allocating overhead costs to products. Compute the unit product cost for one unit of each model.

2. An intern suggested that the company use activity-based costing to cost its products. A team was formed to investigate this idea, and it came back with the recommendation that four activity cost pools be used. These cost pools and their associated activities follow:

Activity Cost Pool and Activity Measure	Estimated Overhead Cost	Activity		
		Deluxe	Regular	Total
Purchase orders (number of orders)	$ 476,800	1,184	1,200	2,384
Rework requests (number of requests)	562,400	810	1,440	2,250
Product testing (number of tests)	908,000	5,000	6,350	11,350
Machine related (machine-hours)	3,236,800	15,240	25,220	40,460
	$5,184,000			

Compute the activity rate (i.e., predetermined overhead rate) for each of the activity cost pools.

3. Assume that actual activity is as expected for the year. Using activity-based costing, do the following:
   a. Determine the total amount of overhead that would be applied to each model for the year.
   b. Compute the unit product cost for one unit of each model.

4. Can you identify a possible explanation for the company's declining profits? If so, what is it?

PROBLEM 5–3
Computing Unit Product Costs in ABC and Cost Flows (LO2 – CC6, 7; LO4 – CC10^A, 11^A)

Hunter Corporation uses ABC to determine product costs for external financial reports. At the beginning of the year, management made the following cost and activity estimates in the company's five activity cost pools:

> **CHECK FIGURE**
> (2d) Total overhead overapplied: $22,500

Activity Cost Pool	Activity Measure	Estimated Overhead Cost	Expected Activity
Labour related	Direct labour-hours	$ 405,000	45,000 DLHs
Production orders	Number of orders	90,000	1,125 orders
Materials receipts	Number of receipts	270,000	1,800 receipts
Relay assembly	Number of relays	480,000	12,000 relays
General factory	Machine-hours	1,260,000	90,000 MHs
		$2,505,000	

Required:

1. Compute the activity rate (i.e., predetermined overhead rate) for each of the activity cost pools.

2. During the year, actual overhead cost and activity were recorded as follows:

Activity Cost Pool	Actual Overhead Cost	Actual Activity
Labour related	$ 418,500	48,000 DLHs
Production orders	87,000	1,050 orders
Materials receipts	285,000	1,950 receipts
Relay assembly	480,000	11,850 relays
General factory	1,270,500	91,500 MHs
Total overhead cost	$2,541,000	

   a. Prepare a journal entry to record the incurrence of actual manufacturing overhead cost for the year (credit accounts payable). Post the entry to the company's manufacturing overhead T-account.

   b. Determine the amount of overhead cost applied to production during the year.

   c. Prepare a journal entry to record the application of manufacturing overhead cost to work in process for the year. Post the entry to the company's manufacturing overhead T-account.

   d. Determine the amount of underapplied or overapplied manufacturing overhead for the year.

3. The actual activity for the year was distributed among the company's four products as in the table below.

   a. Determine the total amount of overhead cost applied to each product.

   b. Does the total amount of overhead cost applied to the products above tie in to the T-accounts in any way? Explain your answer.

Activity Cost Pool	Actual Activity	Product A	Product B	Product C	Product D
Labour related	48,000 DLHs	12,000	16,500	6,000	13,500
Production orders	1,050 orders	240	300	195	315
Materials receipts	1,950 receipts	150	690	360	750
Relay assembly	11,850 relays	4,050	–0–	7,800	–0–
General factory	91,500 MHs	19,500	27,000	21,000	24,000

PROBLEM 5–4
Contrasting Activity-Based Costing and Traditional Product Costs [LO1 – CC1; LO2 – CC3, 6, 7]

Case Construction Company, a three-year-old business, provides contracting and construction services to a variety of clients. Given that each construction job is different from any other, company accountant Susan Kalagnanam decided that it was best to use a job-order costing system to allocate costs to the different jobs. She decided to use construction labour-hours as the basis for overhead allocation. In December 20X4, she estimated the following amounts for the year 20X5:

CHECK FIGURE

(2b) Total cost of the cinema job: $2,472,892

Direct materials	$14,560,000
Construction labour	9,800,000
Overhead	7,510,000
Construction labour-hours	500,000

Kalagnanam recorded the following for the first quarter of 20X5 for the three jobs that the company started and completed during the quarter:

	School	Residential	Cinema
Direct materials	$824,000	$1,034,600	$1,425,000
Construction labour-hours	66,400	37,200	18,500

Required:

1. Compute the cost of each job using the current system of cost allocation.

2. Tyler Case, the company's CEO, recently returned from a seminar on activity-based costing and instructed Kalagnanam to consider implementing the new system. As a first step, he instructed her to analyze the overhead costs for 20X5. Through her research she was able to derive the following breakdown of the estimated overhead costs for 20X5:

Activity	Amount	Activity Measure	Activity Volume
Foundation laying	$1,685,000	Foundation-laying hours	421,250
Building construction	1,740,000	Construction labour-hours	500,000
Painting	1,760,000	Painting-hours	550,000
Finishing	2,325,000	Finishing-hours	750,000

She also documented the following activity on the three jobs during the first quarter of 20X5 (*in addition* to the construction labour-hours consumed by the three jobs):

	School	Residential	Cinema
Foundation-laying hours	39,550	38,500	44,250
Painting-hours	49,380	36,120	47,660
Finishing-hours	41,460	60,600	94,000

Calculate the following:
   a. The activity rates for each of the five activities.
   b. The total cost of each job using activity-based costing.

3. Both Kalagnanam and Case are wondering if using activity-based costing will eliminate the existence of under- or overapplied overhead. As a managerial accountant, explain to them whether the use of activity-based costing will always result in *zero* under- or overapplied overhead.

PROBLEM 5–5
Computing Activity-Based Costing Cost Flows (LO2 – CC6, 7; LO4 – CC10^A, 11^A)

Munoz Corporation uses ABC to determine product costs for external financial reports. At the beginning of the year, management made the following cost and activity estimates in the company's five activity cost pools:

Activity Cost Pool	Activity Measure	Estimated Overhead Cost	Expected Activity
Labour related	Direct labour-hours	$ 214,200	29,750 DLHs
Purchase orders	Number of orders	55,080	765 orders
Product testing	Number of tests	121,380	1,200 tests
Template etching	Number of templates	321,300	8,950 templates
General factory	Machine-hours	892,500	59,500 MHs
		$1,604,460	

Required:

1. Compute the activity rate (i.e., predetermined overhead rate) for each of the activity cost pools.
2. During the year, actual overhead cost and activity were recorded as follows:

Activity Cost Pool	Actual Overhead Cost	Actual Activity
Labour related	$ 202,130	30,200 DLHs
Purchase orders	56,610	760 orders
Product testing	122,400	1,105 tests
Template etching	316,030	8,775 templates
General factory	911,625	57,800 MHs
Total overhead cost	$1,608,795	

a. Prepare a journal entry to record the incurrence of actual manufacturing overhead cost for the year (credit accounts payable). Post the entry to the company's manufacturing overhead T-account.

b. Determine the amount of overhead cost applied to production during the year.

c. Prepare a journal entry to record the application of manufacturing overhead cost to work in process for the year. Post the entry to the company's manufacturing overhead T-account.

d. Determine the amount of underapplied or overapplied manufacturing overhead for the year.

3. The actual activity for the year was distributed among the company's four products as follows:

Activity Cost Pool	Actual Activity	Product A	Product B	Product C	Product D
Labour related	30,200 DLHs	3,200	8,800	9,500	8,700
Purchase orders	760 orders	140	205	120	295
Product testing	1,105 tests	310	160	145	490
Template etching	8,775 templates	3,750	1,270	860	2,895
General factory	57,800 MHs	16,580	12,590	6,800	21,830

a. Determine the total amount of overhead cost applied to each product.

b. Does the total amount of overhead cost applied to the products above relate to the T-accounts in any way? Explain.

PROBLEM 5–6
Contrasting ABC and Traditional Product Costs [LO2 – CC3, 6, 7]

Chomyn Corporation provides a variety of consulting services to a diverse range of clients. The company has three support departments and two operating departments, whose cost details for a typical quarter are presented below:

> **CHECK FIGURE**
> (4) Total cost of Job L342: $144,473

Support Departments	
Information systems	$ 268,000
Administration	347,000
Legal	192,000
Operating Departments	
Research	822,000
Preparation	590,000
	$2,219,000

The existing cost allocation system is designed as follows: (1) the support department costs are allocated to the two operating departments, and (2) the operating department costs are allocated to individual jobs. The support department costs are allocated to the operating departments as follows: (1) information systems department costs are allocated to research and preparation using a 60:40 ratio, (2) administration department costs are allocated using a 30:70 ratio, and (3) legal department costs are allocated using a 50:50 ratio. The costs accumulated in the two operating departments are allocated to individual jobs using research-hours and preparation-hours, respectively. The research and preparation departments recorded 9,000 and 7,500 hours, respectively, for the quarter.

Required:

1. Compute the predetermined cost allocation rates for the two operating departments.
2. Using the rates computed in part (1) above, assign the costs to jobs L123 and L342. The two jobs consumed 340 and 480 research-hours, respectively, and 600 and 750 preparation-hours, respectively.
3. You have recently learned about activity-based costing and decide to use five activity cost pools, one for each department. The additional information you have collected is as follows:

Activity Cost Pool	Cost Driver (allocation base)	Allocation Base Quantity
Information systems (IS)	IS time	14,970 hours
Administration	Number of consultants	40
Legal	Sales value	$8,000,000
Research	Research-hours	9,000 hours
Preparation	Preparation-hours	7,500 hours

Compute the predetermined allocation rate for each activity cost pool.

4. In addition to the research-hours and preparation-hours specified in part (2) above, the two jobs consumed the following additional resources:

Resource	Job L123	Job L342
Information systems time	350	150
Number of consultants	2	2
Sales value	$1,350,000	$900,000

Assign the costs to the two jobs using activity-based costing.

PROBLEM 5–7
Computing and Using Activity Rates to Determine the Costs of Serving Customers
[LO1 – CC1; LO2 – CC3, 6, 7, 8]

Jordan's Lakeside is a popular restaurant located on Lake Muskoka in Ontario. The owner of the restaurant has been trying to better understand costs at the restaurant and has hired a student intern to conduct an ABC study. The intern, in consultation with the owner, identified the following major activities:

CHECK FIGURE
(3b) $13.20 per diner

Activity Cost Pool	Activity Measure
Serving a party of diners	Number of parties served
Serving a diner	Number of diners served
Serving drinks	Number of drinks ordered

One or more diners who ask to sit at a table are counted as a party. Some costs, such as the costs of cleaning linen, are the same whether one person is at a table or the table is full. Other costs, such as washing dishes, depend on the number of diners served.

 Data concerning these activities are displayed below.

	A	B	C	D	E	F	G	H
1		Serving a Party		Serving a Diner		Serving Drinks		Total
2	Total cost	$58,000		$161,000		$35,000		$254,000
3	Total activity	7,250	parties	17,500	diners	14,000	drinks	
4								
5								

Prior to the ABC study, the owner knew very little about the costs of the restaurant. She knew that the total cost for the month was $254,000 and that 17,500 diners had been served. Therefore, the average cost per diner was approximately $14.51 (= $254,000 ÷ 17,500 diners).

Required:

1. Compute the activity rate for each of the three activities.
2. According to the ABC system, what is the total cost of serving each of the following parties of diners?
   a. A party of four diners who order three drinks in total.
   b. A party of two diners who do not order any drinks.
   c. A lone diner who orders two drinks.
3. Convert the total costs you computed in part (2) to costs per diner. In other words, what is the average cost per diner for serving each of the following parties of diners?
   a. A party of four diners who order three drinks in total.
   b. A party of two diners who do not order any drinks.
   c. A lone diner who orders two drinks.
4. Why do the costs per diner for the three different parties differ from each other and from the overall average cost of $14.51 per diner?

PROBLEM 5–8
Assigning Costs to Product Lines [LO2 – CC7]

Brown Inc. manufactures and distributes two types of household items. The items, Mops and Dusters, are manufactured on a common assembly line by the same direct labourers. Different direct materials are used in each type, and the machinery is retooled for each product. Until now, manufacturing overhead costs have been allocated on the basis of direct labour-hours using a plantwide rate. However, the production manager has been reading about ABC and wishes to institute it for Brown's production operations. To that end, she has assembled the following information regarding production activities and manufacturing overhead costs for the month of September:

> **CHECK FIGURE**
>
> (1) Total overhead costs allocated to Mops using ABC, $6,800

Activity Cost Pool	Cost Driver (activity base)	Allocation Rate	Activity Usage Mops	Activity Usage Dusters
Materials handling	Number of parts	$1.00 per part	2,000 parts	1,300 parts
Machining	Machine-hours	$15.00 per machine-hour	200 machine-hours	300 machine-hours
Assembly	Units started	$1.60 per unit	1,000 units	1,125 units
Inspection	Units tested	$2.00 per unit	100 units	1,200 units
Direct materials			$ 5,200	$ 2,600
Direct labour			$12,000	$12,000

Each product consumed 600 direct labour-hours.

Required:

1. Using ABC, determine the total manufacturing cost and cost per unit for each of the two product lines for September, assuming that all units were started and completed in September.
2. Using the plantwide rate to allocate manufacturing overhead, determine the total manufacturing cost per unit for each of the two product lines for September, assuming that all units were started and completed in September.
3. With reference to the results of the analysis in parts (1) and (2), briefly explain the implications of using the ABC costing approach instead of using the plantwide rate to determining the cost of Mops and Dusters.
4. Briefly explain how the allocation rate for materials handling would have been calculated. Is it true that the planned number of parts to be handled is 3,300 parts? Explain.
5. Will you recommend that the activity rate be calculated using actual cost in each cost pool and the actual activity usage? Explain.

(Adapted © CPA Canada)

PROBLEM 5–9
Contrasting ABC and Traditional Product Costs [LO1 – CC1; LO2 – CC3, 6, 7]

MotoMover makes three models of motorized skateboards. At present, all indirect costs are applied to production using a single predetermined overhead (OH) rate based on direct labour-hours. Management would like you to provide an analysis of the costs of manufacture of the three models that compares the present approach to costing with the ABC approach to costing. Management is not confident that its products are priced appropriately relative to its competitors. The following information has been assembled regarding the activity cost pools and cost drivers.

CHECK FIGURE

Overhead allocated to Deluxe using ABC, $33,120

Activity	Recommended Activity Measure	Estimated Overhead Cost	Annual Expected Volume of Activity Measure
Order processing	Number of orders	$ 160,000	100 orders
Materials handling	Materials used (kilograms)	514,920	122,600 kilograms
Machine depreciation and maintenance	Machine-hours	322,000	16,100 hours
Quality control	Number of inspections	64,000	40 inspections
		$1,060,920	

In addition, management estimates that 40,000 DLHs will be used in the upcoming year, at a rate of $16 per hour. Assume that the following activity took place in the first month of the upcoming year:

	Economy	Deluxe	Supreme
Number of units produced	22,000	9,000	3,000
Direct materials costs	$22,880	$14,600	$8,000
Direct labour-hours	550	1,125	2,000
Number of orders	6	4	3
Number of production runs	2	2	3
Kilograms of materials used	9,000	3,600	1,500
Machine-hours	1,320	340	200
Number of inspections	3	3	3
Number of units shipped	19,000	8,250	2,250

Required:

Assume that the data provided is reliable and accurate. Prepare a brief memorandum to management of less than one page in which you compare the costs of each model of skateboard as computed using the two alternative costing approaches. Explain why the costs are the same or not the same and which costing approach you would recommend.

(Adapted © CPA Canada)

PROBLEM 5–10
Contrasting ABC and Traditional Product Costs [LO1 – CC1; LO2 – CC3, 6, 7]

AnoDigi Inc. (ADI) uses a traditional approach to overhead allocation. The company produces two different models of weight scales for use in homes: Analog (an analog scale) and Digital (a digital weight scale with readout). Prices for the two products are based on full costs of production (i.e., inclusive of allocated manufacturing overhead). In 20X4, ADI incurred

CHECK FIGURE
(1) $200,000 to model A

$300,000 of factory overhead and produced 40,000 units of Analog model and 20,000 units of Digital model. Overhead was applied based on a predetermined overhead rate per direct labour-hour. The wage rate is $20 per direct labour-hour and total labour cost is $600,000. Based on this rate, the cost per unit of each product in 20X4 was as follows:

	Model A	Model D
Direct materials	$ 6	$10
Direct labour	10	10
Factory overhead	?	?
Total	$?	$?

The market is becoming more competitive, and ADI is looking into refining its costing system by introducing ABC next year. Analysis of the 20X4 data showed that the $300,000 of overhead costs could be assigned to three activities as follows:

Overhead Costs Assigned in 20X4	
Setup	$ 20,000
Materials handling	60,000
Equipment operations	220,000
	$300,000

Management determined that the following activity drivers were appropriate for the overhead categories:

Activity	Driver	20X4 Activity Level
Setups	Number of setups	160 setups
Materials handling	Quantity of materials (kilograms)	120,000 kilograms
Equipment operations	Machine-hours (MHs)	44,000 MHs

Activity drivers and units produced in 20X4 for each model are as follows:

	Analog	Digital
Number of units	40,000	20,000
Number of setups	100	60
Quantity of material handled (in kilograms)	60,000	60,000
Machine-hours	14,000	30,000

Required:

1. In 20X4, ADI used a single predetermined overhead rate based on DLHs to allocate overhead. Calculate the rate. How much factory overhead was allocated to the Analog model product line and how much to the Digital model product line? What is the product cost per unit of each model?

2. In 20X4, if ADI had been using ABC, how much factory overhead would have been allocated to the Analog product line and how much to the Digital model product line? Calculate the total unit cost for each model under ABC.

(Adapted © CPA Canada)

PROBLEM 5–11
Assigning Overhead Cost to Products in ABC [LO2 – CC3, 6, 7]

Manson Co. produces two products—Model S and Model T—and allocates its fixed manufacturing costs using a predetermined overhead rate based on estimated total overhead for the year and estimated machine-hours for the year. The estimates are as follows:

> **CHECK FIGURE**
> Overhead allocation rate for inspection, $100 per hour

Estimated total overhead for the year	$2,000,000
Estimated total machine-hours to be worked in the year	20,000

The controller is not sure that the estimated costs of the two products reflect the actual costs for which each product is responsible. She is thinking about switching to ABC. The accounting department came up with the following information about activities and associated cost drivers for the two products:

Activity	Activity Measure	Estimated Activity Cost	Estimated Volume of Activity Measure
Materials purchasing	Quantity of materials (kilograms)	$240,000	120,000 kilograms
Machine setups	Number of machine setups	800,000	400 setups
Inspection	Inspection-hours	360,000	3,600 hours
Machine operations	Machine-hours	600,000	20,000 MHs

The following data pertain to Manson for October, the most recent month:

	Model S	Model T
Purchasing materials	6,000 kilograms	4,000 kilograms
Machine setups	10	30
Inspection	200 hours	200 hours
Machine operations	1,500 hours	500 hours

Required:

1. Prepare an analysis of the overhead costs allocated to the products for October, using the ABC method.
2. Will there be over- or underapplied manufacturing overhead under the ABC costing system?
3. Is inspection a unit-level or a batch-level activity? How can you tell?
4. Is it possible for inspection activity to be a batch-level activity? Why or why not?

(Adapted © CPA Canada)

PROBLEM 5–12
Assigning Overhead Cost to Products in ABC [LO1 – CC1, 2; LO2 – CC3, 6, 7]

"A dollar of gross margin per briefcase? That's ridiculous!" roared Art Dejans, president of CarryAll, Inc. "Why do we go on producing those standard briefcases when we're able to make over $15 per unit on our specialty items? Maybe it's time to get out of the standard line and focus the whole plant on specialty work."

CHECK FIGURE

(2) Standard model unit product cost: $30.11 per unit

Dejans is referring to a summary of average unit costs and revenues that he had just received from the company's accounting department:

	Standard Briefcases	Specialty Briefcases
Selling price per unit	$36.00	$50.00
Unit product cost	35.00	32.50
Gross margin per unit	1.00	17.50

CarryAll produces briefcases from leather, fabric, and synthetic materials in a single plant. The basic product is a standard briefcase made from leather lined with fabric. The standard briefcase is a high-quality item and has sold well for many years.

Last year, the company decided to expand its product line and produce specialty briefcases for special orders. These briefcases differ from the standard in that they vary in size, contain the finest synthetic materials, and have the buyer's name embossed on them. To reduce labour costs on the specialty briefcases, most of the cutting and stitching is done by automated machines. These machines are used to a much lesser degree in the production of standard briefcases.

"I agree that the specialty business is looking better and better," replied Sally Henrie, the company's marketing manager. "And there seems to be plenty of specialty work out there, particularly since the competition hasn't been able to touch our price. Did you know that Armour Company, our biggest competitor, charges over $65 a unit for its specialty items? Now that's what I call gouging the customer!"

A breakdown of the manufacturing cost for each of CarryAll's product lines follows:

		Standard Briefcases			Specialty Briefcases
Units produced each month		9,000			2,250
Direct materials:					
Leather	1.0 m^2	$15.00	0.5 m^2		$ 7.50
Fabric	1.0 m^2	5.00	1.0 m^2		5.00
Synthetic		—			5.00
Total materials		20.00			17.50
Direct labour	0.5 h @ $12	6.00	0.5 h @ $12		6.00
Manufacturing overhead	0.5 h @ $18	9.00	0.5 h @ $18		9.00
Unit product cost		$35.00			$32.50

Manufacturing overhead is applied to products on the basis of direct labour-hours. The rate of $18 per direct labour-hour is determined by dividing the total manufacturing overhead cost for a month by the direct labour-hours:

$$\frac{\text{Manufacturing overhead cost, } \$101{,}250}{\text{Direct labour-hours, } 5{,}625} = \$18 \text{ per DLH}$$

The following additional information is available about the company and its products.

a. Standard briefcases are produced in batches of 200 units, and specialty briefcases are produced in batches of 25 units. Thus, the company does 45 setups for the standard items each month and 90 setups for the specialty items. A setup for the standard items requires one hour, whereas a setup for the specialty items requires two hours.

b. All briefcases are inspected to ensure that quality standards are met. A total of 300 hours of inspection time is spent on the standard briefcases and 500 hours of inspection time is spent on the specialty briefcases each month.

    (Adapted from a case written by Harold P. Roth and Imogene Posey, "Management Accounting Case Study: CarryAll Company," *Management Accounting Campus Report,* Montvale, NJ: Institute of Management Accountants, Fall 1991, p. 9. Used by permission.)

c. A standard briefcase requires 0.5 hours of machine time, and a specialty briefcase requires 2 hours of machine time.

d. The company is considering using ABC as an alternative to its traditional costing system for computing unit product costs. Since these unit product costs will be used for external financial reporting, all manufacturing overhead costs are to be allocated to products, and nonmanufacturing costs are to be excluded from product costs. The ABC system has already been designed and costs allocated to the activity cost pools. The activity cost pools and activity measures follow:

Activity Cost Pool	Activity Measure	Estimated Overhead Cost
Purchasing	Number of orders	$ 12,750
Materials handling	Number of receipts	15,000
Production orders and setup	Setup-hours	22,500
Inspection	Inspection-hours	16,000
Frame assembly	Assembly-hours	8,000
Machine related	Machine-hours	27,000
		$101,250

	Expected Activity		
Activity Measure	Standard Briefcase	Specialty Briefcase	Total
Number of orders:			
Leather	24	46	70
Fabric	51	79	130
Synthetic material	—	100	100
Number of receipts:			
Leather	46	14	60
Fabric	70	10	80
Synthetic material	—	160	160
Setup-hours	?	?	?
Inspection-hours	?	?	?
Assembly-hours	800	800	1,600
Machine-hours	?	?	?

Required:

1. Using ABC, determine the amount of manufacturing overhead cost that would be applied to each standard briefcase and each specialty briefcase.

2. Using the data computed in part (1) and other data from the case as needed, determine the unit product cost of each product line from the perspective of the ABC system.

3. Within the limitations of the data that have been provided, evaluate the president's concern about the profitability of the two product lines. Would you recommend that the company shift its resources entirely to production of specialty briefcases? Explain.

4. Henrie stated that "the competition hasn't been able to touch our price" on specialty business. What do you think is the reason?

Building Your Skills

COMPREHENSIVE PROBLEM [LO1 – CC1, 2; LO2 – CC3, 6, 7]

Classic Windows is a small company that builds specialty wooden windows for local builders. For the year 20X4, Lori Newman prepared the following profitability statement for two of the company's major customers:

CHECK FIGURE

(1) Overhead allocated to Kusczik Builders, $115,640

	Kusczik Builders	Western Homes
Sales revenues	$125,000	$680,000
Less:		
Direct materials	$42,000	$185,000
Direct labour	$54,000	$360,000
Overhead	$41,100	$274,000
Net income (loss)	$(12,100)	$(139,000)
Number of orders	50	50

For years, the small company has relied on a simple costing system that allocated all overhead costs using direct labour-hours (DLH). The company paid $18 per hour to its direct labour employees.

However, the company's president became interested in activity-based costing (ABC) after reading an article about ABC in a trade journal. An ABC design team was put together, and within a few months a simple system consisting of four activity cost pools had been designed. The activity cost pools and their activity measures appear below:

Activity Cost Pool	Activity Measure	Activity Volume for the Year
Window making	Direct labour-hours	100,000 DLH
Order processing	Number of orders	2,000 orders
Customer relations	Number of customers	100 customers
Other	None	Not applicable

Direct materials and labour costs are easily traceable to individual jobs. The total overhead costs for the year are budgeted to be $1.37 million, as follows:

Overhead:	
Wages and salaries	$400,000
Depreciation	300,000
Insurance	80,000

Rental	300,000	
Supplies	40,000	
Travel	250,000	$1,370,000

Largely on the basis of interviews with employees, the above overhead costs were assigned to the four activity cost pools as follows:

Activity Cost Pool	Amount	
Window making	$535,000	
Order processing	232,000	
Customer relations	284,000	
Other	319,000	$1,370,000

Required:

1. Compute the profitability of the two customers using the proposed ABC system. Show all the steps in your calculation.
2. Why is there a difference in the profitability of the two customers under the two costing systems? Be specific.
3. What steps (if any) would you take based on the information obtained from the two systems?
4. Katherine Lukey, CEO of Classic Windows, is wondering whether it is appropriate *not to* allocate "other" costs to customers. Analyze the costs of the "other" category and advise Lukey what she should do. If you advise her that these costs should be allocated to individual customers, identify the allocation base(s) you would use.

THINKING ANALYTICALLY [LO1 – CC1, 2; LO2 – CC3, 6, 7]

"Does charging a uniform price to all customers really make sense?" This was the question that Lori Peters, founder and CEO of One Stop Shop (OSS), asked her management team. "Charging a uniform price assumes that all customers are the same in terms of the resources they consume; this can't possibly be true." Ralph Goodwin, the chief operations officer, couldn't agree more. Sarah Price, the accountant, jumped in to add that her new activity-based costing system accounts for the differences in the resources consumed by different customers. "Our new costing system does not allocate costs based on the dollar value of orders; we now capture the number of transactions, by customer, of the four major activities involved in satisfying our customers." While acknowledging the new system, Goodwin still did not believe that the new system actually captured the resources required to cater to the different customers' needs. "The resources required to cater to each customer's needs vary considerably, and the number of transactions is at best a somewhat poor proxy for this." The meeting ended with Price agreeing to review her costing system.

Upon returning to her office, she went through the data for the previous year (20X4) and listed the following information pertaining to OSS's four major customers (A, B, C, and D), who account for well over 85% of the company's orders:

Activity	Amount	Transactions
Order taking	$ 1,685,000	28,720 (number of orders received)
Inspection	1,740,000	36,810 (number of inspections)
Packaging	1,760,000	452,500 (number of packages)
Shipping	2,325,000	186,450 (number of shipments)
	$ 7,510,000	

	A	B	C	D
Number of orders received	9,560	7,400	5,200	6,560
Number of inspections	6,500	9,120	7,450	13,740
Number of packages	98,600	125,680	84,600	143,620
Number of shipments	51,000	40,900	56,350	38,200

Upon further reflection, she decided to investigate the four activities to determine whether number of transactions is really a poor proxy, as Goodwin had commented. After completing her investigation, she prepared the following additional table, which captured the time consumed for each activity:

	A Hours	B Hours	C Hours	D Hours	Total Hours
Order-taking time	80,200	130,800	110,460	99,790	421,250
Inspection time	88,290	123,870	101,200	186,640	500,000
Packaging time	95,460	185,460	125,420	143,660	550,000
Shipping time	206,100	162,940	226,700	154,260	750,000

Required:

Sarah Price has approached you to help her prepare a response to the concerns raised by Peters and Goodwin. Analyze the costing system and report whether using different measures of activity volume will lead to differences in the costs allocated to the four customers. Explain the reasons for any differences. What will you recommend to senior management with respect to improving the costing system?

COMMUNICATING IN PRACTICE [LO1 – CC1, 2]

You often provide advice to Maria Graham, a client who is interested in diversifying her company. Maria is considering the purchase of a small manufacturing concern that assembles and packages its many products by hand. She plans to automate the factory, and her projections indicate that the company will once again be profitable within two to three years. During her review of the company's records, she discovered that the company currently uses direct labour-hours to allocate overhead to its products. Because of its simplicity, Maria hopes that this approach can continue to be used.

Required:

Write a memorandum to Maria that addresses whether DLHs should continue to be used as an allocation base for overhead.

ETHICS CHALLENGE [LO1 – CC1; LO2 – CC8]

Sherri Rowland had recently been transferred to the home security systems division of National Home Products. Shortly after taking over her new position as divisional accountant, she came to know that each of the three division presidents had a lot of autonomy in decision making and reporting. In her first meeting with one division president, Harry Irving, the following conversation took place.

Irving: It is good to have you on our team, Sherri. I am sure we can report better profits to the bosses in "the White House" (I mean, head office).

Rowland: What exactly are you thinking about? I have reviewed some files and see that there are inconsistencies.

Irving: Are you talking about the poor information system and our estimation techniques? We do that so that we look good at the end of the year.

Rowland: How so?

Irving: Head office allocates overhead costs on the basis of machine-hours. I have always had an agreement with your predecessor to shave 5% or so off the estimated machine-hours every year. That way, we kept a reserve that usually resulted in a big boost to net income at the end of the fiscal year in December. We called it our holiday bonus. Corporate headquarters always seemed pleased as punch that we could pull off such a miracle at the end of the year. But, recently, they have been asking too many questions.

Rowland: So what do you want me to do?

Irving: Looking good in the eyes of our bosses is extremely important in this company. Can we find ways to look good without being the centre of attention?

Rowland: I am not too sure about what we can do.

Irving: I have heard that the accounting standards offer flexibility to users. Can you somehow produce cost information that will always show us in a positive light?

After returning to her office, Sherri Rowland looked up the standards and came across the following:

> *The cost of inventories shall comprise all costs of purchase, costs of conversion, and other costs incurred in bringing the inventories to their present location and condition.*

She was confident about materials cost but wanted more clarification regarding conversion costs. She read on and came to the following paragraph:

> *The costs of conversion of inventories include costs directly related to the units of production, such as direct labour. They also include a systematic allocation of fixed and variable production overheads that are incurred in converting materials into finished goods.*

Required:

1. Explain how shaving 5% off the estimated direct labour-hours in the base for the predetermined overhead rate usually results in a big boost in net income at the end of the fiscal year.
2. Assume the role of Sherri Rowland. What would you do?

TEAMWORK IN ACTION [LO1 – CC2]

This activity requires teamwork to reinforce the understanding of the hierarchy of activities commonly found in ABC systems in manufacturing companies.

Required:

1. The team should discuss and then draft a brief description of how the ABC system allocates overhead to products. All team members should agree with and understand the description.

2. Without referring to the related section in the text, each member of the team should choose one of the following levels of activities, define the level of activity chosen, and provide one or more examples of tasks performed at that level of activity in a manufacturing firm:
   a. Unit-level activities.
   b. Batch-level activities.
   c. Product-level activities.
   d. Facility-level activities.

3. Each team member should present the answers from part (2) to the other teammates, who should confirm or correct those answers.

Endnotes

1. P. Clarke, P. Juras, and P. Dierks, "The Dublin Shirt Company," in W. Bremser, ed., *Cases from Management Accounting Practice* (Montvale, NJ: Institute of Management Accountants, 2002), pp. 27–35.

2. S. Ansari, and J. Bell, "Activity-Based Management in Shell Gabon," *IMA Education Case Journal,* 1(4), 2008.

3. K. Benzacar, "A New Look at Profitability," *CMA Management Magazine,* August/September 2006, pp. 17–19.

4. D. Swenson, "The Benefits of Activity-Based Cost Management to the Manufacturing Industry," *Journal of Management Accounting Research,* 7, Fall 1995, pp. 167–180.

5. E. Noreen and N. Soderstrom, "The Accuracy of Proportional Cost Models: Evidence from Hospital Service Departments," *Review of Accounting Studies, 2,* 1997; E. Noreen and N. Soderstrom, "Are Overhead Costs Proportional to Activity? Evidence From Hospital Service Departments," *Journal of Accounting and Economics,* January 1994, pp. 253–278.

Cost Behaviour: Analysis and Use

LEARNING OBJECTIVES AND CHAPTER COMPETENCIES		
After studying Chapter 6, you should be able to demonstrate the following competencies:		

COMPETENCY		Know	Apply
LO1	**UNDERSTAND COST BEHAVIOUR.**		
CC1	Describe the behaviour of variable costs.	●	
CC2	Describe the behaviour of step-variable costs.	●	
CC3	Describe the behaviour of fixed costs.	●	
CC4	Explain committed and discretionary fixed costs.	●	
CC5	Explain the importance of relevant range in understanding fixed costs.	●	
CC6	Describe the behaviour of mixed costs.	●	
LO2	**ANALYZE AND ESTIMATE COSTS.**	●	
CC7	Construct a basic linear cost equation, and explain the individual elements of the cost equation.	●	●
CC8	Explain the importance of separating mixed costs into fixed and variable portions.	●	
CC9	Describe the high–low method of analyzing mixed costs, and set up a cost equation using this method.	●	●
CC10	Explain the scattergraph method of analyzing mixed costs, and set up a cost equation using this method.	●	●
CC11	Explain the least-squares regression method of analyzing mixed costs, and set up a cost equation using this method.	●	●
LO3	**COMPUTE CONTRIBUTION MARGIN AND INCOME.**		
CC12	Explain the concept of contribution margin, and prepare a contribution margin income statement.	●	●

ON THE JOB

DRAGON HELPS BUILD THE CONTAINER BUSINESS

Imagine getting more than the "ask" (the amount you asked for) from a dragon on CBC's *Dragons' Den!* This is what Bryan McCrea and Evan Willoughby of Saskatoon-based 3twenty Modular experienced after impressing the investors with their solution for temporary accommodations and site office trailers. For many large corporations (such as Enbridge Pipelines, Gibsons Energy, and Cameco Corporation) that are looking to accommodate employees temporarily in remote locations, building and then tearing down housing or offices is expensive and inconvenient. 3twenty Modular offers a more cost-effective and headache-free solution.

McCrea and Willoughby got together in 2009 to convert used shipping containers into modular structures for offices and accommodations. The units come fully insulated and equipped with lighting, heating, and water, providing a comfortable private bedroom in a remote location! Customers can order a single unit or a large multi-unit complex. The plant's 25 production workers have built projects all over Canada and the Arctic, including an accommodation complex for 180 people for the Department of National Defence.

As a co-owner and the accountant, McCrea is pleased that the company exceeded revenue and profit expectations in its very first full year of operation, and he is clearly optimistic about the future. "The learning curve was steep," explains McCrea, and he knows that there is much more to learn. But one thing is clear—3twenty understands the importance of a quality product, and that quality comes at a price. McCrea knows that cost control is critical to realizing the budgeted profit margins. A significant variable cost is direct material; however, controlling fixed costs is McCrea's goal. "We are trying to operate as a lean outfit although our fixed costs have grown significantly over the last few years," McCrea says. 3twenty subcontracts the spray foam and plumbing work and pays by the unit (a variable cost); hiring a full-time spray foamer and plumber will change this cost from variable to fixed regardless of the number of containers built. Direct labour is also a fixed cost. "Our production workers are efficient, but we often have a small period of downtime between jobs. Although we don't regret having to pay our workers during transitions, it is important that we find alternative ways to generate revenues to cover the downtime costs." This has come to fruition; 3twenty now generates additional revenue by renting out its own office and washcar trailers.

3twenty Modular

According to McCrea, being on *Dragons' Den* was a great experience. Having one of Canada's top oil and gas investors—dragon W. Brett Wilson—on board adds credibility to the business and provides a comfort level to the young entrepreneurs. "We can turn to him for advice when we need it; he can also help us fill any shortfalls in our working capital," adds McCrea.

Sources: http://3twenty.ca/; conversation with Bryan McCrea, co-founder.

Critical thinking question *How does the knowledge of cost behaviour help businesses control costs?*

Note to student: See **Guidance Answers** *online.*

◀◀ A Look Back	▶ A Look at This Chapter	▶▶ A Look Ahead
We briefly introduced cost concepts in Chapter 2, followed by cost accounting and cost allocation methods in Chapters 3, 4 and 5.	After reviewing the behaviour of variable and fixed costs introduced in Chapter 2, we will discuss mixed costs—a third type of behavioural pattern—and provide an overview of the methods that can be used to break a mixed cost into its variable and fixed components. We also introduce the contribution format income statement, which is used for internal decision making.	Chapters 7, 8, and 9 focus on planning and decision making. Specifically, Chapter 7 describes the process of budgeting, whereas both Chapters 8 and 9 focus on decision making. Chapter 8 introduces the concept of cost–volume–profit analysis and break-even. Chapter 9 discusses relevant costs and their use in decision making.

In our discussion of cost terms and concepts in Chapter 2, we stated that one way to classify costs is by behaviour. We defined cost behaviour as the way a cost reacts or changes as changes take place in the level of business activity. As we will see in later chapters, an understanding of cost behaviour is important for the purposes of planning, making decisions, and controlling costs. Managers who understand how costs behave are better able to predict costs under varying operating conditions. Attempts at planning and decision making without a thorough understanding of the costs involved—and how these costs may change with the activity level—can lead to disaster. For example, a decision to cut back a particular product line might result in far less cost savings than managers may have estimated if they confuse variable and fixed costs, thereby leading to a decline in profits. To avoid such problems, a manager must be able to accurately predict costs at different activity levels. In this chapter, we will find that the key to effective cost prediction lies in understanding variable and fixed costs.

In this chapter, we briefly review the definitions of variable costs and fixed costs and then discuss the behaviour of these costs in greater depth than we were able to do in Chapter 2. After this review and discussion, we turn our attention to the analysis of mixed costs. We conclude the chapter by introducing a new income statement format—called the *contribution format*—in which costs are organized by behaviour rather than by the traditional functions of production, sales, and administration.

MANAGERIAL ACCOUNTING IN ACTION

THE ISSUE

Dr. Derek Chalmers, the chief executive officer of Mid-Town Medical Centre (MMC), motioned Kinh Nguyen, the chief financial officer of the hospital, to come into his office.

M I D - T O W N
M E D I C A L
CENTRE

Chalmers: Kinh, come on in.

Nguyen: What can I do for you?

Chalmers: Actually, I wanted to talk to you about our maintenance expenses. I don't usually pay attention to such things, but these expenses seem to be bouncing around a lot. Over the last half-year or so, they have been as low as $7,400 and as high as $9,800 per month.

Nguyen: Actually, that's a pretty normal variation in those expenses.

Chalmers: Well, we budgeted a constant $8,400 a month. Can't we do a better job of predicting what these costs are going to be? And how do we know when we've spent too much in a month? Shouldn't there be some explanation for these variations?

Nguyen: Now that you mention it, we are in the process right now of tightening up our budgeting process. Our first step is to break all of our costs down into fixed and variable components.

Chalmers: How will that help?

Nguyen: Well, that will permit us to predict what the level of costs will be. Some costs are fixed and shouldn't change much. Other costs go up and down as our activity level goes up and down. The trick is to figure out what is driving the variable component of the costs.

Chalmers: What about the maintenance costs?

Nguyen: My guess is that the variations in maintenance costs are being driven by our overall level of activity. When we treat more patients, our equipment is used more intensively, which leads to more maintenance expense.

Chalmers: How would you measure the level of overall activity? Would you use patient-days?

Nguyen: I think so. Each day a patient is in the hospital counts as one patient-day. The greater the number of patient-days in a month, the busier we are. Besides, our budgeting is all based on projected patient-days.

Chalmers: Okay, so suppose you are able to break the maintenance costs down into fixed and variable components. What will that do for us?

Nguyen: Basically, I will be able to predict what maintenance costs should be as a function of the number of patient-days.

Chalmers: I can see where that would be useful. We could use it to predict costs for budgeting purposes.

Nguyen: We could also use it as a benchmark. On the basis of the actual number of patient-days for a period, I can predict what the maintenance costs should have been. We can compare this with the actual spending on maintenance.

Chalmers: Sounds good to me. Let me know when you get the results.

Before we go any further in answering the question posed by Dr. Derek Chalmers, let us review the different patterns of cost behaviour.

Types of Cost Behaviour Patterns

In Chapter 2, we mentioned only variable and fixed costs. In this chapter, we will discuss a third behaviour pattern, generally known as *mixed* cost. All three cost behaviour patterns—variable, fixed, and mixed—are found in most organizations. The relative proportion of each type of cost present in a firm determines its **cost structure**. For example, a firm might have a higher proportion of fixed costs and a relatively lower proportion of variable or mixed costs. A firm's cost structure can have a significant impact on decisions. In this chapter, we will concentrate on getting a better understanding of the different types of cost behaviour.

Variable Costs

LO1   • **Know**

CC1: Describe the behaviour of variable costs.

We explained in Chapter 2 that a variable cost is a cost whose total dollar amount varies in direct proportion to changes in the activity level. For example, if the activity level increases by 10%, then the total dollar amount of the variable cost will also increase by 10%.

We also found in Chapter 2 that a variable cost remains constant when expressed on a *per-unit* basis. To provide an example, consider 50 Plus Expeditions, a Toronto-based company that organizes adventure travel for people over the age of 50. Among other things, the company provides all of the necessary equipment and experienced guides and serves meals to its guests. Assume that the meals cost $30 per guest for a daylong excursion; the total cost of meals will vary depending upon the number of guests, as illustrated in the table.

Number of Guests	Cost of Meals per Guest	Total Cost of Meals
100	$30	$ 3,000
500	30	15,000
1,000	30	30,000

The idea that a variable cost is *constant per unit*, but *varies in total* with the activity level, is crucial to an understanding of cost behaviour patterns; Exhibit 6–1 provides a graphic illustration of variable cost behaviour. We shall return to this concept repeatedly in this chapter and in the chapters ahead.

THE ACTIVITY BASE

For a cost to be variable, it must be variable *with respect to something*. That "something" is its *activity base*. An **activity base** is a measure of whatever causes the incurrence of a variable cost. An activity base is also sometimes referred to as a *cost driver*. Activity bases may be output-based or input-based. Common output-based activity measures are volume of goods or services sold, number of customers served, and number of patients treated. Common input-based activity measures include direct labour-hours, machine-hours, number of customer service calls, and kilograms of raw materials used.

To plan and control variable costs, a manager must be well acquainted with the various activity bases within the firm. People sometimes think that if a cost does not vary with production or with sales, then it is not really a variable cost. This is not correct. As suggested by the range of bases listed above, costs are caused by many different activities within an organization. Whether a cost is considered to be variable depends on whether it is caused by the activity under consideration. For example, if a manager is analyzing the cost of service calls, the relevant activity measure will be the number of service calls made. Those costs that vary in total with the number of service calls made are the variable costs of making service calls.

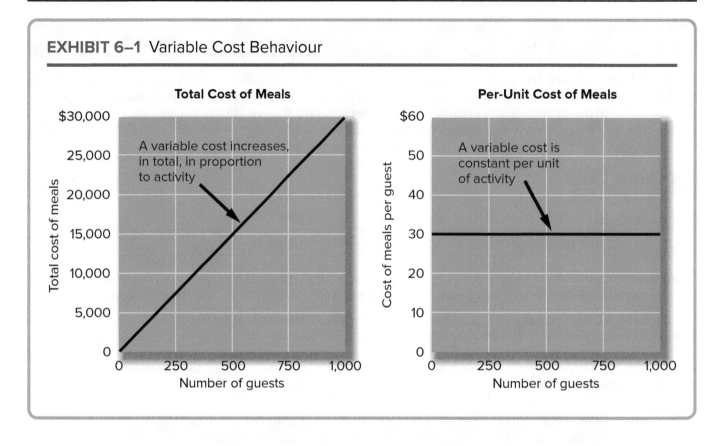

EXHIBIT 6–1 Variable Cost Behaviour

Total Cost of Meals

A variable cost increases, in total, in proportion to activity

Per-Unit Cost of Meals

A variable cost is constant per unit of activity

Generally, most organizations are interested in classifying costs as variable or fixed using an appropriate output-based activity measure as the base (e.g., volume of goods or services sold). Doing this allows management to make crucial decisions and assess profitability using output as the basis; we will elaborate on this in later chapters.

DECISION POINT

BUDGET ANALYST

You are the budget analyst for a firm that provides janitorial services to other companies. You have been asked to estimate the costs that will be incurred on the janitorial jobs that will be performed next year. What types of costs would you expect? How would you characterize these costs in terms of behaviour? What activity would you need to measure in order to estimate the costs?

*Note to student: See **Guidance Answers** online.*

EXTENT OF VARIABLE COSTS

The number and type of variable costs present in an organization will depend, in large part, on the organization's structure and purpose. A public utility such as BC Hydro, with large investments in equipment, will tend to have few variable costs. Most of the costs are associated with its plant, and these costs tend to be insensitive to changes in levels of service provided. A manufacturing company such as Black & Decker, in contrast, will often have many variable costs. These costs will be associated with both manufacturing and distributing its products to customers.

A merchandising company, such as Walmart or Canadian Tire, will usually have a high proportion of variable costs in its cost structure. In most merchandising companies, the cost of merchandise purchased for resale—a variable cost—constitutes a large component of total cost. Service companies, by contrast, have diverse cost structures. On the one hand, some service companies, such as the Pizza Pizza restaurant chain, have fairly large variable costs because of the costs of their raw materials. On the other hand, service companies involved in consulting, auditing, engineering, dental, medical, and architectural activities have very large fixed costs in the form of expensive facilities and highly trained salaried employees.

Some of the more frequently encountered variable costs are listed in Exhibit 6–2. This exhibit is not a complete listing of all costs that can be considered variable. Moreover, some of the costs listed in the exhibit may behave more like fixed costs than like variable costs in some firms. We will see some examples of this later in the chapter. Nevertheless, Exhibit 6–2 provides a useful listing of many of the costs that normally would be considered variable with respect to the volume of output.

EXHIBIT 6–2 Examples of Variable Costs

Type of Organization	Costs That Are Normally Variable With Respect to Volume of Output
Merchandising company	Cost of goods (merchandise) sold
Manufacturing company	Manufacturing costs:
	Direct materials
	Direct labour*
	Variable portion of manufacturing overhead:
	Indirect materials
	Lubricants
	Supplies
Both merchandising and manufacturing companies	Selling, general, and administrative costs:
	Commissions
	Clerical costs, such as invoicing
	Shipping costs
Service organizations	Supplies, travel, clerical

*Direct labour may or may not be variable in practice (see the On the Job box at the beginning of this chapter). Also see the discussion later in this chapter.

True Variable Versus Step-Variable Costs

LO1 • **Know**

CC2: Describe the behaviour of step-variable costs.

Not all variable costs have exactly the same behaviour pattern. Some variable costs behave in a *true variable* or *proportionately variable* pattern. Other variable costs behave in a *step-variable* pattern. Let us examine these costs, using Pizza Pizza as an example.

TRUE VARIABLE COSTS

True variable costs are those that vary in direct proportion to changes in the level of activity. The cost of direct materials is a true variable cost because the amount used during a period will vary in direct proportion to the number of customers served or pizzas served. Moreover, any amounts purchased but not used can be stored and carried forward to the next period as inventory (remember that just-in-time purchasing is extremely important in the restaurant business because direct materials are perishable items).

STEP-VARIABLE COSTS

A cost that increases or decreases only in response to more than a unit change in the activity level is known as a **step-variable cost**. The behaviour of a step-variable cost, contrasted with the behaviour of a true variable cost, is illustrated in Exhibit 6–3.

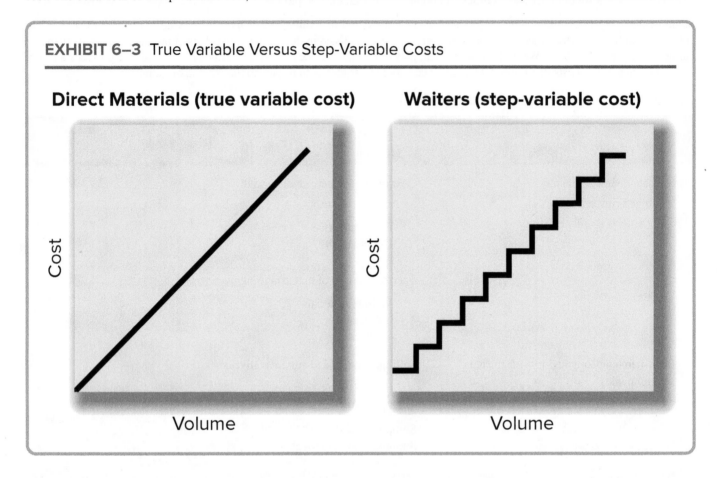

EXHIBIT 6–3 True Variable Versus Step-Variable Costs

Direct Materials (true variable cost)

Waiters (step-variable cost)

For example, one waiter at Pizza Pizza might be able to serve a total of 80 customers in a four-hour shift. However, when the number of customers is expected to be between 80 and 160, management must plan to have two waiters, and three if the number of customers expected is between 160 and 240. Thus, the number of waiters required depends on *block changes* in the number of customers. Moreover, when additional waiter time is obtained, it usually comes in indivisible blocks of, say, four or eight hours. It is reasonable to expect that Pizza Pizza will require additional waiters on weekends due to the higher number of customers typically expected. The strategy of management in dealing with step-variable costs must be to obtain the fullest use of services possible for each step. Great care must be taken in working with these kinds of costs in order to prevent "fat" (or excess) from building up in an organization. There may be a tendency to employ additional help more quickly than needed, and there is a natural reluctance to lay staff off when volume declines.

CONCEPT CHECK

1. Which of the following cost behaviour assumptions are false? (You may select more than one answer.)
   a. Variable cost per unit increases as the activity level increases.
   b. The average fixed cost per unit decreases as the activity level increases.
   c. Total variable costs decrease as the activity level decreases.
   d. Total fixed costs remain the same as the activity level changes (within the relevant range).

*Note to student: See **Guidance Answers** online.*

The Linearity Assumption and the Relevant Range

In dealing with variable costs, we have assumed a strictly linear relationship between cost and volume, except in the case of step-variable costs. Economists correctly point out that many costs classified as variable by the accountant actually behave in a *curvilinear* fashion. This is because the marginal productivity of variable inputs (e.g., direct materials and direct labour) is not constant. Instead, it shows an increasing trend that tapers off after some time and picks up again. The behaviour of a **curvilinear cost** is shown in Exhibit 6–4.

EXHIBIT 6–4 Curvilinear Costs and the Relevant Range

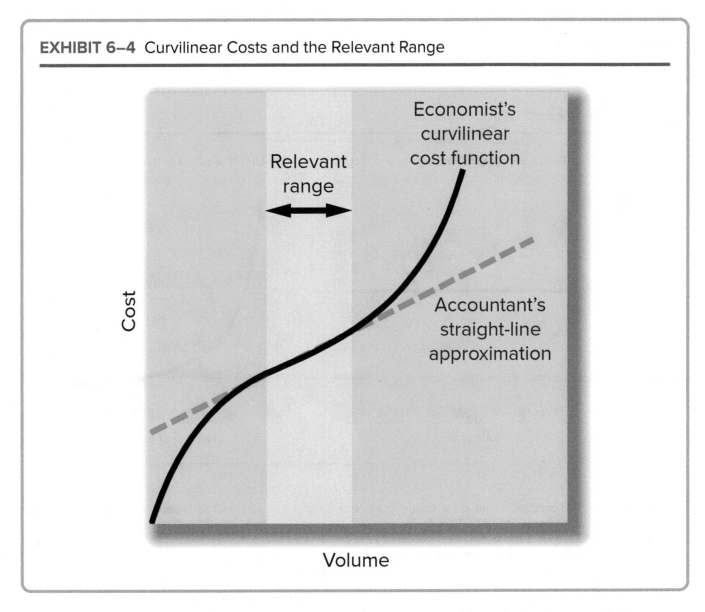

Although many costs are not strictly linear when plotted as a function of volume, a curvilinear cost can be satisfactorily approximated as a straight line within a narrow band of activity known as the *relevant range*. The **relevant range** is the range of activity within which the assumptions made about cost behaviour by the manager are valid. For example, note that the dashed line in Exhibit 6–4 can be used as an approximation to the curvilinear cost with little loss of accuracy within the relevant range (*grey area*). However, outside of the relevant range, this particular straight line is a poor approximation to the curvilinear cost relationship. Managers should always keep in mind that a particular assumption made about cost behaviour may be inappropriate if activity falls outside of the relevant range.

Fixed Costs

LO1 • **Know**

CC3: Describe the behaviour of fixed costs.

In our discussion of cost behaviour patterns in Chapter 2, we stated that fixed costs remain constant in total dollar amount within the relevant range of activity. To continue the 50 Plus Expeditions example, assume the company decides to rent a building for $5,000 per month to store its equipment. The *total* amount of rent paid is the same, regardless of the number of guests the company takes on its expeditions during any given month. This cost behaviour pattern is shown graphically in Exhibit 6–5.

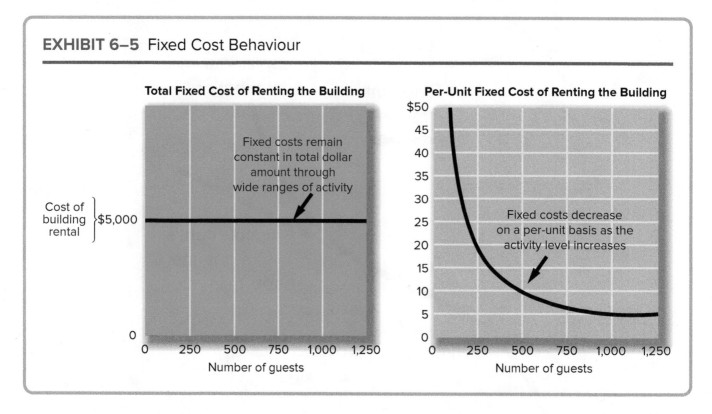

EXHIBIT 6–5 Fixed Cost Behaviour

Since fixed costs remain constant in total, the amount of fixed costs computed on a *per-unit* basis becomes progressively smaller as the level of activity increases. If 50 Plus Expeditions has only 250 guests in a month, the $5,000 fixed rental cost will amount to $20 per guest. If there are 1,000 guests, the fixed rental cost will amount to only $5 per guest. This aspect of the behaviour of fixed costs is also displayed in Exhibit 6–5. Observe that as the number of guests increases, the average unit cost drops, but it drops at a decreasing rate. The first guests have the biggest impact on unit costs.

Fixed costs are sometimes expressed on a per-unit basis (i.e., unitized). In such situations, users of the information must be cautioned that fixed costs have been unitized and should not be mistaken for variable costs. For example, if Pizza Pizza allocates building rent at $0.25 per pizza, this does not mean that rent cost will increase by $0.25 every time a pizza is served. The amount of $0.25 per pizza is simply an average cost based on a certain volume of pizzas served and really has no meaning for decision-making purposes. This amount is allocated so that managers understand that the total cost of a pizza is *more than* the sum of all the variable costs. From a decision-making angle, this information can be useful for pricing purposes; from an analysis perspective, total cost information is useful for understanding profitability.

IN BUSINESS

R&D SPENDING CRITICAL AT AVAYA

Developing new products and new technologies is what sustains the telecommunications industry; this is especially true for Markham-based Avaya Canada, which acquired a division of Nortel Networks in the fall of 2009. Research and development (R&D) is a carefully planned activity at Avaya, with staff working on an average of 30 projects in any given year. Avaya invests considerable R&D resources into four broad cost categories: (1) employee-related costs (60% of total R&D costs), (2) contract partnership costs (15%), (3) direct project expenses (25%), and (4) capitalization costs (<1%). Close to two-thirds of the annual costs are relatively constant (fixed), and the remaining one-third is fluctuating (variable) depending upon the number and types of projects. Actual expenses are compared with the planned levels on a monthly basis to ensure that things are happening according to plan.

Source: Personal conversation with Gordon Adamyk, director, Avaya Networking R&D/Biz Ops.

Types of Fixed Costs

LO1 • Know

CC4: Explain committed and discretionary fixed costs.

Fixed costs are sometimes referred to as *capacity costs,* since they result from outlays made for buildings, equipment, skilled professional employees, and other items needed to provide the basic capacity for sustained operations. For planning purposes, fixed costs can be viewed as being either *committed* or *discretionary*.

COMMITTED FIXED COSTS

Committed fixed costs relate to the investment in facilities, equipment, and the basic organizational structure of a firm. Examples include depreciation of buildings and equipment, taxes on real estate, insurance, and salaries of key personnel.

Committed fixed costs are long-term in nature and cannot be reduced to zero even for short periods without seriously impairing the profitability or long-term goals of the organization. Even if operations are interrupted or cut back, the committed fixed costs will still continue largely unchanged. During a recession, for example, a firm will not usually discharge key executives or sell off key facilities. The basic organizational structure and facilities are generally kept intact. The costs of restoring them later are likely to be far greater than any short-term savings that might be realized. Since it is difficult to change a committed fixed cost once the commitment has been made, management should approach these decisions with particular care. Management should make such commitments only after careful analysis of the available alternatives.

DISCRETIONARY FIXED COSTS

Discretionary fixed costs (often referred to as *managed fixed costs*) usually arise from *annual* decisions by management to spend in certain areas. Examples of discretionary fixed costs include advertising, research, public relations, management development programs, management retreats, and internships for students.

Basically, two key differences exist between discretionary fixed costs and committed fixed costs. First, the planning horizon for a discretionary fixed cost is short—usually a single year. By contrast, committed fixed costs have a longer planning horizon. Second, discretionary fixed costs can be cut for short periods with minimal damage to the long-term goals of the organization. For example, spending on management retreats can be cut back because of poor economic conditions.

Whether a particular cost is regarded as committed or discretionary may depend on management's strategy. For example, during recessions when the level of home building is down, some construction companies lay most of their workers off and virtually disband operations. Other construction companies retain large numbers of employees on the payroll, even though the workers have little or no work to do. While these latter companies may be faced with short-term cash flow problems, it will be easier for them to respond quickly when economic conditions improve. The improved morale and loyalty of their employees may also give these companies a significant competitive advantage.

The most important characteristic of discretionary fixed costs is that management is not locked into a decision regarding such costs. The costs can be adjusted from year to year, or even perhaps during the course of a year, if circumstances demand such a modification.

HELPFUL HINT

Committed fixed costs are those that organizations (or individuals) are committed to for a period of time, whereas discretionary fixed costs are those for which no such commitments exist. As an example, an individual who enters into a rental agreement is committed to paying the monthly rent. In contrast, going to see a movie or buying an additional pair of shoes is more likely a discretionary expense (i.e., there is no commitment of any sort to incur these expenses).

THE TREND TOWARD FIXED COSTS

The trend in many industries is toward greater fixed costs relative to variable costs. Chores that used to be performed manually have been taken over by machines. For example, an H&R Block employee used to fill out tax returns for customers by hand, and the advice given to a customer largely depended on the knowledge of that particular employee. Now, sophisticated computer software is used to complete tax returns, and the software provides the customer with tax planning and other advice tailored to the customer's needs on the basis of the accumulated knowledge of many experts. The move toward online banking and shopping has also necessitated more investment in technology and the required support structure.

As machines take over more and more of the tasks that used to be performed by humans, the overall demand for human workers has not diminished. The demand for *knowledge workers,* those who work primarily with their minds rather than their muscles, has grown tremendously. Knowledge workers tend to be salaried, highly trained, and difficult to replace. As a consequence, the costs of compensating knowledge workers are often relatively fixed and are committed, rather than discretionary.

IS LABOUR A VARIABLE COST OR A FIXED COST?

As the preceding discussion suggests, wages and salaries may be fixed or variable. The behaviour of wage and salary costs will differ from one country to another, depending on labour regulations, labour contracts, and custom. In some countries, such as France, Germany, China, and Japan, management has little flexibility in adjusting the labour force to changes in business activity. In such countries as Canada, management typically has much greater latitude. However, even in less restrictive environments, managers may choose to treat employee compensation as a fixed cost.

Classifying direct labour as variable or fixed really depends on the employment terms and how employees are paid. If wages are paid strictly on the basis of the volume of output, then direct labour is truly a variable cost. However, in many organizations (including those that are unionized), direct labour is paid either a weekly or a monthly salary. On top of that, employees may receive incentive compensation in the form of performance-based bonuses, provided they achieve predetermined output targets. In situations like this, direct labour cost is more likely fixed.

Many major organizations have undergone waves of downsizing in recent years, in which large numbers of employees—particularly middle managers—have lost their jobs. This downsizing might seem to prove that even management salaries should be regarded as variable costs, but this would not be a valid conclusion. Downsizing has been the result of attempts to automate and/or reengineer business processes and cut costs, rather than a response to a decline in sales activity. This underscores an important, but subtle, point: Fixed costs can change—they just do not change in response to small changes in activity.

In summary, we cannot provide a clear-cut answer to the question, "Is labour a variable or fixed cost?" It depends on how much flexibility management has and on management's strategy. *Nevertheless, we will assume in this text that unless otherwise stated, direct labour is a variable cost.*

IN BUSINESS

AIRLINES FACE INCREASING LABOUR COSTS

Rising labour costs and employee benefits are a concern to the entire airline industry since these expenditures have been identified as the second largest cost to be borne by airlines. Over the years, WestJet's labour costs have increased by almost 50%. This and the increasing maintenance costs due to its aging fleet have resulted in a tighter cost situation for the airline. Through the involvement of labour unions in the industry, these challenges have only intensified. WestJet's American counterpart—American Airlines Group Inc.—was seeing a higher increase in labour costs in 2015 due to its two agreements with union groups: a $200 million increase in pay for flight attendants, and a potential $650 million increase in labour costs from proposed contracts with pilots. An interesting trend for both the airlines was a steady decrease in the quarterly average closing stock price during the first three quarters of 2015. WestJet's quarterly averages were $30.47, $26.83, and $23.75, whereas American Airlines' quarterly averages were $50.76, $45.60, and $41.06, respectively.

Sources: M. Esterl, "Labor Demands Cloud AMR Outlook," *The Wall Street Journal*, April 14, 2009, p. B1; S. Deveau, "WestJet Looking to Cut Costs as 'Cushion' Over Air Canada Shrinks," *Financial Post (online)*, December 6, 2012; T. Maxon, "Proposed Pilot Contract Would Raise American's 2015 Labor Costs by $650 Million," *The Dallas Morning News*, January 12, 2015; T. Cederholm, "Why Investors Should Track Labor Cost in the Airline Industry," *Market Realist*, October 30, 2014; http://www.nasdaq.com/symbol/aal/historical; https://ca.finance.yahoo.com/q/hp?s=WJA.TO&a=00&b=1&c=2014&d=09&e=20&f=2015&g=d.

Fixed Costs and the Relevant Range

LO1 ● **Know**

CC5: Explain the importance of relevant range in understanding fixed costs.

The concept of relevant range, introduced in the discussion of variable costs, is also important in understanding fixed costs. The relevant range of activity for a fixed cost is the range of activity over which the graph of the cost is flat, as shown in Exhibit 6–6. As a company expands its level of activity, it may outgrow its present facilities, or the key management team may need to be expanded. The result, of course, will be increased committed fixed costs as larger facilities are built and as new management positions are created. For example, if Pizza Pizza doubles its capacity, more space, additional equipment, and more people will be required.

One reaction to the step pattern depicted in Exhibit 6–6 is to say that fixed costs are really just step-variable costs. To some extent, this is true, since almost *all* costs can be adjusted in the long run. There are two major differences, however, between the step-variable costs depicted in Exhibit 6–3 and the fixed costs depicted in Exhibit 6–6.

The first difference is that the step-variable costs can often be adjusted quickly as conditions change, whereas once fixed costs have been set they often cannot be changed easily. A step-variable cost, such as the cost of employing waiters, can be adjusted upward or downward by hiring and laying waiters off. In contrast, once an organization has signed a lease for a building, it is locked into that level of lease cost for the life of the contract.

The second difference is that the *width of the steps* depicted for step-variable costs is much narrower than the width of the steps depicted for the fixed costs in Exhibit 6–6. The width of the steps relates to volume or level of activity. For step-variable costs, the width of a step might be 40 hours of activity or less for clerical labour cost. For fixed costs, however, the width of a step might be *thousands* or even *tens of thousands* of hours of activity. In essence, the width of the steps for step-variable costs is generally so narrow that these costs can be treated essentially as variable costs for most purposes. The width of the steps for fixed costs, in contrast, is large enough that these costs must generally be treated as entirely fixed within the relevant range.

EXHIBIT 6–6 Fixed Costs and the Relevant Range

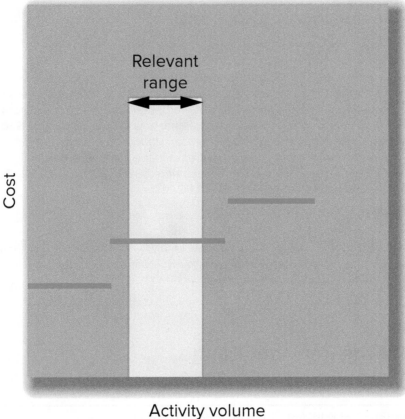

Cost

Relevant range

Activity volume

IN BUSINESS

MANAGING SALES AND MARKETING

CEL Packaging Pvt. Limited is based in western India and provides total packaging solutions to its customers. As with every organization, CEL has also been finding ways to reduce costs across various functions. A thorough cost analysis suggested that there was some scope for reducing sales and marketing costs by at least 25%. After additional analysis, CEL decided to close its sales offices in some locations and employ sales agents on a commission basis. As a result, the company eliminated the large fixed costs of maintaining sales offices. It now incurs only variable costs by way of commissions paid to the sales agents on the basis of sales revenues. (CEL uses the Indian rupee (₹) as its base currency, and $1 = ₹50 at the time of writing.) CEL saved about ₹23,000 per month on sales of ₹200,000, which translated into a reduction of about 31%. CEL has not stopped its cost reduction efforts with these savings; instead, it continues to find other areas where costs can be saved.

Source: Personal correspondence with the executive director of CEL Packaging Pvt. Limited; http://www.coreemb.com.

Mixed Costs

LO1   • Know

CC6: Describe the behaviour of mixed costs.

A **mixed cost** is one that contains both variable and fixed cost elements. To continue the 50 Plus Expeditions example, assume that the company must pay a licence fee of $25,000 per year plus $3 per rafting party to provincial authorities. If the company runs 1,000 rafting parties this year, then the total fees paid to the province will be $28,000, made up of $25,000 in fixed cost plus $3,000 in variable cost. The behaviour of this mixed cost is shown graphically in Exhibit 6–7.

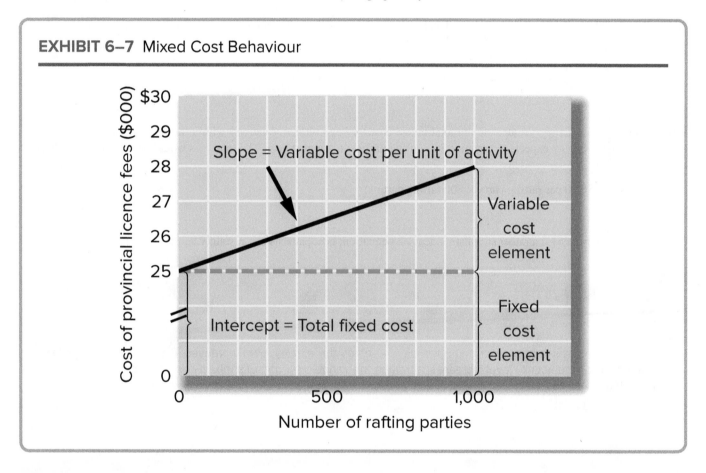

EXHIBIT 6–7 Mixed Cost Behaviour

LO2   • Apply   • Know

CC7: Construct a basic linear cost equation, and explain the individual elements of the cost equation.

Even if 50 Plus fails to attract any customers, the company will still have to pay the licence fee of $25,000. This is why the cost line in Exhibit 6–7 intersects the vertical cost axis at the $25,000 point. For each rafting party the company organizes, the total cost of the provincial fees will increase by $3. Therefore, the total cost line slopes upward as the variable cost element is added to the fixed cost element.

Since the mixed cost in Exhibit 6–7 is represented by a straight line, the following equation for a straight line can be used to express the relationship between mixed cost and the volume of activity:

$$Y = a + bX$$

In this equation,

Y = Total mixed cost

a = Total fixed cost (the vertical intercept of the line)

b = Variable cost per unit of activity (the slope of the line)

X = Level of activity

In the case of the provincial fees paid by 50 Plus Expeditions, the equation is written as follows:

$$Y = \$25{,}000 + \$3.00 \times X$$

Total mixed cost	Total fixed cost	Variable cost per unit of activity	Activity Volume

This equation makes it easy to calculate the total mixed cost for any volume of activity within the relevant range. For example, suppose that the company expects to organize 800 rafting parties in the next year. The total fees would be $27,400, calculated as follows:

Y = $25,000 + ($3.00 per rafting party × 800 rafting parties)
   = $27,400

Note that we have presented a rather simplistic linear cost equation; cost patterns can certainly be more complicated.

HELPFUL HINT

A mixed cost expressed on a per-unit basis decreases as the activity level increases. Do you know why? On a per-unit basis as the activity level increases, although the variable portion of a mixed cost stays constant, the fixed portion of a mixed cost decreases. This occurs because the fixed cost is being spread across more units.

CONCEPT CHECK

2. Which of the following statements are false? (You may select more than one answer.)
    a. The planning horizon for discretionary fixed costs is longer than the planning horizon for committed fixed costs.
    b. Discretionary fixed costs can be cut in the short term if necessary, while committed fixed costs cannot be cut for short periods.
    c. As companies increasingly rely on knowledge workers, the labour cost associated with employing these workers is often committed fixed as opposed to discretionary.
    d. A mixed cost contains both committed fixed and discretionary elements.

Note to student: See **Guidance Answers** *online.*

The Analysis of Mixed Costs

LO2 • **Know**

CC8: Explain the importance of separating mixed costs into fixed and variable portions.

In practice, mixed costs are quite common. For example, the cost of providing X-ray services to patients at the Toronto General Hospital is a mixed cost. There are substantial fixed costs for equipment depreciation and for salaries of radiologists and technicians, but there are also variable costs for X-ray film, power, and supplies. At WestJet Airlines, maintenance costs are mixed costs. The company must incur fixed costs for renting maintenance facilities and for keeping skilled mechanics on the payroll, but the costs of replacement parts, lubricating oils, tires, and so on are variable with respect to how often and how far the company's aircraft are flown.

The fixed portion of a mixed cost represents the basic, minimum cost of just having a service *ready and available* for use (i.e., capacity cost). The variable portion represents the cost incurred for *actual consumption* of the service. The variable element varies in proportion to the amount of service consumed.

Why should management be interested in separating the fixed and variable portions of a mixed cost? The simple answer is that a mixed cost is a combination of two cost types with exactly opposite behaviours. While one cost type varies in proportion to changes in activity volume, the other type does not. Therefore, when activity volume changes within the organization, only the variable portion of the mixed cost will be affected (in terms of total cost going up or down). Approximating a mixed cost to one or the other will distort planning and decision making. For example, budgeting is an important activity in most organizations and requires a good understanding of cost behaviour. Managers who are unable to separate variable costs from fixed costs will not be able to make accurate predictions of future costs—this is not a desirable situation.

Now we know why separating the fixed and variable portions is important, but how does management go about estimating the fixed and variable elements? That really depends on the availability of historical data to guide the process. *Account analysis* and the *engineering approach* are commonly used when there is little or no historical data available for analysis. However, when a considerable amount of historical data is available, managers can choose from the following three methods: *high–low, scattergraph,* and *regression analysis.*

Nonquantitative Approaches to Cost Analysis

In **account analysis**, each account under consideration is classified as either variable or fixed on the basis of the analyst's knowledge of how the cost in the account behaves. For example, direct materials would be classified as variable, and a building lease cost would be classified as fixed, because of the nature of those costs.

Account analysis works best when analyzing costs at a fairly aggregated level, such as the cost of serving patients in the emergency room (ER) of your local hospital. The costs of drugs, supplies, forms, wages, equipment, and so on can be roughly classified as variable or fixed, with respect to the number of patients, and a mixed cost formula for the overall cost of the ER can be estimated fairly quickly.

The **engineering approach** to cost analysis involves a detailed analysis of what the cost behaviour should be, based on an industrial engineer's evaluation of the production methods to be used, the materials specifications, labour requirements, equipment usage, efficiency of production, power consumption, and so on. For example, Pizza Hut might use the engineering approach to estimate the cost of serving a particular takeout pizza. Once we know the types of resources required, we can attempt to classify them as fixed or variable.

Quantitative Approaches to Cost Analysis

This section will focus on how to separate fixed and variable costs using quantitative methods. We do this using the example presented at the beginning of this chapter (see Managerial Accounting in Action).

We will examine three methods that Kinh Nguyen could use to break mixed costs down into their fixed and variable elements—the *high–low method,* the *scattergraph method,* and the *least-squares regression method.* All three methods are based on analyzing historical cost and activity data. In the case of Mid-Town Medical Centre (MMC), we will use the following records of maintenance costs and patient-days for the previous year to estimate the fixed and variable elements of maintenance costs:

Month	Activity Volume (patient-days)	Maintenance Cost Incurred
January	5,600	$7,900
February	7,100	8,500
March	5,000	7,450
April	6,500	8,200
May	7,300	9,070
June	8,000	9,800
July	6,200	7,800
August	7,200	8,600
September	6,100	8,000
October	5,900	7,950
November	6,200	8,120
December	5,800	7,970

The High–Low Method

LO2 ● **Know** ● **Apply**

CC9: Describe the high–low method of analyzing mixed costs, and set up a cost equation using this method.

To analyze mixed costs with the **high–low method**, begin by identifying the period with the lowest level of activity (March) and the period with the highest level of activity (June). The difference in cost corresponding to the two extreme activity levels is divided by the difference between the high and low activity levels to estimate the variable cost per unit of activity (the calculation is shown below).

	Patient- Days	Maintenance Cost Incurred
High activity level (June)	8,000	$9,800
Low activity level (March)	5,000	7,450
Change	3,000	$2,350

$$\text{Variable cost} = \frac{\text{Change in cost}}{\text{Change in activity}} = \frac{\$9,800 - \$7,450}{8,000 - 5,000} = \frac{\$2,350}{3,000 \text{ patient-days}} = \$0.783 \text{ per patient-day}$$

We can now determine the amount of fixed cost. This is done by taking the total cost at *either* the high or the low activity level and deducting the variable cost element. In the computation that follows, total cost at the high activity level is used in computing the fixed cost element:

$$\text{Fixed cost element} \quad = \quad \text{Total cost} - \text{Variable cost element}$$

$$= \quad \$9,800 - (\$0.783 \text{ per patient-day} \times 8,000 \text{ patient-days})$$

$$= \quad \$3,536$$

Both the variable and fixed cost elements have now been isolated. The cost of maintenance can be expressed as $3,536 per month plus 78.3 cents per patient-day.

The cost of maintenance can also be expressed in terms of the equation for a straight line as follows:

$$Y = \$3,536 \quad + \quad \$0.783X$$

Total   Number of

maintenance cost   patient-days

The data used in this illustration are shown graphically in Exhibit 6–8. Three things should be noted in relation to this exhibit:

1. The total maintenance cost, Y, is plotted on the vertical axis. Cost is known as the **dependent variable**, since the amount of cost incurred during a period depends on the volume of activity for the period. (That is, as the volume of activity increases, total cost will also increase.)

2. The activity, X (patient-days in this case), is plotted on the horizontal axis. Activity is known as the **independent variable**, since it causes variations in the cost.

3. A straight line has been drawn through the two points corresponding to the low and high levels of activity. (The formula for the variable cost is the same as the formula for the slope of the line.) It is important to note that by drawing a straight line we are assuming linearity of costs. Managers must be made aware that approximating a cost formula to a linear function may result in a misstatement of costs.

EXHIBIT 6–8 High–Low Method of Cost Analysis

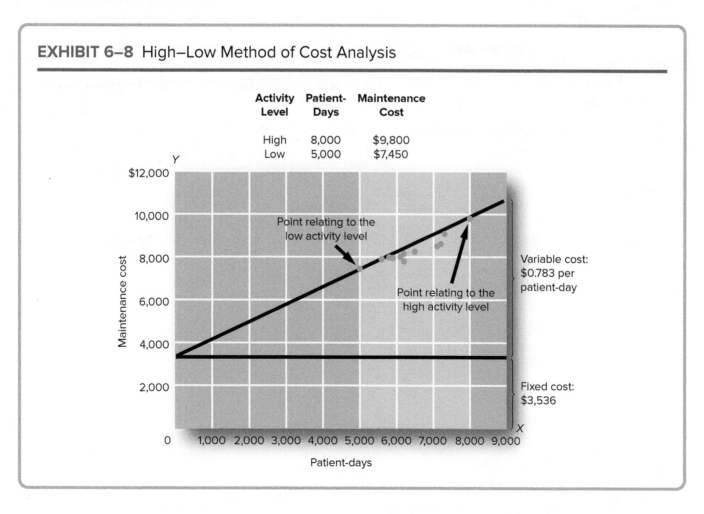

Activity Level	Patient-Days	Maintenance Cost
High	8,000	$9,800
Low	5,000	$7,450

Sometimes, the high and low levels of activity *do not coincide* with the high and low amounts of cost. For example, the period that has the highest level of activity might not have the highest amount of cost. Nevertheless, the highest and lowest levels of *activity* and the costs *corresponding* to these two activity levels are used to analyze a mixed cost under the high–low method. The activity is the independent variable (i.e., the factor that presumably causes costs); therefore, the analyst would like to use data that reflect the greatest possible variation in activity.

WORKING IT OUT

Assume a hotel rented 400, 480, and 420 rooms in the months of April, May, and June, respectively; the total housekeeping costs for the three months in question were $6,000, $6,800, and $6,200.

Required:

Using the high–low method, what is the amount of monthly fixed housekeeping costs?

SOLUTION TO WORKING IT OUT

We use the following five-step process to perform the high–low method calculations:

Step 1: Select the two periods with the highest and lowest levels of activity.
In our question, the highest level of activity occurs in May and the lowest level of activity occurs in April.

Step 2: Compute the change in cost and the change in activity between the two periods.
The activity levels and corresponding costs in those two months are 480 rooms and $6,800, and 400 rooms and $6,000, respectively. Therefore, the change in cost is $800 and the change in activity level is 80.

Step 3: Divide the change in cost by the change in activity to derive your estimate of the variable cost per unit.

$$\text{Variable cost} = \frac{\text{Change in cost}}{\text{Change in activity}} = \frac{\$6,800 - \$6,000}{480 - 400} = \$10 \text{ per } room$$

Step 4: Multiply the low (or high) level of activity by the variable cost per unit. Subtract this amount from the total cost at the low (or high) level of activity to derive the fixed portion of the mixed cost.

$$\text{Total variable cost at the low level of activity} = 400 \text{ rooms} \times \$10 \text{ per room} = \$4,000$$

Therefore,

$$\text{Fixed cost} = \$6,000 - \$4,000 = \$2,000$$

Step 5: Use the equation $Y = a + bX$ to estimate the total mixed cost for any level of activity within the relevant range.
Cost equation is as follows: $Y = \$2,000 + \$10X$, where
$$Y = \text{Monthly housekeeping costs}$$
$$X = \text{Number of rooms}$$

The Scattergraph Method

CC10: Explain the scattergraph method of analyzing mixed costs, and set up a cost equation using this method.

A more accurate method of analyzing mixed costs is the **scattergraph method**, which takes into account all of the activity volume and cost data. A graph like the one that we used in Exhibit 6–8 is constructed, in which costs observed at various levels of activity are plotted and a line is fitted to the plotted points. However, rather than just fitting the line to the high and low points, all points are considered when the line is drawn. This is done through simple visual inspection of the data, with the analyst taking care that the line is representative of all points, not just the high and low ones. Typically, the line is drawn such that approximately equal numbers of points fall above and below it. A graph of this type is known as a *scattergraph,* and the line *fitted* to the plotted points is known as a **regression line**.

The scattergraph approach using the MMC maintenance data is illustrated in Exhibit 6–9. Note that the regression line has been placed in such a way that approximately equal numbers of points fall above and below it. Since the regression line intersects the vertical cost axis at $3,750, this amount represents the fixed cost element.

EXHIBIT 6–9 Scattergraph Method of Cost Analysis

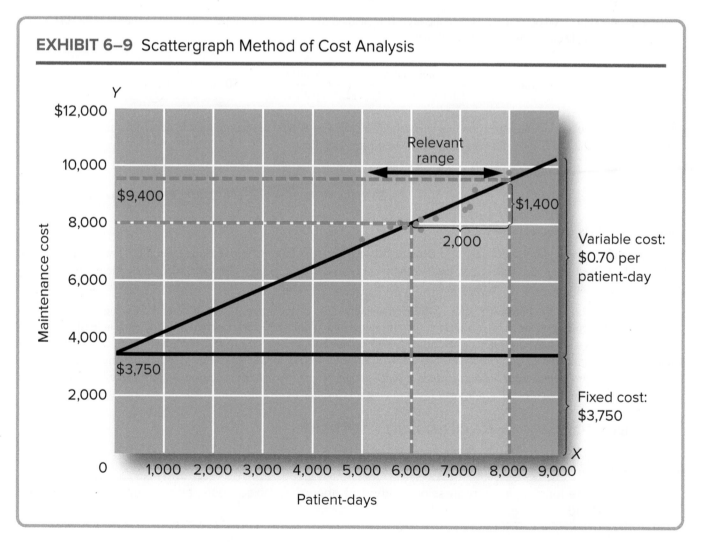

The variable cost element can be computed by determining the slope of the regression line, *within the relevant range,* which can be done as follows. First, select any two activity levels on the X-axis that lie within the relevant range of 5,000 to 8,000 patient-days;

we have selected 6,000 and 8,000 patient-days. Next, draw vertical lines from these two activity levels to intersect the regression line. From the two points where the just-drawn vertical lines intersect the regression line, draw horizontal lines to the Y-axis. Note that the horizontal line corresponding to the 8,000-patient-day activity level intersects the Y-axis at the $9,400 cost level, whereas the horizontal line corresponding to the 6,000-patient-day activity level intersects the Y-axis at the $8,000 cost level. We capture these two data points as follows:

	Patient-Days	Maintenance Cost Incurred
Activity level 1	8,000	$9,400
Activity level 2	6,000	8,000
Change	2,000	$1,400

It is important to note that the amount of $9,400 shown in the table above is different from $9,800 as mentioned in the data table. This is because the amounts shown in the data table are actual recorded amounts, whereas the amounts shown in the table above are estimates based on the graph shown in Exhibit 6–9. *These estimated amounts can change depending upon the slope of the line that the analyst draws.*

We now use the same method that we used in the high–low method to calculate the slope of the line or the variable cost, which will result in a variable cost of $0.70 per patient-day.

$$\text{Variable cost} = \frac{\text{Change in cost}}{\text{Change in activity}} = \frac{\$1,400}{2,000 \text{ patient-days}} = \$0.70 \text{ per patient-day}$$

Thus, the cost formula using the regression line in Exhibit 6–9 would be $3,750 per month plus 70 cents per patient-day. In terms of the linear equation $Y = a + bX$, the cost formula can be written as follows:

$$Y = \$3,750 + \$0.70X$$

where activity (X) is expressed in patient-days.

In this example, there is not a great deal of difference between the cost formula derived using the high–low method and the cost formula derived using the scattergraph method (only 8.3 cents per patient-day). However, sometimes, there *could* be a big difference. In such situations, more reliance should ordinarily be placed on the results of the scattergraph approach.

Also, observe that all of the points in Exhibit 6–9 lie reasonably close to the straight line. In other words, the estimates of the fixed and variable costs are reasonably accurate within this range of activity, and so the relevant range extends at least from 5,000 to 8,000 patient-days. It may also be accurate below 5,000 patient-days and above 8,000 patient-days—we cannot tell for sure without looking at more data. *If the activity level consistently falls below 5,000 patient-days, it may be possible for MMC to reduce the level of fixed costs. Similarly, if the activity level consistently increases above 8,000 patient-days, MMC may have to increase its level of fixed costs. Both these situations will result in new cost formulas.*

The Least-Squares Regression Method

LO2   • Know   • Apply

CC11: Explain the least-squares regression method of analyzing mixed costs, and set up a cost equation using this method.

The basic idea underlying the **least-squares regression** method is illustrated in Exhibit 6–10 using hypothetical data points. Note that the deviations from the plotted points to the regression line are measured vertically on the graph. These vertical deviations, called the *regression errors,* are the key to understanding least-squares regression. There is nothing mysterious about the least-squares regression method. It simply computes the regression line that minimizes the sum of these squared errors. The formulas that accomplish this are fairly complex and involve numerous calculations, but the principle is simple.

EXHIBIT 6–10 The Concept of Least-Squares Regression

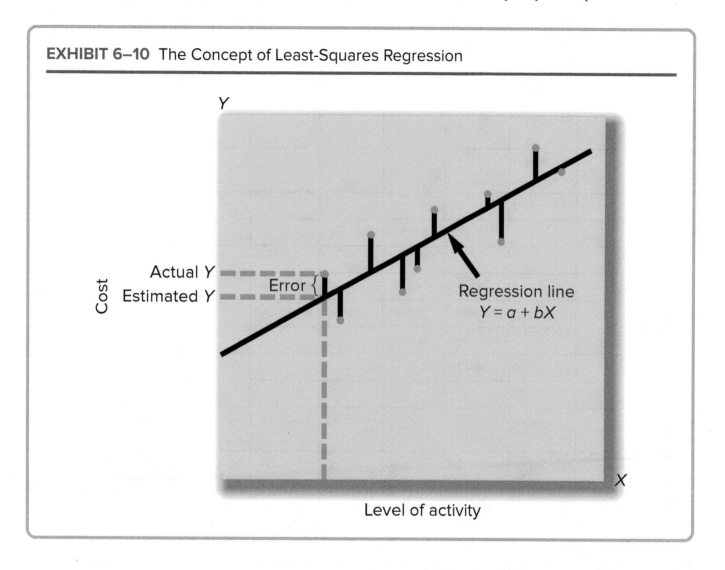

Using Excel to Do Regression Analysis

Basic regression analysis can be done using the following simple steps in Excel.

1. Enter data for the Y (dependent) variable and the X (independent) variable in two separate columns.
2. Click on the Data tab in Excel.
3. In the Data menu, click on Data Analysis, which appears on the far right.
4. Scroll down the Data Analysis menu and click on Regression.
5. Enter the data range for the Y and the X variables (e.g., A3:A15).
6. Enter the range where you want the output to be displayed (e.g., A31:H50).
7. Click OK; results will be displayed in the output range specified.

Results from a regression analysis of MMC's maintenance cost data will appear as follows:

	A	B	C	D	E	F	G	H	I
1	*Regression Statistics*								
2	Multiple R	0.939225444							
3	R Square	0.882144434							
4	Adjusted R Square	0.870358877							
5	Standard Error	229.3805547							
6	Observations	12							
7									
8	ANOVA								
9		*df*	*SS*	*MS*	*F*	*Significance F*			
10	Regression	1	3938245.611	3938246	74.84962	5.89323E-06			
11	Residual	10	526154.3889	52615.44					
12	Total	11	4464400						
13									
14		*Coefficients*	*Standard Error*	*t Stat*	*P-value*	*Lower 95%*	*Upper 95%*	*Lower 95.0%*	*Upper 95.0%*
15	Intercept	3752.265765	527.5150675	7.113097	3.24E-05	2576.888948	4927.642582	2576.888948	4927.642582
16	X Variable 1	0.706538502	0.081665953	8.651567	5.89E-06	0.52457542	0.888501584	0.52457542	0.888501584

The intercept term (3,752) represents the fixed cost per month, whereas the coefficient for the X variable 1 (0.707) represents the slope of the regression line—which is also the variable cost per patient-day. Therefore, using the least-squares regression method, the cost equation can be written as

$$Y = \$3{,}752 + \$0.707\,X$$

where activity (X) is expressed in patient-days.

One very important statistic generated as part of the regression analysis is R square (R^2). The R^2 in this example is 0.88 or 88%. This simply means that 88% of the variation in maintenance costs is explained by the variation in patient-days. In other words, only 12% of the variation in maintenance cost is not explained by the variation in patient-days. Knowing this helps the managers to decide whether the cost estimates have been developed on a reliable basis (e.g., patient-days). In other words, if the R^2 is low, the manager must look for some other base to estimate costs.

Comparing the Three Methods

Which of the three methods is most useful? Exhibit 6–11 compares the three methods.

EXHIBIT 6–11 Comparison of the Three Methods of Cost Data Analysis

Method	Advantages	Limitations
High–low	It is easy to understand and apply.	It utilizes only two points in the analysis; these could be abnormal observations. The cost formula may seriously misrepresent the true cost relationship that holds during normal periods.
Scattergraph	It can be an extremely useful tool in the hands of an experienced analyst. Quirks in cost behaviour due to strikes, bad weather, breakdowns, and so on become immediately apparent to the trained observer.	The line drawn is subjective. No two analysts who look at the same scattergraph are likely to draw exactly the same regression line. The cost estimates are not as precise as they are with other more sophisticated methods.
Least-squares regression	It is an objective and precise approach. It uses all data points in the analysis. It mathematically fits the regression line. It provides other useful statistics (e.g., R^2). Analysis can be done using computer software.	

MANAGERIAL ACOUNTING IN ACTION

THE WRAP-UP

After completing the analysis of maintenance costs, Kinh Nguyen met with Dr. Derek Chalmers to discuss the results.

MID-TOWN MEDICAL CENTRE

Nguyen: We used least-squares regression analysis to estimate the fixed and variable components of maintenance costs. According to the results, the fixed cost per month is $3,752, and the variable cost per patient-day is 70.7 cents.

Chalmers: Okay, so if we plan for 7,800 patient-days next month, what is your estimate of the maintenance costs?

Nguyen: That will take just a few seconds to figure out. [He wrote the following calculations on a pad of paper.]

Fixed costs	$3,752
Variable costs:	
7,800 patient-days × $0.707 per patient-day	5,515
Total expected maintenance costs	$9,267

Chalmers: Nine thousand two hundred sixty-seven dollars ... isn't that a bit *too* precise?

Nguyen: Sure. I don't really believe the maintenance costs will be exactly this figure. However, on the basis of the information we have, this is the best estimate we can come up with.

Chalmers: Don't let me give you a hard time. Even though it is an estimate, it will be a lot better than just guessing like we have done in the past. It will surely help us in our budgeting efforts. Thanks. I hope to see more of this kind of analysis.

DECISION POINT

ENTREPRENEUR

You are the owner of a small manufacturing firm. You are thinking about expanding your production capacity and are wondering about the implications of this on your costs. You therefore need a better understanding of your costs. How do you proceed?

*Note to student: See **Guidance Answers** online.*

Contribution Margin

LO3   ● **Know**   ● **Apply**

CC12: Explain the concept of contribution margin, and prepare a contribution margin income statement.

What do you do after separating costs on the basis of behaviour? We have already partially answered this question by saying that this separation can be used to estimate costs. Another important use of the separation of costs into fixed and variable is that managers can use the information to compute the contribution margin and prepare a contribution margin income statement (see Exhibit 6–12), which is different from the traditional income statement presented in Chapter 2. **Contribution margin** is the difference between sales revenues and all variable costs based on an output measure of activity; it is the amount remaining once all the variable costs have been deducted from sales revenues.

EXHIBIT 6–12 Traditional and Contribution Margin Income Statements for a Merchandising Company (all numbers given)

Traditional Format			Contribution Format		
Sales		$12,000	Sales		$12,000
Cost of goods sold*		6,000	Variable expenses:		
Gross margin		6,000	Cost of goods sold	$6,000	
Selling and administrative expenses:			Variable selling	600	
Selling	$3,100		Variable administrative	400	7,000
Administrative	1,900	5,000	Contribution margin		5,000
Net operating income		$ 1,000	Fixed expenses:		
			Fixed selling	2,500	
			Fixed administrative	1,500	4,000
			Net operating income		$ 1,000

*For a manufacturing company, the cost of goods sold would include some variable costs, such as direct materials, direct labour, and variable overhead, and some fixed costs, such as fixed manufacturing overhead.

The unique thing about the contribution margin approach is that it provides managers with an income statement that clearly distinguishes between fixed and variable costs, and therefore aids planning and decision making. For example, a merchandising company will price its product in such a way that it covers all its costs and earns a certain level of income. However, competitive pressures may force it to drop its price for a short period, at which time management will want to ensure that the lower price covers at least the variable costs. We will revisit the concepts of variable and fixed costs and contribution margin in later chapters.

CONCEPT CHECK

3. A company's contribution margin income statement showed net operating income of $4,000 and fixed expenses of $10,000. How much contribution margin did the company earn?
   a. $29,000
   b. $15,000
   c. $19,000
   d. $14,000

*Note to student: See **Guidance Answers** online.*

Learning Objectives Summary

LO1   UNDERSTAND COST BEHAVIOUR.

Understanding cost behaviour is important for planning, decision making, and reporting. A variable cost varies in direct proportion to changes in activity. A step-variable cost increases or decreases only in more than a unit change in activity. A fixed cost remains constant in total within a relevant range of activity (the range of activity for which assumptions about cost behaviour are valid). Two types of fixed costs exist: committed and discretionary. A mixed cost is one that contains variable and fixed portions.

LO2   ANALYZE AND ESTIMATE COSTS.

A basic cost equation is written in terms of $Y = a + bX$, where Y is the total cost, a is the total fixed cost, b is the variable cost per unit of activity, and X is the activity level. Y is mixed in nature, and it is useful to separate the fixed and variable portions for the purposes of cost analysis and estimation. The most common quantitative methods used to analyze mixed costs are the high–low method, scattergraph method, and least-squares regression method.

LO3   COMPUTE CONTRIBUTION MARGIN AND INCOME.

Contribution margin is the difference between sales revenue and total variable costs. Companies often prepare a contribution margin income statement for internal use. Such a statement shows sales revenues, variable costs, contribution margin, fixed costs, and income. This income statement format is quite different from the traditional format, which does not separate costs by behaviour.

Application Competency Summary

APPLICATION COMPETENCY	DELIVERABLE	SOURCE DOCUMENTS AND KEY INFORMATION	STEPS	KNOWLEDGE COMPETENCY
Construct a basic linear cost equation. ● **LO2–CC7**	*Key Information* Cost equation *Report/ Document* No specific report Can be used in preparing other reports for planning and decision making (e.g., flexible budget performance report)	*Cost Records* Fixed portion of the total cost (constant term) Variable portion of the total cost (slope of the equation) Activity causing costs (independent variable)	1. Identify the fixed and variable portions of the cost, and express the cost equation in the form $Y = a + bX$	Mixed costs ● **LO1–CC6**

APPLICATION COMPETENCY	DELIVERABLE	SOURCE DOCUMENTS AND KEY INFORMATION	STEPS	KNOWLEDGE COMPETENCY
Set up a cost equation using the high–low method. ● **LO2–CC9**	*Key Information* Cost equation *Report/ Document* No specific report Can be used in preparing other reports for planning and decision making (e.g., standard cost card)	*Historical Cost Records* Actual historical data of the volume of the independent variable (*X*-values) and the corresponding cost (*Y*-values) over a period (e.g., daily, weekly, monthly)	1. Identify the high and low observations of the independent variable and the corresponding costs associated with each observation. 2. Compute the slope (*b*) as follows: Divide the difference in the two cost numbers by the difference between the quantity of the high and low observations of the independent variable. 3. Compute the intercept (*a*) as follows: Multiply the slope by the high (or low) observation of the independent variable, and deduct this amount from the total cost corresponding to the independent variable. 4. Using the slope and the intercept, construct a cost equation to estimate future costs.	Mixed costs ● **LO1–CC6** Elements of the cost equation ● **LO2–CC7** High–low method ● **LO2–CC9**
Set up a cost equation using the scattergraph method. ● **LO2–CC10**	*Key Information* Cost equation *Report/ Document* No specific report Can be used in preparing other reports for planning and decision-making situations (e.g., profitability report)	*Historical Cost Records* Actual historical data of the volume of the independent variable (*X*-values) and the corresponding cost (*Y*-values) over a period (e.g., daily, weekly, monthly)	1. Plot the data with the *X*-axis representing the independent variable and the *Y*-axis representing the cost. 2. Visually, draw a straight line that best fits the data through the points on the plot, and extend it to intersect the *Y*-axis. The above intersection point on the *Y*-axis represents the intercept (fixed portion) of the cost equation. 3. Draw vertical lines from any two points on the *X*-axis such that they intersect the *Y*-axis. Draw lines from the intersecting points on the line to the *Y*-axis. Compute the slope as follows: Divide the difference between the two points on the *Y*-axis by the difference between the two points on the *X*-axis.	Mixed costs ● **LO1–CC6** Elements of the cost equation ● **LO2–CC7** Scattergraph method ● **LO2–CC10**

APPLICATION COMPETENCY	DELIVERABLE	SOURCE DOCUMENTS AND KEY INFORMATION	STEPS	KNOWLEDGE COMPETENCY
			4. Using the slope and the intercept, construct a cost equation to estimate future costs.	
Set up a cost equation using the least-squares regression method. • LO2–CC11	*Key Information* Cost equation *Report/ Document* No specific report Can be used in preparing other reports for planning and decision-making situations (e.g., budget)	*Historical Cost Records* Actual historical data of the volume of the independent variable (*X*-values) and the corresponding cost (*Y*-values) over a period (e.g., daily, weekly, monthly)	1. Enter the data using statistics software or a spreadsheet, then run the least-squares regression method. 2. Identify the value of the slope and the intercept from the output generated by the software. 3. Using the slope and the intercept, construct a cost equation to estimate future costs.	Mixed costs • LO1–CC6 Elements of the cost equation • LO2–CC7 Least-squares regression technique • LO2–CC11
Prepare a contribution margin income statement. • LO3–CC12	*Key Information* Contribution margin and net income *Report/ Document* Contribution margin income statement	*Sales Ledger* Actual sales revenue *Various Cost Ledgers* Actual variable and fixed costs	1. Obtain the sales revenue from the sales ledger and the variable and fixed costs from various cost ledgers. 2. Deduct all variable costs from sales revenues to compute the contribution margin, and deduct fixed costs to compute net income.	Variable and fixed costs • LO1–CC1, 3 Mixed costs • LO1–CC6 • LO2–CC8

Review Problem 1: Cost Behaviour

Neptune Rentals offers a boat rental service. Consider the following costs of the company over the relevant range of 5,000 to 8,000 hours of operating time for its boats:

	Hours of Operating Time			
	5,000	**6,000**	**7,000**	**8,000**
Total costs:				
Variable costs	$ 20,000	$?	$?	$?
Fixed costs	168,000	?	?	?
Total costs	$ 188,000	$?	$?	$?
Cost per hour:				

	Hours of Operating Time			
	5,000	6,000	7,000	8,000
Variable cost	$?	$?	$?	$?
Fixed cost	?	?	?	?
Total cost per hour	$?	$?	$?	$?

Required:

Compute the missing amounts, assuming that cost behaviour patterns remain unchanged within the relevant range of 5,000 to 8,000 hours.

SOLUTION TO REVIEW PROBLEM 1

The variable cost per hour can be computed as follows:

$$\$20,000 \div 5,000 \text{ hours} = \$4 \text{ per hour}$$

Therefore, in accordance with the behaviour of variable and fixed costs, the missing amounts are as follows:

	Hours of Operating Time			
	5,000	6,000	7,000	8,000
Total costs:				
Variable costs	$ 20,000	$ 24,000	$ 28,000	$ 32,000
Fixed costs	168,000	168,000	168,000	168,000
Total costs	$188,000	$192,000	$196,000	$200,000
Cost per hour:				
Variable cost	$ 4.00	$ 4.00	$ 4.00	$ 4.00
Fixed cost	33.60	28.00	24.00	21.00
Total cost per hour	$ 37.60	$ 32.00	$ 28.00	$ 25.00

Observe that the total variable costs increase in proportion to the number of hours of operating time but that these costs remain constant at $4 if expressed on a per-hour basis.

In contrast, the total fixed costs do not change with changes in the level of activity. They remain constant at $168,000 within the relevant range. With increases in activity, however, the fixed costs decrease on a per-hour basis, dropping from $33.60 per hour when the boats are operated 5,000 hours a period to only $21 per hour when the boats are operated 8,000 hours a period. *Because of this troublesome aspect of fixed costs, they are most easily (and most safely) dealt with on a total basis, rather than on a per-unit basis, in cost analysis work.*

Review Problem 2: High–Low Method

The manager of Golf Warehouse would like a cost formula linking the costs involved in processing orders to the number of orders received during a month. The order entry department's costs and the number of orders received during the immediately preceding eight months are given in the following table:

Month	Number of Orders Received	Order Entry Department Costs
May	1,000	$11,980
June	1,700	16,000
July	1,400	14,200
August	1,650	15,500
September	900	11,520
October	1,150	12,500
November	1,200	13,000
December	1,320	13,800

Required:

1. Use the high–low method to establish the fixed and variable components of order processing costs.
2. Express the fixed and variable components of order processing costs as a cost formula in the linear equation form $Y = a + bX$.

SOLUTION TO REVIEW PROBLEM 2

1. The first step in the high–low method is to identify the periods of the highest and lowest activity. Those periods are June (1,700 orders received) and September (900 orders received).

   The second step is to compute the variable cost per unit using those two points:

Month	Number of Orders Received	Order Entry Department Costs
High activity level (June)	1,700	$16,000
Low activity level (September)	900	11,520
Change	800	$ 4,480

$$\text{Variable cost} = \frac{\text{Change in cost}}{\text{Change in activity}} = \frac{\$4,480}{800 \text{ orders received}} = \$5.60 \text{ per order received}$$

The third step is to compute the fixed cost element by deducting the variable cost element from the total cost at either the high or low point of activity. In the computation below, the high point of activity is used:

Fixed cost element = Total cost − Variable cost element

= $16,000 − ($5.60 per order received × 1,700 orders received)

= $6,480 per month

2. The cost formula expressed in the linear equation form is $Y = \$6,480 + \$5.60X$.

Questions

6–1   Distinguish among (a) variable cost, (b) fixed cost, and (c) mixed cost.

6–2   What effect does an increase in activity volume have on

   a.   Unit fixed costs?

   b.   Unit variable costs?

   c.   Total fixed costs?

   d.   Total variable costs?

6–3   Define the following terms: (a) cost behaviour and (b) relevant range.

6–4   What is meant by an *activity base* when dealing with variable costs? Give several examples of activity bases.

6–5   Distinguish among (a) a variable cost, (b) a mixed cost, and (c) a step-variable cost. Chart the three costs on a graph, with activity plotted horizontally and cost plotted vertically.

6–6   Managers often assume a strictly linear relationship between cost and activity volume. How can this practice be defended in light of the fact that many cost relationships are curvilinear?

6–7   Distinguish between discretionary fixed costs and committed fixed costs.

6–8   Classify the following fixed costs as normally being either committed or discretionary:

   a.   Depreciation on buildings.

   b.   Advertising.

   c.   Research.

   d.   Long-term equipment leases.

   e.   Pension payments to the firm's retirees.

   f.   Management development and training.

6–9   Does the concept of the relevant range apply to fixed costs? Explain your answer.

6–10   What is the major disadvantage of the high–low method?

6–11   What methods are available for separating a mixed cost into its fixed and variable elements using past records of cost and activity data? Which method is considered to be most accurate? Why?

6–12   What is a regression line? Give the general formula for a regression line. Which term represents the variable cost? The fixed cost?

6–13   Once a regression line has been drawn, how do you determine the fixed cost element? The variable cost element?

6–14   What is least-squares regression?

6–15   Why is the least-squares regression method preferred to the high–low method when analyzing mixed costs?

6–16   What is the difference between the scattergraph method and the least-squares regression method?

6–17   "The higher the R^2 of a regression equation, the better the likelihood that X is an appropriate cost driver for Y." Is this true or false? Explain your answer.

6–18   What is the contribution margin?

6–19   What is the difference between the contribution margin approach to the income statement and the traditional approach to the income statement?

The Foundational 15

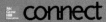

[LO1 – CC1, 3, 6; LO2 – CC7, 9; LO3 – CC12]

Consider the following data for Magnimus Corporation.

	July	August	September
Sales in units	4,000	4,200	4,800
Sales revenue	$400,000	$420,000	$480,000
Direct materials	74,000	77,700	88,800
Direct labour	88,600	93,030	106,320
Manufacturing overhead	63,480	65,160	70,680
Sales commission	30,000	31,500	36,000
Other selling expenses	41,960	43,620	44,360
Administrative expenses	31,550	31,550	31,550

Required:

6–1   What is the average price per unit sold?
6–2   Write the cost equation for direct materials.
6–3   Write the cost equation for direct labour.
6–4   Write the cost equation for manufacturing overhead.
6–5   Write the cost equation for sales commission.
6–6   Write the cost equation for other selling expenses.
6–7   Write the cost equation for administrative expenses.
6–8   Compute the total variable product costs per unit.
6–9   Compute the total variable selling and administrative costs per unit.
6–10   If 4,100 units are sold, what is the sales commission expense?
6–11   If 4,500 units are sold, what is the manufacturing overhead cost?
6–12   If 4,700 units are sold, what is the total cost?
6–13   What is the contribution margin per unit?
6–14   If 4,000 units are sold, what is the total contribution margin?
6–15   If 4,600 units are sold, what is the income?

Brief Exercises

BRIEF EXERCISE 6–1
Identifying Fixed and Variable Cost Behaviour [LO1 – CC1, 3]

Espresso Express operates a number of espresso coffee stands in busy suburban malls. The fixed weekly expense of a coffee stand is $2,200, and the variable cost per cup of coffee served is $0.18.

Required:

1. Complete the following table with your estimates of total costs and cost per cup of coffee at the indicated levels of activity for a coffee stand. Round the cost of a cup of coffee to the nearest tenth of a cent.

	Cups of Coffee Served in a Week		
	3,000	3,200	3,400
Fixed cost	?	?	?
Variable cost	?	?	?
Total cost	?	?	?
Cost per cup of coffee served	?	?	?

2. Does the cost per cup of coffee served increase, decrease, or remain the same as the number of cups of coffee served in a week increases? Explain.

BRIEF EXERCISE 6–2
Applying the High–Low Method [LO2 – CC9]

The Royal Canadian Lodge in Banff, Alberta, has accumulated records of the total electrical costs of the hotel and the number of occupancy-days over the last year. An occupancy-day represents a room rented out for one day. The hotel's business is highly seasonal, with peaks occurring during the ski season and in the summer.

Month	Occupancy-Days	Electrical Costs
January	1,736	$4,127
February	1,407	3,207
March	2,536	5,383
April	960	2,857
May	630	2,871
June	744	2,696
July	2,108	4,670
August	1,406	3,148
September	480	1,391
October	224	1,988
November	720	2,454
December	1,364	3,529

Required:

1. Using the high–low method, estimate the fixed cost of electricity per month and the variable cost of electricity per occupancy-day. Round the fixed cost to the nearest whole dollar and the variable cost to the nearest whole cent.

2. What factors other than occupancy-days are likely to affect the monthly variation in electrical costs?

BRIEF EXERCISE 6–3
Applying the Scattergraph Method [LO2 – CC10]

Oki Products, Ltd. has observed the following processing costs at various levels of activity over the past 10 months:

Month	Units Produced	Processing Cost
1	2,500	$28,000
2	11,000	52,000
3	15,000	59,000
4	5,500	38,000
5	9,000	47,000
6	8,500	52,000
7	7,500	44,000
8	7,000	41,000
9	11,500	52,000
10	6,000	41,000

Required:

1. Prepare a scattergraph by plotting these data on a graph. Plot cost on the vertical axis and units produced on the horizontal axis. Fit a line to your plotted points by visual inspection.

2. What is the approximate monthly fixed cost? The approximate variable cost per unit processed? Show your computations.

BRIEF EXERCISE 6–4
Applying the Least-Squares Regression Method [LO2 – CC11]

Required:

Using the data in Brief Exercise 6–3, repeat part (2) using least-squares regression (using any spreadsheet software). Is units produced a reliable basis for estimating processing costs?

BRIEF EXERCISE 6–5
Understanding Cost Behaviour and Contribution Margin [LO1 – CC1, 3; LO3 – CC12]

Murugan Ltd. had the following results for the year:

Sales	$45,000
Less: Operating expenses	39,000
Net operating income	$ 6,000

The average selling price for the units sold was $15 per unit and average variable cost $9 per unit.

Required:

Prepare a contribution margin income statement.

BRIEF EXERCISE 6–6
Understanding Cost Behaviour: Mixed Costs [LO1 – CC6; LO2 – CC7, 8]

Which of the following are linear cost functions? Which are mixed cost functions? Given: Y = total costs, X_1 = production volume, and X_2 = number of batches produced.

1. $Y = 4,000 + 3X_1 + 45X_2$
2. $Y = 1,500 + 6X_1 + 4X_2$
3. $Y = 16,780$
4. $Y = 4.5X_2$
5. $Y = 12,450 + 3.20X_2$

BRIEF EXERCISE 6–7
Applying the High–Low Method [LO2 – CC9]

The utility costs for Pizza Parlour (PP) amounted to $12,520 and $16,040 in April and December respectively; during these months PP sold 24,000 and 32,000 pizzas (these were the lowest and highest recorded sales). Using the high–low method, develop a cost equation for utility costs.

BRIEF EXERCISE 6–8
Preparing a Contribution Margin Income Statement [LO3 – CC12]

The Alpine House, Inc. is a large retailer of winter sports equipment. Here is an income statement for the company's ski department for a recent quarter:

THE ALPINE HOUSE, INC. Income Statement—Ski Department For the Quarter Ended March 31	
Sales	$560,000
Less: Cost of goods sold	390,000
Gross margin	170,000

THE ALPINE HOUSE, INC.
Income Statement—Ski Department
For the Quarter Ended March 31

Less: Operating expenses:		
Selling expenses	$60,000	
Administrative expenses	20,000	80,000
Net income		$ 90,000

On average, skis sell for $700 per pair. Variable selling expenses are $50 per pair of skis sold. The remaining selling expenses are fixed. The administrative expenses are 20% variable and 80% fixed. The company does not manufacture its own skis; it purchases them from a supplier for $450 per pair.

Required:

1. Prepare a contribution margin income statement for the quarter.
2. For every pair of skis sold during the quarter, what was the contribution toward covering fixed expenses and toward earning profits?

Exercises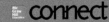

EXERCISE 6–1
Applying the High–Low Method; Predicting Cost [LO2 – CC9]

The Lakeshore Hotel's occupancy-days and custodial supplies expense over the last seven months were as follows:

Month	Occupancy-Days	Custodial Supplies Expense
March	18,000	$22,500
April	12,500	19,250
May	15,000	20,900
June	28,500	28,850
July	24,000	27,100
August	19,000	22,750
September	14,500	20,750

Occupancy-days are a measure of the overall activity at the hotel. For example, when a guest stays at the hotel for three days, it is counted as three occupancy-days.

Required:

1. Using the high–low method, estimate a cost formula for custodial supplies expense.
2. Using the cost formula you derived above, what amount of custodial supplies expense would you expect to be incurred at an occupancy level of 13,000 occupancy-days?

EXERCISE 6–2
Applying the Least-Squares Regression Method [LO2 – CC11]

Required:

Repeat parts (1) and (2) of Exercise 6–1 using least-squares regression (you may use a spreadsheet to compute the fixed and variable costs). Comment on the reliability of using occupancy-days as an allocation base.

EXERCISE 6–3
Applying the High–Low and Scattergraph Methods [LO2 – CC8, 9, 10]

Refer to the data in Exercise 6–1.

Required:

1. Prepare a scattergraph by plotting custodial supplies expense on the vertical axis and occupancy-days on the horizontal axis. Fit a regression line to your plotted points by visual inspection.
2. What is the approximate monthly fixed cost? The approximate variable cost per occupancy-day?
3. Scrutinize the points on your graph, and explain why the high–low method would or would not yield an accurate cost formula in this situation.

EXERCISE 6–4
Applying the High–Low and Scattergraph Methods [LO2 – CC9, 10]

The following data relating to units shipped and total shipping expense have been assembled by Archer Company, a manufacturer of large, custom-built air-conditioning units for commercial buildings:

Month	Units Shipped	Total Shipping Expense
January	3	$1,800
February	6	2,300
March	4	1,700
April	5	2,000
May	7	2,300
June	8	2,700
July	2	1,200

Required:

1. Estimate a cost formula for shipping expense using the high–low method.
2. For the scattergraph method, do the following:
   a. Prepare a scattergraph using the data given above. Plot total shipping expense on the vertical axis and units shipped on the horizontal axis. Fit a regression line to your plotted points by visual inspection.
   b. Using your scattergraph, estimate the approximate variable cost per unit shipped and the approximate fixed cost per month.
3. What factors, other than the number of units shipped, are likely to affect the company's total shipping expense? Explain your reasoning.

EXERCISE 6–5
Applying the High–Low Method; Predicting Cost [LO2 – CC7, 9]

Hoi Chong Transport, Ltd. operates a fleet of delivery trucks in Singapore. The company has determined that if a truck is driven 105,000 kilometres during a year, the average operating cost is 12.665 cents per kilometre. If a truck is driven only 70,000 kilometres during a year, the average operating cost increases to 14.5 cents per kilometre. (The Singapore dollar is the currency used in Singapore.) Note: Please do not round the decimal places of cost per kilometre.

Required:

1. Using the high–low method, estimate the variable and fixed cost elements of the annual cost of truck operation.
2. Express the variable and fixed costs in the form $Y = a + bX$.
3. If a truck were driven 80,000 kilometres during a year, what total cost would you expect to be incurred?

EXERCISE 6–6
Examining Cost Behaviour and Contribution Margin [LO1 – CC1, 3; LO2 – CC7; LO3 – CC12]

Bikes Manufacturing produces and sells children's bikes at an average price of $60. Its costs are as follows: direct materials, $12; direct labour, $7; variable overhead, $3; sales commission, 5% of price. Its fixed monthly costs are $38,000.

Required:

1. Using the above cost data, set up a monthly cost equation.
2. What is the company's contribution margin percentage?

EXERCISE 6–7
Understanding Cost Behaviour and Contribution Margin Income Statement [LO1 – CC1, 3; LO3 – CC12]

Harris Company manufactures and sells a single product. A partially completed schedule of the company's total and per-unit costs over the relevant range of 30,000 to 50,000 units produced and sold annually is given below:

| | Units Produced and Sold | | |
	30,000	40,000	50,000
Total costs:			
Variable costs	$180,000	?	?
Fixed costs	_____	?	?
Total costs	?	?	?
Cost per unit:			
Variable cost	?	?	?
Fixed cost	?	7.50	?
Total cost per unit	?	?	?

Required:

1. Complete the schedule of the company's total and unit costs.

2. Assume that the company produces and sells 45,000 units during a year at a selling price of $16 per unit. Prepare a contribution margin income statement for the year.

Problems

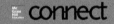

PROBLEM 6–1
Applying the High–Low Method; Predicting Cost [LO2 – CC9]

St. Mark's Hospital contains 450 beds. The occupancy rate varies between 50% and 90% per month, but the average occupancy rate is generally 80%. In other words, on average, 80% of the hospital's beds are occupied by patients. At this level of occupancy, the hospital's operating costs are $32 per occupied bed per day, assuming a 30-day month. This $32 figure contains both variable and fixed cost elements. This average cost figure drops to $29 when the occupancy rate is 90% (typically during the months of July and August).

CHECK FIGURE

(1) $294,637 per month plus $4.75 per bed-day

During June, the hospital's occupancy rate was only 50% and a total of $326,700 in operating costs was incurred during the month.

Required:

1. Using the high–low method, estimate
   a. The variable cost per occupied bed on a daily basis.
   b. The total fixed operating costs per month.

2. Assume an occupancy rate of 70% per month. What amount of total operating cost would you expect the hospital to incur?

PROBLEM 6–2
Applying the Scattergraph Method [LO2 – CC10]

Molina Company is a value-added computer reseller that specializes in providing services to small companies. The company owns and maintains several vehicles for use by its sales staff. All expenses of operating these vehicles have been entered into an automobile expense account on the company's books. Along with this record of expenses, the company has also kept a careful record of the number of kilometres the vehicles have been driven each month.

CHECK FIGURE

(2) Approximately $11,300 per month plus $0.476 per kilometre driven

The company's records of kilometres driven and total vehicle expenses over the past 10 months are given below:

Month	Kilometres Driven (000)	Total Cost
January	4	$13,000
February	8	15,700
March	7	15,300
April	12	17,000
May	6	14,300
June	11	16,500
July	14	18,000
August	10	15,000
September	13	18,100
October	15	18,400

Molina Company's president wants to know the cost of operating the fleet of vehicles in terms of the fixed monthly cost and the variable cost per kilometre driven.

Required:

1. Prepare a scattergraph using the data provided. Place cost on the vertical axis and activity (kilometres driven) on the horizontal axis. Fit a regression line to the plotted points by simple visual inspection.

2. By analyzing your scattergraph, estimate fixed cost per month and the variable cost per kilometre driven.

PROBLEM 6–3
Applying the High–Low, Scattergraph, and Least-Squares Regression Methods [LO2 – CC8, 9, 10]

Mountain View Hospital in Alberta has just hired a new chief administrator, who is anxious to employ sound management and planning techniques in the business affairs of the hospital. Accordingly, she has directed her assistant to summarize the cost structure existing in the various departments to secure data for planning purposes.

CHECK FIGURE

(1) $2,113 per month plus $53.41 per scan

The assistant is unsure how to classify the utilities costs in the radiology department, since these costs do not exhibit either strictly variable or strictly fixed cost behaviour. Utilities costs are very high in the department due to a CT scanner that draws a large amount of power and is kept running at all times. The scanner cannot be turned off due to the long warm-up period required for its use. When the scanner is used to scan a patient, it consumes an additional burst of power. The assistant has accumulated the following data on utilities costs and use of the scanner since the first of the year:

Month	Number of Scans	Utilities Cost
January	40	$ 4,250
February	85	6,300
March	100	7,000
April	150	10,400
May	200	14,000
June	110	8,500
July	260	16,000
August	160	11,700
September	210	15,100
October	180	13,500

The chief administrator has informed her assistant that the utilities cost is probably a mixed cost that will have to be broken down into its variable and fixed cost elements by use of a scattergraph. The assistant feels, however, that if an analysis of this type is necessary, the high–low method should be used because it is easier and quicker to use than other methods. The controller has suggested that there might be a better approach.

Required:

1. Using the high–low method, estimate a cost formula for utilities. Express the formula in the form $Y = a + bX$. (The variable rate should be stated in terms of cost per scan.)

2. Prepare a scattergraph by plotting the above data on a graph. (The number of scans should be placed on the horizontal axis, and utilities cost should be placed on the vertical axis.) Fit a regression line to the plotted points by visual inspection, and estimate a cost formula for utilities.

3. Estimate a cost formula using least-squares regression (use a spreadsheet).

4. Comment on the differences among the three cost formulas estimated above. Which one would you use?

PROBLEM 6–4

Examining Cost Behaviour; High–Low Analysis; Contribution Margin Income Statement [LO1 – CC1, 3, 6; LO2 – CC9; LO3 – CC12]

Morrisey & Brown, Ltd., of Sydney, Australia, is a merchandising firm that is the sole distributor of a product that is increasing in popularity among Australian consumers. The company's income statements for the three most recent months follow:

<table>
<tr><td colspan="4">MORRISEY & BROWN, LTD.
Income Statements
For the Three Months Ending September 30</td></tr>
<tr><td></td><td>July</td><td>August</td><td>September</td></tr>
<tr><td>Sales in units</td><td>4,000</td><td>4,500</td><td>5,000</td></tr>
<tr><td>Sales revenue</td><td>A$400,000</td><td>A$450,000</td><td>A$500,000</td></tr>
<tr><td>Less: Cost of goods sold</td><td>240,000</td><td>270,000</td><td>300,000</td></tr>
<tr><td>Gross margin</td><td>160,000</td><td>180,000</td><td>200,000</td></tr>
<tr><td>Less: Operating expenses:</td><td></td><td></td><td></td></tr>
<tr><td>Advertising expense</td><td>21,000</td><td>21,000</td><td>21,000</td></tr>
<tr><td>Shipping expense</td><td>34,000</td><td>36,000</td><td>38,000</td></tr>
<tr><td>Salaries and commissions</td><td>78,000</td><td>84,000</td><td>90,000</td></tr>
<tr><td>Insurance expense</td><td>6,000</td><td>6,000</td><td>6,000</td></tr>
<tr><td>Depreciation expense</td><td>15,000</td><td>15,000</td><td>15,000</td></tr>
<tr><td>Total operating expenses</td><td>154,000</td><td>162,000</td><td>170,000</td></tr>
<tr><td>Net income</td><td>A$ 6,000</td><td>A$ 18,000</td><td>A$ 30,000</td></tr>
</table>

> **CHECK FIGURE**
> (2) Shipping: A$18,000 per month plus A$4 per unit

(*Note:* Morrisey & Brown, Ltd.'s Australian-formatted income statement has been recast into the format common in Canada. The Australian dollar is denoted by A$.)

Required:

1. Identify each of the company's expenses (including cost of goods sold) as being variable, fixed, or mixed.
2. Using the high–low method, separate each mixed expense into variable and fixed elements. State the cost formula for each mixed expense.
3. Redo the company's income statement at the 5,000-unit level of activity using the contribution format.

PROBLEM 6-5
Identifying Cost Behaviour Patterns [LO1 – CC1, 2, 3, 6]

A number of graphs displaying cost behavior patterns are shown below. The vertical axis on each graph represents total cost and the horizontal axis represents the level of activity (volume).

Required:

1. For each of the following situations, identify the graph below that illustrates the cost pattern involved. A graph may be used more than once.
   a. Cost of raw materials used.
   b. Electricity bill—a flat fixed charge, plus a variable cost after a certain number of kilowatt-hours are used.
   c. City water bill, computed as follows:

First 1,000,000 litres or less	$1,000 flat fee
Next 10,000 litres	0.003 per litre used
Next 10,000 litres	0.006 per litre used
Next 10,000 litres	0.009 per litre used

   d. Depreciation of equipment, where the amount is computed by the straight-line method. When the depreciation rate was established, it was anticipated that the obsolescence factor would be greater than the wear-and-tear factor.
   e. Rent on a factory building donated by the city, wherein the agreement calls for a fixed fee payment unless 200,000 labour-hours or more are worked, in which case no rent need be paid.
   f. Salaries of maintenance workers, where one maintenance worker is needed for every 1,000 machine-hours or less (i.e., 0 to 1,000 machine-hours requires one maintenance worker, 1,001 to 2,000 machine-hours requires two maintenance workers, etc.).
   g. Cost of raw materials, where the cost starts at $7.50 per unit and then decreases by 5 cents per unit for each of the first 100 units purchased, after which it remains constant at $2.50 per unit.
   h. Rent on a factory building donated by the city, where the agreement calls for rent of $100,000 less $1 for each direct labour-hour worked in excess of 200,000 hours, but a minimum rental payment of $20,000 must be paid.
   i. Use of a machine under a lease, where a minimum charge of $1,000 is paid for up to 400 hours of machine time. After 400 hours of machine time, an additional charge of $2 per hour is paid up to a maximum charge of $2,000 per period.

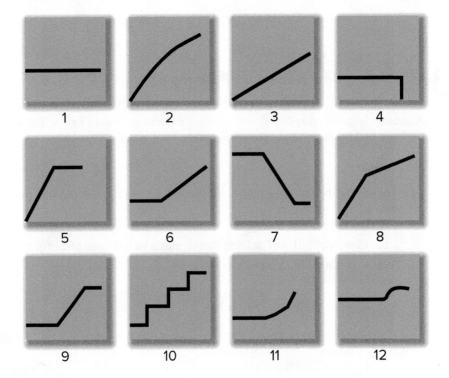

2. How would knowing cost behaviour patterns, such as those above, be of help to a manager in analyzing the cost structure of the firm?

(Adapted © AICPA)

PROBLEM 6–6
Applying the High–Low Method and Cost Behaviour [LO2 – CC9]

Sawaya Co., Ltd., of Japan, is a manufacturing company whose total factory overhead costs fluctuate considerably from year to year according to increases and decreases in the number of direct labour-hours worked in the factory. Total factory overhead costs (in Japanese yen, denoted ¥) at high and low levels of activity for recent years, are provided below:

CHECK FIGURE

(2) ¥1,300,000 per year plus ¥14.50 per DLH

	Level of Activity	
	Low	High
Direct labour-hours	100,000	150,000
Total factory overhead costs	¥12,450,000	¥15,275,000

The factory overhead costs above consist of indirect materials, rent, and maintenance. The company has analyzed these costs at the 100,000-hour level of activity as follows:

Indirect materials (V)	¥ 4,200,000
Rent (F)	5,500,000
Maintenance (M)	2,750,000
Total factory overhead costs	¥12,450,000

V = variable; F = fixed; M = mixed.

To have data available for planning, the company wants to break down the maintenance cost into its variable and fixed cost elements.

Required:

1. Estimate how much of the ¥15,275,000 factory overhead cost at the high level of activity consists of maintenance cost. (*Hint:* To do this, it may be helpful to first determine how much of the ¥15,275,000 consists of indirect materials and rent. Think about the behaviour of variable and fixed costs!)
2. By means of the high–low method of cost analysis, estimate a cost formula for maintenance.
3. What total factory overhead costs would you expect the company to incur at an operating level of 70,000 direct labour-hours?

PROBLEM 6–7
Applying the High–Low Method and Predicting Cost [LO2 – CC9]

Nova Company's total overhead costs at various levels of activity follow:

> **CHECK FIGURE**
> (2) $9,000 per month plus $1.60 per machine-hour

Month	Machine-Hours	Total Overhead Costs
April	70,000	$198,000
May	60,000	174,000
June	80,000	222,000
July	90,000	246,000

Assume that the total overhead costs consist of utilities, supervisory salaries, and maintenance. The breakdown of these costs at the 60,000 machine-hour level of activity is as follows:

Utilities (V)	$ 48,000
Supervisory salaries (F)	21,000
Maintenance (M)	105,000
Total overhead costs	$174,000

V = variable; F = fixed; M = mixed.

Nova Company's management wants to break down the maintenance cost into its basic variable and fixed cost elements.

Required:

1. As shown, overhead costs in July amounted to $246,000. Determine how much of this consisted of maintenance cost. (*Hint:* To do this, it may be helpful to first determine how much of the $246,000 consisted of utilities and supervisory salaries. Think about the behaviour of variable and fixed costs!)

2. By means of the high–low method, estimate a cost formula for maintenance.

3. Express the company's *total* overhead costs in the linear equation form $Y = a + bX$.

4. What *total* overhead costs would you expect to be incurred at an operating activity level of 75,000 machine-hours?

 PROBLEM 6–8

Applying the High–Low Method; Cost of Goods Manufactured [LO2 – CC9; CHAPTER 2 LO6 – CC12]

Amfac Company manufactures a single product. The company keeps careful records of manufacturing activities, from which the following information has been extracted:

> **CHECK FIGURE**
>
> (2) $114,000 per month plus $6 per unit

	Level of Activity	
	March	June
Number of units produced	5,000	9,000
Cost of goods manufactured	$268,000	$397,000
Work-in-process inventory, beginning	29,000	52,000
Work-in-process inventory, ending	15,000	21,000
Direct materials cost per unit	10	10
Direct labour cost per unit	12	12
Manufacturing overhead cost, total	?	?

The company's manufacturing overhead cost consists of both variable and fixed cost elements. To have data available for planning, management wants to determine how much of the overhead cost is variable with units produced and how much of it is fixed per month.

Required:

1. For both March and June, determine the amount of manufacturing overhead cost added to production. (*Hint:* A useful way to proceed might be to construct a schedule of cost of goods manufactured.)

2. By means of the high–low method of cost analysis, estimate a cost formula for manufacturing overhead. Express the variable portion of the formula in terms of a variable rate per unit of product.

3. If 7,000 units are produced during a month, what will be the cost of goods manufactured? (Assume that work-in-process inventories do not change for the month.)

PROBLEM 6–9
Applying the High–Low Method; Least-Squares Regression [LO1 – CC5; LO2 – CC9, 11]

Dylan Flaherty, marketing clerk for TipTop Marketing Agency, recorded the following information for last year:

CHECK FIGURE

(2) $125,664 + $1,112 per customer

Month	Number of Customers	Customer Service Costs
January	341	$524,908
February	402	542,010
March	318	479,280
April	496	698,340
May	385	528,250
June	442	654,660
July	351	541,970
August	480	678,900
September	330	468,540
October	498	679,440
November	428	626,780
December	400	540,500

He would like to be able to estimate customer service costs using the number of customers as the basis for estimation. However, because he has never taken a course in managerial accounting, he does not know how to set up a cost equation. He has therefore approached you for help.

Required:

1. Set up a cost equation for monthly customer service costs using the high–low method.
2. Using the equation from part (1), compute the estimated customer service costs if the number of customers is expected to be 550.
3. You also used the least-squares regression method to do the analysis of the costs; the analysis resulted in the following output:

Intercept:	82,231.04
Coefficient of X-variable:	1,227.02
Adjusted R square:	0.91

- Set up a cost equation using the above numbers.
- Explain the significance of R square.

PROBLEM 6–10
Preparing a Contribution Margin Income Statement [LO3 – CC12]

Gallop Corporation prepared the following report for the first quarter of this year:

CHECK FIGURE

(2) Contribution margin, $4,280,000

Sales (2,500 units @ $2,800 per unit)		$7,000,000
Less: Cost of goods sold		3,840,000
Gross margin		3,160,000
Less:		
Selling expenses	$1,024,000	
Administrative expenses	1,000,000	2,024,000
Income		$1,136,000

Gallop's controller, Nancy Johnstone, studied the costs in detail, particularly focusing on cost behaviour. Her analysis revealed the following:

- Sixty-five percent of the cost of goods sold was variable with respect to the number of units.
- Of the selling expenses, $800,000 was fixed; the remaining was variable with respect to the number of units.
- All of the administrative expenses were fixed.

Required:

1. Express the cost of goods sold and the selling expenses in terms of cost equations.
2. Redo the above income statement using a contribution margin approach.

PROBLEM 6–11
Cost Behaviour, Analysis of Mixed Costs, Contribution Margin Income Statement
[LO1 – CC1, 3, 6; LO2 – CC7, 9; LO3 – CC12]

The Central Valley Company is a manufacturing firm that produces and sells a single product. The company's revenues and expenses for the last four months are given below.

CHECK FIGURE

(2) Contribution margin, $269,500

Central Valley Company Comparative Monthly Income Statements				
	March	April	May	June
Sales in units	5,000	4,500	5,250	6,000
Sales revenue	$ 700,000	$ 630,000	$735,000	$840,000
Less: Cost of goods sold	370,000	342,000	379,000	426,000

Central Valley Company
Comparative Monthly Income Statements

	March	April	May	June
Gross margin	330,000	288,000	356,000	414,000
Less: Operating expenses				
Shipping expense	61,500	56,000	65,000	71,000
Advertising expense	70,000	70,000	70,000	70,000
Salaries & commissions	160,800	143,000	161,500	180,500
Insurance expense	9,000	9,000	9,000	9,000
Depreciation expense	42,000	42,000	42,000	42,000
Total operating expenses	343,000	320,000	347,500	372,500
Net income	$(13,300)	$(32,000)	$ 8,500	$ 41,500

Required:

1. Management is concerned about the losses experienced during the spring and would like to know more about the cost behaviour. Develop a cost equation for each of the costs.

2. Using the cost equations, prepare a contribution margin income statement (in good form) for September when 5,500 units are expected to be sold.

Building Your Skills

COMPREHENSIVE PROBLEM [LO1 – CC5; LO2 – CC9, 10]

Coral, Inc. manufactures a variety of products. The following data pertains to its plant in Chennai, India, which is relatively new and manufactures auto parts. Management wants to better understand the behaviour of overhead costs in order to better estimate and manage these costs. Management believes that direct labour-hours are a good driver of overhead costs; moreover labour hours-data is readily available. Historical data for the past two years is available and is as follows:

> **CHECK FIGURE**
>
> (1) Cost formula, $Y =$ $455,590 + $5.40X (using data for the two-year period)

	Year 1		Year 2	
	Direct Labour-Hours	Overhead Cost	Direct Labour-Hours	Overhead Cost
January	70,000	$840,000	73,500	$860,450
February	84,000	990,450	87,500	928,450
March	77,000	855,000	80,500	940,400
April	80,500	902,250	77,000	870,000

	Year 1		Year 2	
	Direct Labour-Hours	Overhead Cost	Direct Labour-Hours	Overhead Cost
May	70,000	815,000	70,000	800,000
June	66,500	735,850	63,000	775,000
July	49,000	745,000	42,000	675,000
August	35,000	645,000	45,500	700,900
September	42,000	690,000	52,500	735,000
October	59,500	750,000	59,500	725,850
November	56,000	695,000	52,500	710,000
December	66,500	780,000	63,000	718,000

All equipment in the Chennai plant is leased under an arrangement calling for a flat fee up to 70,000 direct labour-hours of activity in the plant, after which lease charges are assessed on an hourly basis. Lease expense is a major item of overhead cost.

Required:

Complete requirements 1 and 2 using data for each year as well as the full two-year period.

1. Using the high–low method, estimate the cost formula for overhead in the Chennai plant.
2. Using the least-squares regression method, estimate the cost formula for overhead in the Chennai plant.
3. Assume that the Chennai plant works 78,750 and 54,500 direct labour-hours respectively during two different months. Compute the expected overhead cost for the month using the cost formulas developed for the two-year period with
   a. The high–low method.
   b. The regression method.
4. Of the two proposed methods, which one should Coral, Inc. use to estimate monthly overhead costs in the Chennai plant? Explain fully, indicating the reasons why the other method is less desirable.
5. How is the concept of relevant range applicable to the Chennai plant?

THINKING ANALYTICALLY [LO2 – CC9, 11]

Kilpauk Corporation, located in London, Ontario, has gathered data on its overhead activities and associated costs for the past 12 months. Nancy Cruder, a member of the controller's department, has convinced management that the purchasing department's overhead costs can be better estimated and controlled if the fixed and variable components of each overhead activity are known. Nancy has identified two possible variables (activity bases) that influence costs: (1) number of purchase orders and (2) kilograms of materials purchased. She does not know which activity base will be a better predictor of costs. Therefore, she decides to gather data over a one-year period (see below).

CHECK FIGURE

(1) Monthly cost equation:
$3,000 per month +
$13.333 per purchase
order

Month	Number of Purchase Orders	Kilograms of Materials	Overhead Cost
1	1,000	30,000	$15,980
2	900	25,000	15,000
3	1,500	45,000	24,200
4	1,100	32,000	17,000
5	1,300	44,000	22,150
6	1,100	28,000	18,000
7	1,600	55,000	25,500
8	1,400	39,000	23,660
9	1,650	23,500	25,000
10	950	23,000	15,240
11	1,250	37,500	21,900
12	1,150	35,000	19,500

Required:

1. Using the high–low method, develop a cost formula for the purchasing department's overhead costs using the number of purchase orders as the activity base. Repeat using kilograms of materials as the activity base.

2. Using the least-squares regression method, develop a cost formula for the purchasing department's overhead costs using the number of purchase orders as the activity base. Repeat using kilograms of materials as the activity base. You may use Excel or another spreadsheet to compute the answer.

3. For the next two months, the company expects to issue 1,200 orders per month. However, it expects to buy 40,000 kilograms in the first month and 50,000 kilograms in the following month. Compute the estimated costs for each of the two months using all the cost formulas that you have developed in parts (1) and (2).

4. Comment on the differences in costs that you have estimated in part (3), above. Which of the two methods (high–low versus regression) would you prefer in developing a cost formula? Why? Which of the two activity bases would you prefer to use? Why?

COMMUNICATING IN PRACTICE [LO1 – CC1, 2, 3, 5, 6]

Maria Chavez owns a catering company that serves food and beverages at parties and business functions. Chavez's business is seasonal, with a heavy schedule during the summer months and holidays and a lighter schedule at other times.

One of the major events requested by Chavez's customers is a cocktail party. She offers a standard cocktail party and has estimated the total cost per guest as follows:

Food and beverages	$15.00
Labour (0.5 hours @ $10 per hour)	5.00
Overhead (0.5 hours @ $13.98 per hour)	6.99
Total cost per guest	$26.99

The standard cocktail party lasts three hours, and she hires one worker for every six guests, which works out to one-half hour of direct labour per guest. The servers work only as needed and are paid only for the hours they actually work.

When bidding on cocktail parties, Chavez adds a 15% markup to yield a price of $31 per guest. Chavez is confident about her estimates of the costs of food, beverages, and labour, but is not as comfortable with the estimate of overhead cost. The overhead cost per guest was determined by dividing total overhead expenses for the last 12 months by total labour-hours for the same period. Her overhead includes such costs as annual rent for office space, administrative costs (including those relating to hiring and paying workers), and so on.

Chavez has received a request to bid on a large fundraising cocktail party to be given next month by an important local charity. (The party would last three hours.) She would really like to win this contract—the guest list for this charity event includes many prominent individuals she would like as future clients.

Other caterers have also been invited to bid on the event, and she believes that one, if not more, of those companies will bid less than $31 per guest. She is not willing to lose money on the event and needs your input before making any decisions.

Required:

Write a memorandum to Ms. Chavez that addresses the validity of her concern about her estimate of overhead costs and whether she should base her bid on the estimated cost of $26.99 per guest. (*Hint:* Start by discussing the need to consider cost behaviour when estimating costs. You can safely assume that she will not incur any additional fixed costs if she wins the bid on this cocktail party.)

ETHICS CHALLENGE [LO1 – CC1, 3; LO2 – CC9, 10, 11; LO3 – CC12]

"I truly think that we should use the scattergraph method to analyze mixed costs," said Suzanne Arthur to her accountant Jane Golding. "It gives us the flexibility to manage the proportion of variable and fixed costs according to the decisions that we are required to make."

Jane wondered whether this would offer flexibility or the ability to manipulate the data as individual managers saw fit. "How can this so-called flexibility be good, when I can compute 10 different amounts for contribution margin and claim that they are all correct?" she asked herself. She turned to her handbook of the International Financial Reporting Standards (IFRS), but found no reference to this in the standards.

Required:

1. Do you believe that the scattergraph method gives managers the ability to manipulate costs?
2. Do you believe that the use of a particular method can lead to an ethical dilemma? Why or why not?

TEAMWORK IN ACTION [LO1 – CC1, 3, 5]

Assume that your team is going to form a company that will manufacture chocolate chip cookies. The team is responsible for preparing a list of all product components and costs necessary to manufacture this product.

Required:

1. The team should discuss and then write a brief description of the definitions of variable, fixed, and mixed costs. All team members should agree with and understand the definitions.
2. After preparing a list of all product components and costs necessary to manufacture your cookies, identify each of the product costs as direct materials, direct labour, or factory overhead. Then identify each of those costs as variable, fixed, or mixed.
3. Prepare to report this information in class. (Each teammate can assume responsibility for a different part of the presentation.)

7

Budgeting

LEARNING OBJECTIVES AND CHAPTER COMPETENCIES

After studying Chapter 7, you should be able to demonstrate the following competencies:

COMPETENCY		Know	Apply
LO1	**UNDERSTAND THE CONCEPT OF BUDGETS AND BUDGETING.**		
CC1	Explain the role of budgeting.	●	
CC2	Explain why organizations budget.	●	
CC3	Describe a master budget and the relationships among its components.	●	
CC4	Explain zero-based budgeting.	●	
LO2	**PREPARE EACH COMPONENT BUDGET OF THE MASTER BUDGET.**		
CC5	Prepare a sales budget, including a schedule of cash collections.		●
CC6	Prepare a production budget.		●
CC7	Prepare a direct materials budget, including a schedule of cash disbursements for purchases of raw materials.		●
CC8	Prepare a direct labour budget.		●
CC9	Prepare a manufacturing overhead budget.		●
CC10	Prepare an ending finished goods inventory budget.		●
CC11	Prepare a selling and administrative expense budget.		●
CC12	Prepare a cash budget.		●
LO3	**DEVELOP BUDGETED FINANCIAL STATEMENTS FROM THE COMPONENT BUDGETS OF THE MASTER BUDGET.**		
CC13	Prepare a budgeted income statement.		●
CC14	Prepare a budgeted balance sheet.		●
LO4	**UNDERSTAND THE BUDGETING PROCESS AND THE ROLE OF THE BEYOND BUDGETING MODEL.**		
CC15	Describe the practical issues in the budgeting process, including participative budgeting and responsibility accounting.	●	
CC16	Explain the beyond budgeting model and its approach to budgeting.	●	

Note: Appendix 7A is available on Connect.

ON THE JOB

"BIG BUDGET, SMALL BUDGET": ACHIEVING COST CONTROL IN THE PRODUCTION OF ANIMATED MOVIES

"Big budget, small budget" is a phrase often used in conversations when referring to movies coming out of Hollywood and other film-making capitals of the world. With such references, *budget* is often tied to judgment or speculation about whether the movie provides entertainment value commensurate with its cost (think *Heaven's Gate; Cleopatra; Waterworld;* and, most recently, *John Carter*). However, for managerial accountants, *budget* is used in the context of cost control and planning. Occasionally the managerial accounting usage of *budget* surfaces in discussions of the process of film-making.

Back in 1999, Disney released the animated version of *Tarzan;* the reported cost was $150 million and the movie made about $450 million worldwide. At that time, it was thought that the main reason for the $150 million price tag was uncontrolled production costs led by a production strategy that focused on meeting a predetermined release date no matter the cost. To compound this, during production, drawings were made more complex and rich than had been planned, resulting in an estimate of 190,000 drawings to complete the film as compared to the 130,000 required to complete *The Lion King.* The mandate to meet the release date caused cost overruns in terms of overtime expenses and a near doubling of the film crew. It seemed that a poor production management strategy and lack of override prevention in the control system spelled doom for the usefulness of the budget as a planning and control device.

With the next feature, *Lilo & Stitch,* released in 2002, Disney management set out to address the challenge of producing a movie at a dramatically reduced cost while making sure that the audience would not notice any decline in quality. This meant prioritizing where and how money would be spent. For *Lilo & Stitch,* the music budget was kept generous and animation costs were tightly controlled. For example, the studio decided not to add cute drawings to the clothes worn by Nani, Lilo's big sister, and saved nearly a quarter of a million dollars in animation costs without affecting the quality of the images and the story appearing on-screen. The film was completed on time and with a cost of $70 million—much less than the cost of *Tarzan.*

It would seem that the key to success is knowing what elements of the product are essential for its success and ensuring that money is spent only on those elements—and only in the amount required. Striking a balance between achieving creative success and controlling costs is the main challenge facing producers of animated movies. These aspects are not mutually exclusive, as has been demonstrated by the financial success of *Lilo & Stitch* and more recent animated films such as *Ice Age, Despicable Me,* and *Hop.* According to Christopher Meledandri, the person behind these recent movies, "Very few management layers, clear decision-making, shortening the length of time you spend developing a movie—it can be done." The key production elements in animated movies are the animation technology, the associated labour, the music, and the vocal talent. The art of balancing creative sense with business sense appears to be working for Illumination Entertainment, Meledandri's company. With *Despicable Me,* the company reaped gross revenues of $544 million globally against a budget of $69 million. Similarly, the company earned an opening weekend gross revenue of $38 million for its movie *Hop,* which had a budget of $63 million. And most recently its 2012 release, *The Lorax,* contributed in spurring Universal Pictures to achieve the highest annual revenue from its filmed entertainment releases in its 100-year history. It would seem that budgets play a critical role in enabling management to achieve the ideal balance between creativity and cost control, providing that the budget reflects the chosen strategy.

Walt Disney Productions/Photofest

Sources: "For Illumination Entertainment, Animation Meets Economic Reality." *The New York Times,* April 3, 2011, http://www.nytimes.com/2011/04/04/business/media/04illumination.html?pagewanted=all; "Universal Pictures' Box Office Hits 100 Year High," *The Hollywood Reporter,* September 24, 2012, http://www.hollywoodreporter.com/news/universal-pictures-box-office-hits-one-billion-373928; Bruce Orwall, "Comics Stripped: At Disney, String of Weak Cartoons Leads to Cost Cuts," *The Wall Street Journal,* June 18, 2002, pp. A1, A8.

 Critical thinking question   *How does the experience of Disney in managing the production of* Tarzan *and* Lilo & Stitch *suggest that there is a strong intrinsic value to budgeting for an organization?*

Note to student: See **Guidance Answers** *online.*

◀◀ A Look Back	▶ A Look at This Chapter	▶▶ A Look Ahead
In Chapter 6, we discussed cost behaviour and learned about mixed costs. You learned about methods to break costs into fixed and variable portions.	After discussing why organizations prepare budgets, Chapter 7 provides an overview of each of the individual budgets that constitute a firm's master budget. We also address the preparation of the cash budget, the budgeted income statement, and the budgeted balance sheet. The chapter concludes with a discussion of the processes organizations use to create budgets and some of the issues that arise in practice.	In Chapter 8, we focus on management accounting tools and concepts for making decisions—such as cost–volume–profit analysis, breakeven concepts, and operating leverage, which focuses on the how the cost structure of a production system can determine how vulnerable a business's profits can be to the volatility of its sales volume.

LO1   ● **Know**

CC1: Explain the role of budgeting.

Budgeting is the process used by businesses to describe, in financial terms, how they intend to achieve their desired financial and nonfinancial objectives—in other words, their strategy. The key tool in the budgeting process is the **budget**. A budget is a quantitative **plan** for acquiring and using financial and other resources. It is a medium to communicate—quantitatively—management's objectives for sales, production, purchasing, distribution, and financing activities. It is also the instrument that guides and coordinates (i.e., implements **controls**around) the firm's activities among all of these areas. Budgeting is accomplished through the preparation of a number of budgets, which collectively form an integrated business plan known as the **master budget**. The budgeting process culminates with the preparation of a cash budget, detailing the planned cash receipts and disbursements, including short-term borrowing requirements, a budgeted income statement, and a budgeted balance sheet. In short, the budget proclaims what the organization intends to achieve financially during the upcoming operations period. This is **planning**. And, in doing so, the budget becomes the basis for management's actions, as well as the reference point for performance measurement (*what* is measured) and performance evaluation (*how* the measures are used). This is **control**, which means taking steps to increase the likelihood that the objectives and targets described in the budgets are attained and all parts of the organization function in a manner consistent with organizational policies. Thus, the budget is the key element of both planning and control, the two main aspects of implementing an organization's strategy.

MANAGERIAL ACCOUNTING IN ACTION

THE ISSUE

Tom Wills is the majority shareholder and chief executive officer of Hampton Freeze, Inc., a company he started in 2017. The company makes premium popsicles using only natural ingredients and featuring exotic flavours such as tangy tangerine and minty mango. The company's business is highly seasonal, with most of the sales occurring in spring and summer.

In 2018, the company's second year of operations, a major cash crunch in the first and second quarters almost forced the company into bankruptcy. In spite of this cash crunch, 2018 was turning out to be a very successful year in both overall cash flow and net income. Partly as a result of that harrowing experience, Wills decided to hire a professional financial manager toward the end of 2018. Wills interviewed several promising candidates for the job and settled on Larry Giano, who had considerable experience in the packaged foods industry. In the job interview, Wills questioned Giano about the steps he would take to prevent a recurrence of the 2018 cash crunch:

Wills: As I mentioned earlier, we are going to wind up 2018 with a very nice profit. What you may not know is that we had some very big financial problems this year.

Giano: Let me guess. You ran out of cash some time in the first or second quarter.

Wills: How did you know?

Giano: Most of your sales are in the second and third quarters, right?

Wills: Sure, everyone wants to buy popsicles in the spring and summer, but nobody wants them when the weather turns cold.

Giano: So you don't have many sales in the first quarter?

Wills: Right.

Giano: And in the second quarter, which is the spring, you are producing like crazy to fill orders?

Wills: Sure.

Giano: Do your customers, the grocery stores, pay you the day you make your deliveries?

Wills: Are you kidding? Of course not.

Giano: So, in the first quarter, you don't have many sales. In the second quarter, you are producing like crazy, which eats up cash, but you aren't paid by your customers until long after you have paid your employees and suppliers. No wonder you had a cash problem. I see this pattern all the time in food processing because of the seasonality of the business.

Wills: What can we do about it?

Giano: The first step is to predict the magnitude of the problem before it occurs. If we can predict early in the year what the cash shortfall is going to be, we can go to the bank and arrange for credit before we really need it. Bankers tend to be leery of panicky people who show up begging for emergency loans. They are much more likely to make the loan if you look like you know what you are doing, you have done your homework, and you are in control of the situation.

Wills: How can we predict the cash shortfall?

Giano: You can put together a cash budget. While you're at it, you might as well do a master budget. You'll find it is well worth the effort.

Wills: I don't like budgets. They are too confining. My wife budgets everything at home, and I can't spend what I want.

Giano: Can I ask you a personal question?

Wills: What?

Giano: Where did you get the money to start this business?

Wills: Mainly from our family's savings. I get your point. We wouldn't have had the money to start the business if my wife hadn't been forcing us to save every month.

Giano: Exactly. I suggest you use the same discipline in your business. It is even more important here because you can't expect your employees to spend your money as carefully as you would.

Wills: I'm sold. Welcome aboard! Get ready: Your first project is to develop our 2019 master budget and projected financial statements!

Giano: All right, let's go!

As should be evident from Wills and Giano's conversation, without the benefit of a tool like the budget and the experience of developing it, an organization is likely to be functioning in the dark, lacking direction for its operating activities, and blind to the outcomes of actions taken and progress achieved on decisions made. Overspending, resource shortages, inefficiencies, and waste are likely negative consequences of operating without a plan and not knowing what is needed and what must be done. It is important for accountants to know how to prepare budgets, what advantages and disadvantages they confer on organizations, and the implications of budgeting for influencing behaviours and attitudes in an organization. That is what this chapter will focus on.

IN BUSINESS

EXECUTING STRATEGY WITH BUDGETS

Robert DeMartini, the CEO of New Balance since 2007, wants New Balance to become a truly international, multisport athletic brand like its competitors Nike and Adidas. The company wants to boost its annual sales growth, which averaged 15% over the past five years. To that end, New Balance has planned a global advertising campaign with a budget that is twice as big as any in its 109-year history.

To further diversify its offerings, New Balance branched out into sports such as soccer by signing endorsement deals with players including Vincent Kompany of Manchester City, one of the world's most popular clubs, in Liverpool FC. These decisions represented a strategic shift for New Balance, which usually spends less than $20 million per year in advertising, compared to competitors such as Nike and Adidas, which annually invest $184 million and $80 million, respectively.

One reason companies prepare budgets is to allocate resources across departments in a manner that supports strategic priorities. DeMartini used the budget to send a clear signal that his marketing department was expected to play a huge role in achieving the company's revenue growth targets. As time progresses, he will compare the company's actual revenue growth from young consumers to the marketing department's expenditures to see if his strategy is working or requires adjustment.

Sources: S. Kang, "New Balance Steps Up Marketing Drive," *The Wall Street Journal*, March 21, 2008, p. B3; Matthew Townsend, "New Balance to Challenge Nike With Its Biggest Ad Campaign Ever," *Bloomberg*, June 30, 2015, http://www.bloomberg.com/news/articles/2015-07-01/new-balance-to-challenge-nike-with-its-biggest-ad-campaign-ever

Budgets and Budgeting

Responsibility for Budgets

To be effective, a good budgeting system must provide for both planning and control. Good planning without effective control is time wasted. As a consequence, budgeting is one of the most important managerial activities in an organization. Given their importance, budgets are not typically the responsibility of a single individual. Depending on the organizational level at which the budget is developed (departmental, divisional, etc.), budget preparation is usually the responsibility of a standing **budget committee**. The budget committee will usually be responsible for overall policy matters relating to the budget program, resolving disputes, and coordinating the preparation of the budget itself. The budget committee approves the final budget and receives periodic reports on the progress of the company in attaining budgeted goals.

At the highest levels of an organization, this committee generally will consist of the president; vice-presidents in charge of various functions such as sales, production, and purchasing; and the controller. At the lower levels, membership and composition of the committee will vary but will likely involve organizational unit leaders and key decision makers—anyone with the authority and responsibility for resource acquisition and/or spending decisions.

Advantages of Budgeting

LO1 ● **Know**

CC2: Explain why organizations budget.

Why should we budget? The simplest answer is, "Because resources are scarce." If resources were unlimited and free, we would be unconcerned about waste and there would be no need for planning and control. There would be no need for communication of plans throughout the organization, and there would be no impediments to achieving our objectives. In short, there would be no need to think about how our objectives can be achieved in a systematic, organized, and coordinated manner.

But scarcity of resources is a fundamental reality confronting businesses and individuals. Therefore, organizations and individuals must:

- think about and plan for the future systematically
- uncover potential impediments to achieving goals and objectives, such as resource constraints and bottlenecks
- communicate plans carefully and clearly
- coordinate the planned actions across the various parts of the organization
- ensure that scarce resources are employed to best benefit the organization
- define goals and objectives that can serve as benchmarks for subsequent performance

Budgeting and budgets enable organizations to accomplish all of these items.

How can organizations ensure that the potential benefits from budgeting and preparing budgets are actually realized? This is an extremely important question. We need to consider the *individuals* involved in budgeting and those affected by the budget, the *steps* taken to accomplish the budgeting, and the manner in which the organization *intends to use* the budgets. We must also consider how the organization communicates those intentions and whether the budgets are, in fact, used as intended. To fully appreciate these important issues, it is important that you are first shown the process of budgeting. Therefore, we will address these issues after we have illustrated the preparation of the master budget.

IN BUSINESS

BUDGETS, STRATEGY, AND RECOVERY PLANS AT RESEARCH IN MOTION

During 2012, the stock of Research In Motion (RIM) went on a roller coaster ride in terms of a decline in per-share value and company value, on the heels of consistent delays in the launch of the new BlackBerry operating system and next generation of smart phones—while the competition was making positive strides. In response to the decline in the stock price, the company underwent a change in leadership at the highest level and embarked on a recovery plan to stem the hemorrhaging of value and investor confidence. In its report filed with the Securities and Exchange Commission in 2012, the company listed several ways it planned to repair its business. Two specific initiatives mentioned in the report are the Cost Optimization Program and the CORE Program.

The Cost Optimization Program was "designed to eliminate redundancies and reallocate resources to focus on areas that offer the highest growth opportunities and alignment with RIM's strategic objectives." This would be through "headcount reductions and elimination of facilities redundancies." The CORE Program was "expected to drive significant improvements and efficiencies across all functions in RIM's organization." Targeted areas included "product lifecycle management, supply chain management and business support services." These measures were included to help RIM attain "a more efficient cost structure [that] will better enable it to respond to new market opportunities and changes in the competitive environment." These two programs were aimed at improving all key operational metrics and effectively managing the risks related to RIM's production strategy. These risks involved RIM's reliance on outsourcing for the majority of its manufacturing "to specialized global Electronic Manufacturing

Services ('EMS') companies who are positioned to meet the volumes, scale, cost and quality requirements of the Company."

RIM's tactic in this regard was to diversify the outsourcing among several suppliers, obtain access to the suppliers' facilities, audit the production processes, and take control of the financial parameters by negotiating the prices of the materials and services. On September 28, 2012, *The Globe and Mail* reported that cost-cutting was positively affecting the company's fortunes. Although RIM was reported to have incurred costs of $93 million in severance and other expenses from 5,000 job cuts, RIM's stock price rose by 20% to $8.55 on the heels of the news release in after-hours trading.

Sources: http://ca.blackberry.com/content/dam/bbCompany/Desktop/Global/PDF/Investors/Documents/2012/2012rim_ar_40F.pdf; "Cost-Cutting Stems RIM Losses," *The Globe and Mail*, September 28, 2012. p. B1; "BlackBerry's Future Comes Undone," *Canadian Business*, July 16, 2012, p. 12.

An Overview of the Master Budget

LO1 ● **Know**

CC3: Describe a master budget and the relationships among its components.

The master budget is the principal output of the budgeting process. Exhibit 7–1 provides an overview of the various parts of the master budget and how they are related. The type of organization—manufacturer, merchandiser, or service provider—will determine if some of the component budgets are necessary. A merchandiser will not require a *production budget*, for example. Instead, the merchandising company will prepare a *merchandise purchases budget*. A service provider will require neither a production budget nor a merchandise purchases budget. Service organizations, such as law offices and health services departments, will rely on the *operating expenses budget*.

THE SALES BUDGET

A **sales budget** is a detailed schedule showing the expected sales—expressed both in dollars and in units of product (or service)—for the budget period. The sales budget is usually based on the company's *sales forecast*. In addition, the manager may examine the company's unfulfilled back orders, the company's pricing policy and marketing plans, trends in the industry, and general economic conditions. Sophisticated statistical tools may be used to analyze data and build models that are helpful in predicting key factors influencing the company's sales. These tools and models are more appropriately covered in marketing courses, so we will not go into the details of how sales forecasts are made.

Service organizations must estimate the demand for their services. Professional accountants, for example, have to estimate the revenues they expect to earn from their consulting practice. These estimates are typically derived from projections of the number of consulting engagements and the nature (tax advice, auditing engagements, business consulting) of the service to be provided. The projections will also depend on the rates to be charged. These rates, in turn, might be established on a cost-plus basis, where the exact figure is set on the basis of the desired margin over the costs. In such cases, cost measurement, management, and control will be critical.

An accurate sales budget is the key to the entire budgeting process in for-profit organizations. All of the other parts of the master budget are dependent on the sales budget in some way, as illustrated in Exhibit 7–1. Thus, if the sales budget is sloppily done, then the rest of the budgeting process is largely a waste of time.

Not-for-profit organizations face different challenges. In many of these organizations, the concept of revenue generated from *selling* services will not be relevant. Many of these organizations rely on external sources of funding, such as a parent organization, individual and corporate donors, and/or local and higher levels of government. The programs and services these organizations offer consume financial resources. Budgeting for these organizations controls their operating expenses by controlling the variety and volume of services—the consumers of financial resources—offered so as to be in line with their financial endowments.

The remainder of the discussion will assume that we are concerned with a for-profit manufacturing organization.

EXHIBIT 7–1 Master Budget Interrelationships

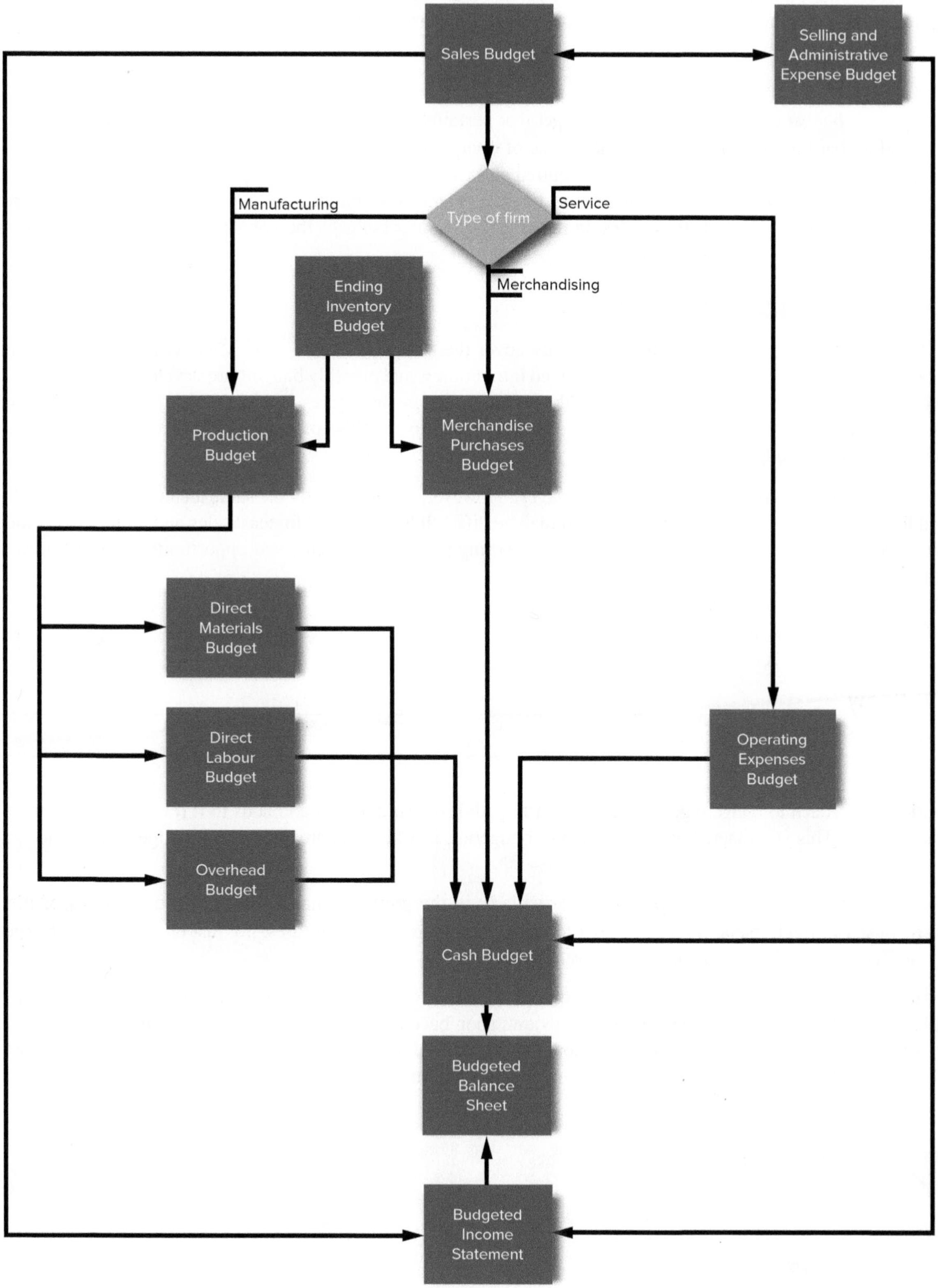

THE INTERDEPENDENCY OF THE BUDGETS

The sales budget will help determine the number of units to be produced. Thus, the production budget is prepared after the sales budget. The production budget, in turn, is used to determine the budgets for the manufacturing costs, including the direct materials budget, the direct labour budget, and the manufacturing overhead budget. These budgets are then combined with the data from the sales budget and the selling and administrative expense budget to determine the cash budget.

THE CASH BUDGET

The term *operating budget* is used to refer to the budget that pertains to such activities as sales, production, purchasing, selling, and administration that the firm undertakes in the course of operating the business. A **cash budget** is a *financial* budget. It is a detailed plan showing how cash resources will be acquired and used over some specified period. Observe from Exhibit 7–1 that all of the operating budgets have an impact on the cash budget. Operations run, ultimately, on money! The sales budget provides the basis for the planned cash receipts from sales. In the case of the other budgets, the impact on the cash budget comes from the planned expenditures described in those budgets.

Choosing a Budget Period

Operating budgets, including the cash budget, ordinarily cover the company's fiscal year. Many companies divide their budget year into four quarters. The first quarter is then subdivided into months, and monthly budgets are developed. The last three quarters are carried in the budget at quarterly totals only. As the year progresses, the figures for the second quarter are broken down into monthly amounts, then the third-quarter figures are broken down, and so on. This approach has the advantage of requiring periodic review and reappraisal of budget data throughout the year.

In this chapter, we will focus on *one-year operating budgets*. However, using basically the same techniques, operating budgets can be prepared for periods that extend over many years. It may be difficult to accurately forecast sales and required data much beyond a year, but even rough estimates can be invaluable in uncovering potential problems and opportunities that would otherwise be overlooked.

Zero-Based Budgeting

In the traditional approach to budgeting, the manager starts with last year's budget and adds to it (or subtracts from it) according to anticipated needs. This is an incremental approach to budgeting in which the previous year's budget is taken for granted as a baseline.

Zero-based budgeting is an alternative approach—particularly in the governmental and not-for-profit sectors of the economy. Under a **zero-based budget**, managers are required to justify *all* budgeted expenditures, not just changes in the budget from the previous year. The baseline is zero, rather than last year's budget.

Critics of zero-based budgeting charge that preparation of zero-based budgets is too time-consuming and too costly to justify on an annual basis. In addition, many argue that annual reviews soon become mechanical and that the whole purpose of zero-based budgeting is then lost. Whether or not a company should use an annual review is a matter of judgment. However, most managers would at least agree that on occasion zero-based reviews can be very helpful.

 DECISION POINT

SALES MANAGER

You were recently hired as the sales manager for a company that designs and manufactures hard-soled casual and dress shoes for sale to department stores. The vice-president of sales recently decided that the company will add athletic footwear to its catalogue and asked you to prepare a sales budget for that product line for the coming year. How would you forecast sales for this product line?

*Note to student: See **Guidance Answers** online.*

Preparing the Master Budget

We will use the situation facing Tom Wills and Larry Giano at Hampton Freeze to illustrate the steps for preparing the master budget and the projected financial statements for 2019. With the full backing of Wills, Giano set out to create a master budget for the company for the year 2019. In his planning for the budgeting process, Giano drew up the following list of documents, which he would have to prepare, that would be a part of the master budget:

1. A sales budget, including a schedule of expected cash collections
2. A production budget (a merchandise purchases budget would be used in a merchandising company)
3. A direct materials budget, including a schedule of expected cash disbursements for raw materials (this would not be needed for a merchandising company)
4. A direct labour budget (this would not be needed for a merchandising company)
5. A manufacturing overhead budget
6. An ending finished goods inventory budget
7. A selling and administrative expense budget
8. A cash budget
9. A budgeted income statement
10. A budgeted balance sheet

Giano felt it was important to have everyone's cooperation in the budgeting process, and so he asked Wills to call a companywide meeting in which the budgeting process would be explained. At the meeting, there was initially some grumbling, but Wills was able to convince nearly everyone of the necessity for planning and getting better control over spending. It helped that the cash crisis earlier in the year was still fresh in everyone's mind.

In the months that followed, Giano worked closely with all of the managers involved in the master budget, gathering data from them and making sure that they understood and fully supported the parts of the master budget that would affect them. In subsequent years, Giano hoped to turn the whole budgeting process over to the managers and to play a more advisory role.

The interdependent documents that Larry Giano prepared for Hampton Freeze are Schedules 1 through 10 of his company's master budget. In this section, we will study these schedules.

 HELPFUL HINT

The 10 schedules that we are about to explain can often be overwhelming to students. To help you see the big picture, keep in mind that Hampton Freeze's master budget is designed to help it estimate the answers to 10 questions for each quarter and the entire year:

1. How much sales revenue will we earn?
2. How much cash will we collect from customers?
3. How much raw material will we need to purchase?
4. How much manufacturing cost (including direct materials, direct labour, and manufacturing overhead) will we need to add to production?

5. How much cash will we pay to our suppliers and our direct labourers, and how much will we pay for manufacturing overhead resources?

6. What is the total cost that will be transferred from finished goods inventory to cost of goods sold?

7. How much selling and administrative expense will we incur, and how much cash will we pay related to those expenses?

8. How much cash will we pay for equipment purchases?

9. How much will we pay in cash dividends?

10. How much money will we borrow from or repay to lenders, including interest?

Estimating the answers to these 10 questions enables Hampton Freeze to prepare a budgeted balance sheet and income statement and to proactively manage its cash flows.

The Sales Budget

LO2 • **Apply**

CC5: Prepare a sales budget, including a schedule of cash collections.

The sales budget is the starting point in preparing the master budget. As shown previously in Exhibit 7–1, all other items in the master budget—including production, purchases, inventories, and expenses—depend on it in some way.

The sales budget is constructed by multiplying the budgeted sales in units by the selling price. Schedule 1 contains the sales budget for Hampton Freeze for the year 2019, by quarter. Note from the schedule that the company plans to sell 100,000 cases of popsicles during the year, with sales peaking in the third quarter.

SCHEDULE OF EXPECTED CASH COLLECTIONS

A schedule of expected cash collections, such as the one that appears in Schedule 1 for Hampton Freeze, is prepared after the sales budget. This schedule will be needed later to prepare the cash budget. Cash collections consist of collections on sales made to customers in prior periods plus collections on sales made in the current budget period. At Hampton Freeze, experience has shown that 70% of sales are collected in the quarter in which the sale is made and the remaining 30% are collected in the following quarter. For example, of the first-quarter sales of $200,000, 70% (or $140,000) are collected during the first quarter, and 30% (or $60,000) are collected during the second quarter.

Schedule 1—Sales Budget and Schedule of Expected Cash Collections

A	B	C	D	E	F
1		HAMPTON FREEZE, INC.			
2		Sales Budget			
3		For the Year Ended December 31, 2019			
4					
5			*Quarter*		
6	*1*	*2*	*3*	*4*	*Year*
7 Budgeted sales in cases	10,000	30,000	40,000	20,000	100,000
8 Selling price per case	$ 20.00	$ 20.00	$ 20.00	$ 20.00	$ 20.00

	A	B	C	D	E	F
9	Total sales	$200,000	$600,000	$800,000	$400,000	$2,000,000
10						
11	Percentage of sales collected in the period of the sale			70%		
12	Percentage of sales collected in the period after the sale			30%		
13		70%	30%			
14	**Schedule of Expected Cash Collections**					
15	Accounts receivable, beginning balance[1]	$ 90,000				$ 90,000
16	First-quarter sales[2]	140,000	$ 60,000			200,000
17	Second-quarter sales[3]		420,000	$ 180,000		600,000
18	Third-quarter sales[4]			560,000	$240,000	800,000
19	Fourth-quarter sales[5]	–	–	–	280,000	280,000
20	Total cash collections[6]	$230,000	$480,000	$740,000	$520,000	$ 1,970,000

[1]Cash collections from last year's fourth-quarter sales. See the beginning-of-year balance sheet.

[2]$200,000 × 70%; $200,000 × 30%

[3]$600,000 × 70%; $600,000 × 30%

[4]$800,000 × 70%; $800,000 × 30%

[5]$400,000 × 70%

[6]Uncollected fourth-quarter sales appear as accounts receivable on the company's end-of-year balance sheet (see Schedule 10).

CONCEPT CHECK

1. March, April, and May sales are $100,000, $120,000, and $125,000, respectively. A total of 80% of all sales are credit sales and 20% are cash sales. A total of 60% of credit sales are collected in the month of the sale and 40% are collected in the next month. There are no bad debt expenses. What is the amount of cash collections for April?
   a. $89,600
   b. $111,600
   c. $113,600
   d. $132,600

2. Referring to the facts in Concept Check 1 above, what is the accounts receivable balance at the end of May?
   a. $40,000
   b. $50,000
   c. $72,000
   d. $80,000

*Note to student: See **Guidance Answers** online.*

The Production Budget

LO2 • Apply

CC6: Prepare a production budget.

The production budget is prepared after the sales budget. The **production budget** lists the number of units that must be produced during each budget period to meet sales needs and to provide for the desired ending inventory. Production needs can be determined as follows:

Budgeted sales in units	XXXX
Add: Desired ending inventory	XXXX
Total needs	XXXX
Deduct: Beginning inventory	XXXX
Required production	XXXX

Schedule 2 contains the production budget for Hampton Freeze.

Note that production requirements for a quarter are influenced by the desired level of the ending inventory. Inventories should be carefully planned. Excessive inventories consume funds and create storage problems. Insufficient inventories can lead to lost sales or crash production efforts in the following period. At Hampton Freeze, management believes that an ending inventory equal to 20% of the next quarter's sales strikes the appropriate balance.

Schedule 2—Production Budget

	A	B	C	D	E	F
3	HAMPTON FREEZE, INC.					
4	Production Budget					
5	For the Year Ended December 31, 2019					
6	(in cases)					
7						Assumed
8				Quarter		
9		1	2	3	4	Year
10	Budgeted sales (Schedule 1)	10,000	30,000	40,000	20,000	100,000
			20%	20%	20%	
11	Add: Desired ending inventory of finished goods[1]	6,000	8,000	4,000	3,000	3,000
12	Total needs	16,000	38,000	44,000	23,000	103,000
13	Deduct: Beginning inventory of finished goods[2]	2,000	6,000	8,000	4,000	2,000
14	Required production	14,000	32,000	36,000	19,000	101,000
15						

[1]20% of the next quarter's sales. The ending inventory of 3,000 cases is assumed.

[2]The beginning inventory in each quarter is the same as the prior quarter's ending inventory.

Inventory Purchases—Merchandising Firm

Hampton Freeze prepares a production budget, since it is a *manufacturing* firm. If it were a *merchandising* firm, it would prepare a **merchandise purchases budget** showing the amount of goods to be purchased from its suppliers during the period. The merchandise purchases budget follows the same basic format as the production budget, as shown:

Budgeted cost of goods sold (in units or in dollars)	XXXX
Add: Desired ending merchandise inventory	XXXX
Total needs	XXXX
Deduct: Beginning merchandise inventory	XXXX
Required purchases (in units or in dollars)	XXXX

A merchandising firm would prepare an inventory purchases budget, such as the preceding one, for each item carried in stock.

The Direct Materials Budget

LO2 ● **Apply**

CC7: Prepare a direct materials budget, including a schedule of cash disbursements for purchases of raw materials.

Returning to Hampton Freeze, after the production requirements have been computed, a direct materials budget can be prepared. The **direct materials budget** details the raw materials that must be purchased to fulfill the production budget and to provide for adequate inventories. The required purchases of raw materials are computed as follows:

Raw materials needed to meet the production schedule	XXXXX
Add: Desired ending inventory of raw materials	XXXXX
Total raw materials needs	XXXXX
Deduct: Beginning inventory of raw materials	XXXXX
Raw materials to be purchased	XXXXX

Schedule 3 contains the direct materials budget for Hampton Freeze. The only raw material included in that budget is high-fructose sugar, which is the major ingredient in popsicles other than water. The remaining raw materials are relatively insignificant and are included in variable manufacturing overhead. Note that materials requirements are first determined in units (kilograms, litres, and so on) and then translated into dollars by multiplying by the appropriate unit cost. Also, note that the management of Hampton Freeze desires to maintain ending inventories of sugar equal to 10% of the following quarter's production needs.

Schedule 3—Direct Materials Budget and Schedule of Expected Cash Disbursements for Materials

	A	B	C	D	E	F
3	**HAMPTON FREEZE, INC.**					
4	**Direct Materials Budget**					
5	**For the Year Ended December 31, 2019**					
6						Assumed
7				*Quarter*		
8		*1*	*2*	*3*	*4*	*Year*
9	Required production in cases (Schedule 2)	14,000	32,000	36,000	19,000	101,000
10	Raw materials needed per case (kilograms)	15	15	15	15	15
11	Production needs (kilograms)	201,000	480,000	540,000	285,000	1,515,000
			10%	10%	10%	
12	Add: Desired ending inventory of raw materials[1]	48,000	54,000	28,500	22,500	22,500
13	Total needs	258,000	534,000	568,500	307,500	1,537,500
14	Deduct: Beginning inventory of raw materials	21,000	48,000	54,000	28,500	21,000
15	Raw materials to be purchased	237,000	486,000	514,500	279,000	1,516,500
16	Cost of raw materials per kilogram	$ 0.20	$ 0.20	$ 0.20	$ 0.20	$ 0.20
17	Cost of raw materials to be purchased	$47,400	$ 97,200	$ 102,900	$55,800	$303,300
18						
19	Percentage of purchases paid for in the period of the purchase			50%		
20	Percentage of purchases paid for in the period after purchase			50%		
21		50%	50%			
22	**Schedule of Expected Cash Disbursements for Materials**					
23						
24	Accounts payable, beginning balance[2]	$25,800				$ 25,800
25	First-quarter purchases[3]	23,700	$ 23,700			47,400
26	Second-quarter purchases[4]		48,600	$ 48,600		97,200
27	Third-quarter purchases[5]			51,450	$51,450	102,900
28	Fourth-quarter purchases[6]	—	—	—	27,900	27,900
29	Total cash disbursements	$49,500	$ 72,300	$ 100,050	$79,350	$301,200

[1]10% of the next quarter's production needs. For example, the second-quarter production needs are 480,000 kilograms. Therefore, the desired ending inventory for the first quarter is 10% × 480,000 kilograms = 48,000 kilograms. The ending inventory of 22,500 kilograms for the quarter is assumed.

[2]Cash payments for last year's fourth-quarter materials purchases. See the beginning-of-year balance sheet.

[3]$47,400 × 50%; $47,400 × 50%

[4]$97,200 × 50%; $97,200 × 50%

[5]$102,900 × 50%; $102,900 × 50%

[6]$55,800 × 50%. Unpaid fourth-quarter purchases appear as accounts payable on the company's end-of-year balance sheet.

HELPFUL HINT

The direct materials budget includes three different units of measure. It begins by defining the number of *units of finished goods* that need to be produced each period. It then defines the *quantity of raw material inputs* (measured in terms such as pounds or kilograms) that need to be purchased to support production. It concludes by translating the quantity of raw materials to be purchased into the *cost of raw materials* to be purchased.

SCHEDULE OF EXPECTED CASH DISBURSEMENTS FOR RAW MATERIALS

The direct materials budget is usually accompanied by a schedule of expected cash disbursements for raw materials. This schedule is needed to prepare the overall cash budget. Disbursements for raw materials consist of payments for purchases on account in prior periods plus any payments for purchases in the current budget period. Schedule 3 contains such a schedule of cash disbursements.

CONCEPT CHECK

3. If a company has a beginning merchandise inventory of $50,000, a desired ending merchandise inventory of $30,000, and a budgeted cost of goods sold of $300,000, what is the amount of required inventory purchases?
   a. $320,000
   b. $280,000
   c. $380,000
   d. $300,000

4. Budgeted unit sales for March, April, and May are 75,000, 80,000, and 90,000 units, respectively. Management desires to maintain an ending inventory equal to 30% of the next month's unit sales. How many units should be produced in April?
   a. 80,000 units
   b. 83,000 units
   c. 77,000 units
   d. 85,000 units

*Note to student: See **Guidance Answers** online.*

The Direct Labour Budget

LO2 • **Apply**

CC8: Prepare a direct labour budget.

The **direct labour budget** is also developed from the production budget. Direct labour requirements must be computed so that the company will know whether sufficient labour time is available to meet production needs and plan accordingly. Firms that neglect to budget labour run the risk of facing labour shortages or having to hire and lay off at awkward times. Erratic labour policies lead to insecurity and inefficiency on the part of employees.

To compute direct labour requirements, the number of units of finished product to be produced each period (month, quarter, and so on) is multiplied by the number of direct labour-hours required to produce a single unit. The direct labour requirements can then be translated into expected direct labour costs. How this is done will depend on the labour policy of the firm. In Schedule 4, the management of Hampton Freeze has assumed that the direct labour force will be adjusted as the work requirements change from quarter to quarter. In that case, the total direct labour cost is computed by simply multiplying the direct labour-hour requirements by the direct labour rate per hour.

However, many companies have employment policies or contracts that prevent them from laying off and rehiring workers, as needed. Suppose, for example, that Hampton Freeze has 50 workers who are classified as direct labour and each of them is guaranteed at least 480 hours of pay each quarter at a rate of $7.50 per hour. In that case, the minimum direct labour cost for a quarter would be as follows:

$$50 \text{ workers} \times 480 \text{ hours per worker} \times \$7.50 \text{ per hour} = \$180,000$$

Schedule 4—Direct Labour Budget

	A	B	C	D	E	F
1	HAMPTON FREEZE, INC.					
2	Direct Labour Budget					
3	For the Year Ended December 31, 2019					
4						
5		*Quarter*				
6		*1*	*2*	*3*	*4*	*Year*
7	Required production in cases (Schedule 2)	14,000	32,000	36,000	19,000	101,000
8	Direct labour-hours per case	0.80	0.80	0.80	0.80	0.80
9	Total direct labour-hours needed	11,200	25,600	28,800	15,200	80,800
10	Direct labour cost per hour	$ 7.50	$ 7.50	$ 7.50	$ 7.50	$ 7.50
11	Total direct labour cost*	$84,000	$192,000	$216,000	$114,000	$606,000

*This schedule assumes that the direct labour workforce will be fully adjusted to the total direct labour-hours needed each quarter.

Note that in Schedule 4, the direct labour costs for the first and fourth quarters would have to be increased to the $180,000 level if Hampton Freeze's labour policy did not allow it to adjust the workforce.

The Manufacturing Overhead Budget

LO2 • **Apply**

CC9: Prepare a manufacturing overhead budget.

The **manufacturing overhead budget** provides a schedule of all costs of production other than direct materials and direct labour. Schedule 5 shows the manufacturing overhead budget for Hampton Freeze. Note how the production costs are separated into variable and fixed components. The variable component is $2 per direct labour-hour. The fixed component is $60,600 per quarter.

Schedule 5 for Hampton Freeze shows its budgeted cash disbursements for manufacturing overhead. Since some of the overhead costs are not cash outflows, the total budgeted manufacturing overhead costs must be adjusted to determine the cash disbursements for manufacturing overhead. At Hampton Freeze, the only significant noncash manufacturing overhead cost is depreciation, which is $15,000 per quarter. These noncash depreciation charges are deducted from the total budgeted manufacturing overhead to determine the expected cash disbursements. Hampton Freeze pays all overhead costs involving cash disbursements in the quarter incurred. Note that the company's predetermined overhead rate for the year will be $5 per direct labour-hour.

Schedule 5—Manufacturing Overhead Budget

	A	B	C	D	E	F
1	**HAMPTON FREEZE, INC.**					
2	**Manufacturing Overhead Budget**					
3	**For the Year Ended December 31, 2019**					
4						
5			*Quarter*			
6		*1*	*2*	*3*	*4*	*Year*
7	Budgeted direct labour-hours (Schedule 4)	11,200	25,600	28,800	15,200	80,800
8	Variable overhead rate	$ 2.00	$ 2.00	$ 2.00	$ 2.00	$ 2.00
9	Variable manufacturing overhead	$22,400	$51,200	$ 57,600	$30,400	$ 161,600
10	Fixed manufacturing overhead	60,600	60,600	60,600	60,600	242,400
11	Total manufacturing overhead	83,000	111,800	118,200	91,000	404,000
12	Less: Depreciation	15,000	15,000	15,000	15,000	60,000
13	Cash disbursement for manufacturing overhead	$68,000	$96,800	$103,200	$76,000	$344,000
14						
15	Total manufacturing overhead (a)					$404,000
16	Budgeted direct labour-hours (b)					80,800
17	Predetermined overhead rate for the year (a) ÷ (b)					$ 5.00

The Ending Finished Goods Inventory Budget

LO2 • **Apply**

CC10: Prepare an ending finished goods inventory budget.

After completing Schedules 1 to 5, Larry Giano had all of the data he needed to compute unit product costs. This computation was needed for two reasons: (1) to determine the cost of goods sold on the budgeted income statement, and (2) to know what amount to put on the balance sheet inventory account for unsold units. The carrying cost of the unsold units is computed on the **ending finished goods inventory budget**.

Giano's next task was to determine what financing, if any, would be required in the year 2019 and then to arrange for that financing from the bank. The unit product cost computations are shown in Schedule 6. For Hampton Freeze, the absorption costing unit product cost is $13 per case of popsicles—consisting of $3 of direct materials, $6 of direct labour, and $4 of manufacturing overhead. Manufacturing overhead is applied to units of product on the basis of direct labour-hours. The budgeted carrying cost of the expected ending inventory is $39,000.

Schedule 6—Ending Finished Goods Inventory Budget

	A	B	C	D	E	F	G	H
1	HAMPTON FREEZE, INC.							
2	Ending Finished Goods Inventory Budget							
3	(absorption costing basis)							
4	For the Year Ended December 31, 2019							
5								
6	*Item*	*Quantity*			*Cost*			*Total*
7	Production cost per case:							
8	Direct materials	15.00	kilograms		$0.20	per kilogram		$ 3.00
9	Direct labour	0.80	hours		7.50	per hour		6.00
10	Manufacturing overhead	0.80	hours		5.00	per hour		4.00
11	Unit product cost							$ 13.00
12								
13	Budgeted finished goods inventory:							
14	Ending finished goods inventory in cases (Schedule 2)							3,000
15	Unit product cost (see above)							$ 13.00
16	Ending finished goods inventory in dollars							$39,000

The Selling and Administrative Expense Budget

LO2 • **Apply**

CC11: Prepare a selling and administrative expense budget.

The **selling and administrative expense budget** lists the budgeted expenses for areas other than manufacturing. In large organizations, this budget would be a compilation of many smaller, individual budgets submitted by department heads and other people responsible for selling and administrative expenses. For example, the marketing manager in a large organization would submit a budget detailing the advertising expenses for each budget period.

Schedule 7 contains the selling and administrative expense budget for Hampton Freeze.

Schedule 7—Selling and Administrative Expense Budget

	A	B	C	D	E	F
1	HAMPTON FREEZE, INC.					
2	Selling and Administrative Expense Budget					
3	For the Year Ended December 31, 2019					
4						
5		Quarter				
6		1	2	3	4	Year
7	Budgeted sales in cases (Schedule 1)	10,000	30,000	40,000	20,000	100,000
8	Variable selling and administrative expense per case	$ 1.80	$ 1.80	$ 1.80	$ 1.80	$ 1.80
9	Total budgeted variable selling and administrative expense	$ 18,000	$ 54,000	$ 72,000	$ 36,000	$ 180,000
10	Budgeted fixed selling and administrative expenses:					
11	Advertising	20,000	20,000	20,000	20,000	80,000
12	Executive salaries	55,000	55,000	55,000	55,000	220,000
13	Insurance*		1,900	37,750		39,650
14	Property taxes*				18,150	18,150
15	Depreciation	10,000	10,000	10,000	10,000	40,000
16	Total budgeted fixed selling and administrative expense	85,000	86,900	122,750	103,150	397,800
17	Total budgeted selling and administrative expenses	103,000	140,900	194,750	139,150	577,800
18	Less: Depreciation	10,000	10,000	10,000	10,000	40,000
19	Cash disbursements for selling and administrative expenses	$ 93,000	$130,900	$184,750	$ 129,150	$537,800.00

*These amounts are shown on a cash basis. Ordinarily, the matching principle would require $39,650 and $18,150 to be allocated equally to the four quarters, if quarterly financial statements were prepared.

IN BUSINESS

MISMATCHED CASH FLOWS—CLIMBING THE HILLS AND VALLEYS

The Washington Trails Association (WTA) is a private, nonprofit organization primarily concerned with protecting and maintaining hiking trails in the state of Washington. Some 2,000 WTA volunteer workers donate more than 80,000 hours per year maintaining trails in rugged landscapes on federal, state, and private lands. The organization is supported by membership dues, voluntary contributions, grants, and some contract work for government.

The organization's income and expenses are erratic—although somewhat predictable—over the course of the year, as shown in the chart. Expenses tend to be highest in the spring and summer when most of the trail maintenance work is done. However, income spikes in December well after the expenses have been incurred. Total income and total expense are approximately equal over the course of the year, but with cash outflows running ahead of cash inflows for much of the year, it is very important for the WTA to carefully plan its cash budget and to maintain adequate cash reserves to be able to pay its bills.

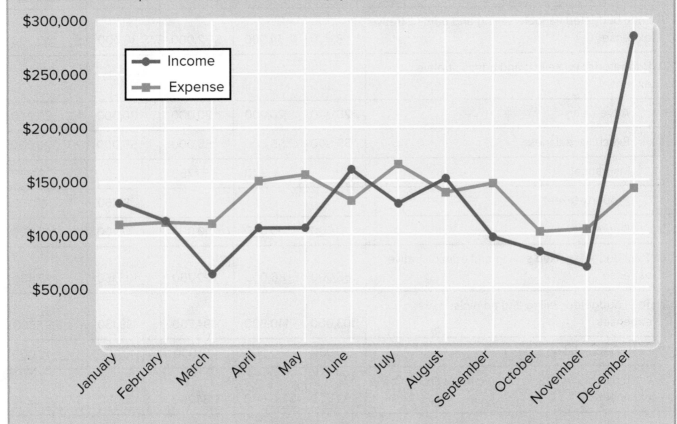

Note: Total income and total expense are approximately equal over the course of the year.

Sources: Conversation with Elizabeth Lunney, president of the Washington Trails Association; WTA documents; and the WTA website http://www.wta.org.

The Cash Budget

LO2 • **Apply**

CC12: Prepare a cash budget.

As illustrated in Exhibit 7–1, the cash budget pulls together much of the data developed in the preceding schedules. It is a good idea to review Exhibit 7–1 once again to get the big picture firmly in mind before moving on.

The cash budget is composed of four major sections:

- Receipts
- Disbursements
- Cash excess or deficiency
- Financing

The receipts section consists of a listing of all of the cash inflows, except for financing, expected during the budget period. Generally, the major source of receipts will be from sales.

The disbursements section consists of all cash payments that are planned for the budget period. These payments will include raw materials purchases, direct labour payments, manufacturing overhead costs, and so on, as contained in their respective budgets. In addition, other cash disbursements—such as equipment purchases, dividends, and other cash withdrawals by owners—are listed. For instance, we see in Schedule 8 that management plans to spend $137,000 during the budget period on equipment purchases and $32,000 on dividends to the owners. This is additional information that does not appear on any of the previous schedules.

Schedule 8—Cash Budget

	A	B	C	D	E	F	G
3	HAMPTON FREEZE, INC.						
4	Cash Budget						
5	For the Year Ended December 31, 2019						
6							
7					Quarter		
8		Schedule	1	2	3	4	Year
9	Cash balance, beginning		$ 42,500	$ 40,000	$ 40,000	$ 40,500	$ 42,500
10	Add: Receipts:						
11	Collections from customers	1	230,000	480,000	740,000	520,000	1,970,000
12	Total cash available before current financing		272,500	520,000	780,000	560,500	2,012,500
13	Deduct: Disbursements:						
14	Direct materials	3	49,500	72,300	100,050	79,350	301,200
15	Direct labour	4	84,000	192,000	216,000	114,000	606,000
16	Manufacturing overhead	5	68,000	96,800	103,200	76,000	344,000
17	Selling and administrative	7	93,000	130,900	184,750	129,150	537,800

	A	B	C	D	E	F	G
18	Equipment purchases		50,000	40,000	20,000	27,000	137,000
19	Dividends		8,000	8,000	8,000	8,000	32,000
20	Total disbursements		352,500	540,000	632,000	433,500	1,958,000
21	Excess (deficiency) of cash available over disbursements		(80,000)	(20,000)	148,000	127,000	54,500
22	Financing:						
23	Borrowings (at beginning)[1]		120,000	60,000	-	-	180,000
24	Repayments (at ending)		-	-	(100,000)	(80,000)	(180,000)
25	Interest[2]		-	-	(7,500)	(6,500)	(14,000)
26	Total financing		120,000	60,000	(107,500)	(86,500)	(14,000)
27	Cash balance, ending		$ 40,000	$ 40,000	$ 40,500	$ 40,500	$ 40,500

[1]The company requires a minimum cash balance of $40,000. Therefore, borrowing must be sufficient to cover the cash deficiency of $80,000 in quarter 1 and to provide for the minimum cash balance of $40,000. All borrowings and repayments of principal are in round $1,000 amounts.

[2]The interest payments relate only to the principal being repaid at the time it is repaid. For example, the interest in quarter 3 relates only to the interest due on the $100,000 principal being repaid from quarter 1 borrowing: $100,000 × 10% per year × 3/4 year = $7,500; the interest paid in quarter 4 is computed as follows:

$20,000 × 10% per year × 1 year	$2,000	(interest on amount repaid from quarter 1)
$60,000 × 10% per year × 3/4 year	4,500	(interest on amount repaid from quarter 2)
Total interest paid	$6,500	

The cash excess or deficiency section is computed as follows:

Cash balance, beginning	XXXX
Add: Receipts	XXXX
Total cash available before financing	XXXX
Deduct: Disbursements	XXXX
Excess (deficiency) of cash available over disbursements	XXXX

If there is a cash deficiency during any budget period, the company will need to borrow funds. If there is a cash excess during any budget period, funds borrowed in previous periods can be repaid or the excess funds can be invested.

The financing section provides a detailed account of the borrowings and repayments projected to take place during the budget period. It also includes the details of interest payments that will be due on money borrowed. Note that the format of the statement of cash flows may also be used for the cash budget.

Generally speaking, the cash budget should be broken down into periods that are as short as feasible. Considerable fluctuations in cash balances may be hidden by looking at a longer period. While a monthly cash budget is most common, many firms budget cash on a weekly or even daily basis. Larry Giano has prepared a quarterly cash budget for Hampton Freeze that can be further refined, as necessary. This budget appears in Schedule 8. Giano has assumed in the budget that an open line of credit can be arranged with the bank and used as needed to bolster the company's cash position. He has also assumed that any loans taken out with this line of credit would carry an interest rate of 10% per year. Giano has assumed that all borrowings and repayments are in round $1,000 amounts and that all borrowing occurs at the beginning of a quarter and all repayments are made at the end of a quarter.

The details on the interest calculation can be found in Appendix 7A, which is available on Connect. Note that interest is calculated separately on each loan being repaid. The company requires a total of $86,500 to completely repay all of the outstanding loans and the accrued interest.

HELPFUL HINT

The calculation of interest payment in a cash budget is where students most often make mistakes. To avoid making errors, consider the following points.

First, borrowings occur at the beginning of a period, so that cash is available to cover the deficit that is being financed.

Second, the amount financed must include all or part of the minimum required cash balance.

Third, start accruing interest on the amount borrowed from the period in which the borrowing occurs—remember that you will owe interest for the period when you borrow since you get the cash on the first day of the period.

Fourth, remember that you make interest payments at the end—on the last day—of a period in which you have funds available. Thus, you will also incur interest for the period in which you are making a repayment. Interest is paid at the same time as the principal is paid, and you must accrue interest on the principal for each period, including the period when you borrowed and the period you make the payment.

Finally, it is very important to calculate the interest for each loan separately before totalling the interest, since each loan will have been outstanding for a different length of time.

In the case of Hampton Freeze, all loans have been repaid by year-end. If all loans are not repaid and a budgeted income statement or balance sheet is being prepared, then interest must be accrued on the unpaid loans. This interest will *not* appear on the cash budget (since it has not yet been paid), but it will appear as part of interest expense on the budgeted income statement and as a liability on the budgeted balance sheet.

IN BUSINESS

EXTERNAL ENVIRONMENT PINCHES CASH FLOWS

The slowdown of the energy sector in Canada in 2014–15 can be traced in part to the drop in oil prices. The contraction in the sector through cutbacks of exploration and development projects and employee layoffs were likely triggered via a re-examination by many of the oil firms of their operating budgets. The impact of the oil price slide on the companies' budgets may be imagined easily since the decline appears to have been unexpected. Prior to the drastic drop in oil prices in June 2014, oil was being traded above $105 per barrel on the West Texas Intermediate. However, the softening demand in Asia, coupled with robust shale-oil production from the United States and OPEC's refusal to reduce production, caused the price to skid below $51 per barrel by March 2015.

The disparity in production costs between OPEC (cheaper) and non-OPEC (more expensive) member countries has meant that, at prices below $51 per barrel, there is very little profit margin. According to Randy Ollenberger, analyst at BMO Nesbitt Burns Inc., the challenge is that "even if they [major oil companies] have investment opportunities that generate returns at sub-$60 oil prices, most don't generate enough cash flow currently to fund those investments, and their balance sheets have always been structured for higher commodity prices."

Accordingly, the hardest hit have been the small developers of oil sands projects as they already struggle to meet rising inflation in labour and materials costs. Paying for the cost overruns requires additional capital, capital which they unfortunately cannot raise because the low oil prices reduce the cash flow from customers.

Source: Jeff Lewis and Jeffrey Jones, "Under Pressure in the Alberta Oil Patch," *The Globe and Mail*, February 20, 2015, http://www.theglobeandmail.com/report-on-business/industry-news/energy-and-resources/the-alberta-oil-squeeze/article23136731/

The Budgeted Income Statement

LO3 ● **Apply**

CC13: Prepare a budgeted income statement.

A budgeted income statement can be prepared from the data developed in Schedules 1 to 8. *The budgeted income statement is one of the key schedules in the budget process.* It shows the company's planned profit for the upcoming budget period, and it serves as a benchmark against which subsequent company performance can be measured.

Schedule 9 contains the budgeted income statement for Hampton Freeze. The cost of goods sold is determined from Schedules 1 and 6 as follows. Hampton Freeze has planned to sell 100,000 cases during 2019. The cost of each case from Schedule 6 is $13. Therefore, the cost of goods sold is $1,300,000. Although this calculation is simple, it is important to realize that it hides many details that may be of interest. For example, detail regarding manufacturing costs incurred and the cost of goods manufactured has been collapsed into the cost of goods sold. It is not difficult to extract this information from the schedules developed. An income statement showing this detail appears below Schedule 9.

Schedule 9—Budgeted Income Statement

	A	B	C
1	HAMPTON FREEZE, INC.		
2	Budgeted Income Statement		
3	For the Year Ended December 31, 2019		
4			
5		*Schedules*	
6	Sales	1	$2,000,000
7	Less: Cost of goods sold	1, 6	1,300,000
8	Gross margin		700,000
9	Less: Selling and administrative expenses	7	577,800
10	Net operating income		122,200
11	Less: Interest expense	8	14,000
12	Net income		$ 108,200

HAMPTON FREEZE, INC.
Income Statement
For the Year Ended December 31, 2019

Sales (Schedule 1)			$2,000,000
Cost of goods sold:			
Beginning finished goods inventory (2,000 cases, Schedule 2 × $13/case, Schedule 6)			26,000
Add: Cost of goods manufactured:			
Total manufacturing costs:			
Direct materials (Schedule 3):			
Beginning inventory of direct materials	$ 4,200		
Add: Purchases of direct materials	303,300		
Deduct: Ending inventory of direct materials	$ 4,500		
Direct materials used in production	303,000		
Direct labour (Schedule 4)	606,000		
Manufacturing overhead (Schedule 5)	404,000		
Manufacturing costs incurred	$1,313,000		
Cost of goods manufactured			1,313,000
Goods available for sale			1,339,000
Deduct: Ending finished goods inventory (3,000 cases, Schedule 2 × $13/case, Schedule 6)			39,000
Cost of goods sold			1,300,000
Gross margin			700,000
Selling and administrative expenses (Schedule 7)			577,800
Net operating income			122,200
Interest expense (Schedule 8)			14,000
Net income			$ 108,200

Hampton Freeze does not have work-in-process inventory; therefore, the cost of goods manufactured and manufacturing costs incurred are equal. Study this income statement carefully and make sure you can see how the information from the various schedules has been used in its construction.

The Budgeted Balance Sheet

LO3 • **Apply**

CC14: Prepare a budgeted balance sheet.

The budgeted balance sheet is developed by beginning with the current balance sheet and adjusting it for the data contained in the other budgets. Hampton Freeze's budgeted balance sheet is presented in Schedule 10. Some of the data on the budgeted balance sheet have been taken from the company's projected end-of-year balance sheet for 2018, which appears in Exhibit 7–2.

EXHIBIT 7–2 Balance Sheet for 2018

HAMPTON FREEZE, INC.
Balance Sheet
December 31, 2018

Assets		
Current assets:		
Cash	$ 42,500	
Accounts receivable	90,000	
Raw materials inventory (21,000 kilograms)	4,200	
Finished goods inventory (2,000 cases)	26,000	
Total current assets		$162,700
Plant and equipment:		
Land	80,000	
Buildings and equipment	700,000	
Accumulated depreciation	(292,000)	
Plant and equipment, net		488,000
Total assets		$650,700
Liabilities and Shareholders' Equity		
Current liabilities:		
Accounts payable (raw materials)		$ 25,800
Shareholders' equity:		
Common shares, no par	$ 175,000	
Retained earnings	449,900	
Total shareholders' equity		624,900
Total liabilities and shareholders' equity		$650,700

Schedule 10—Budgeted Balance Sheet

	A	B	C	D	E
1	**HAMPTON FREEZE, INC.**				
2	**Budgeted Balance Sheet**				
3	**December 31, 2019**				
4					
5	*Assets*				
6	Current assets:				
7	Cash	$ 40,500	(a)		
8	Accounts receivable	120,000	(b)		
9	Raw materials inventory	4,500	(c)		
10	Finished goods inventory	39,000	(d)		
11	Total current assets			$204,000	
12	Plant and equipment:				
13	Land	80,000	(e)		
14	Buildings and equipment	837,000	(f)		
15	Accumulated depreciation	(392,000)	(g)		
16	Plant and equipment, net			525,000	
17	Total assets			$729,000	
18					
19	*Liabilities and Shareholders' Equity*				
20	Current liabilities:				
21	Accounts payable (raw materials)			$ 27,900	(h)
22	Shareholders' equity:				
23	Common share, no par	$ 175,000	(i)		
24	Retained earnings	526,100	(j)		
25	Total shareholders' equity			701,100	
26	Total liabilities and shareholders' equity			$729,000	

The following is an explanation of the December 31, 2019, balance sheet figures in Schedule 10:

a. This is the ending cash balance, as projected by the cash budget in Schedule 8.

b. This is 30% of fourth-quarter sales, from Schedule 1 ($400,000 × 30% = $120,000).

c. From Schedule 3, the ending raw materials inventory will be 22,500 kilograms. This material costs $0.20 per kilogram. Therefore, the ending inventory in dollars will be 22,500 kilograms × $0.20 per kilogram = $4,500.

d. This comes from Schedule 6.

e. This comes from the December 31, 2018, balance sheet (no change).

f. The December 31, 2018, balance sheet indicated a balance of $700,000. During 2019, $137,000 in additional equipment will be purchased (see Schedule 8), bringing the December 31, 2019, balance to $837,000.

g. The December 31, 2018, balance sheet indicated a balance of $292,000. During 2019, $100,000 of depreciation will be taken ($60,000 on Schedule 5 and $40,000 on Schedule 7), bringing the December 31, 2019, balance to $392,000.

h. This represents 50% of the fourth-quarter raw materials purchases, from Schedule 3.

i. This comes from the December 31, 2018, balance sheet (no change).

j.

December 31, 2018, balance	$449,900
Add net income, from Schedule 9	108,200
	558,100
Deduct dividends paid, from Schedule 8	32,000
December 31, 2019, balance	$526,100

The calculation in (j) above highlights how the income statement and the balance sheet connect to one another. The net income from the income statement plugs into retained earnings on the balance sheet. This concept, which is formally referred to as articulated financial statements, is something that all business students must understand.

MANAGERIAL ACCOUNTING IN ACTION

WRAP-UP

After completing the master budget, Larry Giano took the documents to Tom Wills—chief executive officer of Hampton Freeze—for his review.

Giano: Here's the budget. Overall, the net income is excellent, and the net cash flow for the entire year is positive.

Wills: Yes, but I see on this cash budget that we have the same problem with negative cash flows in the first and second quarters that we had last year.

Giano: That's true. I don't see any way around that problem. However, there is no doubt in my mind that if you take this budget to the bank today, they'll approve an open line of credit that will allow you to borrow enough to make it through the first two quarters without any problem.

Wills: Are you sure? They didn't seem very happy to see me last year when I went in for an emergency loan.

Giano: Did you repay the loan on time?

Wills: Sure.

Giano: I don't see any problem. You won't be asking for an emergency loan this time. The bank will have plenty of warning. And, with this budget, you have a solid plan that shows when and how you are going to pay off the loan. Trust me, they'll go for it.

Wills: Fantastic! It would sure make life a lot easier this year.

DECISION POINT

A FISCALLY RESPONSIBLE STUDENT

You are a new student who will be paying part of the bill for your education. You saved quite a bit of money but are sure that you will need to earn more to cover your expenses. Before you look for a part-time job, you need to decide how many hours per week you will work and what hourly wage you will need in order to pay your expenses. You decide to prepare a budget for your postsecondary education. How should you proceed?

*Note to student: See **Guidance Answers** online.*

WORKING IT OUT

The Gazebo Company needs a cash budget. The following schedule describes the quarterly excess or deficiency of cash receipts over cash disbursements for the Gazebo Company. The chief financial officer for Gazebo has stipulated that there should be a minimum of $10,000 in the ending cash balance of each quarter. This requirement is not included in the excess or deficiency provided in the given schedule. Gazebo can borrow funds for the short term at an interest rate of 2% per quarter. The company expects to have an opening cash balance of $10,000 at the beginning of the first quarter. Interest is accrued and due only for the portion of the principal that is repaid at the time of the repayment. All borrowings and repayments of the principal must be in round $1,000 amounts. Borrowings occur at the beginning of a quarter and payments occur at the end of a quarter.

	Quarter				
	1	**2**	**3**	**4**	**Year**
Excess (deficiency) of cash available over disbursements	$(121,140)	$(41,680)	$177,680	$2,160	$17,020

Required:

Prepare a cash budget by quarter and for the year for Gazebo.

SOLUTION TO WORKING IT OUT

The cash budget for Gazebo Company is shown below:

	A	B	C	D	E	F
1		Cash Budget				
2		For the Year Ended December 31				
3			Quarter			
4		**1**	**2**	**3**	**4**	**Year**
5	Cash balance, beginning	$ 10,000	$ 10,860	$ 10,180	$15,900	$ 10,000

	A	B	C	D	E	F
6	Add: Excess (deficiency) of cash available over disbursements	(121,140)	(41,680)	177,680	2,160	17,020
7	Deduct: Minimum desired cash balance	10,000	10,000	10,000	10,000	10,000
8	Balance available (or required) for financing	$ (121,140)	$ (40,820)	$ 177,860	$ 8,060	$ 17,020
9	Financing					
10	Amount borrowed (beginning of period)	$122,000	$ 41,000	$ 0	$ 0	$163,000
11	Principal repaid			163,000	0	$163,000
12	Interest paid			8,960	0	$ 8,960
13	Total financing (or repayments for the period)	$122,000	$ 41,000	$ (171,960)	$ 0	$ (8,960)
14	Cash balance after financing—free cash	$ 860	$ 180	$ 5,900	$ 8,060	$ 8,060
15	Add: Minimum balance	10,000	10,000	10,000	10,000	10,000
16	Cash balance, ending	$ 10,860	$ 10,180	$ 15,900	$18,060	$ 18,060

In quarter 3, a total of $177,860 is available to repay the borrowings made in the previous quarters. Always starting with the oldest loan, Gazebo systematically determines how much of the principal plus accrued interest it is able to pay back. The available funds can accommodate the repayment of the entire principal borrowed in the first quarter plus the three quarters of accrued interest: $122,000 + 2% × 3 × $122,000 = $129,320. This leaves $177,680 − $129,320 = $48,540 available for retiring a portion of or the entire amount borrowed in the second quarter. At the end of the third quarter, there will be two quarters of accrued interest owed on any principal repaid from the second quarter's loan. The total principal that can be repaid using $48,540 is $48,540 ÷ 1.04 = $46,673. Since this is less than the amount borrowed, Gazebo can also retire the second quarter's loan in its entirety. It will thus pay $41,000 + 2% × 2 × $41,000 = $42,640. After both loans from quarters 1 and 2 have been fully paid off, Gazebo has an available cash balance of $5,900 (i.e., $177,860 − $129,320 − $42,640). After adding back $10,000 set aside as the reserve, the actual cash balance for the third quarter is $15,900.

HELPFUL HINT

If a positive difference of cash receipts over cash disbursements (an excess) exists, it must be applied against any minimum balance of cash the company may have set. That is, treat the minimum balance as another disbursement and calculate the resulting cash position. If this position is a positive balance, then no external financing will be required. On the other hand, if the position is negative, then external financing will be required. A negative difference between cash receipts and disbursements—a deficiency—is an automatic signal of the need for external financing. And treating the minimum cash balance required as another disbursement will result in a larger deficiency to be financed.

Master Budget for a Merchandise Company

As was mentioned earlier in referring to Exhibit 7–1, a merchandise company will not require the production, direct labour, direct materials, and overhead budgets. Instead, a merchandise purchases budget is prepared. A fully worked out example is provided in Appendix 7A, available on Connect.

Practical Issues in Budgeting: Use and Abuse

LO4 • Know

CC15: Describe the practical issues in the budgeting process, including participative budgeting and responsibility accounting.

How can organizations ensure that the benefits of budgeting and budgets can be attained in practice? This important question suggests that it is possible for budgeting and budgets to have dysfunctional effects on an organization. In this part of the chapter, we will discuss the issues that organizations must consider in order to attain the advantages of budgeting and avoid the dysfunctional effects.

The example of Larry Giano at Hampton Freeze provides an insightful starting point. Recall how Giano accomplished his mandate to introduce and develop a budgeting system.

1. Giano had the full backing of Tom Wills in developing the budgeting system at Hampton Freeze.
2. At the outset, Giano communicated the need for a budgeting system and obtained the cooperation of those whose involvement was essential to the development and *application* of the budgets.
3. Giano worked closely with all the managers involved and ensured that they understood and supported the parts of the budget that affected them, thus preparing them to take ownership of the budgeting system in the future.

Apparently, Giano knows a thing or two about managing. His experience illustrates the importance of top management support, communication, and cooperation for developing budgets that will be accepted by those who will have to follow them. We now examine these aspects further.

Organizational and Financial Control Using Budgets

Because budgets allocate resources, the budgeting process determines to a large extent which departments get more resources and which get relatively less. Also, the budget sets the benchmarks by which managers and their departments will be at least partially evaluated. Therefore, it should not be surprising that managers take the budgeting process seriously, investing considerable energy and even emotion in ensuring that their departments' interests are protected. Because of this, the success of a budget program will be determined, in large part, by (1) how the budget is developed and (2) how and to what purpose the budget is used. In the most successful budget programs, managers with cost control responsibilities actively participate in preparing their own budgets. The budget that emerges from this approach is called a **participative budget** (or a **self-imposed budget**), and the approach is called **participative budgeting**. This is in contrast to the approach in which budgets are imposed from above.

The participative approach to preparing budgets is particularly important if the budget is to be used to control and evaluate a manager's performance. In such cases, inviting participation by managers helps to hold managers to the plans and targets upon which the budget is based and motivates them to use the budget to guide their activities and decisions. The budget itself is likely to be more accurate since the planning estimates will be based on information from those in the best position to provide that information.

If a budget is imposed on a manager from above, it will probably generate resentment and ill will, rather than cooperation and commitment. A manager who is unable to meet such a budget can always say that the budget was unreasonable or unrealistic to start with and therefore impossible to meet. With a self-imposed budget, this excuse is not available.

Once self-imposed budgets are prepared, and before they are accepted, they must be carefully reviewed by immediate superiors. Top management has a perspective on the company as a whole that is vital, and so top managers participate in the development of the budget. Each level of responsibility in an organization should *cooperate* to develop an integrated budget. If changes seem desirable, the items in question are discussed and modified, as necessary.

Fully participative budgeting is an ideal budgetary process that involves self-imposed budgets prepared by the managers who are directly responsible for revenues and costs. Most companies deviate from this ideal. Typically, top managers initiate the budget process by issuing broad guidelines in terms of overall target profits or sales. Lower-level managers are directed to prepare budgets that meet those targets. The difficulty is that the targets set by top managers may be unrealistically high or may allow too much slack. If the targets are too high and employees know them to be unrealistic, motivation will suffer. If the targets allow too much slack, waste will occur. And, unfortunately, top managers are often not in a position to know whether the targets they have set are appropriate. Admittedly, however, a pure self-imposed budgeting system may lack sufficient strategic direction, and lower-level managers may be tempted to build a great deal of budgetary slack into their budgets. Nevertheless, because of the motivational advantages of self-imposed budgets, top managers should be cautious about setting inflexible targets.

RESPONSIBILITY ACCOUNTING—USING THE BUDGET

The basic idea behind **responsibility accounting** is that a manager should be held responsible for those items—and *only* those items—he or she can actually control significantly. Each line item (i.e., revenue or cost) in the budget is made the responsibility of a manager, and that manager is held responsible for subsequent deviations between budgeted goals and actual results. This concept is central to any effective profit planning and control system. Someone must be held responsible for each cost, or else no one will be responsible and the cost will inevitably grow out of control.

Being held responsible for costs means that if the actual results do not measure up to the budgeted goals, the manager should understand the source of significant favourable or unfavourable discrepancies and should be prepared to explain the reasons for discrepancies to higher management. It also means that the manager should take the initiative to correct any unfavourable discrepancies.

Responsibility accounting does not mean that top management must use the budget as a punishment to pressure employees or as a way to find someone to blame if something goes wrong. Using budgets in such negative ways will simply breed hostility, tension, and mistrust, rather than greater cooperation and productivity. Unfortunately, research suggests that the budget is often used in just this way and that great emphasis is placed on "meeting the budget" under all circumstances.[1] In response to such negative consequences of improperly using budgets, a new movement called *beyond budgeting* has emerged recently. Proponents have argued for doing away with budgets entirely! This idea is considered in the next section.

IN BUSINESS

USING BUDGETS AND FINANCIALS TO ENGAGE EMPLOYEES

According to Robert Meggy, CMA, FMCA, president and CEO of the Great Little Box Company (GLBC), "Being named best place to work in British Columbia is the highlight of my career." This recognition is just one of several honours accorded in recent years to GLBC, which was named one of Canada's 50 best-managed companies for three years in a row. The company under Meggy's leadership has made it a priority to connect with its employees by providing them with the information they need to make decisions and empowering them to make those decisions. The company's budget, financials, and financial statements make up an important element of the information shared with employees. Every two years, the employees are taught the basics of understanding financial statements, using analogies drawn from personal finances. Personal vehicles, homes, and mortgages are used to illustrate balance sheet concepts, and costs and revenues are illustrated in terms of a simple business setting such as a lemonade stand. According to Meggy, "By doing this, I hope to create a sense of trust around our reporting."

As this chapter has illustrated, the budget is a repository of comprehensive information about the financial and operating plans of the company, among other things. Sharing this information with employees can lead to increased identification with the company and commitment to its success. This is borne out by the experience of GLBC: "In our annual survey of employees, when we ask the question 'Do you care about the future of the company?', it garners the highest positive response of any question."

Source: Robert Colman, "Packing the Perfect HR Punch," *CMA Management,* March 2007, pp. 40–43.

Beyond Budgeting[2]

LO4 • Know

CC16: Explain the beyond budgeting model and its approach to budgeting.

Is budgeting worth the trouble that organizations must endure to introduce and apply it successfully? This controversial question is at the heart of a new philosophy about budgeting being developed by the Beyond Budgeting Round Table (BBRT)—a program of a European think tank, the Consortium for Advanced Manufacturing International (Europe). Traditional budgeting is viewed as a tool more appropriate in "command-and-control" organizations. Increased globalization, greater customer involvement, and intense competition have required that firms be more flexible and responsive. This, in turn, requires that firms move away from command-and-control structures and dispense more authority to the front lines. Traditional budgeting is ill suited to this type of organization. It cannot be tweaked or modified. It has to go.

WEAKNESSES OF TRADITIONAL BUDGETING

According to the BBRT, the traditional budgeting model has several weaknesses. Managers tend to look upon a budget as set in stone. Therefore, performance evaluation using the budget as a benchmark is often feared and resented, since the actual performance invariably will differ from planned performance. This fear and resentment can often lead to *gaming:* managers may *lowball* (understate) estimates or overstate the funding needs. Meeting the budget becomes an overarching objective even at the expense of long-term goals. Unnecessary spending can occur where managers end up spending surpluses to zero out the budget to avoid funding clawbacks for the next operating cycle. Finally, managers might understate the actual performance and profits when they exceed targets to avoid the threat of upward ratcheting of performance targets.

Traditional budgets are considered to be financial representations of operational details of the firm's costs and revenues and, as such, are viewed as having little to do with implementing the firm's strategic objectives. It is argued that the traditional budgeting process disconnects the budget participants from the firm's long-term strategic imperatives. Resource allocation is viewed as a zero-sum game, and managers become obsessed with ensuring that they get the funds they need. They end up drowning in the details of the budgeting process and the budgets and lose sight of the goals.

Think back to the master budget for Hampton Freeze. Recall that the various budgets making up the master budget have a *functional* orientation: sales, production, selling and administration, purchasing, and so on. This orientation is considered to be out of step with recent developments in modern management, which emphasize a *process* orientation. Management of processes is the cornerstone of value creation. Where will budgeting fit into this picture?

Finally, keeping with the Hampton Freeze example, note that Larry Giano could not have created the budget *overnight.* Budgets take time and effort to complete. While this is going on, what do you do if the data inputs change? Giano required the involvement and cooperation of many individuals throughout the company. This consumes time and attention. BBRT argues that up to 30% of a senior executive's time can be consumed by the budgeting process. Is this expenditure of resources worthwhile?

So what is the answer? "Get rid of budgets," according to the supporters of the beyond budgeting model. The argument is that budgets have to play many roles. They must capture plans and act as a coordinating mechanism for actions, they must provide benchmarks for performance evaluation, and they must motivate and guide management actions and behaviour. These are conflicting roles. No one knows how these conflicts can be resolved.

THE BEYOND BUDGETING MODEL

If traditional budgeting and budgets are to be discarded, what should fill the gap? BBRT has proposed a model that eschews the fixed, performance-contract–based command-and-control framework of traditional budgeting. It recommends the use of relative performance targets and emphasizes the principles of effective strategic management and empowerment of employees. The following are the key principles of this new model:

1. *Set challenging relative performance targets.* Benchmarks can be relative to industry, specific competitors, internal business units, and so on. The idea is that there is now a basis for evaluating performance. A manager would be hard pressed to explain away poor performance if targets were attained or exceeded by his or her counterparts in similar settings.

2. *Adopt continuous and inclusive planning.* The key here is the *inclusive* aspect. By devolving corporate objectives systematically down the various layers of the organization, a clear link is established between lower-level objectives and targets and the overall strategic imperatives. Now lower-level units of the organization can see and understand the connection

between their actions and the attainment of corporate objectives. Front-line managers can make better-informed decisions because they are aware of the impact these decisions can have on the organization.

3. *Use rolling forecasts.* Forecasts are updated regularly and frequently. As the environment changes, forecasts are modified in response. This allows managers to be aware of the current situation and manage accordingly. In this model, forecasts are separated from performance targets, measures, and rewards.

4. *Use market-like structures for coordination.* The free-market structure is still the best coordinating mechanism. The discipline of the market in promoting efficiency and effectiveness is unequalled. The BBRT model proposes that the centralized coordination be replaced by a set of customer–supplier relationships. On the one hand, there is the external set between the firm and its customers and suppliers. On the other hand, within the firm, central services support operating units through service agreements often based on market prices. Operating units and service units are subject to the discipline of the market.

5. *Decentralize resource management.* The BBRT model proposes that front-line units be allowed the freedom to manage their own resources and be held accountable for their actions. This eliminates many layers of bureaucracy, speeds up resource and funding approval requests, and enables managers to respond quickly to changing circumstances.

6. *Control through self-regulation and transparent information.* This principle advocates that managers be provided with strategic, competitive, and market-based information so they can self-regulate. Information is the basis for making decisions, so it should be available to everyone.

7. *Use low-powered incentives aligned to group or organizational performance.* Rather than emphasizing individually tailored incentive and compensation schemes based on fixed targets negotiated in advance, this principle recommends the use of collective measures and the inclusion of everyone in the reward program. The idea is to promote a holistic view and teamwork, reducing peer pressure.

There is no doubt that the BBRT model will stimulate lively debate as proponents on both sides try to persuade you, and others like you, of the merits of their respective positions. Some organizations, such as Borealis (http://www.borealisgroup.com), have adopted these principles and claimed success. There is still a lot to discover and understand about how budgets are prepared and used. Are organizations and individuals prepared to make the leap without the safety net of budgets and embrace a management model that does not rely on traditional budgets? Theresa Libby and R. Murray Lindsay, the authors of the article on which this discussion is based, have written a major research program to improve our understanding of these issues.

Learning Objectives Summary

LO1   UNDERSTAND THE CONCEPT OF BUDGETS AND BUDGETING.

Organizations budget for a variety of reasons, including to communicate management's plans throughout the organization, to force managers to think about and plan for the future, to allocate resources within the organization, to identify bottlenecks before they occur, to coordinate activities, and to provide benchmarks for evaluating subsequent performance. Budgets should be developed with the full participation of all managers who will be subject to budgetary controls.

LO2   PREPARE EACH COMPONENT BUDGET OF THE MASTER BUDGET.

The sales budget forms the foundation for the master budget. It provides details concerning the anticipated unit and dollar sales. The schedule of expected cash collections is based on the sales budget, the expected breakdown between cash and credit sales, and the expected pattern of collections on credit sales.

The production budget details how many units must be produced each budget period to satisfy expected sales and to provide for adequate levels of finished goods inventories.

The direct materials budget, including a schedule of expected cash disbursements for purchases of raw materials, shows the materials that must be purchased each budget period to meet anticipated production requirements and to provide for adequate levels of materials inventories. Cash disbursements for purchases of materials will depend on the amount of materials purchased in each budget period and the company's policies concerning payments to suppliers for materials bought on credit.

The direct labour budget shows the direct labour-hours that are required to meet the production schedule as detailed in the production budget. The direct labour-hour requirements are used to determine the direct labour cost in each budget period.

The manufacturing overhead budget covers both variable and fixed manufacturing overhead. The variable manufacturing overhead depends on the number of units produced from the production budget. The variable and fixed manufacturing overhead costs are combined to determine the total manufacturing overhead. Any noncash manufacturing overhead, such as depreciation, is deducted from the total manufacturing overhead to determine the cash disbursements for manufacturing overhead.

The ending finished goods inventory budget shows the carrying cost of the unsold units.

The selling and administrative expense budget covers both variable and fixed expenses. The variable expenses depend on the number of units sold or some other measure of activity. The variable and fixed expenses are combined to determine the total selling and administrative expense. Any noncash selling and administrative expenses, such as depreciation, are deducted from the total to determine the cash disbursements for selling and administrative expenses.

The cash budget is a critical piece of the master budget. It permits managers to anticipate and plan for cash shortfalls. The cash budget is organized into a receipts section, a disbursements section, a cash excess or deficiency section, and a financing section. The cash budget draws on information taken from nearly all of the other budgets and schedules, including the schedule of cash collections, the schedule of cash disbursements for purchases of materials, the direct labour budget, the manufacturing overhead budget, and the selling and administrative expense budget.

LO3 DEVELOP BUDGETED FINANCIAL STATEMENTS FROM THE COMPONENT BUDGETS OF THE MASTER BUDGET.

The *budgeted income statement* is constructed using data from the sales budget, the ending finished goods inventory budget, the manufacturing overhead budget, the selling and administrative expense budget, and the cash budget. The *budgeted balance sheet* is constructed using data from virtually all other parts of the master budget.

LO4 UNDERSTAND THE BUDGETING PROCESS AND THE ROLE OF THE BEYOND BUDGETING MODEL.

Some practical issues surrounding the budgeting process include deciding how to develop the budget, and how and to what purpose the budget will be used. One way to ensure a successful budget is to have managers with cost control responsibilities actively participate in preparing their own budgets, instead of having the budgets imposed from above. The beyond budgeting model eschews the fixed command-and-control framework of traditional budgeting and instead recommends the use of relative performance targets.

Application Competency Summary

APPLICATION COMPETENCY	DELIVERABLE	SOURCE DOCUMENTS AND KEY INFORMATION	STEPS	KNOWLEDGE COMPETENCY
Prepare a sales budget, including a schedule of cash receipts. • **LO2–CC5**	*Key Information* Projected quantity of and revenue from sales per period for the planning horizon and projected cash collections per period *Report/Document* Sales budget and schedule of cash receipts	*Sales Forecast Documents* • Projected sales quantities for each period *Pricing Documents* • Selling price of the product/ service *Collection Policy Documents* • Expected collections pattern	1. Compute projected sales revenue as projected sales quantity multiplied by the unit selling price. 2. Compute cash receipts for the current period by multiplying the collection percentages for the sales made in prior periods (including the current period) by the respective summing of the results.	Cash collected in a period need not equal the sales revenue of the period due to timing differences between sales and collections. Accounts receivable represents uncollected sales revenue. Master budget relationships • **LO1–CC3**
Prepare a production budget. • **LO2–CC6**	*Key Information* The number of units budgeted for production or purchase each period to satisfy sales, inventory, and other requirements *Report/Document* Production or purchases budget	*Sales Budget* • Projected sales *Inventory Policy Documents and Inventory Records* • Inventory requirements • Actual inventory balance at the beginning of budget planning period	1. Compute estimated production for each period as follows: • Budgeted sales in units plus desired ending inventory less beginning inventory.	Basic inventory flow equation • **LO6–CC11** (Ch. 2)
Prepare a direct materials (DM) budget, including a schedule of cash disbursements	*Key Information* Raw materials purchases required to support the budgeted production	*Production Budget* • Production quantity for each period	1. Compute the quantity of DM required for production as follows: production quantity	Cash payments in a period need not equal the value of purchases made in the period due to timing difference between

APPLICATION COMPETENCY	DELIVERABLE	SOURCE DOCUMENTS AND KEY INFORMATION	STEPS	KNOWLEDGE COMPETENCY
for purchases of raw materials. ● **LO2–CC7**	Projected cash disbursements for the purchase of DM *Report/Document* DM budget and schedule of expected cash disbursements	*Materials Requirement and Cost Documents* • Direct materials required per unit of product • Cost per unit of DM *Materials Inventory Records* • Actual inventory balance at the beginning of budget planning period *Payables Policy Documents* • Expected payment patterns for materials purchases	multiplied by the units of DM required per unit of production. 2. Add beginning DM inventories to obtain the quantity of DM needs. 3. Subtract the beginning DM inventory balance to obtain the DM quantity to purchase. 4. Compute the cost of DM to be purchased as follows: • Quantity of DM purchase multiplied by the cost per unit of DM. 5. Compute cash payments for the current period by multiplying the payment percentages for the purchases made in prior periods (including the current period) by the respective values and summing the results.	payments made on account and purchases. Accounts payable represents purchases unpaid and remaining on account. Basic inventory flow equation ● **LO6–CC11** (Ch. 2)
Prepare a direct labour (DL) budget. ● **LO2–CC8**	*Key Information* DL hours required to support the planned production	*Production Budget* • Production quantity for each period	1. Multiply the budgeted production quantity by the number of	A budget depends on the assumption of period-by-period adjustment of the workforce to yield

APPLICATION COMPETENCY	DELIVERABLE	SOURCE DOCUMENTS AND KEY INFORMATION	STEPS	KNOWLEDGE COMPETENCY
	and the cost of labour *Report/Document* DL budget	*Labour Requirement Documents* • DL hours (DLHs) required for each unit *Wage Contract Documents* • DL cost per hour	DLHs required per unit to compute the total estimated DLHs for the budget period. 2. Multiply the DLHs by the DL cost per hour to compute the total DL cost.	the required hours. If the firm maintains a constant workforce, this will change the budgeted cost: the cost will be the same for each period.
Prepare a manufacturing overhead (MOH) budget. ● **LO2–CC9**	*Key Information* Budgeted amount of MOH costs per period Cash disbursements for MOH MOH allocation rate per unit of the allocation base *Report/Document* MOH budget	*Activity/Resource Planning Documents* • Budgeted amounts of fixed and variable MOH • Budgeted amounts of overhead allocation base(s)—text example uses DLH as the base but other bases can be used *Plant, Property, and Equipment Budget and the Existing Account in the General Ledger* • Current and estimated depreciation amount	1. Calculate the budgeted variable MOH: quantity of allocation base multiplied by the variable MOH allocation rate. 2. Add the fixed MOH cost to obtain the total MOH cost. 3. Divide the total MOH by total quantity of the allocation base used over the budget period to get the MOH allocation rate per unit of allocation base. 4. Subtract depreciation from total MOH to compute the cash disbursement for MOH.	MOH allocation base Variable MOH allocation rate Predetermined MOH rate ● **LO3–CC6, 7** (Ch. 3)
Prepare an ending finished goods inventory	*Key Information* Budgeted value of ending finished goods inventory at	*Production Budget* • Ending balance of finished goods	1. Calculate cost per unit of product by adding the DM cost, DL cost,	Absorption costing ● **LO1–CC3** (Ch. 3)

APPLICATION COMPETENCY	DELIVERABLE	SOURCE DOCUMENTS AND KEY INFORMATION	STEPS	KNOWLEDGE COMPETENCY
budget. • **LO2–CC10**	year-end (end of budget period) assuming absorption costing *Report/Document* Ending finished goods inventory budget	inventory in units *DM Budget* • DM quantity needed per unit of product • Cost of DM per unit of DM *DL Budget* • DL hours required per unit of product • Cost per DL hour *MOH Budget* • MOH allocation base required per unit of product • Predetermined rate per unit of allocation base	and MOH cost per unit of product. 2. Calculate the value of ending finished goods inventory by multiplying the quantity of goods in ending inventory by the cost per unit calculated, as shown in the previous step.	
Prepare a selling and administrative (S&A) expense budget. • **LO2–CC11**	*Key Information* Budgeted expenses for selling activities, such as advertising, and for administration, such as office salaries, insurance, and property taxes Cash disbursements for S&A expenses *Report/Document* S&A expense budget	*Sales Budget* • Sales quantity and revenues *Documents Estimating the Fixed S&A Expenses* • Fixed expenses budgeted for various fixed S&A items including any depreciation *Documents Describing Computation of Variable S&A Expenses*	1. Calculate the variable S&A expense per period: • Sales quantity multiplied by the variable S&A expense rate. 2. Itemize the budgeted cost of the fixed components of S&A activities and determine the total fixed S&A expense per period. 3. Add the variable and fixed amounts to obtain total	Variable versus fixed costs Depreciation is a noncash expense • **LO1–CC1** (Ch. 2) • **LO2–CC2** (Ch. 2)

APPLICATION COMPETENCY	DELIVERABLE	SOURCE DOCUMENTS AND KEY INFORMATION	STEPS	KNOWLEDGE COMPETENCY
		• Variable S&A rate per unit of sales	budgeted S&A expenses. 4. Subtract depreciation from the total budgeted S&A expense to obtain cash disbursements for S&A expenses.	
Prepare a cash budget. ● **LO2–CC12**	*Key Information* Expected cash receipts per period before financing, expected cash disbursements per period before financing payments, excess of cash or deficiency per period before financing, financing inflows period and payments for financing charges, cash balance at the end of each period projected after financing *Report/Document* Cash budget	*Prior-Period Estimated Balance Sheet* • Estimated cash balance at the beginning of the budget period *Sales Budget and Schedule of Cash Receipts* • Cash receipts per period *DM Budget and Schedule of Disbursements for Materials Purchases* • Cash disbursements for DM purchases *DL, MOH, and S&A Budgets* • DL, MOH, and S&A expenses *Payment Policies Documents* • Disbursement policy for DL, MOH, and S&A related expenses *Capital Purchases Budget*	1. Add cash receipts to the beginning cash balance to obtain the cash available before disbursements. 2. Itemize the disbursements and determine total disbursements for the period including expected payments of dividends and capital investment (equipment, etc.). 3. Calculate the difference between total receipts and disbursements to determine the excess (or deficiency) of cash available over disbursements. 4. If there is a deficiency, calculate the amount of financing required by	Simple and compound interest

APPLICATION COMPETENCY	DELIVERABLE	SOURCE DOCUMENTS AND KEY INFORMATION	STEPS	KNOWLEDGE COMPETENCY
		• Amounts related to capital purchases *Documents Pertaining to Financing Available* • Interest rate on borrowing *Cash Policy Documents* • Minimum cash balance requirements *Dividend Policy Documents* • Expected dividend payments	adding the desired ending cash balance to the amount of the shortfall. 5. If there is an excess of cash, determine the amount to repay on previous borrowings (if any) including interest charges.	
Prepare a budgeted income statement. ● **LO3–CC13**	*Key Information* Projected net income for the budget period *Report/Document* Income statement	*Sales Budget* • Sales revenue *DM, DL, MOH, and Ending Finished Goods Inventory Budgets* • Cost of goods sold (COGS) *S&A Expense Budget* • S&A expenses *Cash Budget* • Interest expense	1. Determine the annual sales revenue from the sales budget. 2. Determine the COGS: multiply the total units sold by the cost per unit obtained from the finished goods ending inventory budget. 3. Calculate gross margin as sales less COGS. 4. Subtract the total S&A expense to obtain operating income. 5. Subtract annual interest expense to	COGS ● **LO5–CC10** (Ch. 2) COGM ● **LO6–CC12** (Ch. 2) Product and period costs ● **LO4–CC7** (Ch. 2)

APPLICATION COMPETENCY	DELIVERABLE	SOURCE DOCUMENTS AND KEY INFORMATION	STEPS	KNOWLEDGE COMPETENCY
			obtain net income. *(Note:* A detailed COGS including cost of goods manufactured [COGM] schedule can also be prepared from this same information.)	
Prepare a budgeted balance sheet. ● **LO3–CC14**	*Key Information* Budgeted balance sheet account information *Report/Document* Balance sheet	*Prior-Period Balance Sheet* • Retained earnings for the prior period *Ending Finished Goods Inventory Budget* • Value of ending finished goods inventory *DM Budget and Schedule of Cash Disbursements for Purchases* • Value of ending balance in raw materials inventory • Unpaid purchases at the end of the budgeting period *Cash Budget* • Cash balance at the end of the budgeting period *Sales Budget and Schedule of Cash Receipts*	1. From the cash budget, obtain the ending cash balance. 2. From the schedule of cash receipts, determine the uncollected sales revenue at year-end—this is accounts receivable. 3. From the DM budget, determine the value of ending balance in raw materials inventory. 4. From the ending finished goods inventory budget, determine the value of ending balance in finished goods inventory. 5. Add the cash disbursements for equipment purchases from the cash budget to the prior-period value of plant	Master budget and its component budgets and the relationships between the budgets ● **LO1–CC3** Understanding how the figures on the balance sheet are derived from the various budgets and schedules Uncollected sales revenue represents accounts receivable. Unpaid purchases represents accounts payable. Total depreciation on the balance sheet includes depreciation in MOH and in S&A expense budgets.

APPLICATION COMPETENCY	DELIVERABLE	SOURCE DOCUMENTS AND KEY INFORMATION	STEPS	KNOWLEDGE COMPETENCY
		• Uncollected sales revenue at the end of the budgeting period *Budgeted Income Statement* • Net income for the year • Total depreciation for the budgeting period *Capital Purchases Budget* • Additions to plant and equipment in the current period *Dividend Policy Documents* • Estimated dividends to be declared during the budgeting period	and equipment to obtain the year-end value of plant and equipment. 6. Add the total depreciation from the MOH budget and the S&A budget to accumulated depreciation from the prior period. 7. Subtract accumulated depreciation from the value of plant and equipment to obtain plant and equipment net. 8. Determine the total assets for the current year. 9. Obtain the amount on account for purchases of DM—this is accounts payable. 10. Add the net income from the income statement to the retained earnings balance from the prior period. 11. Subtract dividends paid from the total above to obtain the year-end	

APPLICATION COMPETENCY	DELIVERABLE	SOURCE DOCUMENTS AND KEY INFORMATION	STEPS	KNOWLEDGE COMPETENCY
			balance of retained earnings. 12. Determine the total liabilities and equity for the current year. (*Note:* The preceding material is based on the text example where all borrowings are paid by year-end; therefore, there is no debt in this example. As well, there are no new share issues or redemptions.)	

Review Problem 1: Budget Schedules

Mylar Company manufactures and sells a product that has seasonal variations in demand, with peak sales coming in the third quarter. The following information concerns operations for year 2—the coming year—and for the first two quarters of year 3:

a. The company's single product sells for $8 per unit. Budgeted sales in units for the next six quarters are as follows:

	Year 2 Quarter				Year 3 Quarter	
	1	2	3	4	1	2
Budgeted sales in units	40,000	60,000	100,000	50,000	70,000	80,000

b. Sales are collected in the following pattern: 75% in the quarter the sales are made and the remaining 25% in the following quarter. On January 1, year 2, the company's balance sheet showed $65,000 in accounts receivable, all of which will be collected in the first quarter of the year. Bad debts are negligible and can be ignored.

c. The company desires an ending inventory of finished units on hand at the end of each quarter equal to 30% of the budgeted sales for the next quarter. This requirement was met on December 31, year 1, in that the company had 12,000 units on hand to start the new year.

d. Five kilograms of raw materials are required to complete one unit of product. The company requires an ending inventory of raw materials on hand at the end of each quarter equal to 10% of the production needs of the following quarter. This requirement was met on December 31, year 1, in that the company had 23,000 kilograms of raw materials on hand to start the new year.

e. The raw material costs $0.80 per kilogram. Purchases of raw material are paid for in the following pattern: 60% paid in the quarter the purchases are made, and the remaining 40% paid in the following quarter. On January 1, year 2, the company's balance sheet showed $81,500 in accounts payable for raw material purchases, all of which will be paid for in the first quarter of the year.

Required:

Prepare the following budgets and schedules for the year, showing both quarterly and total figures:

1. A sales budget and a schedule of expected cash collections
2. A production budget
3. A direct materials purchases budget and a schedule of expected cash payments for material purchases

SOLUTION TO REVIEW PROBLEM 1

1. The sales budget is prepared as follows:

	Year 2 Quarter				
	1	2	3	4	Year 2
Budgeted sales in units	40,000	60,000	100,000	50,000	250,000
Selling price per unit	× $8	× $8	× $8	× $8	× $8
Total sales	$320,000	$480,000	$800,000	$400,000	$2,000,000

On the basis of the budgeted sales above, the schedule of expected cash collections is prepared as follows:

	Year 2 Quarter				
	1	2	3	4	Year 2
Accounts receivable, beginning balance	$ 65,000				$ 65,000
First-quarter sales ($320,000 × 75%, 25%)	240,000	$ 80,000			320,000
Second-quarter sales ($480,000 × 75%, 25%)		360,000	$120,000		480,000
Third-quarter sales ($800,000 × 75%, 25%)			600,000	$200,000	800,000
Fourth-quarter sales ($400,000 × 75%)				300,000	300,000
Total cash collections	$305,000	$440,000	$720,000	$500,000	$1,965,000

2. On the basis of the sales budget in units, the production budget is prepared as follows:

	Year 2 Quarter					Year 3 Quarter	
	1	2	3	4	Year 2	1	2
Budgeted sales (units)	40,000	60,000	100,000	50,000	250,000	70,000	80,000
Add: Desired ending inventory of finished goods*	18,000	30,000	15,000	21,000†	21,000	24,000	
Total needs	58,000	90,000	115,000	71,000	271,000	94,000	
Deduct: Beginning inventory of finished goods	12,000	18,000	30,000	15,000	12,000	21,000	
Required production	46,000	72,000	85,000	56,000	259,000	73,000	

*30% of the following quarter's budgeted sales in units

†30% of the budgeted year 3 first-quarter sales

3. On the basis of the production budget figures, raw materials will need to be purchased as follows during the year:

	Year 2 Quarter				Year 3 Quarter	
	1	2	3	4	Year 2	1
Required production (units)	46,000	72,000	85,000	56,000	259,000	73,000
Raw materials needed per unit (kilograms)	× 5	× 5	× 5	× 5	× 5	× 5
Production needs (kilograms)	230,000	360,000	425,000	280,000	1,295,000	365,000
Add: Desired ending inventory of raw materials (kilograms)*	36,000	42,500	28,000	36,500†	36,500	
Total needs (kilograms)	266,000	402,500	453,000	316,500	1,331,500	
Deduct: Beginning inventory of raw materials (kilograms)	23,000	36,000	42,500	28,000	23,000	
Raw materials to be purchased (kilograms)	243,000	366,500	410,500	288,500	1,308,500	

*10% of the following quarter's production needs in kilograms

†10% of the year 3 first-quarter production needs in kilograms

On the basis of the raw material purchases above, expected cash payments are computed as follows:

| | Year 2 Quarter | | | | |
	1	2	3	4	Year 2
Cost of raw materials to be purchased at $0.80 per kilogram	$194,400	$293,200	$328,400	$230,800	$1,046,800
Accounts payable, beginning balance	$ 81,500				$ 81,500
First-quarter purchases ($194,400 × 60%, 40%)	116,640	$ 77,760			194,400
Second-quarter purchases ($293,200 × 60%, 40%)		175,920	$117,280		293,200
Third-quarter purchases ($328,400 × 60%, 40%).			197,040	$131,360	328,400
Fourth-quarter purchases ($230,800 × 60%)				138,480	138,480
Total cash disbursements	$198,140	$253,680	$314,320	$269,840	$1,035,980

Review Problem 2: Comprehensive Budget Preparation

The balance sheet for the first quarter of Year 20X0 for the One Company is given below:

ONE COMPANY Balance Sheet As at Quarter 1, 20X0			
Assets		**Liabilities and Shareholders' Equity**	
Cash	$ 3,000	Accounts payable	$ 198,000
Accounts receivable	882,000	Note payable	20,000
Inventory	145,510	Common shares	420,000
Buildings, equipment, net	500,000	Retained earnings	892,510
Total assets	$1,530,510	Total liabilities and shareholders' equity	$1,530,510

The company has also developed the following master budget information for the second quarter of 20X0.

Master Budget Information Quarter 2, 20X0	
Revenue @ $40/unit	$1,020,000
Ending inventory, finished goods, units	2,550
Planned production, units	25,550
Ending inventory, direct materials @ $8/kg	$ 81,120
Direct materials required for production	$ 408,800
Beginning inventory, direct materials	$ 81,760
Direct labour cost @ $40/hour	$ 102,200
Manufacturing overhead	
Fixed	$ 75,000
Variable @ $0.625/direct labour dollar	$ 63,875
Total selling and administrative expenses	$ 411,400

Other Information

- Depreciation per quarter: factory, $60,000; selling and administrative: $40,000.
- Note payable due in quarter 2; company will borrow $18,000 in quarter 2 and issue a one-year note payable to the bank for that amount.
- Cash collection and disbursement pattern:

	Percentage of Cash	
	Collected in Current Quarter From Sales	Disbursed in Current Quarter for Inventory Purchases
For sales or inventory purchases occurring last quarter	90%	50%
For sales or inventory purchases occurring in the current quarter	10%	50%

Required:

1. Prepare a schedule showing the cash collections and cash disbursements from operations, and determine the excess or deficit of cash for quarter 2, 20X0.
2. Prepare *in good form* an absorption costing budgeted income statement for quarter 2, 20X0.
3. Prepare *in good form* a quarterly budgeted balance sheet as of the end of quarter 2, 20X0.

SOLUTION TO REVIEW PROBLEM 2

The following notation is used in the answers below: DM is direct materials; MOH is Manufacturing Overhead (F is fixed and V is variable).

1. The schedule of cash collections and disbursements appears below:

Schedule of Cash Collections and Disbursements
For Quarter 2, 20X0

Cash Collections

Current-month sales	$ 102,000[a]	
Prior-month sales	882,000[b]	
New borrowing	18,000	
Total		**$1,002,000**

Cash Disbursements

Direct labour	$ 102,200
FMOH *net* of depreciation	15,000
VMOH	63,875

Direct Materials

Purchases made in current quarter

Used in production	$408,800	
DM ending inventory	81,120	
DM beginning inventory	81,760	
Purchases	408,160	
Current purchases paid this quarter		204,080[c]
Prior quarter purchases paid		198,000[d]
Selling and admin *net* of depreciation		371,400
Note payable paid		20,000
Total		**974,555**
Cash Available (Deficit)		**$ 27,445**

Notes:

[a]0.1 × $1,020,000

[b]20X0 quarter 1 accounts receivable

[c]0.5 × $408,160

[d]Quarter 1 accounts payable

2. To prepare the income statement, the product cost for this quarter must be computed. This will be required in order to value the ending inventory. Without this calculation, it will not be possible to determine the cost of goods sold. The computation of the product cost and the budgeted income statement are shown below:

Production cost:

Direct labour	$102,200
Direct materials	408,800
FMOH	75,000
VMOH	63,875
Total manufacturing cost	$649,875

Product cost = $649,875 ÷ 25,550 = $25.435

THE ONE COMPANY
Budgeted Income Statement
For Quarter 2, 20X0

Sales revenue			$ 1,020,000
Cost of goods sold:			
Direct materials			
Beginning inventory, materials	$ 81,760		
Purchases, direct materials	408,160		
Ending inventory, materials	81,120		
Direct materials used in production		$ 408,800	
Direct labour		102,200	
Manufacturing overhead		75,000	
Manufacturing overhead, variable		63,875	
Manufacturing costs incurred		649,875	
Cost of goods manufactured		649,875	
Add: Beginning inventory, finished goods		63,750*	
Deduct: Ending inventory, 2,550 units @ $25.435		64,860.32	
Cost of goods sold:			648,764.70
Gross margin			$ 371,235.30
Selling and administrative expenses:			
Total selling and administrative expenses			$ 411,400
Net income (loss)			$ (40,164.70)

*Beginning finished goods inventory is total inventory value from balance sheet minus beginning raw materials inventory: $145,510 – $81,760.

3. The budgeted balance sheet is shown below:

THE ONE COMPANY Balance Sheet As at Quarter 2, 20X0		
Assets		
Cash	$ 30,445	(1)
Accounts receivable	918,000	(2)
Inventory		
Direct materials	81,120	(3)
Finished goods	64,860	(4)
Property, plant, and equipment, net	400,000	(5)
Total	$1,494,425	
Liabilities and Shareholders' Equity		
Accounts payable	$ 204,080	(6)
Note payable	18,000	(7)
Common shares	420,000	(8)
Retained earnings	852,345	(9)
Total	$1,494,425	

Notes:
(1) $3,000 + $27,445
(2) 90% × $1,020,000, uncollected sales for this quarter
(3) See income statement
(4) See income statement
(5) $500,000 – $100,000
(6) 50% × $408,160, unpaid purchases made this quarter
(7) Retired note payable of $20,000 and took out new note for $18,000
(8) No change from previous quarter
(9) Opening balance plus net income
For readers who have studied financial accounting, note that the above can be checked as shown below:

Indirect Format Statement of Cash Flow

Net income	($40,164.70)
Add depreciation	$100,000
Increase in AR	($36,000)
Decrease in DM inventory	$640
Increase in FG inventory	($1,110.32)
Change in note payable	($2,000)
Increase in AP	$6,080
Change in cash	$27,445

Questions

7-1   What is a budget? What is budgetary control?

7-2   What are some of the major benefits to be gained from budgeting?

7-3   What is meant by *responsibility accounting*?

7-4   What is a master budget? Briefly describe its contents.

7-5   Why is the sales forecast the starting point in budgeting?

7-6   "As a practical matter, planning and control mean exactly the same thing." Do you agree with this statement? Explain your answer.

7-7   What is a self-imposed budget? What are the major advantages of self-imposed budgets? What caution must be exercised in their use?

7-8   How can budgeting assist a firm in its employment policies?

7-9   "The principal purpose of the cash budget is to see how much cash the company will have in the bank at the end of the year." Do you agree with this statement? Explain your answer.

The Foundational 15

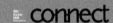

[LO2 – CC5 6, 7, 8, 9, 10, 11, 12; LO3 – CC13, 14]

Morganton Company makes one product and it provided the following information to help prepare the master budget for its first four months of operations:

a.   The budgeted selling price per unit is $70. Budgeted unit sales for June, July, August, and September are 8,400, 10,000, 12,000, and 13,000 units, respectively. All sales are on credit.

b.   40% of credit sales are collected in the month of the sale and 60% in the following month.

c.   The ending finished goods inventory equals 20% of the following month's unit sales.

d.   The ending raw materials inventory equals 10% of the following month's raw materials production needs. Each unit of finished goods requires 5 pounds of raw materials. The raw materials cost $2.00 per pound.

e.   30% of raw materials purchases are paid for in the month of purchase and 70% in the following month.

f.   The direct labour wage rate is $15 per hour. Each unit of finished goods requires two direct labour-hours.

g.   The variable selling and administrative expense per unit sold is $1.80. The fixed selling and administrative expense per month is $60,000.

Required:

7-1   What are the budgeted sales for July?

7-2   What are the expected cash collections for July?

7-3   What is the accounts receivable balance at the end of July?

7-4   According to the production budget, how many units should be produced in July?

7-5   If 61,000 pounds of raw materials are needed to meet production in August, how many pounds of raw materials should be purchased in July?

7-6   What is the estimated cost of raw materials purchases for July?

7-7   If the cost of raw materials purchases in June is $88,880, what are the estimated cash disbursements for raw materials purchases in July?

7-8   What is the estimated accounts payable balance at the end of July?

7-9   What is the estimated raw materials inventory balance at the end of July?

7-10   What is the total estimated direct labour cost for July assuming the direct labour workforce is adjusted to match the hours required to produce the forecasted number of units produced?

7-11   If the company always uses an estimated predetermined plantwide overhead rate of $10 per direct labour-hour, what is the estimated unit product cost?

7–12 What is the estimated finished goods inventory balance at the end of July?

7–13 What is the estimated cost of goods sold and gross margin for July?

7–14 What is the estimated total selling and administrative expense for July?

7–15 What is the estimated net operating income for July?

Brief Exercises 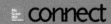 connect

BRIEF EXERCISE 7–1
Examining the Budget Process [LO1 – CC1, 2; LO4 – CC15]

The following terms pertain to the budgeting process:

benchmarks	bottlenecks
budget	budget committee
control	imposed from above
motivation	planning
responsibility accounting	self-imposed budget

Required:

Fill in the blanks with the most appropriate word or phrase from the above list.

1. _____ is generally higher when an individual participates in setting his or her own goals than when the goals are imposed from above.

2. If a manager is not able to meet the budget and it has been _____, the manager can always say that the budget was unreasonable or unrealistic to start with and therefore was impossible to meet.

3. A _____ is a detailed quantitative plan for acquiring and using financial and other resources over a specified period.

4. _____ involves developing objectives and preparing various budgets to achieve those objectives.

5. The budgeting process can uncover potential _____ before they occur.

6. _____ involves the steps taken by management to increase the likelihood that the goals and targets set down in the budgeting stage are attained.

7. Budgets define goals and objectives that can serve as _____ for evaluating subsequent performance.

8. In _____, a manager is held accountable for those items, and only those items, over which he or she has significant control.

9. A _____ is one that is prepared with the full cooperation and participation of managers at all levels of the organization.

10. A _____ is usually responsible for overall policy matters relating to the budget program and for coordinating the preparation of the budget itself.

BRIEF EXERCISE 7–2
Preparing a Schedule of Expected Cash Collections [LO2 – CC5]

Silver Company makes a product that is very popular as a Mother's Day gift. Thus, peak sales occur in May of each year. These peak sales are shown in the following sales budget for the second quarter:

	April	May	June	Total
Budgeted sales	$400,000	$600,000	$300,000	$1,300,000

From past experience, the company has learned that 25% of a month's sales are collected in the month of sale, another 65% are collected in the month following the sale, and the remaining 10% are collected in the second month following the sale. Bad debts are negligible and can be ignored. February sales totalled $380,000, and March sales totalled $360,000.

Required:

1. Prepare a schedule of expected cash collections from sales, by month and in total, for the second quarter.
2. Assume that the company will prepare a budgeted balance sheet as of June 30. Compute the accounts receivable as of that date.

BRIEF EXERCISE 7–3
Preparing a Production Budget [LO2 – CC6]

Down Under Products, Ltd., of Australia, has budgeted sales of its popular boomerang for the next four months as follows:

	Sales in Units
April	50,000
May	75,000
June	90,000
July	80,000

The company is now in the process of preparing a production budget for the second quarter. Past experience has shown that end-of-month inventory levels must equal 10% of the following month's sales. The inventory at the end of March was 5,000 units. (Australia's currency is the Australian dollar.)

Required:

Prepare a production budget for the second quarter; in your budget, show the number of units to be produced each month and for the quarter in total.

BRIEF EXERCISE 7–4
Preparing a Materials Purchases Budget [LO2 – CC7]

Three grams of musk oil are required for each bottle of Mink Caress, a popular perfume made by a small company in western Siberia. (Siberia is located in Russia, whose currency is the rouble.) The cost of the musk oil is 150 roubles per gram. Budgeted production figures of Mink Caress follow by quarters for year 2 and for the first quarter of year 3:

	Year 2 Quarter				Year 3 Quarter
	1	2	3	4	1
Budgeted production, in bottles	60,000	90,000	150,000	100,000	70,000

Musk oil has become so popular as a perfume base that it has become necessary to carry large inventories as a precaution against stock depletion. For this reason, the inventory of musk oil at the end of a quarter must be equal to 20% of the following quarter's production needs. Some 36,000 grams of musk oil will be on hand to start the first quarter of year 2.

Required:

Prepare a materials purchases budget for musk oil, by quarter and in total, for year 2. At the bottom of your budget, show the amount of purchases in roubles for each quarter and for the year in total.

BRIEF EXERCISE 7–5
Preparing a Direct Labour Budget [LO2 – CC8]

The production department of Rordan Corporation has submitted the following forecast of units to be produced by quarter for the upcoming fiscal year:

	1st Quarter	2nd Quarter	3rd Quarter	4th Quarter
Units to be produced	9,000	7,500	8,000	8,500

Each unit requires 0.55 direct labour-hours, and direct labour-hour workers are paid $12 per hour.

Required:

1. Construct the company's direct labour budget for the upcoming fiscal year, assuming that the direct labour workforce is adjusted each quarter to match the number of hours required to produce the forecasted number of units produced.
2. Construct the company's direct labour budget for the upcoming fiscal year, assuming that the direct labour workforce is not adjusted each quarter. Instead, assume that the company's direct labour workforce consists of permanent employees who are guaranteed to be paid for at least 2,800 hours of work each quarter. If the number of required direct labour-hours is less than this number, the workers are paid for 2,800 hours anyway. Any hours worked in excess of 2,800 hours in a quarter are paid at the rate of 1.5 times the normal hourly rate for direct labour.

BRIEF EXERCISE 7–6
Preparing a Manufacturing Overhead Budget [LO2 – CC9]

The direct labour budget of Yuvwell Corporation for the upcoming fiscal year contains the following details concerning budgeted direct labour-hours:

	1st Quarter	2nd Quarter	3rd Quarter	4th Quarter
Budgeted direct labour-hours	8,000	8,200	8,500	7,800

The company's variable manufacturing overhead rate is $3.25 per direct labour-hour and the company's fixed manufacturing overhead is $48,000 per quarter. The only noncash item included in the fixed manufacturing overhead is depreciation, which is $16,000 per quarter. All expenses are paid in the period incurred.

Required:

1. Construct the company's manufacturing overhead budget for the upcoming fiscal year.
2. Compute the company's manufacturing overhead rate (including both variable and fixed manufacturing overheads) for the upcoming fiscal year. Round to the nearest whole cent.

BRIEF EXERCISE 7–7
Preparing a Selling and Administrative Expense Budget [LO2 – CC11]

The budgeted unit sales of Weller Company for the upcoming fiscal year are as follows:

	1st Quarter	2nd Quarter	3rd Quarter	4th Quarter
Budgeted unit sales	15,000	16,000	14,000	13,000

The company's variable selling and administrative expense per unit is $2.50. Fixed selling and administrative expenses include advertising expenses of $8,000 per quarter, executive salaries of $35,000 per quarter, and depreciation of $20,000 per quarter. In addition, the company makes insurance payments of $5,000 in the first quarter and $5,000 in the third quarter. Finally, property taxes of $8,000 are paid in the second quarter.

Required:

Prepare the company's selling and administrative expense budget for the upcoming fiscal year.

BRIEF EXERCISE 7–8
Preparing a Cash Budget [LO2 – CC12]

Garden Depot is a retailer that is preparing its budget for the upcoming fiscal year. Management has prepared the following summary of its budgeted cash flows:

	1st Quarter	2nd Quarter	3rd Quarter	4th Quarter
Total cash receipts	$180,000	$330,000	$210,000	$230,000
Total cash disbursements	260,000	230,000	220,000	240,000

The company's beginning cash balance for the upcoming fiscal year will be $20,000. The company requires a minimum cash balance of $10,000 and may borrow any amount needed from a local bank at an annual interest rate of 12%. The company may borrow any amount at the beginning of any quarter and may repay its loans, or any part of its loans, at the end of any quarter. Interest payments are due on any principal at the time it is repaid.

Required:

Prepare the company's cash budget for the upcoming fiscal year.

BRIEF EXERCISE 7–9
Preparing a Budgeted Income Statement [LO3 – CC13]

Gig Harbour Boating is the wholesale distributor of small recreational catamaran sailboats. Management has prepared the following summary data to use in its annual budgeting process:

Budgeted sales (in units)	460
Selling price per unit	$1,950
Cost per unit	$1,575

Variable selling and administrative expenses (per unit)	$75
Fixed selling and administrative expenses (per year)	$105,000
Interest expense for the year	$14,000

Required:

Prepare the company's budgeted income statement.

BRIEF EXERCISE 7–10
Preparing a Budgeted Balance Sheet [LO2 – CC14]

The management of Mecca Copy, a photocopying centre located on University Avenue, has compiled the following data to use in preparing its budgeted balance sheet for next year:

	Ending Balances
Cash	?
Accounts receivable	$ 8,100
Supplies inventory	3,200
Equipment	34,000
Accumulated depreciation	16,000
Accounts payable	1,800
Common shares	5,000
Retained earnings	?

The beginning balance of retained earnings was $28,000, net income is budgeted to be $11,500, and dividends are budgeted to be $4,800.

Required:

Prepare the company's budgeted balance sheet.

BRIEF EXERCISE 7–11
Tracking Cash Collections and Disbursements [LO2 – CC5, 7, 12]

The following information relates to Old Company for September of this year:

Opening cash balance	$16,000
Depreciation expense	4,000
Dividends declared	6,000

Cash collections	36,000
Equipment, loss on sale (original cost $14,000)	3,200
Cash operating expenses	15,800
Cash purchases of merchandise	22,000

Required:

What will be Old's cash balance on September 30? Assume current book value of equipment is $10,000.

(Adapted © CPA Canada)

BRIEF EXERCISE 7–12
Preparing a Production Budget [LO2 – CC6]

A company has the following incomplete production budget data for the first quarter:

	January	February	March
Expected unit sales	4,000	12,000	16,000

Ending inventory is budgeted at 5% of projected sales units in the coming month.

Required:

What is the expected production in February?

BRIEF EXERCISE 7–13
Using a Cash Budget [LO2 – CC5, 7, 12]

At the end of August, there was $90,000 in inventory. The change in inventory balance for September was (10,000). The following entries were posted to the GL at the end of September:

Cost of sales	Dr $420,000	
Inventory		Cr $420,000
To record the cost of sales for September		
Accounts payable	Dr $110,000	
Cash		Cr $110,000
To record payments for purchases in August and prior months		
The company pays for 80% of a month's purchases in the month of the purchase.		

Required:

1. Calculate the purchases made in September.
2. What is the total amount of cash disbursements made in September for purchases?
3. What amount will be reported for inventory on the September 30 balance sheet?

BRIEF EXERCISE 7–14

Preparing a Cash Budget [LO2 – CC5, 7, 12]

A company has the following excess (deficiency) of cash receipts over cash disbursements projected for the next year on a quarterly basis. It will not have any cash at the start of the year. The quarterly interest rate is 2%, and any borrowing and repayment of principal must be in round $1,000 amounts. There is no cash reserve requirement. Assume borrowings and repayments of principal are in round $1,000 amounts.

	Quarter				
	1	**2**	**3**	**4**	**Year**
Excess (deficiency) of cash available over disbursements	$(121,140)	$(41,680)	$177,680	$2,160	$17,020

Required:

Prepare a cash budget by quarter and for the year.

Exercises

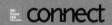

EXERCISE 7–1

Preparing Schedules of Expected Cash Collections and Disbursements [LO2 – CC5, 7, 12]

You have been asked to prepare a December cash budget for Ashton Company, a distributor of exercise equipment. The following information is available about the company's operations:

a. The cash balance on December 1 will be $40,000.

b. Actual sales for October and November and expected sales for December are as follows:

	October	November	December
Cash sales	$ 65,000	$ 70,000	$ 83,000
Sales on account	400,000	525,000	600,000

Sales on account are collected over a three-month period in the following ratio: 20% collected in the month of sale, 60% collected in the month following sale, and 18% collected in the second month following sale. The remaining 2% are uncollectible.

c. Purchases of inventory will total $280,000 for December. 30% of a month's inventory purchases are paid during the month of purchase. The accounts payable remaining from November's inventory purchases total $161,000, all of which will be paid in December.

d. Selling and administrative expenses are budgeted at $430,000 for December. Of this amount, $50,000 is for depreciation. These are paid in the period incurred.

e. A new web server for the marketing department costing $76,000 will be purchased for cash during December, and dividends totalling $9,000 will be paid during the month.

f. The company must maintain a minimum cash balance of $20,000. An open line of credit is available from the company's bank to bolster the cash position, as needed.

Required:

1. Prepare a schedule of expected cash collections for December.
2. Prepare a schedule of expected cash disbursements for materials during December to suppliers for inventory purchases.
3. Prepare a cash budget for December. Indicate in the financing section any borrowing that will be needed during the month.

EXERCISE 7–2
Preparing Sales and Production Budgets [LO2 – CC5, 6]

The marketing department of Jessi Corporation has submitted the following sales forecast for the upcoming fiscal year:

	1st Quarter	2nd Quarter	3rd Quarter	4th Quarter
Budgeted sales (units)	8,000	10,000	12,000	11,000

The selling price of the company's product is $20 per unit. Management expects to collect 65% of sales in the quarter in which the sales are made and 30% in the following quarter; 5% of sales are expected to be uncollectible. The beginning balance of accounts receivable, all of which are expected to be collected in the first quarter, is $80,500.

The company expects to start the first quarter with 2,000 units in finished goods inventory. Management desires an ending finished goods inventory in each quarter equal to 15% of the next quarter's budgeted sales. The desired ending finished goods inventory for the fourth quarter is 2,250 units.

Required:

1. Prepare the company's sales budget and schedule of expected cash collections.
2. Prepare the company's production budget for the upcoming fiscal year.

EXERCISE 7–3
Preparing Production and Direct Materials Budgets [LO2 – CC6, 7]

The marketing department of Gaeber Industries has submitted the following sales forecast for the upcoming fiscal year:

	1st Quarter	2nd Quarter	3rd Quarter	4th Quarter
Budgeted sales (units)	8,000	7,000	6,000	7,000

The company expects to start the first quarter with 1,600 units in finished goods inventory. Management desires an ending finished goods inventory in each quarter equal to 20% of the next quarter's budgeted sales. The desired ending finished goods inventory for the fourth quarter is 1,700 units.

In addition, the beginning raw materials inventory for the first quarter is budgeted to be 3,120 kilograms and the beginning accounts payable for the first quarter are budgeted to be $14,820.

Each unit requires two kilograms of raw material that costs $4 per kilogram. Management desires to end each quarter with an inventory of raw materials equal to 20% of the following quarter's production needs. The desired ending inventory for the fourth quarter is 3,140 kilograms. Management plans to pay for 75% of raw material purchases in the quarter acquired and 25% in the following quarter.

Required:

1. Prepare the company's production budget for the upcoming fiscal year.
2. Prepare the company's direct materials budget and schedule of expected cash disbursements for materials for the upcoming fiscal year.

EXERCISE 7–4
Preparing Direct Materials and Direct Labour Budgets [LO2 – CC7, 8]

The production department of Hareston Company has submitted the following forecast of units to be produced by quarter for the upcoming fiscal year:

	1st Quarter	2nd Quarter	3rd Quarter	4th Quarter
Units to be produced	7,000	8,000	6,000	5,000

In addition, the beginning raw materials inventory for the first quarter is budgeted to be 1,400 kilograms and the beginning accounts payable for the first quarter are budgeted to be $2,940.

Each unit requires two kilograms of raw material that costs $1.40 per kilogram. Management desires to end each quarter with an inventory of raw materials equal to 10% of the following quarter's production needs. The desired ending inventory for the fourth quarter is 1,500 kilograms. Management plans to pay for 80% of raw material purchases in the quarter acquired and 20% in the following quarter. Each unit requires 0.60 direct labour-hours, and direct labour-hour workers are paid $14 per hour.

Required:

1. Prepare the company's direct materials budget and schedule of expected cash disbursements for materials for the upcoming fiscal year.
2. Prepare the company's direct labour budget for the upcoming fiscal year, assuming that the direct labour workforce is adjusted each quarter to match the number of hours required to produce the forecasted number of units produced.

EXERCISE 7–5
Preparing Direct Labour and Manufacturing Overhead Budgets [LO2 – CC8, 9]

The production department of Raredon Corporation has submitted the following forecast of units to be produced by quarter for the upcoming fiscal year:

	1st Quarter	2nd Quarter	3rd Quarter	4th Quarter
Units to be produced	24,000	28,000	26,000	22,000

Each unit requires 1.4 direct labour-hours, and direct labour-hour workers are paid $21 per hour.

In addition, the variable manufacturing overhead rate is $1.30 per direct labour-hour. The fixed manufacturing overhead is $160,000 per quarter. The only noncash element of manufacturing overhead is depreciation, which is $44,000 per quarter.

Required:

1. Prepare the company's direct labour budget for the upcoming fiscal year, assuming that the direct labour workforce is adjusted each quarter to match the number of hours required to produce the forecasted number of units produced.

2. Prepare the company's manufacturing overhead budget.

EXERCISE 7–6
Inferring Cash Budget Relations [LO2 – CC12]

A cash budget, by quarters, follows for a retail company. Fill in the missing amounts (000 omitted). The company requires a minimum cash balance of at least $5,000 to start each quarter.

	Q1	Q2	Q3	Q4	Year
Cash balance, beginning	$ 6	$?	$?	$?	$?
Add: Collections from customers	?	?	96	?	323
Total cash available before current financing	71	?	?	?	?
Deduct: Disbursements:					
Purchase of inventory	35	45	?	35	?
Operating expenses	?	30	30	?	113
Equipment purchases	8	8	10	?	36
Dividends	2	2	2	2	?
Total disbursements	?	85	?	?	?
Excess (deficiency) of cash available over disbursements	(2)	?	11	?	?
Financing:					
Borrowings	?	15	—	—	?
Repayments (including interest)*	=	=	(?)	(17)	(?)
Total financing	?	?	?	?	?
Cash balance, ending	$?	$?	$?	$?	$?

*Interest will total $1,000 for the year.

EXERCISE 7–7
Preparing a Cash Budget [LO2 – CC12]

The controller of Arrowroot Company wishes to improve the company's control system by preparing a monthly cash budget. The following information relates to the month ending July 31, 20X1:

June 30, 20X1, cash balance	$ 90,000
Dividends to be declared on June 15*	24,000
Cash expenditures to be paid in July for operating expenses	73,600
Depreciation expense	9,000
Cash collections to be received	178,000
Merchandise purchases to be paid in cash	112,400
Equipment to be purchased for cash	41,000
Arrowroot Company wishes to maintain a minimum cash balance of	30,000

*Dividends are payable to shareholders of record on declaration date, 30 days after declaration.

Required:

1. Prepare a cash budget for the month ended July 31, 20X1, indicating how much, if anything, Arrowroot will need to borrow to meet its minimum cash requirement.
2. Explain how cash budgeting can facilitate cash management at Arrowroot.

(Adapted © CPA Canada)

EXERCISE 7–8
Interpreting a Cash Budget and a Materials Purchase Budget [LO2 – CC5, 7, 12]

All sales of Aegan Electronics Supply are made on credit. Sales are billed twice monthly, on the 10th of the month for sales made in the last half of the prior month, and on the 20th of the month for sales made in the first half of the current month. When payments are made in the month of the sale, the sale qualifies for a 2% discount. The expected collection experience of accounts receivable is as follows:

Within the discount period	80%
In the second month	18%
Uncollectible	2%

Sales for the month of May were $750,000. Forecast sales for the next four months are as follows:

June	$400,000
July	450,000
August	450,000
September	300,000

Aegan's cost of sales is 75% of revenue. Aegan purchases sufficient merchandise for resale to meet the current month's sales and to have an ending inventory of 25% of the next month's forecast sales. All purchases are on credit. Aegan pays for one-half of a month's purchases in the month of purchase and the other half in the month following purchase. All purchases and sales occur evenly throughout the month.

Required:

1. How much will be collected in September?
2. What is the amount of expected collections during August for sales made in July?
3. How much merchandise should be purchased in July and in August?
4. What is the amount of disbursements in August?
5. Calculate the net cash flow from sales and purchases in August.

(Adapted © CPA Canada)

EXERCISE 7–9
Preparing a Cash Budget [LO2 – CC7]

The following schedule shows the excess of cash receipts over cash disbursements projected for the Zoptic Company for 20X1:

> **CHECK FIGURE**
>
> Interest paid in Q3 to retire $2,300 = $368
> Ending cash balance Q3: $608
> Q1 borrowing repaid in Q3: $111,700

	Q1	Q2	Q3	Q4	Year
Excess (deficiency) of cash available over disbursements	$(123,300)	$(41,680)	$127,780	$42,300	$5,100

The company borrows and repays from an open line of credit in round $100 amounts. The current balance (principal plus accrued interest) in the line of credit account is $2,392 for the borrowing that occurred in the last quarter of the previous year. The annual interest rate is 16%. A minimum cash reserve of $600 must be maintained each quarter. The opening balance for the year is expected to be $780.

Required:

Prepare a cash budget for each quarter and for the year in total and calculate the annual interest expense on the line of credit that would appear on the budgeted income statement for the year 20X1

Problems

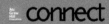

PROBLEM 7–1
Preparing a Schedule of Expected Cash Collections and a Cash Budget [LO2 – CC5, 7, 12]

Janus Products, Inc. is a merchandising company that sells binders, paper, and other school supplies. The company is planning its cash needs for the third quarter. In the past, Janus Products has had to borrow money during the third quarter to support peak sales of back-to-school materials, which occur during August. The following information has been assembled to assist in preparing a cash budget for the quarter:

> **CHECK FIGURES**
>
> (1) August collections: $47,760
> (3) July ending cash balance: $8,410c.

a. Budgeted monthly absorption costing income statements for July to October are as follows:

	July	August	September	October
Sales	$40,000	$70,000	$50,000	$45,000
Cost of goods sold	24,000	42,000	30,000	27,000
Gross margin	16,000	28,000	20,000	18,000
Selling and administrative expenses:				
Selling expense	7,200	11,700	8,500	7,300
Administrative expense*	5,600	7,200	6,100	5,900
Total selling and administrative expenses	12,800	18,900	14,600	13,200
Net operating income	$ 3,200	$ 9,100	$ 5,400	$ 4,800

*Includes $2,000 depreciation each month.

b. Sales are 20% for cash and 80% on credit.

c. Credit sales are collected over a three-month period, with 10% collected in the month of sale, 70% in the month following sale, and 20% in the second month following sale. May sales totalled $30,000, and June sales totalled $36,000.

d. Inventory purchases are paid for within 15 days. Therefore, 50% of a month's inventory purchases are paid for in the month of purchase. The remaining 50% are paid in the following month. Accounts payable for inventory purchases at June 30 total $11,700.

e. The company maintains its ending inventory levels at 75% of the cost of the merchandise to be sold in the following month. The merchandise inventory at June 30 is $18,000.

f. Land costing $4,500 will be purchased in July.

g. Dividends of $1,000 will be declared and paid in September.

h. The cash balance on June 30 is $8,000; the company must maintain a cash balance of at least this amount at the end of each month.

i. The company has an agreement with a local bank that allows it to borrow in increments of $1,000 at the beginning of each month, up to a total loan balance of $40,000. The interest rate on these loans is 1% per month, and for simplicity, we will assume that interest is not compounded. The company would, as far as it is able, repay the loan plus accumulated interest at the end of the quarter.

Required:

1. Prepare a schedule of expected cash collections for July, August, and September and for the quarter in total.
2. Prepare the following for merchandise inventory:
   a. A merchandise purchases budget for July, August, and September.
   b. A schedule of expected cash disbursements for merchandise purchases for July, August, and September and for the quarter in total.
3. Prepare a cash budget for July, August, and September and for the quarter in total.

PROBLEM 7–2
Preparing Production and Purchases Budgets [LO2 – CC6, 7]

Daisy Products Limited of Shenzhen, China, manufactures and distributes toys throughout Southeast Asia.

CHECK FIGURE
(1) July: 45,000 units

Three cubic centimetres (cc) of solvent Q80 are required to manufacture each unit of Fineclay, one of the company's products. The company is now planning raw materials needs for the third quarter, the quarter in which peak sales of Fineclay occur. To keep production and sales moving smoothly, the company has the following inventory requirements:

a. The finished goods inventory on hand at the end of each month must be equal to 3,750 units of Fineclay plus 20% of the next month's sales. The finished goods inventory on June 30 is budgeted to be 12,500 units.

b. The raw materials inventory on hand at the end of each month must be equal to one-half of the following month's production needs for raw materials. The raw materials inventory on June 30 is budgeted to be 67,500 cc of solvent Q80.

c. The company maintains no work-in-process inventories.

A sales budget for Fineclay for the last six months of the year follows:

	Budgeted Sales in Units
July	43,750
August	50,000
September	62,500
October	37,500
November	25,000
December	12,500

Required:

1. Prepare a production budget for Fineclay for the months of July to October.

2. Examine the production budget that you prepared in part (1). Why will the company produce more units than it sells in July and August, and fewer units than it sells in September and October?

3. Prepare a budget showing the quantity of solvent Q80 to be purchased for July, August, and September, and for the quarter in total.

 ## PROBLEM 7–3
Preparing a Cash Budget, Income Statement, and Balance Sheet [LO2 – CC5, 7, 12; LO3 – CC13, 14]

Minden Company is a wholesale distributor of premium European chocolates. The company's balance sheet on April 30 is as follows:

CHECK FIGURES
(1) May 31 cash balance: $8,900
(2) NI: $15,900

MINDEN COMPANY
Balance Sheet
April 30

Assets

Cash	$ 9,000
Accounts receivable, customers	54,000
Inventory	30,000
Buildings and equipment, net of depreciation	207,000
Total assets	$300,000

Liabilities and Shareholders' Equity

Accounts payable, suppliers	$ 63,000
Note payable	14,500
Capital shares, no par	180,000
Retained earnings	42,500
Total liabilities and shareholders' equity	$300,000

The company is in the process of preparing budget data for May. A number of budget items have already been prepared, as follows:

a. Sales are budgeted at $200,000 for May. Of these sales, $60,000 will be for cash; the remainder will be credit sales. One-half of a month's credit sales are collected in the month the sales are made, and the remainder are collected in the following month. All of the April 30 receivables will be collected in May.

b. Purchases of inventory are expected to total $120,000 during May. These purchases will all be on account. 40% of all purchases are paid for in the month of purchase; the remainder are paid in the following month. All of the April 30 accounts payable to suppliers will be paid during May.

c. The May 31 inventory balance is budgeted at $40,000.

d. Operating expenses for May are budgeted at $72,000, exclusive of depreciation. These expenses will be paid in cash. Depreciation is budgeted at $2,000 for the month.

e. The note payable on the April 30 balance sheet will be paid during May, with $100 in interest. (All of the interest relates to May.)

f. New refrigerating equipment costing $6,500 will be purchased for cash during May.

g. During May, the company will borrow $20,000 from its bank by giving a new note payable to the bank for that amount. The new note will be due in one year.

Required:

1. Prepare a cash budget for May. Support your budget with schedules showing budgeted cash receipts from sales and budgeted cash payments for inventory purchases.

2. Prepare a budgeted income statement for May. Use the traditional income statement format.

3. Prepare a budgeted balance sheet as of May 31.

PROBLEM 7–4
Integration of the Sales, Production, and Purchases Budgets [LO2 – CC5, 6, 7]

Milo Company manufactures beach umbrellas. The company is now preparing detailed budgets for the third quarter and has assembled the following information to assist in the budget preparation:

CHECK FIGURE

(2) July: 36,000 units

a. The marketing department has estimated sales as follows for the remainder of the year (in units):

July	30,000
August	70,000
September	50,000
October	20,000
November	10,000
December	10,000

The selling price of the beach umbrellas is $12 per unit. Sales in June were 25,000 units.

b. All sales are on account. On the basis of past experience, sales are collected in the following pattern:

30% in the month of sale

65% in the month following sale

5% uncollectible

c. The company maintains finished goods inventories equal to 15% of the following month's sales. This requirement will be met at the end of June.

d. Each beach umbrella requires four metres of Gilden, a material that is sometimes hard to get. Therefore, the company requires that the inventory of Gilden on hand at the end of each month be equal to 50% of the following month's production needs. The inventory of Gilden on hand at the beginning and end of the quarter will be as follows:

June 30	72,000	metres
September 30	?	metres

e. Gilden costs $0.80 per metre. One-half of a month's purchases of Gilden are paid for in the month of purchase; the remainder are paid for in the following month. The accounts payable on July 1 for purchases of Gilden during June will be $76,000.

Required:

1. Prepare a sales budget, by month and in total, for the third quarter. (Show your budget in both units and dollars.) Also, prepare a schedule of expected cash collections, by month and in total, for the third quarter.

2. Prepare a production budget for each of the months July to October.

3. Prepare a materials purchases budget for Gilden, by month and in total, for the third quarter. Also, prepare a schedule of expected cash payments for Gilden, by month and in total, for the third quarter.

PROBLEM 7–5
Preparing a Cash Budget With Supporting Schedules [LO2 – CC5, 7, 12]

Garden Sales, Inc. sells garden supplies. Management is planning its cash needs for the second quarter. The company usually has to borrow money during this quarter to support peak sales of lawn care equipment, which occur during May. The following information has been assembled to assist in preparing a cash budget for the quarter:

CHECK FIGURES

(2a) May purchases: $459,200

(3) June 30 cash balance: $57,880

a. Budgeted monthly income statements for April to July are as follows:

	April	May	June	July
Sales	$480,000	$720,000	$400,000	$320,000
Cost of goods sold	336,000	504,000	280,000	224,000
Gross margin	144,000	216,000	120,000	96,000
Less: Operating expenses:				
Selling expense	63,200	96,000	49,600	40,800
Administrative expense*	36,000	41,600	32,800	30,400
Total operating expenses	99,200	137,600	82,400	71,200
Net income	$ 44,800	$ 78,400	$ 37,600	$ 24,800

*Includes $20,000 in depreciation each month.

b. Sales are 20% for cash and 80% on account.

c. Sales on account are collected over a three-month period in the following ratio: 10% collected in the month of sale, 70% collected in the first month following the month of sale, and the remaining 20% collected in the second month following the month of sale. February's sales totalled $160,000, and March's sales totalled $240,000.

d. Inventory purchases are paid for within 15 days. Therefore, 50% of a month's inventory purchases are paid for in the month of purchase. The remaining 50% are paid in the following month. Accounts payable at March 31 for inventory purchases during March total $100,800.

e. At the end of each month, inventory must be on hand equal to 20% of the cost of the merchandise to be sold in the following month. The merchandise inventory at March 31 is $67,200.

f. Dividends of $39,200 will be declared and paid in April.

g. Equipment costing $12,800 will be purchased for cash in May.

h. The cash balance at March 31 is $41,600; the company must maintain a cash balance of at least $32,000 at all times.

i. The company can borrow from its bank, as needed, to bolster the cash account. Borrowings and repayments must be in multiples of $800. All borrowings take place at the beginning of a month, and all repayments are made at the end of a month. The annual interest rate is 12%. Compute interest on whole months (1/12, 2/12, and so forth).

Required:

1. Prepare a schedule of expected cash collections from sales for each of the months April, May, and June, and for the quarter in total.

2. Prepare the following for merchandise inventory:
   a. An inventory purchases budget for each of the months April, May, and June.
   b. A schedule of expected cash disbursements for inventory for each of the months April, May, and June, and for the quarter in total.

3. Prepare a cash budget for the third quarter, by month as well as in total for the quarter. Show borrowings from the company's bank and repayments to the bank, as needed, to maintain the minimum cash balance.

 PROBLEM 7–6

Preparing a Cash Budget With Supporting Schedules [LO2 – CC5, 7, 11, 12]

Westex Products is a wholesale distributor of industrial cleaning products. When the treasurer of Westex Products approached the company's bank in late 2019 seeking short-term financing, he was told that money was very tight and that any borrowing over the next year would have to be supported by a detailed statement of cash receipts and disbursements. He was also told that it would be very helpful to the bank if borrowers would indicate the quarters in which they would be needing funds, as well as the amounts that would be needed, and the quarters in which repayments could be made.

CHECK FIGURES
(2) First-quarter net payments: $75,000
(3) First-quarter ending cash balance: $12,000

Since the treasurer is unsure as to the particular quarters in which the bank financing will be needed, he has assembled the following information to assist in preparing a detailed cash budget:

a. Budgeted sales and merchandise purchases for the year 2020, as well as actual sales and purchases for the last quarter of 2019, are as follows:

	A	B	C
1			
2		Sales	Merchandise Purchases
3	2019:		
4	Fourth-quarter actual	$200,000	$126,000
5	2020:		
6	First-quarter estimated	300,000	186,000
7	Second-quarter estimated	400,000	246,000
8	Third-quarter estimated	500,000	305,000
9	Fourth-quarter estimated	200,000	126,000
10			

b. The company normally collects 65% of a quarter's sales before the quarter ends and another 33% in the following quarter. The remainder are uncollectible. This pattern of collections is now being experienced in the 2019 fourth-quarter actual data.

c. 80% of a quarter's merchandise purchases are paid for within the quarter. The remainder are paid in the following quarter.

d. Operating expenses for the year 2020 are budgeted quarterly at $50,000 plus 15% of sales. Of the fixed amount, $20,000 each quarter is depreciation.

e. The company will pay $10,000 in dividends each quarter.

f. Equipment purchases of $75,000 will be made in the second quarter, and purchases of $48,000 will be made in the third quarter. These purchases will be for cash.

g. The cash account contained $10,000 at the end of 2019. The treasurer feels that this represents a minimum balance that must be maintained.

h. Any borrowing will take place at the beginning of a quarter, and any repayments will be made at the end of a quarter at an annual interest rate of 10%. Interest is paid only when the principal is repaid. All borrowings and all repayments of the principal must be in round $1,000 amounts. Interest payments can be in any amount. (Compute interest on whole months, e.g., 1/12, 2/12.)

i. At present, the company has no loans outstanding.

Required:

1. Prepare the following by quarter and in total for the year 2020:
    a. A schedule of expected cash collections.
    b. A schedule of budgeted cash disbursements for merchandise purchases.

2. Compute the expected cash payments for operating expenses, by quarter and in total, for the year 2020.

3. Prepare a cash budget, by quarter and in total, for the year 2020. In your budget, clearly show the quarter(s) in which borrowing will be necessary and the quarter(s) in which repayments can be made, as requested by the company's bank.

PROBLEM 7–7
Comprehensive Master Budget [LO2 – CC5, 7, 11, 12; LO3 – CC13, 14]

Hillyard Company, an office supplies specialty store, prepares its master budget on a quarterly basis. The following data have been assembled to assist in preparation of the master budget for the first quarter:

a. As of December 31 (the end of the prior quarter), the company's general ledger showed the following account balances:

CHECK FIGURES

(2a) February purchases: $315,000

(4) February ending cash balance: $30,800

	Debits	Credits
Cash	$ 48,000	
Accounts receivable	224,000	
Inventory	60,000	
Buildings and equipment (net)	370,000	
Accounts payable		$ 93,000
Capital shares		500,000
Retained earnings		109,000
	$702,000	$702,000

b. Actual sales for December and budgeted sales for the next four months are as follows:

December (actual)	$280,000
January	400,000
February	600,000
March	300,000
April	200,000

c. Sales are 20% for cash and 80% on credit. All payments on credit sales are collected in the month following sale. The accounts receivable at December 31 are a result of December credit sales.

d. The company's gross margin is 40% of sales.

e. Monthly expenses are budgeted as follows: salaries and wages, $27,000 per month; advertising, $70,000 per month; shipping, 5% of sales; depreciation, $14,000 per month; other expenses, 3% of sales.

f. At the end of each month, inventory is to be on hand equal to 25% of the following month's sales needs, stated at cost.

g. One-half of a month's inventory purchases are paid for in the month of purchase; the other half are paid for in the following month.

h. During February, the company will purchase a new copy machine for $1,700 cash. During March, other equipment will be purchased for cash at a cost of $84,500.

i. During January, the company will declare and pay $45,000 in cash dividends.

j. The company must maintain a minimum cash balance of $30,000. An open line of credit is available at a local bank for any borrowing that may be needed during the quarter. All borrowing is done at the beginning of a month, and all repayments are made at the end of a month. Borrowings and repayments of principal must be in multiples of $1,000. Interest is paid only at the time of payment of principal. The annual interest rate is 12%. (Figure interest on whole months, e.g., 1/12, 2/12.)

Required:

Using the preceding data, complete the following statements and schedules for the first quarter:

1. Schedule of expected cash collections.
2. a. Inventory purchases budget.
    b. Schedule of cash disbursements for purchases.
3. Schedule of cash disbursements for expenses.
4. Cash budget.
5. Income statement for the quarter ending March 31 as shown in Schedule 9 in the chapter.
6. Balance sheet as of March 31.

PROBLEM 7–8
Preparing a Comprehensive Master Budget [LO2 – CC5, 7, 11, 12; LO3 – CC13, 14]

Following is selected information relating to the operations of Shilow Company, a wholesale distributor:

CHECK FIGURES
(2) May purchases: $64,800
(4) May 31 cash balance: $4,590

Current assets as of March 31:	
Cash	$ 8,000
Accounts receivable	20,000
Inventory	36,000
Plant and equipment, net	120,000
Accounts payable	21,750
Capital shares	150,000
Retained earnings	12,250

a. Gross margin is 25% of sales.
b. Actual and budgeted sales data are as follows:

March (actual)	$50,000
April	60,000
May	72,000
June	90,000
July	48,000

c. Sales are 60% for cash and 40% on credit. Credit sales are collected in the month following sale. The accounts receivable at March 31 are a result of March credit sales.

d. At the end of each month, inventory is to be on hand equal to 80% of the following month's sales needs, stated at cost.

e. One-half of a month's inventory purchases are paid for in the month of purchase; the other half are paid for in the following month. The accounts payable at March 31 are a result of March purchases of inventory.

f. Monthly expenses are as follows: salaries and wages, 12% of sales; rent, $2,500 per month; other expenses (excluding depreciation), 6% of sales. Assume that these expenses are paid monthly. Depreciation is $900 per month (includes depreciation on new assets).

g. Equipment costing $1,500 will be purchased for cash in April.

h. The company must maintain a minimum cash balance of $4,000. An open line of credit is available at a local bank. All borrowing is done at the beginning of a month, and all repayments are made at the end of a month; borrowing must be in multiples of $1,000. The annual interest rate is 12%. Interest is paid only at the time of repayment of principal; figure interest on whole months (1/12, 2/12, and so forth).

Required:

Using the preceding data:

1. Prepare a schedule of expected cash collections.
2. Prepare a schedule of inventory purchases and a schedule of expected cash disbursements for purchases.
3. Prepare a schedule of expected cash disbursements for operating expenses.
4. Prepare a cash budget by month and for the quarter in total.
5. Prepare an income statement for the quarter ended June 30. (Use the functional format in preparing your income statement, as shown in Schedule 9.)
6. Prepare a balance sheet as of June 30.

PROBLEM 7–9
Preparing Merchandise Purchases and Cash Budgets [LO2 – CC7, 12]

Kat Ltd.'s September balance sheet contains the following information:

Cash	$ 37,500 (dr)
Accounts receivable	126,000 (dr)
Allowance for doubtful accounts	2,800 (cr)
Merchandise inventory	26,250 (dr)

Management has designated $37,500 as the firm's minimum monthly cash balance. Other information about the firm and its operations is as follows:

a. Sales revenues of $350,000, $420,000, and $312,500 are expected for October, November, and December, respectively. All goods are sold on account.

b. The collection pattern for accounts receivable is 60% in the month of sale, 39% in the month following the month of sale, and 1% uncollectible, which is set up as an allowance.

c. Cost of goods sold is 60% of sales revenues.

d. Management's target ending balance of merchandise inventory is 10% of the current month's budgeted cost of goods sold.

e. All accounts payable for inventory are paid in the month of purchase.

f. Other monthly expenses are $49,250, which includes $3,500 of depreciation and $2,000 of bad debt expense.

g. In the event of a shortfall, the company borrows money. In contrast, in the event of excess cash, the company invests in short-term investments. Borrowings and investments are assumed to be made at the end of a month in increments of $6,250.

h. Interest on borrowings is 10% per year, payable every quarter, on the accumulated amount of the loan; similarly, interest earned on investments is 8% per year on the accumulated investments and is received every quarter. Investments can be matured and the principal amount redeemed in June or December of a year.

Required:

1. Prepare a merchandise purchases budget for October and November.

2. Prepare the cash budgets for October and November, including the effects of financing (borrowing or investing). Interest is earned or paid quarterly.

(Adapted © CPA Canada)

PROBLEM 7–10
Creating a Schedule of Cash Collections and Disbursements [LO2 – CC5, 7, 12]

It is mid-February and a company has just approached its bank with a request for a $300,000 90-day loan to meet its working capital requirements. Inventories peak in April in anticipation of spring sales, and the treasurer believes the company can repay the loan in full by the end of the 90-day loan period. In support of the loan application, the bank has requested a three-month cash budget for March, April, and May. If the loan

is granted, it will be made in March and repaid in May and have an interest cost of $24,000 payable at the time of repayment. The following data are available to assist in the preparation of the cash budget:

a. The loan will be granted on March 1. The cash balance at the beginning of March is $520,000. Of the accounts receivable on February 28, the company expects to collect $2,660,000 in March and $144,000 in April. These expected collections are estimated after allowing that some of the receivables will be uncollectible.

b. Past collection experience indicates that 20% of a month's sales will be collected in the month of the sale, 75% the next month, and 4% the second month after the sale, and that 1% will never be collected and represents bad debts.

c. Merchandise purchases are paid in full on the 15th of each month for any purchases made between the 15th of the previous month and the 14th of the current month. The company has estimated the following amounts will be purchased during the budget period:

February 15 to March 14	March 15 to April 14	April 15 to May 14
$2,160,000	$2,400,000	$3,200,000

d. Equipment will be sold in March. The terms of the sale are such that a loss on sale of $60,000 will be reported on the income statement for March. The carrying amount of the asset to be disposed of is $220,000.

e. The following are budgeted sales and expenses for the three-month loan period:

	March	April	May
Sales	$4,000,000	$6,000,000	$5,000,000
Period expenses	2,040,000	2,080,000	1,660,000
Depreciation	200,000	200,000	200,000

Required:

1. Prepare a schedule of expected cash collections for the months of March, April, and May, and for the three months in total.

2. Prepare a cash budget, by month and in total, for the three-month period.

3. Explain whether the loan can be repaid as planned if the company needs a minimum starting cash balance of $400,000 each month.

4. What is the impact on the cash flow of the policy regarding paying for purchases? Will it make a difference to pay for purchases over two months? Do not redo the cash budget and provide a brief qualitative answer.

PROBLEM 7–11
Comprehensive Cash Budgeting From Accounting Records [LO2 – CC5, 7, 12]

You have been asked to prepare the monthly cash budget for June and July for the Merchandise and Mercantile Company. The company sells a unique product that is specially made for it by a major product manufacturer. The selling price is $16 per unit. All sales are on account.

Merchandise purchases are also on account. The policy of the company is to purchase sufficient quantity of product to ensure that each month's ending inventory is 50% of the following month's expected sales quantity.

The assignment file contains extracts from the general journal showing the journal entries pertaining to certain relevant transactions that have occurred and a set of entries the bookkeeper has provided that indicate the transactions expected to occur affecting cash, accounts payable, accounts receivable, and merchandise inventory accounts due to the projected sales revenues and projected merchandise purchases on the master budget. This

CHECK FIGURES

(1) $4

(2) Purchases in May, 3,500 units

(4) Collection percentage in month of sales, 49%

(5) Disbursement percentage in month of purchase, 75%

(7) June cash balance $33,330

(8) July ending cash balance $66,600

analysis, with other additional data, is shown below. Assume today is May 31, 20X1, and that all dollar amounts are in thousands of dollars.

Information From Accounting Records and Planning Documents		
	Dr	**Cr**
Extracts From the May 31 Adjusted Trial Balance		
May 31 Cash	3,500	
Merchandise inventory	8,000	
Accounts receivable	27,200	
Accounts payable		3,500
Extracts From the General Journal		
April 30 Accounts receivable, April sales	32,000	
Revenue		32,000
Cash	15,680	
Accounts receivable, April sales		15,680
Bad debt expense, percentage of April sales	1,280	
Allowance for doubtful accounts		1,280
May 31 Accounts receivable, May sales	48,000	
Revenue		48,000
Cash	36,320	
Accounts receivable, April sales		12,800
Accounts receivable, May sales		23,520
Merchandise inventory	14,000	
Accounts payable, May purchases		$14,000
Accounts payable, May purchases	10,500	
Cash, payment May purchases		10,500
Projected Entries to the General Journal for Selected Anticipated Transactions as per Master Budget		
June 30 Accounts receivable, June sales	64,000	
Revenue		64,000
Cost of sales for June	16,000	
Inventory		16,000

Information From Accounting Records and Planning Documents		
	Dr	**Cr**
Accounts payable, May purchases	3,500	
Cash, May purchases		3,500
Cash	2,240	
Accounts receivable, April sales		2,240
July 31 Accounts receivable, July sales	56,000	
Sales revenue		56,000
August 31 Accounts receivable, August sales	72,000	
Sales revenue		72,000
Period fixed expenses, August	2,000	
Accumulated depreciation, August		500
Cash		1,500
Variable operating expenses (percent of sales)	7,560	
Cash		7,560

Required:

1. Calculate the cost per unit of merchandise inventory
2. Prepare a schedule showing the quantity of sales, ending inventory, beginning inventory and the quantity of product purchased in May, June, and July.
3. Use the price per unit of inventory purchased and the quantity purchased to determine the expenditure for purchases in May, June, and July.
4. Calculate the percentages of sales the company expects to collect in the month of the sale and in the two months following the sale. What is the percentage of uncollectible sales? Assume that the percentages calculated for the month for which data is provided also apply to sales for any month of the year.
5. Calculate the percentages of May and June merchandise purchases the company expects to pay in June.
6. Calculate the balance in the accounts receivable on June 30. Assume all receivables are due to sales on account.
7. Calculate the balance in the cash account on June 30, based on the transactions projected to occur in June. Use the collection and disbursement percentages previously calculated. Assume that fixed expenses occur evenly in each month of the year.
8. Prepare a cash budget for July, in good form. Use the collection and disbursement percentages previously calculated.

PROBLEM 7–12
Preparing a Budgeted Income Statement and Manufacturing Cash Flows [LO2 – CC5, 7, 9; LO3 – CC13]

The Red Company is a relatively new company. The company's accountant has assembled the following information pertaining to the company's operations budget for the year ended December 31, 20X0:

Sales price	$40 per unit
Direct materials cost	$8 per unit of direct materials
Direct materials required for production	2 units per unit of product
Budgeted direct labour cost	$40 per hour
Variable manufacturing overhead rate	$25 per direct labour-hour
Depreciation (non-mfg)	$160,000
Factory depreciation	$240,000
Budgeted fixed manufacturing overhead	$140,000 excluding depreciation

	Previous Year (Actual) Quarter 4	Quarter 3	20X0 Quarter 4	Year
Direct materials inventory:				
Quantity	9,820	9,820	9,820	9,820
Cost	$ 78,560	$ 78,560	$ 78,560	$ 78, 650
Finished goods inventory:				
Quantity	2,450		2,500	
Cost	$ 62,475		$?	
Direct labour:				
Hours	2,400	2,535	2,455	10,000
Dollars	$ 96,000	$ 101,400	$ 98,200	$ 400,000
Production quantity	24,000	25,350	24,550	100,000
Sales revenue	$960,000	$1,020,000	$978,000	$3,998,000
	$407,200	$ 411,400	$408,460	$1,639,860

Required:

1. Calculate the predetermined overhead rate per direct labour-hour for the year and the overhead cost per unit.

2. Calculate the total manufacturing cost for 20X0, the budgeted production cost per unit of finished goods for 20X0, and the value of the 20X0 ending finished goods inventory for the year.

3. Calculate the cash disbursement relating to the manufacturing activity for the fourth quarter. Assume that the purchases made in a quarter are paid in the quarter of the purchase and the following quarter in equal proportion. Also assume that the fixed overhead cash expenditures occur evenly throughout the year.

4. Your friend responds to the previous question by calculating the cost of goods sold. Explain if you agree with your friend's approach.

5. Prepare, in good form, the budgeted annual income statement for the year ended December 31, 20X0, including the schedule of the cost of goods manufactured.

PROBLEM 7–13
Using a Cash Budget to Change Assumptions [LO2 – CC5, 9, 12]

Refer to the data for Janus Products, Inc. in Problem 7–1. The company's president is interested in knowing how reducing inventory levels and collecting accounts receivable sooner will impact the cash budget. He revises the cash collection and ending inventory assumptions as follows:

> **CHECK FIGURES**
> (1) August collections: $52,960
> (3) July ending cash balance: $13,710

a. Sales continue to be 20% for cash and 80% on credit. However, credit sales from July, August, and September are collected over a three-month period, with 25% collected in the month of sale, 60% collected in the month following sale, and 15% in the second month following sale. Credit sales from May and June are collected during the third quarter using the collection percentages specified in Problem 7–1.

b. The company maintains its ending inventory levels for July, August, and September at 25% of the cost of merchandise to be sold in the following month. The merchandise inventory on June 30 remains $18,000, and accounts payable for inventory purchases on June 30 remain $11,700.

All other information from Problem 7–1 that is not referred to above remains the same.

Required:

1. Using the president's new assumptions in (a) above, prepare a schedule of expected cash collections for July, August, and September and for the quarter in total.

2. Using the president's new assumptions in (b) above, prepare the following for merchandise inventory:
   a. A merchandise purchases budget for July, August, and September.
   b. A schedule of expected cash disbursements for merchandise purchases for July, August, and September and for the quarter in total.

3. Using the president's new assumptions, prepare a cash budget for July, August, and September, and for the quarter in total.

4. Prepare a brief memorandum for the president explaining how his revised assumptions affect the cash budget.

Building Your Skills

COMPREHENSIVE PROBLEM [LO2 – CC5, 7, 12; LO3 – CC13, 14]

You have just been hired as a management trainee by Cravat Sales Company, a nationwide distributor of a designer's silk ties. The company has an exclusive franchise on the distribution of the ties, and sales have grown so rapidly over the last few years that it has become necessary to add new members to the management team. You have been given responsibility for all planning and budgeting. Your first assignment is to prepare a master budget for the next three months, starting April 1. You are anxious to make a favourable impression on the president and have assembled the information below.

CHECK FIGURES

(2) June ending cash balance: $10,730;

(3) Net income: $151,880

The company desires a minimum ending cash balance each month of $10,000. The ties are sold to retailers for $8 each. Recent and forecasted sales in units are as follows:

January (actual)	20,000
February (actual)	24,000
March (actual)	28,000
April	35,000
May	45,000
June	60,000
July	40,000
August	36,000
September	32,000

The large buildup in sales before and during June is due to Father's Day. Ending inventories are supposed to equal 90% of the next month's sales in units. The ties cost the company $5 each.

Purchases are paid for as follows: 50% in the month of purchase and the remaining 50% in the following month. All sales are on credit, with no discount, and payable within 15 days. The company has found, however, that only 25% of a month's sales are collected by month-end. An additional 50% are collected in the following month, and the remaining 25% are collected in the second month following sale. Bad debts have been negligible.

The company's monthly selling and administrative expenses are given below:

Variable:	
Sales commissions	$1 per tie
Fixed:	
Wages and salaries	$22,000

Utilities	$14,000
Insurance	$1,200
Depreciation	$1,500
Miscellaneous	$3,000

All selling and administrative expenses are paid during the month, in cash, with the exception of depreciation and insurance expired. Land will be purchased during May for $25,000 cash. The company declares dividends of $12,000 each quarter, payable in the first month of the following quarter. The company's balance sheet at March 31 is given below:

Assets

Cash	$ 14,000
Accounts receivable ($48,000 February sales; $168,000 March sales)	216,000
Inventory (31,500 units)	157,500
Prepaid insurance	14,400
Fixed assets, net of depreciation	172,700
Total assets	$574,600

Liabilities and Shareholders' Equity

Accounts payable	$ 85,750
Dividends payable	12,000
Common shares	300,000
Retained earnings	176,850
Total liabilities and shareholders' equity	$574,600

The company has an agreement with a bank that allows it to borrow in increments of $1,000 at the beginning of each month, up to a total loan balance of $140,000. The interest rate on these loans is 1% per month, and for simplicity, we will assume that interest is not compounded. At the end of the quarter, the company would pay the bank all of the accumulated interest on the loan and as much of the loan as possible (in increments of $1,000), while still retaining at least $10,000 in cash.

Required:

Prepare a master budget for the three-month period ending June 30. Include the following detailed budgets:

1. a. A sales budget by month and in total.
   b. A schedule of expected cash collections from sales, by month and in total.
   c. A merchandise purchases budget in units and in dollars. Show the budget by month and in total.
   d. A schedule of expected cash disbursements for merchandise purchases, by month and in total.
2. A cash budget. Show the budget by month and in total.
3. A budgeted income statement for the three-month period ending June 30. Use the contribution approach.
4. A budgeted balance sheet as of June 30.

THINKING ANALYTICALLY [LO1 – CC1, 2, 3, 4; LO4 – CC15]

Granger Stokes, managing partner of the venture capital firm of Halston and Stokes, was dissatisfied with the top management of PrimeDrive, a manufacturer of computer disk drives. Halston and Stokes had invested $20 million in PrimeDrive, and the return on their investment had been below expectations for several years. In a tense meeting of the board of directors of PrimeDrive, Stokes exercised his firm's rights as the major equity investor in PrimeDrive and fired PrimeDrive's chief executive officer (CEO). He then quickly moved to have the board of directors of PrimeDrive appoint him as the new CEO.

Stokes prided himself on his hard-driving management style. At the first management meeting, he asked two of the managers to stand and fired them on the spot, just to show everyone who was in control of the company. At the budget review meeting that followed, he ripped up the departmental budgets that had been submitted for his review and yelled at the managers for their "wimpy, do-nothing targets." He then ordered everyone to submit new budgets calling for at least a 40% increase in sales volume and announced that he would not accept excuses for results that fell below budget.

Keri Kalani, an accountant working for the production manager at PrimeDrive, discovered toward the end of the following year that her boss had not been scrapping defective disk drives that had been returned by customers. Instead, he had been shipping them in new cartons to other customers to avoid booking losses. Quality control had deteriorated during the year as a result of the push for increased volume, and returns of defective disk drives were running as high as 15% of the new drives shipped. When she confronted her boss with her discovery, he told her to mind her own business. And then, to justify his actions, he said, "All of us managers are finding ways to hit Stokes's targets."

Required:

1. Is Stokes using budgets as a planning and control tool?
2. What are the behavioural consequences of the way budgets are being used at PrimeDrive?
3. What, if anything, do you think Kalani should do?

COMMUNICATING IN PRACTICE [LO1 – CC1, 2; LO2 – CC12]

Risky Rolling, Inc. is a rapidly expanding manufacturer of skateboards that have been modified for use on ski slopes during the off-season. This year's sales are considerably higher than last year's sales, and sales are expected to double next year. The unexpected growth in sales has presented numerous challenges to the company's management team, and the stress is really starting to show. Laura Dennan, the company's president, believes that the management time required to prepare a cash budget should be devoted to other, more pressing matters.

Required:

Write a memorandum to the president that states why cash budgeting is particularly important to a rapidly expanding company such as Risky Rolling.

ETHICS CHALLENGE [LO1 – CC1, 2; LO4 – CC15]

Is the use of budgetary slack unethical? Consider a hypothetical conversation between you and the sales and production managers of your company that you recently joined about how the managers estimated their sales and production numbers which drive the budget of your company.

Sales Manager: We have a systematic process that incorporates our recent experience and what we know about our customers and the economic conditions to develop initial estimates. Then we add that usual dose of intuition to come up with the best forecast we can.

Production Manager: The sales projections that are given to me are the basis for my production planning. Of course, we have to make an estimate of what this year's ending inventories will be, which is sometimes difficult.

You: Why does that present a problem? There must have been an estimate of ending inventories in the budget for the current year.

Production Manager: Those numbers aren't always reliable, since Sales makes some adjustments to the sales numbers before passing them on to me.

You: What kind of adjustments?

Sales Manager: Well, my department is evaluated on how well we hit the sales targets and we don't want to fall short of the sales projections, and so we generally give ourselves a little breathing room by lowering the initial sales projection anywhere from 5% to 10%.

Production Manager: So you can see why this year's budget is not a very reliable starting point. We always have to adjust the projected production rates as the year progresses, and, of course, this changes the ending inventory estimates. By the way, we make similar adjustments to expenses by adding at least 10% to the estimates. I think everyone around here does the same thing.

Required:

1. The practice followed by the managers as described illustrates *budgetary slack*.
   a. Why do managers behave in this manner? Describe the benefits they expect to realize from the use of budgetary slack.
   b. Explain how the use of budgetary slack can adversely affect these managers.
2. As a professional accountant, explain why the use of budgetary slack may be unethical. When formulating your response, consider the following enabling competencies expected of a professional accountant: professional competence; integrity; and objectivity. You may refer to any published Code of Professional Conduct from professional accounting organizations like CPA-Canada or one of its legacy organizations like CGA-Canada or CMA-Canada or the AICPA in the United States.

TEAMWORK IN ACTION [LO1 – CC1, 2; LO4 – CC15]

Tom Emory and Jim Morris strolled back to their plant from the administrative offices of Ferguson & Son Mfg. Company. Emory is manager of the machine shop in the company's factory; Morris is manager of the equipment maintenance department.

The men had just attended the monthly performance evaluation meeting for plant department heads. These meetings had been held on the third Tuesday of each month since Robert Ferguson, Jr., the president's son, had become plant manager a year earlier.

As they were walking, Emory spoke: "Boy, I hate those meetings! I never know whether my department's accounting reports will show good or bad performance. I'm beginning to expect the worst. If the accountants say I saved the company a dollar, I'm called 'Sir,' but if I spend even a little too much—boy, do I get in trouble. I don't know if I can hold on until I retire."

Emory had just been given the worst evaluation he had ever received in his long career with Ferguson & Son. He was the most respected of the experienced machinists in the company. He had been with Ferguson & Son for many years and was promoted to supervisor of the machine shop when the company expanded and moved to its present location. The president (Robert Ferguson, Sr.) had often stated that the company's success was due to the high quality of the work of machinists like Emory. As supervisor, Emory stressed the importance of craftsmanship and told his workers that he wanted no sloppy work coming from his department.

When Robert Ferguson, Jr., became the plant manager, he directed that monthly performance comparisons be made between actual and budgeted costs for each department. The departmental budgets were intended to encourage the supervisors to reduce inefficiencies and to seek cost reduction opportunities. The company controller was instructed to have his staff tighten the budget slightly whenever a department attained its budget in a given month; this was done to reinforce the plant manager's desire to reduce costs. The young plant manager often stressed the importance of continued progress toward attaining the budget; he also made it known that he kept a file of these performance reports for future reference when he succeeded his father.

Emory's conversation with Morris continued as follows:

Emory: I really don't understand. We've worked so hard to meet the budget, and the minute we make it, they tighten the budget on us. We can't work any faster and still maintain quality. I think my men are ready to quit trying. Besides, those reports don't tell the whole story. We always seem to be interrupting the big jobs for all those small rush orders. All that setup and machine adjustment time is killing us. And quite frankly, Jim, you were no help. When our hydraulic press broke down last month, your people were nowhere to be found. We had to take it apart ourselves and got stuck with all that idle time.

Morris: I'm sorry about that, Tom, but you know my department has had trouble making budget, too. We were running well behind at the time of that problem, and if we'd spent a day on that old machine, we would never have made it up. Instead, we made the scheduled inspections of the forklift trucks because we knew we could do those in less than the budgeted time.

Emory: Well, Jim, at least you have some options. I'm locked into what the scheduling department assigns to me, and you know they're being harassed by sales for those special orders. Incidentally, why didn't your report show all the supplies you guys wasted last month when you were working in Bill's department?

Morris: We're not out of the woods on that deal yet. We charged the maximum we could to other work and haven't even reported some of it yet.

Emory: Well, I'm glad you have a way of getting out of the pressure. The accountants seem to know everything that's happening in my department, sometimes even before I do. I thought all that budget and accounting stuff was supposed to help, but it just gets me into trouble. It's all a big pain. I'm trying to put out quality work; they're trying to save pennies.

Required:

The team should discuss and then respond to the following two questions. All team members should agree with and understand the answers and be prepared to explain the solutions in class. (Each teammate can assume responsibility for a different part of the presentation.)

1. Identify the problems that appear to exist in Ferguson & Son Mfg. Company's budgetary control system, and explain how the problems are likely to reduce the effectiveness of the system.
2. Explain how Ferguson & Son Mfg. Company's budgetary control system could be revised to improve its effectiveness.

(Adapted © CPA Canada)

Endnotes

1. Paul J. Carruth, Thurrell O. McClendon, and Milton R. Ballard, "What Supervisors Don't Like About Budget Evaluations," *Management Accounting, 64(8)*, February 1983, p. 42.
2. This section is based on a two-part article by Theresa Libby and R. Murray Lindsay, "Budgeting—An Unnecessary Evil: How the BBRT Envisions a World Without Traditional Budgeting," *CMA Management,* March 2003 and April 2003.

8

Cost–Volume–Profit Relationships

LEARNING OBJECTIVES AND CHAPTER COMPETENCIES		
After studying Chapter 8, you should be able to demonstrate the following competencies:		

COMPETENCY		Know	Apply
LO1	**UNDERSTAND THE COST–VOLUME–PROFIT ANALYSIS FRAMEWORK.**		
CC1	Explain the basics of cost–volume–profit (CVP) analysis.	●	
CC2	Explain and compute the contribution margin and the contribution margin ratio.	●	●
CC3	Explain how changes in activity affect contribution margin, contribution margin ratio, and net income.	●	
CC4	Explain, prepare, and interpret a CVP graph.	●	●
LO2	**APPLY THE CVP ANALYSIS FRAMEWORK AND EXPLAIN THE ANALYSIS.**		
CC5	Apply the CVP framework to different managerial decisions.		●
CC6	Compute break-even sales using different approaches.		●
CC7	Compute the sales needed to achieve a target profit, including the effect of income tax on this analysis.		●
CC8	Explain and compute the margin of safety.	●	●
CC9	Explain the effect of cost structure on a company's profitability.	●	
CC10	Compute the degree of operating leverage and explain its usefulness.	●	●
CC11[A]	Explain the concept of sales mix.	●	
CC12[A]	Compute break-even sales in a multi-product environment.		●

COMPETENCY		Know	Apply
LO3	**COMPARE AND CONTRAST ABSORPTION COSTING AND VARIABLE COSTING.**		
CC13^B	Differentiate between absorption and variable product costing.	●	
CC14^B	Prepare absorption and variable costing income statements and reconcile the operating incomes from the two statements.		●

Note: The superscripts "A" and "B" refer to Appendix 8A and Appendix 8B, respectively; both appendices are available on Connect.

◀◀ **A Look Back**	▶ **A Look at This Chapter**	▶▶ **A Look Ahead**
In Chapter 7, we discussed the topic of budgeting and learned how to prepare budgets.	This chapter begins our discussion of decision making. Here we describe the basics of cost–volume–profit (CVP) analysis, an essential management accounting tool for decision making.	In Chapter 9, we discuss the core of decision making by introducing the concept of relevant costs and their application to various managerial decisions.

ON THE JOB

COST–VOLUME–PROFIT ANALYSIS AND BUSINESS FUNDAMENTALS

You wouldn't think that someone who has worked for big companies like Cameco and Hitachi for most of their career would switch over to creating a startup company. But Naqsh Kochar did just that. With a background in computer science and business strategy, Kochar founded Refresh Inc. in 2009. Now, with a core team of four marketing gurus and project managers, Refresh has established itself as a marketing, strategy, and innovation technology firm based in Saskatoon, Saskatchewan. Refresh is armed with big ideas that help its clients—such as Lawson Heights Mall in Northern Saskatoon, 4-H Saskatchewan, and Meridian Developments—grow and prosper. Its marketing successes come from an innate understanding of the art and science of building a brand. The ability to combine current technology with innovative strategies helps its clients achieve business success; this is what sets Refresh apart.

Refresh

Just like any service company, Refresh goes through peaks and valleys of client work. There are times when the amount of work that is to be done exceeds the company's capacity. There are other times where the number of people exceeds the amount of work that is on the table, thereby creating excess capacity. During peaks and valleys of client work, Refresh must leverage its variable costs. The organizational structure at Refresh is unique compared to other companies, which, in turn, reflects a higher variable cost in its cost structure. The core team of four people at Refresh who project manage client work hire experts in designated fields based on need. The company outsources work to designers, copywriters, and web developers especially during peak times in the company. "We align our extended team members to our clients' needs, not the other way around," says Kochar. "This enables Refresh to align each project with the right people with the right skills." These subcontractors work on a project-by-project basis with Refresh, which is why there is no design team in-house.

Although this works at the current time, it also introduces the risk of not finding the right subcontractor when needed. The question, "Should we expand the core team with a suite of designers, copywriters, or web developers?" has often crossed Kochar's mind. He knows that hiring full-time employees will change Refresh's cost structure by increasing its committed fixed costs, regardless of the number of projects and amount of client work coming through the door. This, in turn, will increase the number of projects that Refresh must work on during a time period just to break even.

Source: Personal conversation with Naqsh Kochar, founder, Refresh Inc.

 Critical thinking question *Why is the understanding of variable and fixed costs especially important for small organizations?*

*Note to student: See **Guidance Answers** online.*

Cost–volume–profit (CVP) analysis is one of the most powerful tools managers have. It helps them understand the interrelationships among cost, volume, and profit in an organization in order to determine, for example, the products to manufacture or sell, the pricing policy to follow, the marketing strategy to employ, and the type of production facilities to acquire. To help understand the role of CVP analysis in business decisions, consider the case of Acoustic Concepts, Inc.

MANAGERIAL ACCOUNTING IN ACTION

THE ISSUE

Prem Narayan, an engineer, started Acoustic Concepts, Inc. to market a radically new speaker he had designed for automobile sound systems. The speaker, called the Sonic Blaster, uses an advanced microprocessor chip to boost amplification to awesome levels. Narayan contracted with an Indian electronics manufacturer to produce the speaker. With seed money provided by his family, Narayan placed an order with the manufacturer and ran advertisements in auto magazines.

The Sonic Blaster was a success. Sales grew to the point that Narayan moved the company's headquarters out of his apartment and into a neighbouring industrial park. He also hired a receptionist, an accountant, a sales manager, and a small sales staff to sell the speakers to retail stores. The accountant, Bob Luchinni, had worked for several small companies as a business advisor, accountant, and bookkeeper.

The following discussion occurred soon after Luchinni was hired:

Narayan: Bob, I've got a lot of questions about the company's finances that I hope you can help answer.

Luchinni: We're in great shape. The loan from your family will be paid off within a few months.

Narayan: I know, but I am worried about the risks I've assumed by expanding operations. What would happen if a competitor entered the market and our sales slipped? How far could sales drop before we started to lose money? Another question I've been trying to resolve is, how much would our sales have to increase in order to justify the big marketing campaign the sales staff is pushing for? The production manager wants to assemble the speaker components using a new method that is supposed to take less time than our present method, and wants me to spend money on a training program to train our workers in the new method.

Luchinni: The marketing department always wants more money for advertising, and the production department is keen to keep up with the latest techniques.

Narayan: Marketing is always pushing me to drop the selling price on the speaker. I agree with them that a lower price will boost our volume, but I'm not sure the increased volume will offset the loss in revenue from the lower price. I am also not convinced that the new assembly method will reduce our production costs sufficiently to pay for the training program.

Luchinni: It sounds like these questions are all related in some way to the relationships among our selling prices, our costs, and our volume. I know of a way to come up with the answers. I'll need a day or two, though, to gather some data.

Narayan: Why don't we set up a meeting for three days from now? That would be Thursday.

Luchinni: That'll be fine. I'll have some preliminary answers for you, as well as a model you can use for answering similar questions in the future.

Narayan: Good. I'll be looking forward to seeing what you come up with.

The Basics of CVP Analysis

The Contribution Margin Income Statement

LO1 ● **Know**

CC1: Explain the basics of cost–volume–profit (CVP) analysis.

Bob Luchinni returned to his office and set about getting ready for his next meeting with Prem Narayan. Luchinni knew that, in order to provide answers for Narayan, he needed an analysis tool to show how profits would be affected by the different decisions and operating choices that Narayan was considering. This tool is the contribution margin income statement, first presented in Chapter 6. The contribution margin approach—also called the *variable costing approach*—is useful for decision making because it gives the manager a better understanding of costs under different situations—exactly what Narayan needs. Luchinni realized that his first task would be to prepare a contribution margin format income statement for June.

CHARACTERISTICS OF A CONTRIBUTION MARGIN INCOME STATEMENT

The contribution margin income statement is different from the absorption costing income statement. The chart below shows a high-level view of the income statements obtained from the two approaches. Note that we have used abbreviations for cost of goods sold (COGS), selling and general and administrative costs (SG&A), variable costs (VC), fixed costs (FC), and operating income (OI).

The Structure of Operating Income Statements

Contribution Margin Format		Gross Margin Format	
Variable Costing		*Absorption Costing*	
Sales Revenue	Revenue	Sales Revenue	
VC { Less: Variable COGS / Less: Variable SG&A	Costs I	Less: Variable COGS / Less: Fixed COGS } Mfg cost	
Contribution margin		Gross margin	
FC { Less: Fixed COGS / Less: Fixed SG&A	Costs II	Less: Variable SG&A / Less: Fixed SG&A } Non-mfg. cost	
Net OI	Net OI	Net OI	

Looking down the middle of the chart, you will see the basic structure of an operating income statement: two sets of costs are deducted from revenue to obtain net operating income. Margin is the result of deducting Costs I from revenue. Net operating income is obtained when the Costs II amount is deducted from the margin. The two approaches differ with respect to how Costs I and II are made up.

Contribution Margin Format	Absorption Costing Format
Costs are grouped according to *cost behaviour:* • costs that change in response to changes in the volume of activity (variable costs) • costs that are fixed with respect to the change in the activity driver (fixed costs) Cost drivers are • production activity for variable product costs • sales level for the selling and general administrative costs	Costs are grouped by *function:* • manufacturing • nonmanufacturing
Product costs include *only the variable* cost elements: direct materials, direct labour, and variable manufacturing overhead.	Products costs include *all* manufacturing costs: variable manufacturing cost elements plus the fixed cost per unit.
Fixed manufacturing cost is expensed as a period cost without being assigned to the products. The cost of the inventory of products will not include fixed costs of manufacturing.	Fixed costs must be converted to a per-unit basis to assign these costs to units in production.
Units in inventory will carry only the variable cost of manufacturing.	Units in inventory will carry the full cost of manufacturing (i.e., variable as well as fixed cost per unit).
Margin is calculated from sales revenue after charging all of the variable costs against revenue. The result is called the contribution margin.	Margin is calculated from sales revenue after deducting the cost of goods sold. The result is called gross margin. The key is that selling and administrative costs are not deducted when computing the gross margin.

Fixed costs are deducted from the contribution margin to determine the net operating income.	Selling and administrative costs are deducted from gross margin to determine the absorption costing operating income.
The net operating income from the contribution margin approach need not equal the net operating income from the absorption costing approach.	The net operating income from the contribution margin approach need not equal the net operating income from the absorption costing approach.

The contribution margin income statement is an ideal tool to explore how profits will change when different operating decisions are made. Why? The quick answer is, "Because operating decisions are short-term in focus and they impact activities performed, such as sales or production." Consider some examples of an operating decision and its potential cost or profit impact:

Decision	Potential Cost Impact
Increase production.	Higher total variable cost of production
Change the procedure to assemble this component.	Lower variable cost per unit
Introduce a two-for-one promotional program.	Higher variable selling cost per unit
Hire a better-qualified person to train the workers.	Higher fixed cost
Reduce the selling price.	Depends on the response of sales volume

As you can see, each decision is expected to affect profits because cost and volume are affected. A good decision or a bad decision, in this context, is defined in terms of the decision's impact on profits (*this does not mean that impact on other factors or variables is irrelevant*). This impact is easier to trace and explain using the contribution margin income statement because of its presentation format.

On the other hand, the absorption costing format is ideal for *external* financial reporting, where the goal is to give an accounting of the costs and expenses to the company's stakeholders. As noted earlier, the costs are classified by function, indicating how much money was spent on manufacturing, IT, marketing, finance and administration, and so on. But the absorption costing format is ill suited for decision making because in this approach the fixed manufacturing costs are allocated to units of production. This requirement will cause distortions in operating income, which, if unrecognized, can lead to poor decisions. For example, fixed manufacturing cost is applied to production after being converted to a per-unit basis. This has the undesirable effect of making the product cost appear to be a variable cost with respect to the number of units made. But the product cost per unit is actually a mixture of the variable cost per unit and the fixed cost per unit, and thus it is not a true variable cost. Misinterpreting the product cost as a variable cost can lead to mistakes in pricing, or a mistaken decision to drop or keep a product, and so on. This and other potential distortions in operating income from using the absorption costing format income statement for decision making are discussed fully in Appendix 8B.

To conclude, the contribution margin format income statement is the ideal tool to use for decision making and internal reporting.

PREPARING A CONTRIBUTION MARGIN INCOME STATEMENT

To prepare the contribution margin income statement for June, Bob Luchinni gathered the sales and operating data he would require. The data appear below:

	A	B	C
1	**ACOUSTIC CONCEPTS, INC.**		
2	**Selected Sales and Operating Data for Month of June**		
3	Beginning inventory	50	units (speakers)
4	Production during the month	410	units
5	Sales during the month	400	units

	A	B	C
6	Ending inventory	60	units
7	Selling price per speaker	$250	
8	Variable costs per speaker		
9	Direct materials	$40	
10	Direct labour	60	
11	Manufacturing overhead	20	
12	Selling and administrative expenses	30	
13	Fixed costs per month		
14	Manufacturing overhead	$25,000	
15	Selling and administrative expenses	10,000	

In addition to the above data, Luchinni noted from the accounting records that the cost information for June was also valid for the month of May. There were no work-in-process inventories in May and June, and the company followed the first-in-first-out (FIFO) method of controlling inventory flow. Acoustic Concepts, Inc. used an actual costing system. The following steps describe the procedure followed by Luchinni to prepare the income statement.

Step 1: Calculate the product cost for each speaker.

The product cost must include only the *variable* costs of manufacturing. Product cost should not include any selling or administrative cost. Luchinni calculated the product cost as follows:

	A	B
24	**Product Cost per Speaker—Contribution Margin Approach**	
25		
26	Direct materials (DM)	$ 40
27	Direct labour (DL)	$ 60
28	Variable manufacturing overhead (VMOH)	$ 20
29	Total	$120
30		

Thus, $120 is the *variable* product cost per speaker.

Step 2: Compute the variable cost of goods sold.

When there are beginning inventories, and sales and production are not equal, a preliminary step is required to account for the flow of units through inventory, production, and sales. Acoustic Concepts, Inc. began the month of June with 50 speakers in inventory. Planned production is 410 speakers, and the company expects to sell 400 speakers. Therefore, accounting for the flow of units, we see that inventory at the end of June will be 60 speakers:

$$\text{Beginning inventory} \quad + \quad \text{Production} \quad - \quad \text{Quantity sold} \quad = \quad \text{Ending inventory}$$

$$50 \quad + \quad 410 \quad - \quad 400 \quad = \quad 60$$

With this information, the variable cost of goods sold is computed as follows:

		K	L	M	N
1					
2		**Variable Cost of Goods Sold for June**			
3			**Units**	**Cost/Unit**	**Value**
4	Beginning inventory		50	$120	$ 6,000
5	Add: Variable cost of goods manufactured		410	$120	$49,200
6	Deduct: Ending inventory		60	$120	$ 7,200
7	Variable cost of goods sold*		400	$120	$48,000
8					
9	*Variable cost of goods sold can also be calculated directly: 400 × $120 = $48,000.
10	This is acceptable as long as the cost per unit in beginning inventory is equal to
11	the cost per unit for units manufactured in the current period. This assumes
12	that the company follows the FIFO method for controlling inventory flow. Note that
13	LIFO is not an option under ASPE or IFRS.

HELPFUL HINT

When the variable cost per unit is unchanged between periods, as in this case, or if there are no inventories, then the variable cost of goods sold can be calculated directly as

Variable cost of goods sold = Variable product cost per unit × Units sold

A separate schedule of cost of goods manufactured and sold will not be necessary *unless* there are beginning inventories *and* the product cost has changed between periods. Why? Because units in beginning inventory will have a different cost per unit than units produced during the period. And under FIFO, the assumption is that units in beginning inventory are among the units sold. Therefore, we must calculate the cost of the units sold from beginning inventory separately from the cost of the units sold from current production. Valuing all the units sold using a single cost per unit is not appropriate. Note that LIFO (last-in-first-out) is not permitted under IFRS and ASPE.

Step 3: Compute the variable selling and administrative expense.

The variable selling and administrative cost per speaker *sold* is $30. The total cost for 400 speakers works out to be $30 × 400 = $12,000.

Step 4: Determine the total fixed costs.

The total of manufacturing fixed costs (FMOH) and the fixed selling and general and administrative cost (FSG&A) is

$$FMOH + FSG\&A = \$25,000 + \$10,000 = \$35,000$$

Step 5: Putting it all together.

We put all of the pieces together by following the structure shown above for the contribution format income statement:

	A	B
1	**ACOUSTIC CONCEPTS, INC.**	
2	**Contribution Format Income Statement**	
3	**for the Month of June**	
4	Sales (400 units @ $250/unit)	$100,000
5	Less: Variable costs	
6	Variable cost of goods sold (400 @ $120)*	$ 48,000
7	Variable selling and administrative expense (400 @ $30)†	12,000
8	Total variable costs	$ 60,000
9	Contribution margin	$ 40,000
10	Less: Fixed costs	
11	Fixed manufacturing cost	$ 25,000
12	Fixed selling and administrative cost	10,000
13	Total fixed costs	$ 35,000
14	Net operating income	$ 5,000
15	Notes:	
16	*The variable product cost (i.e., cost of manufacturing) *per speaker* is the total of per-	
17	unit cost of direct material, direct labour, and variable manufacturing overhead. This	
18	is $40 (DM) + $60 (DL) + $20 (VMOH) = $120.	
19	†Note that variable selling expenses are based on the quantity of speakers *sold* and	
20	not on the quantity of production.	

A CONDENSED FORMAT FOR ANALYSIS

Luchinni leaned back and considered the contribution margin income statement he had just prepared. He had broken down the variable and the fixed costs into manufacturing and nonmanufacturing categories. He looked at the notes from his meeting with Narayan. Luchinni realized that the information Narayan wanted revolved around the relationship between sales volume, costs, and profits. Therefore, Luchinni decided to simplify the presentation of the income statement by combining all the variable costs into a single line item and the fixed costs into a single cost line item. The result of doing this simplification is shown below:

ACOUSTIC CONCEPTS, INC. Contribution Margin Income Statement for the Month of June			
	Total	Per Unit	Percentage
Sales (400 speakers)	$100,000	$250	100
Less: Variable expenses	60,000	150	60
Contribution margin	40,000	$100	40
Less: Fixed expenses	35,000		
Net income	$ 5,000		

Notice that the condensed format emphasizes the behaviour of costs and is therefore extremely helpful to a manager in judging the impact on profits of changes in selling price, cost, or volume—such an analysis is known as **cost–volume–profit analysis** or simply **CVP analysis**. Note that sales, variable expenses, and contribution margin are expressed in total, on a per-unit basis, and as a percentage. This is a good idea on income statements prepared for management's own use because it facilitates profitability analysis.

Contribution Margin and CVP Analysis

LO1 • **Know**   • **Apply**

CC2: Explain and compute the contribution margin and the contribution margin ratio.

Contribution margin is the difference between sales revenue and variable expenses. The contribution margin can be expressed on a per-unit basis, and in that form it is referred to as the *unit contribution margin*. Contribution margin may also be expressed as a percentage of sales. This is called the *contribution margin ratio*—or CM ratio. For Acoustic Concepts, the CM ratio is 40%. The interpretation of the CM ratio is discussed further below.

LO1 • **Know**

CC3: Explain how changes in activity affect contribution margin, contribution margin ratio, and net income.

Contribution margin is the amount available to cover fixed expenses and then to provide profits for the period. Note the sequence here—contribution margin is used *first* to cover the fixed expenses, and then whatever remains goes toward profits. If the contribution margin is not sufficient to cover the fixed expenses, a loss occurs for the period. To illustrate with an extreme example, assume that Acoustic Concepts sells only one speaker during a particular month. The company's income statement will then appear as follows:

	Total	Per Unit	Percentage
Sales (1 speaker)	$ 250	$250	100
Less: Variable expenses	150	150	60
Contribution margin	100	$100	40
Less: Fixed expenses	35,000		
Net loss	$ (34,900)		

For each additional speaker that the company is able to sell during the month, $100 more in contribution margin will become available to help cover the fixed expenses. If a second speaker is sold, for example, then the total contribution margin will increase by $100 (to a total of $200) and the company's loss will decrease by $100, to $34,800:

	Total	Per Unit	Percentage
Sales (2 speakers)	$ 500	$250	100
Less: Variable expenses	300	150	60
Contribution margin	200	$100	40
Less: Fixed expenses	35,000		
Net loss	$ (34,800)		

If enough speakers can be sold to generate $35,000 in contribution margin, all of the fixed costs will be covered and the company will at least have managed to *break even* for the month—that is, to show neither profit nor loss, simply to cover all of its costs. In order to break even, the company will have to sell 350 speakers in a month, since each speaker sold yields $100 in contribution margin:

	Total	Per Unit	Percentage
Sales (350 speakers)	$ 87,500	$250	100
Less: Variable expenses	52,500	150	60
Contribution margin	35,000	$100	40
Less: Fixed expenses	35,000		
Net income	$ –0–		

The quantity 350 is the company's **break-even point**—that is, the level of sales at which profit (net income) is zero. Computation of the break-even point is discussed in detail later in the chapter. Note that at the break-even point, the total contribution margin equals the total fixed expenses—both are $35,000.

Once the break-even point has been reached, net income will increase by the amount of the unit contribution margin for each additional unit sold. For example, if 351 speakers are sold in a month, we can expect that the net income for the month will be $100, since the company will have sold one speaker more than the number needed to break even:

	Total	Per Unit	Percentage
Sales (351 speakers)	$ 87,750	$250	100
Less: Variable expenses	52,650	150	60
Contribution margin	35,100	$100	40
Less: Fixed expenses	35,000		
Net income	$ 100		

If 352 speakers are sold (two speakers above the break-even point), we can expect that the net income for the month will be $200, and so on. To know what the profits will be at various levels of activity, therefore, it is not necessary to prepare a whole series of income statements. The manager can, instead, simply take the number of units to be sold over the break-even point and multiply that number by the unit contribution margin ($100 in our example). The result represents the anticipated profits for the period. Or, to estimate the effect of a planned increase in sales on profits, the manager can simply multiply the increase in units sold by the unit contribution margin. The result will be the expected increase in profits. To illustrate, if Acoustic Concepts is currently selling 400 speakers per month and plans to increase sales to 425 speakers per month, the anticipated impact on profits can be computed as follows:

Increased number of speakers to be sold	25
Contribution margin per speaker	× $100
Increase in net income	$2,500

These calculations can be verified as follows:

	Sales Volume			
	400	**425**	**Difference,**	
	Speakers	**Speakers**	**25 Speakers**	**Per Unit**
Sales	$100,000	$106,250	$6,250	$250
Less: Variable expenses	60,000	63,750	3,750	150
Contribution margin	40,000	42,500	2,500	$100
Less: Fixed expenses	35,000	35,000	–0–	
Net income	$ 5,000	$ 7,500	$2,500	

To summarize these examples, if there were no sales, the company's loss would equal its fixed expenses. Each unit sold reduces the loss by the amount of the unit contribution margin. Once the break-even point has been reached, each additional unit sold increases the company's profit by the amount of the unit contribution margin. The assumption about fixed expenses remaining unchanged is that any increase in sales is within the relevant range of operations.

Contribution Margin Ratio and CVP Analysis

The contribution margin as a percentage of sales is referred to as the **contribution margin (CM) ratio**. The CM ratio is computed as follows:

$$\text{CM ratio} = \frac{\text{Contribution margin}}{\text{Sales}}$$

For Acoustic Concepts, the CM ratio is

$$\text{CM ratio} = \frac{\text{Contribution margin}}{\text{Sales}}$$

$$= \frac{\$40,000}{\$100,000}$$

$$= 40\%$$

For a single-product company such as Acoustic Concepts, the CM ratio can also be computed as follows:

$$\text{CM ratio} = \frac{\text{Per-unit contribution margin}}{\text{Per-unit sales revenue}}$$

$$= \frac{\$100}{\$250}$$

$$= 40\%$$

The effect of changes in sales can also be measured using the CM ratio. To illustrate, a CM ratio of 40% for Acoustic Concepts means that, for each dollar increase in sales, total contribution margin will increase by 40 cents (= $1 sales × CM ratio of 40%). As this example suggests, *the impact on contribution margin of any given dollar change in total sales can be computed in seconds by simply applying the CM ratio to the dollar change*. If, for example, Acoustic Concepts plans a $30,000 increase in sales during the coming month, management can expect the contribution margin to increase by $12,000 (= $30,000 increased sales × CM ratio of 40%).

If fixed costs do not change, the change in the contribution margin will flow through to change net income. Each dollar increase in sales will increase net income by 40 cents (= $1 sales × CM ratio of 40%). And a $30,000 increase in sales will increase net income by $12,000.

Similarly, if you know the *level* of sales, then the level of contribution margin is sales multiplied by the CM ratio. Thus, for a sales level of $130,000, the CM will be 0.40 × $130,000 = $52,000. This is verified by the following table:

	Sales Volume			Percentage
	Current	Expected	Increase	of Sales
Sales	$100,000	$130,000	$30,000	100
Less: Variable expenses	60,000	78,000*	18,000	60
Contribution margin	40,000	52,000	12,000	40
Less: Fixed expenses	35,000	35,000	—0—	
Net income	$ 5,000	$ 17,000	$12,000	

*$130,000 expected sales ÷ $250 per unit = 520 units. 520 units × $150 per unit = $78,000.

The CM ratio is particularly valuable when the manager must make trade-offs between more dollar sales of one product and more dollar sales of another. Generally speaking, when trying to increase sales, products that yield the greatest amount of contribution margin per dollar of sales should be emphasized.

IN BUSINESS

CVP AND BUSINESS VALUE

Cascades Inc. is a $4 billion manufacturer of paper and packaging products catering to a variety of industries and uses. A pioneer in recycling paper, it has added a number of products during its half century of existence. The following remarks, made by Alain Lemaire, executive chairman of the board, following the release of a recent quarter's financial results, illustrate the power of the CVP framework for understanding and explaining financial operating performance: "On a segmented basis, maintenance expenses and lower average prices due to increased promotional activities in Canada and increased competition in the U.S. affected our tissue papers sector. On the containerboard front, the operating rate of our containerboard mills has improved during the first quarter. However, the current weakness of the Canadian economy impacted our corrugated product business as order levels in Eastern Canada were lower than expected. This group was also impacted by the production of lower margin products by our boxboard manufacturing mills in North America. In Europe, lower energy prices and higher volumes more than offset the impact of lower selling prices. As for fibre, costs for brown grades and virgin pulp were higher than during the previous quarter which also impacted our results."

Evidently, performance was affected by lower than expected volume of sales, higher input prices, lower selling price due to promotional activities and increased competition, and a shift in sales mix to lower-margin products.

Sources: "Cascades Makes Moving Easy," http://www.theglobeandmail.com/globe-investor/news-sources/?mid=PRNEWS.20130515.MO829; "Cascades Releases Financial Results for the First Quarter of 2013," http://www.theglobeandmail.com/globe-investor/news-sources/?mid=CNW.20130509.C4585; R. Gibbens, "Cascades Boosts Profit in Challenging Climate," *CanWest News*, May 11, 2007, p. 1.

CVP Relationships in Equation Form

The contribution format income statement can be expressed in equation form as follows (for brevity, we use *profit* to stand for *net operating income* in equations):

$$\text{Profit} = (\text{Sales} - \text{Variable expenses}) - \text{Fixed expenses}$$

When a company has only a *single* product, as at Acoustic Concepts, we can further refine the equation as follows:

$$\text{Sales} = \text{Selling price per unit} \times \text{Quantity sold} = P \times Q$$
$$\text{Variable expenses} = \text{Variable expenses per unit} \times \text{Quantity sold} = V \times Q$$
$$\text{Profit} = (P \times Q - V \times Q) - \text{Fixed expenses}$$

We can do all of the calculations of the previous section using this simple equation. For example, we previously computed the net operating income (profit) at sales of 351 speakers as $100. We can arrive at the same conclusion using the above equation as follows:

$$
\begin{aligned}
\text{Profit} &= (P \times Q - V \times Q) - \text{Fixed expenses} \\
&= (\$250 \times 351 - \$150 \times 351) - \$35,000 \\
&= (\$250 - \$150) \times 351 - \$35,000 \\
&= (\$100) \times 351 - \$35,000 \\
&= \$35,100 - \$35,000 \\
&= \$100
\end{aligned}
$$

It is often useful to express the simple profit equation in terms of the unit contribution margin (unit CM) as follows:

$$
\begin{aligned}
\text{Unit CM} &= \text{Selling price per unit} - \text{Variable expenses per unit} = P - V \\
\text{Profit} &= \left(P \times Q - V \times Q\right) - \text{Fixed expenses} \\
\text{Profit} &= \left(P - V\right) \times Q - \text{Fixed expenses} \\
\text{Profit} &= \text{Unit CM} \times Q - \text{Fixed expenses}
\end{aligned}
$$

We could also have used this equation to determine the profit at sales of 351 speakers as follows:

$$
\begin{aligned}
\text{Profit} &= \text{Unit CM} \times Q - \text{Fixed expenses} \\
&= \$100 \times 351 - \$35,000 \\
&= \$35,100 - \$35,000 \\
&= \$100
\end{aligned}
$$

The relation between profit and the CM ratio can also be expressed using the following equation:

$$
\text{Profit} = \text{CM ratio} \times \text{Sales} - \text{Fixed expenses}
$$

This equation can be derived using the basic profit equation and the definition of the CM ratio as follows:

$$
\begin{aligned}
\text{Profit} &= (\text{Sales} - \text{Variable expenses}) - \text{Fixed expenses} \\
&= \text{Contribution margin} - \text{Fixed expenses} \\
&= \frac{\text{Contribution margin}}{\text{Sales}} \times \text{Sales} - \text{Fixed expenses} \\
&= \text{CM ratio} \times \text{Sales} - \text{Fixed expenses}
\end{aligned}
$$

For example, at sales of $130,000, the profit is expected to be $17,000, as shown below:

$$
\begin{aligned}
\text{Profit} &= \text{CM ratio} \times \text{Sales} - \text{Fixed expenses} \\
&= 0.40 \times \$130,000 - \$35,000 \\
&= \$52,000 - \$35,000 \\
&= \$17,000
\end{aligned}
$$

If you are comfortable with algebra, this approach will often be quicker and easier than constructing contribution format income statements.

CVP Relationships in Graphical Form

LO1 • **Know**   • **Apply**

CC4: Explain, prepare, and interpret a CVP graph.

The relationships among revenue, cost, profit, and volume can be expressed graphically by preparing a **CVP graph**. A CVP graph highlights CVP relationships over wide ranges of activity, giving managers a perspective that can be obtained in no other way. To help explain his analysis to Prem Narayan, Bob Luchinni decided to prepare a CVP graph for Acoustic Concepts.

PREPARING THE CVP GRAPH

In a CVP graph (sometimes called a *break-even chart*), unit volume is commonly represented on the horizontal (*X*) axis and dollars on the vertical (*Y*) axis. Preparing a CVP graph involves three steps. These steps are keyed to the graph in Exhibit 8–1.

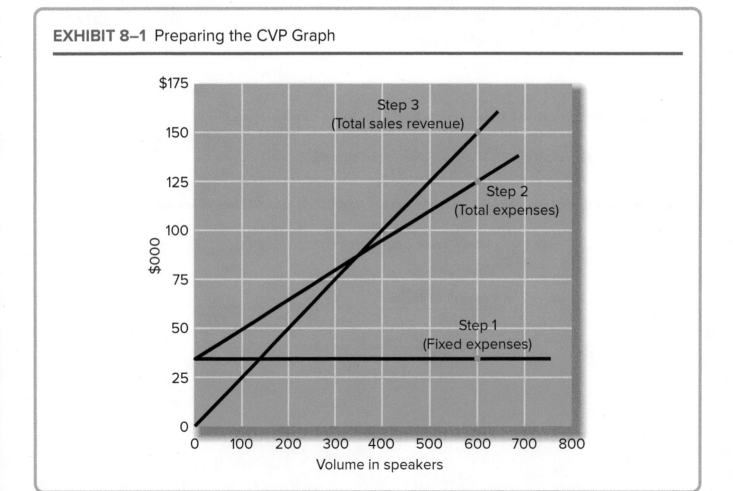

EXHIBIT 8–1 Preparing the CVP Graph

1. Draw a line parallel to the volume axis to represent total fixed expenses. For Acoustic Concepts, total fixed expenses are $35,000.

2. Choose some volume of sales and plot the point representing total expenses (fixed and variable) at the activity level you have selected. In Exhibit 8–1, Luchinni chose a volume of 600 speakers. Total expenses at that activity level would be as follows:

Fixed expenses	$ 35,000
Variable expenses (600 speakers × $150 per speaker)	90,000
Total expenses	$125,000

After the point has been plotted, draw a line through it back to the point where the fixed expenses line intersects the dollar axis.

3. Again, choose a volume of sales and plot the point representing total sales dollars at the activity level you have selected. In Exhibit 8–1, Luchinni again chose a volume of 600 speakers. Sales at that activity level total $150,000 (= 600 speakers × $250 per speaker). Draw a line through this point back to the origin.

The interpretation of the completed CVP graph is given in Exhibit 8–2. The anticipated profit or loss at any given level of sales is measured by the vertical distance between the total revenue line (sales) and the total expenses line (variable expenses plus fixed expenses).

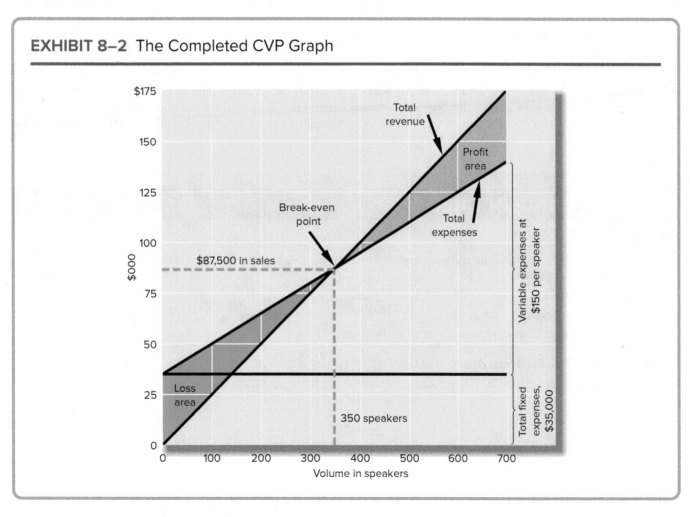

EXHIBIT 8–2 The Completed CVP Graph

Break-even occurs at the intersection point of the total revenue and total expenses lines. Thus, the break-even point of 350 speakers in Exhibit 8–2 agrees with the break-even point computed earlier.

As discussed previously, when sales are below the break-even point—in this case, 350 units—the company suffers a loss. Note that the loss (represented by the vertical distance between the total expense and total revenue lines) worsens as sales decline. When sales are above the break-even point, the company earns a profit and the size of the profit (represented by the vertical distance between the total revenue and total expense lines) increases as sales increase.

Assumptions of CVP Analysis

A number of assumptions underlie CVP analysis:

- Selling price is constant. The price of a product or service will not change as volume changes.
- Costs are linear and can be accurately divided into variable and fixed elements. The variable element is constant per unit, and the fixed element is constant in total over the entire relevant range.
- In multi-product companies, the sales mix is constant.
- In manufacturing companies, inventories do not change. The number of units produced equals the number of units sold.

While some of these assumptions may be violated in practice, the violations are usually not serious enough to compromise the basic validity of CVP analysis. For example, in most multi-product companies, the sales mix is constant enough that the results of CVP analysis are reasonably valid.

Perhaps the greatest danger lies in relying on simple CVP analysis when a manager is contemplating or experiencing significant changes in price, costs, or volume. For example, a manager might consider increasing the level of sales far beyond what the company has ever achieved before. However, even in these situations, a manager can adjust the model, as we have done in this chapter, to take into account anticipated changes in selling prices, fixed costs, and the sales mix that would otherwise violate the assumptions. For example, in a decision that would affect fixed costs, the change in fixed costs can be explicitly taken into account, as illustrated previously in the Acoustic Concepts example.

As another example, a manager may be forced to sell below the planned (or assumed) sales price due to variations in critical factors such as demand, season, competition, location, economy, interest rate, inflation, and customer willingness to pay. In such situations, continuing to rely on the results of a CVP analysis performed using a different set of numbers would be too risky (and perhaps a little naive).

CONCEPT CHECK

1. The contribution margin ratio always increases when (you may select more than one answer):
    a. Sales increase.
    b. Fixed costs decrease.
    c. Total variable costs decrease.
    d. Variable costs as a percentage of sales decrease.

*Note to student: See **Guidance Answers** online.*

Some Applications of CVP Concepts

LO2   ● **Apply**

CC5: Apply the CVP framework to different managerial decisions.

Bob Luchinni, the accountant at Acoustic Concepts, wanted to demonstrate to the company's president, Prem Narayan, how the CVP concepts developed so far can be used in planning and decision making. The CVP framework provides management with the following *levers:* unit variable costs, fixed costs, and selling price. These levers can be used either singly or in combination to influence the sales volume and thereby affect the company's profitability. The objective of CVP analysis is to determine this impact on profits, which will depend on the effect of the policy on total contribution margin and how that effect flows through to profits. The challenge for managers is that many proposed policies can involve changes to both revenues and costs. The ultimate impact on the bottom line—the company's profits—is rarely transparent without a careful analysis. In the following examples, let us see which combination of levers management is proposing to pull, the nature of trade-offs facing management, and the effect of a proposed policy on the company's profits.

We will use the following approach: (1) Determine the impact of a proposed policy on the *total* contribution margin. (2) Determine the impact of a proposed policy on fixed costs, if necessary. (3) Compare these two impacts to determine the effect on the company's profits, that is, net income.

Recall the basic data for Acoustic Concepts, which are captured in the table below:

ACOUSTIC CONCEPTS, INC. Basic Data	
Sales (number of speakers per month)	400
Selling price per speaker	$ 250
Variable costs per speaker	$ 150
Fixed expenses per month	$35,000

Example 1: Increase in Fixed Cost, Leading to an Increase in Sales Volume

The sales manager feels that a $10,000 increase in the monthly advertising budget will increase monthly sales by 30% to 520 speakers, increasing sales revenues by $30,000 from $100,000 to $130,000. Should the advertising budget be increased?

The policy proposes to pull the fixed cost lever—increase the advertising budget. Volume is predicted to increase as a result. Before a decision can be made to pull the lever, the expected impact on net income must be determined. The following table shows the effect of the proposed change in monthly advertising budget on net income:

	Current Sales	Sales With Additional Advertising Budget	Difference	Per Unit	Percentage of Sales
Sales	$100,000	$130,000	$30,000	$250	100
Less: Variable expenses	60,000	78,000*	18,000	150	60

	Current Sales	Sales With Additional Advertising Budget	Difference	Per Unit	Percentage of Sales
Contribution margin	40,000	52,000	12,000	$100	40
Less: Fixed expenses	35,000	45,000†	10,000		
Net income	$ 5,000	$ 7,000	$ 2,000		

*520 units × $150 per unit = $78,000

†$35,000 plus additional $10,000 monthly advertising budget = $45,000

The increase in the advertising budget should be approved, since it would lead to an increase in net income of $2,000. There are two shorter ways to present this solution. The first alternative solution follows:

ALTERNATIVE SOLUTION 1

	Using Sales Dollars and CM Ratio	Using Sales Units and CM per Unit
Expected total contribution margin	$130,000 × 40% = $52,000	520 × $100 = $52,000
Present total contribution margin	$100,000 × 40% = $40,000	400 × $100 = $40,000
Incremental contribution margin	$12,000	$12,000
Change in fixed costs:		
Incremental advertising expense	$10,000	$10,000
Incremental net income	$ 2,000	$ 2,000

Since in this case only the fixed costs and the sales volume change, the solution can be presented in an even shorter format, as follows:

ALTERNATIVE SOLUTION 2

	Using Sales Dollars and CM Ratio	Using Sales Units and CM per Unit
Incremental contribution margin	$30,000 × 40% = $12,000	120 × $100 = $12,000
Change in fixed costs:		
Incremental advertising expense	$10,000	$10,000
Incremental net income	$ 2,000	$ 2,000

Note that this approach does not depend on the knowledge of previous sales. Also, observe that it is unnecessary under either alternative to prepare an income statement. Both of the preceding solutions involve an **incremental analysis**, considering only those items of revenue, cost, and volume that will change if the new program is implemented. Although in each case a new income statement could have been prepared, most managers would prefer the incremental approach. It is simpler and more direct, focusing attention on the specific items involved in the decision. Finally, note that the expected impact on volume from the change in the advertising budget must be provided before the decision to implement the proposed change to the advertising budget can be made.

Example 2: Increase in Unit Variable Costs, Leading to an Increase in Sales Volume

Management is contemplating the use of higher-quality components, which would increase variable costs per unit from $150 to $160 (thereby reducing the unit contribution by $10 per speaker). The sales manager predicts that the higher quality would increase sales by 20% to 480 speakers per month. Should the higher-quality components be used?

In this example, the proposal is to pull the variable cost per unit lever. The predicted impact on sales is an increase of 80 units. Now management must determine the impact on net income of the proposed policy. The way to do this is to determine the impact on total contribution and the impact on fixed costs, and then to compare the two impacts.

The $10 increase in the unit variable costs will cause the unit contribution margin to drop from $100 to $90. The total contribution margin is expected to change as follows:

Expected total contribution margin with higher-quality components:	
480 speakers × $90 contribution margin per speaker	$43,200
Present total contribution margin:	
400 speakers × $100 contribution margin per speaker	40,000
Increase in total contribution margin	$ 3,200

Since fixed costs will not change, net income should increase by the $3,200 increase in total contribution shown previously. The higher-quality components should be used.

Example 3: Increase in Fixed Cost, Decrease in Selling Price, Leading to an Increase in Sales Volume

The sales manager would like to cut the selling price by $20 per speaker to $230 and increase the advertising budget by $15,000 per month. The sales manager argues that if these two steps are taken, unit sales will increase by 50% to 600 speakers per month. Should the changes be made?

Management is proposing to pull two levers—sales price and fixed costs—together to increase sales. A decrease of $20 per speaker in the selling price will reduce the unit contribution margin from $100 to $80. The increase in the advertising budget by $15,000 will cause fixed cost to increase by this amount. To determine the impact of these changes on net income, the effect on total contribution margin must be compared with the effect on fixed cost. This is shown in the following table:

Expected total contribution margin with higher volume due to a lower selling price and an increase in the advertising budget:	
600 speakers × $80 contribution margin per speaker	$48,000
Present total contribution margin:	
400 speakers × $100 contribution margin per speaker	40,000
Incremental contribution margin (1)	8,000
Change in fixed costs:	
Increase in advertising budget (2)	15,000
Increase (decrease) in net income (1) – (2)	($7,000)

On the basis of the information above, the changes should not be made.

Example 4: Increase in Variable Cost per Unit and Decrease in Fixed Cost, Leading to an Increase in Sales Volume

The sales manager would like to pay sales staff a commission of $15 per speaker sold, rather than pay them flat salaries that now total $6,000 per month. The sales manager is confident that the change will increase monthly sales by 15% to 460 speakers. Should the change be made?

In this example, management proposes to pull the variable cost and fixed cost levers, which is predicted to lead to an increase in sales. Paying a commission for each speaker sold instead of a flat salary will increase variable cost per speaker by $15 to $165 per speaker and reduce fixed cost by $6,000. Unit contribution margin will decrease by $15 to $85 per speaker. The impact of these changes on total contribution margin and fixed cost is shown in the following table:

Expected total contribution margin with higher volume due to a higher variable cost per unit and a decrease in fixed cost:	
460 speakers × $85 contribution margin per speaker	$39,100
Present total contribution margin:	
400 speakers × $100 contribution margin per speaker	40,000
Incremental contribution margin (1)	(900)
Change in fixed costs:	
Decrease in fixed cost from salaries avoided (2)	(6,000)
Increase (decrease) in net income (1) – (2)	$ 5,100

On the basis of the preceding analysis, the changes should be made. The company stands to increase net income by $5,100 by switching to a commission-based compensation system from the present policy of paying flat salaries.

The same conclusion can be obtained by preparing comparative income statements. This approach is shown in the following table:

	Present 400 Speakers per Month		Expected 460 Speakers per Month		Difference: Increase (Decrease) in Net Income
	Total	Per Unit	Total	Per Unit	
Sales	$100,000	$250	$115,000	$250	$15,000
Less: Variable expenses	60,000	150	75,900	165	(15,900)
Contribution margin	40,000	$100	39,100	$ 85	(900)
Less: Fixed expenses	35,000		29,000		6,000
Net income	$ 5,000		$ 10,100		$ 5,100

Example 5: Calculation of Selling Price to Meet Profit Target

Acoustic Concepts has an opportunity to make a special-order bulk sale of 150 speakers to a wholesaler if an acceptable price can be worked out. This sale will not affect the company's regular sales or its fixed cost. Variable cost is $150 per speaker. Acoustic Concepts would like to make a profit of $3,000 from this sale. What price per speaker should be quoted?

Since the special sale will not affect fixed costs, the company's profits from the sale will be $3,000 if the total contribution margin from the sale is also $3,000. Since the sale is for 150 speakers, the contribution margin per speaker has to be $3,000 ÷ 150 = $20. Given a variable cost of $150 per speaker, the desired selling price per speaker will be the variable cost per speaker plus the contribution margin per speaker, that is, $150 + $20 = $170. The company should quote a price of $170 per speaker. The calculation is summarized as follows:

Variable cost per speaker	$150
Desired profit per speaker:	
$3,000 ÷ 150 speakers	20
Quoted price per speaker	$170

This example is different from the previous examples because it does not involve tracing the impact of pulling a combination of levers on profits. Instead, it illustrates the use of the CVP framework to determine a pricing policy for a special sales order, given costs and a profit target. The CVP framework is flexible and can aid management in planning and decision making.

Importance of the Contribution Margin

CVP analysis seeks the most profitable combination of variable cost per unit, fixed cost, and selling price. These are levers available for management to pull to influence first volume and ultimately the company's profits. The examples we presented show that, without a framework to analyze the effect of pulling the levers, management cannot determine if a proposed policy to improve profits should be adopted.

The challenge is that using a combination of levers involves trade-offs: you have to spend money to make money. Whether you come out ahead at the end will depend on whether the incremental total contribution compares favourably with the incremental fixed cost. Exhibit 8–3, a summary of Examples 1 to 4, illustrates this point.

EXHIBIT 8–3 Summary of CVP Examples Illustrating the Use of the CVP Framework for Decision Making

	Example 1	Example 2	Example 3	Example 4
Revenue lever: Selling price	Unchanged	Unchanged	Decrease by $20	Unchanged per speaker
Cost lever: Variable cost per unit	Unchanged	Increase by $10	Unchanged	Increase by $15 per speaker
Cost lever: Fixed cost	Increase by $10,000	Unchanged	Increase by $15,000	Decrease by $6,000
Predicted impact on volume	Increase by 120 speakers	Increase by 80 speakers	Increase by 200 speakers	Increase by 60 speakers
Calculated impact on total contribution margin	Increase by $12,000	Increase by $3,200	Increase by $8,000	Decrease by $900
Calculated impact on net income	Increase by $2,000	Increase by $3,200	Decrease by $7,000	Increase by $5,100

In Example 1, management predicts an increase in volume from increasing the fixed cost. The increase in volume causes the total contribution margin to increase. Profits increase because the increase in contribution margin is greater than the increase in the fixed cost. In this example, management spends money (increases fixed cost) to make money (increase profits).

In Example 2, a volume increase is obtained because of an increase in variable cost per unit. Although the unit contribution margin decreased, the *total* contribution margin increased because of the increase in volume. The increase in the total contribution margin flows through to income because the fixed costs are unchanged.

In Example 3, management decreases unit price and increases fixed cost. The increase in volume from taking these steps does not increase the total contribution margin sufficiently to cover the increase in fixed costs. Profits are reduced. Therefore, the proposed policy is rejected. Note here that simply looking at the total contribution margin alone is not enough if fixed costs are also changed. The correct conclusion can only be reached if the impact on the total contribution margin is compared with the impact on fixed cost.

In Example 4, management decreases fixed expenses and simultaneously increases variable cost per unit. The unit contribution margin is reduced. Management predicts an increase in volume from the steps taken. But the total contribution margin *decreases* from its current level because the increase in volume cannot offset the effect of the reduction in the unit contribution margin. Nonetheless, profits increase because fixed expense is reduced by more than the decrease in the total contribution margin. This example illustrates that a decline in contribution margin need not cause too much distress, provided fixed costs are reduced even more.

In general, these examples illustrate that careful analysis of a policy using the CVP framework is important to determining the impact on profits, especially when there are increases (or decreases) to both costs and revenue. The key is that the effect of a policy on the total contribution margin must be compared with the effect of the policy on fixed cost. This is clear from Exhibit 8–3, where you can see that the impact on the bottom line follows from subtracting the impact on the total contribution margin from the impact on the fixed cost.

Finally, note that the size of the unit contribution margin (or the size of the CM ratio) will heavily influence the steps a company is willing to take to improve profits. For example, the greater the unit contribution margin for a product, the greater the amount a company will spend to increase sales volume by a given percentage (look at Example 1 again). This explains why companies with high unit contribution margins (like car makers) advertise so heavily, while companies with low unit contribution margins (such as appliance makers) tend to spend much less on advertising.

IN BUSINESS

MORENO TURNS THE LOS ANGELES ANGELS AROUND

When Arturo Moreno bought Major League Baseball's Los Angeles Angels (now called the Los Angeles Angels of Anaheim) in 2003, the team was drawing 2.3 million fans and losing $5.5 million per year. Moreno immediately cut prices to attract more fans and increase profits. For his first spring training game, he reduced the price of selected tickets from $12 to $6. By increasing attendance, Moreno understood that he would sell more food and souvenirs. He dropped the price of draft beer by $2 and cut the price of a baseball cap from $20 to $7.

The Angels now consistently draw about 3.4 million fans per year. This growth in attendance helped double stadium sponsorship revenue to $26 million, and it motivated the Fox Sports Network to pay the Angels $500 million to broadcast all of their games for the next 10 years. The team is now valued at $718 million, according to *Forbes*.

Source: Matthew Craft, "Moreno's Math," *Forbes*, May 11, 2009, pp. 84–87; http://www.forbes.com/teams/los-angeles-angels-of-anaheim/.

Break-Even Analysis

LO2   • **Apply**

CC6: Compute break-even sales using different approaches.

CVP analysis is sometimes referred to simply as *break-even analysis*. This is unfortunate because break-even analysis is just a special case of CVP analysis. Break-even analysis is designed to answer such questions as those asked by Prem Narayan, the president of Acoustic Concepts, concerning how far sales could drop before the company began to lose money.

Break-Even Computations

Previously in the chapter, we defined the break-even point as the level of sales at which the company's profit is zero. The break-even point can be computed using either the *equation method* or the *contribution margin method*—the two methods are equivalent.

THE EQUATION METHOD

The **equation method** centres on the contribution approach to the income statement illustrated previously. Recall that the format of this income statement can be expressed in equation form as follows:

$$\text{Profits} = \text{Sales} - (\text{Variable expenses} + \text{Fixed expenses})$$

Rearranging this equation slightly yields the following equation, which is widely used in CVP analysis:

$$\text{Sales} = \text{Variable expenses} + \text{Fixed expenses} + \text{Profits}$$

At the break-even point, profits are zero. Therefore, the break-even point can be computed by finding that point where sales equal the total of variable expenses and fixed expenses. For Acoustic Concepts, the break-even point in unit sales, Q, can be computed as follows:

$$\text{Sales} = \text{Variable expenses} + \text{Fixed expenses} + \text{Profits}$$

$$
\begin{aligned}
\$250Q &= \$150Q + \$35{,}000 + \$0 \\
\$100Q &= \$35{,}000 \\
Q &= \$35{,}000 \div \$100 \text{ per speaker} \\
Q &= 350 \text{ speakers}
\end{aligned}
$$

where

$$
\begin{aligned}
Q &= \text{Number (quantity) of speakers sold} \\
\$250 &= \text{Unit sales price} \\
\$150 &= \text{Unit variable expenses} \\
\$35{,}000 &= \text{Total fixed expenses}
\end{aligned}
$$

The break-even point in sales dollars can be computed by multiplying the break-even level of unit sales by the selling price per unit:

$$350 \text{ speakers} \times \$250 \text{ per speaker} = \$87{,}500$$

The break-even in total sales dollars, X, can also be directly computed as follows:

$$
\begin{aligned}
\text{Sales} &= \text{Variable expenses} + \text{Fixed expenses} + \text{Profits} \\
X &= 0.60X + \$35{,}000 + \$0 \\
0.40X &= \$35{,}000 \\
X &= \$35{,}000 \div 0.40 \\
X &= \$87{,}500
\end{aligned}
$$

where

$$
\begin{aligned}
X &= \text{Total sales dollars} \\
0.60 &= \text{Variable expense ratio } (= \text{Variable expenses} \div \text{Sales}) \\
\$35{,}000 &= \text{Total fixed expenses}
\end{aligned}
$$

Firms often have data available only in percentage or ratio form, and the approach we have just illustrated must then be used to find the break-even point. Note that the use of ratios in the equation yields a break-even point in sales dollars, rather than in units sold. The break-even point in units sold is the following:

$$\$87{,}500 \div \$250 \text{ per speaker} = 350 \text{ speakers}$$

 DECISION POINT

RECRUIT

Assume that you are being recruited by Connexus Corp. and have an interview scheduled for later this week. You are interested in working for this company for a variety of reasons. In preparation for the interview, you did some research and gathered the following information.

Connexus is a company set up by two young engineers, George Searle and Humphrey Chen, to allow consumers to order music CDs on their cellphones. Suppose you heard on the radio a track from a CD that you would like to own. If you subscribed to the Connexus service, you would pick up your cellphone, type "*CD" and the radio station's frequency and the time you heard the song, and the CD would be on its way to you.

Connexus charges about $17 for a CD, including shipping. The company pays its supplier about $13, leaving a contribution margin of $4 per CD. Because of the fixed costs of running the service (about $1,850,000 a year), Searle expects the company to lose about $1.5 million in its first year of operations on sales of 88,000 CDs.

What are your initial impressions of this company on the basis of the information you gathered? What other information would you want to obtain during the job interview?

Source: Adapted from Peter Kafka, "Play It Again," *Forbes*, July 26, 1999, p. 94.

*Note to student: See **Guidance Answers** online.*

THE CONTRIBUTION MARGIN METHOD

The **contribution margin method** is actually just a shortcut version of the equation method already described. The approach centres on the idea that each unit sold provides a certain amount of contribution margin that goes toward covering fixed costs. To find how many units must be sold to break even, divide the total fixed expenses by the unit contribution margin:

$$\text{Break-even point in units sold} = \frac{\text{Fixed expenses}}{\text{Unit contribution margin}}$$

Each speaker generates a contribution margin of $100 (= $250 selling price − $150 variable expenses). Since the total fixed expenses are $35,000, the break-even point is computed as follows:

$$\frac{\text{Fixed expenses}}{\text{Unit contribution margin}} = \frac{\$35,000}{\$100 \text{ per speaker}} = 350 \text{ speakers}$$

A variation on this method uses the CM ratio instead of the unit contribution margin. The result is the break-even in total sales dollars, rather than in total units sold:

$$\text{Break-even point in total sales dollars} = \frac{\text{Fixed expenses}}{\text{CM ratio}}$$

In the Acoustic Concepts example, the calculations are as follows:

$$\frac{\text{Fixed expenses}}{\text{CM ratio}} = \frac{\$35,000}{0.40} = \$87,500$$

This approach, based on the CM ratio, is particularly useful when a company has multiple product lines and wishes to compute a single break-even point for the company as a whole. More is said on this in Appendix 8A.

IN BUSINESS

COST OVERRUNS INCREASE THE BREAK-EVEN POINT

When Airbus launched the A380 800-seat jetliner in 2000, the company said it would need to sell 250 units to break even on the project. By 2006, Airbus was admitting that more than $3 billion of cost overruns had raised the project's break-even point to 420 airplanes. Although at that time Airbus had fewer than 170 orders for the A380, the company remained optimistic that it would sell 751 units by 2026. Affected by internal and external factors, both Airbus and its rival, Boeing, have been struggling to acquire new sales for their superjumbo planes. Despite facing difficulties in securing orders for the A380, Airbus had reassured its investors that A380 would meet production break-even in 2015. As of May 2016, the company had 319 firm orders and delivered 190 of them (just under 60%).

Sources: Daniel Michaels, "Embattled Airbus Lifts Sales Target for A380 to Profit," *The Wall Street Journal*, October 20, 2006, p. A6; http://www.airbus.com/company/market/orders-deliveries/; Robert Wall, "Ten Years of the Airbus A380, but Demand Remains Soft," *The Wall Street Journal*, April 26, 2015, http://www.wsj.com/articles/ten-years-of-the-airbus-a380-but-demand-remains-soft-1430052393; David Kaminski-Morrow, "Airbus Assures on A380 Break-Even This Year," *Flight Global*, February 27, 2015, https://www.flightglobal.com/news/articles/airbus-assures-on-a380-break-even-this-year-409534/; http://www.reuters.com/article/airbus-group-a-idUSP6N12L01H; http://www.airbus.com/tools/airbusfor/analysts/

IN BUSINESS

LEAN MANUFACTURING HELPS BREAK EVEN

What does lean manufacturing have to do with breaking even? Recall from Chapter 1 that implementing lean business principles can help companies reduce costs, which means lower sales revenues are required to break even. This is exactly what 60-year-old Groupe Bocenor Inc. did. The company, which had three plants in Quebec and over 500 employees, was a leading manufacturer of doors and windows, with customers in Canada and the United States. Groupe Bocenor used a number of different strategies to improve its earnings, including implementing elements of a lean manufacturing program, which helped substantially lower the break-even point of its manufacturing operation. However, due to other factors, the company posted negative earnings before interest, income taxes, depreciation, and amortization (EBITDA) in 2007.

The company went bankrupt in 2011 when it was unable to pay its suppliers due to a cash crunch from which it could not recover. The lesson here is that even if improvement in costs through innovative cost management techniques is achieved, without volume and adequate revenues, it is impossible to repaint a red bottom line and make it black.

Sources: "Fiscal 2006–2007: Groupe Bocenor Completes Its Restructuring and Intensifies Its Product and Market Development," *Canada NewsWire,* May 17, 2007, p. 1; http://www.winnipegfreepress.com/business/quebec-window-door-firm-bankrupt-131910558.html?story=Quebec%20window,%20door%20firm%20bankrupt.

CONCEPT CHECK

2. Assume the selling price per unit is $30, the contribution margin ratio is 40%, and the total fixed cost is $60,000. What is the break-even point in unit sales?
   a. 2,000
   b. 3,000
   c. 4,000
   d. 5,000

*Note to student: See **Guidance Answers** online.*

Target Profit Analysis

LO2 • **Apply**

CC7: Compute the sales needed to achieve a target profit, including the effect of income tax on this analysis.

CVP formulas can be used to determine the sales volume needed to achieve a target profit. Suppose that Prem Narayan would like Acoustic Concepts to earn a target profit of $40,000 per month. How many speakers would have to be sold?

THE CVP EQUATION

One approach is to use the equation method. Instead of solving for the unit sales where profits are zero, you solve for the unit sales where profits are $40,000, as follows:

$$\text{Sales} = \text{Variable expenses} + \text{Fixed expenses} + \text{Profits}$$

$$\$250Q = \$150Q + \$35,000 + \$40,000$$

$$\$100Q = \$75,000$$

$$Q = \$75,000 \div \$100 \text{ per speaker}$$

$$Q = 750 \text{ speakers}$$

where

$$Q = \text{Number of speakers sold}$$

$$\$250 = \text{Unit sales price}$$

$$\$150 = \text{Unit variable expenses}$$

$$\$35,000 = \text{Total fixed expenses}$$

$$\$40,000 = \text{Target profit}$$

Thus, the target profit can be achieved by selling 750 speakers per month, which represents $187,500 in total sales (= $250 per speaker × 750 speakers).

THE CONTRIBUTION MARGIN APPROACH

A second approach involves expanding the contribution margin formula to include the target profit, as follows:

$$\text{Unit sales to attain the target profit} = \frac{\text{Fixed expenses} + \text{Target profit}}{\text{Unit contribution margin}}$$

$$= \frac{\$35,000 + \$40,000}{\$100 \text{ per speaker}}$$

$$= 750 \text{ speakers}$$

This approach gives the same answer as the equation method, since it is simply a shortcut version of the equation method. Similarly, the dollar sales needed to attain the target profit can be computed as follows:

$$\text{Dollar sales to attain target profit} = \frac{\text{Fixed expenses} + \text{Target profit}}{\text{CM ratio}}$$

$$= \frac{\$35,000 + \$40,000}{0.40}$$

$$= \$187,500$$

Likewise, this approach gives the same answer as the equation method, since it is simply a shortcut version of the equation method.

Often, companies will state their desired target profit level as a percentage of sales rather than in dollars. For example, assume that Acoustic Concepts wishes to earn a profit equivalent to 20% of its sales. What should the sales be?

THE CVP EQUATION

We can use the following equation to compute the required sales:

$$\text{Sales} = \text{Variable expenses} + \text{Fixed expenses} + \text{Profits}$$

$$X = 0.60X + \$35{,}000 + 0.20X$$

$$X = 0.80X + \$35{,}000$$

$$0.20X = \$35{,}000$$

$$X = \$35{,}000 \div 0.20$$

$$X = \$175{,}000$$

At this level of sales, variable expenses will be \$105,000 (= 60% of \$175,000), which means that total expenses will be \$140,000 (= \$105,000 + \$35,000). The resulting profit will amount to \$35,000 (= the required 20% of \$175,000).

The Effect of Income Tax

We did not include taxes in our discussion of target profit analysis; however, most organizations (definitely for-profit businesses) are required to pay income tax.

Assume a 40% income tax rate. How will this change the analysis? In order to conduct the analysis, we must first convert the target after-tax income into before-tax income, and then compute the required sales level exactly as we did before (in the no-tax situation). Why should we convert the target profit into before-tax numbers? We do this because our first measure of income on an income statement is a before-tax measure. Sales minus costs results in a before-tax measure of income, which then attracts income tax.

How do we convert after-tax income into its before-tax equivalent? The formula is simple:

$$\text{After-tax income or ATI} = (1 - t) \times \text{Before-tax income (or BTI)}$$

$$\text{BTI} = \text{ATI} \div (1 - t)$$

Recall our example in which the unit selling price was \$250, the unit variable cost was \$150, and annual fixed expenses were \$35,000. We will use this basic data in illustrating the effect of income taxes on target profit analysis, that is, computing the sales level required to achieve a certain target profit. For the purpose of this analysis, we will use an income tax rate of 40%.

- *Case 1.* Assume that the company's target ATI is \$40,000. We convert this amount into the target BTI as follows:

$$\text{BTI} = \$40{,}000 \div (1 - 0.40)$$

$$= \$66{,}667$$

The unit sales required to achieve the target profit can now be computed as follows:

$$\text{(Fixed expenses + BTI)} \div \text{Unit contribution margin}$$

$$= \quad (\$35,000 + \$66,667) \div \$100$$

$$\approx \quad 1,017 \text{ units}$$

We can compute the sales in dollars by multiplying 1,017 units by the sales price of $250, which will result in $254,250.

- *Case 2.* Assume that the company's ATI is 20% of sales revenue (X). We convert this into the target BTI as follows:

$$\text{BTI} \quad = \quad 0.20X \div (1 - 0.40)$$

$$= \quad 0.333X$$

The sales revenue (X) required to achieve the target profit can now be computed as follows:

$$X \quad = \quad 0.60X + \$35,000 + 0.33X$$

$$0.067X \quad = \quad \$35,000$$

$$X \quad = \quad \$35,000 \div 0.067$$

$$X \quad = \quad \$522,388$$

We can compute the sales in units by dividing $522,388 by the sales price of $250, which will result in approximately 2,090 units.

Note that when we consider taxes, the sales required to achieve the target profit increase significantly compared with the previous *tax-free* situation. Tax is a real expense for organizations that they must consider in their planning and decision making.

The Margin of Safety

LO2 • **Know** • **Apply**

CC8: Explain and compute the margin of safety.

The **margin of safety** is the excess of budgeted (or actual) sales over the break-even volume of sales. It is the amount by which sales can drop before losses begin to be incurred. The higher the margin of safety, the lower the risk of not breaking even. The formula for its calculation is as follows:

$$\text{Margin of safety} = \text{Total budgeted (or actual) sales} - \text{Break-even sales}$$

The margin of safety can also be expressed in percentage form. This percentage is obtained by dividing the margin of safety in dollars by total sales, as follows:

$$\text{Margin of safety percentage} = \frac{\text{Margin of safety in dollars}}{\text{Total budgeted or actual sales}}$$

The calculations for the margin of safety for Acoustic Concepts are as follows:

Sales (at the current volume of 400 speakers) (a)	$100,000
Break-even sales (at 350 speakers)	87,500
Margin of safety (in dollars) (b)	$ 12,500
Margin of safety as a percentage of sales, (b) ÷ (a)	12.5%

This margin of safety means that, at the current level of sales and with the company's current prices and cost structure, a reduction in sales of $12,500, or 12.5%, would result in just breaking even.

In a single-product firm such as Acoustic Concepts, the margin of safety can also be expressed in terms of the number of units sold by dividing the margin of safety in dollars by the selling price per unit. In this case, the margin of safety is 50 speakers (= $12,500 ÷ $250 per speaker = 50 speakers).

DECISION POINT

LOAN OFFICER

Ketan Trivedi and Bharat Shah, former oil merchants from Ahmedabad, India, opened a fast-food restaurant in Calgary, in hopes of establishing a chain in Canada. They called their restaurant Chai and Snacks. For $6 per serving, Chai and Snacks offers 12 homemade snacks every day. Trivedi and Shah report that in their first year of operation, they netted $210,000 on sales of $700,000. They report that it costs about $2 per serving to make the snacks.

Assume that Trivedi and Shah have approached your bank for a loan. As the loan officer, you should consider a variety of factors, including the company's margin of safety. Assuming that other information about the company is favourable, would you consider the company's margin of safety to be comfortable enough to extend the loan?

*Note to student: See **Guidance Answers** online.*

MANAGERIAL ACCOUNTING IN ACTION

THE WRAP-UP

It is Thursday morning, and Prem Narayan and Bob Luchinni are discussing the results of Luchinni's analysis.

Narayan: Bob, everything you have shown me is pretty clear. I can see what impact some of the sales manager's suggestions would have on our profits. Some of those suggestions are quite good, and some are not so good. I also understand that our break-even is 350 speakers, and so we have to make sure we don't slip below that level of sales. What really bothers me is that we are only selling 400 speakers a month now. What did you call the 50-speaker buffer?

Acoustic Concepts, Inc.

Luchinni: That's the margin of safety.

Narayan: Such a small buffer makes me very nervous. What can we do to increase the margin of safety?

Luchinni: We have to increase total sales or decrease the break-even point or both.

Narayan: And to decrease the break-even point, we have to either decrease our fixed expenses or increase our unit contribution margin?

Luchinni: Exactly.

Narayan: And to increase our unit contribution margin, we must either increase our selling price or decrease the variable cost per unit?

Luchinni: Correct.

Narayan: So, what do you suggest?

Luchinni: Well, the analysis doesn't tell us which of these we should do, but it does indicate that we have a potential problem here.

> **Narayan:** If you don't have any immediate suggestions, I would like to call a general meeting next week to discuss ways we can work on increasing the margin of safety. I think everyone will be concerned about how vulnerable we are to even small downturns in sales.
>
> **Luchinni:** I agree. This is something everyone will want to work on.

CONCEPT CHECK

3. Assume a company produces one product that sells for $55, has a variable cost per unit of $35, and has fixed costs of $100,000. How many units must the company sell to earn a target profit of $50,000?
   a. 7,500 units
   b. 10,000 units
   c. 12,500 units
   d. 15,000 units

4. Given the same facts as in Concept Check 3 above, if the company exactly meets its target profit, what will be its margin of safety in sales dollars?
   a. $110,000
   b. $127,500
   c. $137,500
   d. $150,000

*Note to student: See **Guidance Answers** online.*

CVP Considerations in Choosing a Cost Structure

As stated in Chapter 6, cost structure refers to the relative proportion of fixed and variable costs in an organization. An organization often has some latitude in trading off between these two types of costs. For example, fixed investments in automated equipment can reduce variable labour costs. In this section, we discuss the choice of a cost structure. We focus on the impact of cost structure on profit stability, in which *operating leverage* pays a key role.

Cost Structure and Profit Stability

LO2 • **Know**

CC9: Explain the effect of cost structure on a company's profitability.

When a manager has some latitude in trading off between fixed and variable costs, which cost structure is better: high variable costs and low fixed costs, or vice versa? No single answer is possible; there might be advantages either way, depending on the circumstances. For example, refer to the income statements given below for two blueberry farms. Flat Farm depends on temporary foreign workers to pick its berries by hand, whereas Balloon Farm has invested in expensive berry-picking machines. Consequently, Flat Farm has higher variable costs, but Balloon Farm has higher fixed costs:

	Flat Farm		Balloon Farm	
	Amount	Percentage	Amount	Percentage
Sales	$100,000	100%	$100,000	100%
Less: Variable expenses	60,000	60	30,000	30
Contribution margin	40,000	40%	70,000	70%
Less: Fixed expenses	30,000		60,000	
Net income	$ 10,000		$ 10,000	

Determining which farm has the better cost structure depends on many factors, including the long-term trend in sales, year-to-year fluctuations in the level of sales, and the attitude of the owners toward risk. If sales are expected to be above $100,000 in the future, then Balloon Farm probably has the better cost structure. The reason is that its CM ratio is higher, and its profits will therefore increase more rapidly as sales increase. To illustrate, assume that each farm experiences a 10% increase in sales without any increase in fixed costs. The new income statements would be as follows:

	Flat Farm		Balloon Farm	
	Amount	Percentage	Amount	Percentage
Sales	$110,000	100%	$110,000	100%
Less: Variable expenses	66,000	60	33,000	30
Contribution margin	44,000	40%	77,000	70%
Less: Fixed expenses	30,000		60,000	
Net income	$ 14,000		$ 17,000	

Balloon Farm has experienced a greater increase in net income due to its higher CM ratio even though the increase in sales was the same for both farms.

What if sales drop below $100,000 from time to time? What are the break-even points of the two farms? What are their margins of safety? The computations needed to answer these questions are carried out using the contribution margin method, as shown below:

	Flat Farm	Balloon Farm
Fixed expenses	$ 30,000	$ 60,000
Contribution margin ratio	÷ 40%	÷ 70%
Break-even in total sales dollars	$ 75,000	$ 85,714
Total current sales (a)	$100,000	$100,000
Break-even sales	75,000	85,714
Margin of safety in sales dollars (b)	$ 25,000	$ 14,286
Margin of safety as a percentage of sales, (b) ÷ (a)	25.0%	14.3%

This analysis makes it clear that Flat Farm is less vulnerable to downturns than is Balloon Farm. We can identify two reasons why it is less vulnerable: (1) Due to its lower fixed expenses, Flat Farm has a lower break-even point and a higher margin of safety, as shown by the preceding computations. Therefore, it will not incur losses as quickly as Balloon Farm will in periods of sharply declining sales. (2) Due to its lower CM ratio, Flat Farm will not lose contribution margin as rapidly as Balloon Farm will when sales fall off. Thus, Flat Farm's income will be less volatile. We saw previously that this is a drawback when sales increase, but it provides more protection when sales drop.

To summarize, without knowing the future, it is not obvious which cost structure is better. Both have advantages and disadvantages. Balloon Farm, with its higher fixed costs and lower variable costs, will experience wider swings in net income as changes take place in sales, with greater profits in good years and greater losses in bad years. Flat Farm, with its lower fixed costs and higher variable costs, will enjoy greater stability in net income and will be more protected from losses during bad years, but at the cost of lower net income in good years.

IN BUSINESS

MANAGING RISK IN THE BOOK PUBLISHING INDUSTRY

CreateSpace is a self-publishing company that offers print-on-demand service. It allows for greater accessibility to authors who want to self-publish their work with lower costs and risk by efficiently bypassing traditional routes to printing books. Additionally, self-publishing provides authors with the advantage of timing, which can be a crucial factor in a book's success. The Espresso Book Machine by Oscar's Art Books is an even less expensive option for aspiring self-publishers. It is a machine that can print a high quality 100-page book in five minutes from two PDF submissions. The advantage for a modern, non-traditional self-publisher can be illustrated as follows.

Assume a typical publisher prints 10,000 copies of a new book that sells for $12.50 per unit. The publisher pays the author an advance of $20,000 to write the book and then incurs $60,000 in expenses to edit, market, and print the book. The publisher also has to pay the author a 20% royalty (or $2.50 per unit) on each book sold above 8,000 units. In this scenario, the publisher must sell 6,400 books to break even (= $80,000 in fixed costs ÷ $12.50 per unit). If all 10,000 copies are sold, the author earns $25,000 (= $20,000 advance + 2,000 copies × $2.50) and the publisher earns $40,000 (= $125,000 − $60,000 − $20,000 − $5,000).

With self-publishing platforms such as CreateSpace available, authors such as Stephen Jagger were seeing greater profits. He pays between $4 and $5 to print a book and makes a profit of $11 per book, as opposed to $2 he will receive from a traditional publisher. Books will only be printed after receiving payment from the customer online, thereby effectively doing away with inventory space requirements. Based on the level of services desired, an author could incur setup fees anywhere from $0 to $4,999. It is a small price to pay for greater control and efficiency over the process of delivering an author's work to the hands of customers.

Sources: Christopher Steiner, "Book It," *Forbes*, September 7, 2009, p. 58; Emily Jackson, "Cut the Cost Out of Self-Publishing; Espresso Book Machine Lets Writers Who Want to Avoid Traditional Publishers Print Their Work," *The Vancouver Sun*, August 16, 2010, http://search.proquest.com.cyber.usask.ca/docview/744526901/EA9FAC86FE964ED9PQ/1?accountid=14739

IN BUSINESS

A WINNING COST STRUCTURE?

The wireless telecom industry has been booming recently, especially in the developing countries. India alone had close to 430 million wireless subscribers in 2009. Given the nature of the business, the telecom industry has traditionally been a capital-intensive industry with a high proportion of fixed costs. However, with ever-increasing competition, the tariffs are low, which means that wireless operators must depend on large volumes to first break even and then earn some profits. Consequently, India's wireless operators are constantly finding ways to reduce their high dependence on fixed costs through outsourcing certain activities such as network management, and through infrastructure sharing. In doing so, companies are changing fixed costs into variable costs (usage-based costing), which has the potential of lowering unit contribution margins and therefore profits. However, the reduction in fixed costs can offset the lower contribution margins. In any case, "All's well that ends well," and that is the case of the Indian telecom industry in that carriers have delivered over 40% EBITDA margins.

Sources: M. Agrawal, "How Can Carriers Make 40% EBITDA Margin at 2 Cents/Min Tariff?" 2009, Telecom Circle site, http://www.telecomcircle.com/2009/02/carriers-ebidta, accessed August 13, 2010; B. Ramakrishna, "Redefining Business Transactions—Increasing Speed and Reducing Costs," 2009, presentation at Indian Institute of Management, Kozhikode, India, October 10, 2009.

Operating Leverage

LO2 ● **Know** ● **Apply**

CC10: Compute the degree of operating leverage and explain its usefulness.

A **lever** is a tool for multiplying force. With a lever, you can move a massive object with only a modest amount of force. In business, *operating leverage* serves a similar purpose. **Operating leverage** is a measure of sensitivity based on a company's cost structure. Operating leverage acts as a multiplier. If operating leverage is high, a small percentage increase in sales can produce a much larger percentage increase in net income.

Operating leverage can be illustrated by returning to the data for the two blueberry farms. We previously showed that a 10% increase in sales (from $100,000 to $110,000 in each farm) results in a 70% increase in the net income of Balloon Farm (from $10,000 to $17,000) and only a 40% increase in the net income of Flat Farm (from $10,000 to $14,000). Thus, for a 10% increase in sales, Balloon Farm experiences a much greater percentage increase in profits than does Flat Farm. Therefore, we can conclude that Balloon Farm has greater operating leverage than Flat Farm has.

The **degree of operating leverage (DOL)** at a given level of sales is computed by the following formula:

$$\text{Degree of operating leverage} = \frac{\text{Contribution margin}}{\text{Net income}}$$

The degree of operating leverage is a measure, at a given level of sales, of how a percentage change in sales volume will affect profits. To illustrate, the degree of operating leverage for the two farms at a $100,000 sales level would be computed as follows:

$$\text{Flat Farm:} \quad \frac{\$40,000}{\$10,000} = 4$$

$$\text{Balloon Farm:} \quad \frac{\$70,000}{\$10,000} = 7$$

Since the degree of operating leverage for Flat Farm is 4, the farm's net income grows four times as fast as its sales. Similarly, Balloon Farm's net income grows seven times as fast as its sales. Thus, if sales increase by 10%, then we can expect the net income of Flat Farm to increase by four times the current amount, or by 40%, and the net income of Balloon Farm to increase by seven times the current amount, or by 70%.

	(1)	(2)	(3)
	Percentage Increase in Sales	Degree of Operating Leverage	Percentage Increase in Net Income (1) × (2)
Flat Farm	10%	4	40%
Balloon Farm	10%	7	70%

What is responsible for the higher operating leverage at Balloon Farm? The only difference between the two farms is their cost structure. If two companies have the same total revenue and same total expense but different cost structures, then the company with the higher proportion of fixed costs in its cost structure will have higher operating leverage. Referring to our original data, when both farms have sales of $100,000 and total expenses of $90,000, one-third of Flat Farm's costs are fixed but two-thirds of Balloon Farm's costs are fixed. As a consequence, Balloon's degree of operating leverage is higher than Flat's.

The degree of operating leverage is not constant; it is greatest at sales levels near the break-even point and decreases as sales and profits rise. This can be seen from the following tabulation, which shows the degree of operating leverage for Flat Farm at various sales levels:

Sales	$75,000	$80,000	$100,000	$150,000	$225,000
Less: Variable expenses	45,000	48,000	60,000	90,000	135,000
Contribution margin (a)	30,000	32,000	40,000	60,000	90,000
Less: Fixed expenses	30,000	30,000	30,000	30,000	30,000
Net income (b)	$ –0–	$ 2,000	$ 10,000	$ 30,000	$ 60,000
Degree of operating leverage, (a) ÷ (b)	∞	16	4	2	1.5

Thus, a 10% increase in sales would increase profits by only 15% (= 10% × 1.5) if the company were operating at a $225,000 sales level, as compared with the 40% increase we computed earlier at the $100,000 sales level. The degree of operating leverage will continue to decrease the farther the company moves from its break-even point. At the break-even point, the degree of operating leverage will be infinitely large (= $30,000 contribution margin ÷ $0 net income = ∞).

A manager can use the degree of operating leverage to quickly estimate what impact various percentage changes in sales will have on profits, without the necessity of preparing detailed income statements. As shown by our examples, the effects of operating leverage can be dramatic. If a company is near its break-even point, then even small percentage increases in sales can yield large percentage increases in profits. *This explains why management will often work very hard for only a small increase in sales volume.* If the degree of operating leverage is 5, then a 6% increase in sales would translate into a 30% increase in profits. One key assumption is that the sales increases are within the relevant range of operations so that the fixed expenses remain constant.

IN BUSINESS

BOEING'S 787 DREAMLINER BATTERY WOES AND ITS PROSPECTS

In mid-January 2013, the brand new Boeing 787 airliner was grounded following unexplained incidents of fire breaking out in the lithium-ion batteries used to power the plane's electrical systems. Grounding the planes meant that airlines that relied on the planes to service various routes would have to substitute other aircraft or cancel flights and routes. Until the problem was solved, Boeing could not deliver new planes to waiting customers, who in turn would have to change plans for servicing passengers and operating on the routes intended for the 787. In the face of this problem, Boeing was maintaining that it did not expect adverse financial consequences. Indeed, the company reported that it beat analysts' earnings expectations on January 30.

How can we explain this? CVP analysis tells us to look at the possible impact on volume first. The company stated that it intended to be able to meet its production targets for 2013 of between 635 and 645 aircraft, including 60 of the 787s. So overall volume was not expected to be affected and the production volume of 787s was expected to be only marginally affected. Also, airlines had not cancelled orders already placed and were seemingly prepared to wait for Boeing to fix the problem, which speaks to the attractiveness of the airplane to meet the airlines' requirements effectively.

Will costs be affected? Recall that the costs of fixing the problem have to be absorbed by Boeing and will not factor into the operating costs of manufacturing the plane. Assuming only marginal increases in production cost from implementing the repair, the break-even point is unlikely to be affected, but the break-even point will be affected if you include the repair costs in the fixed cost base.

What about operating costs for the airlines? Boeing, logically, is saying that batteries are a replaceable component and that about 2,000 batteries are replaced across the Boeing fleet annually; the company promised it would look for opportunities to extend the service of replaceable units. It would thus seem that Boeing is confident that its volume will be relatively unaffected; its operating cost with fixes in place will be marginally affected. The airlines' operating cost will also likely not be too different and thus will not affect Boeing's margin (from airlines demanding a price break). Looked at this way, we can see why there has yet to be any significant adverse effect on Boeing's financial prospects. It will certainly be interesting to watch how this story plays out in the coming months.

Sources: http://www.foxbusiness.com/news/2013/01/30/boeing-profit-drops-sees-no-significant-impact-from-787-in-2013/; http://www.reuters.com/article/2013/02/04/boeing-dreamliner-jal-idUSL4N0B41L520130204; http://www.cnbc.com/id/100416146/ Boeing_Profit_Beats_Sees_No_2013_Impact_From_787_Grounding.

Learning Objectives Summary

LO1   UNDERSTAND THE COST–VOLUME–PROFIT ANALYSIS FRAMEWORK.

The basic tool of cost–volume–profit analysis is the contribution format income statement (also called the variable costing income statement). In the standard *absorption costing format,* the income statement groups costs into cost of goods sold (includes only production costs, both variable and fixed) and selling and administrative costs (also variable and fixed). In the *contribution margin format,* fixed costs are treated as period costs and do not flow through inventory. In the short run, when a company cannot alter the asset base and thus its fixed cost due to commitments already made for the operating year, the fixed costs become irrelevant to decision making. Thus, the analysis focuses on the contribution margin. The unit contribution margin, which is the difference between a unit's selling price and its variable cost, indicates how net operating income will change as a result of selling one more or one less unit. The contribution margin ratio is the unit contribution margin divided by the unit selling price, or the total contribution margin divided by the total sales. The contribution margin ratio (CM ratio) is used to compute changes in contribution margin and net operating income resulting from changes in sales volume. Contribution margin concepts can be used to estimate the effects of changes in various parameters, such as variable costs, fixed costs, selling prices, and volume, on net operating income.

LO2   APPLY THE CVP ANALYSIS FRAMEWORK AND EXPLAIN THE ANALYSIS.

The CVP analysis framework provides information on sales, margins, and profitability. At the break-even level of sales, a business just covers the fixed costs. The sales needed for a desired target profit are determined by summing the desired target profit and the fixed expenses and then dividing the result by the unit contribution margin. The margin of safety is the difference between the total budgeted (or actual) sales dollars of a period and the break-even sales dollars. The cost structure is expressed by the level of the fixed costs that must be covered. The key is the mix between the fixed cost and the variable costs at a given level of sales. The degree of operating leverage is the total contribution margin divided by the net operating income and can be used to determine the impact on net operating income of a given percentage change in sales. A company with a high degree of operating leverage is especially vulnerable to loss when sales are expected to decline from the current level. But when sales are expected to increase, this company will benefit because all of the margin goes to the operating income, with the fixed cost having already been covered. The CVP framework can also be used to determine the break-even point for a multi-product company and understand the effects of shifts in the sales mix on contribution margin and the break-even point. The break-even point for a multi-product company can be computed by dividing the company's total fixed expenses by the overall contribution margin ratio, assuming that the sales mix is constant. If the sales mix shifts toward products with a lower contribution margin ratio, then more total sales are required to attain any given level of profits.

LO3   COMPARE AND CONTRAST ABSORPTION COSTING AND VARIABLE COSTING

Under absorption costing, fixed and variable product costs are assigned to products. In contrast, only variable product costs are assigned to products under variable costing. IFRS requires that both fixed and variable product costs must be assigned to products for the purposes of inventory valuation. Variable costing, on the other hand, is relevant for the purposes of decision making and includes only the variable cost of goods sold. Typically, fixed costs are irrelevant, especially for short-term decisions. The absorption costing income statement includes sales revenue, cost of goods sold, gross margin, selling and administrative expenses, and net income, whereas the variable costing income statement includes sales revenue, variable cost of goods sold, variable selling and administrative expenses, contribution margin, fixed costs, and net income. The difference between the two income amounts is due to the change in finished goods inventory level from one period to the next, multiplied by the fixed product cost per unit.

Application Competency Summary

APPLICATION COMPETENCY	DELIVERABLE	SOURCE DOCUMENTS AND KEY INFORMATION	STEPS	KNOWLEDGE COMPETENCY
Compute the contribution margin ratio. • **LO1–CC2**	*Key Information* Contribution margin to sales ratio *Report/ Document*	*Sales, Cost/ Expense Accounts in the General Ledger* Actual sales, variable and fixed costs	1. Divide the contribution margin by the sales revenue (either in total or per unit) to compute the contribution margin ratio.	Contribution margin • **LO3–CC12** (Ch. 6)

APPLICATION COMPETENCY	DELIVERABLE	SOURCE DOCUMENTS AND KEY INFORMATION	STEPS	KNOWLEDGE COMPETENCY
	No specific report	*Master Budget* Budgeted sales, variable and fixed costs		
Prepare and interpret a CVP graph. ● **LO1–CC4**	*Key Information* Cost and sales patterns Break-even point Profit and loss areas *Report/ Document* CVP graph	*Sales, Cost/ Expense Accounts in the General Ledger* Actual sales, variable and fixed costs *Master Budget* Budgeted sales, variable and fixed costs	1. Using the number of units sold as the *X*-axis and the total cost/sales (in dollars) as the *Y*-axis, draw three lines. 2. Draw a horizontal line representing the fixed cost line—this will intersect the *Y*-axis at the fixed cost point. 3. Draw a total cost line originating from the fixed cost point on the *Y*-axis—this upward-sloping straight line will increase correspondingly with the number of units sold. 4. Draw an upward-sloping sales revenue line from the origin. 5. Label the point where the total cost and sales revenue lines meet as the break-even point and the area between the two lines above (below) the break-even point as the profit (loss) area.	Variable and fixed cost behaviour ● **LO1–CC1, 3** (Ch. 6)
Apply the CVP framework to different managerial decisions. ● **LO2–CC5**	*Key Information* Impact of decision on sales, costs, and profitability *Report/ Document* No specific report	*Sales, Cost/ Expense Accounts in the General Ledger* Actual sales, variable and fixed costs *Master Budget* Budgeted sales, variable and fixed costs	1. Set up the basic profit equation using the base data, and then alter the equation by plugging in the revised numbers to assess the impact of different decisions on profitability.	Basic profit equation ● **LO1–CC1**
Compute break-even sales using different approaches. ● **LO2–CC6**	*Key Information* Sales required to incur no profit and no loss	*Sales, Cost/ Expense Accounts in the General Ledger* Actual sales,	1. Set up the basic profit equation, equate profit to zero. 2. Manipulate the two sides of the equation to group the	Basic profit equation ● **LO1–CC1** Contribution margin ratio ● **LO1–CC2**

APPLICATION COMPETENCY	DELIVERABLE	SOURCE DOCUMENTS AND KEY INFORMATION	STEPS	KNOWLEDGE COMPETENCY
	Report/ Document No specific report	variable and fixed costs *Master Budget* Budgeted sales, variable and fixed costs	fixed costs into one side of the equation. 3. Divide the fixed expenses by the contribution margin per unit (or contribution margin ratio) to compute break-even sales in units (or dollars).	
Compute the sales needed to achieve a target profit, including the effect of income tax on this analysis. ● **LO2–CC7**	*Key Information* Sales required to achieve a specified before-tax target profit *Report/ Document* No specific report	*Sales, Cost/ Expense Accounts in the General Ledger* Actual sales, variable and fixed costs *Master Budget* Budgeted sales, variable and fixed costs	1. Set up the basic profit equation, and compute the sales units by manipulating the two sides of the equation. 2. Where necessary convert the after-tax profit to its equivalent before-tax amount. 3. Divide fixed expenses plus target before-tax profit by the contribution margin per unit to compute the sales units.	Basic profit equation ● **LO1–CC1**
Explain and compute the margin of safety. ● **LO2–CC8**	*Key Information* Sales above break-even point *Report/ Document* No specific report	*Sales, Cost/ Expense Accounts in the General Ledger* Actual sales, variable and fixed costs *Master Budget* Budgeted sales, variable and fixed costs	1. Deduct the break-even sales from the actual or budgeted sales to compute the margin of safety in dollars.	Break-even point ● **LO2–CC6**
Compute the degree of operating leverage and explain its usefulness. ● **LO2–CC10**	*Key Information* Ratio of contribution margin to net income *Report/ Document* No specific report	*Contribution Margin Income Statement* Contribution margin Net income	1. Divide the contribution margin by the net income to compute the degree of operating leverage.	Contribution margin ● **LO1–CC2** Cost structure ● **LO2–CC9**

Review Problem 1: CVP Relationships

Voltar Company manufactures and sells a wireless router signal booster. The company's contribution margin income statement for the most recent year is given below:

	Total	Per Unit	Percentage of Sales
Sales (20,000 units)	$1,200,000	$60	100
Less: Variable expenses	900,000	45	?
Contribution margin	300,000	$15	?
Less: Fixed expenses	240,000		
Net operating income	$ 60,000		

Management is anxious to improve the company's profit performance and has asked for an analysis of a number of items.

Required:

1. Compute the company's CM ratio and variable expense ratio.
2. Compute the company's break-even point in both units and sales dollars. Use the equation method.
3. Assume that sales increase by $400,000 next year. If cost behaviour patterns remain unchanged, by how much will the company's net operating income increase? Use the CM ratio to determine your answer.
4. Refer to the original data. Assume that next year management wants the company to earn a minimum profit of $90,000. How many units will have to be sold to meet this target profit figure?
5. Refer to the original data. Compute the company's margin of safety in both dollar and percentage terms.
6. a. Compute the company's degree of operating leverage at the present level of sales.
   b. Assume that, through a more intense effort by the sales staff, the company's sales increase by 8% next year. By what percentage would you expect net income to increase? Use the operating leverage concept to obtain your answer.
   c. Verify your answer to part (b) by preparing a new income statement showing an 8% increase in sales.
7. In an effort to increase sales and profits, management is considering the use of a higher-quality antenna. The higher-quality antenna would increase variable costs by $3 per unit, but management could eliminate one quality inspector, who is paid a salary of $30,000 per year. The sales manager estimates that the higher-quality antenna would increase annual sales by at least 20%.
   a. Assuming that changes are made as described above, prepare a projected income statement for next year. Show data on total, per-unit, and percentage bases.
   b. Compute the company's new break-even point in both units and dollars of sales. Use the contribution margin method.
   c. Would you recommend that the changes be made?

SOLUTION TO REVIEW PROBLEM 1

1.

$$\text{CM ratio} = \frac{\text{Contribution margin}}{\text{Selling price}} = \frac{\$15}{\$60} = 25\%$$

$$\text{Variable expense ratio} = \frac{\text{Variable expense}}{\text{Selling price}} = \frac{\$45}{\$60} = 75\%$$

2.

Sales	=	Variable expenses + Fixed expenses + Profits
$60Q	=	$45Q + $240,000 + $0
$15Q	=	$240,000
Q	=	$240,000 ÷ $15 per unit
Q	=	16,000 units; or at $60 per unit, $960,000

Alternative solution:

X	=	0.75X + $240,000 + $0
0.25X	=	$240,000
X	=	$240,000 ÷ 0.25
X	=	$960,000; or at $60 per unit, 16,000 units

3.

Increase in sales	$400,000
Multiply by the CM ratio	× 25%
Expected increase in contribution margin	$100,000

Since the fixed expenses are not expected to change, net operating income will increase by the entire $100,000 increase in contribution margin computed above.

4. *Equation method:*

Sales	=	Variable expenses + Fixed expenses + Profits
$60Q	=	$45Q + $240,000 + $90,000
$15Q	=	$330,000
Q	=	$330,000 ÷ $15 per unit
Q	=	22,000 units

Contribution margin method:

$$\frac{\text{Fixed expenses + Target profit}}{\text{Contribution margin per unit}} = \frac{\$240,000 + \$90,000}{\$15 \text{ per unit}} = 22,000 \text{ units}$$

5.

$$\text{Margin of safety in dollars} = \text{Total sales} - \text{Break-even sales}$$

$$= \$1,200,000 - \$960,000 = \$240,000$$

$$\text{Margin of safety percentage} = \frac{\text{Margin of safety in dollars}}{\text{Total sales}} = \frac{\$240,000}{\$1,200,000} = 20\%$$

6.   a. $$\text{Degree of operating leverage} = \frac{\text{Contribution margin}}{\text{Net operating income}} = \frac{\$300,000}{\$60,000} = 5$$

b.

Expected increase in sales	8%
Degree of operating leverage	× 5
Expected increase in net operating income	40%

c.   If sales increase by 8%, then 21,600 units (= 20,000 × 1.08 = 21,600) will be sold next year. The new income statement will be as follows:

	Total	Per Unit	Percentage of Sales
Sales (21,600 units)	$1,296,000	$60	100
Less: Variable expenses	972,000	45	75
Contribution margin	324,000	$15	25
Less: Fixed expenses	240,000		
Net operating income	$ 84,000		

Thus, the $84,000 expected net operating income for next year represents a 40% increase over the $60,000 net operating income earned during the current year:

$$\frac{\$84,000 - \$60,000}{\$60,000} = \frac{\$24,000}{\$60,000} = 40\% \text{ increase}$$

Note from the income statement that the increase in sales from 20,000 to 21,600 units has resulted in increases in *both* total sales and total variable expenses. It is a common error to overlook the increase in variable expenses when preparing a projected income statement.

7. a. A 20% increase in sales would result in 24,000 units being sold next year: 20,000 units × 1.20 = 24,000 units.

	Total	Per Unit	Percentage of Sales
Sales (24,000 units)	$1,440,000	$60	100
Less: Variable expenses	1,152,000	48*	80
Contribution margin	288,000	$ 12	20
Less: Fixed expenses	210,000†		
Net operating income	$ 78,000		

*$45 + $3 = $48; $48 ÷ $60 = 80%
†$240,000 − $30,000 = $210,000

Note that the change in per-unit variable expenses results in a change in both the per-unit contribution margin and the CM ratio.

$$\text{Break-even point in unit sales} = \frac{\text{Fixed expenses}}{\text{Contribution margin per unit}}$$

$$= \frac{\$210,000}{\$12 \text{ per unit}} = 17,500 \text{ units}$$

b.

$$\text{Break-even point in dollar sales} = \frac{\text{Fixed expenses}}{\text{CM ratio}}$$

$$= \frac{\$210,000}{0.20} = \$1,050,000$$

c. Yes, on the basis of these data, the changes should be made. The changes will increase the company's net operating income from the present $60,000 to $78,000 per year. Although the changes will also result in a higher break-even point (17,500 units as compared with the present 16,000 units), the company's margin of safety will actually be wider than before:

$$\text{Margin of safety in dollars} = \text{Total sales} - \text{Break-even sales}$$

$$= \$1,440,000 - \$1,050,000$$

$$= \$390,000$$

As shown in part (5), the company's present margin of safety is only $240,000. Thus, several benefits will result from the proposed changes.

Questions

8–1   What is a product's CM ratio? How is this ratio useful in planning business operations?

8–2   Often, the most direct route to a business decision is to make an incremental analysis on the basis of the information available. What is meant by *incremental analysis?*

8–3   Company A's cost structure includes costs that are mostly variable, whereas company B's cost structure includes costs that are mostly fixed. In a time of increasing sales, which company will tend to realize the most rapid increase in profits? Explain.

8–4   What is meant by *operating leverage?*

8–5   "A 10% decrease in the selling price of a product will have the same impact on net income as a 10% increase in the variable expenses." Do you agree? Why, or why not?

8–6   Define *break-even point.*

8–7   Name three approaches to break-even analysis. Briefly explain how each approach works.

8–8   In response to a request from your immediate supervisor, you have prepared a CVP graph portraying the cost and revenue characteristics of your company's product and operations. Explain how the lines on the graph and the break-even point would change if (a) the selling price per unit decreased, (b) fixed costs increased throughout the entire range of activity portrayed on the graph, and (c) variable costs per unit increased.

8–9   Al's Auto Wash charges $4 to wash a car. The variable costs of washing a car are 15% of sales. Fixed expenses total $1,700 monthly. How many cars must be washed each month for Al to break even?

8–10   What is meant by *margin of safety?*

The Foundational 15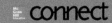

[LO1 – CC2, 3; LO2 – CC5, 6, 7, 8, 10]

Oslo Company prepared the following contribution format income statement based on a sales volume of 1,000 units (the relevant range of production is 500 units to 1,500 units):

Sales	$20,000
Variable expenses	12,000
Contribution margin	8,000
Fixed expenses	6,000
Net operating income	$ 2,000

Required:

(Answer each question independently and always refer to the original data unless instructed otherwise.)

8–1   What is the contribution margin per unit?

8–2   What is the contribution margin ratio?

8–3   What is the variable expense ratio?

8–4   If sales increase to 1,001 units, what would be the increase in net operating income?

8–5   If sales decline to 900 units, what would be the net operating income?

8–6   If the selling price increases by $2 per unit and the sales volume decreases by 100 units, what would be the net operating income?

8–7   If the variable cost per unit increases by $1, spending on advertising increases by $1,500, and unit sales increase by 250 units, what would be the net operating income?

8–8   What is the break-even point in unit sales?

8–9   What is the break-even point in sales dollars?

8–10   How many units must be sold to achieve a target profit of $5,000?

8–11   What is the margin of safety in dollars? What is the margin of safety percentage?

8–12   What is the degree of operating leverage?

8–13   Using the degree of operating leverage, what is the estimated percent increase in net operating income of a 5% increase in sales?

8–14   Assume that the amounts of the company's total variable expenses and total fixed expenses were reversed. In other words, assume that the total variable expenses are $6,000 and the total fixed expenses are $12,000. Under this scenario and assuming that total sales remain the same, what is the degree of operating leverage?

8–15   Using the degree of operating leverage that you computed in the previous question, what is the estimated percent increase in net operating income of a 5% increase in sales?

Brief Exercises

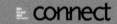

BRIEF EXERCISE 8–1
Preparing a Contribution Margin Income Statement [LO1 – CC1]

Whirly Corporation's most recent income statement is shown below:

	Total	Per Unit
Sales (12,500 units)	$450,000	$36.00
Less: Variable expenses	250,000	20.00
Contribution margin	200,000	$16.00
Less: Fixed expenses	185,000	
Net income	$ 15,000	

Required:

Prepare a new income statement under each of the following conditions (consider each case independently):

1. The sales volume increases by 1,000 units.

2. The sales volume decreases by 1,000 units.

3. The sales volume is 9,250 units.

BRIEF EXERCISE 8–2
Computing and Using the CM Ratio [LO1 – CC2, 3]

Last month, when Holiday Creations, Inc. sold 50,000 units, total sales were $200,000, total variable expenses were $120,000, and total fixed expenses were $65,000.

Required:

1. What is the company's CM ratio?
2. Estimate the change in the company's net income if it were to increase its total sales by $1,100.

BRIEF EXERCISE 8–3
Proposing Changes in Variable Costs, Fixed Costs, Selling Price, and Volume [LO2 – CC5]

Data for Hermann Corporation are shown below:

	Per Unit	Percentage of Sales
Sales price	$90	100
Less: Variable expenses	63	70
Contribution margin	$27	30

Fixed expenses are $40,000 per month, and the company is selling 2,000 units per month.

Required:

1. The marketing manager argues that a $4,000 increase in the monthly advertising budget would increase monthly sales by $9,000. Should the advertising budget be increased?
2. Refer to the original data. Management is considering using higher-quality components that would increase the variable cost by $2.00 per unit. The marketing manager believes the higher-quality product would increase sales by 10% per month. Should the higher-quality components be used?

BRIEF EXERCISE 8–4
Computing the Break-Even Point [LO2 – CC6]

Mauro Products has a single product, a woven basket whose selling price is $54, and variable cost is $45 per unit. The company's monthly fixed expenses are $26,550.

Required:

1. Compute the company's break-even point in unit sales using the equation method.
2. Compute the company's break-even point in sales dollars using the equation method and the CM ratio.
3. Compute the company's break-even point in unit sales using the contribution margin method.
4. Compute the company's break-even point in sales dollars using the contribution margin method and the CM ratio.

BRIEF EXERCISE 8–5
Preparing a CVP Graph [LO1 – CC4]

Karlik Enterprises has a single product, whose selling price is $24, and variable cost is $18 per unit. The company's monthly fixed expenses are $24,000.

Required:

1. Prepare a CVP graph for the company up to a sales level of 8,000 units.
2. Estimate the company's break-even point in unit sales using your CVP graph.

BRIEF EXERCISE 8–6
Computing Level of Sales for Target Before-Tax Profit [LO2 – CC7]

Lin Corporation has a single product, whose selling price is $180 and whose variable cost is $100 per unit. The company's monthly fixed expenses are $60,000.

Required:

1. Using the equation method, compute the unit sales that are required to earn a target before-tax profit of $10,000.
2. Using the contribution margin approach, compute the dollar sales that are required to earn a target before-tax profit of $15,000.

BRIEF EXERCISE 8–7
Computing Level of Sales for Target After-Tax Profit [LO2 – CC7]

Refer to the data in Brief Exercise 8–6. Assume a 40% tax rate, and assume that the profits in the figures shown in parts (1) and (2) are after-tax amounts.

Required:

Redo Brief Exercise 8–6.

BRIEF EXERCISE 8–8
Computing the Margin of Safety [LO2 – CC8]

Molander Corporation sells a sun umbrella used at resort hotels. Data concerning the next month's budget are given below:

Selling price	$48	per unit
Variable expense	$28	per unit
Fixed expense	$30,000	per month
Unit sales	2,000	units per month

Required:

1. Compute the company's margin of safety.
2. Compute the company's margin of safety as a percentage of its sales.

BRIEF EXERCISE 8–9
Computing Margin of Safety [LO1 – CC2; LO2 – CC8]

Brewer Corporation estimated its quarterly break-even sales for 2017 to be 45,800 units, priced at $38 each. Its actual sales for the year amounted to $7,752,000 and actual quarterly fixed expenses were $618,250.

Required:

1. Compute the annual margin of safety in units and dollars.
2. Compute the contribution margin per unit.

BRIEF EXERCISE 8–10
Computing and Using the Degree of Operating Leverage [LO2 – CC10]

Engberg Company's most recent monthly income statement is given below:

	Amount	Percentage of Sales
Sales	$96,000	100
Less: Variable expenses	57,600	60
Contribution margin	38,400	40
Less: Fixed expenses	28,000	
Net income	$10,400	

Required:

1. Compute the company's degree of operating leverage.
2. Using the degree of operating leverage, estimate the impact on net income of a 10% decrease in sales.
3. Verify your estimate from part (2) by constructing a new income statement for the company assuming a 10% decrease in sales.

BRIEF EXERCISE 8–11
Calculating Contribution Margin [LO2 – CC8]

Craig Company Inc. earns a contribution margin ratio of 36% on its main product sold at $120 per unit. Assume that the annual break-even point is 80,000 units.

Required:

1. Compute the annual fixed costs.
2. What is the contribution margin for every unit sold beyond the break-even point?

BRIEF EXERCISE 8–12
Performing a Break-Even Analysis; Calculating Fixed Costs [LO1 – CC1; LO2 – CC6]

In 2018, Paton Ltd.'s margin of safety was 24% of the break-even sales level of $2,450,000 (at $49 per unit). The (actual) annual fixed costs amounted to $860,000.

Required:

What was the annual income in 2018?

Exercises   ⁐ connect

EXERCISE 8–1
Using a Contribution Margin Format Income Statement [LO1 – CC1, 3, 4]

Miller Company's most recent income statement follows:

	Total	Per Unit
Sales (20,000 units)	$300,000	$16
Less: Variable expenses	180,000	9
Contribution margin	120,000	$ 6
Less: Fixed expenses	70,000	
Net income	$ 50,000	

Required:

Prepare a new income statement under each of the following conditions (consider each case independently):

1. The sales volume increases by 15%, and the selling price decreases by $1.00.
2. The selling price decreases by $2.50 per unit, and the sales volume increases by 25%.
3. The selling price increases by $0.50 per unit, fixed expenses increase by $20,000, and the sales volume decreases by 5%.
4. The selling price increases by 5%, variable expenses increase by 60 cents per unit, and the sales volume decreases by 10%.

EXERCISE 8–2
Calculating Break-Even Sales [LO1 – CC1; LO2 – CC6]

Klinken Corporation's contribution margin ratio on the sale of its most popular product is 42%. The product is priced at $80, annual fixed expenses are $800,000. Management is evaluating two options: (1) lowering variable costs by 10% and (2) reducing fixed expenses by 10%.

Required:

Calculate the current level of break-even sales in dollars, as well as the break-even sales for the two options.

EXERCISE 8–3
Determining Operating Leverage [LO1 – CC1; LO2 – CC10]

Magic Realm, Inc. has developed a new fantasy board game. The company sold 15,000 games last year at a selling price of $20 per game. Fixed costs associated with the game total $182,000 per year, and variable costs are $6 per game. Production of the game is entrusted to a printing contractor. Variable costs consist mostly of payments to this contractor.

Required:

1. Prepare an income statement for the game last year, and compute the degree of operating leverage.
2. Management is confident that the company can sell 18,000 games next year (an increase of 3,000 games, or 20%, over last year). Compute the following:
   a. The expected percentage increase in net income for next year.
   b. The expected total dollar net income for next year. (Do not prepare an income statement; use the degree of operating leverage to compute your answer.)

EXERCISE 8–4
Computing Break-Even Point; Creating a CVP Graph [LO2 – CC5, 6]

The Hartford Symphony Guild is planning its annual dinner and dance. The committee has assembled the following expected costs for the event:

Dinner (per person)	$ 28
Favours and program (per person)	2
Band	4,000
Rental of ballroom	1,900
Professional entertainment during intermission	2,000
Tickets and advertising	2,300

The committee members would like to charge $55 per person for the evening's activities.

Required:

1. Compute the break-even point for the dinner and dance (in terms of the number of people who must attend).
2. Assume that last year 300 people attended the dinner and dance. If the same number attend this year, what price per ticket must be charged in order to break even?
3. Refer to the original data ($55 ticket price per person). Prepare a CVP graph for the dinner and dance from a zero level of activity up to 700 tickets sold, in increments of 100. Number of people should be put on the horizontal (X) axis, and dollars should be put on the vertical (Y) axis.

EXERCISE 8–5
Calculating Break-Even Point, Target Profit, Margin of Safety, and CM Ratio [LO1 – CC2, 3; LO2 – CC6, 7, 8]

Wesley Company manufactures and sells a single product. The company's sales and expenses for last quarter follow:

	Total	Per Unit
Sales	$600,000	$40
Less: Variable expenses	420,000	28
Contribution margin	180,000	$12
Less: Fixed expenses	146,520	
Net operating income	$ 33,480	

Required:

1. What is the monthly break-even point in units sold and in sales dollars?
2. Without resorting to computations, calculate the total contribution margin at the break-even point.
3. How many units would have to be sold each quarter to earn a target profit of $18,000? Use the formula method. Verify your answer by preparing a contribution format income statement at the target level of sales.
4. Refer to the original data. Compute the company's margin of safety for the quarter in both dollar and percentage terms.
5. What is the company's CM ratio? If quarterly sales increase by $80,000 and there is no change in fixed expenses, by how much would you expect quarterly net operating income to increase? (Do not prepare an income statement; use the CM ratio to compute your answer.)

EXERCISE 8–6
Performing Break-Even and Target Profit Analysis [LO2 – CC5, 6, 7]

Krait Products sells camping equipment. One of the company's products, a camp lantern, sells for $90 per unit. Variable expenses are $63 per lantern, and fixed expenses associated with the lantern total $135,000 per month.

Required:

1. Compute the company's break-even point in number of lanterns and in total sales dollars.
2. If the variable expenses per lantern increase as a percentage of the selling price, will it result in a higher or a lower break-even point? Why? (Assume that the fixed expenses remain unchanged.)
3. At present, the company is selling 8,000 lanterns per month. The sales manager is convinced that a 10% reduction in the selling price will result in a 25% increase in the number of lanterns sold each month. Prepare two contribution format income statements: one under present operating conditions, and one as operations would appear after the proposed changes. Show both total and per-unit data on your statements.
4. Refer to the data in part (3) above. How many lanterns would have to be sold at the new selling price to yield a minimum net operating income of $72,000 per month?

EXERCISE 8–7
Interpreting the CVP Graph [LO1 – CC4]

A CVP graph, such as the one shown below, is useful for showing relationships among costs, volume, and profits in an organization.

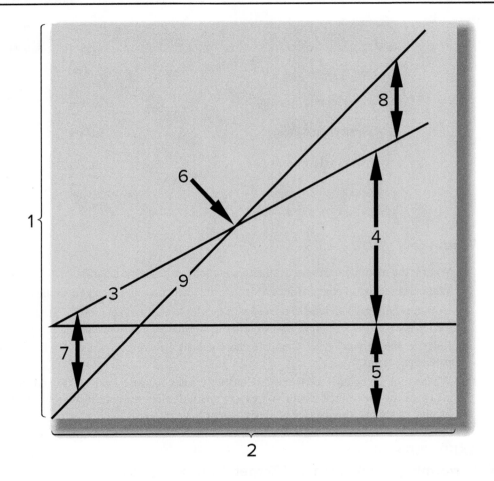

Required:

1. Identify the numbered components in the CVP graph.
2. State the effect of each of the following actions on line 3, line 9, and the break-even point. For line 3 and line 9, state whether the action will cause the line to

   - Remain unchanged.
   - Shift upward.
   - Shift downward.
   - Have a steeper slope (i.e., rotate upward).
   - Have a flatter slope (i.e., rotate downward).
   - Shift upward *and* have a steeper slope.
   - Shift upward *and* have a flatter slope.
   - Shift downward *and* have a steeper slope.
   - Shift downward *and* have a flatter slope.

In the case of the break-even point, state whether the action will cause the break-even point to

   - Remain unchanged.
   - Increase.
   - Decrease.
   - Probably change, but the direction is uncertain.

Treat each case independently.

Example. Fixed costs are increased by $20,000 each period.

Answer (see choices above):   Line 3: Shift upward.

                                                 Line 9: Remain unchanged.

                                                 Break-even point: Increase.

a. The unit selling price is decreased from $30 to $27.
b. The per-unit variable costs are increased from $12 to $15.
c. The total fixed costs are reduced by $40,000.
d. Five thousand fewer units are sold during the period than were budgeted.
e. Due to purchasing a robot to perform a task that was previously done by workers, fixed costs are increased by $25,000 per period, and variable costs are reduced by $8 per unit.
f. As a result of a decrease in the cost of materials, both unit variable costs and the selling price are decreased by $3.
g. Advertising costs are increased by $50,000 per period, resulting in a 10% increase in the number of units sold.
h. Due to paying sales staff a commission rather than a flat salary, fixed costs are reduced by $21,000 per period, and unit variable costs are increased by $6.

EXERCISE 8–8
Performing a Break-Even Analysis [LO2 – CC5, 6]

Sultan Corporation operated at its normal capacity during the current year, producing 60,000 units of its single product. Sales totalled 50,000 units at an average price of $30 per unit. Variable cost of goods sold amounted to $10 per unit, and sales commissions were paid out at $5 per unit sold. Fixed product costs, incurred uniformly throughout the year, amounted to $208,000 and fixed period costs, incurred uniformly, amounted to $18,000 per quarter.

Required:

1. Compute Sultan's break-even point in sales dollars for the current year.
2. If Sultan's fixed product costs unexpectedly increase by 10%, what is the new unit selling price that would yield the same break-even sales as before the cost increase (rounded to the nearest dollar)?

EXERCISE 8–9
Preparing a Contribution Margin Income Statement [LO1 – CC1, 4]

Fletcher Corporation prepared the following income statement for the fourth quarter in 2018.

Sales revenue (30,000 units)	$930,000
Less: Costs of goods sold	586,600
Gross margin	343,400
Less: Selling & administrative expenses	184,600
Net income	$158,800

Fletcher's annual fixed manufacturing expenses, incurred uniformly each quarter, amount to $834,400; it also pays a sales commission of $2 per unit to its sales personnel.

Required:

Prepare a contribution margin income statement for the third quarter in 2018. Include columns for total dollars, per-unit dollars, and percentages of sales.

EXERCISE 8–10
Performing a Break-Even Analysis; Tax Calculation [LO2 – CC5, 6, 7]

Carter Manufacturing Company manufactures exclusive pens which sell for $60 per unit. Its unit variable costs are $28 and fixed expenses are $384,000. The company pays income tax at the rate of 30%.

Required:

1. How many units must Carter sell to earn an after-tax income of $22,400?
2. Re-compute the sales level to earn the above-mentioned after-tax income if the tax rate changes to 40%.

EXERCISE 8–11
Calculating the CM Ratio, Margin of Safety and Degree of Operating Leverage [LO1 – CC2; LO2 – CC8, 10]

Croftsman Company recorded the following information for its main product:

Selling price per unit	$200
Costs per unit (at the normal capacity of 20,000 units):	
Direct material	50
Direct labour	30
Variable overhead	25
Fixed overhead	50
Sales commission	7.5% of sales

Required:

1. Compute the contribution margin ratio and break-even sales.
2. What is the margin of safety in dollars and units, and the degree of operating leverage?

EXERCISE 8–12
Performing Break-Even and Target Profit Analysis [LO2 – CC5, 6, 7]

Krueger Ltd. wishes to earn a before-tax profit equal to 20% of sales revenue. Its monthly fixed costs are $40,000 and contribution margin ratio is equal to 40%.

Required:

1. Determine the annual break-even sales.
2. Compute the sales level required to achieve the desired profit level.

Problems

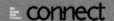

 PROBLEM 8–1
Performing Basic CVP Analysis [LO1 – CC4; LO2 – CC6, 7, 10]

Stratford Company distributes a lightweight lawn chair that sells for $15 per unit. Variable expenses are $6 per unit, and fixed expenses total $180,000 annually.

> **CHECK FIGURE**
> (2) Break-even: $300,000

Required:

Answer the following independent questions:

1. What is the product's CM ratio?
2. Use the CM ratio to determine the break-even point in sales dollars.
3. The company estimates that sales will increase by $45,000 during the coming year due to increased demand. By how much should net operating income increase?
4. Assume that the operating results for last year were as follows:

Sales	$360,000
Less: Variable expenses	144,000
Contribution margin	216,000
Less: Fixed expenses	180,000
Net operating income	$ 36,000

    a. Compute the degree of operating leverage at the current level of sales.

    b. The president expects sales to increase by 15% next year. By how much should net operating income increase?

5. Refer to the original data. Assume that the company sold 28,000 units last year. The sales manager is convinced that a 10% reduction in the selling price, combined with a $70,000 increase in advertising expenditures, would increase annual unit sales by 50%. Prepare two contribution format income statements: one showing the results of last year's operations, and one showing what the results of operations would be if these changes were made. Would you recommend that the company do as the sales manager suggests?

6. Refer to the original data. Assume again that the company sold 28,000 units last year. The president feels that it would be unwise to change the selling price. Instead, he wants to increase the sales commission by $2 per unit. He thinks that this move, combined with some increase in advertising, would double annual unit sales. By how much could advertising be increased with profits remaining unchanged? Do not prepare an income statement; use the incremental analysis approach.

PROBLEM 8–2
Performing Basic CVP Analysis; Determining Cost Structure [LO1 – CC3; LO2 – CC5, 6, 7, 9]

Memofax, Inc. produces memory enhancement software for computers. Sales have been very erratic, with some months showing a profit and some months showing a loss. The company's contribution format income statement for the most recent month is given below:

CHECK FIGURES
(1) CM ratio: 30%
(4) 17,500 units
(5) Operating income with automation: $52,000

Sales (13,500 units at $20 per unit)	$270,000
Less: Variable expenses	189,000
Contribution margin	81,000
Less: Fixed expenses	90,000
Net operating loss	$ (9,000)

Required:

1. Compute the company's CM ratio and its break-even point in both units and dollars.

2. The sales manager feels that an $8,000 increase in the monthly advertising budget, combined with an intensified effort by the sales staff, will result in a $70,000 increase in monthly sales. If the sales manager is right, what will be the effect on the company's monthly net operating income or loss? (Use the incremental approach in preparing your answer.)

3. Refer to the original data. The president is convinced that a 10% reduction in the selling price, combined with an increase of $35,000 in the monthly advertising budget, will double unit sales. What will the new contribution format income statement look like if these changes are adopted?

4. Refer to the original data. The company's advertising agency thinks that a new package would help sales. The new package being proposed would increase packaging costs by $0.60 per unit. Assuming no other changes, how many units would have to be sold each month to earn a profit of $4,500?

5. Refer to the original data. By automating, the company could slash its variable expenses in half. However, fixed costs would increase by $118,000 per month.
   a. Compute the new CM ratio and the new break-even point in both units and dollars.
   b. Assume that the company expects to sell 20,000 units next month. Prepare two contribution format income statements: one assuming that operations are not automated, and one assuming that they are.
   c. Would you recommend that the company automate its operations? Explain.

 ## PROBLEM 8–3
Performing Basic CVP Analysis and Graphing [LO1 – CC4; LO2 – CC6]

The Fashion Shoe Company operates a chain of women's shoe shops around the country. The shops carry many styles of shoes that are all sold at the same price. Sales personnel in the shops are paid a substantial commission on each pair of shoes sold (in addition to a small basic salary) in order to encourage them to be aggressive in their sales efforts.

CHECK FIGURES
(1) 12,500 pairs of shoes
(3) $6,000 loss

The following cost and revenue data relate to Shop 48 and are typical of one of the company's many outlets:

	A	B	C	D
1		*Per Pair*		
2		*of Shoes*		
3	Sales price	$ 30.00		
4				
5	Variable expenses:			
6	Invoice cost	$ 13.50		
7	Sales commission	4.50		
8	Total variable expenses	$ 18.00		
9				
10		*Annual*		
11	Fixed expenses:			
12	Advertising	$ 30,000		
13	Rent	20,000		
14	Salaries	100,000		
15	Total fixed expenses	$150,000		

Required:

1. Calculate the annual break-even point in dollar sales and in unit sales for Shop 48.

2. Prepare a CVP graph showing cost and revenue data for Shop 48 from a zero level of activity up to 20,000 pairs of shoes sold each year. Clearly indicate the break-even point on the graph.

3. If 12,000 pairs of shoes are sold in a year, what would be Shop 48's net income or loss?

4. The company is considering paying the store manager of Shop 48 an incentive commission of 75 cents per pair of shoes (in addition to the salesperson's commission). If this change is made, what will be the new break-even point in dollar sales and in unit sales?

5. Refer to the original data. As an alternative to part (4), the company is considering paying the store manager 50 cents in commission on each pair of shoes sold in excess of the break-even point. If this change is made, what will be the shop's net income or loss if 15,000 pairs of shoes are sold?

6. Refer to the original data. The company is considering eliminating sales commissions entirely in its shops and increasing fixed salaries by $31,500 annually. If this change is made, what will be the new break-even point in dollar sales and unit sales for Shop 48? Would you recommend that the change be made? Explain.

 PROBLEM 8–4

Computing Break-Even Sales and Degree of Operating Leverage [LO2 – CC6, 10]

Klyne Corporation manufactures pharmaceutical products that are sold through a network of sales agents. The agents are paid a commission of 18% of sales. The income statement for the year ending December 31, 2017, is as follows:

CHECK FIGURE

(2) $18.6 million

KLYNE CORPORATION
Income Statement
For the Year Ending December 31, 2017

Sales		$26,000,000
Cost of goods sold		
Variable	$11,700,000	
Fixed	2,870,000	14,570,000
Gross margin		11,430,000
Selling and marketing expenses		
Commissions	4,680,000	
Fixed costs	3,420,000	8,100,000
Operating income		$ 3,330,000

Klyne is considering hiring its own sales staff to replace the network of agents. Klyne will pay its salespeople a commission of 10% and incur fixed costs of $2,080,000.

Required:

1. Calculate Klyne Corporation's break-even point in sales dollars for the year 2017.
2. Calculate Klyne Corporation's break-even point in sales dollars for the year 2017 if the company had hired its own sales force to replace the network of agents.
3. Calculate the degree of operating leverage at sales of $26,000,000, considering (a) Klyne uses sales agents and (b) Klyne employs its own staff. Describe the advantages and disadvantages of each alternative.
4. If Klyne increases the commission paid to its sales staff to 15%, keeping all other costs the same, how much revenue (in dollars) would Klyne have to generate to earn the same operating income it did in 2017?

PROBLEM 8–5
Various CVP Questions: Break-Even Point; Cost Structure; Target Sales [LO1 – CC2, 3; LO2 – CC5, 6, 7]

Tyrene Products manufactures recreational equipment. One of the company's products, a skateboard, sells for $37.50. The skateboards are manufactured in an antiquated plant that relies heavily on direct labour workers. Thus, variable costs are high, totalling $22.50 per skateboard, of which 60% is direct labour cost.

Over the past year the company sold 40,000 skateboards, with the following operating results:

CHECK FIGURES
(2) Break-even: 40,000 skateboards;
(6a) 43,000 skateboards

Sales (40,000 skateboards)	$1,500,000
Variable expenses	900,000
Contribution margin	600,000
Fixed expenses	480,000
Net operating income	$ 120,000

Management is anxious to maintain and perhaps even improve its present level of income from the skateboards.

Required:

1. Compute (a) the CM ratio and the break-even point in skateboards, and (b) the degree of operating leverage at last year's level of sales.

2. Due to an increase in labour rates, the company estimates that variable costs will increase by $3 per skateboard next year. If this change takes place and the selling price per skateboard remains constant at $37.50, what will be the new CM ratio and the new break-even point in skateboards?

3. Refer to the data in (2) above. If the expected change in variable costs takes place, how many skateboards will have to be sold next year to earn the same net operating income, $120,000, as last year?

4. Refer again to the data in (2) above. The president has decided that the company may have to raise the selling price of its skateboards. If Tyrene Products wants to maintain *the same CM ratio as last year,* what selling price per skateboard must it charge next year to cover the increased labour costs?

5. Refer to the original data. The company is considering the construction of a new, automated plant. The new plant would slash variable costs by 40%, but it would cause fixed costs to increase by 90%. If the new plant is built, what would be the company's new CM ratio and new break-even point in skateboards?

6. Refer to the data in (5) above.

   a. If the new plant is built, how many skateboards will have to be sold next year to earn the same net operating income, $120,000, as last year?

   b. Assume that the new plant is constructed and that next year the company manufactures and sells 40,000 skateboards (the same number as sold last year). Prepare a contribution format income statement, and compute the degree of operating leverage.

   c. If you were a member of top management, would you have been in favour of constructing the new plant? Explain.

PROBLEM 8–6
Graphing CVP; Incremental Analysis; Operating Leverage [LO1 – CC4; LO2 – CC5, 6, 7, 10]

Angie Silva has recently opened The Sandal Shop in Brisbane, Australia. The store specializes in fashionable sandals. Angie has just earned a business degree and is anxious to apply business principles to her company. In time, she hopes to expand into a chain of sandal shops. As a first step, she has prepared the following analysis for her new store:

CHECK FIGURES

(1) Break-even: 2,500 pairs
(5a) Leverage: 6

Sales price per pair of sandals	$40
Variable expenses per pair of sandals	16
Contribution margin per pair of sandals	$24
Fixed expenses per month:	
Building rental	$15,000
Equipment depreciation	7,000
Selling	20,000
Administrative	18,000
Total fixed expenses	$60,000

Required:

1. How many pairs of sandals must be sold each month to break even? What does this represent in total dollar sales?

2. Prepare a CVP graph for the store from a zero level of activity up to 5,000 pairs of sandals sold each month. Indicate the break-even point on your graph.

3. Angie has decided that she must earn at least $108,000 the first year to justify her time and effort. How many pairs of sandals must be sold on average per month to reach this target profit?

4. Angie now has two salespeople working in the store—one full-time and one part-time. It will cost her an additional $36,000 per year to convert the part-time position to a full-time position. Angie believes that the change would bring in an additional $60,000 in sales each year. Should she convert the position? Use the incremental approach (do not prepare an income statement).

5. Refer to the original data. During the first year, the store sold 36,000 pairs of sandals and reported the following operating results:

Sales (36,000 pairs)	$1,440,000
Less: Variable expenses	576,000
Contribution margin	864,000
Less: Fixed expenses	720,000
Net income	$ 144,000

  a. What is the store's degree of operating leverage?

  b. Angie is confident that, with a more intense sales effort and a more creative advertising program, she can increase sales by 20% next year. What would be the expected percentage increase in net income? Use the degree of operating leverage to compute your answer.

PROBLEM 8–7
Computing Break-Even and Margin of Safety [LO2 – CC6, 8]

Draaksh Corporation sells premium quality wine for $50 per bottle. Its direct materials and direct labour costs are $9 and $6 respectively per bottle. It pays its direct labour employees a wage of $12 per hour.

The company performed a regression analysis using the past 12 months' data and established the following monthly cost equation for manufacturing overhead costs using direct labour hours as the overhead allocation base:

$$y = \$148,200 + \$16.50x$$

Draaksh believes that the above cost estimates will not substantially change for the next fiscal year. Given the stiff competition in the wine market, Draaksh budgeted an amount of $32,000 per month for sales promotions; additionally, it has decided to offer a sales commission of $2.75 per bottle to its sales personnel. Administrative expenses are expected to be $24,000 per month.

Required:

1. Compute the expected total variable cost *per bottle* and the expected contribution margin ratio.
2. Compute the *annual* break-even sales in units and dollars.
3. Draaksh has budgeted sales of $7.5 million for the next fiscal year. What is the company's margin of safety in dollars and as a percentage of budgeted sales?
4. As the marketing manager of Draaksh, how can you use the information regarding the margin of safety in your planning?

PROBLEM 8–8
Performing a Comprehensive CVP Analysis [LO2 – CC5, 6]

The Central Valley Company is a manufacturing firm that produces and sells a single product. The company's revenues and expenses for the last four months are given below.

Central Valley Company Comparative Income Statement				
	March	*April*	*May*	*June*
Sales in units	5,000	4,500	5,250	6,000
Sales revenue	$ 700,000	$ 630,000	$ 735,000	$ 840,000
Less: Cost of goods sold	370,000	342,000	379,000	426,000
Gross margin	$ 330,000	$ 288,000	$ 356,000	$ 414,000
Less: Operating Expenses				
Shipping expense	$ 61,500	$ 56,000	$ 65,000	$ 71,000

Central Valley Company
Comparative Income Statement

	March	April	May	June
Advertising expense	70,000	70,000	70,000	70,000
Salaries and commissions	160,800	143,000	161,500	180,500
Insurance expense	9,000	9,000	9,000	9,000
Amortization expense	42,000	42,000	42,000	42,000
Total operating expenses	$ 343,000	$ 320,000	$ 347,500	$ 372,500
Net income	$ (13,300)	$ (32,000)	$ 8,500	$ 41,500

Required:

1. Management is concerned about the losses experienced during the spring and would like to know more about the cost behaviour. Develop a cost equation for each of the costs.
2. Assume that fixed costs are incurred uniformly throughout the year. Compute the annual break-even sales, and the profit if 66,000 units are sold during the year.
3. Calculate the change in profit if the selling price were reduced by $4 each and annual sales were to increase by 5,000 units.
4. Determine the change in profit if the company were to increase advertising by $100,000 and if this were to increase sales by 5,000 units.

PROBLEM 8–9
Changes in Cost Structure; Break-Even Analysis; Operating Leverage; Margin of Safety [LO1 – CC3; LO2 – CC5, 6, 8, 9, 10]

Frieden Company's contribution format income statement for the most recent month is given below:

CHECK FIGURE

(2c) Present margin of safety: $160,000

Sales (40,000 units)	$800,000
Variable expenses	560,000
Contribution margin	240,000
Fixed expenses	192,000
Net operating income	$ 48,000

The industry in which Frieden Company operates is quite sensitive to cyclical movements in the economy. Thus, profits vary considerably from year to year according to general economic conditions. The company has a large amount of unused capacity and is studying ways of improving profits.

Required:

1. New equipment has come on the market that would allow Frieden Company to automate a portion of its operations. Variable expenses would be reduced by $6 per unit. However, fixed expenses would increase to a total of $432,000 each month. Prepare two contribution format income statements: one showing present operations, and one showing how operations would appear if the new equipment were purchased. Show an Amount column, a Per Unit column, and a Percent column on each statement. Do not show percentages for the fixed expenses.

2. Refer to the income statements in (1) above. For both present operations and the proposed new operations, compute (a) the degree of operating leverage, (b) the break-even point in dollars, and (c) the margin of safety in both dollar and percentage terms.

3. Refer again to the data in (1) above. As a manager, what factor would be paramount in your mind in deciding whether to purchase the new equipment? (Assume that ample funds are available to make the purchase.)

4. Refer to the original data. Rather than purchase new equipment, the marketing manager argues that the company's marketing strategy should be changed. Instead of paying sales commissions, which are included in variable expenses, the marketing manager suggests that salespeople be paid fixed salaries and that the company invest heavily in advertising. The marketing manager claims that this new approach would increase unit sales by 50% without any change in selling price; the company's new monthly fixed expenses would be $240,000; and its net operating income would increase by 25%. Compute the break-even point in dollar sales for the company under the new marketing strategy. Do you agree with the marketing manager's proposal?

 PROBLEM 8–10

Performing a Break-Even Analysis [LO1 – CC1, 3; LO2 – CC6, 12^A]

Required:

Fill in the missing amounts in each of the following eight case situations. *Treat each case independently.* (*Hint:* One way to find the missing amounts would be to prepare a contribution margin income statement for each case, enter the known data, and then compute the missing items.)

CHECK FIGURES

(a) Case 2, Variable expenses: $60,000

(b) Case 4, Fixed expenses: $185,000

a. Assume that only one product is being sold in each of the following four case situations:

Case	Units Sold	Sales	Variable Expenses	Contribution Margin per Unit	Fixed Expenses	Net Income (Loss)
1	15,000	$180,000	$120,000	$?	$ 50,000	$?
2	?	100,000	?	10	32,000	8,000
3	10,000	?	70,000	13	?	12,000
4	6,000	300,000	?	?	100,000	(10,000)

b. Assume that more than one product is being sold in each of the following four case situations:

Case	Sales	Variable Expenses	Average Contribution Margin (Percentage)	Fixed Expenses	Net Income (Loss)
1	$500,000	$?	20	$?	$ 7,000
2	400,000	260,000	?	100,000	?
3	?	?	60	130,000	20,000
4	600,000	420,000	?	?	(5,000)

Building Your Skills

COMPREHENSIVE PROBLEM [LO1 – CC3; LO2 – CC5, 6, 7]

Allen Moving and Storage prepared the following income statement for 2018:

CHECK FIGURE
(2) Break-even sales
 = $4,838,485

Revenues:

Local	$1,433,500
Intra-province	510,000
Inter-province	2,490,500
Containers	333,000
Packing	437,000
Storage	289,000
Total revenues	$5,493,000

Less expenses:

Outside vehicle repair	$ 220,000
Fuel	352,000
Sales commissions	102,000
Tires, oil, lube	20,500
Wages (driver and helper)	1,584,000

Internal maintenance	293,000
Advertising	88,000
Equipment rental	422,000
Packing materials	557,000
Salaries	821,000
Cargo loss claims	234,000
Utilities	16,700
Insurance	44,000
Fuel taxes and tariffs	132,000
Bad debt	193,000
Depreciation	205,000

Total expenses	5,284,200
Operating income	$ 208,800
Less: Taxes (42%)	87,696
Net income	$ 121,104

Upon reviewing the income statement for 2018, chief financial officer Suzie Allen called a meeting to discuss the company's financial status. She invited sales manager Heidi Strom and controller Gautam Singh.

Allen: Our before-tax income has dropped from a high of 12% of sales to about 4% this last year. I know that both of you are aware of our problem and have some suggestions on how we can improve the situation.

Strom: Suzie, competition has become quite intense in our industry. I have two suggestions to help improve sales. First, we need to increase our advertising budget. We have a good reputation, and I think we need to capitalize on it. I suggest that we emphasize our expertise in crating electronic equipment and other sensitive instruments. Our losses in this area are minuscule. We have a much better record than any of our competitors, and we need to let customers and potential customers know about the quality of our services.

Allen: That sounds good. How much more do you need for advertising, and what kind of increase in sales would you predict?"

Strom: To do it right, I would need to double our current advertising budget. I would guess that sales would increase by 20%. I also have another suggestion. I think we should look at the international goods and freight-moving market. Many firms ship goods internationally, and I believe that they would switch to us if we entered that market. My preliminary analysis reveals that we could pick up $500,000 of sales during the first year.

Allen: Both suggestions seem to offer some potential for improving our profitability. Gautam, would you gather the data needed to estimate the effect of each of these two alternatives on our profits?

Singh: Sure. I have a suggestion also—I plan to install a cost accounting system. At this point, we have no real idea how much each of our services is costing. I believe that there is some hope of reducing costs without affecting the quality of our services.

Allen: I'm all for reducing costs where possible. However, keep in mind that I don't want to lay off any employees yet. I like the idea of providing security to our employees. I would rather see everyone take a pay cut before we reduce our workforce. So far, we have been able to keep everyone despite the drop in our sales. I think it's a good policy. If these two ideas of Heidi's work out, no new hires may be necessary, and we have trained, loyal employees ready for the new business.

Required:

1. Classify all expenses in the 2018 income statement as either variable or fixed. Assume that each expense is strictly variable or strictly fixed with respect to sales revenue. Once the classification is completed, prepare a contribution margin income statement.

2. Using the information obtained in Requirement 1, compute the revenue that Allen Moving and Storage needs to generate to break even. Now compute the revenue that is needed to earn operating income equal to 12% of sales revenue.

3. What is the maximum amount that Suzie can spend on additional advertising assuming that profits remain unchanged for 2019 and sales will increase by 20%, as predicted by Heidi? Suppose that Suzie spends the amount Heidi requested and sales increase by 20%; what will be the change in profits? Should Heidi's suggestion be adopted?

4. Suppose that the directly traceable fixed expenses associated with entry into the international market are $200,000. Assume that the variable-cost ratio for this segment is the same as that computed in the 2018 income statement prepared in Requirement 1. How much revenue must be generated from international shipping for this segment to break even? What is the expected margin of safety? Would you recommend entry into the international market? Why?

5. Suppose that Suzie Allen decides both to increase advertising and to enter the international market. Assume that actual sales increase by 10%, with $340,000 of the increase coming from international sales and the remainder from the increased advertising. Using data from Requirements 1 and 4, answer the following questions:

   a. How much did operating income change because of these two decisions?

   b. What is the profit change attributable to the advertising campaign? The international market? What is your recommendation for the coming year? Should the company continue these two strategies? Or should it do only one or neither? Explain.

   c. Suppose that the company achieved its target profit of 12% of sales in spite of the less-than-expected increase in profits from the advertising campaign and the international market. The remaining increase in profits was achieved by cutting variable costs. What is the new variable-cost ratio?

THINKING ANALYTICALLY [LO1 – CC2; LO2 – CC5, 6, 9, 10]

The marketing manager, Raj Mehta, picked up the phone to call Susan Ahmed, the company's cost accounting assistant and Raj's personal friend.

Mehta: Hi, Susan. Can you help me understand something that came up at a meeting earlier today? It was about break-even when we were discussing cost structure and operating leverage.

Ahmed: What's the problem?

Mehta: The president was talking about automating certain parts of the operations and was throwing out different alternatives.

Ahmed: What's new about that?

Mehta: Well, he was saying something about the changes to the cost structure as a result of that, and that our break-even points might change. As the marketing guy, I would like to better understand the implications of all these proposals for me. How will these potential changes affect my function in the company? Can we meet tomorrow afternoon about this? In the meantime, I will provide you with enough details to compute some numbers for me.

Ahmed: Sounds good, Raj. Now you owe me one!

Ahmed worked with the following documents to conduct her analysis:

- The contribution margin income statement for the most recent year
- Rough notes regarding three new proposals being considered

> **CHECK FIGURE**
> (1) Operating leverage: 2.725

Contribution Margin Income Statement	
Sales revenues (300,000 units)	$78,000,000
Less: Variable costs	
Variable cost of goods sold	35,100,000
Variable selling and administrative expenses	23,400,000
Contribution margin	$19,500,000
Less: Fixed costs	
Manufacturing	9,560,000
Selling and administrative	2,783,000
Net income	$ 7,157,000

The following are notes regarding the new proposals:

- Invest in automation in three areas of sales and marketing: (1) order entry, (2) sales administration, and (3) sales distribution. As a result of this proposal, the contribution margin ratio is expected to increase by 8% and annual fixed costs are expected to increase by $9,570,500.
- Invest in automation in three areas of the organization: (1) sales administration, (2) human resources and corporate office, and (3) manufacturing operations. This move is expected to increase the contribution margin ratio by 11% and simultaneously increase annual fixed costs by $11,280,000. The total cost savings will be divided equally between the manufacturing and nonmanufacturing functions.
- Invest in an ABC system and a new performance measurement system, which will increase the annual fixed costs by $1,800,000. This move will eliminate the need for a total of 33 accounting and administrative clerical staff at an average cost of $32,000 per year per person, and streamline operations.

Required:

Assume the role of Susan Ahmed, and do the following for Raj Mehta:

1. Recreate the preceding contribution margin income statement with additional columns for per-unit amounts and cost percentages (except for fixed costs). Also, compute the break-even point and operating leverage for the year.
2. Prepare three new contribution margin income statements to reflect the three proposals (assuming there is no effect on sales). Ensure that your statements contain columns for per-unit amounts and percentages.
3. Describe how the three proposals will affect the break-even sales for the company. Which proposal will result in the highest increase in income from increases in sales (within the relevant range of operations)? Support your answer with computations.

 ## COMMUNICATING IN PRACTICE [LO1 – CC1, 3, 4; LO2 – CC5, 6]

Marston Corporation manufactures disposable thermometers that are sold to hospitals through a network of independent sales agents located in the United States and Canada. These sales agents sell a variety of products to hospitals in addition to Marston's disposable thermometer. The sales agents are currently paid an 18% commission on sales, and this commission rate was used when Marston's management prepared the following budgeted absorption income statement for the upcoming year:

CHECK FIGURE

(2c) Break-even:
$26,875,000

MARSTON CORPORATION
Budgeted Income Statement

Sales		$30,000,000
Cost of goods sold:		
Variable	$17,400,000	
Fixed	2,800,000	20,200,000
Gross margin		9,800,000
Selling and administrative expenses:		
Commissions	5,400,000	
Fixed advertising expense	800,000	
Fixed administrative expense	3,200,000	9,400,000
Net operating income		$ 400,000

Since the completion of the above statement, Marston's management has learned that the independent sales agents are demanding an increase in the commission rate to 20% of sales for the upcoming year. This would be the third increase in commissions demanded by the independent sales agents in five years. As a result, Marston's management has decided to investigate the possibility of hiring its own sales staff to replace the independent sales agents.

Marston's controller estimates that the company will have to hire eight salespeople to cover the current market area, and the total annual payroll cost of these employees will be about $700,000, including fringe benefits. The salespeople will also be paid commissions of 10% of sales. Travel and entertainment expenses are expected to total about $400,000 for the year. The company will also have to hire a sales manager and support staff whose salaries and fringe benefits will come to $200,000 per year. To make up for the promotions that the independent sales agents had been running on behalf of Marston, management believes that the company's budget for fixed advertising expenses should be increased by $500,000.

Required:

1. Assuming sales of $30,000,000, construct a budgeted contribution format income statement for the upcoming year for each of the following alternatives:
   a. The independent sales agents' commission rate remains unchanged at 18%.
   b. The independent sales agents' commission rate increases to 20%.
   c. The company employs its own sales force.
2. Calculate Marston Corporation's break-even point in sales dollars for the upcoming year assuming the following:
   a. The independent sales agents' commission rate remains unchanged at 18%.
   b. The independent sales agents' commission rate increases to 20%.
   c. The company employs its own sales force.
3. Refer to your answer to part (1b) above. If the company employs its own sales force, what volume of sales would be necessary to generate the net operating income the company would realize if sales are $30,000,000 and the company continues to sell through agents (at a 20% commission rate)?
4. Determine the volume of sales at which net operating income would be equal regardless of whether Marston Corporation sells through agents (at a 20% commission rate) or employs its own sales force.
5. Prepare a graph on which you plot the profits for both of the following alternatives:
   a. The independent sales agents' commission rate increases to 20%.
   b. The company employs its own sales force.

On the graph, use total sales revenue as the measure of activity.

6. Write a memo to the president of Marston Corporation in which you recommend whether the company should continue to use independent sales agents (at a 20% commission rate) or employ its own sales force. Fully explain the reasons for your recommendation in the memo.

(CMA Adapted)

TEAMWORK IN ACTION [LO1 – CC1; LO2 – CC9]

Revenue from major intercollegiate sports is an important source of funds for some colleges and universities. Most of the costs of putting on a football or basketball game may be fixed and may increase very little as the size of the crowd increases. Thus, the revenue from every extra ticket sold may be almost pure profit.

Choose a sport played at school that generates significant revenue. Talk with the business manager of the school's sports programs before answering the following questions:

Required:

1. What is the maximum seating capacity of the venue in which the sport is played? During the past year, what was the average attendance at the games? On average, what percentage of the venue's capacity was filled?

2. The number of seats sold often depends on the opponent. The attendance for a game with a traditional rival is usually substantially above the average. Also, games against conference foes may draw larger crowds than other games. As a consequence, the number of tickets sold for a game is somewhat predictable. What implications does this have for the nature of the costs of putting on a game? Are most of the costs really fixed with respect to the number of tickets sold?

3. Estimate the variable cost per ticket sold.

4. Estimate the total additional revenue that would be generated in an average game if all of the tickets were sold at their normal prices. Estimate how much profit is lost because these tickets are not sold.

5. Estimate the ancillary revenue (parking and concessions) per ticket sold. Estimate how much profit is lost in an average game from these sources of revenue as a consequence of not having a sold-out game.

6. Estimate how much additional profit would be generated for your school if every game were sold out for the entire season.

9

Relevant Costs: The Key to Decision Making

LEARNING OBJECTIVES AND CHAPTER COMPETENCIES		

After studying Chapter 9, you should be able to demonstrate the following competencies:

COMPETENCY		Know	Apply
LO1	**UNDERSTAND AND APPLY THE RELEVANT COSTING APPROACH TO DECISION MAKING.**		
CC1	Explain the relevant cost analysis framework as it applies to managerial decision making, and distinguish between relevant and irrelevant costs.	●	
CC2	Apply the relevant cost analysis framework to an equipment replacement decision.		●
CC3	Apply the relevant cost analysis framework to a business addition/deletion decision.		●
CC4	Apply the relevant cost analysis framework to a make-or-buy (outsourcing) decision.		●
CC5	Apply the relevant cost analysis framework to a special-order decision.		●
CC6	Explain target costing.	●	
LO2	**UNDERSTAND DECISION MAKING IN A CONSTRAINED SETTING.**		
CC7	Explain decision making in a constrained resource environment.	●	
CC8	Compute the contribution margin per unit of a constrained resource.		●
CC9	Explain how constraints are managed.	●	
LO3	**UNDERSTAND COST CONCEPTS AND DECISION MAKING FOR JOINT PRODUCTS.**		
CC10	Understand the pitfalls of allocation for decision making.	●	
CC11	Apply the relevant cost analysis framework to a sell-or-process-further decision.		●

ON THE JOB

RELEVANT COSTS AND THE F-35 AIRPLANE PURCHASE PROGRAM

The concept of relevant costs can be very useful to us as citizens when our government reports the costs of various public expenditures. A case in point is the proposal from the Government of Canada to replace its aging CF-18 fighter aircraft with Lockheed Martin's F-35 jet fighter.

In 2010, the government-estimated cost of replacing the current CF-18 fleet with 65 F-35s was $25.1 billion over 20 years. At the end of 2012, controversy erupted with KPMG's publication of an independent review of the program's life cycle cost. The review pegged the "cradle to grave" cost of the program at $44.8 billion over 42 years as follows: $9 billion for acquisition, $15.2 billion for sustainment, $20 billion for operations, and $600 million for development and disposal. Furthermore, it was also revealed that, of the $565 million estimated for development, the government had already put $280 million toward development of the jets.

Critics allege that the government has not provided adequately for escalation of acquisition costs above $9 billion. The government's contingency fund of $660 million is much less than the $2.5 billion estimated by KPMG. There is also the issue of what costs are included in the estimates; here, the issue is of relevance. Should costs be included that will exist regardless of whether the plane is the F-35 or some other plane? What is the appropriate time frame over which to estimate the costs: 20 years, or the full life cycle of 42 years? Unless there is agreement over the answers to these types of questions, there is not likely to be any agreement over the costs of the program, and the argument over what is the true cost will continue unabated.

The Canadian Press/Adrian Wyld

The lesson to learn about the concept of relevance is always to ask, "Relevance with respect to what?" Is the goal to report the costs that will be incurred, or to consider the costs that will matter for decision making?

Sources: http://www.winnipegfreepress.com/canada/cost-analysis-could-spell-end-for-f-35-program-183305621.html; http://www.cbc.ca/news/canada/story/2012/04/02/f-f35-cost-concerns.html.

? **Critical thinking question** *Consider the $280 million the government has spent for the development of the F-35 in conjunction with other partner nations. A decision must be made about whether to select the F-35 or a different airplane. The parliamentary budget committee has asked the defence department for an accounting of the costs related to the F-35 airplane. Explain how you will treat the $280 million with respect to the above two objectives of making a decision and accounting for costs.*

*Note to student: See **Guidance Answers** online.*

◀◀ A Look Back	▶ A Look at This Chapter	▶▶ A Look Ahead
We began our discussion of decision making in Chapter 8 by introducing CVP analysis.	We continue our coverage of the decision-making process here by focusing on the use of relevant cost data when analyzing alternatives. This is also called differential analysis. In general, only those costs and benefits that differ between alternatives are relevant when making a decision. This basic idea is applied in a wide variety of situations in this chapter.	The common approaches to making major investment decisions, which can have significant long-term implications for any organization, are discussed in Chapter 10.

Making decisions is one of the basic functions of a manager. Every decision involves choosing between at least two alternatives, after comparing the *relevant* costs and benefits of the alternatives.

Costs that differ between alternatives are called **relevant costs**. Successful decision makers must distinguish between relevant and irrelevant data, ignore the irrelevant data, and base the final choice on only the relevant costs and other nonfinancial and qualitative information.

The purpose of this chapter is to develop these skills by illustrating their use in a wide range of decision-making situations. We hasten to add that these decision-making skills are as important in your personal life as they are to managers in the business world. After completing your study of this chapter, you should be able to think more clearly about decisions in all facets of your life. You may find it helpful to refresh your memory concerning different cost concepts from Chapter 2 before reading on.

MANAGERIAL ACCOUNTING IN ACTION

THE ISSUE

It is Wednesday night at the Diving Duck, the campus pub at the University of Western Alberta. Billy Zane has arrived early for his meeting with his friend Kit Walker, with whom he will graduate with a bachelor of commerce degree in accounting. Both Zane and Walker have lined up jobs with accounting firms in western Canada and are planning to start work in August after taking a couple of months off to depressurize after their studies. Walker arrives a few minutes later and sits down.

Walker: Well, I've got it figured out. I'm going to take a bicycling tour of selected portions of the route of the 2010 Tour de France this summer before starting work!

Zane: Really?

Walker: I've done the research, man. A company called Javelin Cycling Vacations is offering an escorted tour for the price of $2,250 per person, and it sure looks exciting.

Zane: I'm surprised—I think of you as more of a do-it-yourself guy, and I figured you would have wanted to organize your own tour instead of paying someone else.

Walker: Well, you're right about me! But I've looked at the numbers and brought them with me. Let me show you!

Cost Concepts for Decision Making

Identifying Relevant Costs and Benefits

LO1 • Know

CC1: Explain the relevant cost analysis framework as it applies to managerial decision making, and distinguish between relevant and irrelevant costs.

Before we present and analyze Kit Walker's data, we want to introduce several important cost terms and concepts. Only those costs and benefits that differ in total between alternatives are relevant in a decision. The difference in costs between the two alternatives is known as the **differential cost** (or *incremental cost*). For example, suppose a family is deciding between the alternatives of renting a movie and going to the theatre. The relevant costs, those that differ between the two alternatives, include (1) the cost of renting a movie, (2) the ticket price at the theatre, and (3) the cost of popcorn and drinks at the theatre. Each cost is associated with only one of the two alternatives and is incurred only when that alternative is chosen. The cost of the movie ticket is incurred only if the alternative of going to the movie theatre is chosen. If the alternative of staying home and renting a movie is chosen instead, the cost of the movie ticket will not be incurred and thus will be avoided. However, the cost of the movie rental will be incurred instead. In other words, when one alternative is chosen, costs associated with the other alternative are not incurred, which means they are avoidable. An **avoidable cost** is one that can be eliminated in whole or in part by choosing one alternative over the other. The concept of an avoidable cost is an equivalent way of defining a relevant cost because these costs are differential costs. Finally, note one other aspect of the costs mentioned above: these are all costs yet to be incurred. In other words, each is a future cost associated with one of the alternatives. This aspect is another feature of relevant costs.

In contrast, if costs do not differ between alternatives, they are irrelevant to the decision. The monthly rent (or mortgage) for the family's home will be the same under each alternative. Since this expense will not differ between the two alternatives, it is irrelevant to the decision. Equivalently, note that the mortgage expense must be incurred regardless of the alternative chosen. In this sense, the mortgage cost is unavoidable. Any cost that is unavoidable across the alternatives being considered is irrelevant.

Let us add a slight twist to the decision. Assume that instead of going to the theatre with your family, you could instead mow your neighbour's lawn and earn $35. If you choose to go to the theatre, you must forgo the *opportunity* to earn some money. This amount, $35, is an **opportunity cost**—the benefit given up when one alternative is selected over another. Opportunity costs are relevant costs. Now suppose that the family has already purchased your movie ticket when you learn of the opportunity to mow the lawn. Given that the ticket has already been purchased, and assuming it cannot be returned for a refund, the ticket cost is considered a sunk cost. A **sunk cost** is one already incurred that cannot be avoided. A sunk cost is an irrelevant cost.

In conclusion, as a general rule, there are two important characteristics of relevant costs: (1) they differ among alternatives, and (2) they are costs that will be incurred in the future. Consequently, sunk costs and costs that do not differ among alternatives are not considered relevant. In contrast, avoidable, incremental, and differential costs are always relevant, as are opportunity costs.

To identify the costs that are avoidable (differential) in a particular decision situation and are therefore relevant, you should follow these steps:

1. Eliminate costs and benefits that do not differ between alternatives. These irrelevant costs consist of (a) sunk costs and (b) future costs that do not differ between alternatives.

2. Use the remaining costs and benefits that *do* differ between alternatives in making the decision. The costs that remain are the differential, or avoidable, costs.

IN BUSINESS

THE RELEVANT COST OF EXECUTIVE PERKS

Identifying relevant costs is often tricky. Consider the case of CEOs who use company-owned airplanes for personal travel. This is a perk, and the Securities and Exchange Commission in the United States has expressed concern about what is reported as a charge for this perk. Statistics suggest that the personal use of corporate jets is increasing and this has raised scrutiny among many investors. Fortune 100 companies saw a 25.83% increase in personal use of corporate jets in 2012, and the 50 largest companies on the S&P 500 saw a 3.14% increase in 2013.

For example, consider a CEO who uses his employer's Gulfstream V luxury airplane to transport his family from New York City to Orlando, Florida, and back, a distance of 2,000 miles (about 3,200 kilometres). The standard practice among companies with personal travel reimbursement policies would be to charge their CEO $1,500 for this flight based on a per-mile reimbursement rate meant to approximate the per-mile cost of a first-class ticket on a commercial airline—a practice allowed by the U.S. Internal Revenue Service (IRS). However, critics argue that using IRS reimbursement rates grossly understates the flight costs that are borne by shareholders. Some of these critics claim that the $11,000 incremental cost of the flight—including fuel, landing fees, and crew hotel charges—should be reimbursed by the CEO. Still others argue that even $11,000 understates the true cost of a flight because fixed costs such as the cost of the airplane, crew salaries, and insurance should be included. These costs are relevant because the excessive amount of personal travel by corporate executives essentially requires their companies to purchase, insure, and staff additional airplanes. This latter group of critics argues that the relevant cost of travelling between New York City and Orlando is $43,000—the market price that would have to be paid to charter a comparable size airplane for this flight. What is the relevant cost of this flight? Should shareholders expect their CEO to reimburse $0 (as is the practice at some companies), $1,500, $11,000, or $43,000? Or, should all companies disallow personal use of corporate assets? These are interesting questions. Some companies have referred to nonmonetary reasons such as the security of the CEOs and time-savings to justify nonbusiness trips.

Sources: Mark Maremont, "Amid Crackdown, the Jet Perk Suddenly Looks a Lot Pricier," *The Wall Street Journal,* May 25, 2005, pp. A1, A8; Joann S. Lublin, "Highflying CEO Perk: Private Trips on Company Jet," *The Wall Street Journal,* May 27, 2014, http://www.wsj.com/articles/highflying-ceo-perk-private-trips-on-company-jet-1401229423; Thomas Black, "What Stigma? U.S. CEOs Flying in Style Again; Personal Use of Corporate Jets Is Growing," *The Ottawa Citizen,* May 3, 2014, retrieved from http://search.proquest.com/docview/1520610625?accountid=14739

AN EXAMPLE OF IDENTIFYING RELEVANT COSTS AND BENEFITS

Cynthia is currently a student in an MBA program in Saskatoon and would like to visit a friend in Regina over the weekend. She is trying to decide whether to drive or take the bus. Because she is on a tight budget, she wants to carefully consider the costs of the two alternatives. If one alternative is far less expensive than the other, that may be decisive in her choice. By car, the distance between her apartment in Saskatoon and her friend's apartment in Regina is 230 kilometres. Cynthia has compiled the following list of items to consider:

		Automobile Costs	
	Item	**Annual Cost of Fixed Items**	**Cost per Kilometre (based on 10,000 km per year)**
(a)	Annual straight-line depreciation on car [($24,000 original cost − $10,000 estimated resale value in 5 years)/5 years]	$2,800	$0.280
(b)	Cost of gasoline ($1.30/L ÷ 13 km/L)		0.100
(c)	Annual cost of auto insurance and licence	$1,380	0.138

		Automobile Costs	
	Item	Annual Cost of Fixed Items	Cost per Kilometre (based on 10,000 km per year)
(d)	Maintenance and repairs		0.065
(e)	Parking fees at school ($45 per month × 8 months)	$ 360	0.036
(f)	Total average cost per kilometre		$0.619

	Additional Data	
Item		
(g)	Reduction in the resale value of car due solely to wear and tear	$0.026/km
(h)	Cost of round-trip bus ticket from Saskatoon to Regina	$104
(i)	Benefit of relaxing and being able to study during the bus ride rather than having to drive	?
(j)	Cost of kennel fees for the dog	$40
(k)	Benefit of having a car available in Regina	?
(l)	Hassle of parking the car in Regina	?
(m)	Cost of parking the car in Regina	$25/day

Which costs and benefits are relevant in this decision? Remember, only those costs and benefits that differ across alternatives are relevant. Everything else can be ignored.

Start at the top of the list with item (a): the original cost of the car is a sunk cost. This cost has already been incurred and therefore can never differ across alternatives. Consequently, it should be ignored. The same is true of the accounting depreciation of $2,800 per year, which simply spreads the sunk cost across five years.

Item (b), the cost of gasoline consumed by driving to Regina, is a relevant cost. If Cynthia takes the bus, this cost will not be incurred. Hence, the cost differs across alternatives and is therefore relevant.

Item (c), the annual cost of auto insurance and licence, is not relevant. Whether Cynthia takes the bus or drives on this particular trip, her annual auto insurance premium and her auto licence fee will remain the same.

Item (d), the cost of maintenance and repairs, is relevant. While maintenance and repair costs have a large random component, over the long run they should be more or less proportional to the number of kilometres the car is driven. Thus, the average cost of $0.065 per kilometre is a reasonable estimate to use.

Item (e), the monthly fee that Cynthia pays to park at her school during the academic year, is not relevant. Regardless of which alternative she selects—driving or taking the bus—she will still need to pay for parking at school.

Item (f) is the total average cost of $0.619 per kilometre. As discussed above, some elements of this total are relevant, but some are not relevant. Because it contains some irrelevant costs, it would be incorrect to estimate the cost of driving to Regina and back by simply multiplying the $0.619/km by 460 km (230 km each way × 2). This erroneous approach would yield a cost of driving of $284.74. Unfortunately, such mistakes are often made both in personal life and in business. Because the total cost is stated on a per-kilometre basis, people are easily misled. Often people think that if the cost is stated as $0.619 per kilometre, the cost of driving 100 km is $61.90. But it is not. Many of the costs included in the $0.619 cost per kilometre are sunk and/or fixed and will not increase if the car is driven another 100 km. The $0.619 is an average cost, not an incremental cost. Beware of such unitized costs (i.e., costs stated in terms of a dollar amount per unit, per kilometre, per direct labour-hour, per machine-hour, and so on)—they are often misleading.

Item (g), the decline in the resale value of the car that occurs as a consequence of driving more kilometres, is relevant in the decision. Because she uses the car, its resale value declines, which is a real cost of using the car that should be taken into account. Cynthia estimated this cost by accessing the Kelly Blue Book website. The reduction in resale value of an asset through use or over time is often called *real* or *economic depreciation.* This is different from accounting depreciation, which attempts to match the sunk cost of an asset with the periods that benefit from that cost.

Item (h), the $104 cost of a round-trip ticket by bus, is relevant in this decision. If she drives, she will not have to buy the ticket.

Item (i) is relevant to the decision, even if it is difficult to put a dollar value on relaxing and being able to study while on the bus. It is relevant because it is a benefit that is available under one alternative but not the other.

Item (j), the cost of kennel fees for her dog while Cynthia is gone, is irrelevant in this decision. Whether she takes the bus or drives to Regina, she will still need to pay to board her dog in a kennel.

Like item (i), items (k) and (l) are relevant to the decision even if it is difficult to measure their dollar impacts.

Item (m), the cost of parking in Regina, is relevant to the decision.

Bringing together all of the relevant data, Cynthia would estimate the relevant costs of driving and of taking the bus as follows:

Relevant Financial Cost of Driving to Regina	
Gasoline (460 km × $0.100/km)	$ 46.00
Maintenance and repairs (460 km × $0.065/km)	29.90
Reduction in the resale value of car due solely to wear and tear (460 km × $0.026/km)	11.96
Cost of parking the car in Regina (2 days × $25/day)	50.00
Total	$137.86
Relevant Financial Cost of Taking the Bus to Regina	
Cost of round-trip bus ticket from Saskatoon to Regina	$104.00

What should Cynthia do? From a purely financial standpoint, it would be cheaper by $33.86 (= $137.86 − $104.00) to take the bus than to drive. Cynthia has to decide whether the convenience of having a car in Regina outweighs the additional cost and the disadvantages of being unable to relax and study and the hassle of finding parking in the city.

In this example, we focused on identifying the relevant costs and benefits—everything else was ignored. In the next example, we include all of the costs and benefits—relevant or not. Nonetheless, we will still get the correct answer because the irrelevant costs and benefits will cancel out when we compare the alternatives.

IN BUSINESS

MASSAGING THE NUMBERS

How do politicians justify enormous investments in public projects like convention or community centres or sports stadiums and hockey arenas? For example, there has been much discussion about building a football stadium in Regina, Saskatchewan, and a new hockey arena in Edmonton, Alberta. Politicians and sports franchise owners frequently rely on consultants who produce studies that purport to show the favourable economic impact of the proposed investment on the area.

These economic impact studies can be bogus in two respects: (1) A large portion of the so-called favourable economic impact that is cited by consultants would be realized by a city even if it did not invest in a new or expanded facility, and unless costs differ between alternatives they are not relevant. (2) Substantial economic incentives (such as waiving rental or other fees, or tax concessions) are frequently offered to attract investment. The cost of these concessions, although often excluded from consultants' projections, can further erode the genuine economic viability of building or expanding a facility.

Little evidence exists to support the argument that sporting events are better at attracting tourism dollars to a city than other activities. Sports economist Craig Depken from the University of North Carolina says that discussions between sports economists on the subject of publicly funded stadiums often reach the conclusion that "generally speaking, the broader benefits seem to be outweighed by the costs."

How much of the money spent by residents would have been spent in a city even if the new stadium or convention centre had not been built? We don't know, but in all likelihood much of this money could have been spent anyway at the zoo, the art museum, the theatre, local restaurants, and so on. This portion of the "favourable" economic impact, usually cited by consultants and used by politicians to justify expanding convention centres, should be ignored because of its irrelevance.

Sources: Victoria Murphy, "The Answer Is Always Yes," *Forbes,* February 28, 2005, pp. 82–84; Jaime Hellman, "Money for Nothing: How Taxpayers Foot the Bill for Pro Sports Stadiums," *Al Jazeera America,* August 10, 2015, http://america.aljazeera.com/watch/shows/Ali-Velshi-On-Target/articles/2015/8/10/stadiums-bult-with-taxpayer-dollars-not-nfl.html.

Common Mistakes to Avoid in Relevant Cost Analysis

DIFFERENT COSTS FOR DIFFERENT PURPOSES

In *every* decision situation, you have to examine the data and isolate the relevant costs. Otherwise, you might easily be misled by irrelevant data. It is important to recognize that costs that are relevant in one situation are not necessarily relevant in another. For example, suppose you have plans to go out for a late evening dinner. The cost of dining out will depend on the choice of the restaurant; therefore, the dining costs at alternative restaurants will be relevant to your choice of restaurant. However, the cost of a movie ticket and the rental cost of a DVD are not relevant in this situation. Simply put, you require *different costs for different purposes.* The costs you require to decide between buying a movie ticket and renting a DVD are different from those you require for deciding which restaurant to choose for a late evening dinner.

The concept of "different costs for different purposes" is basic to managerial accounting; we shall see its application frequently in the discussion that follows.

 IN BUSINESS

RELEVANT COSTS FOR A FRANCHISE PURCHASE DECISION

Suppose you wanted to become a franchisee of a fast food restaurant chain such as Tim Hortons, Pizza Pizza, or Robin's Donuts. There would be many costs to consider, including the initial cost of the franchise and regular royalty, rental, and other fees. These are explicit costs, and most companies will provide this information to prospective investors. However, there are additional opportunity costs that you will not find itemized on company websites or in franchise brochures, since these will differ from investor to investor. Examples of such costs are the investor's forgone salary, forgone returns on the money initially invested to buy the franchise, and money used as working capital.

SUNK COSTS ARE NOT RELEVANT COSTS

LO1 • **Apply**

CC2: Apply the relevant cost analysis framework to an equipment replacement decision.

One of the most difficult conceptual lessons for managers is that sunk costs are never relevant in decision making. Take the example of Peter Kronski, production manager of Soaring Wings Inc., a small manufacturer of high-quality hang gliders, who is trying to explain why the company should replace an old brazing machine purchased several years ago for $175,000. Pete's boss, J. J. Marker, is resistant to the idea because comparing the remaining book value of the old machine to its disposal value today shows that a loss will be incurred upon disposal as shown below:

Old Machine	
Remaining book value	$140,000
Disposal value now	90,000
Loss if disposed of now	$ 50,000

However, this analysis is wrong. The investment in the old machine is a sunk cost. The portion of this investment that remains on the company's books (the book value of $140,000) should not be considered in a decision about whether to buy the new machine. It is *not* a cost of any kind. The firm has not incurred it. It is merely an artifact of an accounting policy, which apportions the original (sunk) cost of $175,000 to future periods.

To determine whether to replace the old machine or not, Pete gathers the following data concerning the old machine and the proposed new machine to perform a relevant cost analysis:

Old Machine		Proposed New Machine	
Original cost	$175,000	List price new	$200,000
Remaining book value	$140,000		
Remaining life	4 years	Expected life	4 years
Disposal value now	$ 90,000		
Disposal value in four years	$ 0	Disposal value in four years	$ 0
Annual variable expenses to operate	$345,000	Annual variable expenses to operate	$300,000
Annual revenue from sales	$500,000	Annual revenue from sales	$500,000

What costs are relevant in the decision concerning whether to buy the new machine? To determine the relevant costs, we should eliminate (1) the sunk costs and (2) the future costs and benefits that do not differ between the alternatives at hand:

1. The sunk costs:
   a. The original investment, $175,000, is a sunk cost, and therefore the remaining book value of the old machine ($140,000) is also irrelevant.
2. The future costs and benefits that do not differ:
   a. The sales revenue ($500,000 per year).
   b. The variable expenses (to the extent of $300,000 per year).

The costs and benefits that remain will form the basis for a decision. The analysis is as follows:

	Differential Costs and Benefits, Four Years
Reduction in variable expense promised by the new machine: ($45,000* per year × 4 years)	$ 180,000
Cost of the new machine	(200,000)
Disposal value of the old machine	90,000
Net advantage of the new machine	$ 70,000

*$345,000 – $300,000 = $45,000

The analysis of the machine replacement decision makes the simplifying assumptions that (1) the depreciation treatment for the two machines is identical, (2) there are no taxes, (3) the two machines are assumed to last for the same length of time, and (4) there is no time value of money. The relevance of the time-value-of-money concept for decision making is considered in Chapter 10. (A separate procedure exists for situations where the useful lives of equipment are different. This text does not consider such situations.) The above analysis can also be presented in the following format:

	Total Cost and Revenues, Four Years		
	Keep Old Machine	Purchase New Machine	Differential Costs and Benefits (new – old)
Sales	$ 2,000,000	$ 2,000,000	$ 0
Variable expenses	(1,380,000)	(1,200,000)	180,000
Cost of the new machine	—	(200,000)	(200,000)
Depreciation of the old machine or book value writeoff	(140,000)	(140,000)*	0
Disposal value of the old machine	—	90,000*	90,000
Total net operating income over the four years	$ 480,000	$ 550,000	$ 70,000

*For external reporting purposes, the $140,000 remaining book value of the old machine and the $90,000 disposal value would be netted together and deducted as a single $50,000 loss.

Looking at all four years together, the analysis reveals that the firm will be $70,000 better off by purchasing the new machine. The $140,000 book value of the old machine had *no effect* on the outcome of the analysis. If the old machine is kept and used, then the $140,000 book value is deducted in the form of depreciation. If the old machine is sold, the $140,000 book value is deducted in the form of a lump-sum writeoff. Either way, the differential cost is zero.

Also, observe that all of these figures represent *cash flows*. The company pays out or receives these amounts. Armed with this analysis, Pete can confidently explain the financial advantages of the new machine to the president of the company.

CONCEPT CHECK

1. Which of the following statements are false? (You may select more than one answer.)
   a. Under some circumstances, a sunk cost may be a relevant cost.
   b. Future costs that do not differ between alternatives are irrelevant.
   c. The same cost may be relevant or irrelevant depending on the decision context.
   d. Only variable costs are relevant costs. Fixed costs cannot be relevant costs.

2. Assume that in October you bought a $450 nonrefundable airline ticket for a five-day/four-night winter ski vacation in Lake Louise, Alberta. The price of your lift ticket for the Lake Louise vacation would be $300. The price of a hotel room in Lake Louise would be $180 per night. You now have an opportunity to buy, for $400, a winter ski vacation package that includes airfare and a lift ticket in Mont Sainte Anne, Quebec. The price of a hotel room in Mont Sainte Anne is $150 per night. The trip length is the same for both destinations. Which of the following costs is not relevant in deciding whether to proceed with the planned trip to Lake Louise, or to change the destination to Mont Sainte Anne?
   a. The $450 airline ticket to Lake Louise
   b. The $400 airline ticket to Mont Sainte Anne
   c. The $300 lift ticket for Lake Louise
   d. The $180 per night hotel room in Lake Louise

3. Based on the facts in Concept Check 2 above, does a differential cost analysis favour Lake Louise or Mont Sainte Anne, and by how much?
   a. Mont Sainte Anne, by $470
   b. Mont Sainte Anne, by $20
   c. Lake Louise, by $70
   d. Lake Louise, by $20

*Note to student: See **Guidance Answers** online.*

FUTURE COSTS THAT DO NOT DIFFER ARE NOT RELEVANT COSTS

We stated previously that people often have difficulty accepting the idea that sunk costs are never relevant in a decision. Some people also have difficulty accepting the principle that future costs that do not differ between alternatives are never relevant in a decision.

Let us look at an example of irrelevant future costs. A company is contemplating the purchase of a new labour-saving machine that will cost $30,000 and have a 10-year useful life. Data concerning the company's annual sales and costs with and without the new machine follow:

	Current Situation	Situation With the New Machine
Units produced and sold	5,000	5,000
Selling price per unit	$ 40	$ 40
Direct materials cost per unit	14	14
Direct labour cost per unit	8	5

	Current Situation	Situation With the New Machine
Variable overhead cost per unit	2	2
Fixed costs, other	62,000	62,000
Fixed costs, new machine	—	3,000

The new machine promises a saving of $3 per unit in direct labour costs ($8 − $5 = $3), but it will increase fixed costs by $3,000 per year. All other costs, as well as the total number of units produced and sold, will remain the same. Following the steps outlined previously, our analysis is as follows:

1. Eliminate the sunk costs. (No sunk costs are included in this example.)
2. Eliminate the future costs and benefits that do not differ between the alternatives.
    a. The selling price per unit and the number of units sold do not differ between the alternatives. (Therefore, total future sales revenues will not differ.)
    b. The direct materials cost per unit, the variable overhead cost per unit, and the number of units produced do not differ between the alternatives. (Therefore, total future direct materials costs and variable overhead costs will not differ.)
    c. The other fixed costs do not differ between the alternatives.

The remaining costs—direct labour costs and the fixed costs associated with the new machine—are the only relevant costs.

Savings in direct labour costs (5,000 units at a cost saving of $3 per unit)	$15,000
Less: Increase in fixed costs	3,000
Net annual cost savings promised by the new machine	$12,000

This solution can be verified by looking at *all* of the cost data (both those that are relevant and those that are not) under the two alternatives. This is done in Exhibit 9–1. Note from the exhibit that the net advantage in favour of buying the machine is $12,000—the same answer we obtained by focusing on just the relevant costs. Thus, we can see that future costs that do not differ between alternatives are indeed irrelevant and can be safely eliminated from the analysis.

EXHIBIT 9–1 Differential Cost Analysis

	5,000 Units Produced and Sold		
	Current Situation	Situation With New Machine	Differential Costs and Benefits (new – old)
Sales	$200,000	$200,000	$ –0–
Variable expenses:			
Direct materials	70,000	70,000	–0–
Direct labour	40,000	25,000	15,000
Variable overhead	10,000	10,000	–0–

	5,000 Units Produced and Sold		
	Current Situation	Situation With New Machine	Differential Costs and Benefits (new – old)
Total variable expenses	120,000	105,000	
Contribution margin	80,000	95,000	
Less: Fixed expenses:			
Other	62,000	62,000	–0–
New machine	–0–	3,000	(3,000)
Total fixed expenses	62,000	65,000	
Net operating income	$ 18,000	$ 30,000	$12,000

In conclusion, mingling irrelevant costs with relevant costs may cause confusion and distract attention from the matters that are really critical. Furthermore, the danger always exists that an irrelevant piece of information may be used improperly, resulting in an incorrect decision. The best approach is to ignore irrelevant data, basing the decision entirely on relevant data.

Using the contribution margin approach (see Chapter 6), the unit contribution margin (unit price less unit variable cost) improves by $3, thereby increasing the total contribution margin for a sales volume of 5,000 units by $15,000. Since fixed costs increase by only $3,000, net income will increase by $15,000 – $3,000 = $12,000. Relevant cost analysis, combined with the *contribution approach* to the income statement, provides a powerful tool for making decisions. We will investigate various uses of this tool in the remaining sections of this chapter.

IN BUSINESS

COSTS AND DECISION MAKING AT ROGERS AND LANTIC SUGAR LTD.

Rogers and Lantic Sugar Ltd. has secured contracts with many candy makers, food companies, and other industrial customers. However, the company has faced the choice of becoming a value-added manufacturer by expanding beyond its existing packaging and refining duties.

A lucrative contract proposed by Kraft Foods Inc. has attracted Rogers and Lantic's attention. Basically, Kraft has moved its entire LifeSavers production line to a Montreal plant in an effort to reduce substantial production costs, and a supplier is needed. Since LifeSavers are composed of 99% sugar, the sugar-laden company can anticipate an additional 25,000 tonnes of sugar sales per year. Instead of just supplying sugar to Kraft, Rogers and Lantic has the option to operate and manage the LifeSavers production line from mixing to packaging the candy. The company would have to acquire new facilities in order to carry out this plan. As well, to move up in the value chain, Rogers and Lantic would have to expand its operations.

For Kraft, the decision to allow Rogers and Lantic to take over the LifeSavers manufacturing and packaging is a make-or-buy decision. For Rogers and Lantic, this is an opportunity to add a new line of business. The disadvantage to Rogers and Lantic is the risk of competing against its own customers in an effort to procure higher profit margins. Furthermore, observers believe that many companies that have gone beyond their core business in hopes of more rewards end up in ruins. If Rogers and Lantic is not careful, it could end up being flattened by its customers-turned-competitors.

However, if Rogers and Lantic can find a winning strategy to add value to its products and become a multibillion dollar company, it may have a leading edge in the industry.

Source: Brian Banks, "How Sweet It Is," *Canadian Business,* April 1, 2002, pp. 54–57. Reprinted with permission of Brian Banks.

Adding and Dropping Product Lines and Other Segments

LO1 • **Apply**

CC3: Apply the relevant cost analysis framework to a business addition/deletion decision.

Among the most difficult decisions a manager has to make are decisions relating to whether old product lines or other segments of a company should be dropped and new ones added. In such decisions, many qualitative and quantitative factors must be considered. Ultimately, however, any final decision to drop an old segment or to add a new one is going to hinge primarily on the impact the decision will have on net operating income. To assess this impact, you must make a careful analysis of the costs involved.

IN BUSINESS

ROUTE EXPANSION IN THE AIRLINE INDUSTRY

Have you ever wondered how airlines like WestJet and Air Canada decide to add or remove an airline route from their route network? The concept of relevant costs is particularly important to this type of decision. Relevant costs will include expenses such as fuel costs, flight crew and ground crew wages, landing fees, passenger baggage handling costs, air cargo handling costs (receiving, weighing, sorting, and storage), costs of servicing aircraft at the terminal, and so on. Airlines must determine and analyze such costs carefully when making decisions. The business model of Southwest Airlines, emulated by WestJet and other providers of low-cost airfare travel, are examples of effective cost management in the airline industry. Using a fleet made up of a single model of aircraft, reducing layover times in terminals, restricting the number of pieces of checked baggage per passenger, and eliminating in-flight meals are means by which the relevant costs of providing passenger and air transport services can be reduced or controlled.

An Illustration of Cost Analysis

Consider the three major product lines—drugs, cosmetics, and housewares—of the Discount Drug Company. Sales and cost information for the preceding month for each separate product line and for the store in total are given in Exhibit 9–2.

EXHIBIT 9–2 Discount Drug Company Product Lines

	Product Line			
	Drugs	**Cosmetics**	**Housewares**	**Total**
Sales	$125,000	$75,000	$50,000	$250,000
Less: Variable expenses	50,000	25,000	30,000	105,000
Contribution margin	75,000	50,000	20,000	145,000
Less: Fixed expenses:				
Salaries	29,500	12,500	8,000	50,000
Advertising	1,000	7,500	6,500	15,000
Utilities	500	500	1,000	2,000
Depreciation—fixtures	1,000	2,000	2,000	5,000
Rent	10,000	6,000	4,000	20,000
Insurance	2,000	500	500	3,000
General administrative	15,000	9,000	6,000	30,000
Total fixed expenses	59,000	38,000	28,000	125,000
Net operating income (loss)	$ 16,000	$12,000	$ (8,000)	$ 20,000

What can be done to improve the company's overall performance? One product line—housewares—shows a net operating loss for the month. Perhaps dropping this line would cause profits in the company as a whole to improve. In deciding whether the line should be dropped, management should reason as follows. If the housewares line is dropped, the company will lose $20,000 per month in contribution margin. By dropping the line, however, it may be possible to avoid some fixed costs, perhaps by discharging certain employees or reducing advertising costs. If by dropping the housewares line the company is able to avoid more in fixed costs than it loses in contribution margin, it would be better off to eliminate the line, since overall net income should improve. However, if the company is not able to avoid as much in fixed costs as it loses in contribution margin, the housewares line should be retained. In short, the manager should ask, "What costs can I avoid if I drop this product line?"

As we have seen from our previous discussion, not all costs are avoidable. For example, some of the costs associated with a product line may be sunk costs. Other costs may be allocated as fixed costs that will not differ in total, regardless of whether the product line is dropped or retained.

To show how the manager should proceed in a product-line analysis, suppose that the management of the Discount Drug Company has analyzed the costs being charged to the three product lines and determined the following:

1. The salaries expense represents salaries paid to employees working directly in each product-line area. All of the employees working in housewares would be discharged if the line were dropped.
2. The advertising expense represents direct advertising of each product line and is avoidable if the line is dropped.
3. The utilities expense represents utilities costs for the entire company. The amount charged to each product line is an allocation based on space occupied and is not avoidable if the product line is dropped.
4. The depreciation expense represents depreciation on fixtures used for display of the various product lines. Although the fixtures are nearly new, they are custom-built and will have little resale value if the housewares line is dropped.
5. The rent expense represents rent on the entire building housing the company; it is allocated to the product lines on the basis of sales dollars. The monthly rent of $20,000 is fixed under a long-term lease agreement.

6. The insurance expense represents insurance carried on inventories within each of the three product-line areas.

7. The general administrative expense represents the costs of accounting, purchasing, and general management, which are allocated to the product lines on the basis of sales dollars. Total administrative costs will not change if the housewares line is dropped.

With this information, management can identify costs that can and cannot be avoided if the product line is dropped:

	Not Avoidable*	Avoidable	Total Cost
Salaries		$ 8,000	$ 8,000
Advertising	$ 6,500	6,500	
Utilities	1,000		1,000
Depreciation—fixtures	2,000		2,000
Rent	4,000		4,000
Insurance		500	500
General administrative	6,000		6,000
Total fixed expenses	$13,000	$15,000	$28,000

*These costs represent either sunk costs or future costs that will not change whether the housewares line is retained or discontinued.

To determine how dropping the line will affect the overall profits of the company, we can compare the contribution margin that will be lost with the costs that can be avoided if the line is dropped:

Contribution margin lost if the housewares line is discontinued (see Exhibit 9–2)	$(20,000)
Less: Fixed costs that can be avoided if the housewares line is discontinued (see above)	15,000
Decrease in overall company net operating income	$ (5,000)

In this case, the fixed costs that can be avoided by dropping the product line are less than the contribution margin that will be lost. Therefore, based on the data provided, the housewares line should be retained unless a more profitable use can be found for the floor and counter space it is occupying. (The issue of opportunity cost of floor space is considered later in the chapter.)

A COMPARATIVE FORMAT

Some managers prefer to approach decisions of this type by preparing comparative income statements showing the effects on the company as a whole of either keeping or dropping the product line in question. A comparative analysis of this type for the Discount Drug Company is shown in Exhibit 9–3. As shown in the rightmost column, overall company net operating income will decrease by $5,000 each period if the housewares line is dropped. This is, of course, the same answer as we obtained in our previous analysis.

EXHIBIT 9–3 A Comparative Format for Product-Line Analysis

	Keep Housewares	Drop Housewares	Difference: (Drop – Keep) Net Income Increase (Decrease)
Sales	$50,000	$ –0–	$ (50,000)
Less: Variable expenses	30,000	–0–	30,000
Contribution margin	20,000	–0–	(20,000)
Less: Fixed expenses:			
Salaries	8,000	–0–	8,000
Advertising	6,500	–0–	6,500
Utilities	1,000	1,000	–0–
Depreciation—fixtures	2,000	2,000	–0–
Rent	4,000	4,000	–0–
Insurance	500	–0–	500
General administrative	6,000	6,000	–0–
Total fixed expenses	28,000	13,000	15,000
Net operating income (loss)	$ (8,000)	$ (13,000)	$ (5,000)

Beware of Allocated Fixed Costs

Our conclusion that the housewares line should not be dropped seems to conflict with the data shown previously in Exhibit 9–2. Recall from that exhibit that the housewares line is showing a loss rather than a profit. Why keep a line that is showing a loss? The explanation for this apparent inconsistency lies, at least in part, with the *common fixed costs* that are being allocated to the product lines. A **common fixed cost** supports the operations of more than one segment of an organization and is not avoidable in whole or in part by eliminating any one segment. For example, the salary of the CEO of a company ordinarily would not be cut if any one product line were dropped, and so it is a common fixed cost of the product lines. In fact, if dropping a product line is a good idea that results in higher profits for the company, the compensation of the CEO is likely to increase, rather than decrease, as a result of dropping the product line. One of the great dangers in allocating common fixed costs is that such allocations can make a product line (or other segment of a business) *look* less profitable than it really is. By allocating the common fixed costs among all product lines, the housewares line has been made to *look* as if it were unprofitable, whereas, in fact, dropping the line would result in a decrease in overall company net operating income. This point can be seen clearly if we recast the data in Exhibit 9–2 and eliminate the allocation of the common fixed costs. This recasting of data is shown in Exhibit 9–4.

EXHIBIT 9–4 Discount Drug Company Product Lines—Recast in Contribution Format (from Exhibit 9–2)

| | Product Line | | | |
	Drugs	Cosmetics	Housewares	Total
Sales	$125,000	$75,000	$50,000	$250,000
Less: Variable expenses	50,000	25,000	30,000	105,000
Contribution margin	75,000	50,000	20,000	145,000
Less: Traceable fixed expenses:				
Salaries	29,500	12,500	8,000	50,000
Advertising	1,000	7,500	6,500	15,000
Depreciation—fixtures	1,000	2,000	2,000	5,000
Insurance	2,000	500	500	3,000
Total traceable fixed expenses	33,500	22,500	17,000	73,000
Product-line segment margin	$ 41,500	$27,500	$ 3,000*	72,000
Less: Common fixed expenses:				
Utilities				2,000
Rent				20,000
General administrative				30,000
Total common fixed expenses				52,000
Net operating income				$ 20,000

*The impact of dropping the housewares line will be the $3,000 segment margin plus $2,000 representing depreciation expense. The depreciation expense must be added back to obtain the impact on profits because it represents a noncash charge. In other words, the company does not actually *incur* this expense. Thus, it can be seen that if the housewares line is dropped, the company will *lose* $5,000.

Note that the common fixed expenses have not been allocated to the product lines in Exhibit 9–4. Only the fixed expenses that are traceable to the product lines and that could be avoided by dropping the product lines are assigned to them. For example, the fixed expenses of advertising the housewares product line can be traced to that product line and can be eliminated if that product line is dropped. However, the general administrative expenses, such as the CEO's salary, cannot be traced to the individual product lines and would not be eliminated if any one product line were dropped. Consequently, these common fixed expenses are not allocated to the product lines in Exhibit 9–4 as they were in Exhibit 9–2. The allocations in Exhibit 9–2 provide a misleading picture that suggests that portions of the fixed common expenses can be eliminated by dropping individual product lines—this is not the case.

Exhibit 9–4 gives us a much different perspective of the housewares line than does Exhibit 9–2. As shown in Exhibit 9–4, the housewares line is covering all of its own traceable fixed costs and is generating a $3,000 *segment margin* toward covering the common fixed costs of the company. The **segment margin** is the difference between the revenue generated by a segment and its own traceable costs. Unless another product line can be found that will generate more than a $3,000 segment margin, the company would be better off keeping the housewares line. By keeping the line, the company's overall net operating income is higher than if the product line were dropped.

Additionally, we should note that managers may choose to retain an unprofitable product line (when considered by *itself*) if the line is necessary to the sale of other products or if it serves as a *magnet* to attract customers. Bread, for example, is not an especially profitable line in food stores, but customers expect it to be available, and many would undoubtedly shift their buying elsewhere if a particular store decided to stop carrying it. In other words, bread may be profitable if its impact on sales of other items is included in the analysis.

Finally, note that this issue of common fixed costs and the distortions introduced by allocating such costs lies at the heart of the rationale for an ABC management system. This was covered in Chapter 5. You can see that the analysis in Exhibit 9–4 could not have been done if it was not possible to *trace* the fixed expenses to the various segments. The ability to carry out this type of tracing is clearly the key.

IN BUSINESS

THE TRAP LAID BY FULLY ALLOCATED COSTS: A DEATH SPIRAL

A bakery distributed its products through route salespeople, each of whom loaded a truck with an assortment of products in the morning and spent the day calling on customers in an assigned territory. Believing that some items were more profitable than others, management asked for an analysis of product costs and sales. The accountants allocated all manufacturing and marketing costs to products to obtain a net profit for each product. The resulting figures indicated that some of the products were being sold at a loss, and management discontinued these products. However, when this change was put into effect, the company's overall profit declined. Dropping some products caused sales revenues to decline with no commensurate reduction in costs, because the common manufacturing costs and route sales costs had to be continued in order to make and sell the remaining products. This phenomenon is called the "death spiral" by some.

The Make-or-Buy Decision

LO1   ● **Apply**

CC4: Apply the relevant cost analysis framework to a make-or-buy (outsourcing) decision.

A decision about whether to produce a fabricated part internally or buy the part externally from a supplier is called a **make-or-buy decision**. This is also known as an *outsourcing* or *subcontracting decision*. As an illustration of a make-or-buy decision, consider Mountain Goat Cycles. The company is now producing the heavy-duty gear shifters used in its most popular line of mountain bikes. The company's accounting department reports the following costs of producing the shifter internally:

	Per Unit	8,000 Units
Direct materials	$ 6	$ 48,000
Direct labour	4	32,000
Variable overhead	1	8,000

	Per Unit	8,000 Units
Supervisor's salary	3	24,000
Depreciation of special equipment	2	16,000
Allocated general overhead	5	40,000
Total cost	$21	$168,000

An outside supplier has offered to sell Mountain Goat Cycles 8,000 shifters a year at a price of only $19 each. Should the company stop producing the shifters internally and start purchasing them from the outside supplier? To approach the decision from a financial point of view, the manager should again focus on the differential costs. As we have seen, the differential costs can be obtained by eliminating the unavoidable costs—that is, by eliminating (1) the sunk costs and (2) the future costs that will continue regardless of whether the shifters are produced internally or purchased outside. The costs that remain are the costs that are avoidable to the company by purchasing outside. If these avoidable costs are less than the outside purchase price, the company should continue to manufacture its own shifters and reject the outside supplier's offer. That is, the company should purchase outside only if the outside purchase price is less than the costs that can be avoided internally as a result of stopping production of the shifters.

Looking at the cost data for producing the shifter internally, note first that depreciation of special equipment is listed as one of the costs of producing the shifters internally. Since the equipment has already been purchased, this depreciation is a sunk cost and therefore irrelevant. If the equipment could be sold, its salvage value would be relevant. Or if the machine could be used to make other products, this might be relevant as well. However, we will assume that the equipment has no salvage value and that it has no other use than making the heavy-duty gear shifters.

Also, note that the company is allocating a portion of its general overhead costs to the shifters. Any portion of this general overhead cost that would actually be eliminated if the gear shifters were purchased, rather than made, would be relevant in the analysis. However, it is likely that the general overhead costs allocated to the gear shifters are, in fact, common to all items produced in the factory and would continue unchanged even if the shifters were purchased from outside. Such allocated common costs are not differential costs (since they do not differ between the make-or-buy alternatives) and should be eliminated from the analysis along with the sunk costs.

The variable costs of producing the shifters (materials, labour, and variable overhead) are differential costs, since they can be avoided by buying the shifters from the outside supplier. If the supervisor can be discharged and his or her salary avoided by buying the shifters, then it too will be a differential cost and relevant to the decision. Assuming that both the variable costs and the supervisor's salary can be avoided by buying from the outside supplier, the analysis takes the form shown in Exhibit 9–5.

EXHIBIT 9–5 Mountain Goat Cycles' Make-or-Buy Analysis

	Production Cost per Unit	Per-Unit Differential Costs		Total Differential Costs, 8,000 Units	
		Make	Buy	Make	Buy
Direct materials	$ 6	$ 6		$ 48,000	
Direct labour	4	4		32,000	
Variable overhead	1	1		8,000	
Supervisor's salary	3	3		24,000	
Depreciation of special equipment	2	—		—	
Allocated general overhead	5	—		—	
Outside purchase price	—	—	$19	—	$152,000
Total cost	$21	$14	$19	$112,000	$152,000
Difference in favour of continuing to make		$5		$40,000	

Since it costs $5 less per unit to continue to make the shifters, Mountain Goat Cycles should reject the outside supplier's offer. However, there is one additional factor that the company may wish to consider before coming to a final decision: the opportunity cost of the space now being used to produce the shifters.

IN BUSINESS

THE GROWING POPULARITY OF OUTSOURCING: TASKS, JOBS, AND PRODUCTS

Change seems to be the only constant in today's business world! A significant trend in Canada and the United States is the outsourcing of manufacturing and other processing activities to countries such as Vietnam, India, and China.

In car manufacturing, GM, BMW, and other manufacturers have long outsourced the production of car components to international manufacturers. However, starting in 2016, GM will import between 30,000 and 40,000 Buick Envision crossovers annually from a plant in Shandong Province, China. This effectively makes GM the first US firm to import a vehicle made in China to the United States.

The Envision is just the beginning of GM's plans in China: it is increasingly making China a hub for new vehicle development and global exports. More important is that GM's pioneering Chinese import could help diminish consumer stigma attached to Chinese cars. The next generation of GM's small and medium-sized vehicles will be fitted with new technology co-developed with its Chinese partner, the Shanghai Automobile Industry Corporation.

When thinking about relevant costs, consider if all of the costs and benefits are accounted for, including strategic advantages of vertical integration and better control over quality and expenditures. Outsourcing is not without risks. The key question is whether the risks and the financial impacts have been recognized.

Sources: Edward Niedermeyer, "How GM's Bailout Became China's Bonanza," *BloombergView*, November 13, 2015, http://www.bloombergview.com/articles/2015-11-13/how-gm-s-bailout-became-china-s-bonanza; "As Labor Costs Rise, GM to Sell Chinese-Made Buick SUV in U.S.," *FOX Business*, November 12, 2015, http://www.foxbusiness.com/industries/2015/11/12/as-labor-costs-rise-gm-to-sell-chinese-made-buick-suv-in-us/

Opportunity Cost

If the space now being used to produce the shifters *would otherwise be idle,* then Mountain Goat Cycles should continue to produce its own shifters and the supplier's offer should be rejected, as stated previously. Idle space that has no alternative use has an opportunity cost of zero.

But what if the space now being used to produce shifters could be used for some other purpose? In that case, the space would have an opportunity cost that would have to be considered in assessing the desirability of the supplier's offer. What would this opportunity cost be? It would be the segment margin that could be derived from the best alternative use of the space.

To illustrate, assume that the space now being used to produce shifters could be used to produce a new cross-country bike that would generate a segment margin of $60,000 per year. Under these conditions, Mountain Goat Cycles would be better off to accept the supplier's offer and to use the available space to produce the new product line, as shown below:

	Make	Buy
Differential cost per unit (see prior example)	$ 14	$ 19
Number of units needed annually	× 8,000	× 8,000
Total annual cost	112,000	152,000
Opportunity cost—segment margin forgone on a potential new product line	60,000	
Total cost	$172,000	$152,000
Difference in favour of purchasing from the outside supplier		$ 20,000

Opportunity costs are not recorded in the accounts of an organization. They do not represent actual dollar outlays. Rather, they represent economic benefits that are *forgone* as a result of pursuing some course of action. The opportunity costs of Mountain Goat Cycles are sufficiently large in this case to make continued production of the shifters very costly from an economic point of view.

KIT WALKER'S MAKE-OR-BUY DECISION

Make-or-buy decisions are frequently encountered in both our business and personal lives. In fact, you can now see that the decision facing Kit Walker, whom we introduced at the beginning of the chapter, is actually a make-or-buy decision: Walker has to decide whether to take an escorted bicycle tour (the *buy* alternative) or to organize his own tour (the *make* alternative). The data Walker has gathered from his research is given in Exhibit 9–6.

EXHIBIT 9–6 Expenses Related to Bicycle Tour

Javelin's Escorted Tour Costs	
Price:*	$2,250

*Price includes meals and accommodations for seven nights, insurance, and a bicycle fitted to the rider's physical characteristics. It does not include airfare to Paris. Kit Walker has put down a nonrefundable deposit of $200. He plans to arrive the night before the tour starts and depart the night after its conclusion.

Projected Costs If Kit Walker Organizes His Own Tour	
Airfare to Paris	$2,350
Bicycle upgrades[1]	750
Meals (9 days @ $50)[2]	450
Hotel (9 nights @ $75)[2]	675
Trip insurance	
Health[3]	270
Bicycle[4]	50
Bicycle maintenance	
Labour[5]	165
Equipment[6]	140
Bike and equipment transport[7]	150

[1]Walker has to upgrade his bicycle to withstand the rigours of the tour.

[2]The daily cost of the meals and accommodations is the same as that of Javelin. The "nine days" estimate is for the day prior to the start of the tour, the day after the final day of the tour, and the seven days of the tour.

[3]The cost of health insurance includes a $170 premium over the group insurance cost per person paid by tour operators.

[4]This is for insuring the bicycle against damage or theft during the tour.

[5]The labour cost estimate for bicycle maintenance is for potential repairs that might be needed on the road.

[6]The equipment cost is for a bicycle support company. This company is responsible for transporting bicycle parts along the tour route and providing a mechanic if one is needed.

[7]The airfare does not include the cost of transporting the bike to Paris. Since the shipping box is oversized, excess baggage charges will be incurred.

To decide if Walker should buy the escorted tour or organize his own tour, he has to compare the relevant cost of the make alternative with that of the buy alternative. This analysis is shown below:

	Make	Buy	Difference: Make – Buy
Cost to buy[1]	$ —	$2,050	$(2,050)
Airfare[2]	2,350	2,350	0
Bicycle upgrades	750	0	750
Health upcharge[3]	170	0	170
Meals[4]	450	100	350
Accommodations[4]	675	150	525
Bike insurance	50	0	50
Bike maintenance	305	0	305
Bike transport	150	0	150
Total	$4,900	$4,650	$ 250

[1]The deposit of $200 is a sunk cost and irrelevant to the make-or-buy decision; therefore, the cost to buy is $2,250 − $200 = $2,050.

[2]Since the airfare is not included in the tour price, it is a common cost for both alternatives.

[3]This represents the $170 additional expense over and above what the tour operator provides, the cost of which is included in the price.

[4]Walker will incur nine days of meals and accommodation expenses if he plans his own trip instead of taking the escorted tour. Since the tour price includes meals and accommodations for seven days, he will be responsible for two days of meals and hotel if he buys the tour.

On the basis of the analysis, Walker should not organize his own tour; he should instead purchase the escorted tour because the relevant cost is $250 less than the relevant cost of organizing his own tour.

MANAGERIAL ACOUNTING IN ACTION

THE WRAP-UP

Walker: So now you can see why I have decided to take the escorted tour.

Zane: Yeah, I understand the math. In fact, I think you might be underestimating the savings, because there is a cost to the time that you will end up having to spend managing the many details around the tour, which you'd expect the tour operator will be taking care of.

Walker: You're right about that! All the planning and research has already taken up a lot of my time. Well ... another round?

DECISION POINT

VICE-PRESIDENT OF PRODUCTION

You are faced with a make-or-buy decision. The company currently makes a component for one of its products, but it is considering whether it should purchase the component instead. If the offer from an outside supplier were accepted, the company would no longer need to rent the machinery currently being used to manufacture the component. You realize that the annual rental cost is a fixed cost but recall some sort of warning about fixed costs. Is the annual rental cost relevant to this make-or-buy decision?

Special Orders

LO1 ● **Apply**

CC5: Apply the relevant cost analysis framework to a special-order decision.

Managers often must evaluate whether a *special order* should be accepted, and if the order is accepted, the price that should be charged. A **special order** is a one-time order that is not considered part of the company's normal ongoing business.

To illustrate, suppose Mountain Goat Cycles has just received a request from the Charlottetown Police Service to produce 100 specially modified mountain bikes at a price of $740 each. The bikes would be used to patrol some of the more densely populated residential sections of the city. Mountain Goat Cycles can easily modify its City Cruiser model to fit the specifications of the Charlottetown Police. The normal selling price of the City Cruiser bike is $930, and its unit product cost is $750, as shown below:

Direct materials	$400
Direct labour	225
Manufacturing overhead	125
Unit product cost	$750

The variable portion of the manufacturing overhead is $25 per unit. The order would have no effect on the company's total fixed manufacturing overhead costs. The modifications to the bikes consist of welded brackets to hold radios, nightsticks, and other gear. These modifications would require $50 in incremental variable costs. In addition, the company would have to pay a graphic design studio $2,000 to design and cut stencils that would be used for spray painting the Charlottetown Police Service's logo and other identifying marks on the bikes.

This order should have no effect on the company's other sales. The production manager says that she can handle the special order without disrupting any of the regularly scheduled production. What effect would accepting this order have on the company's net operating income?

Only the incremental costs and benefits are relevant. Since the existing fixed manufacturing overhead costs would not be affected by the order, they are not incremental costs and are therefore not relevant. The incremental net operating income can be computed as follows:

	Per Unit	Total, 100 Bikes
Incremental revenue	$740	$74,000
Incremental costs:		
Variable costs:		
Direct materials	400	40,000
Direct labour	225	22,500
Variable manufacturing overhead	25	2,500
Special modifications	50	5,000
Total variable cost	$700	70,000
Fixed cost:		
Purchase of stencils		2,000
Total incremental cost		72,000
Incremental net operating income		$ 2,000

Therefore, even though the price on the special order ($740) is below the normal unit product cost ($750) and the order would require incurring additional costs, the order would result in an increase in net operating income. In general, a special order is profitable as long as the incremental revenue from the special order exceeds the incremental costs of the order. We must ensure, however, that there is indeed idle capacity and that the special order does not cut into normal sales. For example, if the company was operating at capacity, opportunity costs would have to be taken into account as well as the incremental costs already detailed.

IN BUSINESS

SPECIAL ORDERS OF JEWELLERY

Generally, managers accept special orders that generate additional (or incremental) profits and reject those that do not. However, managers sometimes accept a special order if they believe that doing so could lead to additional future sales; this is also the case with jewellers.

Producing a custom jewellery order can be costly as there are many steps involved in producing the jewellery—the jeweller must locate and order the raw materials, and communicate with the customer until the design is finalized. Moreover, they incur additional shipping costs and discounts are not usually available. Finally, this can be risky because the customer may not return to pick up the jewellery and pay for it. Luxury Bazaar, an online jewellery retailer based in Philadelphia, USA, provides an online channel in conjunction with its Philadelphia showroom, for customers to preview prior to purchasing luxurious and rare jewellery from all over the world.

Luxury Bazaar's customers are able to check the availability of a pre-crafted piece through either visiting the store or accessing a real-time database online. If the piece is in the store, the customer is shown the piece with the option of purchasing it then and there. Otherwise custom orders can be placed where the item is handcrafted in-house prior to delivery. Customers satisfied with their custom orders are likely to be returning customers. Rather than being risky, special orders immediately generate cash for the company: a non-refundable deposit or full payment is due when the order is placed. The decision to accept or reject special orders is no longer the issue it once was for the managers.

Sources: Michelle Brown, "Custom Orders for High-End Items Are Crafted in-House at Luxury Bazaar," *SBWire*, October 21, 2015; http://www.sbwire.com/press-releases/custom-orders-for-high-end-items-are-crafted-in-house-at-luxury-bazaar-634938.htm; Luxury Bazaar http://www.luxurybazaar.com/other/aboutUs.aspx; A. Nash, "Handling Custom Jewelry Orders," *Jewelry Making Journal*, http://jewelrymakingjournal.com/custom-jewelry-orders/

Pricing New Products: Target Costing

LO1   ● **Know**

CC6: Explain target costing.

Target costing provides an alternative, market-based approach to pricing new products. In the target costing approach, management estimates how much the market will be willing to pay for the new product even before the new product has been designed. The company's required profit margin is subtracted from the estimated selling price to determine the target cost for the new product. A cross-functional team consisting of designers, engineers, cost accountants, marketing personnel, and production personnel is charged with the responsibility of ensuring that the cost of the product is ultimately less than the target cost. If, at some point in the product development process, it becomes clear that meeting the target cost will not be possible, the new product is abandoned.

The target costing approach to pricing has a number of advantages over the cost-plus mark-up approach. First, a product is not made unless the company is reasonably confident that customers will be willing to buy the product at a price that provides the company with an adequate profit. Second, the target costing approach inspires a much higher level of cost-consciousness than the cost-plus approach and probably results in less expensive products that are more attractive to customers. The target cost lid creates relentless pressure to drive out unnecessary costs. In the cost-plus approach, this pressure to control costs is absent, since whatever the costs turn out to be, the price will be higher; this allows designers and engineers to create products with expensive features that customers may not actually be willing to pay for. Consequently, many companies are abandoning the cost-plus approach to new product pricing in favour of the target costing approach.

 DECISION POINT

TUTOR

Your financial accounting instructor has suggested that you should consider working with selected students in her class as a tutor. Should you adopt a cost-plus or target costing approach to setting your hourly fee?

*Note to student: See **Guidance Answers** online.*

Utilization of a Constrained Resource

CC7: Explain decision making in a constrained resource environment.

Managers are routinely faced with the problem of deciding how constrained resources are going to be utilized. A department store, for example, has a limited amount of floor space and therefore cannot stock every product that may be available. A manufacturing firm has a limited number of machine-hours and a limited number of direct labour-hours at its disposal. When a limited resource of some type restricts the company's ability to satisfy demand, the company is said to have a **constraint**. Because of the constrained resource, the company cannot fully satisfy demand, and so the manager must decide how the constrained resource should be used. Fixed costs are usually unaffected by such choices, and so the manager should select the course of action that will maximize the firm's *total* contribution margin.

Contribution in Relation to a Constrained Resource

CC8: Compute the contribution margin per unit of a constrained resource.

To maximize total contribution margin, a firm should promote those products or accept those orders that provide the highest unit contribution margin *per unit of the constrained resource*. To illustrate, Mountain Goat Cycles makes a line of panniers—saddlebags for bicycles. Two models are offered—a touring model and a mountain model. Cost and revenue data for each pannier model are provided below:

	Model	
	Mountain Pannier	**Touring Pannier**
Selling price per unit	$25	$30
Variable cost per unit	10	18
Contribution margin per unit	$15	$12
Contribution margin (CM) ratio	60%	40%

The mountain pannier appears to be much more profitable than the touring pannier. It has a $15 per unit contribution margin, compared to only $12 per unit for the touring model, and it has a 60% CM ratio, against only 40% for the touring model.

But now let us add one more piece of information—the plant that makes the panniers is operating at capacity. At Mountain Goat Cycles, the machine or process that is limiting overall output is called the **bottleneck**—it is the constraint. The bottleneck is a particular stitching machine. The mountain pannier requires two minutes of stitching time, while the touring pannier requires one minute of stitching time. In this situation, if additional time becomes available on the stitching machine, which product is more profitable to produce? To answer this question, the manager should look at the *contribution margin per unit of the constrained resource*. This figure is computed by dividing the contribution margin by the amount of the constrained resource that a unit of product requires. These calculations are carried out below for the mountain and touring panniers:

	Model	
	Mountain Pannier	Touring Pannier
Contribution margin per unit (above) (a)	$15	$12
Time on the stitching machine required to produce one unit (b)	2 min	1 min
Contribution margin per unit of the constrained resource, (a) ÷ (b)	$7.50/min	$12/min

Every minute of processing time on the stitching machine devoted to the touring pannier results in an increase of $12 in contribution margin and profits. The comparable figure for the mountain pannier is only $7.50 per minute. Therefore, more units of the touring model should be made using the additional time. Even though the mountain model has the larger per-unit contribution margin and the larger CM ratio, the touring model provides the larger contribution margin in relation to the constrained resource.

To verify that the touring model is, indeed, the more profitable product, suppose an hour of additional stitching time is available and that there are unfilled orders for both products. Total contribution margin will increase by $7.50/min × 60 min = $450 if the mountain pannier is made, and by $12/min × 60 min = $720 if the touring pannier is made.

This clearly shows that looking at unit contribution margins alone is not enough; the contribution margin has to be viewed in relation to the amount of the constrained resource each product requires.

Managing Constraints

LO2 • Know

CC9: Explain how constraints are managed.

Profits can be increased by effectively managing the organization's constraints. One aspect of managing constraints is to decide how best to utilize them. As discussed previously, if the constraint is a bottleneck in the production process, the manager should select the product mix that maximizes the total contribution margin. In addition, the manager should take an active role in managing the constraint itself. Management should focus efforts on increasing the efficiency of the bottleneck operation and on increasing its capacity. Such efforts directly increase the output of finished goods and will often pay off in an almost immediate increase in profits.

It is often possible for a manager to effectively increase the capacity of the bottleneck, which is called **relaxing the constraint** (or **elevating the constraint**). For example, the stitching machine operator could be asked to work overtime. This would result in more available stitching time and hence more finished goods that can be sold. The benefits from relaxing the constraint in such a manner are often enormous and can easily be quantified. The manager should first ask, "What would I do with additional capacity at the bottleneck if it were available?" In the example, if there are unfilled orders for both the touring and mountain panniers, the additional capacity would be used to process more touring panniers, since that would be a better use of the additional capacity. In that situation, the additional capacity would be worth $720 per hour. Since overtime pay for the operator is likely to be much less than $720 per hour, running the stitching machine on overtime would be an excellent way to increase the profits of the company while satisfying customers as well.

To reinforce this concept, suppose that making touring panniers has already been given top priority and consequently there are only unfilled orders for the mountain pannier. How much would it be worth to the company to run the stitching machine overtime in this situation? Since the additional capacity would be used to make the mountain pannier, the value of that additional capacity would drop to $7.50 per minute or $450 per hour. Nevertheless, the value of relaxing the constraint would still be quite high.

These calculations indicate that managers should pay great attention to bottleneck operations. If a bottleneck machine breaks down or is ineffectively utilized, the losses to the company can be quite large. In our example, for every minute the stitching machine is down due to breakdowns or setups, the company loses between $7.50 and $12. The losses on an hourly basis are between $450 and $720! In contrast, there is no such loss of contribution margin if time is lost on a machine that is not a bottleneck—such machines have excess capacity anyway.

The implications are clear. Managers should focus much of their attention on managing bottlenecks. As we have discussed, managers should emphasize products that most profitably utilize the constrained resource. They should also make sure that products are processed smoothly through the bottlenecks, with minimal lost time due to breakdowns and setups. And, they should try to find ways to increase the capacity at the bottlenecks.

The capacity of a bottleneck can be effectively increased in a number of ways, including:

- Working overtime on the bottleneck
- Subcontracting some of the processing that would be done at the bottleneck
- Investing in additional machines at the bottleneck
- Shifting workers from processes that are not bottlenecks to the process that is a bottleneck
- Focusing business process improvement efforts, such as TQM and business process reengineering, on the bottleneck
- Reducing defective units (each defective unit processed through the bottleneck and subsequently scrapped takes the place of a good unit that could be sold)

The last three methods of increasing the capacity of the bottleneck are particularly attractive, since they are essentially free and may even yield additional cost savings.

Finally, note that the analysis considered a single constraint. When there are multiple bottlenecks, the method of analysis is more complicated. The basic idea, however, is the same.

CONCEPT CHECK

4. A company has received a special order from a customer to make 5,000 units of a customized product. The direct materials cost per unit of the customized product is $15, the direct labour cost per unit is $5, and the manufacturing overhead per unit is $18, including $6 of variable manufacturing overhead. If the company has sufficient available manufacturing capacity, what is the minimum price that can be accepted for the special order?
    a. $24
    b. $26
    c. $32
    d. $38

5. Refer to the facts from Concept Check 4; however, in answering this question, assume that the company is operating at 100% of its capacity without the special order. If the company normally manufactures only one product that has a contribution margin of $20 per unit and that consumes two minutes of the constrained resource per unit, what is the opportunity cost (stated in terms of forgone contribution margin) of taking the special order? Assume the special order would require 1.5 minutes of the constrained resource per unit.
    a. $25,000
    b. $50,000
    c. $75,000
    d. $100,000

*Note to student: See **Guidance Answers** online.*

HELPFUL HINT

Use the following four steps to help determine the most profitable use of a constrained resource:

Step 1: Calculate each product's contribution margin per unit.

Step 2: Identify the constraining resource, and calculate the quantity of that resource used to make one unit of each product.

Step 3: Calculate each product's contribution margin per unit of the constraining resource (step 1 ÷ step 2).

Step 4: Rank the products from the highest contribution margin per unit of the constraining resource to the lowest.

Joint Product Costs and the Contribution Approach

LO3 ● Know

CC10: Understand the pitfalls of allocation for decision making.

In some industries, a number of end products are produced from a single raw material input. For example, in the petroleum refining industry a large number of products are extracted from crude oil, including gasoline, jet fuel, home heating oil, lubricants, asphalt, and various organic chemicals. In meat processing, various cuts of meat and meat products are produced from the cow, pig, chicken, or turkey. In these industries, the production process begins with a common input—for example, crude oil or a chicken. The raw material goes through processing, and at a particular stage in the production process called the **split-off point**, various products are identified. For example, in chicken processing, a whole chicken is processed to yield chicken legs, chicken breasts, and wings. These products are called **joint products**. An important decision for the producer at the split-off point is whether to sell the products identified or to process some of these products further. A partially finished product is called an *intermediate product,* and a fully finished product is an *end product*. Markets exist for intermediate products, which is why at the split-off point a company must assess the profitability of selling the intermediate product against the profitability of processing the intermediate product further and then selling it. The cost incurred up to the split-off point is called **joint cost**. The central question in a decision to sell or process further is whether the costs incurred up to the split-off point are relevant to the decision.

Joint costs are *common* costs that are incurred to simultaneously produce a variety of end products. These joint costs are traditionally *allocated* among the different products. A typical approach is to allocate the joint costs according to the relative sales value of the products. Although allocation of joint product costs is needed for some purposes, such as balance sheet inventory valuation, allocations of this kind are extremely misleading for decision making. Think back to the earlier discussion in this chapter regarding allocating fixed costs. The same basic lesson applies here as well. Allocating costs to products or to a decision alternative although the cost is not traceable to that alternative should be avoided in the analysis of alternatives.

Sell-or-Process-Further Decisions

LO3 ● Apply

CC11: Apply the relevant cost analysis framework to a sell-or-process-further decision.

When joint products are identified at the split-off point, management has to decide if any of the joint products should be processed further, at additional cost, and sold for a price higher than the price at the split-off point. Decisions of this type are known as **sell-or-process-further decisions**. It is profitable to continue processing a joint product after the split-off point *so long as the incremental revenue from such processing exceeds the incremental processing cost incurred after the split-off point*. Joint costs that have already been incurred up to the split-off point are always irrelevant in decisions concerning what to do from the split-off point forward.

Once the split-off point is reached, the joint costs have already been incurred and nothing can be done to avoid them. Even if a joint product was disposed of at the split-off point without any further processing, *all* of the joint costs must be incurred and no part is avoidable by disposing of any one of the products that emerge from the split-off point. Therefore, none of the joint costs are traceable to any one of the intermediate or end products. The joint costs are a *common* cost of all of the intermediate and end products and should not be allocated to them *for the purpose of making decisions about the individual products.*

The situation of Maple Creek Wool Cooperative of Saskatchewan will be used to illustrate these points. The company buys raw wool from local sheep farmers, separates the wool into three grades—coarse, fine, and superfine—and then dyes the wool using traditional methods that rely on pigments from local materials. Exhibit 9–7 contains a diagram of the production process. The joint costs are made up of $200,000 for the raw wool and $40,000 for separating the wool. The undyed wool is the intermediate product because it is not finished at this point. Nevertheless, a market does exist for undyed wool—although at a significantly lower price than finished, dyed wool. The sales value of each type of undyed wool at the split-off point, the additional cost to dye each type of wool, and the final sales value of each type of dyed wool are shown in Exhibit 9–7.

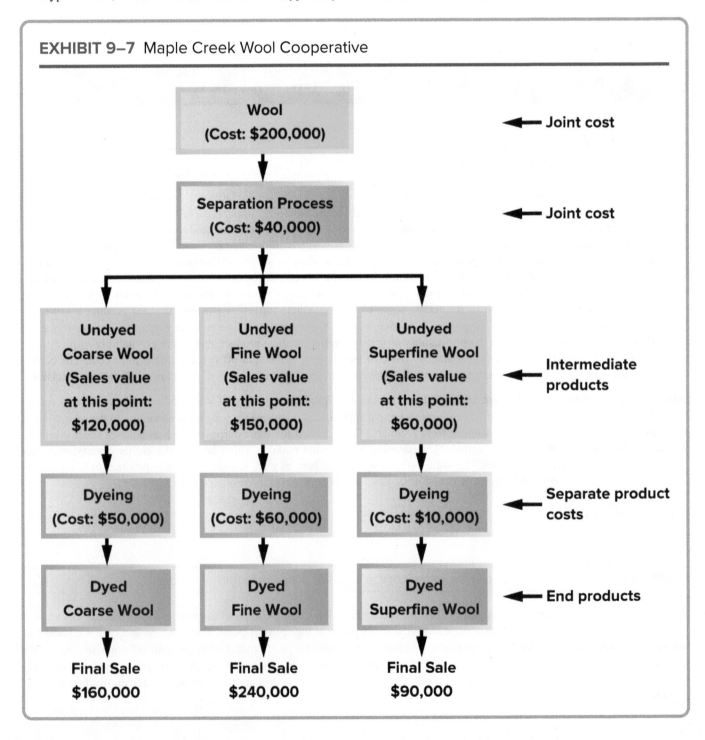

EXHIBIT 9–7 Maple Creek Wool Cooperative

Using the data, we can address two key questions for management. First, is the company making money if it runs the entire process from beginning to end? Assuming there are no costs other than those displayed in Exhibit 9–7, the company is indeed making money, as follows:

Analysis of the profitability of the overall operation:

Combined final sales value ($160,000 + $240,000 + $90,000)		$490,000
Less: Costs of producing the end products:		
Cost of wool	$200,000	
Cost of separating wool	40,000	
Combined costs of dyeing ($50,000 + $60,000 + $10,000)	120,000	360,000
Profit		$130,000

Note that the joint costs of buying the wool and separating the wool *are* relevant when considering the profitability of the *entire* operation. This is because these joint costs *could* be avoided if the entire operation were shut down. However, these joint costs are *not* relevant when considering the profitability of any *one* product. As long as the process is being run to make the other products, no additional joint costs are incurred to make the specific product in question.

Even though the company is making money overall, it may be losing money on one or more of the products. If the company buys wool and runs the separation process, it will get all three intermediate products. Nothing can be done about that. However, each of these products can be sold *as is* without further processing. It may be that the company would be better off selling one or more of the products prior to dyeing to avoid the dyeing costs. This is the second question for management: Should it process each type of undyed wool further (i.e., dye it), or should the wool be sold at the split-off point? The appropriate way to make this choice is to compare the incremental revenues to the incremental costs from further processing as follows:

Analysis of Sell-or-Process-Further Question			
	Coarse Wool	Fine Wool	Superfine Wool
Final sales value after further processing	$160,000	$240,000	$90,000
Less: Sales value at the split-off point	120,000	150,000	60,000
Incremental revenue from further processing	40,000	90,000	30,000
Less: Cost of further processing (dyeing)	50,000	60,000	10,000
Profit (loss) from further processing	$ (10,000)	$ 30,000	$20,000

As this analysis shows, the company would be better off selling the undyed coarse wool rather than processing it further. The other two products should be processed further and dyed before selling them. The sell-or-process-further question should have been answered first because, even though the overall operation is profitable, had the company known that coarse wool should be sold without being dyed, its profit would have been $10,000 greater.

Note that the joint costs of the wool ($200,000) and of the wool separation process ($40,000) play no role in the decision to sell or further process the intermediate products. These joint costs are relevant in a decision of whether to buy wool and to run the wool separation process, but they are not relevant in decisions about what to do with the intermediate products once they have been separated.

HELPFUL HINT

For each end product, use the following three steps to make sell-or-process-further decisions:

   Step 1: Calculate the sales value if processed further minus the sales value at the split-off point. The sales value is quantity of product times the unit price of each unit.

   Step 2: Determine the cost of further processing beyond the split-off point.

   Step 3: Take the amount in step 1 and subtract from it the amount in step 2. If the result is a positive number, then choose to process further. If it is a negative number, then choose to sell at the split-off point.

While you may need to add additional steps when solving complex problems, these three steps will help organize your analysis.

WORKING IT OUT

Narmada Company manufactures three products from a common input in a joint processing operation. Joint processing costs up to the split-off point total $100,000 per year. The company allocates these costs to the joint products on the basis of their total sales value at the split-off point. These sales values are as follows: product X, $50,000; product Y, $90,000; and product Z, $60,000.

Each product may be sold at the split-off point or processed further. Additional processing requires no special facilities. The additional processing costs and the sales value after further processing for each product (on an annual basis) are shown below:

Product	Additional Processing Costs	Sales Value After Further Processing
X	$35,000	$ 80,000
Y	$40,000	$150,000
Z	$12,000	$ 75,000

Required:

1. Which product(s) should be sold at the split-off point, and which should be processed further? Show computations.

2. What is the relevance, if any, of the costs of production up to the split-off point?

3. Calculate the maximum amount the company would be prepared to pay for the joint cost of production.

SOLUTION TO WORKING IT OUT

1. Product X should be sold at the split-off point and not be processed further. Products Y and Z should be processed further. The incremental benefit to further processing is $18,000.

	Product X	Product Y	Product Z
Sales value after further processing	$80,000	$150,000	$75,000
Sales value at split-off point	50,000	90,000	60,000
Incremental revenue	30,000	60,000	15,000
Cost of further processing	35,000	40,000	12,000
Incremental profit (loss)	$ (5,000)	20,000	3,000

2. The joint cost of production is only relevant for the *decision to operate the joint production process* that yields the joint products at the split-off point. It is relevant for answering the question, "Should the company operate the production process or shut down?"

3. The maximum amount the company would be willing to incur as the joint cost of production will be an amount that makes the overall profitability of the operation zero:

Total revenue after further processing	$305,000
Total cost of additional processing	87,000
Amount available to cover joint cost	$ 218,000

The maximum cost of joint production the company will pay is $218,000. Note that the maximum amount is not $200,000, which is the total sales value ($50,000 + $60,000 + $90,000) at the split-off point, because we know there is additional benefit to processing further of $18,000, which is available to cover the joint cost of production.

Learning Objectives Summary

LO1 UNDERSTAND AND APPLY THE RELEVANT COSTING APPROACH TO DECISION MAKING.

Every decision involves a choice from among at least two alternatives. Only those costs and benefits that differ in total between the alternatives are relevant; costs and benefits that are the same for all alternatives are not affected by the decision and can be ignored. Only future costs that differ between alternatives are relevant. Sunk costs are always irrelevant. This is the *relevant cost analysis framework*. Since a decision is made following an analysis of the costs and revenues that differ between alternatives, this approach is also called *differential cost analysis*.

When deciding whether or not to replace an asset like a piece of equipment, compare the costs of retaining the existing asset with the costs of the proposed replacement. One important consideration is that the remaining life of the existing equipment should equal the life of the new equipment. In this chapter we omit the complications arising due to the time value of money.

When deciding whether a product line or other segment should be dropped, focus on the differences in the costs and benefits of dropping or retaining the product line or segment. Be careful when using reports in which common fixed costs have been allocated among segments. If these common fixed costs are unaffected by the decision of whether to add or drop the segment, they are irrelevant and should be removed before determining the real profitability of a segment.

When deciding whether to make or buy a component, focus on the costs and benefits that differ between those two alternatives. As in other decisions, sunk costs—such as the depreciation on old equipment—should be ignored. Future costs that do not differ between alternatives—such as allocations of common fixed costs like general overhead—should be ignored.

When deciding whether to accept or reject a special order, focus on the benefits and costs that differ between those two alternatives. Specifically, a special order should be accepted when the incremental revenue from the sale exceeds the incremental cost. As always, sunk costs and future costs that do not differ between the alternatives are irrelevant.

LO2   UNDERSTAND DECISION MAKING IN A CONSTRAINED SETTING.

When demand for a company's products and services exceeds its ability to supply them, the company has a bottleneck. The bottleneck—whether it is a particular material, skilled labour, or a specific machine—is a constrained resource. Since the company is unable to make everything it could sell, managers must decide what to make and what not to make. In this situation, the profitability of a product is best measured by its contribution margin per unit of the constrained resource. The products with the highest contribution margin per unit of the constrained resource should be favoured.

Managers should focus their attention on effectively managing the constraint. This involves making the most profitable use of the constrained resource and increasing the amount of the constrained resource that is available. The value of relaxing the constraint is determined by the contribution margin per unit of the constrained resource for the work that would be done if more of the resource were available.

LO3   UNDERSTAND COST CONCEPTS AND DECISION MAKING FOR JOINT PRODUCTS.

Managers should recommend further processing of an intermediate product so long as the incremental revenue from such processing exceeds the incremental processing cost incurred after the split-off point. Joint costs are irrelevant in decisions regarding what to do with a product from the split-off point forward. Once the split-off point is reached, the joint costs have already been incurred and nothing can be done to avoid them.

Application Competency Summary

APPLICATION COMPETENCY	DELIVERABLE	SOURCE DOCUMENTS AND KEY INFORMATION	STEPS	KNOWLEDGE COMPETENCY
Apply the relevant cost analysis framework to an equipment replacement decision. ● **LO1–CC2**	*Key Information* The different alternatives Avoidable costs and benefits Net incremental benefit	Asset/Cost/ *Expense Accounts in the General Ledger* Operating costs of existing equipment	1. List the costs and benefits associated with keeping the existing equipment and purchasing new equipment. 2. Eliminate sunk costs and future costs that are identical between	Variable and fixed costs ● **LO1–CC1** (Ch. 2) Direct and indirect costs ● **LO2–CC2** (Ch. 2)

APPLICATION COMPETENCY	DELIVERABLE	SOURCE DOCUMENTS AND KEY INFORMATION	STEPS	KNOWLEDGE COMPETENCY
	Report/ Document No specific document (report structure may vary from company to company)	Salvage value of existing equipment *Quotes From Potential Suppliers of Equipment* Estimated purchase price of new equipment Estimated operating costs of new equipment *Sales/Production Reports* Production and sales quantities	alternatives (e.g., book value of old equipment, allocated common costs). 3. Compute the net incremental benefit of replacing existing equipment.	Differential, opportunity, and sunk costs ● **LO3–CC3** (Ch. 2) Relevant and irrelevant costs ● **LO1–CC1**
Apply the relevant cost analysis framework to a business addition/ deletion decision. ● **LO1–CC3**	*Key Information* The different alternatives Avoidable costs and benefits Net incremental benefit *Report/ Document* No specific document (report structure may vary from company to company)	*Various Accounts in the General Ledger* Current revenues and costs associated with the operations of existing segments *Planning Documents* Estimated revenues and costs associated with a proposed new segment	1. List the costs associated with existing segments/ product lines. 2. Identify (and list) the benefits and costs associated with adding a new segment. 3. In the decision to drop a segment, identify the costs that can be avoided by dropping the segment. 4. Compute the net incremental benefit to the company of adding or dropping a segment.	Variable and fixed costs ● **LO1–CC1** (Ch. 2) Direct and indirect costs ● **LO2–CC2** (Ch. 2) Differential, opportunity, and sunk costs ● **LO3–CC3** (Ch. 2) Relevant and irrelevant costs ● **LO1–CC1**
Apply the relevant cost analysis framework to a make-or-buy (outsourcing) decision. ● **LO1–CC4**	*Key Information* The different alternatives Avoidable costs and benefits Net incremental benefit	*Cost/Expense/ Inventory Accounts in the General Ledger* Existing production-related costs *Master Budget*	1. Compute the total purchasing-related costs (including the purchase costs and incremental, receiving, inspection, storage and handling, and supplier-related administrative costs).	Variable and fixed costs ● **LO1–CC1** (Ch. 2) Direct and indirect costs ● **LO2–CC2** (Ch. 2)

APPLICATION COMPETENCY	DELIVERABLE	SOURCE DOCUMENTS AND KEY INFORMATION	STEPS	KNOWLEDGE COMPETENCY
	Report/ Document No specific document (report structure may vary from company to company)	Estimated price, quantity, and costs *Planning Documents* Estimated additional costs of receiving, inspection, storage and handling, and other supplier-related administrative costs	2. List the avoidable production costs (or the estimated directly traceable incremental production costs). 3. Compute the net incremental benefit of make versus buy (or vice versa).	Differential, opportunity, and sunk costs • **LO3–CC3** (Ch. 2) Relevant and irrelevant costs • **LO1–CC1**
Apply the relevant cost analysis framework to a special-order decision. • **LO1–CC5**	*Key Information* The different alternatives Avoidable costs and benefits Net incremental benefit *Report/ Document* No specific document (report structure may vary from company to company)	*Schedule of Cost of Goods Manufactured* Existing production costs *Master Budget* Estimated production costs (including a breakdown of the variable and fixed components) *Customer Inquiry Documents (Requests for Quotes, Orders)* Order quantity and price per unit	1. Compute the revenues associated with the special order. 2. Compute the total variable costs and the total incremental (new) fixed costs associated with the order. 3. Compute the net incremental benefit from the order.	Variable and fixed costs • **LO1–CC1** (Ch. 2) Direct and indirect costs • **LO2–CC2** (Ch. 2) Differential, opportunity, and sunk costs • **LO3–CC3** (Ch. 2) Relevant and irrelevant costs • **LO1–CC1**
Compute the contribution margin per unit of a constrained resource. • **LO2–CC8**	*Key Information* Contribution margin per unit of product/ service Contribution margin per unit of the constrained resource *Report/ Document*	*Resource Capacity Documents (e.g., Budgets)* Capacity of constrained resource *Production Reports, Standard Cost Card* Estimated or actual consumption of	1. Compute the contribution margin per unit for each product/service. 2. Divide the contribution margin by the quantity of the constrained resource consumed per unit by each product/service.	Decision making in a constrained resource environment • **LO2–CC7** Unit contribution margin • **LO3–CC12** (Ch. 6)

APPLICATION COMPETENCY	DELIVERABLE	SOURCE DOCUMENTS AND KEY INFORMATION	STEPS	KNOWLEDGE COMPETENCY
	No specific document (report structure may vary from company to company)	constrained resource per unit of a product/service *Variable Cost Report, Budget* Contribution margin per unit of individual product/service		Contribution margin ratio • **LO1–CC2** (Ch. 8)
Apply the relevant cost analysis framework to a sell-or-process-further decision • **LO3–CC11**	*Key Information* Profit from processing a joint product beyond the split-off point *Report/Document* No specific document	*Production Documents* Production costs to manufacture joint products *Marketing and Sales Analyses* Selling prices at the split-off point Selling prices after further processing	1. Calculate the sales value if processed further minus the sales value at the split-off point. The sales value is the quantity of product times the unit price of each unit. 2. Determine the cost of further processing beyond the split-off point. 3. Take the amount in step 2 and subtract it from the amount in step 1. If the result is a positive number, then choose to process further. If it is a negative number, then choose to sell at the split-off point.	Variable and fixed costs • **LO1–CC1** (Ch. 2) Direct and indirect costs • **LO2–CC2** (Ch. 2) Differential, opportunity, and sunk costs • **LO3–CC3** (Ch. 2) Relevant and irrelevant costs • **LO1–CC1**

Review Problem 1: Relevant Costs

Charter Sports Equipment manufactures round, rectangular, and octagonal trampolines. Data on sales expenses for the past month follow:

		Trampoline		
	Total	Round	Rectangular	Octagonal
Sales	$1,000,000	$140,000	$500,000	$360,000
Less: Variable expenses	410,000	60,000	200,000	150,000

| | Total | Trampoline | | |
		Round	Rectangular	Octagonal
Contribution margin	590,000	80,000	300,000	210,000
Less: Fixed expenses:				
Advertising—traceable	216,000	41,000	110,000	65,000
Depreciation of special equipment	95,000	20,000	40,000	35,000
Line supervisors' salaries	19,000	6,000	7,000	6,000
General factory overhead*	200,000	28,000	100,000	72,000
Total fixed expenses	530,000	95,000	257,000	178,000
Net operating income (loss)	$ 60,000	$ (15,000)	$ 43,000	$ 32,000

*A common cost that is allocated on the basis of sales dollars.

Management is concerned about the continued losses shown by the round trampolines and wants a recommendation as to whether the line should be discontinued. The special equipment used to produce the trampolines has no resale value. If the round trampoline model is dropped, the two line supervisors assigned to the model will be discharged.

Required:

1. Should production and sale of the round trampolines be discontinued? You may assume that the company has no other use for the capacity now being used to produce the round trampolines. Show computations to support your answer.
2. Recast the preceding data in a format that would be more usable to management in assessing the long-term profitability of the various product lines.

SOLUTION TO REVIEW PROBLEM 1

1. No, production and sale of the round trampolines should not be discontinued. Computations to support this answer follow:

Contribution margin lost if the round trampolines are discontinued		$(80,000)
Less: Fixed costs that can be avoided:		
Advertising—traceable	$41,000	
Line supervisors' salaries	6,000	47,000
Decrease in net operating income for the company as a whole		$(33,000)

The depreciation of the special equipment represents a sunk cost; therefore, it is not relevant to the decision. The general factory overhead is allocated and will presumably continue regardless of whether the round trampolines are discontinued; thus, it is also not relevant to the decision.

2. If management wants a clear picture of the profitability of the segments, the general factory overhead should not be allocated. It is a common cost and therefore should be deducted from the total product line segment margin, as shown in Exhibit 9–4. A more useful income statement format is as follows:

| | Trampoline | | | |
	Round	Rectangular	Octagonal	Total
Sales	$140,000	$500,000	$360,000	$1,000,000
Less: Variable expenses	60,000	200,000	150,000	410,000
Contribution margin	80,000	300,000	210,000	590,000
Less: Traceable fixed expenses:				
Advertising—traceable	41,000	110,000	65,000	216,000
Depreciation of special equipment	20,000	40,000	35,000	95,000
Line supervisors' salaries	6,000	7,000	6,000	19,000
Total traceable fixed expenses	67,000	157,000	106,000	330,000
Product-line segment margin	$ 13,000	$143,000	$104,000	260,000
Less: Common fixed expenses				200,000
Net operating income (loss)				$ 60,000

ALTERNATIVE SOLUTION TO REVIEW PROBLEM 1, PART (1)

	Keep Round Trampolines	Drop Round Trampolines	Difference: Net Income Increase (Decrease)
Sales	$ 140,000	$ –0–	$(140,000)
Less: Variable expenses	60,000	–0–	60,000
Contribution margin	80,000	–0–	(80,000)
Less: Fixed expenses:			
Advertising—traceable	41,000	–0–	41,000
Depreciation of special equipment	20,000	20,000	–0–
Line supervisors' salaries	6,000	–0–	6,000
General factory overhead	28,000	28,000	–0–
Total fixed expenses	95,000	48,000	47,000
Net operating income (loss)	$ (15,000)	$(48,000)	$ (33,000)

Review Problem 2: Adding a Product Line

Compton Products makes and sells two products, Miss and Mister. The financial results for the year ended December 31, 20X5, are as follows:

	Miss	Mister	Total
Unit sales	350,000	131,250	481,250
Revenues	$700,000	$ 603,750	$1,303,750
Cost of sales:			
Variable	245,000	157,500	402,500
Fixed	202,300	116,760	319,060
Gross margin	252,700	329,490	582,190
Selling and administrative expenses:			
Variable	140,000	84,000	224,000
Fixed	70,700	124,740	195,440
Product line profit	$ 42,000	$120,750	$ 162,750
Organization-wide costs:			
Fixed costs			226,940
Equipment lease expense			70,000
Equipment rental revenue			84,000
Income			$ (50,190)

To address the poor financial performance in 20X5, the company is considering adding a new product, Master.

a. The company expects to sell 7,000 units of Master at a price of $92.50 per unit. The variable manufacturing cost per unit will be $39.90, and the variable selling and general administrative expense per unit will be $37.80.

b. The introduction of Master is expected to add $60,060 to the fixed manufacturing costs of Master.

c. Of the present fixed organization-wide costs of $226,940, $86,940 will be allocated to the fixed manufacturing cost of Master and $70,000 will be allocated towards its marketing.

d. Currently, the company is earning rental revenue of $84,000 by renting equipment that it did not require for either Miss or Mister. The company is leasing this equipment for $70,000 per year. This equipment will now be used for making Master.

e. The product manager of Mister has indicated that the sales of Mister will decline by one-third from its present level with the addition of Master, as these products compete in the same market. Due to this decline, the company will no longer require leased space that is being used for the purpose of selling and administrative activities of Mister, and the company will allow the lease to expire. The annual payments for leasing the space have been $70,000.

Required:

Determine whether the company should introduce Master. Show all calculations.

SOLUTION TO REVIEW PROBLEM 2

Three alternative solution approaches will be illustrated. Regardless of the approach, the recommendation is to not introduce Master. The company's profit will decline by $91,210.

1. Nonincremental approach, absorption format (relevant costs only):

	Master	Miss	Mister	Total
Unit sales	7,000	350,000	87,500	444,500
Revenues	$ 647,500	$700,000	$402,500[3]	$1,750,000
Cost of sales:				
Variable	279,300	245,000	105,000	629,300
Fixed	130,060[1]	202,300	116,760	449,120
Gross margin	238,140	252,700	180,740	671,580
Lease rental revenue				0
Selling and administrative expenses:				
Variable	264,600	140,000	56,000	460,600
Fixed	0[2]	70,700	54,740[4]	125,440
Product-line profit	$ (26,460)	$ 42,000	$ 70,000	$ 85,540
Organization-wide costs				
Fixed costs				226,940[5]
Income				$ (141,400)

[1]$60,060 +70,000 (equipment lease)

[2]Marketing and selling expense

[3]Sales of Master product are reduced by one-third.

[4]$124,740 – $70,000 (savings from expiry of lease of space)

[5]Represents the remaining untraceable cost from before the introduction of Master

2. The above analysis can also be presented in the contribution format (relevant costs only):

	Master	Miss	Mister	Total
Revenues	$647,500	$700,000	$402,500	$1,750,000
Variable manufacturing	279,300	245,000	105,000	629,300
Variable selling and administrative	264,600	140,000	56,000	460,600
Contribution margin	103,600	315,000	241,500	660,100
Fixed manufacturing	130,060	202,300	116,760	449,120
Fixed selling and administrative	0	70,700	54,740	125,440
Product line profit	$ (26,460)	$ 42,000	$ 70,000	$ 85,540
Organization-wide costs (fixed)				226,940
Net income				$ (141,400)

3. Incremental (differential) cost analysis:

Revenue (Master)	$ 647,500
Variable manufacturing	279,300
Variable selling and administrative	264,600
Contribution margin	103,600
Incremental fixed manufacturing	(60,060)
Loss of lease revenue	(84,000)
Loss of Mister contribution	(120,750)*
Saving from lease expiry	70,000
Incremental profit (loss)	$ (91,210)

*1/3 × ($603,750 − $157,500 − $84,000) = $120,750

Questions

9–1   What is a relevant cost?

9–2   Define the following terms: *incremental cost, opportunity cost,* and *sunk cost.*

9–3   Are variable costs always relevant costs? Explain.

9–4   The original cost of a machine the company already owns is irrelevant in decision making. Explain why this is so.

9–5   "Sunk costs are easy to spot—they're simply the fixed costs associated with a decision." Do you agree? Explain your reasoning.

9–6   "Variable costs and differential costs mean the same thing." Do you agree? Explain your reasoning.

9–7   "All future costs are relevant in decision making." Do you agree? Why, or why not?

9–8   Prentice Company is considering dropping one of its product lines. What costs of the product line would be relevant to this decision? Irrelevant?

9–9   "If a product line is generating a loss, that's pretty good evidence that the product line should be discontinued." Do you agree? Explain your reasoning.

9–10 What is the danger in allocating common fixed costs among product lines or other segments of an organization?

9–11 How does opportunity cost enter into the make-or-buy decision?

9–12 Give four examples of possible constraints.

9–13 How will relating product contribution margins to the constrained resource they require help a company ensure that profits will be maximized?

9–14 Airlines sometimes offer reduced rates during certain times of the week to members of a businessperson's family if they accompany him or her on trips. How does the concept of relevant costs enter into the decision to offer reduced rates of this type?

The Foundational 15

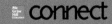

[LO1 – CC1, 3, 4, 5; LO2 – CC8]

Cane Company manufactures two products called Alpha and Beta that sell for $120 and $80, respectively. Each product uses only one type of raw material that costs $6 per pound. The company has the capacity to annually produce 100,000 units of each product. Its unit costs for each product at this level of activity are given below:

	Alpha	Beta
Direct materials	$ 30	$ 12
Direct labour	20	15
Variable manufacturing overhead	7	5
Traceable fixed manufacturing overhead	16	18
Variable selling expenses	12	8
Common fixed expenses	15	10
Total cost per unit	$ 100	$ 68

The company considers its traceable fixed manufacturing overhead to be avoidable, whereas its common fixed expenses are deemed unavoidable and have been allocated to products based on sales dollars.

Required:

(Answer each question independently unless instructed otherwise.)

9–1   What is the total amount of traceable fixed manufacturing overhead for the Alpha product line and for the Beta product line?

9–2   What is the company's total amount of common fixed expenses?

9–3   Assume that Cane expects to produce and sell 80,000 Alphas during the current year. One of Cane's sales representatives has found a new customer that is willing to buy 10,000 additional Alphas for a price of $80 per unit. If Cane accepts the customer's offer, how much will its profits increase or decrease?

9–4   Assume that Cane expects to produce and sell 90,000 Betas during the current year. One of Cane's sales representatives has found a new customer that is willing to buy 5,000 additional Betas for a price of $39 per unit. If Cane accepts the customer's offer, how much will its profits increase or decrease?

9–5   Assume that Cane expects to produce and sell 95,000 Alphas during the current year. One of Cane's sales representatives has found a new customer that is willing to buy 10,000 additional Alphas for a price of $80 per unit. If Cane accepts the customer's offer, it will decrease Alpha sales to regular customers by 5,000 units. Should Cane accept this special order?

9–6   Assume that Cane normally produces and sells 90,000 Betas per year. If Cane discontinues the Beta product line, how much will profits increase or decrease?

9–7   Assume that Cane normally produces and sells 40,000 Betas per year. If Cane discontinues the Beta product line, how much will profits increase or decrease?

9–8   Assume that Cane normally produces and sells 60,000 Betas and 80,000 Alphas per year. If Cane discontinues the Beta product line, its sales representatives could increase sales of Alpha by 15,000 units. If Cane discontinues the Beta product line, how much would profits increase or decrease?

9–9   Assume that Cane expects to produce and sell 80,000 Alphas during the current year. A supplier has offered to manufacture and deliver 80,000 Alphas to Cane for a price of $80 per unit. If Cane buys 80,000 units from the supplier instead of making those units, how much will profits increase or decrease?

9–10   Assume that Cane expects to produce and sell 50,000 Alphas during the current year. A supplier has offered to manufacture and deliver 50,000 Alphas to Cane for a price of $80 per unit. If Cane buys 50,000 units from the supplier instead of making those units, how much will profits increase or decrease?

9–11   How many pounds of raw material are needed to make one unit of Alpha and one unit of Beta?

9–12   What contribution margin per pound of raw material is earned by Alpha and Beta?

9–13   Assume that Cane's customers would buy a maximum of 80,000 units of Alpha and 60,000 units of Beta. Also assume that the company's raw materials available for production is limited to 160,000 pounds. How many units of each product should Cane produce to maximize its profits?

9–14   If Cane follows your recommendation in requirement 13, what total contribution margin will it earn?

9–15   If Cane uses its 160,000 pounds of raw materials as you recommended in requirement 13, up to how much should it be willing to pay per pound for additional raw materials?

Brief Exercises   connect

BRIEF EXERCISE 9–1
Identifying Relevant Costs [LO1 – CC1]

Following are a number of costs that may be relevant in decisions faced by the management of Svahn, AB, a Swedish manufacturer of sailing yachts:

	Item	Case 1 Relevant	Case 1 Not Relevant	Case 2 Relevant	Case 2 Not Relevant
a.	Sales revenue				
b.	Direct materials				
c.	Direct labour				
d.	Variable manufacturing overhead				
e.	Depreciation—Model B100 machine				
f.	Book value—Model B100 machine				
g.	Disposal value—Model B100 machine				
h.	Market value—Model B300 machine (cost)				
i.	Depreciation—Model B300 machine				
j.	Fixed manufacturing overhead (general)				
k.	Variable selling expense				
l.	Fixed selling expense				
m.	General administrative overhead				

Required:

Copy the preceding costs onto your answer sheet and place an X in the appropriate column to indicate whether each cost is relevant or not relevant in the following situations (part (1) relates to case 1; part (2) relates to case 2):

1. Management is considering purchasing a Model B300 machine to use in addition to the company's present Model B100 machine. This would increase the company's production and sales. The increase in volume would be large enough to require increases in fixed selling expenses and in general administrative overhead but not in fixed manufacturing overhead.

2. Management is instead considering replacing its present Model B100 machine with a new Model B300 machine. The Model B100 machine would be sold. This change would have no effect on production or sales, other than some savings in direct materials costs due to reduced waste.

BRIEF EXERCISE 9–2
Making an Equipment Replacement Decision [LO1 – CC2]

Waukee Railroad is considering the purchase of a powerful, high-speed wheel grinder to replace a standard wheel grinder now in use. Selected information on the two machines follows:

	Standard Wheel Grinder	High-Speed Wheel Grinder
Original cost new	$45,000	$62,500
Accumulated depreciation to date	$18,000	$ 0
Current salvage value	$21,750	$ 0
Estimated cost per year to operate	$26,250	$12,250
Remaining years of useful life	5 years	5 years

Required:

Prepare a computation covering the five-year period that will show the net advantage or disadvantage of purchasing the high-speed wheel grinder. Use only relevant costs in your analysis.

BRIEF EXERCISE 9–3
Dropping or Retaining a Segment [LO1 – CC3]

Bed & Bath, a retailing company, has two departments: hardware and linens. A recent monthly income statement for the company follows:

	Department		
	Hardware	Linens	Total
Sales	$3,000,000	$1,000,000	$4,000,000
Less: Variable expenses	900,000	400,000	1,300,000
Contribution margin	2,100,000	600,000	2,700,000
Less: Fixed expenses	1,400,000	800,000	2,200,000
Net operating income (loss)	$ 700,000	$ (200,000)	$ 500,000

A study indicates that $340,000 of the fixed expenses being charged to linens are sunk costs or allocated costs that will continue even if the linens department is dropped. In addition, the elimination of the linens department will result in a 10% decrease in the sales of the hardware department.

Required:

If the linens department is dropped, what will be the effect on the net operating income of the company as a whole?

BRIEF EXERCISE 9–4
Determining Whether to Make or Buy [LO1 – CC4]

For many years, Futura Company has purchased the starters that it installs in its standard line of farm tractors. Due to a reduction in output of some of its products, the company has idle capacity that could be used to produce the starters. The chief engineer has recommended against this move, however, pointing out that the cost to produce the starters would be greater than the current $12.60 per unit purchase price:

	Per Unit	Total
Direct materials	$ 4.65	
Direct labour	4.05	
Supervision	2.25	$90,000
Depreciation	1.50	60,000
Variable manufacturing overhead	0.90	
Rent	0.45	18,000
Total production cost	$13.80	

A supervisor would have to be hired to oversee production of the starters. However, the company has sufficient idle tools and machinery that no new equipment would have to be purchased. The rent charge above is based on space utilized in the plant. The total rent on the plant is $148,000 per period. Depreciation is due to obsolescence, rather than wear and tear.

Required:

Prepare computations to show the dollar advantage or disadvantage per period of making the starters.

BRIEF EXERCISE 9–5
Determining Whether to Accept a Special Order [LO1 – CC5]

Delta Company produces a single product. The cost of producing and selling a single unit of this product at the company's normal activity level of 60,000 units per year is as follows:

Direct materials	$6.10
Direct labour	3.80
Variable manufacturing overhead	2.00
Fixed manufacturing overhead	4.20
Variable selling and administrative expense	2.50
Fixed selling and administrative expense	2.40

The normal selling price is $25 per unit. The company's capacity is 75,000 units per year. An order has been received from a mail-order house for 15,000 units at a special price of $16 per unit. This order would not affect regular sales.

Required:

1. If the order is accepted, by how much will annual profits be increased or decreased? (The order will not change the company's total fixed costs.)
2. Assume the company has 1,000 units of this product left over from last year that are vastly inferior to the current model. The units must be sold through regular channels at reduced prices. What unit cost figure is relevant for establishing a minimum selling price for these units? Explain your answer.

BRIEF EXERCISE 9–6
Determining the Utilization of a Constrained Resource [LO2 – CC7, 8]

Benoit Company produces three products, A, B, and C. Data concerning the three products follow (per unit):

	Product		
	A	B	C
Selling price	$132.00	$92.40	$115.50
Less: Variable expenses:			
Direct materials	39.60	24.75	14.85
Other variable expenses	39.60	44.55	66.00
Total variable expenses	79.20	69.30	80.85
Contribution margin	$ 52.80	$23.10	$ 34.65
CM ratio	40%	25%	30%

Demand for the company's products is very strong, with far more orders each month than the company has raw materials available to produce. The same material is used in each product. The material costs $4.95 per kilogram with a maximum of 8,230 kilograms available each month.

Required:

How would you advise the company to prioritize the orders for A, B, and C?

BRIEF EXERCISE 9–7
Deciding Whether to Accept or Reject a Special Order [LO1 – CC5]

Cora Limited's normal monthly production output is 3,800 units of a product that sells for $30 per unit. Its total variable costs amount to $22 per unit and total monthly fixed costs amount to $10,250, A special order is received for 100 units at a price of $25 per unit.

Required:

Assume that Cora Ltd.'s current level of capacity utilization is 90%. Should Cora accept the special order?

BRIEF EXERCISE 9–8
Identifying Relevant Costs [LO1 – CC1]

Coral Corporation is evaluating a proposal to supply warehouse space to a potential customer as well as maintain all the required warehouse records. Coral has a storage barn not currently in use; however it will require the installation of additional shelving and a special concrete pad for delivery truck access. Coral's existing accountant will assume the additional accounting duties and receive an additional $8,000 per annum. The potential customer will pay a fee to Coral based on the volume of product stored.

Required:

Which of the following items is not a relevant consideration in deciding whether Coral should provide the warehouse space to the potential customer?

1. Original purchase price of the storage barn.
2. Projected volume of product for storage
3. The 8,000 increase in the accountant's annual salary.
4. Allocation of administrative salaries.

BRIEF EXERCISE 9–9
Determining Whether to Make or Buy [LO1 – CC4]

Montreal Corporation (MC) has received an offer from an outside supplier to supply 10,000 units of parts used annually in the manufacture of its main product at $36 per unit. The following current cost data is available in the manufacture of the product:

	Cost to Make (per unit)
Direct materials	$15
Direct labour	12
Variable overhead	4
Allocated common costs	4
Supervision	6

Supervision cost of $7 per unit consists entirely of the salary of the production supervisor, who will be transferred to another department if the company decides to accept the supplier's offer.

Required:

Should MC continue to manufacture the part or accept the outside supplier's offer? (Show necessary calculations.)

BRIEF EXERCISE 9–10
Determining Whether to Sell or Process Further [LO3 – CC11]

Logan Company produces several products from processing wolvotron, a rare mineral. Joint processing costs total $30,000 per tonne, one-third of which is allocated to the product evamantium. The evamantium produced from a tonne of wolvotron can either be sold at the split-off point for $40,000, or be processed further at a cost of $13,000 into adamantium and then sold for $60,000.

Required:

Should the company sell evamantium or adamantium?

Exercises

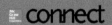

EXERCISE 9–1
Identifying Relevant Costs [LO1 – CC1]

Bill has just returned from a duck-hunting trip. He has brought home eight ducks. Bill's friend John disapproves of duck hunting, and to discourage Bill from further hunting, John has presented him with the following cost estimate per trip:

Camper and equipment:	
Cost, $12,000; usable for 8 seasons; 10 hunting trips per season	$150

Travel expense (pickup truck):

    100 kilometres at $0.12 per kilometre (gas, oil, and tires—$0.07 per kilometre;   12
        depreciation and insurance—$0.05 per kilometre)

Shotgun shells (two boxes)   20

Boat:

    Cost, $2,320; usable for 8 seasons; 10 hunting trips per season   29

Hunting licence:

Cost, $30 for the season; 10 hunting trips per season   3

Money lost playing poker:

    Loss, $18 (Bill plays poker every weekend)   18

A bottle of Old Grandad:

    Cost, $8 (used to ward off the cold)   <u>8</u>

Total cost   <u>$240</u>

Cost per duck ($240 ÷ 8 ducks) $ 30

Required:

1. Assuming that the duck-hunting trip Bill has just completed is typical, what costs are relevant to a decision as to whether Bill should go duck hunting again this season?
2. Suppose that Bill gets lucky on his next hunting trip and shoots ten ducks in the amount of time it took him to shoot eight ducks on his last trip. How much would it have cost him to shoot the last two ducks?
3. Which costs are relevant in a decision of whether Bill should give up hunting? Explain.

EXERCISE 9–2
Identifying Relevant Costs [LO1 – CC1]

Hollings Company sells office furniture in the Rocky Mountain area. As part of its service, Hollings delivers furniture to customers. The costs associated with the acquisition and annual operation of a delivery truck are given below:

Insurance	$2,320.00
Licences	362.50
Taxes (vehicle)	217.50
Garage rent for parking (per truck)	1,740.00
Depreciation ($13,050 ÷ 5 years)	2,610.00*
Gasoline, oil, tires, and repairs	0.10 per kilometre

*Based on obsolescence, rather than on wear and tear

Required:

1. Assume that Hollings Company has purchased one truck and that the truck has been driven 72,500 kilometres during the first year. Compute the average cost per kilometre of owning and operating the truck.

2. At the beginning of the second year, Hollings Company is unsure whether to use the truck or leave it parked in the garage and have all hauling done commercially. (The province requires the payment of vehicle taxes even if the vehicle is not used.) What costs from the previous list are relevant to this decision? Explain.

3. Assume that the company decides to use the truck during the second year. Near year-end, an order is received from a customer over 1,450 kilometres away. What costs from the previous list are relevant in a decision between using the truck to make the delivery and having the delivery done commercially? Explain.

4. Occasionally, the company could use two trucks at the same time. For this reason, some thought is being given to purchasing a second truck. The total kilometres driven would be the same as if only one truck were owned. What costs from the previous list are relevant to a decision about whether to purchase the second truck? Explain.

EXERCISE 9–3
Deciding Whether to Drop or Retain a Segment [LO1 – CC3]

Thalassines Kataskeves, S.A., of Greece, makes marine equipment. The company has been experiencing losses on its bilge pump product line for several years. The most recent quarterly income statement for the bilge pump product line follows:

THALASSINES KATASKEVES, S.A. Income Statement—Bilge Pump For the Quarter Ended March 31		
Sales		€950,000
Less: Variable expenses:		
Variable manufacturing expenses	€340,000	
Sales commissions	46,000	
Shipping	14,000	
Total variable expenses		400,000
Contribution margin		550,000
Less: Fixed expenses:		
Advertising	290,000	
Depreciation of equipment (no resale value)	90,000	
General factory overhead	115,000*	
Salary of product-line manager	38,000	
Insurance on inventories	18,000	
Purchasing department expenses	65,000[†]	
Total fixed expenses		616,000
Net operating loss		€(66,000)

*Common costs allocated on the basis of machine-hours

[†]Common costs allocated on the basis of sales dollars

The currency in Greece is the euro, denoted by €. The discontinuance of the bilge pump product line would not affect sales of other product lines and would have no noticeable effect on the company's total general factory overhead or total purchasing department expenses.

Required:

Would you recommend that the bilge pump product line be discontinued? Support your answer with appropriate computations.

EXERCISE 9–4
Determining Whether to Make or Buy [LO1 – CC4]

Han Products manufactures 55,500 units of part S-6 each year for use on its production line. At this level of activity, the cost per unit for part S-6 is as follows:

Direct materials	$ 6.66
Direct labour	18.50
Variable overhead	4.44
Fixed overhead	16.65
Total cost per part	$46.25

An outside supplier has offered to sell 55,500 units of part S-6 each year to Han Products for $38.85 per part. If Han Products accepts this offer, the facilities now being used to manufacture part S-6 could be rented to another company at an annual rental of $148,000. However, Han Products has determined that two-thirds of the fixed overhead being applied to part S-6 would continue even if part S-6 were purchased from the outside supplier.

Required:

Prepare computations to show the net dollar advantage or disadvantage of accepting the outside supplier's offer.

EXERCISE 9–5
Evaluating a Special Order [LO1 – CC5]

Imperial Jewellers is considering a special order for 20 handcrafted gold bracelets for a major upscale wedding. The gold bracelets are to be given as gifts to members of the wedding party. The normal selling price of a gold bracelet is $199.95 and its unit product cost is $169, as shown:

Materials	$ 84.00
Direct labour	45.00
Manufacturing overhead	40.00
Unit product cost	$169.00

The manufacturing overhead is largely fixed and unaffected by variations in how much jewellery is produced in any given period. However, 20% of the overhead is variable with respect to the number of bracelets produced. The customer interested in the special bracelet order would like special filigree applied to the bracelets. This would require additional materials costing $2 per bracelet and would also require acquisition of a special tool costing $250 that would have no other use once the special order was completed. This order would have no effect on the company's regular sales, and the order could be fulfilled using the company's existing capacity without affecting any other order.

Required:

What effect would accepting this order have on the company's net operating income if a special price of $169.95 is offered per bracelet for this order? Should the special order be accepted at this price?

EXERCISE 9–6
Utilizing a Constrained Resource [LO2 – CC7, 8]

Barlow Company manufactures three products: A, B, and C. The selling price, variable costs, and contribution margin for one unit of each product follow:

| | Product | | |
	A	B	C
Selling price	$90	$135	$120
Less: Variable expenses:			
Direct materials	12	36	16
Other variable expenses	51	45	74
Total variable expenses	63	81	90
Contribution margin	$27	$ 54	$ 30
Contribution margin ratio	30%	40%	25%

The same raw material is used in all three products. Barlow Company has only 5,000 kilograms of material on hand and will not be able to obtain any more material for several weeks due to a strike in its supplier's plant. Management is trying to decide which product(s) to concentrate on next week in filling its backlog of orders. The material costs $4 per kilogram.

Required:

1. Compute the amount of contribution margin that will be obtained per kilogram of material used in each product.
2. Which orders would you recommend that the company work on next week—the orders for product A, product B, or product C? Show computations.
3. A foreign supplier could furnish Barlow with additional stocks of the raw material at a substantial premium over the usual price. If there is unfilled demand for all three products, what is the highest price that Barlow Company should be willing to pay for an additional kilogram of materials?

EXERCISE 9–7
Determining Whether to Make or Buy [LO1 – CC4]

Golfers, Inc. (GI) manufactures golf related equipment including golf balls. This year's expected production of golf balls is 100,000 packs (each consisting of four golf balls). Cost data are as follows:

	Per Pack	100,000 Packs
Product costs directly traceable to balls:		
Direct materials	$1.00	$100,000
Direct labour	0.40	50,000
Variable manufacturing overhead	0.25	25,000
Fixed manufacturing overhead		12,000
General allocated overhead		35,000
		$212,000

The full cost of one pack of golf balls is $2.12. GI has received an offer from an outside supplier to supply any desired quantity of balls at a price of $1.80 per pack of four golf balls. The cost accounting department has provided the following information:

a. The direct fixed manufacturing overhead is the cost of leasing the machine that stamps out the balls. The machine can produce a maximum of 500,000 balls per year. If the balls are bought, the machine will no longer be needed.

b. No other costs will be affected.

Required:

1. Prepare an analysis showing whether GI would be better off making or buying the balls at a projected volume of 100,000 packs (400,000 golf balls).

2. At what volume would GI be indifferent between making and buying? What does the indifference point indicate?

3. List other quantitative and/or qualitative factors that GI should consider before making the final decision.

EXERCISE 9–8
Deciding Whether to Drop or Keep a Product Line [LO1 – CC3]

Your Retail Store's accountant prepared the following income statement for the ladies' accessories product line:

Sales		$2,800,000
Less: Variable expenses		1,200,000
Contribution margin		1,600,000
Less: Fixed expenses:		
Wages	$1,100,000	
Insurance on inventory	60,000	
Advertising	600,000	1,760,000
Net operating income (loss)		($ 160,000)

Management is concerned about the loss and is considering dropping the product line. If the product line is dropped, a job has to be created elsewhere for a long-term employee currently earning an annual salary of $80,000.

Required:

Should the ladies' accessories product line be dropped? Show the required computations.

EXERCISE 9–9
Determining Whether to Outsource [LO1 – CC4]

We Make Company has traditionally manufactured a number of different standard machine parts. It is now exploring an outsourcing decision for several of the parts that it currently produces. Cost information for one such machine part is given below:

Variable cost/unit	$ 28.00
Fixed manufacturing costs (total)	4,250.00
Allocated corporate overhead	6,560.00
Unit product cost (based on 500 units)	$ 49.62

Fifty percent of the fixed manufacturing costs are directly traceable to this specific machine part and therefore avoidable. An outside supplier will sell the part at a price of $45 per unit if 500 units are purchased.

Required:

Assess whether We Make should continue to manufacture this machine part or whether it should purchase it from the outside supplier.

EXERCISE 9–10
Determining Whether to Sell or Process Further [LO3 – CC11]

Hearty Dairy is trying to decide whether it should sell the milk that it processes "as is" or further process it into butter. Management has collected the following data pertaining to milk:

Wholesale selling price ($5.30 per 4 litres)	$5.30
Less: Joint costs incurred up to the split-off point where milk can be identified as a separate product	4.40
Profit per 4-litres	$0.90

A 4-litre container of milk, when further processed, can yield 0.5 kilogram of butter. The cost of further processing is $3 per kilogram of butter. One kilogram of butter can be sold at a price of $15.60.

Required:

1. What data items are relevant when deciding whether to sell milk "as is" or process further into butter? How should the remaining cost items be classified?
2. Should milk be sold "as is" or processed further into butter?

Problems

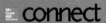

 PROBLEM 9–1
Making an Equipment Replacement Decision [LO1 – CC2]

Murl Plastics Inc. purchased a new machine one year ago at a cost of $30,000. Although the machine operates well, the president of Murl Plastics is wondering if the company should replace it with a new electronic machine that has just come on the market. The new machine would slash annual operating costs by two-thirds, as shown in the comparative data below:

> **CHECK FIGURE**
> (2) Net advantage: $30,000

	Present Machine	**Proposed New Machine**
Purchase cost new	$30,000	$45,000
Estimated useful life new	6 years	5 years
Annual operating costs	$21,000	$ 7,000
Annual straight-line depreciation	5,000	9,000
Remaining book value	25,000	—
Salvage value now	5,000	—
Salvage value in five years	–0–	–0–

In trying to decide whether to purchase the new machine, the president has prepared the following analysis:

Book value of the old machine	$25,000
Less: Salvage value	5,000
Net loss from disposal	$20,000

"Even though the new machine looks good," said the president, "we can't get rid of that old machine if it means taking a huge loss on it. We'll have to use the old machine for at least a few more years."

Sales are expected to be $100,000 per year, and selling and administrative expenses are expected to be $63,000 per year, regardless of which machine is used.

Required:

1. Prepare a summary income statement covering the next five years, assuming:
   a. The new machine is not purchased.
   b. The new machine is purchased.
2. Determine the desirability of purchasing the new machine using only relevant costs in your analysis.

PROBLEM 9-2
Deciding Whether to Add or Drop a Product [LO1 – CC3]

Tracey Douglas is the owner and managing director of Heritage Garden Furniture Ltd., a South African company that makes museum-quality reproductions of antique outdoor furniture. Tracey would like advice concerning the advisability of eliminating the model C3 lawn chair. These lawn chairs have been among the company's best-selling products, but they seem unprofitable.

CHECK FIGURE

(2) Minimum sales: R60,000

A condensed statement of operating income for the company and for the model C3 lawn chair for the quarter ended June 30 follows:

	Model C3 Lawn Chair	All Products
Sales	R300,000*	R2,900,000
Cost of sales:		
Direct materials	122,000	759,000
Direct labour	72,000	680,000
Fringe benefits (20% of direct labour)	14,400	136,000
Variable manufacturing overhead	3,600	28,000
Building rent and maintenance	4,000	30,000
Depreciation	19,100	75,000
Total cost of sales	235,100	1,708,000
Gross margin	64,900	1,192,000
Selling and administrative expenses:		
Product managers' salaries	10,000	75,000
Sales commissions (5% of sales)	15,000	145,000
Fringe benefits (20% of salaries and commissions)	5,000	44,000
Shipping	10,000	120,000
General administrative expenses	48,000	464,000
Total selling and administrative expenses	88,000	848,000
Net operating income (loss)	R(23,100)	R344,000

*The currency in South Africa is the rand, denoted here by R.

The following additional data have been supplied by the company:

a. Direct labour is a variable cost at Heritage Garden Furniture.

b. All of the company's products are manufactured in the same facility and use the same equipment. Building rent, maintenance, and depreciation are allocated to products using various bases. The equipment does not wear out through use; it eventually becomes obsolete.

c. There is ample capacity to fill all orders.

d. Dropping the model C3 lawn chair would have no effect on sales of other product lines.

e. Inventories of work in process or finished goods are insignificant.

f. Shipping costs are traced directly to products.

g. General administrative expenses are allocated to products on the basis of sales dollars. There would be no effect on the total general administrative expenses if the model C3 lawn chair were dropped.

h. If the model C3 lawn chair were dropped, the product manager would be laid off.

Required:

1. Given the current level of sales, would you recommend that the model C3 lawn chair be dropped? Prepare appropriate computations to support your answer.

2. What would sales of the model C3 lawn chair have to be, at minimum, in order to justify retaining the product? (*Hint:* Set this up as a break-even problem, but include only the relevant costs from part (1).)

PROBLEM 9–3
Deciding Whether to Discontinue a Flight [LO1 – CC3]

Profits have been decreasing for several years at Pegasus Airlines. In an effort to improve the company's performance, consideration is being given to dropping several flights that appear to be unprofitable.

A typical income statement for one such flight (Flight 482) follows:

CHECK FIGURE

(1) Decrease in profits: $6,400

Ticket revenue (175 seats × 40% occupancy × $200 ticket price)	$ 28,000	100.0%
Less: Variable expenses ($15 per person)	2,100	7.5
Contribution margin	25,900	92.5%
Less: Flight expenses:		
Salaries, flight crew	3,600	
Flight promotion	1,500	
Depreciation of aircraft	3,100	
Fuel for aircraft	13,600	
Liability insurance	8,400	
Salaries, flight attendants	1,000	
Baggage loading and flight preparation	3,400	
Overnight costs for flight crew and attendants at destination	600	
Total flight expenses	35,200	
Net operating loss	$ (9,300)	

The following additional information is available about Flight 482:

a. Members of the flight crew are paid fixed annual salaries, whereas the flight attendants are paid by the flight.

b. One-third of the liability insurance is a special charge assessed against Flight 482 because, in the opinion of the insurance company, the destination is in a high-risk area. The remaining two-thirds would be unaffected by a decision to drop Flight 482.

c. The baggage loading and flight preparation expense is an allocation of ground crew's salaries and depreciation of ground equipment. Dropping Flight 482 would have no effect on the company's total baggage loading and flight preparation expenses.

d. If Flight 482 is dropped, Pegasus Airlines has no authorization at present to replace it with another flight.

e. Depreciation of aircraft is due entirely to obsolescence. Depreciation due to wear and tear is negligible.

f. Dropping Flight 482 would not allow Pegasus Airlines to reduce the number of aircraft in its fleet or the number of flight crew on its payroll.

Required:

1. Prepare an analysis showing what impact dropping Flight 482 would have on the airline's profits.

2. The airline's scheduling officer has been criticized because only about 50% of the seats on Pegasus's flights are being filled, compared with an average of 60% for the industry. The scheduling officer has explained that Pegasus's average seat occupancy could be improved considerably by eliminating about 10% of the flights but that doing so would reduce profits. Explain how this could happen.

PROBLEM 9–4
Determining Whether to Make or Buy [LO1 – CC4]

Troy Engines Ltd. manufactures a variety of engines for use in heavy equipment. The company has always produced all of the necessary parts for its engines, including all of the carburetors. An outside supplier has offered to produce and sell one type of carburetor to Troy Engines Ltd. for a cost of $35 per unit. To evaluate this offer, Troy Engines Ltd. has gathered the following information relating to its own cost of producing the carburetor internally:

CHECK FIGURE

(1) The part can be made inside the company for $6 less per unit.

	Per Unit	15,000 Units per Year
Direct materials	$14	$210,000
Direct labour	10	150,000
Variable manufacturing overhead	3	45,000
Fixed manufacturing overhead, traceable	6*	90,000
Fixed manufacturing overhead, allocated	9	135,000
Total cost	$42	$630,000

*One-third supervisory salaries; two-thirds depreciation of special equipment (no resale value)

Required:

1. Assuming that the company has no alternative use for the facilities that are now being used to produce the carburetors, should the outside supplier's offer be accepted? Show all computations.

2. Suppose that if the carburetors were purchased, Troy Engines Ltd. could use the freed capacity to launch a new product. The segment margin of the new product would be $150,000 per year. Should Troy Engines Ltd. accept the offer to buy the carburetors for $35 per unit? Show all computations.

 PROBLEM 9–5

Determining Whether to Accept or Reject a Special Order [LO1 – CC5]

Polaski Company manufactures and sells a single product called a Ret. Operating at capacity, the company can produce and sell 30,000 Rets per year. Costs associated with this level of production and sales are as follows:

> **CHECK FIGURE**
> (1) Net increase in profits: $65,000

	Unit	Total
Direct materials	$15	$ 450,000
Direct labour	8	240,000
Variable manufacturing overhead	3	90,000
Fixed manufacturing overhead	9	270,000
Variable selling expense	4	120,000
Fixed selling expense	6	180,000
Total cost	$45	$1,350,000

The Rets normally sell for $50 each. Fixed manufacturing overhead is constant at $270,000 per year within the range of 25,000 through 30,000 Rets per year.

Required:

1. Assume that, due to a recession, Polaski Company expects to sell only 25,000 Rets through regular channels next year. A large retail chain has offered to purchase 5,000 Rets if Polaski is willing to accept a 16% discount off the regular price. There would be no sales commissions on this order; thus, variable selling expenses would be slashed by 75%. However, Polaski Company would have to purchase a special machine to engrave the retail chain's name on the 5,000 units. This machine would cost $10,000. Polaski Company has no assurance that the retail chain will purchase additional units any time in the future. Determine the impact on profits next year if this special order is accepted.

2. Refer to the original data. Assume again that Polaski Company expects to sell only 25,000 Rets through regular channels next year. The Canadian Forces would like to make a one-time-only purchase of 5,000 Rets. The Forces would pay a fixed fee of $1.80 per Ret, and in addition it would reimburse Polaski Company for all costs of production (variable and fixed) associated with the units. Since the Forces would pick up the Rets with its own trucks, there would be no variable selling expenses of any type associated with this order. If Polaski Company accepts this order, by how much will profits be increased or decreased for the year?

3. Assume the same situation as that described in part (2), except that the company expects to sell 30,000 Rets through regular channels next year. Thus, accepting the Canadian Forces' order would require giving up regular sales of 5,000 Rets. If the Forces' order is accepted, by how much will profits be increased or decreased from what they would be if the 5,000 Rets were sold through regular channels?

PROBLEM 9–6

Utilizing a Constrained Resource [LO2 – CC7, 8]

Soft and Cuddly Friends (SCF) produces soft dolls. Demand for the dolls is increasing, and management wants you to identify an economical sales and production mix for the coming year. The following information is available:

CHECK FIGURE

(1) Total direct labour-hours: 125,000

	Softy	Friendly	Goody	Besty	Lovey
Demand (units)	70,000	58,800	49,000	56,000	100,000
Price per unit	$ 26.00	$ 11.00	$ 42.00	$ 20.00	$ 16.00
Variable costs:					
Direct materials	10.75	2.75	16.10	5.00	8.00
Direct labour	4.80	3.00	8.40	6.00	2.40

The following additional information is available:

a. The company's plant has a capacity of 100,000 direct labour-hours per year on a single-shift basis. The company's present employees and equipment can produce all five products.

b. The direct labour rate is $12 per hour; this rate is expected to remain unchanged during the coming year.

c. Fixed manufacturing costs amount to $680,000 per year. Variable overhead costs are $4 per direct labour-hour.

d. All of the company's sales and administrative costs are fixed.

Required:

1. How many total direct labour-hours will be required to produce the units estimated to be sold during the coming year? Show your computations.

2. Keeping in mind the direct labour-hour capacity, what should be the company's product mix for the upcoming year? Prepare a schedule in support of your recommendation.

3. What is the highest price, in terms of a rate per hour, that SCF would be willing to pay for additional capacity (i.e., for added direct labour time)?

4. Assume again that the company does not want to reduce sales of any product. Identify ways the company could obtain the additional output.

PROBLEM 9–7

Preparing a Make-or-Buy Analysis and Making an Equipment Replacement Decision [LO1 – CC2, 3]

"In my opinion, we ought to stop making our own drums and accept that outside supplier's offer," said Wim Niewindt, managing director of Antilles Refining, N.V., of Aruba. "At a price of 36 florins per drum, we would be paying 10 florins less than it costs us to manufacture the drums in our own plant. (The currency in Aruba is the florin, denoted by Afl.) Since we use 120,000 drums a year, we would save 600,000 florins on an annual basis."
Antilles Refining's present cost to manufacture one drum follows (based on 120,000 drums per year):

CHECK FIGURE

(1) Advantage to make: Afl126,000

Direct material	Afl20.70
Direct labour	12.00
Variable overhead	3.00
Fixed overhead (Afl5.60 general company overhead, Afl3.20 depreciation, and Afl1.50 supervision)	10.30
Total cost per drum	Afl46.00

A decision about whether to make or buy the drums is especially important at this time, since the equipment being used to make the drums is completely worn out and must be replaced. The choices facing the company are as follows:

- *Alternative 1:* Purchase new equipment and continue to make the drums. The equipment would cost Afl1,620,000; it would have a six-year useful life and no salvage value. The company uses straight-line depreciation.

- *Alternative 2:* Purchase the drums from an outside supplier at Afl36 per drum under a six-year contract.

The new equipment would be more efficient than the equipment that Antilles Refining has been using and, according to the manufacturer, would reduce direct labour and variable overhead costs by 30%. The old equipment has no resale value. Supervision cost (Afl180,000 per year) and direct materials cost per drum would not be affected by the new equipment. The new equipment's capacity would be 180,000 drums per year. The company has no other use for the space being used to produce the drums.

The company's total general company overhead would be unaffected by this decision.

Required:

1. To assist the managing director in making a decision, prepare an analysis showing the total cost and the cost per drum under each of the two alternatives stated previously. Assume that 120,000 drums are needed each year. Which course of action would you recommend to the managing director?

2. Would your recommendation in part (1) be the same if the company's needs were (a) 150,000 drums per year? (b) 180,000 drums per year? Show computations to support your answer, with costs presented on both a total and a per-unit basis.

3. What other factors would you recommend that the company consider before making a decision?

PROBLEM 9–8
Deciding Whether to Shut Down or Continue to Operate a Plant [LO1 – CC3]

(*Note:* This type of decision is similar to that of dropping a product line.)

Birch Company normally produces and sells 30,000 units of RG-6 each month. RG-6 is a small electrical relay used in the automotive industry as a component part in various products. The selling price is $22 per unit, variable costs are $14 per unit, fixed manufacturing overhead costs total $150,000 per month, and fixed selling costs total $30,000 per month.

CHECK FIGURE

(1) Disadvantage to close: $40,000

Employment contract strikes in the companies that purchase the bulk of the RG-6 units have caused Birch Company's sales to temporarily drop to only 8,000 units per month. Birch Company estimates that the strikes will last for about two months, after which time sales of RG-6 should return to normal. Due to the current low level of sales, however, Birch Company is thinking about closing its own plant during the two months that the strikes are on. If Birch Company does close its plant, it is estimated that fixed manufacturing overhead costs can be reduced to $105,000 per month and that fixed selling costs can be reduced by 10%. Startup costs at the end of the shutdown period would total $8,000. Since Birch Company uses just-in-time production methods, no inventories are on hand.

Required:

1. Assuming that the strikes continue for two months, as estimated, would you recommend that Birch Company close its own plant? Show computations in good form.

2. At what level of sales (in units) for the two-month period should Birch Company be indifferent between closing the plant and keeping it open? Show computations. (*Hint:* This is a type of break-even analysis, except that the fixed cost portion of your break-even computation should include only those fixed costs that are relevant [i.e., avoidable over the two-month period].)

PROBLEM 9–9
Analyzing Relevant Costs in a Variety of Situations [LO1 – CC1, 4, 5]

Andretti Company has a single product called a Dak. The company normally produces and sells 60,000 Daks each year at a selling price of $32 per unit. The company's unit costs at this level of activity follow:

CHECK FIGURES
(1) Incremental net income: $130,000 unit costs
(2) Break-even price: $22.15

Direct materials	$10.00	
Direct labour	4.50	
Variable manufacturing overhead	2.30	
Fixed manufacturing overhead	5.00	$300,000 total
Variable selling expenses	1.20	
Fixed selling expenses	3.50	$210,000 total
Total cost per unit	$26.50	

A number of questions relating to the production and sale of Daks follow. *Consider each question separately.*

Required:

1. Assume that Andretti Company has sufficient capacity to produce 90,000 Daks every year without any increase in fixed manufacturing overhead costs. The company could increase its sales by 25% above the present 60,000 units each year if it were willing to increase the fixed selling expenses by $80,000. Would the increased fixed expenses be justified?

2. Assume again that Andretti Company has sufficient capacity to produce 90,000 Daks every year. A customer in a foreign market wants to purchase 20,000 Daks. Import duties on the Daks would be $1.70 per unit, and costs for permits and licences would be $9,000. The only selling costs that would be associated with the order would be $3.20 per unit shipping cost. You have been asked by the president to compute the per-unit break-even price on this order.

3. The company has 1,000 Daks on hand that have some irregularities and are therefore considered to be *seconds*. Due to the irregularities, it will be impossible to sell these units at the normal price through regular distribution channels. What unit cost figure is relevant for setting a minimum selling price?

4. Due to a strike in its supplier's plant, Andretti Company is unable to purchase more materials for the production of Daks. The strike is expected to last for two months. Andretti Company has enough materials on hand to continue to operate at 30% of normal levels for the two-month period. As an alternative, Andretti could close its plant down entirely for the two months. If the plant were closed, fixed overhead costs would continue at 60% of their normal level during the two-month period; the fixed selling costs would be reduced by 20% while the plant was closed. What would be the dollar advantage or disadvantage of closing the plant for the two-month period?

5. An outside manufacturer has offered to produce Daks for Andretti Company and to ship them directly to Andretti's customers. If Andretti Company accepts this offer, the facilities that it uses to produce Daks would be idle; however, fixed overhead costs would be reduced by 75% of their present level. Since the outside manufacturer would pay all the costs of shipping, the variable selling costs would be only two-thirds of their present amount. Compute the unit cost figure relevant for comparison to whatever quoted price is received from the outside manufacturer.

PROBLEM 9–10
Determining Whether to Make or Buy [LO1 – CC4]

The Hyatt Company is trying to decide whether it should purchase new equipment so that it can continue to make its engines, a key component of its final product, internally or whether production should be discontinued and the engines purchased from an outside supplier.

> **CHECK FIGURE**
> (1) Relevant cost of the make option = $89 per engine.

New equipment for producing the engines can be purchased at a cost of $4,000,000. The equipment would have a five-year useful life (the company uses straight-line depreciation) and a $1,000,000 salvage value. Alternatively, the engines could be purchased from an outside suppler. The supplier has offered to provide the engines for $90 each under a five-year contract.

Hyatt Company's present costs per unit of producing the engines internally (with the old equipment) are given below. The costs are based on a current activity level of 40,000 engines per year:

Direct materials	$ 30.00
Direct labour (hourly employees)	42.00
Overhead	43.00
Total cost per unit	$115.00

The overhead amount of $43 per unit includes both variable and fixed items as follows:

Supplies (variable)	$ 6.00
Supervision	8.00
Depreciation	9.00
General overhead	20.00

Supervision was directly traceable to the manufacturing activity and primarily involved supervising the hourly labour and overseeing production.

The new equipment would be more efficient and would reduce direct labour costs and variable overhead costs by 25%. Supervision cost ($320,000 per year) and direct materials cost per unit would not be affected by the new equipment. The company has no other use for the space now being used to produce the engines. The company's total general overhead would not be affected by this decision.

Required:

1. Assume that 40,000 engines are needed each year. Should Hyatt purchase new equipment and continue manufacturing the engines, or should it buy the engines from the outside supplier? Provide all necessary calculations.

2. At what level of activity will the company be indifferent between the two options? Present all the necessary calculations.

3. The manager believes demand might drop in the future years and feels it is better to buy the engines rather than make them. Explain the rationale for such a decision.

PROBLEM 9–11
Equipment Replacement Decision [LO1 – CC1, 2]

Standard Machine Parts Ltd. makes specialized machine parts for several customers, all of whom are major manufacturers. Standard is considering replacing one of the special machines used in the production of a specific product; this machine was purchased eight years ago for $750,000 and has seven years of useful life remaining. The new machine, costing $400,000, is expected to have a useful life equal to the remaining useful life of the current machine and a zero disposal value. Standard incurs annual operating costs equal to $72,000 with the existing equipment, but the new equipment is expected to result in operating costs equal to $36,000. Standard expects to incur additional maintenance expense on the existing machine over the remainder of its seven year life as follows: $5,000 per year in the first three years, $7,000 per year in years 4 and 5, and $9,000 per year in years 6 and 7.

> **CHECK FIGURE**
>
> Differential cost of new machine = ($20,000)

Despite the significant reduction in annual operating costs, as well as the increase in maintenance costs, the controller is hesitant because the machine is a specialized piece of equipment and, due to the limited second-hand market for such a machine, the current one could only be sold for 50% of its current book value of $350,000, resulting in a loss on disposal of $175,000.

Required:

Ignoring income taxes and time value of money, prepare a quantitative analysis of the best course of action for Standard, with regard to the two alternatives.

PROBLEM 9–12
Deciding Whether to Accept or Reject an Order [LO1 – CC5]

Anchor Company manufactures a variety of tool boxes. The firm is currently operating at 80% of its full capacity of 7,500 machine-hours per month. Each unit requires 30 minutes of machine time. Its sales manager has been looking for special orders to make productive use of the excess capacity. JCL Ltd., a potential customer, has offered to buy 10,000 tool boxes at $7.50 per box, provided that the entire quantity is delivered in two months. The current per-box cost data are as follows:

> **CHECK FIGURE**
>
> (1) Contribution margin if special order accepted: $87,500

Direct materials	$2.50
Direct labour (½ hour at $6.00/hour)	3.00
Total manufacturing overhead	2.00
Total unit product cost	$7.50

Both fixed and variable overhead are allocated using direct labour-hours as a base. Variable overhead is $1.50 per direct labour-hour. Without the order, Anchor would have enough business to operate at 6,000 direct labour-hours in each of the next two months. The regular selling price of the tool boxes is $10.50. A sales commission of 50 cents per unit is paid to sales representatives on all regular sales.

No additional selling or administrative expenses are anticipated on account of accepting this special order and no commissions will be paid on this special order.

The production manager is concerned about the labour time that 10,000 boxes would require. She cannot schedule overtime because Anchor has a policy against it. JCL will not accept fewer than 10,000 tool boxes. Therefore, in order to fill the special order, it would be necessary for Anchor Company to divert some of its regular sales to the special order.

Required:

1. Prepare contribution margin income statements for the two-month period both with and without the special order. Based on financial considerations, should Anchor accept the order?
2. List and briefly discuss at least two qualitative issues regarding this order. Should Anchor accept the order?

PROBLEM 9–13
Making a Replacement Decision [LO1 – CC2]

SpeedCar Corporation makes toy cars that it can sell for $25 per car. Production manager Alex Carvahllo is considering whether to refurbish or replace the moulds that SpeedCar uses in the manufacturing process. The original cost of the moulds, purchased three years ago, was $600,000. They have an expected useful life of three more years, a terminal disposal value of $0, current disposal value of $100,000, and a book value of $300,000. Refurbishing the mould will not change its terminal disposal value (the expected disposal value of the new mould is also $100,000). The following additional information is available for the two alternatives:

> **CHECK FIGURE**
>
> (1) Differential savings over three years from replacing: $60,000

1. Refurbishing will cost $400,000, whereas replacing will cost $800,000; both options will result in an expected useful life of four years.
2. Variable costs of production will be higher by $2 when using the refurbished mould, compared to the new mould.
3. Annual production of cars is expected to be 60,000 units.

The new equipment would be depreciated on a straight-line basis.

Required:

1. Should SpeedCar refurbish or replace the moulds? Show all calculations and explain.
2. The capital expenditure to replace the moulds is $800,000, but the demand is not known for certain. At what level of annual sales of cars will SpeedCar be indifferent between refurbishing and purchasing new moulds?

PROBLEM 9–14
Determining Whether to Expand a Product Line [LO1 – CC3]

Cora Corporation produces refrigerator units. The company's normal production and sales volume of Standard units is 3,000 units per month, and units sell for $800 each. The costs of manufacturing and marketing a Standard model are as follows:

> **CHECK FIGURE**
>
> (1) Operating income with Economy and Deluxe included: $592,250

Variable manufacturing cost per unit	$ 250
Variable marketing cost per unit	50
Fixed product cost	350,000
Fixed period cost	400,000

The company is considering diversifying the product line to include two additional models, Economy and Deluxe, which would sell for $670 and $900 per unit, respectively. The costs of manufacturing these new models are as follows:

	Economy	Deluxe
Variable manufacturing cost	40% below Standard	$490
Variable marketing cost	10% above Standard	Twice Standard

Total fixed product and period costs are expected to remain unchanged. Cora expects to sell 1,250 units of the Economy model and 600 units of Deluxe model per month. The company cannot expand its production capacity beyond its current level of 3,000 units.

Required:

1. What combination of production and sales will result in the highest profit? Support your answer with relevant calculations.
2. Suppose that a supplier is willing to supply 600 units of the Standard model at a price of $250 per unit. Also assume that the company can sell all that it can produce of the remaining two models. Explain whether the supplier's offer should be accepted, and determine how many Economy and Deluxe models should be produced.

PROBLEM 9–15
Determining Whether to Accept a Special Order and Whether to Make or Buy [LO1 – CC4, 5]

The Engine Guys produces specialized engines for "snow climber" buses. The company's normal monthly production volume is 1,000 engines, whereas its monthly production capacity is 2,000 engines. The current selling price per engine is $1,260. The cost per unit of manufacturing and marketing the engines at the normal volume is as follows:

CHECK FIGURE

(1) Incremental benefit of contract: $48,000

	Costs per Unit for Engines
Manufacturing costs:	
Direct materials	$160
Direct labour	200
Variable overhead	40
Fixed overhead	200
Subtotal	$600
Marketing costs:	
Variable	$ 60
Fixed	140
Subtotal	200
Total unit cost	$800

Required:

Answer the following *independent* questions.

1. The Provincial Bus Company wishes to purchase 300 engines in October. The bus company is willing to pay a fixed fee of $480,000 and reimburse The Engine Guys for all manufacturing costs incurred to manufacture 300 motors. October is a busy month for The Engine Guys, and there are sufficient orders to operate at 100% capacity utilization. There will be no variable marketing costs on this government contract. Indicate whether the Provincial Bus Company's contract should be accepted. Provide all supporting calculations.

2. An outside contractor is willing to supply 500 engines at a price of $600 per unit. If the offer is accepted, the company will make 500 engines in-house and buy 500 engines from the contractor. The company's fixed manufacturing costs will decline by 20% and the variable marketing costs per unit on the 500 engines purchased will decline by 40%. Determine whether the contractor's offer should be accepted. Provide all supporting calculations.

PROBLEM 9–16
Determining Whether to Make or Buy [LO1 – CC4]

The Brain Teasers (TBT) specializes in creating and manufacturing board games for youth. Each game has a unique game board to accompany the other pieces of the game. The company is at the final development stage of a new game called "Inverted World" based on a recent fictional book and subsequent film of the same name. Since it is important that the game be on the shelves quickly to capitalize on the advertising and promotion done by the movie studio for the film, the manager of TBT is considering an offer from another game manufacturer to supply the game boards for $5.60 per board. This is a common practice in the game industry as the life of a toy is very short and there is a need to act quickly to get the product to market before demand shifts.

CHECK FIGURE

Relevant cost of making the Inverted World board: $4.99

TBT's cost accountant has developed the following cost estimates for the production of the game board:

	Cost per Unit of Inverted World
Direct material	$3.20
Direct labour	0.80
Production overhead	1.98
Corporate overhead	0.48
Cost of game board	$6.46

The accountant has also provided the following information:

- The board can be produced using current machinery that has a capacity to produce 500,000 units per month and is 50% utilized.
- The anticipated demand for the game will not exceed 50,000 units a month, according to the sales team.
- Half of the production overhead is fixed.
- The corporate overhead allocation is based on 15% of the direct materials charge.

Required:

State whether TBT should make the game boards or buy them from the supplier. Please support your decision with the required calculations.

PROBLEM 9–17
Determining Whether to Add a Product Line [LO1 – CC3]

Javelin Cycling Vacations Ltd. offers cycling tours in Canada and France. Each year a single tour is offered. For 20X5, the company is offering a tour of the Continental Divide. Following is an estimate of the revenues and costs for this tour:

CHECK FIGURES

(1) Operating income without tour: loss of $3,800
(2) $167,200

JAVELIN CYCLING VACATIONS LTD. Continental Divide Tour Revenue and Expenses Forecast for 20X5	
Revenue	$170,000
Expenses:	
Tour guide salaries[1]	$ 48,000
Promotion[2]	12,000
Gratuities	8,000
Office and equipment insurance[3]	2,000
Group accident and life insurance[4]	7,000
Depreciation	8,000
Tour support employee salaries[1]	28,000
Bicycle maintenance	7,000
Customer meals	20,000
Hotel and camping costs	20,000
Administrative and office expense[5]	3,000
Tour coordinator salary	30,000
Total expenses	193,000
Net operating income (loss)	$ (23,000)

[1]Javelin will incur a cost of 5% of the salaries in severance costs when employees are terminated.
[2]Promotion costs have already been incurred.
[3]Office and equipment insurance is paid in advance of commencement of the tour.
[4]Insurance is payable only if the tour is confirmed.
[5]These expenses are for booking accommodations, arranging meals, and providing communication services during the tour.

Required:

1. Indicate whether the tour should be offered. Provide calculations in support of your response.
2. Calculate the minimum revenue required to justify offering the tour.

PROBLEM 9–18
Determining Whether to Sell or Process Further [LO3 – CC11]

Tischler the Honey Man (THM) purchases honeycombs from beekeepers for $4.40 per kilogram. THM produces two main products from the honeycombs—honey and beeswax. Honey is drained from the honeycombs, and then the honeycombs are melted down to form cubes of beeswax. The beeswax is sold for $3.30 per kilogram.

The honey can be sold in raw form for $6.60 per kilogram. However, some of the raw honey is used by THM to make honey drop candies. The candies are packed in a decorative container and are sold in gift and specialty shops. A container of honey drop candies sells for $9.70.

CHECK FIGURES
(1) Incremental contribution margin = $2.07
(2) Avoidable fixed costs = $6,930

Each container of honey drop candies contains three-quarters of a kilogram of honey. The other variable costs associated with making the candies are as follows:

Decorative container	$0.50
Other ingredients	0.30
Direct labour	0.35
Variable manufacturing overhead	0.15
Total variable manufacturing cost	$1.30

The monthly fixed manufacturing overhead costs associated with making the candies follow:

Master candy maker's salary	$4,180
Depreciation of candy-making equipment	460
Total fixed manufacturing cost	$4,640

The master candy maker has no duties other than to oversee production of the honey drop candies. The candy-making equipment is special-purpose equipment that was constructed specifically to make this particular candy. The equipment has no resale value and does not wear out through use.

A salesperson is paid $2,750 per month plus a commission of 5% of sales to market the honey drop candies.

The company had enjoyed robust sales of the candies for several years, but the recent entrance of a competing product into the marketplace has depressed sales of the candies. The management of the company is now wondering whether it would be more profitable to sell all of the honey rather than converting some of it into candies.

Required:

Should THM further process the honey into candies? What is the minimum number of containers of candy that must be sold each month to justify the continued processing of honey into candies? Support your answer with relevant computations.

Building Your Skills

THINKING ANALYTICALLY [LO1 – CC1, 3, 4]

Storage Systems, Inc. sells a wide range of drums, bins, boxes, and other containers that are used in the chemical industry. One of the company's products is a heavy-duty corrosion-resistant metal drum, called the XSX drum, used to store toxic wastes. Production is constrained by the capacity of an automated welding machine that is used to make precision welds. A total of 2,000 hours of welding time is available annually on the machine. Because each drum requires 0.8 hours of welding time, annual production is limited to 2,500 drums. At present, the welding machine is used exclusively to make the XSX drums. The accounting department has provided the following financial data concerning the XSX drums:

XSX Drums		
Selling price per drum		$154.00
Cost per drum:		
Direct materials	$44.50	
Direct labour ($18 per hour)	4.50	
Manufacturing overhead	3.15	
Selling and administrative expense	15.40	67.55
Margin per drum		$ 86.45

Management believes 3,000 XSX drums could be sold each year if the company had sufficient manufacturing capacity. As an alternative to adding another welding machine, management has looked into the possibility of buying additional drums from an outside supplier. Metal Products, Inc., a supplier of quality products, would be able to provide up to 1,800 XSX-type drums per year at a price of $120 per drum, which Storage Systems would resell to its customers at its normal selling price after appropriate relabelling.

Jasmine Morita, Storage Systems' production manager, has suggested that the company could make better use of the welding machine by manufacturing premium mountain bike frames, which would require only 0.2 hours of welding time per frame. Jasmine believes that Storage Systems could sell up to 3,500 mountain bike frames per year to mountain bike manufacturers at a price of $65 per frame. The accounting department has provided the following data concerning the proposed new product:

Mountain Bike Frames		
Selling price per frame		$65.00
Cost per frame:		
Direct materials	$17.50	
Direct labour ($18 per hour)	22.50	
Manufacturing overhead	15.75	
Selling and administrative expense	6.50	62.25
Margin per frame		$ 2.75

The mountain bike frames could be produced with existing equipment and personnel. Manufacturing overhead is allocated to products on the basis of direct labour-hours. Most of the manufacturing overhead consists of fixed common costs such as rent on the factory building, but some of it is variable. The variable manufacturing overhead has been estimated at $1.05 per XSX drum and $0.60 per mountain bike frame. The variable manufacturing overhead cost would not be incurred on drums acquired from the outside supplier.

Selling and administrative expenses are allocated to products on the basis of revenues. Almost all of the selling and administrative expenses are fixed common costs, but it has been estimated that variable selling and administrative expenses amount to $0.85 per XSX drum and would be $0.40 per mountain bike frame. The variable selling and administrative expenses of $0.85 per drum would be incurred when drums acquired from the outside supplier are sold to the company's customers.

All of the company's employees—direct and indirect—are paid for full 40-hour workweeks, and the company has a policy of laying workers off only in major recessions.

Required:

1. Given the margins of the two products as indicated in the reports submitted by the accounting department, does it make any sense to even consider producing the mountain bike frames? Explain your answer.
2. Compute the contribution margin per unit for
    a. Purchased XSX drums.
    b. Manufactured XSX drums.
    c. Manufactured mountain bike frames.
3. Determine the number of XSX drums (if any) that should be purchased and the number of XSX drums and/or mountain bike frames (if any) that should be manufactured. What is the improvement in net income that would result from this plan over current operations?

As soon as your analysis was shown to the top management team at Storage Systems, several managers got into an argument concerning how direct labour costs should be treated when making this decision. One manager argued that direct labour is always treated as a variable cost in textbooks and in practice and has always been considered a variable cost at Storage Systems. After all, "direct" means you can directly trace the cost to products. If direct labour is not a variable cost, what is? Another manager argued just as strenuously that direct labour should be considered a fixed cost at Storage Systems. No one had been laid off in over a decade, and for all practical purposes, everyone at the plant is on a monthly salary. Everyone classified as direct labour works a regular 40-hour workweek, and overtime has not been necessary since the company adopted lean production techniques. Whether the welding machine were used to make drums or frames, the total payroll would be exactly the same. There is enough slack, in the form of idle time, to accommodate any increase in total direct labour time that the mountain bike frames would require.

4. Redo requirements (2) and (3) above, making the opposite assumption about direct labour from the one you originally made. In other words, if you treated direct labour as a variable cost, redo the analysis treating it as a fixed cost. If you treated direct labour as a fixed cost, redo the analysis treating it as a variable cost.
5. What do you think is the correct way to treat direct labour in this situation—as a variable cost or as a fixed cost? Explain.

COMMUNICATING IN PRACTICE [LO1 – CC4, 5; LO3 – CC11]

Rasoi Equipment manufactures a variety of cooking equipment and related accessories. The data given below is for a special heavy-duty exhaust fan.

CHECK FIGURES

Profit (loss) if capacity used to make ovens and fans are purchased, $1,140,000; Difference in profit (loss), $540,000.

Annual production capacity (units)	10,000
Price (per unit)	$240.00
Variable cost of manufacturing	120.00
Fixed manufacturing cost	36.00
Fixed selling and administrative cost	24.00
Profit	$ 60.00

The company is evaluating how best to use its production capacity. One option is that it can use the existing capacity to manufacture industrial ovens. This option is attractive because a competitor has offered to supply 10,000 exhaust fans at a price of $150 per fan. The following information pertains to the manufacture of industrial ovens:

Annual production capacity (units)	7,000
Price (per unit)	$360.00
Variable cost of manufacturing	240.00

There will be no change in the fixed manufacturing and selling and administrative costs.

A government agency is looking to purchase industrial ovens that will meet additional standards for quality and reliability. The agency has offered to pay $400 for each oven and is prepared to purchase up to 7,000 oven. The ovens, if made by Rasoi, will require a special finishing process to meet the agency's standards. The special finishing process will cost $60 per oven in variable production cost. The additional processing will result in production decreasing to 6,500 units (i.e., a loss of 500 units). The additional processing will *increase* fixed manufacturing costs by $12 per oven based on a volume of 6,500 ovens.

Required:

Write a memorandum to the president of Rasoi Equipment outlining the options, and recommending an appropriate course of action. Include all supporting computations as an appendix to your memo.

ETHICS CHALLENGE [LO1 – CC3]

Haley Romeros had just been appointed vice-president of the Great Lakes Region of the Bank Services Corporation (BSC). The company provides cheque-processing services to small banks. The banks send cheques presented for deposit or payment to BSC, which records the data on each cheque in a computerized database. BSC then sends the data electronically to a Canadian Payments Association cheque-clearing centre where the appropriate transfers of funds are made between banks. The Great Lakes Region has three cheque-processing centres, which are located in Burlington, Kingston, and Owen Sound, Ontario. Prior to her promotion to vice-president, Haley Romeros had been the manager of a cheque-processing centre in Nova Scotia.

Immediately upon assuming her new position, Haley requested a complete financial report for the just-ended fiscal year from the region's controller, John Littlebear. Haley Romeros specified that the financial report should follow the standardized format required by corporate headquarters for all regional performance reports. That report follows:

BANK SERVICES CORPORATION (BSC)
Great Lakes Region Financial Performance

| | Cheque-Processing Centres | | | |
	Kingston	Burlington	Owen Sound	Total
Sales	$20,000,000	$18,000,000	$12,000,000	$50,000,000
Operating expenses:				
Direct labour	12,500,000	11,000,000	8,500,000	32,000,000
Variable overhead	350,000	310,000	190,000	850,000
Equipment depreciation	1,300,000	1,400,000	1,200,000	3,900,000
Facility expense	900,000	800,000	1,100,000	2,800,000
Local administrative expense*	140,000	160,000	150,000	450,000
Regional administrative expense†	600,000	540,000	360,000	1,500,000
Corporate administrative expense‡	1,900,000	1,710,000	1,140,000	4,750,000
Total operating expense	17,690,000	15,920,000	12,640,000	46,250,000
Net operating income	$ 2,310,000	$ 2,080,000	$ (640,000)	$ 3,750,000

*Local administrative expenses are the administrative expenses incurred at the cheque-processing centres.

†Regional administrative expenses are allocated to the cheque-processing centres on the basis of sales.

‡ Corporate administrative expenses are charged to segments of the company, such as the Great Lakes Region and the cheque-processing centres, at the rate of 9.5% of their sales.

Upon seeing this report, Haley Romeros summoned John Littlebear for an explanation.

Romeros: What's the story on Owen Sound? It didn't have a loss the previous year, did it?

Littlebear: No, the Owen Sound facility has had a nice profit every year since it opened six years ago, but Owen Sound lost a big contract this year.

Romeros: Why?

Littlebear: One of our national competitors entered the local market and bid very aggressively on the contract. We couldn't afford to meet the bid. Owen Sound's costs—particularly their facility expenses—are just too high. When Owen Sound lost the contract, we had to lay a lot of employees off, but we could not reduce the fixed costs of the Owen Sound facility.

Romeros: Why is Owen Sound's facility expense so high? It's a smaller facility than either Kingston or Burlington, yet its facility expense is higher.

Littlebear: The problem is that we are able to rent suitable facilities very cheaply in Kingston and Burlington. No such facilities were available at Owen Sound; we had them built. Unfortunately, there were big cost overruns. The contractor we hired was inexperienced at this kind of work and, in fact, went bankrupt before the project was completed. After hiring another contractor to finish the work, we were way over budget. The large depreciation charges on the facility didn't matter at first, because we didn't have much competition at the time and could charge premium prices.

Romeros: Well, we can't do that any more. The Owen Sound facility will obviously have to be shut down. Its business can be shifted to the other two cheque-processing centres in the region.

Littlebear: I would advise against that. The $1,200,000 in depreciation at the Owen Sound facility is misleading. That facility should last indefinitely with proper maintenance. And, it has no resale value; there is no other appropriate commercial activity around Owen Sound.

Romeros: What about the other costs at Owen Sound?

Littlebear: If we shifted Owen Sound's business over to the other two processing centres in the region, we wouldn't save anything on direct labour or variable overhead costs. We might save $90,000 or so in local administrative expense, but we would not save any regional administrative expense, and corporate headquarters would still charge us 9.5% of our sales as corporate administrative expense. In addition, we would have to rent more space in Kingston and Burlington in order to handle the work transferred from Owen Sound; that would probably cost us at least $600,000 a year. And don't forget that it will cost us something to move the equipment from Owen Sound to Kingston and Burlington. And the move will disrupt service to customers.

Romeros: I understand all that, but a money-losing processing centre on my performance report is completely unacceptable.

Littlebear: But if you shut down Owen Sound, you are going to throw some loyal employees out of work.

Romeros: That's unfortunate, but we have to face hard business realities.

Littlebear: And you would have to write off the investment in the facilities at Owen Sound.

Romeros: I can explain a writeoff to corporate headquarters. Hiring an inexperienced contractor to build the Owen Sound facility was my predecessor's mistake. But they'll have my head at headquarters if I show operating losses every year at one of my processing centres. Owen Sound has to go. At the next corporate board meeting, I am going to recommend that the facility be closed.

Required:

1. From the standpoint of the company as a whole, should the Owen Sound processing centre be shut down and its work redistributed to other processing centres in the region? Explain.

2. Do you think Haley Romeros's decision to shut down the Owen Sound facility is ethical? Explain.

3. What influence should the depreciation on the facilities at Owen Sound have on prices charged by Owen Sound for its services?

TEAMWORK IN ACTION [LO1 – CC4; LO2 – CC7, 8]

Autoway Inc. is a wholesale Winnipeg-based distributor supplying a wide range of moderately priced auto equipment to large chain stores. Autoway manufactures about 40% of these products and the rest are purchased from other manufacturers. One department of Autoway currently manufactures side view mirrors. Autoway has the capacity to make and sell 40,000 pairs of mirrors on an annual basis. This production volume consumes 100% of the department's capacity of direct labour at available workstations. Following are the selling price and costs associated with Autoway's mirrors:

Selling price per pair		$188.00
Cost per box:		
Moulded plastic	$ 17.60	
Glass	19.80	
Direct labour ($15 per hour)	41.25	
Manufacturing overhead	27.50	
Selling and administrative cost	37.40	143.55
Net operating income per pair		$ 44.45

Autoway could easily sell 50% more volume but current production capacity is a major constraint. Waterloo based Krueger Company has offered to supply up to 25,000 pairs of mirrors annually at a delivery price of $150 per pair.

Autoway's production manager, Radha Balan, believes that this capacity can be better used by manufacturing high quality floor mats (pack of 4), and has collected the following supporting information:

Estimated sales volume		75,000
Selling price per floor mat pack		$ 90.00
Cost per floor mat pack:		
Moulded plastic	$25.50	
Direct labour ($15 per hour)	16.50	
Manufacturing overhead	11.00	
Selling and administrative cost	16.00	69.00
Net operating income per floor mat pack		$ 21.00

Autoway uses direct labour-hours as the application base for manufacturing overhead. Included in the manufacturing overhead for the current year is $440,000 of fixed overhead costs, of which 40% is traceable to the plastics department and 60% is allocated to factorywide manufacturing overhead cost. The remaining manufacturing overhead cost is variable with respect to direct labour-hours. The floor mats could be produced with existing equipment and personnel in the moulded plastics department.

For each unit of product that Autoway sells, regardless of whether the product has been purchased or is manufactured in-house, there is an allocated $10 fixed cost per unit for distribution. This $10 per unit is included in the selling and administrative cost for all products. The remaining amount of selling and administrative cost for all products—purchased or manufactured—is variable. The total selling and administrative cost figure for the purchased pairs of mirrors is $18 per unit.

Required:

Your team should discuss and then respond to the following questions. All team members should agree with and understand the answers (including the calculations supporting the answers) and be prepared to report to the class. (Each teammate can assume responsibility for a different part of the presentation.)

1. Determine the number of direct labour-hours per year being used to manufacture mirrors.
2. Compute the contribution margin per unit for
   a. Mirrors purchased from outside supplier.
   b. Mirrors manufactured in-house
   c. Floor mats manufactured in-house.
3. Determine the best combination of production and purchase, and compute the increase in net income that would result from this product mix over current operations.

10

Capital Budgeting Decisions

LEARNING OBJECTIVES AND CHAPTER COMPETENCIES		
After studying Chapter 10, you should be able to demonstrate the following competencies:		
COMPETENCY	**Know**	**Apply**
LO1 **UNDERSTAND THE BASICS OF CAPITAL BUDGETING ANALYSIS.**		
CC1 Describe some business decisions that rely on capital budgeting analysis.	●	
CC2 Explain the distinction between screening decisions and preference decisions.	●	
CC3[A] Compute the present value of a series of cash flows.		●
CC4 Determine the acceptability of an investment project using the net present value (NPV) method.		●
CC5 Describe the typical cash flows in a capital budgeting analysis without taxes.	●	
CC6 Outline the simplifying assumptions made in a capital budgeting analysis.	●	
CC7 Explain the logic of ignoring financing-related cash flows and the choice of the appropriate discount rate in capital budgeting analysis.	●	
LO2 **UNDERSTAND AND APPLY ALTERNATIVE METHODS TO ANALYZE CAPITAL INVESTMENTS.**		
CC8 Prepare an NPV analysis of two competing projects using either the total cost approach or the incremental cost approach.		●
CC9 Compute the NPV of a project when no revenues are involved.		●
CC10 Rank projects in order of preference using the profitability index.		●
CC11 Compute the internal rate of return (IRR) of a project, interpret it, and explain its use for project selection.	●	●
CC12 Compare and contrast the IRR and NPV methods in project selection.	●	
CC13 Calculate the payback period of an investment project.		●
CC14 Explain the payback method and its potential to mislead a manager.	●	

COMPETENCY		Know	Apply
CC15	Calculate the simple rate of return (SRR) of an investment project.		●
CC16	Explain the disadvantages of the SRR method for project selection.	●	
LO3	**UNDERSTAND AND INCORPORATE THE EFFECTS OF INFLATION ON CASH FLOWS IN CAPITAL BUDGETING.**		
CC17^B	Explain the distinction between real and nominal cash flows.	●	
CC18^B	Compute the price index number for a future year given the annual rate of inflation.		●
CC19^B	Explain the distinction between real and nominal rates of return.	●	
LO4	**UNDERSTAND AND INCORPORATE THE EFFECTS OF TAXES ON CASH FLOWS IN CAPITAL BUDGETING.**		
CC20^C	Explain the impact of tax-deductibility of depreciation (i.e., capital cost allowance [CCA]).	●	
CC21^C	Compute the present value of CCA tax shields.		●
CC22^C	Compute the NPV of a project when cash flows related to the ownership and disposal of depreciable property are included in the analysis.		●

Note: The superscripts "A," "B," and "C" refer to Appendices 10A, 10B, and 10C respectively; all are available on Connect.

ON THE JOB

A FRAMEWORK FOR SUSTAINABLE GROWTH

Capital investments are among the most important decisions a company can make. These investments both enable a company to continue to operate in the future and position the company to exploit new opportunities—called growth opportunities—to anchor its competitive position in the marketplace. So how do companies allocate scarce funds to these two purposes? The process underlying such decisions is the capital budgeting process, and every company will have its own set of policies and procedures that managers must follow when seeking approval and funding for capital projects. At Calgary-based Suncor Energy, for example, the decisions are based on expected returns, short-term cash flows, and risk. At Cintas Corporation—a supplier of uniforms to various corporations—the capital proposals must be accompanied by a financial analysis that estimates the project's cash inflows and outflows. In addition, the assumptions underlying the cash flow estimates are carefully scrutinized

Stockbyte/Getty Images

so that the company can channel its limited capital funds toward the most profitable opportunities. Capital investments are good news stories because they signal expansions in enterprises. Conversely, in downturns, capital disinvestment occurs. Indeed, following the precipitous fall in oil prices in 2015, Suncor stepped back its capital investments and laid off personnel, as did much of the oil sector in Alberta.

Sources: "Suncor Energy Board Approves 2010 Capital Spending Plan," press release, November 13, 2009, Suncor Energy website, http://www.suncor.com/en/newsroom/2418.aspx?id=1076131; personal conversation between Peter C. Brewer and Paul Carmichael, senior controller, Cintas Corporation.

Critical thinking question *Given a number of investment opportunities, how should Suncor decide which projects should receive funding?*

*Note to student: See **Guidance Answers** online.*

◄◄ A Look Back	▶ A Look at This Chapter	▶▶ A Look Ahead
Chapter 9 presented a basic framework for the decision-making process, centred on the notion of relevant costs and benefits, and used it in a wide variety of situations.	Chapter 10 expands the coverage of the decision-making process by focusing on decisions about significant outlays on long-term projects. A variety of techniques used by managers faced with these decisions are reviewed and illustrated.	Standard costs and variance analysis are covered in Chapter 11. This chapter introduces management control and performance measurement.

The term **capital budgeting** is used to describe how managers plan significant outlays on projects that have long-term implications, such as the purchase of new equipment and the introduction of new products. Most companies have many more potential projects than can actually be funded. Hence, managers must carefully select those projects that promise the greatest return. How well managers make these capital budgeting decisions is a critical factor in the long-term profitability of the company.

Capital budgeting involves *investment*—a company must commit funds now in order to receive a return in the future. Investments are not limited to shares and bonds. Purchase of inventory or equipment is also an investment. For example, Yum! Brands, Inc. makes an investment when it opens a new Pizza Hut restaurant. Mountain Equipment Co-op makes an investment when it installs a new computer to handle customer billing. Chrysler makes an investment when it redesigns a product, such as the Jeep Compass, and has to retool its production lines. Merck & Co. invests in medical research. Amazon.ca makes an investment when it redesigns its website. All of these investments are characterized by a commitment of funds today in the expectation of receiving a return in the future in the form of additional cash inflows or reduced cash outflows.

Capital Budgeting—Planning Investments

Typical Capital Budgeting Decisions

LO1   • **Know**

CC1: Describe some business decisions that rely on capital budgeting analysis.

The types of business decisions that require capital budgeting analysis are virtually any decisions that involve an outlay now in order to obtain some return (increase in revenue or reduction in costs) in the future. Typical capital budgeting decisions include the following:

- Cost reduction decisions: Should new equipment be purchased to reduce costs?
- Expansion decisions: Should a new plant, warehouse, or other facility be acquired to increase capacity and sales?
- Equipment selection decisions: Which of several available machines would be the most cost effective to purchase?
- Lease-or-buy decisions: Should new equipment be leased or purchased?
- Equipment replacement decisions: Should old equipment be replaced now or later?

LO1   • **Know**

CC2: Explain the distinction between screening decisions and preference decisions.

Capital budgeting decisions tend to fall into two broad categories—*screening decisions* and *preference decisions*. **Screening decisions** are those relating to whether a proposed project meets some preset standard of acceptance. For example, a firm might have a policy of accepting projects only if they promise a return of, say, 20% on the investment. The required rate of return is the minimum rate of return a project must yield to be acceptable.

Preference decisions, by contrast, are those in which you select from among several *competing* courses of action. To illustrate, a firm might be considering several different machines to replace an existing machine on the assembly line. The choice of which machine to purchase is a *preference* decision.

In this chapter, we initially discuss ways of making screening decisions. Preference decisions are discussed toward the end of the chapter.

The Time Value of Money

As stated previously, business investments commonly involve returns that extend over fairly long periods. Therefore, in approaching capital budgeting decisions, you must employ techniques that recognize the *time value of money:* (1) A dollar today is worth more than a dollar a year from now. (2) Projects that promise returns earlier in time are preferable to those that promise returns later in time. The capital budgeting techniques that involve *discounted cash flows* recognize the preceding two characteristics of business investments most fully.

We will spend most of this chapter illustrating the use of discounted cash flow methods in making capital budgeting decisions. If you are not already familiar with discounting and the use of present value tables, you should read Appendix 10A on Connect before proceeding any further; present value tables are provided in Exhibits 10–1 and 10–2. (*Note:* Future value tables are available in Appendix 10D.)

EXHIBIT 10–1 Present Value of $1

$$P = \frac{F_n}{(1 + r)^n}$$

Period	4%	5%	6%	8%	10%	12%	14%	16%	18%	20%	22%	24%	26%	28%	30%	40%
1	0.962	0.952	0.943	0.926	0.909	0.893	0.877	0.862	0.847	0.833	0.820	0.806	0.794	0.781	0.769	0.714
2	0.925	0.907	0.890	0.857	0.826	0.797	0.769	0.743	0.718	0.694	0.672	0.650	0.630	0.610	0.592	0.510
3	0.889	0.864	0.840	0.794	0.751	0.712	0.675	0.641	0.609	0.579	0.551	0.524	0.500	0.477	0.455	0.364
4	0.855	0.823	0.792	0.735	0.683	0.636	0.592	0.552	0.516	0.482	0.451	0.423	0.397	0.373	0.350	0.260
5	0.822	0.784	0.747	0.681	0.621	0.567	0.519	0.476	0.437	0.402	0.370	0.341	0.315	0.291	0.269	0.186
6	0.790	0.746	0.705	0.630	0.564	0.507	0.456	0.410	0.370	0.335	0.303	0.275	0.250	0.227	0.207	0.133
7	0.760	0.711	0.665	0.583	0.513	0.452	0.400	0.354	0.314	0.279	0.249	0.222	0.198	0.178	0.159	0.095
8	0.731	0.677	0.627	0.540	0.467	0.404	0.351	0.305	0.266	0.233	0.204	0.179	0.157	0.139	0.123	0.068
9	0.703	0.645	0.592	0.500	0.424	0.361	0.308	0.263	0.225	0.194	0.167	0.144	0.125	0.108	0.094	0.048
10	0.676	0.614	0.558	0.463	0.386	0.322	0.270	0.227	0.191	0.162	0.137	0.116	0.099	0.085	0.073	0.035
11	0.650	0.585	0.527	0.429	0.350	0.287	0.237	0.195	0.162	0.135	0.112	0.094	0.079	0.066	0.056	0.025
12	0.625	0.557	0.497	0.397	0.319	0.257	0.208	0.168	0.137	0.112	0.092	0.076	0.062	0.052	0.043	0.018
13	0.601	0.530	0.469	0.368	0.290	0.229	0.182	0.145	0.116	0.093	0.075	0.061	0.050	0.040	0.033	0.013
14	0.577	0.505	0.442	0.340	0.263	0.205	0.160	0.125	0.099	0.078	0.062	0.049	0.039	0.032	0.025	0.009
15	0.555	0.481	0.417	0.315	0.239	0.183	0.140	0.108	0.084	0.065	0.051	0.040	0.031	0.025	0.020	0.006
16	0.534	0.458	0.394	0.292	0.218	0.163	0.123	0.093	0.071	0.054	0.042	0.032	0.025	0.019	0.015	0.005
17	0.513	0.436	0.371	0.270	0.198	0.146	0.108	0.080	0.060	0.045	0.034	0.026	0.020	0.015	0.012	0.003
18	0.494	0.416	0.350	0.250	0.180	0.130	0.095	0.069	0.051	0.038	0.028	0.021	0.016	0.012	0.009	0.002
19	0.475	0.396	0.331	0.232	0.164	0.116	0.083	0.060	0.043	0.031	0.023	0.017	0.012	0.009	0.007	0.002
20	0.456	0.377	0.312	0.215	0.149	0.104	0.073	0.051	0.037	0.026	0.019	0.014	0.010	0.007	0.005	0.001
21	0.439	0.359	0.294	0.199	0.135	0.093	0.064	0.044	0.031	0.022	0.015	0.011	0.008	0.006	0.004	0.001
22	0.422	0.342	0.278	0.184	0.123	0.083	0.056	0.038	0.026	0.018	0.013	0.009	0.006	0.004	0.003	0.001
23	0.406	0.326	0.262	0.170	0.112	0.074	0.049	0.033	0.022	0.015	0.010	0.007	0.005	0.003	0.002	
24	0.390	0.310	0.247	0.158	0.102	0.066	0.043	0.028	0.019	0.013	0.008	0.006	0.004	0.003	0.002	
25	0.375	0.295	0.233	0.146	0.092	0.059	0.038	0.024	0.016	0.010	0.007	0.005	0.003	0.002	0.001	
26	0.361	0.281	0.220	0.135	0.084	0.053	0.033	0.021	0.014	0.009	0.006	0.004	0.002	0.002	0.001	
27	0.347	0.268	0.207	0.125	0.076	0.047	0.029	0.018	0.011	0.007	0.005	0.003	0.002	0.001	0.001	
28	0.333	0.255	0.196	0.116	0.069	0.042	0.026	0.016	0.010	0.006	0.004	0.002	0.002	0.001	0.001	
29	0.321	0.243	0.185	0.107	0.063	0.037	0.022	0.014	0.008	0.005	0.003	0.002	0.001	0.001		
30	0.308	0.231	0.174	0.099	0.057	0.033	0.020	0.012	0.007	0.004	0.003	0.002	0.001	0.001		
40	0.208	0.142	0.097	0.046	0.022	0.011	0.005	0.003	0.001	0.001						

EXHIBIT 10–2 Present Value of an Annuity of $1

$$P_n = \frac{1}{r}\left[1 - \frac{1}{(1 + r)^n}\right]$$

Period	4%	5%	6%	8%	10%	12%	14%	16%	18%	20%	22%	24%	26%	28%	30%	40%
1	0.962	0.952	0.943	0.926	0.909	0.893	0.877	0.862	0.847	0.833	0.820	0.806	0.794	0.781	0.769	0.714
2	1.886	1.859	1.833	1.783	1.736	1.690	1.647	1.605	1.566	1.528	1.492	1.457	1.424	1.392	1.361	1.224
3	2.775	2.723	2.673	2.577	2.487	2.402	2.322	2.246	2.174	2.106	2.042	1.981	1.923	1.868	1.816	1.589
4	3.630	3.546	3.465	3.312	3.170	3.037	2.914	2.798	2.690	2.589	2.494	2.404	2.320	2.241	2.166	1.879
5	4.452	4.330	4.212	3.993	3.791	3.605	3.433	3.274	3.127	2.991	2.864	2.745	2.635	2.532	2.436	2.035
6	5.242	5.076	4.917	4.623	4.355	4.111	3.889	3.685	3.498	3.326	3.167	3.020	2.885	2.759	2.643	2.168
7	6.002	5.786	5.582	5.206	4.868	4.564	4.288	4.039	3.812	3.605	3.416	3.242	3.083	2.937	2.802	2.263
8	6.733	6.463	6.210	5.747	5.335	4.968	4.639	4.344	4.078	3.837	3.619	3.421	3.241	3.076	2.925	2.331
9	7.435	7.108	6.802	6.247	5.759	5.328	4.946	4.607	4.303	4.031	3.786	3.566	3.366	3.184	3.019	2.379
10	8.111	7.722	7.360	6.710	6.145	5.650	5.216	4.833	4.494	4.192	3.923	3.662	3.465	3.269	3.092	2.414
11	8.760	8.306	7.887	7.139	6.495	5.938	5.453	5.029	4.656	4.327	4.035	3.776	3.544	3.335	3.147	2.438
12	9.385	8.863	8.384	7.536	6.814	6.194	5.660	5.197	4.793	4.439	4.127	3.851	3.606	3.387	3.190	2.456
13	9.986	9.394	8.853	7.904	7.103	6.424	5.842	5.342	4.910	4.533	4.203	3.912	3.656	3.427	3.223	2.468
14	10.563	9.899	9.295	8.244	7.367	6.628	6.002	5.468	5.008	4.611	4.265	3.962	3.695	3.459	3.249	2.477
15	11.118	10.380	9.712	8.559	7.606	6.811	6.142	5.575	5.092	4.675	4.315	4.001	3.726	3.483	3.268	2.484
16	11.652	10.838	10.106	8.851	7.824	6.974	6.265	5.669	5.162	4.730	4.357	4.033	3.751	3.503	3.283	2.489
17	12.166	11.274	10.477	9.122	8.022	7.120	6.373	5.749	5.222	4.775	4.391	4.059	3.771	3.518	3.295	2.492
18	12.659	11.690	10.828	9.372	8.201	7.250	6.467	5.818	5.273	4.812	4.419	4.080	3.786	3.529	3.304	2.494
19	13.134	12.085	11.158	9.604	8.365	7.366	6.550	5.877	5.316	4.844	4.442	4.097	3.799	3.539	3.311	2.496
20	13.590	12.462	11.470	9.818	8.514	7.469	6.623	5.929	5.353	4.870	4.460	4.110	3.808	3.546	3.316	2.497
21	14.029	12.821	11.764	10.017	8.649	7.562	6.687	5.973	5.384	4.891	4.476	4.121	3.816	3.551	3.320	2.498
22	14.451	13.163	12.042	10.201	8.772	7.645	6.743	6.011	5.410	4.909	4.488	4.130	3.822	3.556	3.323	2.498
23	14.857	13.489	12.303	10.371	8.883	7.718	6.792	6.044	5.432	4.925	4.499	4.137	3.827	3.559	3.325	2.499
24	15.247	13.799	12.550	10.529	8.985	7.784	6.835	6.073	5.451	4.937	4.507	4.143	3.831	3.562	3.327	2.499
25	15.622	14.094	12.783	10.675	9.077	7.843	6.873	6.097	5.467	4.948	4.514	4.147	3.834	3.564	3.329	2.499
26	15.983	14.375	13.003	10.810	9.161	7.896	6.906	6.118	5.480	4.956	4.520	4.151	3.837	3.566	3.330	2.500
27	16.330	14.643	13.211	10.935	9.237	7.943	6.935	6.136	5.492	4.964	4.525	4.154	3.839	3.567	3.331	2.500
28	16.663	14.898	13.406	11.051	9.307	7.984	6.961	6.152	5.502	4.970	4.528	4.157	3.840	3.568	3.331	2.500
29	16.984	15.141	13.591	11.158	9.370	8.022	6.983	6.166	5.510	4.975	4.531	4.159	3.841	3.569	3.332	2.500
30	17.292	15.373	13.765	11.258	9.427	8.055	7.003	6.177	5.517	4.979	4.534	4.160	3.842	3.569	3.332	2.500
40	19.793	17.159	15.046	11.925	9.779	8.244	7.105	6.234	5.548	4.997	4.544	4.166	3.846	3.571	3.333	2.500

Several approaches can be used to evaluate investments using discounted cash flows. The easiest method to use is the *net present value method,* which is the subject of the next several sections.

HELPFUL HINT

We discount two types of cash flows in this chapter:

1. *A single sum of money that is received (or paid) at a single point in the future.* For example, if a company expects to sell a piece of equipment five years from today for $10,000, this amount represents a single sum of money that we assume the company will receive on the last day of the fifth year from now. Exhibit 10–1 is used to discount a single sum of money that will be received or paid in the future to its value as of today, also known as its present value.

2. *An annuity.* An annuity refers to a series of identical sums of money that will be received or paid in consecutive future periods. For example, if a company expects to receive $20,000 from customers annually for each of the next five years, this amount represents an annuity that we assume the company will receive on the last day of five consecutive years. Exhibit 10–2 is used to discount an annuity that will be received or paid in consecutive future periods to its lump sum value as of today.

IN BUSINESS

ECONOMIC CONDITIONS DICTATE CAPITAL BUDGETS

When the health of the economy is uncertain, capital spending declines. Rite Aid CEO Mary Sammons cut her company's capital budget by $50 million due to uncertain economic conditions. Estée Lauder tightened its belt by challenging managers to defend what they must have and define what they can give up. Yum! Brands (owner of Pizza Hut, KFC, and Taco Bell) navigated the difficult economy by abandoning projects that might come true in favour of a must-have capital budgeting mentality.

Look at the recent news stories out of the Canadian oil patch. In 2015–2016, they spell out the woes of the oil firms—including large oil refiners and oil exploration companies, and the many companies that rely on these enterprises to pull activity and value along the value chain. Emphasis during lean times will be on essentials just sufficient to maintain the enterprise until the turnaround occurs. In some cases companies may indeed exit an industry entirely.

In contrast to these firms, for companies whose fuel costs are a significant fraction of their total operating costs, the low oil prices represent good news. In February 2016, Air Canada announced plans to purchase 45 C-Series jets from Bombardier with options for another 30. For Bombardier, this comes as welcome news because the manufacturer had only 243 firm orders as of early 2016.

Sources: Matthew Boyle, "The Budget Knives Come Out," *BusinessWeek*, October 13, 2008, p. 30. For the Air Canada announcement, visit, for example, http://newssaskatchewan.ca/2016/02/17/air-canada-says-cseries-fits-into-expansion-plans/. Note that virtually every business news outlet reported Air Canada's announcement.

The Net Present Value Method

CC4: Determine the acceptability of an investment project using the net present value (NPV) method.

Under the net present value method, the present value of a project's cash inflows is compared with the present value of the project's cash outflows. The difference between the present values of these cash flows, called the **net present value (NPV)**, determines whether the project is an acceptable investment. To illustrate, let us assume the following data:

EXAMPLE A

Harper Company is contemplating the purchase of a machine capable of performing certain operations that are now performed manually. The machine will cost $5,000, and it will last for five years. At the end of the five-year period, the machine will have a zero scrap value. Use of the machine will reduce labour costs by $1,800 per year. Harper Company requires a minimum return of 20% before taxes on all investment projects. (For simplicity, we ignore taxes and inflation.)

Should the machine be purchased? Harper Company must determine whether a cash investment now of $5,000 can be justified if it will result in a cost reduction of $1,800 each year over the next five years. It may appear that the answer is obvious, since the total cost savings is $9,000 (= 5 years × $1,800). However, the company can earn a 20% return by investing its money elsewhere. It is not enough that the cost reductions cover the original cost of the machine; they must also yield at least a 20% return, or the company would be better off investing the money elsewhere.

To determine whether the investment is desirable, management must discount the stream of annual $1,800 cost savings to its present value and then compare it with the cost of the new machine. Since Harper Company requires a minimum return of 20% on all investment projects, this rate is used in the discounting process. Exhibit 10–3 shows how this analysis is done.

EXHIBIT 10–3 NPV Analysis of a Proposed Project

Initial cost				$5,000
Life of the project (years)				5
Annual cost savings				$1,800
Salvage value				–0–
Required rate of return				20%

Item	Year(s)	Amount of Cash Flow	20% Factor	Present Value of Cash Flows
Annual cost savings	1–5	$ 1,800	2.991*	$5,384
Initial investment	Now	(5,000)	1.000	(5,000)
Net present value				$ 384

*From Exhibit 10–2 above

According to the analysis, Harper Company should purchase the new machine. The present value of the cost savings is $5,384, compared to a present value of only $5,000 for the investment required (cost of the machine). Deducting the present value of the investment required from the present value of the cost savings gives a *net present value* of $384. Whenever the net present value is zero or greater, as in our example, an investment project is acceptable. Whenever the net present value is negative (the present value of the cash outflows exceeds the present value of the cash inflows), an investment project is not acceptable. In summary:

If the Net Present Value Is	Then the Project Is
Positive	Acceptable, since it promises a return greater than the required rate of return
Zero	Acceptable, since it promises a return equal to the required rate of return
Negative	Not acceptable, since it promises a return less than the required rate of return

Emphasis on Cash Flows

LO1 ● **Know**

CC5: Describe the typical cash flows in a capital budgeting analysis without taxes.

In capital budgeting decisions, the focus is on cash flows, not on accounting net income. This is because accounting net income is based on accrual concepts that ignore the timing of cash flows into and out of an organization. From a capital budgeting standpoint, the timing of cash flows is important, since a dollar received today is more valuable than a dollar received in the future. Therefore, even though the accounting net income figure is useful for many things, it is not ordinarily used in discounted cash flow analysis. (Under certain conditions, capital budgeting decisions can be correctly made by discounting appropriately defined accounting net income. However, this approach requires advanced techniques that are beyond the scope of this text. Accounting net income can, in some situations, be the starting point for determining the cash flows of a project. In these cases, the manager must make appropriate adjustments to net income (like adding back depreciation) to arrive at the project's cash flows. We will not consider this approach further in this chapter.)

What kinds of cash flows should the manager look for? Although they will vary from project to project, certain types of cash flows tend to recur, as explained in the following paragraphs.

TYPICAL CASH OUTFLOWS

Most projects will have an immediate cash outflow in the form of an initial investment in equipment or other assets. In addition, some projects require that a company expand its working capital. **Working capital** is current assets (cash, accounts receivable, and inventory) less current liabilities. When a company takes on a new project, the balances in the current asset accounts will often increase. For example, opening a new Ikea store would require additional cash in sales registers, increased accounts receivable for new customers, and more inventory to stock the shelves. These additional working capital needs should be treated as part of the initial investment in a project. Also, many projects require periodic outlays for repairs and maintenance and for additional operating costs. These should all be treated as cash outflows for capital budgeting purposes.

TYPICAL CASH INFLOWS

On the cash inflow side, a project will normally either increase revenues or reduce costs. Either way, the amount involved should be treated as a cash inflow for capital budgeting purposes. *A reduction in costs is equivalent to an increase in revenues.* Cash inflows are also frequently realized from salvage of equipment; this can occur at the start of a project when old equipment is replaced and at the end of a project when equipment is sold. In addition, any working capital that was tied up in the project can be released for use elsewhere at the end of the project and should be treated as a cash inflow. Working capital is released, for example, when a company sells off its inventory or collects its receivables.

In summary, the following types of cash flows are common in business investment projects:

- Cash outflows: initial investment (including installation costs), increased working capital needs, repairs and maintenance, incremental operating costs
- Cash inflows: incremental revenues, reduction in costs, salvage value, release of working capital

Simplifying Assumptions

CC6: Outline the simplifying assumptions made in a capital budgeting analysis.

A number of assumptions underlie our treatment of the NPV method.

TIMING OF CASH FLOWS

All cash flows are assumed to occur at the end of the period. Typically cash flows will occur throughout a period, but our assumption will make calculations easier.

REINVESTMENT OF CASH INFLOWS

All surplus cash inflows generated by the project are assumed to be immediately reinvested at a rate of return equal to the discount rate, until the end of the project. Without this assumption (e.g., if the cash flows from a project are simply kept locked up in a safe until the project ends), the net present value will not be accurate.

PROJECTS ARE CARBON COPIES OF THE FIRM

The risk of investing in a project is assumed to be identical to the risk you would face if you bought the company outright—that is, if you purchased all of the outstanding securities of the company. This means that projects are basically clones of the company in so far as risk is concerned. This assumption is very important to the choice of the discount rate in NPV analysis and to the procedure for handling financing-related cash flows. This is explained below.

TREATMENT OF INFLATION

Although this is somewhat unrealistic, inflation is assumed not to be a factor. When inflation exists, we will need to adjust either the cash flows or the discount rate. A brief discussion of these adjustments is provided in Appendix 10B on Connect.

INCOME TAXES

The NPV method usually considers cash flows only on an *after-tax* basis. This, in turn, requires that we use an after-tax discount rate and that we focus on after-tax cash flows. The effect of income taxes on revenues and costs should be fully reflected in the analysis. As an example, if we assume a 30% tax rate, the after-tax amount of a cash inflow of $100 is $70 (= $100 × [1 − 0.30]). Similarly, we must also take into account the tax-deductibility of depreciation. Recall that depreciation is an expense item when calculating income (it may be buried in the cost of goods sold or selling and administrative expenses on an income statement). Therefore, although depreciation in itself is not a cash flow, it is treated as an expense when calculating income taxes and hence results in tax savings. These tax savings—called *tax shields*—are cash inflows and must be treated as such in any NPV analysis involving depreciable property. In Canada, a complex set of rules governs the calculation of depreciation for tax purposes. The amount allowed as a deduction is called the **capital cost allowance (CCA)**. These rules, as well as the techniques for calculating CCA, after-tax discount rates, and after-tax cash flows, are discussed briefly in Appendix 10C on Connect. A more complete treatment can be found in advanced texts on corporate finance.

Choosing a Discount Rate

The discount rate should be the company's minimum required rate of return. What is a company's minimum required rate of return? The company's *cost of capital* is usually regarded as the minimum required rate of return. The **cost of capital** is the average rate of return the company must pay to its long-term creditors and to shareholders for the use of their funds. The cost of capital is the minimum required rate of return, because if a project's rate of return is less than the cost of capital, the company does not earn enough of a return to compensate its creditors and shareholders. Therefore, any project with a rate of return less than the cost of capital should not be accepted.

The cost of capital serves as a *screening device* in net present value analysis. When the cost of capital is used as the discount rate, any project with a negative net present value does not cover the company's cost of capital and therefore should be discarded as unacceptable.

Financing-Related Cash Flows

LO1 • **Know**

CC7: Explain the logic of ignoring financing-related cash flows and the choice of the appropriate discount rate in capital budgeting analysis.

A common source of confusion for students is how to handle cash inflows from borrowing and cash outflows for making interest payments and principal repayments. Given our simplifying assumptions and our choice of the company's cost of capital for the discount rate, the rule is very simple: *ignore all financing-related cash flows*. The impact on the project of the financing decisions made to fund the project is captured in the company's cost of capital—the discount rate. More advanced discussions of this topic will consider specific cases where our simple rule requires modification. For our purposes, this rule will suffice.

An Extended Example of the Net Present Value Method

To conclude our discussion of the net present value method, we present the following extended example of how it is used to analyze an investment proposal. This example will also help tie together (and reinforce) many of the ideas developed thus far.

EXAMPLE B

Under a special arrangement with a large customer, Swinyard Company has an opportunity to produce a new product in western Canada for a five-year period. Swinyard Company will be responsible for all costs of production. The special arrangement could be renewed at the end of the five-year period at the option of the customer. After careful study, Swinyard Company has estimated the following costs and revenues for the new product:

Cost of equipment needed	$ 60,000
Working capital needed	100,000
Overhaul of the equipment in four years	5,000
Salvage value of the equipment in five years	10,000
Annual revenues and costs:	
Sales revenues	200,000
Cost of goods sold (cash)	125,000
Out-of-pocket operating costs (for salaries, advertising and other direct costs)	35,000

At the end of the five-year period, the working capital would be released for investment elsewhere if the manufacturer decided not to renew the licensing arrangement. Swinyard Company's discount rate and cost of capital is 20%. Would you recommend that the new product be introduced?

This example involves a variety of cash inflows and cash outflows. The solution is given in Exhibit 10–4.

EXHIBIT 10–4 The NPV Method—An Extended Example

Sales revenues (cash)	$200,000
Less: Cost of goods sold (cash)	125,000
Less: Out-of-pocket costs for salaries, advertising, etc.	35,000
Annual net cash inflows	$ 40,000

Item	Amount of Year(s)	20% Cash Flows	Factor	Present Value of Cash Flows
Purchase of equipment	Now	$ (60,000)	1.000	$ (60,000)
Working capital needed	Now	(100,000)	1.000	(100,000)
Overhaul of equipment	4	(5,000)	0.482*	(2,410)
Annual net cash inflows from sales of the product line	1–5	40,000	2.991†	119,640
Salvage value of the equipment	5	10,000	0.402*	4,020
Working capital released	5	100,000	0.402*	40,200
Net present value				$ 1,450

*From Exhibit 10–1
†From Exhibit 10–2

Note in particular how the working capital is handled in this exhibit. It is counted as a cash outflow at the beginning of the project and as a cash inflow when it is released at the end of the project. Also, note how the sales revenues, cost of goods sold, and out-of-pocket costs are handled. **Out-of-pocket costs** are actual cash outlays for salaries, advertising, and other operating expenses. Cost of goods sold is also assumed to be cash costs. Depreciation involves no current cash outlay and hence is not considered here.

Since the overall net present value is positive, the new product should be added, assuming the company has no better use for the investment funds.

HELPFUL HINT

Microsoft® Excel® is often used to perform net present value analysis. For example, the solution depicted in Exhibit 10–4 might be depicted in Excel as follows:

	A	B	C	D	E	F	G
1	Item	Now	Year 1	Year 2	Year 3	Year 4	Year 5
2	Purchase of equipment	$ (60,000)					
3	Working capital needed	$(100,000)					
4	Overhaul of equipment					$ (5,000)	
5	Annual net cash inflows		$40,000	$40,000	$40,000	$40,000	$ 40,000
6	Salvage value of equipment						$ 10,000
7	Working capital released	$ -	$ -	$ -	$ -	$ -	$100,000
8	Annual net cash flows (a)	$(160,000)	$40,000	$40,000	$40,000	$35,000	$150,000
9	Discount rate (b)	1.000	0.833	0.694	0.579	0.482	0.402
10	Present value of cash flows (a) × (b)	$(160,000)	$33,320	$ 27,760	$ 23,160	$ 16,870	$ 60,800
11	Net present value	$ 1,410					

This approach creates one column in the spreadsheet for "Now" and one for each year (year 1 through year 5). All cash flows are inserted into the column of the spreadsheet that corresponds to when they occur. For example, the $60,000 purchase of equipment appears in the "Now" column because the cash outflow takes place immediately. In addition, all cash flows, including annuities, are discounted using the factors from Exhibit 10–1. For example, although the $40,000 annual net cash inflows that are shown above represent an annuity, each of these five $40,000 amounts is discounted using factors from Exhibit 10–1.

The net present value of $1,410 that is shown in cell B11 is computed by adding together cells B10 through G10. This amount is $40 lower than the net present value shown in Exhibit 10–4; however, this difference exists solely because the discount factors in Exhibits 10–1 and 10–2 have been rounded to three decimal places.

IN BUSINESS

ASIAN BUSINESSES INVESTING IN CANADA

Foreign investment in Canada is not new, with many American businesses having set up shop in Canada. More recently, the Canadian resource sector has attracted Asian interest. Chinese energy giants CNOOC and Sinopec have expressed interest in investing billions of dollars in the potash, fertilizer, and oil sectors. Quite in contrast to the resource sector, another group of Chinese investors is planning the development of a mega-mall in Dundurn, Saskatchewan. The proposed mall, when fully constructed, is expected to be larger than the West Edmonton Mall in terms of square footage. As another example, Indian company Central Pulp & Paper Inc. will build a wheat straw-based paper plant in Manitoba for Winnipeg-based Prairie Pulp & Paper Inc. (PPPI). While the investment will exceed $500 million, it is expected to reduce PPPI's annual costs by $5 million.

But, in a delicate balancing act, Canada must weigh the influx of capital against loss of control of potentially strategic resources which could impact national interest. This was seen by Saskatchewan's rejection of a bid for the province's potash business by BHP Billiton, which abandoned its plan to buy a stake in PotashCorp of Saskatchewan. On the West Coast, Asian interests have flocked to participate in the boom experienced in Vancouver's technology, digital entertainment, interactive, and green-economy sectors. The favourable exchange rate for the Canadian dollar against its US counterpart and a competitive tax regime are a couple of factors complementing the strengths in these sectors in Canada.

Sources: Jason Fekte, "Chinese Energy Giants Set Sights on Potash; Documents Show Canada a Target for Investment in Resource Sector," *The Ottawa Citizen,* November 2, 2012, p. A.1, http://www2.canada.com/ottawacitizen/news/story.html?id=30f4c684-b1b5-46a3-8d63-bdfb3659d5cc; Jeff Davis, "Dundurn Mega-Mall Plan Gets Official Launch Date," *Leader Post* [Regina, Sask], March 16, 2013, p. B.4, http://www.leaderpost.com/news/Dundurn+megamall+plan+gets+official+launch+date/8108522/story.html; "14 Canada–India Deals in the Spotlight," *CBC News,* posted November 5, 2012, http://www.cbc.ca/news/business/story/2012/11/05/pol-trade-deals-india.html. For news of the fate of Billiton's plan to buy PotashCorp. see https://search.yahoo.com/yhs/search?p=BHP+Billiton+loss+of+Potash+bid&ei=UTF-8&hspart=mozilla&hsimp=yhs-004. http://www.worldeyereports.com/reports/article/asian-business-and-investment-flocks-to-vancouver/.

Expanding the Net Present Value Method

CC8: Prepare an NPV analysis of two competing projects using either the total cost approach or the incremental cost approach.

So far, our examples have involved only a single investment alternative. We will now expand the NPV method to include two alternatives. Note that if all projects have a negative net present value, *none* should be accepted. In addition, we will integrate the concept of relevant costs into the discounted cash flow analysis.

The NPV method can be used to compare competing investment projects in two ways. One is the *total cost approach,* and the other is the *incremental cost approach.* Each approach is illustrated below.

The Total Cost Approach

The total cost approach is the most flexible method for comparing projects. To illustrate the mechanics of this approach, let us assume the following data.

EXAMPLE C

Don Ferry Company provides a ferry service across the Don River. One of its ferries is in poor condition. This ferry can be renovated at an immediate cost of $200,000. Further repairs and an overhaul of the motor will be needed five years from now at a cost of $80,000. In all, the ferry will be usable for 10 years if this work is done. At the end of 10 years, the ferry will have to be scrapped at a salvage value of approximately $60,000. The scrap value of the ferry right now is $70,000. It will cost $300,000 each year to operate the ferry, and revenues will total $400,000 annually.

As an alternative, Don Ferry Company can purchase a new ferry at a cost of $360,000. The new ferry will have a life of 10 years, but it will require some repairs at the end of five years. It is estimated that these repairs will amount to $30,000. At the end of 10 years, it is estimated that the ferry will have a scrap value of $60,000. It will cost $210,000 each year to operate the ferry, and revenues will total $400,000 annually.

Don Ferry Company requires a minimum return of 18% before taxes on all investment projects. Should the company purchase the new ferry or renovate the old ferry?

Exhibit 10–5 gives the solution using the total cost approach.

EXHIBIT 10–5 The Total Cost Approach to Project Selection

	New Ferry	Old Ferry
Annual revenues	$400,000	$400,000
Annual cash operating costs	210,000	300,000
Net annual cash inflows	$190,000	$100,000

Item	Year(s)	Amount of Cash Flows	18% Factor*	Present Value of Cash Flows
Buy the new ferry:				
Initial investment	Now	$(360,000)	1.000	$(360,000)
Repairs in five years	5	(30,000)	0.437	(13,110)
Net annual cash inflows	1–10	190,000	4.494	853,860

Item	Year(s)	Amount of Cash Flows	18% Factor*	Present Value of Cash Flows
Salvage of the old ferry	Now	70,000	1.000	70,000
Salvage of the new ferry	10	60,000	0.191	11,460
Net present value				562,210
Keep the old ferry:				
Initial repairs	Now	(200,000)	1.000	(20,000)
Repairs in five years	5	(80,000)	0.437	(34,960)
Net annual cash inflows	1–10	100,000	4.494	449,400
Salvage of the old ferry	10	60,000	0.191	11,460
Net present value				225,900
Net present value in favour of buying the new ferry				$ 336,310

*All factors are from Exhibits 10–1 and 10–2.

Two points should be noted from the exhibit. First, observe that *all* cash inflows and *all* cash outflows are included in the solution under each alternative. No effort has been made to isolate those cash flows that are relevant to the decision and those that are not relevant. The inclusion of all cash flows associated with each alternative gives the approach its name—the *total cost* approach.

Second, note that a net present value figure is computed for each of the two alternatives. This is a distinct advantage of the total cost approach in that an unlimited number of alternatives can be compared side by side to determine the best action. For example, another alternative for Don Ferry Company would be to get out of the ferry business entirely. If management desired, the net present value of this alternative could be computed to compare with the alternatives shown in Exhibit 10–5. Still other alternatives might be open to the company. Once management has determined the net present value of each alternative, it can select the course of action that promises to be the most profitable. In the case at hand, given only the two alternatives, the best alternative is to purchase the new ferry. The alternative with the highest NPV is not always the best choice, although it is the best choice in this case. For further discussion, see the upcoming section, "Preference Decisions—The Ranking of Investment Projects."

The Incremental Cost Approach

When only two alternatives are being considered, the incremental cost approach offers another route to a decision. Unlike the total cost approach, it focuses only on differential costs. (Technically, the incremental cost approach is misnamed, since it focuses on differential costs (i.e., on both cost increases and cost decreases), rather than just incremental costs. As used here, the term *incremental costs* should be interpreted broadly to include both cost increases and cost decreases.) The procedure is to include in the discounted cash flow analysis only those costs and revenues that *differ* between the two alternatives being considered. To illustrate, refer again to the data in Example C relating to Don Ferry Company. The solution using only differential costs is presented in Exhibit 10–6.

EXHIBIT 10–6 The Incremental Cost Approach to Project Selection

Item	Year(s)	Amount of Cash Flows	18% Factor*	Present Value of Cash Flows
Incremental investment required to purchase the new ferry	Now	$(160,000)	1.000	$(160,000)
Repairs in 5 years avoided	5	50,000	0.437	21,850
Increased net annual cash inflows	1–10	90,000	4.494	404,460
Salvage of the old ferry	Now	70,000	1.000	70,000
Difference in salvage value in 10 years	10	–0–	—	–0–
Net present value in favour of buying the new ferry				$ 336,310

*All factors are from Exhibits 10–1 and 10–2.

Note two things from the data in this exhibit: (1) The net present value in favour of buying the new ferry of $336,310 shown in Exhibit 10–6 agrees with the net present value shown under the total cost approach in Exhibit 10–5. This agreement should be expected, since the two approaches are just different roads to the same destination. (2) The costs used in Exhibit 10–6 are just the differences between the costs shown for the two alternatives in the prior exhibit. For example, the $160,000 incremental investment required to purchase the new ferry in Exhibit 10–6 is the difference between the $360,000 cost of the new ferry and the $200,000 cost required to renovate the old ferry from Exhibit 10–5. The other figures in Exhibit 10–6 have been computed in the same way.

Least-Cost Decisions

LO2 • **Apply**

CC9: Compute the NPV of a project when no revenues are involved.

Revenues are not directly involved in some decisions. For example, a company that does not charge for delivery service may need to replace an old delivery truck, or a company may be trying to decide whether to lease or to buy its fleet of executive cars. In such situations, where no revenues are involved, the most desirable alternative will be the one that promises the *least total cost* from the present value perspective. Hence, these are known as *least-cost decisions*. To illustrate a least-cost decision, assume the following data.

EXAMPLE D

Val-Tek Company is considering the replacement of an old threading machine. A new threading machine is available that could substantially reduce annual operating costs. Selected data relating to the old and the new machines are presented below:

	Old Machine	New Machine
Purchase cost when new	$20,000	$25,000
Salvage value now	3,000	—
Annual cash operating costs	15,000	9,000
Overhaul needed immediately	4,000	—
Salvage value in six years	–0–	5,000
Remaining life	6 years	6 years

Val-Tek Company's cost of capital is 10%.

Exhibit 10–7 provides an analysis of the alternatives using the total cost approach.

EXHIBIT 10–7 The Total Cost Approach (least-cost decision)

Item	Year(s)	Amount of Cash Flows	10% Factor*	Present Value of Cash Flows
Buy the new machine:				
Initial investment	Now	$(25,000)	1.000	$(25,000)†
Salvage of the old machine	Now	3,000	1.000	3,000†
Annual cash operating costs	1–6	(9,000)	4.355	(39,195)
Salvage of the new machine	6	5,000	0.564	2,820
Present value of net cash outflows				(58,375)
Keep the old machine:				
Overhaul needed now	Now	(4,000)	1.000	(4,000)
Annual cash operating costs	1–6	(15,000)	4355	(65,325)
Present value of net cash outflows				(69,325)
Net present value in favour of buying the new machine				$ 10,950

*All factors are from Exhibits 10–1 and 10–2.
†These two items could be netted into a single $22,000 incremental cost figure ($25,000 – $3,000 = $22,000).

As shown in the exhibit, the new machine has the lowest total cost when the present value of the net cash outflows is considered. An analysis of the two alternatives using the incremental cost approach is presented in Exhibit 10–8. As before, the data in this exhibit represent the differences between the alternatives as shown under the total cost approach.

EXHIBIT 10–8 The Incremental Cost Approach (least-cost decision)

Item	Year(s)	Amount of Cash Flows	10% Factor*	Present Value of Cash Flows
Incremental investment required to purchase the new machine	Now	$(21,000)	1.000	$(21,000)†
Salvage of the old machine	Now	3,000	1.000	3,000†
Savings in annual cash operating costs	1–6	6,000	4.355	26,130
Difference in salvage value in six years	6	5,000	0.564	2,820
Net present value in favour of buying the new machine				$ 10,950

*All factors are from Exhibits 10–1 and 10–2.

†These two items could be netted into a single $18,000 incremental cost figure ($21,000 − $3,000 = $18,000).

CONCEPT CHECK

1. Which of the following statements are false? (You may select more than one answer.)
   a. The total cost and incremental cost approaches to net present value analysis can occasionally lead to conflicting results.
   b. The cost of capital is a screening mechanism for net present value analysis.
   c. The present value of a dollar increases as the time of receipt extends farther into the future.
   d. The higher the cost of capital, the lower the present value of a dollar received in the future.

*Note to student: See **Guidance Answers** online.*

Preference Decisions—The Ranking of Investment Projects

LO2 • **Apply**

CC10: Rank projects in order of preference using the profitability index.

Recall that when considering investment opportunities, managers have to make two types of decisions—screening decisions and preference decisions. Screening decisions pertain to whether some proposed investment is acceptable. Preference decisions come *after* screening decisions, and they attempt to answer the following question: How do the remaining investment proposals, all of which have been screened and provide an acceptable rate of return, rank in terms of preference? That is, which one(s) would be *best* for the firm to accept?

Preference decisions are more difficult to make than screening decisions because investment funds are usually limited. This often requires that some (perhaps many) otherwise very profitable investment opportunities must be passed up.

Sometimes, preference decisions are called rationing decisions or ranking decisions because they ration limited investment funds among many competing alternatives, or there may be many alternatives that must be ranked.

If the NPV method is used to rank projects, the net present value of one project cannot be compared directly with the net present value of another project unless the investments in the projects are of equal size. For example, assume that a company is considering two competing investments, as shown below:

	Investment	
	A	B
Investment required	$(80,000)	$(5,000)
Present value of cash inflows	81,000	6,000
Net present value	$ 1,000	$ 1,000

Each project has a net present value of $1,000, but the projects are not equally desirable. The project requiring an investment of only $5,000 is much more desirable when funds are limited than the project requiring an investment of $80,000. To compare the two projects on a valid basis, the present value of the cash inflows should be divided by the investment required. The result is called the **profitability index**. The formula for the profitability index follows:

$$\text{Profitability index} = \frac{\text{Present value of cash inflows}}{\text{Investment required}} \qquad (1)$$

The profitability indexes for the two preceding investments are computed as follows:

	Investment	
	A	B
Present value of cash inflows (a)	$81,000	$6,000
Investment required (b)	$80,000	$5,000
Profitability index, (a) ÷ (b)	1.01	1.20

When using the profitability index to rank competing investment projects, the preference rule is as follows: *The higher the profitability index, the more desirable the project.* Applying this rule to the two preceding investments, investment B should be chosen over investment A.

The profitability index is an application of the techniques for utilizing scarce resources. In this case, the scarce resource is the limited funds available for investment, and the profitability index is similar to the contribution margin per unit of the scarce resource.

A few details should be clarified with respect to the computation of the profitability index. The "investment required" refers to any cash outflows that occur at the beginning of the project, reduced by any salvage value recovered from the sale of old equipment. It also includes any investment in working capital that the project may need. Finally, we should note that the "present value of cash inflows" is net of all *out*flows that occur after the project starts.

IN BUSINESS

CHOOSING A CAT

Sometimes a long-term decision does not require the use of sophisticated analytical techniques. For example, White Grizzly Cat Skiing of Meadow Creek, British Columbia, needs two snowcats for its powder-skiing operations—one for shuttling guests to the top of the mountain and one to be held in reserve in case of mechanical problems with the first. Bombardier of Canada sells new snowcats for $250,000 and used, reconditioned snowcats for $150,000. In either case, the snowcats are good for about 5,000 hours of operation before they need to be reconditioned. From White Grizzly's perspective, the choice is clear. Since both the new and reconditioned snowcats last about 5,000 hours, the latter will result in a higher net present value due to its lower capital investment. Therefore, the reconditioned snowcats are the obvious choice. They may not have all of the latest bells and whistles, but they get the job done at a price that a small operation can afford.

Bombardier snowcats do not have passenger cabs as standard equipment. To save money, White Grizzly builds its own custom-designed passenger cab for about $15,000, using recycled Ford Escort seats and industrial-strength aluminum for the frame and siding. If purchased retail, a passenger cab would cost about twice as much and would not be as well suited for snowcat skiing.

Source: Brad and Carole Karafil, owners and operators of White Grizzly Cat Skiing, http://www.whitegrizzly.com.

The Internal Rate of Return Method

LO2 • **Know** • **Apply**

CC11: Compute the internal rate of return (IRR) of a project, interpret it, and explain its use for project selection.

The **internal rate of return (IRR)** of a project is defined as the discount rate that makes the net present value of the project equal zero. The internal rate of return is sometimes referred to as the *yield* of the project. It is interpreted as the rate of return promised by the project over the project's useful life. We will consider three aspects of the internal rate of return: (1) its calculation, (2) its interpretation, and (3) its usefulness for decision making about projects as compared with the net present value rule.

Calculating the Internal Rate of Return of a Project

To illustrate the calculation of the internal rate of return, assume the following simplistic data.

EXAMPLE E

Chantal Enterprises is planning to add a new product line during the summer. The net initial investment will be $142,514. The net cash inflow from the sale of the new product line at the end of one year following the purchase is forecast at $149,700. Determine the internal rate of return of this project.

The internal rate of return is the discount rate that will make the project's net present value equal zero. This essentially means that the present value of the net cash inflow at the end of one year must equal the net initial investment. We can illustrate this relationship as follows:

$142,514 =$ Present value of $149,700 received at the end of one year

$142,514 = ($PV factor $\times \$149,700)$

PV factor $= \$142,514 \div \$149,700 = 0.952$

From the present value table in Exhibit 10–1, we can see that 0.952 corresponds to a discount rate of 5% (see the first line corresponding to year 1). We conclude that the proposed investment's internal rate of return is 5%. The present value of 0.952 can also be expressed mathematically as follows (the full calculation is presented in Endnote 1 to this chapter):[1]

$$\frac{1}{(1 + IRR)} = 0.952$$

It was simple to solve for the internal rate of return here because the project had a single cash flow occurring in the first year. Moreover, this was a very simple example to illustrate the principle underlying the calculation of the internal rate of return. The table method will provide a rough estimate within 1% of the internal rate of return, but it will work only for single cash flows or annuities.[2] In practice, a project can last for several years and have nonconstant cash flows. This complicates the *mathematics* (step C of the calculation in Endnote 1), but steps A and B will stay the same. Practitioners use computer programs or spreadsheets to complete step C. To illustrate this, consider the next example.

EXAMPLE F

Rivers Company is considering a project to upgrade its wharves. The project cost is estimated at $2.1 million. The annual savings in maintenance costs and revenue from increased barge traffic is projected as follows:

Cash Flow in				
Year 1	Year 2	Year 3	Year 4	Year 5
$490,000	$445,000	$476,000	$510,000	$435,000

The wharves will require further upgrading after five years; therefore, management is interested in determining if the projected cash flows during the upcoming five-year period are sufficient to warrant proceeding with the proposed upgrade. Determine the internal rate of return of the project.

We can use a spreadsheet program, such as Microsoft Excel. The following screenshot shows the answer:[3]

	A	B	C	D	E	F	G
1				Rivers Company			
2				IRR Calculation for the Wharf Upgrading Project			
3							
4	Year	0	1	2	3	4	5
5	Cash flow	−$2,100,000	$490,000	$445,000	$476,000	$510,000	$435,000
6							
7	IRR	3.9869%					
8							

Interpretation and Use of the IRR

The project's internal rate of return is the rate of return *promised* by the cash flows of the project. If the wharf project at Rivers Company provides the cash flows that have been forecast for each year, *and* if each cash flow is immediately reinvested at the rate of about 4% per year, then the net present value of the project at a discount rate of 4% will be equal to 0.

This, however, does not tell you how the internal rate of return can be used to decide if a project is worthwhile. For example, should Rivers Company go ahead with the wharf upgrade? To decide whether to accept a project, the internal rate of return must be compared with the company's cost of capital. The cost of capital will play the role of a *hurdle rate* (or *minimum required rate of return*).[4] The logic behind this is that if the project cannot yield at least the cost of the funds tied up in it, it will not be profitable. The decision rule using the internal rate of return can be stated as follows: *If the internal rate of return is equal to or greater than the cost of capital, the project should be accepted. If the internal rate of return is less than the cost of capital, the project should be rejected.*

Suppose the cost of the capital for the wharf project is 5%. Since the internal rate of return of 4% is *less* than the hurdle rate of 5%, Rivers Company will reject the project.

The idea that an acceptable project should earn a rate of return greater than the cost of capital is very appealing. This is the basic principle of the internal rate of return method. But the complexity behind the calculation of the internal rate of return can make it look mysterious. Note that the cost of capital in the internal rate of return method is the hurdle rate. In the net present value method, the cost of capital is the *discount rate*.

Comparison of the IRR and NPV Methods

LO2 ● **Know**

CC12: Compare and contrast the IRR and NPV methods in project selection.

Many managers wonder if the IRR and NPV methods provide an identical signal about whether projects should be accepted or rejected. We list the strengths and limitations of the two methods in the table below. Although both methods have strengths and limitations, the net present value will always provide the correct signal regarding acceptance or rejection of a project.

	Internal Rate of Return	**Net Present Value**
Strengths	IRR is a simple way to communicate information about an investment proposal because investors prefer rates to dollars as a measure of evaluation.	NPV is conceptually superior because it assumes that cash flows can be reinvested at the discount rate (which ideally should be the opportunity cost of capital).
	Percentage is a standardized measure; therefore, the IRRs of two different investments can be easily compared.	It can be used even when the cash flow pattern is unconventional (i.e., negative cash flows after the initial investment).
	It can be calculated without the requirement of a pre-established discount rate.	
Limitations	There is a limiting assumption that cash flows are reinvested at the IRR (which may not be the same as the opportunity cost of capital).	It may be difficult to compare two investments of differing magnitudes.
	We cannot easily compute the IRR when the cash flow pattern is unconventional (i.e., negative cash flows after the initial investment).	It requires establishing the discount rate.

WORKING IT OUT

Max Corporation, a recreational company, is considering investing in a new boat that it can use to offer tourists boat rides. After reviewing the features of six different boats, its estimates for the selected option are as follows:

Investment in the boat		$3,000,000
Salvage value after 10 years		125,000
Annual revenue and expense projections:		
Sales revenue		6,400,000
Contribution margin		30% of sales revenue
Fixed expenses		
Marketing, sales, and promotion	$750,000	
Administration	450,000	
Depreciation	287,500	1,400,000

Required:

1. Compute the cash flows over the 10-year period.
2. Using a discount rate of 16%, compute the net present value of the proposed investment. Is this a profitable investment?
3. The second-best boat choice required an investment of $2.4 million and generated a net present value of $820,000. Compute the profitability index of each option.
4. Compute the internal rate of return (IRR) for the company's preferred investment option.

SOLUTION TO WORKING IT OUT

1. The cash flows are as follows:

Year 0 (now)	$3,000,000
Years 1–10	807,500*
Year 10 (salvage value)	125,000
*This amount is calculated as follows:	
Contribution margin (= 30% × $6,400,000)	$1,920,000
Fixed expenses	1,400,000
Net income	$ 520,000
Add back depreciation	287,500
Net annual cash flow	$ 807,500

2. The present values of cash flows are as follows:

	Amount	Discount Factor	Present Value
Year 0	$ (3,000,000)	1.00	$(3,000,000)
Years 1–10	$ 807,500	4.833*	3,902,648
Year 10	$ 125,000	0.227‡	28,375
Total net present value			$ 931,023

*See Exhibit 10–2.
‡See Exhibit 10–1.

The net present value is $931,023; therefore, it is a profitable investment.

3. The profitability index for the preferred boat option is $3,931,023 ÷ $3,000,000 = 1.31. The profitability index for the second-best boat option is $3,220,000 ÷ $2,400,000 = 1.34. The profitability index for the second-best boat option is slightly higher at 1.34.

4. The internal rate of return for the proposed investment is 23.9%:

	A	B	C	D	E	F	G	H	I	J	K	L
1	Year	0	1	2	3	4	5	6	7	8	9	10
2	Cash flow	$(3,000,000)	$807,500	$807,500	$807,500	$807,500	$807,500	$807,500	$807,500	$807,500	$807,500	$932,500
3	IRR	23.9%										

Other Approaches to Capital Budgeting Decisions

The NPV and IRR methods have gained widespread acceptance as decision-making tools. Other methods of making capital budgeting decisions are also used, however, and are preferred by some managers. In this section, we discuss two such methods, known as *payback* and *simple rate of return*. Both methods have been in use for many years, but have been declining in popularity as primary tools for project evaluation.

The Payback Method

LO2 • **Apply**

CC13: Calculate the payback period of an investment project.

The payback method focuses on the **payback period**, the length of time that it takes for a project to recoup its initial cost out of the cash receipts that it generates. This period is sometimes referred to as "the time it takes for an investment to pay for itself."

The basic premise of the payback method is as follows: the more quickly the cost of an investment can be recovered, the more desirable is the investment.

The payback period is expressed in years. *When the net annual cash inflow is the same every year,* the following formula can be used to compute the payback period:

$$\text{Payback period} = \frac{\text{Investment required}}{\text{Net annual cash inflow*}} \tag{2}$$

*If new equipment is replacing old equipment, this becomes incremental net annual cash inflow.

To illustrate the payback method, assume the following data.

EXAMPLE G

York Company needs a new milling machine. The company is considering two machines: machine A and machine B. Machine A costs $15,000 and will reduce operating costs by $5,000 per year. Machine B costs only $12,000, but will also reduce operating costs by $5,000 per year. Which machine should be purchased according to the payback method?

$$\text{Machine A payback period} = \frac{\$15,000}{\$5,000} = 3.0 \text{ years}$$

$$\text{Machine B payback period} = \frac{\$\,12,000}{\$\,5,000} = 2.4 \text{ years}$$

According to the payback calculations, York Company should purchase machine B, since it has a shorter payback period than machine A.

Payback and Uneven Cash Flows

When the cash flows associated with an investment project change from year to year, the simple payback formula that we just outlined is no longer usable, and the computations involved in deriving the payback period can be fairly complex. Consider the following data:

Year	Investment	Cash Inflow
1	$4,000	$1,000
2		2,000
3	2,000	2,000
4		2,000
5		2,500
6		3,000
7		2,000
8		2,000

What is the payback period on this investment? The answer is 3.5 years, but to obtain this figure, you must track the unrecovered investment year by year. The steps involved in this process are shown in Exhibit 10–9. By the middle of the fourth year, sufficient cash inflows will have been realized to recover the entire investment of $6,000 (= $4,000 + $2,000).

EXHIBIT 10–9 Payback and Uneven Cash Flows

Year	(1) Beginning Unrecovered Investment	(2) Investment	(3) Cash Inflow	(4) Ending Unrecovered Investment (1) + (2) − (3)
1	$ –0–	$4,000	$1,000	$ 3,000
2	3,000		2,000	1,000
3	3,000	2,000	2,000	1,000
4	1,000		2,000	–0–
5	2,000		2,500	–0–
6	1,500		3,000	–0–
7	–0–		2,000	–0–
8	–0–		2,000	–0–

An Extended Example of Payback

As shown by formula (2), the payback period is computed by dividing the investment in a project by the net annual cash inflows that the project will generate. If new equipment is replacing old equipment, then any salvage to be received on disposal of the old equipment should be deducted from the cost of the new equipment, and only the *incremental* investment should be used in the payback computation. In addition, any depreciation deducted in arriving at the project's net income must be added back to obtain the project's expected net annual cash inflow. To illustrate, assume the following data.

EXAMPLE H

Goodtime Fun Centres Inc. operates many outlets in the eastern provinces. Some of the vending machines in one of its outlets provide little revenue, and so the company is considering removing the machines and installing equipment to dispense soft ice cream. The equipment would cost $80,000 and have an eight-year useful life. Incremental annual revenues and costs associated with the sale of ice cream would be as follows:

Sales	$150,000
Less: Cost of ingredients	90,000
Contribution margin	60,000
Less: Fixed expenses:	
Salaries	27,000

Maintenance	3,000
Depreciation	10,000
Total fixed expenses	40,000
Net income	$ 20,000

The vending machines can be sold for a $5,000 scrap value. What is the payback period of the proposed project?

An analysis of the payback period of the proposed equipment is given in Exhibit 10–10. Two things should be noted from the data in this exhibit. First, note that depreciation is added back to net income to obtain the net annual cash inflow from the new equipment. As stated previously in the chapter, depreciation is not a cash outlay; thus, it must be added back to net income to adjust net income to a cash basis. Second, note in the payback computation that the salvage value from the old machines has been deducted from the cost of the new equipment and that only the incremental investment has been used in computing the payback period. The proposed equipment has a payback period of 2.5 years.

EXHIBIT 10–10 Computation of the Payback Period

Step 1: *Compute the net annual cash inflow.* Since the net annual cash inflow is not given, it must be computed before the payback period can be determined:

Net income (given above)	$20,000
Add: Noncash deduction for depreciation	10,000
Net annual cash inflow	$30,000

Step 2: *Compute the payback period.* Using the net annual cash inflow figure from step 1, the payback period can be determined as follows:

Cost of the new equipment	$80,000
Less: Salvage value of old equipment	5,000
Investment required	$75,000

$$\text{Payback period} = \frac{\text{Investment required}}{\text{Net annual cash inflow}}$$

$$= \frac{\$75,000}{\$30,000} = 2.5 \text{ years}$$

IN BUSINESS

INVESTING IN AN MBA

"What is the value of an MBA?" This is a key question that potential students might ask. The financial benefit of earning an MBA degree is enhanced earning power; the costs include both tuition and the opportunity cost of lost salary for two years. According to a *Forbes* magazine study published in 2000, the net present value of an MBA using the first five years of post-degree earnings varies a great deal—ranging from over $100,000 at Harvard University to $1,000 or less at some institutions. The payback period of between 3.3 and 5 years shows less variation. This has not changed despite criticisms of the MBA degree. A study published in 2005 suggests that the MBA is still a valuable proposition, providing an average net present value of over $500,000 over one's lifetime, a payback period of less than nine years, and an internal rate of return of over 17%. Finally, a 2011 article suggests that an MBA from a reputable program offers many benefits, including higher compensation, that contribute to a high return on investment.

Sources: Kurt Brandenhausen, "The Bottom Line on B-Schools," *Forbes*, February 7, 2000, pp. 100–104; Antony Davies and Thomas Cline, "The ROI on the MBA," *BizEd*, January/February 2005, pp. 42–45; Denise Deveau, "The ROI of an MBA," *Financial Post*, November 29, 2011, http://business.financialpost.com/2011/11/29/the-roi-of-an-mba/.

Evaluation of the Payback Method

LO2   • Know

CC14: Explain the payback method and its potential to mislead a manager.

The payback period only tells a manager how long it will take for a project to recover its investment. It *does not say anything about a project's profitability*. It is possible for a project to have a shorter payback in comparison with another project *and* not be as profitable. There are three reasons for the payback method to potentially mislead a manager.

DIFFERENT USEFUL LIVES

Consider Example G above. Machine B has a shorter payback period than machine A. This suggests that machine B is preferable. However, the example did not provide any data on the useful lives of the machines. Suppose that machine A has a 10-year useful life, whereas machine B has a five-year useful life. Note that when the useful lives of alternative projects are different, simple comparisons of their net present value or payback period should not be made. Why? It will take two purchases of machine B to provide the same service as machine A. If, on the one hand, a manager is going to use a machine for only five years, the analysis should include the disposal value of machine A. On the other hand, if the manager intends to operate the machine for 10 years, the analysis of machine B should include the cash flow from the second purchase of machine B in year 5. Clearly, an analysis that relies only on the payback period will miss these points.

TIME VALUE OF MONEY

The payback period weighs all cash flows equally, regardless of when the cash flows occur. However, we know that cash flows received in a previous period are more valuable than those received in a later period. This flaw in the payback period method can cause a manager to make a wrong decision. Consider the following simple example. Two alternative projects cost $8,000 each. The cash flows from these projects are shown below:

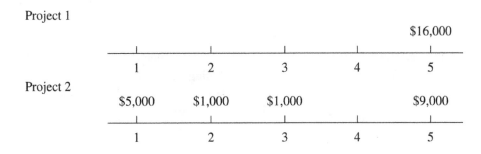

Both projects have a payback period of five years, but project 2 will return most of its cash flows earlier and is, thus, more desirable—a point that will be missed if you rely only on the payback period.

CASH FLOWS BEYOND THE PAYBACK CUTOFF DATE

Sometimes, managers specify that projects have to meet a *cutoff* date criterion for the payback period for the project to be acceptable. Such a policy will discard any project that fails to return its cost by the cutoff date. This can be dangerous, since the cash flows that occur beyond the cutoff date are never considered. Consider the following data:

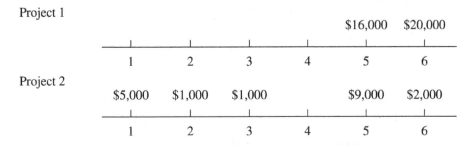

Now, suppose that projects 1 and 2 both have a cost of $7,000 and that management wants a payback period of four years or less. Project 2, which has a payback of three years, will pass this test, but project 1 will fail the test and be rejected. But a net present value analysis will take into consideration all of the cash flows of both projects. Such an analysis will show that project 1 is more profitable than project 2.

In a rapidly changing marketplace, it is not uncommon for managers to demand that projects have small payback periods, because if the cash flows do not materialize in the first two years, they are highly unlikely to surface later. Textbook publishing is a good illustration of this concept. Publishers often tell authors that if a textbook is not adopted for use in its first two years after publishing, it is unlikely to find a market thereafter. This also explains why textbooks undergo revision once every three or four years. But be careful. These instances do *not* justify the unquestioning use of the payback method. Note that when rapid payback is suggested, an assumption is made that cash flows beyond the cutoff date are unlikely to be obtained. Therefore, we hope that it is clear to you that the payback method will not always provide the proper signal for project acceptance or rejection and must be used carefully.

The Simple Rate of Return Method

LO2 • Apply

CC15: Calculate the simple rate of return (SRR) of an investment project.

The **simple rate of return (SRR)** method is another capital budgeting technique that does not involve discounted cash flows. The method is also known as the *accounting rate of return,* the *unadjusted rate of return,* and the *financial statement method.*

Unlike the other capital budgeting methods we have discussed, the simple rate of return method does not focus on cash flows. Rather, it focuses on accounting net income. The approach is to estimate the revenues that will be generated by a proposed investment and then to deduct from these revenues all of the projected operating expenses associated with the project. This net income figure is then related to the initial investment in the project, as shown in the following formula:

$$\text{Simple rate of return} = \frac{\text{Incremental net income} \left(= \text{Incremental revenues} - \text{Incremental expenses, including depreciation on new equipment} \right)}{\text{Initial investment*}} \tag{3}$$

*The investment should be reduced by any salvage from the sale of old equipment.

Or, if a cost reduction project is involved, formula (3) becomes

$$\text{Simple rate of return} = \frac{\text{Cost savings} - \text{Depreciation on new equipment}}{\text{Initial investment*}} \tag{4}$$

*The investment should be reduced by any salvage from the sale of old equipment.

EXAMPLE I

Brigham Tea Inc. is a processor of a low-acid tea. The company is contemplating purchasing equipment for an additional processing line. The additional processing line would increase revenues by $90,000 per year. Incremental cash operating expenses would be $40,000 per year. The equipment would cost $180,000 and have a nine-year life. No salvage value is projected. Compute the simple rate of return.

By applying formula (3), we can compute the following simple rate of return:

$$
\begin{aligned}
\text{Simple rate of return} &= \frac{\left[\begin{array}{c} \$90,000 \\ \text{incremental} \\ \text{revenues} \end{array} \right] - \left[\begin{array}{c} \$40,000 \text{ cash operating expenses} \\ + \$ 20,000 \text{ depreciation} \end{array} \right]}{\$180,000 \text{ initial investment}} \\
&= \frac{\$30,000}{\$180,000} \\
&= 16.7\%
\end{aligned}
$$

EXAMPLE J

Midwest Farms Inc. hires people on a part-time basis to sort eggs using an old egg-sorting machine. The cost of this process is $30,000 per year. The company is investigating the purchase of a new egg-sorting machine that would cost $90,000 and have a 15-year useful life. The machine would have negligible salvage value, and it would cost $10,000 per year to operate and maintain. The egg-sorting equipment currently being used could be sold now for a scrap value of $2,500. Compute the simple rate of return on the new egg-sorting machine.

A cost reduction project is involved in this situation. By applying formula (4), we can compute the simple rate of return as follows:

$$\text{Simple rate of return} = \frac{\$20,000 \text{ * cost savings} - \$6,000^{\dagger} \text{ depreciation on new equipment}}{\$90,000 - \$2,500}$$

$$= 16.0\%$$

*$30,000 − $10,000 = $20,000 cost savings
†$90,000 ÷ 15 years = $6,000 depreciation

Criticisms of the SRR Method

LO2 ● **Know**

CC16: Explain the disadvantages of the SRR method for project selection.

The most damaging criticism of the SRR method is that it does not consider the time value of money. A dollar received 10 years from now is viewed as being just as valuable as a dollar received today. Thus, the manager can be misled if the alternatives being considered have different cash flow patterns.

Additionally, many projects do not have uniform cash flows and incremental revenues and expenses over their useful lives. As a result, the simple rate of return will fluctuate from year to year, with the possibility that a project may appear to be desirable in some years and undesirable in others. In contrast, the NPV method provides a single figure that summarizes all of the cash flows over the entire useful life of the project.

HELPFUL HINT

The simple rate of return has two important limitations when used to make capital budgeting decisions—(1) it does not focus on cash flows, and (2) it does not recognize the time value of money. However, the simple rate of return is important because it can influence how managers perceive investment opportunities. For example, assume that you are the manager of a division within a company that pays or withholds your annual bonus based on whether your division exceeds its historical return on investment (ROI) of 20%. Now assume that your division has an investment opportunity that provides a net present value of $100,000 and a simple rate of return of 16%. Would you make the investment? The company would want you to make the investment because of its positive net present value; however, from your division's standpoint, the investment is undesirable because its simple rate of return is less than the division's historical ROI.

CONCEPT CHECK

2. If a $300,000 investment has a project profitability index of 0.25, what is the net present value of the project?
    a. $75,000
    b. $225,000
    c. $25,000
    d. $275,000

3. Which of the following statements are false? (You may select more than one answer.)
    a. The payback period increases as the cost of capital decreases.
    b. The simple rate of return will be the same for two alternatives that have identical cash flow patterns even if the pattern of accounting for net operating income differs between the alternatives.
    c. The internal rate of return will be higher than the cost of capital for projects that have positive net present values.
    d. If two alternatives have the same present value of cash inflows, the alternative that requires the higher investment will have the higher project profitability index.

*Note to student: See **Guidance Answers** online.*

IN BUSINESS

FEDEX GOES GREEN—WELL, NOT EXACTLY!

In 2003, FedEx announced a 10-year plan to replace 3,000 delivery trucks per year with environmentally friendly hybrid vehicles, thereby eliminating 227,000 tonnes of greenhouse gases per year. The hybrid vehicles cost 75% more than conventional trucks, but over 10 years they generate fuel savings that offset the higher cost. By 2007, FedEx had purchased fewer than 100 hybrid vehicles because management decided that the eco-friendly investment was not the most profitable use of the company's resources. FedEx's environmental director justified the company's actions by saying, "We do have a fiduciary responsibility to our shareholders . . . we can't subsidize the development of this technology for our competitors."

This example illustrates the challenges that companies face when attempting to satisfy the expectations of various stakeholders. Perhaps FedEx shareholders would applaud the company's decision to retreat from its 10-year plan, whereas environmentally conscious customers would criticize the company's actions. What do you think?

Source: Ben Elgin, "Little Green Lies," *BusinessWeek*, October 29, 2007, pp. 45–52.

Postaudit of Investment Projects

A **postaudit** of an investment project involves a follow-up after the project has been approved to see whether expected results are actually realized. This is a key part of the capital budgeting process that provides an opportunity to see if realistic data are being submitted to support capital budgeting proposals. It also provides an opportunity to reinforce successful projects as needed, to strengthen or perhaps salvage projects that are encountering difficulty, to terminate unsuccessful projects before losses become too great, and to improve the overall quality of future investment proposals.

In performing a postaudit, the same technique should be used as was used in the original approval process. That is, if a project was approved on the basis of a net present value analysis, then the same procedure should be used in performing the postaudit. However, the data used in the postaudit analysis should be *actual observed data,* rather than estimated data. This affords management an opportunity to make a side-by-side comparison to see how well the project has worked out. It also helps ensure that estimated data received on future proposals will be carefully prepared, since the people submitting the data will know that their estimates will be given careful scrutiny in the postaudit process. Actual results that are far out of line with original estimates should be carefully reviewed by management. Those managers responsible for the original estimates should be required to provide a full explanation of any major differences between estimated and actual results.[5]

IN BUSINESS

OPERATING DECISIONS CAN AFFECT FUTURE CASH FLOWS

Companies invest in projects based on future cash flows which are derived on the basis of assumptions about the operations of the company and how it intends to execute its business models.

Consider Royal Caribbean Cruises, which invested $1.4 billion to build the *Oasis of the Seas,* a cruise ship that carries 5,400 passengers and stands 20 storeys above the sea. The vessel is one-third larger than any other cruise ship and contains 21 pools, 24 restaurants, 13 retail shops, and 300-foot water slides. The company hopes the ship's extraordinary amenities will attract large numbers of customers willing to pay premium prices.

However, the economic downturn has caused many customers to refrain from spending on lavish vacations. These decisions of customers to cut back on discretionary spending during downturns can affect the speed with which an investment can be recouped and put pressure on the cash flows of the company, especially when the downturn is unexpected.

And what about poor execution of the operations? This can adversely affect customers' experience and the negative publicity can squelch future demand. Again, consider the recent experience of cruise customers who paid for a seven-day cruise from New Jersey to the Bahamas in early February 2016. The ship, *Anthem of the Seas*, sailed out of Bayonne, New Jersey, and into a massive winter storm with 200-kilometre-per-hour winds. The ship was reported to have sailed listing at a 45 degree angle for over four hours during the worst of the storm. Luckily no serious injuries were reported and the ship turned back three days later. While news of this ship's experience has been widely reported, we can only wonder if the lapse in judgment of the ship's operator to sail into the storm will affect how future customers perceive the cruise line's ability to deliver a quality experience which apparently warrants the high prices charged for cruises.

Source: Mike Esterl, "Huge Cruise Ships Prepare for Launch but Face Uncertain Waters," *The Wall Street Journal,* December 4, 2009, pp. B1–B2. The experience of passengers on *Anthem of the Seas* is readily accessed from a variety of news feeds on the net including CNN, NY Times etc.

DECISION POINT

INVESTOR

Each of the following situations is independent. Work out your own solution to each situation, and then check it against the solution provided.
1. John has just reached age 58. He plans to retire in 12 years. Upon retiring, he would like to take an extended vacation, which he expects will cost at least $4,000. What lump-sum amount must he invest now to have the needed $4,000 at the end of 12 years if the rate of return is
   a. 8%?
   b. 12%?
2. The Morgans would like to send their daughter to an expensive music camp at the end of each of the next five years. The camp costs $1,000 a year. What lump-sum amount would have to be invested now to have the $1,000 at the end of each year if the rate of return is
   a. 8%?
   b. 12%?

3. You have just received an inheritance from a relative. You can invest the money and either receive a $20,000 lump-sum amount at the end of 10 years or receive $1,400 at the end of each year for the next 10 years. If your minimum desired rate of return is 12%, which alternative should you select?

*Note to student: See **Guidance Answers** online.*

Learning Objectives Summary

LO1   UNDERSTAND THE BASICS OF CAPITAL BUDGETING ANALYSIS.

Decisions that involve an outlay now in order to obtain some return (increase in revenue or reduction in costs) in the future are usually analyzed using capital budgeting techniques. This usually involves determining the cash flows occurring during the life of the project, discounting the future cash flows to present values using an appropriate discount rate, and assessing how the present values of future net cash inflows compare with cash outflows that must be made at the start of the project. The choice of discount rate is of critical importance when doing the analysis.

LO2   UNDERSTAND AND APPLY ALTERNATIVE METHODS TO ANALYZE CAPITAL INVESTMENTS.

A commonly used method for capital investment analysis includes calculating the net present value (NPV), which is the excess of the present value of future cash flows over the initial cash outlay incurred at the start of the project. A second method involves computing the discount rate at which the NPV is zero; this rate is called the internal rate of return (IRR). The project is considered financially feasible when the IRR exceeds the normally expected return or the normally used discount rate. A third method is the payback period, which is the amount of time it takes for the future cash flows to equal the initial outlay (there is no discounting involved in this method). A fourth method uses a measure of accounting income and divides this income by the investment amount.

Application Competency Summary

APPLICATION COMPETENCY	DELIVERABLE	SOURCE DOCUMENTS AND KEY INFORMATION	STEPS	KNOWLEDGE COMPETENCY

Prepare a net present value (NPV) analysis of two competing projects using either the total cost approach or the incremental cost approach.
 	
• **LO2–CC8**
	Key Information
	
	Total cost approach:
	
	the NPV of each of the alternatives being considered
	
	Incremental cost approach:
	
	the NPV of the differential cash
		Source Documents
		
		Various documents that provide information about the cash flows for each alternative and the company's cost of capital
		
		Required Information
			1. Total cost approach:
			   a. Determine the cash flows of each alternative considered separately.
			   b. Calculate the NPV of each alternative.
			   c. Choose the alternative with the highest NPV.
			
			2. Incremental cost approach:
			   a. Determine the differential cash flows (alternative 1 less alternative 2).
			   b. Calculate the NPV of the differential cash flows.
				Identifying the type and amount of cash flows pertaining to an alternative
				
				• **LO1–CC5**
				
				Cost of capital or the opportunity cost of capital appropriate for the risk of the alternative
				
				• **LO1–CC7**

APPLICATION COMPETENCY	DELIVERABLE	SOURCE DOCUMENTS AND KEY INFORMATION	STEPS	KNOWLEDGE COMPETENCY
	flows—applies only if there are exactly two alternatives *Report/ Document* No specific document; report should contain details of the project's NPV analysis	Cash flows of the alternatives including working capital requirements and recovery; cost of capital	c. Choose alternative 1 if the NPV is positive; otherwise, choose alternative 2.	
Compute the NPV of a project when no revenues are involved. ● **LO2–CC9**	*Key Information* The alternative with the lowest cost on a present value basis *Report/ Document* No specific document	*Source Documents* Various documents with information on expenditures and cost savings pertaining to the alternative *Required Information* Cash flows detailing the expenditures and savings in costs relating to an alternative	1. Use either a total cost or a differential cost approach. (The cost savings of choosing alternative 1 relative to alternative 2 can be used.) See above. 2. Remember that the relevant cash flows are cost flows; the best decision is the one with the lower present value of costs.	Cost savings are also benefits, and certain decision situations will not involve revenues directly. Cost of capital ● **LO1–CC7**
Rank projects in order of preference using the profitability index. ● **LO2–CC10**	*Key Information* Project rankings using the profitability index *Report/ Document* No specific document	*Source Documents* NPV analysis of each project being ranked *Required Information* Present value of cash flows of each project and the corresponding investment required	The profitability index is the ratio of the present value of the cash flows to the investment required. Calculate as follows: 1. Determine the present value of the cash flows. 2. Compute the ratio of the present value of the cash flows to the investment required.	Present value of relevant cash flows and the value of the investment required ● **LO2–CC8**

APPLICATION COMPETENCY	DELIVERABLE	SOURCE DOCUMENTS AND KEY INFORMATION	STEPS	KNOWLEDGE COMPETENCY

Compute the IRR of an alternative, interpret it, and explain its use for project selection.
 	
 ● **LO2–CC11**
	Key Information
	
	 The IRR of an alternative, its interpretation, and its use in recommending a decision to management
	
	 Report/ Document
	
	 No specific document
		(As above)	1. Algebraic method:
			    a. Set up an equation for the NPV calculation using the relevant cash flows and IRR as a discount rate; that is, write out the expression for the NPV using the cash flows and using the expression (1 + IRR) for the discount factor.
			    b. Set the NPV equal to 0.
			    c. Solve the resulting equation for the IRR.
			 2. Spreadsheet method:
			 This is applied when the project life is two or more periods.
			 Follow (a) and (b) as above.
			
			    c. Enter the cash flows on a spreadsheet. Assume that the cell range is B5:G5. Choose a target cell, e.g., B7. In the target cell, enter the formula =IRR(B5:G5, 0). The result in cell B7 will be the IRR.
			 3. Interpretation and use: The IRR is the number, that, if used as the discount rate, will result in an NPV of 0. This means that if the value of the IRR is also the cost of capital, then the NPV of the project will be 0. The use of a higher opportunity cost of capital will logically lead to a negative NPV, and a lower cost of capital than the IRR will yield a positive NPV. Thus, managers should accept projects if the opportunity cost of capital is less than the IRR.
				Identify and determine the relevant cash flows.
				
				 ● **LO1–CC5**
				
				 Cost of capital as a hurdle rate and its role in project selection decisions
				
				 ● **LO1–CC7**

Calculate the payback period of an investment project. ● **LO2–CC13**	*Key Information* The payback period of a project *Report/ Document* No specific document	*Source Documents* Various documents detailing the timing and the amount of cash flows	1. When net annual cash flow is the same for each period, apply the formula Payback period = Investment required ÷ Net annual cash flow. 2. Uneven cash flows: a. Proceeding period by period, calculate the ending unrecovered investment as follows: beginning	Identification and calculation of the amount and timing of relevant cash flows of a project ● **LO1–CC5**

APPLICATION COMPETENCY	DELIVERABLE	SOURCE DOCUMENTS AND KEY INFORMATION	STEPS	KNOWLEDGE COMPETENCY
		Required Information Timing and amount of the project's cash flows including the investment required	unrecovered investment plus any investment made in the period less the cash inflow during the period. b. The payback period is the period at which the unrecovered investment is zero.	
Calculate the SRR of a project. ● LO2–CC15	*Key Information* The simple rate of return of a project *Report/ Document* No specific document	*Source Documents* Various documents detailing cash flows (timing and amount) *Required Information* Project's cash flows	The method is applied using the incremental cash flow approach. 1. Subtract from the cash flows of alternative 1 the cash flow of alternative 2, proceeding period by period, and obtain the differential cash flows. 2. Calculate the simple rate of return as follows: (Incremental revenues − Incremental expenses including depreciation expense) ÷ Initial investment net of any cash inflows from closing down alternative 2.	Accounting net income versus economic profit

Review Problem: Comparison of Capital Budgeting Methods

Lamar Company is studying a project that would have an eight-year life and require a $1,600,000 investment in equipment. At the end of eight years, the project would terminate and the equipment would have no salvage value. The project would provide net income each year as follows:

Sales		$3,000,000
Less: Variable expenses		1,800,000
Contribution margin		1,200,000
Less: Fixed expenses:		
Advertising, salaries, and other fixed out-of-pocket costs	$700,000	
Depreciation	200,000	
Total fixed expenses		900,000
Net income		$ 300,000

The company's discount rate is 18%.

Required:

1. Compute the net annual cash inflow from the project.
2. Compute the project's net present value. Is the project acceptable?
3. Compute the project's payback period. If the company requires a maximum payback of three years, is the project acceptable?
4. Compute the project's simple rate of return.

SOLUTION TO REVIEW PROBLEM

1. The net annual cash inflow can be computed by deducting the cash expenses from sales:

Sales	$3,000,000
Less: Variable expenses	1,800,000
Contribution margin	1,200,000
Less: Advertising, salaries, and other fixed out-of-pocket costs	700,000
Net annual cash inflow	$ 500,000

Or it can be computed by adding back depreciation to net income:

Net income	$300,000
Add: Noncash deduction for depreciation	200,000
Net annual cash inflow	$500,000

2. The net present value can be computed as follows:

Item	Year(s)	Amount of Cash Flows	18% Factor	Present Value of Cash Flows
Cost of new equipment	Now	$(1,600,000)	1.000	$(1,600,000)
Net annual cash inflow	1–8	500,000	4.078	2,039,000
Net present value				$ 439,000

Yes, the project is acceptable, because it has a positive net present value.

3. The formula for the payback period is as follows:

$$\text{Payback} = \frac{\text{Investment required}}{\text{Net annual cash inflow}}$$

$$= \frac{\$1,600,000}{\$500,000}$$

$$= 3.2 \text{ years}$$

No, the project is not acceptable when measured by the payback method. The 3.2-year payback period is greater than the maximum three years set by the company.

4. The formula for the simple rate of return is as follows:

$$\text{Simple rate of return} = \frac{\text{Net income} \left(\begin{array}{ccc} = & \text{Incremental} & - & \text{Incremental expenses,} \\ & \text{revenues} & & \text{including depreciation} \end{array} \right)}{\text{Initial investment}}$$

$$= \frac{\$300,000}{\$1,600,000}$$

$$= 18.75\%$$

Questions

10–1   What is the difference between capital budgeting screening decisions and capital budgeting preference decisions?

10–2   What is meant by the term *time value of money?*

10–3   What is meant by the term *discounting?*

10–4   Why is the NPV method of making capital budgeting decisions superior to other methods, such as the payback and SRR methods?

10–5   What is NPV? Can it ever be negative? Explain.

10–6   "If a firm has to pay interest of 14% on long-term debt, then its cost of capital is 14%." Do you agree? Explain your answer.

10–7   What is meant by "an investment project's internal rate of return"? How is the internal rate of return computed?

10–8   Explain how the cost of capital serves as a screening tool when dealing with the NPV method.

10–9   "As the discount rate increases, the present value of a given future cash flow also increases." Do you agree? Explain your answer.

10–10 Refer to Exhibit 10–3. Is the return on this investment proposal exactly 20%, slightly more than 20%, or slightly less than 20%? Explain your answer.

10–11 Why are preference decisions sometimes called *rationing* decisions?

10–12 How is the profitability index computed, and what does it measure?

10–13 What is the preference rule for ranking investment projects under the NPV method?

10–14 Can an investment with a profitability index of less than 1.00 be an acceptable investment? Explain.

10–15 What is meant by the term *payback period?* How is the payback period determined?

10–16 How can the payback method be useful to the manager?

10–17 What is the major criticism of the payback and SRR methods of making capital budgeting decisions?

The Foundational 15

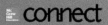

[LO1 – CC3, 4; LO2 – CC10, 13, 14]

Cardinal Company is considering a project that would require a $2,975,000 investment in equipment with a useful life of five years. At the end of five years, the project would terminate and the equipment would be sold for its salvage value of $300,000. The company's discount rate is 14%. The project would provide net operating income each year as follows:

Sales		$2,735,000
Variable expenses		1,000,000
Contribution margin		1,735,000
Fixed expenses:		
Advertising, salaries, and other fixed out-of-pocket costs	$735,000	
Depreciation	535,000	
Total fixed expenses		1,270,000
Net operating income		$ 465,000

Required:

10–1   Which item(s) in the income statement shown above will not affect cash flows?

10–2   What are the project's annual net cash inflows?

10–3   What is the present value of the project's annual net cash inflows?

10–4   What is the present value of the equipment's salvage value at the end of five years?

10–5   What is the project's net present value?

10–6   What is the project profitability index for this project? (Round your answer to the nearest whole percent.)

10–7   What is the project's payback period?

10–8   What is the project's simple rate of return for each of the five years?

10–9   If the company's discount rate was 16% instead of 14%, would you expect the project's net present value to be higher than, lower than, or the same as your answer to question 4? No computations are necessary

10–10   If the equipment's salvage value was $500,000 instead of $300,000, would you expect the project's payback period to be higher than, lower than, or the same as your answer to question 7? No computations are necessary.

10–11   If the equipment's salvage value was $500,000 instead of $300,000, would you expect the project's net present value to be higher than, lower than, or the same as your answer to question 4? No computations are necessary.

10–12   If the equipment's salvage value was $500,000 instead of $300,000, what would be the project's simple rate of return?

10–13   Assume a postaudit showed that all estimates (including total sales) were exactly correct except for the variable expense ratio, which actually turned out to be 45%. What was the project's actual net present value?

10–14   Assume a postaudit showed that all estimates (including total sales) were exactly correct except for the variable expense ratio, which actually turned out to be 45%. What was the project's actual payback period?

10–15   Assume a postaudit showed that all estimates (including total sales) were exactly correct except for the variable expense ratio, which actually turned out to be 45%. What was the project's actual simple rate of return?

Brief Exercises

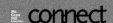

BRIEF EXERCISE 10–1
Using the NPV Method [LO1 – CC4]

The management of Kunkel Company is considering the purchase of a machine that would reduce operating costs. The machine will cost $40,000, and it will last for eight years. At the end of the eight-year period, the machine will have zero scrap value. Use of the machine will reduce operating costs by $7,000 per year. The company requires a minimum return of 12% before taxes on all investment projects.

Required:

1. Determine the net present value of the investment in the machine.
2. What is the difference between the total, undiscounted cash inflows and cash outflows over the entire life of the machine?

BRIEF EXERCISE 10–2
Performing an NPV Analysis of Competing Projects [LO2 – CC8]

Labeau Products Ltd., of Perth, Australia, has $122,500 to invest. The company is trying to decide between two alternative uses for the funds. The alternatives follow:

	Invest in Project X	Invest in Project Y
Investment required	$122,500	$122,500
Annual cash inflows	31,500	—
Single cash inflow at the end of 10 years	—	525,000
Life of the project	10 years	10 years

The company's discount rate is 6%.

Required:

Which alternative would you recommend that the company accept? Show all computations using the NPV approach. Prepare a separate computation for each project.

BRIEF EXERCISE 10–3
Computing the Profitability Index [LO2 – CC10]

Information on four investment proposals is provided below:

	Investment Proposal			
	A	**B**	**C**	**D**
Investment required	$(45,000)	$(50,000)	$(35,000)	$(60,000)
Present value of cash inflows	63,000	45,000	52,500	80,000
Net present value	$ 18,000	$ (5,000)	$ 17,500	$ 20,000
Life of the project	5 years	7 years	6 years	6 years

Required:

1. Compute the profitability index for each investment proposal.
2. Rank the proposals in terms of preference.

BRIEF EXERCISE 10–4
Using the Payback Method [LO2 – CC11]

The management of Unter Corporation is considering an investment with the following characteristics:

Year	Investment	Cash Inflow
1	$15,000	$6,000
2	8,000	5,000
3	—	4,000
4	—	3,000
5	—	4,000
6	—	5,000
7	—	2,000
8	—	3,000
9	—	2,000
10	—	2,500

Required:

1. Determine the payback period of the investment.
2. Would the payback period be affected if the cash inflow in the last year were several times as large?

BRIEF EXERCISE 10–5
Using the SRR Method [LO2 – CC15]

The management of Ballard MicroBrew is considering the purchase of an automated bottling machine for $120,000. The machine would replace an old piece of equipment that costs $30,000 per year to operate. The new machine would have a useful life of 10 years with no salvage value. The new machine would cost $12,000 per year to operate. The old machine currently in use could be sold now for a scrap value of $40,000.

Required:

Compute the SRR on the new automated bottling machine.

BRIEF EXERCISE 10–6
Calculating the Payback Period [LO2 – CC11]

Digger Company is evaluating an investment of $330,000 in earth moving equipment. Management anticipates net cash savings of $100,000 in year 1. The savings will increase by 40% in year 2 and then increase by another 50% in year 3. The minimum desired rate of return is 15%.

(Adapted © CPA Canada)

Required:

What is the payback period for this investment?

BRIEF EXERCISE 10–7
Computing the Internal Rate of Return [LO2 – CC11]

A $100,000 investment is expected to generate $27,740 in cash savings at the end of each year for five years.

(Adapted © CPA Canada)

Required:

What is the approximate internal rate of return?

BRIEF EXERCISE 10–8
Calculating the Payback Period [LO2 – CC11; LO4 – CC20^C]

Manufacturing Division has recommended the purchase of a new model of equipment to save operating costs. Relevant information is shown below:

Equipment cost	$ 70,000
Salvage value of project equipment at the end of the fifth year	20,000
Estimated annual cash savings from the new machine	10,500
Life	5 years
Annual depreciation (straight line)	10,000
Average tax rate	30%

Required:

What is the payback period? [*Hint:* Compute the after-tax cash flow using the average tax rate.]

Exercise

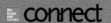

EXERCISE 10–1
Performing an NPV Analysis [LO1 – CC4; LO2 – CC8]

Windhoek Mines Ltd. of Namibia is contemplating the purchase of equipment to exploit a mineral deposit located on land to which the company has mineral rights. An engineering and cost analysis has been made, and it is expected that the following cash flows would be associated with opening and operating a mine in the area:

Cost of new equipment and timbers	R206,250
Working capital required	75,000
Net annual cash receipts	90,000*
Cost to construct new roads in three years	30,000
Salvage value of equipment in four years	48,750

*Receipts from sales of ore, less out-of-pocket costs for salaries, utilities, insurance, and so forth
(The currency in Namibia is the rand, here denoted by R.)

It is estimated that the mineral deposit would be exhausted after four years of mining. At that point, the working capital would be released for reinvestment elsewhere. The company's discount rate is 20%.

Required:

Determine the NPV of the proposed mining project. Should the project be accepted? Explain.

EXERCISE 10–2
Performing NPV Analyses of Competing Projects [LO2 – CC8]

Perrot Industries has $325,000 to invest. The company is trying to decide between two alternative uses of the funds. The alternatives follow:

	Project	
	A	B
Cost of equipment required	$325,000	—
Working capital investment required	—	$325,000
Annual cash inflows	67,650	54,400
Salvage value of equipment in six years	21,200	—
Life of the project	6 years	6 years

The working capital needed for project B will be released at the end of six years for investment elsewhere. Perrot Industries' discount rate is 14%.

Required:

Which investment alternative (if either) would you recommend that the company accept? Show all computations using the NPV method. Prepare a separate computation for each project.

EXERCISE 10–3
Performing NPV Analysis of Competing Projects [LO2 – CC8]

Labeau Products Ltd., of Perth, Australia, has $35,000 to invest. The company is trying to decide between two alternative uses for the funds, as follows:

	Investment Options	
	Project X	**Project Y**
Initial investment	$35,000	$ 35,000
Annual cash inflows	9,000	—
Single cash inflow at the end of 10 years	—	150,000
Life of the project	10 years	10 years

Labeau's discount rate for both projects is 18%.

Required:

(Ignore income taxes.) Which alternative would you recommend that the company accept? Show all computations using the net present value approach. Prepare separate computations for each project.

EXERCISE 10–4
Calculating the Profitability Index [LO2 – CC10]

The management of Revco Products is exploring five different investment opportunities. Information on the five projects under study follows:

	Project Number				
	1	**2**	**3**	**4**	**5**
Investment required	$(270,000)	$(450,000)	$(400,000)	$(360,000)	$(480,000)
Present value of cash inflows at a 10% discount rate	336,140	522,970	379,760	433,400	567,270
Net present value	$ 66,140	$ 72,970	$ (20,240)	$ 73,400	$ 87,270
Life of the project	6 years	3 years	5 years	12 years	6 years

The company's required rate of return is 10%; thus, a 10% discount rate has been used in the preceding present value computations. Limited funds are available for investment, and so the company cannot accept all of the available projects.

Required:

1. Compute the profitability index for each investment project.
2. Rank the five projects according to preference, in terms of
   a. Net present value.
   b. Profitability index.
3. Which ranking do you prefer? Why?

EXERCISE 10–5
Using the Payback and SRR Methods [LO2 – CC11, 15]

A piece of labour-saving equipment has just come onto the market, which Mitsui Electronics Ltd. could use to reduce costs in one of its plants in Japan. Relevant data relating to the equipment follow (currency is in thousands of yen, denoted by ¥):

Purchase cost of the equipment	¥216,000
Annual cost savings that will be provided by the equipment	¥45,000
Life of the equipment	12 years

Required:

1. Compute the payback period for the equipment. If the company requires a payback period of four years or less, will the equipment be purchased?
2. Compute the simple rate of return on the equipment. Use straight-line depreciation based on the equipment's useful life. Will the equipment be purchased if the company requires a rate of return of at least 14%?

EXERCISE 10–6
Utilizing Basic Present Value Concepts [LO2 – CC8]

Kathy Myers frequently purchases shares and bonds, but she is uncertain how to determine the rate of return that she is earning. For example, three years ago she paid $20,000 for 200 common shares of Malti Company. She received a $620 cash dividend on the shares at the end of each year for three years. At the end of three years, she sold the shares for $22,000. Kathy would like to earn a return of at least 14% on all of her investments. She is not sure whether the Malti Company shares provided a 14% return and would like some help with the necessary computations.

Required:

Using the NPV method, determine whether the Malti Company shares provided a 14% return. Round all computations to the nearest whole dollar.

EXERCISE 10–7
Using IRR and NPV Analyses [LO2 – CC8, 13]

Scalia's Cleaning Service is investigating the purchase of an ultrasound machine for cleaning window blinds. The machine would cost $136,700, including invoice cost, freight, and training of employees to operate it. Scalia's has estimated that the new machine would increase the company's cash flows, net of expenses, by $25,000 per year. The machine would have a 14-year useful life with no expected salvage value.

Required:

(Ignore income taxes.)

1. Compute the machine's internal rate of return to the nearest whole percent.
2. Compute the machine's net present value. Use a discount rate of 16%, and use the format shown in Exhibit 10–7. Why do you have a zero net present value?
3. Suppose that the new machine would increase the company's annual cash flows, net of expenses, by only $20,000 per year. Under these conditions, compute the internal rate of return to the nearest whole percent.

EXERCISE 10–8
Calculating the IRR [LO2 – CC13]

Kadalai Company makes metal blanks which it sells to metal fabrication and stamping companies. The sales forecasts for the next four years are 500,000 bars a year. The president estimates that he can save $1,000 per year in fixed cash operating costs plus $0.05/bar during the next four years if he buys a machine to automate the process at a cost of $90,000. A salvage value of $10,000 is expected at the end of the four-year period. The company's minimum desired rate of return is 10%. The company's average tax rate is 20%.

(Adapted © CPA Canada)

Required:

What is the internal rate of return for the investment in the machine? (*Hint:* Calculate the after tax cash flows using the average tax rate.)

EXERCISE 10–9
Calculating the Payback Period, Simple Rate of Return, and NPV [LO2 – CC8, 13, 15]

Nick's Novelties, Inc. is considering the purchase of electronic pinball machines to place in game arcades. The machines would cost a total of $300,000, have an eight-year useful life, and have a total salvage value of $20,000. The company estimated that annual revenues and expenses associated with the machines would be as follows:

Revenues		$200,000
Operating expenses:		
Commissions to game arcades	$100,000	
Insurance	7,000	
Depreciation	35,000	
Maintenance	18,000	160,000
Net operating income		$ 40,000

Required:

1. Assume that Nick's Novelties, Inc. will not purchase new equipment unless it provides a payback period of five years of less. Will the company purchase the pinball machines?
2. Compute the simple rate of return promised by the pinball machines. If the company requires a simple rate of return of at least 12%, will the pinball machines be purchased?
3. If Nick's Novelties, Inc. has a discount rate of 18%, what is the NPV of this investment? (*Hint:* Identify the relevant costs and then perform an NPV analysis.) Should the company purchase the pinball machines?

Problems

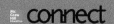

 PROBLEM 10–1
Performing a Basic NPV Analysis [LO2 – CC8]

The Sweetwater Candy Company would like to buy a new machine that would automatically dip chocolates. The dipping operation is currently done largely by hand. The machine the company is considering costs $120,000. The manufacturer estimates that the machine would be usable for 12 years, but would require the replacement of several key parts at the end of the sixth year. These parts would cost $9,000, including installation. After 12 years, the machine could be sold for about $7,500.

> **CHECK FIGURE**
> (1) Annual cash flows: $32,000

The company estimates that the cost to operate the machine will be only $7,000 per year. The present method of dipping chocolates costs $30,000 per year. In addition to reducing costs, the new machine will increase production by 6,000 boxes of chocolates per year. The company realizes a contribution margin of $1.50 per box. A 20% rate of return is required on all investments.

Required:

1. What are the net annual cash inflows that will be provided by the new dipping machine?
2. Compute the new machine's net present value. Use the incremental cost approach, and round all dollar amounts to the nearest whole dollar.

PROBLEM 10–2
Performing an NPV Analysis [LO2 – CC8]

In eight years, Kent Duncan will retire. He has $300,000 to invest, and he is exploring the possibility of opening a self-service car wash. The car wash could be managed in the free time he has available from his regular occupation, and it could be closed easily when he retires. After careful study, Kent has determined the following:

> **CHECK FIGURE**
> (1) Net annual cash receipts: $63,300

a. A building, in which a car wash could be installed, is available under an eight-year lease at a cost of $3,400 per month.

b. Purchase and installation costs of equipment would total $300,000. In eight years, the equipment could be sold for about 10% of its original cost.

c. An investment of an additional $4,000 would be required to cover working capital needs for cleaning supplies, change funds, and so forth. After eight years, this working capital would be released for investment elsewhere.

d. Both a car wash and a vacuum service would be offered, with a wash costing $3 and the vacuum costing 50 cents per use.

e. The only variable costs associated with the operation would be 46 cents per wash for water and 20 cents per use of the vacuum for electricity.

f. In addition to rent, monthly costs of operation would be as follows: cleaning, $900; insurance, $150; maintenance, $1,000.

g. Gross receipts from the car wash would be about $2,700 per week. According to the experience of other car washes, 70% of the customers using the wash would also use the vacuum.

h. Kent will not open the car wash unless it provides at least a 10% return, since this is the amount that could be earned by simply placing the $300,000 in high-grade securities.

Required:

1. Assuming that the car wash will be open 52 weeks a year, compute the expected net annual cash receipts (gross cash receipts less cash disbursements) from its operation. (Do not include the cost of the equipment, the working capital, or the salvage value in these computations.)

2. Would you advise Kent to open the car wash? Show computations using the NPV method of investment analysis. Round all dollar figures to the nearest whole dollar.

PROBLEM 10–3
Employing Total Cost and Incremental Cost Approaches [LO2 – CC8]

Bilboa Freightlines, S.A. of Panama has a small truck that it uses for local deliveries. The truck is in bad repair and must be either overhauled or replaced with a new truck. The company has assembled the following information (Panama uses the U.S. dollar as its currency):

> **CHECK FIGURE**
> (1) NPV: $21,225 in favour of the old truck

	A	B	C
1		*Present Truck*	*New Truck*
2			
3	Purchase cost new	$41,000	$55,000
4	Remaining book value	26,000	–
5	Overhaul needed now	8,000	–
6	Annual cash operating costs	11,000	8,500
7	Salvage value now	14,000	–
8	Salvage value eight years from now	1,000	4,000

If the company keeps and overhauls its present delivery truck, then the truck will be usable for eight more years. If a new truck is purchased, it will be used for eight years, after which it will be traded in on another truck. The new truck would be diesel-fuelled, resulting in a substantial reduction in annual operating costs, as shown above.

The company computes depreciation on a straight-line basis. All investment projects are evaluated using a 16% discount rate.

Required:

1. Should Bilboa Freightlines keep the old truck or purchase the new one? Use the total cost approach to net present value in making your decision. Round to the nearest whole dollar.

2. Redo part (1), this time using the incremental cost approach.

PROBLEM 10–4
Deciding Whether to Keep or Sell Property

Raul Martinas, a professor of languages at Eastern University, owns a small office building adjacent to the university campus. He acquired the property 10 years ago at a total cost of $530,000—that is, $50,000 for the land and $480,000 for the building. He has just received an offer from a realty company that wants to purchase the property; however, the property has been a good source of income over the years, and so Martinas is unsure whether he should keep it or sell it. His alternatives are as follows:

a. *Keep the property.* Martinas's accountant has kept careful records of the income realized from the property over the past 10 years. These records indicate the following annual revenues and expenses:

Rental receipts		$140,000
Less: Building expenses:		
Utilities	$25,000	
Depreciation of building	16,000	
Property taxes and insurance	18,000	
Repairs and maintenance	9,000	
Custodial help and supplies	40,000	108,000
Net operating income		$ 32,000

Professor Martinas makes a $12,000 mortgage payment each year on the property. The mortgage will be paid off in eight more years. He has been depreciating the building by the straight-line method, assuming a salvage value of $80,000 for the building, which he still thinks is an appropriate figure. He feels sure that the building can be rented for another 15 years. He also feels sure that 15 years from now the land will be worth three times what he paid for it.

b. *Sell the property.* A realty company has offered to purchase the property by paying $175,000 immediately and $26,500 per year for the next 15 years. Control of the property would go to the realty company immediately. To sell the property, Professor Martinas would need to pay the mortgage off, which could be done by making a lump-sum payment of $90,000.

Required:

Assume that Professor Martinas requires a 12% rate of return. Would you recommend that he keep or sell the property? Show computations using the total cost approach to net present value.

PROBLEM 10–5
Determining the Ranking of Projects [LO2 – CC8, 10]

Oxford Company has limited funds available for investment and must ration the funds among five competing projects. Selected information on the five projects follows:

Project	Investment Required	Net Present Value	Life of the Project (years)
A	$480,000	$132,969	7
B	405,000	126,000	12
C	300,000	105,105	7
D	525,000	114,408	3
E	450,000	(26,088)	6

The net present values above have been computed using a 10% discount rate. The company wants your assistance in determining which project to accept first, which to accept second, and so on.

Required:

1. Compute the profitability index for each project.
2. In order of preference, rank the five projects in terms of
   a. Net present value.
   b. Profitability index.
3. Which ranking do you prefer? Why?

 PROBLEM 10–6
Using the SRR and Payback Methods [LO2 – CC11, 15]

Sharkey's Fun Centre contains a number of electronic games, as well as a miniature golf course and various rides located outside the building. Paul Sharkey, the owner, would like to construct a water slide on one portion of his property. Paul has gathered the following information about the slide:

CHECK FIGURE

(2) Return: 15.0%

a. Water slide equipment could be purchased and installed at a cost of $330,000. According to the manufacturer, the slide would be usable for 12 years, after which it would have no salvage value.
b. Paul would use straight-line depreciation on the slide equipment.
c. To make room for the water slide, several rides would be dismantled and sold. These rides are fully depreciated, but they could be sold for $60,000 to an amusement park in a nearby city.
d. Paul has concluded that about 50,000 more people would use the water slide each year than have been using the rides. The admission price would be $3.60 per person (the same price that the Fun Centre has been charging for the rides).
e. On the basis of experience at other water slides, Paul estimates that incremental operating expenses each year for the slide would be as follows: salaries, $85,000; insurance, $4,200; utilities, $13,000; maintenance, $9,800.

Required:

1. Prepare an income statement showing the expected incremental net income each year from the water slide.
2. Compute the SRR expected from the water slide. On the basis of this computation, would the water slide be constructed if Paul requires an SRR of at least 14% on all investments?
3. Compute the payback period for the water slide. If Paul requires a payback period of five years or less, should the water slide be constructed?

PROBLEM 10–7

Performing SRR and Payback Analyses of Two Machines [LO2 – CC11, 15]

Westwood Furniture Company is considering the purchase of two different machines, as described below:

Machine A. A compacting machine has just come onto the market that would permit Westwood Furniture Company to compress sawdust into various shelving products. At present the sawdust is disposed of as a waste product. The following information is available on the machine:

  a. The machine would cost $420,000 and would have a 10% salvage value at the end of its 13-year useful life. The company uses straight-line depreciation and considers salvage value in computing depreciation deductions.

  b. The shelving products manufactured from use of the machine would generate revenues of $300,000 per year. Variable manufacturing costs would be 20% of sales.

  c. Fixed expenses associated with the new shelving products would be as follows (per year): advertising, $40,000; salaries, $110,000; utilities, $5,200; insurance, $800.

Machine B. A second machine has come onto the market that would allow Westwood Furniture Company to automate a sanding process that is now done largely by hand. The following information is available:

  a. The new sanding machine would cost $234,000 and would have no salvage value at the end of its 13-year useful life. The company would use straight-line depreciation on the new machine.

  b. Several old pieces of sanding equipment that are fully depreciated would be disposed of at a scrap value of $9,000.

  c. The new sanding machine would provide substantial annual savings in cash operating costs. It would require an operator at an annual salary of $16,350 and $5,400 in annual maintenance costs. The current, hand-operated sanding procedure costs the company $78,000 per year in total.

Westwood Furniture Company requires a simple rate of return of 15% on all equipment purchases. Also, the company will not purchase equipment unless the equipment has a payback period of four years or less.

Required:

  1. For machine A:
    a. Prepare an income statement showing the expected net income each year from the new shelving products. Use the contribution format.
    b. Compute the simple rate of return.
    c. Compute the payback period.
  2. For machine B:
    a. Compute the simple rate of return.
    b. Compute the payback period.
  3. According to the company's criteria, which machine, if either, should the company purchase?

 PROBLEM 10–8

Performing an NPV Analysis of Securities [LO2 – CC8]

Linda Clark received $175,000 from her mother's estate. She placed the funds into the hands of a broker, who purchased the following securities on Linda's behalf:

a. Common shares were purchased at a cost of $95,000. The shares paid no dividends, but they were sold for $160,000 at the end of three years.

b. Preferred shares were purchased at their par value of $30,000. The shares paid a 6% dividend (based on par value) each year for three years. At the end of three years, the shares were sold for $27,000.

c. Bonds were purchased at a cost of $50,000. The bonds paid $3,000 in interest every six months. After three years, the bonds were sold for $52,700. (*Note:* In discounting a cash flow that occurs semiannually, the procedure is to halve the discount rate and double the number of periods. Use the same procedure in discounting the proceeds from the sale.)

The securities were all sold at the end of three years so that Linda would have funds available to open a new business. The broker stated that the investments had earned more than a 16% return, and he gave Linda the following computation to support his statement:

Common shares:	
Gain on sale ($160,000 − $95,000)	$65,000
Preferred shares:	
Dividends paid (6% × $30,000 × 3 years)	5,400
Loss on sale ($27,000 − $30,000)	(3,000)
Bonds:	
Interest paid ($3,000 × 6 periods)	18,000
Gain on sale ($52,700 − $50,000)	2,700
Net gain on all investments	$88,100

$$\frac{\$88,100 \div 3 \text{ years}}{\$175,000} = 16.8\%$$

Required:

1. Using a 16% discount rate, compute the net present value of *each* of the three investments. On which investment(s) did Linda earn a 16% rate of return? (Round computations to the nearest whole dollar.)

2. Considering all three investments together, did Linda earn a 16% rate of return? Explain.

3. Linda wants to use the $239,700 (= $160,000 + $27,000 + $52,700) from the sale of the securities to open a retail store under a 12-year franchise contract. What net annual cash inflow must the store generate for Linda to earn a 14% return over the 12-year period? Round computations to the nearest whole dollar.

PROBLEM 10–9
Calculating IRR and Performing a Sensitivity Analysis [LO2 – CC13]

Dr. Helen Floss is the managing partner of the Crestwood Dental Clinic. Floss is trying to determine whether the clinic should move patient files and other items out of a spare room in the clinic and use the room for dental work. She has determined that it would require an investment of $358,950 for equipment and related costs to prepare the room for use. On the basis of receipts being generated from other rooms in the clinic, Floss estimates that the new room would generate a net cash inflow of $87,500 per year. The equipment purchased for the room would have a seven-year estimated useful life.

CHECK FIGURE

(1) IRR = 16%

Required:

(Ignore income taxes.)

1. Compute the IRR on the equipment for the new room to the nearest whole percent. Verify your answer by computing the NPV of the equipment using the IRR you have computed as the discount rate.

2. Although seven years is the average life for dental equipment, Floss knows that due to changing technology, this life can vary substantially. Compute the IRR to the nearest whole percent if the life of the equipment is (a) five years and (b) nine years, rather than seven years. Is there any information provided by these computations that you would be particularly anxious to show Floss?

3. Refer to the original data. Assume that the equipment is purchased and that the room is opened for dental use. However, due to an increasing number of dentists in the area, the clinic is able to generate only $60,000 per year in net cash receipts from the new room. At the end of five years, the clinic closes the room and sells the equipment to a newly licensed dentist for a cash price of $101,375. Compute the IRR (to the nearest whole percent) that the clinic earned on its investment over the five-year period. Round all dollar amounts to the nearest whole dollar. (*Hint:* A useful way to proceed is to find the discount rate that will cause the net present value of the investment to be equal to, or near, zero).

PROBLEM 10–10
Computing the SRR, Payback, and IRR [LO2 – CC11, 13, 15]

Château Beaune is a family-owned winery located in the Burgundy region of France, headed by Gerard Despinoy. The harvesting season in early fall is the busiest time of the year for the winery, and many part-time workers are hired to help pick and process grapes. Despinoy is investigating the purchase of a harvesting machine that would significantly reduce the amount of labour required in the picking process. The harvesting machine is built to straddle grapevines, which are laid out in low-lying rows. Two workers are carried on the machine just above ground level, one on each side of the vine. As the machine slowly crawls through the vineyard, the workers cut bunches of grapes from the vines, and the grapes fall into a hopper. The machine separates the grapes from the stems and other woody debris. The debris is then pulverized and spread behind the machine as a rich ground mulch. Despinoy has gathered the following information relating to the decision of whether to purchase the machine (the French currency is the euro, denoted by €):

> **CHECK FIGURE**
> (1) SRR = 14.2% (rounded)

a. The winery would save €190,000 per year in labour costs with the new harvesting machine. In addition, the company would no longer have to purchase and spread ground mulch—at an annual savings of €10,000.

b. The harvesting machine would cost €480,000. It would have an estimated 12-year useful life and zero salvage value. The winery uses straight-line depreciation.

c. Annual out-of-pocket costs associated with the harvesting machine would be insurance, €1,000; fuel, €9,000; and a maintenance contract, €12,000. In addition, two operators would be hired and trained for the machine, and they would be paid a total of €70,000 per year, including all benefits.

d. Despinoy feels that the investment in the harvesting machine should earn at least a 16% rate of return.

Required:

(Ignore income taxes.)

1. Determine the annual net savings in cash operating costs that would be realized if the harvesting machine were purchased.

2. Compute the SRR expected from the harvesting machine. (*Hint:* This is a cost reduction project.)

3. Compute the payback period on the harvesting machine. Despinoy will not purchase equipment unless it has a payback period of five years or less. Under this criterion, should the harvesting machine be purchased?

4. Compute (to the nearest whole percent) the IRR promised by the harvesting machine. On the basis of this computation, does it appear that the SRR is an accurate guide in investment decisions?

PROBLEM 10–11
Performing an NPV Analysis of a Lease or Buy Decision [LO2 – CC8]

The Wrongway Ad Agency provides cars for its sales staff. In the past, the company has always purchased its cars from a dealer and then sold the cars after three years of use. The company's present fleet of cars is three years old and will be sold very shortly. To provide a replacement fleet, the company is considering two alternatives as follows:

Purchase Alternative. The company can purchase the cars, as in the past, and sell the cars after three years of use. Ten cars will be needed, which can be purchased at a discounted price of $17,000 each. If this alternative is accepted, the following costs will be incurred on the fleet as a whole:

Annual cost of servicing, taxes, and licensing	$3,000
Repairs, year 1	1,500
Repairs, year 2	4,000
Repairs, year 3	6,000

At the end of three years, the fleet could be sold for one-half of the original purchase price.

Lease Alternative. The company can lease the cars under a three-year lease contract. The lease cost would be $55,000 per year (with the first payment due at the end of year 1). As part of this lease cost, the owner would provide all servicing and repairs, license the cars, and pay all the taxes. Wrongway would be required to make a $10,000 security deposit at the beginning of the lease period, which would be refunded when the cars were returned to the owner at the end of the lease contract.

Wrongway's required rate of return is 18%.

Required:

(Ignore income taxes.)

1. Use the total cost approach to determine the present value of the cash flows associated with each alternative. Round all dollar amounts to the nearest whole dollar.
2. Which alternative should the company accept based on the calculations in part (1)? What other factors might be important for Wrongway to consider?

PROBLEM 10–12
Calculating the Simple Rate of Return and Payback [LO2 – CC13, 15]

Joe Swanson has an opportunity to acquire a franchise from The Yogurt Place, Inc. to dispense frozen yogurt products under the name The Yogurt Place. Swanson has assembled the following information relating to the franchise:

a. A suitable location in a large shopping mall can be rented for $3,500 per month.
b. Remodelling and necessary equipment would cost $270,000. The equipment would have a 15-year life and an $18,000 salvage value. Straight-line depreciation would be used.
c. On the basis of similar outlets elsewhere, Swanson estimated that sales would total $300,000 per year. Ingredients would cost 20% of sales.
d. Operating costs would include $70,000 per year for salaries, $3,500 per year for insurance, and $27,000 per year for utilities. In addition, Swanson would have to pay a commission to The Yogurt Place of 12.5% of sales.

Required:

(Ignore income taxes.)

1. Prepare a contribution format income statement that shows the expected net operating income each year from the franchise outlet.
2. Compute the simple rate of return promised by the outlet. If Swanson requires a simple rate of return of at least 12%, should he acquire the franchise?
3. Compute the payback period on the outlet. If Swanson wants a payback of four years or less, will he acquire the franchise?

Building Your Skills

COMPREHENSIVE PROBLEM [LO2 – CC8, 10, 11, 13; Chapter 9 LO1 – CC3]

Marlon Plastics purchased a new machine one year ago at a cost of $750,000. Although the machine operates well, the president of the company is considering replacing it with a new electronic machine that has just entered the market. The new machine would slash the annual operating costs by two-thirds, as shown in the data provided below:

CHECK FIGURE

(2) IRR = approx. 22%

	A	B	C
1		Present Machine	Proposed New Machine
2	Estimated useful life in years	6	5
3	Purchase cost new	$750,000	$1,125,000
4	Annual operating costs	525,000	175,000
5	Annual straight-line depreciation	125,000	225,000
6	Remaining book value	625,000	–
7	Salvage value now	125,000	–
8	Salvage value in five years	–	–

The president's assistant prepared the following analysis:

	A	B
1	Book value of the old machine	$625,000
2	Less: Salvage value	125,000
3	Net loss from disposal	$500,000

"Even though the new machine looks good," said the president, "we can't get rid of that old machine if it means taking a huge loss on it. We'll have to use that old machine for at least a few more years."

Sales are expected to be $2.5 million per year, and selling and administrative expenses are expected to be $1,575,000 per year, regardless of which machine is used.

Required:

1. Prepare a summary income statement covering the next five years, assuming that
   a. The new machine is not purchased.
   b. The new machine is purchased.

2. Using three capital investment analysis methods, determine whether the company should purchase the new equipment. Use only the incremental costs in your analysis. The company likes a 16% return on all its investments. What is the profitability index of this investment?

THINKING ANALYTICALLY [LO2 – CC8]

Top-Quality Stores Inc. owns a nationwide chain of supermarkets. The company is going to open another store soon, and a suitable building site has been located in an attractive and rapidly growing area. In discussing how the company can acquire the desired building and other facilities needed to open the new store, Sam Watkins, the company's vice-president in charge of sales, stated, "I know most of our competitors are starting to

> **CHECK FIGURE**
> (1) NPV: $78,001 in favour of leasing

lease facilities, rather than buy, but I just can't see the economics of it. Our development people tell us that we can buy the building site, put a building on it, and get all the store fixtures we need for just $850,000. They also say that property taxes, insurance, and repairs would run $20,000 a year. When you figure that we plan to keep a site for 18 years, that's a total cost of $1,210,000. But then when you realize that the property will be worth at least a half million in 18 years, that's a net cost to us of only $710,000. What would it cost to lease the property?"

"I understand that Beneficial Insurance Company is willing to purchase the building site, construct a building and install fixtures to our specifications, and then lease the facility to us for 18 years at an annual lease payment of $120,000," replied Lisa Coleman, the company's executive vice-president.

"That's just my point," said Watkins. "At $120,000 a year, it would cost us a cool $2,160,000 over the 18 years. That's three times what it would cost to buy, and what would we have left at the end? Nothing! The building would belong to the insurance company!"

"You're overlooking a few things," replied Coleman. "For one thing, the treasurer's office says that we could only afford to put $350,000 down if we buy the property, and then we would have to pay the other $500,000 off over four years at $175,000 a year. So there would be some interest involved on the purchase side that you haven't figured in."

"But that little bit of interest is nothing compared with over two million bucks for leasing," said Watkins. "Also, if we lease, I understand we would have to put up an $8,000 security deposit that we wouldn't get back until the end. And besides that, we would still have to pay all the yearly repairs and maintenance costs just like we owned the property. No wonder those insurance companies are so rich if they can swing deals like this."

"Well, I'll admit that I don't have all the figures sorted out yet," replied Coleman. "But I do have the operating cost breakdown for the building, which includes $7,500 annually for property taxes, $8,000 for insurance, and $4,500 for repairs and maintenance. If we lease, Beneficial will handle its own insurance costs, and of course the owner will have to pay the property taxes. I'll put all this together and see if leasing makes any sense with our required rate of return of 16%. The president wants a presentation and recommendation in the executive committee meeting tomorrow. Let's see, Development said the first lease payment would be due now and the remaining ones due in years 1 to 17. Development also said that this store should generate a net cash inflow that's well above average for our stores."

Required:

1. Using the NPV approach, determine whether Top-Quality Stores Inc. should lease or buy the new facility. Assume that you will be making your presentation before the company's executive committee, and remember that the president detests sloppy, disorganized reports.

2. What reply will you make in the meeting if Watkins brings up the issue of the building's future sales value?

COMMUNICATING IN PRACTICE [LO1 – CC4; LO2 – CC13, 15]

Use an online directory, such as http://www.yellowpages.ca or http://www.411.ca, to find a manufacturer in your area that has a website. Make an appointment with the controller or chief financial officer of the company. Before your meeting, find out as much as you can about the organization's operations from its website.

Required:

After asking the following questions about a capital budgeting decision that was made by the management of the company, write a brief memorandum to your instructor that summarizes the information obtained from the company's website and addresses what you found out during your interview.

1. What was the nature of the capital project?
2. What was the total cost of the capital project?
3. Did the project costs stay within budget (or estimate)?
4. What financial criteria were used to evaluate the project?

TEAMWORK IN ACTION [LO1 – CC4; LO2 – CC8, 10]

Kingsley Products Ltd. is using a model 400 shaping machine to make one of its products. The company is expecting to have a large increase in demand for the product and is anxious to expand its production capacity. Two possibilities are under consideration, as follows:

> **CHECK FIGURE**
> (1) NPV: $30,046 in favour of the model 400 machine

- *Alternative 1.* Purchase another model 400 shaping machine to operate along with the currently owned model 400 machine.
- *Alternative 2.* Purchase a model 800 shaping machine and use the currently owned model 400 machine as standby equipment. The model 800 machine is a high-speed unit with double the capacity of the model 400 machine.

The following additional information is available on the two alternatives:

a. Both the model 400 machine and the model 800 machine have a 10-year life from the time they are first used in production. The scrap value of both machines is negligible and can be ignored. Straight-line depreciation is used.
b. The cost of a new model 800 machine is $300,000.
c. The model 400 machine now in use cost $160,000 three years ago. Its present book value is $112,000, and its present market value is $90,000.
d. A new model 400 machine costs $170,000 now. If the company decides not to buy the model 800 machine, then the currently owned model 400 machine will have to be replaced in seven years at a cost of $200,000. The replacement machine will be sold at the end of the tenth year for $140,000.
e. Production over the next 10 years is expected to be as follows:

Year	Production in Units
1	40,000
2	60,000
3	80,000
4–10	90,000

f. The two models of machines are not equally efficient. Comparative variable costs per unit are as follows:

	Model	
	400	**800**
Materials per unit	$0.25	$0.40
Direct labour per unit	0.49	0.16
Supplies and lubricants per unit	0.06	0.04
Total variable cost per unit	$0.80	$0.60

g. The model 400 machine is less costly to maintain than the model 800 machine. Annual repairs and maintenance costs on a model 400 machine are $2,500.

h. Repairs and maintenance costs on a model 800 machine, with a model 400 machine used as standby, would total $3,800 per year.

i. No other factory costs will change as a result of the decision between the two machines.

j. Kingsley Products requires a 20% rate of return on all investments.

Required:

The team should discuss and then respond to the questions below. All team members should agree with and understand the answers (including the calculations supporting the answers) and be prepared to report the information developed in class. (Each teammate can assume responsibility for a different part of the presentation.)

1. Which alternative should the company choose? Use the NPV approach.

2. Suppose that the cost of labour increases by 10%. Would this make the model 800 machine more or less desirable? Explain your reasoning. No computations are needed.

3. Suppose that the cost of materials doubles. Would this make the model 800 machine more or less desirable? Explain your reasoning. No computations are needed.

Endnotes

1. The mathematical expression of the internal rate of return computation is illustrated in three steps:

Step A (set up the NPV calculation using the IRR as the discount rate):

$$\text{NPV} = -\$142,514 + \frac{1}{1 + \text{IRR}} \times \$149,700$$

Step B (set the NPV equal to zero):

$$0 = -\$142,514 + \frac{1}{1 + \text{IRR}} \times \$149,700$$

Step C (solve for the IRR):

$$0 = -\$142{,}514 + \frac{\$149{,}700}{1 + \text{IRR}}$$

$$\$142{,}514 = \frac{\$149{,}700}{1 + \text{IRR}}$$

$$\$142{,}514 \times (1 + \text{IRR}) = \$149{,}700$$

$$1 + \text{IRR} = \frac{\$149{,}700}{\$142{,}514} = 1.0504$$

$$\text{IRR} = 1.0504 - 1 = 0.0504 = 5.04\%$$

2. If the single cash flow occurs in year n, the present value factor is written as $1/(1 / \text{IRR})^n$. Locate the present value factor in the n-period line of Exhibit 10–1 to find the rate of return. When cash flows are an annuity, calculate the annuity factor as follows:

    Annuity factor = Investment required ÷ Net annual cash inflow

    Then consult Exhibit 10–2. If the number of periods is 5, look in the 5-period line for the annuity factor you calculated to see what rate of return it represents.

    We used the formula = IRR(B5:G5,0) in cell B7 to compute the internal rate of return. The syntax of the formula is = IRR(cell range for the cash flows, initial guess value for IRR)

    We used a value of 0 for the initial guess. The default is 0.1. The internal rate of return is approximately 4%.

3. Mathematically we can express the computation as follows:

    Step A (set up the NPV calculation using the IRR as the discount rate):

    $$\text{NPV} = -\$2{,}100{,}000 + \frac{\$490{,}000}{(1 + \text{IRR})} + \frac{\$445{,}000}{(1 + \text{IRR})^2} + \frac{\$476{,}000}{(1 + \text{IRR})^3} + \frac{\$510{,}000}{(1 + \text{IRR})^4} + \frac{\$435{,}000}{(1 + \text{IRR})^5}$$

    Step B (set the NPV equal to zero):

    $$0 = -\$2{,}100{,}000 + \frac{\$490{,}000}{(1 + \text{IRR})} + \frac{\$445{,}000}{(1 + \text{IRR})^2} + \frac{\$476{,}000}{(1 + \text{IRR})^3} + \frac{\$510{,}000}{(1 + \text{IRR})^4} + \frac{\$435{,}000}{(1 + \text{IRR})^5}$$

    Step C (solve for the IRR): This is complex to solve by hand; the result is shown in the Excel screenshot below:

	A	B	C	D	E	F	G
1	Rivers Company						
2	IRR Calculation for the Wharf Upgrading Project						
3							
4	Year	0	1	2	3	4	5
5	Cash flow	22,100,000	$490,000	$445,000	$476,000	$510,000	$435,000
6							
7	IRR	3.9869%					
8							

4. Rates of return will vary by industry (sector). Information about rates of return is available online from various sources, such as TD Asset Management (https://www.tdwaterhouse.ca/markets-research/markets/index.jsp?referer=https://www.tdcanadatrust.com/markets/index.jsp).

5. For further discussion, see Lawrence A. Gordon and Mary D. Myers, "Postauditing Capital Projects," *Management Accounting, 72(7)* (January 1991), pp. 39–42. This study of 282 large U.S. companies states that "an increasing number of firms are recognizing the importance of the postaudit stage" (p. 41).

11

Standard Costs and Variance Analysis

LEARNING OBJECTIVES AND CHAPTER COMPETENCIES			
After studying Chapter 11, you should be able to demonstrate the following competencies:			
COMPETENCY		**Know**	**Apply**
LO1	**UNDERSTAND STANDARD COSTING AND COMPUTE STANDARD COSTS.**		
CC1	Explain the concept of standards and standard costs.	●	
CC2	Distinguish between ideal and practical standards.	●	
CC3	Develop standard costs for direct materials.		●
CC4	Develop standard costs for direct labour.		●
CC5	Develop standard costs for variable overhead.		●
CC6	Prepare a standard cost card.		●
LO2	**PREPARE AND USE STATIC AND FLEXIBLE BUDGETS FOR PERFORMANCE ANALYSIS.**		
CC7	Prepare a static budget.		●
CC8	Prepare a static budget performance report.		●
CC9	Explain the concept of variances.	●	
CC10	Explain the deficiency of a static budget for performance analysis.	●	
CC11	Distinguish the static budget from the flexible budget.	●	
CC12	Prepare a flexible budget.		●
CC13	Prepare a flexible budget performance report.		●
CC14	Distinguish between price and quantity variances.	●	
LO3	**COMPUTE AND INTERPRET VARIABLE COST FLEXIBLE BUDGET VARIANCES.**		
CC15	Compute and explain direct materials variances.	●	●
CC16	Compute direct materials variances when the quantities of materials purchased and used for production are not equal.		●

CC17	Compute and explain direct labour variances.		•	•
CC18	Compute and explain variable overhead variances.		•	•
LO4	**PERFORM AN ANALYSIS OF FIXED OVERHEAD COSTS.**			
CC19	Explain the nature of fixed costs of manufacturing.		•	
CC20	Explain the control issues pertaining to fixed overhead costs and the distinction between normal and standard costing systems.		•	
CC21	Explain the concept of denominator activity level, and compute the predetermined fixed overhead allocation rate.		•	•
CC22	Explain and compute fixed overhead cost budget variance.		•	•
CC23	Explain and compute fixed overhead cost volume variance.		•	•
CC24	Explain overhead variances, and compute the over- or underapplied overhead.		•	•
LO5	**UNDERSTAND MANAGEMENT CONTROL IN A STANDARD COSTING ENVIRONMENT.**			
CC25	Describe the principle of management by exception.		•	
CC26	Describe the benefits and limitations of using standard costing for the purposes of control.		•	
LO6	**UNDERSTAND COST FLOWS IN A STANDARD COSTING ENVIRONMENT.**			
CC27[A]	Explain the cost flows in a standard costing system.		•	
CC28[A]	Prepare journal entries to record standard costs and variances.			•

Note: The superscript "A" refers to Appendix 11A, which is available on Connect.

ON THE JOB

AUTO SERVICE STANDARDS

Keith & Herb Alignment & Brake is a Saskatoon auto service business founded by Keith Atchinson and Herb Friesen. In 2000, Richard Semchyshen (then a young mechanic with eight years of experience at Keith & Herb) purchased the business along with Heather, his partner and wife.

Semchyshen fully understands the importance of Keith & Herb's reputation and works hard to maintain it by providing value to the customer—quality service at a reasonable price. Being profitable is also important, however, and this is where standards come into the picture. For most jobs, customers are billed according to standard times that Semchyshen has developed over the years; for some jobs, he uses the standard times published in labour guides. For all jobs, Semchyshen and his employees pay close attention to the standards—completing a job in less than the standard time means more money for the business.

Although his primary source of learning is on-the-job training and experience, Semchyshen attends training seminars organized by parts dealers and even contacts other mechanics when he needs a second opinion (especially on less frequent jobs). Knowing that his time is valuable and is best spent on work he can complete quickly and confidently, he is very careful about accepting jobs outside of his specialty areas, especially complicated ones.

According to Semchyshen, "There is never a dull moment in the shop." Semchyshen is as passionate about his work as he is about hockey and, above all, his family!

Source: Personal conversations with Richard Semchyshen.

Blend Images/Getty Images

 Critical thinking question *Is it necessary for Semchyshen to implement a costing system based on standards?*

Note to student: See **Guidance Answers** *online.*

◀◀ A Look Back	▶ A Look at This Chapter	▶▶ A Look Ahead
Chapter 7 discussed the budgeting process and the budget as a planning tool. In Chapters 8 and 9, cost information developed from the planning/budgeting processes was used for making decisions. Chapter 10 focused on capital budgeting decisions, such as whether or not to invest in long-lived assets such as plant and equipment.	Chapter 11 introduces the topic of management control: ensuring that the business is being operated as intended and achieving desired results. Controlling is one of the most important functions performed by an accountant, and a budget is a key tool for control because it provides a framework for measuring and reporting financial performance. This chapter will explore this role of the budget, considering static and flexible budgets, standard costs and standard costing systems, and variance analysis.	Chapter 12 continues the discussion of management control by focusing on the management challenges in decentralized organizations. It introduces the concept of responsibility centres and considers issues in motivation and control of managers.

Chapter 7 showed that budgeting was essential to planning and demonstrated how to prepare a budget from given planning data. In this chapter, the budget is used for measuring and evaluating financial performance. To fully understand this aspect of budgeting, consider the planning data upon which the budget is based and how the budget can be used by management. This is not a simple task.

After a budget for a period has been prepared, it guides the activities performed by the business during the period. Managers have the authority to make decisions regarding use of the business's resources to perform activities and are accountable for how those resources are consumed. Costs are incurred, products are made and sold, and revenues are earned; meanwhile, the budget is the reference point for what the organization is supposed to be achieving. At the end of the operating cycle, actual results are reported and compared to what was planned: this is the process of performance measurement and evaluation.

Because the company's activities and results derive from its people's decisions and actions, the activities of employees and managers alike will be observed, measured, and evaluated. Effective managers will want to observe *appropriately,* measure *accurately,* and evaluate *fairly,* but how? Performance measurement and evaluation breeds tension. People might fear being thought irresponsible or unable to properly account for their performance. Employees and management might disagree about control; an employee might express concern that something was not measured properly, or an irrelevant (and thus inappropriate) aspect of an activity was observed, or an unfair comparison was made, making their performance look bad. Consequently, if the budget is the guide for actions, and a basis for evaluating performance, people will question the budget.

To minimize tension and disagreements, managers will logically begin with the planning data used to prepare the budget. These data contain important *standards* in addition to the forecasts of various business variables, like sales volume, interest rates, business tax rules, and so on. Effective managers will ensure that these data are accurate, are reasonable, and reflect both the company's objectives and the abilities of the personnel who must carry out their duties and responsibilities.

For example, a pizzeria manager knows that, on average, seven minutes elapse between receiving a customer's order and placing the pizza in the oven. She uses this average time to compute the total time that should be budgeted for the *order-processing activity* given the volume of orders projected to occur during a certain period (week, month, quarter, or year). In this case, seven minutes is the accepted *standard* time for the order-processing activity. The manager has done two things: (1) decided that observing the order-processing activity was important in order to know whether it was being performed in a timely fashion and (2) determined a benchmark—a standard—by which she would be able to say whether the activity was being performed in a timely manner. If there is disagreement over the standard, everything else that depends on this standard will be questioned. Thus, selecting the activities to observe and developing the standards to use when evaluating performance are key first steps for management controllers.

After standards have been developed, the budget is prepared and will become the basis for evaluation of actual results. Now the concern will be whether the comparison of the standard and the actual result is fair. Imagine that you have just been hired to work part-time in the pizzeria and your job is to take customer orders. The manager is expecting 16 orders for Friday evening between 8:00 p.m. and 10:00 p.m. (the hours you are working) and has budgeted 112 minutes for you, or 7 minutes per pizza. Now suppose that you took a total of 130 minutes to process 20 orders. At the end of your shift, the manager fires you for poor performance because you spent 130 minutes instead of 112 minutes—you exceeded the budgeted time you were allotted. Do you think you were fairly evaluated?

We hope you answered with a resounding "No!" Why? For one thing, the manager's budget was based on a volume of 16 pizza orders; the actual number of orders was 20. More orders to process means more time, and your exceeding the allotted time was to be expected. Thus, comparing 112 minutes with 130 minutes was unfair. The standard of 112 minutes is the time based on a *planned* activity or budgeted volume level of 16 pizzas. A budget developed from a single *planned* level of activity is called a *static budget.*

To evaluate your performance fairly, we have to compare your actual time with *the time the standard will have predicted for the actual volume of 20 pizza orders.* This is 140 minutes (= 7 minutes × 20 pizza orders). Comparing 130 minutes with 140 minutes is fair and correct. The proper conclusion about your work is that your performance (130 minutes) was superior to expectations (140 minutes) by 10 minutes, which reflects positively on you as an employee—an ending radically different from being fired! The time of 140 minutes is in fact a budgeted time for a *budget based on a volume of 20 pizza orders.* A budget developed by using a volume level equal to that *actually* observed is called a *flexible* budget. Comparison between the actual time and the flexible budget yields a difference of 130 minutes − 140 minutes = −10 minutes.

The 10-minute difference when expressed in dollar terms is called a *variance*. Analyzing the variance enables us to reach a conclusion—an evaluation of the performance. In this case it is a favourable variance, because you took 10 minutes less than the time you were allowed by the standard for the actual volume observed. An attentive manager will want to know why you used less time than the allowed time.

The above situation shows the issues involved when budgets are used in performance measurement and evaluation. There are three things to watch for:

1. The data (the activities being monitored and the standards used to evaluate performance) upon which a budget is based must be appropriate and accurate. This is the topic of *standards*.
2. Actual results must be compared to the proper benchmark; the wrong benchmark will lead to wrong comparisons and wrong decisions. To make meaningful comparisons the actual results have to be recorded, and the static budget and the flexible budget must be prepared. Learning to construct these budgets is the topic of *static and flexible budgets*.
3. To evaluate performance, a variance is computed and interpreted. In the pizzeria, you took 10 minutes less than what was expected; therefore, you generated a *favourable* variance. The manager should study what you did and how you did it. She will want to understand whether what happened was a fluke or whether it can be repeated regularly. If it is concluded that your achievement was a fluke, no change in the standard will be needed. But if you have discovered a way to speed up order processing, then the manager will likely want the other employees to follow your procedure and will change the standard to 6.5 minutes instead. This is the topic of *variance analysis*—computation, interpretation, and formulation of appropriate follow-up action. It is important to note that many different variances can be computed and analyzed. We will describe the important ones in the chapter. Also note that it is common practice to express variance in dollars instead of physical units like minutes. You will see this later.

We now turn to a detailed look at each of the three aspects of performance measurement and evaluation using budgets: (1) standard setting, (2) preparing flexible budgets and the static budget, and (3) computing and interpreting variances. Our first topic is standard costs and their use for planning and control.

MANAGERIAL ACCOUNTING IN ACTION

THE ISSUE

The Colonial Pewter Company was organized a year ago. The company's only product is a set of reproduction 18th-century pewter bookends. The bookends are made largely by hand, using traditional metalworking tools. Consequently, the manufacturing process is labour intensive and requires a high level of skill.

Colonial Pewter recently expanded its workforce to take advantage of unexpected demand for the bookends as gifts. The company started with a small cadre of experienced pewter workers but has had to hire less experienced workers as a result of the expansion. Colonial's president, J. D. Wriston, has called a meeting to discuss production problems. Attending the meeting are production manager Tom Kuchel, purchasing manager Janet Warner, and corporate controller Terry Sherman.

Wriston: I've got a feeling that we aren't getting the production that we should out of our new people.

Kuchel: Give us a chance. Some of the new people have been on board for less than a month.

Warner: Let me add that production seems to be wasting an awful lot of material—particularly pewter. That stuff is very expensive.

Kuchel: What about the shipment of defective pewter you bought a couple of months ago—the one with iron contamination? That caused us major problems.

Warner: That's ancient history. How was I to know it was off-grade? Besides, it was a great deal.

Wriston: Calm down, everybody. Let's get the facts before we start sinking our fangs into each other.

Kuchel: I agree. The more facts we have, the better off we'll be.

Wriston: Okay, Terry, it's your turn. Facts are the controller's department.

Sherman: I'm afraid I can't provide the answers off the top of my head, but it won't take me too long to set up a system that can routinely answer questions relating to worker productivity, material waste, and input prices.

Wriston: How long is "too long"?

Sherman: I will need all of your cooperation, but how about a week from today?

Wriston: That's okay with me. What about everyone else?

Kuchel: Sure.

Warner: Fine with me.

Wriston: Let's mark it on our calendars.

Terry Sherman is referring to a standard costing and variance analysis system. This is a useful control tool for managers because it captures the financial impact of deviations from the plan. However, before we get into variances, it would be useful to understand how standards are established and how standard costs are computed.

Standard Costs

LO1   ● **Know**

CC1: Explain the concept of standards and standard costs.

A standard is a benchmark for measuring performance. *Quantity standards* specify how much of a resource should be used to make *one* unit of a product or provide *one* instance of a service. Throughout this chapter and the next, we will label a quantity standard as *SQI*. *Price standards* specify the price that is expected to be paid for a unit of a resource. We will label the standard price *SP*. The **standard cost** of a *resource* is the cost of the input required for a single performance of an activity or to make one unit of output. It is the standard quantity of input required multiplied by the standard price of the input (i.e., $SQI \times SP$). The standard cost of the single performance of an *activity* or a single unit of *output* made is the sum of the standard costs of every input necessary to perform the activity or make one unit of output. There are two different cost objects here: (1) the standard cost of an input to make one unit of a product and (2) the standard cost of making one unit of product or providing one instance of a service.

To illustrate, let us go back to your pizzeria. Imagine making a 10-inch pepperoni pizza that is supposed to have 10 slices of pepperoni in addition to cheese, sauce, and dough. The pepperoni is an input. The 10 slices of pepperoni (say, 50 grams) are a standard quantity. The standard price (assumed) is $2.20 per 100 grams of pepperoni. The *standard cost of pepperoni* to make one 10-inch pizza is $1.10 (= $2.20 \times 50/100$). The standard cost of *one pizza* is the sum of the standard costs of all the inputs required to make it.

Standards are found everywhere and are by no means restricted to businesses. Colleges and universities use admission standards to decide which students are eligible for admission into their programs. Your doctor evaluates your weight using standards that have been established for individuals of your age, height, and gender. Similarly, the foods we eat in restaurants are prepared using standardized recipes. Actual quantities and actual costs of inputs are compared to the standards. If either the quantity or the cost of inputs departs *significantly* from the standards, managers will investigate the discrepancy to find the cause of the problem and eliminate it.

IN BUSINESS

ENVIRONMENTAL STANDARDS FOR AUTO MAKERS: WILL THEY COMPLY?

Standards have been used for centuries and serve as benchmarks against which managers can compare actual performance at the end of a given period. In an effort to address threats to the global environment, to save fuel, and to curtail carbon gas emissions, governments (including those of Canada and the United States) have legislated environmental standards. Automakers are obliged to make increasingly fuel efficient cars that produce less pollution, hopefully improving fuel consumption and resulting in cleaner air.

Against this backdrop, in 2015 a major scandal broke involving Volkswagen. It was learned that this company's diesel cars had software cheats installed that would misreport the emissions coming out of the tailpipe and indicate that the car was in compliance with the emission standards. However, once the test mode had been exited, the software would set the engine controls to maximize fuel economy and override the settings for limiting the emissions. The automaker has been ordered to fix the problem and this will involve millions of the cars it has sold worldwide. The specific steps that will be taken are yet unknown as of early 2016.

Source: "Automakers, Obama Announce Fuel Consumption, Pollution Ratings," *The Associated Press,* May 19, 2009, http://www.cbc.ca/consumer/story/2009/05/19/emissions.html. Used with permission of The Associated Press © 2013. All rights reserved.

The Standard Cost Card

The **standard cost card** is a list of every input required to make one unit of output, along with the corresponding standard quantity, standard price, and standard cost. The standard cost card will also show the standard cost of one unit of the product, which is computed as the sum of the standard costs of all the inputs. Although it is possible to imagine a large number of inputs, in order to better explain the concepts and illustrate the computations, we will focus on the following variable cost inputs—direct materials, direct labour, and variable manufacturing overhead.

Standard setting is more an art than a science. It requires the combined expertise of all those who have responsibility over input prices and over the effective use of inputs. In a manufacturing setting, this might include accountants, purchasing managers, engineers, production supervisors, line managers, and production workers. Historical data (that is, past records of purchase prices and input usage) can be helpful in setting standards. In addition to prior experience, knowing the current and future expected conditions in the environment (including what competitors are doing, if you can find out) is useful when developing standards. However, the standards should be designed to encourage efficient *future* operations, not a repetition of past inefficient operations. The company must consider the effects of any changes with respect to factors such as competition, economy, demand/supply, and technology when estimating the standard quantities and prices of inputs.

Ideal Versus Practical Standards

LO1 ● **Know**

CC2: Distinguish between ideal and practical standards.

Disagreements can arise when individuals are being monitored and evaluated, and standards can be the first cause of disagreements. Employees will worry that the standards being applied are unreasonable in that they are difficult to attain or sustain. Managers, on the other hand, will be concerned that standards are too lax in that the abilities of the employees are not fully recognized and that expected achievement levels are much lower than what is desired. This point leads to the concepts of ideal and practical standards.

Ideal standards can be attained only under the best circumstances. They allow for no machine breakdowns or other work interruptions, and they call for a level of effort that can be provided only by the most skilled and efficient employees working at peak performance 100% of the time. **Practical standards** are *tight but attainable*. They allow for normal machine downtime and employee rest periods and can be attained through reasonable, though highly efficient, efforts by the average worker.

Ideal standards are rarely achievable and certainly not sustainable. Even so, certain managers, especially those from lean organizations, see value in developing and implementing ideal standards—which are the ultimate *stretch targets*—because they want to remind everyone of the need for ever-increasing efficiency and effort. There are three issues with ideal standards and stretch targets in general: (1) Managers must make a conscious effort to ensure that employees are not discouraged by standards/targets that might ruin the morale within the organization. (2) Deviations from ideal standards may be hard to interpret and these must therefore be used with caution and not acted upon hastily. (3) Ideal standards cannot be used in forecasting and planning; they do not allow for normal inefficiencies, and therefore they result in unrealistic planning and forecasting figures.

Practical standards are easier to convince employees to adopt. Even so, judgment will always be involved in any standard-setting exercise. For example, different people may have different answers to the question, "What is 'normal' downtime for machines?" Therefore, practical standards should be developed with care and should balance the objectives of the organization against the abilities of those who will be evaluated against the standard.

Practical standards can serve multiple purposes. Departures from a practical standard represent deviations that fall outside of normal operating conditions and signal a need for management attention. Since practical standards represent normal operating expectations, they can be used in forecasting cash flows and production planning and inventory management. In other words, they provide the planning parameters for budgeting. Throughout this chapter we assume that practical standards are used, and exceptions will be noted explicitly.

DECISION POINT

HOCKEY COACH

During the winter, you coach a team of 10-year-olds in your neighbourhood. One of the parents has approached you with a list of NHL records that he believes should be used as benchmarks or standards of performance for the kids. The parent suggests that players who meet the benchmarks be recognized and rewarded for their efforts. How do you respond?

*Note to student: See **Guidance Answers** online.*

Setting Direct Materials Standards

LO1   ● **Apply**

CC3: Develop standard costs for direct materials.

Terry Sherman's first task was to prepare price and quantity standards for the company's only significant raw material, pewter ingots. The **standard price per unit** (*SP*) for direct materials will be the best possible price in light of the internal and external operating circumstances of the company—which is why it is a *standard*. The price should be the final, delivered cost of the materials, net of any discounts taken.

After consulting with purchasing manager Janet Warner, Sherman determined that the standard price for 1 kg of pewter was $8.80. Note that the standard price is for 1 kg of pewter even though it is purchased in particular lot sizes (18-kilogram ingots).

The **standard quantity per unit** (*SQI*) for direct materials is the amount of material that should be going into each unit of finished product, as well as an allowance for *unavoidable* waste, spoilage, rejects, and other *normal* inefficiencies. This is usually determined from consultation with engineering and operating personnel and from taking into account the pertinent internal and external operating circumstances of the company. After consulting with the production manager, Terry Sherman determined the standard quantity of pewter in a pair of bookends as 1.25 kg.

Waste and spoilage refers to materials that are wasted as a normal part of the production process or that spoil before they are used. *Rejects* refers to the direct material contained in units that are defective and must be scrapped. When allowances for waste, spoilage, and rejects are built into the standard cost, the levels of those allowances should be periodically reviewed and reduced over time to reflect improved processes, better training, and better equipment.

Once the price and quantity standards have been set, *the standard cost of material* per unit of finished product can be computed as follows:

$$1.25 \ \text{kg} / \text{unit} \times \$8.80 / \text{kg} = \$11 / \text{unit}$$

Setting Direct Labour Standards

LO1 • **Apply**

CC4: Develop standard costs for direct labour.

Direct labour price and quantity standards are usually expressed in terms of a labour rate and labour-hours. The standard is developed around a variety of factors, including the skills required and the pay rates being paid in the labour market. Without a good understanding of the labour market, management cannot be assured that an appropriate *standard* wage rate has been developed. The **standard rate per hour (SP)** for direct labour should include not only wages earned but also fringe benefits and other labour costs. Using last month's wage records and in consultation with the production and human resources personnel, Terry Sherman determined the standard rate per hour at the Colonial Pewter Company as $14. When companies prepare a single standard rate for all employees in a department, like Colonial Pewter has done, the standard rate reflects the expected "mix" of workers, even though the actual wage rates may vary somewhat from individual to individual due to differing skills or seniority. A single standard rate simplifies the use of standard costs.

The standard direct labour time required to complete a unit of product (generally called the **standard hours per unit**) is perhaps the single most difficult standard to determine. It reflects management's expectation regarding the productivity of its workforce, with allowances for breaks, downtime, and cleanup. It is determined by considering a multitude of factors, such as the skills required, the training and knowledge expected in the workforce, and any other operating circumstances that might be relevant. The field of operations and process analysis uses a number of techniques (e.g., time-and-motion studies) to develop appropriate labour time standards. After consulting with the production manager, Sherman determined the standard hours (*SQI*) per unit as 2.5 hours.

Once the rate and time standards have been set, the standard labour cost per unit of product can be computed as follows:

$$SQI \times SP = 2.5 \ \text{hours} / \text{unit} \times \$14 / \text{hour} = \$35 / \text{unit}$$

Over time, attentive managers would strive to reduce the allowances included in computing the labour standards and to assure themselves that the standards are still relevant.

Setting Variable Manufacturing Overhead Standards

LO1 • **Apply**

CC5: Develop standard costs for variable overhead.

As with direct labour, the price and quantity standards for variable manufacturing overhead are generally expressed in terms of rate and the quantity of the base (usually direct labour-hours or machine-hours) that is used to allocate variable overhead. The rate represents *the variable portion of the predetermined overhead rate* discussed in Chapter 3. At Colonial Pewter, labour-hours are used as the base to allocate variable overhead; the predetermined variable overhead rate (*SP*) is $3 per labour-hour. Therefore, the standard variable manufacturing overhead cost per unit is computed as follows:

$$SQI \times SP = 2.5 \quad \text{labour-hours} / \text{unit} \times \$3 / \text{hour} = \$7.50 / \text{unit}$$

Notice that the standard for variable manufacturing overhead is *derived* from another standard: the quantity standard for labour-hours. This standard specifies that 2.5 labour-hours should be allowed to make one unit of output. Also note that the rate of $3/hour is another standard: management has specified how much it should be spending on variable manufacturing overhead expenses in total. This is the numerator for the calculation of the overhead rate. The denominator, labour-hours, will be the total labour-hours management has estimated it will devote to the production in the operating period: 2.5 × planned output level (*SQI* for direct labour × planned *Q*).

Preparing the Standard Cost Card

LO1   • **Apply**

CC6: Prepare a standard cost card.

The standard cost card for Colonial Pewter is shown in Exhibit 11–1.

As you can see, the standard cost card lists the standard quantity required of each *input* resource (i.e., direct materials, direct labour, and variable overhead), the price paid to acquire one unit of that resource, and the cost per unit of the output. As mentioned previously with regard to the standard cost of a pizza, observe that the **standard cost per unit** (of the output) is computed by multiplying the standard quantity and the standard price of all the input resources and adding them up. The standard cost card informs the manager concerned that the standard variable production cost of one pewter bookend is $53.50.

EXHIBIT 11–1 Standard Cost Card—Variable Production Cost

Inputs	(1) Standard Quantity (*SQI*) or Hours	(2) Standard Price (*SP*) or Rate	(3) Standard Cost (*SC*) (1) × (2) *SQI* × *SP*
Direct materials	1.25 kg	$ 8.80	$11.00
Direct labour	2.5 hours	14.00	35.00
Variable manufacturing overhead	2.5 hours	3.00	7.50
Total standard cost per unit			$53.50

FIXED COSTS ON THE STANDARD COST CARD

Where are the fixed manufacturing costs? Only the standard variable cost of making one pewter bookend is shown on the standard cost card. Fixed manufacturing overhead cost should *not* be driven by the volume of output, and a cost per unit has no economic meaning in the sense that a unit of product "causes" a certain cost to be incurred. For the purpose of product costing, however, management may want to allocate the fixed cost of manufacturing to the product. To do this, the total fixed cost must be expressed on a per-unit basis; this is called the *unitization of fixed overhead cost*. Unitizing fixed costs can mislead one to think that the cost is a variable cost when making operating decisions. Indeed, this is a very common mistake that anyone, even a seasoned manager, can make. As a result, bad pricing decisions and poorly designed job bids can occur, and erroneous profitability results may be reported. The main question to answer is, should fixed costs even be presented on the standard cost card and, if so, should the cost be presented as a total figure or on a unitized basis? Because this topic must be studied carefully, we are going to postpone the consideration of this question and that of analyzing performance with respect to fixed overhead cost until later in the chapter. Until then, we will work with the standard cost card as developed above.

The Static Budget

After developing the standard cost card, Terry Sherman turned to the preparation of the static budget for June using the information on the standard cost card. A **static budget** is a budget developed for a *single planned activity level*. For the month of June, Sherman knew that Colonial Pewter had expected to sell 1,800 bookends at the price of $110 per bookend and had also planned for a production activity level of 1,800 bookends. Remember that the static budget will be prepared *before* the start of the operating year. In this case, because Sherman is trying to figure out what happened at Colonial Pewter, he prepared the static budget after the fact.

Preparing the Static Budget

LO2 • **Apply**

CC7: Prepare a static budget.

The static budget for June is shown in Exhibit 11–2. The information from the standard cost card from Exhibit 11–1 is the key to preparing the budget, along with the planned activity level of 1,800 bookends. The exhibit shows that two equivalent budget cost drivers can be used to calculate the variable costs (see column 7). One driver is the planned activity level of $Q = 1,800$ bookends. The alternative cost driver is *the total quantity of input required for making the planned production quantity* of 1,800 bookends. The two drivers give rise to the two alternative cost formulas shown at the top of column 7 in the exhibit.

EXHIBIT 11–2 Static Budget for June

	A	B	C	D	E	F	G	H	I	J
1						COLONIAL PEWTER COMPANY				
2						Static Budget for Planned Activity Level of Q = 1,800, June				
3				(1)	(2)	(3)	(4)	(5)	(6)	(7)
4					Standard Cost Card			Budget Cost Drivers		Static Budget†
5				Price	Standard Price	Standard Quantity	Standard Cost	Driver 1: Q	Driver 2: SQ*	
6				P	SP	SQI	SC = SP × SQI	Q	SQ = SQI × Q	(SC) × (Q) or (SP) × (SQ)
7	Sales			$110				1,800	n/a	$198,000
8	*Variable costs:*									
9	Direct materials (kilograms of pewter)				$8.8/kg	1.25 kg/unit	$11/unit	1,800	2,250 kg	19,800
10	Direct labour (hours)				$14/h	2.5 h/unit	$35/unit	1,800	4,500 hours	63,000
11	Variable overhead (hours)				$3/h	2.5 h/unit	$7.5/unit	1,800	4,500 hours	13,500
12	Other variable expenses				$4 per Q	1 per unit	$4/unit	1,800	1,800 bookends	7,200
13		Contribution margin								$ 94,500
14	*Fixed costs:*									
15	Fixed manufacturing overhead							1,000 to 3,000		$ 22,000

	A	B	C	D	E	F	G	H	I	J
16	Fixed administrative and selling							1,000 to 3,000		7,200
17		Operating income								$ 65,300
18										
19										
20	*SQ is the standard quantity of input allowed for the budgeted output level. SQ = SQI × Output level.									
21	SQ for direct materials: SQ = SQI × Q = 1.25 kg/unit × 1,800 units = 2,250 kg									
22	SQ for direct labour: SQ = SQI × SQ = 2.5 h/unit × 1,800 units = 4,500 h									
23	SQ for variable overhead cost: Same as that for direct labour because the overhead allocation base is direct labour-hours.									
24										
25										
26	Budgeted cost for inputs can be calculated using either of the two cost drivers, Q or SQ:									
27		Cost = SP × SQ or Cost = SC × Q								
28	Example: Budgeted cost for direct materials: Cost = SQ × SP = 2,250 kg × $8.80/kg = $19,800 or Cost = SC × Q $11/unit × 1,800 units = $19,800									

Calculating the Budgeted Variable Manufacturing Costs: Two Alternative Cost Formulas

Cost Formula 1: Standard Cost Times Output Level Approach ($C = SC \times Q$). In this approach, the budgeted variable production cost of each input is prepared using the standard cost of the input from the standard cost card. And the budgeted costs will be driven by the level of output, Q. The calculation of the standard cost is essentially copied over from the standard cost card and is laid out in columns 2 through 4 of Exhibit 11–2, with the *standard cost* per unit of output shown in column 4. The cost driver—the level of output, Q—is shown in column 5. Column 7 is the static budget.

Using direct materials as an example, the standard cost of pewter for one bookend is $SC = \$11$ (= 1.25 kg × \$8.80/kg); Q is 1,800 bookends. Therefore, the budgeted cost of pewter (direct materials) to make $Q = 1,800$ bookends is $\$11Q$ or \$11/unit × 1,800 units = \$19,800.

Cost Formula 2: Standard Price Times Standard Quantity Approach ($C = SP \times SQ$). In this approach, the cost driver is the total quantity of an input required to make a given volume of output. This total quantity of an input—labeled as "SQ"—must be calculated using the information on the standard quantity of input (SQI) on the standard cost card.

You must be careful not to confuse SQ with SQI. Recall that the quantity standard specifies the amount of an input to make one unit of output. This is SQI. The standard cost card will not show SQ, the total quantity of an input, because SQ will vary with the level of production planned. Since the company may choose whatever production quantity it wishes to make in any given period, the total quantity of an input needed for that production level will change from period to period, and it is impossible to capture this changing information on a single standard cost card.

Using direct labour to illustrate how SQ is calculated, notice that *each* bookend is supposed to use 2.5 hours, that is, $SQI = 2.5$, and given the plan to make 1,800 bookends, the total number of hours (SQ) needed to achieve the desired production quantity is

$$SQ = SQI \times Q = 2.5 \text{ hours/unit} \times 1,800 \text{ units} = 4,500 \text{ hours}$$

The standard wage rate is $14 per hour and the budgeted cost for direct labour is

$$C = SP \times SQ = \$14/\text{hour} \times 4,500 \text{ hours} = \$63,000$$

In the case of direct materials, 1.25 kg will be needed for each bookend produced. Therefore, SQI is 1.25. And since $Q = 1,800$,

$$SQ \text{ of direct materials} = SQI \times Q = 1.25 \text{ kg/unit} \times 1,800 \text{ units} = 2,250 \text{ kg of pewter}$$

The budgeted direct materials cost for June will be the cost of the 2,250 kg of pewter. The standard price for 1 kg of pewter is $8.80 ($SP = \$8.8$). The budgeted cost as per cost formula 2 is

$$C = SP \times SQ = \$8.8/\text{kg} \times 2,250 \text{ kg} = \$19,800$$

Finally, let us look at the variable overhead cost. Given the variable overhead rate of $3 per labour-hour (the SP) and SQ of 4,500 hours (since overhead is driven by direct labour-hours), the budgeted cost for variable overhead is

$$C = SP \times SQ = \$3/\text{hour} \times 4,500 \text{ hours} = \$13,500$$

The above procedure is illustrated in Exhibit 11–2. In column 3, the standard quantity of each input (SQI), the amount needed to make one unit of output, is shown. Column 5 shows the output level, Q, driving the budget. In Column 6 we calculate SQ—the standard quantity of input allowed for the budgeted output level. For each variable input, this is the standard quantity times the output level upon which the budget is based ($SQI \times Q$). Column 7 of the exhibit shows the budgeted cost.

HELPFUL HINT

The most important thing to remember about the second cost formula is that SQ is a *derived* figure; it represents the *total* quantity of an input required for making a given level, Q units, of output. SQ is thus derived from the output level Q and SQI (the standard quantity). For this reason, SQ is referred to as the "standard quantity of input allowed for making the level of output of Q units." You will see this phrase (with slight modifications) used repeatedly in this chapter, and it will be very helpful for you to understand its meaning thoroughly.

There are some additional points to understand regarding the static budget and the information shown in Exhibit 11–2. Note that the budget is presented using the contribution margin format. Also note that, for simplicity, we will assume that sales will equal production; this helps avoid clutter and also the unnecessary distraction of having to account for inventory changes. Given the plan to make and sell 1,800 bookends at a unit price of $110, the budgeted sales revenue is $110/unit \times 1,800/\text{units} = \$198,000$. This is shown in column 7 of the exhibit.

HELPFUL HINT

Why have two cost formulas to calculate the same thing? Because management's intention might be more than simply to calculate the budgeted costs. When the goal is simply to prepare a budget, choosing the activity level, Q, to be the cost driver and using cost formula 1 will make the calculation easy and quick. But if the goal is to analyze performance, then knowing how much of an input the standard allows for an output level can be handy because you can compare the actual usage of an input to the allowed standard. This was the key lesson of our pizzeria example. You took 130 minutes to process 20 orders. The SQ for 20 orders is 140 minutes ($SQI \times Q = 7$ minutes/order $\times$ 20 orders). Thus, you were efficient in the use of time, having used only 130 minutes, which is less time than you were supposed to. Using cost formula 2 to develop the budget makes this type of analysis easier to do, whereas cost formula 1 does not allow for this type of understanding of performance.

BUDGETED FIXED COSTS

The static budget in Exhibit 11–2 shows that Sherman has estimated the fixed manufacturing cost per month to be $22,000. Furthermore, Sherman has estimated that this cost will not vary with the output level as long as the planned production (i.e., activity) level is within the range of 1,000 to 3,000 bookends per month. This is consistent with the point we made back in Chapter 6, that fixed costs can be expected to remain fixed with respect to changes in the level of the cost driver only over a certain range called the *relevant range*. As long as the activity level driving a budget is within the range of 1,000 to 3,000 bookends, Sherman will use $22,000 as the estimate of the fixed cost of manufacturing in *that* budget.

NONMANUFACTURING COSTS

Sherman has allowed for "other (nonmanufacturing) variable costs" that the company expects to incur, without showing the details of these costs or the standards associated with them. A standard cost of $4 per bookend (which also equals the standard price) has been assumed. And, with regard to nonmanufacturing fixed costs, Sherman has estimated the costs at $7,200 per month.

We have shown these types of costs to remind you that budgets are supposed to itemize and estimate all the relevant costs of operating the business. But we will not consider these nonmanufacturing costs further in the ensuing discussion because they are not the focus of Sherman's analysis.

Static Budget Performance Report

LO2 ● **Apply**

CC8: Prepare a static budget performance report.

With the static budget for June completed, Sherman was now in a position to prepare a report showing the actual results for June compared with the planned budget for June. The actual results for June are shown in Exhibit 11–3.

Note that, for simplicity, we are assuming that there is only one type of material and labour. In reality, there will likely be many types of inputs and classes of labour in a production organization. In these cases, the input prices should be interpreted as an average of the prices for different types of materials, labour, and overhead elements. Typically, such prices are not observable directly and will not be found in a costing system; instead, the accountant would have to compute them from the records on the prices of each individual type of input. The analysis becomes more complex in these situations, so we will not consider this topic of *input mix* further in this book.

EXHIBIT 11–3 Actual Results for June

	Actual Quantity (AQ)	Actual Price (AP)	Actual Cost or Revenue
Sales and production	2,000 bookends	$101.50	$203,000
Direct materials	3,000 kg	$ 8.50	$ 25,500
Direct labour	5,400 hours	$ 13.75	$ 74,250
Variable overhead			$ 15,390
Fixed manufacturing overhead			$ 21,100
Other variable expenses			$ 6,500
Fixed selling and administrative expense			$ 7,200

Using the information in Exhibit 11–3, Sherman prepared the static budget performance report shown in Exhibit 11–4. The budget figures are based on the planned volume of 1,800 bookends from Exhibit 11–2.

EXHIBIT 11–4 Static Budget Performance Report, June

COLONIAL PEWTER COMPANY Static Budget Performance Report, June Actual Activity Level Was 2,000 and Planned Activity Level Was 1,800				
	Actual **(Q = 2,000)**	**Static Budget** **(Q = 1,800)**	**Variance**	
Sales revenue	$203,000	$198,000	$ 5,000	F
Variable costs:				
Direct materials	25,500	19,800	5,700	U
Direct labour	74,250	63,000	11,250	U
Variable overhead	15,390	13,500	1,890	U
Other variable expenses	8,000	7,200	800	U
Contribution margin	$ 79,860	$ 94,500	$(14,640)	U
Fixed manufacturing overhead	21,100	22,000	(900)	F
Fixed administrative and selling	7,200	7,200	0	F
Operating income before tax	$ 51,560	$ 65,300	$(13,740)	U

THE CONCEPT OF A VARIANCE

LO2   • **Know**

CC9: Explain the concept of variances.

The difference between an actual financial result and the corresponding budgeted amount is called a **variance**. The static budget performance report compares the actual result with the budgeted amount by calculating the difference, Actual – Budgeted, for each line in the report. In the present situation, since the actual result is compared to the static budget, the variances are called the **static budget variances**.

The variances are shown in the variance column of the report. Each variance is evaluated as either favourable (F) or unfavourable (U). A favourable variance has caused operating income to be higher than it would have been if there had been no variance. An unfavourable variance has caused operating income to be lower than it would have been had there been no variance (i.e., if the budget had been met).

To decide if a variance is favourable or unfavourable, first determine if the variance is a revenue variance or a cost variance. If the variance concerns revenue, margin, or income, then a positive difference is a favourable variance (actual income is higher than the budgeted income). If the variance concerns expenditures, a positive difference is an unfavourable variance (actual expenditures exceeded the budgeted amount). Similarly, negative revenue, margin, or income variances are unfavourable (actual profit is less than budgeted), and negative cost variances are favourable (actual expenditure is less than the budgeted amount).

ANALYZING A STATIC BUDGET PERFORMANCE REPORT

Sherman is troubled by information in the static budget performance report. Looking at the bottom line, it is evident that the actual operating income before tax is less than the budgeted operating income by $13,740. Furthermore, the contribution margin variance is also unfavourable by $14,640. This is all despite the fact that the company made and sold more bookends than it had planned. Sherman decided to analyze the performance report more closely.

Looking at the variances, Sherman realized that they were what one would expect when comparing costs and revenues based on one activity level (2,000 bookends) with costs and revenues at a different activity level (1,800 bookends). Gross revenue was higher with the higher activity level. But there were unanswered questions. Sherman knew that further study would be needed on the revenue variance. While it was true that the revenue was higher at a sales level of 2,000 bookends compared to the budgeted revenue at the sales level of 1,800 bookends, the actual price per bookend was lower ($101.50 instead of the expected price of $110 per bookend). The cause for the price decrease would have to be investigated further. And then there was the puzzle of why the contribution margin and operating income were both lower despite the increase in sales. Finally, he noted that the static budget variances were unhelpful because they only confirmed a basic fact: if more is produced, more variable cost is incurred.

Volume-driven variable expenditures were also higher at the higher activity level. To see what more he might be able to learn from the static budget, Sherman decided to look more closely at a worksheet he had created when preparing the static budget performance report. This worksheet is shown in Exhibit 11–5. The information for the worksheet was obtained from the standard cost card and the data on actual results in Exhibits 11–1 and 11–2. Sherman used cost formula 2 to express the actual costs in terms of the total quantity of inputs used to make the actual production quantity of 2,000 bookends and to express the static budget variable costs in terms of the quantity of input that was allowed to make the *planned activity level of* 1,800 bookends (cost formula 2). The actual costs and the static budget costs were placed on opposite ends of the spreadsheet, and the variances were placed in the middle of the spreadsheet. By being able to break the actual results and the budget numbers into the relevant constituent values as per cost formula 2, Sherman was able to learn some important things about the performance of the company in June.

EXHIBIT 11–5 Static Budget Performance Worksheet

	A	B	C	D	E	F	G	H	I	J	K	L
1	COLONIAL PEWTER COMPANY											
2	Static Budget Performance Report: WORKSHEET, June											
3												
4–5		Actual Cost Card		Actual Activity	Actual Quantity	Actual Results	Static Budget Variances	Static Budget	Standard Quantity	Budgeted Activity	Standard Cost Card	
6		AP	AQI*	Q	AQ*	AP × AQ	Actual – Budget	SP × SQ	SQ′	Q	SQI′	SP
7	Sales	$101.50	n/a	2,000	n/a	$203,000	$ 5,000 (F)	$198,000	n/a	1,800	n/a	$ 110
8	*Variable costs:*											
9	Direct materials	8.50	1.5	2,000	3,000	25,500	5,700 (U)	19,800	2,250	1,800	1.25	8.80
10	Direct labour	13.75	2.7	2,000	5,400	74,250	11,250 (U)	63,000	4,500	1,800	2.5	14
11	Variable overhead	2.85	2.7	2,000	5,400	15,390	1,890 (U)	13,500	4,500	1,800	2.5	3
12	Other variable expenses					8,000	800 (U)	7,200				
13	Contribution margin					$ 79,860	$(14,640) (U)	$ 94,500				
14	*Fixed costs:*											
15	Manufacturing overhead					21,100	(900) (F)	22,000				
16	Administrative and selling					7,200	0	7,200				
17	Operating income					$ 51,560	$ (13,740) (U)	$ 65,300				
18												
19												
20	*AQI is the quantity of input used *per unit of output* produced: AQI = AQ ÷ Q.*											
21	AQ is the actual *total* quantity of input used to achieve the actual production level of 2,000 bookends, calculated from AQI and Q: AQ = AQI × Q.											
22	The cost accounting system must provide the level of Q and at least one of AQI or AQ to create a performance report.											
23												
24	′SQI is the standard quantity of input per unit of output, given on the standard cost card.											
25	SQ is the standard quantity of input allowed for making the budgeted level of production, calculated after the activity level Q is specified: SQ = SQI × SQ.											

Sherman began by comparing the two outermost columns and then systematically moved to the middle, comparing a column from the actual side with the corresponding column on the budget side. The first comparison between *AP* and *SP* immediately showed that the company paid less per unit of input than the standard price (*AP* < *SP*): Colonial Pewter paid $8.50/kg instead of $8.80/kg of pewter, and direct labour was paid at the rate of $13.75 instead of $14 for each hour used during June. This *price difference,* taken on its own, is good news. But how much has operating income been helped by this result when compared against the budget? Sherman could not answer this question yet because all he had was a difference between the actual and budgeted prices. It was not possible to determine the impact on operating income of this difference by looking at the price difference alone. Sherman needed to calculate a variance from the price difference, since only a cost variance tells us the amount by which operating income is higher or lower than what it would have otherwise been in the absence of the variance.

Next, Sherman wanted to look at how the inputs were used in comparison to the budget. Sherman realized that he could not compare *AQ* and *SQ* since *AQ* was based on *Q* = 2,000 bookends and *SQ* was based on *Q* = 1,800 bookends. He therefore decided to compare the actual quantity of input used *per unit of output* (*AQI*) with the standard quantity of input *per unit of output* from the standard cost card (*SQI*). The values for *AQI* had to be calculated on the worksheet because this is a productivity measure and is not directly observable. Therefore, this type of information is not tracked by an accounting information system and thus is not in Exhibit 11–1. The total quantity of an input used for production in a given period (*AQ*), on the other hand, is observable and is normally tracked and thus reported regularly. You can see this information in Exhibit 11–3.

Comparing *AQI* and *SQI,* Sherman realized that Colonial Pewter had used more pewter and labour-hours *per unit of output* than the corresponding amounts on the standard cost card (*AQI* of 1.5 versus *SQI* of 1.25 for direct materials, and *AQI* of 2.7 versus *SQI* of 2.5 for direct labour). This is not good news; it is a signal of inefficiency in production operations. Sherman wondered by how much operating income was hurt by this result when compared to the budget. All he had at this point was another difference, that between *AQI* and *SQI;* this difference was not a variance.

Finally, how did the good news on the price balance out with the bad news on the usage of the inputs? What was the overall impact on operating income? Sherman could not say. The main problem was that the only meaningful comparisons between the actual result and the static budget he was able to do were on a per-unit basis. But the prices were per unit of *input* (kilograms, hours), and the quantities were per unit of *output* (bookends), and it was not possible to combine the two differences into a single value. This made it hard to aggregate the results and to develop a total picture. In other words, Sherman had no idea how much the operating income was hurt or helped in total. Furthermore, Sherman could not easily conclude anything about the overhead costs. Knowing that there was a favourable input price difference and an unfavourable productivity difference provided only partial insights into the company's performance. Sherman was not able to express his findings in terms of the financial impact on operating income. He realized that the static budget was not helping him very much, despite allowing a closer look at some of the numbers behind the results and the budget.

WHY A STATIC BUDGET IS NOT AN IDEAL BASIS FOR PERFORMANCE ANALYSIS

LO2 • **Know**

CC10: Explain the deficiency of a static budget for performance analysis.

The problem with the static budget performance report is the inability to distinguish *control over activity* from *control over costs.* The variance arising from a difference between the actual activity level and the planned activity level is relevant to the objective of controlling activity. But when an activity is performed, costs are incurred. Concern about how an activity was performed, the quantity of resources consumed to perform the activity, and the prices paid for these resources—all of which contribute to the costs incurred—on the other hand, is related to the objective of cost control. Did costs change simply because of the activity level change, or was it because of the manner in which activities were performed and managed? It is impossible to properly focus on cost control when an activity level change has occurred at the same time. This was the lesson with our pizzeria example at the beginning of the chapter. Like in the pizzeria, the increase in activity was good for Colonial Pewter, but the increase in activity at Colonial Pewter has apparently had a negative impact on the costs (in the same way that you seemed to have taken more time to process the pizza orders).

In conclusion, the fundamental flaw of using the static budget as the basis for evaluating the actual results was that the budget was based on *Q* = 1,800, while the actual production was *Q* = 2,000. A change in activity level from the budget had occurred, and Sherman, who was interested in cost control, now needed to adjust for this change to properly evaluate the June results from a cost control perspective. This was the reason that the price difference and the productivity difference, both of which are relevant to cost control, could not be re-expressed as a cost variance from an analysis of the static budget.

HELPFUL HINT

Many students create a worksheet like Sherman did in Exhibit 11–5, but they go on to compare the *AP* with *SP* or *AQI* with *SQI* and reach a conclusion about the performance. These students mistakenly think that *AP − SP* is a variance and that *AQI − SQI* is also a variance. These differences are *not* variances and should not be reported or interpreted as such. A properly calculated variance will always allow you to describe the impact of that variance on net income. Avoid the temptation to compare the actual performance against the budget *on a per-unit basis*. While such comparisons can help to show what is happening, they will not allow you to reach a complete and proper assessment of performance. The static budget is not an ideal basis for performance evaluation.

The Flexible Budget

To overcome the difficulties of comparing performance at one level of activity with the budget based on a different level of activity, Sherman decided he must let go of the static budget, which was based on an output level of 1,800 bookends, and instead create a budget based on the output level achieved in June—2,000 bookends. This budget would be the ideal comparison budget for evaluating performance from the perspective of cost control, since the same activity level would drive actual results as well as the budget.

This decision meant that Sherman would *flex* the original planning budget by using the same standard cost card information as before, but drive (i.e., flex) the budget using a different activity level. This new budget is called a flexible budget.

Preparing the Flexible Budget for Evaluating Actual Performance

LO2   • **Know**

CC11: Distinguish the static budget from the flexible budget.

• **Apply**

CC12: Prepare a flexible budget.

A **flexible budget** is any budget based on an activity level *different* from the planned activity level, and is prepared using the *same* budget data and standard cost card information as the static budget. This is the meaning behind the concept of flexing a budget: only the volume of activity is changed or flexed, and a different budget is prepared. Notice that, in the rare circumstance where the actual activity level is the same as the planned activity, there will be no need to flex the budget to enable comparison.

The flexible budget, using both cost formulas, for June is shown in Exhibit 11–6. The layout of the exhibit is identical to that of Exhibit 11–2 for the static budget. The *only* difference is that the activity level of 2,000 bookends is used here to develop the budget. In other words, as stipulated in the definition of a flexible budget, we have used the same standard cost card information as before but now we use $Q = 2,000$ and also calculate SQ using Q of 2,000. Fixed costs are the same as before because they are expected to remain constant for any activity level in the range of 1,000 to 3,000 bookends. As was just mentioned, it is very important to realize that the root of the flexible budget is the *output volume*. This is what gets flexed. All direct cost inputs—materials and labour—are volume driven; variable overhead and fixed overhead are applied using some driver that correlates with output volume and thus are also indirectly driven by production volume. Because of this, we distinguish different budgets like the static budget from a flexible budget in terms of the output volume driving each budget.

EXHIBIT 11–6 The Flexible Budget for June

	A	B	C	D	E	F	G	H
1				COLONIAL PEWTER COMPANY				
2				The Flexible Budget for an Activity Level of *Q* = 2,000: June				
3		(1)	(2)	(3)	(4)	(5)	(6)	(7)
4		Price	Standard Cost Card			Budget Cost Drivers		Flexible Budget†
5			Standard Price	Standard Quantity	Standard Cost	*Driver 1: Q*	*Driver 2: SQ**	
6		*P*	*SP*	*SQI*	*SC = SP × SQI*	*Q*	*SQ = SQI × Q*	*(SC) × (Q)* or *(SP) × (SQ)*
7	Sales	$110				2,000	n/a	$220,000
8	*Variable costs:*							
9	Direct materials (kilograms of pewter)		$8.8/kg	1.25 kg/unit	$11/unit	2,000	2,500 kg	22,000
10	Direct labour (hours)		$14/h	2.5 h/unit	$35/unit	2,000	5,000 hours	70,000
11	Variable overhead (hours)		$3/h	2.5 h/unit	$7.5/unit	2,000	5,000 hours	15,000
12	Other variable expenses		$4/Q	1/unit	$4/unit	2,000	2,000 bookends	8,000
13	Contribution margin							$105,000
14	*Fixed costs:*							
15	Manufacturing overhead					1,000 to 3,000		22,000
16	Administrative and selling					1,000 to 3,000		7,2000
17	Operating income							$ 75,800
18								
19								
20	*SQ is the standard quantity of input allowed for the budgeted output level and equals, for each input, SQ = SQI × Output level.							
21	SQ for direct materials: Standard allows 2,500 kg (SQ = 1.25 kg/unit × 2,000 units) to manufacture 2,000 bookends.							
22	SQ for direct labour: Standard allows 5,000 h (SQ = 2.5 h/unit × 2,000 units) to manufacture 2,000 bookends.							
23	SQ for variable overhead cost is the same as that for direct labour because the allocation base is direct labour-hours.							
24								
25	† The budgeted cost for inputs can be calculated using either of the two cost drivers, Q or SQ: Budgeted cost = SP × SQ or Budgeted cost = SC × Q.							
26	*Example:* The budgeted cost for direct materials is C = SQ × SP = 2,500 kg × $8.80/kg = $22,000 or C = SC × Q = $11/unit × 2,000 units = $22,000.							

HELPFUL HINT

It is easy to become confused about how the word *flexible* is used. On the one hand, the word describes an attribute of volume-driven budgets: change the output volume (this is "flexing"), and you get a different budget. Do you remember the budget cost formula 1 in Exhibit 11–2, where $C = SC \times Q$? Once flexed, the resulting budget will be different from the original planning budget (i.e., the static budget). There are now two different budgets. To distinguish the two budgets, the "flexed" budget is labelled as "the flexible budget."

Comparing the Flexible Budget and the Static Budget: Sales Volume Variances

Since the flexible budget and the static budget share the same standard cost information, the difference between these budgets exists only because each budget is based on a different activity level. The variances that arise from this comparison are called **sales volume variances** to indicate that the source of the variance is activity level differences and not cost control. The sales volume variances are shown in the table below. Analysis of the sales volume *cost* variances will tell us nothing because they will be unfavourable if the flexible budget volume is greater than the static budget volume and favourable if the flexible budget volume is less than the static budget volume. That is, you will spend more if you produce more, and you will spend less if you make less. Analysis of the revenue variance, on the other hand, is important to conduct since the reasons for selling more or less than planned and selling at a higher or lower price than planned will be important for managers to know and understand. This topic is more complex, however, and is not covered in this book.

	A	B	C	D	E	F	G	H	I
1	COLONIAL PEWTER COMPANY								
2	Comparison of Static and Flexible Budgets for the Month of June								
3	Sales Volume Variances								
4	Sales and production levels (bookends): Q			2,000		1,800		Sales Volume Variances	
5		SP	SQI	SQ#	Flexible Budget	SQ*	Static Budget		
6	Sales	$110	n/a	n/a	$220,000	n/a	$198,000	$22,000	F
7									
8	*Variable costs:*								
9	Direct materials	8.80	1.25	2,500	22,000	2,250	19,800	2,200	U
10	Direct labour	14.00	2.50	5,000	70,000	4,500	63,000	7,000	U
11	Variable overhead	3.00	2.50	5,000	15,000	4,500	13,500	1,500	U
12	Other variable expenses	4.00	1.00	2,000	8,000	1,800	7,200	800	U
13	Contribution margin				$105,000		$ 94,500	$10,500	F
14									

	A	B	C	D	E	F	G	H	I
15	Fixed manufacturing overhead				22,000		22,000	0	
16	Fixed administrative and selling				7,200		7,200	0	
17	Operating income before tax				$ 75,800		$ 65,300	$10,500	F
18									
19									
20	*SQ is the standard quantity of input allowed for the output level achieved: SQ/ Output level.								

The Flexible Budget Performance Report: Flexible Budget Variances

LO2 ● **Apply**

CC13: Prepare a flexible budget performance report.

After Sherman prepared the flexible budget to use as the comparison budget for evaluating the actual results, he prepared the flexible budget performance report, shown in Exhibit 11–7. This report compares the actual results against the flexible budget. The variances in this report are called **flexible budget variances** and are calculated and evaluated as either favourable or unfavourable in exactly the same way as was done in the static budget performance report. Some accountants also refer to the flexible budget variances as spending variances. This practice originates from the interpretation of the variance as a spending difference relative to a budget that controls for the volume difference between the original volume planned and the actual volume achieved.

EXHIBIT 11–7 Flexible Budget Performance Report

	A	B	C	D	E
1	COLONIAL PEWTER COMPANY				
2	Flexible Budget Performance Report, June				
3	Actual Activity Level Was 2,000 and Flexible Budget Activity Level Was 2,000				
4		Actual	Flexible Budget	Variance	
5	Activity level (bookends)	2,000	2,000	–	
6	Sales revenue	$203,000	$220,000	$(17,000)	U
7	*Variable costs:*				
8	Direct materials	25,500	22,000	3,500	U
9	Direct labour	74,250	70,000	4,250	U
10	Variable overhead	15,390	15,000	390	U
11	Other variable expenses	8,000	8,000	0	
12	Contribution margin	$ 79,860	$105,000	$(25,140)	U
13	*Fixed costs:*				
14	Manufacturing overhead	21,100	22,000	(900)	F
15	Administrative and selling	7,200	7,200	0	
16	Operating income before tax	$ 51,560	$ 75,800	$(24,240)	U

Flexible budget variances are pure descriptions of the success or failure of cost control; these variances are not contaminated by any effect due to the difference between the activity level achieved and that which was planned. For example, the flexible budget variance for direct materials is $3,500 U. We can conclude from this that the variance is entirely due to the manner in which the purchase *and* the use of direct materials were managed in June. No part of this variance is due to the fact that the company made 2,000 bookends instead of the planned quantity of 1,800 bookends.

Looking at the bottom line of the performance report, you can see that the actual operating income was less than the budgeted figure—by the amount of $24,240. The ultimate objective of performance evaluation for management is to learn why this result occurred. They made and sold 2,000 bookends in June and yet lost money relative to the budget for the same volume level.

To understand why operating income is less by $24,240 when compared against the income that should have been earned given the activity level of 2,000 bookends, let us look at the revenue variance and the cost variances.

Starting at the top line, sales revenue variance is $17,000 U, meaning the actual operating income was $17,000 lower when compared against the income it should have earned had revenues met the budget. Since sales revenue is a function of two variables, selling price and the number of bookends sold (i.e., output volume), the variance must be due to the difference between the prices, or the difference between numbers of bookends sold, or differences in both price and quantity. But since the budget is based on the same sales quantity as the actual sales quantity, there is no quantity difference here. Therefore, the flexible budget revenue variance must be solely due to the difference between the actual and the budgeted selling prices. Colonial's budgeted selling price was $110 per unit (= $220,000 ÷ 2,000), whereas its actual selling price was only $101.50 (= $203,000 ÷ 2,000). This is the source of the variance. Management of Colonial should identify and investigate the factors behind the price decrease.

Turning to the variable costs of production, Exhibit 11–7 also shows that actual variable costs were higher than the budgeted amounts. All of the variable manufacturing cost variances are unfavourable. Why? How can we explain, for example, why Colonial spent $3,500 more on direct materials than it should have, in order to make 2,000 bookends? What happened? Perhaps Colonial paid more for pewter than it should have, or used more pewter than it should have as specified by a budget driven by the identical activity level as the actual level achieved in June. Further analysis is needed to develop a more complete understanding.

Flexible Budget Variance Analysis: Price and Quantity Variances

LO2 • **Know**

CC14: Distinguish between price and quantity variances.

Like sales revenue, the variable cost of an input is also a function of two variables—the quantity of an input and the price of the input. Therefore, to understand the source of the flexible budget cost variance, we must consider two differences: (1) between the price paid for an input (AP) and the price specified by the standard cost card (SP) and (2) between the quantity of input used (AQ) and the quantity of input allowed for the activity level in the flexible budget (SQ). The price difference gives rise to a price variance, and the quantity difference gives rise to a quantity variance. Together, these two variances will add up to the total flexible budget variance.

We need to learn how the price and quantity variances are calculated from a price or a quantity difference in order to fully understand the reasons behind a cost variance. Since the output level is identical (2,000 bookends) between the actual result and the flexible budget, the quantity difference $AQ - SQ$ *cannot* be due to an activity level difference! The quantity difference tells us that the total amount of an input actually used is more than or less than the total quantity of input allowed by the standard. It implies that actual productivity in the use of an input differed from expectations. The quantity variance describes the impact on operating income of a productivity difference in use of an input and provides information on the efficiency of operations. An input price difference tells us that the price we paid for each unit of an input was different from the price we had expected to pay. This result can be due to good or bad purchasing practices, altered market conditions, or other reasons. Thus, input price variances can provide information about the performance and management of the purchasing function.

For example, returning to the unfavourable direct materials flexible budget variance, consider the following questions concerning the purchase and use of direct materials during June when compared against the (flexible) budget. Did Colonial spend $3,500 more than it should have because the price it paid for pewter was different from the price it expected to pay, and/or because it used more pewter than it should have when making 2,000 bookends? How much of the $3,500 is due to each factor, the price difference and the quantity difference? Similar questions can be asked about direct labour and variable manufacturing overhead. Finding answers to these questions is what **variance analysis** is all about.

It is important from a cost control point of view to be able to isolate and distinguish price variances from quantity variances, because different managers are usually responsible for acquiring resources and for using the resources. You want to make sure that managers are held accountable only for their responsibilities. Price deviations should be the responsibility of the purchasing manager, and quantity differences should be the responsibility of the production manager.

The task of computing the price variance and the quantity variance for each type of manufacturing cost and properly interpreting the results is called **flexible budget variance analysis**.

CONCEPT CHECK

1. Which of the following statements are false? (You may select more than one answer.)
   a. A flexible budget is used for control purposes, and a static budget is used for planning purposes.
   b. A flexible budget is prepared at the end of the period, and a static budget is prepared at the beginning of the period.
   c. A flexible budget is not useful for controlling variable costs.
   d. A static budget provides budgeted estimates for one level of activity.

2. A five-star hotel buys bouquets of flowers to decorate its common areas and guest rooms. Its flexible budget for flowers is $325 per day of operations plus $7.20 per room-day. (A room-day is a room rented for one day; a room is decorated with flowers only if it is occupied.) If the hotel operated for 30 days this month and it had 7,680 room-days, what would be the flexible budget amount for flowers for the month?
   a. $55,296   c. $9,750
   b. $65,046   d. $332.20

3. Refer to the data in Concept Check 2. If the actual spending on flowers for the month was $61,978 and the hotel originally budgeted for 30 operating days and 7,500 room-days, what would be the flexible budget variance for the month?
   a. $3,068 favourable   c. $1,772 favourable
   b. $3,068 unfavourable   d. $1,772 unfavourable

*Note to student: See **Guidance Answers** online.*

A General Model for Standard Cost Flexible Budget Variance Analysis

The information to perform the variance analysis for Colonial Pewter is in the worksheet shown in Exhibit 11–8. The worksheet is a tabular framework for organizing the information needed to do the variance calculations and understand the procedure involved. The worksheet is based on the standard cost card in Exhibit 11–1 and the actual results in Exhibit 11–3.

EXHIBIT 11–8 Flexible Budget Performance Report Worksheet, June

	A	B	C	D	E	F	G	H	I	J	K	L
1	COLONIAL PEWTER COMPANY											
2	Flexible Budget Performance Report: WORKSHEET, June											
3												
4				Actual Results, Q = 2,000			Flexible Budget Variances		Flexible Budget, Q = 2,000			
5		Actual Cost Card		Actual Activity	Actual Quantity	Actual Results		Flexible Budget	Standard Quantity	Budgeted Activity	Standard Cost Card	
6		AP	AQI*	Q	AQ*	AP × AQ	Actual – Budget	SP × SQ	SQ#	Q	SQI†	SP
7	Sales	$101.50	n/a	2,000	n/a	$203,000	$(17,000) (U)	$220,000	n/a	2,000	n/a	$110
8	*Variable costs:*											
9	Direct materials	8.50	1.5	2,000	3,000	25,500	3,500 (U)	22,000	2,250	2,000	1.25	$8.80
10	Direct labour	13.75	2.7	2,000	5,400	74,250	4,250 (U)	70,000	4,500	2,000	2.5	$14
11	Variable overhead	2.85	2.7	2,000	5,400	15,390	390 (U)	15,000	4,500	2,000	2.5	$3
12	Other variable expenses					8,000	0	8,000				
13	Contribution margin					$ 79,860	$(25,140) (U)	$105,000				
14	*Fixed costs:*											
15	Manufacturing overhead					21,100	900 (F)	22,000				
16	Administrative and selling					7,200	0	7,200				
17	Operating income					$ 51,560	$(24,240) (U)	$ 75,800				
18												
19												
20	*AQI is the quantity of input used *per unit of output* produced: AQI = AQ ÷ Q.											
21	AQ is the actual *total* quantity of input used to achieve the actual production level of 2,000 bookends, calculated from AQI and Q: AQ = AQI × Q.											
22	Note that the cost accounting system must provide the level of Q and at least one of AQI or AQ to create a performance report.											
23												

	A	B	C	D	E	F	G	H	I	J	K	L
24	*SQI* is the standard quantity of input per unit of output, given on the standard cost card.											
25	*SQ* is the standard quantity of input allowed for making the budgeted level of production, calculated after the activity level *Q* is specified: *SQ* = *SQI* × *SQ*.											

The layout of this worksheet is identical to that shown earlier for the static budget. And just like before, our approach will be to start by comparing the two outermost columns and then work toward the middle. The reason to start from the outside and work inward is that, when you look at the middle of the worksheet where the variance is calculated as the difference between the Actual column and the Flexible Budget column, it is easy to see the point we just made. A variance will arise because there is a difference between the actual price paid for an input and the budgeted price (*AP* is different from *SP*), or because there is a difference between the actual *total* quantity of an input used and the *total* quantity of the input budgeted (*AQ* is different from *SQ*), or because there is a difference between the input prices as well as a difference between quantities.

The information on the worksheet can also be organized and presented diagrammatically. Exhibit 11–9 presents the diagram illustrating the general approach. Column (1) is the actual results for the period, *AQ* × *AP*, and corresponds to the actual results column in Exhibit 11–8. Column (3) corresponds to the flexible budget column in Exhibit 11–8. The difference between columns (1) and (3) is the total variance for each variable production input: the flexible budget variance. This is the variance that we are trying to decompose into the quantity and price variance. The decomposition is achieved by inserting column (2) in the diagram. A comparison of columns (1) and (2) results in a price variance because of the difference between the actual price, *AP*, and the standard price, *SP*. The quantity difference is kept constant since *AQ* is used in both columns. The actual quantity is involved (and not *SQ*) because the total cost difference from the price difference should be based on the quantity of resource actually purchased given that the purchasing manager is being evaluated on whether or not too much was paid for the resource in total.

EXHIBIT 11–9 A General Model for Variance Analysis—Variable Production Costs

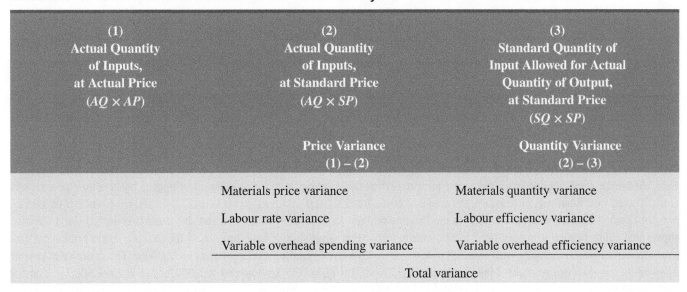

A comparison of columns (2) and (3) will result in a quantity variance because of the quantity difference, *AQ* − *SQ*. The price element is kept constant. The standard price is used as opposed to the actual price, because the production manager should be evaluated on the basis of the cost of the materials used when compared to the budget, and we do not want to be distracted by the effects related to good or bad decisions in the purchasing function.

Notice that Exhibit 11–9 depicts a general variance analysis in that a price variance and a quantity variance can be computed for *all three* variable cost elements—direct materials, direct labour, and variable manufacturing overhead—even though the variance will *not* be called by the *same name* in all cases. For example, a price variance is called a *materials price variance* in the case of direct materials, but a *labour rate variance* in the case of direct labour, and an *overhead spending variance* in the case of variable manufacturing overhead.

With this general model in Exhibits 11–8 and 11–9 as a foundation, we will now examine the price and quantity variances in more detail for each variable manufacturing cost input.

Variance Analysis: Direct Materials Variances

LO3 • **Know** • **Apply**

CC15: Compute and explain direct materials variances.

The analysis of the direct materials flexible budget variance involves calculating the price variance and the quantity variance for this input.

DIRECT MATERIALS PRICE VARIANCE

The flexible performance report worksheet in Exhibit 11–8 shows that the company paid only $8.50 ($AP$) for a kilogram of pewter instead of $8.80 ($SP$), the amount specified on the standard cost card. Therefore, Sherman concluded that one source for the observed variance must be the price difference, $AP - SP = \$8.50 - \$8.80 = \$(0.30)$.

For Colonial Pewter, this meant that it saved $0.30 on every kilogram of pewter that was purchased for use in production. This difference between the price of the input that was paid and the price that should have been paid gives rise to the price variance, which is the impact of the price difference on operating income. This impact (i.e., the variance) is found by multiplying the price difference ($AP - SP$) by the quantity of materials purchased, which is AQ.

For direct materials, the **materials price variance** is calculated by the following formula:

$$
\begin{aligned}
\text{Materials price variance} \quad &= \quad \left(AP - SP\right) \times AQ \\[2mm]
&= \quad \left(\$8.80 \,/\, \text{kg} - \$8.50 \,/\, \text{kg}\right) \times 3{,}000 \text{ kg} \\[2mm]
&= \quad \$900 \text{ F}
\end{aligned}
$$

Thus, the net income is higher by $900 as compared to the budget because of the savings of $0.30 on each kilogram of pewter purchased.

DIRECT MATERIALS QUANTITY VARIANCE

Next, Sherman remembered from the static budget performance report that, on a *per-unit-of-output* basis, more pewter was actually used than what was indicated in the standard cost card (i.e., AQI of 1.5 kg *per bookend* was different from SQI of 1.25 kg *per bookend*). This information was also in the flexible budget performance worksheet. But the worksheet in Exhibit 11–8 also shows that more pewter was used *on a total quantity basis* than what should have been used for making 2,000 bookends. The total amount of pewter actually used was $AQ = AQI \times Q = 1.5$ kg/bookend $\times 2{,}000$ bookends $= 3{,}000$ kg. The quantity of pewter *allowed by the standard* to make 2,000 bookends is $SQ = SQI \times Q = 1.25$ kg/bookend $\times 2{,}000$ bookends $= 2{,}500$ kg. The SQ in the quantity variance calculation is the **standard quantity of an input allowed for the actual quantity of output**. This is the proper benchmark against which to compare the actual usage of an input.

The company used $AQ - SQ = 3{,}000$ kg $- 2{,}500$ kg $= 500$ kg more pewter than it *should have*. When you use 500 kg more material than called for by the budget, the spending will of course be higher. Sherman concluded that the quantity difference ($AQ - SQ$) must be a second source for the unfavourable observed variance of $3,500.

The variance that arises from the *quantity difference* between AQ and SQ is the *quantity variance*. Remember that the quantity difference by itself is not the variance, however; the variance is obtained by multiplying the quantity difference ($AQ - SQ$) by the standard price (SP).

For the direct materials, the **materials quantity variance** is calculated by the following formula:

$$\text{Materials quantity variance} = (AQ - SQ) \times SP$$

$$= (3{,}000 \text{ kg} - 2{,}500 \text{ kg}) \times \$8.80 \Big/ \text{kg}$$

$$= \$4{,}400 \text{ U}$$

This result tells us that operating income is lower by $4,400 than what it otherwise would have been, because the company used more pewter—500 kg more—to make 2,000 bookends than what the budget stipulated it should have used.

The total variance (the flexible budget variance) is the sum of the individual variances:

$$\text{Total variance} = \text{Price variance} + \text{Quantity variance}$$

$$= \$900 \text{ F} + \$4{,}400 \text{ U}$$

$$= \$3{,}500 \text{ U}$$

Turning to Exhibit 11–10, we show the above computations on the variance diagram. In this picture, the formula for the price variance appears in the following form:

$$\text{Direct materials price variance} = (AP - SP) \times AQ$$

$$= AP \times AQ - SP \times AQ$$

$$= \$25{,}500 - \$26{,}400$$

$$= \$900 \text{ F}$$

EXHIBIT 11–10 Direct Materials Price and Quantity Variances

	A	B	C	D	E	F
1		**Actual Quantity of Input at Actual Price**		**Actual Quantity of Input at Standard Price**		**Standard Quantity of Input Allowed for Actual Output at Standard Price**
2		**AQ × AP**		**AQ × SP**		**SQ × SP**
3	**Direct Materials**	3,000 kg × $8.50/kg		3,000 kg × $8.80/kg		2,500 kg* × $8.80
4		$25,500	Price variance	$26,400	Efficiency variance	$22,000
5			$(900)		$4,400	
6			F	Total variance, $3,500 U	U	
7	*SQ allowed for actual output: 2,000 units × 1.25 kg/unit = 2,500 kg					
8	F = Favourable; U = Unfavourable					

The quantity variance appears in the following form:

$$\text{Direct materials quantity variance} \ = \ \left(AQ - SQ\right) \times SP$$

$$= \ AQ \times SP - SQ \times SP$$

$$= \ \$26{,}400 - \$22{,}000$$

$$= \ \$4{,}400 \ U$$

Now that you have seen how a typical variance calculation is performed, you should be able to understand why you were asked to learn the two different cost formulas for preparing the static and flexible budgets. The concept of a quantity variance arises from the quantity difference between the amount of an *input* used and the amount of that *input* allowed by the standard. This is all about inputs. The *output* quantity is the same in the flexible budget and the actual results: both are based on the same Q. Cost formula 1, on the other hand, is based on the output quantity: $C = SC \times Q$; we cannot isolate input quantity variances when costs are expressed in this way.

In conclusion, the analysis shows that the company saved $900, relative to the flexible budget, when it paid less than what it had budgeted to pay for each kilogram of pewter. But this is before considering how much pewter was consumed to make 2,000 bookends. With regard to direct materials used in the production process, operations consumed 500 kg more pewter than it should have and thus Colonial Pewter ended up spending $4,400 more than it should have. The total (i.e., net) effect is that Colonial Pewter spent $3,500 more than it should have, thus causing its actual operating income to be lower by this amount than what it would have been otherwise.

HELPFUL HINT

The key to doing variance analysis correctly is to be properly organized. A worksheet like the one in Exhibit 11–8 or the variance diagram is an example of usefully organizing the information. Remember that cost formula 2 is the appropriate formula. Consequently, you must correctly identify *AP, SP, AQ,* and *SQ* from the available information. The calculation of *SQ* is especially important for you to understand correctly since this information will rarely be provided. It is calculated by the accountant as a part of preparing the flexible budget.

Direct Materials Price Variance When the Quantity Purchased Does Not Equal the Quantity Used

LO3 ● **Apply**

CC16: Compute direct materials variances when the quantities of materials purchased and used for production are not equal.

The budget data for Colonial Pewter reflect the fact that all of the materials purchased during June were also used during June. The calculation of the materials price variance is based on this assumption. How are the variances computed if the amount of materials purchased is different from the amount used? To illustrate the procedure in this situation, assume that, during June, the company purchased 3,000 kilograms of materials, as before, but that it used only 2,800 kilograms during the month to produce the 2,000 units. In this case, the materials price variance is based on the *purchased quantity,* and the quantity variance is based on the 2,800 kilograms used:

$$\text{Materials price variance} = (AP - SP) \times AQ \text{ purchased}$$

$$= \left(\$8.50 / \text{kg} - \$8.80 / \text{kg}\right) \times 3{,}000 \text{ kg}$$

$$= \$900 \text{ F}$$

$$\text{Materials quantity variance} = (AQ \text{ used} - SQ) \times SP$$

$$= \left(2{,}800 \text{ kg} - 2{,}500 \text{ kg}\right) \times \$8.80 / \text{kg}$$

$$= \$2{,}640 \text{ U}$$

The price variance will be observed when the materials are purchased and the purchase cost is incurred. The quantity variance will be observed when materials are introduced into work in process and when the cost of direct materials actually used is compared to the budgeted cost indicated in the flexible budget. Note that the actual inventory of direct materials will not equal the inventory of direct materials in the flexible budget.

Since each variance occurs at a different point in time and impacts operating income at a different place on the income statement, the variances *cannot be combined*. A total direct materials variance cannot be computed in this situation. This point is illustrated in Exhibit 11–11. Note the use of $AQ = 3{,}000$ kg when the price variance is calculated and $AQ = 2{,}800$ kg for the calculation of the quantity variance.

EXHIBIT 11–11 Direct Materials Variances When Quantity Purchased Differs From Quantity Used

	A	B	C	D	E	F
1		**Actual Quantity of Input at Actual Price**			**Actual Quantity of Input at Standard Price**		**Standard Quantity of Input Allowed for Actual Output at Standard Price**
2		**AQ × AP**			**AQ × SP**		**SQ × SP**
3	**Direct Materials**	3,000 kg × $8.50/kg			3,000 kg × $8.80/kg		
4		$25,500	Price variance		$26,400		
5			$(900)				
6			F	2,800 kg × $8.80/kg			2,500 kg* × $8.80/kg
7				$24,640		Quantity variance	$22,000
8						$2,640	
9						U	
10	Note: AQ for the price variance is the quantity of direct materials purchased (3,000 kg), and the AQ for the quantity variance is the amount of direct materials used (2,800 kg). A total variance cannot be computed in this situation.					
11	*SQ allowed for actual output: 1.25 kg/bookend × 2,000 bookends = 2,500 kg					

Management Control Using Direct Materials Variances

Now that you know how to calculate the direct materials variances, let us turn to the issue of controlling an organization from knowledge of these variances. There are three control issues: (1) timing of the isolation of variances, (2) responsibility for the variances, and (3) eliminating variances in the future.

TIMING OF THE ISOLATION OF VARIANCES

When should variances be isolated and brought to the attention of management? The answer is, "The sooner, the better." The sooner deviations from standards are brought to the attention of management, the sooner problems can be evaluated and corrected. The price variance should be identified when the purchasing function has completed its responsibilities.

The materials quantity variance is best isolated at the time that materials are placed into production. Materials are drawn for the number of units to be produced, according to the standard **bill of materials**, which is a listing of every component and the quantity of that component required to make the desired quantity of units. Any additional materials are usually drawn with an excess materials requisition slip, which is usually in a different colour from normal requisition slips. The use of the excess material requisition slip calls attention to the excessive usage of materials *while production is still in process* and provides an opportunity for early control of any developing problem. Excessive use of materials can result from many factors, including faulty machines, inferior quality of materials, untrained workers, and poor supervision. Management should consider these factors when deciding on the steps to take for eliminating an unfavourable quantity variance.

RESPONSIBILITY FOR THE VARIANCES

The materials price variance should be the responsibility of the individual who has the decision rights over the price—that is, the person who approves a price to be paid to suppliers. Generally speaking, the purchasing manager has control over the price paid for goods and is therefore responsible for any price variances. To fully understand why a variance occurred, the many factors that influence the prices paid for goods (including lot sizes, how the order is delivered, whether the order is a rush order, and the quality of materials purchased) should all be studied and understood. A deviation in any of these factors from what was assumed when the standards were set can result in a price variance. For example, purchase of second-grade rather than top-grade materials may result in a favourable price variance, since the lower-grade materials would generally be less costly (but perhaps less suitable for production). Although this may result in a favourable purchase price variance, it can lead to an unfavourable quantity variance, as explained later. Thus, it is important to also find out why the decision was made to accept a lower-grade material in the first place and whether a proper study of the implications of using lower-grade material was made.

There may be circumstances, however, when someone other than the purchasing manager is responsible for a materials price variance. Consider the situation in which a sales representative, in order to please a customer (and meet personal sales targets), promises a shorter delivery schedule. What is the effect of this? The production department will be required to juggle its schedule to accommodate this request, which will have a cascading effect on all the input resources required for production—materials, labour, and overhead. Consequently, the purchasing manager might be required to order materials in a hurry and pay a significantly higher price than planned. Who should be held responsible for the resulting unfavourable materials price variance? The sales department should be held responsible. Responsibility cannot be determined until the full story is uncovered, however, and sometimes no responsibility may be assigned. For example, it might be that this is a much sought after customer who is expected to place large orders in the future if the first order is handled satisfactorily, and, consequently, the company might decide to accept the price variance without making any changes to its operations.

With regard to quantity standards, it is generally the responsibility of the production department to see that materials usage is kept in line with standards. There may be times, however, when the *purchasing* department instead may be responsible for an unfavourable materials quantity variance. If the purchasing department obtains inferior-quality materials in an effort to economize on price, the materials may be unsuitable for use and may result in excessive waste. Thus, purchasing, rather than production, would be responsible for the quantity variance. At Colonial Pewter, production manager Tom Kuchel said that second-grade materials were the cause of the unfavourable materials quantity variance for June.

A word of caution: variance analysis should not be used as an excuse to punish line managers and workers. The goal of the control function should be to support the line managers and *assist* them in meeting the goals that they have participated in setting for the company. Dwelling excessively on the past, particularly in order to find someone to blame, can destroy morale and kill any cooperative spirit.

CONCEPT CHECK

4. The standard and actual prices per kilogram of raw material are $4.00 and $4.50, respectively. A total of 10,500 kilograms of raw material was purchased and then used to produce 5,000 units. The quantity standard allows two kilograms of the raw material per unit produced. What is the materials quantity variance?
   a. $5,000 unfavourable
   b. $5,000 favourable
   c. $2,000 favourable
   d. $2,000 unfavourable

5. Referring to the facts in Concept Check 4 above, what is the materials price variance?
   a. $5,250 favourable
   b. $5,250 unfavourable
   c. $5,000 unfavourable
   d. $5,000 favourable

*Note to student: See **Guidance Answers** online.*

Variance Analysis—Direct Labour Variances

LO3 • **Know** • **Apply**

CC17: Compute and explain direct labour variances.

The next task for Sherman was to compute the price and quantity variances for direct labour. The information for making the calculation was on his worksheet presented in Exhibit 11–8. Remember, if such a worksheet has not already been prepared, you may either prepare one or alternatively use the information from the standard cost card in Exhibit 11–1 and the actual results in Exhibit 11–3.

Direct Labour Rate Variance

The price variance for direct labour is commonly termed **labour rate variance**. The difference, $AR - SR$, between the actual (average) wage rate (AR) and the standard wage rate (SR) gives rise to this variance. From Exhibit 11–8 we can calculate the rate difference to be $(AR - SR) = (\$13.75 - \$14.00) = -\$0.25$. The company saved $0.25 per hour it used. The labour rate variance (i.e., the impact on operating income from saving 25 cents per hour) is calculated by the following formula:

$$
\begin{aligned}
\text{Labour rate variance} &= (AR - SR) \times AH \\
&= \left(\$13.75\,/\,\text{hour} - \$14.00\,/\,\text{hour}\right) \times 5{,}400\ \text{hours} \\
&= \$1{,}350\ \text{F}
\end{aligned}
$$

Alternatively, we have the following:

$$\text{Labour rate variance} = AR \times AH - SR \times AH$$

$$= \$13.75\,/\,\text{hour} \times 5{,}400\ \text{hours} - \$14.00\,/\,\text{hour} \times 5{,}400\ \text{hours}$$

$$= \$74{,}250 - \$75{,}600$$

$$= \$1{,}350\ \text{F}$$

During June, the company paid its direct labour workers $74,250, including employment taxes and fringe benefits, for 5,400 hours of work. This implies an average wage of $13.75 per hour. If the rate paid had been as per the standard cost card, the company would have paid $14 per hour. The cost for 5,400 hours would have been 5,400 × $14 = $75,600. Thus, the company saved a total of $1,350 because of the savings of 25 cents on each hour. The impact on operating income is that it is higher by $1,350 due to this favourable rate difference from what it would have been otherwise.

The variance computation is shown in Exhibit 11–12. Again, note that the information to calculate the variance can also be found on the worksheet in Exhibit 11–8 or in Exhibits 11–1 and 11–3.

Note that the column headings in Exhibit 11–12 are the same as those used in the prior two exhibits, except that in Exhibit 11–12, the terms *hours* and *rate* are used in place of *quantity* and *price*. On the worksheet in Exhibit 11–8, the more general labels of *price* and *quantity* are used for convenience.

EXHIBIT 11–12 Variance Analysis—Direct Labour, Colonial Pewter Company

	A	B	C	D	E	F
1		**Actual Quantity of Input at Actual Rate**		**Actual Quantity of Input at Standard Rate**		**Standard Quantity of Input Allowed for Actual Output at Standard Rate**
2		**AH × AR**		**AH × SR**		**SH × SR**
3	**Direct Labour**	5,400 hours × $13.75/hour		5,400 hours × $14/hour		5,000 hours* × $14/hour
4		$74,250	Spending variance	$75,600	Efficiency variance	$70,000
5			$(1,350)		$5,600	
6			F	Total variance, $4,250 U	U	
7						
8	*SQ allowed for actual output: 2,000 bookends × 2.5 hours/bookend = 5,000 hours					
9	F = Favourable; U = Unfavourable					

MANAGEMENT CONTROL USING THE LABOUR RATE VARIANCE

In most organizations, the rates paid to workers are quite predictable. Nevertheless, rate variances can arise through the way labour is used. Skilled workers with high hourly rates of pay may be given duties that require little skill and low hourly standard rates of pay. This will result in unfavourable labour rate variances, since the actual hourly rate of pay will exceed the standard rate specified for the particular task being performed. The reverse situation exists when unskilled or untrained workers are assigned to jobs that require some skill or training. The lower pay scale for these workers will result in favourable rate variances, although the workers may be inefficient. Finally, unfavourable rate variances can arise from overtime work at premium rates *if any portion of the overtime premium is added to the direct labour account.*

Who is responsible for controlling the labour rate variances? This is a tricky question because the question itself contains a trap: namely that a single rate can be identified, and that control over that single rate can be traced to a single individual. Remember that both the actual and the standard wage rates are averages taken over the many classes of labour a department might be employing. The average rate will depend not just on the number of different labour classes used but also on the particular mix of these classes. Because of this, the labour rate variance must be carefully analyzed for the causes before any action is taken.

Labour Efficiency Variance

The quantity variance for direct labour is called the **labour efficiency variance**. It measures the productivity of labour time. No other variance is more closely watched by management due to the belief that increasing the productivity of direct labour time is vital to reducing costs. This is particularly true in the case of labour-intensive operations and may not be relevant in highly automated environments. The formula for the labour efficiency variance is expressed as follows:

$$\text{Labour efficiency variance} = (AH - SH) \times SR$$

The information for using the formula is found on the worksheet in Exhibit 11–8. Note that the variance arises from the difference between actual hours used in production (denoted as AH—5,400 hours in June) and the standard hours allowed by the standard for producing 2,000 bookends (denoted as SH, which is SQI = 2.5 hours per bookend multiplied by Q = 2,000 bookends: SH = 2.5 hours/bookend × 2,000 bookends = 5,000 hours). The standard wage rate is $14/hour. Plugging into the formula, we have the following:

$$(5,400 \text{ hours} - 5,000 \text{ hours}) \times \$14 \,\big/\, \text{hour} = \$5,600 \text{ U}$$

The calculation of the variance is shown in Exhibit 11–12. This exhibit shows the above calculation in the following form:

$$
\begin{aligned}
\text{Labour efficiency variance} \quad &= \quad AH \times SR - SH \times SR \\
&= \quad 5,400 \text{ hours} \times \$14 \,/\, \text{hour} - 5,000 \text{ hours} \times \$14 \,/\, \text{hour} \\
&= \quad \$75,600 - \$70,000 \\
&= \quad \$5,600 \text{ U}
\end{aligned}
$$

The analysis reveals that the company, in producing 2,000 bookends, used a total of 5,400 hours at a cost of $75,600. But the company was only allowed a total of 5,000 hours to make 2,000 bookends and consequently only allowed for an expenditure of 5,000 × $14 = $70,000 on the flexible budget. In other words, the company used 400 more hours than it should have according to the standard, and consequently incurred 400 × $14 = $5,600 in additional expenditure on labour over the budget, resulting in operating income being reduced by this amount relative to the flexible budget.

What can management do about this variance?

MANAGEMENT CONTROL OF THE LABOUR EFFICIENCY VARIANCE

The possible causes of an unfavourable labour efficiency variance are poorly trained or poorly motivated workers; poor-quality materials, requiring more labour time in processing; faulty equipment, causing breakdowns and work interruptions; poor supervision of workers; and inaccurate standards. The managers in charge of production would generally be responsible for controlling the labour efficiency variance. However, the variance might be chargeable to purchasing if the acquisition of poor materials resulted in excessive labour processing time.

When the labour force is essentially fixed in the short term, another important cause of an unfavourable labour efficiency variance is insufficient demand for the output of the factory. There is idle time, which must be paid for but does not yield any output. In some firms, the labour-hours worked are fixed—particularly in the short term. It is difficult, and perhaps even unwise, to constantly adjust the workforce in response to changes in the workload.

When an unfavourable labour efficiency variance occurs because of idle time (excess of available hours for the activity level required to satisfy the demand), the work centre manager has two options: (1) accept the variance because it is not a symptom of poor operations but a mismatch between the available labour capacity and the need for that capacity, or (2) build inventory by producing more than the demand. But building inventory is a bad idea. Inventory—particularly work-in-process inventory—can lead to high defect rates, obsolete goods, and generally inefficient operations. Large finished goods inventory ties up valuable capital and can cause cash flow problems. As a consequence, when the workforce is fixed in the short term, managers must be cautious about how labour efficiency variances are used. Some managers advocate dispensing with labour efficiency variances entirely in such situations—at least for the purposes of motivating and controlling workers on the shop floor.

CONCEPT CHECK

6. Last month, a company worked 4,500 direct labour-hours, incurring direct labour costs of $38,250 in manufacturing 2,500 units of output. The plan was to manufacture 2,800 units using 5,600 hours at a cost of $44,800. What is the direct labour efficiency variance?
   a. $4,000 favourable
   b. $4,000 unfavourable
   c. $4,500 unfavourable
   d. $4,500 favourable

*Note to student: See **Guidance Answers** online.*

DECISION POINT

DEPARTMENT MANAGER

You are the manager of the computer-generated special effects department for a company that produces special effects for high-profile films. You receive a copy of this month's performance report for your department and discover a large labour efficiency variance that is unfavourable. What factors might have contributed to this unfavourable variance?

*Note to student: See **Guidance Answers** online.*

Variance Analysis—Variable Overhead Variances

LO3 ● **Know** ● **Apply**

CC18: Compute and explain variable overhead variances.

The final step in Terry Sherman's analysis of Colonial Pewter's variances for June was to compute the variable manufacturing overhead variances. The variable portion of manufacturing overhead can be analyzed using the same basic formulas that are used to analyze direct materials and direct labour.

Variable Overhead Spending (Rate) Variance

The **variable overhead spending variance** (or rate variance) arises because of the difference between the actual variable overhead cost and the cost from applying the standard rate to the actual quantity of the allocation base consumed during production. The company consumed 5,400 hours and incurred $15,390 in variable overhead cost. The implied actual rate paid for variable overhead per hour is $15,390 \div 5,400$ hours = $2.85/hour. The standard rate is $3 per hour. Thus, the difference $AR - SR = \$2.85 - \$3.00 = -\$0.15$ gives rise to the variance:

$$\text{Variable overhead rate variance} = (AR - SR) \times AH$$

$$= \$0.15 / \text{hour} \times 5,400 \text{ hours} = \$810 \text{ F}$$

Note that we have used AH for actual quantity as opposed to AQ to remind you that the variable overhead is allocated using a cost base such as labour-hours or machine-hours or something else.

An alternative approach does not calculate the implied actual rate. Instead, the actual cost is kept as a total and the cost from applying the standard rate to the actual quantity of the base is calculated. Then, the variance is computed as follows:

$$\text{Variable overhead rate variance} = \text{Actual cost} - SR \times AH$$

$$= \$15,390 - SR \times AH$$

$$= \$15,390 - \$3 / \text{hour} \times 5,400 \text{ hours}$$

$$= \$810 \text{ F}$$

The interpretation of the variable overhead rate variance is not easy; it simply indicates that more was spent on variable overhead than would be indicated from applying the predetermined allocation rate to the actual quantity of the base. Because of this, the variance is also referred to as spending variance. Since the predetermined rate is calculated by dividing the budgeted total variable overhead cost for the planned activity level by the budgeted quantity of the base, any errors in determining these two amounts will lead to the variance being observed. Assuming that there is confidence in the standard rate, an unfavourable spending variance would lead management to scrutinize the various components of the cost, such as indirect materials; labour used for support activities; and time spent on setups, ordering supplies, and so on.

It should not be surprising that the variable overhead spending variance is difficult to control, and identifying and holding one specific manager responsible and accountable is not easy. One strategy for a company is to break the variable overhead into various components and calculate the variance for each component separately, assuming that a predetermined allocation rate for each variable overhead cost element is available. This may help the company to identify appropriate individuals to whom the responsibility for the cost can be assigned.

Variable Overhead Efficiency Variance

The concept of efficiency in managing variable overhead is directly related to whether the resource being used as the cost driver has been used efficiently. Efficiency has little or nothing to do with how the resources constituting the various overhead elements were used and the associated costs. For Colonial Pewter, variable overhead is allocated using labour-hours. Therefore, if direct labour has an unfavourable efficiency variance, the **variable overhead efficiency variance** will also be unfavourable. But, because the labour wage rate and the variable overhead allocation rate are different, the magnitude of the labour efficiency variance and that of the variable overhead efficiency variance will not be equal.

The efficiency variance will arise due to the difference $(AQ - SQ)$ or, in this case, $(AH - SH)$, since the cost driver is labour-hours. The standard rate is $3 per hour. The variance is given by the following formula:

$$\text{Variable efficiency variance} \;=\; AQSQ \times SR$$

$$=\; (5{,}400 \text{ hours} - 5{,}000 \text{ hours}) \times \$3 \,/\, \text{hour}$$

$$=\; \$1{,}200 \text{ U}$$

Alternatively, we have the following:

$$\text{Variable overhead efficiency variance} \;=\; AQ \times SR - SQ \times SR$$

$$=\; 5{,}400 \text{ hours} \times \$3 \,/\, \text{hour} - \$5{,}000 \text{ hours} \times \$3 \,/\, \text{hour}$$

$$=\; \$16{,}200 - \$15{,}000$$

$$=\; \$1{,}200 \text{ U}$$

Exhibit 11–13 (which uses the more general label AQ instead of AH) lays out the computation of the variable overhead variances. The total variable overhead variance is \$810 F + \$1,200 U = \$390 U, which agrees with the amount in the flexible budget performance report in Exhibit 11–7.

EXHIBIT 11–13 Variable Overhead Variances, Colonial Pewter Company

	A	B	C	D	E	F
1		**Actual Quantity of Input at Actual Rate**		**Actual Quantity of Input at Standard Rate**		**Standard Quantity of Input Allowed for Actual Output at Standard Rate**
2		**$AQ \times AR$***		**$AQ \times SR$**		**$SQ \times SR$**
3	**Variable overhead**			5,400 hours × \$3/hour		5,000 hours[†] × \$3/hour
4		\$15,390	Spending variance	\$16,200	Efficiency variance	\$15,000
5			\$(810)		\$1,200	
6			F	Total variance, \$390 U	U	
7	*Note that AR is usually not observable and is an average rate. Thus, actual variable overhead costs are observed as a total.					
8	[†]SQ allowed for actual output: 2,000 bookends × 2.5 hours/bookend = 5,000 hours					
9	F = Favourable; U = Unfavourable					

INTERPRETATION AND CONTROL OF THE VARIABLE OVERHEAD EFFICIENCY VARIANCE

As just explained, efficiency in the case of variable overhead cost will pertain to the cost driver—the labour resource—and not to the overhead resources themselves (e.g., power-hours, lubricant quantities, efficiencies in the setup times, etc.). This makes assigning the accountabilities to managers difficult. You want managers to manage the activities giving rise to the consumption of the underlying overhead resources, but the variance is being based on the use of labour-hours. The management of labour may not be the primary responsibility of the manager who is responsible for the overhead. In such cases, there will be a problem because the overhead manager is being evaluated for the management of a resource over which he or she has no control. A strong correlation between labour-hours consumption and overhead resource consumption would reduce concerns that management's attention is not properly focused on the underlying causes of inefficiency in the use of variable overhead.

At Colonial Pewter, the company used 400 more hours than it should have; therefore, the variable overhead efficiency variance is unfavourable. The responsibility appropriately should reside with the manager who controls the allocation and the use of direct labour. It is inappropriate to draw conclusions about efficiency in using variable overhead resources simply from looking at the efficiency variance. The only conclusion possible is that the underlying variable overhead cost allocation base has or has not been used efficiently.

CONCEPT CHECK

7. During the previous month, 4,500 direct labour-hours were actually worked and 2,500 units were produced. Each unit is supposed to take two direct labour-hours, and the plan was to make 2,800 units. In the plan, the budget for variable overhead was $14,000. What is the variable overhead efficiency variance?
   a. $5,000 favourable
   b. $5,000 unfavourable
   c. $2,500 unfavourable
   d. $2,500 favourable

*Note to student: See **Guidance Answers** online.*

Summary of Variable Cost Variances

Before proceeding further, it might be useful to summarize the standard and actual costs and the variances for Colonial Pewter Company; this is done in Exhibit 11–14. Comparing the total actual and standard variable costs for 2,000 units simply tells us that Colonial incurred an additional $8,140 in variable costs over what was budgeted (slightly more than 7.6% of variable standard cost). The numbers in Exhibit 11–14 clearly indicate that the cost increase was due to excessive use of the two inputs: direct materials and direct labour. Remember that variable overhead is allocated using labour-hours as the base; therefore, the variable overhead efficiency variance is a reflection of the inefficiency in the use of direct labour-hours. Note also that managers at Colonial were able to acquire all three inputs at lower than standard prices.

EXHIBIT 11–14 Summary of Standard Costs and Variances for Colonial Pewter Company

	Direct Materials	Direct Labour	Variable Overhead	Total
Standard cost/unit of output	$ 11.00	$ 35.00	$ 7.50	$ 53.50
Standard cost/2,000 units	$22,000	$70,000	$15,000	$107,000
Actual cost/2,000 units	$25,500	$74,250	$15,390	$115,140
Price-related variance	$ 900 F	$ 1,350 F	$ 810 F	$ 3,060 F
Quantity-related variance	$ 4,400 U	$ 5,600 U	$ 1,200 U	$ 11,200 U
Total variance	$ 3,500 U	$ 4,250 U	$ 390 U	$ 8,140 U

IN BUSINESS

INTERNAL STANDARDS OR EXTERNAL BENCHMARKS?

Some critics argue that standard costing systems have become obsolete in the modern business environment, which is characterized by shortened product life cycles, rapid design, and process changes. However, a review of research pertaining to managerial accounting practices suggests that standard costing is very much alive, although standards do not have to be internally developed. Many organizations (manufacturing and nonmanufacturing) use external standards (or *benchmarks*), rather than internal ones, to assess their performance along various dimensions. A recent survey of facilities management (FM) divisions within North American universities suggests that 54% benchmark their FM operations largely by comparing themselves with other universities on measures such as cleaning costs, maintenance costs, and energy expenditures. In addition, they may also use benchmarks established by the International Facilities Management Association.

Sources: R. Faruquee, *Performance Measurement and Benchmarking in Facilities Management: A Survey of North American Universities*, MBA thesis, University of Saskatchewan, 2003; A. Zoysa and S. Herath, "Standard Costing in Japanese Firms: Re-examination of Its Significance in the New Manufacturing Environment," *Industrial Management and Data Systems, 107(2)* (2007): 271–283.

MANAGERIAL ACCOUNTING IN ACTION

THE WRAP-UP

In preparation for the scheduled meeting to discuss his analysis of Colonial Pewter's standard costs and variances, Terry Sherman distributed Exhibits 11–1 through 11–14, with supporting explanations, to the management group of Colonial Pewter. This included company president J. D. Wriston, production manager Tom Kuchel, and purchasing manager Janet Warner. Wriston opened the meeting with the following question:

Wriston: Terry, I think I understand the report you distributed, but just to make sure, would you mind giving the highlights of what you found?

Sherman: As you can see, the biggest problems are the unfavourable materials quantity variance of $4,400 and the unfavourable labour efficiency variance of $5,600.

Wriston: Tom, you're the production boss. What do you think is responsible for the unfavourable labour efficiency variance?

Kuchel: It pretty much has to be the new production workers. Our experienced workers shouldn't have much problem meeting the standard of 2.5 hours per unit. We all knew that there would be some inefficiency for a while as we brought new people on board.

Wriston: No one is disputing that, Tom. However, $5,600 is a lot of money. Is this problem likely to go away very soon?

Kuchel: I hope so. If we were to contrast the last two weeks of June with the first two weeks, I'm sure we would see some improvement.

Wriston: I don't want to beat up on you, Tom, but this is a significant problem. Can you do something to accelerate the training process?

Kuchel: Sure. I could pair up each of the new guys with one of our old-timers and have them work together for a while. It would slow down our older guys a bit, but I'll bet the new workers would learn a lot.

Wriston: Let's try it. Now, what about that $4,400 unfavourable materials quantity variance?

Kuchel: Are you asking me?

Wriston: Well, I would like someone to explain it.

Kuchel: Don't look at me. It's that iron-contaminated pewter that Janet bought on her "special deal."

Warner: We got rid of that stuff months ago.

Wriston: Hold your horses. We're not trying to figure out whom to blame here. I just want to understand what happened. If we can understand what happened, maybe we can fix it.

Sherman: Tom, are the new workers generating a lot of scrap?

Kuchel: Yeah, I guess so.

Wriston: I think that might be part of the problem. Can you do anything about it?

Kuchel: I can watch the scrap closely for a few days to see where it's being generated. If it is the new workers, I can have the old-timers work with them on the problem when I team them up.

Wriston: What about the overhead?

Sherman: Well, variable overhead consists of a number of different items all captured in a single cost pool and allocated using labour-hours.

Wriston: And I see that we have used more labour-hours than the standard allowed.

Kuchel: It is partly the new workers and partly a result of unexpected breakdowns perhaps due to the poor-quality materials. I'll look into it.

Wriston: Good. Let's reconvene in a few weeks and review what has happened. Hopefully, we can get those unfavourable variances under control.

Fixed Overhead Cost Variances

The Nature of Fixed Costs of Manufacturing

LO4 ● **Know**

CC19: Explain the nature of fixed costs of manufacturing.

It is natural when analyzing costs to focus on the behaviour of those costs in response to changes in their cost drivers. We tend to think of costs being incurred due to causes, and during analysis we gravitate toward the notion of a cost driver and how that driver induces the incurrence of costs. Since fixed costs, in total, by their very nature are fixed over a range of values for any volume-based cost driver, managing volume drivers will not help to control the fixed costs. A different way of thinking is needed.

Fixed costs of manufacturing include facility costs such as property taxes, insurance, heating and power costs, costs for supplies that are periodically purchased in lump-sum quantities, salaries of factory managers and production personnel, lease costs of machinery and equipment, and so on. Such costs occur because we have purchased or rented or leased plant, equipment, buildings, and facilities that must be powered regardless of the level of activity in them. We have acquired services or resources in lump-sum amounts at the outset of the operating cycle or throughout the operating cycle and are contractually obligated to make a fixed payment. Such costs have nothing to do with how much or how little output is produced.

Control of Fixed Overhead Costs

LO4 • **Know**

CC20: Explain the control issues pertaining to fixed overhead costs and the distinction between normal and standard costing systems.

Now let's consider managing the fixed costs of manufacturing. At the beginning of the planning/budgeting cycle, management must estimate and budget the total amount of these costs that the company is expecting to incur. The budgeted amount will stay fixed over the range of values for the main activity level driver.

LO4 • **Know** • **Apply**

CC21: Explain the concept of denominator activity level, and compute the predetermined fixed overhead allocation rate.

During the period, management will allocate the fixed cost to production using a predetermined overhead allocation rate, which will result in a total amount of allocated cost. The predetermined overhead rate is used to apply fixed overhead cost to the cost allocation base. It is calculated as follows:

$$\text{Predetermined fixed overhead application rate} = \frac{\text{Budgeted fixed manufacturing overhead cost}}{\text{Estimated activity level of the allocation base}}$$

Also, during the operating period, management will make payments for the various fixed cost items. At the end of the period, there will be the total amount of fixed overhead cost actually paid.

There are, in sum, three distinct amounts pertaining to fixed manufacturing cost:

1. Actual fixed overhead cost
2. Budgeted fixed overhead cost
3. Allocated (i.e., applied) fixed overhead cost.

Performance evaluation with respect to managing fixed overhead costs is essentially comparing the above three distinct fixed overhead cost amounts as shown in the diagram below:

	A	B	C	D	E	F	G	H	I	J
1	Actual Fixed Overhead Cost				Budgeted Fixed Overhead Cost				Applied Fixed Overhead Cost	
2										
3										
4			Budget variance				Volume variance			
5		(Exists because the actual cost differs from the cost in the numerator in the predetermined overhead rate calculation)				(Exists because the denominator activity level differs from the activity level of the allocation base to which the predetermined rate is applied)				
6										
7			Total variance, under- or overapplied fixed overhead							
8										

Comparing the actual fixed overhead cost to the applied fixed overhead, as was explained in Chapter 3, results in under- or overapplied fixed overhead. Why? It exists because the fixed overhead cost is applied to production units using the predetermined rate. Because this rate is a quotient of the numerator divided by the denominator, looking at each of these will help explain why the actual cost will be different from the allocated cost. When the actual cost is different from the numerator of the rate (the budgeted fixed overhead cost), the difference is called the **fixed overhead budget variance**. The analysis of the budget variance involves understanding why the actual spending on fixed overhead was different from the planned expenditure.

Next, consider the denominator in the rate calculation. This is the estimated activity level of the allocation base for the operating period and is called the **denominator activity level**. The denominator activity level will typically be set to equal the "normal" volume of activity. This is sometimes also referred to as the practical capacity of the facility. When the predetermined rate is applied to allocate fixed overhead, the quantity of the allocation base to which the rate is applied will be different from the denominator activity level. This difference gives rise to the difference between the budgeted cost and the allocated cost and is called the **fixed overhead volume variance** or **production volume variance**.

The analysis of the **volume variance** involves understanding why the quantity of the allocation base to which the predetermined rate is applied is different from the denominator activity level. This is an analysis of the utilization of the production capacity (i.e., the difference between the planned or normal activity level and the actual activity level). This is not an easy topic to learn because it deals with *activity control* and not *cost control*. Until now, all of the variances we have calculated have been related to how costs are managed in terms of purchasing and productivity. The volume variance, however, has nothing to do with either spending on resources or productivity of operations.

We can conclude that cost control over fixed manufacturing overhead has two parts. The first part concerns whether actual spending for fixed overhead cost compares favourably with the amount budgeted in the static as well as the flexible budget. The second part concerns the implications of a *volume difference* between the quantity of the allocation base to which the predetermined overhead rate is applied to allocate the fixed overhead and the denominator activity level of the allocation base. We consider each of these two parts in more detail next.

Fixed Overhead Budget Variance

LO4 • **Know** • **Apply**

CC22: Explain and compute fixed overhead cost budget variance.

The **budget variance** is the difference between the actual fixed overhead cost and the amount budgeted in the flexible budget. We reference the flexible budget because it is the *comparison* budget for performance evaluation, as was explained before, even though in the case of fixed costs the budgeted amount is unchanged between the static and the flexible budget. To avoid giving the mistaken impression that the fixed cost in the flexible budget is different from the fixed cost originally estimated in the planning (static) budget, we will refer to the fixed cost in the flexible budget simply as "Budgeted fixed overhead cost."

At Colonial Pewter, the actual overhead cost for June was $21,100. (See Exhibit 11–3.) The budgeted amount is $22,000. The comparison of these two amounts yields the budget variance:

$$\text{Budget variance} \quad = \quad \text{Actual fixed overhead cost} - \text{Budgeted fixed overhead cost}$$
$$= \quad \$21{,}100 - \$22{,}000$$
$$= \quad \$900 \text{ F}$$

The favourable variance indicates that the company spent less on fixed overhead than it had expected. And therefore net income is higher by this amount than it would otherwise have been. This good news needs to be investigated further and the reasons understood.

ANALYSIS OF THE BUDGET VARIANCE

There can be numerous reasons for a budget variance, some under the control of the manager responsible and some not. For example, facility costs may exceed the budget because more money was spent on cleanups or fixing unforeseen problems to the facilities, or bills were consistently paid late, incurring late charges, or there was a tax reassessment that required the payment of an amount different from that budgeted, and so on.

Remember also that there can be correlation between the variable cost variances and the budget variance. Suppose, for example, that workers are not properly trained and thus use more time than specified by the standard. Now, also suppose that the poorly trained workers waste materials and make a mess of the facilities that requires unanticipated cleanup costs, etc. This can show up as an unfavourable budget variance and unfavourable materials quantity variance. In this type of situation, problems from one area—the poor training of workers—spread to a number of other areas and lead to correlating variances. A careful investigation of all the variances will help managers understand what is happening and take appropriate corrective actions.

For Terry Sherman, the above discussion suggests some potential avenues for further investigation if he wants to know the reasons for the favourable budget variance in June.

Overhead Application in a Standard Costing System and the Volume Variance

LO4   ● **Know**   ● **Apply**

CC23: Explain and compute the fixed overhead cost volume variance.

Recall that the volume variance arises because the denominator level of activity that is used to compute the predetermined overhead application rate is different from the quantity of the allocation base to which that rate is applied. To properly compute and interpret the volume variance, you should know how to calculate the quantity of the allocation base to which the predetermined rate is *applied* and understand why it will be different from the denominator activity level. For this, you need to learn how overhead is applied in a standard costing system and how it is different from the procedure in a normal costing system. We will first explain each costing system and then, using an example, illustrate how overhead is applied in each system.

NORMAL COSTING SYSTEM

A normal costing system is one where the overhead allocation is based on a predetermined overhead application rate, and the rate is applied to the *actual quantity of the allocation base consumed during a period.*

STANDARD COSTING SYSTEM

A standard costing system is one where the overhead allocation is based on a predetermined overhead application rate, and the rate is applied to the *standard quantity of the allocation base allowed for the actual quantity of output produced in a period.* Exhibit 11–15 illustrates the distinction between these costing systems and is applicable to both variable and fixed overhead cost.

EXHIBIT 11–15 Applied Overhead Costs: Normal Costing System versus Standard Costing System

Normal Costing System Manufacturing Overhead		Standard Costing System Manufacturing Overhead	
Actual overhead costs incurred	Applied overhead costs: Actual activity level × Predetermined overhead rate	Actual overhead costs incurred	Applied overhead costs: Standard activity level allowed for actual output × Predetermined overhead rate
Under- or overapplied overhead		Under- or overapplied overhead	

EXAMPLE

Consider a small manufacturing company where the overhead costs are allocated to products using direct labour-hours as the allocation base. The budgeted amount of fixed overhead costs is $9,600. The standard cost card has specified that each unit of product should use two labour-hours. The planned production level, also the normal volume, is 1,200 units. Thus, the planned (*SQ* for 1,200 units) total labour-hours will be 2,400 hours. This is the denominator activity level. The predetermined fixed overhead rate will thus be $9,600 ÷ 2,400 hours = $4 per hour. The actual results show a total of 2,200 hours were consumed in producing 1,300 units, and the fixed manufacturing overhead was $9,400.

Calculate the amount of the allocated fixed overhead cost under each of the following two assumptions: (1) the company uses a normal costing system, and (2) the company uses a standard costing system. Calculate the difference between the denominator activity level and the quantity of the allocation base used to allocate the fixed cost in each of the two costing systems:

1. *Fixed overhead application in a normal costing system.* Overhead is allocated on the basis of *actual hours* consumed in the production of 1,300 units using the predetermined rate. Given the predetermined fixed overhead rate of $4 per hour and 2,200 actual hours, the total fixed overhead cost allocated equals $4 × 2,200 hours = $8,800. The denominator activity level is 2,400 hours, the quantity of the allocation base is 2,200 hours, and the *volume difference* is 200 hours. The overhead cost is allocated to 200 fewer hours than planned.

2. *Fixed overhead application in a standard costing system.* The overhead cost is allocated on the basis of the *standard number of hours allowed to produce 1,300 units* (i.e., 1,300 units × 2 hours/unit = 2,600 hours). The total fixed overhead cost allocated is $4/hour × 2,600 hours = $10,400. The denominator activity level is 2,400 hours, and the quantity of the allocation base is 2,600 hours, so the difference is −200 hours, implying that cost was allocated to more hours than the denominator activity level.

The normal cost system allocates $8,800, whereas the standard costing system allocates $10,400. The allocated cost is not the same because the quantity of the allocation base to which the predetermined rate is applied is not the same in both systems. The original budgeted fixed overhead cost was $9,600. You can immediately see that in each system there is a difference between the budgeted cost and the cost allocated. In the standard costing system, the difference is $9,600 − $10,400 = −$800; for the normal costing system, the difference is $9,600 − $8,800 = $800.

The difference of −$800 in the standard costing system is the volume variance. It is evaluated as favourable because there was an overallocation relative to budget. Net income calculated using the *budgeted* fixed overhead cost will be greater by $800 than the net income calculated using the *allocated* fixed overhead cost. The company operated at an activity level above that planned for the period. This means that the fixed overhead cost was spread over more units of the allocation base than was originally budgeted, with each unit of product "absorbing" less cost than what was planned. We will explore this interpretation in more depth below after we calculate the volume variance for Colonial Pewter.

The $800 difference between the budgeted cost and the allocated cost in the normal costing system is *not* a volume variance. Since fewer hours were used to make more units than was planned (2,200 hours for 1,300 units, instead of 2,400 hours for 1,200 units), the $800 difference in the normal costing system reflects *both* the volume (i.e., the activity level difference of 1,300 units made versus 1,200 units planned) *and* the efficiency in the actual use of the allocation base (used 2,200 hours instead of the planned 2,400 hours). Consequently, the difference between the budgeted fixed overhead and the allocated fixed overhead is not analyzed by management of companies using the normal costing system.

The main point of this example is to understand the overhead application process and to realize that the quantity of the allocation base to which the predetermined rate is applied to determine total allocated fixed overhead cost will differ from the denominator activity level, and that this is the source of the overhead volume variance. The quantity of the allocation base in the standard costing system is $SQ = SQI × Q$, the standard quantity of the allocation base allowed for the actual output.

HELPFUL HINT

Remember that the concept of the denominator activity level (2,400 hours) is distinct from the concept of the *SQ* of the allocation base (2,600 hours). The denominator activity level is used to calculate the predetermined rate, whereas the *SQ* for actual output is the quantity of the allocation base to which the rate is applied. Notice that the actual hours *never enter into the calculation of the volume variance!* In other words, it is irrelevant to the calculation of the volume variance that more units were made using fewer hours (2,200 hours) than either the number of hours budgeted originally (2,400 hours) or the actual number of units made (2,600 hours).

Volume Variance for Colonial Pewter

Colonial Pewter estimated that, for the month of June, the fixed costs would be $22,000. The allocation base for fixed overhead was chosen to be direct labour-hours. To estimate the number of direct labour-hours to use in the denominator, Sherman proceeded in two steps. First, he determined the planned activity level of the output for the period. This was 1,800 bookends. Second, from the standard cost card, which specified that each bookend should require 2.5 hours (the standard quantity per unit), he calculated the total planned number of hours as 1,800 units × 2.5 hours/unit = 4,500 hours. This is the denominator level of activity. It is very important to realize that this calculation recognizes that the 4,500 hours figure is *derived* from the *planned* activity level of production. The predetermined overhead rate for June (as well as for the entire year) is as follows:

$$PDR = \frac{\text{Estimated fixed overhead cost}}{\text{Estimated activity level of the allocation base for the period}}$$

$$= \frac{\$22,000}{4,500 \text{ hours}} = \$4.889 \text{ per direct labour-hour}$$

Note that *PDR* denotes "predetermined overhead rate." This calculation is made before the start of the year, and the predetermined overhead rate is used to apply overhead to product via the allocation base throughout the year. The rate is fixed throughout the operating cycle even if the actual activity level changes during the period from the amount estimated in the denominator of the rate formula. The reason is that if the denominator activity level is changed, the rate will change and then the cost allocation to the product will change, and this will lead to a change in product cost and, possibly, price. Managers dislike introducing volatility into product costing and thus seek to avoid it if possible. To maintain stable allocations, a single calculation is made at the beginning and the calculated rate is used throughout the year. This is the practice followed at Colonial Pewter.

With the calculation of the predetermined rate completed, Sherman applied the rate to the standard quantity of labour-hours allowed for making 2,000 bookends: 2.5 hours/bookend × 2,000 bookends = 5,000 hours. The cost allocated is $4.889/hour × 5,000 hours = $24,445. Now the volume variance can be calculated:

$$\text{Volume variance} = \text{Budgeted fixed overhead cost} - \text{Applied fixed overhead cost}$$

$$= \$22,000 - \$24,445$$

$$= \$2,445 \text{ F}$$

There is an alternative formula for the volume variance:

Volume variance = (Quantity of allocation base used to calculate the predetermined rate − Standard quantity of allocation base allowed for the actual output made) × Predetermined rate

That is,

$$\text{Volume variance} = (\text{Denominator activity level of the allocation base}$$

$$- SQ \text{ of the allocation base allowed for actual Q}) \times \text{Predetermined rate}$$

$$= (4,500 \text{ hours} - 5,000 \text{ hours}) \times \$4.889 \big/ \text{ hour} = \$2,445 \text{ F}$$

The variance is favourable because the overhead cost is applied to 5,000 hours as opposed to the planned activity level of 4,500 hours, meaning the overhead rate was applied to more hours than was originally planned. This point is explained below. The above computation of the two fixed overhead cost variances is illustrated in Exhibit 11–16.

EXHIBIT 11–16 Fixed Overhead Variances, Colonial Pewter Company

	A	B	C	D	E	F
2		**Actual Fixed Overhead Cost**		**Budgeted Fixed Overhead Cost**		**Applied Fixed Overhead Cost**
3						5,000 h† × $4.889/h
4	**Fixed overhead**	$21,100	Budget variance	$22,000*	Volume variance	$24,445
5			$900 F		$2,445 F	
6				Total variance = $ 3,345 F		
7	*As originally budgeted in the static (or planning budget). This will also be the amount in the flexible budget					
8	since fixed cost will not vary with output volume in the relevant range. This figure can also be expressed as follows:					
9	Budgeted fixed overhead cost = *PDR* × Denominator activity level = $4.889/hour × 4,500 hours = $22,000					
10	†SQ allowed for actual output = *SQI* × Actual *Q* = 2.5 h/bookend × 2,000 bookends = 5,000 h					
11	F = Favourable; U = Unfavourable					

HELPFUL HINT

Students often mistakenly calculate the fixed overhead cost in the flexible budget using the actual quantity of the allocation base. Recall that the actual hours for June were 5,400 hours. Applying the rate to this amount gives $4.889/hour × 5,400 hours = $26,400. A common error is to think that this is the amount of the fixed overhead in the flexible budget. But remember that the fixed cost will not vary across budgets as long as the budgeted output levels are within the relevant range. Therefore, $26,400 is *not* the budgeted fixed overhead cost. It is also *not* the applied fixed overhead cost in a *standard* costing system. It is the applied fixed overhead in a *normal* costing system and thus has no role to play here and should not be calculated to obtain a volume variance.

CONCEPT CHECK

8. Puzzle Company is transitioning to a standard costing system from a normal costing system. During the transition phase, management is receiving information from both systems. In the previous month, the normal costing system reported that fixed overhead cost was overapplied by $8,000 relative to the actual fixed overhead for the month of $32,000. Fixed overhead is applied on the basis of direct labour-hours, and in

the last month a total of 16,000 hours were worked and 5,000 units were made. The original budget for the month called for a production quantity of 5,600 units using 16,800 hours. What amount will the standard costing system report as the volume variance for the previous month?

a. $4,500 F

c. $8,000 F

b. $4,500 U

d. $8,000 U

Note to student: See **Guidance Answers** *online.*

Interpretation of the Volume Variance

The volume variance does not measure over- or underspending. The variance arises because 200 more bookends were produced during the budget period than planned and, as a consequence, overhead cost was applied to 2.5 hours/bookend × 200 bookends = 500 more hours than the hours in the denominator of the predetermined rate formula. That is, instead of overhead being applied to 4,500 hours as planned, it was applied to 5,000 hours.

This means that we spread the total budgeted fixed costs over a greater number of units; each unit of product "absorbs" a lesser portion of the overhead than planned. The original predetermined rate was $4.889 per direct labour-hour. With 5,000 hours allowed for making 2,000 bookends, the budgeted fixed overhead cost will be driven onto the units of production at the rate of $22,000 ÷ 5,000 hours = $4.40 per direct labour-hour instead. Fixed overhead cost for each hour is priced at $4.889 − $4.40 = $0.489 less than before. The "benefit" of this is 5,000 hours − $0.489/hour = $2,445, the favourable volume variance.

Alternatively, if you were to determine net income based on the budgeted fixed overhead cost ($22,000), and then determine net income using the allocated fixed overhead cost ($24,445) while keeping all other data the same, then net income based on budgeted fixed overhead cost would be higher by $2,445 than the net income using the allocated fixed overhead cost. This is why the variance is evaluated as favourable. Now you can see that the favourable nature of the variance arises solely from the overallocation relative to the budget triggered by a higher than planned level of activity. The true cause of this variance is the higher activity level than the planned level. Managers have to focus their attention on understanding why 200 more bookends were produced. There can be many reasons, such as an increase in orders (perhaps due to an improvement in the economy or due to increased marketing effort), or an increase in production to build inventory or take advantage of lower input prices. Each possible reason should be studied carefully to ensure that the organization truly benefited. For example, building inventory is not necessarily a good thing because it ties up funds that might be used for other activities. For plans to be truly effective in guiding operations, an effort must be made to ensure that planned production levels are achieved.

A CAUTIONARY NOTE REGARDING FIXED OVERHEAD COST

Expressing the lump-sum fixed overhead cost on a per-unit basis by the predetermined allocation rate is a necessary step for the purpose of product costing. Beyond this purpose, it is not recommended that fixed cost be considered on a per-unit basis because it can mislead someone to believe that each additional unit of activity will cause cost to increase by the amount of the predetermined rate. For example, Terry Sherman would be mistaken if he thought that for every additional hour of labour used, fixed cost would increase by $4.889.

The manager has to keep clearly in mind that fixed overhead costs come in large, indivisible pieces. Expressing fixed costs on a per-unit or per-hour basis, though necessary for product costing for external reports, is artificial. Increases or decreases in activity, in fact, have no effect on total fixed costs within the relevant range of activity. Even though fixed costs are expressed on a per-unit or per-hour basis, they are not proportional to activity. In a sense, the volume variance is the error that occurs, *relative to the flexible budget,* as a result of treating fixed costs as variable costs in the costing system. In other words:

- If the normal and actual production levels are the same, then the denominator activity level and standard hours allowed for the output of the period are the same, and there is no volume variance.

- If actual production is less than normal production, then the denominator activity level is greater than the standard hours allowed for the output of the period, and the volume variance is unfavourable. This signals that the available facilities are underutilized.

- If actual production is greater than normal production, as in the example, then the denominator activity is less than the standard hours allowed for the output of the period, and the volume variance is favourable. This signals that utilization levels are higher than planned.

A Note on the Denominator Activity Level

As was mentioned earlier, the denominator activity level should be based on the normal volume of activity that represents the practical capacity of the facilities and the volume of activity that on average the business will plan to produce. Therefore, in most periods, normal volume and planned volume will be the same. But they can be different. For example, consider a firm with a practical capacity of 2,000 units per period. The theoretical capacity (i.e., the maximum capacity) is 2,700 units. For the next period, due to a fire at a competitor's factory, the firm expects to be able to step in to supply some of the shortfall and thus *plans to make 2,300* units. The actual production volume was 2,500 units for the period. Assuming that the standard calls for 1.2 machine-hours per unit produced and that fixed overhead is allocated using machine-hours, what will be the denominator activity level of machine-hours to use to calculate the predetermined rate?

The answer is found by using the normal volume of output: 2,000 units × 1.2 hours/unit = 2,400 hours. The logic is that the company planned to make more than 2,000 units only as a short-term response to the supply shortage expected in the market. Since the planned increase to production was only a short-term phenomenon, there is no need to revise the predetermined allocation rate. The volume variance will be based on the difference between 2,000 units and 2,500 units (i.e., 500 units). When analyzing the volume variance, management will note that 300 units of the 500-unit difference result from the company *intentionally* increasing production from the normal volume level. Thus, the volume difference, which will require further explanation, is the 200-unit difference between 2,300 units and 2,500 units. The volume variance will be favourable regardless of whether it is based on the difference of 500 units or 200 units.

Because of the confusion that can arise concerning the interpretation of the volume variance, some companies present the volume variance in physical units (e.g., labour-hours) rather than in dollars. These companies feel that stating the variance in physical units gives management a clearer signal concerning the cause of the variance, or at least leads to the right questions being asked. In other words, remember what we said earlier: volume variance is about control over activity, and not control over resource spending or resource deployment and use (i.e., productivity).

DECISION POINT

VICE-PRESIDENT OF PRODUCTION

One of the company's factories produces a single product. The factory recently reported a significant unfavourable volume variance for the year. Sales for that product were less than anticipated. What should you do?

*Note to student: See **Guidance Answers** online.*

Overhead Variances and Under- or Overapplied Overhead Cost

LO4   • **Know**   • **Apply**

CC24: Explain overhead variances, and compute the over- or underapplied overhead.

Four variances relating to overhead cost have been computed for Colonial Pewter Company in this chapter. They are as follows:

Variable overhead spending variance	$ 810 F
Variable overhead efficiency variance	1,200 U
Fixed overhead budget variance	900 F
Fixed overhead volume variance	2,445 F
Total overhead variance	$2,955 F

Recall from Chapter 3 that over- or underapplied overhead is the difference between the actual overhead costs incurred during a period and the amount of overhead applied to products during a period. The overhead variances we have computed in this chapter partition the under- or overapplied overhead. Consequently, *the sum of the overhead variances equals the under- or overapplied overhead cost for a period.*

Furthermore, in a standard costing system, unfavourable variances are equivalent to underapplied overhead, and favourable variances are equivalent to overapplied overhead. Unfavourable variances occur because more was spent on overhead than the standards allow. Underapplied overhead occurs when more was spent on overhead than was applied to products during the period. But in a standard costing system, the standard amount of overhead allowed and the amount of overhead applied to products are exactly the same (see column F in Exhibits 11–13 and 11–16). Therefore, in a standard costing system, unfavourable total overhead variance and underapplied overhead are the same thing, and favourable total overhead variance and overapplied overhead are the same thing. Managers seeking to know why overhead was over- or underapplied will want to look at the overhead cost variances for the answers.

For Colonial Pewter Company, the total overhead variance was $2,955 favourable. Therefore, its overhead cost was overapplied by $2,955 for June. The main contributors to this were the favourable variable overhead spending variance, the budget variance, and the volume variance.

WORKING IT OUT

VCT Corporation has estimated in its static budget that it expects to incur $800,000 in fixed manufacturing overhead. The volume of activity budgeted in the static budget is 50,000 units. The company actually produced 40,000 units. Overhead is allocated on the basis of direct labour-hours, and the static budget estimated that 50,000 labour-hours will be required. Actual hours expended in the year amounted to 35,000. The budgeted labour rate is $40 per hour.

Required:

1. Calculate the overhead volume variance.
2. Determine if the variable overhead efficiency variance is favourable or unfavourable.
3. Consider the statement, "Fixed overhead volume variance does not relate to efficiency with which the allocation base was used by the company. Instead, it is a manifestation of overhead cost allocation variance due to the difference between the planned level of production activity and the actual level of production activity." Using the calculation made earlier, explain if the statement is true or false.
4. What is the meaning of "unfavourable" or "favourable" in the context of the overhead volume variance? Respond by referring to the calculations made in parts (1) and (2).

SOLUTION TO WORKING IT OUT

1. The predetermined fixed overhead allocation rate is $800,000 ÷ 50,000 hours = $16/hour. The static budget quantity of labour-hours of 50,000 is used as the denominator volume.

   To calculate the SQ for the actual volume of output, the standard quantity of labour-hours per unit of output must be calculated. This is SQI = 50,000 hours ÷ 50,000 units = 1 hour per unit of output.

   Thus, the standard quantity of hours allowed for the actual output achieved is $SQ = SQI \times Q$ = 1 hour/unit × 40,000 units = 40,000 hours. This is the quantity of the allocation base to which the predetermined rate will be applied to allocate fixed overhead cost.

Budgeted fixed overhead cost:	$800,000
Allocated fixed overhead cost	
(SQ × allocation rate):	40,000 hours × $16/hour = 640,000
Fixed overhead volume variance:	$160,000 U

Alternative derivation:

Overhead volume variance = (Denominator activity level − SQ) × Predetermined rate

$$= (50,000 \text{ hours} - 40,000 \text{ hours}) \times \$16/\text{hour}$$

$$= \$160,000 \text{ U}$$

2. **Variable overhead efficiency variance** = **(Actual hours−Standard hours allowed for the actual output) × Standard rate**

= **(35,000 hours − 40,000 hours) × Standard rate**

= **− 5,000 hours × SR**

This is a favourable variance since actual hours are less than the standard hours allowed for the actual output. It is *not* necessary to know the variable overhead application rate to determine if the variance will be favourable or unfavourable. The rate will be needed, however, to compute the magnitude of the variance.

3. The statement is true. The calculation made in part (1) demonstrates that the volume variance arises only because 40,000 units were made instead of the planned 50,000 units, or equivalently that 40,000 hours were used instead of 50,000 hours. The difference of 10,000 hours does not signal the inefficient use of labour because the use of 40,000 hours is exactly what is expected for an output level of 40,000 units. Indeed, since actual labour-hours used are 35,000 for 40,000 units, showing that labour has been used efficiently, it can be seen that the volume variance is unrelated to the concept of efficiency.

4. The overhead volume variance is unfavourable because the allowed quantity of the driver for the actual production quantity achieved does not absorb all of the fixed overhead being allocated. Think of the variance as an indicator of whether the *cost allocation* is favourable or not. The manager had planned to fully allocate $800,000 to the planned production quantity of units. In actuality, only $640,000 was allocated since the allocation rate was based on the expectation of a higher volume of activity than what was achieved. This leaves $160,000 in underallocated fixed overhead, *relative to the budget*. This is the meaning of *unfavourable:* the inability to fully allocate the fixed overhead to the actual volume of activity.

The Flexible Budget Cost Variance Analysis Report

With the calculation of all the variances completed, let us turn to how this analysis might be presented to management. Exhibit 11–17 illustrates one possible way to organize and present your analysis. Each total flexible budget cost variance is decomposed into a price variance and the quantity variance. The columns labelled D, G, and J correspond to the three columns in the variance diagrams in the previous exhibits. Notice one important point regarding fixed costs: the fixed costs in the flexible budget should be equal to the budgeted costs since fixed costs will not vary with the activity level, assuming that the activity level is within the allowable range of levels for which the fixed costs will stay fixed. When fixed costs are applied to production, applied fixed costs will not equal the budgeted cost if the denominator activity level is different from the standard quantity allowed for actual output. This is shown in the very last column.

EXHIBIT 11–17 Flexible Budget Cost Variance Analysis Report

	A	B	C	D	E	F	G	H	I	J	K	L	M
1				COLONIAL PEWTER COMPANY									
2				Flexible Budget Cost Variance Analysis Report									
3				for the Month of June									
4		Standard Quantity (SQI)	Standard Price (SP)	Actual	PRICE VARIANCE		AQ X SP	QUANTITY VARIANCE		Flex Budget SQ × SP			Applied Cost SQ × SP
5					Activity Level: Q = 2,000 units								
6				Cost Drivers: Actual Input Quantity Used for Q = 2,000 units			Cost Drivers: Standard Quantity of Input Allowed for Q = 2,000 units					
7	Sales:		$110.00	$203,000	$ 17,000	U	$ 220,000	$ –	–	$ 220,000			$ 220,000
8	*Variable costs:*												
9	Direct materials	1.25	$ 8.80	$ 25,500	$ 900	F	$ 26,400	$ 4,400	U	$ 22,000			$ 22,000
10	Direct labour	2.5	$ 14.00	$ 74,250	$ 1,350	F	$ 75,600	$ 5,600	U	$ 70,000			$ 70,000
11	Variable overhead	2.5	$ 3.00	$ 15,390	$ 810	F	$ 16,200	$ 1,200	U	$ 15,000			$ 15,000
12	Other variable expenses			$ 8,000	$ –	-	$ 8,000	$ -		$ 8,000			$ 8,000
13	Total variable overhead cost			$ 123,140	$ 3,060	F	$ 126,200	$ 11,200	U	$ 115,000			$ 115,000
14	Contribution margin			$ 79,860	$ 13,940	U	$ 93,800	$ 11,200	U	$ 105,000			$ 105,000
15											VOLUME VARIANCE		
16	*Fixed costs:*												
17	Manufacturing overhead			$ 21,100	BUDGET VARIANCE = $900 (F)					$ 22,000	$ 2,444	U	$ 24,444
18	Administrative and selling			$ 7,200						$ 7,200	$ –		$ 7,200
19	Total fixed cost			$ 28,300						$ 29,200	$ 2,444	U	$ 31,644
20	Operating income			$ 51,560						$ 75,800	$ 2,444	U	$ 73,356
21	*Note: This format of presentation is based on cost formula 2. The cost driver for*				Price Variance		Budget Variance	Quantity Variance			Volume Variance		
22	*each variable cost element is the input quantity used in production or allowed for production. Also, all amounts in the actual column are lump sums.*												
23					= $3,060 (F)		= $900 (F)	= $11,200 (U)			= $2,444 (U)		
24													

With regard to the variable costs, there will be no difference between the costs in the flexible budget column and the amounts in the applied cost column. This is because variable costs in the flexible budget are *applied costs* to begin with; remember that the flexible budget cost for a variable input is SQ allowed × SP. But the fixed cost in the budget is a lump sum ($22,000). The fixed cost in the applied column is not a lump sum; rather, it is an amount SQ allowed × Predetermined rate ($24,444 = 5,000 hours × $4.889/hour). Comparison of the budgeted fixed cost and the applied fixed cost yields *only* the volume variance. To make this clear, the top portion of the volume variance column has been left blank.

In the bottom left-hand corner, we have provided a reminder that cost formula 2 has been used because cost formula 1 ($C = SC$ × Q) will not help to isolate the price and quantity variances. You can see that the volume level driving both the actual result and the flexible budget is the actual level of 2,000 units. Since Q is the same across the board in all the columns, using cost formula 1 will be unhelpful. The cost drivers for the budget are the standard quantities of the input allowed for 2,000 bookends. The cost driver for the actual results (column D) and the $AQ × SP$ column (column G) is the actual quantity of input used for making 2,000 bookends (AQ).

You should realize that this exhibit is the *result* of having made all the calculations earlier. It is not intended to explain how the numbers were calculated. Too much of the earlier detail is hidden. You can use this format to present and interpret the calculations made.

At the very bottom, all the variances are gathered together. The price, budget, and quantity variances add up to $3,060 F + $900 F + $11,200 U = $7,240 U. This is the total flexible budget cost variance. When the sales revenue variance is added we get $17,000 U + $ $7,240 U = $24,240 U. This is the bottom-line variance we identified way back in Exhibit 11–7. The volume variance is not part of the flexible budget variance since it arises as a difference between budgeted fixed cost and applied fixed cost. In a standard costing system, this variance is isolated and recorded because only costs that are applied to work in process are recorded in the ledgers. Refer to Appendix 11A for a detailed discussion of the cost flows and transaction recording in a standard costing system.

Standard Costing and Variance Analysis in an Activity-Based Costing Environment

Our example in this chapter uses labour-hours as the base to allocate overhead; we have used this simple method to compute the standard variable as well as the fixed overhead cost and to compute variable overhead variances. Using a single allocation base makes the computation much simpler. However, using a single allocation base may not provide information as accurately as desired by managers.

The accuracy of standard costs can be improved by using a more complex system (such as activity-based costing, which we covered in Chapter 5) to develop them. However, moving to ABC is not a simple extension of the single overhead allocation base setting used in this chapter. Two main reasons underlie this complexity: (1) ABC uses multiple allocation bases, and (2) only the unit-level activities are directly proportional to production volume. The use of multiple allocation bases means that standards must be developed for costs pertaining to each activity (allocation base). Moreover, the existence of non-unit-level activities means that the costs pertaining to these activities will not change proportionately in response to a change in volume. Consequently, developing standards for a single unit of production is conceptually more challenging in settings where ABC is used.

DECISION POINT

BUDGET ANALYST

Your company is in the process of implementing an ABC program and plans to use the flexible approach to budgeting. To aid in the analysis of the factory overhead once these plans are in place, how should the under- or overapplied overhead be analyzed? Who should be held responsible for each of the variances?

*Note to student: See **Guidance Answers** online.*

Variance Analysis and Management by Exception

LO5 ● **Know**

CC25: Describe the principle of management by exception.

Are all variances worth investigating? The answer is no. The causes of the variances might be known to management and judged to be beyond its control and not investigated. Factors external to the firm—economic downturns or upturns, natural or human-made disasters, and exchange rate fluctuations—are examples.

How should managers decide which variances are worth investigating? One clue is the size of the variance either in absolute dollar figures or as percentage figures. For example, it may not be worth management's time to pay attention to a 0.5% variance from the standard. Management must decide when a variance is significant and when it is not. For example, if a variance is 5% or more, it may be considered to be significant. Once this is decided, management should investigate only those variances that are classified as significant as per the criteria. This rule of prioritization is the concept of **management by exception**—a management philosophy where a manager directs attention toward those parts of the organization where the variances are significant as defined by the organization. By focusing on the more significant variances, the hope is to achieve significant gains from any improvements. But as with any benchmarks and criteria that reflect managerial judgment, they must be reviewed regularly. What is and is not significant can change with time, and thus management must be sure that the criteria being used remain relevant.

In addition to watching for significant variances, managers must also pay attention to the pattern of variances. For example, if the labour efficiency variance is steadily increasing period after period, this should trigger an investigation, even though none of the variances are large enough by themselves to warrant investigation. Timely attention to the pattern of variances can help in arresting the problem before it gets out of hand. For example, a rising trend of materials quantity and labour efficiency variances may suggest the existence of problems with the process or equipment used, which need to be looked into. In summary, variance analysis is a useful tool for managers and facilitates management by exception.

If actual performance is close to the plans, there is little cause for immediate worry. Nonetheless, it is important to examine the standards (and budgets) regularly. Organizations must continuously look for ways to improve; a significant benefit of improvements is that they can result in reducing the level of input resources required by the organization (e.g., fewer materials, less labour, and less overhead). Any reduction in input requirements will directly impact standard costs; when this happens, organizations have to revise the standard costs to reflect such improvements.

Evaluation of Controls Based on Standard Costs

Advantages of Standard Costs

LO5 • **Know**

CC26: Describe the benefits and limitations of using standard costing for the purposes of control.

Standard costing systems have a number of advantages:

1. Standard costs are a key element in a management-by-exception approach. So long as costs remain within the standards, managers can focus on other issues. When costs fall significantly outside the standards, managers are alerted that there may be problems requiring attention. This approach helps managers focus on important issues. The standards themselves should be reviewed periodically for their continued relevance.

2. As long as standards are viewed by employees as being reasonable, they can promote economy and efficiency. They provide benchmarks that individuals can use to judge their own performance.

3. Standard costs can greatly simplify bookkeeping. Instead of recording actual costs for each job, the standard costs for materials, labour, and overhead can be charged to jobs.

4. Standard costs fit naturally in an integrated system of *responsibility accounting*. The standards establish what costs should be, who should be responsible for them, and whether actual costs are under control.

Potential Problems With Standard Costs

The use of standard costs can present a number of potential problems. Most of these problems result from the improper use of standard costs and the failure to follow the management-by-exception principle, or from using standard costs in situations where they are not appropriate.

1. Standard cost variance reports are usually prepared on a monthly basis and often are released days or even weeks after the end of the month. As a consequence, the information in the reports may be so stale that it is almost useless. Timely, frequent reports that are approximately correct are better than infrequent reports that are very precise but out of date by the time they are released. Some companies are now reporting variances and other key operating data daily or even more frequently.

2. If managers are insensitive and use variance reports as a club, morale may suffer. Employees should receive positive reinforcement for work well done. Management by exception, by its nature, tends to focus on the negative. If variances are used as a club, subordinates may be tempted to cover up unfavourable variances or take actions that are not in the best interests of the company to make sure the variances are favourable. For example, workers may make a frenzied effort to increase output at the end of the month to avoid an unfavourable labour efficiency variance. In the rush to produce output, quality may suffer.

3. Labour quantity standards and efficiency variances make two important assumptions. First, they assume that the production process is labour-paced; if labour works faster, output will go up. However, output in many companies is no longer determined by how fast labour works; rather, it is determined by the processing speed of machines. Second, the computations assume that labour is a variable cost. However, direct labour may be essentially fixed. If labour is fixed, then an undue emphasis on labour efficiency variances creates pressure to build excess work-in-process and finished goods inventories.

4. In some cases, a favourable variance can be as bad as (or worse than) an unfavourable variance. For example, McDonald's has a standard for the amount of hamburger meat that should be in a Big Mac. A favourable variance means that less meat was used than the standard specifies. The result is a substandard Big Mac and possibly a dissatisfied customer.

5. There may be a tendency with standard cost reporting systems to emphasize meeting the standards to the exclusion of other important objectives, such as maintaining and improving quality, on-time delivery, and customer satisfaction. This tendency can be reduced by using supplemental performance measures that focus on these other objectives. (This is discussed in Chapter 12.)

6. Just meeting standards may not be sufficient; continuous improvement may be necessary to survive in the current competitive environment. For this reason, some companies focus on the trends in the standard cost variances—aiming for continuous improvement, rather than just meeting the standards. In other companies, engineered standards are being replaced either by a rolling average of actual costs, which is expected to decline, or by very challenging target costs.

In conclusion, managers should exercise considerable care in their use of a standard costing system. It is particularly important that managers go out of their way to focus on the positive, rather than on just the negative, and to be aware of possible unintended consequences.

Learning Objectives Summary

LO1 UNDERSTAND STANDARD COSTING AND COMPUTE STANDARD COSTS.

Standard costs are benchmarks against which to compare actual costs and evaluate performance. Standards are developed for the amount of resources (materials, labour, overhead) needed to make one unit of product, and for the price to pay for one unit of a resource. Standards are established using time and motion studies from operations analysis, prior experience of the business, knowledge of industry norms and practices, and other factors. The outcome of setting standards is the standard cost card, which specifies the standard quantities, prices, and cost of the resources required to make the product. Setting standards is challenging for managers because it requires them to strike a balance between too lax and too ambitious levels. Standard costs are the key information upon which budgets are developed.

LO2 PREPARE AND USE STATIC AND FLEXIBLE BUDGETS FOR PERFORMANCE ANALYSIS.

A static budget is a budget developed for a single planned level of activity. It is the basis for planning the business's activities and is formulated prior to the start of the operating period. A flexible budget is any budget based on an activity level *different* from the planned activity level and is prepared using the *same* budget data and standard cost card information as the static budget. A static budget is not an ideal comparison for actual performance, since the planned activity level (the basis for the static budget) will usually differ from the actual activity level achieved and, consequently, it will not be possible to know if the variance resulted from the difference in the activity levels or from management operating decisions regarding prices paid for resources and quantities of resources used.

Comparing an actual result to the budget leads to a variance, which is the difference between the actual and budgeted amounts of revenue and costs. A variance is evaluated as either favourable (if it signals that actual net income is higher than the budget) or unfavourable (if it implies that actual net income is lower than the budget). A variance traced to an activity level difference is a signal that management should investigate its control over activity. A variance due to operating decisions signifies control issues in cost management.

The flexible budget is the proper comparison budget for analyzing controls over costs. The variance between the actual results and the flexible budget is called a flexible budget variance. Variance analysis is the process of decomposing a flexible budget variance into its constituent parts.

LO3   COMPUTE AND INTERPRET VARIABLE COST FLEXIBLE BUDGET VARIANCES.

The actual cost of resources used to make a given volume of output is calculated as the product of the actual quantity of resource used and the price paid for the resource: $AQ \times AP$. The cost for the same resource in the flexible budget is the product of the standard quantity of the resource allowed by the standard to make the quantity of the product actually produced and the standard price per unit of the resource: $SQ \times SP$. The variance between the actual cost and the flexible budget can be due to the quantity difference between AQ and SQ and/or the price difference between AP and SP. The quantity difference leads to a quantity variance when multiplied by the standard price, and the price difference leads to a price variance when multiplied by the actual quantity. A quantity variance is calculated for each direct cost and variable overhead (the variance is called by different names for each type of input), and a price variance is also calculated for each type of cost.

A favourable quantity variance is a signal that actual net income is higher than budget because the business used less resources to produce the period's output than the quantity allowed by the standard for that level of output. It means that the business was efficient in the use of resources. An unfavourable quantity variance means that actual net income is lower than the budget because the business used more resources than allowed by the standard for the level of output made for the period. Regardless of whether a variance is favourable or unfavourable, if management concludes that the magnitude of the variance is significant, the causes for the variance should be determined, investigated, and understood.

LO4   PERFORM AN ANALYSIS OF FIXED OVERHEAD COSTS.

Because fixed costs, by their very nature, do not vary with volume-based cost drivers, controlling such costs can be a challenge. Two types of variances are computed for fixed overhead cost: the budget variance and the volume variance. The budget variance is the difference between the actual cost and the budgeted cost. The volume variance is the difference between the budgeted cost and the cost that is applied to the units produced. In a standard costing system, fixed cost is applied to production using a predetermined overhead allocation rate, which is itself calculated by dividing the budgeted fixed overhead by the quantity of the allocation base the company estimated it would consume (also known as the denominator activity level). The volume variance arises because the denominator activity level used to calculate the rate is different from the quantity of the allocation base to which the rate is applied. When the actual volume is higher than the planned volume, overhead is overapplied, and this signals a higher utilization of the fixed resources of the firm, while an underutilization of the fixed resources is implied when actual volume is less than the planned volume.

LO5   UNDERSTAND MANAGEMENT CONTROL IN A STANDARD COSTING ENVIRONMENT.

The introduction of a standard costing system in an organization has important implications for management control. Management must set standards appropriately: overly tight standards cause employees to resent being evaluated against them; overly lax standards allow workers to underachieve relative to their true potential. Since standards enable the calculation of variances (which are signals of departures of actual results from expectations), managers must determine which variances are worthy of investigation and which can be ignored. Criteria must be developed to classify a variance as either significant or insignificant. Prioritizing variances in this way is the principle of management by exception and allows managers to conserve their valuable time and ensure that this time is not wasted in the analysis of insignificant variances.

Standard costing systems have many advantages, including simplifying recordkeeping and transaction processing, clarifying expectations and responsibilities, and revealing control weaknesses and strengths. Although these advantages might imply that a standard costing system should be adopted by most organizations, there are also some potential problems. Standards should be reviewed regularly for relevance and appropriateness as benchmarks for performance evaluation. Out-of-date standards will cause problems and mislead management into taking wrong actions. If variances are interpreted as mistakes made by personnel and result in punishment for employees, the effectiveness of the system as a method for performance evaluation will be lost. There is a risk of dysfunctional behaviour by employees, who may not report unfavourable variances and might take unplanned action to try to avoid discovery of problems, and in so doing may cause problems elsewhere in the firm. Variances should be analyzed and investigated in an integrated manner, since they can be correlated.

Application Competency Summary

APPLICATION COMPETENCY	DELIVERABLE	SOURCE DOCUMENTS AND KEY INFORMATION	STEPS	KNOWLEDGE COMPETENCY
Develop standard costs for direct materials. ●LO1–CC3	*Key Information* Ideal and practical quantity standards of direct materials per unit of output Standard price of direct materials per unit of output, including other purchase-related costs Standard cost of direct materials per unit of output *Report/Document* No specific document	*Bill of Materials* Historical data of direct materials consumed per unit of output Historical records of direct materials cost *Purchase Orders* Price quotes from potential suppliers Purchase terms and conditions *Quality Records* Historical records of scrap, rejects, and other allowances	1. Determine the ideal quantity of direct materials required per unit of output based on historical data and product and process design. 2. Add the normal waste allowed due to quality and other production considerations to determine the (practical) standard quantity of direct materials. 3. Determine the average price of the materials based on historical data and quotes from potential suppliers. 4. Add delivery and other purchase-related costs; deduct any discounts to determine the standard price of direct materials. 5. Multiply the standard quantity by the standard price to compute the standard cost of direct materials per unit of output.	Ideal and practical standards, price standards, quantity standards, and cost standards ●LO1–CC1, 2

APPLICATION COMPETENCY	DELIVERABLE	SOURCE DOCUMENTS AND KEY INFORMATION	STEPS	KNOWLEDGE COMPETENCY
Develop standard costs for direct labour. ●LO1–CC4	*Key Information* Ideal and practical direct labour-hours per unit of output Standard rate of direct labour per unit of output including benefits and taxes Standard cost of direct labour per unit of output *Report/Document* No specific document	*Annual Budget Documents* Direct labour required per unit of output Allowances for quality and other production considerations *Wage Agreement Documents* Direct labour wage rate	1. Determine the ideal direct labour-hours required per unit of output based on historical data, and product and process design. 2. Add the normal allowance for rests and breaks, and additional time allowed due to normal quality and other production considerations to determine the (practical) standard quantity of direct labour-hours. 3. Determine the average wage rate based on historical data and labour market conditions. 4. Add benefit expenses, taxes, and other expenses to determine the standard wage rate. 5. Multiply the standard labour-hours by the standard rate to compute the standard cost of direct labour per unit of output.	Ideal and practical standards, price standards, quantity standards, and cost standards ●LO1–CC1, 2
Develop standard costs for variable overhead. ●LO1–CC5	*Key Information* Ideal and practical quantity of overhead allocation base per unit of output Standard overhead allocation rate per unit of output	*Annual Budget Documents* Variable overhead allocation base Estimated variable overhead for the period Estimated quantity of the allocation base for the period	1. Identify the base used to allocate variable overhead. 2. Determine the standard quantity of the allocation base required per unit of output. 3. Compute the predetermined overhead allocation rate based on estimated overhead	Ideal and practical standards, price standards, quantity standards, and cost standards ●LO1–CC1, 2

APPLICATION COMPETENCY	DELIVERABLE	SOURCE DOCUMENTS AND KEY INFORMATION	STEPS	KNOWLEDGE COMPETENCY
	Standard cost of variable overhead per unit of output *Report/Document* No specific document	Quantity of allocation base required per unit of output	costs and the estimated quantity of the allocation base. 4. Multiply the standard quantity of the overhead allocation base by the predetermined overhead allocation rate to compute the standard cost of variable overhead per unit of output.	
Prepare a standard cost card. ●**LO1–CC6**	*Key Information* Standard costs of direct materials, direct labour, overhead, and total standard costs *Report/Document* Standard cost card	*Annual Budget and Other Internal Documents* Standard price and quantity for direct materials, direct labour, and variable overhead	1. List the standard costs of direct materials, direct labour, and variable overhead per unit of output. 2. Add the three amounts to determine the total standard cost per unit of output.	Standard costs for direct materials, direct labour, and variable overhead ●**LO1–CC3, 4, 5**
Prepare a static budget. ●**LO2–CC7**	*Key Information* Total variable and fixed costs at different levels of activity *Report/Document* Flexible budget	*Standard Cost Cards* Standard cost per unit of activity volume for variable costs *Annual Budget Documents* Expected fixed costs *Historical Activity and Cost Records* Relevant range of operations	1. Choose the planned activity level within the relevant range. 2. Compute total variable costs for the chosen activity level by multiplying the cost per unit of activity volume by the activity level. Use cost formula 1 or cost formula 2. 3. List the estimated total fixed cost.	Variable and fixed cost behaviour ●**LO1–CC1 (Ch. 2)** Relevant range of operations ●**LO1–CC5 (Ch. 6)**
Prepare a static budget performance report. ●**LO2–CC8**	*Key Information* Actual and budgeted revenues and costs, and variances	*Budgets* Budgeted volume of activity and corresponding revenues and costs	1. List the actual and budgeted activity volumes, revenues, and costs. 2. Deduct the budgeted revenues	Role of budgeting ●**LO1–CC1 (Ch. 7)** Master budget ●**LO1–CC3 (Ch. 7)**

APPLICATION COMPETENCY	DELIVERABLE	SOURCE DOCUMENTS AND KEY INFORMATION	STEPS	KNOWLEDGE COMPETENCY
	Report/Document Static budget performance report	*Revenue and Expense Ledgers* Actual volume of activity and corresponding revenues and costs	and costs from the corresponding actual amounts to compute variances. 3. For revenues, label positive differences as favourable (F); for costs, label positive differences as unfavourable (U).	
Prepare a flexible budget. ●**LO2–CC12**	*Key Information* Total variable and fixed costs at different levels of activity *Report/Document* Flexible budget	*Standard Cost Cards* Standard cost per unit of activity volume for variable costs *Annual Budget Documents* Expected fixed costs *Historical Activity and Cost Records* Relevant range of operations	1. Choose and list the activity levels within the relevant range for which a budget must be prepared. 2. Compute total variable costs for each activity level by multiplying the cost per unit of activity volume by the activity level. Use cost formula 2 if a performance report is also going to be prepared. 3. List the estimated total fixed cost for each activity level (fixed amount). If all the levels for which the budget is being flexed are in the relevant range, the fixed cost should be the same at each level.	Variable and fixed cost behaviour ●**LO1–CC1 (Ch. 2)** Relevant range of operations ●**LO1–CC5 (Ch. 6)**
Prepare a flexible budget performance report. ●**LO2–CC13**	*Key Information* Actual and flexible budget revenues and costs, and variances *Report/Document* Flexible budget performance report	*Flexible Budget* Budgeted revenues and costs corresponding to the actual activity level *Sales/Production Records*	1. List the actual activity volumes and the corresponding actual and flexible budget revenues and costs. 2. Deduct the flexible budget revenues and costs from the corresponding actual amounts to compute variances.	Variances ●**LO2–CC9, 10, 11**

APPLICATION COMPETENCY	DELIVERABLE	SOURCE DOCUMENTS AND KEY INFORMATION	STEPS	KNOWLEDGE COMPETENCY
		Actual sales/ production volume

Revenue and Expense Ledgers

Actual revenues and costs | 3. For revenues, label positive differences as favourable (F); for costs, label positive differences as unfavourable (U). | |
| Compute direct materials variances.
●**LO3–CC15, 16** | *Key Information*

Actual and standard price, quantity, and cost of direct materials purchased/used

Price and quantity variances

Report/Document

Performance report | *Production Reports*

Actual output quantity

Bill of Materials

or

Direct Materials Account in the General Ledger

Quantity of direct materials used in production

Purchase Orders

Actual price of direct materials purchased

Standard Cost Card

Standard quantity of direct materials required for actual output, and standard price of direct materials | 1. Determine the actual cost of direct materials purchased by multiplying the actual price by the actual quantity.
2. Compute the standard cost of the actual quantity purchased (used) by multiplying the standard price by the actual quantity.
3. The difference between the actual and standard costs of the actual quantity purchased is the price variance.
4. Compute the standard cost of the standard quantity required to produce the actual output by multiplying the standard price by the standard quantity.
5. The difference between the standard costs of the actual quantity used and the standard quantity that should have been used is the quantity variance. | Price and quantity variances, direct materials variances
●**LO2–CC14** |
| Compute direct labour variances.
●**LO3–CC17** | *Key Information* | *Production Reports* | 1. Determine the actual cost of direct labour purchased | Price and quantity variances, direct |

APPLICATION COMPETENCY	DELIVERABLE	SOURCE DOCUMENTS AND KEY INFORMATION	STEPS	KNOWLEDGE COMPETENCY
	Actual and standard rate, quantity, and cost of direct labour Rate and efficiency variances *Report/Document* Performance report	Actual output quantity *Labour Time Sheets* or *Direct Labour Account in the General Ledger* Direct labour-hours used in production *Payroll Records* Actual wage rate of direct labour used *Standard Cost Card* Standard direct hours required for actual output, and standard wage rate price of direct labour	by multiplying the actual rate by the actual hours used. 2. Compute the standard cost of the actual hours (used) by multiplying the standard rate by the actual hours. 3. The difference between the actual and standard costs of the actual hours used is the rate variance. 4. Determine the standard cost of the standard hours required to produce the actual output by multiplying the standard rate by the standard hours. 5. The difference between the standard costs of the actual hours used and the standard hours that should have been used is the efficiency variance.	labour variances ●**LO2–CC14**
Compute variable overhead variances. ●**LO3–CC18**	*Key Information* Actual and standard rate, quantity and cost of direct labour Rate and efficiency variances *Report/Document* Performance report	*Production Reports* Actual output quantity Actual quantity of the overhead allocation base used *Variable Overhead Account in the General Ledger* Actual variable overhead expenses	1. Determine the actual cost of variable overhead from the overhead account ledgers. 2. Compute the standard cost of the actual quantity of the allocation base consumed by multiplying the standard rate by the actual quantity. 3. The difference between the actual and standard costs is the spending variance.	Price and quantity variances, variable overhead variances ●**LO2–CC14**

APPLICATION COMPETENCY	DELIVERABLE	SOURCE DOCUMENTS AND KEY INFORMATION	STEPS	KNOWLEDGE COMPETENCY
		Standard (allocated) variable overhead amount for actual output *Standard Cost Card* Standard quantity of allocation base that should have been used to produce actual output	4. Compute the standard cost of the standard quantity of the allocation base required to produce the actual output by multiplying the standard rate by the standard quantity. 5. The difference between the standard costs of the actual quantity of the allocation base and the standard quantity that should have been used is the efficiency variance.	
Compute a predetermined fixed overhead rate. ●**LO4–CC21**	*Key Information* Predetermined overhead rate *Report/Document* No specific report	*Annual Budget Documents* Denominator activity level and corresponding fixed overhead cost	1. Divide the fixed overhead cost corresponding to the denominator activity level by the activity level to compute the predetermined overhead rate.	Overhead allocation ●**LO2–CC9, 14** ●**LO4–CC19, 20** ●**LO1–CC2, 3 (Ch. 3)**
Compute fixed overhead budget variance. ●**LO4–CC22**	*Key Information* Fixed overhead budget variance *Report/Document* Overhead performance report	*Flexible Budget* Budgeted fixed overhead costs at actual activity level *Fixed Overhead Expense Ledger* Actual fixed overhead costs	1. List the actual cost and the flexible budget fixed overhead cost corresponding to the actual activity volume of the overhead allocation base (not the applied fixed cost). 2. Deduct the flexible budget amount from the actual amount to compute the fixed overhead budget variance.	Variances ●**LO2–CC9, 14** ●**LO4–CC19, 20**
Compute fixed overhead volume variance. Compute the over- or	*Key Information* Fixed overhead volume variance *Report/Document*	*Flexible Budget* Budgeted fixed overhead	1. Compute the applied overhead amount by multiplying the standard quantity of the activity volume	Variances ●**LO2–CC9, 14** ●**LO4–CC19, 20**

APPLICATION COMPETENCY	DELIVERABLE	SOURCE DOCUMENTS AND KEY INFORMATION	STEPS	KNOWLEDGE COMPETENCY
underapplied overhead. ●LO4–CC23, 24	Overhead performance report	*Sales/Production Records* Actual sales/ production volume Actual consumption of overhead allocation base *Fixed Overhead Expense Ledger* Applied fixed overhead	allowed for actual output by the predetermined overhead rate. (This is not the budgeted cost.) 2. Specify the flexible budget fixed overhead costs. It is assumed that the actual volume of activity is within the allowable range of activity volumes. The budgeted fixed overhead will not vary with the volume. 3. Deduct the applied overhead from the flexible budget amount to compute the volume variance. 4. Calculate the over- or underapplied overhead as the sum of all of the overhead variances.	

Review Problem 1: Standard Costs and Variance Analysis

Xavier Company manufactures a single product. The following information is available regarding the standards for the product:

- Each saleable finished unit consists of 5 grams of direct materials.
- As a result of the nature of the direct materials used and the production process, 12.25% of the direct materials used in production are lost.
- The ideal direct labour time required to produce one saleable finished unit is 1.5 hours.
- Direct labour is paid for 8 hours, which includes an hour for breaks and cleanup.
- 5% of the units produced have to be scrapped (at zero value) due to poor quality.
- Direct materials cost $400 per kilogram plus an additional 25% for customs and excise duties and shipping costs.
- Direct labour is paid at $20 per hour.
- Variable overhead is allocated using direct labour-hours as a base, at a rate of $5 per hour.

During June, 2,000 units were produced. The costs associated with June's operations were as follows:

Materials purchased: 18 kilograms at $600/kg	$10,800
Materials used in production: 14 kilograms	—
Direct labour: 4,000 hours at $19.50 per hour	$78,000
Variable manufacturing overhead costs incurred	$20,800

Required:

1. Develop a standard cost card for the product produced by Xavier Company (use Exhibit 11–1 as a guide).
2. Compute the materials, labour, and variable manufacturing overhead variances for the month of June.

SOLUTION TO REVIEW PROBLEM 1

1. **Standard Cost Card Inputs (1)**

Inputs	(1) Standard Quantity or Hours	(2) Standard Price or Rate	(3) Standard Cost (1) × (2)
Direct materials	6.0 grams	$ 0.50	$ 3.00
Direct labour	1.8 hours	20.00	36.00
Variable manufacturing overhead	1.8 hours	5.00	9.00
Total standard cost per unit			$48.00

Explanation of calculations:

Direct Materials

Each unit of good (saleable) finished product consists of 5 grams; this is equivalent to 87.75% of the materials used (remember that 12.25% is lost).

Direct materials required to be used to produce one finished unit = 5 grams ÷ 0.8775 = 5.7 grams (rounded)

Also, remember that 5% of the finished units are scrapped due to poor quality. This means that to obtain 95 good (saleable) units, 100 must be produced. Therefore, additional direct materials must be used to account for quality problems.

Thus, the *standard quantity of direct materials* used to produce one *good* (saleable) finished unit is

$$5.7 \text{ grams} \div 0.95 = 6 \text{ grams}$$

Standard price of direct materials = $400 + ($100 × 25%) = $500 per kilogram, or $0.50 per gram

Direct Labour

Each unit of finished product requires 1.5 hours of direct labour.

Direct labour is paid for 8 hours per day, which includes 1 hour for breaks, cleanup, and so on. This means labour is paid 8/7 times the amount of time actually worked to produce a product.

Paid labour-hours required per unit $= 1.5 \times (8/7) = 1.714$ hours

Also, remember that 5% of the finished units are scrapped due to poor quality. This means that to obtain 95 good (saleable) units, 100 must be produced. Therefore, additional direct labour must be used to account for quality problems.

Thus, the *standard quantity of direct labour* required to produce one *good* (saleable) finished unit is

$$1.714 \div 0.95 = 1.8 \text{ hours (rounded)}$$

Variable Overhead

Variable overhead is allocated using direct labour-hours (DLH) as the allocation base at $5 per DLH.

2. **Variance Analysis**

Materials Variances

Actual Quantity of Inputs, at Actual Price	Actual Quantity of Inputs, at Standard Price	Standard Quantity Allowed for Output, at Standard Price
$(AQ \times AP)$	$(AQ \times SP)$	$(SQ \times SP)$
18 kg × $600/kg	18 kg × $500/kg	12 kg* × $500/kg
= $10,800	= $9,000	= $6,000
Price variance, $1,800 U		
	14 kg × $500 per kg	
	= $7,000	
	Quantity variance, $1,000 U	

*2,000 units × 6 g/unit = 12 kg

A total variance cannot be computed in this situation, since the amount of materials purchased (18 kilograms) differs from the amount of materials used in production (14 kilograms).

Using the formulas in the chapter, the same variances would be computed as

$$\text{Materials price variance} = AQ \times (AP - SP)$$

$$18 \text{ kg} \times (\$600 \,/\, \text{kg} - \$500 \,/\, \text{kg}) = \$1,800 \text{ U}$$

$$\text{Materials quantity variance} = SP \times (AQ - SQ)$$

$$\$500 \,\big/\, \text{kg} \times (14 \text{ kg} - 12 \text{ kg}) = \$1,000 \text{ U}$$

Labour Variances

Actual Hours of Input, at the Actual Rate $(AH \times AR)$		Actual Hours of Input, at the Standard Rate $(AH \times SR)$		Standard Hours Allowed for Output, at the Standard Rate $(SH \times SR)$
4,000 hours × $19.50/hour		4,000 hours × $20/hour		3,600 hours* × $20/hour
= $78,000		= $80,000		= $72,000
	Rate variance, $2,000 F		Efficiency variance, $8,000 U	
		Total variance, $6,000 U		

*2,000 units × 1.8 hours/unit = 3,600 hours

Using the formulas in the chapter, the same variances would be computed as

$$\text{Labour rate variance} = AH \times \left(AR - SR\right)$$

$$4{,}000 \text{ hours} \times \left(\$19.50 \,/\, \text{hour} - \$20 \,/\, \text{hour}\right) = \$2{,}000 \text{ F}$$

$$\text{Labour efficiency variance} = SR \times \left(AH - SH\right)$$

$$\$20 \,/\, \text{hour} \times \left(4{,}000 \text{ hours} - 3{,}600 \text{ hours}\right) = \$8{,}000 \text{ U}$$

Variable Manufacturing Overhead Variances

Actual Quantity of Input, at the Actual Rate $(AQ \times AR)$	Actual Quantity of Input, at the Standard Rate $(AQ \times SR)$	Standard Quantity Allowed for Output, at the Standard Rate $(SQ \times SR)$
	4,000 hours × $5/hour	3,600 hours* × $5/hour
$20,800	= $20,000	= $18,000

Actual Quantity of Input, at the Actual Rate $(AQ \times AR)$	Actual Quantity of Input, at the Standard Rate $(AQ \times SR)$	Standard Quantity Allowed for Output, at the Standard Rate $(SQ \times SR)$
	Spending variance, $800 U	Efficiency variance, $2,000 U
	Total variance, $2,800 U	

*2,000 units $\times$ 1.8 hours/unit = 3,600 hours

Using the formulas in the chapter, the same variances would be computed as

$$\text{Variable overhead spending variance} = AH \times (AR - SR)$$

$$4,000 \text{ hours} \times \left(\$5.20 / \text{hour}^* - \$5 / \text{hour}\right) = \$800 \text{ U}$$

$$^* \$20,800 \div 4,000 \text{ hours} = \$5.20 \text{ per hour}$$

$$\text{Variable overhead efficiency variance} = SR \times (AH - SH)$$

$$\$5 / \text{hour} \times (4,000 \text{ hours} - 3,600 \text{ hours}) = \$2,000 \text{ U}$$

Review Problem 2: Overhead Cost Variances

Aspen Company manufactures a single product. Manufacturing overhead costs are allocated to the product using machine-hours. Five machine-hours are required per unit of product. The company has set denominator activity for the coming period at 6,000 machine-hours derived from the planned output volume of 1,200 units. Data for the manufacturing overhead cost portion in the static budget of Aspen Company follow:

Overhead Costs	Static Budget (Q = 1,200 units)
Variable overhead costs:	
Supplies	$ 1,200
Indirect labour	1,800
Total variable overhead cost	3,000
Fixed overhead costs:	

Depreciation	4,000
Supervision	5,000
Total fixed overhead cost	9,000
Total overhead cost	$12,000

Assume the following *actual* results for the period:

Number of units produced	1,300 units
Actual machine-hours	6,800 machine-hours
Actual variable overhead cost	$4,200
Actual fixed overhead cost	$9,400

Required:

1. Compute the predetermined overhead rates for (a) total overhead cost; (b) variable overhead cost, in total; and (c) fixed overhead cost, in total.

2. How many machine-hours would the flexible budget show as being necessary to achieve the actual output of 1,300 units? What is this quantity of machine-hours called?

3. Compute the following variances:
   a. The variable overhead spending variance, in total.
   b. The variable overhead efficiency variance, in total.
   c. The fixed overhead budget variance, in total.
   d. The fixed overhead volume variance, in total.

4. Verify that the total overhead variance agrees with the amount of over- or underapplied overhead cost (the balance in the manufacturing overhead cost account).

SOLUTION TO REVIEW PROBLEM 2

1. Since overhead will be applied using machine-hours (MH), the planned output volume of 1,200 units implies a denominator activity level of 6,000 machine-hours using the fact that each unit of output is allowed 5 machine-hours by the standard. The computation of the predetermined overhead rate for the total overhead cost, the variable overhead cost, and the fixed overhead cost is as follows:

   a. Total : $\dfrac{\$12,000}{6,000 \text{ MH}} = \$2$ per MH

   b. Variable element : $\dfrac{\$3,000}{6,000 \text{ MH}} = \$0.50$ per MH

   c. Fixed element : $\dfrac{\$9,000}{6,000 \text{ MH}} = \$1.50$ per MH

2. A flexible budget based on an output level of 1,300 units would show that

$$\text{Standard machine-hours for 1,300 units} = 1,300 \text{ units} \times 5 \text{ MH}\,/\,\text{unit}$$

$$= 6,500 \text{ MH}$$

The quantity of 6,500 machine-hours is called the standard quantity of input allowed for actual output.

3. The variable overhead variances are as follows:

	A	B	C	D	E	F
16		**Actual Quantity of Input at Actual Rate**		**Actual Quantity of Input at Standard Rate**		**Standard Quantity of Input Allowed for Actual Output at Standard Rate**
17		*AQ × AR*		*AQ × SR*		*SQ × SR*
18	**Variable Overhead**			6,800 h × $0.5/h		6,500 h* × $0.5/h
19		$4,200	a. Spending variance	$3,400.00	b. Efficiency variance	$3,250.00
20			$800.00		$150.00	
21			U		U	
22	*SQ allowed for actual output: Calculated above.					

These same variances using the formula format are as follows:

a. Variable overhead spending variance:

$$\text{Spending variance} = (AQ \times AR) - (AQ \times SR)$$

$$(\$4,200\,^*) - (6,800 \text{ hours} \times \$0.50 / \text{hour}) = \$800 \text{ U}$$

$$^*AQ \times AR \text{ equals the total actual cost for the period.}$$

b. Variable overhead efficiency variance:

$$\text{Efficiency variance} = SR \times (AQ - SQ)$$

$$\$0.50 \,/ \text{ hour} \times (6,800 \text{ hours} - 6,500 \text{ hours}) = \$150 \text{ U}$$

The fixed overhead variances are as follows:

	A	B	C	D	E	F
23		**Actual Fixed Overhead**		**Budgeted Fixed Overhead***		**Applied Fixed Overhead**
24						6,500 h† × $1.50/h
25	**Fixed Overhead**	$9,400	c. Budget variance	$9,000	d. Volume variance	$9,750

	A	B	C	D	E	F
26			$400		$(750)	
27			U		F	
28	*Budgeted fixed overhead cost = Denominator activity level × *PDR* = 6,000 denominator hours × $1.50/hour = $9,000					
29	†*SQ* for actual output = *SQI* × Actual *Q* = 3 MH/unit × 1,300 units = 6,500 MH					

These same variances using the formula format are as follows:

c. Fixed overhead budget variance:

$$\text{Budget variance} = \text{Actual fixed overhead cost} - \text{Flexible budget fixed overhead cost}$$

$$= \$9,400 - \$9,000 = \$400 \text{ U}$$

d. Fixed overhead volume variance:

$$\text{Volume variance} = \text{Fixed portion of predetermined overhead rate} \times (\text{Denominator hours} - \text{Standard hours})$$

$$= \$1.50 \Big/ \text{hour} \times (6{,}000 \text{ hours} - 6{,}500 \text{ hours}) = \$750 \text{ F}$$

Note: the computed variances are the only ones we could have possibly calculated, since actual spending on overhead is not broken down into the various variable and fixed overhead cost elements such as supplies or depreciation.

A summary of the four overhead variances is given below:

Variable overhead:	
Spending variance	$800 U
Efficiency variance	150 U
Fixed overhead:	
Budget variance	400 U
Volume variance	750 F
Underapplied overhead	$600 U

4. The underapplied overhead implies a debit balance in the manufacturing overhead cost account. Let us verify that this is indeed the case. The company's manufacturing overhead account would appear as follows at the end of the period:

Manufacturing Overhead		
Actual overhead costs		Applied overhead costs based on standard hours
13,600*	13,000†	
Underapplied overhead 600		

*$4,200 variable + $9,400 fixed = $13,600

†6,500 standard machine-hours × $2 per machine-hour = $13,000 (or $3,250 + $9,750)

Note: In a standard costing system, overhead is applied on the basis of standard hours, not actual hours. The $600 summary variance figure agrees with the debit balance in the company's manufacturing overhead account. This agreement verifies the accuracy of our variance analysis.

Questions

11–1   What is a quantity standard? What is a price standard?

11–2   Distinguish between ideal and practical standards.

11–3   What is meant by *variance?*

11–4   What is meant by *management by exception?*

11–5   Who is generally responsible for the materials price variance? The materials quantity variance? The labour efficiency variance?

11–6   At what two different points in time can the materials price variance be computed? Which point is better? Why?

11–7   What dangers lie in using standards as punitive tools?

11–8   What effect, if any, would you expect poor-quality materials to have on direct labour variances?

11–9   If variable manufacturing overhead is applied to production on the basis of direct labour-hours and the direct labour efficiency variance is unfavourable, will the variable overhead efficiency variance be favourable or unfavourable, or could it be either? Explain your answer.

11–10   Why might undue emphasis on labour efficiency variances lead to excess work-in-process inventories?

11–11   What is a static budget?

11–12   What is a flexible budget, and how does it differ from a static budget?

11–13   In comparing flexible budget data with actual data in a performance report for variable overhead, what variance(s) will be produced if the flexible budget data are based on actual hours worked? On both actual hours worked and standard hours allowed?

11–14   What is meant by *standard hours allowed?*

11–15   How does the variable manufacturing overhead spending variance differ from the materials price variance?

11–16   Why is *overhead efficiency variance* a misnomer?

11–17   What is meant by *denominator level of activity?*

11–18   Why in Chapter 11 do we apply overhead to work in process on the basis of standard hours allowed, when we applied it on the basis of actual hours in Chapter 3? What is the difference in costing systems between the two chapters?

11–19   What does the fixed overhead budget variance measure?

11–20 Under what circumstances would you expect the volume variance to be favourable? Unfavourable? Does the variance measure deviations in spending for fixed overhead items? Explain your answer.

11–21 In Chapter 3, you became acquainted with the concept of under- or overapplied overhead. Into what four variances can the under- or overapplied overhead be broken down?

11–22 If factory overhead is overapplied for August, would you expect the total of the overhead variances to be favourable or unfavourable?

The Foundational 15

[LO2 – CC12; LO3 – CC15, 16, 17, 18; LO4 – CC21, 22, 23, 24]

Preble Company manufactures one product. Its variable manufacturing overhead is applied to production based on direct labour-hours and its standard cost card per unit is as follows:

Direct material: 5 pounds at $8.00 per pound	$40.00
Direct labor: 2 hours at $14 per hour	28.00
Variable overhead: 2 hours at $5 per hour	10.00
Total standard variable cost per unit	$ 78.00

Fixed overhead was budgeted at $585,000. Fixed overhead is applied on the basis of direct labour-hours. The company also established the following cost formulas for its selling expenses:

	Fixed Cost per Month	Variable Cost per Unit Sold
Advertising	$200,000	
Sales salaries and commissions	$100,000	$12.00
Shipping expenses		$3.00

The static (i.e., planning) budget for March was based on producing and selling 25,000 units. However, during March the company actually produced and sold 30,000 units and incurred the following costs:

a. Purchased 160,000 pounds of raw materials at a cost of $7.50 per pound. All of this material was used in production.

b. Direct-labourers worked 55,000 hours at a rate of $15.00 per hour.

c. Total variable manufacturing overhead for the month was $280,500. And fixed manufacturing overhead was $580,000.

d. Total advertising, sales salaries and commissions, and shipping expenses were $210,000, $455,000, and $115,000, respectively.

Required:

11–1 What raw materials cost would be included in the company's flexible budget for March?

11–2 What is the materials quantity variance for March?

11–3 What is the materials price variance for March?

11–4   If Preble had purchased 170,000 pounds of materials at $7.50 per pound and used 160,000 pounds in production, what would be the materials quantity variance for March?

11–5   If Preble had purchased 170,000 pounds of materials at $7.50 per pound and used 160,000 pounds in production, what would be the materials price variance for March?

11–6   What direct labour cost would be included in the company's flexible budget for March?

11–7   What is the direct labour efficiency variance for March?

11–8   What is the direct labour rate variance for March?

11–9   What variable manufacturing overhead cost would be included in the company's flexible budget for March?

11–10   What is the variable overhead efficiency variance for March?

11–11   What is the variable overhead rate variance for March?

11–12   What amounts of advertising, sales salaries and commissions, and shipping expenses would be included in the company's flexible budget for March?

11–13   What fixed overhead cost would be included in the company's flexible budget for March?

11–14   What is the budget (spending) variance related to the fixed overhead cost and the fixed overhead volume variance?

11–15   What is the over- or underapplied fixed overhead cost?

Brief Exercises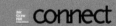

BRIEF EXERCISE 11–1
Determining Standard Costs [LO1 – CC1, 2, 3]

Victoria Chocolates, Ltd. makes premium handcrafted chocolate confections in Victoria, British Columbia. The owner of the company is setting up a standard costing system and has collected the following data for one of the company's products, the Empire Truffle. This product is made with the finest white chocolate and various fillings. The following data pertain only to the white chocolate used in the product:

Material requirements, kilograms of white chocolate per dozen truffles	0.80 kilogram
Allowance for waste, kilograms of white chocolate per dozen truffles	0.04 kilogram
Allowance for rejects, kilograms of white chocolate per dozen truffles	0.02 kilogram
Purchase price, finest-grade white chocolate	$10.50 per kilogram
Purchase discount	5% of purchase price
Shipping cost from the supplier in Belgium	$0.50 per kilogram
Receiving and handling cost	$0.10 per kilogram

Required:

1. Determine the standard price of one kilogram of white chocolate.
2. Determine the standard quantity of white chocolate for a dozen truffles.
3. Determine the standard cost of the white chocolate in a dozen truffles.

BRIEF EXERCISE 11–2
Determining Materials Variance [LO3 – CC15]

Bandar Industries Berhad of Malaysia manufactures sporting equipment. One of the company's products, a football helmet for the North American market, requires a special plastic. During the quarter ending June 30, the company manufactured 70,000 helmets, using 45,000 kilograms of plastic in the process. The plastic cost the company RM342,000. (The currency in Malaysia is the *ringgit,* which is denoted here by RM.)

According to the standard cost card, each helmet should require 0.6 kilograms of plastic, at a cost of RM8 per kilogram.

Required:

1. How much material in kilograms should have been used, and what cost for plastic should have been incurred in the manufacture of the 70,000 helmets? How much does this cost vary from what was incurred?
2. Break the difference computed in part (1) into a materials price variance and a materials quantity variance.

BRIEF EXERCISE 11–3
Computing Direct Labour Variances [LO3 – CC17]

AirCooks, Inc. prepares in-flight meals for a number of major airlines. One of the company's products is grilled salmon in dill sauce with new baby potatoes and spring vegetables. During the most recent week, the company prepared 4,000 of these meals using 960 direct labour-hours. The company paid these direct labourers a total of $9,600 for this work, or $10 per hour.

According to the standard cost card for this meal, it should require 0.25 direct labour-hours at a cost of $9.75 per hour.

Required:

1. How many hours should have been used and what direct labour cost should have been incurred to prepare the 4,000 meals? How much does this cost vary from what was incurred? What is this variance called?
2. Break the difference computed in part (1) into a labour rate variance and a labour efficiency variance.

BRIEF EXERCISE 11–4
Computing Overhead Variances [LO3 – CC18; LO4 – CC21, 22, 23]

Logistics Solutions provides order-fulfillment services for online merchants. The company maintains warehouses that stock items carried by its online clients. When a client receives an order from a customer, the order is forwarded to Logistics Solutions, which pulls the item from storage, packs it, and ships it to the customer. The company uses a predetermined variable overhead rate based on direct labour-hours.

In the most recent quarter, 300,000 items were shipped to customers using 5,800 direct labour-hours. The company incurred a total of $37,860 in variable overhead costs and $23,200 in fixed overhead costs.

According to the company's standards, 0.02 direct labour-hours are required to fulfill an order for one item and the variable overhead rate is $6.25 per direct labour-hour. Total budgeted fixed overhead cost was $23,600 for a planned shipping volume of 295,000 items. Fixed overhead is applied to each item using direct labour-hours.

Required:

1. What variable overhead cost should have been incurred to fill the orders for the 300,000 items? How much does this cost vary from what was incurred?
2. Break the difference computed in part (1) into a variable overhead spending variance and a variable overhead efficiency variance.

3. Compute the predetermined fixed overhead application rate.

4. Compute the fixed overhead budget and the volume variance and assess them.

5. What additional information would you need to conclude that the predetermined rate for fixed cost used by the company is different from the value you calculated in part (3)?

BRIEF EXERCISE 11–5
Explaining Direct Labour Variances [LO3 – CC17]

During the 2016 Republican primary race to be the nominee of the Republican Party for president in the general election for president of the United States, Donald Trump was accused by his opponents of having hired temporary construction workers from Poland instead of American workers during construction of Trump properties. Suppose the direct labour rate variance for the construction project was favourable, and the direct labour efficiency variance was also favourable. Trump was accused of underpaying and overworking the temporary workers. U.S. law stipulated that foreign workers could not change employers once having come to work in the country.

Required:

Explain what Donald Trump's opponents would infer based on the two variances in developing their attacks on his candidacy for the nomination.

BRIEF EXERCISE 11–6
Applying Overhead in a Standard Costing System [LO2 – CC9, 10]

Privack Corporation has a standard costing system in which it applies overhead to products on the basis of the standard direct labour-hours allowed for the actual output of the period. Data concerning the most recent year appear below:

Variable overhead cost per DLH	$2.50
Total fixed overhead cost per year	$350,000
Budgeted standard DLHs (denominator level of activity)	40,000
Actual DLHs	41,000
Standard DLHs allowed for the actual output	42,000

Required:

1. Compute the predetermined overhead rate for the year.
2. Determine the amount of overhead that would be applied to the output of the period.

BRIEF EXERCISE 11–7
Computing Fixed Overhead Variances [LO2 – CC11, 12]

Primara Corporation has a standard costing system in which it applies overhead to products on the basis of the standard direct labour-hours allowed for the actual output of the period. Data concerning the most recent year appear below:

Total budgeted fixed overhead cost for the year	$500,000
Actual fixed overhead cost for the year	$508,000

Budgeted standard direct labour-hours (denominator level of activity)	50,000
Actual direct labour-hours	54,000
Standard direct labour-hours allowed for the actual output	52,000

Required:

1. Compute the fixed portion of the predetermined overhead rate for the year.
2. Compute the fixed overhead budget variance and volume variance.

BRIEF EXERCISE 11–8
Computing Flexible Budget Operating Income [LO1 – CC2, 3]

On January 6, the Nick Company reported that, by earning an actual income of $3,000 in December, the company missed meeting its planned target income by $7,000. Due to the fact that the actual volume of activity in December was different from the original level of activity planned for the month, the company stated that it also missed the flexible budget income by $3,000. The failure to meet each target was considered to be unfavourable.

Required:

Calculate the operating income (loss) that the flexible budget and the static budget would have shown for December.

BRIEF EXERCISE 11–9
Applying Overhead and Computing Overhead Variances [LO2 – CC10, 11, 12]

Taylor Inc. uses a standard cost system. The company has the following results for the current period:

	Budget	Actual
Fixed overhead	$ 160,000	$ 160,000
Units	6,500 units	6,000 units
Direct labour-hours (DLH)	13,333 hours	12,500 hours
Standard quantity of DLH per unit	2.0152 hours	

Variable overhead is applied at $27.50 per direct labour-hour. Actual variable overhead was $310,600.

Required:

1. Compute the fixed overhead budget variance.
2. "Because the actual overhead and the budgeted overhead are the same the volume variance is 0." True or false? Show calculations.
3. Compute the total variable overhead variance and its component variances.

(Adapted © CPA Canada)

Exercises

EXERCISE 11–1
Setting Standards and Preparing a Standard Cost Card [LO1 – CC1, 2, 3, 6]

Martin Company manufactures a powerful cleaning solvent. The main ingredient in the solvent is a raw material called Echol. Information on the purchase and use of Echol follows:

Purchase of Echol: Echol is purchased in 30-litre containers at a cost of $130 per container. A discount of 3% is offered by the supplier for payment within 10 days, and Martin Company takes all discounts. Shipping costs, which Martin Company must pay, amount to $200 for an average shipment of one hundred 30-litre containers of Echol.

Use of Echol: The bill of materials calls for 15.2 litres of Echol per bottle of cleaning solvent. About 5% of all Echol used is lost through spillage or evaporation (the 15.2 litres above is the *actual* content per bottle). In addition, statistical analysis has shown that every 41st bottle is rejected at final inspection because of contamination.

Required:

1. Compute the standard purchase price for one litre of Echol.
2. Compute the standard quantity of Echol (in litres) per saleable bottle of cleaning solvent.
3. Using the data from parts (1) and (2), prepare a standard cost card showing the standard cost of Echol per bottle of cleaning solvent.

EXERCISE 11–2
Computing All Variances [LO3 – CC15, 17, 18; LO4 – CC22, 23]

Huron Company produces a commercial cleaning compound known as Zoom. The direct materials and direct labour standards for one unit of Zoom follow:

	Standard Quantity or Hours	Standard Price or Rate	Standard Cost
Direct materials	4.2 kilograms	$2 per kilogram	$8.20
Direct labour	0.4 hour	$12 per hour	4.80
Variable overhead	0.4 hour	$2 per hour	0.80

The budgeted fixed overhead cost is $15,800 per month. The denominator activity level of the allocation base is 800 direct labour-hours.

During the most recent month, the following activity was recorded:

a. 9,000 kilograms of material were purchased at a cost of $2.20 per kilogram.
b. All of the material purchased was used to produce 2,000 units of Zoom.
c. A total of 850 hours of direct labour time was recorded at a total labour cost of $9,265.
d. The variable overhead cost was $1,650, and the fixed overhead cost was $15,890.

Required:

1. Compute the direct materials price and quantity variances for the month.
2. Compute the direct labour rate and efficiency variances for the month.

3. Compute the variable overhead spending and efficiency variances for the month.

4. Compute the fixed overhead budget and the volume variances for the month.

5. Compute the underapplied or overapplied overhead for the month.

EXERCISE 11–3
Computing Material Variances [LO3 – CC16]

Refer to the data in Exercise 11–2. Assume that instead of producing 2,000 units during the month, the company produced only 1,500 units, using 6,500 kilograms of material in the production process. (The rest of the material purchased remained in inventory.)

Required:

1. Compute the direct materials price and quantity variances for the month.

2. Will the overhead volume variance be different now from its value in Exercise 11–2?

EXERCISE 11–4
Computing Labour and Overhead Variances [LO3 – CC17, 18; LO4 – CC22, 23, 24]

Erie Company manufactures an MP3 player called the Jogging Mate. The company uses standards to control its costs. The labour and variable overhead standards that have been set for one Jogging Mate MP3 player are as follows:

	Standard Hours	Standard Rate per Hour	Standard Cost
Direct labour	18 minutes	$12	$3.60
Variable overhead	18 minutes	$4	$1.20

Budgeted fixed overhead was estimated to be $31,500 per month. Fixed overhead cost is applied using direct labour-hours. During August, 5,750 hours of direct labour time was recorded in the manufacture of 20,000 units of the Jogging Mate. The direct labour cost totalled $73,600 for the month. Actual variable overhead and fixed overhead costs were $21,850 and $32,000, respectively.

Required:

1. What direct labour cost should have been incurred in the manufacture of the 20,000 units of the Jogging Mate? By how much does this differ from the cost that was incurred?

2. Break the difference in cost from part (1) into a labour rate variance and a labour efficiency variance.

3. Compute the variable overhead spending and efficiency variances for the month.

4. Suppose the static budget volume is 19,000 players—this is the denominator volume. Compute the volume variance for fixed overhead cost.

5. Ignore the data in part (4). Suppose that the static budget volume is also the normal volume and that the budgeted *variable* overhead cost in the static budget is $25,200. Given the standard cost card data in the question, calculate the under- or overapplied fixed overhead for August.

EXERCISE 11–5
Performing an All-Variance Analysis [LO3 – CC16, 17, 18; LO4 – CC22, 23]

Dawson Toys, Ltd. produces a toy called the Maze. The company has recently established a standard costing system to help control costs with the following standards for the Maze toy:

Direct materials: 8 microns per toy at $0.75 per micron

Direct labour: 0.9 hours per toy at $12 per hour

Variable overhead: 0.9 hours per toy at $3.05 per hour

During July, the company planned to make 4,100 toys, the normal volume, and produced 4,200 Maze toys. Production data for the month on the toy follow:

Direct materials: 25,000 microns were purchased for use in production at a cost of $0.60 per micron. 5,000 of these microns were still in inventory at the end of the month.

Direct labour: 4,000 direct labour-hours were worked at a cost of $52,000.

Variable overhead cost was $12,340, and fixed overhead cost was $44,000. The budget variance for July was $0.

Required:

1. Compute the following variances for July:
   a. Direct materials price and quantity variances.
   b. Direct labour rate and efficiency variances.
2. Prepare a brief explanation of the significance and possible causes of each variance.
3. Compute the variable overhead cost variances. Based on your calculation, is it possible to conclude that there were inefficiencies in operations causing excessive variable overhead to be incurred?
4. Compute the fixed overhead volume variance.
5. Is there over- or underapplied overhead? How much?

EXERCISE 11–6
Performing an All-Variance Analysis [LO3 – CC15, 17; LO4 – CC22, 23]

The following standard costing data, per unit, are for Black Ltd. for January:

Direct materials	45 kilograms at $8 per kilogram
Direct labour	6 hours at $30 per hour
Variable overhead	6 hours at $10 per hour
Fixed overhead	$45

For January, Black's flexible budget volume of output was 720 units. Budgeted (planned) output was 750 units. Direct materials purchased and used were 31,000 kilograms at a total cost of $251,720. Direct labour used was 4,800 hours at $28.50 per hour. Variable overhead cost was $42,700. Actual fixed overhead cost was $38,000. Fixed overhead cost is applied using direct labour-hours. The normal volume is the same as the planned volume for January.

Required:

1. Without doing any calculations, complete a table like the following, adding as many rows as needed, and then answer the question. To illustrate the format, we show you three rows. Because fixed overhead cost variances have a different structure, we show the information you need to fill out. The question marks indicate the information you must provide. Can you tell for each variance if it will exist and its nature, F or U, from the table?

Variance	AR	SR	AQ	SQ
DM, price variance	$251,720/ 31,000	$8/kg	N/A	N/A
DM, quantity variance	N/A	N/A	31,000 kg	?
Fixed overhead variances	Actual cost = ?	Budgeted cost = ?	Planned volume of labour-hours = ?	Standard volume of direct labour-hours for actual output 6 hours × ? units

2. Calculate the direct labour flexible budget variances.
3. Calculate the direct materials variances.
4. Compute the variable overhead variances.
5. Compute the fixed overhead variances.

EXERCISE 11–7
Preparing Flexible Budgets [LO2 – CC12]

ToasToe Inc. (TI) is a manufacturer of heating elements for toaster overs. To improve control over operations, the president wants to install a flexible budgeting system, rather than the single master budget being used at present. The following data are available for expected costs for production. The relevant range of production levels for fixed overhrad costs is 75,000 to 170,000 units:

Variable costs:	
Manufacturing	$6/unit
Administrative	$3/unit
Selling	$1/unit
Fixed costs:	
Manufacturing	$100,000
Administrative	$ 80,000

Required:

Prepare a flexible budget for each of the three sales levels of: 90,000, 100,000, and 110,000 units. Each heating element is expected to sell for $12.

EXERCISE 11–8
Performing a Basic Variance Computation [LO2 – CC8]

The following data were collected by Bemidji Co. for the month of June:

Static budget data:

Sales	9,000 units @ $30/unit
Variable costs	$23 per unit
Total fixed costs	$18,800

Actual results:

Sales	9,600 units @ $29/unit
Variable costs	$24 per unit
Total fixed costs	$18,200

Required:

1. Prepare the static budget.
2. Prepare the flexible budget. Explain its usefulness for management control in one or two sentences.
3. Compute the static budget variance and decompose it into its component variances.

Note: It is recommended that you prepare a single schedule to answer all three parts.

(Adapted © CPA Canada)

EXERCISE 11–9
Computing Fixed and Variable Overhead Variances [LO3 – CC18; LO4 – CC22, 23]

Consider a manufacturer that makes a certain product. Variable manufacturing overhead and fixed manufacturing overhead are allocated to each unit made based on budgeted direct labour-hours. The following are the production data. (There were no beginning or ending inventories.)

Budgeted variable overhead rate per DLH	$12
Budgeted DLHs per unit	4

Data for May are as follows:

Budgeted production volume	1,000 units
Actual direct labour-hours	4,540 DLHs
Actual variable overhead costs	$52,200
Actual production volume	1,100 units
Budgeted fixed overhead costs	$60,000
Actual fixed overhead costs	$63,000

Required:

1. Calculate all the variable overhead variances.
2. Calculate all the fixed overhead variances.

(Adapted © CPA Canada)

EXERCISE 11–10
Classifying Fixed Overhead Variances [LO4 – CC23]

Selected operating information on three different companies for a recent year is shown below:

	Company		
	A	B	C
Full-capacity MHs	15,000	27,000	30,000
Budgeted MHs*	12,500	25,000	30,000
Actual MHs	12,500	26,000	28,000
Standard MHs allowed for actual production	13,000	23,000	30,000

*Denominator activity level for computing the predetermined overhead rate

Required:

For each company, state whether the company would have a favourable or unfavourable volume variance, and why.

Problems

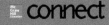

PROBLEM 11–1
Performing Variance Analysis in a Hospital [LO3 – CC15, 17, 18]

John Fleming, chief administrator for a district hospital, is concerned about costs for tests in the hospital's lab. Fleming has asked you to evaluate costs for the past month. The following information is available:

> **CHECK FIGURES**
> (1) Materials quantity variance: $5,250 U
> (2a) Labour rate variance: $2,300 F

a. Basically, two types of tests are performed in the lab—blood tests and smears. During the past month, 1,800 blood tests and 2,400 smears were performed in the lab.

b. Small glass plates are used in both types of tests. During the past month, the hospital purchased 12,000 plates at a cost of $28,200. This cost is net of a 6% quantity discount. 1,500 of these plates were still on hand unused at the end of the month; there were no plates on hand at the beginning of the month.

c. During the past month, 1,150 hours of labour time were recorded in the lab. The cost of this labour time was $13,800.

d. Variable overhead cost last month in the lab for utilities and supplies totalled $7,820.

The hospital has never used standard costs. By searching industry literature, however, you have determined the following nationwide averages for hospital labs:

Plates: Two plates are required per lab test. These plates cost $2.50 each and are disposed of after the test is completed.

Labour: Each blood test should require 0.3 hour to complete, and each smear should require 0.15 hour to complete. The average cost of this lab time is $14 per hour.

Overhead: Overhead cost is based on direct labour-hours. The average rate for variable overhead is $6 per hour.

Fleming would like a complete analysis of the cost of plates, labour, and overhead in the lab for the last month so that he can get to the root of the lab's cost problem.

Required:

1. Compute a materials price variance for the plates purchased last month and a materials quantity variance for the plates used last month.

2. a. For labour cost in the lab, compute a labour rate variance and a labour efficiency variance.

   b. In most hospitals, one-half of the workers in the lab are senior technicians and one-half are assistants. In an effort to reduce costs, the hospital employs only one-fourth senior technicians and three-fourths assistants. Would you recommend that this policy be continued? Explain.

3. Compute the variable overhead spending and efficiency variances. Is there any relationship between the variable overhead efficiency variance and the labour efficiency variance? Explain.

 PROBLEM 11–2

Performing an All-Variance Analysis [LO3 – CC15, 17, 18; LO4 – CC22, 23, 24]

Becton Labs Inc. produces various chemical compounds for industrial use. One compound, called Fludex, is prepared by means of an elaborate distilling process. The company has developed standard costs for one unit of Fludex, as follows:

CHECK FIGURES
(1a) Materials price variance:
$15,000 F
(2a) Labour efficiency
variance: $4,375 U

Direct materials	2.5 mL at $20 per millilitre
Direct labour	1.4 hours at $12.50 per hour
Variable overhead	1.4 hours at $3.50 per hour

During November, the following activity was recorded by the company relative to production of Fludex:

a. Materials were purchased, 12,000 millilitres at a cost of $225,000.

b. There was no beginning inventory of materials on hand to start the month; at the end of the month, 2,500 millilitres of material remained in the warehouse unused.

c. The company employs 35 lab technicians to work on the production of Fludex. During November, each worked an average of 160 hours at an average rate of $12 per hour.

d. Variable manufacturing overhead is assigned to Fludex on the basis of direct labour-hours. Variable manufacturing overhead costs during November totalled $18,200.

e. Fixed overhead is also allocated on the basis of direct labour-hours. The company had budgeted $14,000 for the month but underapplied it by $675.

f. During November, 3,750 good units of Fludex were produced. The normal volume for the month is 4,000 good units.

The company's management is anxious to determine the efficiency of the activities surrounding the production of Fludex. The company's policy is to investigate any variance more than 2% different from the relevant standard.

Required:

1. a. For materials used in the production of Fludex, compute the price and quantity variances.

    b. The materials were purchased from a new supplier who is anxious to enter into a long-term purchase contract. Would you recommend that the company sign the contract? Explain.

2. a. For direct labour employed in the production of Fludex, compute the rate and efficiency variances.

    b. In the past, the 35 technicians employed in the production of Fludex consisted of 20 senior technicians and 15 assistants. During November, the company experimented with only 15 senior technicians and 20 assistants in order to save costs. Would you recommend that the new labour mix be continued? Explain.

3. Compute the variable overhead spending and efficiency variances. What relationship can you see between this efficiency variance and the labour efficiency variance?

4. Compute the fixed overhead cost variances for November.

PROBLEM 11–3
Performing a Comprehensive Variance Analysis [LO2 – CC14; LO3 – CC15, 16, 17, 18; LO4 – CC22, 23, 24]

Miller Toy Company manufactures a plastic swimming pool at its Westwood Plant. The standard cost for one pool is as follows:

CHECK FIGURES

(1a) Materials price variance: $3,000 F

(2) Net variance: $16,290 U

	Standard Quantity or Hours	Standard Price or Rate	Standard Cost
Direct materials	1.5 kilograms	$4 per kilogram	$ 6.00
Direct labour	0.8 hours	$6 per hour	4.80
Variable manufacturing overhead	0.4 machine-hours	$3 per machine-hour	1.20
Total standard cost			$12.00

The plant has been experiencing problems for some time, as is shown by its June income statement when it made and sold 15,000 pools; the normal volume is 15,150 pools per month. Fixed costs are allocated using machine-hours.

	Flexible Budgeted	Actual
Sales (15,000 pools)	$450,000	$450,000
Less: Variable expenses:		
Variable cost of goods sold*	180,000	196,290
Variable selling expenses	20,000	20,000
Total variable expenses	200,000	216,290
Contribution margin	250,000	233,710

	Flexible Budgeted	Actual
Less: Fixed expenses:		
Manufacturing overhead	130,290	130,290
Selling and administrative	84,000	84,000
Total fixed expenses	214,290	214,290
Net income	$ 35,710	$ 19,420

*Contains direct materials, direct labour, and variable manufacturing overhead

Janet Dunn, the general manager of the Westwood Plant, wants to get things under control. She needs information about the operations in June since the income statement signalled that the problem could be due to the variable cost of goods sold. Dunn learns the following about operations and costs in June:

a. 30,000 kilograms of materials were purchased at a cost of $3.90 per kilogram.

b. 24,600 kilograms of materials were used in production. (Finished goods and work-in-process inventories are insignificant and can be ignored.)

c. 11,800 direct labour-hours were worked at a cost of $7 per hour.

d. Variable manufacturing overhead cost totalling $18,290 for the month was incurred. A total of 5,900 machine-hours was recorded.

It is the company's policy to close all variances to cost of goods sold on a monthly basis.

Required:

1. Compute the following variances for June:
    a. Direct materials price and quantity variances.
    b. Direct labour rate and efficiency variances.
    c. Variable overhead spending and efficiency variances.

2. Summarize the variances you computed in part (1) by showing the net overall favourable or unfavourable variance for the month. What impact did this figure have on the company's income statement? Show your computations.

3. Pick out the two most significant variances you computed in part (1). Explain to Dunn the possible causes of these variances.

4. Compute the fixed overhead cost variances and explain their significance to Dunn.

5. Do you agree that the budget shown above is the proper comparison for the actual results for June, or do you think that the correct budget should be based on a volume of 15,150 pools? Explain.

PROBLEM 11–4
Performing a Variable Cost Variances Analysis and Preparing Journal Entries [LO2 – CC14; LO3 – CC15, 17, 18; LO6 – CC27^A, 28^A]

Trueform Products Inc., a U.S. company, produces a broad line of sports equipment and uses a standard costing system for control purposes. Last year, the company produced 8,000 varsity footballs. The standard costs associated with this football, along with the actual costs incurred last year, follow (per football):

CHECK FIGURES

(2a) Labour rate variance: $3,200 U
(3) Variable overhead efficiency variance: $2,000 F

	Standard Cost	Actual Cost
Direct materials:		
Standard: 3.7 feet at $5.00 per foot	$18.50	
Actual: 4.0 feet at $4.80 per foot		$19.20
Direct labour:		
Standard: 0.9 hour at $7.50 per hour	6.75	
Actual: 0.8 hour at $8 per hour		6.40
Variable manufacturing overhead:		
Standard: 0.9 hour at $2.50 per hour	2.25	
Actual: 0.8 hour at $2.75 per hour	_____	2.20
Total cost per football	$27.50	$27.80

The president was elated when he saw that actual costs exceeded standard costs by only $0.30 per football. He stated, "I was afraid that our unit cost might get out of hand when we gave out those raises last year in order to stimulate output. But it's obvious our costs are well under control."

There was no inventory of materials on hand to start the year. During the year, 32,000 feet of materials were purchased and used in production.

Required:

1. For direct materials:
    a. Compute the price and quantity variances for the year.
    b. Prepare journal entries to record all activity relating to direct materials for the year.
2. For direct labour:
    a. Compute the rate and efficiency variances.
    b. Prepare a journal entry to record the incurrence of direct labour cost for the year.
3. Compute the variable overhead spending and efficiency variances.
4. Was the president correct in his statement that "our costs are well under control"? Explain.
5. State possible causes of each variance that you have computed.

PROBLEM 11–5
Setting Standards [LO1 – CC1, 2, 3, 4, 5, 6]

Canuck Maple makes maple syrup. It is based in a small town between Montreal and Quebec City. The owner uses a special recipe handed down through several generations in his family to make the highly popular brand of maple syrup. Due to recent growth of the company, the owner wants to develop a standard cost for the syrup. The following information is available on the production of the syrup:

CHECK FIGURES
(1) Syrup: 18.0 kg
(3) Standard cost: $97.20

a. Syrup is made by combining the base syrup with a secret ingredient called X. The syrup and ingredient X are brought together in a specific proportion and boiled for a specific time at a specific temperature. This process results in a 20% loss in volume for both ingredients. After boiling, the mixture consists of 9.6 litres of syrup and 12 kilograms of X per 10-litre batch of syrup.

b. After the boiling process is complete, the solution is cooled slightly before 5 kilograms of a second ingredient, Y, are added per 10-litre batch of syrup. There is no loss of volume during this process. The resulting solution is then bottled in 10-litre containers.

c. The finished product is undergoes strict quality testing. The syrup is unstable and easily spoils, and one 10-litre batch out of six is rejected at final inspection. In other words, after every five good batches, the sixth one is rejected. Rejected batches have no commercial value and are thrown out.

d. It takes a worker 35 minutes to process one 10-litre batch of syrup. Employees work an eight-hour day, including one hour per day for rest breaks and cleanup.

Required:

1. Determine the amount of syrup that must be processed to yield one batch of finished product, considering only the loss during processing.
2. Determine the amount of syrup that is lost due to failure to pass the quality test.
3. Determine the standard quantity of syrup that will be required to make one 10-litre batch of finished syrup.
4. Determine the standard quantity of ingredients X and Y needed to produce an acceptable 10-litre batch of syrup.
5. How many batches of syrup are processed in a day?
6. Determine the standard labour time to produce an acceptable 10-litre batch of syrup.
7. Assuming the following purchase prices and costs, prepare a standard cost card for materials and labour for one acceptable 10-litre batch of syrup:

Syrup	$1.50 per litre
Ingredient X	$2.80 per kilogram
Ingredient Y	$3.00 per kilogram
Direct labour cost	$9.00 per hour

PROBLEM 11–6
Working Backward From Labour Variances [LO3 – CC17]

The auto repair shop of Quality Motor Company uses standards to control the labour time and labour cost in the shop. The standard labour cost for a motor tune-up follows:

CHECK FIGURE
(1) Actual hours: 171

Job	Standard Hours	Standard Rate	Standard Cost
Motor tune-up	3	$9	$27

The record showing the time spent in the shop last week on motor tune-ups has been misplaced. However, the shop supervisor recalls that 50 tune-ups were completed during the week, and the controller recalls the following variance data relating to tune-ups:

Labour rate variance	$90 F
Total labour variance	96 U

Required:

1. Determine the number of actual labour-hours spent on tune-ups during the week.
2. Determine the actual hourly rate of pay for tune-ups last week.

(*Hint:* A useful way to proceed would be to work from known to unknown data either by using the variance formulas or by using the columnar format shown in Exhibit 11–5.)

PROBLEM 11–7
Performing Computations From Incomplete Data [LO3 – CC15, 17]

Sharp Company manufactures a product for which the following standards have been set:

CHECK FIGURES
(1a) Actual cost: $5.43/m
(2a) Standard labour rate: $8.11

	Standard Quantity or Hours	Standard Price or Rate	Standard Cost
Direct materials	3 metres	$7 per metre	$21
Direct labour	? hours	? per hour	?

During March, the company purchased direct materials at a cost of $55,650, all of which were used in the production of 3,200 units of product. In addition, 4,900 hours of direct labour time was worked on the product during the month. The cost of this labour time was $36,750. The following variances have been computed for the month:

Materials quantity variance	$4,500 U
Total labour variance	2,000 F
Labour efficiency variance	1,000 U

Required:

1. For direct materials:
    a. Compute the actual cost per metre for materials for March.
    b. Compute the materials price variance and a total variance for materials.
2. For direct labour:
    a. Compute the standard direct labour rate per hour.
    b. Compute the standard hours allowed for the month's production.
    c. Compute the standard hours allowed per unit of product.

(*Hint:* To answer the problem, it may be helpful to organize the information in a variance diagram (Exhibit 11–9) along with with the variance formulas, and then solve for the unknown values.)

PROBLEM 11-8

Performing a Variance Analysis—Working Backward [LO1 – CC6; LO3 – CC15, 16, 17, 18, LO4 – CC21, 22]

JigSaw Puzzle Company makes a certain product using materials measured in metres, labour-hours, and overhead costs.. The company uses a standard costing system. The following information is available regarding the standard variable costs of producing one unit:

CHECK FIGURE

(1b) Standard direct labour rate per hour: $30

Standard variable overhead cost per direct labour-hour	$ 6
Standard direct materials cost per metre	16
Total standard variable cost per unit	63

In the month of June, 3,000 units were produced and sold. Also in June, all materials purchases made in the month were consumed in production. Selected information for June follows:

Standard cost of direct labour to produce 3,000 units	$48,000
Standard cost of variable manufacturing overhead to produce 3,000 units	9,600
Actual direct materials cost	$130,000
Actual variable overhead cost	$9,720
Actual direct labour-hours	1,700
Total materials variance	$1,400 F
Materials quantity variance	$2,400 U
Variable overhead spending variance	$480 F
Actual variable cost per unit produced	$63.42
Actual fixed overhead cost	$33,200

Required:

1. Based on the above information:
   a. What is $9,600/$6?
   b. What is the standard wage rate per direct labour-hour?
   c. Calculate the standard cost of the materials required for June production.
   d. What is $63.42 × 3,000?
   e. Calculate the total actual direct labour cost incurred.
   f. Calculate materials price variance.
   g. Calculate the labour rate variance.
   h. Calculate the labour efficiency variance.
2. Prepare the standard cost card.

3. Subsequent to the preparation of the analyses required above, you learn that the predetermined fixed overhead allocation rate is $20 per direct labour-hour and that the static budget volume of output was 3,200 units. Compute the fixed overhead cost variances.

(Adapted © CPA Canada)

 PROBLEM 11–9

Performing a Comprehensive Variance Analysis With Incomplete Data; Preparing Journal Entries [LO3 – CC15, 16, 17, 18; LO6 – CC27[A], 28[A]]

Maple Products Ltd., a U.S. company, manufactures hockey sticks that are used worldwide. The standard cost of one hockey stick is as follows:

> **CHECK FIGURES**
>
> (1a) Materials price variance: $6,000 F
> (3) Variable overhead spending variance: $1,650 F

	Standard Quantity or Hours	Standard Price or Rate	Standard Cost
Direct materials	? feet	$3.00 per foot	$?
Direct labour	2 hours	? per hour	?
Variable manufacturing overhead	? hours	1.30 per hour	?
Total standard cost			$27.00

Last year, 8,000 hockey sticks were produced and sold. Selected cost data relating to last year's operations follow:

	Dr	Cr
Direct materials purchased (60,000 feet)	$174,000	
Wages payable (? hours)		$79,200*
Work in process—direct materials	115,200	
Direct labour rate variance		3,300
Variable overhead efficiency variance	650	

*Relates to the actual direct labour cost for the year

The following additional information is available for last year's operations:

a. No materials were on hand at the start of last year. Some of the materials purchased during the year were still on hand in the warehouse at the end of the year.

b. The variable manufacturing overhead rate is based on direct labour-hours. Total actual variable manufacturing overhead cost for last year was $19,800.

c. Actual direct materials usage for last year exceeded the standard by 0.2 foot per stick.

Required:

1. For direct materials:
   a. Compute the price and quantity variances for last year.
   b. Prepare journal entries to record all activities relating to direct materials for last year.
2. For direct labour:
   a. Verify the rate variance given above and compute the efficiency variance for last year.
   b. Prepare a journal entry to record activity relating to direct labour for last year.
3. Compute the variable overhead spending variance for last year and verify the variable overhead efficiency variance given above.
4. State possible causes of each variance that you have computed.
5. Prepare a completed standard cost card for one hockey stick.

PROBLEM 11–10
Developing Standard Costs [LO1 – CC2, 3, 4, 5, 6; LO3 – CC15, 17]

Canadian Lawn and Yard Services (CLYS) recently decided to implement a standard costing system for all the different kinds of yard and lawn services it provides to customers. For its "standard" service, it determined the following *ideal* standards:

CHECK FIGURE

(2) Standard cost: $623

| Direct materials | 47 kilograms of soil; 20 bunches of foliage |
| Direct labour | 10.8 hours |

The following additional information is available:

a. Six percent of the soil transported to the customer's work site is blown away during transportation.
b. For every 10 kilograms of usable soil, half a kilogram is considered unusable and thrown away.
c. For every 10 usable bunches of foliage, one is considered unusable and thrown away.
d. On an average yard, labourers spend 10% of their total work time redoing portions of the work.
e. Yard workers put in seven-hour days including three breaks of 20 minutes each for rest, nutrition, and cleanup.
f. The standard price of direct materials is soil, $7.20 per kilogram, and foliage, $3.50 per bunch.
g. Yard labour is paid at the rate of $12 per hour including benefits.

Required:

1. Compute the practical quantity standards for direct materials and direct labour required to provide "standard" service to a customer. Show all the steps in your calculation.
2. Compute the standard costs of providing "standard" service to a customer.
3. As part of the implementation of a standard costing system at CLYS, John Wakefield (a cost accountant) plans to train those responsible for maintaining the standards on how to use variance analysis. Wakefield is particularly concerned with the causes of unfavourable variances.
   a. Discuss possible causes of unfavourable materials price variances, and identify the individual(s) who should be held responsible for these variances.
   b. Discuss possible causes of unfavourable labour efficiency variances, and identify the individual(s) who should be held responsible for these variances.

PROBLEM 11–11

Working Backward, Comprehensive Variance Analysis [LO2 – CC14; LO3 – CC15, 16, 17, 18; LO4 – CC22, 23, 24]

You have been given the following list of variances for the Pennadi Company:

Direct materials price variance	$14,000 U
Direct materials quantity variance	10,000 U
Direct labour rate variance	8,320 F
Direct labour efficiency variance	48,000 U
Variable overhead spending variance	1,920 U
Variable overhead efficiency variance	4,000 U
Fixed overhead budget variance	3,000 U
Fixed overhead volume variance	43,800 F

You have also been given the following information:

Actual units produced	20,000
Budgeted units of production (normal volume)	16,000
Standard labour-hours for actual output	10,000
Standard material units for actual output	200,000
Actual direct labour costs	$199,680
Actual cost of direct materials	$264,000

Overhead is applied using direct labour-hours. Variable overhead is applied at the rate of $10 per direct labour-hour. The materials purchase price was $0.528.*(Attempt the following questions in the order listed.)*

Required:

1. What was the actual number of units of direct materials purchased?
2. What was the standard cost of the actual number of units of direct materials purchased and the standard price of direct materials?
3. What cost for direct materials will be reported in the flexible budget?
4. What is the standard cost of direct materials used in production?
5. How much direct materials were consumed in production?
6. How many actual direct labour-hours were worked?
7. What was the standard cost per unit of output produced, assuming that variable costing was used?

8. Calculate the budgeted fixed overhead cost allocation rate.
9. Calculate the actual, budgeted, and allocated fixed overhead costs.
10. Calculate the underapplied or overapplied fixed overhead cost.

(Adapted © CPA Canada)

PROBLEM 11–12
Performing a Labour Variance Analysis [LO3 – CC17]

Zinn Corporation recently agreed to a union contract provision that guarantees a minimum wage of $1,250 per month to each direct labour employee equivalent to 125 hours of work each month. Currently, 125 employees are covered by this provision. All direct labour employees are paid $10 per hour. Thus, until an employee works 125 hours, the remenuration is a fixed $1,250 per employee each month. Rusty Zinn, the assistant to the accountant was given the task of budgeting for the direct labour cost. Because of the contract provision, Rusty decided that the $156,250 (= 125 × $1,250 per month) should be treated as a fixed monthly cost. Rusty was instructed to calculate each month's budget using the following formula: $156,250 + $7 per direct labour-hour.

CHECK FIGURE

(2) May: $0 F

Figures for the first three months of the fiscal year are as follows:

	April	May	June
Direct labour-hours planned and worked	27,500	40,000	60,000
Direct labour costs budgeted	$348,750	$436,250	$576,250
Direct labour costs incurred	$275,000	$400,000	$600,000
Variance	$73,750F	$36,250F	$23,750U

These figures are a source of concern because they show unfavourable variances when production is high, and favourable variances during slow months. The factory manager is certain that this trend does not reflect reality.

Required:

1. Explain why the variance is favourable during slow months and unfavourable in months when production is high. A diagram may help you to develop an explanation.
2. Develop a formula for direct labour costs more appropriate to the actual cost behaviour, then recalculate the variances for April, May, and June.

PROBLEM 11–13
Variance Analysis and the Impact of Variances on Unit Costs [LO3 – CC15, 16, 17]

Landers Company manufactures a number of products. The standards relating to one of these products are shown below, along with actual cost data for May.

CHECK FIGURES

(1b) Labour rate variance: $6,840 F

(1c) Variable overhead efficiency variance: $3,000 U

	Standard Cost per Unit	Actual Cost per Unit
Direct materials:		
Standard: 1.80 feet at $3.00 per foot	$ 5.40	
Actual: 1.75 feet at $3.20 per foot		$ 5.60
Direct labour:		
Standard: 0.90 hours at $18.00 per hour	16.20	
Actual: 0.95 hours at $17.40 per hour		16.53
Variable overhead:		
Standard: 0.90 hours at $5.00 per hour	4.50	
Actual: 0.95 hours at $4.60 per hour	_____	4.37
Total cost per unit	$26.10	$26.50
Excess of actual cost over standard cost per unit	$0.40	

The production superintendent was pleased when he saw this report and commented: "This $0.40 excess cost is well within the 2% limit management has set for acceptable variances. It's obvious that there's not much to worry about with this product."

Actual production for the month was 12,000 units. Variable overhead cost is assigned to products on the basis of direct labour-hours. There were no beginning or ending inventories of materials.

Required:

1. Compute the following variances for May:
   a. Materials quantity and price variances.
   b. Labour efficiency and rate variances.
   c. Variable overhead efficiency and rate variances.
2. How much of the $0.40 excess unit cost is traceable to each of the variances computed in (1) above.
3. How much of the $0.40 excess unit cost is traceable to apparent inefficient use of labour time?
4. Do you agree that the excess unit cost is not of concern?

PROBLEM 11–14
Performing a Basic Variance Analysis [LO3 – CC15, 17, 18; LO4 – CC22, 23]

Aaha Inc. produces premium protective automotive covers. The direct materials and direct labour standards for one car cover are as follows:

CHECK FIGURES

(1) Total direct materials cost variance, $6,000 F

(3) Volume variance = $1,498.63 U; Spending variance = $125 U

	Standard Quantity or Hours	Standard Price or Rate	Standard Cost
Direct materials	6.0 metres of cloth	$9 per metre	$54.00
Direct labour	0.25 hours	$15 per hour	$ 3.75
Variable overhead	0.25 hours	$7 per hour	$ 1.75

Budgeted fixed overhead cost is $17,700, and the normal production volume is 2,185 car covers. Overhead is applied on the basis of direct labour-hours.

In September, the following activity was recorded:

- 12,000 metres of cloth were purchased at a cost of $8.50 per metre.
- All of the purchased material was used to produce 2,000 car covers.
- 525 direct labour-hours were recorded at a total labour cost of $7,875.

Actual variable overhead cost was $3,800, and fixed overhead cost was $17,500.

Required:

1. Compute all direct materials variances for September.
2. Compute all direct labour cost variances for September.
3. Calculate the total under- or overapplied overhead. Show all the variances calculated and indicate if each variance is favourable or unfavourable.
4. Suppose the standard price per metre for cloth increases by $1. "The quantity variance is unaffected, but the price variance will become more favourable than before, all else equal." True or false?
5. When the productivity in the use of direct materials improves, where will the impact be first measured? Select from the three choices below:
   a)   In the actual cost of direct materials used.
   b)   In the standard cost of direct materials used.
   c)   In the cost of the direct materials reported on the flexible budget.

(Adapted © CPA Canada)

PROBLEM 11–15
Comparing Static versus Flexible Budget Analysis [LO2 – CC10, 11, 12, 13]

The St. Lucia Blood Bank, a private charity partly supported by government grants, is located on the Caribbean island of St. Lucia. The blood bank has just finished its operations for September, which was a particularly busy month due to a powerful hurricane that hit neighbouring islands, causing many injuries. The hurricane largely bypassed St. Lucia, but the residents of St. Lucia willingly donated their blood to help people on other islands. As a consequence, the blood bank collected and processed 24% more blood than had been originally planned for the month.

CHECK FIGURE

(1) Flexible budget total cost at 620 litres: $32,290

A report prepared by a government official comparing actual costs to budgeted costs for the blood bank appears below. (The currency on St. Lucia is the East Caribbean dollar.) Continued support from the government depends on the blood bank's ability to demonstrate control over its costs.

ST. LUCIA BLOOD BANK Cost Control Report For the Month Ended September 30			
	Actual	**Budget**	**Variance**
Litres of blood collected	620	500	120 F
Variable costs:			
Medical supplies	$ 9,350	$ 7,500	$1,850 U
Lab tests	6,180	6,000	180 U
Refreshments for donors	1,340	1,000	340 U
Administrative supplies	400	250	150 U
Total variable cost	17,270	14,750	2,520 U
Fixed costs:			
Staff salaries	10,000	10,000	—
Equipment depreciation	2,800	2,500	300 U
Rent	1,000	1,000	—
Utilities	570	500	70 U
Total fixed cost	14,370	14,000	370 U
Total cost	$31,640	$28,750	$2,890 U

The managing director of the blood bank was very unhappy with this report, claiming that his costs were higher than expected due to the emergency on the neighbouring islands. He also pointed out that the additional costs had been fully covered by payments from grateful recipients on the other islands. The government official who prepared the report countered that all of the figures had been submitted by the blood bank to the government; he was just pointing out that actual costs were a lot higher than promised in the budget.

Required:

1. Prepare a new performance report for September using the flexible budget approach. (*Note:* Even though some of these costs might be classified as direct costs rather than overhead, the flexible budget approach can still be used to prepare a flexible budget performance report.) Organize your report using the format of Exhibit 11–7. Show four columns (actual, flexible budget, variance, and static budget).

2. Do you think any of the variances in the report you prepared should be investigated? Why?

 PROBLEM 11–16

Computing Comprehensive Standard Cost Variances [LO1 – CC6; LO3 – CC15, 17, 18; LO4 – CC22, 23]

Flandro Company uses a standard costing system and sets predetermined overhead rates on the basis of direct labour-hours. The following data are taken from the company's budget for the current year:

CHECK FIGURES

(1) Standard cost: $48
(3) Volume variance: $54,400 U

Denominator activity (direct labour-hours)	20,000
Variable manufacturing overhead cost	$60,000
Fixed manufacturing overhead cost	$86,000

The standard cost card for the company's only product is as follows:

Direct materials, 3 metres at $4.80/m	$14.40
Direct labour, 2 hours at $7/h	14.00
Manufacturing overhead, 140% of direct labour cost	19.60
Standard cost per unit	$48.00

During the year, the company produced 6,000 units of product and incurred the following costs:

Materials purchased, 24,000 metres at $5.10/m	$122,400
Materials used in production (in metres)	18,500
Direct labour cost incurred, 11,600 hours at $7.50/h	$87,000
Variable manufacturing overhead cost incurred	$34,580
Fixed manufacturing overhead cost incurred	$69,400

Required:

1. Redo the standard cost card in a clearer, more usable format by detailing the variable and fixed overhead cost elements.
2. Prepare an analysis of the variances for materials and labour for the year.
3. Prepare an analysis of the variances for variable and fixed overhead for the year.
4. What effect, if any, does the choice of a denominator activity level have on unit standard costs? Is the volume variance a controllable variance from a spending point of view? Explain.

PROBLEM 11–17
Applying Overhead and Computing Overhead Variances [LO3 – CC18; LO4 – CC21, 22, 23, 24]

Chilczuk, S.A. of Gdansk, Poland, is a major producer of classic Polish sausage. The company uses a standard costing system to help control costs. Overhead is applied to production on the basis of labour-hours. According to the company's flexible budget, the following manufacturing overhead costs should be incurred at an activity level of 70,000 labour-hours (the denominator activity level) (the currency in Poland is the zloty, denoted here by PZ):

CHECK FIGURE

(3) Spending variance: PZ6,000 U; Budget variance: PZ1,200 F

Variable overhead costs	PZ175,000
Fixed overhead costs	420,000
Total overhead cost	PZ595,000

During the most recent year, the following operating results were recorded:

Activity:	
Actual labour-hours worked	60,000
Standard labour-hours allowed for output	64,000
Cost:	
Actual variable overhead cost incurred	PZ156,000
Actual fixed overhead cost incurred	PZ418,800

At the end of the year, the company's manufacturing overhead account contained the following data:

Manufacturing Overhead

Actual	574,800	Applied	544,000
	30,800		

Management would like to determine the cause of the PZ30,800 underapplied overhead.

Required:

1. Compute the predetermined overhead rate. Break the rate into variable and fixed cost elements.
2. Show how the PZ544,000 applied figure in the manufacturing overhead account was computed.
3. Analyze the PZ30,800 underapplied overhead figure in terms of the variable overhead spending and efficiency variances and the fixed overhead budget and volume variances.
4. Explain the meaning of each variance you computed in part (3).

PROBLEM 11–18
Computing Comprehensive Standard Cost Variances [LO3 – CC15, 17, 18; LO4 – CC22, 23, 24]

"Wonderful! Not only did our salespeople do a good job in meeting the sales budget this year, but our production people did a good job in controlling costs as well," said Kim Clark, president of Martell Company. "Our $18,000 overall manufacturing cost variance is only 1.5% of the $1,200,000 standard cost of products sold during the year. That's well within the 3% parameter set by management for acceptable variances. It looks like everyone will be in line for a bonus this year."

CHECK FIGURES
(3a) Efficiency variance: $7,500 U
(3b) Volume variance: $42,000 F

The company produces and sells a single product. A standard cost card for the product follows:

Standard Cost Card—Per Unit of Product	
Direct materials, 2 metres at $8.45 per metre	$16.90
Direct labour, 1.4 hours at $8 per hour	11.20
Variable overhead, 1.4 hours at $2.50 per hour	3.50
Fixed overhead, 1.4 hours at $6 per hour	8.40
Standard cost per unit	$40.00

The following additional information is available for the year just completed:

a. The company manufactured 30,000 units of product during the year.
b. A total of 64,000 metres of material was purchased during the year at a cost of $8.55 per metre. All of this material was used to manufacture the 30,000 units. There were no beginning or ending inventories for the year.
c. The company worked 45,000 direct labour-hours during the year at an average cost of $7.80 per hour.
d. Overhead is applied to products on the basis of direct labour-hours. Data relating to manufacturing overhead costs follow:

Denominator activity level (direct labour-hours)	35,000
Budgeted fixed overhead costs (from the overhead flexible budget)	$210,000
Actual variable overhead costs incurred	108,000
Actual fixed overhead costs incurred	211,800

Required:

1. Compute the direct materials price and quantity variances for the year.
2. Compute the direct labour rate and efficiency variances for the year.
3. For manufacturing overhead, compute the following:
    a. The variable overhead spending and efficiency variances for the year.
    b. The fixed overhead budget and volume variances for the year.
4. Total the variances you have computed, and compare the net amount with the $18,000 mentioned by the president. Do you agree that bonuses should be given to everyone for good cost control during the year? Explain your answer.

PROBLEM 11–19
Using Fixed Overhead Variances [LO4 – CC22, 23]

The standard cost card for the single product manufactured by Cutter, Inc. is provided below:

CHECK FIGURE
(1) Standard hours allowed:
28,500 hours

Standard Cost Card—Per Unit	
Direct materials, 3 metres at $7.50 per metre	$22.50
Direct labour, 3 hours at $7.75 per hour	23.25
Variable overhead, 3 hours at $1.50 per hour	4.50
Fixed overhead, 3 hours at $5 per hour	15.00
Total standard cost per unit	$65.25

Manufacturing overhead is applied to production on the basis of direct labour-hours. During the year, the company worked 27,000 hours and manufactured 9,500 units of product. Selected data relating to the company's fixed manufacturing overhead cost for the year are shown below:

Actual Fixed Overhead Cost	Flexible Budget Fixed Overhead Cost	Applied Fixed Overhead Cost
$148,700	?	__?__ hours × $?
Budget variance, $?	Volume variance, $7,500 U	= $?

Required:

1. What were the standard hours allowed for the year's production?
2. What was the amount of fixed overhead cost contained in the flexible budget for the year?
3. What was the fixed overhead budget variance for the year?
4. What denominator activity level did the company use in setting the predetermined overhead rate for the year?

PROBLEM 11–20
Finding Relations Among Fixed Overhead Variances [LO4 – CC22, 23]

Selected information relating to Yost Company's operations for the most recent year is as follows:

CHECK FIGURE
(3) Volume variance:
$54,000 F

Activity:	
Denominator activity level (machine-hours)	30,000
Standard hours allowed per unit	3
Number of units produced	12,000
Cost:	
Actual fixed overhead costs incurred	$267,000
Fixed overhead budget variance	$3,000 F

The company applies overhead cost to products on the basis of machine-hours.

Required:

1. What were the standard hours allowed for the actual production?
2. What was the fixed portion of the predetermined overhead rate?
3. What was the volume variance?

 PROBLEM 11–21

Creating a Flexible Budget and Overhead Performance Report [LO2 – CC12, 13; LO3 – CC18; LO4 – CC22, 23]

You have just been hired by FAB Company, the manufacturer of a revolutionary new garage door opening device. John Foster, the president, has asked that you review the company's costing system and "do what you can to help us get better control of our manufacturing overhead costs." You find that the company has never used a flexible budget, and you suggest that preparing such a budget would be an excellent first step in overhead planning and control.

> **CHECK FIGURE**
> (2) Total of spending and budget variances: $800 U

After much effort and analysis, you are able to determine the following cost formulas for the company's normal operating range of 10,000 to 20,000 units each month:

Overhead Costs	Cost Formula
Utilities	$0.90 per machine-hour
Maintenance	$1.60 per machine-hour plus $40,000 per month
Machine setup	$0.30 per machine-hour
Indirect labour	$0.70 per machine-hour plus $130,000 per month
Depreciation	$70,000 per month

To show the president how the flexible budget concept works, you have gathered the following actual cost data for the most recent month, March, in which the company produced 13,000 units:

Utilities	$ 24,200
Maintenance	78,100
Machine setup	8,400
Indirect labour	149,600
Depreciation	71,500
Total cost	$331,800

The only variance in the fixed costs for the month was with depreciation, which increased as a result of a purchase of new equipment.

The company had originally planned to work 17,000 units during March using the standard quantity of 34,000 machine-hours.

Required:

1. Prepare flexible budgets for the company in increments of 2,500 units from 10,000 units to 15,000 units.
2. Prepare a flexible budget overhead performance report for the company for March. (Use the format illustrated in Exhibit 11–7.)
3. What additional information would you need to compute an overhead efficiency variance for the company?

PROBLEM 11–22
Performing an Analysis of Variances [LO2 – CC12, 13; LO3 – CC15, 17, 18; LO4 – CC22, 23]

Frank Western, supervisor of the machining department of Freemont Company, was visibly upset after being reprimanded for his department's poor performance over the prior month. The department's performance report is given below.

CHECK FIGURE
(2) Total variance: $36,500 F

"I just can't understand all the red ink," said Western to Sarah Mason, supervisor of another department. "When the boss called me in, I thought he was going to give me a pat on the back because I know for a fact that my department worked more efficiently last month than it has ever worked before. Instead, he tore me apart. I thought for a minute that it might be over the supplies that were stolen out of our warehouse last month. But they only amounted to a couple of thousand dollars, and just look at this report. Everything is unfavourable, and I don't even know why."

	A	B	C	D	E	F
1		FREEMONT COMPANY				
2		Performance Report—Machining Department				
3						
4		Cost				
5		Formula				
6		(per				
7		machine-				
8		hour)	Actual	Budget	Variance	
9	Machine-hours		38,000	35,000		
10						
11	Variable overhead costs:					
12	Utilities	$ 0.40	$ 15,700	$ 14,000	$ 1,700	U
13	Indirect labour	2.30	86,500	80,500	6,000	U
14	Supplies	0.60	26,000	21,000	5,000	U
15	Maintenance	1.20	44,900	42,000	2,900	U
16	Total variable overhead cost	$ 4.50	$173,100	$157,500	$ 15,600	U
17						

	A	B	C	D	E	F
18	Fixed overhead cost:					
19	Supervision		38,000	38,000		
20	Maintenance		92,400	92,000	400	U
21	Depreciation		80,000	80,000	—	
22	Total fixed overhead cost		210,400	210,000	400	U
23	Total overhead cost		$ 383,500	$ 367,500	$ 16,000	U
24						

The budget for the machining department had called for production of 14,000 units last month, which is equal to a budgeted activity level of 35,000 machine-hours (at a standard time of 2.5 hours per unit). Actual production in the machining department for the month was 16,000 units.

Required:

1. Evaluate the overhead performance report given above, and explain why the variances are all unfavourable.

2. Prepare a new overhead performance report that will help Western's superiors assess efficiency and cost control in the machining department. (*Hint:* Exhibit 11–7 may be helpful in structuring your report.)

3. Would the supplies stolen out of the warehouse be included as part of the variable overhead spending variance or as part of the variable overhead efficiency variance for the month? Explain.

PROBLEM 11–23
Applying Overhead and Computing Overhead Variances [LO3 – CC18; LO4 – CC22, 23]

Lane Company manufactures a single product that requires a great deal of hand labour. Overhead cost is applied on the basis of direct labour-hours. The company's condensed flexible budget for manufacturing overhead follows:

CHECK FIGURES

(2) Standard cost: $46
(4) Volume variance: $24,000 F

Overhead Costs	Cost Formul (per direct labour-hour)	Denominator Activity Level		
		30,000 (60,000 hours)	40,000 (80,000 hours)	50,000 (100,000 hours)
Variable costs	$2	$120,000	$160,000	$200,000
Fixed costs		480,000	480,000	480,000
Total overhead cost		$600,000	$640,000	$680,000

The company's product requires 1.5 kilograms of material that has a standard cost of $14 per kilogram and 2 hours of direct labour time that has a standard rate of $4.50 per hour.

The company's facility has a practical capacity of 40,000 units. This was also the planned volume of production for the most recent year. Actual activity and costs for the year were as follows:

Number of units produced	42,000
Actual direct labour-hours worked	85,000
Actual variable overhead cost incurred	$163,500
Actual fixed overhead cost incurred	$483,000

Required:

1. Compute the predetermined overhead rate for the year for the variable and fixed overhead costs. What is the total overhead allocation rate?
2. Prepare a standard cost card for the company's product; show the details for all manufacturing costs on your standard cost card.
3. Do the following:
   a. Compute the standard hours allowed for the year's production.
   b. Complete the following manufacturing overhead T-account for the year:

Manufacturing Overhead

?	?
?	?

4. Determine the reason for any under- or overapplied overhead for the year by computing the variable overhead spending and efficiency variances and the fixed overhead budget and volume variances.
5. Suppose the company had chosen 85,000 direct labour-hours as the denominator activity level, rather than 80,000 hours. State which, if any, of the variances computed in part (4) would have changed, and explain how the variance(s) would have changed. No computations are necessary.

PROBLEM 11–24
Selection of a Denominator; Overhead Analysis; Standard Cost Card [LO4-CC21,22,23]

Scott Company is based in the United States. Its variable manufacturing overhead should be $2.50 per standard direct labour-hour and fixed manufacturing overhead should be $320,000 per year.

The company produces a single product that requires 2.5 direct labour-hours to complete. The direct labour wage rate is $20 per hour. Three yards of raw material are required for each unit of product, at a cost of $5 per yard.

CHECK FIGURE

(4a) 46,250 standard hours

(4c) Volume variance:
$50,000 F

Demand for the company's product differs widely from year to year. Expected activity for this year is 50,000 direct labour-hours; normal activity is 40,000 direct labour-hours per year.

Required:

1. Assume that the company chooses 40,000 direct labour-hours as the denominator level of activity. Compute the predetermined overhead rate, breaking it down into fixed and variable cost components.
2. Assume that the company chooses 50,000 direct labour-hours as the denominator level of activity. Repeat the computations in (1) above.

3. Complete two standard cost cards as outlined below.

Denominator Activity: 40,000 DLHs	
Direct materials, 3 yards at $5 per yard	$15.00
Direct labour, ?	?
Variable manufacturing overhead, ?	?
Fixed manufacturing overhead, ?	?
Total standard cost per unit	$?

Denominator Activity: 50,000 DLHs	
Direct materials, 3 yards at $5 per yard	$15.00
Direct labour, ?	?
Variable manufacturing overhead, ?	?
Fixed manufacturing overhead, ?	?
Total standard cost per unit	$?

4. Assume that 48,000 actual hours are worked during the year, and that 18,500 units are produced. Actual manufacturing overhead costs for the year are as follows:

Variable manufacturing overhead cost	$124,800
Fixed manufacturing overhead cost	321,700
Total manufacturing overhead cost	$446,500

a. Compute the standard hours allowed for the year's actual output.
b. Compute the missing items from the Manufacturing Overhead account below. Assume that the company uses 40,000 direct labour-hours (normal activity) as the denominator activity figure in computing overhead rates, as you have used in requirement 1.

Manufacturing Overhead

Actual costs	446,500		?
?			?

c. Analyze your underapplied or overapplied overhead balance in terms of variable overhead efficiency and rate variances and fixed overhead budget and volume variances.

5. Looking at the variances that you have computed, what appears to be the major disadvantage of using normal activity rather than expected actual activity as a denominator in computing the predetermined overhead rate? What advantages can you see to offset this disadvantage?

PROBLEM 11–25
Computing Overhead Variances [LO3 – CC18; LO4 – CC22, 23]

Begum Company has developed the following standard overhead costs based on a capacity of 400,000 direct labour-hours:

CHECK FIGURE

(1) Variable overhead spending variance: $84,000 F

Variable overhead costs (2 hours at $4)	$ 8
Fixed overhead costs (2 hours at $5)	10
	$18

During May, 170,000 units were scheduled for production; however, only 160,000 units were actually produced. The following information relates to May's production:

a. Actual direct labour cost incurred was $1,288,000 for 330,000 actual hours of work.

b. Actual overhead costs incurred totalled $2,956,000 ($1,236,000 variable and $1,720,000 fixed).

c. All inventories are carried at standard cost.

Required:

1. Compute the variable overhead variances for May.
2. Compute the fixed overhead variances for May.
3. Explain the variable overhead efficiency and production volume variances.

(Adapted © CPA Canada)

PROBLEM 11–26
Applying Overhead; Overhead Variances [LO4 – CC 21, 22, 23]

Highland Shortbread, Ltd., of Aberdeen, Scotland, produces a single product and uses a standard cost system to help control costs. Manufacturing overhead is applied to production on the basis of standard machine-hours. According to the company's flexible budget, the following overhead costs should be incurred at an activity level of 18,000 machine-hours (the denominator activity level chosen for the year):

CHECK FIGURES

(2) Overhead applied: £92,000
(3) Volume variance: £8,000 U

Variable manufacturing overhead cost	£ 31,500
Fixed manufacturing overhead cost	72,000
Total manufacturing overhead cost	£103,500

During the year, the following operating results were recorded:

Actual machine-hours worked	15,000
Standard machine-hours allowed	16,000
Actual variable manufacturing overhead cost incurred	£26,500
Actual fixed manufacturing overhead cost incurred	£70,000

At the end of the year, the company's Manufacturing Overhead account contained the following data:

Manufacturing Overhead

Actual costs	96,500		Applied costs	92,000
	4,500			

Management would like to determine the cause of the £4,500 underapplied overhead.

Required:

1. Compute the predetermined overhead rate for the year. Break it down into variable and fixed cost elements.
2. Show how the £92,000 "Applied costs" figure in the Manufacturing Overhead account was computed.
3. Analyze the £4,500 underapplied overhead figure in terms of the variable overhead efficiency and rate variances and the fixed overhead budget and volume variances.
4. Explain the meaning of each variance that you computed in (3) above.

PROBLEM 11–27
Comprehensive Standard Cost Variances [LO3 – CC15, 16, 17, 18; LO4 –CC21, 22, 23]

Dresser Company uses a standard cost system and sets predetermined overhead rates on the basis of direct labour-hours. The following data are taken from the company's budget for the current year:

> **CHECK FIGURES**
> (2) Materials price variance
> $3,000 F
> (3) $4,200 F

Denominator activity (direct labour-hours)	9,000
Variable manufacturing overhead cost at 9,000 direct labour-hours	$34,200
Fixed manufacturing overhead cost	$63,000

The standard cost card for the company's only product is given below:

Direct materials, 4 pounds at $2.60 per pound	$10.40
Direct labour, 2 direct labour-hours at $9.00 per direct labour-hour	18.00
Overhead, 120% of direct labour cost	21.60
Standard cost per unit	$50.00

During the year, the company produced 4,800 units of product and incurred the following costs:

Materials purchased, 30,000 pounds at $2.50 per pound	$75,000
Materials used in production (in pounds)	20,000
Direct labour cost incurred, 10,000 direct labour-hours at $8.60 per direct labour-hour	$86,000
Variable manufacturing overhead cost incurred	$35,900
Fixed manufacturing overhead cost incurred	$64,800

Required:

1. Redo the standard cost card in a clearer, more usable format by detailing the variable and fixed overhead cost elements.
2. Prepare an analysis of the variances for materials and labour for the year.
3. Prepare an analysis of the variances for variable and fixed overhead for the year.
4. What effect, if any, does the choice of a denominator activity level have on standard unit costs? Is the volume variance a controllable variance from a spending point of view? Explain.

PROBLEM 11–28
Computing Variable Cost Variance [LO3 – CC15, 17, 18; LO4 – CC22, 23]

Winterfell Inc., a manufacturing company, has the following standard costs for one unit of production:

CHECK FIGURE

(1) Total variance, $46,800 U

Direct materials	(5 kg @ $6/kg)	$ 30
Direct labour	(3 h @ $15/h)	45
Factory overhead:		
Variable	(3 DLHs @ $6/DLH)	18
Fixed	(3 DLHs @ $12/DLH)	36
Total standard cost		$129

The planning budget for the quarter was based on 6,200 units.

Actual results for the last quarter were as follows:

Production volume		6,000 units
Direct materials	(36,000 kg @ $6.30/kg)	$226,800
Direct labour	(17,800 h @ $15.60/h)	277,680

Factory overhead:	
Variable	102,000
Fixed	186,000

Required:

Calculate all the possible variances.

(Adapted © CPA Canada)

Building Your Skills

COMPREHENSIVE PROBLEM 11–1 [LO2 – CC12, 13; LO3 – CC15, 17, 18; LO4 – CC22, 23]

Chennai Manufacturing Company (CMC) is a small manufacturer based in southern India. CMC's controller, Asha Pandey, recently implemented a standard costing system and has decided to use it as a planning and control tool. The following information is available for two of its products (A and B):

CHECK FIGURES

(1) Actual profit level: $26,396,686; static budget profit level: $86,200,400
(2) Flexible budget profit level $82,795,932
(3) Direct materials price variance, product A: $5,529,792 F; Efficiency variance, product B: $7,575 U

	Product A		Product B	
	Standard	**Actual**	**Standard**	**Actual**
Direct materials:				
Kilograms/unit (*SQI*)	12.00	12.80	90.00	84.00
Price/kilogram (*SP*)	$38.50	$38.20	$4.60	$4.90
Direct labour				
Hours/unit (*SQI*)	0.022	0.018	0.440	0.470
Wage rate/hour (*SR*)	$12.00	$11.80	$12.00	$13.40
Machine-hours/unit (*SR*)	0.80	0.85	2.40	2.40
Units budgeted to be produced	1,500,000		20,000	
Units produced and sold		1,440,050		21,040
Selling price/unit		$510.00		$459.00

Total overhead was budgeted at $4,618,000, 32.5% of which accounted for the fixed portion. Actual variable overhead incurred during the year amounted to $3,122,620, which accounted for exactly 70% of the total overhead incurred. The production system is highly machine intensive, and overhead was allocated accordingly. Standard/budgeted price is computed by adding a 12% markup to the standard product cost and then rounding it up to the nearest dollar. Assume that there were no changes in inventory levels for direct materials, WIP, and finished goods.

Required:

(*Hint:* You may wish to combine requirements (1) and (2) into a single report.)

1. Prepare a performance report that compares the actual results with the static budget. What is the static budget profit variance for the year?

2. Prepare a performance report that compares the actual results with the flexible budget for the year.

3. How much of the flexible budget profit variance is accounted for by the individual manufacturing variances? Show all the calculations, and label each variance as favourable or unfavourable.

 COMPREHENSIVE PROBLEM 11–2 [LO1 – CC3, 4, 5, 6; LO3 – CC15, 17, 18]

Highland Company produces a lightweight backpack that is popular with students. Standard variable costs relating to a single backpack follow:

CHECK FIGURES
(1) Standard cost: $31.50
(3) 2.8 metres

	Standard Quantity or Hours (*SQI*)	Standard Price or Rate (*SP*)	Standard Cost (*SC*)
Direct materials	?	$6 per metre	$?
Direct labour	?	?	?
Variable manufacturing overhead	?	$3 per hour	?
Total standard cost			$?

Fixed overhead is applied using direct labour-hours. During March, 1,000 backpacks, the practical capacity of the facility, were manufactured and sold. Selected information relating to the month's production follows:

	Materials Used	Direct Labour	Variable Manufacturing Overhead
Total standard cost allowed*	$16,800	$10,500	$4,200
Actual costs incurred	$15,000	?	$3,600
Materials price variance	?		
Materials quantity variance	1,200 U		
Labour rate variance		?	
Labour efficiency variance		?	

	Materials Used	Direct Labour	Variable Manufacturing Overhead
Variable overhead spending variance			?
Variable overhead efficiency variance			?

*For the month's production

The following additional information is available for March's production:

Actual direct labour-hours	1,500
Standard overhead rate per hour	$ 3
Standard price of one metre of materials	$ 6
Price difference between standard and actual cost per backpack produced during March	$ 0.15 F
Applied fixed overhead cost	$17,300
Underapplied fixed overhead	$ 2,700

Overhead is applied to production on the basis of direct labour-hours.

Required:

1. What is the standard cost of a single backpack?
2. What was the actual cost per backpack produced during March?
3. How many metres of material are required at standard per backpack?
4. What was the materials price variance for March?
5. What is the standard direct labour rate per hour?
6. What was the labour rate variance and the labour efficiency variance for March?
7. What was the variable overhead spending variance and the variable overhead efficiency variance for March?
8. Prepare a standard cost card for one backpack.
9. Did the company overspend or underspend on fixed overhead relative to budget? Calculate the actual amount of spending on fixed overhead.

THINKING ANALYTICALLY 11–1 [LO3 – CC15, 17, 18; LO4 – CC22, 23]

Linda Trueblood, president of ProSkate, was staring at the most recent quarterly performance report and was not pleased. "How can this be possible?" she asked of her senior management team. "I thought the market for our products had improved and that all we needed to do was maintain our budgeted market share. But this report tells me that our profits are below expectations, and I do not understand that." She then turned her attention to the manufacturing manager, wondering what story was going to emerge from his side. The performance report she was reviewing contained the following information:

> CHECK FIGURE
>
> Total direct labour variance: $1,080 U

Sales		$2,880,000
Less: Cost of goods sold		
Variable	$617,256	
Fixed	992,750	1,610,006
Gross margin		$1,269,994
Less: Selling and administration		
Variable	$172,800	
Fixed	450,000	622,800
Operating income		$ 647,194

Other information is as follows:

a. Overall profit variance was $107,294 U.
b. Sales revenues were $144,000 lower than the budgeted amount.
c. Contribution margin was $105,144 lower than the budgeted amount.
d. Actual market share was about 0.535% lower than the budgeted 10%.

ProSkate manufactures two types of skates: professional and amateur. The following additional information is available:

e. The company sold 7,200 pairs of professional skates and 18,000 pairs of amateur skates during the quarter, compared with the budgeted quantities of 8,000 and 17,600, respectively.
f. Budgeted unit contribution margins for the professional and amateur models were $185.55 and $40.38, respectively.
g. Direct materials were purchased at the budgeted price of $28 per kilogram; all materials purchased were used during the period. Direct labour was paid $0.50 per hour higher than the budgeted amount of $14 per hour.
h. Total direct materials variance amounted to $5,040 (unfavourable).
i. Direct materials and direct labour used for the amateur model were the same as the budgeted quantity (0.28 kilograms per unit and 0.40 hours per unit, respectively).
j. The total direct materials and direct labour used for the professional model during the quarter were 3,060 kilograms and 5,040 hours, respectively.
k. Direct labour-hours used for the professional model were less than the budgeted quantity by 0.05 hours per unit.
l. The predetermined allocation rate for variable overhead was 130% of direct labour cost; the total (i.e., flexible budget) variable overhead variance amounted to $16,344 (favourable).
m. Fixed manufacturing overhead was underallocated by $35,527; the actual amount incurred during the quarter was $992,750. The predetermined overhead rate for fixed manufacturing overhead was based on 13,040 labour-hours.

Required:

Copy and complete the following variance table. Be sure to label each of the variances as favourable (F) or unfavourable (U).

Direct Materials Variances

Price variance

Usage (quantity) variance

Total direct materials variance

Direct Labour Variances

Rate variance

Efficiency variance

Total direct labour variance

Variable Manufacturing Overhead Variances

Spending variance

Efficiency variance

Total variable manufacturing overhead variance

Fixed Manufacturing Overhead Variances

Spending variance

Production volume variance

Total fixed manufacturing overhead variance

THINKING ANALYTICALLY 11–2 [LO1 – CC3, 4, 6; LO3 – CC15, 16, 17, 18; LO6 – CC27^A, 28^A]

You are employed by Olster Company, which manufactures products for the health and nutrition market. As a rising executive in the company, you are scheduled to make a presentation in a few hours to your superior. This presentation relates to last week's production of Maxitol, Olster's popular health tonic. Unfortunately, while you were near the pool in your company's fitness centre, studying ledger sheets and variance summaries, somebody bumped into you and you dropped the papers into the water. In desperation, you fished the papers out of the pool, but you have discovered that only the following fragments are legible:

> **CHECK FIGURES**
> (1)   120 batches
> (2a) Actual cost: $7,700

Maxitol—Standard Cost Card			
	Standard Quantity or Hours	Standard Price or Rate	Standard Cost
Material A	24 litres	$2 per litre	$
Material B		per kilogram	
Direct labour		per hour	0
Standard cost per batch			$99.50

You remember that the accounts payable are for purchases of materials A and B. You also remember that only 10 direct labour workers are involved in the production of Maxitol and that each worked 40 hours last week. The wages payable are for wages earned by these workers.

You realize that, to be ready for your presentation, you must quickly reconstruct all data relating to Maxitol. As a start, you have called purchasing and found that 4,000 litres of material A and 400 kilograms of material B were purchased last week.

Required:

1. How many batches of Maxitol were produced last week? (This is a key figure; be sure it is right before going on.)
2. For material A:
    a. What was the cost of material A purchased last week?
    b. How many litres were used in production last week?
    c. What was the quantity variance?
    d. Prepare journal entries to record all activity relating to material A for last week.

Maxitol—General Ledger Accounts

Raw Materials—A

Bal. March 1	0		
Bal. March 7	2,000		

Material A—Price Variance

		300	

Raw Materials—B

Bal. March 1	70	2,500	
Bal. March 7	1,400		

Material B—Quantity Variance

100			

Work in Process

Bal. March 1	0		
Material A	5,760		
Bal. March 7	0		

Wages Payable

	4,100

Labour Rate Variance

500	

Accounts Payable

	11,460

3. For material B:
   a. What is the standard cost per kilogram for material B?
   b. How many kilograms of material B were used in production last week? How many kilograms should have been used at standard?
   c. What is the standard quantity of material B per batch?
   d. What was the price variance for material B last week?
   e. Prepare journal entries to record all activity relating to material B for last week.

4. For direct labour:
   a. What is the standard rate per direct labour-hour?
   b. What are the standard hours per batch?
   c. What were the standard hours allowed for last week's production?
   d. What was the labour efficiency variance for last week?
   e. Prepare a journal entry to record all activity relating to direct labour for last week.

5. Complete the standard cost card previously shown for one batch of Maxitol.

COMMUNICATING IN PRACTICE [LO1 – CC1, 2; LO2 – CC9; LO5 – CC26]

Make an appointment to meet with the manager of an auto repair shop that uses standards. In most cases, this would be an auto repair shop that is affiliated with a chain, such as Petro-Canada or Canadian Tire, or the service department of a new-car dealer.

Required:

At the scheduled meeting, find out the answers to the following questions and write a memo to your instructor describing the information obtained during your meeting.

1. How are standards set?
2. Are standards practical or ideal?
3. Is the actual time taken to complete a task compared with the standard time?
4. What are the consequences of unfavourable variances? Of favourable variances?
5. Do the standards and variances create any potential problems?

ETHICS CHALLENGE [LO1 – CC1; LO2 – CC9; LO5 – CC26]

Stacy Cummins, the newly hired controller at Merced Home Products, Inc., was disturbed by what she had discovered about the standard costs at the home security division. In looking over the past several years of quarterly earnings reports from the home security division, she noticed that the first-quarter earnings were always poor, the second-quarter earnings were slightly better, the third-quarter earnings were again slightly better, and then the fourth quarter and the year always ended with a spectacular performance in which the home security division always managed to meet or exceed its target profit for the year. She also was concerned to find letters from the company's external auditors to top management warning about an unusual use of standard costs in the home security division.

When Cummins saw these letters, she asked the assistant controller, Gary Farber, if he knew what was going on in the home security division. Farber said that it was common knowledge in the company that the vice-president in charge of that division, Preston Lansing, had rigged the standards there in order to produce the same quarterly earnings pattern every year. According to company policy, variances are taken directly to the income statement as an adjustment to cost of goods sold.

Favourable variances have the effect of increasing net income, and unfavourable variances have the effect of decreasing net income. Lansing had rigged the standards so that there were always large favourable variances. Company policy was a little vague about when these variances have to be reported on the divisional income statements. While the intent was clearly to recognize variances on the income statement in the period in which they arose, nothing in the company's accounting manuals explicitly required this. So, for many years, Lansing had followed a practice of saving up the favourable variances and using them to create a nice smooth pattern of earnings growth in the first three quarters, followed by a big "holiday present" of an extremely good fourth quarter. (Financial reporting regulations forbid carrying variances forward from one year to the next on the annual audited financial statements, and so all of the variances must appear on the divisional income statement by the end of the year.)

Cummins was concerned about these revelations and attempted to raise the subject with the president of Merced Home Products, but she was told, "We all know what Lansing's doing, but as long as he continues to turn in such good reports, don't bother him." When Cummins asked if the board of directors was aware of the situation, the president somewhat testily replied, "Of course they are aware."

Required:

1. How did Preston Lansing probably rig the standard costs—are the standards set too high or too low? Explain.
2. Should Lansing be permitted to continue his practice of managing reported earnings?
3. What should Stacy Cummins do in this situation?

TEAMWORK IN ACTION [LO2 – CC 9, 11, 12, 13]

The Munchkin Theatre is a nonprofit organization devoted to staging plays for children. The theatre has a very small full-time professional administrative staff. Through a special arrangement with the actors' union, actors and directors rehearse without pay and are paid only for actual performances.

The costs from the current year's planning budget appear below. The Munchkin Theatre had tentatively planned to put on five different productions with a total of 60 performances. For example, one of the productions was *Peter Rabbit,* which had five performances.

The Munchkin Theatre Costs From the Planning Budget For the Year Ended December 31	
Budgeted number of productions	5
Budgeted number of performances	60
Actors' and directors' wages	$144,000
Stagehands' wages	27,000
Ticket booth personnel and ushers' wages	10,800
Scenery, costumes, and props	43,000
Theatre hall rent	45,000
Printed programs	10,500
Publicity	13,000
Administrative expenses	43,200
Total	$336,500

Some of the costs vary with the number of productions, some with the number of performances, and some are fixed and depend on neither the number of productions nor the number of performances. The costs of scenery, costumes, props, and publicity vary with the number of productions. It doesn't make any difference how many times *Peter Rabbit* is performed; the cost of the scenery is the same. Likewise, the cost of publicizing a play with posters and radio commercials is the same whether there are 10, 20, or 30 performances of the play. On the other hand, the wages of the actors, directors, stagehands, ticket booth personnel, and ushers vary with the number of performances. The greater the number of performances, the higher the wage costs will be. Similarly, the costs of renting the hall and printing the programs will vary with the number of performances. Administrative expenses are more difficult to pin down, but the best estimate is that approximately 75% of the budgeted costs are fixed, 15% depend on the number of productions staged, and the remaining 10% depend on the number of performances.

After the beginning of the year, the board of directors of the theatre authorized changing the theatre's program to four productions and a total of 64 performances. Actual costs were higher than the costs from the planning budget. (Grants from donors and ticket sales were also correspondingly higher, but are not shown here.) Data concerning the actual costs appear below:

The Munchkin Theatre Actual Costs For the Year Ended December 31	
Actual number of productions	4
Actual number of performances	64
Actors' and directors' wages	$148,000
Stagehands' wages	28,600
Ticket booth personnel and ushers' wages	12,300

The Munchkin Theatre Actual Costs For the Year Ended December 31	
Scenery, costumes, and props	39,300
Theatre hall rent	49,600
Printed programs	10,950
Publicity	12,000
Administrative expenses	41,650
Total	$342,400

Required:

Your team should prepare the analyses required below and then use the results to discuss the remaining issues. All team members should know and agree on the quantitative analyses as well as on the issues and be prepared to present to the class.

1. Prepare a flexible budget for The Munchkin Theatre based on the actual activity of the year.
2. Prepare a report that summarizes the flexible budget variances for all expense items.
3. The president of the board of directors of the theatre has asked for your opinion as to how well costs were controlled during the year. What would be your response? Explain.
4. The president of the board has asked you to report how accurately you think these figures would predict the cost of a new production or of an additional performance of a particular production. What will be your response? You realize that the cost formulas provide figures for the average cost per production and average cost per performance.

12

Organizational Structure and Performance Measurement

LEARNING OBJECTIVES AND CHAPTER COMPETENCIES			
After studying Chapter 12, you should be able to demonstrate the following competencies:			
COMPETENCY		**Know**	**Apply**
LO1	**UNDERSTAND DECENTRALIZATION AND REPORTING IN A DECENTRALIZED ORGANIZATION.**		
CC1	Explain the role, strengths, and weaknesses of decentralization in organizations.	●	
CC2	Explain cost, profit, and investment centres.	●	
CC3	Explain segmented reporting and prepare a segmented performance report.	●	●
LO2	**EXPLAIN KEY FINANCIAL PERFORMANCE METRICS REPORTED IN A DECENTRALIZED ORGANIZATION.**		
CC4	Define and compute the return on investment (ROI) measure.	●	●
CC5	Explain how changes in sales, expenses, and operating assets can influence the ROI.	●	
CC6	Define and compute the residual income (RI) measure.	●	●
CC7	Explain the advantage of the RI measure over ROI to motivate managers.	●	
CC8	Explain the concept of transfer pricing.	●	
LO3	**UNDERSTAND MULTI-DIMENSIONAL PERFORMANCE REPORTING.**		
CC9	Explain the concept of multi-dimensional performance reporting.	●	
CC10	Describe the balanced scorecard, outlining its strengths and weaknesses.	●	
CC11[A]	Construct a balanced scorecard.		●

Note: The superscript "A" refers to Appendix 12A, which is available on Connect.

ON THE JOB

MANAGING THE SPREAD

Conexus Credit Union—founded in 2003 through a merger of Assiniboia Credit Union, Moose Jaw Credit Union, and Sherwood Credit Union—is Canada's sixth-largest credit union, with an asset base of approximately $3.7 billion. As a credit union, it is a cooperative with close to 120,000 members, who are equal owners and have the right to participate in important decisions such as electing the board of directors.

With 68 locations spread across Saskatchewan, managing the spread is quite a task. Conexus takes a decentralized approach to planning and decision making; however, it is not a 100% decentralized organization; each location (branch) relies on the corporate office for guidance. The corporate office's planning team is still heavily involved in long-term planning, target setting, and budgeting.

With decentralization comes accountability. Approximately seven years ago, Conexus decided to use the balanced scorecard model to "ensure we successfully deliver on our strategies." The balanced scorecard is used for the purposes of planning, establishing targets, and identifying key initiatives. Conexus's balanced scorecard includes four dimensions: (1) customer, member, and

Conexus Credit Union

community value; (2) internal and operational effectiveness; (3) employee/employer of choice; and (4) financial strength. Each dimension includes no fewer than two performance measures, with a weight assigned to each measure. The financial dimension includes "return on assets" as one of its four measures, and this is assigned the highest weighting of all the measures.

The balanced scorecard is a key planning and performance measurement tool; nothing happens without considering the impact of individual actions/decisions on the different dimensions.

Sources: Conexus website, http://www.conexus.ca; company's internal documents; discussions with a manager

Critical thinking question *Why is accountability important in a decentralized setting?*

*Note to student: See **Guidance Answers** online.*

◀◀ A Look Back	▶ A Look at This Chapter	▶▶ A Look Ahead
We first discussed the budgeting process in Chapter 7. We then introduced management control and performance measures in Chapter 11, with a discussion of standard costs and variance analysis.	Chapter 12 continues our coverage of performance measurement by introducing the concept of decentralization and the associated concept of responsibility centres. We will look at the challenges in reporting the financial performance of decentralized business units and deciding on the appropriate performance measures to motivate managers and monitor progress toward achieving the company's goals. These topics constitute the area of managerial accounting called management control systems.	In the chapters that follow, which are available on Connect, we take up financial performance measurement and address the key question that every manager should ask and be able to answer: "How well am I doing?" This will involve learning the basic tools of financial statement analysis and the construction of the cash flow statement.

P erformance management is an important task for managers, as it helps them in ensuring that the organization's overall objectives are met (or even exceeded). The previous chapter introduced variance analysis, which is one tool that can be used by managers for the purpose of performance management. In a broader context, performance management includes specifying how individual units within an organization will be evaluated, what measures will be used to evaluate these units, and what actions will be taken to ensure continuous progress. We will discuss these issues in this chapter.

MANAGERIAL ACCOUNTING IN ACTION

THE ISSUE

Canadian Foods Corporation makes different kinds of ready-to-eat snacks in various sizes. Over the years, Canadian Foods has grown significantly, and Taylor Keegan, its president, is considering restructuring the company. She has called a meeting of her key senior executives—Bob McKintosh (general counsel), Brandy Gerspacher (operations vice-president), Noreen Peters (chief financial officer), and Keith Randall (personnel vice-president)—to discuss her concerns.

Keegan: Our company has grown rapidly over the last few years, and I am concerned that managing the company might become a challenge for the handful of us.

Peters: How so? I have continued to manage in the same way from day one, and it has produced the desired results. We just have to do more of what we did earlier. I am not suggesting that there are no issues, but we have to learn to deal with them.

Gerspacher: I don't know about you, Noreen, but since the time we have scaled up our operations, I am certainly finding it challenging to coordinate plans and activities. Decision making is not as straightforward as it used to be.

> ***Randall:*** I agree with Brandy; managing the larger scale and the broader scope of our operations and business has become harder. There is much more to do by way of human resources. I cannot be involved in each and every hiring decision. I can only set broad guidelines and let some others make the actual hiring (and firing) decisions.
>
> ***McKintosh:*** I agree with both Keith and Brandy. I am sure the expansion poses coordination, communication, and evaluation challenges. We have more managers with decision-making authority, and this means we ought to have a mechanism to assess their decision-making ability.
>
> ***Keegan:*** I am sure we can put our heads together and devise a system that will allow us to be more organized, allowing for better communication, coordination, and performance assessment at various levels.

Decentralization in Organizations

LO1   ● **Know**

CC1: Explain the role, strengths, and weaknesses of decentralization in organizations.

When an organization is relatively small, as in the case of Canadian Foods Corporation (CFC) when it started out, a single manager or a small management team will be able to make most decisions, including strategic and day-to-day operating decisions. This is known as a **centralized organization**. However, as organizations grow larger, it often becomes ineffective for the top manager (or management team) to make all decisions regarding all aspects of business. For example, it would be better if the top management team of the Real Canadian Superstore did not make hiring decisions about cashiers for a store in British Columbia. Such decisions are best left to the store managers, who know their personnel needs best. Top management would, however, likely be involved in establishing hiring policies and establishing the overall strategic direction for the retailer. An organization in which decision making is not confined to a few top executives but rather is spread throughout the organization, with managers at various levels making decisions that pertain to their area of responsibility, is called a **decentralized organization**.

Centralization and *decentralization* refer to the *dimension* of the business for which the decision making is either held closely or delegated. For example, some companies might centralize a business function like information technology or purchasing, while others might delegate decision-making authority over these functions. Some companies might decentralize along a product line (like pick-up trucks or crossover vehicles) or a geographic area (like Ontario or western Canada). Factors that will play into determining how an organization is decentralized and the extent of decentralization include the number of distinct business lines; the geographic spread of the organization; and the complexity and scale of various business functions like operations, purchasing, accounting and finance, and information systems.

When an organization is decentralized, it is divided into different units or *segments*. Depending on the dimension of segmentation, individual segments may represent different divisions, product lines, market territories, or even individual departments (e.g., marketing, purchasing, and production). There can be multiple levels of segmentation in an organization. For example, in a university, the first line of segmentation would be the different colleges or faculties (e.g., business, nursing, education), and the second line might be the individual departments within each college or faculty (e.g., within the faculty of business, the departments of accounting, marketing, and so on).

It is important to remember that segments within an organization are not usually independent of one another. They often have to work closely to achieve the objectives of the organization. Consequently, coordination and communication among the individual segments are important and sometimes challenging issues for top management.

Advantages and Disadvantages of Decentralization

Decentralization has many benefits, including the following:

- Top management is relieved of much day-to-day problem solving and is left free to concentrate on strategy, higher-level decision making, and coordinating activities.
- Decentralization provides lower-level managers with vital experience in making decisions. Without such experience, they would be ill prepared to make decisions when they are promoted to higher-level positions.
- Added responsibility and decision-making authority often result in increased job satisfaction. They make the job more interesting and motivate people to put out their best efforts.
- Lower-level managers generally have more detailed and up-to-date information about conditions in their own area of responsibility than do top managers. Therefore, the decisions of lower-level managers are often based on better information.
- Lower-level managers will likely act in a more responsible manner when they are held accountable for their actions as well as the results.

Decentralization has four major disadvantages:

1. Lower-level managers may make decisions without fully understanding the big picture. While top-level managers typically have less detailed information about operations than do lower-level managers, they usually have more information about the company as a whole and may have a better understanding of the company's strategy.
2. In a truly decentralized organization, there may be a lack of coordination among autonomous managers. This problem can be reduced by clearly defining the company's strategy and communicating it effectively throughout the organization.
3. Managers' objectives may be different from those of the owners of an organization as a whole; this suggests a lack of goal congruence between owners and managers. For example, some managers may be more interested in increasing the size of their departments and showing off their prestige and influence than in increasing the profits of the company. If these managers are left unchecked, valuable company resources can be squandered, possibly leading to a fall in the value of the company, and culminating in loss of jobs. The issue of how to ensure that managers act in the best interests of the owners of the company continues to puzzle experts. To some degree, this problem can be overcome by designing performance evaluation systems that motivate managers to make decisions that are in the company's best interests.
4. In a highly decentralized organization, it may be more difficult to disseminate innovative ideas effectively. Someone in one part of the organization might have a terrific idea that would benefit other parts of the organization, but without strong central direction the idea may not be shared with, or adopted by, other parts of the organization. This would be especially true when rewards are a zero-sum game.

DECISION POINT

A FRIEND

One of your friends from school started a business that designs websites, which has become a wildly successful startup. On the way to meet your friend for lunch, you think how great it would be to be your own boss—to be able to come and go as you please. At lunch, you hardly recognize her. She is tired and stressed, complains a lot about the hours she has been putting in to supervise various projects, and is puzzled by the high turnover that she has experienced at the managerial level. After all, as she notes, she keeps her hand in all of the major projects. What advice do you have for her?

*Note to student: See **Guidance Answers** online.*

IN BUSINESS

SONY ATTEMPTS TO REBOUND

In the past, Sony has delighted customers with its Walkman, the Trinitron TV, the PlayStation, and the CD. However, in the digital media era, Sony has lost ground to many better-managed competitors, such as Microsoft, Apple, Sharp, and Nokia. Sony is attempting to rebound by discontinuing unprofitable segments such as Aibo, a line of robotic pets; Qualia, a line of boutique electronics; 1,220 cosmetic salons; and 18 Maxim de Paris restaurants. In addition, the company has closed nine plants, sold $705 million worth of assets, and eliminated 5,700 jobs.

The next step for Sony is to improve communications across its remaining business units. For example, at one point, Sony had three business units unknowingly competing against one another by developing their own digital music players. Sony's challenge is to encourage decentralized decision making to spur product innovation, while centralizing control of communications across the company so that engineers do not create competing or incompatible products.

Source: Marc Gunther, "The Welshman, the Walkman, and the Salarymen," *Fortune*, June 12, 2006, pp. 70–83.

Responsibility Centres

 LO1   ● **Know**

CC2: Explain cost, profit, and investment centres.

From a performance management perspective, there are two key issues relating to decentralization: (1) clarifying the decentralized segment manager's scope of responsibilities, and (2) deciding how the manager's performance will be evaluated. In order to resolve these issues, top management categorizes the individual segments into **responsibility centres**, which are segments of an organization whose manager is responsible and accountable for costs, profits, or investments. The three primary types of responsibility centres are cost centres, profit centres, and investment centres.

COST CENTRE

A **cost centre** is a business function or a department such as accounting, finance, general administration, human resources, production, and so on that provides valuable support to the other segments *but does not have the capability to directly generate revenue or profit*. The manager of a cost centre is responsible for costs but not revenues, profits, or investments. Managers of cost centres are expected to minimize costs while ensuring that the outputs they provide to other segments within the organization meet the needs of these "consumer" segments (e.g., quality). The performance of these managers is evaluated by comparing actual costs against standard costing information and annual budgets using variance analysis (discussed in Chapter 11).

PROFIT CENTRE

The manager of a **profit centre** is responsible for both revenues and costs and thus profits. The manager will have the authority to influence both costs and revenues but not the use of investment funds. This means he or she does not need top management's approval for production, operations, and pricing decisions but does need approval for spending money on capital acquisition or disposal. Managers of individual stores of a major retail chain would usually be responsible for profits and would likely be evaluated on the basis of profitability. Consequently, a report such as the income statement would be useful for the purpose of management control.

INVESTMENT CENTRE

The manager of an **investment centre** is responsible for and has control over cost, revenue, profit, and investment in operating assets. The vice-president of a product division of a large corporation, such as Honeywell International Inc., would have the responsibility for allotting funds to research and development, to modernization of production equipment, and to production and sales of new products. Once the investment proposals were approved by the board of directors, the vice-president would be responsible for how the money was invested and would ensure that the assets were utilized in such a manner that they provided the targeted returns. Investment centre managers are usually evaluated using return on investment (ROI) or residual income (RI) measures.

An Example of Responsibility Centres

We now go back to Canadian Foods Corporation (CFC). After much deliberation, the four senior managers decided to create an organization structure and a responsibility accounting system. A partial organization chart for CFC appears in Exhibit 12–1. This partial organization chart indicates how the various business segments of the company are classified in terms of responsibility. Note that the cost centres do not generate revenues on their own. These are staff departments (such as finance, legal, and human resources) and operating units (such as the bottling plant, warehouse, and beverage distribution centre). The profit centres are business segments that generate revenues and include the beverage, salty snacks, and confections product lines. The vice-president of operations oversees allocation of investment funds across the product segments, is responsible for revenues and costs, and thus is treated as an investment centre. Finally, corporate headquarters is an investment centre, since it is responsible for all revenues, costs, and investments.

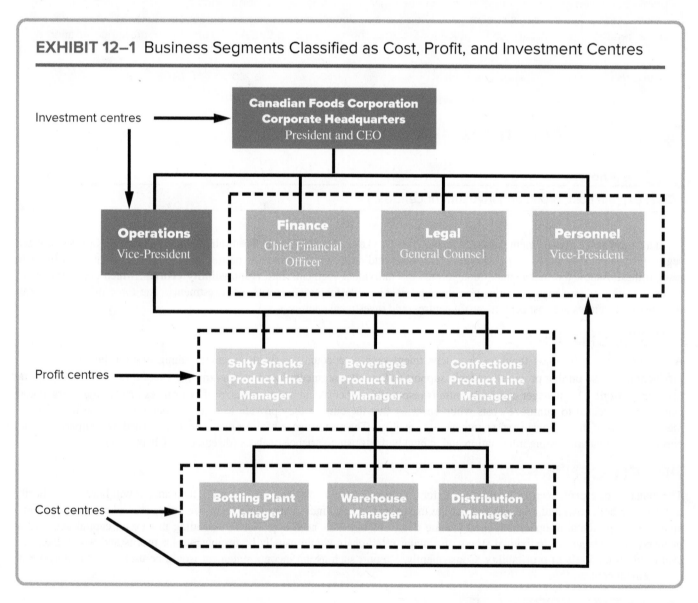

EXHIBIT 12–1 Business Segments Classified as Cost, Profit, and Investment Centres

Segmented Reporting

LO1   ● **Know**   ● **Apply**

CC3: Explain segmented reporting and prepare a segmented performance report.

The performance of decentralized segments is often reported using segment reports. A **segment** is an individual unit within an organization whose manager has the responsibility to carry out its activities. A company's operations can be segmented in many ways. For example, Canadian Foods Corporation can be segmented by its individual plants, geographic sales territories, or product lines. Exhibit 12–2 illustrates the different forms (dimensions) of segmenting a company. Note that additional levels of segmenting are possible. For example, the beverages line can be broken down into fruit juices and soft drinks subsegments. The fruit juices subsegment can be further broken into apple juice, orange juice, and so on. Dividing a segment into subsegments facilitates profitability analysis at lower levels of segmentation.

EXHIBIT 12–2 Segmenting a Company

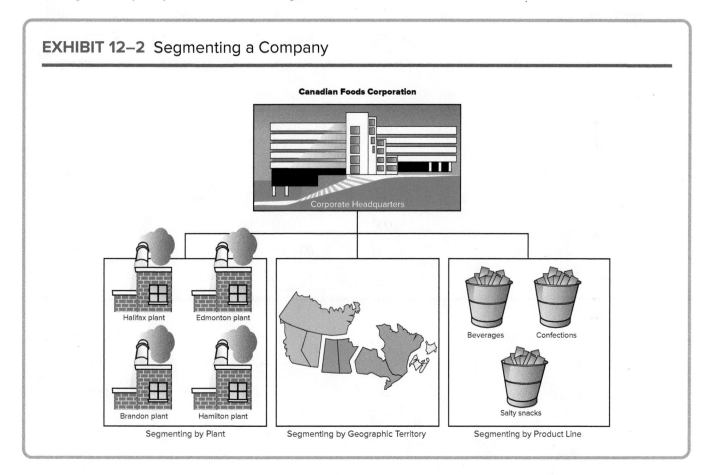

Individual segment managers are responsible for their segments and are interested in knowing the performance of their segments. Similarly, senior management responsible for all three segments will be interested in the performance of the individual segments, as well as the operations in total. Exhibit 12–3 presents a report containing the performance of the three product segments, as well as the total of the three. The exhibit reports the sales revenues, variable expenses, and directly traceable fixed expenses for each of the three segments and the combined total.

EXHIBIT 12–3 Profit Centre Segmented Report: Canadian Foods Corporation

	Profit Centres			
	Salty Snacks	Beverages	Confections	Total Company
Sales	$2,320,000	$2,000,000	$1,500,000	$5,820,000
Less: Variable expenses:				
Direct materials	400,000	360,000	240,000	1,000,000
Direct labour	250,000	200,000	140,000	590,000
Manufacturing overhead	150,000	140,000	120,000	410,000
Selling and other	250,000	200,000	150,000	600,000
Total variable expenses	$1,050,000	$ 900,000	$ 650,000	$2,600,000
Contribution margin	$1,270,000	$1,100,000	$ 850,000	$3,220,000
Less: Traceable fixed expenses:				
Salaries and benefits	400,000	210,000	130,000	740,000
Office equipment	190,000	120,000	80,000	390,000
Building rent	120,000	80,000	50,000	250,000
Selling and administrative	160,000	120,000	90,000	370,000
Other	130,000	70,000	50,000	250,000
Total fixed expenses	$1,000,000	$ 600,000	$ 400,000	$2,000,000
Segment margin	$ 270,000	$ 500,000	$ 450,000	$1,220,000
Less: Common fixed expenses:				
Senior management salaries				$ 500,000
Corporate office building				140,000
Legal and accounting				210,000
Other				50,000
Total common fixed expenses				900,000
Net income				$ 320,000
Segment margin %	11.64%	25.00%	30.00%	20.96%

Before proceeding further, it would be useful to distinguish between *traceable* fixed expenses and *common* fixed expenses. A **traceable fixed expense (or cost)** of a segment is an expense that is incurred because of the existence of the segment and would generally be avoided if the segment were eliminated (assuming that all assets were sold). Exhibit 12–3 lists several traceable fixed expenses. A **common fixed expense (or cost)** is an expense that supports the operations of more than one segment but is not traceable in whole or in part to any individual segment.

Some costs that would be treated as a traceable (direct) cost at the segment level may be classified as a common cost at the subsegment level; this is because we are dealing with two different cost objects (recall from Chapter 2 that we classify costs as direct or indirect [common] with respect to a specific cost object). For example, building rent cost is directly traceable to the beverages product line but common to the fruit juice and soft drinks subsegments.

According to the exhibit, the overall segment margin percentage of the company is just under 21% (= $1,220,000 ÷ $5,820,000). Although the beverages segment reports the highest margin in terms of dollars ($500,000), the confections segment provides a higher margin in terms of percentage (30%). The salty snacks segment generates the lowest margin in terms of both dollars and percentage.

Note, however, that the overall segment margin of $1.22 million is *not* the profit generated by the company. This is because the company incurs additional expenses of $900,000, which are not directly traceable to any one of the three product segments—these are the *common fixed expenses.* The net income of the company is $320,000.

One question to ask is whether the common fixed expenses must be allocated among the individual segments. One argument against this is that any allocation will be at best arbitrary and will unfairly penalize individual segment managers. Another argument against any such allocation is that segment managers have no control over the common fixed expenses; therefore, holding them accountable for net profit after deducting a proportion of the common expenses goes against the principle of responsibility accounting. But proponents of allocation argue that debate is useful and necessary to control common costs because it forces an examination of both the spending side and the consumption side.

For instance, assume that senior management decides to allocate common fixed expenses equally among the three segments. As is shown in Exhibit 12–4, this results in the salty snacks segment showing a loss of $30,000, which can result in negative consequences for the segment. Presumably, both reports will be studied and the wisdom and consequences of equally distributing the common costs will be debated and the value derived from spending $900,000 will be questioned.

EXHIBIT 12–4 Revised Profit Centre Segmented Report Following Common Cost Allocation to Segments: Canadian Foods Corporation

	Profit Centres			
	Salty Snacks	Beverages	Confections	Total Company
Segment margin	$ 270,000	$500,000	$450,000	$1,220,000
Less: Common fixed expenses				
Allocated portion	300,000	300,000	300,000	900,000
Net income	$(30,000)	$200,000	$150,000	$ 320,000

In general, traceable costs should be assigned to segments, but common fixed costs should not be assigned to segments for the reasons mentioned above.

IN BUSINESS

DECENTRALIZED OPERATIONS AT THE BANK

The Royal Bank Financial Group (RBFG) started reorganizing its management team and business structure in 1995 in an attempt to decentralize its operations. The flat, market-focused organization enabled each business-unit manager to be held accountable for his or her own performance. When valuing loans and deposits and distributing costs of shared services, transfer pricing was used to ensure that the company still controlled its centralized processes (such as corporate services) and gained economies of scale. Transfer pricing is based on the principles of activity-based costing.

RBFG established priorities, allocated resources, and measured performance on the basis of a "financial standard." Being successful in the market entails understanding the interests of many stakeholders—customers, employees, and shareholders. For example, the company used shareholder value growth as the governing objective, and the "value-added" metric for making strategic decisions, acquisitions, and so on.

Source: Paul A. Sharman and John Shaw, "Royal Bank of Canada—Ahead of the Rest: Deploying Value-Based Management," *Focus Magazine* website, 2003. Adapted with permission from Focused Management, Inc.

CONCEPT CHECK

1. In which of the following responsibility centres are managers held responsible for profits? (You may select more than one answer.)
   a. Cost centres
   b. Profit centres
   c. Investment centres
   d. All of the above
2. Which of the following statements are false? (You may select more than one answer.)
   a. The same cost can be traceable or common depending on how the segment is defined.
   b. In general, common fixed costs should be assigned to segments.
   c. If a company eliminates a segment of its business and sells the segment's assets, the costs that were traceable to that segment should disappear.
   d. If four segments share $1 million in common fixed costs and one segment is eliminated, the common fixed costs will decrease by $250,000.

*Note to student: See **Guidance Answers** online.*

Measuring and Controlling Investment Centre Performance

In decentralized organizations, individual segments are usually classified as investment centres when they are run like independent businesses. The segment managers are responsible for all aspects of running the segment, including investing in assets. One important investment centre performance metric is the rate of return that investment centre managers are able to generate on their assets. This rate of return is called the *return on investment*.

Measuring Performance: The Return on Investment Formula

LO2 • Know • Apply

CC4: Define and compute the return on investment (ROI) measure.

The **return on investment (ROI)** is defined as net operating income divided by average operating assets:

$$ROI = \frac{\text{Net operating income}}{\text{Average operating assets}}$$

The higher the ROI of a business segment, the greater the profit generated per dollar invested in the segment's operating assets. There are some issues about how to measure net operating income and average operating assets, but the formula in itself seems clear enough.

NET OPERATING INCOME AND OPERATING ASSETS DEFINED

Note that *net operating income,* rather than net income, is used in the ROI formula. **Net operating income** is income before interest and taxes and is sometimes referred to as *EBIT* (*earnings before interest and taxes*). The reason for using net operating income in the formula is that the income figure used should be consistent with the base (i.e., denominator) to which it is applied, which is *operating assets.*

Operating assets include cash, accounts receivable, inventory, plant, equipment, and all other assets held for productive use in the organization. Some might argue that current liabilities should be offset against the current assets so as to include only the net working capital in the computation of operating assets. However, for our purposes, we will use total current assets to compute operating assets. Examples of assets that would *not* be included in the operating assets category (i.e., examples of nonoperating assets) are land held for future use, an investment in another company, or a factory building rented to someone else. The operating assets base used in the formula is typically computed as the average of the operating assets between the beginning and the end of the year.

PLANT AND EQUIPMENT: NET BOOK VALUE OR GROSS COST?

What dollar amount of plant and equipment should the company include with its operating assets in computing ROI? One widely used approach is to include only the plant and equipment's *net book value*—that is, the plant's original cost less accumulated depreciation. A second approach is to ignore depreciation, including the plant's entire *gross cost* in the operating assets base. Arguments can be made to support either approach:

Measure Operating Assets in ROI Computations Using	
Net Book Value Method	**Gross Cost Method**
• This is consistent with how plant and equipment are reported on the balance sheet (i.e., cost less accumulated depreciation to date).	• This method eliminates both the age of equipment and the method of depreciation as factors in ROI computations.
• ROI will tend to increase over time as net book value declines due to depreciation.	• It does not discourage replacement of old, worn-out equipment.
• It is consistent with the computation of operating income, which includes depreciation as an operating expense.	
• Replacing fully depreciated equipment with new equipment can have a dramatic, adverse effect on ROI.	

The two approaches will obviously yield very different operating asset and ROI figures. Managers generally view consistency as the most important of the considerations above. As a result, a majority of companies use the net book value approach in ROI computations. *In this text, we will also use the net book value approach unless a specific exercise or problem directs otherwise.*

Controlling the Rate of Return

LO2 • Know

CC5: Explain how changes in sales, expenses, and operating assets can influence the ROI.

Controlling the performance of an investment centre will require managers to focus on decisions that would lead to an increase in the ROI. When we first defined the return on investment, we used the following formula:

$$\text{ROI} = \frac{\text{Net operating income}}{\text{Average operating assets}}$$

This suggests that managers should increase income—this seems reasonable. But mathematically ROI can also be increased by decreasing the denominator—average operating assets. This approach should make you uneasy; reducing the asset base is a risky move unless the assets are old, unproductive, etc. But we cannot perceive whether our assets are of poor quality simply from the formula. To make it easier to see possible control options available, we can modify this formula slightly by introducing sales as follows:

$$\text{ROI} = \frac{\text{Net operating income}}{\text{Sales}} \times \frac{\text{Sales}}{\text{Average operating assets}}$$

The first term on the right-hand side of the equation is the *margin,* which is defined as follows:

$$\text{Margin} = \frac{\text{Net operating income}}{\text{Sales}}$$

The **margin** is a measure of management's ability to control operating expenses in relation to sales. The lower the operating expenses per dollar of sales, the higher the margin earned. This in itself can be a useful measure even for a profit centre manager.

The second term on the right-hand side of the preceding equation is *turnover,* which is defined as follows:

$$\text{Turnover} = \frac{\text{Sales}}{\text{Average operating assets}}$$

Turnover is a measure of the utilization of the operating assets in terms of the sales that are generated for each dollar invested in operating assets.

The following alternative form of the ROI formula, which we will use most frequently, combines margin and turnover:

$$\text{ROI} = \text{Margin} \times \text{Turnover}$$

Rewriting the formula for ROI as the product of the margin and the turnover provides additional insights. For example, a small jewellery company will likely focus on margin to generate its ROI; for each sales dollar, it captures a relatively large proportion as income. A high sales volume company like Walmart, on the other hand, will focus on turnover. Walmart relies on a very large number of sales transactions, each with relatively small margin.

You already know that increasing margin is a good objective and can be a valuable indicator of a manager's performance. Focusing on margin alone, however, overlooks one crucial area of an investment centre manager's responsibility—the investment in operating assets. Deploying capital funds to operating assets is an important responsibility of an investment centre's manager, and the manager should be held accountable for that responsibility. Excessive funds tied up in operating assets, which reduce turnover, can be just as much of a drag on profitability as excessive operating expenses, which reduce margin. One of the advantages of ROI as a performance measure is that it forces the manager to control the investment in operating assets, as well as to control expenses and the margin. Investment in assets is wasteful if the assets are not employed to increase sales or if they are not properly used to maximize the sales. This point is explained further below.

The ROI Levers for Controlling Performance: The DuPont Approach

DuPont pioneered the ROI concept and recognized the importance of looking at both margin and turnover in assessing the performance of a manager. The ROI formula is now widely used as the key measure of the performance of an investment centre. The ROI formula blends many aspects of the manager's responsibilities into a single figure that can be compared with the returns of competing investment centres, with the returns of other firms in the industry, and with the past returns of the investment centre itself.

DuPont's approach appears in Exhibit 12–5. This exhibit helps managers understand how they can control ROI. An investment centre manager can increase ROI in three ways: (1) increase sales, (2) reduce expenses, or (3) reduce assets.

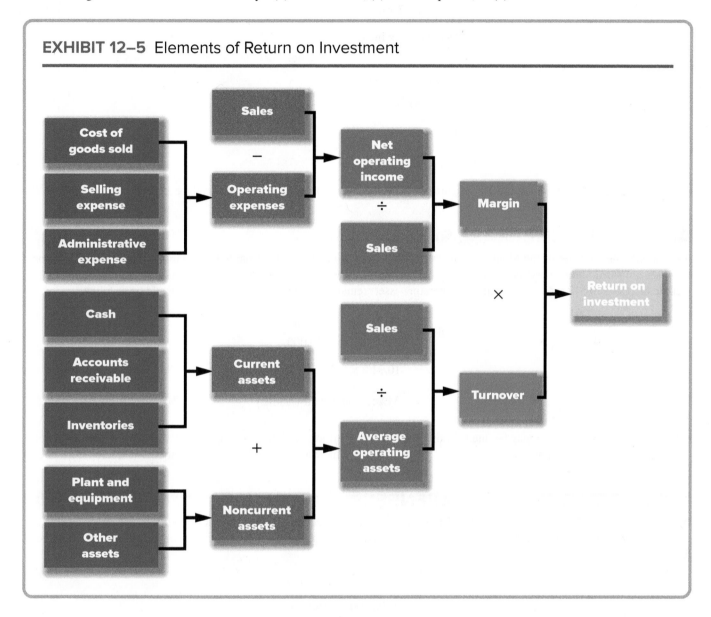

EXHIBIT 12–5 Elements of Return on Investment

To illustrate how the rate of return can be improved by each of these three actions, consider how the manager of the Monthaven Burger Grill is evaluated. Burger Grill is a small chain of upscale casual restaurants that has been rapidly adding outlets via franchising. The Monthaven franchise is owned by a group of local surgeons who have little time to devote to management and little expertise in business matters. Therefore, they delegate operating decisions—including decisions concerning investment in operating assets, such as inventories—to a professional manager whom they have hired. The manager is evaluated largely on the basis of the ROI the franchise generates.

The following data represent the results of operations for the most recent month:

Net operating income	$ 10,000
Sales	100,000
Average operating assets	50,000

The rate of return generated by the Monthaven Burger Grill investment centre is as follows:

$$
\begin{aligned}
\text{ROI} \quad &= \quad \text{Margin} \times \text{Turnover} \\[2mm]
&= \quad \frac{\text{Net operating income}}{\text{Sales}} \times \frac{\text{Sales}}{\text{Average operating assets}} \\[2mm]
&= \quad \frac{\$10,000}{\$100,000} \times \frac{\$100,000}{50,000} \\[2mm]
&= \quad 10\% \times 2 \\[2mm]
&= \quad 20\%
\end{aligned}
$$

As stated previously, to improve the ROI figure, the manager can (1) increase sales, (2) reduce expenses, or (3) reduce the operating assets.

APPROACH 1: INCREASE SALES

Assume that the manager of the Monthaven Burger Grill is able to increase sales from $100,000 to $110,000. Given that some expenses are fixed, the increase in sales is likely to result in an increase in net operating income. Assume that the net operating income increases to $12,000. Assume that the operating assets remain constant. Then the new ROI would be as follows:

$$
\begin{aligned}
\text{ROI} \quad &= \quad \frac{\$12,000}{\$110,000} \times \frac{\$110,000}{\$50,000} \\[2mm]
&= \quad 10.91\% \times 2.2 \\[2mm]
&= \quad 24\% \left(\text{as against 20\% above}\right)
\end{aligned}
$$

However, an increase in sales may be due to additional marketing efforts (which may be costly). This may result in the income decreasing or staying the same. In such situations, the ROI will not increase. This is because the margin will decrease despite an increase in the turnover.

APPROACH 2: REDUCE EXPENSES

Assume that the manager of the Monthaven Burger Grill is able to reduce expenses by $1,000 so that net operating income increases from $10,000 to $11,000. Assume that both sales and operating assets remain constant. Then the new ROI would be as follows:

$$
\begin{aligned}
\text{ROI} \quad &= \quad \frac{\$11,000}{\$100,000} \times \frac{\$100,000}{\$50,000} \\[2mm]
&= \quad 11\% \times 2 \\[2mm]
&= \quad 22\% \ (\text{as against 20\% above})
\end{aligned}
$$

APPROACH 3: REDUCE ASSETS

Assume that the manager of the Monthaven Burger Grill is able to reduce operating assets from $50,000 to $40,000, but that sales and net operating income remain unchanged. Then the new ROI would be as follows:

$$
\begin{aligned}
\text{ROI} \quad &= \quad \frac{\$10,000}{\$100,000} \times \frac{\$100,000}{\$40,000} \\[2mm]
&= \quad 10\% \times 2.5 \\[2mm]
&= \quad 25\% \ (\text{as against 20\% above})
\end{aligned}
$$

A clear understanding of these three approaches to improving the ROI figure is critical to the effective management of an investment centre. We will now look at each approach in more detail.

Increase Sales to Improve ROI

When first looking at the ROI formula, one is inclined to think that the sales figure is neutral, since it appears as the denominator in the margin computation and as the numerator in the turnover computation. We *could* cancel out the sales figure, but we do not do so for two reasons. First, this would tend to draw attention away from the fact that the rate of return is a function of *two* variables, margin and turnover. And, second, it would tend to conceal the fact that a change in sales can affect both the margin and the turnover in an organization. A change in sales can affect the *margin* if expenses increase or decrease at a different rate from sales. For example, a company may be able to keep a tight control on its costs as its sales increase, with the result that net operating income increases more rapidly than sales and increases the margin. Or a company may have fixed expenses that remain constant as sales increase, resulting in an increase in the net operating income and in the margin. Either (or both) of these factors might have been responsible for the increase in the margin percentage from 10% to 10.91% illustrated in approach 1.

Further, a change in sales can affect the *turnover* if sales either increase or decrease without a proportionate increase or decrease in the operating assets. In the first approach above, for example, sales increased from $100,000 to $110,000, but the operating assets remained unchanged. As a result, the turnover increased from 2 to 2.2 for the period. Therefore, although mathematically sales in the denominator and sales in the numerator cancel each other out, a change in sales can lead to an increase or decrease in operating income that ultimately leads to a change in ROI.

Reduce Expenses to Improve ROI

Often, the easiest route to increased profitability and to a stronger ROI figure is to simply cut the fat through a concerted effort to control expenses. When margins begin to be squeezed, this is generally the first line of attack. Discretionary fixed costs (i.e., fixed costs that arise from annual decisions by management to spend in certain fixed cost areas) usually come under scrutiny first, and various programs are either curtailed or eliminated in an effort to cut costs. Managers have to be careful, however, not to cut out muscle and bone along with the fat. Also, they must remember that frequent cost-cutting binges can destroy morale. Most managers now agree that it is best to stay lean and mean.

Reduce Assets to Improve ROI

Managers have always been sensitive to the need to control sales, operating expenses, and operating margins. However, they have not always been equally sensitive to the need to control investment in operating assets. Firms that have adopted the ROI approach to measuring managerial performance report that one of the first reactions of investment centre managers is to trim their investment in operating assets. Managers soon realize that an excessive investment in operating assets reduces turnover and hurts the ROI. As these managers reduce their investment in operating assets, funds are released that can be used elsewhere in the organization.

How can an investment centre manager control the investment in operating assets? One approach is to eliminate unneeded inventory. Just-in-time (JIT) purchasing and JIT manufacturing have been extremely helpful in reducing inventories of all types, with the result that ROI figures have improved dramatically in some companies. Another approach is to devise various methods of speeding up the collection of receivables. For example, many firms now employ the lockbox technique, which enables customers in distant regions to send their payments directly to post office boxes in their area. The funds are received and deposited by a local bank on behalf of the payee firm. This speeds up the collection process, since the payments are not delayed in the postal system. The advent of Internet banking has reduced the time for receipt of payments even further. As a result of the expedited collection, the accounts receivable balance is reduced and the asset turnover is increased.

IN BUSINESS

INVEST IN SOCIAL NETWORKING?

What do Facebook, Twitter, YouTube, Orkut, LinkedIn, and other such sites have in common? They are all networking tools through which connections can be made. Should businesses encourage the use of such tools as a marketing vehicle to promote their products and services? Authors of a recent article state that CEOs may be able to discover the power of social networking sites in terms of potentially developing customer relationships, and in the process achieve their return on investment. This can be particularly true when tough financial conditions require low-cost, innovative solutions.

The thinking from 2009 was that the use of social networking sites may require little investment but may provide large benefits—the mathematics appears simple! The world in 2016 is more complex, especially in regard to the proliferation of ecommerce-oriented business models and customer value propositions. The use of social networking and having a presence on social media is now ubiquitous, and knowing if there is a comparative advantage is increasingly becoming a challenge and a mystery.

When investing in information technology, businesses have had to rethink their business processes and carefully evaluate the costs and benefits of the investment, including the use of social media networking-based strategies to reach customers and close sales. Two issues can be isolated. First, how is ROI measured when contemplating social media investments? Both measuring benefits and choosing the investment base (site visits, clicks, online purchases, downloads, registrations, etc.) have to be resolved. Second, the ROI metric itself has to be examined for relevance. Are there other metrics that do a better job of connecting the investment to the payoff? Simple math has become anything but simple.

Source: R. Angel and J. Sexsmith, "Social Networking: The View From the C-Suite," *Ivey Business Journal Online*, July/August 2009, http://www.iveybusinessjournal.com/topics/the-organization/the-art-of-business-relationships-through-social-media#.Ud2TkdLkvso. Examples of ROI calculations in social media and ecommerce settings are many: http://www.socialmediaexaminer.com/measure-social-media-roi/. For one view that examines alternatives to ROI for measuring success in social media see: http://www.hugeinc.com/ideas/report/social-roi.

IN BUSINESS

ROI FROM HUMAN CAPITAL

Come financial troubles, discretionary expenses are first on the chopping block, and training is one of these expenses. Many organizations do not regard training as an investment activity. But as some authors point out, investing in training *especially* during downturns can be very beneficial in the long run. Acquiring specialized skills, attending conferences, enhancing educational qualifications, and other such activities can strengthen the knowledge base of an organization, allowing it to stay ahead of the competition. Unfortunately, employers in Canada are less committed to job-related education than those in the United Kingdom and the United States. An attitudinal shift among employers to regard job-related education and training as an investment, not as an expense, is the first step to generating returns from the investment!

Sources: J. Brownlee, "There's ROI in Workplace Training Investments," *Plant*, May 2009, p. 22; M. Gupta-Sunderji, "Training as an Investment," *CGA Magazine*, May/June 2009, p. 14.

Criticisms of ROI

Although ROI is widely used in evaluating performance, it is not a perfect tool. The method is subject to the following criticisms:

- Just telling managers to increase ROI may not be enough. Managers may not know how to increase ROI, they may increase ROI in a way that is inconsistent with the company's strategy, or they may take actions that increase ROI in the short run but harm the company in the long run (such as cutting back on research and development).

- A manager who takes over a business segment typically inherits many committed costs over which the manager has no control. These committed costs make it difficult to assess the performance of the manager fairly relative to other managers.

- As discussed in the next section, a manager who is evaluated on the basis of ROI may reject investment opportunities that are profitable for the company as a whole.

DECISION POINT

STORE MANAGER

You were recently hired as the manager of a chain of jewellery stores that are located in downtown Toronto. You are excited about the high level of autonomy that you have been given to run the stores but are nervous because you have heard rumours that the previous manager was let go because the ROI of the stores was unacceptable. What steps should you consider to improve ROI?

*Note to student: See **Guidance Answers** online.*

IN BUSINESS

MICROSOFT MANAGES IN AN ECONOMIC DOWNTURN

Microsoft responded to tough economic times by lowering its prices, thereby accepting lower margins per unit sold in exchange for higher turnover. For example, Microsoft lowered the price of its Office software from $150 to $100 (after promotional discounts) and realized a 415% increase in unit sales. In China, the company combatted huge piracy problems by dropping the price of Office to $29, resulting in an 800% increase in sales. Microsoft established a selling price of $200 for its Windows 7 PC operating system, which was $40 less than the price the company charged for its predecessor Vista PC operating system.

Source: Peter Burrows, "Microsoft's Aggressive New Pricing Strategy," *BusinessWeek,* July 27, 2009, p. 51.

Residual Income—Another Measure of Investment Centre Performance

LO2 ● **Know** ● **Apply**

CC6: Define and compute the residual income (RI) measure.

Another measure of an investment centre's performance is *residual income.* **Residual income (RI)** is the net operating income that an investment centre earns above the minimum required return on its operating assets. Residual income is computed as follows:

$$\text{Residual income} = \text{Net operating income} - (\text{Required rate of return} \times \text{Average operating assets})$$

For the purpose of illustration, consider the following data for an investment centre—the Lethbridge division of Western Canada Services Corporation.

WESTERN CANADA SERVICES CORPORATION Lethbridge Division Basic Data for Performance Evaluation	
Average operating assets	$100,000
Net operating income	$20,000
Minimum required rate of return	15%

Western Canada Services Corporation has long had a policy of evaluating investment centre managers on the basis of ROI but is considering a switch to residual income. The controller of the company, who is in favour of the change to residual income, has provided the following table, which shows how the performance of the division would be evaluated under each of the two methods:

WESTERN CANADA SERVICES CORPORATION Lethbridge Division		
	Alternative Performance Measures	
	ROI	**Residual Income**
Average operating assets (a)	$100,000	$100,000
Net operating income (b)	$ 20,000	$ 20,000
ROI, (b) ÷ (a)	20%	
Minimum required return (15% × $100,000)		15,000
Residual income		$ 5,000

The reasoning underlying the residual income calculation is straightforward. The company is able to earn a rate of return of at least 15% on its investments. Since the company has invested $100,000 in the Lethbridge division in the form of operating assets, the company should be able to earn at least $15,000 (= 15% × $100,000) on this investment. Since the Lethbridge division's net operating income is $20,000, the residual income above and beyond the minimum required return is $5,000. If residual income is adopted as the performance measure to replace ROI, the manager of the Lethbridge division will be evaluated on the basis of the growth from year to year in residual income.

IN BUSINESS

MEETING TARGETS THE WRONG WAY

Putting too much emphasis on meeting financial targets can lead to undesirable behaviour. Michael C. Jensen reports, "I once watched the management of a manufacturing company struggle to reach their year-end targets. In late fall, they announced a price increase of 10% effective January 2. Now, it may be that a price increase was needed, but it was not in line with the competition, nor was it likely that January 2, of all dates, was the best time for the increase. A price increase on January 2, would, however, cause customers to order before year-end and thereby help managers reach their targets." The short-term boost in sales comes at the cost of lost future sales and possible customer ill will.

Source: Michael C. Jensen, "Why Pay People to Lie?" *The Wall Street Journal,* January 8, 2001, p. A32.

Motivation and Residual Income

LO2 • Know

CC7: Explain the advantage of the RI measure over ROI to motivate managers.

One of the primary reasons why the controller of Western Canada Services Corporation would like to switch from ROI to RI has to do with how managers view new investments under the two performance measurement schemes. The residual income approach encourages managers to make investments that are profitable for the entire company, but that would be rejected by managers who are evaluated by the ROI formula.

To illustrate this problem, suppose that the manager of the Lethbridge division is considering purchasing a computerized diagnostic machine to aid in servicing marine diesel engines. The machine would cost $25,000 and is expected to generate additional operating income of $4,500 a year. From the company's standpoint, this would be a good investment, since it promises a rate of return of 18% (= $4,500/$25,000), which is in excess of the company's minimum required rate of return of 15%.

If the manager of the Lethbridge division is evaluated on the basis of residual income, she will be in favour of the investment in the diagnostic machine as shown below:

WESTERN CANADA SERVICES CORPORATION Lethbridge Division Performance Evaluated Using RI			
	Present	**New Project**	**Overall**
Average operating assets	$100,000	$25,000	$125,000
Net operating income	$ 20,000	$ 4,500	$ 24,500
Minimum required return	15,000	3,750*	18,750
Residual income	$ 5,000	$ 750	$ 5,750

*$25,000 × 15% = $3,750

Since the project would increase the residual income of the Lethbridge division, the manager would want to invest in the new diagnostic machine.

Now suppose that the manager of the Lethbridge division is evaluated on the basis of ROI. The effect of the diagnostic machine on the division's ROI is computed as follows:

WESTERN CANADA SERVICES CORPORATION Lethbridge Division Performance Evaluated Using ROI			
	Present	**New Project**	**Overall**
Average operating assets (a)	$100,000	$25,000	$125,000
Net operating income (b)	$ 20,000	$ 4,500	$ 24,500
ROI, (b) ÷ (a)	20%	18%	19.6%

The new project reduces the division's ROI from 20% to 19.6%. This happens because the 18% rate of return on the new diagnostic machine, while above the company's 15% minimum rate of return, is below the division's present ROI of 20%. Therefore, the new diagnostic machine would drag the division's ROI down, even though it would be a good investment from the standpoint of the company as a whole. If the manager of the division is evaluated on the basis of ROI, she will be reluctant even to propose such an investment, especially if her annual bonus is based on her ability to meet or exceed her current result.

Basically, a manager evaluated on the basis of ROI will tend to reject any project whose rate of return is below the division's current ROI, *even if the rate is above the minimum required rate for the entire company.* In contrast, any project whose rate of return is above the minimum required rate for the company will result in an increase in residual income. Since it is in the best interests of the company as a whole to accept any project whose rate of return is above the minimum, managers evaluated on the basis of residual income will tend to make better decisions concerning investment projects than ones evaluated on the basis of ROI. Thus, the use of residual income as a performance measure can offer a win–win situation.

Divisional Comparison and Residual Income

The residual income approach has one major disadvantage: it cannot be used to compare the performance of divisions of different sizes. You would expect larger divisions to have a greater residual income than smaller divisions, not necessarily because they are better managed but simply because of the bigger numbers involved.

As an example, consider the following residual income computations for Division X and Division Y:

	Division	
	X	Y
Average operating assets (a)	$1,000,000	$250,000
Net operating income	120,000	40,000
Minimum required return: 10% × (a)	100,000	25,000
Residual income	$ 20,000	$ 15,000

Observe that Division X has slightly more residual income than Division Y, but that Division X has $1,000,000 in operating assets compared to Division Y's $250,000 in operating assets. Thus, Division X's greater residual income is probably more a result of its size than the quality of its management. In fact, it appears that the smaller division is better managed, since it has been able to generate nearly as much residual income with only one-fourth as much in operating assets to work with. This problem can be reduced to some degree by focusing on the percentage change in residual income from year to year, rather than on the absolute amount of the residual income. In contrast, ROI is a standardized measure and lends itself to comparisons regardless of size.

Computing Profitability of Non-Revenue-Generating Segments

LO2 • **Know**

CC8: Explain the concept of transfer pricing.

In some decentralized organizations, individual segments are treated as profit or investment centres, even if they do not generate revenues from sales to external customers. Consider the information technology (IT) department of a large organization, which services other segments in the organization and has been classified as a profit centre by top management. Given its classification as a profit centre, IT must show revenues so that its profitability can be computed. In such a setting, the IT department (the selling segment) must *sell* its services to other segments (the buying segments) within the organization in order to *generate* revenues. The term used for such an internal sale is *transfer;* all transfers occur at a predetermined price known as the **transfer price**. It is easy to see that on the one hand, the *buying* segment would like a low transfer price because it is a cost for the segment; on the other hand, the *selling* segment would prefer a high transfer price because the price determines the segment's revenue.

How should the transfer price be determined? There are many complications in arriving at an acceptable transfer price. For example, should transfer prices include just the variable costs, or will they include fixed costs as well? What about common costs? Most organizations establish guidelines that govern the determination of transfer prices, including what costs should be considered in determining a transfer price (in the case of cost-based pricing). Transfer pricing is often a source of real tension between segment managers that organizations must deal with to ensure that no dysfunctional consequences result from the transfer-pricing policy established by senior management.

Generally speaking, three methods can be used to establish transfer prices: (1) market-based price, (2) cost-based price, and (3) negotiated price. All three approaches have their benefits and limitations, which are discussed in more advanced texts. Regardless of the methods used, the objective of management must be to motivate the segment managers to do what is in the best interests of both the overall organization and the individual segment.

CONCEPT CHECK

3. Last year, sales were $300,000, net operating income was $75,000, and average operating assets were $500,000. If sales next year remain the same as last year, and expenses and average operating assets are reduced by 5%, what will be the return on investment next year?
   a. 12.2%
   b. 18.2%
   c. 20.2%
   d. 25.2%

4. Referring to the facts in Concept Check 3 above, if the minimum required rate of return is 12%, what will be the residual income next year?
   a. $26,250
   b. $27,250
   c. $28,250
   d. $29,250

*Note to student: See **Guidance Answers** online*

Multi-Dimensional Performance Measurement: The Balanced Scorecard

LO3 • **Know**

CC9: Explain the concept of multi-dimensional performance reporting.

Thus far, we have discussed financial measures of performance such as return on investment, variances, and profits. However, simply using financial measures can be short-sighted, because (1) financial measures are typically *outcome* measures that provide *after-the-fact* information, and (2) financial measures are only one dimension of performance. Critics note that it is at least equally important, if not more important, to know *how* to achieve the desired financial results. They state that an important objective of performance measurement is that it must aid in the implementation of an organization's strategies, and reporting along multiple dimensions is critical in achieving this objective. Managers must know what factors influence financial performance, and must establish measures that inform the organization on how well it is doing with those factors that influence the financial results. Therefore, a multi-dimensional performance measurement system that includes *nonfinancial* performance measures can be useful.

CC10: Describe the balanced scorecard, outlining its strengths and weaknesses.

One such multi-dimensional performance measurement system is the **balanced scorecard**, which contains measures along at least four dimensions: (1) financial, (2) customer, (3) internal business process, and (4) learning and growth. Measures pertaining to the learning and growth dimension are supposed to inform managers about the likely performance along the internal business process dimension. Similarly, measures along the internal business process dimension are supposed to explain or predict potential performance along the customer dimension and ultimately the financial dimension. Thus, a key feature of the scorecard is that measures along the different dimensions are linked to one another or integrated. In this sense, the balanced scorecard is an integrated performance measurement system. This is illustrated in Exhibit 12–6 for AAA Auto Dealership.

EXHIBIT 12–6 AAA Auto Dealership Sample Balanced Scorecard

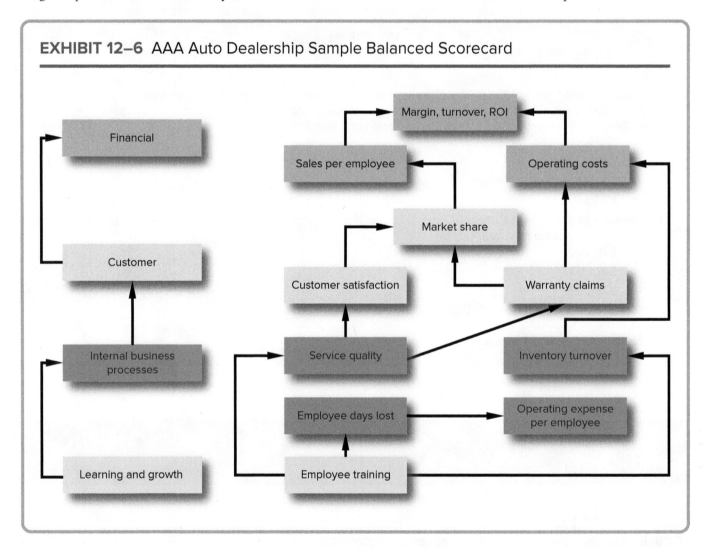

The balanced scorecard provides a way to communicate a company's strategy to managers throughout the organization. A properly designed scorecard should allow managers to answer questions such as the following: Which customers should be targeted, and how can they be attracted and retained at a profit? Which internal business process must be improved to meet customer requirements? In short, a well-constructed balanced scorecard should provide managers with a road map that indicates how the company will achieve its financial objectives. Achieving the financial objectives is important to ensuring the long-term viability of the business.

As an example, think of a car dealership that wants to increase its profitability and growth. A balanced scorecard for this dealership would include measures pertaining to the two objectives, and measures that influence the two objectives (see Exhibit 12–6). Given that the generic profitability equation consists of two variables—sales revenues and costs—the scorecard should measure these two variables. Sales revenue and other sales-related measures, such as customer service, number of referrals, and customer satisfaction, will appear in the customer dimension of the scorecard. Cost and other operational measures that will lead to improvements in the customer and financial measures will appear along the internal business process dimension. Finally, management of the dealership may believe that learning is very important in improving the other measures. Therefore, they may decide to track training hours within the learning and growth perspective.

The key aspect in identifying the right performance measures is that the measures must be linked in a cause-and-effect relationship. Otherwise, the scorecard is simply a collection of ad hoc measures that may result in more confusion, rather than provide any direction to management. The arrows in Exhibit 12–6 starting from the bottom and working up to the top tell a story of how AAA goes about making money through a series of cause-and-effect relationships beginning with employee training. At AAA, well trained employees are a key profit driver. More training hours translate to better service quality, less time lost, and better sales turnover. Better service quality leads to more satisfied customers and reduced warranty claims, which in turn lead to improved market share and lower costs. Ultimately, AAA earns a better margin and a higher rate of return. A scorecard like the one in Exhibit 12–6 is a series of *hypotheses* about how to improve profits and grow the company, and what is important to achieving these goals. Each hypothesis should be testable by measuring the appropriate variables and confirming if there is indeed a cause-and-effect relationship as hypothesized. Managers have a better idea of what to measure and why, of how goals are to be achieved, and of where to look for answers to why the company is either succeeding or failing. A more detailed exploration of these ideas is presented in Appendix 12A.

A multi-dimensional performance measurement system such as the balanced scorecard can provide a more complete picture of an organization's performance. Although the concept is appealing and has been embraced by many types of organizations (including hospitals, universities, government departments, and businesses), there are some key issues that managers must keep in mind when implementing a balanced scorecard within their organizations. First and foremost, top managers must fully support its implementation. Second, individual measures within the different dimensions must be well defined and should flow from the goals and objectives established by senior management. Third, the individual measures must be mutually reinforcing to ensure that employees are not pulled in different directions. Finally, the performance measurement system and the employee evaluation and compensation system must be linked. A system that emphasizes one thing and rewards another is a classic recipe for disaster.

MANAGERIAL ACCOUNTING IN ACTION

THE WRAP-UP

The following week, the senior management team met again to discuss the issue of restructuring.

Peters: I think we have made good progress on the restructuring front.

Keegan: I am excited about this and am looking forward to hearing what you all have to tell me.

CANADIAN FOODS CORPORATION

Randall: I believe we can structure the company into profit and cost centres and give people the responsibility for profits or costs, as the case may be.

Keegan: And how will you evaluate them?

Gerspacher: My three product managers will be evaluated on the basis of their individual segment margins, because they are profit centre managers.

Keegan: And who makes the investment decisions? And what about the balanced scorecard concept?

Peters: Investment decisions would be at Brandy's level, and she would be measured on the basis of return on investment. The balanced scorecard is the responsibility of all of us—the leadership team.

McKintosh: Let me add a word here. Service departments like mine will be evaluated as cost centres, and our responsibility is to maintain costs within the budget.

Keegan: This is good progress that we have made in a short time. I hope that our managers are motivated by the new system and step up to the challenge!

IN BUSINESS

THE WELLNESS SCORECARD

Towers Watson estimates that America's average annual health care spending per employee now exceeds $10,000, up from $5,386 in 2002. However, companies that have implemented high-performing corporate wellness programs have annual health care costs that are $1,800 per employee less than other organizations. These high-performing companies create and track wellness performance measures as an important part of managing their programs.

The wellness scorecard is one framework for measuring corporate wellness performance. It has four categories of measures—attitudes, participation, physical results, and financial results—that are connected on a cause-and-effect basis. If employee attitudes toward the company's wellness program improve, this should increase the rate of employee participation in wellness activities. If employees increase their participation rates, this should produce physical results, such as lower obesity rates, lower incidence of diabetes, and increased smoking cessation rates. These physical improvements should produce positive financial results for the company, such as lower medical, pharmaceutical, and disability disbursements.

Sources: Towers Perrin, "2010 Health Care Cost Survey," www.towerswatson.com; and Peter C. Brewer, Angela Gallo, and Melanie R. Smith, "Getting Fit with Corporate Wellness Programs," *Strategic Finance*, May 2010, pp. 27–33.

IN BUSINESS

MEASURING UP TO THE ENVIRONMENT

After decades of focusing exclusively on reporting financial performance, organizations have realized the need to widen their performance-reporting horizon. Many have adopted multi-dimensional performance measurement systems such as the balanced scorecard. More recently, increased pressure from certain stakeholder groups has resulted in organizations considering performance with respect to environmental and social responsibility issues.

Dow Canada—a subsidiary of the Dow Chemical Company, with plants in Alberta, Ontario, Quebec, and Saskatchewan—is big on environmental stewardship. To reflect its progress with respect to Dow's Global Environment, Health and Safety Goals, Dow Canada annually publishes a report for public consumption, which contains performance indicators such as process safety incidents, waste reduction, wastewater reduction, energy use, chemical emissions, and fines and penalties.

Sources: D. Crawford and T. Scaletta, "The Balanced Scorecard and Corporate Social Responsibility: Aligning Values for Profit," *CMA Management,* October 2005, pp. 20–27; Dow Canada's 2013 public report, http://www.dow.com/sustainability/pdf/23489-Sustainability-Report-interactive.pdf.

Learning Objectives Summary

LO1 UNDERSTAND DECENTRALIZATION AND REPORTING IN A DECENTRALIZED ORGANIZATION.

Decentralization is the act of structuring an organization into segments or subunits such as divisions, departments, and so on. In a decentralized organization, decision making is spread throughout, with managers at various levels making decisions according to their areas of responsibility. A responsibility centre is an organizational unit whose management has decision (i.e., management) rights over a cost, revenue, profit, or asset base. Depending on which financial variable management is accountable for, the organization unit is labelled as a cost centre, a profit centre, or an investment centre. Investment centre managers have the responsibility for the asset base of the organization, meaning that the manager can add or dispose of assets and is responsible for earning an adequate rate of return on the investment. Reporting by an organizational subunit is called segment reporting. Financial performance of a segment of an organization is evaluated on the basis of the segment margin, which is revenues minus all traceable costs of the segment.

LO2 EXPLAIN KEY FINANCIAL PERFORMANCE METRICS REPORTED IN A DECENTRALIZED ORGANIZATION.

The key performance metrics reported in a decentralized organization include return on investment (ROI) and residual income (RI). ROI is defined as net operating income divided by average operating assets. Alternatively, it can be defined as the product of margin and turnover, where margin is net operating income divided by sales, and turnover is sales divided by average operating assets.

The relations among sales, expenses, assets, and ROI are complex. The effect of a change in any one variable on the others will depend on the specific circumstances. Nevertheless, an increase in sales often leads to an increase in ROI via the effect of sales on net operating income. If the organization has significant fixed costs, then a given percentage increase in sales is likely to have an even larger percentage effect on net operating income.

RI is the difference between net operating income and the minimum required return on average operating assets. The minimum required return on average operating assets is computed by applying the minimum rate of return to the average operating assets. A major advantage of RI over ROI is that it encourages investment in projects whose rates of return are above the minimum required rate of return for the entire organization, but below the segment's current ROI.

LO3 UNDERSTAND MULTI-DIMENSIONAL PERFORMANCE REPORTING.

Multi-dimensional performance reporting is the practice of including nonfinancial measures of performance along with the traditional financial performance measures. Proponents of this practice argue that financial measures are short-term outcome measures and are not forward looking. Consequently, focusing on only financial measures would lead managers to miss many important facets of company performance that drive financial performance or are positively correlated with it. A key multi-dimensional performance system is the balanced scorecard, an integrated system of performance measures designed to support an organization's strategy. The various measures in a balanced scorecard should be linked on a plausible cause and effect basis from the very lowest level up through the organization's ultimate objectives. The balanced scorecard is essentially a theory about how specific actions taken by various people in the organization will further the organization's objectives. The theory should be viewed as tentative and subject to change if the actions do not in fact result in improvements in the organization's financial and other goals. If the theory changes, then the performance measures on the balanced scorecard should also change. The balanced scorecard is a dynamic measurement system that evolves as an organization learns more about what works and what doesn't work and refines its strategy accordingly.

Application Competency Summary

APPLICATION COMPETENCY	DELIVERABLE	SOURCE DOCUMENTS AND KEY INFORMATION	STEPS	KNOWLEDGE COMPETENCY
Prepare a segmented performance report. ● LO1–CC3	*Key Information* Profit margin generated by each segment Net income for the whole organization *Report/Document* Segmented performance report	*Sales and Expense Ledgers* Sales revenue, variable costs, and directly traceable fixed costs by segment Common costs for the organization	1. Record the sales revenue, variable costs, and directly traceable fixed expenses for each segment. 2. Deduct variable costs from the sales revenues to compute the segment contribution margin; deduct directly traceable fixed expenses from the contribution margin to compute the segment margin.	Variable and fixed costs ● LO1–CC1 (Ch. 2) Direct and indirect costs ● LO1–CC2 (Ch. 2) Segment margin
Compute return on investment (ROI). ● LO2–CC4	*Key Information* Sales margin Asset turnover ROI *Report/Document* No specific document	*Sales Ledger* Sales revenue *Income Statement* Operating income *Operating Assets Ledgers or Balance Sheet* Operating assets	1. Divide operating income by sales revenue to compute sales margin. 2. Divide sales revenue by average operating assets to compute asset turnover. 3. Multiply sales margin by asset turnover to compute ROI. 4. Alternatively, divide operating income by average operating assets to compute ROI.	Operating income ● LO5–CC9 (Ch. 2) ROI ● LO2–CC4
Compute residual income (RI). ● LO2–CC6	*Key Information* Residual income *Report/Document* No specific document	*Income Statement* Operating income *Operating Assets Ledgers or Balance Sheet* Operating assets *Management Documents* Required rate of return	1. Multiply the required rate of return by the average operating assets and deduct this amount from the operating income to compute RI.	Operating income ● LO5–CC9 (Ch. 2) RI ● LO2–CC6

APPLICATION COMPETENCY	DELIVERABLE	SOURCE DOCUMENTS AND KEY INFORMATION	STEPS	KNOWLEDGE COMPETENCY
Construct a balanced scorecard ● **LO3–CC11**[A]	*Key Information* A balanced scorecard with multiple perspectives that correlate with the financial, customer, and internal business processes, and learning and growth perspectives of the generic balanced scorecard (each perspective must be defined to be consistent with the target organization's specific business model and strategic priorities) Performance measures for each perspective A series of hypotheses that relate the performance measures in a cause and effect relationship	*Income Statement* Operating income *Balance Sheet* Asset account balances *Various Operations and Departmental Reports* Since the number of types of measures are too numerous to be listed, some examples are provided: customer feedback statistics and customer satisfaction reports; operating performance statistics like supplier performance data, time and motion data, etc.; data on training programs offered and registration information for employees	1. Based on the strategy and business model of the company, identify performance perspectives that map to the financial, customer and internal business processes and learning and growth perspectives for the company. 2. Select relevant measures for each perspective (use Exhibit 12A–2 as a guide). 3. Outline a set of hypotheses that summarize your understanding of the cause and effect relationships between the measures (use Exhibit 12A–3 as a guide).	Company mission and strategy Costing systems and production processes (Chs. 4, 5, and 6) Budgeting (Ch. 7) Performance measures ● **LO2–CC4, 5, 6, 7, 8** Variances (Ch. 11) Financial analysis concepts (Chs. 13 and 14 on Connect)

Review Problem: Return on Investment and Residual Income

The magnetic imaging division of Medical Diagnostics, Inc. has reported the following results for last year's operations:

Sales	$25 million
Net operating income	3 million
Average operating assets	10 million

Required:

1. Compute the margin, turnover, and ROI for the magnetic imaging division.
2. Top management of Medical Diagnostics, Inc. has set a minimum required rate of return on average operating assets of 25%. What is the magnetic imaging division's residual income for the year?

SOLUTION TO REVIEW PROBLEM

1. The required calculations are as follows:

$$\text{Margin} = \frac{\text{Net operating income, } \$3,000,000}{\text{Sales, } \$25,000,000}$$

$$= 12\%$$

$$\text{Turnover} = \frac{\text{Sales, } \$25,000,000}{\text{Average operating assets, } \$10,000,000}$$

$$= 2.5$$

$$\text{ROI} = \text{Margin} \times \text{Turnover}$$

$$= 12\% \times 2.5$$

$$= 30\%$$

2. The residual income for the magnetic imaging division is computed as follows:

Average operating assets	$10,000,000
Net operating income	$ 3,000,000
Minimum required return (25% × $10,000,000)	2,500,000
Residual income	$ 500,000

Questions

12–1   What is meant by *decentralization?*
12–2   What benefits result from decentralization?
12–3   Distinguish among a cost centre, a profit centre, and an investment centre.
12–4   Define a segment of an organization. Give several examples of segments.
12–5   What is meant by *margin* and *turnover?*
12–6   What are the three basic approaches to improving return on investment (ROI)?
12–7   What is meant by *residual income?*
12–8   In what way can the use of ROI as a performance measure for investment centres lead to bad decisions? How does the residual income approach overcome this problem?
12–9   What is meant by *transfer price,* and why are transfer prices needed?
12–10 Explain the balanced scorecard.

The Foundational 15

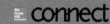

[LO2 – CC4, 5, 6, 7]

Westerville Company reported the following results from last year's operations:

Sales	$1,000,000
Variable expenses	300,000
Contribution margin	700,000
Fixed expenses	500,000
Net operating income	$ 200,000
Average operating assets	$ 625,000

This year, the company has a $120,000 investment opportunity with the following cost and revenue characteristics:

Sales	$200,000
Contribution margin ratio	60% of sales
Fixed expenses	$90,000

The company's minimum required rate of return is 15%.

Required:

12–1   What is last year's margin?
12–2   What is last year's turnover?
12–3   What is last year's return on investment (ROI)?
12–4   What is the margin related to this year's investment opportunity?
12–5   What is the turnover related to this year's investment opportunity?
12–6   What is the ROI related to this year's investment opportunity?

12–7 If the company pursues the investment opportunity and otherwise performs the same as last year, what margin will it earn this year?

12–8 If the company pursues the investment opportunity and otherwise performs the same as last year, what turnover will it earn this year?

12–9 If the company pursues the investment opportunity and otherwise performs the same as last year, what ROI will it earn this year?

12–10 If Westerville's chief executive officer will earn a bonus only if her ROI from this year exceeds her ROI from last year, would she pursue the investment opportunity? Would the owners of the company want her to pursue the investment opportunity?

12–11 What is last year's residual income?

12–12 What is the residual income of this year's investment opportunity?

12–13 If the company pursues the investment opportunity and otherwise performs the same as last year, what residual income will it earn this year?

12–14 If Westerville's chief executive officer will earn a bonus only if her residual income from this year exceeds her residual income from last year, would she pursue the investment opportunity?

12–15 Assume that the contribution margin ratio of the investment opportunity was 50% instead of 60%. If Westerville's chief executive officer will earn a bonus only if her residual income from this year exceeds her residual income from last year, would she pursue the investment opportunity? Would the owners of the company want her to pursue the investment opportunity?

Brief Exercises

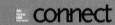

BRIEF EXERCISE 12–1
Recognizing the Principles of Decentralization [LO1 – CC1]

Following are a number of terms associated with decentralization in organizations:

Cost centre	Profit centre
Segment	Investment centre
Responsibility centre	Transfer price
Job satisfaction	

Required:

Fill in the blanks with the appropriate terms from the list provided.

1. A(n) _____ is a part or activity of an organization about which managers would like cost, revenue, or profit data.

2. Added responsibility and decision-making authority often result in increased _____.

3. A(n) _____ is a business segment whose manager is responsible for both cost and revenue but not investment funds.

4. When one segment, such as a division, of a company provides goods or services to another segment of the company, the _____ will determine how much revenue the segment recognizes on the transaction.

5. A(n) _____ is a business segment whose manager is responsible for costs but not revenue or investment funds.

6. A(n) _____ is any segment of an organization whose manager is responsible and accountable for cost, revenue, or investment funds.

7. A(n) _____ is a business segment whose manager is responsible for cost, revenue, and investments in operating assets.

BRIEF EXERCISE 12–2
Preparing a Segment Performance Report [LO1 – CC3]

Klinker Corporation consists of three segments: North America, Europe, and Asia. Revenues during 20X3 for the three segments were $1,200,000, $3,800,000, and $800,000, respectively. Variable costs amounted to 30% of sales for all three segments, whereas the fixed expenses for each segment were $270,000, $900,000, and $600,000, respectively. The common fixed expenses for the company amounted to $1,590,000 for the year.

Required:

Prepare a segmented performance report for Klinker Corporation.

BRIEF EXERCISE 12–3
Computing the ROI [LO2 – CC4]

Crawford Company's plans for a new product require a target cost per unit of $50. It plans to sell 20,000 units at $60 per unit. The average investment, including design and development, is $900,000.

Required:

1. Compute the expected margin for Crawford Company.
2. Compute the expected turnover for Crawford Company.
3. Compute the ROI for Crawford Company.

BRIEF EXERCISE 12–4
Computing Effects of Changes in Sales, Expenses, and Assets on ROI [LO2 – CC4, 5]

CommercialServices.com Corporation provides business-to-business services on the Internet. Data concerning the most recent year follow:

Sales	$3,000,000
Net operating income	450,000
Average operating assets	1,800,000

Required:

Consider each question below independently. Carry out all computations to two decimal places.

1. Compute the company's ROI.
2. The entrepreneur who founded the company is convinced that sales will increase next year by 50% and that net operating income will increase as a result by 200%, with no increase in average operating assets. What would be the company's ROI?
3. The chief financial officer of the company believes a more realistic scenario would be a $1,000,000 increase in sales, requiring a $200,000 increase in average operating assets, with a resulting $150,000 increase in net operating income. What would be the company's ROI in this scenario?

BRIEF EXERCISE 12–5
Computing Residual Income [LO2 – CC6]

Eucalyptus Design Ltd. of Canberra, Australia, is a company specializing in providing design services to residential developers. Last year, the company had net operating income of $604,000 on sales of $3,000,000. The company's average operating assets for the year were $2,800,000, and its minimum required rate of return was 18%.

Required:

Compute the company's residual income for the year.

(Adapted © CPA Canada)

BRIEF EXERCISE 12–6
Calculating ROI [LO2 – CC4]

The following information relates to Lionel Manufacturing Company for 20X7:

Original cost of assets as of January 1, 20X6	$200,000
Useful life of assets	10 years
Years of depreciation taken as of January 1, 20X7 (straight-line)	1 year
Operating income gross of depreciation for 20X6	$ 40,000
Estimated salvage value	$ 0

Required:

What is the ROI for 20X7, using the beginning-of-year book value of the assets?

(Adapted © CPA Canada)

BRIEF EXERCISE 12–7
Calculating RI [LO2 – CC6]

Xylo Co. reported the following statistics and results for 20X9:

ROI	14%
Invested capital (average operating assets)	$200,000
Cost of capital	10%

Required:

What was Zhao's residual income for 20X9?

(Adapted © CPA Canada)

BRIEF EXERCISE 12–8
Calculating Net Investment [LO2 – CC4, 5, 6]

Bajaj Ltd. reported the following statistics and results for 20X9:

Net operating income	$54,000
Return on sales	9.5%
Asset turnover	2.4
Residual income	$10,000

Required:

What was the value of Bajaj's average operating assets in 20X9?

(Adapted © CPA Canada)

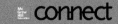

Exercises

EXERCISE 12–1
Preparing a Segment Performance Report [LO1 – CC3]

Indi Services Corporation, headquartered in Bengaluru, India, provides specialized information technology (IT) services and consists of three divisions: (1) financial services, (2) health services, and (3) transportation services. For 2014, it recorded the following data:

	Financial Services	Health Services	Transportation Services	Total
Sales revenues	$3,956,000	$5,594,000	$1,970,000	$11,520,000
Variable costs (% of sales)	28%	40%	45%	
Traceable fixed costs	2,145,320	2,768,450	730,560	5,644,330
Common fixed costs				1,590,000

Required:

1. Prepare a segment performance report showing the segment margin in dollars and percentages for all three divisions. Use Exhibit 12–3 as a guide.
2. Which segment is most profitable? Why?

EXERCISE 12–2
Computing and Interpreting ROI [LO2 – CC4]

Selected operating data for two divisions of Outback Brewing, Ltd. of Australia are as follows:

	Division	
	Queensland	New South Wales
Sales	$3,500,000	$6,000,000
Average operating assets	1,000,000	3,000,000
Net operating income	420,000	360,000
Property, plant, and equipment (net)	400,000	1,900,000

Required:

1. Compute the rate of return for each division using the ROI formula stated in terms of margin and turnover.
2. Using the data, identify which divisional manager seems to be doing the better job. Why?

EXERCISE 12–3
Contrasting ROI and RI [LO2 – CC4, 6]

Meiji Isetan Corp. of Japan has two regional divisions with headquarters in Osaka and Yokohama. Selected data on the two divisions follow (in millions of yen, denoted by ¥):

	Division	
	Osaka	Yokohama
Sales	¥4,500,000	¥13,500,000
Net operating income	315,000	1,080,000
Average operating assets	1,500,000	6,000,000

Required:

1. For each division, compute the ROI in terms of margin and turnover. Where necessary, carry computations to two decimal places.
2. Assume that the company evaluates performance by use of RI and that the minimum required return for any division is 15%. Compute the RI for each division.
3. Is Yokohama's greater amount of RI an indication that it is better managed than Osaka? Explain.

EXERCISE 12–4
Evaluating New Investments With ROI and RI [LO2 – CC4, 6]

Selected sales and operating data for three divisions of a multinational structural engineering firm are provided below:

	Division		
	Asia	Europe	North America
Sales	$12,000,000	$14,000,000	$25,000,000
Average operating assets	$ 3,000,000	$ 5,000,000	$10,000,000
Net operating income	$ 420,000	$ 400,000	$ 1,000,000
Minimum required rate of return	14%	10%	16%

Required:

1. Compute the ROI for each division using the formula stated in terms of margin and turnover.
2. Compute the RI for each division.
3. Assume that each division is presented with an investment opportunity that would yield a 13% rate of return.
   a. If performance is being measured by ROI, which division(s) will probably accept the opportunity? Reject the opportunity? Why?
   b. If performance is being measured by RI, which division(s) will probably accept the opportunity? Reject the opportunity? Why?

EXERCISE 12–5
Studying Effects of Changes in Profits and Assets on ROI [LO2 – CC4, 5]

Pecs Alley is a regional chain of health clubs. The managers of the clubs, who have authority to make investments as needed, are evaluated based largely on ROI. The Vancouver club reported the following results for the past year:

Sales	$2,400,000
Net operating income	480,000
Average operating assets	1,080,000

Required:

The following questions are to be considered independently. Carry out all computations to two decimal places:

1. Compute the club's ROI.
2. Assume that the manager of the club is able to increase sales by $120,000, and, as a result, net operating income increases by $25,600. Further assume that this is possible without any increase in operating assets. What would be the club's ROI?
3. Assume that the manager of the club is able to reduce expenses by $24,000 without any change in sales or operating assets. What would be the club's ROI?
4. Assume that the manager of the club is able to reduce operating assets by $120,000 without any change in sales or net operating income. What would be the club's ROI?

EXERCISE 12–6
Analyzing ROI [LO2 – CC4]

Images.com is a small Internet retailer of high-quality posters. The company has $800,000 in operating assets and fixed expenses of $160,000 per year. With this level of operating assets and fixed expenses, the company can support sales of up to $5 million per year. The company's contribution margin ratio is 10%, which means that an additional dollar of sales results in additional contribution margin, and net operating income, of 10 cents.

Required:

Complete the following table showing the relationship between sales and return on investment (ROI):

Sales	Net Operating Income	Average Operating Assets	ROI
$4,500,000	$290,000	$800,000	?
$4,600,000	?	$800,000	?
$4,700,000	?	$800,000	?
$4,800,000	?	$800,000	?
$4,900,000	?	$800,000	?
$5,000,000	?	$800,000	?

EXERCISE 12–7
Evaluating Performance Using ROI and RI [LO2 – CC4, 6]

One division of a company has reported the following operating results for the year just ended:

Sales	$600,000
Operating income	72,000
Average operating assets	300,000

Required:

1. Compute the margin percentage, turnover, and ROI for this division.
2. If management sets a minimum required rate of return on average operating assets of 20%, what is the RI for this division for the year?
3. Explain the meaning of RI, and identify one strength and one weakness of measuring performance using RI.

(Adapted © CPA Canada)

Problems

connect

PROBLEM 12–1
Preparing a Segmented Performance Report [LO1 – CC2, 3]

Prairie Electronics, located in Regina, manufactures three product lines: (1) high-end speakers, (2) personal computers, and (3) handheld devices. For 20X5, it compiled the following budgeted data:

CHECK FIGURE

(2) Segment margin percentage, personal computers, 5.1%

	High-End Speakers	Personal Computers	Handheld Devices	Total
Sales (in units)	340,000	550,000	440,000	
Price (per unit)	$1,500	$1,250	$375	
Variable costs per unit:				
Direct materials	$ 426	$ 384	$ 40	
Direct labour	120	210	48	
Overhead	80	110	37	
Shipping	30	30	4	
Sales commissions	20	20	2	
Direct fixed costs:				
Salaries	$61,560,000	70,250,000	40,330,000	
Utilities	41,250,000	55,005,000	12,500,600	
Depreciation	59,000,250	112,600,000	30,250,000	
Common fixed costs:				
Corporate salaries				$33,460,000
Building depreciation				27,900,800
Legal & accounting				41,380,640
Other				11,340,760

Required:

1. Prepare a segmented performance report; use Exhibit 12–3 as your guide.

2. Compute the contribution margin percentage (contribution margin divided by sales) and segment margin percentage. On the basis of the dollar amounts and percentages, how would you assess the performance of the three segments (i.e., the three product lines)?

3. Allocate the common fixed expenses equally to the three segments and prepare a performance report similar to the one in Exhibit 12–3. As a manager overseeing all three segments, how would you react to the report?

PROBLEM 12–2
Calculating ROI Relations [LO2 – CC4]

Required:

Provide the missing data in the following tabulation:

> **CHECK FIGURE**
> Bravo: 2.4 turnover

	Division		
	Alpha	**Bravo**	**Charlie**
Sales	?	$12,000,000	?
Net operating income	?	$ 1,200,000	210,000
Average operating assets	$1,600,000	?	?
Margin	8%	?	7%
Turnover	6	?	?
ROI	?	24%	14%

PROBLEM 12–3
Inferring Data Based on ROI and RI Relations [LO2 – CC4, 6]

A family friend has asked for your help in analyzing the operations of three anonymous companies.

> **CHECK FIGURE**
> Company B residual income: ($40,000)

Required:

Supply the missing data in the tabulation below:

	Company		
	A	**B**	**C**
Sales	$10,800,000	$7,000,000	$9,000,000
Net operating income	?	$ 280,000	?
Average operating assets	$ 4,200,000	?	$6,000,000
Return on investment	18%	14%	20%

Minimum required rate of return:			
Percentage	16%	?	?
Dollar amount	?	$ 320,000	?
Residual income	?	?	$ 180,000

PROBLEM 12–4
Comparing Performance Using ROI [LO2 – CC4, 6]

Guenther Corporation uses the return on investment (ROI) measure to evaluate its managers. A summary of the performance of two divisions is given below:

CHECK FIGURE

(1) Division A ROI 20%;
Division B ROI 18%

	Division A	Division B
Average operating assets	$240,000	$400,000
Net income	48,000	72,000

The minimum required return on operating assets for Guenther Corporation is 14%.

Required:

1. According to Guenther's senior management, which division is the better performer? Why?
2. Can Guenther's management use a different measure to evaluate performance? How will using a different measure affect management's evaluation of the two divisions?
3. Suppose the manager of Division A were offered a one-year project that would increase his average operating assets by $100,000 and increase profit by $15,000.
   a. Would the manager accept the project under the current method of performance evaluation? Why, or why not?
   b. Using your alternative measure of performance evaluation (as in part (2) above), do you think the manager should accept the project? Why, or why not?
4. Comment on the value of using only financial metrics to evaluate performance. Is there any other performance measurement model available that provides a more holistic view of an organization's performance? Explain this performance measurement model in detail.

 ## PROBLEM 12–5
Computing ROI and RI [LO2 – CC4, 6]

Financial data for Joel de Paris Inc. for last year follow:

CHECK FIGURE

(1) ROI, 25%

JOEL DE PARIS INC.
Balance Sheet

	Ending Balance	Beginning Balance
Assets		
Cash	$ 120,000	$ 140,000
Accounts receivable	530,000	450,000
Inventory	380,000	320,000
Plant and equipment, net	620,000	680,000
Investment in Buisson, S.A.	280,000	250,000
Land (undeveloped)	170,000	180,000
Total assets	$2,100,000	$2,020,000
Liabilities and Shareholders' Equity		
Accounts payable	$ 310,000	$ 360,000
Long-term debt	1,500,000	1,500,000
Shareholders' equity	290,000	160,000
Total liabilities and shareholders' equity	$2,100,000	$2,020,000

JOEL DE PARIS INC.
Income Statement

Sales		$4,050,000
Less: Operating expenses		3,645,000
Net operating income		405,000
Less: Interest and taxes:		
Interest expense	$ 150,000	
Tax expense	110,000	260,000
Net income		$ 145,000

The company paid dividends of $15,000 last year. The "Investment in Buisson, S.A." on the balance sheet represents an investment in the shares of another company.

Required:

1. Compute the company's margin, turnover, and ROI for last year.
2. The board of directors of Joel de Paris Inc. has set a minimum required return of 15%. What was the company's residual income last year?

PROBLEM 12–6
Calculating ROI and RI [LO2 – CC4, 5, 6]

"I know headquarters wants us to add on that new product line," said Dell Havasi, manager of Billings Company's office products division. "But I want to see the numbers before I make any move. Our division has led the company for three years, and I don't want any letdown."

Billings Company is a decentralized organization with five autonomous divisions. The divisions are evaluated on the basis of the return that they are able to generate on invested assets, with year-end bonuses given to the divisional managers who have the highest ROI figures. Operating results for the company's office products division for the most recent year are as follows:

Sales	$10,000,000
Less: Variable expenses	6,000,000
Contribution margin	4,000,000
Less: Fixed expenses	3,200,000
Net operating income	$ 800,000
Divisional operating assets	$ 4,000,000

The company had an overall ROI of 15% last year (considering all divisions). The office products division has an opportunity to add a new product line that would require an additional investment in operating assets of $1,000,000. The cost and revenue characteristics of the new product line per year would be as follows:

Sales	$2,000,000
Variable expenses	60% of sales
Fixed expenses	$ 640,000

Required:

1. Compute the office products division's ROI for the most recent year; also compute the ROI if the new product line were added.
2. If you were in Dell Havasi's position, would you be inclined to accept or reject the new product line? Explain.
3. Why do you suppose headquarters is anxious for the office products division to add the new product line?
4. Suppose that the company views a return of 12% on invested assets as being the minimum that any division should earn and that performance is evaluated by the RI approach.
   a. Compute the office products division's RI for the most recent year; also compute the RI as it would appear if the new product line were added.
   b. Under these circumstances, if you were in Dell Havasi's position, would you accept or reject the new product line? Explain.

PROBLEM 12–7
Analyzing ROI [LO2 – CC4, 5]

The income statement for Huerra Company for last year is provided below:

CHECK FIGURE
(2b) ROI: 23%
(2e) ROI: 13.41%

	A	B	C	D
1			Total	Unit
2	Sales		$4,000,000	$80.00
3	Less: Variable expenses		2,800,000	56.00
4	Contribution margin		1,200,000	24.00
5	Less: Fixed expense		840,000	16.80
6	Net operating income		360,000	7.20
7	Less: income taxes @	30%	108,000	2.16
8	Net income		$ 252,000	$ 5.04

The company had average operating assets of $2,000,000 during the year.

Required:

1. Compute the company's ROI for the period using the ROI formula stated in terms of margin and turnover.
2. For each of the following questions, indicate whether the margin and turnover will increase, decrease, or remain unchanged as a result of the events described, and then compute the new ROI figure. Consider each question separately, starting in each case from the data used to compute the original ROI in part (1).
   a. By using JIT, the company is able to reduce the average level of inventory by $600,000. (The released funds are used to pay off short-term creditors.)
   b. The company achieves a savings of $2 per unit by using cheaper materials.
   c. The company issues bonds and uses the proceeds to purchase machinery and equipment, thus increasing the average assets by $600,000. Interest on the bonds is $60,000 per year. Sales remain unchanged. The new more efficient equipment reduces fixed production costs by $30,000 per year.
   d. As a result of a more intense effort by the sales staff, sales are increased by 10%; operating assets remain unchanged.
   e. Obsolete items of inventory carried on the records at a cost of $120,000 are scrapped and sold for 10% of the book value.
   f. The company uses $200,000 in cash (received on accounts receivable) to repurchase and retire some of its common shares.
   g. The company pays a cash dividend to its shareholders, which results in a $300,000 change in average operating assets.

PROBLEM 12–8
Computing ROI and RI in a Decentralized Company [LO1 – CC2, 3; LO2 – CC4, 5, 6]

Wally Steel Division is a unit of Wally Industries which produces tool and die machinery for manufacturers. The steel division operates as one of several separate investment centres of Wally Industries.

The investment centres are evaluated on the basis of ROI. Management bonuses are also based on ROI. All investments in operating assets are expected to earn a minimum rate of return of 10%.

Divisional ROI of the steel division has ranged from 12% to 15% since it was acquired by the parent company. During the past year, the steel division had an investment opportunity that would yield an estimated rate of return of 12%. But the divisional management decided against the investment because it believed the investment would decrease the division's overall ROI.

Last year's income statement for Wally Steel Division is given below. The division's operating assets employed were $19,440,000 at the end of the year, which represents an 8% increase over the previous year-end balance.

WALLY STEEL DIVISION Divisional Income Statement For the Year Ended December 31		
Sales		$28,600,000
Cost of goods sold		12,450,000
Gross margin		16,150,000
Less: Operating expenses:		
Selling expenses	$5,280,000	
Administrative expenses	8,206,000	13,486,000
Net operating income		$ 2,664,000

Required:

1. Compute the average operating assets for the year.
2. Compute the ROI of the division. State the ROI in terms of margin and turnover.
3. Compute the residual income for the steel division.
4. Did the management of Wally Steel Division err in rejecting the investment opportunity it had last year? Why?
5. Would last year's investment opportunity have been rejected if RI were used as a performance measure instead of ROI? Explain.
6. Wally Steel Division is a separate investment centre within Wally Industries. Identify the items the division must be free to control if it is to be evaluated fairly by either the ROI or RI performance measure.

PROBLEM 12–9
Computing Operating Income, ROI, and RI [LO1 – CC2; LO2 – CC4, 5, 6]

Auto Parts is a division of MPI International, located in Wadena, Saskatchewan. Auto Parts manufactures various automobile parts, such as bumpers, fenders, and axles, and sells them to major auto manufacturers. The division and its management are evaluated by senior corporate management on the basis of investment centre concepts. The following information pertains to operations of the Auto Parts division for 20X4:

> **CHECK FIGURE**
> (3) $132,000

Operating results:	
Total revenues	$21,250,000
Less: Direct variable costs	8,750,000
Contribution margin	12,500,000
Less: Direct fixed costs	7,500,000
Segment margin	5,000,000
Less: Allocated corporate costs	3,938,000
Operating income	$ 1,062,000

	Book Values		Market Values	
	December 31, 20X3	December 31, 20X4	December 31, 20X3	December 31, 20X4
Current assets	$ 1,250,000	$ 1,800,000		
Fixed assets	10,250,000	11,700,000		
Accumulated depreciation	(1,250,000)	(1,750,000)		
Total operating assets	$10,250,000	$11,750,000	$9,500,000	$10,500,000
Liabilities	$ 3,000,000	$ 3,500,000		
Net assets	$ 7,250,000	$ 8,250,000		

Required:

1. Compute the margin, turnover, and ROI using operating income and the book value of average total operating assets.

2. Compute ROI replacing net income with segment margin when calculating the margin and average market value of operating assets.

3. Compute RI using operating income and the book value of average net assets. Assume that the required rate of return is 12%.

(Adapted © CPA Canada)

PROBLEM 12–10
Calculating ROI and RI Relationships [LO2 – CC4, 6]

Mushi Heavy Industries manufactures primarily heavy machinery and drilling installations for mining, oil wells, and other similar industries. The vice-president of the transport division, newly created for bulk transportation of raw materials, is preparing a capital budget for the coming year for inclusion in the companywide capital budget. The managers of the

six subdivisions of the transport division have each submitted a capital investment proposal to the vice-president, who must decide which project(s) to include in the submission to corporate head office. The proposals are listed below. All are considered equally risky.

Project	Investment Required	Expected Return
1	$4,800,000	$1,200,000
2	1,900,000	627,000
3	1,400,000	182,000
4	950,000	152,000
5	650,000	136,000
6	300,000	90,000

The vice-president has to decide which of the proposed projects to include in the transport division's submission. Mushi has a cost of capital of 15%. The transport division has been allocated $7 million for capital investment purposes.

Required:

1. Calculate, for each project, the expected ROI and the RI.
2. Which projects will be funded and what will be the total investment, total return, ROI, and total RI?

(Adapted © CPA Canada)

PROBLEM 12–11
Preparing Segment Performance Reports [LO1 – CC2, 3]

Bharat Curry Foods (BCF) prepares and sells frozen curry dinners. The company reported the following operating results for 20X1, in which there were no inventories of dinners at the beginning and end of the year:

BHARAT CURRY FOODS Income Statement For the Year Ended December 31, 20X1	
Sales	$1,560,000
Cost of goods sold	900,000
Gross margin	660,000

Selling and administrative expenses	420,000
Operating income	$ 240,000

BCF sells two types of curry foods—chicken and lamb—and operates in Ontario and western Canada. Information on sales and costs is as follows:

	Chicken	Lamb	Total
Regional sales percentage of national sales:			
Ontario	37%	28%	65%
Western Canada	20	15	35
Total	57%	43%	100%
Costs as percentage of regional sales:			
Variable production costs	46%	36.75%	
Variable selling expenses	11.4%	12%	
Fixed costs by product:			
Traceable fixed expenses	$75,000	$45,000	$120,000
Common fixed costs	Remainder of total costs		

The following information is for lamb products only:

	Ontario	Western Canada	
Costs as percentage of regional lamb sales:			
Variable production costs	38%	34.42%	
Variable selling expenses	10.92%	14%	
Fixed costs by region:			
Traceable fixed expenses	$20,000	$25,000	$45,000

Required:

1. Prepare, in good form, an income statement segmented by product line, showing the corresponding company totals. Use Exhibit 12–3 as a guide.
2. Prepare, in good form, a segmented performance report for lamb curry dinners by region.
3. What inferences can you draw from the segmented performance report prepared above in part (2)? How can the manager get more insight into this?

(Adapted © CPA Canada)

Building Your Skills

THINKING ANALYTICALLY [LO1 – CC1, 2; LO2 – CC4, 5, 6]

The valve division of Bendix Inc. produces a small valve that is used by various companies as a component part in their products. Bendix Inc. operates its divisions as autonomous units, giving its divisional managers great discretion in pricing and other decisions. Each division is expected to generate a rate of return of at least 14% on its operating assets. The valve division has average operating assets of $700,000. The valves are sold for $5 each. Variable costs are $3 per valve, and fixed costs total $462,000 per year. The division has a capacity of 300,000 valves each year.

Required:

1. How many valves must the division sell each year to generate the desired rate of return on its assets?
   a. What is the margin earned at this level of sales?
   b. What is the turnover at this level of sales?

2. Assume that the division's current ROI is just equal to the minimum required 14%. In order to increase the division's ROI, the divisional manager wants to increase the selling price per valve by 4%. Market studies indicate that an increase in the selling price would cause sales to drop by 20,000 units each year. However, operating assets could be reduced by $50,000 due to decreased needs for accounts receivable and inventory. Compute the margin, turnover, and ROI if these changes are made.

3. Refer to the original data. Assume again that the valve division's current ROI is just equal to the minimum required 14%. Rather than increase the selling price, the sales manager wants to reduce the selling price per valve by 4%. Market studies indicate that this would fill the plant to capacity. In order to carry the greater level of sales, however, operating assets would increase by $50,000. Compute the margin, turnover, and ROI if these changes are made.

4. Refer to the original data. Assume that the normal volume of sales is 280,000 valves each year at a price of $5 per valve. Another division of the company is currently purchasing 20,000 valves each year from an overseas supplier, at a price of $4.25 per valve. The manager of the valve division has adamantly refused to meet this price, even though he has the production capacity to accommodate the production, pointing out that it would result in a loss for his division:

Selling price per valve		$ 4.25
Cost per valve:		
Variable	$3.00	
Fixed ($462,000 ÷ 300,000 valves)	1.54	4.54
Net loss per valve		$(0.29)

The manager of the valve division also points out that the normal $5 selling price barely allows his division the required 14% rate of return. "If we take on some business at only $4.25 per unit, then our ROI is obviously going to suffer," he reasons, "and maintaining that ROI figure is the key to my future. Besides, taking on these extra units would require us to increase our operating assets by at least $50,000 due to the larger inventories and receivables we would be carrying." If the manager of the valve division accepts the transfer price of $4.25 for 20,000 units, how would that decision impact the valve division's ROI? Should the manager of the valve division accept the price of $4.25 per valve? Why, or why not?

COMMUNICATING IN PRACTICE [LO3 – CC10, 11^A]

Weierman Department Store is located in the downtown area of Edmonton, Alberta. While the store had been profitable for many years, it is facing increasing competition from large national chains that have set up outlets in the city's suburbs. Recently, the downtown area has been undergoing revitalization, and the owners of Weierman Department Store are somewhat optimistic that profitability can be restored.

In an attempt to accelerate the return to profitability, the management of Weierman Department Store is in the process of designing a balanced scorecard for the company. Management believes the company should focus on two key problems:

a. Customers are taking longer and longer to pay the bills they incur on the department store's charge card, and they have far more bad debts than are normal for the industry. If this problem were solved, the company would have more cash to make much-needed renovations. Investigation has revealed that much of the problem with late payments and unpaid bills is apparently due to disputed bills that are the result of incorrect charges on the customer bills. These incorrect charges usually occur because sales clerks enter data incorrectly on the charge card reader.

b. The company has been incurring large losses on unsold seasonal apparel. Such items are ordinarily resold at a loss to discount stores that specialize in such distressed items.

The meeting in which the balanced scorecard approach was discussed was disorganized and ineffectively led—possibly because no one other than one of the vice-presidents had read anything about how to create a balanced scorecard. Nevertheless, a number of potential performance measures were suggested by various managers. These potential performance measures are

- Total sales revenue
- Percentage of sales clerks trained to correctly enter data on the charge card reader
- Customer satisfaction with accuracy of charge account bills from monthly customer survey
- Sales per employee
- Travel expenses for buyers for trips to fashion shows
- Average age of accounts receivable
- Courtesy shown by junior staff members to senior staff members based on surveys of senior staff
- Unsold inventory at the end of the season as a percentage of total cost of sales
- Sales per square foot of floor space
- Percentage of suppliers making just-in-time deliveries
- Quality of food in the staff cafeteria based on staff surveys
- Written-off accounts receivable (bad debts) as a percentage of sales
- Percentage of charge account bills containing errors
- Percentage of employees who have attended the city's cultural diversity workshop
- Total profit
- Profit per employee

Required:

1. You have been asked to build an integrated balanced scorecard. In your scorecard, use only performance measures that were suggested by the managers. You do not have to use all of the performance measures suggested by the managers, but you should build a balanced scorecard that reveals a strategy for dealing with the problems with accounts receivable and with unsold merchandise. Construct the balanced scorecard following the format used in Exhibit 12–6. Do not be particularly concerned with whether a specific performance measure falls within the learning and growth, internal business process, customer, or financial perspective. However, clearly show the causal links between the performance measures and explain whether the performance measures should show increases or decreases.

2. Assume that the company adopts your balanced scorecard. After operating for a year, there are improvements in some performance measures but not in others. What should management do next?

3. a. Suppose that customers express greater satisfaction with the accuracy of their charge account bills, but the performance measures for the average age of accounts receivable and for bad debts do not improve. Explain why this might happen.

   b. Suppose that the performance measures for the average age of accounts receivable, bad debts, and unsold inventory improve, but total profits do not. Explain why this might happen. Assume in your answer that the explanation lies within the company.

TEAMWORK IN ACTION [LO3 – CC10, 11ᴬ]

There is often more than one way to improve a performance measure. Unfortunately, some of the actions taken by managers to make their performance look better may actually harm the organization. For example, suppose the marketing department is held responsible only for increasing the performance measure "total revenues." Increases in total revenues may be achieved by working harder and smarter, but they can also usually be achieved by simply cutting prices. The increase in volume from cutting prices almost always results in greater total revenues; however, it does not always lead to greater total profits. Those who design performance measurement systems need to keep in mind that managers who are under pressure to perform may take actions to improve performance measures that have negative consequences elsewhere.

Required:

Form teams and, for each of the following situations, discuss and describe actions that managers might take to show improvement in the performance measure but that do not actually lead to improvement in the organization's overall performance. Each member of the team should be prepared to present the team's conclusions in a class discussion. When there is no consensus among the team members, be prepared to present the points on which the team could not reach consensus.

1. Concerned with the slow rate at which new products are brought to market, top management of a consumer electronics company introduces a new performance measure—speed-to-market. The research and development department is given responsibility for this performance measure, which measures the average amount of time a product is in development before it is released to the market for sale.

2. The CEO of a telephone company has been under public pressure from city officials to fix the large number of public pay phones that do not work. The company's repair people complain that the problem is vandalism and damage caused by theft of coins from coin boxes—particularly in high-crime areas in the city. The CEO says she wants the problem solved and has pledged to city officials that there will be substantial improvement by the end of the year. To ensure that this is done, she makes the managers in charge of installing and maintaining pay phones responsible for increasing the percentage of public pay phones that are fully functional.

3. A manufacturing company has been plagued by the chronic failure to ship orders to customers by the promised date. To solve this problem, the production manager has been given the responsibility of increasing the percentage of orders shipped on time. When a customer calls in an order, the production manager and the customer agree to a delivery date. If the order is not completed by that date, it is counted as a late shipment.

4. Concerned with the productivity of employees, the board of directors of a large multinational corporation has dictated that the manager of each subsidiary will be held responsible for increasing the revenue per employee of his or her subsidiary.

INDEX